John R. Hinnells studied at King's College, London, and the School of Oriental and African Studies before taking up lectureships at Newcastle-upon-Tyne and Manchester universities. He was Visiting Senior Lecturer at the Open University (1975-7) and is Professor of Comparative Religion at Manchester University.

His publications include *Persian Mythology, Spanning East and West* and *Parsis and the British.* He is editor of *The Penguin Dictionary of Religions* and *The Penguin Handbook of Living Religion* and is currently working on a three-volume text on Zoroastrians in Modern History.

WHO'S WHO OF WORLD RELIGIONS

WHO'S WHO OF WORLD RELIGIONS

Editor
John R. Hinnells

SIMON & SCHUSTER
A Paramount Communications Company
New York London Toronto Sydney Tokyo Singapore

First published 1991
by The Macmillan Press Ltd.
London and Basingstoke

And in the USA by
Academic Reference Division
Simon & Schuster
15 Columbus Circle
New York, NY 10023
A Paramount Communications Company

Library of Congress Cataloging-in-Publication Data

Who's who of world religions/editor, John R. Hinnells.
p. cm.
Includes bibliographical references and index.
ISBN 0-13-952946-2
1. Religious biography. I. Hinells. John R.
BL72.W54 1992
291′.092′2—dc20
[B]

91-36866
CIP

Typeset and printed in Great Britain

Contents

Editors

General Editor: John Hinnells, *University of Manchester*

Area Editors:
Buddhism & East Asia – Paul Griffiths, *University of Chicago*
Christianity – Terence Thomas, *Open University*
Hinduism – Simon Weightman, *School of Oriental & African Studies, London*
Islam – Andrew Rippin, *Calgary University*

Contributors

A. H. Armstrong **(A.H.A.)**
formerly Classical Studies, Liverpool and Dalhousie Universities.

Anne Bancroft **(A.B.)**
writer on mysticism

Eileen Barker **(E.B.)**
Sociology of Religion, London School of Economics

Robert M. Baum **(R.M.B.)**
Ohio State University

Roger Beck **(R.B.)**
Classical Studies, Erindale College, University of Toronto

C. Edmond Bosworth **(C.E.B.)**
Arabic Studies, University of Manchester

Mary Boyce **(M.B.)**
formerly Iranian Studies, School of Oriental and African Studies, London

Demitri Brady **(D.B.)**
Interdisciplinary Studies, Manchester Polytechnic

Jan van Bragt **(J.V.B.)**
Nanzan Institute for Religion and Culture, Nagoya

George Brooke **(G.J.B.)**
Intertestamental Literature Studies, University of Manchester

Norman Calder **(N.C.)**
Arabic Studies, University of Manchester

David Carrasco **(D.C.)**
Religious Studies, University of Colorado at Boulder

Steven Collins **(S.C.)**
Department of Religion, Concordia University, Montreal

A. Rosalie David **(A.R.D.)**
Egyptology, University of Manchester Museum

Paul Dundas **(P.D.)**
Sanskrit, University of Edinburgh

Gary Ebersole **(G.E.)**
Divinity School, University of Chicago

Hilda Ellis-Davidson **(H.E.D.)**
formerly Vice-Principal, Lucy Cavendish Hall, Cambridge

Paul Jo Griffiths **(P.J.G.)**
Divinity School, University of Chicago

Janet Gyatso **(J.G.)**
Department of Religion, Amherst College, Massachusetts

Rosalind Hackett **(R.H.)**
Religious Studies, University of Tennessee at Knoxville

Charles Hallisey **(C.H.)**
Theology, Loyola University, Chicago

John Hinnells **(J.R.H.)**
Comparative Religion, University of Manchester

Jack Irwin **(J.I.)**
Sydney

Roger Jackson **(R.J.)**
Department of Religion, Carleton College, Minnesota

Michael Kalton **(M.Kal.)**
Department of Religion, Wichita State University, Kansas

Matthew Kapstein **(M.Kap.)**
Department of Religion, Columbia University, New York

John Keenan **(J.K.)**
Religious Studies, Middlebury College, Vermont

John P. Kane **(J.P.K.)**
Comparative Religion, University of Manchester

Dermot H. Killingley **(D.H.K.)**
Religious Studies, University of Newcastle

Jan Knappert **(J.Kn.)**
formerly School of Oriental and African Studies, London

Per Kvaerne **(P.K.)**
Institutt for Religionshistorie og Kristendomkunnskap, University of Oslo

B. Todd Lawson **(B.T.L.)**
Middle East and Islamic Studies, University of Toronto

Harry Lesser **(H.L.)**
Philosophy, University of Manchester

Sam Lieu **(S.L.)**
Classics, University of Warwick

Donald S. Lopez **(D.L.)**
Asian Languages and Cultures, University of Michigan

Tanya Luhrman **(T.L.)**
Anthropology, University of California, San Diego

Dennis MacEoin **(D.M.)**
formerly Religious Studies, University of Newcastle

Hew McLeod **(W.H.M.)**
History, Dunedin University

John R. McRae **(J.M.)**
Department of Religion, Case Western Reserve University, Ohio

Elizabeth Manning **(E.M.)**
Senior Councillor and Tutor, Open University

John Marr **(J.R.M.)**
Tamil and Indian Art Studies, School of Oriental and African Studies, London

David J. Melling **(D.J.M.)**
Dean of Humanities, Manchester Polytechnic

T. Mukherjee **(T.M.)**
Bengali Studies, School of Oriental and African Studies, London

Keith Munning **(K.M.)**
bookseller and tutor, Bristol

Gordon Neil **(G.R.N.)**
Classics, University of Manchester

Harban Singh Oberoi **(H.S.O.)**
Asian Studies, University of British Columbia, Vancouver

Ken Parry **(K.P.)**
Theological Studies, University of Manchester

Iain M. P. Raeside **(I.M.P.R.)**
Marathi and Gujarati, School of Oriental and African Studies, London

Reginald Ray **(R.R.)**
Naropa Institute, Colorado

Stephen Reno **(S.R.)**
Dean of Academic Affairs, South Oregon State College

Mervyn Richardson **(M.R.)**
Middle Eastern Studies, University of Manchester

Andrew Rippin **(A.R.)**
Religious Studies, Calgary University, Alberta

Valerie Roebuck **(V.J.R.)**
Comparative Religion, University of Manchester

Christopher Shackle **(C.S.)**
South Asian Language and Literature, School of Oriental and African Studies, London

A. Christopher Smith **(A.C.S.)**
Centre for the Study of Christianity in the non-Western World, University of Edinburgh

Richard Snell **(R.S.)**
Hindi Studies, School of Oriental and African Studies, London

Laurence Sullivan **(L.S.)**
Center for the Study of World's Religions, Harvard University

Terry Swain **(T.S.)**
Religious Studies, Sydney University

Paul L. Swanson **(P.L.S.)**
Nanzan Institute for Religion and Culture, Nagoya

Mark Tatz **(M.T.)**
California Institute of Integral Studies, San Francisco

Terence Thomas **(T.T.)**
Religious Studies, Open University

Larry G. Thompson **(L.T.)**
University of Southern California

Gary Trompf **(G.W.T.)**
Religious Studies, Sydney University

Allan Unterman **(A.U.)**
Comparative Religion, University of Manchester

Andrew Walls **(A.F.W.)**
Centre for the Study of Christianity in the non-Western World, University of Edinburgh

Simon Weightman **(S.C.R.W.)**
Hindi Studies, School of Oriental and African Studies, London

Geoffrey Wigoder **(G.W.)**
Director of Oral History Studies, Hebrew University, Jerusalem

Katherine Williams **(K.W.)**
Arts Education, University of Warwick

Dedication

The editor wishes to dedicate his work behind this volume to the Revd Prof. C. F. Evans, the first teacher to give both encouragement and stimulation to study further, and whose friendship means a great deal.

Introduction

Regardless of what one's own religion may be, Buddhist or Christian, Muslim, or atheist, it is beyond dispute that religions have been major factors in the development of all societies ancient and modern. One cannot understand what occurs in Iran or Israel, India or Britain, America or Japan, without taking into account the religious forces at work, both past and present. As peoples migrate from one continent to another, as the media brings different parts of the world into contact with each other, so there is a growing awareness of the varieties of religions and an increasing fascination with their diverse roles in all societies. For the sake of international understanding it is vital that knowledge concerning other people's traditions, their heroes and their role models, is spread.

It may well be said that religions do not exist apart from the people who practice them. In historical, as opposed to theological, terms religions are what they are by what human beings have made them. Because dictionaries and encyclopedias tend to focus on movements and 'isms' rather than details of individual people there is a need for a reference work collecting data on the men and women who have shaped the world's religions in the past and in the present. This book is about some of those people who have made the religions what they were and are.

Who's Who of World Religions places religions in a truly global setting, with materials on ancient Egypt and modern Africa, from Brazil (both ancient and modern) to China and Australia. It is concerned with the formally established churches and the new religious movements, especially in North America, with the occult and with the magical. It also seeks to understand individual religions in a world wide perspective. So, for example, the entries on Christianity are concerned not only with the western world, but also with the Eastern Orthodox churches, and Christians in Africa, Latin America, Asia and on Pacific islands. Other religions are similarly considered in a broad perspective with Buddhism not only in South Asia but also in Tibet, China and Japan; Islam is not merely restricted to the Middle East but appears also in its African and Asian contexts.

Who's Who of World Religions is the outcome of scholarly collaboration on an international scale, with entries by 68 scholars who live and write in different continents. A number of the traditions are so vast and complex that many contributors representing a range of specialisms were required. To coordinate this work Area Editors were appointed who were responsible for the 'subject areas' of Buddhism (together with East Asia as a whole, because in that region there are often no clear division between religions), Christianity, Hinduism and Islam. The General Editor would like to express his profound gratitude to these editors who ensured a balanced scholarly treatment from a team of authors.

It is important to state clearly the presuppositions which lie behind the structures of the work. Other editors would undoubtedly have made some different choices. Although seeking to present a balanced overall picture, this book exercises a degree of positive discrimination in favour of subjects which tend to be neglected in general books, for example Christianity in the non-western world. Traditional approaches might have emphasized more the contributions of the great, and mainly western, theologians (though many examples of these figures have been included here also). Where a substantial body of literature is already available then entries tend to be shorter with bibliographical references pointing to the published works. But in other areas where it is difficult to find material, for example with the Jains, or some modern Parsis, the entries tend to be longer, especially in the cases where there is no material in a European language. Inclusion of a figure does not necessarily indicate 'approval' of that person, e.g. few would wish to justify the work of Charles Manson but, for better or worse, he, like many others who have encouraged the taking of life, is part of the history of religions and it was thought proper to include such entries. In short, care has been taken to cover many of the perceived gaps in the readily available literature, although the well known, the 'great and the glorious', have, obviously, all been included.

There are many different types of people who are important in religions. The *Who's Who of World Religions* has sought to give a balanced picture of the range of religious types in the various traditions. It does not deal simply with the 'founders' and the major thinkers but with many other religious roles also. For some groups the great teachers are crucial, not least in Protestant Christianity, as too are the missionaries. But the visionary and the mystic, the miracle worker, the ascetic, the artist and musician, even the good ruler, tyrant or oppressor can be important types of religious figure and who are found in this book. Contributors have focussed on people who are thought to have actually lived. This is not, therefore, a *Who's Who* of the mythological figures of the various religions, that would be a very different book (although it has to be recognized that the boundaries between history, legend and myth are at times difficult, if not impossible, to draw). Where possible, note has also been taken of the role of women in religion. While it is sometimes easy to decide who should be included – Islam could hardly be covered without an entry on Muḥammed – this is not always the case. There is an on-going debate in Religious Studies as to whether Marxism should be classified as a form of religious movement. For the purposes of this book 'religious' people are generally understood to be those who thought of themselves as, or who have been thought by their followers to be, religious. Marx is not, therefore, included. But once again, it is difficult to draw a clear dividing line on who does, or does not, qualify for inclusion.

A difficult task for any editor is to maintain a balance in the allocation of space to the various traditions. That is especially true in this book because some religions have a stronger sense of history and biography than others do. Christianity in its different forms, and in most eras, has a strong historical sense and has left more records than, for example, certain forms of Indian tradition. In some instances it is extremely difficult to uncover much biographical material for historical figures in non-literate societies. The *Who's Who of World Religions* focuses mostly upon the 'living religions' of Christianity, Islam, Buddhism, Hinduism and Judaism, but ancient societies cannot be ignored both because of their own inherent historical significance and interest (as in the case of Egypt, or the Aztecs and Incas) and because of the influence many have had upon later cultures (for example the Greeks and the Romans). It was also thought important, in principle, to include material from non-literate societies (e.g. in Africa or the North American Indians), utilizing what sources exist (such as oral history) because of their importance, numbers and interest.

There are, in addition to the main text, three important 'tools' in the book: the index, the maps and the bibliography. An index was thought essential because writing about one person commonly involves an account of others. It is often the case that figures referred to in the body of the texts do not appear under a separate head word. Such references, together with some alternative forms or spelling of the headword names, are listed in the index. The maps cannot be exhaustive because so many places are mentioned in the text, but where a place is mentioned in association with an important moment in the life of individuals, or which may have become the focus of pilgrimage, these are generally included.

The language and style of the text makes this *Who's Who of Religions* accessible to the general reader. But in many places it incorporates new, original research. In order to make it a more useful 'tool' for the scholar there is an extensive bibliographical section which provides a substantial guide to large bodies of material. Contributors were asked to provide a bibliography of works written by, and about, their subjects so that there is not only an account of the subject's history, insofar as this can be reconstructed, it also includes references to literature about the position that person has come to play within the respective traditions (as a role model, as a source of authority or inspiration, or as the perceived founder or reformer). In order to avoid wasting space by having individual contributors providing full bibliographical references in their own entries, which would inevitably have resulted in much repetition where a religion is covered by many authors (e.g. Buddhism and Islam), the bibliographies have been conflated and given a numerical reference which is explained below (*see* **Using this Book**). Very occasionally, where a subject does not fit under any of the sub-divisions of the bibliography, the references are given at the end of the entry (e.g. that on Mānī).

Because this is a work both for the general reader and for the specialist it was decided to use diacritical marks. The academic reason for them is strong. Often more than one non-English letter is referred to by one English letter, for example a short and long vowel, or for 's' there are numerous letters in, say, Sanskrit which are indicated by s, ṣ or ś. Many scholars would argue that diacritics are the only way to spell some non-English terms correctly; they have not, however, been generally used in this book for names, since these are usually anglicized in common use.

As there are religious assumptions underlying the abbreviations 'BC' and 'AD' ('Before Christ' and 'Anno Domini', which assume acceptance of Jesus as Messiah or Lord), these are unacceptable to many religious people of traditions other than Christianity. In this *Who's Who* the letters BCE (Before the Christian [or Common] Era) and CE (Christian [or Common] Era) are used throughout. These make no assumption about a person's religious position. For readers not familiar with this usage it may be said that AD 1991 refers to the same year as 1991 CE: the date is constant, only the nomenclature changes.

Finally, the editor wishes to place on record his deep appreciation of the in-house editing carried out with care and understanding by Dr David Roberts; to Kate Alexander, Robert Houghton and Rachel Pike for help with proof reading, to Jeanne Lockett for help with the correspondence and to Nora Firby for help with the maps on Christianity and with the index.

John R. Hinnells
Professor of Comparative Religion, Manchester University.

Using this book

Alphabetization of headings is based on the principle that words are read continuously, ignoring spaces, hyphens, accents, bracketed matter etc. up to the first comma; the same principle applies thereafter. Names beginning 'Mc' are listed as though they began 'Mac'. Arabic names beginning with the article 'al-' are listed under the first capital letter.

Cross-references to other headings are shown in small capitals, with a large capital to indicate the letter under which the corresponding article will be found in the alphabetical sequence. Thus the cross-reference LEONARDO DA VINCI reminds the reader that the article appears under L (and not D or V), similarly AL-JUNAYD and DAYANDAD SARASVATI appear under J and D respectively.

Subject areas are indicated by the roman numerals that appear in square brackets immediately after the heading to each article. The 26 areas are as follows:

[I]	African Religions
[II]	Ancient Near Eastern Religions
[III]	Bahā'ī
[IV]	Buddhism
[V]	Chinese Religions, excluding Buddhism
[VI]	Christianity
[VII]	Egyptian Religion, Ancient
[VIII]	European Religions, Ancient
[IX]	Gnosticism
[X]	Greek Religion, Ancient
[XI]	Hinduism
[XII]	Islam
[XIII]	Jainism
[XIV]	Japanese Religions, excluding Buddhism
[XV]	Judaism
[XVI]	Korean Religions, excluding Buddhism
[XVII]	Magic and the Occult
[XVIII]	Meso-American Religions
[XIX]	New Religious Movements in the West
[XX]	North American Indian Religions
[XXI]	Pacific Religions
[XXII]	Roman Religion
[XXIII]	Sikhism
[XXIV]	South American Religions
[XXV]	Tibetan and Central Asian Religions, excluding Buddhism
[XXVI]	Zoroastrianism

It should be remembered that boundaries around religions are open to question, and it is sometimes arbitrary whether an entry is listed under one subject area rather than another, for example certain African figures might equally well be placed under [I] African Religions or [VI] Christianity.

The **bibliography** is divided into sections corresponding to the 26 subject areas. Some of the sections are subdivided, in which case a letter is appended to the roman numerals indicating the area; thus the very long bibliography on Christianity is divided into two parts – [VI.A] and [VI.B]. The number of the relevant bibliography section appears in square brackets immediately after the heading to each article. Each section of the bibliography is arranged in alphabetical order, with items numbered in arabic numbers. An arabic number in square brackets in the body of an article indicates an item in the relevant bibliography section; if more than one bibliography item is referred to, they are shown separated by semicolons. If a number is followed by a colon, however, the information that follows (up to the next semicolon or closing bracket) indicates relevant pages, chapters or other subdivisions of the work. Thus, [5: 19–21, 25] refers to pages 19, 20, 21 and 25 of bibliography item 5; [33: X–XII] refers to chapters 10 to 12 of bibliography item 33; that is to say, arabic numerals after the colon indicate page numbers, whereas roman numerals show chapter numbers.

The **maps**, though not exhaustive, show the more important places mentioned in the text.

The **synoptic index** is a list showing how articles are distributed among the 26 subject areas.

The **general index** enables the reader to retrieve information that might otherwise be difficult to find. For example, certain important figures are referred to in articles other than their own, and some other figures who do not have their own articles are discussed under another heading: the general index will locate these references. It also records religious movements associated with an individual, etc. discussed in various entries in the volume.

A

Aaron [xv] (*c.*13th century BCE). First Israelite high priest and ancestor of the Jewish priestly line. He was the elder brother of MOSES, for whom he acted as spokesman (in view of Moses' stammer) before Pharaoh and the Israelites in the events leading up to the Exodus from Egypt (described in *Exodus* 4–14). At this period he is often coupled with Moses as a miracle worker and leader of the people. Subsequently his role diminished. When Moses was on Mount Sinai, the people of Israel – doubting his return – appealed to Aaron to make them an alternative god. Succumbing to their pressures, he constructed a golden calf for them to worship. Despite his obvious guilt, he was saved from death and punishment at the intercession of Moses.

Subsequently, with the establishment of the sanctuary, Aaron was selected as its first high priest, being anointed and clothed in priestly garments – together with his sons – by Moses. The priesthood was made hereditary in his family while his tribe, the Levites, was consecrated to serve in the sanctuary. Aaron died at the age of 123 in the wilderness (on Mount Hor) in the last year of the Israelites' wanderings. [45: 175–200]

In Jewish tradition, Aaron is described as embodying the love and pursuit of peace [28; vol. 2: IV]. Critical scholars have suggested that the biblical narrative combines the biographies of two different personalities. (G.W.)

ʿAbd al-Bahā' [III] [ʿAbbās Effendi, Sir Abdul-Baha Abbas] (1844?–1921). 'The Servant of Bahā'', oldest son and successor of BAHĀ' ALLĀH, founder of the Bahā'ī religion. According to modern Bahā'ī accounts, he was born in Tehran, Iran, on 23 May 1844, the day of the 'Declaration' of Sayyid ʿAlī-Muḥammad Shīrāzī (later to be THE BĀB). In 1853 ʿAbbās left Tehran in the company of his father, who had opted for exile in Baghdad along with a number of other converts to the Bābī movement.

In Baghdad he received a good Arabic education whose effects are readily visible in the fluent and intelligent style of much of his later writing. Transferred to Edirne in Turkey in 1863 and to Acre in Palestine in 1868, he was able to familiarize himself with currents of modernism in Ottoman society. Association with progressive thinkers and wide reading (including reformist journals and translations of European works) laid the basis for the ideas developed in the books, letters and lectures of his mature years. Such ideas first appear in the essentially reformist work *Risāla-yi madaniyya* ('The Secret of Divine Civilization'), written before 1875.

Appointed the inspired expounder of his father's teachings, he became head of the movement on his father's death in 1892. Despite rival claims from a younger brother, Muḥammad ʿAlī, ʿAbbās won widespread acceptance, and from the late 1890s began to receive Western converts in Palestine.

Released from technical confinement in 1908, he travelled abroad to Egypt (1910), Europe (1911), the United States and Europe again (1912–13). In the course of these tours, he lectured on Baha'ism to large audiences and became widely known for his views on such subjects as world peace, race equality and female emancipation. His life was threatened by the Ottomans during the war years in Palestine, but in 1920 he was knighted for his 'consistently loyal service to the British cause since the occupation' [16: 344]. He died in Haifa on 28 November 1921.

A charismatic and patriarchal figure, ʿAbd al-Bahā' attracted favourable attention within certain circles in the West, and his presence was undeniably the primary factor that helped Baha'ism establish a successful mission there. He himself began the process of formally organizing the movement, later energetically furthered by his grandson and successor, SHOGHI EFFENDI.

His chief contribution to the development of Baha'ism was, however, the systematization and extension of his father's teachings, a task notably executed during his Western lecture-tours. Among the concepts he introduced or gave particular prominence were those of sexual equality, the oneness of religions, the harmony of religion and science, and the solution of economic problems by the application of spiritual laws. His talks and letters also deal extensively with themes such as scientific and social progress, labour relations, socialism, education, biblical prophecy and topics of a more occult nature; all of these contributed enormously to the popularity of Baha'ism in the West during the 1900s and 1920s.

The writings of ʿAbd al-Bahā' are chiefly collections of letters. A historical text has been translated into English as *A Traveller's Narrative*. His lectures and table-talks have been collected and published in numerous editions and languages. [1; 2; 3; 16; 25] (D.M.)

ʿAbd al-Jabbār, Abū'l-Ḥasan ibn Muḥammad al-Hamdhānī al-Asadābādī [XII] (935?–1025?). Major Muslim Muʿtazilite theologian. Born in central Iran, he was educated in the tradition of law from AL-SHĀFIʿĪ and the theology of AL-ASHʿARĪ. Moving to Baṣra, he embraced the rationalist school of the Muʿtazilites and spent much of his life in his native Iran writing works on law and theology. He was appointed to the position of highest judge of Rayy in Iran by the Būyid rulers of the time. His most famous work is his *al-Mughnī fī abwāb al-tawḥīd wa'l-ʿadl*, some 20 volumes (of which 14 are published) on theology, although this is only one of his many books. His influence on later intellectuals was limited by the gradual disappearance of the Muʿtazilites but in more modern times, with an increasing influence once again on rationalism, his place in the development of Islamic thought is becoming more appreciated. [53] (A.R.)

ʿAbd Allāh ibn Yāsīn [XII] (*d.*1059). Founder of the Murābiṭūn (the Almoravid movement). ʿAbd Allāh was probably born in Sijilmāsa in what is now south-east Morocco. He went to study in Kairouan in Tunisia, which was a great centre of scholarship. There he was met by Yaḥyā ibn Ibrāhīm, the paramount chief of the Ṣanhāja Berbers, who took him home, but the Berbers did not admire ʿAbd Allāh's austerity, so he withdrew to the Atlantic coast where he founded a *ribāṭ*, a retreat or hermitage, where he soon surrounded himself with hundreds of disciples who were attracted by his religious doctrine and fervent practice. With force of words and swords he carved out a dominion in what is now Mauritania and Wādī'l-dhahab (Rio de Oro) in the western Sahara. He conquered Awdughast in southern Mauritania, then marched north to his native Sijilmāsa, which he also took, but did not destroy. From there he rode west over the Atlas mountains and conquered the fertile plain of Morocco. Soon afterwards, in 1059, he was killed in battle against yet another Berber tribe rebelling against his austerity.

ʿAbd Allāh was succeeded by Abū Bakr ibn ʿUmar al-Lamtūnī, who subdued southern and central Morocco and founded the city of Marrakesh. Rebellion in the south forced him to reconquer the western Sahara, leaving Morocco in charge of his cousin, Yūsuf ibn Tashufīn, who soon made himself master of Algeria, Tunisia and even Andalusia. Thus the movement of religious reform which ʿAbd Allāh ibn Yāsīn had started, resulted in the conquest of a vast double empire. [34: 'Almoravids'] (J.K.)

ʿAbd al-Ra'ūf ibn ʿAlī [XII] [of Singkel, or al-Sinkilī] (*c.*1620–1693). Mystic and teacher of Islam in Indonesia. Born on the west coast of Sumatra in what was then the Sultanate of Acheh, ʿAbd al-Ra'ūf studied for 19 years in Arabia and was initiated into the religious order of the Shaṭṭāriyya by his teacher Aḥmad al-Qushāshī. After 1660 he returned to his native land and began preaching the doctrine of the order which was in accordance with the orthodox dogmas, avoiding extremist views. His teachings and his fame as a mystic and ascetic spread along the coasts and across the islands, and became especially popular in Java. He is the author of a number of books in Malay, written in a period of history when the Malay language was only just beginning to be used for theological and philosophical prose. His best known work is *ʿUmdat al-muḥtājīn ilā sulūk maslak al-mufridīn* ('Support for those who are in need of travelling forth on the path of those who are absorbed in the unity of being'). This title refers to the Ṣūfī doctrine of the seven steps or stages along which the ardent student must climb moving toward becoming the image of God.

ʿAbd al-Ra'ūf also translated the Qur'ān into Malay; although its literalness makes it difficult to read for modern Indonesians it is of great interest to the history of Islamic literature in Indonesia. He also wrote works on the personal duties of Muslims (*fiqh*), on Islamic law and mystic lore. After his death he was venerated as a saint and his tomb became a centre of pilgrimage such that he became known as Teungku di-Kuala (Achenese: 'My lord of the estuary'). [75; 35: s.v.] (J.K.)

ʿAbduh, Muḥammad [XII] (1849–1905). Egyptian reformer, regarded as the founder of Islamic modernism. He studied theology at Ṭanṭā before moving (1866) to the Azhar seminary in Cairo, where he devoted himself to Ṣufism. From 1872, he came under the influence of the radical pan-Islamist AL-AFGHĀNĪ. When Afghānī was expelled from Egypt in 1879, ʿAbduh was dismissed from his teaching post at the Dār al-Funūn. In 1880, however, he was made editor of the government gazette, which he used as a forum for his liberal views. This experiment came to an end in 1882, when he was exiled for suspected involvement in an attempted *coup* led by ʿArābī Pāshā.

He joined Afghānī in Paris (1884), forming a reformist society and publishing a short-lived but influential journal, *al-ʿUrwa al-wuthqā* ('The Firm Cord'). Soon after, he left for Beirut, where he taught theology, urging education and gradual reform instead of outright revolution. Returning to Egypt in 1889, he was appointed to a number of legal posts, including (1899) that of chief mufti, in which capacity he introduced numerous changes in the Islamic legal code. He also served on the state legislative council and the supreme council of Al-Azhar university, where he moved several curricular and administrative reforms.

ʿAbduh's writings include the *Risālat al-tawḥīd* ('Treatise on the Divine Unity', Cairo, 1897), *al-Islām wa'l-Naṣrāniyya* ('Islam and Christianity', Cairo, 1902), and an incomplete but important commentary on the Qur'ān (later revised and completed by his pupil RASHĪD RIḌĀ). The main thrust of his work was to synthesize the desirable features of Western civilization with the essential truths of Islam. To achieve this, he sought to maintain the religious elements of Islam against Western secularism, while abandoning many non-religious elements of Islamic culture. His emphases on the rationality of Islam and its adaptability to modern conditions have been major influences on later reformers. [69; 71] (D.M.)

Abelard, Peter [VI.A] (1079–1142). Christian theologian and philosopher. In early life he experienced a love affair with Héloïse, the daughter of a canon of Nôtre-Dame, Paris, who bore him a son. He was punished with castration but retained a life-long contact with Héloïse as mentor and protector. He taught in Paris when not forced to take refuge in monasteries because of opposition to his teaching. His rational interpretation of traditional doctrines brought condemnation from BERNARD OF CLAIRVAUX and official condemnation at the Councils of Soissons (1121) and Sens (1140). His writings include *Christian Theology*, *Ethics* and his letters to Héloïse on moral, theological and doctrinal topics. Later reconciled to Bernard, he died in a Cluniac monastery. [134; 135; 501] (T.T.)

Abhayākaragupta [IV] (11th–12th century). According to Tibetan tradition Abhayākaragupta was a Brahman of Orissa, who in response to a prophetic vision became a Buddhist monk. Though fully initiated in the esoteric disciplines of the Buddhist tantras, he chose not to adopt the lifestyle of a tantric yogin, and remained throughout his career a monastic scholar, based probably at Vikramaśīla in eastern Bihar, where he is known to have been active during the reign of Rāma Pāla (*c*1100). A prolific author, Abhayākaragupta wrote on all aspects of Buddhist monastic discipline and scholastic philosophy, as well as on Buddhist tantric ritual, iconography and interpretation. The preservation of large numbers of Sanskrit manuscripts of his works in India, Nepal and

Tibet demonstrates his importance for later Indian Buddhism and the Newari Buddhist traditions of the Kathmandu Valley; and the translation of his writings into Tibetan was begun during his lifetime under his personal guidance. Despite this, only Abhayākaragupta's contributions to the study of Buddhist tantric iconography have so far been made the object of sustained contemporary research. [16; 17; 47: 82–92; 184: 1046–7; 186] (M.K.)

Abiodun, (Capt.) Christianah [I.A.] [Mrs Emmanuel; Akinsowon] (1907–). Co-founder and spiritual head of the Cherubim and Seraphim Society, one of Nigeria's earliest independent, faith-healing (*Aladura*) churches (*See* ORIMOLADE MOSES). A Yoruba from Lagos, and educated at several mission schools, Abiodun was originally a member of the Anglican Church. Following a series of spiritual experiences, beginning in 1925, which drew widespread attention, she and Orimolade began leading prayer meetings which later developed into the Seraphim Society. She began to travel throughout Nigeria, drawing many people because of her physical presence and preaching capabilities, and eventually establishing all the major branches of the Society. She also published *Celestial Vision History Book*, *Order of Service* and *First C & S Hymn Book*. In 1929 she broke away with a youth faction. Despite the fact that Orimolade continues to be viewed by most sections of the Society as the incontestable founder, Abiodun has continually described herself as the 'living' and 'co-founder' of the church. [25: 39–43, 201] (R.H.)

Abraham [XV] [originally Abram] (*c.*19th century BCE). First patriarch of the Jewish people and traditional originator of monotheism. His story is related in *Genesis* 11:26 – 25:10; like other biblical narratives it is written with strong didactic, religious and national motivations.

Born in Ur in southern Mesopotamia, Abraham was taken by his father, Terah, to Haran in north-western Mesopotamia. After his father's death, Abraham was divinely instructed to leave his homeland for another country. Arriving in the Land of Canaan with his wife, Sarah, his nephew, Lot, and a large company of servants, he lived a nomadic life, mainly in the southern part of the country, making agreements with local rulers and propounding his belief in the One God.

In a succession of theophanies, God promised to grant him a multitude of descendants who would become a great nation; to make him the father of many nations and a blessing to all peoples on earth; and to give him and his descendants the Land of Canaan (but only after a period of bondage in a foreign land). Abraham, for his part, undertook to recognize and serve the One God. A formal covenant was made; its sign was circumcision, which Abraham performed on himself, his family and his entourage.

After a dispute between the followers of Lot and Abraham, Lot and his camp moved to the Dead Sea area while Abraham remained in the mountainous region and the Negeb. There he was visited by three angel-messengers who brought the tidings that he and Sarah (now both aged around 100) would at last have a son; Sarah treated this as a joke (providing a folk etymology for the name of their son when he was born – ISAAC, i.e. 'he will laugh'). They also informed Abraham that they were on a divine errand to destroy the cities of Sodom and Gomorrah for their wickedness. Abraham pleaded with God not to punish indiscriminately the righteous with the wicked; but when God agreed to relent should there be ten righteous men in the cities, Abraham failed to locate them.

Previously Abraham had fathered a son, Ishmael, by Sarah's handmaiden, Hagar, but after the birth of Isaac, Sarah insisted upon their expulsion from the household. They were cast into the wilderness but miraculously saved. The episode legitimizes the divine heritage of Isaac (to whom the covenant was later reaffirmed) and his descendants in preference to the neighbouring peoples, traditionally of Ishmaelite descent.

When Isaac was still 'a young lad' (according to the text, although to go by the chronology he was already in his thirties), God instructed Abraham to sacrifice him. Abraham unhesitatingly followed the divine dictate and prepared to slaughter the boy on an altar on Mount Moriah (many centuries later, identified with the site of Solomon's Temple in Jerusalem). At the last moment Abraham's hand was stayed by an angel who explained that God did not in fact want such a sacrifice but had been testing his faith. The story of the Sacrifice (or Binding) of Isaac provided a major theme of Jewish theology, with its message of absolute trust in God; it provided a prototypal inspiration for Jewish martyrdom. Some scholars have seen it as a veiled condemnation of the practice of human sacrifice. It was also an influential theme in Christianity (seen as a prefiguration of the sacrifice of JESUS on the cross) and in Islam. (For an account of Abraham in the Islamic tradition, *see* IBRĀHĪM.)

Abraham died at the age of 175 and was buried by his two sons, Isaac and Ishmael, in the Cave of Machpelah, which he had initially purchased as a burial plot for Sarah. In Arabic, Hebron is called al-Khalīl ('beloved [of God]', see 2 *Chronicles* 20: 7), which was a favourite epithet for Abraham in later tradition. [68: IV–X].

In Jewish religious thought Abraham is especially associated with the concept of monotheism, the covenant with God including the promise of the Land of Canaan to his descendants and his complete devotion, as evidenced in his willingness to sacrifice his son and heir. For his gracious treatment of the three angels (while he still thought them only chance passing wayfarers) he is regarded as the symbol of hospitality. [28; vol. 1: V]

Critical views which saw Abraham in terms of a local god or demigod have now been generally discarded. The biblical background to his biography has received striking confirmation in recent archaeological discoveries (especially at Nuzi and Mari). However, the historicity of Abraham is impossible to authenticate and some scholars regard him as an eponymous figure, symbolizing the emergence of the Israelite people (*See also* HAMMURABI.) (G.W.)

Abraham ben David of Posquières [xv] (*c*1125–1198). Talmudist in southern France. He was regarded as the outstanding rabbinic authority in western Europe. Pupils came from far and wide to attend his academy. Legal problems were referred to him from many countries and his decisions were accepted as standard.

The wide corpus of law contained in the diffuse Talmud required systematization and this work had begun in previous centuries, notably by ISAAC ALFASI. Abraham (better known as Ravad, an acronym of Rabbi Abraham ben David) wrote incisive critiques of his predecessors. The codification of MOSES MAIMONIDES' *Mishneh Torah* reached him in his latter years; he wrote a detailed criticism, coupled with praise of those parts of which he approved. He objected to Maimonides' pronouncement of legal decisions on controversial issues without indicating his sources, and attacked his pioneering formulation of religious dogmas as contrary to the spirit of Judaism. Although he himself composed a partial code of Jewish law, he was concerned that study of the codes would displace study of the basic sources, notably the Talmud. His critique of Maimonides was often published alongside the original. Regarded as one of the outstanding Talmudists of all time, Abraham was admired for his deep understanding of the text and his original definition of Talmudic concepts. [78] (G.W.)

Abravanel [Abarbanel], **Isaac** [xv] (1437–1508). Statesman, Jewish philosopher and Bible exegete. He succeeded his father as Treasurer to the King of Portugal. Following a change of regime he had to flee to Spain (1483), where he became advisor to Ferdinand and Isabella but failed to move them to quash the decree expelling the Jews from Spain (1492) [5: vol. 2: XIII, XV]. He himself left with the refugees, living first in Naples and then in Venice, serving in both places as financial advisor to the monarch.

Abravanel wrote diffuse, largely philosophical, commentaries on the Bible (except for the Hagiographa). Noteworthy were his commentaries on the often neglected Former Prophets, in which he drew on his own political experience. He divided the Bible into sections, providing a prolix discussion of the topics of each section rather than commenting verse by verse as had his predecessors. His approach was commonsensical but he was critical of the rational explanations of other commentators, notably MAIMONIDES, and although he opposed Kabbalah he allowed for esoteric interpretations alongside the literal. His messianic views (especially in his commentary on *Daniel*) were influential, even after the Messiah failed to arrive in 1503 as he predicted. He found ready ears for his teaching that the world was approaching its end and that the great Jewish suffering of his time could be equated with the pangs preceding the advent of the Messiah. His exposition of the messianic theme had an impact on the messianic movements of the 16th–17th centuries [18: XIII].

He was a Jewish pioneer in the world of Renaissance humanism and the first Jewish commentator to adduce social and political factors for understanding the Bible. Abravanel was the last of the medieval Jewish philosophers, although his philosophy lacked originality and had little influence on Jewish thought, which as a result of the expulsion from Spain was growingly centred on mysticism. However, in Latin translation, his Bible commentaries were widely quoted by Christian scholars in the 16th–18th centuries. [56] (G.W.)

Abū Bakr [xii] (*c*580–634). Companion of MUḤAMMAD and one of his earliest converts in Mecca; at the end of his life, the first Caliph. Stemming from the Meccan clan of Taym, he always remained one of Muḥammad's closest and most faithful associates. He accompanied Muḥammad on his *hijra* or migration from Mecca to Medina in 622 (Qur'ān 9: 40), and his young daughter ʿĀISHA was early betrothed to the Prophet and became his favourite wife. During Muḥammad's last illness in 632, Abū Bakr was designated leader of the corporate Muslim worship (the *ṣalāt*), and on the former's death succeeded as first Caliph (literally, 'Successor [of Muḥammad]'), temporal head of the new Muslim community and its war leader. His two years' tenure of this office was filled with the so-called *ridda* wars, when outlying Arabian tribes threw off the suzerainty of Medina; he successfully directed military operations for the reimposition of the political control of Medina over western Arabia and imposition of its authority for the first time over the eastern and southern parts of the peninsula. He may thus be regarded as the man who made firm the fabric of the nascent Islamic community and who laid the bases for the expansion of the faith by Arab arms outside Arabia during the caliphate of his successor ʿUMAR IBN AL-KHAṬṬĀB. Later popular tradition emphasized Abū Bakr's unquestioning faith and devotion – he is said to have expended his fortune in Mecca buying up believing slaves from pagan owners, and acquired the sobriquet of *al-Ṣiddīq*, the one testifying to the truth of Muḥammad's mission – and his mild and God-fearing nature earned him the further designation of *al-Bakka'* ('the Copious Weeper'), a touch probably added under the influence of the ascetic traditions of the Eastern Christian Church. [35: s.v.; 70: III] (C.E.B.)

Abū Dāwūd al-Sijistānī, Sulaymān ibn al-Ashʿath [xii] (812 or 817–889). Muslim Traditionist and scholar, compiler of one of the six canonical collections of Prophetic *ḥadīth*, of which those of AL-BUKHĀRĪ and MUSLIM are the most famous. Abū Dāwūd was born in Sijistān, travelled much in search of *ḥadīth*, and finally settled in Baṣra. He is reported to have learnt 500,000 *ḥadīth*, from which he selected 4,800 for his collection. In fact, the collection is available in a number of versions, exhibiting some differences in content. Among his teachers was IBN ḤANBAL, and both the Ḥanbalī and the Shāfiʿī school traditions claim his loyalty. He is said to have shown his collection to Ibn Ḥanbal, who declared himself pleased with it. A certain Ibn al-Aʿrābī is reported to have said that if a man had no other book than the Qur'ān and the book of Abū Dāwūd, he would need no further knowledge; Zakariyya al-Sājī declared the Qur'ān the foundation of Islam and Abū Dāwūd's work its pillar. Abū Dāwūd made similar claims on his own behalf. His work, known as the *Sunan*, is more narrowly focused than those of al-Bukhārī and Muslim, being almost exclusively devoted to juristic matters. It is more liberal in accepting *ḥadīth*, and contains therefore more, and more specialized, juristic material than al-Bukhārī or Muslim. The conditions for accepting *ḥadīth* relate exclusively to the chains of transmitters and not to the substantive content of the report. Criticism was based on historical considerations (could A have met B?) and on the moral and technical reliability of transmitters. Abū Dāwūd's collection contains *ḥadīth* recognized as reliable (*ṣaḥīḥ*) and some which are only nearly so. When the latter is the case he frequently adds justificatory comments, explaining why he has included them. The principle of commenting on the quality of a *ḥadīth* was significantly developed by AL-TIRMIDHĪ, pupil and follower of Abū Dāwūd. [35: 'Abū Dā'ūd; 41: 229–34] (N.C.)

Abū Ḥanīfa, al-Nuʿmān ibn Thābit ibn Zūṭā [xii] (*d c*767). Muslim jurist of Kufa and eponymous patron of the Ḥanafī school of law. Early records of his life are sparse and later ones, creative. His biography is neatly contained between two visions: a youthful dream in which he saw himself digging into the tomb of MUḤAMMAD (prefiguring a life dedicated to reviving the Prophet's practice) and a death-bed vision of the Prophet and Paradise. The only significant public event attached to him is his rejection of judicial office, concerning which there are many anecdotes. He rejected the post, saying, 'I am not suitable.' The Caliph said, 'You lie,' to which Abū Ḥanīfa responded, 'The Caliph has confirmed my unsuitability, for liars are not suitable for this office.' These skills were of no avail: he was imprisoned and shortly died. The biography of his pupil, ABŪ YŪSUF, exhibits a different approach to judicial office. As a jurist Abū Ḥanīfa prefigures the characteristics of his school, in which cleverness, skilful public display and even juristic trickery were not incompatible with a serious concern for divine law. Criticized once, in a story, for his failure to control unruly students, he commended their commitment to argument as a means to knowledge of the law. Outside the Ḥanafī tradition, he was vilified for a loose approach to the law, based on opinion rather than Prophetic tradition. In the realm of theology too he was associated with dogmatic positions contrary to orthodoxy, notably denial of the eternity of the Qur'ān. Other reports confirm the soundness of his views and, wherever his school dominates, the basic version of the creed is attributed to him. Abū Ḥanīfa has left no written law-books. Western scholars dispute whether he has left any theological tracts. In later legal works, he serves, together with his pupils, AL-SHAYBĀNĪ and Abū Yūsuf, to justify diverse views. This tripartite division of authority kept the Ḥanafī tradition open, alive and committed to debate. [35: s.v.; 137: VII] (N.C.)

Abū Yūsuf, Yaʿqūb ibn Ibrāhīm al-Anṣārī [XII] (*d*798). Muslim jurist of Kūfa and pupil to ABŪ ḤANĪFA; he became Chief Judge of Baghdad under the Caliph Hārūn al-Rashīd. From poor origins, he was spotted by Abū Ḥanīfa, provided with a bursary, and studied until he became an astute and wily courtier and jurist. His religious credentials were vouched for by Abū Ḥanīfa, who predicted that he would be the most learned person (in divine law) in the world and by IBN ḤANBAL, who seemed to approve of his knowledge of Prophetic Traditions. Together with Abū Ḥanīfa and AL-SHAYBĀNĪ, Abū Yūsuf is recognized as one of the three primary authorities of the Ḥanafī school of law. He represents (in contrast to Abū Ḥanīfa) the willing and capable servant of the state thereby providing the school with two models of approach to political power. He represents also the school's commitment to Prophetic Traditions. The role of Traditions in relation to juristic skill is neatly depicted in a story where, on replying to a juristic problem, Abū Yūsuf relates his response to a Tradition which he had heard from the questioner himself. The point is clear: knowing Traditions is one thing, knowing their interpretation another. Not all circles recognized either the learning or the skills of Abū Yūsuf. Such negative views were dispelled on his death when a vision was granted to a popular mystic in Baghdad. He saw a splendid pavilion built in Paradise for Abū Yūsuf, who had merited this for his teaching and for all the slander he had suffered. Of works attributed to him only one survives, namely the *Kitāb al-Kharāj* ('The Book of Taxation'). Some scholars recognize the authenticity of other works. The subject matter of the *Book of Taxation* suits the political career of Abū Yūsuf. It has been described as an administrative handbook, but it is also an exploration of moral and religious problems, worked out in a political context. In later works Abū Yūsuf figures as an authority in all fields of the law, confirming the views of other authorities or guaranteeing variant views. [35: s.v.] (N.C.)

Acosta, José de [VI.A] (1540–1600). Spanish Jesuit missionary. He was born in Medina del Campo, Spain and was admitted to the Society of Jesus in 1552. After studying in various Iberian schools, he was ordained in 1566, teaching theology both before and after he sailed for Peru in 1571. As Jesuit Provincial based in Lima, he made an extensive visit into the Andes (1573–74) to assess the evangelistic and ecclesiastical scene. With help from Quechua linguists, this enabled him to produce his monumental mission-manual, *De procuranda Indorum salute* (1577), which was translated as *Predicación del Evangelio en las Indias* ('Preaching the Gospel in the Indies', 1588) and his cross-cultural *Historia natural y*

Moral de las Indias (Seville, 1590). Though censored heavily, they were major contributions to missiology and the history of science. He played an influential missio-theological role in the Church's Third Lima Council before leaving for Europe, via Mexico, in 1586. He was convinced that wherever Catholics evangelized, they should emulate non-coercive, apostolic precedents. Scholastic and Aristotelian in much of his thinking, he had done his best in Lascasian style to provide guidelines for the colonization process and to lay a firm foundation for making Christians of the Andean peoples. During the last decade of his life he became embroiled in controversial ecclesiastical politicking between Spain and Rome. Nevertheless, his remarkable scriptural legacy from earlier days perdured in Catholic missions for many centuries and may have penetrated significantly into Dutch Protestant circles. [2; 203: 26–31; 493] (A.C.S.)

Adam and **Eve** [xv]. The progenitors of the human race, according to the biblical tradition. The word *adam* in Hebrew is used for 'man' generically, while a folk etymology explains Eve as meaning 'mother of all living things'. The Bible gives two accounts of their creation, ascribed by critics to two different sources. In the first (*Genesis* 1), God created them, male and female, on the sixth day of creation in his own image, granting them the blessings of fertility and rule over other forms of life, plant and animal. In the second (*Genesis* 2–3), Adam was created first, made from the dust of the earth, and God breathes into him the spirit of life. He is placed in the Garden of Eden, which is to be enjoyed freely with the exception of the tree of the knowledge of good and evil. God then decides man should not be alone and creates Eve from his rib as a 'fitting helper'. The Bible comments that this explains why a man leaves his parents and becomes as of one flesh with his wife.

The idyll ends when Eve succumbs to the wiles of the serpent and persuades her husband to eat of the forbidden fruit. The three guilty parties are all divinely punished: the snake condemned to move on its belly, the woman to suffer the pangs of childbirth and to be subject to her husband (presumably as against the original intention of sexual equality), and the man condemned to a life of toil. Lest they should eat of the tree of life and obtain immortality, Adam and Eve are expelled from the Garden of Eden. Little is related of their subsequent lives. They had three children – Cain, Abel and Seth – and Adam died at the age of 930. [68: 1]

While other Middle Eastern mythologies contain parallels to certain aspects of this story, the biblical account has unique features. These include its monotheism (in other cultures, many gods are involved and in some man is the direct offspring of a god), the concepts of obedience to the will of God, sin and punishment, and the implication of the equality of all men. The last is stressed in rabbinic legend, which relates that God gathered dust from all parts of the world to create Adam so that no place or people could claim a natural superiority. [28: II] (G.W.)

Adejobi, Emmanuel Adeleke [I.A.] (1919–). Current Primate of the Church of the Lord (Aladura) and one of Africa's most able independent church leaders. An Oshogbo Yoruba born in Nigeria, he received both his secular and religious instruction from the Anglican Church, although he was to continue his earlier studies at the Glasgow Bible Training Institute in the early 1960s. After leaving the Anglican Church, where he served for a time as a teacher, he became an influential member within Oshitelu's Church of the Lord (Aladura). He introduced the church to Sierra Leone (1947), Ghana (1953) and London (1964), and founded the Aladura Theological Seminary in Lagos with the aid of the Mennonite Church. He became leader of the church following Oshitelu's death in 1966 and has published widely, including *The Bible Speaks on the Church of the Lord*. [37] (R.H.)

Adret, Solomon ben Abraham [xv] [Known as Rashba from the acronym of Rabbi Shelomo Ben Adret] (*c*1235–*c*1310). Rabbinic authority in Spain. He lived all his life in Barcelona, where he served as rabbi for over 40 years. Because of his learning and personality, he was regarded as the intellectual leader of Spanish Jewry and was called 'the rabbi of Spain'. His reputation spread throughout the Jewish world. Queries were sent to him on matters of Jewish law and learning; his replies – numbering many thousands – were assiduously collected. They covered all legal aspects of Judaism – ritual, family and civil law – and provided lucid explanations of even the most complicated subjects. He had complete mastery of the writings of earlier authorities and his works were a major source for subsequent codifiers on whom he had a great influence. He himself wrote a code called *Torat ha-Bayit* ('Law of the House'), dealing primarily with Jewish home life, notably the dietary laws and laws concerning the ritual purity of women. His novellae on the Talmud, reconciling apparent contradictions, were carefully studied by later generations of scholars.

Adret was the author of polemical works against Christianity and Islam. The former was a result of his disputation with the Dominican friar Raymond Martini (or with his disciple), and deals mainly with allegorical interpretations of the Bible and the eternity of the Law. The latter, replying to the polemics of IBN ḤAZM, attacks the dogmas of Islam, notably the divine origin of the Qur'ān.

In response to demands by other rabbis, he issued an edict restricting the study of secular literature. While refusing the request for an outright ban applying to all students under the age of 30, he prohibited works on physics and metaphysics (except medicine) to those under 25, although permitting the writings of MAIMONIDES and other Jewish philosophers. [21] (G.W.)

Advayavajra. *See* MAITRĪPA.

Aelius Aristides [XXII] (mid-2nd century CE). Greek sophist (i.e. professional public speaker and intellectual), active in Asia Minor. Aristides' career was thwarted by a debilitating series of illnesses, to control which he spent most of his adult life in close contact with the temple precinct of the healing god Asclepius at Pergamum, which functioned as medical centre, hospital and spa as well as religious shrine. More important, Aristides entered a life-long relationship of dependence on the god of the centre, Asclepius himself [11: 39–45; 15: 85–104]. He felt himself under the special personal protection of the god, who prescribed his cures through the medium of dreams (the standard method at such precincts) and advanced his interests in other ways. The record of this relationship, and especially of the dreams and their outcomes, is preserved in Aristides' own journal, the *Sacred Discourses* (*Hieroi logoi*) [4; 23: 160–63]. Behind the somewhat unattractive character of a self-obsessed hypochondriac there lies at the heart of this work the real and touching devotion of a man who felt himself saved by the love of a god and in some sense united with that god. Hence the importance of Aelius Aristides and his *Sacred Discourses*: they afford a rare insight into the texture of the *personal* religious life of Graeco-Roman paganism (*compare* MARCUS AURELIUS). (R.B.)

al-Afghānī, Sayyid Jamāl al-Dīn (Asadābādī) [XII] (1839–1897). Outstanding Iranian Muslim reformer and propagandist, best known for his propagation of 'pan-Islamism'. He was born in Iran. Much of his early life was spent in neighbouring Afghanistan, where he was briefly involved in politics until 1869. He later travelled widely, visiting India, Egypt, Turkey, Iran, England, France, Russia and the United States. In Islamic countries, he became embroiled in political activity, stirring up controversy with predictable regularity.

In Cairo (1871–9), he profoundly influenced a young generation of religious and political reformers, including MUḤAMMAD ʿABDUH and Saʿd Zaghlūl. His activities there led the British authorities to demand his deportation to India. While there (1879–82), he started his main work, later published in Arabic (1886) as *Al-Radd ʿalaʾl-dahrīyīn* ('Refutation of the Materialists'). In Paris (1883–6), he wrote on Eastern topics for the newspapers, engaged in a famous debate with the philosopher Ernest Renan, and edited with ʿAbduh a short-lived but influential journal, *al-ʿUrwa al-wuthqā* ('The Firm Cord'). During the second of two stays in Iran (1889–91), where he had gone as a guest of Nāṣir al-Dīn Shāh, he quickly became a determined opponent of the regime. Forcibly expelled to Turkey, he made for England, where he agitated against Iranian despotism. His hand was behind the Iranian Tobacco Revolution of 1891, and it was one of his followers who assassinated Nāṣir al-Dīn in 1896. In 1892, he was invited by Sulṭān ʿAbd al-Ḥamīd to settle in Istanbul, where he died of cancer five years later.

Al-Afghānī is still regarded as the most influential figure in the creation of the modern Muslim response to Western colonialism and secularism. His aim of reviving and uniting Islam against the Western powers has gained much relevance in recent years, and many modern proponents of Islamic revivalism regard him as a precursor. [68; 69] (D.M.)

Agbebi, Mojola [I.A.] [David Brown Vincent] (1860–1917). One of the most impressive leaders of the early independent church movement in Africa. The son of a Nigerian (Yoruba) Anglican catechist, Agbebi had a varied ecclesiastical career of three decades, being associated with the Anglican, Methodist and Baptist churches as well as facilitating the emergence of a number of separatist churches. While in Dahomey, 1882–5, he had a vision of the independent African church of the future. In Lagos he helped found the Native Baptist Church and later the first Anglican secession, the United Native African Church. In 1894 he left his post as minister in that church to go to Sierra Leone and Liberia, where he became a Baptist pastor and assumed his African name. He facilitated another Anglican secession, the African Church (Incorporated), before leading his own Africanizing schism within the Native Baptist Church. Agbebi spent time in the United States and Britain, and became an important spokesman for the African churches and the defence of African culture. Despite his predominantly Baptist convictions, Agbebi possessed an ecumenical and transnational vision, and in 1913, under his leadership, the African Communion was founded as a fellowship uniting all the African churches that had emerged. Before that, in 1898, he had founded the African Baptist Union of West Africa. [2; 40] (R.H.)

Aggrey, James Emman Kwegyir [VI.A] (1875–1927). African Christian apologist. He was born at Anamabu, Gold Coast, lived in a Methodist missionary's house and became a schoolteacher. A connection with the African Methodist Episcopal Zion Church took him to the United States for education. He graduated from Livingstone College, North Carolina, and taught there. He married an American wife, was pastor of a church and studied at Columbia University. His reputation grew as a speaker on African and race issues; white audiences were attracted by his emphasis on co-operation between Blacks and Whites. His international status was confirmed by service on the Phelps–Stokes Commissions of 1920–21 and 1924. The commissions travelled throughout Africa and greatly influenced later educational and mission policy. Aggrey also became a celebrated speaker at student conferences in Europe and North America. Some of his sayings and figures ('Only the best is good enough for Africa'; 'Africa is shaped like a question mark'; 'The black and white keys of the piano') passed into common currency. He returned to live in his own country in 1924 as Vice-Principal of the new Achimota School which was to pave the way to higher education in Ghana. The time left to him was short; his work had been as the spokesman of a hopeful future for Africa. [204; 407; 408; 736] (A.F.W.)

Aglipay y Labayan, Gregorio [VI.A] (1860–1940). First leader of the Philippine Independent Church. He was born into a Roman Catholic farming family in Batac, in northern Luzon, Philippines. He studied theology in Vigan and Manila and was ordained in Manila in 1889. He was involved with other Filipino clergy in the revolution against Spain in 1896. Following American occupation from 1898 he led guerilla expeditions and became Vicar-General of the insurgent army against American occupation from 1898. In 1899, having assumed episcopal authority, he was summoned before an ecclesiastical court and was excommunicated when he failed to appear. The Philippine Independent Church (PIC) was formed and Aglipay unwillingly became its leader in 1902. In 1903 he was consecrated *Obispo Maximo* by a group of 12 priests. He and other patriotic Filipino clergy tried to persuade the pope to reorganize the church under Filipino bishops. This move failed and the Supreme Court restored all properties to the Roman Catholic Church in 1906. Other churches refused to collaborate and the church was led in a Unitarian direction. In 1927 affiliation with American Unitarians was established. In 1935 Aglipay published *Tres discursos notables*. He was successful in holding together the PIC, though with some secessions, from 1903 until his death. [676; 860] (T.T.)

Agnihotri [XI] [Shiv Narayan; Satya Nand; Dev Atma] (1859–1928). Founder of the Dev Samaj, who changed his given first name from

Shiv Narayan to Satya Nand, and later bestowed on himself the title Dev Atma or 'Divine Spirit'. These changes of name reflect a spiritual career equally remarkable for its sudden changes of direction, frequently caused by an intolerance of any authority other than his own which was to involve him in several protracted periods of bitter litigation. Born near Kanpur into an orthodox Brahman family, he received a college education and was appointed a teacher in Lahore in 1873. There he quickly became a leading member of the Brahmo Samaj and a bitter opponent of DAYANAND and his Arya Samaj. In 1887 he broke with KESHUB CHUNDER SEN and attracted many local Brahmos to his Dev Samaj, which originally added little to typical Brahmo theistic doctrines and concerns with social reform other than an emphasis on its leader's divine status. In the 1890s, however, Agnihotri's ideas were radically changed by his discovery of British materialist philosophy, notably Drummond's *Natural Law in the Spiritual World* and the writings of Herbert Spencer. He was thus led to formulate a religious atheism reminiscent of Comtism [32: 181], which viewed the human soul as a mechanical life-force, and had as its ideals the attainment of *mokṣa* through abandonment of the pleasure-principle and of *vikās* through the evolution of altruistic feelings. These ideals were perfectly exemplified in the record of Agnihotri's own life in his Hindi autobiography and laid down in his *Dev śāstra* (1917), whose regulations emphasize scrupulous financial probity and strict vegetarianism. Continuing to have a loyal if limited following among Punjabi Hindus, the Dev Samaj is particularly noted for its active involvement in female education, a tradition which goes back to Agnihotri's first wife Lilavati (1852–1880). [32: 173–82; 54; 55] (C.S.)

Agrippa von Nettesheim, Henricus Cornelius [XVII.A] (1486–1535). An important figure in the history of Renaissance Hermetic-kabbalistic magical philosophy. His *De occulta philosophia* (1531–3) presents a clear, essentially popular survey of the magical philosophy of FICINO and PICO DELLA MIRANDOLA among others. The work describes three worlds, the elemental (earthly), the celestial (the stars) and the intellectual (the angels). These worlds are interdependent, and Agrippa describes the way magicians may draw down the virtues and powers of the higher worlds by manipulating elements of the lower ones. It is not a deeply learned work but it is accessible, and it was produced in many editions during the period. The surprising feature of the work is that previous Hermetic-kabbalistic philosophers had gone to some lengths to demonstrate the spiritual purity of their philosophy; Agrippa allows the possibility of conjuring demons and producing religious miracles, although the truly powerful magician is also presented as a religious man. [11; 24: vol. 5: VIII; 25; 26] (T.L.)

Aḥmad al-Badawī [XII] (*c*1199–1276). The greatest of the Egyptian Ṣūfī saints. Born in Fez in Morocco, at about 11 years of age he accompanied his father to Mecca, where the latter died. After the reckless youth typical of Ṣūfī conversion tales, he underwent a radical transformation about 1230 and withdrew from the world. Following a succession of visions, he travelled to Iraq, where he is said to have visited the tombs of numerous Ṣūfī saints. Here he was initiated into the Rifāʿī Ṣūfī order, within which he received his spiritual training. In 1236, following the death of the Rifāʿī representative in Egypt, he was sent there to take his place, settling in Ṭanṭā, where he established his own order and remained until his death.

In Ṭanṭā, Aḥmad led an ascetic existence much in the manner of Indian yogis, being accredited with miracles and gathering a large following which became the nucleus for the Aḥmadī brotherhood, the largest Ṣūfī order in North Africa. His tomb in Ṭanṭā grew into a major pilgrimage centre, with the celebration of his birthday considered the most popular of the mass religious festivals in Egypt. The cult based around al-Badawī, himself a character of little importance who has left no literary legacy, seems to owe much to its incorporation of pre-Islamic elements. [35: s.v.; 115] (D.M.)

Aḥmad al-Tijānī [XII] (1737–1815). Founder of the militant North and West African Ṣūfī order of the Tijāniyya. Born at ʿAyn Mādī in southern Algeria, he was attracted early to the mystical life and travelled to Fez in Morocco, where he joined several Ṣūfī orders. From Fez he retired to a desert monastery in Algeria, remaining five years before undertaking a pilgrimage to Mecca. Initiated there into the Khalwatī order, he was sent to preach in the Maghrib.

In Tlemcen in 1781 he experienced a daylight vision of the Prophet, who instructed him to found his own order. For several years he gathered followers around him at a desert retreat, but in 1789 returned to Fez, the religious capital of the region. Given royal patronage and protection, he built a large Ṣūfī centre and established his new order as an effective rival to the existing brotherhoods.

The Tijāniyya attracted large numbers of Moroccan dignitaries and by the end of the founder's life had begun to spread in neighbouring countries. After his death, a complex system of succession preserved the order, particularly in Algeria, where the Tijānīs became allies of the French, who at one point aimed to turn it into a 'National Church' as a tool of French policy.

The order spread rapidly, notably in Senegal and elsewhere, where AL-ḤAJJ ʿUMAR IBN SAʿĪD AL-FŪTĪ and others established Tijānī states and launched *jihāds* against the French, animists and non-Tijānī Muslims in the latter part of the 19th century.

In religion, al-Tijānī introduced several innovations. He considered himself the highest embodiment of sainthood in Islam and a channel of grace between God and His creation. The Tijānī order is the last Ṣūfī brotherhood, to which exclusive allegiance is owed. These teachings, combined with Tijānī militancy, have made the order generally unpopular with orthodox Muslims. [3] (D.M.)

Aḥmad Khān [XII] (1817–1898). Indian Muslim reformist, commonly referred to by his double title 'Sir Sayyid'. Born into a noble Sayyid family of Delhi, he entered the service of the British, to whom his loyalty was demonstrated during the Mutiny of 1857. On his early retirement, he devoted himself to the advancement of the Muslims in British India, particularly through the modern system of higher education imparted at the Muslim Anglo-Oriental College he founded at Aligarh in 1875. His services were recognized by the conferral of a knighthood in 1888. Sayyid Aḥmad Khān was throughout his long life a tireless writer on all manner of subjects in Urdu, whose subsequent unchallenged status as the premier language of South Asian Islam indeed owes much to his example. The character of his major contribution to the reformist debate so hotly pursued among the Muslims of 19th-century India was determined as much by his unswerving loyalism to the British, for whose cultural values and scientific achievements his admiration was further increased by a visit to London in 1869–70, as by an increasingly rationalist approach to received Muslim doctrines going considerably beyond the position taken by such earlier thinkers as SHĀH WALĪ ALLĀH, to whom he acknowledged his indebtedness [19a: 141–2]. Sayyid Aḥmad Khān's openness to Christianity and his awareness of contemporary critical approaches are demonstrated in his partial biblical commentary, *Tabyīn al-kalām* (1862), but his most substantial achievement is his incomplete *Tafsīr al-Qur'ān* (1880–95), in which he attempted to establish complete conformity between revelation (*waḥy*) and the mechanistic Victorian conception of the laws of nature (*necar*) [6: 42–8]. The hostility generally aroused by this attempted rationalization of scripture led to his opprobrious dismissal as a *necarī*, but the reliance upon *ijtihād* which it implied was to prove more lastingly influential in South Asian Islam. [6: II; 19a; 131a] (C.S.)

Aḥmad Sirhindī [XII] (1564–1624). Shaykh of the Naqshbandī order generally regarded as the pivotal figure in the restoration of Islamic orthodoxy in Mughal India. Born in Sirhind in the Punjab, he was trained in the traditional religious sciences. An invitation to the court of AKBAR resulted in his spending some years in Agra assisting the emperor's liberal favourite Abu'l-Faḍl in his literary work, while he himself wrote two rigorously Sunni treatises, one attacking the Shiʿas, the other upholding the doctrine of prophecy (*nubuwwah*). Sirhindī's spiritual life was radically changed in 1600 on becoming the disciple of Khwāja Bāqī biʿllāh, a Naqshbandī shaykh from Afghanistan who brought to India a Sufi message closely based on orthodoxy, and who rapidly brought him to an advanced state of spiritual awareness. Succeeding his teacher as Shaykh in 1603, Sirhindī claimed for himself a unique spiritual authority. Considerable opposition was thereby aroused, and he was for a period imprisoned by Akbar's successor Jahāngīr, but his enthusiastic followers bestowed on him the title *Mujaddid-i alf-i* *thānī* ('Renewer') of the second Muslim millennium which began in 1591 CE. Sirhindī's teachings were chiefly expressed in his letters, collected in the three volumes of his Persian *maktūbāt*. Particular importance attaches to his arguments against the ontological monism (*waḥdat al-wujūd*) of Ibn ʿArabī long so popular with the Sufis, but which in India could appear so dangerously close to Vedantic monism, in favour of a phenomenological monism (*waḥdat al-shuhūd*) recognizing the existence of man separate from God [7: 186–8]. Always a fierce upholder of the *sharīʿah*, Sirhindī is also noteworthy for his vehement hostility to Hinduism [2: VII]. Caution is however to be exercised in fully accepting the 20th-century view of his special role in stemming the tide of Mughal syncretism which reached its high-water mark in the writings of Dārā shikoh [36a: IX]. [7: VII; 36a; 92: 243–7] (C.S.)

Aḥmad Yasawī [xii] (*d.*1166). Turkic Ṣūfī shaykh of Central Asia. His life story is shrouded in legend. He was born in Sayrām, which is now in China just north of Kuldja (Yining) and just south of the Djungarski Alatau mountains, which form the border with the USSR, in the second half of the 11th century; his father died when he was seven and his family subsequently moved to Yasī. There he studied with the famous Arslan Baba; later he went to Bukhārā, which was then a great centre of learning, and he studied with Shaykh Yūsuf Hamadhānī whom he succeeded as master when the latter died in 1160. Eventually Aḥmad returned to Yasī where he taught for the last few years of his life, dying in 1166. His tomb soon became a place of pilgrimage even for kings and princes, visited by devotees from all over Central Asia. The emperor Timur erected a mausoleum on Aḥmad's grave which is still visited by pilgrims.

Aḥmad Yasawī adapted the Islamic religion to his native Uyghur-Turkic beliefs and practices. His brand of Islam thence spread all across Turkic-speaking Central Asia and even as far as the Volga region. He wrote poetry in his native Turkic dialect in the old syllabic metre in order to spread his lore in a traditional form which the people, still mostly nomadic, could easily recite and remember. These verses have been collected in a book entitled *Dīwān-i-Ḥikmet*, although some of the poems in it may have been added later. This early Yasawī poetry created a new genre, that of popular, mystic songs with a strong didactic element, which continued to flourish side-by-side with the classical literature and the secular folk traditions. [35: s.v.] (J.K.)

al-Aḥsāʾī, Shaykh Aḥmad ibn Zayn al-Dīn [xii] (1753–1826). Founder of Shaykhism, an important 19th-century school of Shiʿite Islam, from which the messianic Bābī movement emerged. Al-Aḥsāʾī was born in the Shiʿite province of al-Ahsā' in the eastern Arabian peninsula. He studied there and later at the theological schools of Iraq. In 1806 he travelled to Iran, where he remained almost until the end of his life.

While in Iran, he acquired a considerable reputation as one of the leading Shiʿite clerics of his day, attracting the attention of the king and various notables, and acquiring a large following among religious scholars, many of whom studied under him. He was a prolific writer and is credited with over 100 titles, among which the best known are the *Sharḥ al-ziyāra al-jāmiʿa al-kabīra*, his commentaries on the *Mashāʿir* and *ʿArshiyya* of Mullā Ṣadr, and the short *Ḥayāt al-nafs*, all written in Arabic.

In 1822, al-Aḥsāʾī was for the first time publicly condemned as a heretic, on the grounds of his stated views on such matters as resurrection, the ascent of the prophet Muḥammad, and the status of the Shiʿite Imāms. Of possibly equal importance in his condemnation may have been the shaykh's belief that he was privy to direct, infallible guidance from the Imāms, communicated to him in dreams and visions.

He died on 27 June 1826 in the course of a pilgrimage to Mecca, and was buried in Medina. His Iranian successor, Sayyid Kāẓim Rashtī, undertook the defence of his master's teachings from his headquarters in Karbalāʾ, Iraq, and in so doing brought into being a distinct school of Shiʿism known as al-Shaykhiyya and based around the teachings of al-Aḥsāʾī and Rashtī himself. Headship of the school later passed to the Ibrāhīmī family in Kerman, south-east Iran, where it remained until shortly after the Islamic Revolution of 1979. [28: vol. 4; 33: 'Shaykh Aḥmad ibn Zayn al-Dīn Aḥsāʾī'] (D.M.)

ʿĀ'isha [XII] (*c*.614–678). The daughter of the first Caliph ABŪ BAKR and the favourite wife of MUḤAMMAD, the only wife whom he married as a virgin, consummating the marriage when ʿĀ'isha was about ten years old. During Muḥammad's lifetime, she remained very close to him but produced no children for him, and after his death in 632, she was to spend nearly half a century as a widow, since retention of her honoured status as one of the 'Mothers of the Faithful' precluded remarriage. As the early unity of the caliphate began to show signs of breaking up during the caliphate of ʿUTHMĀN IBN ʿAFFĀN, ʿĀ'isha became drawn into politics, and after ʿUthmān's death, openly declared her opposition to his rival ʿALĪ IBN ABĪ ṬĀLIB, whom she regarded as indirectly responsible for the murder. She took part in the rebellion against ʿAlī, which culminated in the 'Battle of the Camel' (thus called because ʿĀ'isha's camel was a rallying-point for her side) in 656, but after the rebels' defeat she retired to a quiet life in Medina. ʿĀ'isha's closeness to Muḥammad during his lifetime subsequently made her a great source of traditions from him, amounting in number allegedly to 1,210; but only one-eighth of these were accepted as authentic by the compilers of the two canonical collections of traditions, the *Ṣaḥīḥayn* of AL-BUKHĀRĪ and MUSLIM, some two centuries later. [2; 35: s.v.; 39: 149–51; 82: LXIV–LXV] (C.E.B.)

Ajuoga, Abednego Matthew [I.A.] (1925–). Founder and Presiding Bishop of the Church of Christ in Africa (or JoHera, People of Love). A Kenyan of Luo birth, orginally baptized within the Anglican Church in 1945, he later served as a pastor before breaking away with 16,000 followers to found his own independent church in 1957. He has written several works (*African Tuned Hymn Book* and denominational booklets) and travelled extensively, including two years of study at Union Theological Seminary in New York during the early 1960s. Under his direction the church has constructed several supporting institutions including a homecraft training centre, a commercial school and a Bible school. [41: 42, 45–71, 130–31, 135–6] (R.H.)

Akalaṅka [XIII] (8th century CE). Prominent Digambara Jain logician. The accounts of Akalaṅka's life, while written several centuries after his death, reflect the strongly anti-Buddhist stance he adopted in many of his philosophical writings. According to the standard version of his biography, Akalaṅka and his brother studied clandestinely in a Buddhist monastery in order to master the intricacies of Buddhist doctrine so that the Jains could confute their greatest intellectual opponents. They were discovered, however, and during the ensuing flight Akalaṅka's brother was killed. Akalaṅka fled on alone and arrived at the court of the king of Kalinga in eastern India, where he was persuaded to engage in philosophical debate with the Buddhist teacher, Saṅghaśrī. Having become alarmed at Akalaṅka's obvious intellectual prowess, Saṅghaśrī summoned the Buddhist goddess Tārā who debated with Akalaṅka invisibly while hidden in a pot. Nonetheless, despite this supernatural intervention, Akalaṅka easily held his own against the Buddhist opposition until eventually a Jain goddess appeared to show Akalaṅka how to defeat Tārā completely, at which the truth of the Jain religion became popularly established.

Akalaṅka's significance lies in his organizing of the disparate materials relating to epistemology and logic found in the early Jain scriptures and in subsequent writings, thus enabling the Jains to launch an assault upon both Hindu intellectual orthodoxy and, in particular, upon the ideas of figures such as DHARMAKĪRTI, who defended the standard Buddhist doctrine of impermanence, abhorrent to the Jains, by the use of sophisticated logical techniques. Akalaṅka should therefore be seen as moving beyond UMĀSVĀTI's contribution through his virtually definitive systematization of Jain epistemology, which he correctly saw as being the area in which Jainism was most liable to controversion by rival religio-philosophical groups. [26].

Akalaṅka's most important works are: the 'Eight Hundred' (*Aṣṭāśatī*), a commentary on a work by Samantabhadra (5th century), which deals with the enlightened Jain teacher as an omniscient being and which also demonstrates how Jain relativism can overthrow the absolutism of other philosophical schools; the 'Investigation into Logic' (*Nyāyaviniścaya*), a work modelled on Dharmakīrti's *Pramāṇaviniścaya*, which deals in the main with the nature of perception but also addresses itself to other matters such as the Vedic doctrine of the non-createdness of scripture, and the *Rājavārttika*, a commentary on Umāsvāti's *Tattvārthasūtra*, which itself became the object of a vast commentary by the 9th-century Digambara writer Vidyānandin. None of Akalaṅka's writings has been translated into a Western language. (P.D.)

Akbar [xii] (1542–1605). Emperor of the Mughal dynasty in India, reigned 1556–1605 over the most extensive and powerful Islamic state ever constituted in the subcontinent. Akbar's religious policy marks him out from all other Indo-Muslim rulers. Reigning as he did over an empire whose peoples were in majority non-Muslim, above all Hindu, he arrived at a policy of conciliation and understanding with the non-Muslims, if only as a means of strengthening the fabric of the state, rather than a policy of confrontation and the forcible imposition of Islamic law and discriminatory practices. He married Hindu wives and declared a policy of toleration for non-Muslim faiths; he abolished the poll-tax on non-Muslims, regarded as the cardinal feature of humiliation for the unbelievers; he adopted certain Hindu food practices and participated in their festivals. Though himself illiterate, a lively intellectual curiosity about religions led him to found an *ʿIbādat-khāna* ('House of Worship'), where religious leaders of all persuasions, including Hindus, Jains, Jews, Zoroastrians and Jesuit Fathers could discuss their faiths; sessions in this house are illustrated in contemporary miniature paintings. Then in 1581 he founded a new religion of his own, the *Dīn-i Ilāhī* or 'Divine Faith', which involved a solar monotheism drawing eclectically on such influences as Zoroastrianism and Hinduism as well as Muslim Ṣufism; but this was always meant by him as the faith of a small élite circle rather than as one for the masses, and was combined with Akbar's affirmation that he remained a sincere, if unorthodox, Muslim. Controversy has in fact raged up to modern times as to whether Akbar should be regarded merely as a heretic or as an apostate from Islam. Though his policies disappeared with him and, indeed, provoked a conservative Islamic reaction after his death, they illustrate how Islam in India has had on occasion willy-nilly to adapt itself to, or to be influenced by, the pervading strength of the indigenous Indian religious and philosophical tradition. [7: II, vi; 35: s.v. and 'Dīn-i Ilāhī'; 124: V–X, XII] (C.E.B.)

Akhenaten [vii] [Amenophis IV] (1367–1350 BCE). King of Egypt of Dynasty 18. Amenophis IV, the son of Amenophis III and Tiye, changed his name to Akhenaten ('Servant of the Aten') as an indication of his allegiance to the Aten, a creator god symbolized by the sun's disc. According to one theory, Akhenaten effected a religious 'revolution' through his introduction of the sole worship of the Aten. Others evaluate his heresy as a restatement of an earlier belief in a supreme deity. The Aten, orginally an aspect of the sun-god Re, increased in importance throughout Dynasty 18 and particularly in the reign of Amenophis III. However, Akhenaten's unique contribution was to elevate the cult to a form of monotheism. The Aten was henceforth regarded as a universal creator god, a supreme and loving deity.

In the early years of his reign, Akhenaten resided at the old capital of Thebes, and allowed the worship of the Aten to flourish there alongside that of the great state-god, Amun (Amen-Re); in general the Egyptians honoured many gods. However, Akhenaten then moved in several ways to change the status of the Aten to an unprecedented degree. First, the king changed his own name; he closed the temples of the many gods and disbanded their priesthoods; and finally he moved the political and religious capital from Thebes to a previously undeveloped site. Known today as Amarna, Akhenaten's city was named Akhetaten (the 'Horizon of the Aten'); here, Akhenaten built great temples for the god's worship, several royal palaces, and official and administrative headquarters [23].

Akhenaten worshipped the life-giving power of the sun, symbolized by the Aten; he regarded himself as the god's sole earthly representative and he and his deity became virtually interchangeable in concept. However, political motives may have strongly influenced his 'revolution', for his actions effectively terminated the overreaching powers of the priesthoods, particularly of Amen-Re, which had come to rival the king's position in previous reigns.

The king's body has never been discovered, but, on the basis of sculptures and art representations, scholars have discussed and disputed theories relating to his suggested physical abnormalities. Sometimes he is represented in an almost caricatured form and his apparent physical peculiarities are even extended to all other persons shown in the scenes. This is a distinctive feature which identifies the art now practised at Amarna and elsewhere, inspired by the religious innovations which enabled art forms to break away from the traditional mould. The art also emphasized the Aten's creativity, expressed through a naturalistic representation of plants, birds and animals and extolling the joy and beauty of life.

In this cult, the importance of Akhenaten's wife NEFERTITI, is underlined. The royal couple lived at Akhetaten with their six daughters, one of whom married TUTANKHAMUN. At his death, Akhenaten lacked a direct male heir, thus weakening the position of his new cult, and his two young successors (drawn from a secondary branch of the family), Smenkhkare and Tutankhamun, were unable to perpetuate the Aten's status. Additionally, the cult had failed to gain support outside the royal court and, under Tutankhamun, the traditional deities were reintroduced. A successor, HOREMHEB, sought to eradicate all traces of Atenism and Akhenaten; he reinstated Thebes as the capital city, together with the multitude of gods and their priesthoods.

The city of Akhetaten, partly excavated in recent years, has provided much information about Akhenaten who remains a controversial figure. The Great Hymn to the Aten, preserved in texts carved in courtiers' tombs at Amarna [7], incorporates the tenets of Atenism and appears to have influenced the Biblical *Psalm* 104. (A.R.D.)

Akinyele, Isaac Babalola [VI] (1882–1964). Olubadan of Ibadan and Nigerian Independent church leader. He was born in Ibadan and attended Anglican schools locally and in Lagos. He rose steadily in the local administration, was an Ibadan councillor and eventually chief judge of the Native Court with a knighthood. He became Ikolaba of Ibadan in 1935, Balogun in 1953, and Olubadan, the supreme office for a traditional ruler, in 1955. He wrote a history of Ibadan.

He began as a zealous Anglican, and was a member of the synod when he joined the Precious Stone prophet-healing group in 1925. This led him eventually to association with JOSEPH BABALOLA's revival in 1930, and an active part in first the Apostolic, and then the Christ Apostolic Church, of which he became 'Chairman, head and father' in 1957. Committed to healing by faith, he rejected all medicines, African and European, and wrote books on prayer and spirituality. He originally refused the office of Olubadan because installation required non-Christian sacrifices; he was installed without the rites to which he objected. His brother became the Anglican bishop of Ibadan. [813] (A.F.W.)

Akiva [XV] (mid-1st century CE–*c.*135). One of the most influential figures in the formative stage of rabbinic Judaism. His early history is clothed in legend, which relates that until the age of 40 he was an unlettered shepherd. After marrying the daughter of a rich merchant, he left her to study; 24 years later he returned together with thousands of disciples. What is clear historically is that he had emerged before the end of the 1st century as one of the great teachers of his time, establishing an academy at B'nai B'rak (not far from present-day Tel Aviv). As a leader of the Jewish community in Palestine, he travelled extensively to solicit help from Diaspora communities and was a member of a mission to Emperor Domitian in Rome to plead for the cancellation of anti-Jewish legislation.

Akiva collected and organized the large body of oral traditions that had accumulated down the centuries, laying the foundation for its codification by JUDAH HA-NASI in the Mishnah. He was a major influence on the development of Jewish law, introducing innovations in the methods of its exposition which evoked the statement: 'What was not revealed to Moses was discovered by Akiva.' He maintained that Scripture, as God-given, contained no superfluous word or letter, and he derived conclusions from every unusual or apparently redundant spelling in the Bible. His chief opponent in this approach was Rabbi Ishmael ben Elisha, who held 'the Bible speaks in human terms' and should be understood in a straightforward, literal manner, and not through expositions that tended to be homiletic and far-fetched. Akiva's approach had a strong influence on *Targum Onkelos*, the standard Aramaic translation of the Pentateuch.

Akiva taught that man's own deeds would determine his ultimate reward or punishment. This stress on human free-will may have been directed against determinist elements in early Christian teaching.

Following the destruction of the Temple and the loss of independence (70 CE), he was convinced of the imminence of national redemption. This led him to hail Bar Kokhba, leader of the rebellion against Rome (132–5 CE), as the 'messiah-king', and it has been suggested that Akiva was one of the spiritual instigators of that revolt. However, after its suppression, he was arrested, not as a revolutionary, but for refusing to accept Emperor Hadrian's interdict on teaching the Torah. Even in prison he continued to teach his disciples; for this – despite his advanced age – he was cruelly tortured and martyred in Caesarea. [22] (G.W.)

Albo, Joseph [xv] (*c.*1380–*c.*1444). Spanish Jewish religious philosopher; pupil of Ḥasdai Crescas. In 1413–14 he was one of the chief spokesmen in the Disputation of Tortosa imposed on the Jews by the Christian authorities. The disputation, with its discussion of religious dogma, was followed by widespread conversions among Jews; Albo sought to stem the resultant crisis and strengthen the wavering faith of those who adhered to their religion. Accordingly he wrote *Sefer ha-Ikkarim* ('Book of Principles'), which was an attempt to determine the dogmatic roots of Judaism and their divine origin. [5: XI].

The need to define dogmas was felt in Judaism only in the Middle Ages. Albo's version, influenced by Crescas and Albo's contemporary, Simon ben Zemaḥ Duran, postulated three basic dogmas: the existence of God, divine revelation and the doctrine of reward and punishment. From these are derived corollaries or 'roots', belief in which is essential for a share in the world to come. The existence of God implies his unity, incorporeality, independence of time and perfection; revelation implies his omniscience and the gift of prophecy to his authentic messengers, especially Noah, Abraham and Moses; while from reward and punishment may be inferred divine and individual providence. These 'roots' in turn have 'branches', namely belief in creation *ex nihilo*, the recognition of Moses as the greatest of the prophets, the immutability of the Pentateuch, the attainment of blessedness through the observance of even one of the Commandments, resurrection and the coming of the Messiah. The secondary place assigned to the Messiah may be a reaction to the teachings of Christianity. Only Judaism, Albo stresses, may be ascribed to revelation and certainly not Christianity, whose theology contradicts the basic doctrine of God's unity [39: XVIII].

Albo's book featured prominently in subsequent Jewish–Christian polemics. (G.W.)

Alexander of Abonuteichos [xxii] (*c.*150 CE). Charismatic figure and cult founder, active in Asia Minor. His life and mission are known almost entirely from a single very hostile source, the humorous and satirical *Alexander, or the False Prophet* by the great essayist Lucian, with whom Alexander clashed personally. Alexander founded an oracle and mystery cult in the city of Abonuteichos in Paphlagonia [14: 187–9; 23: 241–50]. The cult was centred on an avatar of the healing god Asclepius in the form of a huge serpent named Glycon. Alexander himself acted as the god's interpreter, the principal celebrant and initiator into the cult's rites, and the interpreter of its oracles. Lucian portrays Alexander as a complete charlatan (though a shrewd entrepreneur) and his followers as credulous dupes. But the cult enjoyed a more widespread and sustained success than mere fraud would likely have produced. The contemporary coinage of Abonuteichos, featuring Glycon, attests the cult's official acceptance. Alexander is of some interest as a type of local religious leader and cultic innovator not otherwise well represented in the records of the paganism of the times. *Compare* Peregrinus, likewise the target of Lucian's pen. (R.B.)

Alfasi, Isaac [xv] [known by the acronym Rif] (1013–1103). Rabbinic scholar in North Africa and Spain. Born in what is today Algeria, he settled in Fez (the name 'Alfasi' means 'man of Fez'). He taught there until he was 75 when he was maligned to the rulers and had to flee to Spain. There he established an academy in Lucena and, as the first major rabbinic authority in Spain, laid the foundations for that country's distinguished rabbinical centre. He was therefore a major link in the shift in the focus of Jewish learning from

Babylonia to Spain via North Africa. [7: vol. 6: 84–90].

Alfasi's classic work is his *Sefer Halakhot* ('Book of Laws', also known as *Alfas*), an abridgement of the Talmud which was one of the most influential codifications of Jewish law. It extracted from the Talmud the legal material – civil, criminal and religious – organized it logically and systematically and determined the final rulings. It constituted a digest of the Talmud and was referred to as 'the little Talmud', becoming itself the subject of a considerable literature, and was studied even more widely than the Talmud itself. [81: X] (G.W.)

ʿAlī ibn Abī Ṭālib [XII] (*c*.600–661). Cousin and son-in-law of MUḤAMMAD, first Imām of the Shiʿites, and fourth Caliph of Islam. According to some Shīʿī accounts, ʿAlī became the first to believe in Muḥammad's prophetic mission while still a child. His father, Abū Ṭālib, was head of the Hashimite clan of Mecca, but had become impoverished. ʿAlī was, therefore, adopted by Muḥammad, then aged about 30.

In adulthood he became one of the prophet's most devoted supporters, being selected by him to carry out several important tasks on his behalf. When Muḥammad fled to Medina in 622, ʿAlī volunteered to sleep in his bed in order to mislead his enemies. He acted as one of the prophet's scribes, and was present at all his military campaigns, except for Tabūk, when he remained in Medina as his representative. His own military exploits became legendary.

ʿAlī was chosen as the prophet's 'brother' during a ceremony intended to establish formal links of brotherhood between the believers, and was afterwards married to Muḥammad's eldest daughter, FĀṬIMA. According to Shiʿite accounts, Muḥammad publicly named him his successor in an address delivered at Ghadīr Khumm about three months before his death in 632. This episode – recorded by Sunnī as well as Shīʿī sources – is crucial for Shiʿites as the central event on which their claim to legitimacy rests.

Following Muḥammad's death, ʿAlī was ignored in favour of ABŪ BAKR, ʿUMAR, and ʿUTHMĀN IBN ʿAFFĀN, the first three caliphs. However, a small group of ʿAlid loyalists, the *shīʿat ʿAlī* ('party of ʿAlī'), persisted in the belief that he was the rightful leader of the community. During the period of the first caliphs, he lived in retirement, devoted to religious pursuits.

On ʿUthmān's assassination in 656, ʿAlī was persuaded to accept the caliphate. The first trial of his strength came in the same year, when a triumvirate including ʿĀʾisha, a widow of the prophet, challenged his rule. The Battle of the Camel followed, in which he was victorious. He then established his capital in Kūfa, and prepared for conflict with Muʿāwiya, the governor of Syria. Following the abortive Battle of Siffīn (657) and subsequent negotiations, Muʿāwiya was declared Caliph by a section of the community and began to wage war against ʿAlī.

In January 661 ʿAlī was stabbed to death in a mosque in Kūfa by a member of the Kharijite sect, a group that had earlier broken from his allegiance and which he had treated harshly. The alleged site of his burial near Kufa subsequently became a shrine, around which the town of al-Najaf later grew up. It is today a place of pilgrimage for Shiʿites.

A large number of sayings, sermons, letters, and political discourses attributed to ʿAlī were collected in a single volume in the 10th century by the Shiʿite scholar Sharīf al-Raḍī. The authenticity of his collection, known as the *Nahj al Balāgha*, has been questioned, but its influence, both as an authoritative text for Shīʿī theology, ethics, and political theory, and as a work of Arabic literature has been considerable.

ʿAlī has always enjoyed great veneration among Muslims, whether Sunnī or Shīʿī. For the former, he comes second only to the prophet in holiness, while for the latter he is not only the first Imām but also the father of ḤASAN and ḤUSAYN, and the husband of Fāṭima.

As an Imām, he possesses superhuman, even quasi-divine qualities, chiefly as a recipient of divine inspiration and a repository of esoteric knowledge. Among some extremist Shiʿite sects (notably the ʿAlawīs [Nuṣayrīs] of Syria), he is worshipped as an incarnation of the universal soul and a divine emanation. Some groups have taught that he, rather than Muḥammad, was the intended recipient of the Qurʾanic revelation, while others have maintained that it was he who sent Muḥammad to mankind. According to certain Shiʿite mystical philosophers, he embodies the inner reality of all religion; he existed before the rest of humanity and was sent by God with every prophet before appearing openly with Muḥammad.

ʿAlī plays a central role in Ṣufism as the nominal progenitor of many orders and a transmitter of esoteric knowledge. Among the Turkish Bektashis, he forms a trinity with God and Muḥammad. [33: s.v.; 64; 67; 92] (D.M.)

Alinesitoué [I.A] (*c.*1915–). A prophetess among the Diola of Senegal, the Gambia and Portuguese Guinea during the Second World War. She had a series of visions of the Diola supreme being, Emitaï, which led her to introduce several new spirit shrines (*ukine*) that would help procure rain, but whose ritual offices would be open to all, regardless of wealth, age or sex. Alinesitoué taught of a renewed commitment to community, a stripping away of social and religious hierarchies, and a reaffirmation of many customs that had fallen into disuse. Despite her arrest and subsequent disappearance in 1943, Alinesitoué provided a series of new teachings that helped the Diola meet the crisis generated by the French occupation. Her emphasis on the supreme being revitalized traditional religions in this area of West Africa against the challenge of a colonial order, Christianity and Islam. [10] (R.M.B.)

Allen, Richard [VI.A] (1760–1831). American clergyman; a founder of the African Methodist Church. He was born in slavery in Philadelphia and sold with his family to a slave owner in Delaware. Following religious conversion under Methodist influence he borrowed money to buy his freedom at the age of 20. In 1786 he returned to Philadelphia as a preacher to a growing black Methodist community and tried to organize a separate black Methodist church. He led a group of his fellow Blacks out of the predominantly white St George's Methodist Church. However, in 1794, FRANCIS ASBURY, the local Methodist bishop dedicated Bethel Church; five years later Asbury ordained Allen as a deacon. In 1816 the African Methodist Episcopal Church was formed with Allen as its first bishop. He was influential in forming the Negro Convention Movement. [9; 294; 852] (T.T.)

Allen, Roland [VI.A] (1868–1947). English missionary. He was born in Bristol, the son of a priest of the Church of England. He studied at St John's College, Oxford and came under Anglican high church influence. Later he attended the Anglo-Catholic Leeds Clergy Training School. In 1892 he applied to the Society for the Propagation of the Gospel to be accepted as a missionary. After some time as an assistant curate in Darlington he was accepted by the Society and was sent to the North China Mission in 1895. In Peking he was caught in the Boxer Rebellion of 1900 and published a diary he kept entitled *The Siege of the Peking Legations* (1901). He returned to England and married Mary Beatrice Tarlton. In 1902 they went to China, Allen as priest-in-charge of a rural mission in Yung Ching. His health soon broke and they were forced to return to England. He was a parish priest for a time in Chalfont St Peter, Buckinghamshire but resigned over the question of 'baptism on demand' required of clergy of the Church of England and never held any living after that. Thereafter he published his famous work *Missionary Methods: St Paul's or Ours?* (1912), in which he attacked current Western missionary policies. Other works on missionary policy followed but his ideas were not taken seriously by missionary bodies until long after his death in Nairobi, Kenya, whither he had moved in 1932 to be near his son. [561; 625; 626] (T.T.)

A-lo-pen [VI.B]. The Chinese name of a Persian monk who, according to a stele erected *c.*781 and discovered by Jesuit missionaries in 1625 at Sian-fu in Shensi province, received approval from Emperor Tai-tsung (627–50) to promote Christianity in China. The stele records the Emperor receiving A-lo-pen in 635 and names 67 missionaries who worked in Sian-fu.

Nestorian missions to China were remarkably successful. From 1280 to 1317 a Uigur Bishop from China reigned over the Nestorian Church as Catholicos Yahballaha III. Rabban Sauma, also a Uigur, Bishop of Khan Baliq, visited King Edward I of England and Pope Nicholas IV during 1288. Ming persecutions eliminated Nestorian Christianity from China.

There were, for centuries, strong Nestorian communities across central Asia and into Tibet. Under Timur (1396–1405) most of these communities were annihilated. [5: XIII; 56: 180–81] (D.J.M.)

Āḻvār [XI]. The collective name for the ten Tamil Śrī Vaiṣṇava devotees – to which two further were later added – whose religious poetry forms the collection called *Nālāyira ppirapantam*, the '4,000 compositions', which celebrate 96 Viṣṇu temples, mostly in Tamil Nadu. Most scholars now agree on 7th to 9th centuries for these authors. The term *āḻvār* means 'deep (in devotion)', and is suffixed to the names of most of them. Best known of their number is the one female among them, ĀṆṬĀL: *See also* NAMMĀḺVĀR; TIRUMAṄKAIY ĀḺVĀR; TŌṆṬARAṬIPPŌṬIY ĀḺVĀR. [17; 43; 118] (J.R.M.)

Alves, Rubém [VI.A] (1933–). Brazilian exponent of liberation theology. He was born into a small town in the Brazilian interior but moved to the city as a teenager and took refuge in fundamentalist Christianity. At the Presbyterian Seminary in Campinas, he encountered professors such as Richard Shaull and awoke to the grim realities of Brazilian society. Repressive church leaders turned his early pastoral ministry into a very difficult experience. Like many contemporaries in the late 1950s, he left the organized church and has declared ever since: 'I belong to a frustrated generation and it is out of this experience that I think and speak.' [11: 551] In his doctoral thesis at Princeton Theological Seminary, he identified closely with the political theology of Europeans such as Jürgen Moltmann. His work was published in 1969 as *A Theology of Human Hope* [260: 27–29]. It was published in Uruguay as *Religión: ¿Opio o instrumento de liberación?* (1970). Having spent decades living under repressive regimes, he makes much of a suffering God, wrestles with capitalist affluence-for-the-few, and has explored what is required 'to establish a future society that is truly worthy of human beings' [297: 306]. His major works include *Tomorrow's Child: Imagination, Creativity and Rebirth of Culture* (1972) and penetrating sociological critiques of Latin American Christianity such as *Protestantism and Repression: A Brazilian Case Study* (1985). He is a professor at the University of Campinas in Brazil and is *the* philosopher of Protestant liberation theology – which he believes is presently being done not in an Exodus situation but 'in a situation of captivity'. [874: 61] (A.C.S.)

Amar Dās, Gurū [XXIII] (1479–1574). Third Gurū of the Sikhs. Although sources are very few the outline of his life can be determined. He was born in Basarke (near Amritsar), the son of Tej Bhān Bhallā. According to tradition he was a pious Vaishnava, prompted to search for a gurū by another pilgrim when proceeding on a visit to the Gaṅgā. GURŪ AṄGAD's daughter had married into his brother's family and he happened to overhear her singing a hymn. So captivated by it was he that he insisted on being taken to her father in the village of Khaḍūr and there became a Sikh.

Amar Dās greatly impressed Gurū Aṅgad by his devotion and although well advanced in years he was appointed to succeed him as third Gurū of the Panth. When Amar became Gurū he was already 73, remaining in the position until he died at the age of 95. While Aṅgad was still alive Amar was sent to the neighbouring village of Goindvāl, and when he succeeded as Gurū this became the new centre of the Panth. He continued the tradition of married Gurūs, his family numbering two sons and either one or two daughters.

As Gurū he assumed responsibility for the Panth at a time when it was settling down after the first flush of its early years. It had spread geographically and so pious followers were appointed by Amar Dās as *mañjīs*, looking after each congregation in the absence of the Gurū. The anti-caste *langar* (refectory in which all may dine) was apparently inaugurated in his time; and at least three rituals were introduced for the Sikhs. A sacred well was dug as a pilgrimage centre in Goindvāl; three festival days were designated; and a sacred scripture was recorded in four volumes (the so-called *Mohan Pothīs* or *Goindvāl Pothīs*). When he died he was succeeded as fourth Gurū by his son-in-law, GURŪ RĀM DĀS. [14: II–VIII] (W.H.M.)

Ambedkar, Bhimrao Ramji [IV] [Babasaheb] (1891–1956). Political leader, social reformer and founder of a new Buddhist movement in independent India. He was a member of the *mahār* caste in Maharashtra, a group which traditionally worked at menial labour, though some had used new economic opportunities in colonial India to change their social status. Only the second high school graduate from among the *mahārs*, Ambedkar eventually earned a doctoral degree in the United States and the title of barrister in England. His public life in India was devoted to building a movement which would encourage self-respect among untouchables and create new social and political opportunities for them in the face of opposition from caste Hindus.

Gradually Ambedkar and his movement became associated with Buddhism. In 1935 he stated that although he had been born a Hindu he would not die a Hindu, but it was not until 1956, two months before his death, that he formally became a Buddhist in a public conversion ceremony. Following Ambedkar's example, 4 million other Indians, most of them from oppressed social groups, also became Buddhists. In this continuing movement, in which Ambedkar is affectionately known as Babasaheb, his life is taken to represent that of an ideal Buddhist.

Ambedkar's Buddhist writings are significant in two respects. First, he argued that untouchables were originally Buddhists, and that they have been degraded and subjugated in Hindu society because they held fast to their Buddhism when other Indians turned to Brahmanical Hinduism. Second, in his book *The Buddha and his Dhamma*, he presented a rationalist, humanist and egalitarian Buddhism, supported by extracts from the Pali literature. He felt that a secular and social interpretation of Buddhism – a Buddhist social gospel, so to speak – would have wide appeal in India, even among caste Hindus. [1; 144] (C.H.)

Ambrose [VI.A] (*c*.339–97). Bishop of Milan. He was born in Trier, the son of a Roman imperial official, and governed a Roman province centred on Milan. In 374, after the death of the previous bishop, the Christians of Milan demanded that Ambrose be made bishop though he was not yet baptized. He accepted, was swiftly baptized and consecrated bishop. He became a champion of orthodoxy, attacking Arianism and paganism. He maintained the church's independence of the state and condemned emperors for what he considered immoral acts. His best known works are theological, *On the Sacraments* and *On Penance*, and moral, *On the Duties of the Clergy*. [12; 13; 219] (T.T.)

Amenemmes I [VII] [Amenemhet I] (20th century BCE). King of Egypt of Dynasty 12. As vizier of King Mentuhotep Nebtowy, Amenemmes seized the throne and inaugurated a new era (1991–1962 BCE). He restored pyramid-building, and established his favourite god, Amun (Amen-Re), as a great state-deity. His assassination is described in the text of an Instruction with which he is accredited, addressed to his son, Sesostris I. This is a treatise on regicide and was probably actually composed in Sesostris I's reign. [19: vol. 1: 135–9] (A.R.D.)

Amenemope [VII]. Ancient Egyptian author. The Instruction of Amenemope is preserved completely in British Museum Papyrus 10474, as well as in other sources. Although these are all of a later date, the text was probably composed in the Ramesside period (*c*.1300 BCE) [19: vol. 2: 146–63]. In contrast to earlier Wisdom Texts, this Instruction emphasizes the virtues of contemplation and endurance; man must now attempt to develop modesty, quietude and humility rather than seek worldly success. The individual is expected to follow a course of rightful action and to live his life according to the Egyptian principle of truth, order and correct balance (*maʿat*). Self-control is highly esteemed, and the 'heated man' is contrasted with the 'silent man'. However, a man can no longer aspire to perfection, since only the gods can attain this state. The text is important because of its alleged influence on the Biblical Book of *Proverbs* [9; 24; 29], and also because it reflects changed attitudes within Egypt. (A.R.D.)

Amenhotep I [VII] (16th century BCE). An early king of Egypt of Dynasty 18 (1550–1528 BCE). He was the son of Ahmose-Nefertari who, together with other early queens of this dynasty, wielded considerable political power. Amenophis I received an important temple cult, aimed to ensure the king's continuance as a god, a royal ancestor, and a ruler in the afterlife. However, in the village of the royal necropolis workers at Thebes (Deir el Medina), the craftsmen and their families worshipped Amenhotep I and his mother as the founders of the community, even when they were dead. Deification of individual human rulers was rare in Egypt, and the personal nature of this cult seems to have been unique. Amenhotep I was buried nearby, in the vicinity of the Valley of the Kings. [5] (A.R.D.)

Amoghavajra [IV] [Pu-k'ung Chin-kang] (705–774). The most celebrated master of esoteric Buddhism during its golden age in 8th-century China. Amoghavajra came to China (from, according to different sources, India, Central Asia or Sri Lanka) at the age of ten and studied under the Indian master Vajrabodhi (Chih-kang-chih, 671–741). Together with Śubhakarasimha (Shan-wu-wei, 637–735), these two monks were the major figures in the transmission of the esoteric Buddhist tradition to China.

Amoghavajra went to India in 741 and returned to Chang-an, the capital, in 746, where he received imperial support to perform esoteric rituals, build temples, teach and translate esoteric texts. He enjoyed an illustrious career in the centre of Chinese civilization for 30 years, during which time he received the support and favour of three emperors and was active in disseminating esoteric Buddhism. Through his activity esoteric Buddhism merged with indigenous Taoist practices to reach its height of prominence in China. Among his many disciples was Hui-ko (746–805), through whom the esoteric tradition was transmitted to KŪKAI and thence to Japan.

Amoghavajra's religious worldview was based on the *Vajraśekhara-sūtra*, an esoteric text which serves as the basis for the Vajradhātu maṇḍala, and which emphasizes the importance of the Buddha's wisdom. He also promoted faith in Mañjuśrī, the bodhisattva of wisdom.

Amoghavajra is credited with the translation of about 150 texts, placing him along with KUMĀRAJĪVA, PARAMĀRTHA and HSÜAN-TSANG as one of the most prolific and influential translators of Buddhist texts into Chinese. He was also famous as an accomplished performer of esoteric rites and prayers, and many of the magic formulae that he translated were used extensively in East Asia. [31: 335–6; 101; 197: 361, 500] (P.L.S.)

Amos [XV] (8th century BCE). Hebrew prophet. The first of the literary prophets of the Bible, he was also the first whose utterances have survived in a single book, called after him. He was a herdsman from the town of Tekoa, near Bethlehem in the southern kingdom of Judah, but his prophecies were uttered in the northern kingdom of Israel, notably at the sanctuary of Bethel and probably also at that of Samaria. He prophecied during a period of national prosperity and expansion, denouncing moral complacency and self-satisfaction at military achievement. He condemned the King of Israel, Jeroboam II, and his nobles for the social ills of the kingdom, castigating their oppression of the underprivileged as well as their hedonistic life of luxury. Amos' emphasis on morality as the supreme criterion for determining Israel's destiny marked a new epoch in the development of Judaism. His prophecies are filled with forecasts of calamities and doom unless Israel mends its ways. He was the first to express the possibility of the punishment of exile. God, he stresses, is responsible for the fate of all nations, but Israel bears a special responsibility by virtue of its covenant which imposes on it unique obligations, particularly in the ethical realm. Sacrifice is useless unless linked to morality.

Amos spoke of the 'Day of the Lord' when Israel would be saved and its enemies judged. Israel too would be judged and punished for its sins and is urged to repent in anticipation of this climactic event. His recorded prophecy concludes on a note of optimism foretelling the restoration of Israel and its glorious future. [38: II; 45: 363–7] (G.W.)

Amvrosy Grenkov [VI.B] (1812–1891). A teacher from Tambov, he joined the *starets* Leonid at Optina Wilderness in 1839, where monks had gathered round the ascetic brothers Moses and Antony in the 1820s. In 1860 he succeeded the ailing Makary as *starets*. Those who sought his guidance included Dostoyevsky, Tolstoy and the theologian Solovyev. In 1884 Amvrosy founded the Shamordino Convent. The lineage of Optina *startsi* survived to the Russian Revolution, prominent amongst them the elders Anatoly and Barsanuphy. [27; 30; 48; 49] (D.B.)

Anan ben David [XV] (8th century). Jewish schismatic; traditional founder of Karaism. Little is known of his life except that he was a rabbinical scholar of a distinguished family who founded a sect known after him as the Ananites. He lived in Babylonia, probably in Baghdad. Various accounts, most of them hostile, explain his rebellion, the best known ascribing it to jealousy of his younger brother's being chosen leader of the community. He did not have many followers, but brought together a number of small groups who rejected the Jewish establishment and rabbinic tradition, teaching a return to biblical fundamentalism. His followers were later assimilated into the broader movement of Karaism which looked back on Anan as its founder. [7: vol. 5: XXVI]

Anan's book, *Sefer ha-Mitzvot* ('Book of Commandments') became the basis of the Karaite schism. A legal-religious work, written in Aramaic, it rejected the Oral Law which normative Jewry (the 'Rabbanites') regarded as stemming from divine revelation to MOSES on Mount Sinai and which had been committed to writing in the Mishnah (the basis of the Talmud). The Karaites (who exist to this day in Israel, Egypt and Lithuania) accepted only biblical law to which they gave a rigorous, even ascetic, interpretation, including stringent Sabbath observance, the addition of fast days to those already stipulated in the Jewish calendar, severe rules on forbidden degrees of propinquity for purposes of marriage, and a rejection of medicine in as much as healing is in God's hands. [57: 3–20] (G.W.)

Ānanda [IV]. A first cousin of the BUDDHA, said to have been born on the same day though the details of his birth and death are known only from 5th century CE commentaries. He became a monk soon after the Buddha's awakening, and was chosen 20 years later to be his personal attendant. He performed his tasks with great devotion, taking care of the Buddha's needs, admitting and keeping away visitors, and at one point even risking his life to save his master's. It was through Ānanda's intervention that the Buddha granted the wish of his stepmother MAHĀPAJĀPATI and allowed the founding of the order of nuns. Some later texts reproach Ānanda for this, and also reproach him for his failure to ask the Buddha to postpone his entry into final *nirvāṇa*. Although he was renowned as a great preacher, he was still unawakened at the time of the Buddha's death, and so wept bitterly; but he attained release soon after, on the eve of the First Buddhist Council, where his unparalleled knowledge of the Buddha's sermons allowed him to recite almost all of the second section of the scriptures, the *Sutta Piṭaka*. Each text begins with the words 'Thus I have heard', which is taken to have been Ānanda's way of introducing the sermon he remembered. He died at the age of 120. [150: vol. 1: 249–68] (S.C.)

Anandamurti, Shrii Shrii [XIX] [Prabhat Rainjan Sarkar; Baba] (1923–1990). Founder of Ananda Marga. He was born Prabhat Rainjan Sarkar, in Jamalpur, Bihar, the eldest son of a railway accounts clerk. When his father died he became a railway clerk. Stories are circulated about his childhood – his having ridden a tiger, his command of languages, his extraordinary ability to recite long passages of scripture and his miraculous knowledge of distant events.

In 1954 Sarkar formed Brahma Ista Marga, later renamed Ananda Marga (Path of Bliss), as an international socio-spiritual organization, teaching Tantra Yoga. Sarkar's political ideas, formulated in PROUT (PROgressive Utilization Theory), criticize the materialism of both capitalism and socialism, and advocate change through voluntary movements and a fairer redistribution of income and wealth [53]. Other organizations associated with Sarkar's thought include AMURT, ERAWS, RU and RAWA, which have been responsible for the establishment of numerous schools (particularly in India), social and relief work (especially in the developing countries) and providing yoga and meditation classes around the world.

Sarkar and his movement have been the subject of considerable controversy and persecution [50]. In 1971 Sarkar was imprisoned on charges that included abetment to murder. While he was in prison there is said to have been an attempt to poison him [50: 53]; he began a long fast, becoming seriously ill. Following Indira Gandhi's 1975 Declaration of Emergency, Ananda Marga was banned as a 'terrorist organization'. A number of Margiis set fire to themselves as a protest against Sarkar's imprisonment [50: 19, 47]. After a retrial in 1978 he was found not guilty and released.

Sarkar has written over 100 volumes on economics, linguistics, education, correct conduct, philosophy, science, history and spirituality [1; 2]. He is also said to have written over 5,000 songs within a five-year period on the theme of 'neo-humanism', a social ethic to enable humanity to overcome racial, religious, linguistic, national and other divisions. (E.B.)

Anaxagoras [x] (*c.*500–428 BCE). Philosopher from Clazomenae, who worked mainly at Athens. His most important doctrine was that the world is set in order and governed by *Nous* (Mind or Intellect), for which he was praised by ARISTOTLE [46: 984b] as the first sober thinker, but criticized by SOCRATES and PLATO for not going on to give a complete teleological explanation of the world, in terms of why it is good for things to be as they are [62: 97–100]. He was also the first to deny the divinity of the heavenly bodies, for which, in a rare departure from the Athenian ideal of *parrhesia* (freedom of speech), he was prosecuted for impiety (like Socrates, and possibly Protagoras), and sent into exile. However, no attempt was made to suppress his book, which according to Plato [62: 26d] could be bought 'for a drachma at most'. [20: vol. 2; 48; 62] (H.L.)

Andrei Rublev, St [VI.B] (*c.*1360–1430). Russian iconographer. His name is closely linked to that of Theophan the Greek with whom he worked in 1405 but their styles are different. A spiritual son of Nikon of Radonezh, Andrei was a monk of the Trinity–St Sergei Monastery then of Andronikov Monastery near Moscow. He and his assistant Daniil Cherny worked on the Vladimir Dormition Cathedral (1408) and throughout the Moscow region. His icon of the Trinity caused a sensation when restored in 1904. Dionisiy (1450–1508) had a comparable impact on Russian iconography. The Stoglav Council declared Andrei's icons the canon others should follow. [85: V] (D.B.)

Andrew [VI.A] (1st century). An early disciple and later an apostle of Jesus Christ. According to one Gospel tradition he was called from sea fishing with his brother (Simon) PETER by JESUS to be 'fishers of men', hence he is associated in some Christian traditions with the missionary work of the church. Though not prominent among the followers of Jesus he was present at significant events such as the miracle of the feeding of the five thousand. Unreliable tradition maintains he was martyred on an X-shaped cross, hence the flag which denotes him as patron saint of Scotland. [228; 267; 644] (T.T.)

Andrews, Charles Freer [VI.A] (1871–1940). He was born in Newcastle-upon-Tyne, England, into a family of members of the Catholic Apostolic Church, founded by EDWARD IRVING. He was educated in Birmingham and in 1890 entered Pembroke College, Cambridge, graduating in classics in 1893. In Cambridge Andrews came under Anglican High Church influence and in 1895 became a member of the Church of England. He took up lay parish work in Monkwearmouth in the diocese of Durham. He was made a deacon in 1896 and priested in 1897. During this period, as a Christian socialist, he worked in the Pembroke College Mission among the poor of Walworth, London. In 1899 he returned to his Cambridge college as a lecturer and remained there until 1903. Thereafter, for ten years he taught at St Stephen's College, Delhi, as a member of the brotherhood of the Cambridge Mission and became acquainted with SADHU SUNDAR SINGH, who became a major influence on him. He soon became identified with the Indian nationalist movement and critical of missionary policy. He also changed his theological stance in a liberal direction which led to him leaving the Anglican priesthood for 22 years. Having met RABINDRANATH TAGORE in London in 1912 he joined him in his ashram at Shantiniketan in 1914. In the same year he also met Mahatma GANDHI, with whom he maintained close links. For the rest of his life he participated in Indian nationalist work and sought for reconciliation between the imperial authorities and the Indian nationalists. He died in Calcutta. [15; 596; 801] (T.T.)

Aṅgad, Gurū [XXIII] (1504–1552). Second Gurū of the Sikhs. He was born as Lahiṇā, probably in the village of Harike in central Punjab. He married Khīvī, the daughter of a Khatrī of Khaḍūr, and had three children. While leading a group on pilgrimage to Jvālāmukhī he encountered GURŪ NĀNAK in Kartārpur and was converted to the Sikh way. Before GURŪ NĀNAK's death in 1539 Aṅgad was chosen to succeed him in preference to either of Nānak's sons and was renamed Aṅgad to indicate his closeness to the first Gurū [53: 165–9]. His works, which are recorded in the *Ādi Granth*, testify to his reputation for austerities and loyal obedience. (W.H.M.)

Angelico, Fra [VI.A] [Guido di Pietro; Giovanni da Fiesole] (1387–1455). Florentine painter. He was a friar of the Dominican Order at their house in Fiesole and a painter of the Florentine school. Among his masterpieces are about 50 frescos, probably intended as aids to meditation, an altarpiece in the San Marco convent in Florence, taken over by his order in 1436, and frescos in two chapels in the Vatican. There are two of his frescos in Orvieto Cathedral. His work is mainly of a didactic nature as befits an Order of Preachers. His altarpiece in San Marco depicting the Madonna surrounded by Saints is important in the development of the type of altarpiece known as *sacra conversazione*. [656] (T.T.)

Ani (VII] (16th century BCE). A scribe in the palace of Queen Ahmose-Nefertari, wife of Amosis and mother of AMENHOTEP I (*c*.1560 BCE). He is accredited with a Book of Wisdom which imitates earlier examples such as PTAH-HOTEP. The text is preserved on Papyrus Boulaq 4 (Dynasty 22, *c*.850 BCE) in Cairo Museum, on a writing board, and on ostraca and other fragments, and was probably originally composed in Dynasty 18 (*c*.1400 BCE). It was copied as an exercise by schoolboys and displays many scribal errors [12: 234–42; 19: vol. 2: 135–46]. Ani gives advice to his son on suitable conduct and behaviour, but, although they retain many traditional concepts, these maxims basically reflect current middle-class values rather than the aristocratic concepts of earlier Instructions. (A.R.D.)

Ankhsheshonq [VII]. Even in later historical times, new Egyptian Wisdom Instructions were composed. British Museum Papyrus 10508 dates to the late Ptolemaic period (*c*.50 BCE) and provides the Demotic text of the Instructions of Ankhsheshonq, although the original composition may be of an earlier date. Probably written by an anonymous scribe, the maxims are set in the context of a story and are attributed to Ankhsheshonq, a priest of Re at Heliopolis. Visiting an old friend at Memphis (Harsiese, the chief royal physician), Ankhsheshonq becomes implicated (although he is innocent) in a plot to kill the king, and is thrown into prison, where he writes his Wisdom Instructions. [13; 19: vol. 3: 159–84] (A.R.D.)

Anklesaria, Tahmuras D. [XXVI] (1842–1903). Parsi priest and scholar. Born at Anklesar in rural Gujarat, he received a traditional upbringing and at ten years of age was a fully qualified priest. His brilliant intellectual gifts and eagerness to learn induced his uncle to send him at the age of 18 to Bombay. There, while working as a priest, he studied English, French and German, Persian, Sanskrit, Avestan and above all Pahlavi, the last both on traditional lines at the Sir J. JEEJEEBHOY Madressa and on modern principles under K. R. CAMA. In 1874 he was appointed lecturer at the MULLA FEROZE Madressa. He came to be a leading authority on Pahlavi, and was much consulted by Western scholars on that and on ritual matters. Married in traditional fashion at the age of four, he had 11 children and was never financially well-off, but succeeded in building up a valuable library. This included some unique and very important Pahlavi manuscripts which through friendships with Irani priests in Bombay he managed to obtain from Iran. These texts would otherwise almost certainly have perished, for conditions were still bad for Zoroastrians there. Tahmuras set up his own press to print works in Avestan and Pahlavi scripts, helping halt the growing tendency to neglect these for Gujarati. He himself prepared some admirable editions of unpublished texts, but diffidence prevented him bringing them out, and they were published posthumously by his son Bahramgore (1873–1944). Bahramgore was a considerable Pahlavi scholar in his own right. He studied Avestan and Pahlavi at Bombay University, and published numerous learned editions and English translations of Pahlavi texts. He was lecturer in Avestan and Pahlavi at the Jeejeebhoy and Mulla Feroze Madressas, and then principal of these combined institutions. He took an active part in the public life of his community, wrote articles and lectured on religious matters, and strove to defend orthodoxy against theosophy (*see* BLAVATSKY, HELENA PETROVNA) [20: vol. 2: 96–7] (M.B.)

Anselm [VI.A] (*c*.1033–1109). Archbishop of Canterbury. A native of Lombardy, he was educated in the Benedictine monastery of Bec, Normandy, under the tutelage of prior Lanfranc, whom he succeeded both as prior and as Archbishop of Canterbury. His accession to the see was delayed due to his refusal to accept control over the church by kings William II and Henry I. He rejected the right of kings to choose bishops and to invest him as Archbishop of Canterbury. During a period of exile in Rome he wrote *Cur Deus Homo*, on the theology of the Atonement. He maintained that belief was the prerequisite of reason, hence his famous dictum, 'credo ut intelligam' ('I believe that I may understand'). He argued in his *Proslogion* (originally titled *Fides quaerens intellectum* – 'Faith seeking insight') the ontological 'proof' of the existence of God. [712; 744] (T.T.)

Anskar [VIII] (801–865). The first Archbishop of the twin dioceses of Hamburg and Bremen, who devoted his life to the conversion of Scandinavia to Christianity. He was a monk in the Benedictine monastery of New Corbey, and about 825 was sent to Denmark to assist the Danish king, Harald Haraldson, who had just been baptized at Ingelheim, to establish the church there. Anskar began a small school for Christian boys, probably at Hedeby, but Harald was soon driven out by the Danes, and Anskar went on a mission to Sweden. He stayed two years in Birka, a prosperous market town where many Christians came to trade, and was then consecrated Bishop and later Archbishop of Hamburg and Bremen, with special responsibility for missionary work in the North. In 845 the first Swedish bishop was driven out, and the Danes raided Hamburg, destroying nearly all the churches and Anskar's library. However, he still made visits to Denmark and Sweden, and built churches at Schleswig and Ribe, although he failed to win over the people as a whole. Anskar constantly opposed slavery, and managed to free a number of Christian slaves; he showed great courage in his untiring work as a missionary. His Latin *Life* was written not long after his death, by his disciple and successor Rimbert, and was rediscovered in the 17th century. It gives a vivid and on the whole realistic picture of life around the Baltic in the early Viking Age, and of the difficulties of the early Christian missionaries. [8: introduction] (H.E.D.)

Āṇṭāḷ [XI]. A girl devotee of Lord Viṣṇu in his form of Kṛṣṇa. She composed *Tiruppāvai* and *Nāycciyār tirumŏḻi*, the third and the fourth works in the first Thousand of *Nālāyira ppirapantam* (*see* ĀḺVĀR). Āṇṭāḷ is said to have been found under a Tulasī bush, Tulasī being basil, sacred to the followers of Viṣṇu. Pĕriyāḻvār, another Āḻvār, found her, and raised her at Śrīvilliputtūr as his own daughter. She grew up refusing any mortal husband, regarding the god Kṛṣṇa as her Lord. She infuriated her foster-father, a priest of the god, by donning the garlands destined for his worship thereby, in Pĕriyāḻvār's eyes, polluting the offerings. Finally the god indicated acceptance of her as his bride and she vanished within his shrine. *Tiruppāvai* is of 30 stanzas and celebrates a midwinter festival for girls of the cowherd caste, who, desirous of husbands, bathe in the river. The ceremony also ensures abundant rain. The poem takes its name from the refrain at the end of each stanza: *orĕmpāvāy*, meaning, almost certainly, 'O my sole Idol' [33]. *Nāycciyār tirumŏḻi*, 'The sacred words of the dancer', is of 143 stanzas. In it she tells of her childhood, when her doll's house was destroyed by the mischievous Kṛṣṇa, and of her later marriage to him. One of its sections is sung to this day as a wedding hymn in Vaiṣṇava houses. [17; 33; 43; 118] (J.R.M.)

Antiochus of Ascalon [VI.B] (*c.*130–68 BCE). A Platonist, he studied with the sceptical Scholarch of the Academy, Philo of Larissa, and also studied Stoic philosophy. He rejected the sceptical tradition and led the Platonic school back to what he saw as the doctrinal position of the first generations of Platonists, believing their philosophy to be in harmony with the teachings of Aristotle and with the fundamental doctrines of Stoicism. He gave the Platonic school a strongly ethical orientation, opening the door to the eclecticism that marked Middle Platonism, and to the focus on the soul and its destiny. Eudorus of Alexandria, for example, in the 1st century BCE presents the end of human life as 'becoming like God in so far as possible', and sees the life of virtue and wisdom as the path to this end. The writings of Plutarch (45–125 CE) reflect an equally strong ethical concern and present a pure and refined doctrine of God. He defends the immortality of the soul and the freedom of human choice. His works have a religious tone, accepting the reality of divine revelation to individuals. Apuleius of Madaura (*b c*124 CE) belongs to the same Platonist tradition. His novel *The Golden Ass* shows a genuine religious devotion to the cult of Isis which Apuleius combined with his Platonistic philosophy. His philosophical theology is expounded in his work *On Plato*. His *On the God of Socrates* contains an important discussion of the daemons, eternal intelligent air-spirits with which he associates the human soul.

Celsus's *True Discourse* (*c*.179), the arguments of which can be reconstructed from Origen's magisterial reply, is an attack on Christianity based on Platonist philosophical positions.

Neo-Pythagorean philosophers of the 2nd century CE such as Numenius of Apamea, Nicomachus of Gerasa and Moderatus of Gedes revived interest in Pythagorean number mysticism: they drew freely on Platonic tradition, seeing Plato as standing in the Pythagorean tradition. Their views on theology tend to emphasize the plurality within the Divine, prefiguring Neo-Platonism. Numenius believed that the god, in the making of the world had to combat and reorder the world's evil soul.

Ammonius Saccas (*d c*240 CE), a convert from Christianity, taught both Plotinus and Origen: the distinct forms of Platonism they represent make it virtually impossible to reconstruct his doctrine. Given that both were interested in practical mysticism, it may be that an emphasis on mystical practice is part of their common debt to him.

In the Roman period Stoic philosophers such as Seneca (*d*.65 CE), Epictetus (*d c*138 CE) and the Emperor MARCUS AURELIUS (121–180 CE) also exhibit a strongly ethical interest, and a genuine religious feeling. Stoicism generally believed only in the temporary survival of the human soul until it returned to god in the great conflagration which ended each world cycle. [24; 42; 67] (D.J.M.)

Antonio the Counsellor. *See* MACIEL, ANTONIO.

Antony the Great [VI.A] (251–356). The father of Christian monasticism. He was born in Middle Egypt. When his parents died he retired into solitude, eventually moving off into the desert to live a life of prayer and penance. Others followed and formed a loose community accepting him as Elder. He taught them a life of prayer supported by their own manual labour, developing teaching he had received from St Paul of Thebes, the hermit. ATHANASIUS, who wrote his life, knew him well. He twice returned to Alexandria to confront the pagans (311) and to confute the Arians (355). Even when he moved much further into the desert, visitors and letters came from all over the Roman world, including a letter from the Emperor CONSTANTINE (337). [4; 5: III] (D.B.)

Aoko, Gaudencia [I.A] (*c*.1943–). Charismatic preacher of an African Catholic faith. Following the mysterious death of two of her children in 1963, this Luo Catholic woman received a prophetic call to reject traditional magic and create (together with Simon Ondeto) an all-African church named Maria Legio (after the Catholic Legion of Mary), offering free healing and exorcism by prayer. Her natural preaching skills drew thousands of Luo followers from Kenya and Tanzania. Despite her short-lived appeal and unsuccessful attempt to create a breakaway church, she inspired many women to seek release from sorcery and marital domination, and her movement challenged the structure of the Catholic Church by developing a married lay clergy. (R.H.)

Apollinaris [VI.A] (*c*.310–*c*.390). Born in Laodicaea, he received an early classical education. In 360 he was made bishop of Laodicaea. He was a close friend of ATHANASIUS but was later condemned as one of the arch-heretics of Christianity. His teaching has been compiled from the writings of his detractors or from fragments published under other persons' names. His teaching on Christology was challenged at the Council of Alexandria in 362, when he was able to persuade his critics of his orthodoxy. He seceded from the church after he was outrightly condemned at a succession of synods held in Rome in 374–80. The Council of Constantinople in 381 confirmed his condemnation. Apollinaris held that a human person was made up of body, soul and spirit; JESUS had a human body and soul but the human spirit was replaced with the Divine Logos. [473; 666; 663: vol. 3, 377–83] (T.T.)

Apollonius of Tyana [XXII] (*fl.* late 1st century CE). Itinerant Greek philosopher, moral teacher, religious reformer and holy man, active in the Roman empire [13; 14: 181–3]. Apollonius' career is known to us from a biography written over a century after his death, the *Life of Apollonius* by Philostratus [21]. This source is problematic since, apart from the lapse of time between subject and author, its tone and intention are frankly hagiographic: to establish Apollonius as the perfect type of holy man. Nevertheless, despite its marvels the work rests on the life of a real enough individual. There is also extant a collection of letters attributed to Apollonius, some of which are probably genuine [27]. These letters are addressed to both individuals and communities and are for the most part exhortations to personal and civic virtue. In the brief compass of what follows no distinction will be drawn between the 'real' Apollonius and the hagiographic figure. In any case, it is the latter that is the more important: Apollonius is one of the very few highly visible pagan 'saints' to set against the plethora of Christian counterparts within the same social framework of the Roman empire. Obvious differences set aside, his story resonates, sometimes quite strikingly, with that of another preacher and wanderer, the PAUL of Tarsus of *Acts*. And a century on from Philostratus, another pagan author, Hierocles, a zealous official during the Great Persecution, was to present Apollonius as a superior model to the Christians' JESUS. (The work, unfortunately, is totally lost.)

Apollonius identified himself with the Pythagorean school of philosophy (*see* PYTHAGORAS), a somewhat mystical sect enjoying a recrudescence at the time. Apollonius trained himself within this tradition through a long period of asceticism and silence. Since the Pythagoreans believed in the transmigration of souls, blood sacrifice of living creatures was repugnant to them, and Apollonius became a lifelong critic of this practice which was fundamental to pagan cult. Apollonius taught at no fixed centre but instead toured the cities of the empire giving philosophical and moral instruction (often of a practical nature fitting the local social situation, e.g. on the evils of grain hoarding and profiteering during a famine) and performing miracles (e.g. healing, expelling demons). He was always particularly interested in local religious practices and would offer advice for their reform. He undertook two great foreign journeys to acquire the wisdom of other cultures, to India to learn from the Brahmans, whose spiritual superiority he ever afterwards maintained, and far up the Nile to study with the Gymnosophists ('naked philosophers'), who disappointed him with their fractiousness. He seems himself to have been of a rather quarrelsome nature, feuding bitterly with his philosophical rivals and sometimes challenging the political authorities. He was imprisoned by the emperor Domitian, but escaped miraculously by teleportation. His death too was surrounded by marvels, and for many years after he received semi-divine cult worship, especially in his home city of Tyana. (R.B.)

Appar [XI] [Tirunāvukk'aracar] (late 6th century). One of the 63 NĀYAṈMĀR and author of books 4 to 6 of *Tirumuṟai*. He was born at Tiruvārūr into a Vĕḷḷāḷa family and was named Maru'ṇīkkiyār. He became a Jain, with the name Dharmasena, and was made an abbot, but he later came back to Śaivism through the intercession of his sister. Around 620 he 'converted' the Pallava king Mahendravarman I to Śaivism. Of his poems, some 3,100 stanzas are extant. Called Appar, 'father', by the youthful TIRUÑĀṈACAMPANTAR, he acquired the title Tirunāvukk'aracar, 'King of divine speech'. He was 81 years old at the time of his death. Appar's poetry is supremely that of the convert. Emotional, it is full of self-castigation for his Jain past. In his first hymn in *Tirumuṟai* book 4, Appar laments: 'I realized not the many wickednesses I had done.' He recalls with contempt his naked asceticism, self-denial and personal habits as a Jain, and now, as a Śiva devotee, expatiates on the glorious loving relationship between the god Śiva and himself. [28; 73; 118]. (J.R.M.)

Apuleius [XXII] [Lucius Apuleius of Madauros] (*fl.* mid-2nd century CE). A sophist and rhetorician active in Roman North Africa. Apuleius' significance as a religious figure rests on his authorship of a strange and brilliant novel, the *Metamorphoses* or *Golden Ass*, which tells the story of a man transformed into a donkey but finally restored to human form by the providence of the goddess Isis, whose cult he then joins [15: 68–84; 20; 25:

138–55; 36; 40]. Some suppose the book to be autobiographical, not of course in the literal sense (although AUGUSTINE OF HIPPO toyed with that idea), but in the sense of a spiritual Odyssey of fall and redemption. The description of the retransformed hero's initiation into the cult of Isis, *if* it can be trusted as a reasonably close record of the author's own experience, is our best – indeed our only – account of the objective act and the subjective experience of initiation into one of the Graeco-Roman mystery religions.

In contrast, another significant work of Apuleius is indisputably rooted in his experience. This is his *Apology*, a courtroom speech which he delivered in his own defence against a charge of magic brought by the relatives of his wife, a wealthy and attractive widow whom they claimed he had lured into remarriage by sorcery [36: 105–19]. The work is a mine of information on the magic and superstition of the times. (R.B.)

Āqā [Āgā; Āghā] **Khān I** [XII] [Sayyid Ḥasan ʿAlī Shāh Āqā Khān I Maḥallātī] (1804–1881). Last of the Nizārī Ismāʿīlī Imāms to reside in Iran, and the first of the modern line of Āqā Khāns. Born near Maḥallāt in central Iran, then the seat of the Ismāʿīlī imamate, he became Imām following his father's murder in Yazd in 1817. In reparation for his father's death, he was given a daughter of the reigning monarch, Fatḥ-ʿAlī Shāh, in marriage and appointed governor of Qumm, receiving the title 'Āqā Khān'. On the accession of Muḥammad Shāh in 1834, he was made governor of the south-eastern province of Kermān. Dismissed in 1836, in part because of internal dissension within the Niʿmatallāhī Ṣūfī order to which he was affiliated, he rebelled unsuccessfully against the government on two occasions and finally decided to flee to India, possibly in agreement with the British authorities.

Accompanied by about 1,000 followers, he moved to Qandahār, where he provided mercenary services for the British forces. Finally settling in Bombay in 1848, he reorganized the large Ismāʿīlī community there and grew both wealthy and politically influential. His increased central control over the social and financial affairs of his followers was much assisted by litigation in the British courts, culminating in a famous judgment in his favour by Sir Joseph Arnould in 1866. This laid the basis for the enormous wealth of his descendants, derived in the main from tribute given by believers.

The first Āqā Khān's successors, Āqā ʿAlī Shāh (1830–1885) and Sulṭān Muḥammad Shāh (1877–1957), continued the sect's close association with the British in India, while raising its prestige within the Muslim community generally. The latter, in particular, played a role on the international stage, affecting economic and social reform among Ismāʿīlīs while remaining conservative in matters of doctrine. [33: s.v.] (D.M.)

Aquinas, Thomas. *See* THOMAS AQUINAS.

Ardašīr I [XXVI] (3rd century). Founder of the Sasanian dynasty (reigned *c.*224–*c.*240 CE), which ruled Iran till the Arab conquest in the 7th century, and was noted for its zealous and authoritarian upholding of the Zurvanite form of Zoroastrianism [14: 149–55; 9: 112–13, 118–20] (*see also* KIRDĒR). Ardašīr founded fire temples, and probably launched the campaign, pursued by his successors, to replace cult images by sacred fires [9: 106–8]. Under him the priest TANSAR established the canon of Zoroastrian holy texts, and it appears to be in his reign that the 360-day Zoroastrian calendar was officially reformed by the addition of five extra days [9: 104–6]. All his innovations were claimed to be restorations of old ways, neglected by his predecessors, the Arsacids. [7; 10.3.1; 14: 86–96] (M.B.)

Aristeas of Proconnesus [X]. Aristeas fell dead in a fuller's shop, but when the fuller returned with his relatives to see the body it had disappeared, and a stranger from Clazomenae insisted that he had just met and spoken with Aristeas on his road. The Greeks of Metapontum (home of PYTHAGORAS) also saw him briefly over two centuries afterwards, when he demanded that they set up an altar to Apollo and a statue to himself, saying that he had visited them together with the god, though he himself had adopted the form of a raven. His poem *Tales of the Arimaspians*, lost to us, told how he went – whether in the body or out of it is not clear – to the land of the Issedones, where he learned of the one-eyed Arimaspians, the griffins which guard gold and the Hyperboreans (tales known elsewhere in Central Asiatic folklore). The shamanistic features of these stories – trance, journey of the soul which leaves the body in visible form, bilocation, connection with divination (Apollo) – can be no accident. They appear at the time when Greek colonists had settled on the Dead Sea, and met the Scythians of the North; and they embody experiences claimed by the modern Siberian *shaman*. Pliny *Natural History* 7.52, 174 preserves an even more interesting version than HERODOTUS 4.13–6: 'the soul [*anima*] of Aristeas was seen *flying out of his mouth* at Proconnesus in the form of a crow'. Sir James Frazer in the *Golden Bough* collected such tales of the soul which leaves the body in visible form, sometimes as a psychic double (Greek: *psychē*, 'soul'), sometimes in animal form. A further parallel in Greek sources is Hermotimus of Clazomenae, whose soul travelled and ranged far and wide while his body remained inanimate at home; but his enemies burned the body and his soul could not return. In PLATO's *Republic* [67: book X] the soul of Er the Pamphylian was away for 12 days from his apparently dead but unchanging body; it returned as the body was about to be burned with a tale of flying to a place of Judgement, from where evil souls were banished to Tartarus. [3: 110–11; 6: 140–41; 9: 36–7; 19: 193–6] (J.P.K.)

Aristotle [x] (384–322 BCE). Greek philosopher, pupil of PLATO, founder and head of the Peripatetic school in Athens. Aristotle is a key figure in the Western intellectual tradition who marked out the major divisions of science and philosophy (physics, psychology, ethics, logic, metaphysics etc.). His arguments for the existence of God and his discussions of the nature of the soul, while more humanistic than religious in inspiration (if the distinction is meaningful), were to prove profoundly influential in the late Middle Ages (especially the 12th century) within Judaism, Christianity and Islam. His writings consist of terse but lucid treatises debating the fundamental principles of particular areas of knowledge: best known are perhaps *De anima, Categories, Metaphysics, Nicomachean Ethics, Physics, Poetics, Politics* and *Prior Analytics*. He had little or no influence on religious belief and practice in his own day.

Aristotle was born in Stagira (on the North Aegean peninsula of Chalkidike, part of modern Turkey), the son of the court physician Nicomachus. He studied in Plato's Academy in Athens from 368 to 348 BCE, was appointed tutor to Alexander the Great in 342, and after his accession, founded his own school, the Lyceum, in Athens in 335 in opposition to the Academy. He died in Euboia, having left Athens after Alexander's death (323) to escape anti-Macedonian hostility.

His genius for exploring the assumptions, implications and hence inevitably the inconsistencies and ambiguities, of commonly held views concerning nature, society and the individual produced valuable clarification of an enormous range of problems. So incisive, however, were his analyses of the questions, that later writers often mistook them for authoritative answers. His proof of the existence of God, for instance, in *Metaphysics* bk. 12 (ch. 6–9) proceeds by marrying Plato's version of the cosmological argument (there must be an eternal first cause of motion) with an ontological argument based on the actuality–potentiality distinction of which he made extensive use throughout his philosophy. The resultant Unmoved Mover, eternally fulfilled in self-contemplation, is the product of reason rather than faith, and as such was later enthusiastically assimilated (with alterations) into theology, into Islam by (e.g.) IBN SĪNĀ (Avicenna) and, through the Muslim schools, into Christianity by (e.g.) THOMAS AQUINAS, and Judaism by (e.g.) MAIMONIDES. As pure form, however, the concept of the Unmoved Mover infringes Aristotle's own first principles of being, and in any case, he finds himself unable to pronounce (for reasons arising from his astronomy) on whether there are 55 prime movers or only one.

His position on immortality was similarly ambiguous. *De anima* bk. 2 follows a line of argument leading to a definition of *psyche* (soul) as a function of physical body (namely, being alive): this rules out survival after the body dies. However, *De anima* 3 argues that a mind which can comprehend eternal objects must (at least in part) be eternal, though perhaps not individual. The inconclusiveness of this analysis led to claim and counter-claim being laid to Aristotelian authority both in support of personal immortality – e.g. Ibn Sīnā – and against it – e.g. IBN RUSHD (Averroes).

Aristotle's formulation of rules for valid (syllogistic) argument is a solid achievement in logic, his exploration of different 'categories' of being (and meanings of the verb 'to be') is useful but well short of definitive. The attempt in ethics to base a moral code on the ideal of human fulfilment (*eudaimonia* – often mistranslated 'happiness') and the moderation of character (virtue as 'a mean') required to achieve it is ultimately unsuccessful. In physics the analysis of four 'modes' of inquiry (doctrine of 'four causes') he found a more universal key to progress than we do: in particular, while matter, form, and efficient cause (mover) are rightly distinguished as subjects of investigation, he failed to give an adequate account of any of them, and the fourth, the 'final cause' or ultimate goal of action, is far too problematic to bear the weight which Aristotle wishes to give it as linchpin linking cosmology, biology, physics, theology and ethics. But if asking the right questions rates more highly than giving the right answers, Aristotle stands squarely in the tradition of SOCRATES, and fully deserves his reputation as 'the master of those who think' (Dante). He also stands, with Greek medicine, at the source of the tradition of empirical science. In every area Aristotle tackled, he invariably began his investigations with a painstaking collection of detailed factual evidence. [10; 20: vol. 6; 46; 47] (G.R.N.)

Arius [VI.A] (*c*.250–*c*.336). Arius gave his name to a prominent early Christian heresy. He was probably born in Alexandria. He became priest in Baucalis in Alexandria and made his name as a preacher. He became involved in a theological dispute with the bishop of Alexandria. Only fragments of his work have survived, mostly in the form of popular songs, the *Thaleia*. The heresy concerned Christology. Arius found it impossible that any other being could share absolutely in the being of God. If it were maintained that Christ was divine or God then it could only be true in the sense that Christ had derived his divinity from God, not that he was co-eternally God; Christ was subordinate to God. Arius had supporters at Antioch who carried on his teaching for many years, even after Arianism was explicitly outlawed at the Council of Nicaea in 325. [418; 419] (T.T.)

Arjan, Gurū [XXIII] (1563–1606). Fifth Gurū of the Sikhs, was the youngest of the three sons of the fourth Gurū, RĀM DĀS. In 1581 he succeeded his father, the two older brothers having been passed over. When he died in 1606 he was followed as Gurū by his only son, HARGOBIND.

Throughout the years of Gurū Arjan and his predecessors the Sikh Panth had been steadily extending its popularity in the Punjab, particularly among the rural population and in particular amongst the people who were Jaṭ by caste. It was, however, still an exclusively religious Panth, preaching liberation through remembrance of the divine Name. The decision of Gurū Rām Dās to select Arjan as his successor had not been welcomed by his oldest son, Prithī Chand, who sought to find recognition amongst a portion of the Sikhs.

According to tradition Prithī Chand's followers were circulating spurious hymns; this led Gurū Arjan to decide that a definitive scripture (the *Ādi Granth*) was needed. For this purpose the four volumes collected under instructions from GURŪ AMAR DĀS (the *Mohan* or *Goindvāl Pothīs*) were used as a basis, and the work was carried out in Amritsar in 1603–4. The recording of all the hymns of his four predecessors together with his own substantial works and those of approved Sant poets was of critical importance, particularly after the death of the tenth Gurū, when the sacred volume came to be accepted as the literal embodiment of the eternal Gurū when the line of personal Gurūs had ceased. [38: 41–50]

Gurū Arjan's death marks the bridge between an exclusively religious Panth and one with political and military features. The Mughal rulers of the Punjab were evidently concerned with the growth of the Panth and in 1606 Arjan died in their custody. [5: 6] (W.H.M.)

Arminius, Jacobus [VI.A] (1560–1609). Originator of the theological movement of Arminianism. He was born in Oudewater, Holland and raised in the Dutch Reformed tradition. After studying theology at Marburg, Leiden and Geneva he became a pastor at Amsterdam in 1587, and later professor at Leiden in 1603. Although his theological training was in the Calvinist tradition his own studies led him to question the Calvinist view of predestination. Arminius argued that the full sovereignty of God was compatible with human free will and that through Christ humans received universal 'sufficient' grace as opposed to CALVIN's limited 'effective' grace. [44; 585] (T.T.)

Arnot, Frederick Stanley [VI.A] (1858–1914). Missionary in Central Africa. He was born in Glasgow. As a young man he joined the (Plymouth) Brethren and in 1881 began missionary work on that movement's strictly biblicist principles. He travelled alone, through large areas of what are now known as Zimbabwe, Zambia, Angola and Zaire. He did little by way of establishing churches, but opened the way for later missions. His journeys had unexpected political importance. He influenced Lewanika of Barotseland to ally with the Christian chief KHAMA III of the Ngwato rather than with Lobengula of the Ndebele, and in Katanga he warned chiefs about dealings with Europeans involving papers. [24; 252; 696; 697] (A.F.W.)

Asaṅga [IV] (late 4th century CE?). With VASUBANDHU the most important and influential theoretical thinker of the Indian Buddhist Yogācāra school, and, in effect, its founder. Little is known about his life, and his dates are a matter of conjecture. The tradition tells us that he was the elder (half-)brother of Vasubandhu; that he was born into a Brahmanical family in Puruṣapura (modern Peshawar); and that he took the name Asaṅga ('without attachment') only when he had penetrated to and understood the Mahāyāna Buddhist doctrine of emptiness (*śūnyatā*). Asaṅga was not able to achieve this understanding by himself. The celestial bodhisattva Maitreya, resident in the Tuṣita heaven – one of the many heavenly realms described in Buddhist cosmology – expounds the doctrine to him, and later promulgates through him certain texts of key importance to the Yogācāra tradition, texts that in the Tibetan tradition are called the 'five books of Maitreya'. Asaṅga writes commentaries on these texts, later converts his younger half-brother Vasubandhu to the Mahāyāna, and dies leaving the final systematization of Yogācāra scholasticism to Vasubandhu. [214: 273–4; 14: 247–58; 38: 154ff.; 171: 137ff.]

It is no longer possible to go behind this semi-legendary account and reconstruct the lineaments of the 'historical Asaṅga'. All that can be said for certain is that he was a scholar-monk active during the Gupta dynasty's unification of northern and central India, a period in which Buddhist intellectual life, like most other aspects of Indian cultural life, flourished. Asaṅga's importance for the tradition lies both in the works that he wrote and in the paradigm he provides for later Buddhists of the devout and scholarly life. There is considerable debate about precisely which of the many works attributed to Asaṅga by the later tradition can properly be said to have been written by him [76: 348–54]; most of these texts are not yet available in English translation in any case. It must suffice here to notice Asaṅga's *Compendium of the Great Vehicle (Mahāyānasaṅgraha)*, perhaps the most influential of all his works, especially in East Asia. [77; 137] (P.J.G.)

Asbury, Francis [VI.A] (1745–1816). He was sent by JOHN WESLEY to America in 1771 and soon took over the informal supervision of Methodist work in that country. In 1784 he was joined by THOMAS COKE, who had been ordained by John Wesley as a superintendent with a commission to pass on ordination to Asbury and others. Asbury and Coke began to call themselves bishops, much to Wesley's annoyance. The usage was officially confirmed in 1787 and the Methodist society became the Methodist Episcopal Church. Asbury's journal, begun in 1771, contains much of historical importance. [42; 226] (T.T.)

Asclepius [X] [Aesculapius]. The 'blameless physician' (*Iliad* 4: 194), whose sons Machaon and Podalirius, lords of Tricca in Thessaly, were in HOMER healers to the Greek heroes at Troy (*Iliad* 2: 729–33; 4: 192–219; 11: 504–20). So too in HESIOD's *Ehoiai* and Pindar's third *Pythian Ode* (475 BCE) [58a] he is a god-born hero (*see* HOMER), son of Coronis by Apollo. Taught to heal by the wise Centaur Chiron, he was struck dead by the bolt of Zeus when he raised the dead to life, so overstepping the limit set by the gods for man (*see* HOMER; HERODOTUS). Aeschylus and Euripides follow the same tradition of a mortal hero. But an Athenian inscription of *c*.420 BCE refers to him as a god, and from that time on there is abundant evidence of cult to him as a god, and of a most notable shrine at Epidaurus (*see* ISYLLUS), where the sick slept and were healed through dreams. Six tablets dedicated by the priests at Epidaurus to proclaim the god's cures and other wonders were seen by Pausanias *c.*180 CE. Two of these and parts of a third have been excavated by Kavvadias, and studied with great insight by Herzog [24], who notes parallels with Christian cures performed by the saints. Such parallels are also the subject of Hamilton's book [22]. (J.P.K.)

al-Ashʿarī, Abū'l-Ḥasan ʿAlī ibn Ismāʿīl [XII] (873–935). Muslim theologian instrumental in the enunciation of Muslim doctrinal orthodoxy. Born in Baṣra in 873, al-Ashʿarī was a pupil of al-Jubbā'ī (849–915), a prominent Muʿtazilite thinker, until the proverbial age of 40, when it is related that he had visions of MUḤAMMAD urging him to return to adherence to the authority of the Qur'ān and *ḥadīth*, rather than following the dictates of reason. Al-Ashʿarī came to hold that where conflicts occurred between these two sources and reason, things must be held to be the way the sources proclaimed, *bilā kayf*, 'without knowing how' this can be.

Various lists of al-Ashʿarī's works exist, some tabulating as many as 300 tracts having been composed by him. Many of these appear to have been polemical tracts written against 'heretics', but they also include works on the Qur'ān, tradition and dogma. Among his surviving works is his book *al-Ibāna* for example, in which he uses the *kalām* style of argumentation, setting up questions to be posed to his opponents who are stipulated to be especially the Muʿtazilites who 'interpret the Qur'ān according to their opinions with an interpretation for which God has neither revealed authority nor shown proof'. Al-Ashʿarī's method was based upon extensive use of the Qur'ān and the *sunna*, the 'example' of Muḥammad as found in the *ḥadīth* material, in order to formulate his rational arguments. He fully supported the position of predestination, God being pictured in the Qur'ān clearly as all-powerful and all-knowing; that God should not know and not be in control of what people were doing is clearly a problem if the free will position is embraced. For al-Ashʿarī, God creates the power for people to act at the moment of action (God being the only one who actually has the power to create) yet the individual is responsible for all he or she does. This responsibility is referred to as 'acquisition', that is that people 'acquire' the ramifications of their actions. God's attributes are real for al-Ashʿarī because the Qur'ān clearly states them and so it must be meaningful to speak of God's hand and God's face; de-anthropomorphization was one of the central elements of Muʿtazilite thought which al-Ashʿarī denounced, for he saw it as a symbol of rationalist excesses and wilful ignorance of the sense of the Qur'anic text. Still, he did not wish to deny that reason indicates that speaking of these attributes of God would seem problematic when put in conjunction with an infinite God. His solution was to speak of the reality of the attributes but that these are not attributes in the same way that humans have such: God does have a hand, but we just 'do not know how' this is to be conceived.

Al-Ashʿarī saw the Qur'ān as the eternal and uncreated word of God, precisely because it was the word of God and, therefore, must partake in the character of His attributes. Those attributes (most importantly knowing, powerful, living, hearing, seeing, speech and will) are all strongly affirmed by al-Ashʿarī, who argued that if God does not have these attributes in reality, then He is somehow deficient and that, of course, cannot be the case. All these positions are to be associated with traditional orthodoxy in Islam and have existed since the time of al-Ashʿarī, only being seriously brought into question in the 20th century. [17; 74; 105: v] (A.R.)

Asher ben Jehiel [XV] [known by the acronym Rosh] (*c.*1250–1327). Jewish rabbinic scholar and codifier. He studied in his native Germany and taught in Worms, succeeding MEIR OF ROTHENBURG as leader of the Jews of Franco-Germany (Ashkenaz). However, fearing the fate of Meir, who was imprisoned for years as he refused to allow his community to pay the blackmail ransom so as not to create a precedent, Asher left Germany and went to Spain in 1304, becoming rabbi of the prestigious community of Toledo. Jewish communities from all parts of Spain and beyond submitted their queries to him for decision while students flocked to his academy from as far away as Russia. The combination of learning, towering personality and noble character made him the outstanding rabbi of the time. [5: vol. 1: 297–301, 316–25]

He contributed to every branch of rabbinic study. His major work is his code of Jewish law, which abstracts the legal sections of the Talmud adding the views of later authorities. His main predecessors, ISAAC ALFASI and MOSES MAIMONIDES, had in their codes usually given the decisions of the authors (without the sources), and, moreover, had not reflected Franco-German scholarship and traditions. Asher gave expression to the Ashkenazi scholarship and also supplied the Talmudic sources that his predecessors had omitted. Thus, although the work was written in Spain, it combined the Spanish (Sephardi) and Franco-German (Ashkenazi) traditions. It constituted the foundation for the *Turim*, the definitive code compiled by his son, JACOB BEN ASHER. [81: vol. 2: 137–39]

Over 1,200 of Asher's responsa (replies to queries on matters of religious law and custom) are extant. They throw much light on conditions of Jewish communal life in 14th-century Spain. (81: vol. 2: 167–69] (G.W.)

Ashi [xv] (*c*.335–*c*.427). Main editor of the Babylonian Talmud. He headed the rabbinical academy at Sura in Babylonia for over 50 years; under his direction it was the leading and authoritative focus of Jewish learning in the Diaspora. Twice a year he conducted study months to which Jews flocked from far and wide to join the Sura scholars and students in the study of a tractate of the Mishnah. It is said that over the course of almost 60 years, Rav (i.e., Rabbi) Ashi guided students twice through the entire talmudic material.

Some two centuries earlier, the traditions of the Oral Law had been redacted by JUDAH HA-NASI in the Mishnah. Immediately the rabbinic academies in both Palestine and Babylonia began to discuss the Mishnah, sentence by sentence. The Palestinian traditions and discussions were edited in the Palestinian Talmud, *c*.400. About that time Ashi and his colleague Ravina undertook a similar organization of the parallel Babylonian material. For over 30 years they collected and arranged the vast corpus of legislative discussion and rabbinic lore that had accumulated. Ashi did not complete the work, which was largely concluded several decades after his death by scholars from the Sura academy following the patterns he had established [58: vol. 5] (G.W.)

Aśoka [IV] (3rd century BCE). King of a vast empire in North and Central India, *c*.268–239 BCE, the third monarch of the Maurya dynasty, founded *c*.324 by his grandfather Candragupta. This was the first really large-scale political unit that India had seen. Aśoka is known to us through two quite different sets of evidence. On the one hand, he left many inscriptions, on rocks and pillars, recording details of his biography and policies, religious exhortations etc. On these inscriptions is based the 'historical' Aśoka. One of them, Rock Edict 13, mentions the names of five Greek kings, ruling over areas of the old empire of Alexander the Great; they can be dated fairly accurately, and so it has been deduced that the edict must have been written *c*.256 BCE. This piece of knowledge is the basis not only for the dating of Aśoka's reign, but also for that of the whole of ancient Indian history. On the other hand, Buddhist tradition has preserved many stories of him, in a variety of kinds of text. Although we may say that these texts show us the 'legendary' Aśoka as opposed to the historical one (the inscriptions were only rediscovered in the 19th century, and seem to have been unknown to the Buddhist tradition), it would be wrong to forget the undoubted historical importance of the 'legendary' figure in Buddhist culture. The pictures which emerge from these two sources are, nonetheless, quite different from each other.

From Aśoka's own inscriptions one sees a committed lay Buddhist, tolerant of other religious groups, and concerned with the moral and social aspects of *dharma* rather than doctrines and soteriology. (He does not, for example, mention *nirvāṇa*.) One inscription records that in the early part of his reign, *c*.260, he waged a bloody war in Kaliṅga (modern Orissa); he felt remorse over the suffering it caused, and resolved in future to conquer only by 'righteousness' (*dharma*). Others show that he encouraged non-violence, banning animal sacrifice, discouraging hunting and fishing, and encouraging vegetarianism; opinions differ as to whether he abolished the death penalty. He appointed 'ministers of righteousness' (*dhamma-mahāmattas*) to spread awareness of his policies, and instituted a number of social services, such as medical care, and wells and resting-places on roads. Two of his edicts concern the Buddhist monkhood directly. One recommends the reading of certain texts (some of which have been identified with extant works); the other warns monks or nuns against causing splits in the Order, and threatens to expel them.

Two Rock Edicts (5 and 13) record *dharma* missions sent out by Aśoka, and it is this issue which connects the evidence of the inscriptions with the Aśoka who appears in Buddhist tradition. Naturally scholars have differed as to the precise correspondence (if any) between the two, since, for example, the term *dharma* in Aśoka's usage seems to have had a general moral sense wider than the specific doctrines and institutions of Buddhism.

The Aśoka depicted in Buddhist texts is a 'Defender of the Faith', siding with one or another school (depending on whose chronicles are telling the tale: *see* MOGGALLIPUTTA TISSA and UPAGUPTA), expelling miscreants and sending out missions to introduce the true Teaching and legitimate monastic lineage to other areas (*see* MAHINDA). The conversion from cruelty to righteousness is exaggerated on both sides: before, he murders his 99 brothers, hundreds of ministers and concubines, and wages war mercilessly; after, he constructs 84,000 stūpas, goes on extensive pilgrimages, actively 'purifies' the faith, and provides the perfect paradigm of the 'Universal Emperor' (*cakravartin*) who in Buddhist ideology is the social and political counterpart of the 'Universal Saviour' (i.e., the BUDDHA). These two 'Universal' figures co-operate in the work of instantiating the cosmic order of truth and salvation in space and time. [13; 167] (S.C.)

Aśvaghoṣa [IV] (2nd century CE?). Buddhist poet traditionally associated with the Kuṣāna king KANIṢKA; the dates of Kaniṣka and therefore also of Aśvaghoṣa are uncertain. Very little is known of his life.

Aśvaghoṣa was learned both in the literary and philosophical traditions of Buddhism and in those of Brahmanical Hinduism; he is perhaps the earliest Buddhist writer in India to have composed texts in beautiful, mellifluous, classical Sanskrit, and one of the earliest and best examples of the enrichment of the Buddhist intellectual and literary tradition by its entry into the mainstream of Indian intellectual life.

His most famous work is the *Buddhacarita* ('Life of the Buddha') [111], a complete biography of the Buddha from conception to death (*parinirvāṇa*), including also an account of the disputes over the relics of the Buddha, the first council, and the reign of the emperor AŚOKA. The work is of great literary beauty, as well as of great interest to the student of the development of the Buddha legend. (P.J.G.)

Atahuallpa. *See* 'ATA WALLPA 'INKA.

ʿAtallah [VI.B] [Aithalaha; Ahattallah] (*d* *c*1653). Ignatius Mar ʿAtallah was sent as bishop for the Syrian Christians of South India who were under the dominance of Roman Catholic bishops: he was captured, and despite petitions for his release, handed to the Inquisition. Many believe he was burned in Goa, but there is strong evidence he was sent to Lisbon, dying in Paris on the way.

Tradition claims the ancient Church in South India was founded by THOMAS THE APOSTLE. It became part of the Nestorian Catholicate of the East. Medieval European visitors record the presence of the St Thomas Christians in India. They formed a distinct and, like the Jews, a privileged community.

The arrival of Portuguese colonists brought dedicated Roman Catholic clergy, horrified by Nestorian elements in the liturgy used by St Thomas Christians and by customs they saw as Hindu. Under the Archbishop of Goa Alexis de Menezis the St Thomas Christians were brought into communion with Rome: at the Synod of Diamper (1599) their liturgical books were reformed in a Catholic direction, and all their ancient writings consigned to the flames. While most Syrian Christians stayed loyal to Rome, many longed for Syrian bishops to lead them. The terrible fate of Ignatius Mar ʿAtallah, who had arrived as 'Patriarch of India', led the anti-Roman community to swear an oath (the Coonen Cross oath) never to submit to Rome. Syrian bishops did arrive, but from the Jacobite church, not from the Nestorians. After centuries of external and internal difficulties, not helped by the readiness of certain missionaries to promote the establishing of schismatic reformed groups, Syrian Orthodox tradition is flourishing in South India and undergoing a spiritual and intellectual revival.

Malabarese Catholics are now the largest community descending from the Nestorian tradition: the Syrian Orthodox Jacobites of South India are the largest community of the Syrian Orthodox tradition. [5: XXI] (D.J.M.)

Atatürk, Mustafa Kemal [XII] (1881–1938). Turkish nationalist leader, founder of the modern Turkish republic and its first President. Born in Salonica and a professional soldier, it was he who, after the First World War, successfully raised Turkey out of the ruins of the defeated Ottoman empire, expelled the Greek invaders from its soil and set it on the path of secularization and westernization. Atatürk is thus significant not as a religious figure himself, but as the catalyst for the processes which transformed what had been a cosmopolitan, traditionalist Islamic society into a forward-facing, largely self-sufficient nation state. This was achieved by abolishing the Islamic caliphate, the moral and spiritual focus for Muslims, a role which had never been formally conferred but tacitly assumed by the Ottoman Sultans (1924), and by suppressing the Islamic legal and educational system, the dervish orders and other Islamic institutions which Atatürk and his followers regarded as forces for reaction and brakes on Turkey's transition into the modern world. Mention of Islam as the state religion was removed from the new constitution; above all, the change from writing Turkish in the old Arabic script – the vehicle for the Islamic sacred writings – to the adoption of the Latin alphabet was made (1928), a change of both religious and cultural significance, signalling a deliberate break with much of Turkey's past. Although post-1950 state policies towards religion have moderated, Atatürk remains the outstanding example in the Middle East of a forceful national leader able to wreak a radical religious change in his country. [35: s.v.; 79: VIII; 80: vi–xvi] (C.E.B.)

'Ataw Wallpa 'Inka [XXIV] [Atahuallpa] (*c.*1502–1533). Thirteenth Inca emperor, 1532–3. For several reasons, the brief reign of 'Ataw Wallpa 'Inka, bastard son of Huayna Capac, the eleventh Inca emperor, is significant. 'Ataw Wallpa 'Inka (known to 16th century Spanish chroniclers as Atahuallpa) was the last Inca emperor before the Conquest. He made the first official contact with the Spanish conquistador Francisco Pizarro in 1532. At the time of contact with the Spanish, 'Ataw Wallpa 'Inka had gained the upper hand in a civil war against his half-brother Washkar (Huascar). In April 1532 'Ataw Wallpa 'Inka's forces had captured Washkar, killed his family in public executions along the highway, and burned the sacred mummy bundle of the ancestor Thupa 'Inka Yupanki. His fortunes, along with those of the entire native population of the Andes, were to change dramatically in an instant. Invading Spaniards kidnapped 'Ataw Wallpa 'Inka when he came forward in his ceremonial litter to confer with them at Cajamarca on 16 November 1532. The emperor directed his subordinates to meet the Spanish demands for ransom and also ordered his brother Washkar killed. Pizarro used the murder of Washkar as a pretext for the continued incarceration of the emperor even after the ransom was paid.

'Ataw Wallpa 'Inka was garrotted by the Spaniards. His death is a most significant event in Andean history and is commemorated in popular theatre, myth, folklore and eschatology. According to these lively traditions, 'Ataw Wallpa 'Inka was beheaded, not strangled. His death was tantamount to the death of the cosmos, the plunging of the world into utter darkness and chaos (*pachakuti*, 'the world turned upside down'). 'Ataw Wallpa 'Inka is now an invisible force deep within the earth of the Andes. His head, buried and unseen, is revitalizing itself, sprouting a new body. When the head has grown a completely new body, Atahuallpa will reappear as the saviour, the Inkarri (from *inca*, meaning emperor, and *rey*, the Spanish word for king). His appearance will mark the onset of a new age, an end of colonial time. At that time, all evidence of Spanish overlordship will be destroyed and the Andes will return to the glories of the Inca Golden Age. From time to time, messiahs, prophets and military leaders have appeared in the Andes and declared themselves re-embodiments of 'Ataw Wallpa 'Inka and manifestations of Inkarri. The belief in the eventual resurrection of 'Ataw Wallpa 'Inka and the restoration of an eschatological kingdom under the leadership of Inkarri is a fundamental theme of Andean eschatology and soteriology. [6; 10; 16: 602–14 *et passim*] (L.S.)

Atcho, Albert [I.A] (1903–). Prophet, official healer and most famous layman in the Harrist Church in Côte d'Ivoire. Born into a Bregbo family of herbal doctors, he joined the Harrist Church (*see* HARRIS, WILLIAM WADÉ) in the 1940s and played a major role in its expansion, chiefly because of his renown as a healer. In 1967 he became chairman of the national committee that determines church policy. His herbalistic and anti-witchcraft activities have not only strengthened the healing function of the Harrist Church, but also widened its appeal. [1; 39: 112, 130, 134, 173 (n. 7)] (R.H.)

Athanasius [VI.A] (*c.*298–373). The champion of Christian orthodoxy against the Arian heresy. A native of Alexandria, he was made deacon by bishop Alexander just before the Council of Nicaea in 325 which he attended with his bishop. He was elected to succeed Alexander in 328, though opposed by Arianizing clergy and Eastern bishops. Between 328 and 334 he engaged in pastoral visits over a wide area of North Africa. In 335 a majority of pro-Arians at the Synod of Tyre deposed him. He was exiled by CONSTANTINE but returned to Alexandria after Constantine's death. Constantius II, son of Constantine, was persuaded by the Eastern bishops to exile Athanasius again in 338. He fled to Rome, where the local synod rehabilitated him. His position was ratified by a synod in Serdica (Sofia) in 342 but he was not able to return to Alexandria until 346. Again he was made to flee and he remained in seclusion from 356 to 361. In 366 he was recognized by a new emperor, regained office and held it until his death. Athanasius was influential at the Councils of Nicaea (325) and Alexandria (362) and his influence was felt at the Council of Constantinople (381) after his death. These Councils dealt with Arian Christology and its attack on orthodoxy. His Christology is found in *De Incarnatione, Against the Heathens* and in his *Discourse against the Arians*. [172; 417; 689] (T.T.)

Athenagoras [VI.A] (2nd century). One of a group of early Christian thinkers known as Apologists, who defended the doctrines of the Christian faith against non-Christian philosophers and detractors using the methods of classical philosophy. Athenagoras lived in Athens. He addressed his apology titled *Legatio* (late 170s) to the emperor MARCUS AURELIUS, who espoused a form of Stoicism and tried to force the church to recognize the state religion. Athenagoras tried to build a bridge between the Christian faith and Stoicism. He was the first to offer a philosophical defence of the doctrine of the Trinity. [27; 713] (T.T.)

Athenagoras I [VI.B] (1886–1964). Ecumenical Patriarch. Athenagoras came from Epirus to study in the Patriarchal Academy on Halki in 1903. In 1910 he was sent to assist the bishop of Pelagonia and in 1922 consecrated Metropolitan of Corfu. He became Archbishop of America in 1930, and in 1948 was elected Patriarch of Constantinople. Believing the Oecumenical Patriarchate too closely enmeshed in Greek politics, Athenagoras sought to find a modern expression of its primacy in the Orthodox communion. Anti-Greek riots in Turkey in 1955 damaged his policy, but contacts with JOHN XXIII, PAUL VI and Archbishop Ramsey made him a major figure in the Ecumenical movement. In 1960 he convened a pan-Orthodox synod to bring the Orthodox churches closer and focus them on contemporary issues. In 1964 he and Pope Paul VI revoked the anathemas of 1054 issued by the Papal Legate Humbert and Patriarch Michael Caerularius. [61: V. 3] (D.B.)

Atiśa [IV] [Dīpaṅkara Śrījñāna] (982–1054). Indian Buddhist monk. The place of his birth is not definitely known. He entered the Buddhist monastic order at the age of 29 in Bodhgaya, after extensive study of Mahāyāna Buddhist philosophy, and of tantra. His name is connected with that of NĀROPA, who may have been his teacher. Atiśa is also said to have studied in Sumatra for ten or twelve years (perhaps 1012–22), then a major Buddhist monastic centre with close ties to Bengal. When he returned to India Atiśa taught at the monastic centres of Vikramaśīla and Odantapuri, composing there several of his influential philosophical works.

At the age of 60, in 1042, Atiśa travelled to Tibet, and spent the rest of his life there. He, more than any other single figure, is associated with the 'second spread' of Buddhism into Tibet. His career there is treated by

Tibetan historians as of very great significance in the history of the establishment of Buddhism in their country, and he is effectively responsible, through the work of his disciple 'BROM-STON RGYAL-BA'I 'BYUNG-GNAS, for the establishment of the bka'-gdams-pa school in Tibet. [192: xi–xiii; 197: 479–81]. Atiśa's most influential work is probably the *Bodhipathapradīpa* ('A Lamp for the Path Towards Awakening' [192]), a short summary of the bodhisattva's path towards awakening in which the gradualist tradition of KAMALAŚĪLA is taken up and elaborated, and the monastic life presented as the ideal way of attaining the desired goal. [37] (P.J.G.)

Augustine of Canterbury [VI.A] (*d.*604/5). First Archbishop of Canterbury. He was sent in 596 by Pope GREGORY I (the Great) to re-establish the church in England following the invasion of the Saxons. He succeeded in converting Ethelbert, king of Kent, to Christianity. Having succeeded in his immediate task, he was consecrated bishop in Arles and in 601 was appointed first Archbishop of Canterbury. Shortly before his death he tried unsuccessfully to persuade the bishops of the old Celtic Church in other parts of Britain to submit to Rome. [68: book 1, cc. 23–33, book 2, cc. 1–3; 196; 376] (T.T.)

Augustine of Hippo [VI.A] (354–430). Bishop of Hippo Regius, a region of North Africa of which he was a native. He was born of a pagan father and a Christian mother, Monica, who like her son also achieved sainthood. Though introduced into the catechumenate by his mother at an early age, he was not converted to Christianity and baptized until the age of 33. Until this age he had been a student of law, literature and philosophy, had a mistress for 15 years and spent nine years as a member of the Manichaean sect (*see* MĀNĪ), which held dualistic beliefs concerning the creation of the world and practised severe asceticism. Having become disillusioned with Manichaeism, he went to Rome and Milan, where he came under the influence of AMBROSE. For much of this time he was attracted to the Christian life but could not forego his licentious existence. Finally he submitted and was baptized. He returned to North Africa in 388, was ordained at the behest of the people of Hippo Regius, continued a monastic existence, held great influence in the African church, became coadjutor bishop and eventually succeeded to the see. He fought against three heresies, the Manichaean, of which he had been part, the Donatist and the Pelagian. Augustine's teaching on the Fall, Original Sin and Predestination became acceptable to the Catholic and, later, to the Protestant traditions. [31; 38; 739] (T.T.)

Augustus [XXII] (63 BCE – 14 CE). First of the Roman emperors [35]. Born C. Octavius, he was adopted posthumously in the will of his great-uncle, the assassinated (44 BCE) dictator C. Julius Caesar – hence his personal name C. Julius Caesar Octavianus ('Caesar' to his contemporaries, 'Octavian' to historians). He immediately aspired to avenge his murdered father and to seize his control of the state, ambitions both of which he realized in a series of brutal civil wars both against the assassins (the 'liberators' of the 'Republican' faction) and against his principal rival among the Caesarians, Marcus Antonius. He achieved final victory over Antony and unchallengeable power throughout the empire at the naval battle of Actium [31 BCE]. In 27 BCE he consolidated that power constitutionally in a settlement which formally restored the Republic but in effect inaugurated the system of rule by an emperor, which was to last as long as the empire itself. Among the honours he received at the time was the name or title 'Augustus' (assumed by all subsequent emperors), a word of primarily religious connotations meaning something like 'the revered'.

Augustus' new name is an indication of the fundamental role that religion played in his personal and public agenda [16: XIX; 24: II; 26: VIII; 31: 254–72; 35: XXX; 38: III]. In reordering the state and society after the political and (as some saw it) moral collapse of the preceding half century Augustus sought to restore also the religious values and institutions on which, it was believed, the goodwill of the gods and thus the well-being of the state depended. He repaired many temples and founded magnificent new ones, such as that of Mars the Avenger (celebrating thereby his own filial 'piety' as his father's avenger). The public cult of the gods was carefully maintained. (Note, for example, the prominence given to the celebration of the 'Secular

Games', a great festival of state renewal, in 17 BCE.) The regime's religious ideology, essentially a conservative one, is reflected (though not in the form of obvious propaganda) in the great poets of the age (especially VIRGIL), and in some of its art, e.g. the Altar of Peace dedicated in 9 BCE.

Augustus' own person was hedged with a superhuman aura [37]. Since his father Julius Caesar was deified, he himself became officially 'the god's son' (*divi filius*). He received divine honours, gradated from (e.g.) the pouring of libations to his 'genius' at banquets in the capital to outright worship in the provinces (temples, priesthoods, festivals, etc. – usually in conjunction with the goddess Roma). At his death he too was definitively deified, becoming a god of the state cult. All these honours, including the position of high priest (*pontifex maximus*) to which Augustus was elected in 12 BCE, were routinely conferred on his successors.

Although Augustus was not a particularly 'religious' person in any spiritual sense, it would be a mistake to dismiss his policy and his honours as the cynical manipulation of religion for personal ends or the mere consolidation of his rule. His views on the centrality of public religion to the state's welfare were sincere, as was his sense of a personal mission and destiny with a religious dimension. He had a deep appreciation of the traditional religion of his people and a real flair for the institutional means through which their religious aspirations might be realized. (R.B.)

Aulén, Gustav Emanuel Hildebrand [VI.A] (1879–1978). Swedish Lutheran theologian (professor of systematic theology at the University of Lund) and successively Bishop of Lund and Strängnäs. He was one of the leaders of the *motivsforschung* school in theology which concentrates on the essential truth which underlies a particular doctrine rather than on the way in which the doctrine is articulated. His important works included studies on the Catholic Christian faith, the Christian idea of God and the Atonement of Christ. The last work was translated and published in English in an abridged form under the title *Christus Victor* (1931). [32] (T.T.)

Aurobindo, Sri [XI] [Aurobindo Ghose; Aravinda Ghose] (1872–1950). Indian nationalist and Hindu philosopher. He was born in Calcutta; his father was an atheist doctor, and his mother the daughter of Rajnarain Bose, leader of the Adi Brahmo Samaj (*see* TAGORE, DEBENDRANATH). He was educated in English surroundings at Loretto Convent, Darjeeling, St Paul's School, London, and King's College, Cambridge, where he gained first class honours in the Part I Classical Tripos, but did not complete his degree. Avoiding the Indian Civil Service career intended by his father, he joined instead the service of Baroda State, where he worked in education from 1893 to 1907. On his return to India in 1893 he immersed himself in Indian culture and politics; he was a leading opponent of the partition of Bengal (1905). Arrested for seditious journalism in 1908, he was acquitted after nearly a year in prison, during which he underwent a spiritual change. He started his own paper, *Karmayogin*, dedicated to the ideal of disciplined activity presented in the *Bhagavad Gītā*, but in 1910, warned of further official intervention, he fled to Pondicherry, then a French colony, where he began a new life devoted to the spiritual rather than the political regeneration of India. There he wrote the bulk of his work, much of it published in his own journal *Arya*, including *Essays on the Gita* [36: vol. 13] and *The Life Divine* [36: vols. 18, 19]. He developed a new system of Vedanta, called Purnadvaita or Integral Non-dualism, in which Brahman is the sole reality, yet multiplicity and change are included in that reality. Evolution, having passed from inert matter to life and mind, is destined to reach further stages of higher consciousness, in which the human will is united with the divine will. He interpreted the Vedic hymns and the *Bhagavad Gītā* in accordance with these ideas, and saw his earlier nationalism as an attempt to prepare India for the spiritual leadership of the world. A community, Auroville, exists in Pondicherry to carry out his ideals. [88] (D.H.K.)

Averroes. *See* IBN RUSHD.

Avicenna. *See* IBN SĪNĀ.

Avtār Sińgh [XI] (1899–1939). Second guru of the Sant Nirankārīs. By origin a Sikh baker in Peshawar who had been imprisoned as an

Akālī, Avtār Siṅgh became a disciple of Būṭā Siṅgh of Rawalpindi (1873–1943), who founded the Sant Nirankārī movement initiated within Sikhism by BĀBĀ DAYĀL (1783–1855). As systematized by Avtār Siṅgh, Sant Nirankārī teachings have little in common with those of orthodox Sikhism other than such superficial resemblances in terminology as the use of *nirankār* ('Formless') as a preferred name of God. Universal spiritual authority is claimed by the living guru as heir to a prophetic tradition extending from Noah and Rāma to NĀNAK and Dayāl [58: 27]. Avtār Siṅgh was himself given the title Shahinshāh ('Emperor'), while all members of the sect address each other as 'Sant' irrespective of their religious background, which is more likely to be Hindu than Sikh or Muslim. Initiation is through the *gyān*, a personal formula which may be imparted only by the guru or his appointed representative, and the appeal of the Sant Nirankārī Mission has been greatly aided by the liberality of its teachings, which explicitly repudiate the validity of all the dietary restrictions so important in India as markers of religious identity. Rituals include drinking the guru's footwash (*caraṇāmrit*) and congregational singing, particularly of the Punjabi hymns by Avtār Siṅgh and his followers collected in the *Avtār bāṇī* (1957), whose structure recalls that of the Sikh scriptures. Claiming over six million members, the elaborate organization of the mission is centred on the guru in Delhi and those chief disciples nominated as his Seven Stars (*sat sitāre*). In 1963 Avtār Siṅgh transferred the guruship to his son Gurbachan Siṅgh, whose murder in 1980 marked the climax of increasing tensions between the Sant Nirankārīs and orthodox Sikhism, whose mutual relationship is somewhat analogous to that of the Bahā'īs with the official Shiʿism of Iran. [35; 58: IV] (C.S.)

Avvakum [VI.A] (1620/21–1682). An archpriest of the Russian church who was put to death at the stake for attempting to restore what he saw as the primitive Orthodox purity of the church. He sought to revive liturgical and moral behaviour and was the founder of a group known as 'the Old Believers'. Patriarch NIKON of Moscow, following his election in 1652, instituted liturgical changes which drew intense opposition from Avvakum. As a result he was exiled to Siberia. During a further period of exile (1672–3) he wrote an autobiography in which he defended his own beliefs. A new patriarch in Moscow renewed the offensive against the Old Believers and Avvakum along with a number of supporters suffered a martyr's death in 1682. [623; 624] (T.T.)

Azariah, Vedanayagam Samuel [VI.A] (1874–1945). First Indian bishop of the Anglican church. He was born in Tinnevelly, South India, the son of a village pastor. They belonged to a low caste and his father was converted in a 'mass movement' of low and out-caste Hindus. Azariah was educated at a nearby high school and then graduated to a college in Tinnevelly and the Christian College in Madras. For ten years he worked as a secretary in the YMCA. In 1903 he was instrumental in forming the Indian Missionary Society which worked in Dornakal. Azariah himself became a missionary there and was ordained deacon in 1909. When the mission area was made into the diocese of Dornakal in 1912 Azariah became its first bishop and thus the first Indian bishop. He attended the World Missionary Conference in Edinburgh in 1910 and became one of the leading ecumenical figures in India and the world. He died before the inauguration of the Church of South India (1947), a union he worked hard to achieve. [36] (T.T.)

B

Ba'al Shem Tov [xv] [Israel ben Eliezer] (*c.*1700–1760). Founder of Ḥasidism. He was born in Kamenetz, Podolia (now in western Ukrainian SSR). Most information concerning his youth is legendary, but it is clear that from an early age he sought solitude in the woods and fields. When he was in his early thirties he began to achieve a reputation as a wonder-worker, who healed the sick, wrote amulets and exorcized demons. Wonder-workers were known in Hebrew as *ba'al shem* (literally, 'master of the [divine] name') and Israel became known as the Ba'al Shem Tov (i.e. 'the good *ba'al shem*') or from its acronym as *Besht*. From *c.*1740 until his death he lived in Medzibozh, Podolia, to which his admirers flocked. It is estimated that at the time of his death he had over 10,000 followers.

His teachings were influenced by the mystical system of ISAAC LURIA and his school, but with significant innovations. Man's mission is to 'cleave' to the divine and to discover the spiritual within the material. This 'cleaving', which must permeate every human activity, is attained through praying with devotion and enthusiasm which raises the worshipper to the realm of the divine. Torah study can also bring man to unite with the divine, but it must be undertaken with devotion and lead man to the fear of God; it must not be undertaken merely to sharpen the brain or to produce a feeling of intellectual superiority over the unlearned. All man's deeds must be an expression of his worship of God.

The Ba'al Shem Tov placed the emotional before the rational; simple faith before study; joy before asceticism; love before fear; and devotion before discipline. The major factors in the service of God are: religious sensibility, observance of the commandments through joy, trust in God, and love of God, Torah and Israel. The highest level of adherence to the divine is attained by the saint (*tzaddik*), who mediates between the upper and lower worlds. In view of the difficulties experienced by the ordinary man in adhering to the upper world, his requests and thoughts are transmitted on high by the *tzaddik*.

The Ba'al Shem Tov spoke to the masses through stories, anecdotes and parables, emphasizing sincerity and spontaneity, and appealing to his listeners' hearts rather than their intellects. [13: vol. 1: 35–86] He addressed himself in particular to the unlearned; the movement he founded – Ḥasidism – aroused the bitter antagonism of the followers of the rabbinical tradition in which study and knowledge were the ideal. The latter became known as the *Mitnaggedim* (Hebrew: 'opponents') because of their hostility to Ḥasidism (from *ḥasid*, 'pious'). The following century saw a bitter struggle between the two schools in eastern Europe.

The Ba'al Shem Tov did not commit his teachings to writing, and only 20 years after his death were they published by his pupils. [53: 60–105; 87: vol. 9: 27–62] (G.W.)

Bāb, the [III] [Nuqṭā-yi Ūlā ('the Primal Point'), Ḥaḍrat-i Aʿlā ('His Holiness, the Most Exalted')] (1819–1850). Title adopted by the eponymous founder of the Bābī movement in Iran, Sayyid ʿAlī Muḥammad Shīrāzī. He is regarded by his followers (both Azalī Bābīs in Iran and the more numerous Bahāʾīs there and elsewhere) as a manifestation of, or human locus for, the divinity. For the Bahāʾīs, however, he is more particularly viewed as the prophetic forerunner of BAHĀʾ ALLĀH, the founder of the separate Bahāʾī faith.

The Bāb was born in Shiraz in southern

Iran into a family of relatively wealthy merchants and received a basic education suitable for a mercantile career. During his youth, however, he began to show a marked predilection for a religious life. The largely autodidactic study of Shiʿite texts to which he devoted his teens and early twenties left visible traces on his religious writings, particularly those of his final period (*c.*1848–50).

In May or June 1844 (official biographies refer to a single date, 23 May), a group of radical members of the Shaykhī sect of Shiʿism identified Shīrāzī as the new head of their school and as the 'gate' (*bāb*) sent to earth to prepare the way for the imminent advent of the hidden twelfth Imām, MUḤAMMAD AL-MAHDĪ. He himself started work on his first major book, the *Qayyūm al-asmā'*, about this period.

Expectation of his appearance at the Shīʿī shrines in Iraq as a prelude to the parousia of the Imām and the launching of a holy war against all unbelievers (including Sunnī Muslims) led to episodes of chiliastic fervour in the region which abated only when his arrival became unduly delayed. He had, in fact, travelled to Mecca on pilgrimage and had decided to avoid Iraq on receipt of news that his emissary to the region had been imprisoned.

Following his return from pilgrimage in 1845, he was arrested and confined to his home in Shiraz. Escaping in September 1846, he was given asylum by the governor of Iṣfahān, where he met numerous visitors and composed several works, mainly commentaries on parts of the Qur'ān. The governor's death in 1847 allowed the Prime Minister to have the Bāb transferred to prison in the north-west province of Ādharbāyjān, where he remained (first in Mākū, then in Chihrīq) until his execution by firing squad in the provincial capital of Tabriz on 8 or 9 July 1850.

During his imprisonment in Ādharbāyjān the Bāb claimed to be, first, the hidden Imām in person, and, finally, a new manifestation of the eternally reappearing Primal Will or of God in person. As such, he deemed himself empowered to abrogate the Islamic religious dispensation and its laws, replacing these with his own regulations as set out in several important texts.

The chief writings of his later period include the Persian and Arabic *Bayān*s, of which the former is the longer and more significant; the *Kitāb-i panj sha'n*; the shorter *Dalā'il-i sabʿa*; and the lengthy *Kitāb al-asmā'*.

A series of military defeats of the Bāb's followers in several regions of Iran between 1848 and 1852 meant that Babism never obtained a significant constituency in the country. He himself retains his centrality for the small group of Bābīs who followed his successor, MĪRZĀ YAḤYĀ ṢUBḤ-I AZAL. It is through the Bahā'ī movement, however, that he has remained best known, playing an important role as co-founder of the religion and exercising a strong attraction for members through the numerous historical texts devoted to him and his immediate followers.

Manuscripts of the Bāb's extensive Arabic and Persian writings exist in large quantities in several libraries, including the Bibliothèque Nationale, British Library and Cambridge University Library. Several have been published privately in Iran, and a few translated into French and English. They are, in general, difficult to read and understand, the style being markedly idiosyncratic, often to the point of incomprehensibility. Although the influence of Shiʿite esotericism is clear throughout these works, there are numerous passages of great originality and keen intelligence. [4; 5; 10; 15; 16; 20] (D.M.)

Babalola, Joseph [I.A.] (1904–1959). The most famous of the Nigerian Aladura prophets. A Yoruba Anglican, Babalola began preaching in 1930 following a divine revelation while working as a steamroller operator. He became the centre of a mass healing and pentecostal revival, known as the *Aladura* ('praying-people') movement (*see* ABIODUN, CHRISTIANAH; ORIMOLADE, MOSES) which spread throughout much of western Nigeria. Babalola was associated with the American pentecostal organization, the Faith Tabernacle; this was reflected in his advocacy of spiritual healing and rejection of many traditional beliefs and practices. As the movement grew rapidly, help was sought from the British Apostolic Church, until the emergence, in 1939, of a fully independent Christ Apostolic Church. Babalola was to become its General Evangelist. While the movement had no political goals, the colonial government saw such zeal as a potential threat, and imprisoned Babalola in 1932.

Soon released, Babalola continued to be a prominent personality until his death. The church has continued to grow steadily. [15: 83; 36: 126–7] (R.H.)

Bach, Johann Sebastian [VI.A] (1685–1750). German composer of music for the Lutheran church. He was born in Eisenbach and educated in the local grammar school and by his eldest brother. His early training as a chorister in Lüneberg led to posts as organist and choirmaster first at Arnstadt, then at Mühlhausen. His organ works span his whole career, but many of his finest date from his time as organist and court musician at Weimar, where he went in 1708. His move in 1717 to the court at Cöthen enabled him to concentrate on chamber music but it was his last appointment as Kantor at St Thomas's, Leipzig, that saw his greatest activity as a composer of sacred music. His *St Matthew Passion* was revived by Mendelssohn in 1829 and led to the reappraisal of Bach's music. [291; 755; 782] (E.M.)

Baeck, Leo [XV] (1873–1956). Rabbi and theologian. Born in Lissa, Posen (then Prussia), he served as rabbi in Berlin from 1912, with a period as army chaplain on both the western and eastern fronts during the First World War. In 1933 he became president of the Reichsvertretung der Juden in Deutschland, the representative body of German Jewry. In this capacity he led German Jewry during the Nazi era, refusing invitations from abroad as he would not leave the community. In 1943 he was deported to the Theresienstadt concentration camp, where he maintained the morale of the prisoners and wrote the draft of his book *The People of Israel: The Meaning of Jewish Existence.* Having survived the war, he settled in London, acting as chairman of the World Union of Progressive Judaism. He was seen as a saintly symbol of Jewish suffering and spiritual resistance to the Hitler regime.

His best-known work, *The Essence of Judaism* (1905), was a reaction to ADOLF VON HARNACK'S *Essence of Christianity.* The key to Judaism is seen as its polarity between 'mystery' (the manifestation of the divine in man) and 'commandment' (the demands of ethical monotheism). Baeck, who was a Liberal rabbi, stressed morality as the core of Judaism.

Especially well known was his distinction between Judaism as a 'classic religion' of action, which makes demands, and Christianity as a 'romantic religion' of emotion, where all is given. In romantic religion 'tense feelings supply the contents and it seeks its goals in the now mythical, now mystical, visions of the imagination'. As an example, he cites Paul as taking faith, revelation and ecstasy as the ultimate fulfilment of religion. In classical religion, man becomes free through the commandments; in romantic religion, through grace [25; 60: 133–58] (G.W.)

Baëta, Christian Goncalves Kwami [VI.A] (1908–). Ghanaian ecumenical churchman and scholar. He was born at Keta, then lived on the border of Gold Coast and Togo. His father was a minister who became a major leader of the Ewe Protestant Church on the removal of the German missionaries in the First World War. Baëta, educated in the Basel Seminary and at King's College, London, was ordained in 1936, taught at Akropong Training College, and was the chief executive of the Ewe Protestant Church, 1945–9. He also served on the Gold Coast Legislative Council; unprecedentedly, though a commoner, he represented the Trans-Volta chiefs. From 1949 to 1971 he was on the staff of the University of Ghana, from 1962 as its first Professor of the Study of Religions. He was prominent in the Christian Council of Ghana, both in its theological engagement with African culture and its confrontations with Kwame Nkrumah. After Nkrumah's fall, Baëta was appointed to the Constituent Assembly and to a national delegation to seek French and German help (he spoke both languages well).

As a young clergyman, Baëta attended the International Missionary Council meeting in Madras, 1938. In the post-war ecumenical era he was a leading representative of African Christianity, Chairman of the International Missionary Council, a member of the team surveying the whole state of the Christian ministry in Africa, and prominent in the World Council of Churches. He essayed a cautiously sympathetic approach to African Independent churches. [37; 651] (A.F.W.)

Bahā' Allāh [III] [Bahá'u'lláh] (1817–1892). 'The Splendour of God', title adopted by

Mīrzā Ḥusayn ʿAlī Nūrī, the founder of the Bahāʾī religion. Born in Tehran, the son of a government official, he showed little inclination for court life and gravitated from an early age towards mystical pursuits, possibly in association with a Ṣūfī order. In 1844 he was one of the first converts to the new religious movement centred around THE BĀB. Although leadership of the movement was originally restricted to clerics, Ḥusayn ʿAlī played an important role in financing and providing protection for his co-religionists.

In 1852 Bahāʾ Allāh was briefly imprisoned in Tehran following an abortive attempt on the life of Nāṣir al-Dīn Shāh (in which he was not involved). He was released from prison the following year on the intervention of the Russian Minister, and chose to go into exile in neighbouring Iraq. In Baghdad a small Bābī community grew up around his younger half-brother, MĪRZĀ YAḤYĀ ṢUBḤ-I AZAL, appointed head of the movement by the Bāb before his death. But Yaḥyā's reclusiveness left affairs increasingly in the hands of Bahāʾ Allāh, who became the *de facto* head of the Baghdad community.

Bahāʾ Allāh's first major writings date from this period, notably several mystical poems and treatises (*al-Qāṣīda al-warqāʾiyya, Haft vādī, chahār vādī*), a celebrated short ethical work *Kalimāt-i maknūna* ('The Hidden Words'), and a polemic for the Bāb entitled *Kitāb-i Īqān* ('The Book of Certitude'). These and other writings broke new ground, being considerably simpler and more accessible than earlier Bābī texts. In particular, they represent a significant shift from writing by and for a clerical élite to a more popular style with broader appeal.

Forced to leave Baghdad for Edirne in Turkey in 1863, Bahāʾ Allāh soon openly laid claim to leadership of the Bābī faith, proclaiming himself *man yuẓhiruhu ʾllāh* ('he whom God shall manifest'), the Bābī messiah. This led to a rift with Ṣubḥ-i Azal and finally to the division of the Bābī community into rival Bahāʾī and Azalī sects.

In 1868 the Turkish authorities intervened to separate the warring factions, exiling Ṣubḥ-i Azal and his followers to Cyprus and Bahāʾ Allāh with his contingent to Acre in Palestine. At first confined to the barracks of Acre, Bahāʾ Allāh later moved to a house in the city and finally, in the late 1870s, to a mansion in the countryside, where he remained until his death on 29 May 1892. Regarded as the latest manifestation of the divinity, and by some as an incarnation of God himself, his last years were spent in an atmosphere of veneration and increasing seclusion. He was met by a number of Western visitors, including Professor E. G. Browne, who has left a short pen-portrait of him.

During this period, he continued to write prolifically, the products of his pen being regarded as direct revelations of the word of God. Noted works include a series of letters to world rulers, a book of Bahāʾī laws entitled *al-Kitāb al-aqdas* ('The Most Holy Book'), and numerous 'tablets' (*alwāḥ*) in reply to letters from his growing body of followers in Iran and elsewhere. Bahāʾ Allāh's later writings are strongly marked by the influence of modernist ideas, revealed in his increasing concern with issues such as disarmament, world government and inter-religious harmony, which replace the mystical themes of his earlier writing. These later writings are, however, rather jejune and stylistically impoverished, in marked contrast to the vigour of his earlier works.

Bahāʾ Allāh's remains were buried at the mansion of Bahjī, which has become a shrine for Bahāʾī pilgrims and is regarded as the *qibla* or point toward which believers turn in daily formal prayer.

Bahāʾ Allāh married a total of three wives, by all of whom he had children. Before his death, however, he formally appointed his eldest son, ʿAbbās Effendi ʿABD AL-BAHĀʾ, as his successor and the interpreter of his written words. Later divisions within the family led to the disappearance of descendants of Bahāʾ Allāh within the Bahāʾī community.

Bahāʾīs believe that at least 1,000 years must elapse before the appearance of another divine manifestation comparable to Bahāʾ Allāh, and that all future prophets will be sent 'under his shadow'. [6; 7; 8; 11; 24] (D.M.)

Baḥya ibn Pakuda [xv] (11th century). Jewish moral philosopher living in Spain. Nothing is known of his life except that he was a religious judge. His *Ḥovot ha-Levavot* ('Duties of the Heart'), written in Judeo-Arabic (i.e. Arabic in Hebrew characters) was the most popular and influential Jewish ethical work of the Middle Ages. It owed much to Neoplatonism, as well as to Islamic ascetic literature, while remaining thoroughly based in Jewish tradition. He divides man's duties into those 'of the limbs', which involve external actions and are defined as 'visible wisdom', and the duties 'of the heart', which are rational and expressed in man's inner life, being defined as 'hidden wisdom'. The latter, he felt, had been neglected by Jewish writers up to his time. The duties of the heart require prior intellectual knowledge, based in reason, the written law and tradition. Rabbinic learning had confined itself to the external duties, and philosophy must be employed to comprehend the duties of the heart. The basis is the proof of God's essential attributes – his existence, unity and eternity – which, like his proofs of creation, Baḥya largely derives from the Kalam. After the theological chapters, he concentrates on the moral implications: purity of action, humility, repentance, self-examination and abstinence. Although the last is limited in scope, Baḥya's asceticism was unusual in Jewish thought. He suggests that such discipline is required to attain the love of God, the supreme degree of spirituality. Belief in the hereafter plays a prominent role in his system. [50; 39: 80–105] (G.W.)

Banārsīdās [xiii] (1586–1643). Jain mystic and reformer. He was originally a merchant from the city of Agra whose family had links with the Śvetāmbara sect, the Kharatara Gaccha (*see* Jineśvara). At the age of 35 he became disenchanted with the ritual, image-worship and outward trappings of Jainism and was instead drawn to the Adhyātma movement, a loose grouping of like-minded merchants who were interested in the purely spiritual dimensions of the religion. The study of a medieval Digambara doctrinal digest introduced Banārsīdās to the 14 *guṇasthānas*, the stages of spiritual development commencing with false belief and gradually leading to the attainment of enlightenment, and he was persuaded that elements such as image-worship should be integrated into the Jain path only as preliminary adjuncts to the true goal of Jainism which was the experience of the innermost soul (*adhyātma*).

Although the Adhyātma movement had existed before Banārsīdās, he is effectively regarded as its founder. Quasi-fundamentalist in approach, he not only downgraded the practice of ritual but also rejected monastic authority, historically the central and defining element of Jain religious practice. Kundakunda's *Samayasāra* [18] was a major influence upon Banārsīdās, one of his most influential works being a Hindi translation of the epitomizing verses found in Amṛtacandra's commentary on that celebrated scripture, although he does seem also to have drawn on Śvetāmbara as well as Digambara sources in formulating his doctrine.

Banārsīdās's most famous work is his autobiography 'Half-a-Story' (*Ardhkathānak*) [1], so-called because it was written when its author had lived more than half the 110 years which Jainism has traditionally regarded as being the human span, and which has become an important source for the history of North India during the Moghul Empire. In it, the life and spiritual career of Banārsīdās are placed in the context of contemporary events, both mercantile and political. Such an account is virtually unique in Indian literature up to this point. Another important, if hardly positive, source for Banārsīdās is the Śvetāmbara monk Meghavijaya (1652–1730), whose 'Enlightenment through Reason' (*Yuktiprabodha*) is a dyspeptic attack both on Banārsīdās himself and on the doctrine associated with him.

The Adhyātma movement seems to have disappeared about a century after Banārsīdās's death. Among the many Jains influenced by him was the 18th-century Paṇḍit Ṭoḍar Mal, whose digest of Digambara doctrine as seen from an Adhyātma point of view is still of significance today. (P.D.)

Bandā [xxiii] (1670–1716). Sikh military leader and martyr. As one renowned for his bravery against tyrannical rulers Bandā occupies a prominent position in the affections of the Sikhs. Bandā Bahādur or Bandā the Brave was born in Poonch on the northern fringe of the Punjab. His life story is firmly engraved in the Sikh consciousness, but in fact much of it is known only from traditional sources [20: I–XIX]. By tradition he was born Lachhman Dev but became a Vaiśnava bairāgī or ascetic under the name of Mādho Dās. He was dwelling in the Deccan when Gurū Gobind Siṅgh came south; meeting the Gurū shortly before the latter's death in 1708, he was instantly converted to the Sikh faith. Renamed Bandā ('Slave') he was commissioned to return to the Punjab and to wreak vengeance on Vāzīr Khān of Sirhind, who had so cruelly executed the Gurū's two younger sons.

Bandā travelled up to the Punjab and, gathering an army of peasants, he sacked the towns of Samānā and Saḍhaurā. In 1710 he confronted Vāzīr Khān near Sirhind and fighting with great determination defeated and killed him. For five years Bandā's fortunes ebbed and flowed as the leader of peasant armies fighting against the Mughal rulers of the Punjab. Bahādur Shāh, the Emperor, drove him off the plains, and by the end of 1710 Bandā was compelled to hide in the hills. In 1712 Bahādur Shāh's death created renewed opportunity and in the succession struggle Bandā was again able to create havoc on the plains. With the accession of Farrukhsiyār as Emperor he was compelled to withdraw again, this time to the Jammū Hills, where he married. Finally he descended to the plains a last time and was captured after a lengthy siege in the village of Gurdās Naṅgal in Gurdāspur District. He was escorted in chains to Delhi and was there barbarously executed in June 1716. [7: 45–57] (W.H.M.)

Bankei Yōtaku [IV] (1622–1693). Japanese Buddhist monk of the Rinzai Zen school. He was born into a Confucian family in Hamada, a small village on the Inland Sea, but studied Rinzai Zen under Umpo Zenjō (1568–1653) at Zuiō-ji in Akō and with the Ming Chinese monk Tao-che Ch'ao-yüan. During a time of extreme physical illness he experienced the insight that 'all things are resolved in the Unborn (*fushō*)'. He was affiliated with the Zen temple Myōshin-ji but spent most of his time travelling, training disciples and preaching to the people. He tirelessly proclaimed the principle of *fushō*, the Unborn, which for him expressed the essence of Buddhism and the universality of the unborn Buddha mind. He rejected the traditional Rinzai use of the kōan, and was famed as a preacher who spoke to the people in simple, ordinary language. [246] (P.L.S.)

al-Bāqillānī, Abū Bakr Muḥammad ibn al-Ṭayyib [XII] (*d.*1013). Prominent Islamic theologian of Baghdad. Born in Baṣra, he spent some of his life functioning as a judge (*qāḍī*), but he is best known for two works, *al-Tamhīd fī'l-radd ʿalā'l-mulḥida* ('Introduction to the Rejection of the Heretics') and *Kitāb iʿjāz al-Qur'ān* ('The Book concerning the Inimitability of the Qur'ān'). Al-Bāqillānī was the major enunciator of the theology of AL-ASHʿARĪ at his time and is said to have contributed several important elements to the formulation of the orthodox position; at the very least he may be said to have compiled coherent and careful statements of Ashʿarite theology. He also became famous for his incisive discussion of the miraculous character of the Qur'ān, a central principle of Islamic theology, in which he argued for the inferiority of all Arabic literature to the Qur'ān by means of a detailed comparison of the scripture to some of the most famous poetry of the Arabs. [35: 'Bāḳillānī'; 43] (A.R.)

Barclay, Robert [VI.A] (1648–1690). Quaker leader. He was born in Gordonstoun and educated at the Scottish College, Paris. Though raised and educated as a Scottish Roman Catholic he followed his father and became a Quaker at the age of 19. In 1673 he published a *Catechism and Confession of Faith* and followed this in 1676 with *Theologiae verae christianae apologia*. He travelled in Germany and Holland in the same year. Two years later the *Apologia* was published in an English version as *Apology for the True Christian Divinity*. In it he defended the principle of 'the Inner Light' against the authority of all external sources of inspiration, including the Bible. Although imprisoned for his beliefs he was eventually appointed governor of East New Jersey (USA), with its constitution based on Quaker principles. (T.T.)

Bar Hebraeus [VI.B] [Gregory; Abū al-Faraj] (1226–1286). Born at Melitene to a Jewish family, which fled to Antioch to escape the invading hordes of the Mongol Khan Hulagu (1243). Gregory became a Christian and studied in Tripoli. The Jacobite Patriarch Ignatius II consecrated him bishop (1246) and from 1264 to his death in 1286 he was Maphrian of the East.

Bar Hebraeus wrote in Syriac and Arabic. He wrote biblical commentaries, theological, historical, philosophical and grammatical works. His *Cream of Science*, a compendium of contemporary scientific learning, his writings on mathematics and astronomy and his *Book of Splendours* on Syriac grammar were widely used. He practised and wrote on medicine.

Bar Hebraeus, a self-taught mystic, studied Christian and Muslim mystics and recorded his own experiences and theories, making copious use of AL-GHAZĀLĪ's writings. He died at Maradakh, now in Azerbaijan.

The reforming bishop Jacob of Edessa (633–708) wrote widely on theology, biblical exegesis, grammar, philosophy and history. A history continuing EUSEBIUS, now lost, was used by Bar Hebraeus. His *Hexaemeron* on creation was left unfinished. George, Bishop of the Arabs (686–724), completed it as well as writing on logic and philosophy. Moses bar Kepha (813–903) wrote widely in philosophy and theology.

Later Dionysius bar Salibi, Bishop of Mar'ash then from 1156 to his death (1171) of Amida, wrote polemical works against Christian heretics, against Muslims and Jews, commentaries on scripture, on the Fathers and on the mystical writings of EVAGRIUS PONTICUS. Michael the Great, born 1126, Patriarch in 1166 until he died in 1199, wrote a 'Chronicle' from the creation to his own day, which cites valuable sources. He wrote liturgical works and theological works. [5: X] (D.J.M.)

Barrett, Francis [XVII.A] (dates unknown). Primarily known as the London author of *The Magus* (1801), a compendium of spells, invocations and Renaissance magical philosophy often lifted directly from AGRIPPA VON NETTESHEIM's *De occulta philosophia*. Published during the English Gothic revival, the book seems to have attracted some attention and may have encouraged magical practice. Certainly Barrett advertised for students in its pages. Like many Renaissance philosophers he saw magic as a deeply Christian practice – 'the magicians were the first Christians' – and describes the ultimate aim of the magician as 'to know the Creator by the contemplation of the creature . . . for this is the sum and perfection of all learning, to live in the fear of God, and in love and charity with all men'. [2; 9] (T.L.)

Barth, Karl [VI.A] (1886–1968). Swiss theologian. He was born in Basel, received his earliest education in Bern and began his university studies there. In Berlin he studied under ADOLF VON HARNACK. In 1907 he studied in Tübingen and did a final year at Marburg. From 1911 to 1921 he served as a pastor in Safenwil, Switzerland. He came to prominence with the publication of his *Der Römerbrief* in 1919. In this and in later works he rejected the liberalism of much of German Protestantism and turned his back on bourgeois 'cultural-Protestantism'. He was invited to be professor in Göttingen (1921) and Münster (1925). He was in Bonn when Hitler came to power. Barth was instrumental in the publication of the Barmen Declaration which proclaimed the primacy of the Gospel against the demands of the Nazi state. As a result Barth had to leave Germany for his native Switzerland and remained there as professor of theology at Basel. At his death he was still working on his *Church Dogmatics* begun in 1927. [57; 131; 806] (T.T.)

Basava [XI] (1106–1167). He was born, probably at Maṇigavaḷḷi (in modern Karnataka). He was brought up by foster-parents in a Brahmanical Sanskritic tradition, and was himself a keen devotee of Śiva from an early age. By the time he was 16 years of age Basava vowed to spend the rest of his life in the worship and service of Śiva, and to reject his caste and the ritualism thereof as confining and valueless. He removed his sacred thread and went to a place where three rivers meet. Symbolically perhaps, the god worshipped there, Kūḍalasaṅgamadeva, became Basava's chosen deity. We are told that, in a dream, the Lord instructed him to go to the court of King Bijjala at Kalyāṇa. Eventually he became the king's minister there. Basava believed that his followers should be wandering zealots, *Jaṅgamas*, and the term *Vīraśaiva*, 'heroic Śaivite', was and is applied to them. They disregarded caste, class and sex, and were loathed by the orthodox in consequence. Basava lost the king's patronage, left Kalyāṇa, and soon afterwards died. Bijjala in turn was assassinated, and the Vīraśaivas were dispersed. But they never died out, and, under the name *Liṅgāyat*, are a political and religious factor in Karnataka to the present day. [29; 91] (J.R.M.)

Basilides [IX] (2nd century). Christian philosopher and Gnostic, possibly of Syrian origin. He taught at Alexandria in the second quarter of the 2nd century. His followers later reported that he had claimed authority from standing in the tradition of PETER THE APOSTLE [6: 417]. He wrote a Gospel, a lengthy commentary on it, and a collection of Psalms; all these writings are lost but are known about from the works of IRENAEUS, CLEMENT OF ALEXANDRIA, and ORIGEN [2: 39–56].

According to Hippolytus, Basilides taught that a non-existent God created a world by forming a seed of threefold sonship: the first returned to God in the super-celestial realm, the second took the Holy Spirit as a wing and so could not remain with the non-existent God but became a type of human yearning for better things, the third remained in the seed and so in need of restoration to God [10: 124–7]. Basilides held the usual gnostic attitude to matter as alien to the supreme God and seems to have taught that, in order for humanity to be freed from the domination of the God of the Jews, a member of the lowest order of spiritual beings, the supreme God had sent his *Nous* (mind) into the world to dwell in JESUS, who was never crucified [9: 165–6]. Human freedom comes from following the *Nous* and rising to the supreme God but at the time of the restoration of the third sonship most of humanity will remain trapped in the corruptible material world. Basilides taught a form of Stoic ethics. His teachings are represented somewhat differently by Irenaeus [6: 420–25; 9: 311–12]. He is spoken against in the *Testimony of Truth* [8: 413]. (G.J.B.)

Basil of Caesarea [VI.A] [Basil the Great] (*c*.329–379). One of the 'Cappadocian Fathers'. He was born in Cappadocia and educated in Caesarea, Constantinople and Athens. He then chose to live an ascetic life. His experience as a monk and his writings on the vocation are the basis for monastic life in the Eastern tradition. In 370 he was elected bishop of Caesarea. He became involved in theological dispute against the Arians. Much of his writing, polemics and letters have remained. His major contribution, apart from his standards for monasticism, was to Trinitarian doctrine. The Council of Constantinople (381/2), which formally saw the end of Arianism, stands as a memorial to his teaching. [58; 59; 259] (T.T.)

Baur, Ferdinand Christian [VI.A] (1792–1860). German theologian. He was born in Schmiden in Würtemberg and was a student and a professor at Tübingen University and the founder of the Tübingen school of New Testament theology. Hegelian principles were applied to New Testament studies for the first time in his *Untersuchungen über die sog: Pastoral-briefe des Apostels Paulus* (1835). In his *Paulus der Apostel Jesus Christi* (1845) he caused controversy by portraying PAUL THE APOSTLE as being in conflict with all the other early leaders of the church and by questioning the authenticity of most of the epistles bearing his name. [264; 290; 367; 734: vol. 1, 261–89] (T.T.)

Baxter, Richard [VI.A] (1615–1691). Puritan minister. He was born in Rowton, Shropshire. He was educated at Wroxeter, Ludlow and London, where he enjoyed the patronage of the Master of Revels. Though already sympathetic towards dissent he was ordained in the Church of England in 1638. He taught at Bridgnorth for two years and in 1641 he moved to Kidderminster and ministered there until 1660. By this time he had rejected belief in episcopacy. He was a moderate in the period of the Civil War and was prominent in the recall of Charles II. Having refused the bishopric of Hereford he was barred from ecclesiastical office. He took part in the Savoy Conference which tried to reconcile Anglicans and Presbyterians. He veered to the Presbyterian position having prepared a 'Reformed Liturgy'. He welcomed the Toleration Act of William and Mary. His writings, including *Gildas Salvianus, or The Reformed Pastor* (1656), make him one of the leading Puritan divines. [609; 659] (T.T.)

al-Bayḍāwī, Abū'l-Khayr Naṣīr al-Dīn [XII] (*d.* between 1286 and 1316). Muslim religious scholar and judge. Born near Shīrāz, Iran, he spent most of his life as chief justice of the province of Fārs. He wrote about 20 works in Arabic on jurisprudence, law, grammar, theology and Qur'anic sciences. His major fame derives from his commentary on the Qur'ān entitled *Anwār al-tanzīl wa asrār al-ta'wīl* ('The Lights of Revelation and the Secrets of Interpretation'). The work follows the Qur'ān through verse by verse, stating in very concise form the consensus of opinion at al-Bayḍāwī's time regarding the interpretation of the scripture. His main sources were AL-RĀZĪ (*d.*1209) and AL-ZAMAKHSHARĪ (*d.*1144) and what al-Bayḍāwī presents is a simplified and theologically more conservative summary of the opinions of his predecessors. Emphasis in the commentary is placed upon the essentials of grammar, meaning and variant readings; al-Zamakhsharī's rationalist theological leanings are, for the most part, avoided, with emphasis being placed in the interpretations on the dogmatic tradition derived from AL-ASHʿARĪ. Because of its concise nature, the commentary has proven valuable to scholars for quick reference and has been widely read and reproduced throughout the Muslim world; it has been the basic textbook in the field of Qur'anic interpretation for many students through the centuries. As a result, it also became the best known commentary on the Qur'ān in Europe and was published in Germany in 1846–8. [20; 29] (A.R.)

Bdud-'joms rin-po-che [IV] ['jigs-bral ye-shes rdo-rje] (1904–1987). Born in the south-eastern Tibetan district of Padma-bkod, at the age of three Bdud-'joms rin-po-che was recognized to be the rebirth of the far-eastern Tibetan 'treasure-finder' (*gter-bton*) Bdud-'joms gling-pa (1835–1903). He was educated primarily at Smin-grol-gling, the Central Tibetan seat of the Rnying-ma-pa sect, emerging as the leading contemporary exponent of that tradition, particularly in connection with its meditational teachings of the 'Great Perfection' (*rdzogs-pa chen-po*). A 'treasure-finder', poet and scholar, he was well known for his extensive historical writings. Following the Tibetan diaspora of 1959 Bdud-'joms rin-po-che became the Supreme Head of the Rnying-ma-pa sect, and was active in Tibetan refugee educational affairs. His last years were spent mostly in France and the United States, where he had a wide following among Western Buddhists. [56; 113] (M.K.)

Béatrice, Dona [I.A.] [Kimpa Vita] (*c*.1682–1706). Prophetess and founder of perhaps the earliest African Independent Christian movement. Dona Béatrice claimed to be the reincarnation of the Portuguese St Anthony. She founded the Antonian church, through which she espoused an anti-Catholic Christianity, emphasizing traditional Kongo culture and symbolism. She was burned at the stake as a heretic by the Kongo king Pedro IV, under the pressure of missionaries present at his court. Her church survived her death and was to help provide the impetus and focus for a revitalization of the Kongo kingdom in the 1700s. Although she died soon after she began preaching, her politico-religious ideas inspired messianic movements in their struggle against colonial oppression two centuries later. Béatrice is the subject of a three-act opera, *Béatrice du Congo*, by Bernard Dadié, published in Paris in 1970. [36: 116] (R.H.)

Becket, Thomas [VI.A] (?1118–1170). Archbishop of Canterbury. The son of a Norman family settled in England, he studied law in France, was made Archdeacon of Canterbury in 1154 and Chancellor to King Henry II in 1155. As friend to the king he lived a flamboyant life. After his election as Archbishop of Canterbury, however, Thomas changed his lifestyle and became an opponent of the king over matters of taxation and the legal powers of the crown over the clergy. The king summoned bishops and barons to oppose Thomas, who had to flee to France. After an eventual reconciliation Thomas returned to Canterbury but refused to absolve bishops who had sided with the king. Following his assassination in his cathedral on 29 December 1170 his grave became a shrine for pilgrims. [47; 379; 690] (T.T.)

Bede [VI.A] (*c*.673–735). Anglo-Saxon theologian and historian. 'The Venerable', a title conferred on him after his death, was sent at the age of seven to the monastery of Wearmouth and thence to Jarrow, where he carried out his main work as an expositor of the Bible and an historian. He was ordained deacon *c*.692 and priest at about the age of 30. He visited Lindisfarne and York but hardly ventured out of Northumbria. In expounding the Bible he used Greek texts in addition to the more common Vulgate and Old Latin texts. His most famous work is his history of *The Church of the English People*. He worked on a variety of sources and separated facts from unreliable traditions. In 1899 he was pronounced 'Doctor of the Church'. [67; 68; 106] (T.T.)

Behramshah Naoroji Shroff. *See* SHROFF, BEHRAMSHAH NAOROJI.

Benedict of Nursia [VI.A] (*c*.480–547). Born into 'a family of high station' in Nursia in the Province of Umbria, Benedict was educated in Rome in the liberal arts, but at about the age of 20 sought solitude, eventually living in a cave at Subiaco. After a few years he was persuaded to be abbot of a nearby monastery. Later returning to Subiaco he founded 12 small monasteries but finally settled *c*.525 in the monastery which he caused to be built at Monte Cassino on the site of a former pagan shrine. His life is recorded in the *Dialogues* of GREGORY I (the Great). Benedict is best known for the Rule which he gave his order. [352; 830; 831] (T.T.)

Bennett, John Godolphin [XVII.D] (1897–1974). Thinker, writer, teacher and witness to the unconditioned, he was a man of prodigious talents and inner gifts. In his autobiography, *Witness* [1], he does not speak of his early family life, nor his schooldays at King's College, Wimbledon, but begins his life in 1918, when he tasted death in an out-of-body experience when wounded in France. This experience of an unconditioned realm where physical bodies are not required was to transform his life. Invalided back, he recovered and was sent on a Turkish course, which he pursued with great enthusiasm and success, for he was a natural linguist. His first, short-lived, marriage began, bizarrely, on the day his father died. Two months later he was posted to Turkey, where he served in intelligence until 1921, when he resigned from the army. Bennett's years in Turkey were full and rich in experience, but of particular significance were his friendship with Winifred Beaumont, who was later to become his wife and companion for 40 years, and his meeting with GURDJIEFF and OUSPENSKY in 1920. Externally he spent the next year attempting to help sort out the estate of Abdul Hamid, while at the same time attending Ouspensky's meetings and struggling with psychological exercises and Gurdjieff's cosmology. In 1923 he went and worked intensively with Gurdjieff at Fontainebleau, where he was rewarded with very deep inner experiences. However, he did not feel able to commit himself to stay, and spent the next years in a variety of external projects, mainly in the Near East, while working inwardly with Ouspensky when he was in England.

The early 1930s saw him return to England and to science, especially to research on coal, which was to provide him with a position and a livelihood until 1950. He continued to work with Ouspensky until he and his wife left for America in 1941, by which time Bennett already had a group of his own with which he worked on the Gurdjieff system, and was beginning to write his major work, *The Dramatic Universe* [2], which, after being rewritten many times, was finally completed by 1966. In 1946 he established his group as the Institute for the Comparative Study of History, Philosophy and the Sciences, a title chosen deliberately 'to mean little and convey less'. The Institute bought a large house in South London to reproduce the conditions that Gurdjieff had created at Fontainebleau. Ouspensky, with whom relations had become strained owing to Bennett's wish to write about the system, died in 1947, but it then became known that Gurdjieff was still alive in Paris. Bennett and many members of his group were welcomed by Gurdjieff, who worked with them intensively until his death in 1949, during which time Bennett was able to make the progress that had eluded him for many years in his inner transformation, but not without a lot of personal pain. He continued to work with his group, but, feeling in need of a new direction after Gurdjieff's death, in 1953 he left for the Middle East. Amid many experiences, the most significant was to be told that a Messenger of God was on the earth and he must return home, attract more pupils, and prepare his house. He thought nothing more about it until in 1955 he and a few others tried out for themselves what is now known as the Subud *latihan* (*see* SUMOHADIWIDJOJO). Impressed by what they found, they invited Pak Subuh to London in 1957, and for three years Bennett was a central helper in the extraordinary initial expansion of Subud round the world.

In 1957 his wife died and he remarried in 1958. Although never denying the beneficial effects of the Subud *latihan*, nor the great changes it had brought about in himself, by 1961 Bennett felt the need to be his own man again. He resumed working with groups as before; he visited the Śivapuri Baba in Nepal and wrote a book, *Long Pilgrimage*, about him; he became a Roman Catholic; and, in 1965, he gave the house and the care of his pupils to Idries Shah, the representative of an authentic Sufi tradition. He continued his writings and devoted time to developing an educational process called 'Structural Communication' which had evolved from the work he had done on the properties of multi-term systems. By 1970 he felt it his destiny to found a school to prepare people for the New Age. At Sherborne in the Cotswolds he founded the International Academy for Continuous Education and until his death in 1974 taught in annual courses both the need and the techniques required for personal transformation. The range, quality and quantity of his writings is astonishing, but of equal importance to the insights and vision in his written works are the very large number of people whose lives he affected for the better in the various phases of his remarkable life. He saw himself as a witness to deeper realities, but he was also instrumental in enabling many to attain some measure of such realities in themselves. (S.C.R.W.)

Berg, David [XIX] (1919–). Leader of the movement known as the Children of God, the Family of Love, Heaven's Magic, and by several other names. Berg, who is referred to as Moses David, or 'MO' (or 'Dad'), by his followers, grew up in a family of itinerant evangelists in the United States. He was drafted into the army in 1941 but discharged because of a heart condition, and continued the evangelistic mission with his mother. After a short period as the pastor of a Christian Missionary Alliance church in Arizona he decided that he did not wish to be part of any mainstream church [15: 23–5]. He spent some time studying socialism and communism, and then 'personal witnessing' at Fred Jordan's American Soul Clinic, which led to his working on the promotion of Jordan's television programme 'Church in the Home' from 1952 to 1967. Berg then returned to evangelizing and working with the Assemblies of God's Teen Challenge mission to youth in Huntingdon Beach, Southern California. Before long, Berg and his family's success with the hippies led to the establishment of a group called 'Teens for Christ', which then became the Light Club Mission. This, in turn, was to develop into the Children of God after Berg received a revelation that an earthquake would strike California; the group began wandering around North America – like MOSES with the Hebrew children out of Egypt. Over the next few years, the movement grew, with small communes extending eventually all over the world.

Berg's preaching, initially a premillennial and fundamentalist part of the wider Jesus People Revival of the period, grew increasingly opposed to American values and all established authority [15: 45]. 'Revolution for Jesus' was advocated, with the expectation that the Battle of Armageddon will be fought in 1993. Berg's preoccupation with sex increasingly permeated the teachings and organization of the movement. One of his daughters has accused him of having an incestuous relationship with another daughter [15: 28–9], and he introduced 'Flirty Fishing' to the movement – a practice in which attractive members, 'Hookers for Jesus', were enjoined to offer sexual favours to potential recruits. (Fear of AIDS has led to the termination of 'FFing').

Berg, declared to be God's Endtime Prophet [15: 49, 64], disseminates his prophecies and other teachings to his followers through numerous 'MO Letters'. These are written in a crude, flamboyant style with cartoon-type illustrations and titles such as 'SOCK IT TO ME! – THAT'S THE SPIRIT!', 'AMERICA THE WHORE', 'THE LITTLE FLIRTY FISHY', 'COME ON, MA! – BURN YOUR BRA!'. [14: 829, 527, 1359] (E.B.)

Bernadette [VI.A] [Marie-Bernarde Soubirous] (1844–1879). She was the daughter of a miller in Lourdes. At the age of 14 she claimed to have seen a series of eighteen apparitions of the Blessed Virgin MARY near a rock on the outskirts of Lourdes. Mary revealed herself as 'the Immaculate Conception'. A miraculous spring of water appeared and the Virgin asked for a church to be built. Following intense questioning and much publicity Bernadette entered the Order of the Sisters of Notre-Dame at Nevers. She was canonized in 1933. Lourdes has since become a centre for pilgrimage and healing. [646; 810] (T.T.)

Bernardino de Sahagun [XVIII] (*c.*1499–1590 CE). The greatest ethnographer of 16th-century Mexico. His *Historia general de las cosas de Nueva Espana* was the most thorough single account of Aztec religion, society, history and medicine. While not a native Meso-American, his Franciscan training in

Spain prepared him to study, understand and record the cosmology, ritual and social world of the Aztec empire which fell to the Spaniards in the second quarter of the 16th century. His *Historia*, also known as the Florentine Codex, is divided into 12 books, dedicated to (1) the gods; (2) the ceremonies; (3) origins and myths of the gods; (4) the calendar and divination; (5) omens and prophecies; (6) rhetoric and theology; (7) astronomy and renewal ceremonies; (8) kings and lords; (9) merchants and craftsmen; (10) people and medicine; (11) natural history; (12) the conquest of Mexico. His works were banned by the Spanish Inquisition and lost for several centuries. They are now available in several languages and are influencing the interpretation of native American religion more than any other single source. [9] (D.C.)

Bernard of Clairvaux [VI.A] (1090–1153). Cistercian monk. He was born near Dijon and educated at Saint-Vorles, Châillon. In 1113 he entered the monastic life in the abbey of Cîteaux but two years later he was sent to found an abbey at Clairvaux. He attracted so many others that he had to found another abbey, and eventually he was responsible for about 70 new abbeys in the Cistercian Order. Bernard wrote spiritual works on the Virgin MARY, on grace and free will and a large number of sermons on the *Song of Songs*. He also engaged in polemics against his erstwhile friend PETER ABELARD. Much of his work was concerned with church politics and with the reform of the church and monastic life. He campaigned against the Cathars and recruited men for the Second Crusade in 1146. He was canonized in 1174. [248; 466; 467] (T.T.)

Besant, Annie [XVII.A] (1847–1933). English theosophist and social reformer. Born in London, she was married by the age of 20 and separated by 26. She became very active in social reform, one of her more memorable acts being to write a textbook on birth control after a sensational trial which questioned her right to publish on the topic. She became a socialist and for a while at least an atheist, but encountered theosophy and found it to her liking. In 1893 she moved to India, where she founded a Home Rule League, and became one of Nehru's early champions. Her role in colonial Indian politics was considerable. She is also known, however, for her religious views. *Esoteric Christianity* (1902) was a sort of union of BLAVATSKY and KINGSFORD, arguing that Christianity had a hidden esoteric core and that the resurrection could not be understood without it. Besant became president of the Theosophical Society by 1907, and in that position made the search for a 'new' Christ the central feature of a movement devoted to divine wisdom. In this context Christ becomes truth, esoteric knowledge, and divinity. She also discovered KRISHNAMURTI, and although he withdrew from the public role she wished him to have, he has nevertheless played an important role in the lives of many. As it had for many, theosophy seems to have helped Besant to maintain a powerful sense of religious commitment despite her unusual route to faith. [3; 5; 20] (T.L.)

Beschi, Constantine Josephus [VI.A] (1680–1746). Italian Jesuit missionary. After becoming a member of the Society of Jesus he was sent to the Madura Mission in India in 1710. He followed the methods of ROBERTO DE NOBILI by wearing Indian dress and avoiding anything that could give offence to high-caste Hindus. He studied a number of Indian languages, including Tamil. He wrote grammars of classical Tamil and of the vernacular (1732) in impeccable Latin. He wrote many books of classical Tamil poetry and prose, including the epic *Tembarani*, a history of the life of Joseph the husband of Mary interwoven with selections from the Gospel story, which is regarded as a minor classic of Tamil literature. Beschi was a contemporary of ZIEGENBALG and the first Lutheran missionaries at Tranquebar. Beschi attacked them strongly, and in one tract he compares them to the locusts of the *Book of Revelations*, ch. 9. In spite of this, his Tamil grammars were printed at the Lutheran press in Tranquebar. He died at Manapparai. [78] (T.T.)

Bessarion [VI.B] (1403–1472). Metropolitan of Nicaea. At the Council of Florence (1438–45) Emperor John VIII Palaeologus sought Catholic help against the Ottomans threatening Constantinople. He led the Greek delegation which included Bessarion and the Neo-pagan Platonist philosopher Gemistos Plethon, who was received with adulation by Italian intellectuals, into union with the

Papacy; only Mark eugenicus of Ephesus and Plethon did not sign the agreement.

Bessarion, like the Greek Isidore of Kiev, accepted the union with conviction and moved to Italy. Made Cardinal in 1439, he was the principal rival candidate when Alfonso Borgia was elected Pope as Calixtus III. A scholar, patron of the arts and letters, he left his collection of about 500 Greek manuscripts to Venice.

John VIII and his brother, the last Emperor – Constantine XI – remained faithful to the union, though it was unpopular amongst the Orthodox. When Constantinople fell in 1453, Sultan Mehmet II installed Patriarch Gennadios II Scholarios, a Greek Thomist – once a supporter, but now a strong opponent of the union – to replace the uniate patriarch, Gregory Mamas. [36; 37; 45: 267ff.; 63; 75; 76.] (D.J.M.)

Beza, Theodore [vi.a] (1519–1605). Though he was associated mainly with Calvinist Geneva, Beza was French and raised in Paris and originally studied law in Orléans. He became a Protestant in 1548 and because of his conversion had to flee France. He was professor of Greek in Lausanne for ten years but had to flee again, this time to Geneva, on account of his teaching concerning predestination. Until 1599 he was in control of the Academy in Geneva. He wrote on Calvinist doctrines, translated the New Testament from Greek to Latin, interceded between Catholics and Protestants and succeeded john Calvin in Geneva. He discovered what was at the time the oldest manuscript of the New Testament (Codex Bezae), which he presented to Cambridge University, hoping to get Queen Elizabeth I's support for the Protestant cause in France and Geneva. [285; 292] (T.T.)

Bhadrabāhu [xiii] (? 3rd century BCE). In Jain tradition the seventh teacher in succession after Sudharman, the last disciple of Mahāvīra. According to the accounts of the Digambara sect, Bhadrabāhu migrated to the south of India with a large section of the Jain community and the Emperor Candragupta Maurya to escape the effects of a famine in the north. However, this story seems to be late, the first reference to it being an inscription of 600 CE; still later literary accounts which try to present the migration as the cause of the emergence of the Svetāmbara and Digambara sects probably draw on this source. According to Svetāmbara tradition, Bhadrabāhu was the last of the Jain teachers who was fully conversant with the scriptures as handed down by Mahāvīra. While living in Nepal in pursuance of a religious vow, he was visited by Sthūlabhadra, an eminent monk who wished to learn the scriptures from him, but, for mysterious reasons, Bhadrabāhu held back a small part of his knowledge, and from that moment complete familiarity with the scriptures went into decline. [33]

As to the historicity of Bhadrabāhu, we can say little more than that the Jains have preserved the memory of a great teacher who was relatively close to Mahāvīra in terms of pupillary lineage.

We should also note the existence of another important teacher called Bhadrabāhu. This figure, who wrote important mnemonic verse commentaries on canonical texts, must be dated to the 3rd or 4th centuries CE. (P.D.)

Bhajan, Yogi [xix] [Siri Singh Sahib Bhai Sahib Harbhajan Singh Khalsa Yogiji] (1929–). Founder of 3HO (The Healthy, Happy, Holy Organization), the educational branch of Sikh Dharma of the Western Hemisphere, of which he is the leader [5: 196]. The son of a doctor, Yogi Bhajan was raised in the Punjab in an area now in Pakistan. He is said to have mastered Kundalini Yoga at an early age and then proceeded to study White Tantric Yoga [5: 195]. He graduated with a degree in economics from Punjab University of Chandigarh and spent 18 years as an officer in the army and the Indian customs service.

He came to North America in 1968; the following year he began teaching Kundalini yoga and meditation and sharing his Sikh faith with his students. In 1971 he was ordained a minister and authorized to ordain others and initiate individuals into the Khalsa, the Sikh Brotherhood [38: 182]. Beyond orthodox Sikhism, Yogi Bhajan teaches Kundalini [23], Laya and Tantric Yoga, meditation and vegetarian diet. Yogi Bhajan has been a controversial figure, with a certain degree of tension between the Sikh *dharma* and the older Sikh community in America. [38: 185] (E.B.)

Bhāvaviveka [IV] [Bhavya; Legs-Idan 'Byed-pa] (*c.*490–570). Indian Buddhist philosopher-monk. There is no real scholarly consensus as to his dates, but there is little doubt that he was an approximate contemporary of Sthiramati and DHARMAPĀLA [103: 5–10; 58; 59: 15–65; 186: 61–6]. He was probably born in South India, was trained in logic and the Buddhist intellectual tradition generally, and became one of the great systematic thinkers in the Madhyamaka scholastic tradition. He is associated especially with the development of independent arguments (*svatantrānumāna*) for the validity of Mādhyamika positions; this is in contrast with the general absence of such arguments in the negative dialectics of NĀGĀRJUNA and CANDRAKĪRTI.

As did all Madhyamaka thinkers, Bhāvaviveka wrote a commentary on Nāgārjuna's *Basic Verses on the Middle Way*; this is *Prajñāpradīpa* ('The Lamp of Wisdom'). He also wrote a large systematic work of his own called *Tarkajvālā* ('Flame of Reasoning'), in which a systematic exposition and critique of all the important philosophical schools of the time (Buddhist and non-Buddhist) is given [103: 12–16]. This is probably the earliest Buddhist attempt at a complete and systematic philosophical handbook, and was to be of great influence upon later Buddhist intellectual life, both as a model for other such attempts and as a substantive work of reference. [130] (P.J.G.)

Bhavya. *See* BHĀVAVIVEKA.

Bhikṣu, Ācārya [XIII] [Bhīkhanji [20]] (1726–1803). Founder in 1760 and first head (*ācārya*) of the Śvetāmbara Jain reforming sect, the Terāpanthins. Originally an ascetic of the non-idolatrous Sthānakvāsi sect, Ācārya Bhikṣu reacted against what he saw as monastic laxity and in a large number of writings advocated a return to the principles laid down in the scriptures, especially with regard to rules about ascetic dwelling and alms begging. There are different explanations for the name of the sect. According to one view, it was called Terāpanthin because it initially consisted of 13 (*terā*) ascetics and 13 lay followers. Alternatively, the Terāpanthin followers could be regarded as adhering to 13 precepts of Jainism.

Ācārya Bhikṣu was succeeded by a lineage of eight teachers, each of whom, like the founder, was regarded as the exclusive head of the order with sole authority to legislate and appoint a successor. The most famous of these successors is the 20th-century Ācārya Tulsi, the founder of the Aṇuvrata movement, which is committed to raising the moral tone of contemporary Indian public life and to world peace in general. The Terāpanthin sect has always had a very close connection with Rajasthan. (P.D.)

Bhownagree, Muncherji Merwanji [XXVI] (1851–1933). He was born in Bombay the son of a wealthy Parsi merchant. After gaining administrative experience in the State of Bhavnagar he studied law in London and was called to the bar in 1885. In England he rose to positions of office in various social and cultural bodies. In 1887 he returned to India and was responsible for drafting and introducing a constitutional administration in the State of Bhavnagar at the request of the Maharajah. This constitution became a model for that of several princely states. He returned to Britain in 1891 and his public works brought him political attention. In 1895 he was elected Tory Member of Parliament for North East Bethnal Green, the second Indian and Parsi to be so elected (*see also* NAOROJI, DADABHAI; SAKLATVALA, SHAPURJI). He was knighted in 1897. He was in bitter and public conflict with many leaders of the Indian National Congress because of his vigorous defence of British rule in India. In London he was more respected, both by his constituents, who re-elected him for a second term of office, and among members of the Zoroastrian Association. He succeeded Dadabhai Naoroji as President of the Association in 1908. He was responsible for drawing up the formal constitution of the Parsi Association of Europe in 1909 (first formed in 1861), for finding premises for the Association and basically for transforming a loose-knit informal group into a legally constituted, rather high-society, association, the first such South Asian religious association in the Western world. Politically he was very active on behalf of Indians in South Africa, a role for which he has not received due recognition. [1: 475–88; 26; 37: 224–8] (J.R.H.)

Bhūridatto Thera. *See* MUN, ACHARN.

Bihbihānī, Āqā Muḥammad Bāqir [xii] [Vaḥīd-i Bihbihānī, al-Murawwij, Ustād-i Akbar] (1705/7–*c.*1790/91). The most important Shiʿite scholar of the period immediately before the establishment of the Qājār dynasty in Iran. Born in Iṣfahān, he was descended from al-Shaykh al-Mufīd. His father, Muḥammad Akmal, had studied under the great Safavid scholar Muḥammad Bāqir Majlisī. After completing his theological studies in Iraq, he returned to Bihbihān, near Iṣfahān, where he remained for the next 30 years. In 1746, however, he returned to the shrine centre of Karbalāʾ, where he achieved eminence as the outstanding scholar of his day.

Bihbihānī's achievement was twofold. On the one hand, he single-handedly destroyed the influence of the traditionalist Akhbārī school, which had become dominant in Shiʿism in the post-Safavid period. On the other, he established as unassailable the doctrine of the Uṣūlī school, which made the religious scholar (*mujtahid*) and his ability to exercise independent judgement in matters of faith essential ingredients of Shiʿite orthodoxy. Such was his impact on Shīʿī thought that Bihbihānī came to be regarded as the renewer (*mujaddid*) of the faith for the 13th Islamic century.

Uṣūlī Shiʿism has remained the dominant expression of Twelver Islam ever since. Thanks to Bihbihānī, the clerical class grew enormously in social and political importance through the 19th century, culminating in the doctrine of *wilāyat-i faqīh* (government by the clergy) preached by Āyat Allāh Khumaynī and partially implemented by the Islamic Revolution. The power of the *ʿulamāʾ* was much strengthened by Bihbihānī's use of excommunication against Akhbārīs, Ṣūfīs, and other groups deemed heterodox.

Bihbihānī's most celebrated work is the *Risālat al-ijtihād waʾl-akhbār*, a treatise on the role of the *mujtahid*. His pupils numbered many of the leading Shiʿite clerics of the succeeding period, whose work under the newly-created Qājār Shiʿite state consolidated his influence. [35: s.v.; 89: VI] (D.M.)

Bingham, Hiram [vi.a] (1789–1869). A pioneer (and United Church of Christ) missionary to Hawaii. Sent by the American Board of Missioners, Bingham arrived at Maui Island in 1820, from this base establishing schools, building the first church in Honolulu (1821) and completing the translation of the Bible (1839). Due to his efforts the royal house of the Hawaiians leaned towards Christian reforms under Kamehameha III (1825–54). This was during the time that Britain and the United States were contesting the islands, and it provided one pretext for the Americans' securing dominance. Owing to his wife's ill health he returned to the USA in 1841 [287: 37–50]. He is one of the main characters in the famous novel *Hawaii*, by James Michener (1959), who joins with other modern writers in questioning his narrow moralistic views. His descendants, Hiram II and III, continued in his tradition, the former translating the Bible for the Kiribati, the latter famous as the re-discoverer of the Incan city Machu Picchu. [287: 145–55; 572: 72] (G.W.T.)

Bird Jaguar [xviii] (8th century). Aggressive Maya ruler of Yaxchilan, whose career reflects many of the characteristics of sacred warfare and the sacrifice of royal captives. In fact Maya rulers sometimes added the name of their most famous captive to their own title as a sign of valour, conquest and power. Bird Jaguar called himself Captor of Ah Cauac until 755, when he captured Jewelled Skull and transformed his name to Bird Jaguar, Captor of Jewelled Skull. As was typical of Maya temple ritual, following a successful raid or war, captives became the objects of blood-letting rites, ball games and human sacrifice. These events about Bird Jaguar and other Maya kings are recorded on numerous monuments, and in painted scenes which record the narrative, costume, sacred character and political significance of warfare and sacrificial ritual. Bird Jaguar, like his father Shield Jaguar, erected temples with lintel narratives depicting the ritual of warfare and its foundation in religious cosmology [10: 209–11; 3: 93, 166]. For example, Bird Jaguar commissioned Structure 42 and Structure 1 at Yaxchilan depicting his ritual dressing for war, blood-letting, taking a captive and carrying out a blood-letting ceremony with Lady Balam.

The sacred art associated with Bird Jaguar shows the historical significance of warfare among the élites and the legitimation of warfare by cosmology and rites of passage. [10: V] (D.C.)

al-Bīrūnī, Abū Rayḥān [xii] (973–after 1050). Polymath and probably the most original and wide-ranging scholar of the pre-modern period in Islam. Of Iranian origin, he came from Khwārazm in what is now Soviet Central Asia, and spent most of his life at the court of local rulers there, in northern Persia and in Afghanistan, composing a number of works in such diverse fields as chronology and ancient history, mineralogy, pharmacology, astronomy and mathematics. It was his connection with the Sultan of eastern Afghanistan, Maḥmūd of Ghazna (998–1030) which took al-Bīrūnī in the wake of the Muslim plunder raids into northern India, allowing him to imbibe there a knowledge of Sanskrit and contemporary Indian languages and to acquire a deep interest in the religions and philosophies of India. The fruits of his researches there he set forth in a major work, his *Enquiry into what is to be found in India* (1030), one which he expressly wrote without polemical aim, though still regarding Islam as superior to the greater part of the Indians' social and religious practices which he witnessed. Yet he expresses great admiration and sympathy for the philosophical reasoning of the Indians and their scientific achievement, especially that in the fields of astronomy and chronology. Virtually no succeeding Muslim scholar followed al-Bīrūnī's researches into what the orthodox could only regard as an unhealthy concern with infidelity unworthy of the attention of a pious Muslim, if not positively dangerous to his faith; hence al-Bīrūnī remained an isolated intellectual giant, but one with a good claim to be regarded as the pioneer Muslim to be concerned with comparative religion. [22; 23; 35: s.v.] (C.E.B.)

al-Bisṭāmī, Abū Yazīd Ṭayfūr [xii] [Bāyazīd Bisṭāmī] (*d.*874 or 877). Major exponent of early Iranian Ṣufism, frequently referred to in Islamic mystical verse. The grandson of a Zoroastrian convert to Islam, Abū Yazīd began his career, like ʿAbd al-Qādir al-Jīlānī, as a student of Ḥanafī law. One of his students instructed him in the elements of Ṣūfī mysticism, to which he then devoted himself exclusively. Apart from brief periods of enforced exile made necessary by the attacks of orthodox theologians, he passed his entire life in his home town of Bisṭām (Basṭām) in north-west Iran. Almost nothing is known of his mystical career, and much of what has been recorded is manifestly legend.

Of particular interest is his supposedly autobiographical account of a mystical ascension (*miʿrāj*) to paradise, modelled on that of Muḥammad. This was to set something of a fashion for later Ṣūfī writers.

Abū Yazīd himself wrote nothing, but approximately 500 of his mystical sayings have been passed down in works by other writers. Many of these utterances are couched in paradoxical and deliberately shocking language, giving rise to accusations of heresy. A sense of the total loss of self and identification with the divinity impelled him to make statements like: 'Glory be to Me, how great is My majesty.'

Through these sayings Abū Yazīd became identified as the leading representative of one of the two main tendencies of early Ṣufism, Irāqī (Baghdādī) and Khurāsānī. Whereas Irāqī Ṣufism (centred on the figure of Abū'l-Qāsim al-Junayd) was characterized by an emphasis on sobriety (*ṣaḥw*) and accommodation with religious orthodoxy, the Khurāsānī tradition symbolized by Bisṭāmī emphasized intoxication (*sukr*) and a deliberate flouting of convention. This antinomian emphasis became particularly important for Malāmatī and Qalandarī dervishes, and is a motif of much Persian Ṣūfī poetry. [34: s.v.; 35: 'Abū Yazīd al-Bisṭāmī'; 115: 47–51] (D.M.)

Black Elk [xx] (1863–1950). An Oglala Lakota medicine man and shaman who lived in north-central United States. Born at the height of American westward expansion, he witnessed the declining years of Amerindian traditional religion and served as one of its most eloquent spokesmen. At the age of nine, Black Elk received a vision from the Thunder Beings, the powers of the west (Wakinyan), an early omen of his future shamanic powers. In his seventeenth year, he revealed through the 'Horse Dance' the first part of his great vision (the unification of the Lakota: the 'sacred hoop of the nation' in the midst of which would stand the sacred tree) and was accorded recognition as a diviner and curer.

Concerned to learn more of the White culture that was overtaking his people, Black Elk joined Buffalo Bill's Wild West show in 1886 and visited the East Coast of the United States and several European countries. During this period he experienced a decline in his own spiritual powers and turned to Christianity, being baptized in 1886. The Ghost Dance movement passed through Lakota territory in the late 1880s and Black Elk saw in it a call to return to his great vision. The catastrophic climax of the Ghost Dance came with the slaughter of nearly 300 Sioux at Wounded Knee, South Dakota, in 1890. The event convinced Black Elk that he should resume his role as medicine man, a commitment that continued till 1904, at which time he espoused Roman Catholicism. Perhaps the reason for his conversion lay in his fear of the consequences of exercising the destructive power of his great vision to rid Lakota country of the Whites. For several decades he served as a catechist, ever seeking a reconciliation between Christianity and his native beliefs.

Black Elk's vision, the unfulfilled promise of unity, power, and well-being for the Lakota, was dictated to John Neihardt and published as *Black Elk Speaks* (1932). His uneasy compromise between Catholicism and Lakota religion was threatened as he was increasingly perceived by his people, as well as by Whites, as the voice of a vanquished but noble tribe. His dream of a people at harmony with the powers of nature and with one another contributed significantly to the development of the pan-Indian movement of the early 1960s. He died at Manderson, South Dakota, on 19 August 1950. [11] (S.R.)

Blavatsky, Helena Petrovna [XVII.A] (1831–1891). Russian theosophist. She was one of the central religious figures in the late 19th century, who enabled individuals to change the orientation of their religious faith. Like spiritualism and other occult enquiries, theosophy offered a route by which individuals could maintain both the claims of religion and science by presenting a form of religion as a scientific technology.

Born at Ekaterinoslav in the Ukraine to a middle-class family, Blavatsky fled her elderly husband at a young age. It is not clear what she did until she met Colonel HENRY STEEL OLCOTT, with whom she founded the Theosophical Society in New York in 1875, from which it grew until theosophy became a significant cultural presence in middle-class American and British life. Theosophy is an amalgam of Neoplatonic and Eastern ideas. Blavatsky claimed to have been instructed by Tibetan mahatmas, highly evolved human beings who had outgrown their need for bodies but remain as teachers for those on earth. The mahatmas communicated through mediums and sometimes directly to those who sought their aid. Their teaching was to search for the one hidden truth, the secret knowledge, which underlay all religions, which was the teaching of the ancients. In this vision, set out in *Isis Unveiled* (1877), the world is a many-tiered layering of spiritual and earthly reality, in which humans contain within themselves the mirror of the world. God is, as it were, one's Higher Self, and the challenge of the teaching is to evolve into a state of spiritual perfection. There are no Gods to pardon previous sin: the teachings present *karma* as the mechanism to determine one's life course and reincarnation as the process in which one is repeatedly reborn in a struggle to reach *nirvāṇa*, the state of eternal rest.

Blavatsky was among the first to present Eastern philosophy – at least in some form – in a popular way which was accessible to many, and her impact upon the Western awareness of the East has probably been considerable. [4; 5; 8; 20] (T.L.)

Blyden, Edward Wilmot [VI.A] (1832–1912). West African political and religious thinker. He was born in St Thomas, Danish West Indies. After unhappy racial experience in the United States he emigrated at the age of 17 to Liberia, where he studied, and later taught, in a missionary high school. He was ordained a Presbyterian minister in 1858. By 1862 he was a professor at Liberia College, by 1864 Secretary of State. He spent some time in the Middle East, learning some Arabic, which he wanted in the college curriculum. Association with a fallen President forced him to leave Liberia in 1871. He went to Sierra Leone, and made investigative journeys in the hinterland for the government. In 1874 he returned to Liberia, becoming Ambassador in London, Minister of the Interior and President of Liberia College. From 1885 he spent most of his time in Sierra Leone, where he was appointed Director of Mohammedan Education in 1901.

Blyden was a leading West African intellectual of his day, reflecting the outlook of an African community shaped by Protestant missionary effort, Christian education and a humanitarian, anti-slavery philosophy. He preached the inherent dignity of the Black peoples, and advocated a form of pan-Africanism, one aspect of which was a self-governing African church, free of European dominance. (The United Native African Church was inspired by him.) He was more unusual in allocating a major place to Islam in African development, arguing that, not being associated with Europeans, Islam did not undermine African dignity. He enthusiastically endorsed Bosworth Smith's then highly controversial *Mohammed and Mohammedanism*. Despite reports, he never abandoned Christian profession; in late years he was interested in Swedenborgian views (*see* SWEDENBORG, EMANUEL) on the high place of the Black race in the order of redemption. His best essays are collected in *Christianity, Islam and the Negro Race* (1887). [33; 97; 502; 504] (A.F.W.)

Bodhidharma [IV] (*d.*532?). The legendary first patriarch of the Ch'an school of Chinese Buddhism. The traditional version (which has some variations) of his life asserts that Bodhidharma arrived in China 'from the West' in the latter part of the 5th century (some say 520 or 526) and had a brief encounter with the EMPEROR WU of the Liang in which he commented on the vanity of building temples and transcribing sūtras. Bodhidharma then crossed the Yangtze River and sat in meditation facing a wall at the Shao-lin temple for nine years until his legs fell off. During this time of meditation he received a visit by Hui-k'o, who sought to become his follower. Hui-k'o stood in the snow for hours waiting to be accepted, and finally severed his left arm and offered it to Bodhidharma as a sign of his dedication. Hui-k'o eventually became Bodhidharma's most eminent disciple.

Early sources are not consistent, but Bodhidharma and his followers were associated with the *Laṅkāvatāra-sūtra*, a copy of which Bodhidharma is said to have handed to Hui-k'o as a sign of his succession. Only one text, the *Erh-ju ssu-hsing lun* ('Treatise on Two Entrances and Four Practices'), is generally accepted as the work of Bodhidharma. This treatise is a brief exposition of four kinds of practice for entering awakening, and contains a reference to 'wall contemplation' (*pi-kuan*). Its contents and structure are similar to the *Laṅkāvatāra-sūtra* and the *Vajrasamādhi-sūtra* (the latter is an apocryphal Chinese Buddhist text).

There is no compelling reason to doubt the historicity of Bodhidharma, though there is also little solid evidence concerning his actual personality and activity. His importance lies rather in his role as a religious prototype, the legendary founder of the Ch'an movement and model for Buddhist contemplation and denial of worldly fame and status, and as an ideal subject for numerous Ch'an stories, riddles and works of Buddhist art. [63; 155] (P.L.S.)

Boehme, Jakob [VI.A] (1575–1624). The son of a Lutheran farming family from Alt Seidenberg near Görlitz, Saxony, he became a shoemaker after moving to the city of Görlitz, where he also married. In 1600 he experienced a religious conversion and joined a religious group known as the Conventicle of God's Real Servants. His first work, *Aurora*, which dealt with the problem of theodicy, was banned following its condemnation by the local Lutheran pastor. In 1620 he published a number of works including *On the Incarnation, Six Theosophical Points* and *Six Mystical Points*. His many works on Christ, human life, ontology and mysticism caused controversy; for a time he was exiled from Görlitz but returned there before his death. [100; 443; 757] (T.T.)

Boff, Leonardo [VI.A] (1938–). Brazilian exponent of liberation theology. He was born of Italian stock in Concordia, Brazil. He studied philosophy and theology in his own country and in Europe before becoming a Franciscan priest. Since being appointed professor of Systematic Philosophy in Petrópolis, Brazil, he has been a prolific author, displaying in Portuguese the manifold nature of full-blown liberation theology. As if he were a modern Luther opposing 'the Babylonish captivity of the Church', the Vatican issued a stern *Instruction on Certain Aspects of the Theology of Liberation* in 1984 and forbade him to speak publicly for nearly a year. In the 1981 original of his *Church: Charisma and Power: Liberation Theology and the Institutional Church* (1985), he described the relation between the Catholic hierarchy and the laity in terms of class struggle. His creatively provocative publications include *Jesus Christ Liberator: A Critical Christology for Our Time* (1978), *Ecclesiogenesis: The Base Communities Reinvent the Church* (1986;

Portuguese original 1977), *Trinity and Society* (1988), *The Lord's Prayer* (1983), and *Passion of Christ, Passion of the World* (1987). With his erudite brother, Clodovis, who is a Servite priest and professor, he has been co-author of some important text-books. He is renowned for giving a courageous lead to the Third World Church to become truly indigenous in the midst of social turmoil and oppression both at home and abroad. His militant praxis, he declares, derives from his passionate commitment to both the Gospel and the 'popular church'. [168; 260; 297] (A.C.S.)

Boisemenu, Alain de [VI.A] (1870–1953). French missionary of the Sacred Heart and the consolidator of Catholic mission work in Papua. Arriving at Yule Island in 1898, he laboured for 47 years along the coast among the Roro people and inland among the Mekeo, Kuni and Fuyughe. In 1900 he was appointed bishop, and Vicar Apostolic in 1908. Under de Boisemenu the model of small stations manned by single individuals was replaced by district stations, with supporting sisters, schools and catechetical centres, and technical training facilities [811]. At Kubuna, in Kuni country, de Boisemenu founded an indigenous Sisterhood, the Handmaids of our Lord (in 1918), and established the first contemplative monastery in Papua New Guinea by bringing out Carmelite nuns in 1935. As organizer, peacemaker (among warring Fuyughe tribesmen), and as inspirer of faith during the Japanese assaults on Papua, de Boisemenu left an indelible mark as a missionary. [449] (G.W.T.)

Bonaventure [VI.A] [Giovanni di Fidanza] (1221–1274). Franciscan bishop and theologian. Born at Bagnoreggio, near Orvieto, Italy, he joined the Franciscan Order in 1243 and went to study in Paris. From 1248 he taught there and became Master of the Franciscan school in 1253; he continued teaching until 1255. In 1257 he was elected Minister General of the order, which accepted his *Life of St Francis* as the founder's official biography. He became a Cardinal Bishop and was prominent in the Council of Lyons, during whose deliberations he died. In theology he was a traditionalist as against the 'new' theology of THOMAS AQUINAS. He denied the immaculate conception of the Blessed Virgin MARY. His largest work was his *Commentary on the Sentences* of PETER LOMBARD. [103; 303; 775] (T.T.)

Bonhoeffer, Dietrich [VI.A] (1906–1945). German Protestant theologian. He was raised in Berlin and studied theology at Berlin University under ADOLF VON HARNACK but was more deeply influenced by KARL BARTH. From 1930 to 1931 he studied in Union Theological Seminary, New York, under REINHOLD NIEBUHR. He stood against the Nazis as early as 1933 and went to London as a pastor to the German community. Though he could have remained in exile he chose to return to Germany to help train pastors for the Confessing (anti-Nazi) Church. He was forbidden to teach at the University of Berlin. In 1939 he went to teach at the Union Theological Seminary but returned to Germany after four months. He became involved in the plot to assassinate Hitler and was imprisoned in 1943. After the failure of the plot he was executed. His published works include *The Cost of Discipleship*, *Life Together*, *Ethics* and his most famous work, *Letters and Papers from Prison*. [80; 223; 312] (T.T.)

Boniface [VI.A] [Winfrith] (673–754). A monk from Devon, he was the most important English missionary to the Franks, especially after he gained the support of Charles Martell, ruler of the Franks, and his sons Carloman and Pepin. Made bishop and archbishop without a diocese, he eventually became Archbishop of Mainz in 747. He built his reputation on his belief in the central control by Rome of all missionary work and of the establishment of monasteries and convents. Late in life he returned to missionary work in Friesland, where he and his companions were killed by opponents of his work. [218: 339–455; 771; 773] (T.T.)

Boniface VIII [VI.A] [Benedetto Gaetani] (1235–1303). Pope, 1294–1303. He was born in Agnani, studied at Todi and Spoleto, became a canon in Paris and Rome and, following the study of law at Bologna, worked as a notary at the Roman Curia from 1276, as a diplomat in France and England, and became a cardinal in 1291. He instituted many fiscal, legal and clerical reforms as pope from 1294. He was in conflict with Philip IV of France and Edward I of England because he refused to allow the taxation of the clergy.

Boniface issued bulls revoking tax privileges given to the king and summoned the French bishops to a council in Rome. The move was thwarted by the king. Boniface replied with the bull *Unam Sanctam*, which included the statement that: 'It is altogether necessary to salvation for every human creature to be subject to the Roman pontiff.' Philip sent a force to capture the pope but that failed; Boniface died shortly after in Rome. [98; 205; 878] (T.T.)

Booth, William [VI.A] (1829–1912). Founder of the Salvation Army. He was born in Nottingham, the only surviving son of an unsuccessful building contractor. At the age of 15, by which time he had become a Methodist, Booth underwent a religious conversion experience. He worked as a pawnbroker in Nottingham and later in London. In 1825 he became a Methodist minister. He married Catherine Mumford in 1855. In 1865 Booth and his wife established a mission centre in the East End of London which at first was known as the Christian Mission but was later renamed the Salvation Army. He became the first General in 1878. Though Booth maintained an orthodox Methodist theology, these moves effectively cut him off from the Methodist Church. Campaigns to awaken people's conscience to the plight of child prostitution and child labour were launched, and hostels, 'rescue homes' and soup kitchens were established. Booth's major published work was *In Darkest England and the Way Out* (1890). [246] (T.T.)

Boxer [XXI] (*c.*1880–). An exceptional figure in Aboriginal traditions, where individuals are rarely identified as the source of major religious innovation. Today many of the cults that emerged in the post-colonial Kimberley region are attributed to Boxer. He was born in the Gulf country of Queensland but at the age of five or six was brought to the north of Western Australia to live with the famous Durack pastoralist family. Mary Durack describes him as a mysterious man, who frequently stole away from his employers [8: 330ff.]. Aborigines see this as a manifestation of his exceptional powers. It was when his relatives from Queensland came to visit him that he learned the techniques of a 'clever man'. He defeated local traditional healers with his skills, which included the ability to transform into various birds and 'open his guts' without harm [41: 180–83]. He periodically went back to his home and returned to the Kimberley, it is said, with a new concept in social organization and a range of new cults. The latter focused on the 'devil' figure of Djanba who had revealed the ceremonies to Boxer. Diverse historical processes are perhaps here being conflated into the influence of one man, but it has been shown that Djanba, who lived in an iron house, hunted with a rifle, was *au fait* with aeroplanes, cars and ships, and could impart introduced diseases, was a being entirely in keeping with Boxer's life experiences [37: 95–6]. Boxer was jailed at Wyndham but the police could not contain such a man. Three times he escaped, immediately and effortlessly. Oral traditions state he died in Darwin but was subsequently seen in a pub in north Queensland looking younger than ever. When the place where he was buried was checked, the grave was gone and the earth split open. The Aborigine Jack Sullivan reflects: 'Everyone knew what Boxer was, a bloody magic.' [40: 166] (T.S.)

Brahmabandhav Upadhyaya [VI.A] [Bhavani Charan Banerji] (1861–1907). Indian Roman Catholic. He was born and raised as a Bengali Hindu, but was baptized into the Christian faith in 1891 by missionaries of the Church of England. Within months he had joined the Roman Catholic Church, received conditional baptism and had taken the name Theophilus, which he translated as Brahmabandhav ('Friend of Brahma'). Before his baptism he had sought to find ways of reconciling 'pure Hinduism' and 'pure Christianity'. As a Christian he tried to interpret Christian truth through Vedantic categories. He also adopted the role of an itinerant ascetic, or *sannyasi*, and propagated his ideas through a monthly journal *Sophia*. His relations with the Roman Catholic Church deteriorated when he allied himself with the cause of Indian nationalism. He was arrested by the British on charges of sedition but died following surgery before the court case was completed. [18; 111: 63–85; 788: 103–14]. (T.T.)

Brahma Shankar Misra [XI] (1861–1907). The third guru of the Radhasoamis. He was the son of a Bengali Brahman professor of

Sanskrit in Benares. He was himself diverted from an academic career by reading SHIV DAYAL SIṄGH's *Sār bacan.* This led him to become an enthusiastic disciple of RAI SALIGRAM, on whose death in 1898 he became guru with the title Maharaj Sahib. Intellectually he added little to the doctrinal formulations of his great predecessor, and his posthumously published *Discourses on the Radhasoami Faith* (1908), described as 'containing more sound than sense' [32: 165], is chiefly remarkable for its elaborate electromagnetic analogies. His attempts to strengthen the organization of the Radhasoamis through the establishment of a Central Administrative Council 1902 precipitated the schism of the Beas branch led by JAIMAL SIṄGH, and the failure to agree a successor after his death led to a further split [74: VII] in the parent Agra branch between the Soami Bagh and Dayal Bagh groups. [32: 165; 74: VI] (C.S.)

Braide, Garrick [I.A] (*c.*1880–1918). One of Nigeria's great Christian prophets. An Ijo born in the delta region of Nigeria, Braide was responsible in 1915 for a large-scale revival movement in the Anglican Niger Delta Pastorate. He was known as the 'Second Elijah' because of his healing and prophetic powers. He promoted strenuous religious exercises, notably prayer and fasting, and preached against traditional religious shrines and objects. He did, however, encourage an indigenized liturgy and was seen by many Niger Delta Christians as the harbinger of a native church. The movement was originally supported by the Anglican authorities, but it soon broke away to form the Christ Army Church. Following the schism Braide was imprisoned and his church broke into a variety of factions. The major branch of Braide's movement, the Christ Army Church, had a membership of over 40,000 in 1982. His evangelistic activities attracted more converts to the Anglican Church than any other efforts. [35; 36: 122, 123, 138–44] (R.H.)

Bray, Thomas [VI.A] (1656–1730). Anglican clergyman. A native of Shropshire, he was educated at Oswestry School and Oxford. He became rector of a parish in Warwickshire in 1690 but was soon asked to go to Maryland in the American colonies to assist in the organization of the church there. Before leaving he recruited clergy for the colony and organized a free library for the clergy. This became so successful that he decided to do the same thing for England and organized about 80 Bray libraries. There followed the organization of the Society for the Promotion of Christian Knowledge in 1698. He left for Maryland in 1699 but soon returned to set up in 1701 the Society for the Propagation of the Gospel, which sent missionaries overseas. In 1706 he became vicar of St Botolph Without, Aldgate, London. [640] (T.T.)

Brent, Charles Henry [VI.A] (1862–1929). Canadian Anglican clergyman, born in Newcastle, Ontario, studied theology at Trinity College, Toronto and was ordained an Anglican priest in 1887. He worked in a parish in Boston, Mass., from 1888 to 1891. He became Episcopalian bishop of the Philippines in 1901 and of Western New York in 1918. In World War I he was Chief of Chaplains of the American Expeditionary Force in Europe. Arising from his experience in the Philippines he spent many years on international bodies trying to control narcotics traffic. Following the Edinburgh (Missionary) Conference in 1910, he was instrumental in the calling of the ecumenical World Conference on Faith and Order in Lausanne in 1927, over which he presided. [422] (T.T.)

Bridget of Sweden [VI.A] (*c.*1303–1373). Swedish founder of the Brigittine Order. Born to wealthy landowning parents, she was married at the age of 13 and bore eight children, one of whom, Catherine, was also canonized. Following a pilgrimage together to Compostela in 1341–3 her husband died and she turned to a spiritual life. About 1346 she founded the Order of Saint Saviour, known since as the 'Brigittines', and went to Rome in 1349 to seek confirmation of her order. She stayed there until her death. She was a contemporary of CATHERINE OF SIENA, whom she helped in her attempts to restore the papacy from Avignon to Rome. She was canonized in 1391. [393; 670] (T.T.)

Brigid, St [VIII] Although her *Vita* was written by Cogitosus in the 7th century there is no historical proof of her existence. She is reputed to have founded the Abbey of Kildare in the 5th century. Revered as the second patron saint of Ireland, she is regarded as the patroness of cattle and dairy work. Her feast day is 1 February, associated with spring sowing and the opening of the fishing season. It was marked by special practices, such as house visiting by a girl representing the saint, or by youths in fantastic disguises known as the 'Biddies', as well as the hanging up of crosses of reeds or straw in house and stable as a protection against lightning and other dangers. The Christian abbess seems to have taken over many attributes and characteristics of the Celtic goddess Brigit, who may also have been the goddess of the Brigantes in northern England. She was said to have existed in triple form, and to be a daughter of the Dagda, patroness of poetry, learning, healing and craftsmanship. The monastery at Kildare may have replaced an earlier sanctuary of the goddess. The saint's cult is a good example of the assimilation of beliefs and practices of pre-Christian times by the Christian church. [2] (H.E.D.)

Britto, John de [VI.A] (1647–1693). Portuguese Jesuit missionary. He was born in Lisbon, Portugal, to an aristocratic family. While still a page in the royal household he joined the Society of Jesus. Against the wishes of his family he went to the Madura mission in India in 1673. Unlike some of the other missionaries he chose not to evangelize among the Brahmans but among the lower castes as a *Paradre-swami*. He worked in turbulent times in the area of the mission, with wars among the small kingdoms and famines. He was several times imprisoned, beaten and tortured, and finally condemned to death, but was reprieved by the Raja of Marawa (in the Ramnad area) on condition that he no longer preached, so he returned to Portugal in 1687. In 1691 he went back to India, where he was offered the archbishopric of Cranganore, but he refused it and returned to the work which he had left a few years before. He was again arrested by a Raja whose niece was one of the wives of a minor prince who discarded her on his conversion by Britto. He was accused of using magic in the conversion of the prince and was executed by beheading near the small town of Uraiyur. He was one of the first Christian martyrs in India. [79; 209] (T.T.)

'Brom-ston rgyal-ba'i-byung-gnas [IV] ['Brom ston-pa; 'Brom] (1008–1064). A key figure in the period of Tibetan history known as the latter propagation (*phyi dar*) of Buddhism following the suppression ordered by the king Glang-dar-ma, who was assassinated in 842. The subsequent two centuries saw considerable confusion in Tibet concerning Buddhist theory and practice, particularly with regard to tantrism. The pivotal event in the Buddhist renaissance is traditionally regarded to be the arrival in western Tibet in 1042 of the Bengali scholar Dīpaṇkara Śrījñāna, better known as ATIŚA. 'Brom-ston-pa was Atiśa's first and closest Tibetan disciple. He urged Atiśa to visit central Tibet and organized his tour of the area, where he taught and translated until his death in 1054. 'Brom-ston-pa devoted the rest of his life to preserving Atiśa's teachings, establishing the monastery of Rva-sgreng in 1056 and founding the first Tibetan Buddhist monastic order, the Bka'-gdams-pa, which is traditionally etymologized as 'those who take all of the Buddha's words as instructions'. Although 'Brom was a respected scholar and translator, he is best remembered for the rigour and austerity of his Buddhist practice. His instructions are included in compilations of aphorisms and anecdotes of the Bka'-gdams-pa order, such as the *Bka' gdams thor bu* by Btsun-pa-lce-sgom. In these works, 'Brom-ston-pa repeatedly stresses meditation on impermanence, on compassion and on emptiness. He seems to have been wary of the potential for abuse in tantrism and imposed on his followers a strict discipline and devotion to practice for which they became famous. They abstained from marriage, intoxicants, travel and the possession of money. Although later Tibetan orders were not as strict, the Bka'-gdams-pa provided the model for all later Tibetan monasticism. TSONG-KHA-PA (1357–1419) saw himself as re-establishing the tradition of 'Brom-ston-pa, calling his followers, who later were known as Dge-lugs-pa, the 'New Bka'-gdams-pa'. [197: 481–5; 238: 21–3] (D.L.)

Brunner, Emil [VI.A] (1889–1966). Swiss theologian. He was born in Winterthur, Switzerland. After serving as pastor in Obstalden from 1916 to 1922 he taught in Zurich until 1938, when he moved to Princeton University. He reacted against liberal theology and philosophical theology and was subject to the influence of KANT, KIERKEGAARD, LUTHER and CALVIN. His most important work of Christian ethics was *The Divine Imperative* (English trans. 1947). His three volume *Dogmatics* (1946–60) present his complete theology, while *The Mediator* (English trans. 1947) is an important study on the work of Christ. [427] (T.T.)

Bruno, Giordano [XVII.C] (1548–1600). Italian philosopher. He was born Filippo Bruno at Nola, near Naples, the son of a professional soldier. He studied at Naples, and in 1565 entered the Dominican convent there, receiving the name Giordano. By 1572, when he was ordained a priest, he had begun to question accepted ideas, and in 1576, excommunicated for heresy, he ran away from his order [1: 4–10; 2: 1–16].

During the next 16 years he wandered Europe from England to Czechoslovakia, supporting himself by writing and lecturing, and sometimes finding an influential patron [2: iv–vi, viii, ix, xii–xv]. He wrote extensively in both Latin and Italian [7: 184–6]. Bruno's outspoken views scandalized Catholics and Protestants alike. He rejected the authority of ARISTOTLE and developed the heliocentric theory of COPERNICUS: he abandoned the concept, retained by Copernicus, of crystal spheres causing planetary motion, and maintained that some of the stars were Suns while others were inhabited worlds like the Earth [3: 28–9, 87–90, translated 6: 56–8, 94–8; 7: 31–7, 42–4, 135]. He believed that the Universe was infinite, reasoning that the infinite power of God would not have produced a finite creation [7: 132–3, 158].

Bruno finally returned to Italy at the invitation of a Venetian aristocrat, who promised him protection but in 1592 betrayed him to the religious authorities. He spent the rest of his life as a prisoner of the Inquisition, first in Venice and then in Rome [1: 83–91]. The Inquisition tried every means, possibly including torture, to make him recant his views, while Bruno maintained that he had never departed from orthodox Catholic belief. Eventually the theologian BELLARMINO drew up a list of eight allegedly heretical propositions from Bruno's writings and ordered him to abjure them. Bruno, who had previously appeared ready to compromise on certain points, now stood by everything that he had taught. An appeal to the Pope was rejected unread, and he was condemned as an impenitent heretic [1: 103; 7: 26–30].

On 17 February 1600 Giordano Bruno was burned alive at the stake in the Campo de' Fiori, Rome. He faced death steadfastly. He had told his judges: 'Perhaps your fear in passing sentence on me is greater than mine in receiving it.' His books were banned by the Catholic Church [1: 104–6; 2: 298–305].

Bruno has remained a controversial figure. For 19th-century rationalists he was a pioneer of science. Rediscovery of the Hermetic elements in his work has caused some modern scholars – notably Frances Yates – to consider him primarily as a magus [11: 450]. Bruno himself would not have distinguished between science, philosophy and magic: in the age of the Counter-Reformation, he followed the Renaissance ideal of seeking knowledge as a whole. He has become for many a symbol of uncompromising commitment to the truth. (V.J.R.)

Bruno of Cologne [VI.A] (*c.*1032–1101). Founder of the Carthusian order. He studied at Cologne and Rheims, became a canon at St Cunibert's in Cologne and eventually a teacher at the cathedral school at Rheims, where one of his pupils was the future pope Urban II. He came into conflict with the archbishop of Rheims and left, eventually to form his own religious order, the Carthusians, at Grenoble. He assisted Urban II for a time in Rome but again left to found a monastery in La Torre, Calabria. [94; 125] (T.T.)

Buber, Martin [XV] (1878–1965). Jewish philosopher and educator. Born in Vienna, at an early age he joined the emerging Zionist movement, advocating a cultural Zionism which held that Jewish creativity and spirituality would be fully achieved only as the result of the return of a substantial part of the Jewish people to its homeland. From *c.*1905 he immersed himself in the study of Ḥasidism, which decisively influenced his thinking. He took from Ḥasidism the concept of personal piety as the essence of Judaism but selectively rejected those aspects which he felt had no place in true religiosity. His projection of Ḥasidism in a series of works recounting Ḥasidic anecdotes and parables and his adaptation of its thinking to Western thought (known as neo-Ḥasidism) brought this movement to the attention of the Western world. It also brought Buber to his philosophy of encounter, expressed in his best-known work, *Ich und Du* ('I and Thou', 1923), in which he distinguished between two fundamental relationships: 'I–Thou', which is the relation between person and person, implying reciprocity and involving meeting or encounter, and 'I–It', which is the relation of an individual to a thing or a subject to an object, involving domination. 'I–Thou' is a relation of dialogue and is the true teacher–student relationship (developed by Buber in his educational theory). While the 'Thou' can deteriorate into an 'It', the one 'Thou' that never changes is God, who is present in every dialogue and with whom the human has the perfect relationship.

Buber also applied dialogue to the Jewish–Christian relationship. He wrote that what someone else regards as the reality of his faith can be acknowledged as a mystery even if it appears to oppose our own knowledge. This implies the recognition by Jews of the reality of Christianity as a path to God and the demand that Christianity similarly recognize Judaism as an authentic path to God. He distinguished between two types of faith: the Hebrew *emunah*, the biblical pattern which was also the faith of Jesus, and the Greek *pistis*, followed by Paul; the former involves an intellectual act, the latter obedience to God's will. The Jew carries the burden of the unredeemed world in the knowledge that redemption is not an accomplished fact and that history has not yet known a caesura in which a redeemer appeared.

Buber taught in Germany, and after the accession to power of the Nazis in 1933, directed Jewish adult education for all Germany. However, in 1938 when the Nazis forbade him to teach, he emigrated to Palestine, where he was appointed professor of social philosophy at Jerusalem's Hebrew University. There he completed the translation of the Bible into German, which he had begun together with FRANZ ROSENZWEIG, and which was notable for recapturing the original meanings and rhythms of the Hebrew text. [27; 79] (G.W.)

Bucer, Martin [VI.A] (1491–1551). Protestant reformer. He entered the Dominican Order in 1506 and later came under the influence of ERASMUS. In 1518 he began to correspond with MARTIN LUTHER. This led to him seeking dispensation from monastic vows, which was granted in 1521. He married in 1522. In 1523 he began to preach a Lutheran reformed message in Alsace and was excommunicated by the Bishop of Speyer. He led the reforming changes in Strasbourg, which included abolishing the Mass and building a separate church. After 1531 he led the Reformed Churches in Switzerland and South Germany. Having unsuccessfully opposed a religious settlement arranged by Charles V, he went to England, where he became Regius Professor of Divinity at Cambridge. He participated in the revision of *The Book of Common Prayer* and outlined his church reforms in his *De regno Christi*, which he dedicated to Edward VI. He was buried in Great St Mary, Cambridge, but his body was later exhumed and burnt. [236; 628; 763; 764] (T.T.)

Buddha [IV] [Śākyamuni; Siddhārtha Gotama]. The founder of Buddhism. (The word 'Buddhism' is a western term: in the texts the Buddha speaks of his path as 'the Middle Way', or *dharma* (*dhamma*), an untranslatable term meaning 'the Truth', 'the Right Way', etc.; Buddhist monks and nuns are called 'Sons and Daughters of the Buddha' or of 'the Śākyan(s)', and opponents, mainly Hindu or Jain, came to refer to the *Bauddhas*, an adjective meaning 'Buddhist(s)'.) There are two ways of arriving at a date for the Buddha: the so-called 'Long' and 'Short Chronologies'. The Long Chronology, attested from Ceylonese sources (with a revision of about 60 years because of a miscalculation they make), gives a date for his final *nirvāṇa* of 218 years before the consecration of AŚOKA, that is *c.*486 BCE. The Short Chronology, attested from Indian sources and their translations into Tibetan and Chinese, gives a date of 100 years before Aśoka, that is *c.*368 BCE. Since Buddhist texts unanimously say that the Buddha died at the age of 80, his dates can be computed thus as either *c.*566–486 or *c.*448–368 BCE. In the past scholars have usually favoured the earlier date, but the subject is now once again under discussion.

The term *buddha* means simply 'awake', and by extension in the religious context, 'enlightened'. As an adjective it can be and is applied to anyone who has achieved the religious goal in Buddhism, usually termed either *nirvāṇa* or *bodhi*. In Buddhism a longer term *samyaksambuddha* (*sammā sambuddha*), 'Completely, Fully Enlightened', is used to denote specifically those Great Beings who, when knowledge of the saving Truth (*dharma*, *dhamma*) has been lost, rediscover it for themselves and then found a new Teaching (*śāsana*, *sāsana*). The idea can be conveyed in English simply by using the upper-case initial letter B: *the* or *a* Buddha. One early *sutta* in Pali gives a list of six Buddhas before our own; another mentions the next Buddha in the future, Metteyya (Sanskrit: Maitreya); a later Canonical text, the *Buddhavaṃsa* ('Chronicle of Buddhas') gives 24 previous Buddhas. In all Buddhism, the total number of Buddhas in the past and future is logically infinite; the Mahāyāna schools differ from earlier ideas only in making it possible to have more than one Buddha in existence at any one time. In different parts of the Mahāyāna Buddhist world other Buddhas can play important roles in texts and rituals: examples are Akṣobhya, Amitābha (Japanese: Amida), Ratnasambhava, Amoghasiddhi and Vairocana.

The Buddha of our time was born as Siddhārtha Gautama (Pali: Siddhattha Gotama); he was from the Śakya (Sakya) clan, and the title 'Sage of the Sakyans', Śākyamuni, is a particularly common name in Mahāyāna traditions, where the historical career of Siddhārtha Gautama is very much less important. Indeed, in the developed metaphysical doctrine of the Buddha's Three Bodies, the historical Gautama who appeared on this earth is said to have been a magical and unreal 'Transformation Body' (*nirmāṇa-kāya*). But in both iconography and narrative literature, the stories of 'our' Buddha's life and past lives (*see* SUMEDHA and VESSANTARA) remain important, and are ubiquitous in the Theravāda tradition of South and South-east Asia. The outlines of the story are as follows.

In his penultimate life as a god in the Tuṣita heaven, having in countless previous lives fulfilled all the Perfections necessary for Buddhahood, the future Buddha (*Bodhisattva*, *Bodhisatta*; *see* SUMEDHA) chooses to be reborn at a specific time and place (Lumbinī in modern Nepal), and to a specific mother (*see* QUEEN MĀYĀ). At birth it is prophesied that the child will become either a Universal Emperor or a Universal Saviour (*see* AŚOKA for these terms). His father, Suddhodhana, prefers the former, and so surrounds him with luxury. Gautama has three palaces for each of the three Indian seasons. He is married and has a son, Rāhula (*see* YAŚODHARĀ); but at the age of 29 this idyllic existence is interrupted when Gautama goes outside his palace and sees the 'four sights': an old man, a sick man, a corpse and an ascetic (*see* VIPASSI). He renounces the household life, adopts a life of fierce asceticism, so fierce that his body becomes thin and wasted almost to the point of death (this is an occasional subject for iconographic representation). He decides, however, that extreme asceticism is fruitless, and adopts a moderate diet, going to the Bodhi tree (*ficus religiosa*) at what is now Bodh Gāya in Bihar; he finally achieves Enlightenment there after being both tempted and attacked by the demon Māra. He is now 35 years old. At first he hesitates to tell others of his Path to Liberation, but accedes to the request of the chief god Brahmā, and so begins his teaching mission, preaching 'the Middle Way' between the family life of a householder, doomed to rebirth however pleasant the short-term experience, and the celibate life of extreme asceticism, which seeks the right goal – freedom from rebirth – but by the wrong means. He founds the order of monks, and later of nuns (*Saṅgha*), and spends 45 years wandering around North-east India, 'out of compassion for people', accompanied for most of this time by ĀNANDA. As his death, or final *nirvāṇa*, approaches, he goes to the small town Kuśinagara (in modern Uttar Pradesh) and lies down on his side between two trees. His body takes on a golden hue; deities throng the area to take a last look at 'the Teacher of Gods and Men'; and he 'enters' or 'attains' *nirvāṇa* (the usual term is a verb from the compound form *parinirvāṇa*, 'to parinirvanize'). Gods and men who are unenlightened, and not beyond the passions, weep bitterly; those who have mastered their passions take heed of his final admonition: 'Impermanent are all conditioned things; strive (for the Unconditioned) with diligence.' Those Buddhist schools which accept the idea of a final *nirvāṇa* (many Mahāyānist traditions do not) systematically refuse to predicate anything, including 'existence' or 'non-existence', of the Buddha after his *nirvāṇa*.

In previous scholarship, versions of this

story, told realistically, were taken to be historically true. Other Buddhist ideas and treatments of the tale, and of the figure of Gautama Buddha, were said to be 'later, mythological' additions. But many now feel this approach to be wrong-headed: we cannot, it is argued, know that tales with an air – to us – of verisimilitude necessarily precede what seems 'mythological'. At least from the time of the *Lokottaravāda* school (roughly the 'Transcendentalists'), who were an offshoot of the *Mahāsaṅghika*s (*see* MAHĀDEVA), there was a tendency to see the true nature of the Buddha as transcending the impurities and ephemera of this world. Although this did not at first lessen interest in Gautama's biography, the Mahāyāna ideas mentioned earlier, together with the proliferation of other Buddhas, present as well as past, eventually had this effect. [30; 165; 223; 255] (S.C.)

Buddhadāsa [IV] (1906–). Thai Buddhist intellectual and monk who is well known for his innovative and eclectic style of thought. Buddhadāsa was born in Bumrieng, near Chaiya in southern Thailand. The eldest son of a Chinese-Thai trader, his given name was Ñüam. Although as a thinker Buddhadāsa is well known for his appropriation of Ch'an or Zen forms of Buddhism, he apparently did not have any direct contact with Chinese Buddhism through his father's family. He left school at age 14 to work in the family business. At 20 he was ordained in the Buddhist monastic order at the request of his mother, taking the name Indapañño. Buddhadāsa probably expected this ordination to be temporary, in the Thai custom, but he found monastic life congenial. He passed through the various levels of monastic education, eventually going to Bangkok for advanced study. While there, he became increasingly critical of the state of monastic discipline in the capital, and like many other reformers, turned to an intensive study of authoritative texts for guidance about what constitutes an authentic Buddhist life. In 1932 Buddhadāsa returned to his home town, and was supported in a forest hermitage by a lay reformist society called the 'Gift of Dhamma Group'. This society published a journal, *Buddhasāsana*, and 'Buddhadāsa', the pen name he used for articles published there, became the name by which he was generally known.

For over 50 years Buddhadāsa has taught at his meditation centre Suan Mokkh ('Park of Liberation') and produced a large number of publications. In his teaching and writings, Buddhadāsa has often returned to four principle themes: (1) criticism of the conventional practices of Thai Buddhism; (2) advocacy of a return to 'original Buddhism', in which he often appeals to Mahāyāna Buddhist thought and argues for the accessibility of liberation (*nirvāṇa*) to everyone; (3) receptivity to the insights afforded by non-Buddhist thought, especially for dealing with contemporary issues; and (4) the importance of a missionary intention, both towards ordinary Buddhists and non-Buddhists. The last theme is most apparent in Buddhadāsa's writings which are directed to Westerners.

Buddhadāsa's version of Buddhist modernism has been controversial, but at the very least he has stimulated an intensive re-questioning of what it means to be Buddhist in contemporary Thailand [24; 68] (C.H.)

Buddhaghosa [IV] (4th–5th century?). The most famous scholar-monk in Theravāda Buddhism. He is credited with numerous commentaries on the Pali Canon written in Pali (more, certainly, than he can in fact have composed), as well as the monumental *Visuddhimagga* (for a translation of which see [163], a *summa* of the Theravāda tradition). Reliable historical evidence for his life is meagre: there are a few pieces of information in the works attributed to him, an account written in Sri Lanka probably in the 13th century, and a later biography written in Burma, which has been called a 'popular novel' [163: xxiv] and an 'historical romance' [72: title page].

Although there is a late Burmese tradition which holds that he was from that country, this may result from confusion with a later Burmese figure of the same name. There seems no reason to doubt that the general outlines of the traditional biography are correct. This says that he was a monk from India, who had begun to compose treatises and commentaries there, and to have gone to Sri Lanka to gain materials for the work. The tradition that he was a learned Brahman from North India who converted to Buddhism after being defeated in debate by a Buddhist monk is doubtful: although some of his work shows signs of Sanskritic learning, he also sometimes shows ignorance of that language and its texts, and he makes comments which, it is alleged, no one with first-hand knowledge of North India could have made. He stayed at the Mahāvihāra in the capital Anurādhapura for many years, and states on many occasions that his work is meant to preserve the tradition of that monastic lineage. He does mention the views of others, however; sometimes this is to reject them but sometimes it is with apparent approval or without comment. He describes himself as working from the older commentaries written in Sinhalese, which are themselves said to have been continuations of a commentarial tradition brought from India, along with the Canon, by MAHINDA in the 3rd century BCE. This fact lessens somewhat the importance of deciding in this context who 'the author' of any given commentary was, but there has been debate about which of the many commentaries attributed to him can actually have been his work. Stylistic considerations, the fact that some works attributed to him seem to cite the views of his own *Visuddhimagga* only as possible alternatives, and other such criteria are used in this discussion. Perhaps he worked as the supervisor of a group of scholars. Ñāṇamoli (1905–1960), an Englishman who became a Buddhist monk in Sri Lanka and one of the great translators of Pali texts in modern times, referred once to 'The committee called Buddhaghosa'. [164: 235]

Some later Burmese texts, whether or not they think of him as a Burmese native, hold that he went on to Burma after his work in Sri Lanka was finished; but the consensus is that he returned to India. Nothing is reliably recorded of his life after he left Sri Lanka. [163: XV–XXVII; 72] (S.C.)

Buhari Johori [XII] (17th century). Islamic-Malay writer. Johori is best known for his work at rendering *Tāj al-Salāṭīn* ('The Crown of the Princes'), a handbook for young statesmen and princes, into Malay. The work is dated 1603 in the Malay version. The Persian original has not come to light and the possibility does exist that the work is original in Malay, the act of suggesting that a work is being translated from Arabic or Persian into a language of the Islamic periphery while actually composing the work not being that uncommon. The work is divided into 24 chapters dealing with God, life and the proper attitudes and behaviour of those in power. It remained very popular in Malay, such that it was quoted by ʿAbd Allāh Munshī some 200 years later. [175; 140] (J.K.)

al-Bukhārī, Muḥammad ibn Ismāʿīl ibn Ibrāhīm al-Juʿfī [XII] (810–870). Muslim Traditionist and scholar. In the course of the 3rd *hijrī* century (9th century CE) the notion became dominant in the Muslim community that arguments related to juristic and theological matters should be defended and justified by reference to the words or actions of MUḤAMMAD. These were preserved in the form of *ḥadīth*: that is, reports of the Prophet's words or deeds, each report being preceded by a chain of transmitters deemed to have passed on the report successively through two or more centuries. Juristic and theological dispute in the 2nd and early 3rd centuries created a demand for authoritative *ḥadīth* and led to the production of numerous *ḥadīth* collections. Of these, six eventually emerged as dominant, namely those of al-Bukhārī, MUSLIM, ABŪ DĀWŪD, AL-TIRMIDHĪ, AL-NASĀʾĪ and IBN MĀJA. The collection of IBN ḤANBAL is perhaps equally authoritative but less useful as his work is organized on the basis of transmitters, while the canonical six are organized by subject matter. The Muslim tradition recognizes the existence of spurious and doubtful *ḥadīth*, but accepts those contained in the canonical collections as generally reliable. It was acknowledged that there were different degrees of reliability, of which the collections of al-Bukhārī and Muslim represent the highest degree, each being known as *al-Jāmiʿ al-Ṣaḥīḥ* ('The Valid/Reliable Collection'), both together being the Two *Ṣaḥīḥ*s. Western scholars on the other hand see many *ḥadīth*, perhaps the majority, as emerging posterior to and as a result of juristic and theological dispute within the Muslim community.

Al-Bukhārī, like all Traditionists, is reported to have travelled through the Muslim Middle East in order to hear *ḥadīth*. He received training from all the major transmitters of his time, including Ibn Ḥanbal, and had displayed astounding feats of memory even before his travels. It is memory that makes a great Traditionist, and later biographies make much of al-Bukhārī's skills. He is portrayed as claiming knowledge of 600,000 *ḥadīth*, from which he selected those for his work, conventionally assessed to contain about 4,000 *ḥadīth*, but containing in fact less than 3,000 different items. The work is organized in books and chapters, arranged according to the established agenda of juristic and theological problems. Some chapter headings have no *ḥadīth* entries. A handful of works relating to the biographies of *ḥadīth*-transmitters (*ʿilm al-rijāl*) is also attributed to al-Bukhārī.

In biographical sources much is made of al-Bukhārī's piety and devotion. His *Ṣaḥīḥ* is said to be the most noble and superior of books, second only to the Qur'ān itself; similar claims are made for others of the canonical six. Both the Shāfiʿī and the Ḥanbalī law-schools lay claim to al-Bukhārī, though it is not clear he espoused either. He spent his teaching career in Nīshāpūr, but later returned to Bukhāra, where he died, it is said, as a result of some dispute with the local governor. In Ashʿarite sources he represents the theological view that the pronunciation of the Qur'ān is created. [35: s.v.; 41: 216–26] (N.C.)

Bultmann, Rudolf [VI.A] (1884–1976). German New Testament scholar. The son of a German Lutheran pastor and the grandson of a Lutheran missionary to Africa, he was born in Wiefelstede, Oldenburg, where he had his early education. After studying theology at Tübingen, Berlin and Marburg he taught at Breslau and Giessen before settling back at Marburg as professor and, after 1951, emeritus professor. His important critical works are *The History of the Synoptic Tradition* (German original 1921; English trans. 1963); *The Gospel of John* (German original 1941; English trans. 1971); and *Theology of the New Testament*, 2 vols. (German original 1948–53; English trans. 1951, 1955). In New Testament criticism he adopted a radically sceptical view of the historicity of the Gospel story but tried to bring out the significance of the Gospel message for a modern society. [127; 428; 511] (T.T.)

Bunyan, John [VI.A] (1628–1688). English Calvinist. He was a brazier and the son of a brazier born in Elstow, near Bedford. Though possibly lacking formal education he learned to read some of the leading religious works of his day, including Foxe's *Book of Martyrs*. He joined a Baptist congregation in Bedford in 1655, became a preacher but suffered at royalist hands after the Restoration and spent most of the years 1660–72 in Bedford Gaol. It was during this imprisonment that he wrote the first part of his classic *Pilgrim's Progress* (1678), an allegorical work on the Christian life. Among the most important of his other works was *Grace Abounding to the Chief of Sinners* (1666), an autobiography. He was a puritan, a strict Calvinist who untypically rejected the need of water baptism for the faithful. [121; 269; 728] (T.T.)

Burns, William Chalmers [VI.A] (1815–1868). Scottish Presbyterian missionary. He was born at Duns, Scotland, but later became a member of the Presbyterian Church of England. He experienced religious revivals in Britain and Canada and decided on missionary work in China. He reached China in 1847 and began evangelistic and literary work in Amoy, Canton, Swatow and finally in Peking. For seven months in 1855 he was closely associated with JAMES HUDSON TAYLOR. In August 1867, Burns reached Newchwang in Manchuria, and died there nine months later in a narrow room with very few possessions. Before his death he appealed to the Presbyterian Church in Ireland to carry on his work and missionaries were sent from that church within a year of his death. [129; 279] (T.T.)

Buxton, Thomas Fowell [VI.A] (1786–1845). English Christian philanthropist. He was born at Earl's Colne, Essex, and became a prosperous trader and Member of Parliament for Weymouth. He united Evangelical Anglican and Quaker influences, and, after devoting himself to criminal law reform (especially to reducing the number of capital offences), he succeeded William Wilberforce as chief spokesman on slavery matters. He piloted the legislation leading to the emancipation of slaves in the British possessions in 1834, and wrestled with the problem of the continuance of the Atlantic slave trade despite legislative abolition. His book *The African Slave Trade and its Remedy* (1839) enunciated the redemption of Africa by the Bible and the plough, and its recovery by stimulating agricultural development. The government-sponsored Niger Expedition of

1841, sent to further these ideas, was a disaster, but missionary thought in the middle of the 19th century, including that of Henry Venn and DAVID LIVINGSTONE, reflected Buxton's ideals. He gave parliamentary backing to the attempts of JOHN PHILIP to secure justice in South Africa. [19; 132; 133] (A.F.W.)

Byrd, William [VI.A] (1543–1623). English composer. He was probably born in Lincoln and was appointed organist at Lincoln Cathedral in 1563. Towards the end of his period at Lincoln he was for two years also Gentleman of the Chapel Royal in London. He later became co-organist at the Chapel Royal with THOMAS TALLIS. In 1575 Elizabeth I recognized their services by granting them a monopoly of music printing. This patronage is the probable reason why Byrd escaped persecution for being a practising Catholic. His output of music for the Church of England, including many anthems, together with three volumes of *Cantiones sacrae*, preceded a concentration in the 1590s on Latin music for the Roman rite. (E.M.)

C

Caitanya [XI] (1486–1533). Ecstatic devotee of Kṛṣṇa, and inspiration behind the Caitanya or Gauḍīya sect. A mystical experience in early manhood led him to turn away from formal Brahmanical learning in favour of an emotionally informed devotional life, and in 1510 he was initiated as an ascetic, abandoning his given name of 'Viśvambhara' for the ascetic title 'Kṛṣṇa Caitanya'. His charismatic personality and his unrestrained demonstrations of love for Kṛṣṇa through song and dance rapidly attracted a large following in his home town of Nabadwip (Bengal). Detailed hagiographies, such as the important *Caitanya Caritāmṛta* (1615) of Kṛṣṇadās Kavirāj, identify Caitanya as an incarnation of the joint form of Rādhā and Kṛṣṇa. They describe his pilgrimages to various of the Vaiṣṇava centres, including Puri in Orissa and the temples of the South; during a visit to the Braj district, fabled location of Kṛṣṇa's childhood, he joyfully identified certain of the 'lost' sites of Kṛṣṇa's sports, a process whose continuance by his disciples was to lead to the establishment of Vrindaban as a major centre of pilgrimage. Caitanya drew his principal disciples from the province of Gauḍ, which gives the sect its alternative name; but he lived the latter part of his life at Puri, worshipping the deity Jagannāth. Caitanya's ecstatic devotion, involving total absorption in contemplation of Rādhā and Kṛṣṇa, was a distinctly new departure in North Indian devotionalism. Though it has a partial precedent in the *bhakti* of the Tamil ĀLVĀRS (whose emotionalism is reflected in the style of Kṛṣṇa-*bhakti* inculcated by the 9th/10th-century *Bhāgavata Purāṇa*), it is unparalleled in the North even among the other Kṛṣṇaite sects whose origins are contemporary with those of the Caitanya tradition. Caitanya's own devotional frenzies hardly lent themselves to the formation of an analytical theology; as was the case with many a contemporary sect, it was not the so-called 'founder' of the sect but his disciples – especially here the celebrated 'six Gosvāmīs' – who were to put the sect and its teachings on a formal basis. The theology of the sect is based on an adaption of traditional aesthetic theory, *bhakti* being treated in terms of *rasa* or aesthetic sentiment, and the wild abandon of Caitanya's experiential devotionalism is balanced by his disciple RŪPA GOSVĀMĪ's theoretical exposition of the *rasa* 'theory' which allows the devotee to enter the realm of Kṛṣṇa's *līlā* or divine sport by mental association with one or other of its protagonists. Though the finer points of this theory are for sectarian specialists only, its broad approach has been enormously influential in the subsequent development of Kṛṣṇa-*bhakti* generally, and in moulding the conventions of devotional literatures throughout Northern India. The Caitanya sect is notable for its fusion of theological sophistication with popular appeal, and the characteristic public celebrations of Kṛṣṇa's divinity have in recent years attracted an international following in the so-called 'Hare Krishna' movement, based firmly on the devotional attitude of Caitanya. [23; 42; 46] (*See also* PRABHUPADA; CANDĪDĀS.) (R.S.)

Cajetan [VI.A] [Thomas de Vio] (1469–1534). Catholic theologian. A native of Gaeta, he became a Dominican in 1484 and taught philosophy and theology in Padua, Pavia and Rome. In 1508 he became General of the Dominican Order. He was made a cardinal in 1517 and bishop of Gaeta in 1519. He urged reforms at the Lateran Council

(1512) and engaged in discussions with LUTHER in 1518. He opposed the divorce of Henry VIII in 1530. His commentary on the *Summa Theologica* of THOMAS AQUINAS is a classic of scholasticism and revived Thomistic theology in the 16th century. Later he became a biblical critic with 'modern' tendencies. [325] (T.T.)

Cakobau [XXI] [Thakombau] (1817–1883). Fijian chief and champion of the missionaries. He was a chief of Bau, off the main island of Vitu Levu, who led successful wars against neighbouring chieftainships because of a ritual monopoly over (largely salvaged) European firearms. His dominance over most of Fiji occurred between 1830 and 1850, when settlers and missionaries first came to settle in Fiji. Unable to resist a widespread revolt, which drove him back to Bau, Cakobau eventually became Christian in 1854 and a strong supporter of the Wesleyans. King George of Tonga sent 2,000 warriors to relieve him of his military difficulties, and by 1856 he had become paramount chief of western Fiji. His conversion meant Christianization went on apace, and he emerged as King of the Government of Fiji in 1871, with English settler John Woods as his premier and fellow chiefs holding portfolios and councillorships. Manipulation by settlers, however, forced his cession of Fiji to Queen Victoria in 1874. [3: 99–267; 38] (G.W.T.)

Calvin, John [VI.A] [Jean Cauvin] (1509–1564). Protestant theologian. He was born in Noyon and spent his early days as a Roman Catholic in France. He was granted a benefice at the age of 12 and from 1523 to 1528 studied the humanities in Paris. His father died excommunicate and Calvin had difficulty in arranging his father's burial. His association with Lutheran ideas forced him to flee France in 1533. In 1536 he published the first edition of his main work *Institutes of the Christian Religion* in Basel. Soon after, while journeying through Geneva, he was made to stay in the city and help Guillaume Farel to organize Protestant reform. The regime the two men tried to impose on the city caused alienation and they were forced to leave. Calvin spent the next three years in Strasbourg. In 1541 he returned to Geneva and proceeded with further reform. The city became a theocratic state ruled by clergy assisted by a consistory which included laymen. Rules governing worship, belief and morals were strictly enforced. Those who did not conform could be excommunicated and even executed for sins such as heresy. He published further works on the New Testament, the Reformation and Predestination and commentaries on the Old Testament. In 1559 he founded the Academy of Geneva to carry on his form of teaching. [62; 138; 622] (T.T.)

Cama, Kharshedji Rustamji [XXVI] (1831–1909). A Parsi of mercantile family with outstanding intellectual gifts. He early abandoned commerce for learning, and after spending 1857 visiting leading European scholars, introduced in Bombay the study of Avestan and Pahlavi (the Zoroastrian holy languages) on Western philological principles. His classes attracted some remarkably gifted young priests, including TAHMURAS ANKLESARIA, and inspired the founding of the Sir J. JEEJEEBHOY Madressa, which was staffed at first largely by his pupils. When in the 1860s M. Haug expounded his interpretation of ZOROASTER's teachings as strictly monotheistic [9: 202–3], Cama was among the Parsis who accepted this. It provided a defence against Christian missionaries' attacks on their dualism (*see* SANJANA EDAL), but forced them to regard much of their traditional religion as false accretion. The community became therefore deeply divided. Cama sought unity through greater knowledge, and took the lead in sending M. N. DHALLA abroad to study. He himself founded learned societies in Bombay, financed occasional publications and essay-prizes, and was joint owner of the reformist newspaper *Rāst Goftār*. In 1894 he was appointed examiner for Avestan and Pahlavi at Bombay University. Thereafter he studied the two calendars used, divisively, by the Parsis (*see* JĀMĀSP 'VELĀYATĪ'), and finding neither satisfactory, sought to 're-establish' what he deduced had been the original ancient Iranian one. This, called *faṣli*, 'seasonal', is based on the Gregorian calendar and, being adopted only by reformists, created new dissension. Cama's writings on this and other religious matters were published in 1900 in two volumes as his *Collected Works* (reprinted Bombay, 1968). In later life he was attracted to the theosophy expounded by

BLAVATSKY and H. S. OLCOTT, partly, it seems, because of the respect they showed for Zoroastrianism. In 1916 the K. R. Cama Oriental Institute was founded in his memory, and through its fine library, journal and lectures continues his lifework of serving his religion through the pursuit of knowledge. [19; 43; 1: VIII; 25] (J.R.H.)

Câmara, (Dom) Helder Pessoa [VI.A] (1909–). Brazilian Catholic archbishop. He was born in Fortaleza in the 'triangle of hunger' of north-eastern Brazil and entered a conservative Catholic seminary when only 14 years of age. He was ordained priest in 1931 and became deeply involved in the fascist 'Integralist Action' movement. After working in municipal education and administration in Rio de Janeiro, he became Deputy Padre General of 'Catholic Action' in Brazil in 1947. From 1952 to 1964 he was the first Secretary General of the National Conference of Brazilian Bishops and became involved in the Basic Education Movement for the poor. He became Vice-President of the Catholic Latin American Episcopal Conference (CELAM) between 1959 and 1965. In 1955 he was 'converted' from his right-wing ways and decided to devote his life to work for justice for the poor. From 1965, he served as Archbishop of Olinda-Recife in the poverty-stricken North-East. There he set up a non-violent movement called 'Action for Justice and Peace' among 'the submerged masses' and campaigned intrepidly for social reform. For so doing, he was awarded international peace prizes, although in his own land military regimes have subjected him to vicious campaigns of defamation and serious harassment. He retired from his ecclesiastical charge in 1984 and continues to be hailed as a living symbol of God's 'preferential option for the poor'. His radical, eirenic contribution to international Catholic congresses and his assistance in the bringing to birth of 'base ecclesial communities' since the 1960s has been outstanding. His writings have been in practical theology and down-to-earth spirituality; they have been translated into many languages and include among others: *Church and Colonialism* (1969), *Spiral of Violence* (1971), *The Desert is Fertile* (1974) and *Hoping against All Hope* (1984) [120; 163; 339; 874] (A.C.S.)

Campanella, Tommaso [XVII] (1568–1639). Italian philosopher. He was born at Stilo, Calabria, and joined the Dominican Order in 1583. On a number of occasions he came under suspicion of heresy. In 1599 he led a revolutionary movement to overthrow Spanish rule in Southern Italy and create an ideal republic ruled by a magus-priest – himself. Defeated, captured and severely tortured, Campanella escaped execution by feigning madness, but was sentenced to life imprisonment as a heretic. As a prisoner of the Spanish Inquisition at Naples, he spent his time in writing, notably the various versions of *La città del sole* ('The City of the Sun'), his vision of the ideal society [4; 11: 360–7].

Campanella's city was to be governed by a Sun Priest in accordance with natural law and magic. The people would live together in peace, free of crime. Property would be shared, and marriages would be arranged according to astrological compatibility rather than financial interests, to ensure the breeding of healthy children. *La città del sole* shows the influence of PLATO and of More's *Utopia*, but even more of Hermetic and astrological ideas [11: 367–70].

Abandoning his revolutionary aims, Campanella began to look to Spain and the papacy to bring about his ideal state. In 1626 he was released through Spanish influence, though in 1629 he spent a further period in prison in Rome [9: 207–8]. In 1634, having had little success in converting the papacy to his views, he left for Paris, where he spent the rest of his life. His vision of a solar government was welcomed by Louis XIII and was perhaps even a formative influence on the Dauphin, later Louis XIV [11: 389–91, 395–6].

Campanella's philosophical views had much in common with those of his older contemporary GIORDANO BRUNO, with whom, however, he disagreed strongly on matters of religious orthodoxy. He rejected the teachings of ARISTOTLE, who had acquired almost the status of a Christian Father, and defended the heliocentric theory of COPERNICUS. In later life he befriended GALILEO and supported his ideas. However, in an age in which events on Earth were assumed to mirror those in the heavens, Campanella was particularly interested in the social and political implications of the new discoveries. In his search for a heliocentric model of government, he moved from republican and even proto-Communist ideas to providing the philosophical inspiration for the monarchy of Le Roi Soleil [11: 382–3, 361; 9: VII]. (V.J.R.)

Campbell, Alexander [VI.A] (1788–1866). American religious leader. He was born in Northern Ireland, the son of a Presbyterian minister. He joined his father, who had already started his own primitivist New Testament 'Christian Association', in America in 1809. For a time they were Baptists but from the 1830s the son began to organize his 'Reforming Baptist' groups into independent churches. So were born the 'Campbellites', officially known as The Disciples of Christ. Campbell wrote nearly the whole seven volumes of *The Christian Baptist* (1835). He founded Bethany College near his home in Virginia and served as its president until his death. The Disciples formed the American Christian Missionary Society in 1849 with Campbell as President. [139; 486; 681] (T.T.)

Campion, Edmund [VI.A] (1540–1581). English Jesuit martyr. A native of London, the son of a bookseller, he was educated at Oxford and became a Junior Fellow of St John's College. A powerful orator, he was chosen by the university to welcome Queen Elizabeth I to Oxford in 1566. Ordained a deacon of the Church of England in 1569, he soon went to Dublin to follow his Catholic leanings. He was accepted into the Roman Catholic Church in Douai in 1571. At Rome in 1573 he entered the Jesuit Order and was ordained in 1578. He returned to England as a Jesuit missionary in 1580. In 1581 he secretly published *Decem rationes*, a defence of Roman Catholicism. Arrested later that year and refusing to return to the Church of England, he was executed on a charge of conspiracy against the Crown. He was canonized in 1970. [10; 140; 843] (T.T.)

Caṇḍīdās [XI] [Baṛu Caṇḍīdās]. Author of *Śrīkṛṣṇakīrtana*, an important early Bengali Vaiṣṇava text. The name 'Caṇḍīdās' is associated with a wide range of devotional poetry in Bengali, much of it popular to this day as a source of song and aphorism: but this literature does not represent the corpus of any one poet, and the historical position of both the verse and its author(s) is extremely uncertain. The *Śrīkṛṣṇakīrtana*, a work of markedly unreserved eroticism describing various episodes of the Rādhā-Kṛṣṇa myth, was itself discovered only in 1910, and its title also dates from the period of this discovery. Scholarly opinion is divided on the subject of its date: some authorities date it to the late 14th century on linguistic grounds, while others point to such features as Indo-Persian loanwords and posit a date of no earlier than the 16th century. The distinction is an important one because of its implications for the history of Vaiṣṇavism, the question of whether CAITANYA and his followers may have been influenced by the poem being hotly debated. Baṛu Caṇḍīdās, the first part of whose name identifies him as of priestly rank, the second part showing him to be a devotee of 'Caṇḍī' (Durgā), shows a debt to the *Gītagovinda* of JAYADEVA, and also to the quasi-tantric Sahajīya movement. Though it is unlikely that real data will ever emerge to cast light on its author's biography, the *Śrīkṛṣṇakīrtana* remains an important milestone in the development of Bengali and of Vaiṣṇavism. [60] (R.S.)

Candragomin [IV] (*c*.625–*c*.700). Poet and philosopher. He lived several centuries later than the grammarian Cāndra, with whom he is traditionally identified. (For a discussion of Candragomin's date in more detail see [219]; for a list of his literary works see [220].) Born in what is now Bengal, he remained a layman all his life, though relinquishing family ties.

As a philosopher he belongs to the line of VASUBANDHU and Sthiramati. For seven years at the monastic university of Nālandā he engaged in debate with Candrakīrti, upholding Yogācāra against Madhyamaka. He was much favoured by the compassionate deities Tārā and Avalokiteśvara, who rescued him from shipwreck and other dangers, including defeat in that debate.

Candragomin is admired for his versatility, and for his exemplary status as a follower of the bodhisattva's path. He embodies the classical Indian ideal of a cultured, urbane cosmopolitan (*nāgaraka*), learned in art, science and literature. His literary output includes both sacred and secular works.

Modern translations of his works include three didactic texts on the bodhisattva's path [222], a drama [90] and verses of praise in scattered places, including some in praise of Tārā, protectress from the eight dangers. [15:229–30] (M.T.)

Candrakīrti [IV] (*c*.600–650). Buddhist philosopher in the Madhyamaka tradition, perhaps the single most influential commentator upon and expositor of NĀGĀRJUNA's thought. Almost nothing is known about his life; his importance for the Buddhist tradition lies solely in his systematic philosophical works. These were of great influence in both India and Tibet, where Candrakīrti's understanding of Madhyamaka (usually labelled *prāsaṅgika* or 'absurd conclusionist') dominated the systematic thought of the dge-lugs-pa school.

Candrakīrti's two most important works are, first, his commentary on Nāgārjuna's *Basic Verses on the Middle Way* called *Prasannapadā* ('Clear-Worded') [201] and, second, a systematic text called *Madhyamakāvatāra* ('Entry into the Middle Way'). The latter provides a systematic introduction to Madhyamaka, arranged around the structure of the ten perfections developed on the Buddhist path. The former is important for its uncompromising rejection of the need for and possibility of independently valid philosophical arguments to support and establish the Madhyamaka 'position' and for its engagement with BHĀVAVIVEKA's thought [186: 71–81] (P.J.G.)

Carey, William [VI.A] (1761–1834). English Baptist missionary. A native of Northamptonshire, he was baptized into the Church of England but after an experience of conversion in 1779 joined the Baptists. A shoemaker by trade, he also taught at a school and was a pastor of a church. He taught himself Latin, Greek, Hebrew, Dutch and French. In 1792 he was one of the founders of the Baptist Missionary Society. The following year he left for India, eventually settling in Serampore, Bengal. He translated the New Testament into Bengali and with the help of other missionaries it was published in 1801. The whole Bible was published in Bengali in 1809. He continued the translation of the Bible in whole or in part into 24 other Indian languages or dialects and published dictionaries and. grammars in four Indian languages. He became a professor of Indian languages at the new Fort William College in Calcutta. [141; 525; 611] (T.T.)

Caro, Joseph [XV] (1488–1575). Jewish legal codifier. Born in Spain, he was still a child when the Jews were expelled from that country. His family eventually settled in Turkey, where he lived for 40 years. In 1536 he moved to Safed, Palestine, at that time a great centre of Jewish learning and mysticism, where he headed a large academy.

Caro's *Bet Yoseph* ('House of Joseph') and its abridgement, *Shulḥan Arukh* ('The Table is Prepared') were the last of the great Jewish legal codes and had a decisive impact on the final crystallization of the norms of Orthodox Jewry. *Bet Yoseph* is a massive encyclopaedic work following the fourfold division of the *Turim* of JACOB BEN ASHER. It was prompted by the multiplicity of codifications that had been published over the previous centuries and the proliferation of local customs which necessitated the determination of norms. Caro collected and examined the views of dozens of rabbinic authorities, Ashkenazi and Sephardi, and reviewed them in the light of the talmudic sources. His objective was to arrive at 'one law and one Torah'. In particular, he compared the three codes of ISAAC ALFASI, MOSES MAIMONIDES and ASHER BEN JEHIEL; where these three agreed the decision was obvious but where they differed he took the majority view. *Bet Yoseph* became a regular feature of the study of the *Turim*. When study of the Talmud was forbidden in Italy in 1554 Italian Jews turned to *Bet Yoseph*.

The shortened version, *Shulḥan Arukh* (which omitted details of controversies and discussions as well as names and sources) was soon the most popular book of Jewish law (and remains so today in Orthodox circles) and opened rabbinic law to the masses. However, because it was based largely on Sephardi authorities, it was accepted by Sephardim but not immediately by Ashkenazi Jews. Before long, MOSES ISSERLES added Ashkenazi custom in his *Mappah*, and the combined work became the accepted Jewish code among Ashkenazim as well.

Caro also wrote *Keseph Mishneh* ('Double Silver'), an extensive work on Maimonides' classic code *Yad Ḥazakah*, which identifies Maimonides' sources and explains his methodology. This work became an essential companion to the study of Maimonides.

Caro was also a kabbalist and wrote *Maggid Mesharim* ('Preacher of Righteousness') on theoretical and practical Kabbalah. He held that this had been revealed to him by a supernatural being who appeared to him in his dreams and revealed divine mysteries as well as exhorting him to righteous and ascetic deeds and censuring him for moral failings. [82] (G.W.)

Carpocrates [IX] (2nd century). Alexandrian gnostic teacher. He probably did not align himself closely with any standard form of the gnostic myth. His writings do not survive but the opinions attributed by early Christian heresiologists to his followers, the Carpocratians, may be attributed to Carpocrates himself [2: 413–19]. Characteristic of his ideas are an adaptation of Pythagorean teaching on the transmigration of souls, the doctrine that JESUS was born by natural generation, and a view of total separation of matter and spirit which resulted in a licentious ethic, since nothing done in the material world could effect one's standing in the spiritual realm [9: 256, 299]. He may also have espoused the full equality of women [7: 60]. Like many other Gnostics he was heavily influenced by Greek philosophy, especially PLATO. (G.J.B.)

Carroll, John [VI.A] (1735–1815). American Catholic archbishop. A native of Maryland, he was educated in St Omer College in Flanders, became a Jesuit in 1753 and was ordained in 1769. Following the suppression of the Jesuit Order he returned to America, where he led moves to enable the Roman Catholic Church to be independent of the Vicars Apostolic in England. Carroll was made the first Roman Catholic bishop in the United States in 1789. He was consecrated in England to the see of Baltimore. An advocate of the separation of church and state, he argued against states which legally gave Protestantism favoured treatment. He built up the church in his diocese with new parishes, institutions, a seminary and a college for laity. He supported the role of women in the church, particularly the founding of the Daughters of Charity. In 1808 he became first archbishop of Baltimore. [327; 343] (T.T.)

Cartwright, Thomas [VI.A] (1535–1603). English Protestant. From his election as a scholar of St John's College, Cambridge, in 1550, he was involved in the discussions and debates concerning Reformation theology for most of his life. He had to leave Cambridge when Mary came to the throne in 1553 and again in 1571 when he was deprived of his posts of Lady Margaret Professor and Fellow for criticizing the constitution of the Church of England. He spent a year in Geneva. On his return his continued support for Presbyterianism and Puritanism led to arrest in 1590 but he escaped serious charges. In 1603, on the accession of James I he drew up the 'Millenary Petition' by which a thousand clergy asked to be relieved of certain 'catholic' rites and symbols. This action led to the Hampton Court Conference but Cartwright died before it convened. [632; 634] (T.T.)

Castaneda, Carlos [XVII.B] (*b*1925?). Author of a best-selling series of books, the first title published in 1968, lucidly describing his experiences step by step through an apprenticeship to become a Mexican Indian Yacqui sorcerer (*brujo*).

Castaneda's biographical details are somewhat confused, in line with the tenet that a sorcerer has 'no personal history'. One better verified version says he was born in 1925 in the Inca town of Cajamara. The family moved to Lima in 1948, where he graduated in painting and sculpture. Between 1955 and 1959 he enrolled for pre-psychology in Los Angeles City College. It is better documented that from 1960 he joined the University of California to research the field of ethnobotany, the classification of psychotropic plants used by sorcerers. The university awarded a PhD for his second book, *Journey to Ixtlan*.

It was as a graduate student in anthropology, gathering information on various medicinal herbs in Sonara, North Mexico, that he first met the old Yacqui Indian don Juan Matus, and later in the encounters a Mazatec Indian don Genaro Flores. Both are 'men of power', and teach the ways of sorcery through a series of funny and moving conversations, interspersed with beautiful and terrifying experiences. It was the first steps in the training, involving taking the drugs peyote, jimson weed and humito, that caught the interest of the youth cultures of the early 1970s. It emerges in the later books that the use of psychotropics is a preparation for 'seeing' without drugs. The Yacquis themselves are not peyote users, an example of how don Juan's sorcery is a combination of shamanistic beliefs from several cultures. The apprenticeship culminates in the two 'men of knowledge' leading Castaneda to jump from the top of a mountain into an abyss, and survive!

Castaneda portrays himself as desperately clinging to his task as an anthropologist; the books piece together the 'system' he learned. The sorcerer's way is one of 'impeccability', and is described as 'training the left side', the mysterious side, through learning the aspects of ancient knowledge 'awareness, stalking and intent'. The unique state of perceptual clarity attained – 'seeing' – is described as the capacity for human beings to enlarge their perceptual fields until they are capable of knowing the essence of all things. [1; 2] (K.M.)

Castro, Emilio [VI.A] (1927–). Born in Montevideo, Uruguay, he studied in Buenos Aires and under KARL BARTH in Switzerland before becoming a Methodist pastor in 1954, serving in Bolivia, Argentina and Uruguay. From the early 1950s he represented his people at international ecumenical meetings. He went on to become General Secretary of UNELAM (Latin American Protestant Movement for Unity) in 1967 and was Director of the World Council of Churches' Commission for World Mission and Evangelism between 1973 and 1984. He was editor of the *International Review of Missions* during this period. He succeeded the Rev. PHILIP POTTER when called to be the General Secretary of the World Council of Churches in 1984, at which time he also completed a doctoral programme at Lausanne University. He has worked hard at bringing together major groups of Christians which have traditionally held aloof from one another. His many pastor-missiological writings include vital works such as *Hacia una Pastoral Latinamericana* (1974), *Amidst Revolution* (1975), and *Freedom in Mission: The Perspective of the Kingdom of God – An Ecumenical Inquiry* (1985). [166; 590] (A.C.S.)

Catherine of Siena [VI.A] (1347–1380). She was the daughter of a dyer in Siena. At the age of six she received a vision of Christ and took a vow of virginity. She became a Dominican tertiary at 16 and began work among the poor and the sick. Her meditations inspired many followers. She was invited to mediate in the divisions which afflicted the papacy at the time. In 1376 she persuaded Gregory XI to return from Avignon to Rome. When divisions still existed after Urban VI's accession Catherine went to Rome to attempt reconciliation. She believed that the church could survive only with a pope in Rome and with the removal of corruption among the clergy. Her attempt to revitalize the church led her to support a crusade which she thought would give a common purpose to the church and thus unite it. Her thoughts are mainly gathered in a large collection of her letters and the *Dialogo*, an exchange between herself and God. [478; 667] (T.T.)

Cerinthus [IX] (*fl.* 2nd century CE). A Gnostic active in Asia Minor whose ideas are close to those of MARCION. He is known about from the works of Hippolytus and IRENAEUS who thought that the Fourth Gospel had been deliberately written to refute Cerinthus [9: 298–9]. He seems to have believed that the supreme God transcended the world completely, so that the created order was produced by a demiurge or by angels [4: 136]. He taught a form of Docetism that JESUS began his life as a mere man and that a higher divine power entered him at baptism and left him before the crucifixion [2: 433–5; 9: 165]. (G.J.B.)

Chalmers, James [VI.A] (1841–1901). Scottish Congregationalist missionary. He was born at Ardrishaig, Scotland. He joined the London Missionary Society and was trained as a missionary and ordained in the Congregational Church in 1865. He was sent to minister in the South Seas. He married Jane Hercus and they both sailed for Rarotonga in 1866. For ten years Chalmers was a district missionary, organizing and training teachers for the evangelization of New Guinea. In 1877 he and his wife were appointed to New Guinea. They worked from Suau. Chalmers searched for new sites to establish the mission and visited his Rarotongan teachers. He planned a network of stations along the whole coast. Fearing the exploitation of the New Guineans by Europeans he helped to negotiate the annexation of New Guinea by the British Crown. As a result laws were passed which made the deportation of the inhabitants illegal and excluded the importation of intoxicants, drugs and firearms. He advocated indirect rule and government initiative in the education of the population. His wife died in 1879 and in 1899 he married a widow, Eliza Harrison. In 1892 he made his headquarters at Saguane, near the mouth of the Fly River. From here he led and supervised Polynesian and New Guinean teachers in evangelizing the interior and the Torres Strait islands. Chalmers and a missionary colleague along with ten teachers and other assistants were murdered by New Guinean tribesmen on Goaribari Island. [148; 149; 495] (T.T.)

Chāngā Āsā [xxvi] (*fl.* 15th–16th centuries). Eminent Parsi landowner who lived at Navsari, Gujarat. He exerted himself to help his co-religionists, and obtained exemption for them from the oppressive Muslim poll-tax (*jizya*). He encouraged religious observance, and after Sanjan was sacked was influential in bringing its sacred fire to Navsari [27: 37–66]. He persuaded the Parsis to send messengers to Persia to question priests there about rituals and observances. Their answers, the *Persian Rivāyats* [16], preserved at Navsari, are a mine of information on such matters, and shed light on the history of the Zoroastrians of Iran from the 15th to the 18th centuries. [20: vol. 4] (M.B.)

Ch'ang-ch'un. *See* Ch'iu ch'u-chi.

Chang Kuo-lao. One of the Eight immortals of Taoism.

Chang Lu [v] (*fl.* 184–220). Historically, he may be considered the real organizer of the first Taoist 'church', whose founder was his grandfather, the semilegendary Chang tao-ling. Lu successfully established a theocratic state in Shu (the modern Szechwan province), and ruled it for three decades before surrendering to the famous general Ts'ao Ts'ao, founder of the post-Han Wei dynasty (220). The 'Masters Designated by the Heavens' (*t'ien shih*), as he and his successors came to be known, organized their bureaucracy in the form of an hierarchical priesthood; taught that sickness was a manifestation of sin, to be cured by confession in the form of written petitions to the Taoist judges of Heaven, Earth and Waters; set up hostels throughout their domain that provided free food and shelter; followed an annual calendar of religious observances including the remarkable – not to say notorious – sexual ritual called 'Union of Vital Breaths' (*ho ch'i*); trained their followers by a catechism in which the *Tao Te Ching* ('Scripture of the Tao and its Individualizing Power') of Lord Lao (Lao tzu) was interpreted esoterically; and taxed the people five pecks of rice, which led to the vulgar designation 'the Way of Five Pecks of Rice'. The 'Orthodox One' (*cheng-yi*) sect, as it is properly called, has come down to the present day; the successors of Chang Tao-ling and Chang Lu having been granted titles and honours by many rulers. [17; 32; 40) (L.T.)

Chang San-feng [v]. Taoist immortal transcendent, putative originator of the T'ai-chi-ch'üan school of boxing, a 'patron saint' of the Perfection of Truth (*ch'üan chen*) sect. He is one of those Taoist masters about whom little is known historically, but who have had great influence on the religion. He is especially associated with the Taoist centre on Mt Wu-tang in Northern Hupei province. His mortal *vita* is placed mostly in the 14th century, especially in the early years of the Ming dynasty (1368–1644). He is one of the best known examples of the mysterious, wonder-working Taoist eremites who incarnate from time to time and are 'recognized' by those favoured few with eyes to see. [46; 62] (L.T.)

Chang Tao-ling [v] (*fl.* 2nd century?). The prototypical Taoist adept, one who has learned to concoct the elixir of immortal transcendency, to travel through the air, to divide himself into several persons and to exorcize demons – in short, a magician of formidable powers. He enters history as the theocrat of a realm in the far Southwestern region of Shu (modern Szechwan province). This wholly novel polity, although organized on the model of the Han imperium (202 BCE–220 CE), was administered by priestly bureaucrats, and its people were apparently all converts to the new religion of Chang Tao-ling.

How much of the organization of the theocracy was due to Chang Tao-ling, and how much to his grandson Chang lu is not clear. In any case, it is Tao-ling whose *persona* furnishes the essential myth of a sacred being. His powers and legitimacy came directly from Lord Lao (Lao tzu), who thus emerged as the Taoist Divinity in Three Persons. Lord Lao conferred on Chang Tao-ling the title of T'ien

Shih ('Master Designated by the Heavens') and the doctrines of the Orthodox One (*cheng-yi*) sect, secret talismans and registers (*fu* and *lu*), liturgical scriptures, a demon-quelling sword and a seal of office. The line of *t'ien shih* thus starting with Chang Tao-ling is conventionally said to have continued unbroken down to the present day, and its 64th generation representative assumed office (in Taiwan) in 1970. The traditional headquarters of the *t'ien shih* was the Dragon-and-Tiger mountains (Lung-hu-shan) in Kiangsi province, and there the successive holders of the title conferred ordination on Taoist priests over the centuries.

The Orthodox One sect is still the most widespread in China. Chang Tao-ling is frequently depicted in Taoist iconography, wearing his robes with Taoist symbols and the Eight Trigrams, and riding a tiger or sitting on the tiger throne, symbolic of his power over demons which is also shown in the sword he carries. [23: 60–67; 63; 65: 37–41] (L.T.)

Charlemagne [VI.B] (*c*.742–814). King of the Franks (768–814) and Emperor of the West (800–814). His father, Pepin III (714–768) was elected King of the Franks in 751 in succession to the deposed Merovingian Childeric III. Charlemagne succeeded his father in 768. Under the guidance of Alcuin of York (*c*.730–804), Charlemagne's court became the centre of a renascence of Latin scholarship, theology, liturgical revival and church reform. On Christmas Day 800 Pope Leo III crowned Charlemagne Emperor, a title offensive to the Emperor in Constantinople. The reign of Charlemagne marks the emergence of Frankish Christianity as a formative influence on the western church. [44: 10–12; 57; 68: 183–6] (D.J.M.)

Chatterton, Percy [XXI] (1898–1984). Missionary statesman and the most famous expatriate figure in Papua New Guinea's recent history. Growing up in London, Chatterton served as an ambulance bearer in the First World War before resuming his studies in science. During a short period as schoolteacher in a Quaker school at Penketh, he responded to an advertisement by the London Missionary Society (LMS) and was sent to Papua in 1924. There he worked as an educator with the coastal Motu and Roro peoples, eventually being ordained for missionary work as a Congregationalist minister (1943). He entered colonial politics by 1964 and was a key speaker of the Papua and New Guinea House of Assembly. In 1963 he was instrumental in uniting LMS and Methodist work into the Papua Ekalesia, but was disappointed with the later, wide amalgam called of the United Church of Papua New Guinea and the Solomon Islands (1968), because its bishops offended his Congregationalist sensibilities. He turned back to Quakerism, becoming a member just before his death. He was knighted in 1987. Chatterton's best known literary publications include the translation of the whole Bible into pure Motu and an autobiography. In his later years he was contributing to the radio and press almost daily. He is also famous for initiating the Boy Scout movement in Papua. [151] (G.W.T.)

Chaza, Mai [I.A] [Muponesi, Gwayana] (*d*.1960). A Shona healer and church founder born in Rhodesia (now Zimbabwe) sometime around the turn of the century. Raised as a Methodist, Mai Chaza had a traumatic early life, during which she was accused of being mentally deranged. Her spiritual work did not begin until the 1950s, following a grave illness and miraculous recovery which were compared to death and resurrection. Her fame as a healer attracted followers from all over Rhodesia, as well as from neighbouring countries. So large were these groups of followers that they founded 'Villages of Jehova' around her home of Umtali. For a time she attempted to keep the movement within the framework of the Methodist Church, but in 1955 she broke away to found the Church of Mai Chaza. The church's spirituality included elements of Shona tradition. Her death without successor in 1960 led to the church's division into four opposing groups. [24] (R.H.)

Cheops [VII] [Khufu] (26th century BCE). King of Egypt of Dynasty 4. According to Egyptian sources and the account given by HERODOTUS [17: book 2: 125–30], Cheops was a tyrannical ruler; he closed the temples, and forced his subjects to build his tomb, the Great Pyramid, at Giza, even using the income from his daughter's prostitution to meet the enormous cost. However, he is also reputed to have had great wisdom and sacred knowledge. His greatest achievement was the construction of his magnificent pyramid at Giza, which was one of the wonders of the ancient world. The complex also included a surrounding necropolis for his family and courtiers. Nearby, archaeologists have discovered large wooden boats, probably intended for the king's use after death. [10: 97–119] (A.R.D.)

Chephren [VII] [Khafre] (26th century BCE). King of Egypt of Dynasty 4. According to HERODOTUS [17: book 2: 130–31], Chephren was a tyrannical and impious ruler who forced his subjects to build his pyramid at Giza; however, little is known of him as an individual. He is famed for his pyramid which, although slightly smaller than the neighbouring pyramid of his father, CHEOPS, forms part of the best-preserved pyramid complex. It includes a remarkable funerary temple and valley building and the unique feature of the Great Sphinx [10: 119–35]. Represented as a human-headed, crouching lion, this was known to later generations as the god 'Horus-in-the-Horizon', who guarded the burial area. (A.R.D.)

Chi. *See* K'UEI-CHI.

Chih-i [IV] [Japanese: Chisa] (538–597). The third patriarch and effective founder and systematizer of the T'ien-t'ai school, the first and perhaps the most comprehensive of the major Chinese schools of Buddhism.

Chih-i studied and meditated upon the *Lotus Sūtra* under the tutelage of Hui-ssu (515–577) on Mt Ta-su, where he attained his first experience of awakening. After mastering both Buddhist practice and teaching he proceeded to Chin-ling, the capital of the Ch'en, where he taught and lectured on the Buddhist path. Despite his success, or perhaps because of it, he left the capital for Mt T'ien-t'ai in 575, where he dedicated himself once again to study and meditation. This period of seclusion and the insights he gained during it served as the basis for his greatest work, lectures which he gave and which were recorded after his return to Chin-ling in 585. Chih-i retreated again to Mt T'ien-t'ai in 595, and stayed until his death.

Chih-i's principal works (called the 'three great works of T'ien-t'ai'), based on lectures recorded by his disciple Kuan-ting (561–632), are the *Fa-hua wen-chü* (a textual commentary on the *Lotus Sūtra*), the *Fa-hua hsüan-i* (a doctrinal exposition of the 'profound meaning' of the *Lotus Sūtra*), and the *Mo-ho chih-kuan* (an exposition of the theory of Buddhist practice). Numerous textual commentaries and other works are attributed to Chih-i. His manuals for practice, such as the *T'ien-t'ai hsiao chih-kuan* ('Smaller T'ien-t'ai [Manual] on Cessation and Insight') were widely used and influenced the development of the Ch'an movement. His methods of practice included also ideas and techniques which were later developed by the Pure Land movement.

Chih-i's central doctrinal insight is the threefold truth, and his central pattern for practice was, similarly, the concept of threefold contemplation. The threefold truth refers to emptiness (the non-substantiality of all things), conventional existence (the provisional reality of all things) and the middle (the simultaneous emptiness and conventional existence of all things in mutual interdependence). Threefold contemplation is a pattern for the practice of cessation and insight (*chih-kuan*) which follows that of the threefold truth.

Another important aspect of Chih-i's teachings was his schematized classification of Buddhist teachings, which developed later into the 'five periods and eight teachings' classification. This was the most successful and influential of the Chinese attempts to organize and understand the vast and often confusing and contradictory corpus of Buddhist teachings transmitted to China from India.

Chih-i is unique in the history of Chinese Buddhism in his mastery of both the theory and practice of Buddhism; he combined an uncommon scholarly insight with the virtuosity of a dedicated follower and teacher of the Buddhist path. The T'ien-t'ai school which he established incorporated most of the Buddhism which preceded it, and changed the future course of Chinese Buddhism. [52; 100; 213] (P.L.S.)

Chilembwe, John [I.A] (*c*.1860/71–1915). African prophet who led a brief but violent uprising in colonial Nyasaland (now Malawi) during the late 1800s. Chilembwe's legendary and controversial career has inspired a considerable literature. He was originally educated at the mission of the Church of Scotland in southern Malawi. He later joined Joseph Booth's new Baptist mission and travelled to Britain and the United States. While in the US, 1898–1900, he studied at a black Baptist seminary in Virginia. After ordination into the National Baptist Convention he returned to Nyasaland to found the Providence Industrial Mission in 1901–2, renowned for its successful educational system [36: 327]. Over the next few years his following grew, as did his radicalism towards white exploitation. In 1915 he was killed while leading an uprising against the colonial occupation. Despite Chilembwe's death and the suppression of the church following the uprising, the nationalist movement re-emerged in the later 1920s, and in 1962 claimed over 25,000 members. Chilembwe is seen as a national martyr. [32] (R.H.)

Chinggis Khan [IV] [Genghis; Jenghiz] (1167?–1227). Warrior-ruler, born Temujin, who brought about the unification of the Mongol tribes and initiated their conquest of much of Eurasia. While Chinggis was always an adherent of Mongol shamanism, devoted to 'eternal blue heaven' (*köke möngke tengri*), his significance for the history of religions was profound and complex, and may be traced both to the challenge posed by the Mongols' apparently superhuman success to the smugness of medieval religious institutions, and to the ensuing interaction among nations and religions not previously in direct contact with one another. The empire included numerous Muslims, Buddhists, Taoists, Confucianists and Nestorian Christians, and received representatives of the Roman Church as well, who gave Europe its first sustained accounts of Central and East Asian religions. Following the collapse of the empire during the 14th century the Mongols generally retained only their ancient Shamanistic traditions, Chinggis Khan himself being worshipped both as an ancestor and as a divinity. The rapport that had been established with Tibetan Buddhism in the eastern portions of the empire, however, did in some respects pave the way for the conversion of many of the Mongol tribes to that religion under the influence of the Third Dalai Lama Bsod-nams rgya-mtsho (1543–88) and during the two centuries following. [79: 189–90; 95: II, III, V] (M.K.)

Chinmoy, Sri Kumar Ghose [XIX] (1931–). Leader of Sri Chinmoy: The Peace Meditation at the United Nations. He was born in Bengal. At the age of 12 he entered the Sri Aurobindo Ashram in Pondicherry, where, after practising intense spiritual disciplines, he became enlightened. In 1964 he went to the United States and started teaching meditation. He now has some 100 meditation centres around the world. World peace is a recurrent theme in his teachings. His disciples are expected to abstain from drugs, alcohol, tobacco or meat, and great stress is laid on healthy exercise, particularly athletics.

Sri Chinmoy is a prolific writer – he has published over 700 books (e.g. [9; 10]), and written more than 30,000 poems. (On one occasion he is said to have completed 843 poems within 24 hours.) He has also been responsible for a prodigious output of paintings (he reportedly created over 100,000 works of art within one year), as well as composing numerous devotional songs. [28] (E.B.)

Chinul [IV] (1158–1210). One of the most influential representatives of Korean Sŏn (Chinese: Ch'an; Japanese: Zen) Buddhism, and the founder of the indigenous Korean Chogye school. He was born into the gentry class, and was ordained at the age of seven. In 1182 Chinul began to protest against the corrupt state of the Korean Buddhist monastic community of the time, and to advocate the formation of religious societies that would retreat into the mountains and forests to devote themselves exclusively to the cultivation of concentration and insight. Not long after this Chinul experienced his first awakening, his first genuine insight into Buddhist truth, as a result of reading the *Platform Sūtra* of HUI-NENG [261]. This insight led him to attempt a synthesis of Sŏn insight with the Buddhist scriptural tradition, an approach that combined the best of Chinese Ch'an with the theoretical insights of Hwaŏm (Hua-yen), a synthesis evident in his two major works: *The Complete and Sudden Attainment of Buddhahood* [28: 198–237] and *Resolving Doubts about Attaining the Hwadu* [28: 238–61]. Chinul's major importance lies in his firm theoretical and practical grounding of Sŏn as an indigenous Korean tradition. [116] (P.J.G.)

Chisa. *See* CHIH-I.

Chi-tsang [IV] (549–623). Final major scholar and systematizer of the San-lun ('Three Treatises') teachings. Chi-tsang was a disciple of Fa-lang (507–581), under whom he studied the three Mādhyamika treatises *Chung lun* ('Treatise on the Middle'), *Shih êrh mên lun* ('Treatise in Twelve Parts'), and *Pai lun* ('Treatise in 100 Sections'), the basic texts of the San-lun school. He emphasized a correct understanding of emptiness, especially in contradistinction to the teachings of the *Ch'eng shih lun* (*Satyasiddhi*) scholars who focused on the importance of conventional or provisional reality.

Chi-tsang's major writings include *San-lun hsüan-i* ('Profound Meaning of the Three Treatises'), commentaries on the three treatises and most of the major Buddhist sūtras of his day, including influential works on the *Lotus Sūtra* and *Nirvāṇa Sūtra*, and other treatises. His *Erh ti i* ('The Meaning of the Two Truths') presents the San-lun interpretation of the four levels of the two truths (*saṃvṛtisatya* and *paramārthasatya*).

The San-lun (Japanese: Sanron) school never developed a large popular following, but played an important role as an academic tradition. Chi-tsang was a scholar par excellence, and his treatises, especially his commentaries on the *Madhyamakaśāstra* and the *Lotus Sūtra*, were very influential and are recognized as models of Buddhist scholarship. [31: 132–4; 32: 360–69; 125; 182: 23–7, 296–305] (P.L.S.)

Ch'iu Ch'ang Ch'un. *See* CH'IU CH'U-CH'I.

Ch'iu Ch'u-chi [V] [Ch'iu Ch'ang Ch'un] (1148–1227). A native of Shantung province who became the most important disciple of the master WANG CHE. The latter subjected him to the usual lengthy period of apprenticeship, and it is said that for 30 years the disciple never received a single word of instruction. When Wang Che was about to 'grow feathers' (i.e., ascend as an immortal transcendent) he transmitted his secrets to Ch'iu. Having acquired a great reputation as a Taoist master, Ch'iu was summoned to the court of CHINGGIS KHAN, and despite his advanced age of 71 years, made the lengthy and arduous journey far into the desert. His advice to the renowned conqueror was to stop his wholesale slaughter of men and reduce his desires if he wanted to obtain long life. Although this advice was no doubt ignored by Chinggis, he was impressed with Ch'iu's courage and straightforwardness. He bestowed the appellation Ch'ang-ch'un ('Long Spring') on him, and decreed that he was to be head of all Taoists in China. His headquarters was the White Cloud monastery in Peking, still the headquarters of the Perfection of Truth (*ch'üan chen*) sect of which Ch'iu Ch'ang Ch'un was patriarch. Some of his writings are extant; they emphasize cultivation of mind and body over concoction of the elixir. [57: 13–15; 64] (L.T.)

Chŏng Yagyong [XVI] [Chŏng Tasan; Tasan] (1762–1836). Generally considered the outstanding representative of Korea's *sirhak* ('practical learning') movement; he was also involved with the early Christian community in Korea. His very extensive writings are mostly the product of long years in exile after the purge of Christians in 1801 ended his career in government. Modern Koreans see in the experiential and practical orientation of *sirhak* a foreshadowing of modernity, and Chŏng's voluminous writings on everything from Western theories of mechanics to land management techniques and government administrative reforms are avidly studied from this point of view.

Korean Catholicism is unique in that it began with no missionary presence. Chŏng was part of a group of scholars who obtained and pored over the works of the Ming dynasty Jesuit missionary MATTEO RICCI. There they learned not only Western science but also Christianity. In the later persecution of Christians Chŏng's brother was executed, but Chŏng's precise status was less clear, and he escaped with exile. Whether or not he ever became a baptized Catholic, it is clear that his vision of things was deeply influenced by Ricci. Half of his writings deal with the Confucian classics. They carefully review and criticize centuries of interpretation, and then elaborate an equally fully developed theistic Confucianism. In his criticism of neo-Confucian interpretations there is an unexpected maturity in his grasp of the differing systematic ramifications of a non-theistic (i.e. neo-Confucian) vision and the implications of theism. The full potentiality of Chŏng's sophisticated Confucian theism was never realized, however, for his works were little read in the ensuing period of tumultuous change that brought Korea into the modern world. [2; 3] (M.Kal.)

Chos-rgyam Drung-pa. *See* TRUNGPA, CHÖGYAM.

Chuang Tzu [v] (*fl.* 4th century BCE). No reliable details of his life are known, but the book that goes under his name is one of the two basic Taoist classics (the other being the *Tao Te Ching* of LAO TZU). It has traditionally been assumed that Chuang Tzu (i.e., Master Chuang) was a later exponent of the philosophy of the Old Master (i.e., Lao Tzu). The *Chuang Tzu* is, however, a composite collection written by unknown hands at unknown times [59]. Like the *Tao Te Ching*, its thought derives in the last analysis from the *Yi Ching* ('Scripture of Change'). Despite its all-important contribution to the ancient ideas of Taoism, the *Chuang Tzu* did not come into its own until post-Han times, i.e., the Wei-Chin dynasties (220–419), when Taoist religion and Buddhism entered their first period of flourishing. It has ever since been regarded as one of the literary as well as philosophical masterpieces of China, so regarded even by scholars unsympathetic to Taoism. This reputation is the result of its authors' imaginative, poetical, humorous and intellectually challenging ideas. Its importance in Taoism lies in its lengthy, detailed development and exposition of thoughts expressed in extremely terse and often enigmatic form in the *Tao Te Ching* [56]. It is, however, of more significance in the philosophical, rather than the religious, history of Taoism, as Taoist religion tended to more esoteric interpretations of the *Tao Te Ching*.

The earliest attempt at a biography of Master Chuang is found in the 'Historical Records' (*shih chi*) [60] of Ssu-ma Ch'ien (?145–?90 BCE), who says, in part: 'There was nothing he had not studied, but he was firmly rooted in the sayings of the Old Master . . . When he stabbed and flayed the Literati [Confucians] and the Mohists, even the aged scholars of the time were unable to ward off his attacks. His words were as expansive as the sea, unrestrained, phrased to suit himself. Hence no one . . . was able to make a tool of him.' [10; 35; 59] (L.T.)

Chu Hsi [v] (1130–1200). The greatest of the Sung dynasty (960–1280) renewers and systematizers of the Literati (Confucian) tradition, and perhaps the single most influential figure in the development of later Literati thought throughout East Asia. Chu Hsi claimed that the traditional Literati way had been lost with the death of MENG TZU, and had only been recovered by the Ch'eng brothers, Ch'eng Hao and Ch'eng Yi in the 11th century. Chu Hsi was also largely responsible for the establishment of the 'Four Books' as the basis of the Literati Tradition, judging that they should take precedence over the 'Five Classics', and thus for the future direction of the Literati tradition in China and beyond.

Chu Hsi's thought centres upon the idea of 'principle' (*li*), the 'source and fullness of all being and goodness, the One behind the Many' [12: 12], and focuses especially upon *hsing*, which is best understood as principle present in human beings; this latter differs from *hsin* ('mind-and-heart'), which may, if allowed to function improperly, hinder the full manifestation of principle (which is the realization of sagehood) in human beings. Chu Hsi thus claimed that extensive learning and study ('self-cultivation') are necessary in order to attain sagehood. He engaged in extensive polemics against Buddhism, which he saw as nihilistic and destructive of the virtues fostered by self-cultivation [5; 22]; while he was somewhat more sympathetic towards Taoism, it too was always subordinate to the way of the Literati. Chu Hsi commented upon almost all of the Literati classics, and his commentaries became, if anything, more authoritative than the works upon which they commented. [6; 8] (P.J.G.)

Chu-hung [IV] [Yün-chi Chu-hung] (1535–1615). One of the four great teachers of the Ming Dynasty (along with Tz'u-po Chen-k'o, 1543–1603, Han-shan Te-ch'ing, 1546–1623, and Ou-i Chih-hsü, 1599–1655), integrator of various Buddhist traditions (especially Ch'an and Pure Land), and advocate of a lay movement in Buddhism.

Chu-hung studied under T'ien-t'ai, Hua-yen, and Ch'an masters before founding the Yün-ch'i temple, which served as his headquarters. He emphasized adherence to the monastic codes, drew on both the Ch'an and Pure Land traditions while explaining the Buddhist teaching based on the *Hua-yen Sūtra*, and sought to re-establish Buddhism on the basis of a synthesis of all Buddhist traditions. His extensive writings include sayings, rules, treatises and commentaries on all aspects of Buddhism. He also attempted to synthesize the traditional Chinese teachings of Taoism and Confucianism with Buddhism.

In contrast, Chu-hung attacked the teachings of Christianity, which were beginning to gain ground in China. He debated the Catholic missionaries and wrote the *T'ien-shuo ssu-p'ien* ('Four Chapters on the Teachings of Heaven') in which he criticized Christianity and defended Buddhist ideas against Catholic arguments.

Chu-hung was also influential in spreading Buddhism among lay people. His *Tzu-chih lu* ('Writings on Knowing Oneself') incorporated Taoist ideas, taught the idea of karmic retribution, and encouraged lay people to practise chanting the name of the Buddha and lead a moral life. Most significantly, Chu-hung advocated the synthesis of Ch'an and Pure Land (as well as T'ien-t'ai and Hua-yen) Buddhism, encouraging a trend toward harmonization which characterized Ming Buddhism and is still characteristic of Chinese Buddhism today. [31: 437–47; 49: 451–76; 265] (P.L.S.)

Chung-li Ch'üan. One of the EIGHT IMMORTALS of Taoism.

Chung-ni. *See* K'UNG TZU.

Ch'ung-yang Chen-ren. *See* WANG CHE.

Cicero [XXII] [Marcus Tullius Cicero] (106–43 BCE). Roman statesman, orator, philosopher and author [29]. Cicero lived his life in the last, chaotic century of the Roman Republic as one of its foremost politicians and would-be guardians. He achieved the highest office as one of the two annual consuls in 63 BCE. His power rested not on the control of a faction or on military prowess (as did, for example, that of Julius Caesar, his contemporary) but on his influence as the preeminent political and judicial orator of his age. He died the victim of his greatest oratorical target, Marcus Antonius (*see* AUGUSTUS), in the mass 'proscriptions' of 43 BCE.

Cicero's concern with religion was theoretical [24: 29–39; 29: 241–5; 38: 52–62]. One of his self-imposed intellectual tasks (undertaken while side-lined politically) was to give Roman expression to the great philosophical traditions of Greece. To that end, he devoted one of his dialogues (i.e. dramatized philosophical conversations in the manner of PLATO) to theology [9]. Its title, *On the Nature of the Gods*, explains its content. The disengaged and essentially frivolous gods of Epicureanism (*see* EPICURUS) are contrasted with the benign and ordered pantheism of Stoicism (*see* ZENO and KLEANTHES, and the later Stoics EPICTETUS and MARCUS AURELIUS) and both subjected to a sceptical Academic critique. A supplementary dialogue, *On Divination*, deals even more sceptically with the various modes of foreknowledge of the gods' will (astrology, divination, e.g., by the entrails of sacrificial animals, dreams, etc.), which were accepted as real and efficacious in both Stoic philosophy and popular opinion. Paradoxically (from a modern viewpoint), the sceptical Cicero was himself an 'augur', one of the 16 prestigious officials charged with oversight of the lore of public divination that figured so largely in Roman political practice. The maintenance of the traditional rites of public worship, however irrational or bizarre, was for Cicero, as for all responsible Romans, an absolute given, essential for social cohesion (and the control of the lower classes), if not for securing the goodwill of the gods to the state. This principle informs Cicero's *On the Laws*, where he discusses (again in Plato's footsteps) the regulation of an ideal – but very Roman – polity and in particular its religious ordinances.

Beyond a formal adherence to the public religion, Cicero seems to have had, if fitfully, more personal beliefs of a religious sort. For example, devastated by his daughter Tullia's death, he planned to build a shrine to honour that element in her which he was convinced survived as divine. [16: 384–6] (R.B.)

Cleanthes. *See* KLEANTHES.

Clement of Alexandria [VI.A] (150?–215?). A theologian whose works are well known but of whose life we are largely ignorant. He may have been an Athenian and it is possible that he went to Alexandria to study at the catechetical school there. It is claimed that he himself became head of the school but had to flee during the time of Roman persecution in 202 or 203. His works include *The Instructor*, on Christian life and manners, *Stromateis*, miscellaneous studies, and *Quis dives salvetur*, an exposition of the gospel story of the rich man who was told by Jesus to sell all and give to the poor. Clement argued that the Christian truth was a superior form of philosophy. He recognized the importance of *gnosis* (knowledge) but differed from the Gnostics in rejecting esotericism and declaring the knowledge of God to be true knowledge. [147; 485] (T.T.)

Cohen, Hermann [XV] (1842–1918). German Jewish philosopher. From 1873 he taught at the University of Marburg, founding the Marburg School of neo-Kantian philosophy, advocating a radical idealism rooted in reason. Initially he identified Judaism and liberal Christianity, but, stung by Treitschke's anti-Semitism, began to delve more deeply into Judaism, seeking to reconcile its universalism with its particularism. He now stressed Judaism's differences from Christianity, especially the absence of the concept of a mediator between man and God and of a doctrine of original sin. At this stage he saw the supreme message of Judaism in the prophetic concept of God as morality. From the 1890s his objective attitude to Judaism changed to a strong commitment, which even increased after his retirement and move to Berlin in 1912, from which time he devoted himself to Judaism and wrote his posthumously published *Die Religion der Vernunft aus den Quellen des Judentums* ('Religion of Reason from the Sources of Judaism'). He now saw Judaism primarily as a religion of ethical reason. Ethics supplies a universal morality but cannot take cognisance of the individual; that is the contribution of religion. The major ethical concepts were created by the Hebrew prophets; upon these are based the ethics of pure will. Judaism's ethical and religious concepts of God and man are an integrated whole, with the complete fusion of religion and ethics; the messianic era will be one of ethical perfecting. Belief in the messiah means faith in the victory of good and man's attainment of perfection.

Cohen's system of correlations paved the way for the philosophy of dialogue. Thus the correlation between God and man is characterized by the holy spirit, which is *between* man and God and not *in* either and is an attribute of their relationship. (This theory excludes the Christian idea of the hypostasization of the holy spirit). [9: II; 65: 52–105] (G.W.)

Coke, Thomas [VI.A] (1747–1814). He was born in Brecon, Wales. After study in Oxford he became a clergyman in the Church of England. In 1777, having become a Methodist, he was deprived of his living and became a colleague of JOHN WESLEY. In 1784 he was the author of the deed poll which constituted the British Methodist Conference. Having supervised the Irish Methodist societies, he was chosen to superintend the work in America. He received 'ordination' at the hands of John Wesley and was commissioned to hand on the ordination to others. This he did to FRANCIS ASBURY in 1784. They jointly superintended the Methodist Church in America, calling themselves bishops to the annoyance of Wesley, a usage made official in 1787. Thus emerged the Methodist Episcopal Church. Coke went on to evangelize the West Indies and died on the way to a mission in India. [823] (T.T.)

Coker, J. K. [I.A] (1865–1945). One of the leading figures of the early African independent church movement in Nigeria and chief of the founders of the African Church in Lagos in the 1900s. Reared in the Anglican Church, Coker was strongly influenced by the great Nigerian churchman, James Johnson. Coker accrued wealth from his father's cotton estate, but he still gloried in being 'an African'; he campaigned for an enhanced place for women and the laity in the church, local autonomy and an end to bishops and their tyranny. In the early 1900s this radical evangelical began to lose influence because of bankruptcy and family divisions and a major dispute with another leading figure of the African Church, A. W. Thomas. [40: 161–3] (R.H.)

Cokhāmeḷā [XI] (*d.*1338). One of the many minor devotional poets of the Marathi Vārkarī tradition who are attached like satellites to NĀMDEV. He is exceptional only in being a Mahār, one of the lowest Hindu castes, and some of the *abhangas* that he addresses to Viṭṭhala of Pandharpur refer specifically to his lowly status. Tradition has it that he died in 1338, crushed beneath the fallen masonry of a town wall on which he and his caste fellows were working because of the forced labour system to which they were subjected. His *samādhi* or memorial outside the main gate of the Viṭṭhala temple is an object of veneration for all Vārkarīs, but especially for the Mahārs, for whom it once marked the closest point that they were allowed to approach the main shrine. Since the mass conversion of the Mahārs to Buddhism under Dr AMBEDKAR in 1956, Cokhāmeḷā has become a source more of literary than of religious inspiration to his community. The works attributed to him consist almost entirely of short devotional verses which were first published in compendia of the Marathi 'poet saints'. Some have been translated. [112] (I.M.P.R.)

Colenso, John William [VI.A] (1814–1883). Bishop of Natal. He was born in St Austell, Cornwall, educated at Cambridge, was ordained and taught mathematics at Harrow. F. D. MAURICE was a friend and strong influence. After a Norfolk incumbency he became Bishop of Natal in 1853. Controversy filled the next 30 years: over a mission plan to incorporate Christianity into Zulu life rather than extract converts from Zulu society; over tolerance of polygamy; over his 'moral influence' views of the atonement; over his idiosyncratic forays into biblical criticism; over his status in relation to the Bishop of Cape Town, who claimed to be his metropolitan. Colenso won all the legal arguments but became almost isolated in the Anglican church in South Africa. His great work, however, lay in his studies of Zulu, his dictionary and Bible translation, and in his fight with imperial interests over Zulu rights. His last ten years saw a brave championing of Langalibelele and of Cetshwayo and a vain attempt to prevent the dismemberment of Zululand. [235; 331; 364] (A.F.W.)

Comboni, Daniele [VI.A] (1831–1881). Italian organizer of African Catholic missions. He was born in Limone, North Italy. Early occupied by the evangelization of Africa, he studied languages and medicine, and was ordained as a secular priest. After a missionary journey to the White Nile area (1857–9) he produced a *Plan for the Regeneration of Africa* (1864), published in many languages. In 1867 he formed an institute of secular priests, the Verona Fathers; a women's institute followed in 1872. The mission worked extensively in Sudan, Nubia and other parts of North East Africa. Comboni was made Vicar Apostolic of Central Africa in 1877. He was an industrious linguist and an eloquent opponent of the slave trade. [274; 498] (A.F.W.)

Confucius. *See* K'UNG TZU.

Constantine I, St [VI.B] (280?–337). Roman emperor. The son of Constantius Chlorus and St Helena, Constantine was proclaimed Emperor in 306 in York, and fought the decisive battle of the Milvian Bridge, which established his power, under the Christian sign of the Labarum. He reformed and humanized Roman law and adapted civil institutions in a Christian direction. In 321 he established Sunday as a public holiday. He established Constantinople (330) as a new Rome, capital of the new Christian Empire. The foundation column he erected still stands in Divan Yolu. He promoted the building of Christian churches throughout the Empire, especially in Constantinople and in the Holy Land. In his Church of the Twelve Apostles in Constantinople was a cenotaph for each of the twelve and a tomb for himself as the thirteenth Apostle. Although only baptized just before his death, Constantine was committed to the vision of a Christian state in a synergetic relationship with the church. He made religious orthodoxy and conformity a political issue, giving and enforcing judgements in religious disputes. He summoned the First Ecumenical Council, Nicaea (325), to deal with the Arian conflict, creating a new vehicle of ecclesiastical authority. Constantine's relationship with the Church set the precedent for later emperors. [1: XI; 61: II; 68: I; 91] (D.J.M.)

Copernicus, Nikolaus [VI.A] (1473–1543). Polish astronomer. After studying medicine, philosophy, mathematics and law at the University of Cracow and Bologna he became a lecturer in mathematics and astronomy in Rome. In 1512 he settled in Frauenburg, where he was already a canon in the cathedral, and it was there that he developed his theories concerning the universe. He rejected the Ptolemaic earth-centric theory in favour of a helio-centric theory. His first extensive writing on the theory was done in 1541, in the *Commentariolus*, which though not published, received wide circulation. His main work *De revolutionibus orbium caelestium* was published around the time of his death and he was unable to object to a preface which warned the readers against the hypothetical nature of the contents. Because it was held that the work challenged biblical notions of the universe it was outlawed by inclusion in the *Index* of forbidden books in 1616. [694] (T.T.)

Cordovero, Moses [XV] (1522–1570). Theoretician of Jewish mysticism. He lived in Safed, Palestine, the centre of a major school of mystics, where he studied with his brother-in-law, Solomon Alkabetz, and JOSEPH CARO, and where for a short time he was the teacher of ISAAC LURIA. When he was 27 years old he completed his major work, *Pardes Rimmonim* ('Pomegranate Orchard'), a lucid, systematic, encyclopaedic exposition and interpretation of kabbalistic teachings from the classic *Zohar* (*see* MOSES DE LEON) onwards. He explains and seeks to harmonize the various trends that developed in post-Zoharic mysticism.

Cordovero pays special attention to the subject of creation, seeing God as the First Cause. God, the Infinite, reaches the world through a series of emanations, each stage of which constitutes a stage of the divine mind. God is both above these emanations and present in them. They are described as vessels, containing the unchangeable light of God, which thereby penetrates the entire universe. They are both manifestations of God's substance and also his instruments, and apart from their inner content – the light of God – the emanations also contain an outer element, the garments of the inner life of the soul. Nothing exists outside of God, the Infinite, who permeates every particle of the finite, but whereas God is all reality, not all reality is God. In this way, Cordovero escaped a thoroughgoing pantheism by adopting a system of panentheism. [71: 401–4]

His *Tomer Devorah* ('Deborah's Palm-Tree') was the most influential Jewish mystical ethical work for the following centuries. [41] (G.W.)

Cosmas Indicopleustes [VI.B] (*fl.* 6th century). Author of *Topographia Christiana* ('Christian Topography', *c.*548). An Alexandrian merchant, he later became a monk of Mount Sinai. Between 520 and 525 he sailed to the East, visiting India. His book contains useful historical and geographical data as well as an amount of fanciful stuff. It provides evidence of an organized church in India in his day with a bishop in 'Kalliana' and records the conversion of Ethiopia. It is intended to undermine the Ptolemaic system of astronomy in defence of what he regards as Christian orthodoxy. His writings are published and translated in *Sources Chrétiens*, cxli, clix, cxcvii (Paris, 1968–74). [5; 44: II; 60] (D.J.M.)

Costas, Orlando E. [VI.A] (1942–1987). He was born in Ponce, Puerto Rico, but brought up as a teenager in Connecticut, United States. Converted under BILLY GRAHAM, he entered the fundamentalist Bob Jones Academy in Greenville, South Carolina. Ministry among urban Hispanics, further education and trips to Latin America led to his discovering Christ as 'the Lord who identifies with the poor and oppressed'. He and his wife went to Costa Rica in the late 1960s as missionaries with the Latin American Mission. In San José he founded CELEP (the Latin American Evangelical Centre for Pastoral Studies) in conjunction with the Evangelism-in-Depth Movement. His *The Church and its Mission: A Shattering Critique from the Third World* was published in 1974. Doctoral studies followed in Europe, resulting in his missiological *Theology of the Crossroads in Contemporary Latin America* (1976). Thereafter he functioned as 'a minority, Hispanic missiologist' in Central America and the United States in fellowship with the Latin American Theological Fraternity (FTL). As an ecumenically orientated Baptist, he functioned as an evangelical liberation theologian at the cutting edge of radical evangelism and training for practical Christian ministries. During the 1980s, he held posts as Professor of Missiology and Director of Hispanic Studies and produced, among many writings, his prophetic *Christ Outside the Gate: Mission beyond Christendom* (1982). He died in the prime of his influential, international career as a bold, Two-Thirds World missiologist. [137; 735: 320–25] (A.C.S.)

Cranmer, Thomas [VI.A] (1489–1556). Archbishop of Canterbury. A native of Aslacton, Nottinghamshire, he was educated at, and became a fellow of, Jesus College, Cambridge. He was ordained in 1523. His advice to Henry VIII on matrimonial problems brought him to prominence. In 1533 the King persuaded the Pope to consecrate Cranmer as Archbishop of Canterbury. Cranmer annulled Henry's marriage to Catherine and declared the marriage with Anne valid. He was influential in introducing many Protestant features into the worship and practices of the Church of England and his work on the *Book of Common Prayer* of 1549 established his reputation as a reformer and liturgist. Sentenced for high treason under the Catholic Queen Mary, Cranmer at first recanted but later withdrew his recantations and was burned at the stake. [117; 683] (T.T.)

Creme, Benjamin [XIX] (1922–). Leader of the Tara Centers. A Scottish artist, Creme studied the teachings of Madam BLAVATSKY and Alice Bailey. He claims to have been receiving messages from spiritual masters since 1959. In 1975 he proclaimed the imminent appearance of the Christ or Maitreya (the Buddhist bodhisattva who would assist humanity in its next step forward) [36: 737]. Creme says that Maitreya actually incarnated in 1977 and came to live with the Asian community in London. On 24 April 1982 advertisements in the London *Times* and other newspapers around the world proclaimed that Maitreya would make himself known within two months. The media's apathy was given as the cause for the failure of this prediction, but Creme still promises that the Christ will soon appear. Tara Centers were organized to spread Creme's teachings from 1980; several thousand people are on the mailing lists. Many flock to hear Creme talk and buy his books (e.g. [11]). (E.B.)

Crescas, Ḥasdai [XV] (1340–1410). Jewish philosopher. He was born and taught in Barcelona, where he was a leader of the community and eventually of Spanish Jewry as a whole. In his latter years, he lived in Saragossa.

His major work, *Or Adonai* ('Light of the Lord'), represented a reaction against the Aristotelian domination of Jewish religious philosophy, especially through the influence of MOSES MAIMONIDES. Crescas sought to replace what he regarded as alien thought by innate Jewish understanding, based on logical analysis and proof.

His starting point ('the roots of the Torah') is the existence of God, from which derives His unity, incorporeality and uniqueness. Then follow six fundamental dogmas: (1) God's knowledge of all things, including the infinite and the non-existing; (2) God's providence; His provision for individuals depends not on their intellectual excellence but on their love; (3) God's omnipotence; (4) prophecy (in which Crescas reverts to the biblical view that the prophet is chosen for his love of God, rather than Maimonides' psychological explanation); (5) human freedom, which Crescas reconciled with divine omniscience (his writings on this subject strongly influenced Spinoza); (6) the purpose of the Law (spirituality and felicity) and of man (to love God).

In addition, there are obligatory beliefs, denials of which would constitute heresy. These are: creation (*ex nihilo*); immortality; reward and punishment (corporeal and spiritual); resurrection (for the select); the eternity of the Torah; the superiority of Moses to other prophets; the high priest's understanding of the future based on the Urim and Thummim oracles on his breastplate; and the coming of the messiah.

Crescas also wrote polemical works in Catalan combating Christianity. [85] (G.W.)

Crowley, Aleister [XVII.A] (1875–1947). English occultist. He was an unusual man, brilliant, flamboyant, psychologically unstable, probably deeply religious but also deeply unconventional in his religious understanding. Both his parents were members of the Plymouth Brethren, against whose tenets he rebelled. While at Cambridge he began to read about the occult. Later he became involved with the 19th-century magical society, the Hermetic Order of the Golden Dawn (*see* MATHERS, SAMUEL LIDDELL MACGREGOR; WESTCOTT, WILLIAM WYNN). He was a gifted pupil and rose high within the hierarchy, but the Order collapsed in 1903, owing to internal friction partly of his making. By 1908 he had created his own magical system, with a prose-poem entitled *The Book of the Law: Magick in Theory and Practice* (1929), which contains many of his basic ideas. Crowley became involved with a complex system of ritual sexuality (the Ordo Templi Orientis, or OTO) and began to abuse drugs. Crowley's reputation is sinister and salacious, and not unearned. However, many people are inspired by what they perceive to be the lyric beauty of his magical invocations and his philosophy. Crowley had a romantic notion of courage and self-determination: he provided the occult with a famous sentence, 'Do what thou wilt is the whole of the law.' Yet that statement should be set in a philosophical context which asserts that each individual has a 'true will' that they must follow. If all individuals knew and followed their true will, there would be no conflict. Crowley speaks of 'union with God' as the point of magical practice. He has sophisticated theories about the connection between magical practice and scientific theory. He has a Christian concept of the way a 'rational mind' hinders spiritual intensity. Thus he becomes a very attractive author for many, and his books have probably been read by more people than those of any other occultist. [7; 8; 9] (T.L.)

Crowther, Dandeson Coates [VI.A] (1844–1938). Niger Delta Church leader, second son of Bishop Samuel Ajayi Crowther, was born in Freetown, Sierra Leone, and brought up in the Yoruba mission. His education was in Church Missionary Society institutions: the newly opened Lagos Grammar School, Fourah Bay College in Freetown, and Islington Training College. He was ordained in 1870 and appointed to Bonny in the Niger Delta, where the church grew rapidly. In 1877 he became his father's archdeacon in the Delta and Lower Niger. Gradually the Church Missionary Society receded from the policies of Henry Venn, who had aimed at 'self-governing, self-supporting, self-propagating' churches. In 1889–90 its European missionaries removed most of Bishop Crowther's African workers. Archdeacon Crowther was himself suspended.

The response was to constitute a Niger Delta Pastorate Church, led by D. C. Crowther, independently of the missionary society. But Crowther, like JAMES JOHNSON, who many hoped would be bishop of this independent African church, refused to break from the Church of England. When, after some fence-mending, the church was given a new constitution in 1896, Crowther consented to resign and be reappointed by the European bishop. Under Crowther's leadership the Pastorate Church grew immensely and became so self-propagating that it eventually could not remain self-supporting, and was reunited with the missionary society in 1931. Crowther was present, the sole survivor of the rupture 40 years earlier. In 1921 he was made a D.D. of Lambeth and a Vice-President of the Church Missionary Society. He wrote *The Establishment of the Niger Delta Pastorate Church* (1907). [6: 223ff., 253ff.; 33; 34] (A.F.W.)

Crowther, Samuel Adjai (1806?–91). African Christian leader. Adjai [Ajayi] belonged to the Egba section of the Yoruba people. He was captured by slavers at his home town, Ośogun (now in Western Nigeria) when about 15. The slave ship being intercepted, he was taken to Sierra Leone, and became a Christian there, taking the names Samuel Crowther. He became an outstanding teacher for the Church Missionary Society, initiating services in Yoruba. The Society appointed him, with the missionary J. F. Schön, to represent it on BUXTON's 1841 Niger Expedition. Their report stressed the importance of African agency for the evangelization of Africa, and pointed to the presence among the freed slaves of Sierra Leone of able Christians from various parts of West Africa, already equipped with the necessary languages. Ordained in 1843, he was sent to his own Yoruba people. He was the principal translator of the Yoruba New Testament, one of the most durable of all versions in African languages. Through HENRY VENN he was appointed to lead a new mission to the Niger in 1857, with an all-African staff; and in 1864 he became the first African Anglican bishop, his Sierra Leonean missionaries at work from the Upper Niger to its delta.

Crowther's last years were clouded by controversy: Venn was dead, and young European missionaries of a new outlook wrought the dismissal of many of his staff. Although Crowther's probity and sanctity were universally recognized, and despite the presence of outstanding leaders such as his son DANDESON CROWTHER and JAMES JOHNSON, it was long before another African diocesan bishop was appointed. [6; 508A; 617A; 774A] (A.F.W.)

Crummell, Alexander [VI.A]. Afro-American missionary in Liberia. He was born in New York. Unable, even as a well-educated Black, to secure entrance to General Theological Seminary, he nonetheless received Episcopal Church ordination and served several Black congregations. Friends obtained his entrance to Oxford, where he graduated in 1853. For the next 20 years he worked in Liberia, convinced that: 'The children of Africa have been called, in the Divine providence, to meet the demands of civilization, of commerce, and of nationality.' He promoted the cause of Liberia College. On his return to America, when he became Rector of St Luke's, Washington, he established the American Negro Academy with the same concern for Afro-American excellence in scholarship. He wrote *The Future of Africa* (1862), *The Greatness of Christ* (1882) and *Africa and America* (1891). (A.F.W.)

Curl Snout [XVIII] (4th–5th century CE). Ruler of the Maya city of Tikal, *c*.388–425, during a period of interregional trade and communication with the central highlands of Meso-America. Curl Snout [3: 137–8] had himself depicted on his inaugural monument, in a style typical of the élites of Teotihuacan, the great imperial capital of highland central Mexico (100–750). It appears that Curl Snout explored and encouraged new trading and ritual relations with regions distant from Maya culture. [10: 84, 221]. His tomb included imported vessels and other objects reflecting and affirming the Maya-Teotihuacan connection. It appears that this connection reflected political alliances, perhaps marriage ties and ceremonial exchanges of objects, theology and myth. He was succeeded by his son Stormy Sky (reigned 425–455), whose ritual paraphernalia display a waning involvement in the imperial world of Teotihuacan. This period of Maya history indicates attempts to enlarge the political, ritual and mythological world view of the Maya of Tikal and several related ceremonial centres. (D.C.)

Cyprian [VI.A] [Thascius Caecilianus Cyprianus] (*c*.205–258). Bishop of Carthage. He became bishop two years after his conversion to Christianity in 246. He was forced to carry on his work in hiding due to a succession of persecutions by Roman emperors. The persecutions created problems regarding defectors who wished later to be readmitted to the church. He adopted a rigorous approach which led to schism and insisted on the integrity and unity of the Church. His writings include *De catholicae ecclesiae unitate* ('On the Unity of the Catholic Church', 251) in which he wrote: 'No one can have God as Father who does not have the Church as Mother.' In one of his *Letters* he wrote: 'There is no salvation outside the Church.' During the persecution of emperor Valerian, Cyprian was first exiled and then condemned to death and beheaded. [253; 363; 846] (T.T.)

Cyril I Lucaris [VI.B] (1572–1638). Patriarch of Constantinople. He was born in Crete on 13 November 1572. Educated in Venice and Padua, he was ordained by his cousin Meletios Pegas, Greek Patriarch of Alexandria. In 1596, with Nicephorus Cantacuzenus, later killed by the Polish authorities, he was sent to Poland to help the Orthodox opposition to union with Rome, imposed that year at the Council of Brest-Litovsk. He made contact with Lutheran leaders. Summoned to Alexandria in 1601 by Meletius, upon whose death he was made Patriarch of Alexandria, he moved the seat of the patriarchate to Cairo.

Elected Patriarch of Constantinople in 1620, he worked for educational reform and closer association with the reformed churches, especially with the Church of England. His *Confession of Faith*, published in Geneva in 1629, shocked many in the Orthodox Church. In 1633 he was deposed in favour of the pro-Catholic Cyril II Contari, but reinstated almost at once. He was deposed again in 1635 in favour of Cyril II, and condemned as a heretic. Cyril II was deposed in 1636 and Neophytus of Heraclea became Patriarch until Lucaris's re-election in 1637. In 1638 Lucaris was drowned on suspicion of treason. His reign illustrates the impact of Catholic-Protestant rivalries on the Orthodox living under Ottoman rule. [24; 76: VI–X] (D.J.M.)

Cyril VI [VI.B] (1902–1971). Coptic Pope. Considered a saint even in his lifetime, Kirellous Atta became a monk in the Wadi Natrun in 1928 and later studied theology at Helwan. After living as a hermit in the desert near the ancient monastery of Sohag, he became abbot of the Abba Samuel monasteries. In 1959 he became Pope of Alexandria and led a vigorous monastic revival and renewal of Coptic church life. In 1959 he recognized the autonomy of the Ethiopian Church, consecrating its first Catholicos.

His successor, Pope Shenouda, has built on his work. Despite religious and political conflicts, he has played a significant ecumenical role, appointing a bishop to maintain contact with other Christian communities throughout Africa. [5: VI; 8; 11] (D.B.)

Cyril and Methodius [VI.A] (826–869 and *c.*815–885). Apostles of the Slavs. They were brothers from Thessalonica, the younger originally bearing the name Constantine. They followed different careers in early life, Constantine being the librarian of the church of Santa Sophia in Constantinople, Methodius governor of a Slavic-speaking district of Greece. Later they both withdrew to a monastery in Bythinia. Following a successful brief mission to the Khazars, they were sent to Moravia, where they worked in the Slavic language, creating a written alphabet (the later Cyrillic), translating the scriptures into Slavic and creating a Slavic liturgy. Constantine became ill on a visit to Rome, took a vow to remain a monk, adopted the name Cyril, but died two months later. Methodius returned to Moravia and was successful in spite of the opposition of Frankish bishops. He saw the papal authorization of the Slavic (Glagolitic) Mass and the completion of the Slavic Bible. [227; 229] (T.T.)

Cyril of Alexandria [VI.A] (*c.*375–444). He became patriarch of Alexandria in succession to his uncle in 412. He opposed NESTORIUS, patriarch of Constantinople, in the latter's refusal to call Mary *Theotokos* – 'Mother of God'. Cyril accused Nestorius of dividing the Christ into the human and the *logos*. But it was his methods of dealing with Nestorius, apart from the theological dispute, which marks Cyril's character. He succeeded in having Nestorius condemned, partly by argument but also by political manoeuvring. Cyril himself was not entirely free of the taint of heresy for speaking of Christ as having only one *physis* (nature), thus virtually eliminating the human. The later Monophysites, condemned as heretics, claimed Cyril as their mentor. [186; 433; 483] (T.T.)

Cyril of Jerusalem [VI.A] (313–386). A native of the Jerusalem area, he was ordained priest in 343 and became bishop of Jerusalem in 348. The metropolitan of Caesarea had him deposed because of his opposition to Arianism (*see* ARIUS). He was restored by the Council of Seleucia in 359. Later he fled before imperial persecution and was only able to return in 378. His *Catecheses* show the life of the church of his time, in particular the preparation of those to be baptized, and give an insight into the Palestinian liturgy of the 4th century. In his description of the eucharist there is the curious omission of the words of Institution. Doctrinally he avoided the term *homoousios* ('of the same substance') in the reference to the relation of Christ to God the Father. This raised the suspicion for some that he was an Arian. [173; 630; 780] (T.T.)

Cyrus and his successors [XXVI]. The Achaemenian king Cyrus (reigned 550–530 BCE) was the founder of the first Persian Empire and the first western Iranian ruler known to have embraced the religion of ZOROASTER. Magi appear to have prepared for his conquests with both religious and political propaganda, and Zoroastrian elements have been traced accordingly in the works of Second ISAIAH and early Ionian philosophers [5: vol. 2: 43–7, 150–63]. Stone fire-holders were found at Cyrus' capital, Pasargadae, and his tomb was built to conform to Zoroastrian purity laws [5: vol. 2: 54–7; 52: 24–43].

His son Cambyses (reigned 530–522 BCE) instituted daily rites there for his soul, performed by magi [5: vol. 2: 70–71]. He is the first Zoroastrian known to have practised *khvaētvadatha*, next-of-kin marriage [23: III. 31–2; 5: vol. 2: 75–7].

Darius the Great (reigned 522–486 BCE), son of Hystaspes (*see* HYSTASPES), attributed his achievements to the will of Ahuramazda, 'who created this earth, who created yonder sky, who created man, who created happiness for man'. Other religious elements also are to be found in his inscriptions [7: 10.1.1.1–4; 5: vol. 2: 118–22]. He established the funerary iconography of the dynasty [50: 80–87; 5: vol. 2: 112–16], in which the dead king is shown worshipping before fire, sun and moon, the three icons appointed for Zoroastrians. The sun-symbol is the winged disk which at the same time represented *khvarenah*, sun-like heaven-sent glory (*compare* Zoroaster). The rock tombs of Darius and his successors also conform to the purity laws.

Darius' son Xerxes (reigned 486–465 BCE) is recorded as destroying a sanctuary of the *daēvas* (Old Persian: *daiva-*) repudiated by Zoroaster, and establishing Ahuramazda's worship there instead [7: 10.1.1.5; 5: vol. 2: 174–7]. Religious practices during his expedition against Greece, recorded by Herodotus [23: VII.19ff.], are not distinctively Zoroastrian [5: vol. 2. 165–71].

Herodotus himself lived under Artaxerxes I (reigned 465–424 BCE), and described Persian beliefs and observances as he learnt of them in Asia Minor [23: I. 130ff.]. The latter were judged at first by Western scholars to be non-Zoroastrian, but accord in fact with Zoroastrian lay practices maintained till the 20th century [5: vol. 2: 179–83]. Artaxerxes appointed his cup-bearer, the Jew Nehemiah, to govern Palestine [*Nehemiah* 2: 1]; but it is disputed whether it was he or his grandson Artaxerxes II who sent Ezra from Babylon to Jerusalem [*Ezra* 7: 11–26]. Zoroastrian elements appear to have been absorbed by Judaism in the Achaemenian period at both priestly and popular levels [12: 279–325; 5: vol. 3: XI].

Artaxerxes I had Babylonian queens, and his half-Babylonian son Darius II (reigned 423–404 BCE) probably began to use images in private worship. An image cult was imposed on Zoroastrians generally by his son Artaxerxes II (reigned 404–358 BCE), and temples came to be built to house both statues and sacred fires [5: vol. 2: 216ff.]. Previously Zoroastrians had worshipped at their hearth fires or in the open. Other innovations of his reign appear to have been the introduction of a common devotional calendar throughout the Zoroastrian community and the adoption by the royal family of the monotheistic heterodoxy of Zurvanism [5: vol. 2: 231–41]. This, more a philosophy than an effective faith, spread under their influence in the western parts of their empire. It was probably Zurvanite Zoroastrianism which became known to Plato [33: 132].

Aristotle, who lived under Artaxerxes III (reigned 358–338 BCE), regarded the beliefs of the Zoroastrian magi as more ancient even than those of the Egyptians [33: 128–9]. The name Artaxerxes appears as Ahasuerus in the Jewish *Book of Esther*, as Ardašīr in later Persian usage. (M.B.)

D

Dadabhai Nauroji. *See* NAUROJI, DADABHAI.

Dādā Gurus [XIII]. The name of four former chief teachers (*sūri*) of the Śvetāmbara Jain sect, the Kharatara Gaccha, who have become the objects of a devotional cult. Their names and dates are respectively: Jinadatta (1074–1153), Maṇidhāri Jinacandra (1139–1165), Jinakuśala (1279–1331) and Jinacandra (1537–1612). These saints are all credited with enhancing the prestige of the Jain religion through the performance of miracles and conversions; it is because of this that they were given the affectionate title *Dādā*, 'Grand-dad'. The most important of the four is Jinadatta who is regarded by many writers as the real founder of the Kharatara Gaccha rather than JINEŚVARA. As well as writing several works which attempted to establish proper canons of orthodoxy for such matters as temple worship, he also, according to legend, defeated a band of malevolent Hindu witches (*yoginī*). Jinadatta's immediate successor, Jinacandra, was given the epithet 'Maṇidhāri' because he wore a jewel (*maṇi*) in his forehead with which he carried out feats of magic. Jinakuśala is associated with bringing the people of Sindh back into the fold of orthodox Jainism, while the last of the Dādā Gurus, Jinacandra, is credited with having persuaded the great Moghul emperor, AKBAR, to protect Jain holy places from assault by Muslims. Today there is a network of cult spots associated with the Dādā Gurus, mainly in Rajasthan, and the devotees of these saints believe that they have the ability to confer blessings and rewards. (P.D.)

Dādū Dayāl [XI] (1545–1604). Rajasthan poet-saint. The main source for his life is the Hindi biography of Jan Gopāl, the *Dādū janam līla* [14], written about 1620. This work has grown by constant hagiographical accretion, and even its earliest form cannot be too heavily relied upon. Nevertheless, from this and other sources, a fairly certain picture emerges [84]. Dādū was a cotton-carder, a Dhuniyā, belonging to a group that had converted to Islam in Lodi times, and hence was a Muslim by birth. He had a mystical vision of God as an old man when he was 11 years old, and a second vision when he was 18 in which he was told to devote his life to prayer and to leave home. After some years spent as a wandering ascetic, he settled at Sambhar at the age of 25. Here he spent ten years as a married householder, producing, it is said, four children. But he continued his life of prayer and teaching, attracting numerous disciples and offending both Muslims and Hindus with his condemnation of outward religious forms. There is reason to think his own spiritual teacher was the distinguished Muslim saint Shaikh Buddhan of the Qādirī order, but this is seldom mentioned by later followers [84: 45–6]. In 1579, aged 35, Dādū left Sambhar for Amber, where he remained until 1594. During these 14 years he is said to have visited the Emperor AKBAR, but this is unprovable historically. 1580 was spent in Kalyāṇpūr, after which Dādū resumed the life of a wandering ascetic, visiting many parts of Rajasthan and making many disciples. After ten years, physically unable to continue, Dādū settled in the small town of Narainā, where he died in 1604. Dādū's teachings are contained in a substantial body of couplets and hymns which are similar to the works of KABĪR and the other Sants in both form and content. The Dādū-panth, which came into existence soon after Dādū's death, has had a productive and colourful history and still operates in parts of Rajasthan. [84: 191–2] (S.C.R.W.)

Da Free John [XIX] [Franklyn Albert Jones] (1939–). Founder of the Free Daist Communion. He was born as Franklyn Albert Jones in Jamaica, New York. He studied at Columbia and Stanford universities and then at three Christian seminaries. In 1960, after a 'crisis of despair', he received the insights that there is only the one Reality or Transcendent Consciousness and that this Reality or Consciousness is Man's true identity; all else is only a superimposition of the unenlightened mind. [12: 139–40]. He studied with Swami Rudrananda (1928–1973) [36: 874], and in 1968 went to Muktananda's ashram in India, where he attained 'yogic liberation' [12: 140]. Then in 1970 he entered the permanent 'Condition of Sahaj Samadhi' which is coessential with the 'Transcendental Being Consciousness itself' [12: 140–41].

In 1972 he founded the Dawn Horse Communion, which later became the Crazy Wisdom Fellowship, the Johannine Daist Community and, in 1975, the Free Daist Communion. The Laughing Man Institute began making his teaching available in England in 1983. During the mid-1970s Franklyn changed his name to Bubba (brother) Free John; in 1979 he became Da (giver) Free John; then, in the mid-1980s, he became known as Heart-Master Da Love Ananda, or Avadhoota Da Love Ananda Hridayam.

The changes in names were accompanied by different styles of teaching, some intense, involving a number of experiences, including sexual ones, for the purpose of showing their futility. At other times, he has lived in peaceful seclusion. The teachings are known as the Way of Radical Understanding, there being seven stages by which Enlightenment may be realized. [12; 13; 36: 861] (E.B.)

Dalai Lama [IV]. The Dalai Lamas of Tibet, among whom the first was Dge-'dun-grub-pa (1391–1475) and the 14th, the current holder of the office, is Tenzin Gyatso (Bstan-'dzin rgya-mtsho, *b*1935), are regarded by Tibetans as incarnations of the celestial bodhisattva Avalokiteśvara. Avalokiteśvara's main characteristic is that of compassion: his name means, literally, 'the lord who looks down [with compassion upon the world of sentient beings]', and the attribute of compassion is therefore also regarded as the pre-eminent religious characteristic of the Dalai Lamas. As each Dalai Lama dies, so the theory goes, Avalokiteśvara incarnates himself again as a human Tibetan male child; thus each holder of the office holds it from birth until death. A new incarnation is recognized by a combination of astrological and practical tests: astrology points to the region of Tibet in which the new incarnation has been born, and a potential Dalai Lama (still a baby or a very small child) is tested by being asked to recognize items in the paraphernalia of his predecessor.

The first four Dalai Lamas were essentially religious figures without a great deal of political power. But the fifth Dalai Lama (Blo-bzang rgya-mtsho, 1617–1682) was, with the help of the Mongols, able effectively to unite Tibet politically and to become the holder of supreme temporal power. From this period onwards the connections between the political and financial power of the great monasteries – especially those of the 'Yellow Sect' (Dge-lugs-pa) – and the personal prestige and power of the Dalai Lama were many and close. At times, though, the power of individual monasteries came into conflict with that of the Dalai Lama himself, and not infrequently internecine conflict among monasteries was a real obstacle to effective political union, an obstacle that was only partially overcome by the efforts of the Dalai Lamas. This was especially evident during the time of the 13th Dalai Lama (Thub-bstan rgya-mtsho, 1876–1933), who had to contend not only with external pressures from the British and the Chinese, but also with internal pressures from specific monasteries. [235: 161–2]

The current (14th) Dalai Lama was born in Amdo in north-eastern Tibet and was recognized as an incarnation of Avalokiteśvara at the age of three. He was installed as Dalai Lama at the age of five and given the traditional intensive training in Buddhist theory and practice. During the period of his training Tibetan relations with China worsened, and in March 1959 Tenzin Gyatso left Tibet and went into exile in India with thousands of other Tibetans. Since then he has been a campaigner in the West for support for Tibetan independence from China, a prolific writer on matters religious and political [87; 88; 89], and a recipient of the 1989 Nobel Peace Prize. His major concern has been to preserve Tibetan religious culture by ensuring the transmission of teachings and practices which, until now, had been operative only in Tibet. The future of the office of Dalai Lama remains uncertain; since it has historically been so closely linked with the spiritual and physical geography of Tibet, it is possible that the 14th Dalai Lama will also be the last. [145] (P.J.G.)

Damien, Father [VI.A] [Joseph de Veuster] (1840–1889). Belgian priest and missionary. He originally took the name Damien when he became a member of the Fathers of the Sacred Heart of Jesus and Mary in 1859. In 1863 he was sent to the Sandwich Islands and then to Honolulu where he was ordained priest in 1864. He served on the islands of Hawaii and Molokai, making converts and building chapels. He persuaded his superiors to send him to a leprosy settlement in Molokai in 1873 and ministered there alone for many years, caring for the leprosy sufferers until he also caught the disease and was eventually overcome. By this time he was helped by other members of his order and by Sisters of Charity. [257] (T.T.)

Danel [II]. Like KERET, Danel is a heroic figure in Ugaritic religion who has no children. Under the guidance of Baal he makes special preparations with his wife and they duly have a child, who is called Aqhat. The lad is then given a bow as a gift from the gods, and this is coveted by the goddess Anath. The only way she can get the bow is to kill him, and his father is immediately transformed from a strong leader of the people to a desolate mourner. He seeks the boy in the countryside, where the plants have begun to wither with drought. Realizing that vultures have eaten his child, he proceeds to enlist Baal's help to bring the bird that has him in its gizzard down to earth. It turns out to be the mother of all vultures that has eaten him, and the father buries the remains of his son near a spring. Still despondent, he returns home and cannot be comforted for seven years. The end is lost, but presumably he comes to terms with the fact that his dead son, buried as he is at source of water, is a symbol of the seasonal pattern, where fertility is followed by drought as life is followed by death.

Like that of Keret, the story is narrated as history, but clearly is much more of a myth. However, Danel must certainly have epitomized not only faith in the ultimate survival of the adherents of Baalism, but also the origin of opposition to the funerary practice of decarceration in this region of the Middle East. That he is able to rescue the remains of Aqhat from the gizzard of the vulture and bury them in the ground suggests that there was religious opposition to the idea of allowing human bodies to be stripped of flesh by birds of prey. If this was practised further to the north by the Hittites, under whose political domination Ugarit fell, the tale could be seen as one of protest.

The name Danel probably means 'El is the judge' and it was used much later in the Bible in the form 'Daniel'. There it is a pseudonym for a god-fearing man who is threatened with death by a power outside his control and whose faith sustains him. Like Job, whose historical origins are even more obscure, the name was absorbed into Hebrew folklore, where achievements like theirs were presented as human ideals. [1; 3] (M.R.)

Dante Alighieri [VI.A] (1265–1321). Florentine poet. Nothing much is known of his early life except for his love for Beatrice, celebrated in his poem *La vita nuova* (1294). He became involved in Florentine politics and was banned from the city in 1302. He eventually settled in Ravenna in 1317. There he spent his final years composing *La divina commedia*. The poem relates a spiritual journey after death through *Inferno, Purgatorio* and *Paradiso*, and is an indictment of loose morals and corruption in the church. Dante is now memorialized in Santa Croce, Florence, the city which banished him. [192; 733; 864] (T.T.)

Dārā Shikoh [XII] (1615–1659). Eldest son and heir-apparent of the Mughal emperor Shāh Jahān (reigned 1627–58). His spiritual life was first directed by Mullā Shāh Badakhshī (*d.*1661), a Sufi of the Qādirī order with orthodox if liberal views, under whose influence Dārā Shikoh wrote several Persian treatises, beginning with the *Safīnat al-awliyā'* (1640) which has remained a standard work of Sufi hagiography. From about 1650, however, his works reveal an increasingly obsessive search for the common ground he presumed to exist in some essential form between Islam and Hinduism. This quest is first recorded in the conversations on religious topics he had with the Punjabi Hindu ascetic Bābā Lāl [83a: 23–4]. It soon also resulted in translations from Sanskrit into Persian of several major Hindu religious texts, including a version of the *Yoga Vāśiṣṭha* compiled at his instance, besides his own translations of the *Bhagavad Gītā* and of the Upaniṣads. This last, entitled the *Sirr-i akbar* (1657), was to play a major role in introducing Hindu philosophical ideas to Europe, through its Latin translation by Anquetil Duperron (1801–2). Dārā Shikoh's own position, suitably described as 'an intellectualized magical syncretism' [7: 191], is set out in his *Majmaʿ al-baḥrayn* ('The Mingling of the Two Oceans', 1655), whose ambitious title all too clearly indicates the unstructured character of its approach, generally amounting to little more than far-fetched equations between Sufi and Upaniṣadic terminology, e.g. of *rūḥ* with *ātman* [83a: 44–5]. Representing the ultimate development of the liberal attitudes towards Hinduism characteristic of the Mughals since Akbar (reigned 1556–1605), Dārā Shikoh's views were rendered ineffectual by their intellectual shallowness and his own political ineptitude, which led to his defeat in the war of succession by his brother Aurangzeb (reigned 1658–1707), and his subsequent execution on charges including apostasy. His later significance in Indian Islam has been the symbolic one of representing the liberal alternative to the orthodoxy upheld by Aurangzeb. [7: VIII; 45a; 83a] (C.S.)

David [xv] (*c.*1037–*c.*967 BCE). The outstanding king of biblical Israel, who became a Jewish symbol of redemption. Born in Bethlehem, son of Jesse of the tribe of Judah, he spent his early years as a shepherd. According to the biblical account, while still tending the sheep he was anointed by the prophet Samuel as the future king of Israel. David's musical talents first brought him to the court of King Saul, where he achieved military renown by killing the Philistine champion, Goliath, in single combat. He received a military command and married the king's daughter, Michal. His friendship with Jonathan, Saul's son, became proverbial. However, Saul became jealous of David's popularity and, seeing him as a potential threat to his dynasty, sought to kill him. David fled and, with a group of followers, lived the life of an outlaw. He received a religious legitimacy when he was joined by Abiathar, sole survivor of Saul's massacre of the priests at Nob. David remained on good terms with the southern tribes but also sought the protection of Saul's Philistine enemies. He was even prepared to assist them in their attack on the Israelites, but the Philistine chiefs, doubtful of his loyalty, refused his help. In the battle, the Philistines were victorious and Saul and Jonathan were killed; David afterwards composed a famous lament for them.

David now seized his opportunity and returned with his men to Israelite territory, being crowned king at Hebron (*c.*1010) where he ruled for seven and a half years. He defeated an attempt to have Saul's son, Ishbosheth, crowned, and consolidated his position until he united all the tribes and captured the last non-Israelite enclave in his territory, Jerusalem, which had been held by the Jebusites. He made this the capital of his united kingdom ('the city of David' as it was known thereafter), as it was central, strategically located and not associated with any of the tribes. He moved the focus of the cult, the ark of the covenant, to Jerusalem and purchased the land on which his son and successor, Solomon, later built the temple. David also broke the military might of the Philistines in two crucial battles and won victories over other enemies, such as Aram and Edom, leading to a considerable expansion of his territory and the establishment of a minor empire. Other administrative achievements were the creation of a standing army and the systematic organization of the priesthood, with the chief priests serving as royal officials.

Despite the Bible's idealization of David, it does not hesitate to depict his shortcomings. His adultery with Bathsheba and responsibility for the death of her husband earned the severe rebuke of the prophet, Nathan, and divine punishment in the form of the death of the child of their illicit union. His beloved son, Absalom, led a revolt which David suppressed only with great difficulty and which ended with Absalom's death. Before David died, there was a struggle for succession between his sons Adonijah and Solomon. David's story is recorded in 1 *Samuel* 16–31; 2 *Samuel*; 1 Kings 1–2: 12; and 1 *Chronicles* 11–29.

David is depicted as courageous, energetic and wise but also opportunistic and easily swayed by his emotions. He is motivated by deep religious feelings and faith in God. According to tradition the poet and 'sweet singer of Israel' (as he is called) was the author of the Book of *Psalms*. Although many psalms have been shown to date from a later period, some could well have been composed in David's time, possibly by him.

The figure of King David became deeply embedded in the Jewish consciousness. All subsequent legitimate kings had to be descended from him while the messiah too was envisioned as springing from the House of David, destined to bring back the ancient kingdom. The Jewish liturgy frequently prays for the restoration of the house of David, symbol of the link between God and the Jewish people. [17; 64]

David was buried in the 'city of David' but the site is unknown. A grave in Jerusalem venerated since the Middle Ages as the tomb of David owes its identification to a misunderstanding of the site of the original Mount Zion. (G.W.)

David, St [VI.A] [Welsh: Dewi] (*d c*601). The patron saint of Wales. Very little of historical worth is known of him. A *Life of Saint David* written by Rhygyfarch in the 11th century is more of a propaganda document against the primacy of Canterbury than a reliable biography. He was prominent in Wales, having founded 12 monasteries, finally settling in Glyn Rhosyn, Menevia, where the abbey over which he was bishop is the location of the present cathedral of St David's. It is held that in *c*.560 he spoke eloquently, possibly against Pelagianism, at a Synod of Brefi (modern Llanddewi Brefi, Dyfed). [110; 397] (T.T.)

Da Vinci, Leonardo. *See* LEONARDO DA VINCI.

Day, Dorothy [VI.A] (1897–1980). She was born in Brooklyn and lived as a child in San Francisco and Chicago. After studying at the University of Illinois she became a journalist. She engaged in radical causes, but after the birth of her daughter she became a Roman Catholic. Thereafter she promoted the cause of peace, social harmony and world renewal through personal relations and opposed statism and technological oppression. The bases of her personalism were the traditions of the Roman Catholic Church and a literal reading of the Gospels. She organized refuges for destitutes in New York City as well as community farms. She promoted her ideas through lectures and writings, including *The Long Loneliness* (1952). [195; 239; 555] (T.T.)

Dayāl, Bābā [XXIII] (1783–1855). Founder of the Sikh sect of Nirankārīs. Preaching in Rawalpindi in the time of Mahārājā RAÑJĪT SIṄGH and after, Dayāl taught his followers that the contemporary Sikhs had strayed from the way of *nām simaraṇ* (remembrance of the divine Name) and had adopted Hindu practices. Today the Nirankārīs deviate from the orthodox Sikhs only in that they recognize a line of continuing Gurūs, beginning with Bābā Dayāl. They should be distinguished from the Sant Nirankārīs, who currently have hostile relations with orthodox Sikhs. [73: II–V] (W.H.M.)

Dayanand Sarasvati [XI] (1824–1883). Founder of the Arya Samaj, was one of the most notable 19th-century exponents of neo-orthodox Hinduism. Born Mul Shankar, the son of a devout banker in Morvi state in Gujarat, he had a strict Brahmanical upbringing. His early questioning of his family's orthodox Śaivism is, however, illustrated by the well known story of his being taken to a temple at the age of 14 to observe the Śivarātri vigil, only to be horrified, as he remained awake while others fell asleep, to see a mouse crawling over the supposedly omnipotent god's image to nibble at the sweets offered to it [3: 36–7]. Such doubts eventually led him to escape marriage by leaving home, and to repudiate his family's beliefs by being initiated in 1848 as a *sannyāsī* in the Sarasvati Dandi order of yogis with the name Dayanand. A long period as an itinerant yogi ended in 1860 when he settled in Mathura to study with the blind Svami Virajanand, an austere Sanskrit grammarian and Vedic scholar, under whose influence Dayanand came to reject most of post-Vedic Hinduism and its literature as hopelessly corrupt. In 1868 he embarked on a public career of lecturing, writing and engaging in the public disputations then so fashionable in India. His powerful voice and presence gained a wide audience for his call to a return to Vedic values, especially after contact with the

Brahmo Samaj in Calcutta convinced him of the need to communicate in Hindi rather than Sanskrit. In 1875 he announced the formation of the Arya Samaj in Bombay, but a highly successful visit to Lahore in 1877 won many adherents for the new organization, whose chief strength has thereafter lain in the Punjab. Dayanand's aggressive style won him many enemies, and he died through poison. Ample evidence of his uncompromising attitude to other religions is to be found in his best known work, the *Satyārth prakāś* (1874), whose positive teachings emphasize both an absolute monotheism which rejects all idolatry and the eternal truth of the Vedas as the sole repository of all knowledge. 'Never really directed towards the mysteries of God, but rather towards the strivings of man' [51: 278], the main impact of Dayanand's teachings was in their social dimension, which replaced caste-based *dharma* with the teaching that salvation was attainable only through moral action directed by reason, membership of the four classes (*varṇa*) being determined by abilities and behaviour. An active social reformism was thus encouraged, particularly in education, where the Arya Samaj's Dayanand Anglo-Vedic (DAV) institutions have been a formative influence in Punjabi Hindu life for a century. While the austere ceremonies he prescribed for Arya Samaj worship have had less appeal, and his more extreme claims for the Vedas as scientific texts have invited deserved ridicule, Dayanand's rejection of the validity of other religions has proved continuingly important in the ideological underpinning of modern Hindu nationalism. [3; 50; 51] (C.S.)

Dee, John [XVII.A] (1527–1608). English mathematician and occultist. He was among the most remarkable of Elizabethan men. Diplomat, scholar, adviser to the Queen and friend of Philip Sidney, he owned the largest library in England and was for a time at the centre of its intellectual world. He was also deeply immersed in Hermetic-kabbalistic philosophy and may have been the model for Shakespeare's Prospero and Marlowe's Faustus. With Dee, Hermetic-kabbalistic philosophy became even more complex. The work to which he attached greatest significance was his *Monas hieroglyphica* (1564), an alchemical, kabbalistic, mathematical and Christian account of one symbol, which if properly realized and understood could wield great power. Closely connected is his *Propaedeumata aphoristica* (1558). The book probably influenced the creation of the Rosicrucian documents in the early 17th century, and may have been widely disseminated upon the Continent. The first English *Euclide* appeared in 1570 with an important and influential 'Mathematicall Preface' by Dee. He died an outcast, the subject of derision in part generated by his association with the medium Edward Kelley and the growing unease with Hermetic-kabbalistic philosophy. [6; 13; 25; 26; 27; 28] (T.L.)

Deguchi Nao [XIV] (1837–1918). The founder of Ōmotokyō, a Japanese new religion. She had a very difficult early life. When her husband, an alcoholic, died in 1887 she was left with eight children to support and without any readily marketable skills. In the following years her eldest son attempted suicide and two daughters suffered from mental problems. The family lived in dire poverty, with Nao wandering the streets as a ragpicker. In 1892 she began to have visions as she became possessed by a deity who identified himself as Ushitora no Konjin. Gradually she gained local fame as a midwife and a faith-healer, but was jailed by the authorities and disparaged as a crazy woman. In prison she had further visions and there, although she had no formal education, she began to write these down. These teachings of Konjin, revealed to Nao in a trance, were to become part of Ōmoto scripture. They are known as *Ofudesaki* ('The Tip of the Divine Writing Brush') [8].

Ōmoto presents an eschatological religious message, declaring that the present corrupt world is about to end and to be replaced by a world of peace and prosperity. Like some other 19th-century popular religious movements, Ōmoto was critical of the State Shintō imposed by the Meiji government. Because it expressed the discontent and aspirations of the poor and disenfranchised, Nao's message brought Ōmoto into conflict with the political authorities. In 1898 she met Ueda Kisaburō, later to be known as Deguchi Onisaburō. He had himself experienced religious visions and practised Shugendō-inspired mountain asceticism; so Nao's teachings found a receptive ear and he joined Ōmoto, bringing boundless energy, great organizational skill, and his own charismatic personality. Later he married one of Nao's daughters and became the leading figure in Ōmoto, translating the founder's teachings into a more recognizably Shintō idiom. Ōmoto was suppressed by the state in 1921 and its headquarters were destroyed by the police in 1935, but it re-emerged in the post-war period. While it has not shown the phenomenal growth that has characterized some other new religions, it has spawned a number of other new sects. [1: 397–8; 9; 13; 23; 34: 222–4; 59: 127–41] (G.E.)

Dehqani-Tafti, Hassan Barnabas [VI.A] (1920–). Iranian Anglican bishop. He was born in Taft, near Yezd in central Iran, to a Muslim father and a Christian mother, and raised as a Muslim. His mother died when he was five years of age but she had asked Christian friends to ensure that he became a Christian. His father agreed to his entering a Christian school in Isfahan when he was six. He was baptized when he was 18 against his father's wishes. In 1943 he graduated from the University of Teheran. After military service he worked as a layman for the Anglican diocese. In 1947 he began two years as a theological student in Cambridge. He was ordained in Isfahan in 1949. In 1961 he was consecrated Bishop of Iran. Following the Iranian revolution of 1979 his life was threatened, his son was murdered and he was forced into exile in England. [198] (T.T.)

Dengyō Daishi. *See* SAICHŌ.

Devanandan, Paul David [VI.A] (1901–1962). He was born in Madras, India, and was educated at Nizam College, Hyderabad. He taught for a time at Jaffna College, Ceylon (now Sri Lanka) and then studied for an MA at Madras Christian College, graduating in 1924. Later he graduated with a BD from the Pacific School of Theology, Berkeley, and earned a Doctorate in Christian Theology from Yale University. On his return to India he took a teaching post at the United Theological College, Bangalore, where he remained for 17 years. Then he spent eight years as Literature Secretary of the Indian YMCA. In 1957 the Christian Institute for the Study of Religion and Society was set up in Bangalore and he became its first Director. He held the post until his premature death. [111: 186–205; 200; 201; 862] (T.T.)

Dev Atma. *See* AGNIHOTRI.

Dhalla, M. N. [XXVI] (1875–1956). Parsi priest and scholar, who devoted himself to his religion and community. He developed from a strict traditionalist into a modern reformist, and his autobiography [17] sheds much light on Parsi movements in the late 19th to the mid-20th centuries.

Born at Navsari in Gujarat, he was taken in 1878 to Karachi, where his father and uncle, both priests, obtained meagrely paid work. Despite poverty, Dhalla received a strict religious upbringing and good basic education. He was initiated priest at 15, and from 1894 to 1901 worked at the Municipal Library, reading ardently in his spare time. He began to write and lecture and, attracting the notice of K. R. CAMA, was enabled to study in Bombay for a BA in Avesta and Pahlavi, which he obtained in 1904. He was then sent to study with A. V. W. Jackson at Columbia University, New York, obtaining an MA in 1906, a PhD in 1908. His time there revolutionized his ideas, and he became deeply critical of the excessive ritualism which had developed in Zoroastrianism. On his return he was elected *dastūr* (high priest) of Karachi, and thereafter strove, largely by writing and lecturing, to enlarge the devotional life of the Parsis, and their theological understanding. His main books in English are: *Zoroastrian Theology* (1914); *Zoroastrian Civilization* (1920); *Our Perfecting World* (1930); *Homage unto Ahura Mazda* (1942). In these, some orthodox beliefs still find expression, unreconciled with overtly 'reformed' ones. His scholarly work was recognized by an honorary LittD from Columbia in 1929 and the title of Shams-ul-Ulema from the British Government in 1935.

Dhalla was devoted to his wife Cooverbai, by whom he had six children. Admiration for her strengthened his conviction that women should enjoy equality with men; but his liberalism in this and other matters had to be tempered to meet the conservatism of most of his flock. (M.B.)

Dhammaceti [IV] [Dammazedi] (*c.*1412–1492). A Mon king of lower Burma (Pegu), who carried out an important purification of the Buddhist monastic order. Before becoming king, Dhammaceti had been a career monk. He was a tutor of Queen Shinsawbu and accompanied her when she fled from upper Burma to Pegu. She picked Dhammaceti to be her successor on the throne, he disrobed, married her daughter and reigned from 1472 until his death. As a former monk, the king was very familiar with the spiritual state of the Buddhist monastic order, and he began a purification to restore the *saṅgha* to the disciplinary standards of the scriptural code of monastic conduct (*Vinaya*). Key to Dhammaceti's monastic reform was his insistence on the reordination of monks in the Mahāvihāra lineage from Sri Lanka. The idea here was that the Mon monastic lineage had become tainted, but the process of reordination also had the effect of bringing greater unity to the Burmese monastic order, which had become badly fragmented. Dhammaceti's concern for monastic discipline (*Vinaya*), his stress on the strict observance of the rites of ordination, and his admiration for the Mahāvihāra tradition of Sri Lanka all became enduring patterns of emphasis in Burmese Buddhism. [157: I] (C.H.)

Dhammapāla [IV] (*fl.* late 6th century CE?). One of the greatest commentators in the Theravāda Buddhist tradition. He resided in the South Indian town of Badaratittha, which is thought to have been near the southeast coast; some scholars have taken this as an indication that Dhammapāla was ethnically Dravidian. In his commentaries, Dhammapāla says that he made use of the old Sinhala commentaries preserved by the Mahāvihāra, perhaps an indication that he studied in Sri Lanka. Traditionally he is said to be the author of at least 12 works: seven commentaries (*aṭṭhakathā*) on canonical texts belonging to the *Khuddaka Nikāya* and five subcommentaries (*ṭīkā*) on the hermeneutical manual *Nettippakaraṇa*, on Buddhaghosa's systematic treatise, the *Visuddhimagga*, and on three of Buddhaghosa's commentaries on the canonical *Sutta . Piṭaka*. The *Gandhavaṃsa* attributes five other works to Dhammapāla, although this identification is suspect. The illustrative stories in Dhammapāla's commentaries provided rich subject matter for later Buddhist writers, especially in the medieval period. Scholars are increasingly recognizing that Dhammapāla was also a brilliant figure in Theravādin scholasticism, especially with regard to his knowledge of non-Theravādin Buddhist traditions, and because of the systematic rigour so evident in his subcommentary on the *Visuddhimagga*. Most scholarly interest to date, however, has not focused on delineating the outlines of Dhammapāla's thought or his contribution to Theravādin scholasticism. Rather, most attention has been directed towards two questions: Dhammapāla's date and whether all the works traditionally ascribed to Dhammapāla are really the products of more than one author. Some scholars have argued that there were, in fact, two Dhammapālas, the first writing the commentaries in the 6th century and the second writing the subcommentaries in the 9th or 10th centuries. The arguments for such a dual identification are plausible, but by no means conclusive. [51; 151: VI] (C.H.)

Dharmakīrti [IV] (600–660). Indian Buddhist philosopher, perhaps the greatest exponent of the logical-epistemological (*pramāṇa*) school. According to traditional biographies, he was born in South India and mastered Hindu thought before turning to Buddhism. Travelling north, he was introduced to the thought of DIGNĀGA by the latter's disciple, Īśvarasena, but soon surpassed his teacher in understanding. He devoted his life to writing on logic and epistemology and to debating non-Buddhist opponents, eventually settling in Kaliṅga (Orissa).

Dharmakīrti is credited with seven major philosophical works, the most influential of which was his earliest, the *Pramāṇavārttika*. Purportedly a verse commentary on Dignāga's *Pramāṇasamuccaya*, it is, in fact, an independent treatise. Its chapters cover (1) 'inference for oneself' (*svārthānumāna*), as well as Buddhism's nominalist theory of verbal reference (*anyāpoha*); (2) the 'establishment of authority' (*pramāṇasiddhi*), a defence of Buddhist teachings on atheism, rebirth, enlightenment, no-self and karma; (3) perception (*pratyakṣa*), including the details of various perceptual processes and a defence of the Yogācāra idea that external reality is 'percept-only' (*vijñaptimātra*); and (4) 'inference for the sake of others' (*parārthānumāna*), i.e., syllogism. Dharmakīrti's subsequent works further develop the themes of the *Pramāṇavārttika*: the *Pramāṇaviniścaya* and the *Nyāyabindu* reflect his later ideas on inference, perception and syllogism; the *Hetubindu* analyses logical reasons, negative cognition and causality, and includes an important proof of the Buddhist ontology of momentariness (*kṣaṇikatva*); the *Vādanyāya* explains rules of disputation; the *Saṃbandhaparīkṣā* and the *Santānāntarasiddhi* refute, respectively, relationality and solipsism. Though indebted to Dignāga, Dharmakīrti's thought is at once more systematic and wide-ranging, holding forth the promise that virtually every area of human endeavour, from the mundane to the mystical, can be rationally grounded, and therefore mastered. Dharmakīrti's works spawned a huge commentarial tradition in India, and formed the basis of logical and epistemological study among Tibetans, who memorize and comment upon them to this day. [202; 205; 244; 245] (R.J.)

Dharmapāla [IV] (*c*.530–560). Insightful Indian Buddhist commentator and interpreter of Yogācāra philosophy. Tradition reports that he was the son of a minister at Kāñcīpuram, talented in doctrinal study and dispute. He resided at the great monastic university of Nālandā, where, despite his youth, he became abbot. Aware of the imminence of his death, he retired from this post to devote himself to meditative practice.

Only four of his works are extant and only in Chinese translation: a brief commentary on DIGÑĀGA's epistemological ideas entitled *Ālambanaparīkṣā*, a very academic commentary on Vasubandhu's *Viṃśatikāvijñaptimātratāsiddhi* entitled *Vijñaptimātratāsiddhiratnasaṃbhava*, a commentary on Āryadeva's *Catuḥśataka* entitled *Śataśāstravaipulyaṭīkā*, and a commentary on Vasubandhu's *Triṃśatikāvijñaptimātratāsiddhi* entitled *Vijnaptimātratāsiddhi* (Chinese: *Ch'eng wei-shih lun*).

It was apparently Dharmapāla's commentary on the Mādhyamika text of Āryadeva that triggered the split in India between Yogācāra and Mādhyamika. These two schools had previously been seen as alternate but compatible interpretations of emptiness. But Dharmapāla, claiming to defend the Yogācāra interpretation of ultimate meaning from criticism, presents that interpretation as clearly superior to the Mādhyamika, thus eliciting BHĀVIVAVEKA's rejoinder in his *Tarkajvāla*.

Dharmapāla's commentary on VASUBANDHU's *Triṃśatikā* (usually known by its Chinese title of *Ch'eng wei-shih lun*) became the foundational text of the Yogācāra philosophy (the Fa-hsiang school) brought back to China by the Chinese pilgrim scholar, HSÜAN-TSANG. This text purports to be a compendium of ten commentators on Vasubandhu's text and is attributed to 'Dharmapāla and others'. In fact, however, it equates the orthodox view with the opinion of Dharmapāla. This Dharmapāla Fa-hsiang lineage of Yogācāra thought eclipsed the previous Yogācāra interpretations offered in Paramārtha's translations, as well as the teachings of the less influential Ti-lun sect, and became the accepted tradition of East Asian Yogācāra, transmitted by Dōshō (829–710) to Japan as the Hossō school. [77; 117; 240] (J.K.)

Dharmapāla, Anagārika [IV] (1864–1933). Sinhala Buddhist reformer and polemicist whose career both anticipated and provided a charter for much of modern Buddhism in Sri Lanka. Dharmapāla was born Don David Hewavitarne (Hevavitharana), and grew up in Colombo's then small English-speaking middle class. In 1881, under the influence of the Theosophists HENRY STEEL OLCOTT and HELENA PETROVNA BLAVATSKY, he rejected his 'western' name and took the name 'Dharmapāla' ('Guardian of Truth'). At the same time he created and adopted the new religious role of the *anagārika* ('homeless'), which combined the this-worldly activity typical of a social or political reformer with the ascetic renunciation typical of a Buddhist monk. In 1891 he founded the Maha Bodhi society for the restoration of Buddhist sacred sites in India and for the renascence of Buddhism world-wide. He was exiled from Sri Lanka in 1915 for his political activities. In the last years of his life he became an ordained monk, taking the name Devamitta Dharmapāla, but his continuing significance lies not in his role as monk but as *anagārika*.

Dharmapāla is often described as the founder of 'Protestant Buddhism' in Sri Lanka. He gave a new significance to the role of the Buddhist layperson, emphasizing a kind of spiritual egalitarianism which was both more moralistic and narrower than traditional Sinhala Buddhism. Dharmapāla's legacy continues in the Buddhist world-view of Sri Lanka's urban élite, where his brand of this-worldly asceticism is combined with a fundamentalist commitment to Buddhist doctrine, a puritanical moral code, advocacy of the universal practice of meditation, an intolerance towards other religions, and a nationalist identification of Sri Lanka with pure Buddhism. [3; 71] (C.H.)

Diangienda, Joseph Kuntima [I.A] (1918–1971). Spiritual head and legal representative of the Eglise de Jésus-Christ sur la Terre par le Prophète Simon Kimbangu (EJCSK) in Zaïre. Youngest of three sons of SIMON KIMBANGU, Diangienda was designated by his imprisoned father to lead the EJCSK in 1948. The church was harshly repressed by the Belgian authorities until shortly before the granting of independence in 1960. Nonetheless, in 1956 Diangienda successfully united all of the Kimbanguist groups under a single administrative hierarchy. He travelled widely in Europe, the United States and Africa, was a published spiritual author, and was renowned for his healing skills and dedication. (R.H.)

Didymus the Blind [VI.B] (*c*.315–*c*.398). ATHANASIUS made him head of the catechetical school of Alexandria in *c*.335. Though condemned as a heretic at the council of Constantinople (553) Didymus was greatly respected as a theologian and holy man. Blind from the age of four, he invented a raised form of writing for the blind.

The first known head of the catechetical school is Pantaenus (*c*.190) sent by Patriarch Demetrius I as a missionary to India, where he encountered the St Thomas Christians. His successor was the philosopher and theologian CLEMENT OF ALEXANDRIA, who saw elements of divine revelation in Greek philosophy and in the Hindu sages as well as in the Old Testament. ORIGEN succeeded Clement in about 215. [5: 11; 44: II] (D.J.M.)

Dignāga [IV] · [Diṅnaga] (*c*.480–540). Founder of the logical-epistemological (*pramāṇa*) tradition of Indian Buddhism. A native of the Kañci region of South India, Dignāga lived most of his life in Kaliṅga (Orissa), though he also spent time at the Nālandā monastic university. He may have been a student of VASUBANDHU. Originally a proponent of the controversial 'personalism' (*pudgalavāda*) of the Hīnayāna Vātsīputrīya school, he eventually turned to the Mahāyāna Vijñānavāda tradition, whose metaphysical 'idealism' he combined with epistemological insights developed by Sautrāntikas and theories of language and formal inference (*anumāna*) developed by such non-Buddhists as Bhartṛhari. Dignāga is credited with several religious poems and at least 14 philosophical treatises, which are available only in Chinese and/or Tibetan translation, the Sanskrit originals (fragments excepted) having been lost. Important works include the *Prajñāpāramitāpiṇḍārthasaṃgraha*, an 'idealist' interpretation of the Perfection of Wisdom literature; the *Ālambanaparīkṣā*, a refutation of the externality of objects of cognition; the *Hetucakraḍamaru*, which introduces a ninefold 'wheel of reasons' detailing the possible relations between the reason (*hetu*) and thesis (*sādhya*) of a syllogism; and the *Nyāyamukha*, an analysis of modes of argumentation. Dignāga's masterwork is the *Pramāṇasamuccaya*, a synthesis of his views on epistemology and logic. Its chapters cover (1) perception and the radical particularity of its objects, over against the other source of epistemic authority; (2) inference, which apprehends only conceptual generalities; (3) syllogism, which is simplified by Dignāga to comprise just three (rather than five) members; (4) examples to be applied in syllogism; (5) 'exclusion of what is other' (*anyāpoha*), a nominalist theory of verbal reference; and (6) sophistical refutations. Dignāga's influence has been enormous: not only did he set the agenda for most subsequent developments in Buddhist epistemology (including those of DHARMAKĪRTI, ŚĀNTARAKṢITA and RATNAKĪRTI); he also affected non-Buddhists of the Nyāya, Mīmāṃsā and Jaina schools, who often attacked him while incorporating his insights. [65; 93; 94] (R.J.)

Diocletian [XXII] (*c*.245–316). Roman emperor (Augustus) from 284 CE to his retirement in 305. Diocletian effectively ended the anarchy of the late 3rd century and thoroughly reformed the empire, especially in the administrative sphere [39]. He is included here as the author of the Great Persecution which he unleashed against the Christians in

303 through a series of edicts of increasing severity [18: XV; 24: 235–52; 34: 285–9, 293–7; 39: XII–XIV]. He is thus the archetype of the persecuting emperor, although his successors in the east, Galerius (Caesar 293–305, Augustus to 311) and Maximinus (Caesar 305–8, Augustus to 313), were arguably more systematic persecutors and more ideologically motivated. Indeed, it was Galerius who prompted Diocletian to persecute. Measures against the Christians ranged from destruction of churches and seizure of sacred texts to imprisonment, forced labour, mutilation and death. What motivated Diocletian was the sense that the presence and activities of the Christians within the empire endangered its good order and prosperity by compromising the cult of the traditional gods and jeopardizing their goodwill. The Christians, in sum, were religious subversives. On the same grounds Diocletian also persecuted the Manichaeans (*see* Mānī) [34: 282–4], who were additionally suspect for their alien origins in the enemy territory of Persia. (R.B.)

Diodorus Siculus [vii] (1st century BCE). Greek historian. In his *History* [8], Book I in particular deals with aspects of ancient Egypt; comments on religion cover Osiris, animal worship and the cult and burial of the dead. Diodorus visited Egypt briefly *c*.59 BCE, but, although he occasionally draws upon this first-hand experience in his work, his main sources are earlier writers such as Hecataeus of Abdera and Agatharchides of Cnidus, and, extensively, the Histories of Herodotus [17]. Although Diodorus' work is longer than that of Herodotus, it is far less important as a source; nevertheless, it provides additional information on various subjects which is not found elsewhere. (A.R.D.)

Dionysius the Areopagite [vi.b]. The traditional pseudonym of the author of a number of books probably written in Syria in the early 6th century. They present Christian doctrine and mysticism in the thought forms of Neoplatonism, a Platonism different from that in the theology and mystical thought of Origen or Evagrius, though deriving from the same source. Dionysius' writings include mystical exposition of the liturgy and of angelology as well as an account of the mystical path which leads beyond all assertion and denial to the God who transcends all concepts. Paradoxically, the writings of Dionysius were often more influential in the West than the East. They were translated by John Scotus Erigena (*c*.810–*c*.875), an Irish philosopher and theologian, himself an original thinker whose *De divinione naturae* is a major attempt at a Platonistic Christian philosophy of God and creation. [54] (D.J.M.)

Diotima [x] (5th century BCE). Prophetess of Mantinea, who may or may not have existed. Plato, in the *Symposium* [68: 202a–212c], puts into her mouth a course of instruction, supposedly given to Socrates, on the mystical path of love. Love is not itself beautiful or good, but is the stimulus towards goodness and beauty: the person who loves correctly has to begin with mere sexual desire, but to learn to transcend it and to appreciate, stage by stage, physical beauty in general, beauty of character, beauty in human institutions, beauty in the scientific order, and finally absolute Beauty itself, eternal, and incorruptible. This passage has had an enormous influence on artists, such as Michelangelo, and mystics in the Christian, Jewish and Muslim traditions. [68] (H.L.)

Dīpaṅkara Śrījñāna. *See* Atiśa.

Dīp Siṅgh [xxiii] (*d*.1757). Prominent Sikh military leader and martyr. He fought with Bandā against the Mughals and later became chieftain of a group of loyal Sikhs who fought with similar irregular armies against Mughals and Afghāns for control of the Punjab. In old age he was aroused by the desecration in Amritsar of Harimandir Sāhib (the chief Sikh temple) by the Afghāns. He marched on the city at the head of a small army, but before reaching it was defeated and killed by a much larger Afghān army. In Sikh popular art he lives on as the subject of a particularly favoured picture. [43: 121–4; 49: XIX] (W.H.M.)

Dit Siṅgh [xxiii] (1852–1901). Major ideologue of modern Sikh identity [21: 143]. He was educated primarily in traditional religious establishments. Author, publisher, journalist, public speaker, preacher, polemicist *par excellence*, Dit Siṅgh helped formulate and popularize the ideas of the Siṅgh Sabhā movement [6: 23–9]. He wrote over 40 books dealing with such diverse themes as Sikh history, doctrines, rituals, legends of martyrdom and social reform. In his writings he was particularly concerned with demonstrating how Sikhism radically differed from Hinduism and how the folk religious practices prevalent among the Sikh masses had prevented the emergence of a separate Sikh identity. (H.S.O.)

Dōgen [iv] (1200–1253). Transmitter and founder of the Japanese Sōtō school of Zen Buddhism, and one of the most profound thinkers of Japanese Buddhism. Dōgen studied at the Tendai headquarters on Mt Hiei but soon became disillusioned with the corruption he found there, and was unable to resolve his doubts concerning the Tendai teaching that all sentient beings have the Buddha nature. After leaving Mt Hiei he studied under Myōzen (1184–1225), a disciple of Elsai (1141–1215), with whom he left for China in 1223. While in China he met an elderly monk, the chief cook of the monastery of Mt A-yü-wang, who taught Dōgen the importance of discipline and practice in daily life. After visiting numerous monasteries he discovered his 'authentic teacher' in Ju-ching (1163–1268), under whom he was recognized as having attained enlightenment. Dōgen's enlightenment experience occurred when he overheard Ju-ching scolding another monk for drowsing off, saying 'you must drop off body and mind' (Japanese: *shinjin datsuraku*), a phrase which came to have profound implications for Dōgen's philosophy.

Dōgen returned to Japan in 1227, eventually settling at Eihei-ji, a temple in the mountains far from bustle and the centre of secular power, which eventually became the headquarters of the Sōtō school. He spent much of his time maintaining an austere practice and writing the essays which were compiled into the *Shōbōgenzō* ('Treasury-Eye of the Correct Dharma'), a monumental collection of discourses on Buddhist thought and practice. A well-known collection of Dōgen's talks, the *Shōbōgenzō-zuimonki*, was compiled by his disciple Ejō (1198–1280).

Dōgen's approach to practice is summarized in the phrase 'only sit' (*shikan taza*), reflecting Dōgen's teaching that sitting in meditation (*zazen*) is the only true way of enlightenment. He also taught that practice itself is the attainment of enlightenment (*shūshō-ichinyo*). His reinterpretation and rereading of the famous Buddhist phrase that 'all things have the Buddha-nature' to mean that 'all existence is Buddha-nature' is particularly well known.

Dōgen is recognized as one of the most profound Buddhist philosophers in Japanese history. His Sōtō school is still one of the two largest Zen schools in Japan, and his stark and uncompromising approach to life and Buddhist practice has been influential even in the West. [19; 40; 124; 134] (P.L.S.)

Döllinger, Johann [vi] (1799–1890). German Catholic theologian. He was ordained in 1822. As a curate he completed his doctorate and was appointed professor at Aschaffenburg (1823) and from 1826 to 1872 at Munich. He condemned the Protestant schism in two works, *Reformation* (1845–8) and *Luther* (1851). He also wrote a number of important works on ecclesiastical history. In 1863 he convened a conference of Catholic theologians in Munich to seek the independent study of history, free of Roman authority. His views were condemned by the pope in the *Syllabus of Errors* in 1864. Fearing that the First Vatican Council was about to confirm unlimited papal infallibility he spoke out in opposition, with others, in *Letters of Janus* (1869) and *Letters of Quirinius* (1869–70). He was excommunicated but continued to attend Roman Catholic services though denied the sacraments. [162; 447; 580] (T.T.)

Dominic [vi] (1170–1221). Founder of the Dominican Order. He was born in Caleruega, in Old Castile. He studied arts and theology in Palencia between 1186 and 1196 and went to the cathedral of Osma in 1199 as canon and then priest. In 1203 he came into contact with the Albigenses (Cathars), an allegedly heretical sect in Languedoc whose asceticism was a challenge to the Roman Catholic Church. The pope enlisted the Cistercian order of monks to counter the Albigenses. Dominic was sent to join in this preaching mission for nine years (1206–15). This led to his forming the 'Order of Preachers' and receiving papal approval in 1216–17. Dominic died in Bologna following a preaching tour in Lombardy. [472; 822] (T.T.)

Dosabhoy Framjee [xxvi] [later surnamed Karaka] (19th century). Parsi layman who received a Western-type education in Bombay, and conceived a profound admiration for Western culture. He became a journalist, and in 1858 published a book, *The Parsees*, designed to present to Europeans the 'history, beliefs and manners' of his community in what he thought was both a true and favourable light. Knowing little of theology or observance, he confidently presented ZOROASTER's teachings as a simple monotheism with virtually no rituals. This and his longer work *History of the Parsees* [34] contain nevertheless much interesting matter about Parsi history, social customs and outstanding figures. [42: 458] (M.B.)

Dositheos [VI.B] (1641–1707). Patriarch of Jerusalem. A Peloponnesian, Dositheos studied at Corinth. On ordination he went to Constantinople then Jerusalem, where he became Bishop of Caesarea (1666) and at the age of 28 Patriarch of Jerusalem. He refounded monasteries and churches, organized schools and libraries, and reformed the monastic 'Brotherhood of the Holy Sepulchre'. Dositheos toured the Near East and the Balkans to combat Latin propaganda amongst the Orthodox. He repaid the colossal debts of the Patriarchate and set up a printing house in Moldavia. He was respected by the Ottomans and secured 140 firmans protecting Orthodox rights in the Holy Land. In 1672 he published a *Confession* formulating Orthodox doctrine in traditional terms, to counter the Latinizing influences that marked the confession of PETR MOGHILA. [76] (D.B.)

Dov Ber of Mezhirich [XV] (*c.*1704–1772). Ḥasidic leader. He was born in Volhynia, where he pursued talmudic and kabbalistic studies. A brilliant orator and master of parables, he was a travelling preacher (Hebrew: *maggid*), and eventually became known as *Ha-Maggid* (*the* preacher, *par excellence*) [13: vol. 1: 98–113]. He was given to ascetic practices, but fasting and mortifications led to a deterioration in his health, and he turned to the BA'AL SHEM TOV for a cure. He remained as a student and disciple and eventually (1760) succeeded the Ba'al Shem Tov as the leader of Ḥasidism, which he proceeded to organize into a movement. Dov Ber settled in Mezhirich, Volhynia, and sent his own followers (many of whom became among the most famous Ḥasidic masters) far and wide, leading to a great expansion of Ḥasidic centres. Many flocked to Mezhirich to listen to his expositions. In his last years, some of his ideas aroused opposition, even among his followers, brought on by what was regarded as his pantheistic tendencies, his adoption of a Sephardi-influenced liturgy and the neglect by some of his students of traditional rabbinical learning.

He himself tended to the ecstatic, but his teachings were based on a lucid logic and a deep knowledge of Jewish sources. He presented a systematic theology, introducing strong kabbalistic elements, especially as developed by ISAAC LURIA. Wisdom, he stressed, was the basis of knowledge of God. His teaching was panentheistic: God, who is infinite and fills all space, is to be found everywhere, and all material things are suffused with God's wisdom. Man must worship through prayer and Torah study. The highest rank of achievement can only be attained by the *tzaddik* (saintly leader) who mediates between man and God, and for whom the world was created. The doctrine of the *tzaddik* became fundamental in the further history of Ḥasidism. [87: vol. 9: 63–80]

After his death the movement diversified; Dov Ber was its last single leader. (G.W.)

Dubois, Jean Antoine [VI.A] (1765–1848). French Catholic missionary. He was born at Saint-Remèze (Ardèche) France. He was ordained priest in 1792 and joined the Société des Missions Etrangères de Paris. In 1793 he was sent to the Tamil-speaking area of South India and thence to Mysore. He tried to follow the pattern of ROBERTO DE NOBILI's work. He was discouraged in missionary work but wrote the excellent *Moeurs, institutions et cérémonies des peuples de l'Inde* ('Hindu Manners, Customs and Ceremonies', 1825), a comprehensive work based on his own notes and observations. The book was written and revised before he left India but the full text was not published in English until 1897. Between 1815 and 1821, when he left India, he wrote letters in which he pointed to the impracticability of converting Hindus. The letters offer gloomy prospects for the religion in India. In his later years he served at the headquarters of the Société in Paris. [216; 217; 375; 461: vol. 1: 310–18] (T.T.)

Dufay, Guillaume [VI.A] (*c.*1400–1474).

French composer. After an early life as a choirboy in Cambrai Cathedral he went to Bologna, Italy. He was forced to flee to Rome, where he remained for the next five years as a member of the papal chapel. In the 1430s his duties to the new pope Eugenius IV, for whose consecration he provided the music, and the Duke of Savoy, led to difficulties when the former was deposed in favour of the latter, who became Felix V. He returned to Cambrai in 1439 and spent the next decade concentrating on developing his clear melodic style in the cyclic mass. This was based on a *cantus firmus*, often a secular melody, and led to the composition of such masses as *Se la face ay pale* and *L'homme armé*. Felix V relinquished the papacy in 1450, enabling Dufay to return to the Court of Savoy. His influential new ideas marked the transition between the musical styles of the Middle Ages and the Renaissance. [28; 254] (E.M.)

Duff, Alexander [VI.A] (1806–1878). Scottish missionary. He was born in Moulin, Perthshire, into an evangelical farming family. He was educated at Perth Grammar School and later at the University of St Andrews. He graduated in general studies and divinity and felt the influence of Thomas Chalmers. In 1830 he went to India as the first missionary of the Church of Scotland to that country, having the previous year married Anne Scott Drysdale. He set up a school in Calcutta which eventually became the Scottish Church College. Duff's whole emphasis in mission was on an English and Western education, hoping thereby to undermine Hinduism and make way for the Christianizing of India. He scorned any education in or any attention to the languages of India. He returned to Scotland in 1834 and spent six years trying to persuade the Church of Scotland to increase its support for foreign missions. In 1843 after the schism in the Church of Scotland he followed Chalmers into the Free Church, thereby forfeiting all his mission property. He carried on his educational work until he returned to Scotland in 1849. In 1851 he was elected chairman of the General Assembly of the Free Church. In 1856 he returned to India and was engaged in the formation of the University of Calcutta, to which the Scottish Church College became affiliated. On his way back to Britain in 1864 he visited South Africa. He spent the rest of his life in support of missionary work and died in Sidmouth, Devon. [221; 222; 627] (T.T.)

Duns Scotus, John [VI.A] (*c*.1266–1308). Franciscan philosopher and theologian. He was born at Maxton, Roxburgh and began his education at the Franciscan friary in Dumfries. He went to Oxford as a student and later as a teacher. In 1302 he was sent to Paris to lecture at the university. During a dispute between the King and the Pope Duns Scotus sided with the Pope and as a result was exiled but returned after the election of a new pontiff. Around 1305 he became regent master of the University of Paris. In 1307 he went to Cologne to teach at the Franciscan house of studies. He is buried in the Franciscan church next to Cologne Cathedral. Among his most important works is the *Tractate on the First Principle*, on the application of reason to belief in God. [829; 876; 877] (T.T.)

Dürer, Albrecht [VI.A] (1471–1528). German painter and printmaker. A native of Nuremberg, he was the son of a goldsmith. In 1486 he began the study of wood engraving. He travelled extensively in Europe both before and after his marriage in 1494. His religious works, in late Gothic style, consist of some paintings but more important are his woodcuts and copper engravings. He made a lasting contribution to graphic art. His main works were series published under such titles as the *Apocalypse* (1498), the *Great Passion* (1498–1510), the *Little Passion* (1509–11) and the *Life of the Virgin* (1501–11). Though he remained a Catholic his work was appreciated by Protestants. Martin Luther praised him after his death. [73; 620] (T.T.)

Dússel, Enrique D. [VI.A] (1934–). He was born in Mendoza, Argentina. He has degrees in philosophy, history and theology and has lectured, as a Catholic layman, in many countries. Converted from right-wing views in the early 1960s, he developed deep sensitivity to the plight of the poor and became committed to their liberation cause. Because of this, the Argentine professor was exiled, and transferred to the University of Mexico City. Now the dean of Latin American church historians, he is president of the liberationist CEHILA (the ecumenical Commission of the Study of the History of the

Church in Latin America) which is undertaking a vast project to 'reconstruct the historical memory of the people of God in Latin America'. A prolific writer, he has provided a useful framework for understanding the historical growth of Latin American theology, has done seminal work (1988) on the 'Future of Missions in the Third Millennium', and is distinguished by such works as: *Hipótesis para una historia de la Iglesia en América Latina* (1967); *Historia de la Iglesia en América Latina: Coloniaje y Liberación (1492–1973)* (1974); trans. as *A History of the Church in Latin America: Colonialism to Liberation (1492–1973)*, (1981); *Philosophy of Liberation* (1985); *Ethics and Community* (1988). [307; 297: 309–11] (A.C.S.)

Duṭṭhagāmaṇi [IV] [Duṭugämunu] (*fl.* 2nd century BCE). A Sinhala prince who unified Sri Lanka as a Buddhist kingdom and ruled the island for 24 years (*c.*161–137 BCE or 101–77 BCE, depending on how one adjusts the chronology found in the *Mahāvaṃsa*). Duṭṭhagāmaṇi constituted his position as a Buddhist overlord by constructing religious monuments and by making ceremonial donations to the Buddhist monastic order throughout his reign. Thus he came to be perceived as the ideal Buddhist king, in particular, and the ideal Buddhist layperson, in general, since both have a responsibility to protect and promote Buddhist institutions materially.

Duṭṭhagāmaṇi has been an important figure in Sinhala popular culture, where his virtues as a pious king and his exploits as a warrior were embellished and extolled. This folk tradition has been the source for the many versions of the Duṭṭhagāmaṇi story found in the Sri Lankan monastic chronicles and in later Sinhala literature. The classic version is found in the *Mahāvaṃsa*, the most important of the chronicles.

The qualities of piety and violence – antithetical in orthodox Buddhist ethics – are woven together in the *Madāvaṃsa*'s account of Duṭṭhagāmaṇi's military campaign to unify Sri Lanka. He declares that his battles are for the sake of Buddhism and not for the pleasures of sovereignty. He goes into battle accompanied by monks and with a relic of the Buddha on his spear. The dramatic climax comes with Duṭṭhagāmaṇi's battle with the Tamil king Eḷāra, who is described as a just ruler, but is judged to be unfit to rule Sri Lanka because he was not a Buddhist.

Duṭṭhagāmaṇi's story is a critical part of the *dhammadīpa* ('Island of Truth') tradition, emphasizing the necessity of political unity for Sri Lanka to fulfil its religious destiny, as well as the special and exclusive relationship its rulers were to have with Buddhism. The Duṭṭhagāmaṇi story is strongly communalist in its outlook, and has become a virulent element in modern Sri Lanka's ethnic conflicts. [69; 193: I–VI] (C.H.)

Dwags-po Lha-rje. *See* SGAM-PO-PA BSOD-NAMS RIN-CHEN.

E

Eck, Johann [VI.A] [Johann Maier] (1486–1543). German Catholic theologian. He was born in Eck in Swabia. He was educated at the University of Heidelberg, then Tübingen, Cologne and Freiburg, where he received his first doctorate. In 1510 he went to Ingolstadt, where he received his second doctorate and taught in the theology faculty; he remained there for the rest of his life. He became a priest in 1508. He was the leading disputant following the publication of LUTHER's Theses, especially at Leipzig in 1519. In Rome he secured the condemnation of Lutheran theology and was chosen to publicize the bull *Exsurge Domine* which was a condemnation of Luther. Thereafter most of his life was spent in combating Protestantism – in discussions in Augsburg (1530) and Ratisbon (1541), and through publications on papal authority, purgatory, the sacrament of penance and the sacrifice of the Mass. His *Enchiridion* (1537) was a compendium of Protestant errors. He also produced a German translation of the Bible in the same year. [231; 388; 861] (T.T.)

Eckhart, Johannes [VI.A] [Meister Eckhart] (1260–1327?). German theologian and mystic. He was born in Hochheim, Thuringia. He entered the Dominican Order and began studying theology in Cologne about 1280. He went to Paris and was a professor there in 1302. In 1303 and 1307 he was chosen to be the religious superior over a number of Dominican houses. He returned to teach in Paris. His teaching was a combination of scriptural exegesis, theological-philosophical speculation and sermons on the Christian life. In 1314 Eckhart was in Strasbourg, teaching and preaching. He also travelled extensively to Dominican and Cistercian houses, teaching and giving spiritual counsel. By 1322 he was back in Cologne. His teaching and preaching on the divine abyss and the true human self as being the location of a personalized presence of the divine love brought him into conflict with church authorities. In 1326 he was attacked by the Archbishop of Cologne. In 1329 many of his teachings were judged heretical or conducive to heresy. It is not known when or where he died. [232; 233; 598] (T.T.)

Edal Sanjana. *See* SANJANA, EDAL.

Eddy, Mary Baker [VI.A] (1821–1910). Founder of the Christian Science movement. She was a native of New Hampshire, a Calvinist Puritan though she turned against Calvinist predestinarianism in her youth. She suffered much ill health in early life and came to believe that the cause of disease lay in the mind. Following a 'miraculous' recovery from a serious accident after reading of healing by JESUS in the Gospel of Matthew in 1866, and under the influence of Phineas Quimby, a healer, she turned to a study of scripture and offered healing services herself. In 1875 she published *Science and Health with Key to the Scriptures*, and in 1879 she founded Church of Christ, Scientist in Boston. In 1881 she opened the 'Metaphysical College' but in 1889 she suspended the work while she reorganized the movement. It emerged in 1892 as the First Church of Christ, Scientist in Boston and three years later her *Manual of the Mother Church* was published. Two years before she died she founded *The Christian Science Monitor*. [188; 234; 636] (T.T.)

Edwards, Jonathan [VI.A] (1703–1758). American theologian and philosopher. He was born in East Windsor, Connecticut, the son of a Congregationalist minister. In 1716 he went to Collegiate School (Yale College) and studied biblical and classical languages, logic and natural philosophy. He graduated in 1720 and spent two years studying theology in New Haven. In 1726 he became assistant to his maternal grandfather in Northampton, Connecticut and was ordained in 1727. Between 1726 and 1750 he ministered in Northampton and engaged in revivalist preaching. A dispute arose in his Northampton congregation over ministerial authority. He tried to enforce a discipline with respect to communion which brought him into conflict with members of his congregation and led to his dismissal. In 1751 he accepted work in Stockbridge, Massachusetts among a congregation mostly of Indians where he wrote *Original Sin* (published posthumously). In 1758 he became president of the College of New Jersey (later Princeton) but died of smallpox a week after arriving there. [477; 479; 552] (T.T.)

Egeria [VI.B] [Etheria] (4th century). A female pilgrim, probably from Gaul, who visited the Holy Land in the latter part of the 4th century and wrote an account of her travels. It contains important information on the shrines of the Holy Land and the liturgical practices at the holy places during Holy Week and Easter Week. [38] (D.J.M.)

Eight-Deer Tiger Claw [XVIII] (11th century). Mixtec ruler who visited and engaged in ritual activities and conquered over 100 ceremonial communities in the Mixtec territories. Representations of his fabulous career appear in surviving pre-Colombian screenfolds such as the Codex Colombino and the Codex Nutall. In one sequence we see him presenting the captive ruler of Acatepec to another ruler, and initiated into the office of *tecuhtli* ('great lord') in a nose-perforating ceremony. His nose ornament becomes a prominent part of his paraphernalia. He later attempted to conquer a town belonging to his second wife, was defeated, sacrificed and buried by his wife's family. These scenes are vividly depicted in the pictorials. The career of this ruler shows the relationship between rulers, territory, marriage and human sacrifice in Mixtec religions. (D.C.)

Eight Immortals [V] [Immortal Transcendents; Pa Hsien]. These individuals embody the characteristics and occult powers of the 'perfected persons' (*chen ren*) of Taoism in a uniquely popular way. Although several of them are mentioned much earlier, it seems to have been in the Yüan or Mongol period (1264–1368) that they were brought together as a group. From that time until the present their appeal has never diminished, and they have been depicted endlessly in every artistic medium, including poetry and drama. Although they do represent different classes and conditions as well as both sexes, they are not so much symbols as 'living examples' of Chinese conceptions of what the *hsien*, or immortal transcendents, do, of their typical personalities, and of their magical attainments. Stories about them show the playful side of Chinese religion, while on the other hand they have been taken seriously as supernaturals who communicate with their devotees on the planchette, through 'spirit writing'.

Four of the eight are quasi-historical persons. LÜ TUNG-PIN, Han Hsiang-tzu, Chang Kuo-lao and Ts'ao Kuo-chiu. The first three are supposed to have flourished in the mid-T'ang (7th and 8th centuries), while Ts'ao Kuo-chiu belongs to the Northern Sung (11th century). As for Han Hsiang-tzu, he is said to have been a grand-nephew of the famous Literatus Han Yü (768–824). He is represented as a young lad with a flute. Chang Kuo-lao's *persona* is that of so many famous Taoists, a great magician who fascinates emperors but who is difficult to entice to court. He rides a mule which can cover a thousand leagues a day. When he no longer needs him, he folds him up like paper and puts him in his wallet. To revivify him, he sprays him with water from his mouth. Ts'ao Kuo-chiu's appellation indicates that he was a brother of the empress, and he is represented in full court dress. He was admitted to the band when he convinced Chung-li Ch'üan and Lü Tung-pin that he understood the Tao.

Among the other four members of the Eight, who apparently are purely legendary, the most bizarre is Li T'ieh-kuai, or Iron-staff Li. He was a Taoist master who one day hastened off to call on LAO TZU, leaving his mortal form in the care of a disciple with instructions that it should be disposed of if he did not return within seven days. Unfortunately, the disciple had to rush home to see his dying mother after only six days had passed, and so he cremated the body of his master. When Li returned on the seventh day he therefore had to take up residence in the nearest available body, which was that of an ugly lame beggar. Hence it is in this form that he is represented, holding a crutch to support his game leg.

Chung-li Ch'üan is also called Han Chung-li because he is supposed to have lived during the Han period (202 BCE–220 CE). He is reputedly the leader of the Eight. He is pictured wearing an open robe that exposes his great belly (a sign of his cultivation of vital breath or *ch'i*) and holding a fan, symbolic of his mortal career as a military commander, and also of his ability to 'raise the dead'. His most important accomplishment was the conversion and training of Lü Tung-pin.

Lan Ts'ai-ho represents another aspect of *hsien* behaviour, that of the crazy wanderer who despises worldly things. He carries a basket of flowers and is possibly female.

As for Ho Hsien-ku, she is definitely female. As a beautiful young girl she cultivated the Tao to the point she no longer had to eat. She, like the others, represents rejection of the accepted social mores of the Chinese, because she refused to marry. Her attribute is a lotus flower or, earlier, a soup ladle. [16; 65; 68] (L.T.)

Eisai [IV] [Yosai] (1141–1215). Transmitter of the Rinzai school of Zen Buddhism to Japan. Eisai studied Buddhism at the Tendai headquarters on Mt Hiei and travelled to China for five months in 1168. He made a second trip to China in 1187, but his plans to make a pilgrimage to India were thwarted by Chinese officials. Instead Eisai studied the Zen tradition of Lin-chi (Japanese: Rinzai) under Hsu-an Huai-ch'ang.

After his return to Japan in 1191, Eisai began to propagate Rinzai teachings, along with the Tendai and esoteric Buddhist teachings and practice which formed his background. He emphasized the importance of observing the Buddhist precepts. Faced with the opposition of the Tendai establishment, Eisai wrote *Shukke taikō* ('Essentials of the Monastic Life') and *Kōzen-gokoku-ron* ('Dissemination of Zen for the Defence of the Nation'), in which he claimed that the Zen teachings should reform and not threaten Tendai Buddhism and would help strengthen rather than weaken society. In 1199 Eisai went to Kamakura to seek the support of the new shogunate. Eventually he was given charge of Kennin-ji, a new monastery, where he served the shogunate by performing religious services and became involved in the restoration of various temples, such as Tōdai-ji in Nara.

Though he is recognized as the founder of the Rinzai school of Zen Buddhism in Japan, Eisai himself taught an eclectic form of Buddhism which included many elements from the esoteric tradition. He also saw himself as a reformer of Tendai rather than the founder of a new movement. Perhaps he is most famous for his introduction of tea to Japan, which he recommended to monks for their health and as an aid to meditation. [42; 57] (P.L.S.)

Eknāth [XI] [Ekanātha] (*c*.1533–1600). Marathi Brahman poet-saint, composer of *abhangas* to Viṭṭhala of Pandharpur. He was born at Paithan on the Godavari near Aurangabad. As usual the details of his life are known only from pious compilations written down a century later and from the often dubious colophons of the works ascribed to him. He is said to have been the disciple of Janārdansvāmī, a Brahman who combined devotion to the god Dattātreya with being captain of the fort of Daulatabad under a Muslim suzerain. Eknāth thus provides another interesting example of Hindu eclecticism, or perhaps oecumenicism, in that as a major poet and nexus of religious power he is claimed by a number of different sects. Eknāth's *Bhāvārtha Rāmāyaṇa* and *Rukmiṇī Svayaṃvara* are straightforward narrative poems, but the *Ekanāthī Bhāvagata*, supposedly completed in Benares in 1573, is a philosophical commentary on part of the eleventh *skandha* of the *Bhāgavatapurāṇa*. In addition to his more conventional *bhakti* verses, Eknāth is famous for his *bhārūḍa*, short poems in which moral teaching is conveyed in a dramatic monologue, often coarse and scatalogical, put into the mouth of some low-life character: a Mahār perhaps, or a Muslim hunter or an angry peasant woman. Eknāth's other role was as the first editor of *Jñāneśvarī* (*see* JÑĀNEŚVAR). Scandalized by the emendations and scribal errors that had crept into those manuscripts that were known to him, he established a text which remained standard until the days of modern scholarship. Eknāth has a temple dedicated to him in his native town of Paithan, and like all the other saints his *pālakhī* is carried to Pandharpur. [26; 108] (I.M.P.R.)

Eleazar ben Judah of Worms [xv] [Eleazar Roke'aḥ] (*c.*1165–*c.*1230). Jewish scholar, mystic and poet. He was born in Mainz to an outstanding scholarly family and studied with JUDAH BEN SAMUEL HE-ḤASID. He fled from Mainz as a result of Christian anti-Jewish attacks and settled in Worms, where his wife and children were killed before his eyes by Crusaders and he himself was badly wounded. From 1201 he served as rabbi in Worms.

Eleazar was the last major figure in the school of medieval German Jewish mystic pietists (the 'Ashkenaz *Ḥasidim*') whose teachings he brought through his many writings before a wide public. The basis of his thought is the utter spirituality and uniqueness of God, who emanated from his concealed essence his 'glory', which links infinite God to finite creation. All biblical anthropomorphisms refer to this 'glory'. Central to his system is the obligation to repent; the true penitent must inflict himself with pains and punishment to counter the pleasures he derived from his sinfulness.

Eleazar's main mystical theological work is *Sodei Razayya* ('Secrets of Secrets'), which is largely based on alphabet and numeral mysticism. He held that the 22 letters of the Hebrew alphabet and their numerical values were the origin of existence, and that the secrets of life could be solved by word play and mystical letter combinations. His *Sefer ha-Roke'aḥ* (literally 'Book of the Apothecary', but the latter word has the same numerical value as 'Eleazar') is a partial code of religious law and an attempt to codify the ideals of the Ashkenaz Ḥasidim (e.g. prayer, piety and penitence) in terms of Jewish religious law. [72: III]

Eleazar also composed religious poems, many of which entered the Ashkenazi liturgy. They display deep devotion to God but protest the sufferings of the Jewish people. [87: vol. 2: 57–76] (G.W.)

Elijah [xv] (first half of 9th century BCE). Israelite prophet who prophesied in the northern kingdom of Israel during the reigns of Ahab, Ahaziah and Jehoram. He originated from Gilead, east of the Jordan, and belonged to the group of prophets in Israel and Judah who were fighting for the pure worship of God (Yahweh) and resisting polytheistic and idolatrous manifestations. The Bible ascribes to him no settled home but portrays him as wandering the country, making sudden appearances.

Ahab continued the close relations with Tyre initiated by his father, Omri, and this involved toleration of the spread of the Tyrian cult of Baal in Samaria, especially in circles close to Ahab's Tyrian wife, Jezebel. Elijah first clashed with Ahab when he forecast a two-year drought as punishment for Baal worship. He challenged the prophets of Baal to a spectacular confrontation on Mount Carmel, where Elijah's victory was followed by the slaughter of his opponents and the triumphant proclamation 'Yahweh is God' (*see also* KERET). However, in face of Jezebel's wrath, Elijah had to flee to the desert. The divine revelation that he experienced on the mount of God at Horeb (identified with Sinai) follows the pattern of the revelation to Moses, but now God was manifested not in thunder and lightning but in 'a still, small voice'.

Returning to Samaria, Elijah accused the king of injustice and cruelty over the issue of Naboth's vineyard, which harmed the royal image among the people and enhanced Elijah's reputation. He forecast the end of the dynasty (which actually came to pass in the time of Elisha, Elijah's disciple and successor). Elijah's last recorded public act occurred when the ailing King Ahaziah sent to enquire of Baal-Zebub, god of Ekron, concerning his recovery. Elijah condemned this ignoring of the God of Israel and foretold Ahaziah's early death.

Many miraculous acts are ascribed to Elijah and the Bible relates that when his time came to die, he was taken up to heaven in a whirlwind. His powerful and zealous personality, combined with the unique manner of his leaving the world, made him into a legendary figure in Jewish tradition. Already the prophet Malachi said: 'Behold I will send the prophet Elijah to you before the coming of the awesome, fearful day of the Lord. He shall reconcile parents with children and children with their parents.' Consequently Elijah was associated with the messianic age, and by the

1st century was seen as the precursor of the messiah. (In the New Testament some took JESUS to be Elijah, but Jesus rejected this and identified JOHN THE BAPTIST with Elijah.)

Elijah took on a prime role in Jewish eschatology and was even regarded as the partner of the messiah. Insoluble legal disputes were set aside to be solved by Elijah after his return. He was seen as caring for the safety of the Jewish people, and in particular of pious Jews subject to suffering. In folklore he figures prominently as appearing in disguise to fight injustice and help the righteous. A particular role was assigned to him on Passover eve when he would thwart the blood libels to which Jews were subjected at this period, and he would also ensure that the needy were provided for. In the Passover eve ceremony a special cup is placed on the table for Elijah, and in the course of the evening the front door is opened to welcome his expected arrival. A seat, the chair of Elijah, is provided for him at the circumcision ceremony.

The main source for the life of Elijah is 1 *Kings* 17–22 and 2 *Kings* 1–2: 11. [83] (G.W.)

Elijah ben Solomon Zalman of Vilna [XV] [also known as the *Ga'on* (eminent leader) of Vilna and by the acronym *Ha-Gra*] (1720–1797). Rabbinic leader and scholar. A child prodigy, he immersed himself in the study of rabbinic sources and lived most of his life in an austere and reclusive style in Vilna (Vilnius), never accepting an official rabbinic position. His intellectual power and critical mind made him the outstanding rabbinic authority of his time and his methods of study had a deep and lasting impact on the rabbinical academies of Lithuania. His talmudic learning embraced not only the Babylonian Talmud but also the Jerusalem Talmud, on which he wrote a commentary and which he helped rescue from neglect. He compared different manuscripts of the talmudic books so as to establish accurate texts. He was also a profound scholar of the Bible, stressing the need for its intensive study as the source of talmudic decisions. Elijah also studied natural sciences (including mathematics, medicine and astronomy), which was unusual for a rabbinic scholar of that time; he maintained they should be known to pious Jews for the light they throw on traditional literature. He solved complicated issues of Jewish law and initiated fresh methods of Talmud learning, substituting criticism for casuistry. He strongly opposed philosophy as well as the inroads of enlightenment, and applied mystical traditions for the understanding of rabbinic writings.

Elijah vehemently combated the Ḥasidic movement and under his leadership Vilna became the centre of the anti-Ḥasidic forces, known as the *Mitnaggedim* ('opponents'). He was responsible for orders of excommunication being issued against the Ḥasidic leaders. [29: 125–44; 42: 25–30] (G.W.)

Elijah Muhammad [XII] (1897–1975). Leader of the Nation of Islam, the American Black Muslim organization. Born in Georgia, USA, with the name Elijah Poole, he moved to Detroit in 1923. He became a follower of Wallace D. Fard ('Prophet Fard') and his Temple of Islam in 1931 and subsequently became his chief aide. After Fard's death in 1934, Elijah Muhammad (a name given to him by Fard) took a group of followers to Chicago to establish the Nation of Islam, proclaiming Fard to be Allah incarnate and himself a prophet.

Doctrinally, Elijah Muhammad preached Black nationalism combined with elements of Christianity and Islam. The Qur'ān was taken as scripture, supplemented by the decisions of Elijah; God was Allah. His goal was the empowering of the black people, enabling them to become a 'nation' cognisant of their own value as people, a value which had been consistently denied in America.

The movement had its greatest success with the efforts of Elijah's follower MALCOLM X, although his own charismatic personality established a firm basis from which the movement emerged. [81] (A.R.)

Eliot, John [VI.A] (1604–1690). Puritan missionary to the Massachusetts Indians. He was born at Widford, England, and graduated at Jesus College, Cambridge. He taught for a time, but having become a Presbyterian he migrated to Massachusetts Bay Colony in 1632. He became a pastor and teacher at the church in Roxbury, a post he held until his death. In the 1640s he began to take an interest in the conversion of the Indians living nearby, so he began to learn the Algonquin language. In 1646 he preached his first sermon in the language to a band of Massachusetts Indians in Nonantum

(Newton). The English parliament chartered The Society for the Propagation of the Gospel in New England in 1649 to provide the mission with financial support. In 1651 the first baptisms took place. When it became apparent that the converts found it difficult to maintain their new faith while living with those not converted he began to organize separate communities for the converts, the first in Natick in 1651, on land set aside by the Massachusetts General Court. Nonantum (Newton), Ponkapoag (Stoughton) and other towns followed. Each community had its church, school and land for sustenance farming and leaders for church and community government received special training. By 1674 there were 14 such communities. Eliot translated into the Algonquin language the *Catechism* (1653), the *New Testament* (1661), the *Old Testament* (1663) and a *Grammar* (1666). In 1675 various Indian tribes united under King Philip of the Wampanoags in a war to drive out the White man. The conflict lasted more than a year with heavy losses on both sides. The Indian towns were disrupted and gradually disappeared. Eliot's work suffered but in old age he turned his attention to local black slaves. [66; 834; 873] (T.T.)

Emerson, Ralph Waldo [VI.A] (1803–1882). A leading figure among the New England Transcendentalists. He was born in Boston into a distinguished Unitarian family. After graduating from Harvard College in 1817, he studied at Harvard Divinity School. In 1829 he became pastor of the Unitarian Second Church of Boston. The death of his wife of tuberculosis after only two years of marriage may have influenced his thinking. He began to question traditional Christian religion, and broke with the congregation of the Second Church over the administration of the Lord's Supper. In 1833 he visited Europe and met Carlyle, Coleridge and Wordsworth. He gave up preaching altogether in 1838. He had, however, spoken against organized Christianity long before this and declared himself simply 'God's child, a disciple of Christ'. Thereafter he made his name as an essayist, poet and lecturer. [7; 128; 242] (T.T.)

Empedocles [X] (*c.*493–433 BCE). Philosopher, poet, physician and seer, of Acragas in Sicily. His philosophy is expressed in two long poems, of which about 450 lines survive. *On nature* describes a cosmic cycle, in one half of which the force of Love gradually combines everything into a homogeneous mixture, while in the other half Strife gradually breaks everything down into the four eternal and divine elements, Earth, Air, Fire and Water: a world like ours comes into being at a certain stage in both halves of the cycle, once by combination and once by separation. *Purifications* describes the cycle of transmigrations of the soul: we are fallen gods, expelled from heaven for perjury or bloodshed (the ultimate sin), condemned to wander from body to body, including both plant and animal life of all kinds. Empedocles speaks of himself as having completed his own purifying cycle, and therefore to be a god, about to return to heaven. He thus forms part of a Greek philosophical tradition, that to become divine should be the ultimate aim of human life, which is in contrast to the 'orthodox' view that to try to transcend mortality is impious and dangerous. One may compare ARISTOTLE's injunction not to follow those who say that mortals should occupy themselves with mortal things, but 'so far as we can, to make ourselves immortal' [47: 1177b–1178a]. [20, vol. 2; 41; 48] (H.L.)

Ennin [IV] [Jikaku Daishi] (794–864). Japanese Buddhist monk of the Tendai school. Ennin studied Buddhism for many years on Mt Hiei, headquarters of the Tendai school, as a direct disciple of SAICHŌ, the founder of Japanese Tendai. He visited China for nine years from 838, where he studied T'ien-t'ai, esoteric and Pure Land Buddhism. The travel diary of his experiences in T'ang China serves as a major source of information on this period. [177; 178]

Ennin returned to Japan for an illustrious career, firmly establishing the prestige of the Tendai school and enjoying increasing support from the court. His accomplishments include transmitting Pure Land practices from China and establishing halls for the practice of verbal *nenbutsu* (chanting the Buddha's name); consolidation of the Tendai esoteric Buddhism to compete with the Shingon school established by KŪKAI; introduction of *shōmyō*, a melodious method of chanting the scriptures; and generally strengthening the position of the Tendai school. He was granted the posthumous title Jikaku

Daishi at the same time his master SAICHŌ was given the title Dengyō Daishi, the first use of the Daishi title in Japan. (P.L.S.)

En-no-Gyōja [XIV] [En-no-Ozunu] (7th century). The legendary founder and ascetic prototype of Shugendō, an eclectic mountain religion in Japan which combined Buddhist, Shintō, Taoist and shamanistic elements and emphasized ascetic practice in the mountains. He is said to have practised asceticism on Mt Kasuragi, a mountain west of the Yamato plain, and to have attained supernatural powers. Many stories tell of his ability to command spirits and demons, or to blind disobedient ones with a spell. One story relates that he ordered spirits to build a bridge of rock between Mt Katsuragi and Kimpusen in Yoshino. According to the *Nihonshoki* a man named En-no-Ozunu was banished in 699 to the island of Ōshima in Izu on trumped-up charges of using his supernatural powers to control and mislead the people. Legend has it that En-no-Gyōja would fly to Mt Fuji every night to continue his practices. En-no-Gyōja is important mainly as a model of the mountain ascetic. His is a common figure in Japanese lore and literature, and his name and image are found throughout Japan on mountains and places used for ascetic practice. [27; 31] (P.L.S.)

Eno. *See* HUI-NENG.

Ephrem the Syrian [VI.A] (*c.*306–373). A founding father of Syriac spirituality. He is remembered primarily as an hymnographer, but also composed biblical commentaries and a refutation of heresies. He taught at the Christian school at Nisibis, before moving to Edessa and opening his own school, which became just as famous. His reputation for fairness made him the only person the people of Edessa trusted to distribute bread during a famine. It was his final wish to be buried in the plot reserved for strangers. The beauty of his many hymn cycles had a lasting influence on Byzantine hymnography. [15; 16; 58; 78; 92; 93; 94] (K.P.)

Epictetus [XXII] (*c.*55–135 CE). Greek philosopher, teacher and moralist [14: 194–7; 32: 164–70]. Despite his humble status – he was the ex-slave of a Roman bureaucrat – he was greatly admired and much visited for instruction in his eventual home at Nicopolis on the east shore of the Adriatic. One of his pupils, the Roman nobleman Flavius Arrianus (Arrian), preserved some of his lectures in a collection known as the *Discourses* and a summary called the *Manual*. Epictetus was of the Stoic school of philosophy. God, conceived as a beneficent and rational cosmic providence which is yet also 'within' each human, was central to his view of life. Man's highest duty is to honour that providence by aligning with it one's being, one's will and one's moral life, and by respecting it in one's fellows. We should realize that under providence all is for the best, even the harshest misfortunes which we should accept with equanimity as externals beyond our control and thus of no ultimate consequence to us. (Compare Epictetus' admirer and fellow Stoic, the emperor MARCUS AURELIUS). (R.B.)

Epicurus [X] (341–271 BCE). Greek philosopher, adherent of atomism, and founder and head of a philosophical school (the Garden) in Athens. He offered a materialistic, hedonistic explanation of the universe, including a theory of the gods as atomic streams, uniquely immortal beings but with no involvement in the control of the world. Rejecting traditional Greek beliefs in this way, he claimed to represent worship in its purest, most disinterested form [49: book 1, ch. 41, sec. 116]. Of several dozen titles only four of his works survive, three letters (to Herodotus, Menoikeus, and Pythokles) and a summary entitled *Key Doctrines* (*Kuriai Doxai*). He was himself eulogized as a god by his more enthusiastic followers, e.g. the Roman poet Lucretius [58: bk. V line 8].

Born on the Eastern Aegean island of Samos, he adopted the physics of the 5th-century thinkers Leukippos and Demokritos, moving to Athens before 300 BCE to set up his new school. Probably datable to 306, this event may or may not have preceded the founding of the rival Stoic school (*see* KLEANTHES). The Epicurean division of philosophy into three parts – theory of knowledge ('canonic'), physics and ethics – was closely paralleled by the Stoics.

Basing knowledge on the senses but including as a 'sixth sense' a direct apprehension by the soul atoms of certain subliminal data, Epicurus argued from universal consensus for the existence and immortality of the gods. By a suspicious reversal of arguments devised to prove that every other composite object in the universe is destructible [58: bk. V lines 351–79], he emerged with a concept of the gods as exceptions to this rule, their survival guaranteed by steady flows of atoms 'through' their so-called bodies. Uninterrupted enjoyment of pleasure made the gods paragons of the Epicurean good life, measured principally in terms of freedom from bodily pain and mental anxiety, due largely to their freedom from any responsibility for the world. In this they in fact mirrored Epicurus' own withdrawal from society into the harmony of like-minded friends in the Garden. The doctrine also removed from religion the element of fear which traditional beliefs about the gods instilled.

The soul was composed of the smallest, finest atoms: no survival was possible for it outside the body. For Epicurus, this robbed death completely of its terror. His ethics were this-worldly: granted the basic motivation to maximize pleasure, ethics explores how best to achieve this aim without sacrificing long-term loss to short-term gain.

Controversy rages over the element of determinism in Epicurus' philosophy. He regarded the principal processes of nature as the mechanistic results of collisions between the atoms as they fall through the void. An element of chance was introduced into this 'billiard ball universe', however, by his doctrine of the 'swerve' (*parenklisis*), a random deviation of atoms from their established courses necessary to initiate interactions where the only natural movement was downwards and at a constant speed. Lucretius and other successors of Epicurus tried to explain free will in terms of the 'swerve' of soul atoms, but there is a significant absence of any indication that Epicurus used the doctrine himself to such purpose, or that he saw any particular difficulty in the concept of determinism. [1; 12; 26; 27; 34; 49; 58] (G.R.N.)

Epimenides of Crete [x] (*c.* 7th or 6th century BCE). Undoubtedly a historical figure, a Greek ecstatic, a purifier, who gave oracles and had knowledge of mysteries (like the legendary Orpheus and Musaeus). According to ARISTOTLE he purified Athens after Cylon's bid for tyranny. Some of the tales are akin to those about ARISTEAS, whose soul could leave the body. Perhaps he was one of those itinerant purifiers later called *Orpheotelestai* [4], though Guthrie associates him with Apollo, and Plutarch indicates that he was an initiate of Cretan Zeus. Burkert puts him in a list of those whose oracles, historical or invented, were gathered for tyrants or cities by *chresmologoi* or exponents of oracles: Epimenides, Orpheus, Musaeus, Bacis, Sibyls. Forgeries were inserted in these collections, as by Onomacritus [53: 7.6]. Demoulin presents the sources [5]. (J.P.K.)

Erasmus, Desiderius [VI.A] (*c.*1469–1536). Humanist scholar. He was probably born in Rotterdam, and was educated in childhood at Gouda and Deventer and later at the Augustinian monastery at Steyn. He was ordained priest in 1492 and studied theology at the university of Paris, 1495–8. He travelled to Oxford, where he met Thomas More in 1499, to Italy in 1506–9, and to Cambridge before settling in Louvain. Although he was sympathetic to the Lutheran attack on the abuses of the Church he still defended the Church against LUTHER in *De libero arbitrio* (1524). He favoured the 'new learning', being himself anti-scholastic, and adopted a critical approach to the scriptures which led to the first publication of the Greek New Testament. He also brought out new editions of the Greek and Latin Fathers. He is regarded as a Christian 'humanist' and the precursor of later critical Christian scholarship. [39; 245; 602] (T.T.)

Eshin Sōzu. *See* GENSHIN.

Esther [XV]. Heroine of the biblical book bearing her name. It tells of her selection by the Persian king Ahasuerus (Xerxes) to be his queen in his palace in Shushan (Susa). When the king's vizier, Haman, plans to massacre the Jews his plot is frustrated by Esther, with the help of her uncle, Mordecai; Haman is hanged on the gallows he had intended for Mordecai. The anniversary of this deliverance entered the Jewish calendar as the festival of Purim. The previous day is observed as the 'Fast of Esther'; it is, however, of late origin and is not connected with Esther's exhortation to her fellow Jews to observe a three-day fast when she was preparing to appear before Ahasuerus to plead for her people.

The dramatic story of Esther is unconfirmed from any other source, and scholars are divided concerning its historicity. Some have suggested that it is fictional, perhaps with reflections of Persian mythology (Esther = Ishtar; Mordecai = Marduk). However, it became immensely popular among Jews, with Esther's courage regarded as paradigmatic and Haman seen as the archetypal anti-Semite. [54] (G.W.)

Eto, Silas [XXI] [the 'Holy Mama'] (1905–1984). Prophet-leader of the Melanesian Independent Church. From the Roviana culture of New Georgia, the Solomon Islands, Eto trained to be a pastor-teacher under the Methodist missionary J. F. Goldie. Visionary experiences convinced Eto that he was Goldie's successor, and from 1960 he organized the new Christian Fellowship Church, which was marked by ecstatic and glossalalia-looking phenomena. Dressing for worship in white robes, and considered by many of his flock to be a manifestation of God, Eto has provided the closest example to African 'black messiahs' like SIMON KIMBANGU or ISAIAH SHEMBE to be found in Melanesia. His church is marked by a rich hymnology, idiosyncratic prayer techniques, and a mixture of indigenous and Wesleyan-influenced iconography [48]. Following Eto's death Sam Kuku continued the church's organization, which includes schools, a seminary and businesses, while Eto's son, Job Dudley, became Premier of the Western Province of the Solomons. [47: 51–4] (G.W.T.)

Eusebius of Caesarea [VI.A] (*c.*260–*c.*340). Bishop of Caesarea from 314. Little is known of his early life. He engaged in the theological disputes of the time and attended the Councils of Nicaea (325) and Tyre (335). He tried to hold a moderate line in the disputes and presented a creed of Caesarea at Nicaea to prove his own orthodoxy. It did not contain the key term *homoousios* ('of the same substance') which he accepted at the Council. His main literary work is his *Historia ecclesiastica*, which gives the history of the church from apostolic times down to his own. Though not very critical of his sources he was reliable on the events of his own time but stronger on the Eastern church than the Western. [310; 357; 450] (T.T.)

Eutyches [VI.A] (*c.*378–454). Archimandrite of a monastery near Constantinople, the city of his birth. He had a certain amount of influence in the imperial court through acquaintance with the eunuch Chrysaphius. He was a strong opponent of NESTORIUS. In his opposition Eutyches so emphasized the unity of Christ's nature that he was himself accused and condemned for heresy, particularly in the *Tome* of Pope LEO I ('the Great'), on the grounds that he had eliminated the human nature of Christ. He is held to be the originator of Monophysitism – the belief that Christ had only one *physis* (nature). In 451 at Chalcedon he was condemned, deposed and sent into exile. [277; 717] (T.T.)

Evagrius Ponticus [VI.B] (349–399). A pupil of ST BASIL and friend of ST GREGORY OF NAZIANZUS, he abandoned a successful career teaching and preaching in Constantinople to live as a monk in the desert of Nitria from 382 to his death in 399. Although he was condemned for heresy at the Council of Constantinople in 553, his spiritual and mystical writings were treasured by the monastic order. Many were preserved by attributing them to St Neilos (Nilus) the Ascetic. Evagrius teaches a doctrine of pure prayer; a prayer free of imagery, words or concepts, which eventually gives the mind the sapphirine clarity of the sky.

Evagrius represents the impact of Platonist philosophy on Christian spirituality and the rejection of an earlier mysticism, found in many apocryphal writings and, for example, in the writings of Ammonas, the disciple of ST ANTONY, which emphasized the soul's visionary ascent to heaven. The visionary ascent is replaced by Evagrius by the systematic purification of the mind from all impassioned thoughts. Apocalyptic images of the war between heaven and hell are transformed into a subtle psychological account of inner spiritual conflict: his demonology is a penetrating analysis of the psychology of temptation. Evagrius' teaching was a formative influence on Orthodox spirituality, though his intellectualism was later modified to a more incarnationalist approach. (42; 69] (D.J.M.)

Evaristo Asencio. *See* NATOCHÍ.

Ezana [VI.A] (4th century). King of Axum. Greek and Ethiopic sources attribute the conversion of the king and court of Axum (and thus the origins of Ethiopian Christianity) to two Syrian Christian merchants, the brothers FRUMENTIUS and Aedesius, who became palace servants after a shipwreck. Some inscriptions of Ezana use formulae reflecting polytheism and sacral monarchy; others refer solely to 'the Lord of Heaven'. An inscription published in 1970 is in unmistakably Christian terminology. It looks as if the expansionist Ezana, who engaged more in international trade and politics than his predecessors, moved from traditional polytheism to the monotheistic cult of Astar, and then (identifying Astar with the Christian God) to Christianity. There is no reason to doubt the agency of Frumentius and Aedesius. [421] (A.F.W.)

Ezekiel [xv] (early 6th century BCE). Biblical prophet. A member of a priestly family, he was apparently among the élite of the kingdom of Judah exiled to Babylonia by Nebuchadnezzar in 597 BCE. A few years later Ezekiel – then living in a Jewish settlement by the Chebar canal – saw his first vision, the chariot-throne of God, and commenced his prophetic activities among the exiles.

He prophesied over 22 years, which may be divided into two distinct periods. Until the destruction of Jerusalem and its temple by Nebuchadnezzar in 586 he was a prophet of reproof, warning of the inevitability of the fall of Jerusalem. After the event he became a prophet of consolation, foreseeing the restoration of the people to whom God would grant a new heart and bless with eternal bliss.

In the first period, he presented a gloomy picture of the continuous sinfulness of Israel, attacking the popular belief that the Temple itself would protect the people from harm, and denouncing false prophets who were raising vain hopes. His eloquent words and vivid imagery were accompanied by a series of symbolic acts, graphically underlining his message. After the destruction and the further exile, he turned to a message of the return of the exiles, the rebuilding of the Land and the Temple, and a glorious future for God's people. In view of the threat to such a restoration on the part of hostile neighbour states, Ezekiel uttered oracles of doom against foreign nations. In his vision the exiles of all the tribes – of both the northern and southern kingdoms of Israel and Judah – would be reunited in the restored Israel under a ruler of the House of David, never to be separated again. He lays down a detailed plan for the rebuilding of the Temple as well as the tribal division of the people and for the commandments incumbent on the ruler, the priests and the people.

Ezekiel's prophecies had a strong influence on post-exilic Judaism. His vision of the heavenly chariot-throne of God derived elements from other (especially Babylonian) religions, as well as from the Jerusalem Temple with its depiction of bulls and cherubim. Ezekiel's vision was permeated with the image of an all-seeing omnipotent God whose glory fills the entire universe. In turn, it influenced Jewish and Christian apocalypse and later Jewish mysticism (in which 'chariot mysticism' constituted a major topic). [45: 401–46]

Ezekiel's prophecies are contained in the biblical *Ezekiel*. [23] (G.W.)

Ezra [xv] (5th or 4th century BCE). Jewish religious leader. Of priestly origin, he lived in the Babylonian exile, where he was a scribe of holy literature. With the support of King Artaxerxes, he led a large group of exiles back to Jerusalem to join the Jews already settled there. The Bible does not specify which Artaxerxes is referred to; the general presumption has been that it was Artaxerxes I, in which case Ezra went to Jerusalem in 458 BCE. However, some scholars have suggested that it was Artaxerxes II, in which case he would have arrived in 397. Ezra's move was motivated by reports of the depressed state of worship in the temple and the laxity of religious life in Judah. The king granted him wide powers, including the appointment of judicial officials and special concessions concerning the temple.

Ezra travelled with 1,754 other Jews and their families, many of them priests, levites and teachers of a compatible outlook. He also brought many gifts and contributions to the temple. Under Ezra a number of religious reforms were instituted, based on the Pentateuch, which laid the pattern for the development of Judaism in the following centuries.

Appalled at the extent of mixed marriages, which threatened the community's very Jewishness, he ordered the Jews of Judah to put away their non-Jewish wives and their offspring (although he was apparently only partly successful as he had to continue to contend with the practice). His other major action was the reading of the Pentateuch at a mass assembly immediately following the conclusion of the building of the wall around the city. The enthusiasm of the occasion inspired a public fast, congregational confession and the acceptance by the people of a covenant with God to foreswear mixed marriages, not to work on the Sabbath, to support the temple and to obey the Law.

According to the rabbis, Ezra was the father of the Oral Law and a key link in the chain of tradition. They attributed to him the establishment of the Great Assembly, the supreme Jewish spiritual and legislative institution down to the 2nd century BCE. The rabbis also ascribed to Ezra the writing of the Pentateuch, the introduction of the square Hebrew script and several basic ordinances. He was even seen as a prophet and it was said: 'If God had not given the Law through MOSES, he would have given it through Ezra.'

The biblical account of Ezra is contained in *Ezra* 7–10 and *Nehemiah* 8–9. [55] (G.W.)

F

Fanon, Franz [I.B] (1925–1961). He was born in Martinique, in the French West Indies, of mixed race parentage, into a society split along many class and colour lines. He went to France to study medicine, and specialized in psychiatry. He was then sent to work in Algeria during the war for Independence. He saw his duty to try to understand himself, the society in which he lived, and particularly the colonized, the poor and the oppressed. He wrote four major books, which moved from studies of language, consciousness and race, through his disillusionment, to concrete recommendations. The power of his work may be seen in its pervasive influence in Colonial Studies, in the Afro-Caribbean Diaspora, and in Liberation Theology. [5; 6; 7; 8; 10] (K.W.)

al-Fārābī, Abū Naṣr Muḥammad ibn Muḥammad ibn Tarkhān ibn Awzalagh [XII] [Uzlugh?] (*c*.870–950). Known to students of Islamic philosophy as the 'second teacher' (*al-muʿallim al-thānī*), ARISTOTLE being the first. Sources for his biography are not in agreement and sometimes elusive in their indications. He was a Turk by birth, and said to have been something of a Ṣūfī. He came at an early age to Baghdad, where he was associated with a circle of scholars (Nestorian Christians) who represented the philosophical and scientific tradition of the school of Alexandria. For reasons unknown, he left Baghdad in 942. The sources indicate that at one stage he was patronized by the Hamdanid ruler Sayf al-Dawla but that he actually lived in Damascus, where he worked as a gardener during the day and studied philosophy at night by the light of the watchman's torch. He is said to have had boorish manners and enjoyed solitude. He was an outlandish dresser, and a consummate musician in both theory and practice. His *Kitāb al-mūsīqī al-kabīr* established him as medieval Islam's most outstanding music theorist. He is responsible for establishing the foundations of Arabic logic, about which he wrote several works. His best-known metaphysical work is *Fī mabādiʾ ārāʾ ahl al-madīna al-fāḍila* ('The Opinions of the Inhabitants of the Virtuous City'). This book is not only metaphysical but also forms a basis for medieval Islamic political science, stating that the ruler of society must be both a prophet and a philosopher so that people and institutions might be properly encouraged to live in harmony, itself a virtue, with the rest of the cosmos, which is by its very nature rational and harmonious. Its Neoplatonic character is apparent in the first chapter, entitled 'On the First Being'. His emanative cosmology has determined the tone and the substance of virtually all later Islamic philosophy. On the problem of pluralism al-Fārābī said – holding that revelation does not contradict the truths of philosophy, but rather symbolizes them for wide consumption – that because people in different parts of the world differ in language and symbols it may be that some religions differ from each other only in their symbols and not what is symbolized. Al-Fārābī differed from the first Arab philosopher, al-Kindī (*d. c*.870), by upholding the eternity of creation and denying bodily resurrection. Al-Fārābī was also a prolific commentator on Aristotle, and to a lesser extent Ptolemy, Alexander of Aphrodisias, Galen, John Philoponus and al-Rāzī. His studies of Plato and Aristotle and his catalogue of the sciences are the most comprehensive general introduction to Aristotle and PLATO in Arabic. The attainment of happiness appears to be a primary goal of his philosophy. [36: 107–28; 78: pt. 1, I–IV; 102; 132: 18–23, 206–19] (B.T.L.)

Farquhar, John Nicol [VI.A] (1861–1929). He was born in Aberdeen, Scotland. After some initial education he was apprenticed to a draper but returned to education at Aberdeen Grammar School and thence to Aberdeen University. He completed his studies at Oxford University, where under Friedrich Max Müller and Monier Monier-Williams he was introduced to the study of India and Indian religions. He married Euphemia Watson in 1891, and in the same year they went to India, where he taught near Calcutta in a college run by the London Missionary Society. In 1902 he joined the Indian YMCA as its National Student Secretary and from 1912 its Literature Secretary. During this period he wrote *The Crown of Hinduism* (1913), his most famous work, in which he argued that Hinduism found its fulfilment in the Christian gospel. In 1914 appeared *Modern Religious Movements in India*, the published version of lectures delivered in 1913 at Hartford Theological Seminary, Connecticut, USA. He also edited two series of books 'The Religious Quest of India Series' and 'The Religious Life of India Series'. He left India in 1923 owing to ill health and succeeded T. Rhys Davids as the second professor of Comparative Religion in Manchester University, a post he held until his death. [255; 256; 726] (T.T.)

Fāṭima [XII] [al-Zahrā] (*c.*605–633). Daughter of the prophet MUḤAMMAD, wife of his cousin ʿALĪ, and mother of his grandsons ḤASAN and ḤUSAYN. She was Muḥammad's fourth child by his first wife, Khadīja. After Muḥammad's flight to Medina, she was brought there from Mecca and married to ʿAlī after the battle of Badr (624). Following Muḥammad's death in 632, she clashed with the first caliph, ABŪ BAKR and remained hostile to Muḥammad's wife ʿĀ'ISHA, with whom she had already clashed during her father's lifetime. Although her death in the following year put an end to these disagreements, her attitude to Abū Bakr and ʿĀ'isha continued to have profound implications for later Shīʿī views of this period.

Among the Shīʿa, Fāṭima is held in high regard. Her husband ʿAlī and sons Ḥasan and Ḥusayn were the first, second, and third Imāms, and in main-line Shiʿism descent from ʿAlī through Fāṭima rather than any other wives became the basis for legitimation of religious authority.

Particularly among the Shīʿa, a cult of Fāṭima developed, bearing a close resemblance to that of MARY in Christianity (she is even referred to as *al-batūl*, 'the Virgin'). She is one of the 'Fourteen Pure Souls' (*chahārdah maʿṣūm*) of Shiʿism, along with the prophet and twelve Imāms, all of whom are deemed to have preceded and been agents of creation. In this capacity, she is deemed immortal, sinless, and capable of interceding with God on behalf of men. In the 19th century, the Bābī leader ṬĀHIRA QURRAT AL-ʿAYN regarded herself as an incarnation of Fāṭima.

Throughout Islam, Fāṭima is the ideal of perfect womanhood and motherhood. Some modern Shīʿī writing, including that of Dr ʿALĪ SHARĪʿATĪ, has emphasized Fāṭima as a role model for Muslim women in search of an ideal mid-way between rigid traditionalism and Western modernism. [35: s.v.; 89] (D.M.)

Fa-tsang [IV] (643–712). The systematizer of the Hua-yen school, one of the major philosophical schools of Chinese Buddhism, based on the teachings of the *Hua-yen (Avataṃsaka) Sūtra*. Fa-tsang is considered third in the line of Hua-yen founders. The first was Tu-shun (557–640), who expanded on the teachings of the Ti-lun school (based on a section of the *Hua-yen Sutra*) and was a meditation master. Tu-shun's disciple and Fa-tsang's master Chih-yen (602–668) continued this movement and added a stronger theoretical basis with a number of treatises on Hua-yen teachings. Fa-tsang completed the process and is considered the systematizer of the Hua-yen school.

A central teaching of Fa-tsang and the Hua-yen school is the idea of the 'interpenetration of all aspects of reality'. This concept is illustrated in the *Hua-yen Sūtra* by reference to Indra's net, which spreads throughout the universe and contains a perfect jewel in each of its links, each jewel reflecting within itself each and every one of the other jewels. Fa-tsang prepared his famous experiment of the mirrors to illustrate this point. Ten mirrors were placed at the eight points of the compass, above, and below a central Buddha image lit by a torch. Not only the central image but all the mirrors infinitely reflected each other, illustrating the mutual interpenetration and interdependency of all things.

Fa-tsang also developed a comprehensive classification system which sought to surpass the T'ien-t'ai system in incorporating the entire Buddhist tradition by adding, at the pinnacle, the 'perfect' or 'complete' teaching of Hua-yen. This classification is explained in Fa-tsang's *Wu-chiao chang* ('Chapter on the Five Teachings'). He also wrote the *T'an-hsüan chi* (a massive compilation on the *Hua-yen Sūtra*), one of the most influential commentaries on the *Awakening of Faith*, the *Essay on the Golden Lion* in response to queries from Empress Wu Tse-t'ien, and many other commentaries.

Fa-tsang is the most illustrious representative of the Hua-yen tradition, one of the most important philosophical schools of Chinese Buddhism, and a school considered by many to be the 'intellectual' half of the Ch'an tradition. [33; 39; 46] (P.L.S.)

Ficino, Marsilio [XVII.A] (1433–1499). Italian Neoplatonist philosopher. Born near Florence as the eldest son of a physician, he is known for his translation of the *Corpus hermeticum* (1463) and for his translations of PLATO, the first complete renderings of the dialogues in any Western language (begun 1463, completed probably in 1469, first printed in 1484), and for his own interpretive accounts of Neoplatonic 'natural magic'. His chief philosophical works are *Theologica platonica de immortalite animarum* ('Platonic Theology – On the Immortality of Souls', written 1469–74, printed 1482) and *De vita libri tres* (1489), particularly *De vita coelitus comparanda.* He was the founder and for many years the head of the Platonic Academy of Florence, an important centre for Renaissance Platonism and a loosely organized spiritual community.

Ficino's philosophy of 'natural magic' draws upon a Neoplatonic conception of a hierarchical universe, in which each being occupies its place in descending order from God. The soul sits in the middle of the hierarchy, partaking both of that which is above it and that which is below and acting as a link between the two. This is a humanist revision of the traditional Neoplatonic scheme. The magical philosophy based on this interpretation reads like a gentle psychiatry: the human use of lower elements draws down the virtues of the higher ones, so that to feel cheerful, one must surround oneself with flowers and colours which partake of and thus draw down the virtues of the sun. Ficino's writings played an important role in the emergence of Renaissance Hermetic philosophy. [10; 11; 12; 14; 24: vol. 2: LXIII; 25; 26] (T.L.)

Firdausī [XXVI]. Landowner and poet of genius from Ṭus in north-east Iran, who between *c.*975 and 1009/10 composed the huge Persian epic, the *Shāhnāma* ('Book of Kings'). His main source was a Persian translation of the lost Middle Persian chronicle, the *Khwadāy Nāmag* (also meaning 'Book of Kings'), made in 957 by four Zoroastrian priests for a Muslim governor of Ṭus. Firdausī, regarding this as factually sound, aimed at enhancing its contents by versification without altering anything substantial. The epic belongs, therefore, essentially to Zoroastrian Iran. Religious elements are in the main omitted or reduced to a vague monotheism compatible with Islam, but Firdausī incorporated 1,000 verses composed earlier in the 10th century by a Zoroastrian, Daqīqī, on ZOROASTER's conversion of 'Gushtāsp' (*see* HYSTASPES). Firdausī himself shows respect for the old religion, defending its adherents from the charge of fire-worship; and, while avoiding theology, he incorporates a good deal of incidental matter about Zoroastrian customs and institutions, notably festivals and fire temples. This is especially true of the later sections of the epic (the *Khwadāy Nāmag* having been brought down to the reign of the last Sasanian king, Yazdegird III, 632–51 CE).

The *Shāhnāma* is immensely valued by Zoroastrians, preserving as it does in noble verse many of their ancient traditions. But the *Khwadāy Nāmag* was compiled for the Sasanian dynasty, and in it the Macedonians and Arsacids were evidently barely mentioned. Firdausī accordingly virtually omits 500 years of Zoroastrian history. His hugely influential work thus encouraged both Zoroastrians themselves and modern academics to think of Persia as the only region where the faith survived after Alexander's conquest, and helped foster the damaging misconception that great breaks had occurred in its history. The only complete English translation is by the Warners [54], outdated but still valuable, and fully indexed. [11: vol. 4: 624–8] (M.B.)

Fludd, Robert [XVII.A] (1574–1637). English occultist. Born in Kent to Sir Thomas Fludd, paymaster to Queen Elizabeth's forces in France and the Low Countries. Fludd became a physician but he is best known for his abstruse works on Rosicrucian philosophy. Rosicrucian ideas derive from two anonymously published early 17th-century manuscripts which announce intellectual reform and enlightenment through Kabbalistic and alchemical symbology. Fludd developed an elaborate cosmological philosophy, involving both the material and the spiritual world, in works such as *Utriusque cosmi, maioris scilicet et minoris, metaphysica, physica atque technica historia* ('An Account, Metaphysical, Physical and Technical, of Both Worlds, Greater and Lesser', 1617–21). [22; 24: vol. 8: XIV; 27] (T.L.)

Fortune, Dion [XVII.A] [Violet Mary Firth] (1890–1946). Probably the most respected of all 20th century occultists. Her parents, who may have been Christian Scientists, were hotel proprietors. She demonstrated literary talent when young, her parents publishing two small books of her essays. At the age of 23 she called herself a lay analyst. She seems to have worked within a hospital clinic for some years, and to have worked with a clinician whom she perceived to be a magical adept. In her mid-twenties she encountered theosophy (*see* BLAVATSKY, HELENA PETROVNA). She was initiated in 1919 into the well-known 19th-century magical society, the Golden Dawn (*see* WESTCOTT, WILLIAM WYNN), by now reformed as the Stella Matutina. Under her guidance this was transformed into the Society of the Inner Light, an organization that still exists and is quite Christian in its outlook.

Under the pen-name Dion Fortune she produced a variety of books that are still among the first to which an inquiring reader is directed. *The Mystical Qabalah* (1935) is the basic contemporary magical text on the magical kabbala. It describes the kabbala as a practical mysticism, suited to the West, in which the mind uses symbols to explore spiritual experience in realms the mind cannot traverse. The point of the book is to describe these symbols and their use. The novels about magical practice are even more influential than the practical guides. They present magicians as priests and priestesses of unmanifest powers or beings. Fortune particularly stressed the importance of a woman's occult power, asserting that whereas the male is active and the woman passive in the ordinary world, these 'polarities' are reversed on the 'astral', where the magician works. *The Sea Priestess* (1938) and *Moon Magic* (1939/40), her two best-loved novels, describe a priestess of Isis in contemporary England, whose job it is to 'bring through' a particular sort of energy into the world. The novels create a strong sense of the powers of nature, with accounts of the pre-Christian gods of Greece, Egypt and the Celtic countries. In these novels Fortune also relies upon Jungian and Freudian psychology as an explanatory system. The 'archetype' becomes a powerful magical force, and the unconscious becomes a foundation of instinctual energy and the means through which the magic works, for a symbol dropped deeply into one's own unconscious can, as it were, lodge in the collective unconscious, altering the way many people think or feel. The novels are in any event gripping accounts of the ideal practice of magic, and remain among the best fictionalized descriptions ever written. [9; 23] (T.L.)

Foucauld, Charles Eugene de [VI.A] (1858–1916). Desert contemplative in North Africa. Born to a distinguished Strasbourg family, he was commissioned in the army and fought in North Africa. He left the army to study Saharan languages and explore; his *Reconnaissance au Maroc* appeared in 1888. Though he had lost his Christian faith as a young man, the example of Muslim devotion brought about his return to the Church. In 1890 he joined the Trappists in Nazareth. After his ordination in 1901 he returned to the North African desert as a hermit. At Tamanrasset he was respected by the Tuareg as a man of God and a brother. In circumstances not entirely clear he was assassinated in 1916. His spiritual letters have been published. The Orders of the Little Brothers of Jesus and Little Sisters of Jesus derive from his work. [65] (A.F.W.)

Fox, George [IV.A] (1624–1691). Founder of the Society of Friends ('Quakers'). The son of a weaver, he was born in Fenny Drayton, Leicestershire. He was apprenticed to a shoemaker. In 1646 and 1647 he had religious experiences which led him to trust in the 'Inner Light' of the living Christ. Thereafter he rejected formal Christianity and began to preach his new-found experience. He was imprisoned in Nottingham in 1649 on the grounds of blasphemy, an episode that was repeated many times. Each time he was released he continued preaching. In 1652 he settled in Swarthmore Hall, near Ulverstone, where he was supported by Margaret Fell, whom he later married. The movement, 'Friends of the Truth', later the Society of Friends, or 'Quakers', was established. Fox suffered ill health but still built an organization. He collaborated with Oliver Cromwell during the Commonwealth and refused the Oath of Allegiance following the restoration of the monarchy. Fox travelled to Barbados, Jamaica, New England, Virginia and Germany. His *Journal* was published posthumously. [115; 241; 273] (T.T.)

Francis of Assisi St. [VI.A] (1181/2–1226). Founder of the Franciscan Order and a nature mystic. The son of a wealthy cloth merchant, in his youth he lived a life suited to his station. Later, following a period of imprisonment during a border dispute between Assisi and Perugia, he became dissatisfied. A series of experiences – working among leprosy sufferers, repairing the church of S. Damiano, and reading in Matthew's Gospel (10: 7–14) that Christ required his disciples to go out with no personal resources – led him to discard wealth, to dress simply and to serve the poor and preach the Gospel through simplicity. Others joined him. He drew up a simple Rule for himself and his followers which was approved by the Pope in 1209–10. He travelled throughout southern Europe and into Egypt. By 1220 others had taken control of his order, and he devoted his time to consolidating his ideals. He founded the Tertiaries, followers who remained in normal life. He drew up a more settled Rule which received papal approval in 1223. In 1224 he experienced the stigmata, the marks of Christ's crucifixion. He was canonized in 1228. In 1979 the Pope made him patron saint of ecology. [23; 333; 564] (T.T.)

Frank, Jacob [XV] (1726–1791). Jewish sectarian. Born in Podolia, he early came into contact with believers in the messiahship of SHABBETAI TZEVI. After living in the Balkans for 25 years he returned to Poland, claiming leadership of the Shabbateans there. While in Turkey in 1757 he converted to Islam but continued to lead the east European Shabbateans. The rabbis, accusing him and his followers of antinomianism and transgressing the commandments (including sexual restrictions), excommunicated the Frankists, who sought the protection of the Catholic authorities. The latter regarded them as potential converts and the Frankists appeared in public disputations with Jews in which they attacked the Talmud as false and nefarious and indicated their acceptance of basic Christian doctrine. They even expounded the blood libel which alleged that Jews use the blood of a Christian child in their Passover preparations. One consequence of the disputations was the church's order to burn all copies of the Talmud. In 1759 the Frankists accepted Christianity; Frank himself was baptized in Warsaw Cathedral with Emperor Augustus III as his godfather. However, the church did not trust these converts, and when it was discovered that Frank was laying claims to divinity, he was arrested and held captive in Czestochowa for 13 years. Despite his imprisonment, he maintained contact with his followers, who saw him as the 'suffering messiah'. Liberated when the Russians captured Czestochowa in 1772, he re-established his court, first in Brünn (Brno) and then in Offenbach. Although nominally Catholic, he and his followers practised secret rites (reportedly including ritual orgies), with an admixture of Judaism and Christianity. After Frank's death in 1791 the sect continued to exist under his daughter, Eva, but eventually melted away. Many Frankists married into the Polish aristocracy and were absorbed in Polish society. [71: 287–308; 87: vol. 9: 3–26] (G.W.)

Freeman, Thomas Birch [VI.A] (1806–1890). Missionary in the Gold Coast (Ghana). He was born near Winchester, the son of a freed black slave and the daughter of a farm labourer. He became an estate gardener, losing his post for his Methodist allegiance. From 1838 he was a Wesleyan missionary in the Gold Coast, where previous missionaries had soon died. Freeman survived for more than 50 years. Besides consolidating existing work he opened dealings with powerful

African states – Asante, Dahomey, Abeokuta – and set Africans in charge of new Christian congregations. The mission objected to the expanse of his immense activity, and he resigned in 1857, entering the Accra administration. He returned to the mission in 1873. [89] (A.F.W.)

Frumentius [VI.B] [Abba Salama] (4th century). Two boys, Frumentius and Aedesius, journeying to India from Tyre were shipwrecked on the coast of the Red Sea and taken to the royal court of Axum. Aedesius became the king's cup bearer, Frumentius his secretary and tutor to the prince EZANA, whom he converted to Christianity. When Ezana succeeded to the throne, Christianity became the official religion. Frumentius was consecrated Bishop by ST ATHANASIUS. The pro-Arian Emperor Constantius wrote to Ezana in 356 trying to dislodge Frumentius, but in vain. Ethiopian Christians venerate Frumentius as 'Abba Salama' – the Father of Peace.

The work of Frumentius was extended by the 'Nine Saints' who came to Axum in about 480. These Monophysite monastic teachers founded monasteries and churches and translated the bible into Ge'ez. The Ethiopian Church remained closely attached to the Coptic Church, becoming fully independent in 1959 when Abuna Basilios became Patriarch of Ethiopia. [3; 5: III; 60: 118] (D.J.M.)

Fu-Kiau, K. Kia Bunseki [I.A] (1934–). Author of a pioneering study of Kongo religious ethnography and founder of a small private secondary school and Kongo cultural institute [8; 9; 17: 21]. The essays produced by Fu-Kiau's institute have helped systematize and revitalize Kongo thought and culture. Fu-Kiau's 1969 study, which was the first in any language of Kongo cosmology, was entitled 'The N'Kongo and the world that circles around him [or, in which he moves]' [9]. It states the essence of Kongo ritual, the rite of passage, as deriving from a model of divided worlds [21: 107]. Several colleagues and students (Kusikila, Munzele and Diantezila) have been influenced by his thinking. Now based in the United States, he continues to publish on Kongo culture and African thought and traditions. [8] (R.H.)

G

Gairdner, William Henry Temple [VI.A] (1873–1928). Christian missionary to Muslims. He was born in Ardrossan, Scotland, and educated at Oxford. He was active in the movement led by J. R. MOTT to encourage students to volunteer as missionaries. In 1899 he joined the Church Missionary Society in Egypt. He attempted a sympathetic study of Islam, built good personal relations with Muslims, and became a fine linguist (writing Arabic poetry as well as editing a newspaper). He was an innovator in the use of Middle East music for modern Christian hymnody and promoted Christian unity in a divided community, building a congregation of Egyptian, Syrian and European elements. His book *The Reproach of Islam* (later editions called *The Rebuke of Islam*) was widely read in the West. He was closely identified with the aims of the World Missionary Conference, Edinburgh 1910, and was a co-author of the popular report. [617] (A.F.W.)

Galileo Galilei [VI.A] (1564–1642). Italian astronomer, mathematician and physicist. He was born in Pisa, where he received his early education. He then went to the Camaldolese monastery at Vallombroso. His father insisted that he study medicine so he went to Florence but again studied with the Camaldolese monks. He entered the University of Pisa in 1581. In 1585 he turned to lecturing in mathematics and philosophy at the Florentine academy. In 1592 he became professor of mathematics at the University of Padua where he published his work on the laws of motion of falling bodies, *De motu* (1604). In 1610 he announced his first astronomical discoveries. He advocated separate functions for science and philosophy or theology. He published further works and in 1632 his *Dialogue on the Two Great World Systems*, which was intended as a confirmation of the work of COPERNICUS. For this he faced trial and was forced by the church to recant. He escaped imprisonment and was allowed to return to Florence. His final work, *Discourses Concerning Two New Sciences*, was published in 1638. [210; 211; 455] (T.T.)

Gandhi, Mohanadas Karamachand [XI] (1869–1948). Indian political and spiritual leader. He was born in Porbandar on the west coast of Gujarat in a rich and influential family of the *vaiśya* or merchant caste. He studied law in England, took his bar finals in 1891 and worked as a lawyer in South Africa for 21 years, from 1893 to 1915. During this time he developed and tested most of the principles on which the more celebrated latter part of his life was based. His experience of other religions, especially Christianity, made him eager to purge Hinduism of the social evils which had disgusted him from a very early age – especially its oppression of the untouchable castes, its preoccupation with ritual purity rather than with cleanliness, its predilection for elaborate ceremonial. At the same time, because he was a Gujarati and Gujarati Hinduism is much influenced by Jain precepts, he always laid extra stress on non-violence, on pacific methods and on abstinence and self-denial beyond the Hindu norm. Following such principles he served as a stretcher-bearer in the Boer War, and by those same principles became a leader of the Indians in South Africa in their struggles against racial discrimination, developing a highly effective technique of *satyāgraha*, the truth force, sending in wave after wave of passive resisters, often women, to succumb to the blows of the oppressor until the oppressors themselves became sickened by their task and world sympathy was aroused. While in South Africa he founded the Phoenix Community near Durban and Tolstoy Farm near Johannesburg. These were educational institutions and communal experiments on Tolstoyan lines; Gandhi in fact corresponded at some length with Tolstoy at this time.

In 1915 Gandhi returned permanently to India. After a year of silence and acclimatization, following a promise to his mentor, the moderate Maharashtrian leader G. H. Gokhale, he rapidly became one of the most charismatic figures in the Indian National Congress. He subsequently championed a number of peasant causes, starting with the resistance to the indigo planters at Champaran in Bihar, and he launched the non-cooperation movement in 1921. But it was not till the Dandi march of 1930, when he led a flood of protesters to the sea and made salt in defiance of the British ban, that he became a truly international figure and acquired many new disciples, Indian and foreign. One of his first acts after returning to India had been to found the Sabarmati Ashram near Ahmadabad; this, like his South African foundations, became part school, part refuge, but chiefly the headquarters of a powerful movement for independence, for peace, for equality between Hindus and for the tolerance of other religions upon whose hymns and prayers Gandhi would draw freely for his services and for countless moral homilies, spoken and written. He founded the weekly papers *Navajivana* and *Young India* in 1919, and in 1933 *Harijan* and *Harijanabandhu*. Others like *Sarvodaya* were edited by his followers under his general supervision, and for all these he wrote indefatigably in English, in Gujarati and in Hindusthani. At the same time he corresponded endlessly with his followers, who included a growing number of Westerners, and with all manner of religious and political leaders. His growing insistence on rural simplicity, on hand-spun cloth and the burning of Western vanities, brought him increasingly into conflict with the colonial government. Like the other Congress leaders he was imprisoned many times. He frequently undertook fasts, some just for a day or a week, some 'till death', and through these exerted immense moral pressure, whether upon the members of his ashram or on the British government. It is ironic that his last fast was undertaken to stop the terrible communal riots that followed independence and partition in 1947, for Gandhi had always worked tirelessly to preserve amity between Hindu and Muslim and almost until the last minute had opposed the formation of the separate state of Pakistan. It was his determination to see the Indian rather than the Muslim or the Hindu (or the Parsi or the Christian) that made him favour Hindusthani as a national language for India, rather than the divisive and culturally linked Hindi and Urdu. The Hindu nationalists could not forgive him and he was shot by a right-wing Hindu assassin as he walked out to his daily prayer meeting in Delhi on 30 January 1948.

Gandhi's teaching on religion was a constant reassertion of the proposition so frequently advanced by devout Indians, that basically all religions are the same but that it is right and natural to prize above all others the one into which one is born. His thoughts and actions were suffused with the Gujarati Jain and Vaiṣṇava ideals of simplicity and self-denial. He took the word *satya* – truth – and called it God; *ahimsa* – non-violence – he called love. He wrote on almost every conceivable subject with extraordinary fluency and self-confidence in letters, pamphlets and newspaper articles; all this is still being published by the Indian government under the title of *The Collected Works of Mahatma Gandhi* (New Delhi, 1958–). His works in book form are few and were all written first in Gujarati and immediately translated. *Hindavarāja* ('Indian Self-rule') is a booklet or overgrown pamphlet written in South Africa in 1909 advocating not rebellion but a course of purification and de-Westernization which alone would make India fit to rule itself. The *History of Satyagraha in South Africa* was written in 1924, and the much better-known *Autobiography* in 1927–9 [34]. The English translation came out at the same time and there have been many subsequent editions. It gives a self-searching account of Gandhi's inner life but a somewhat random narrative of events.

It would be difficult to exaggerate the importance of Gandhi in the politics of India from 1915 to the moment of his death. His quasi-religious foundations like the Sabarmati Ashram and Sevagram, the village settlement in Wardha District that he set up and used increasingly from 1921, still flourish. Disciples like VINOBA BHAVE continued his work in the villages with the *bhūdān* and then the *grāmdān* movement. The Congress governments of centre and state, especially those of Gujarat, still pay ritual allegiance to handloom cloth and village industries, but in most respects Gandhi's ideology has been neglected in modern India. The depression that he felt in the months that came between independence and his murder would in no way be alleviated if he could see India today. [11; 12; 34; 89] (I.M.P.R.)

Gardner, Gerald Brousseau [XVII.A] (1884–1964). Modern witchcraft was essentially created, at least in its current form, by Gerald Gardner. He spent much of his adult life in the Far East, working as a customs official. He had met ALEISTER CROWLEY, was probably a Freemason, and knew of the Golden Dawn (*see* WESTCOTT, WILLIAM WYNN). His interest in witchcraft was probably sparked by MARGARET MURRAY's historical account of witchcraft as an organized pre-Christian fertility religion, and more generally by the rise of interest in anthropology and folklore. In the early 1950s Gardner published somewhat imaginary ethnographies of supposedly contemporaneous witches (*Witchcraft Today*, 1954; *the Meaning of Witchcraft*, 1959) and a novel, *High Magic's Aid* (1949). The witches were said to practise the secret, ancient rites of their agrarian ancestors and to worship the Great Goddess and her consort in ceremonies beneath the full moon. He claimed to have been initiated into one of these groups, hidden from the authorities since the 'burning times'. From Gardner's initial inspiration – and perhaps from independent sources – the number of covens (the name for an organized group of witches) has increased substantially, and witchcraft, as a pagan, Goddess-oriented religion, is becoming a feasible and serious religion for many thousands of people in England, the United States and continental Europe. [1; 16; 18] (T.L.)

Garīb Dās [XI] (1717–1778). One of the last saint-poets of the medieval Sant tradition of northern India. He is particularly remarkable for the extent to which his works reveal patent debts to the traditions stemming from all three of his greatest predecessors, KABĪR, NĀNAK and DĀDŪ. Garīb Dās was the son of a prosperous Jat farmer of Chhudani, some 30 miles west of Delhi in Haryana, where he spent most of his life and which became the centre of his cult. A fine and prolific poet, his hymns are collected in an extensive *Granth Sāhib*, whose compilation was instigated by a Dādūpanthī scribe [41: 43] and whose organization is clearly modelled on that of the *Ādi Granth*. More recently, the direct influence of Sikh example has encouraged its use among the Garībdāsīs for such ritual purposes as unbroken readings (*akhanḍ pāṭh*). The chief influence on Garīb Dās to be discerned in the hymns themselves is that of Kabīr, who is frequently invoked by name and followed in his use of Nāth yogic terminology. Garīb Dās is, however, less uncompromising than earlier Sants in maintaining the full implications of rigorous *nirguṇ bhakti*, particularly in his Vaiṣṇava sympathies and his enthusiastic upholding of some traditional Hindu practices, including vegetarianism and reverence for the cow. [41] (C.S.)

Garvey, Marcus Mosiah [I.B] (1887–1940). Proponent of black nationalism; an important figure in Rastafarianism. He was born in St Anne's Parish, Jamaica. His youth coincided with a period of stagnation and depression for black people, who were most firmly under the colonial yoke. It was Garvey's destiny to express their aspirations, their repressed desires and unconscious longings. Before he died, his thinking had dynamically changed black self-awareness in Africa and the diaspora.

He was trained as a printer. His ideas were not initially well received at home, where he had founded the Universal Negro Improvement and Conservation Society and African Communities League (UNIA). After two years in London he went to the United States where the UNIA flourished despite the bitter opposition of the NAACP and black leaders such as W. E. du Bois. He built up a membership of more than 2 million establishing the Negro Factories Association, the Black Star Shipping Line and many businesses. In 1920 he hosted an international conference with delegates from 25 countries. This produced 'A

Declaration of the Human Rights of the Negro People of the World'. His ideology had become an economic, political and spiritual movement. In 1922 he served two years in jail for fraud, and when deported went to Toronto, where he created a School for African Philosophy. Garveyism and Zionism ran parallel in politics, and prominent Jews were his patrons.

There is a timelessness about Garvey's thinking, which is divorced from the man, and finds its expression beyond the direct Garveyism of Jamaica. In the 19th century Ethiopianism had developed beyond African Fundamentalism. 'Africa' and 'Ethiopia' became powerful terms in defining and justifying black worth in the face of negative stereotyping created by pseudo-scientific theories of racial inferiority, the implications of Social Darwinism, and the Biblical justification for the subordination of black by white. Believing in the prophecy of *Psalm* 68 that Ethiopia would stretch forth his hands unto God, he helped scholars develop an alternative belief in black history and self-worth. In modernizing Ethiopianism he inspired politicians, especially Kwame Nkrumah of Ghana, and contributed to the Pan-African movement.

Indirectly his influence is most dramatically expressed in Rastafarianism, where he is seen as the greatest prophet. At some time after 1927 it is said that he prophesied the deliverance of black people with the coming of HAILE SELASSIE, their Messiah. In 1939 when he returned to Jamaica after Haile Selassie's coronation, preachers hailed him as a great redeemer, quoting *Revelation* 5: 2 and 19: 20. The transition from Garveyism to Proto-Rastafarianism developed further his ideas on racial superiority, separation and self-sufficiency. Contemporary Rastafarians study his writings, and some dedicate special devotional days to him. [1; 2; 3; 4; 9; 12] (K.W.)

Geiger, Abraham [XV] (1810–1874). German Jewish scholar and pioneer of Reform Judaism. He served as rabbi in Wiesbaden (1832–8), Breslau (1838–63), Frankfurt (1863–70) and Berlin (1870–74). He felt that traditional Judaism was not suited to the world of enlightenment and emancipation, and that a new type of Judaism was required. He criticized traditional Judaism for its national character, finding expression in its laws and ceremonies. Judaism should be within the European tradition, based on modern scientific understandings and express an ethical universalism. The prayerbook he published in 1854 embodied his principles and theology. He excluded all references to angels, the resurrection of the dead, the chosenness of Israel, the restoration of the Temple and the sacrificial system and the return to Zion. Liturgically, he favoured sermons in the vernacular and a choral service. Although privately he supported the abolition of circumcision and the dietary laws, he did not express these views publicly as he believed that Reform – which he saw as an evolution, not a revolution – should advance cautiously. Changes should be based on the spirit of the law with the realization that the letter of the law can become outmoded. As much tradition as feasible should be retained for the sake of a basic continuity. [84]

Geiger was an outstanding representative of the scholarly school of *Wissenschaft des Judentums* ('Science of Judaism'). He mastered all aspects of Jewish studies and made especially noteworthy contributions in the study of the influence of Judaism on Christianity and Islam, medieval literature, Bible, Jewish law, and the history and development of Judaism. [81: vol. 3: x] (G.W.)

Genkū. *See* HŌNEN.

Gennadios Scholarios [VI.A] [Georgios Scholarios] (*c.*1400–1478). Patriarch of Constantinople, 1454–64. He was born in Constantinople and studied under Mark Eugenicus, Metropolitan of Ephesus and an opponent of union with Rome. Scholarios went on to study the humanities, philosophy and theology. He knew Latin and translated some of the works of THOMAS AQUINAS into Greek. He was a schoolteacher, a civil servant and a judge. It would appear that he supported union with Rome unsuccessfully at the Council of Florence (1438–9). Later he became anti-papal and rejected any form of Latin theology. He became a monk and took the name Gennadios. When the Ottomans captured Constantinople in 1453 he was captured but released by the Sultan Mehmed II, who capitalized on Gennadios' anti-papalism by making him patriarch in 1454. They enjoyed cordial relations and an agreement between them set the form of Ottoman and Orthodox Church relations up until 1923. He was not as successful with his own people in relaxing church laws to avoid conversions to Islam. He did succeed in reorganizing the Patriarchal Academy at Serres, thereby improving the training of the clergy. He eventually entered the Monastery of St John the Baptist in Serres. [300; 645; 884] (T.T.)

Genshin [IV] [Eshin Sōzu] (942–1017). Japanese Buddhist monk and scholar of the Tendai school, and forerunner of the Pure Land movement in Japan. Genshin studied Tendai Buddhism on Mt Hiei as a disciple of Ryōgen (912–985), a reformer of the Tendai establishment. Genshin composed many scholarly works, including the *Ichijō yōketsu* ('Essentials of the One Vehicle'), but his major contribution is in the area of Pure Land themes. In 985 he compiled the *Ōjōyōshū* ('Essentials of Birth in the Pure Land'), a collection of passages from various scriptures and texts concerning Pure Land Buddhism. This compilation dealt not only with verbal *nenbutsu*, the chanting of Buddha Amitābha's name, but also with techniques of visualization, meditative *nenbutsu*, contemplation of Amitābha and the Pure Land just before death, and so forth, as well as descriptions of the various realms of existence. These descriptions of the different hells on the one hand and the Pure Land on the other were very influential and were reflected in the literature and arts of medieval Japan, making the *Ōjōyōshū* one of the most popular works of religious literature in Japanese history.

Genshin also established a devotional society for practising *nenbutsu*. Although Pure Land teachings and practices were present in Tendai Buddhism from the beginning and encouraged by ENNIN, an early patriarch of the Tendai school, Genshin is credited with promoting Pure Land practices and the idea of salvation through devotion and the *nenbutsu*, thus influencing the Kamakura founders of Pure Land schools such as HŌNEN and SHINRAN. [4] (P.L.S.)

Gershom ben Judah [XV] [known as Rabbenu Gershom, i.e. 'Our master, Gershom', and as *Me'or ha-Golah*, i.e. 'Light of the Exile'] (*c*.960–1028). Rabbinic authority in Germany. Few details are known of his life. He headed a talmudic academy in Mainz that attracted students from many countries. He was one of the first Ashkenazi rabbinic scholars responsible for bringing to western Europe the scholarship of the academies of Palestine and Babylonia.

His name is associated with a series of ordinances which greatly affected medieval Jewry. It is not certain whether he promulgated all of them or whether some were subsequently ascribed to him to give them authority. Best known was the ban on polygamy, which henceforth was binding on all Ashkenazi communities and was eventually accepted in some non-Ashkenazi communities. Other ordinances in his name restricted a husband's right to divorce without his wife's consent, forbade the opening of mail addressed to others and prohibited the taunting of Jewish apostates who had returned to Judaism.

His extensive literary output covered many aspects of Jewish knowledge. In order to prepare the most accurate texts of the Bible and Talmud, he scoured the Jewish world for reliable copies of both works. He himself commented orally on the entire Talmud to his students, who, over two generations, committed this to writing, with their own additions. Only part survived and it was soon superseded by the commentary of RASHI. His *responsa* (answers to legal queries) and other legal decisions were regarded as authoritative, especially in France and Germany, and influenced the future development of Jewish law. He also wrote poems; his penitential prayers (some of which entered the Ashkenazi liturgy) reflected the troubles facing the Jews in his time. [51: 39–60] (G.W.)

al-Ghazālī, Abū Ḥamīd Muḥammad [XII] (1058–1111). The outstanding theologian of Islam, often regarded as 'the greatest Muslim after MUḤAMMAD'. Born at Ṭūs in eastern Iran, he was educated there, at Gurgān, and, most importantly, at Nīshāpūr, where he studied at the Niẓāmiyya college under al-Juwaynī. On the latter's death in 1085, he joined the retinue of religious scholars at the court of the Seljuk vazir, Niẓām al-Mulk. In 1091, he was appointed to teach at the most important of the Niẓāmiyya schools in Baghdad.

During the four years he taught there, he embarked on a major appraisal of the work of the Islamic philosophers (including AL-FĀRĀBĪ and IBN SĪNĀ), finally writing an important criticism of their views, entitled *Tahāfut al-falāsifa* ('The Inconsistency of the Philosophers'). By 1095, however, he was in the throes of a severe spiritual and intellectual crisis, culminating in a breakdown accompanied by physical symptoms that prevented him from teaching. This crisis was prompted by a religious conversion that called into question the value of worldly success and demanded a life of practical devotion. Several months later, he left Baghdad to make the pilgrimage to Mecca.

The next ten years were spent in travel and in a prolonged period of withdrawal from worldly affairs. During this time, al-Ghazālī associated with Ṣūfī mystics, living the life of an ascetic and eventually gathering a circle of his own disciples. It was in the course of his career as a mystic that he composed his most important work, the *Iḥyā' ʿulūm al-dīn* ('Revival of the Religious Sciences'). This attachment of such an eminent theologian to mystical concerns was later to prove enormously influential in bringing Ṣufism into the mainstream of Islamic life and culture.

In 1105 or early 1106, al-Ghazālī (who had returned to his native town of Ṭūs) was persuaded by the son of Niẓām al-Mulk to return to Nīshāpūr in order to take up a post at the Niẓāmiyya college. He continued there for at least three years, but in 1109 returned to Ṭūs, where he died two years later.

Al-Ghazālī's writings are extensive. One estimate lists 404 titles, but many of these are no longer extant, while others have been considered forgeries [35: s.v.]. As mentioned above, his outstanding contribution to Islamic literature is the *Iḥyā ʿulūm al-dīn.* Written during his period as a Ṣūfī mystic, this massive work represents a turning-point for Islamic spirituality, achieving a synthesis between formal religious practice and the mystical life. Its four volumes deal with worship, social conventions, the vices that lead to hell, and the virtues that assure salvation. It is, therefore, 'a complete guide for the devout Muslim to every aspect of the religious life' [35: s.v.].

We possess a short but profoundly interesting autobiographical account entitled *al-Munqidh min al-ḍalāl* ('Deliverance from Error'), in which al-Ghazālī describes the stages of his intellectual and spiritual search. Other influential works include the *Tahāfut*, mentioned above, and the related *Maqāsid al-falāsifa* ('Aims of the Philosophers'), which were widely read in Europe during the 12th and 13th centuries; the *Mishkāt al-anwār* ('The Niche for Lights'), a short mystical treatise; and the *Kīmiyā' al-saʿāda* ('Alchemy of Happiness'), a Persian synopsis of the *Iḥyā'*.

It is difficult to summarize the significance that al-Ghazālī holds for the development of Islam. By the end of his life, he was regarded by many as the *mujaddid* or renewer of the faith for the 6th Islamic century. Some later writers have seen him as the reviver of Islam *par excellence*, and his life and works as marking a new era in the history of the religion [34: 'Al-Ghazzālī']. His chief contribution was to delineate a broad consensus of Islamic belief and practice, in which philosophical theorizing, theological dogmatism, and jurisprudential systematizing were subordinated to everyday religious experience. In particular, his emphasis on the spiritual life and the possibility of harmonizing mystical practice with the regulations of the religious law guaranteed a place for the emerging Ṣūfī brotherhoods within the mainstream of Islamic life. This, in turn, was to provide orthodox Islam with a source of spiritual and cultural vitality that remained influential down to the early part of this century. [38; 62; 63; 66; 122; 134; 136; 138] (D.M.)

Ghose, Aurobindo. *See* AUROBINDO, SRI.

Gilgamesh [II]. According to ancient tradition in Mesopotamia, there were several famous kings who ruled the land before the Flood, and several others immediately afterwards. For some of them only the legendary length of their reigns is recorded (usually counted in millennia rather than years), and others were famous for just one event. But the most famous of them all was undoubtedly Gilgamesh, who is supposed to have ruled for 126 years, followed by his son Urlugal for 30 years, and his grandson Utulkalamma for 15 years. These were just three of the 12 kings of Uruk, who are said to have reigned for a total of 2,310 years before that city was overthrown and Ur became the centre of power.

The historical circumstances of Gilgamesh's life are probably now shrouded in mystery for ever, but there is little doubt that the folklore associated with him was a powerful influence on shaping the ideals of many a later Assyrian and Babylonian potentate. There are many copies of the long poetic epic about him which have survived in scribal centres from all over the empire. While a few of them may have been simple copying exercises for apprentice scribes, most were written professionally; since it is not primarily a liturgical text it probably functioned as an inspiration to seek under God's guidance what is seemingly impossible, in the same way that the Biblical stories of the Exodus and the patriarchs function as models of behaviour for the one who reveres God.

Of particular interest to the student of comparative religion is the episode in the epic where Gilgamesh journeys across the world to meet a man who was saved from death to eternal life – Atrahasis, the embodiment of ultimate wisdom. When they meet he tells Gilgamesh about the days when the earth was going to be destroyed by divine decree and how the storm god annihilated all life by the Deluge. But he had been forewarned to construct a massive boat and thus survived and was allowed to live for evermore in secret. A close reading of this part of the poem shows time and again identical ideas to those found in the biblical story of Noah's Ark, and it is clear that the Bible story is either a Hebrew version of the same ideas that are reflected in this episode of the Gilgamesh epic, or is a direct borrowing.

Even more intriguing is the way the gift of everlasting life eludes Gilgamesh later in the story. After he has discovered at the bottom of the sea the mysterious plant that would give him the power to live for ever, a serpent steals it from his hand; he is thus, like all mankind, doomed to die. A very similar literary motif occurs in the biblical story of the Garden of Eden. There a mysterious plant is prohibited, but a serpent suggests that by eating it man would be like God and live for ever. In both cases death is shown as the inevitable end for man, whereas snakes seem to have a way of avoiding it.

Gilgamesh appears to be represented in Mesopotamian society as the ideal heroic king. In florid accounts of later military victories it was considered appropriate to quote from the famous text of the Gilgamesh epic in order to add a superhuman and divinely inspired tone to the proceedings. He may not have actually done all that he was supposed to have done, but there is no doubt that he influenced human behaviour wherever ancient Mesopotamian culture spread. [5; 6; 10; 12] (M.R.)

Gilson, Etienne [VI.A] (1884–1978). French philosopher and historian of medieval thought. He was born in Paris and educated there, completing his studies at the Sorbonne. He was a philosopher with an interest in Scholastic theology and philosophy. He held posts at Lille (1913), Strasbourg (1919) and became professor of medieval philosophy at the Sorbonne in 1921 and in 1932 at the Collège de France. From 1929 he also held the post of Director of the Pontifical Institute of Medieval Studies in Toronto. His main publication was *History of Christian Philosophy in the Middle Ages* (1955). He was an apologist for the distinctiveness of Christian philosophy and for the primacy of the philosophy of THOMAS AQUINAS. [302; 303; 520; 539; 730] (T.T.)

Giotto [VI.A] (1266/7–1337). Florentine founder of modern painting who replaced Italo-Byzantine stylization with a naturalism that brought life and passion to his work. Among the paintings that are attributed to him are the frescoes of the lives of S. Joachim and S. Anne and the Virgin, and the Life and Passion of Christ in the Arena Chapel, Padua. He decorated four chapels in the church of Santa Croce in Florence. The *Life of St Francis*, the *Lives of St John the Baptist and St John the Evangelist* and an *Assumption* have survived in three of the chapels. Another of his works, the *Ognissanti Madonna*, hangs now in the Ufizzi in Florence. Giotto was appointed supervisor of the Duomo in Florence in 1334 and began work on the Campanile, but his design was later altered. [304; 802] (T.T.)

Gizur Isleifsson [VIII] (1042–1118). An outstanding bishop of Iceland in the early days of the Christian church there. His father, Isleif, was the first Icelander consecrated as bishop, his predecessors being brought in from abroad. Gizur was educated in Saxony and ordained as priest very young. He probably held the family chieftainship for a time, and he travelled widely before becoming bishop in 1082. He was a skilled administrator who brought about great progress for the new church and the Commonwealth. He established the tithe system by law, and encouraged education; his brother Teit was a gifted scholar and teacher; and the most learned man in Iceland, Saemund the Wise, was his friend and supporter. Gizur made Skalholt the episcopal seat and created a second bishopric in northern Iceland. Under his gifted leadership the priests in various areas took over much of the responsibility formerly held by the chieftains before conversion. Gizur's pattern of administration lasted until the 13th century, but there was no able successor to carry on his work. The Icelanders looked back to his time as bishop as a Golden Age. [7: IV] (H.E.D.)

Gobind Siṅgh, Gurū [XXIII] (1666–1708). Tenth Gurū of the Sikhs. He was born in Paṭnā, the only child of the ninth Gurū, TEGH BAHĀDUR. At the age of five he was brought to Anandpur on the slopes of the Shivalik Hills and was there given a thorough education in Sanskrit and Persian, acquiring the art of poetry and also that of warfare. In 1675 his father was executed in Delhi by the Mughal emperor Auraṅgzeb, an event which understandably made a considerable impression on him. He succeeded him as Gurū and for several more years continued his education in the Shivalik Hills.

Gurū Gobind Siṅgh emerged to adulthood as the ruler of a small Shivalik state. The principal early source for this period is the lengthy poem *Bachitar Nāṭak*, attributed to the Gurū himself, in which he relates his descent, his upbringing, and the wars which he fought as a young ruler against the other chieftains of the hill states. *Bachitar Nāṭak* also tells of the Gurū's great delight in hunting, a sport which was ideally suited to the rugged terrain of his small principality in the Shivalik Hills.

It is generally held that it was on Baisākhī Day in 1699 (the first day of the new year, corresponding to 30 March) that Gobind Siṅgh summoned his Sikhs to Anandpur for what turned out to be the most important event in Sikh history. This was the founding of the Khālsā, the militant order which Sikhs have ever since been encouraged to join. The Gurū held a baptismal ceremony for all who were prepared to enlist in the Khālsā, initiating the five Sikhs who were first to offer themselves and then extending baptism to all members of the Panth who volunteered for the purpose. According to tradition all who accepted baptism were to wear five items beginning with 'k', thereby proclaiming themselves to be Sikhs of the Khālsā.

Much that happened on that 1699 Baisākhī Day is still subject to research, but there appears to be no doubt that thereafter Khālsā Sikhs were required to keep their hair uncut and were commanded to carry arms. The purpose of the occasion is also open to some doubt, the possibilities being that it was to prepare his followers for the onslaught of the Mughals or that it was to mark the disestablishment of the *masands* (vicars who had served the Panth well under early Gurūs but had since become corrupt).

Following the creation of the Khālsā the Gurū was again attacked in Anandpur, this time by the other Shivalik chieftains assisted by troops sent by the Mughal governor of Sirhind. In 1704 the Gurū was compelled to evacuate Anandpur, losing two of his sons in the process, with the remaining two cruelly executed in Sirhind. Gobind Siṅgh escaped to the south, where he inflicted a defeat on his pursuers at Muktsar. After the Mughal emperor Auraṅgzeb died the Gurū agreed to accompany his successor, Bahādur Shāh, to the south, where, in Nandeṛ on the banks of the Godāvarī river, he was assassinated. [30: II–VIII]

Sikh tradition affirms that before his death Gobind Siṅgh declared that there would be no personal Gurū to follow him. Instead his Sikhs should look to the scripture and the community as the Gurū (the Gurū Granth and the Gurū Panth). Every orthodox Sikh accordingly treats the *Ādi Granth* as the Gurū Granth Sāhib, bestowing on it the honour that would be conferred on the living Gurū. In cases where it is possible to make community decisions these are also treated with the same respect as those of the personal Gurū.

The substantial second scripture of the Sikhs, the *Dasam Granth*, is traditionally regarded as the entire work of Gobind Siṅgh. This view is rejected by scholars who accept the *Dasam Granth* has come from Gobind Siṅgh's entourage, but believe that only a part of it is actually by him. [56: 89–92]

Gurū Gobind Siṅgh ranks as the supreme exemplar of all that a Sikh of the Khālsā should be. His bravery is admired, his nobility esteemed, his goodness profoundly revered. The duty of every Khālsā member must be to strive to follow his path and in their lives perform works that would be worthy of him. (W.H.M.)

Gómez, Dionisio Dios [xxiv] (*d.*1924). A prophet of the Toba people of Argentina. When indigenous leaders called a strike in Napalpí in 1924 to protest against government restrictions on labour and travel and exorbitant taxes on already meagre income, Dios Gómez lent the proceedings a distinctly religious tone. He conducted daily seances in the Pampa Aguara, communicating with the spirits of dead ancestors and with God. Speaking through his mouth, these supernatural beings announced the imminent destruction of Whites and their culture and the restoration of the goods of the earth to native peoples. A paradisal state would reign once again, wherein local peoples would live happily forever. If followers wished to see the dawn of this golden age they must follow the restrictions laid down by God. Sickness and death would soon claim all unbelievers but true believers would never succumb to their enemies. Dios Gómez's devotees built a 'temple' in the centre of their encampment, which was set upon by some 150 armed police on 19 July 1924. Believing themselves invincible, the Toba and Mocoví followers responded to the onslaught with intense ritual dancing. Although none of the attackers was wounded, about 50 indigenous people died, including the prophet Dios Gómez. Sporadic outbreaks of messianic fervour have continued since that time. [1; 16: 554, 574] (L.S.)

Gondarra, Djiniyini [xxi] (1945–). The first Aborigine to be a Moderator of the Uniting Church in Australia. He was born at Milingimbi, Arnhem Land, and educated both in a Methodist mission school and by his extended Yolngu family. He was initiated in his clan's ceremonial life and later had the mantle of maintaining his homeland placed upon him by his ageing father. In his early years he trained as a Sunday school teacher and from 1956 to 1968 served as a lay preacher at Galiwin'ku, Elcho Island. In 1964 he completed a. local preacher course in Brisbane, but his main theological training came from Papua New Guinea, where he spent two years at the Malmaluan Training Centre (1969–70) and a further three years at Raronga Theological College (1973–5). He was ordained in 1976 and served in the Galiwin'ku parish (1976–82). He was then appointed as lecturer in theology at Nungalinya college (1983–4) and was vice-president of the Uniting Aboriginal and Islander Christian Congress from its inception in 1983. In 1985 he became Moderator of the northern synod of the Uniting Church. During his term as minister at Galiwin'ku, Christian and Yolngu religious principles were allowed the freedom to converge.

On 14 March 1979 (the Galiwin'ku 'Day of Pentecost') an exuberant Christian revival began, led by Gondarra and others, which has since spread throughout Arnhem Land and into Kimberley and Desert Aboriginal communities [2]. Gondarra has focused his efforts on developing a theology which transcends the captivities of Western church contexts. He emphasizes Christ as the fulfiller of Aboriginal traditions, which are not 'idol worship' but manifestations of a God-given Law comparable with that given to Moses. 'Totems' might be seen to be like the tablets of Mosaic Law, while sacred sites are akin to the temple. This brings Gondarra to his Christian plea for social justice and support for the maintenance of Aboriginal culture, identity and rights to their lands. His is an holistic theology not separating religion from justice, freedom and peace. He also stresses Aboriginal ecumenism and political solidarity under the banner of the words 'Father make us one'. [15; 16; 17] (T.S.)

Gorakhnāth [xi] [Gorakṣanātha]. One of the most potent names in Yogic hagiography, particularly associated with *haṭha yoga*, of which he was a pre-eminent teacher. The balance of probability is that the name does refer to a historical person, but of that person nothing can be established historically. It is customary to give his dates as somewhere between the 9th and the 12th centuries, and to associate him with Eastern India. In many regions of India there are cycles of legends relating to Gorakhnāth, and the sect that takes his name, the Śaivite Nāths, also called the Kānphaṭa Yogīs, are found throughout India. But in addition to featuring in the Nāth hagiography, he is also to be found as one of the 84 Siddhas venerated by the Buddhist Sahajiyās. Two works in Sanskrit are attributed to Gorakhnāth: the *Siddhasiddhānta-paddhati* and the *Gorakśa śataka*, while in early Hindi there are a number of short works, hymns and couplets that also claim his authorship. That these works are genuinely early works is now becoming accepted, but that they were written by Gorakhnāth is unprovable. In spite of, or probably because of, his historical invisibility, Gorakhnāth has come to be regarded as one of the most influential figures in early medieval Hinduism. [10] (S.C.R.W.)

Goreh, Nehemiah Nilakanth [VI.A] (1825–1895). Born at Bundelkhand, near Jhansi, India, of a Brahman family, he moved to Banares as a young child. He learned Marathi, Hindi and Sanskrit, and was educated in the Shastri or Pandit tradition. His first encounter with the Christian religion came when he heard missionaries preaching in the streets of Banares. He entered into fierce discussions with them and was given a Christian apologia written in Sanskrit. In order to refute the missionaries he was obliged to read the Bible. Soon he wrote to one of the missionaries his 'Doubts Concerning Christianity'. After a long personal struggle he accepted the Christian faith and was baptized in 1848. His wife Lakshmibai was baptized five years later. For 20 years he supported himself by literary and translation work but was a tutor to Maharajah Dalīp Singh, who brought him with him to Britain in 1853. He returned to India in 1855. Ordained deacon in 1868 and priest in 1870, he ministered in various centres in central India. In 1876 he was admitted as a novice into the Society of St John the Evangelist (Cowley Fathers), the first Indian member of that society, and spent the rest of his life more or less centred on Pune, where the Society established its house. He was responsible for bringing PANDITA RAMABAI to baptism in 1883. His best known work is the *Shaddarshana Darpana, or Hindu Philosophy Examined by a Benares Pundit.* His daughter Ellen Lakshmi became a deaconess of the Church of England. [111: 40–57; 284; 621; 629] (T.T.)

Graham, Billy [VI.A] [William Franklin] (1918–). American evangelist. He was born on a farm in North Carolina of Scottish-Irish parents. He experienced conversion at an evangelistic meeting in 1934. He graduated from Wheaton College, Illinois, in 1934 and in the same year was ordained as a Southern Baptist minister and married Ruth Bell. He became the first full-time evangelist of the Youth for Christ movement in 1943. In 1947 he became president of Northwestern College, Minneapolis and two years later came to national prominence at a Los Angeles evangelistic crusade. In 1950 he formed the Billy Graham Evangelistic Association. About the same time he began the weekly radio programme *The Hour of Decision.* He resigned his college post in 1952 and devoted himself full-time to world-wide evangelism. His first of many crusades in Britain occurred in 1954. His largest crusade meeting ever, attended by over a million people, was in Seoul, South Korea. He has often been criticized for his conservative social views, and his relationship with Richard Nixon, disgraced president of the USA, showed political naivety. In recent years he has articulated a more sophisticated appreciation of social problems and has distanced himself from such movements as the American Moral Majority. He has always co-operated with a wide diversity of Christian traditions in his evangelism, including more recently the Roman Catholic and Orthodox traditions. His organization also runs the California-based Worldwide Films, and from 1960 *Decision* magazine, and he writes a weekly syndicated newspaper column. He was also prominent in the promotion of two world congresses on evangelism in Berlin (1966) and Lausanne (1974). His books include *Peace with God* (1952), *World Aflame* (1965) and *Angels* (1975). [541; 652; 653] (T.T.)

Gregory I [VI.A] [Gregory the Great] (*c*.540–604). Pope, 590–604. In early life he received a good legal training and was versed in the management of his family's estates. For a time he held the post of prefect of Rome, but gave up public life and took the life of a monk, turning his home into a monastery dedicated to St Andrew. Pope Pelagius II persuaded him to be ordained and to go as his representative to Constantinople, where he remained until about 586. Following the death of Pelagius in 590 Gregory was made pope. He was a good administrator, using papal funds wisely and charitably, and setting the example for church leaders with his *Regula pastoris*. He produced commentaries on the scriptures and *Dialogues*, the most popular being about the life of Benedict. He sent AUGUSTINE OF CANTERBURY to Britain to convert the Anglo-Saxons. He was wise in not interfering in the work of the church's bishops and only took unavoidable corrective action. The 'Gregorian Sacramentary' and 'Gregorian Chant' are not to be ascribed to him. [592; 680; 830] (T.T.)

Gregory V, [VI.B] (*d.*1821). Ecumenical patriarch. He studied in Athens and Smyrna before becoming a monk on Patmos. He became bishop of Smyrna (1785) and was three times Ecumenical Patriarch (1797–8; 1806–8; 1818–21). He founded schools and libraries and translated patristic texts into modern Greek. A conservative churchman, Gregory was horrified by the violence of the Greek Revolution and condemned its leaders. Nonetheless he was executed by the Ottoman authorities as head of the Greek *milet.* On Easter Sunday 1821 he was hanged at the gate of the Patriarchate, still in his vestments. Ex-patriarch Cyril VI and several other bishops died at the same time. (D.B.)

Gregory VII, [VI.B] [Hildebrand] (*c.*1020–1085). Pope, 1073–85. Hildebrand was born in Soano, Tuscany. Educated in Rome, he became chaplain to Gregory VI (1045), following him into virtual exile when Gregory VI abdicated (1046) and joining the Cluniac order. Leo IX (reigned 1049–54) recalled Hildebrand to Rome, where he exercised great influence upon the Pope and on his successors Victor II (1055–7), Stephen IX (1057–8), Nicholas II (1058–61) and Alexander II (1061–73). In 1073 Hildebrand was acclaimed Pope (violating the canons on papal elections) and, reigning as Gregory VII, applied himself to the abolition of clerical abuses, enforcing clerical celibacy, combating simony and freeing the clergy from lay control. Pope Nicholas II (1059) had legislated to free papal elections from lay influence, had forbidden clerical marriages and concubinage, and the lay investiture of clerics. Gregory's attack on lay investiture led him into conflict with Emperor Henry IV. At first Gregory seemed victorious, especially when Henry, threatened with deposition, sought his forgiveness standing three days in snow at Canossa in January 1077. There was no hope of real agreement. In 1080 Gregory VII 'deposed' the emperor. Henry in his turn organized at Brixen a synod which deposed Gregory and elected Guibert (Wibert) of Ravenna as Pope Clement III. When Henry conquered Rome in 1084 the clergy and the people of Rome formally elected Guibert pope. Until his death in 1100 Clement was the effective Bishop in Rome. He was a man of independent spirit and himself a church reformer. However, unlike Gregory VII he was not a defender of the absolute temporal and spiritual supremacy of the papacy that Gregory had proclaimed in his *Dictatus Papae* (1075). In exile, Gregory continued to promote reform and to assert the rights and privileges of the papacy. He died on 25 May 1085, and was canonized in 1606. [47; 55; 71; 89; 100] (D.J.M.)

Gregory of Nazianzus [VI.A] (*c.*329–*c.*391). One of the 'Cappadocian Fathers'. He was born in Nazianzus, Cappadocia, the son of Bishop Gregory. His mother Nonna persuaded him to follow a life of asceticism. He was educated at Caesarea in Cappadocia, Caesarea in Palestine, Alexandria and Athens. Against his will he was ordained priest by his father, and was later (*c.*372) consecrated bishop of Sasima by his friend BASIL OF CAESAREA. He remained in Nazianzus until his father's death as assistant bishop. He then retreated to Seleucia. He was summoned to Constantinople in 379 to preach against the Arian heresy. He was present at the Council of Constantinople (381) but left before the end. During his last years he defended orthodoxy against Apollinarianism through a series of letters. His theology is found in his *Orations*, in his dogmatic letters, and in his poetry. Being one of the 'Cappadocian Fathers' he was an important figure in determining conciliar orthodoxy. [74; 240; 318] (T.T.)

Gregory of Nyssa [VI.A] (*c.*335–*c.*395). One of the 'Cappadocian Fathers'. Little is known of his life beyond the fact that two of his brothers were bishops and his sister Macrina, according to his biography of her, led a saintly ascetic life. He was married to Theosebeia and from 365 was a professional rhetorician. In 371 BASIL OF CAESAREA, seeking support against Arianizing bishops, consecrated him bishop of Nyssa. In 376 he was deposed by the Arian bishops on a charge of maladministration of funds. Following the death of Basil in 379 and the succession of an anti-Arian emperor, Theodosius, Gregory was made metropolitan of Sabeste in 380 but resigned soon after. In 381 he was a key figure at the Council of Constantinople. He was present at a further council of Constantinople in 394 and died soon after. [190; 319] (T.T.)

Gregory Palamas [VI.A] (1296–1359). Orthodox monk, a major figure of the Hesychast tradition. He was born in the Byzantine imperial court. After his father's death when he was aged seven he enjoyed the protection of the Emperor, who provided him with an excellent education. Gregory rejected the offer of public office and went to Mount Athos at the age of 20. He adopted Hesychasm as a form of monasticism and first joined the monastery of the Lavra and later the hermitage of Glossia. In 1325 the Turks invaded the territory and he fled to Thessalonica, where he was ordained priest in 1326. He returned to seclusion at Beroea and Athos. He became engaged in dispute with Barlaam, a monk from Calabria, over the *filioque* clause in the creed. Gregory offered to compromise with Western theology over the clause. He was also engaged in dispute over the idea of the Divine Light, which was part of Hesychastic meditation. Though accused of heresy he survived and was eventually made archbishop of Thessalonica following some imperial politicking. [320; 517; 549] (T.T.)

Gribble, John Brown [VI.A] (1847–1893). An outspoken, dogmatic and influential Anglican missionary to Aborigines. Having begun work in remote New South Wales with the 'broken remnant', in 1885 he established a mission near Carnarvon, Western Australia. Here he aroused intense opposition by publishing a booklet which justifiably claimed that virtual slavery was being practised [322]. He lost the ensuing legal battle and fled, penniless, to New South Wales in 1888 and subsequently established a mission near Brewarrina. In 1892 he again moved to establish the well-known Yarrabah mission in North Queensland. He died soon after and was succeeded by his equally famed son, Ernest. [315: 161–8] (T.S.)

Groote, Gerard [XVII.B] [Gerard the Great] (1340–1383/4). The originator of the Devotio Moderna religious movement in Deventer, Holland, and founder of the communities of the Brothers and Sisters of the Common Life. These movements, and many others inspired by these, spread widely throughout Holland, Belgium and Germany, and all of Europe to some extent, and were responsible for the founding of at least 17 universities available for the first time to the lay community.

Groote was born in Deventer of distinguished parents. Showing great powers of mind he was sent at the age of 15 to the University of Paris and received a Master of Arts, specializing in Theology and Canon Law. After a period of extravagant living, he determined at 34 years of age to lead a Christian life and spent the next three years in the Carthusian Monastery at Monichoysen. He left with a burning zeal to preach. His sermons were powerful and many took up his teachings, but this phase was terminated by an episcopal ruling forbidding him to preach.

He then established the first Society of the Brothers and Sisters of the Common Life. They provided schools for the training of clergy, and set up houses for devoted followers to live the common life and to work together. After a meeting with Ruusbroec, he founded a monastery for the more devout brothers, but the full fruition of the monastery was accomplished only after his death. Groote died a victim of the plague, then spreading through Deventer. He contracted the disease whilst administering help to a friend, Lambert Stuerman. While Stuerman was seized by the raging pestilence he bequeathed enough money to found the monastery according to Groote's directions.

After his death his successor, Florentius Radewin, established many communities of enthusiastic congregations of the Common Life, all practising true obedience, chastity and poverty, without being required to make a vow. One of the best known followers was THOMAS À KEMPIS, whose *The Imitation of Christ* is the best known literary monument of the Devotio Moderna. The aim of all the monasteries and communities was not to overthrow the then scholastically inclined church, but to have it reformed and renewed after its primitive purity. [7; 8; 9] (K.M.)

Grotius, Hugo [VI.A] (1583–1645). Dutch jurist and scholar. He was born in Delft and educated in Leyden university from the age of twelve. He accepted state and diplomatic appointments, including Advocate Fiscal of Holland, Zeeland and West Friesland in

1607. He espoused Arminian theology and fell foul of Prince Mauritz of Nassau, a Calvinist. He was imprisoned for life in 1628 but managed with his wife's assistance to escape. He settled in Paris but remained a Protestant. He returned to Holland in 1621, was banished to Germany and later became the Swedish ambassador in Paris. In later years he tried to encourage theological co-operation between various Protestant churches but did not succeed. He died while travelling from Sweden to France. His most important works were *De jure belli ac pacis* ('On the Law of War and Peace', 1625) and *On the Truth of the Christian Religion* (1622). [293: 93–101; 440; 548] (T.T.)

Gshen-rab Mi-bo-che [XXV] [Ston-pa Gshen-rab, 'The Teacher, Supreme Priest']. Regarded by the adherents of the Bon religion in Tibet as the Enlightened One of the present cosmic period. In this respect Gshen-rab Mi-bo-che ('Supreme Priest, Great Man') occupies the same position in the Bon religion, which claims to be the authentic, pre-Buddhist religion of Tibet, as Śākyamuni BUDDHA does in Buddhism.

According to the chronology which is most widely accepted by the adherents of Bon, Gshen-rab's birth took place more than 18,000 years ago. As one year in his life is believed to correspond to 100 human years, his final entry into *nirvāṇa* is said to have taken place some 10,000 years ago. While Western scholars clearly cannot accept these calculations, they have been at a loss to establish plausible dates for Gshen-rab, and have also hitherto been unsuccessful in disentangling a possible historical figure from the rich enveloping growth of legends and literary motifs.

It has been claimed that the biography of Gshen-rab is a parallel to that of Śākyamuni, but this is only partly true. Like Śākyamuni, Gshen-rab is born into a royal family; the soteriological activity of Gshen-rab, however, consists not only of the preaching of sermons (herein resembling Śākyamuni), for an equally important aspect of this activity is his incessant travels in order to perform elaborate rituals to save repentant evil-doers from prolonged sojourns in purgatory. This Gshen-rab does while still a prince, and as a result of his travels he gradually acquires numerous wives and produces sons and daughters who all play important parts in the dissemination of the doctrine.

A characteristic element in his biography is a prolonged struggle with the host of demons, led by their king, 'The Lord of Darkness'. In this struggle, however, the successes of the demons (seducing Gshen-rab's youngest daughter, stealing his horses, burning his books) are never more than temporary, and the king of demons ends by being converted and becoming Gshen-rab's devoted disciple. In this conflict between good and evil, light and darkness, some scholars have seen Iranian (*see* ZOROASTER) and Manichaean (*see* MĀNĪ) influences at work; but the scenario could just as well have developed from earlier Tibetan mythology. Nevertheless, Iranian influences cannot be entirely ruled out, for the country in which Gshen-rab is claimed to have lived is called Stag-gzig ('Tazik'), which in a vague way designates Persia.

There are three major biographies of Gshen-rab, in one, two and 12 volumes respectively. While the 12-volume version (the *Gzi-brjid*) may be confidently dated to the latter part of the 14th century, the two-volume version (the *Gzer-mig*) may be as early as the 11th century. This vast literary corpus plays a crucial role in the spiritual life of the adherents of Bon, monks and lay people alike, but taken as a whole still awaits exploration. [1: 86–97; 3] (P.K.)

Gurdās, Bhāī [XXIII] [Gurdās Bhallā] (1551–1637). Sikh poet and theologian. He was born in Goindvāl and was related to the third Gurū of the Sikhs, AMAR DĀS. From his earliest days he appears to have been closely associated with the Panth's line of orthodox Gurūs, serving successively Amar Dās, RĀM DĀS, ARJAN and HARGOBIND. Before his death he also acted as teacher of TEGH BAHĀDUR, later to be the ninth Gurū. During these years he served the Gurūs as missionary, steward, and personal messenger on matters of importance, his main task in the latter respect being to conduct negotiations with Prithī Chand, the eldest brother of Gurū Arjan and chief rival for his position as Gurū. His devotion to Gurū Arjan was unbounded and when in 1603 the decision was made to compile a scripture (the *Ādi Granth*) Bhāī Gurdās was chosen as its amanuensis. His puzzled acceptance of the change of atmosphere in the Gurū's entourage is spelt out in a famous verse, the fifth Gurū having been a man of peace and the sixth Gurū surrounding himself with the means of war.

The enduring contribution of Bhāī Gurdās was as a poet and a theologian, his works being collectively known as 'the key to the Gurū Granth Sāhib' (i.e. the *Ādi Granth*). These comprise 556 brief works in Braj known as *kabitts* and the much more popular 39 *vārs* in Punjabi. It is upon the latter that his considerable reputation depends, several of them being poems of a very high order. Some of these relate events from the lives of the Gurūs or from his own time. Others are doctrinal, helping to explain what the Gurūs actually taught. Because of his reputation for both piety and scholarship Gurdās is invariably known as Bhāī Gurdās, or 'Brother' Gurdās. [40: 368–71; 56: 92–4] (W.H.M.)

Gurdjieff, Georgy Ivanovich [XVII.D] (?1877–1949). Modern-day gnostic and enigma. He was born of Armenian mother and Cappadocian Greek father in Alexandrapol, and grew up in Kars in Armenia at a time of great upheaval. Determined to find the explanation to various unusual phenomena such as faith-healing, clairvoyance and telepathy, he began to search from a very early age, sometimes alone, and sometimes with a group he refers to as 'The seekers after truth'. Convinced that long forgotten ancient knowledge still existed he travelled throughout the Middle East, India, Afghanistan, Tibet, Central Asia and Siberia, studying in monasteries, with the Essenes, with various Sufi orders and with the Lamas in Tibet. By the time he was 32 years old he had evolved inwardly, possessing remarkable psychic powers, and he had acquired a body of ideas and techniques for personal development which he sometimes referred to as his 'system'. After some two years working as a professional hypnotist, probably in Tashkent, he moved to Moscow, where he married Countess Ostrowska and, in 1912, established the Institution for the Harmonious Development of Man. Among the many intellectuals who were attracted to work with him at the Institution was OUSPENSKY, who has recorded the content and nature of Gurdjieff's teaching for the years 1915–17 in his book *In Search of the Miraculous* [3]. Fleeing the Russian revolution, Gurdjieff and a number of close disciples made their way through Istanbul to Germany and, finally, to France, where in 1922 the Institute was reopened in the Château du Prieuré at Fontainebleau. Many were drawn to the Institute, including writers such as Orage, Katherine Mansfield, Jane Heap and others, and submitted themselves to its very demanding regime. A serious car crash brought this period of Gurdjieff's life to an end in 1924. When Gurdjieff recovered he decided to preserve his teaching in writing, and, although the Institute continued, his energies went mainly into his writings until he finally abandoned them in 1935. He left three series: the first, *All and Everything, or Beelzebub's Tales to his Grandson*, the second, *Meetings with Remarkable Men*, and the third, *Life is Real Only Then, When 'I Am'*. From 1935 until his death in 1949 Gurdjieff worked very closely and hard with groups and individuals, facilitating their inner transformation and preparing them to be able to interpret his work and carry on when he was gone. Groups still exist that preserve his teaching and the techniques, but the central body of his ideas is buried deep in his unusual but by no means easy books. He saw modern man as a machine, reacting mechanically to events, with minimal being and a fragmented will, and only the possibility of immortality if he worked on himself with 'conscious labour and intentional suffering'. Ahead of his time he saw man as a transformer of energy needed by the biosphere; man could either transform energies consciously and thereby achieve personal immortality, or he could do so unconsciously and 'perish like a dog'. No one who ever met Gurdjieff had any doubt they were in the presence of a most alive, conscious and remarkable man. [4] (S.C.R.W.)

Gurmukh Siṅgh [XXIII] (1849–1898). Born to a humble family of Chandhar Jaṭs, Gurmukh Siṅgh's Western education, a sharp intellect and organizational abilities made him an eminent leader of the Siṅgh Sabhā [6: 23–9], a religious society devoted to redefining Sikh tradition. To promote the Sabhā's new initiatives Gurmukh Siṅgh launched several newspapers and educational institutions. His efforts to dispense with the established religious hierarchy, rejection of caste taboos and critical evaluation of Sikh hagiographic literature embroiled him in endless controversies [21: 139–40]. A strong opposition to his campaign of recasting Sikhism led to his excommunication in 1887. Despite the hostility of religious élites, Gurmukh Singh was eventually vindicated when many of his ideas became the cornerstones of modern Sikhism. (H.S.O.)

Gutiérrez, Gustavo [VI.A] (1928–). Peruvian liberation theologian. A mestizo, he was born to militant socialist parents in Lima, Peru. After studying medicine, he went to Europe in the 1950s to be trained for the priesthood. He was a close friend of CAMILO TORRES. Ordained in Lima in 1959, he has lived in humble surroundings there for most of the time ever since. In the 1960s he broke with the 'dominant theology' he had learned in Europe, and with young fellow-radicals 'developed the epistemological theme of theology as critical reflection on praxis' [297: 312]. Deepening political awareness and involvement in various Latin American theological forums helped to sharpen his focus and to clarify issues. After the epic Latin American Episcopal Conference in Medellín (1968), he produced his *Hacia una teología de la liberación* (1969) and various writings culminating in his *Teología de la Liberación. Perspectivas* (1971), which has been translated into numerous languages. His *A Theology of Liberation: History, Politics and Salvation* (1973, 1988) has rightly been hailed as the *Magna Carta* of liberation theology. High hopes for the transformation of Peruvian society under the socialist regime after Medellín were not fulfilled. Keeping the Peruvian Marxist José Carlos Mariátegui in mind, he endeavoured to articulate his ideological option for indigenous socialism with help from his 'theology from the underside of history'.

Since 1976, the reflection of this 'founding father' of liberation theology has focused on developing a historically mediated 'pastoral of liberation', i.e. a programme of integrally liberating action by the Church in the service of God [569: 5]. Rather than radicalizing further towards the political left in the 1980s, he worked at developing a 'spirituality of liberation' emanating from 'an authentic encounter with the Lord', as can be seen in his *We Drink from Our Own Wells: The Spiritual Journey of a People* (1984) and his beautifully written *Hablar de Dios desde el sufrimiento del inocente* (1986), translated as *On Job: God-Talk and the Suffering of the Innocent* (1987). By 1988 he was at pains to reaffirm the basic orthodoxy of liberation theology, emphasizing that it is by no means Marxism in disguise. This may mark a stage of maturity in his priestly pilgrimage which refutes any attempt to drive a wedge between *orthopraxis* (appropriate Christian social action) and orthodoxy. His study-centre in a run-down area of Lima is deliberately named after LAS CASAS. He has lectured throughout the world and many dissertations have been written on his thought. Noteworthy among a multitude of his recent essays is *The Power of the Poor in History* (1983). [124; 124a: 22–49; 136; 569] (A.C.S.)

Güttmann, Bruno [VI.A] (1876–1966). Missionary in Tanzania and mission theorist. Born in Dresden, he served the Leipzig mission from 1902 to 1938. He lived with the Chagga people in Moshi (Kilimanjaro), and developed a distinctive theory and practice of mission. Affected by contemporary ethnology and by Volkskirche ideas, Güttmann argued that the order of creation required the organic relationship of blood, location and generation groups. It was thus the missionary duty not to break up a society (e.g. by seeking individual conversions) but to regenerate its old forms. Chagga clans, land and age-sets must thus be fully incorporated into the church. Güttmann's work influenced German missions, despite being criticized on theological grounds and as inhibiting African access to education and economic development. Later concern for the integrity of primal cultures revived interest in it. [390; 391; 392; 880] (A.F.W.)

Gyōgi [IV] (668–749). Japanese Buddhist saint who popularized Buddhism and was especially well known for his activities of social welfare. Gyōgi was, technically speaking, a monk of the Hossō school at Yakushi-ji, one of the major Nara temples. However, he travelled extensively, preaching and performing magical signs as well as participating in projects such as building roads, dams and bridges. Gyōgi not only taught but lived the ideal that Buddhism is expressed through action and good deeds in daily life. EMPEROR SHŌMU, aware of Gyōgi's popularity among the people, asked him to raise funds to support construction of the *daibutsu* ('big Buddha'), a huge statue of Vairocana at

Todai-ji in Nara. Gyōgi was also an exponent of the idea that there is no basic opposition between the buddhas and bodhisattvas of Buddhism and the local deities (*kami*) of Japan, an idea which was accepted as standard through most of Japanese history. Gyōgi is usually known as Gyōgi Bosatsu (the bodhisattva) in memory of his selfless service to others and his participation in social welfare projects. [41; 102] (P.L.S.)

H

Hai ben Sherira Ga'on [xv] (939–1038). Jewish religious authority and leader in Babylonia. He assisted his distinguished father, Sherira, head of the great talmudic academy of Pumbedita (at that time situated in Baghdad) in teaching and administration. After his father's retirement in 998, Hai succeeded him as head of the academy with the title of *ga'on* and attracted students from far and near, some coming from western Europe. Although this was a period of decline for Babylonian Jewry, Sherira and Hai raised its prestige so that it was the outstanding centre of Jewish learning and legal decision-making throughout the Jewish world [69]. Many queries were submitted to Hai; his *responsa* (of which about a thousand are known), characterized by the range and depth of the subject matter, were accepted as classic definitions of Jewish legal positions. They were written in Hebrew, Aramaic or Arabic, while his works on civil law, written in Arabic, were translated into Hebrew. He was the author of a commentary on much of the Talmud, of which only parts have survived. He continued to write and teach until his 100th year. [7: vol. 6] (G.W.)

Haile Selassie, Emperor [I.B.] [Tafari Makonnen] (1892–1975). Emperor of Ethiopia (1930–74) and Rastafarian Messiah. The son of the provincial ruler of Harer, his personal name was Tafari Makonnen. In 1917, when Zawditu was made Empress, he was made Ras (Lord), heir to the throne and regent, already having shown qualities of subtlety and ruthlessness which would characterize his life. In 1928 he was made Negus (King), and two years later became Emperor of a world that had remained hidden for 1,000 years.

The country was unique, because despite Italian intentions, it had remained untouched by the scramble for Africa. Haile Selassie's empire possessed an interlocking range of traditional institutions: monarchy, nobility and church, bound into a scripturally based mesh. The people were held together by Amharic expansion and Shoan hegemony, together with a vigorous policy of amharization. The Amharas are vigorous Christians, so there was nevertheless tension with the Muslims.

The coronation brought rulers and dignitaries from all over the world and drew attention to Ethiopia. Even before the coronation he had decided to modernize his country. He set up a printing press, established schools and hospitals, and introduced a first decree for the abolition of slavery.

In 1934 the Fascist Italians invaded, and he pleaded for help from the League of Nations: 'God and history will remember your verdict.' His cry went unanswered, and he was forced into exile, to return to Ethiopia in 1941.

The Orthodox Church gained its first Ethiopian Patriarch in 1951. In real terms Haile Selassie controlled both Church and State. The constitutions of 1931–55 confirmed traditional religious freedoms, but in 1959 the power of the Coptic patriarchate was reduced; it pressed the non-Chalcedonian churches into regrouping. In 1969 relations with the papacy, broken off in 1632, were sanctioned, and the Pope had a meeting with Haile Selassie. Additionally the Emperor tried to persuade the churches to conserve the many priceless old illuminated documents and manuscripts from churches and monasteries, most national treasures then being in a state of frightful deterioration. The artefacts have both a mythical and religious significance: they represent Ethiopian–Christian nationalism.

The ceremonies and legends of the Church, and Haile Selassie's dazzling regality failed to reinforce each other when the Emperor was deposed by a military *coup* in 1974. He died, a palace prisoner, a year later.

Haile Selassie and Ethiopia had a vast, mythical impact on the outside world. Just as Ethiopianism developed, so he became the focus for cults. In Rastafarianism he became the returned Messiah, the divinity of a religion. Haile Selassie ('Might of the Trinity'), King of Kings, Lion of the Tribe of Judah, legendary direct descendant from the marriage of Solomon and Sheba, validates the honourable origins of many black people in the diaspora. For proto-Rastafari, his coronation was the fulfilment of Bible prophecy.

In 1955 Haile Selassie gave Jamaicans wishing to repatriate to Ethiopia 500 acres near Shasemama. He asserted the sincerity of his Christianity. It seemed that he was both displeased and flattered by the notion of his 'divinity'. When he visited Jamaica in 1966, it was the Rastafari who overwhelmed him with their greetings.

By 1968 the Ethiopian Orthodox Church had established branches in Trinidad, New York, Jamaica and London, which have friendly relations with many Rastafarian groups. In particular, books in the Ethiopian Bible help validate their belief in their legendary descent. After Haile Selassie's death, the Church has come to an accommodation with the new regime. The Rastafarians, too, have rationalized the death of their Messiah. [11; 13; 14; 16; 18] (K.W.)

Ḥājjī Bektāsh Valī [XII] (1247?–1338?). The traditional founder of the Bektāshiyya, a Ṣūfī order widespread in Turkey until the modern period. Traditional accounts of Ḥajjī Bektāsh are exceptionally ahistorical, with a preponderance of legendary information. Even the dates of his birth and death are unreliable, being based on numerological correspondences rather than any established fact. His father is said to have been the ruler of a state in the eastern Iranian province of Khurāsān, and accounts of his childhood and youth are chiefly concerned with miracles performed by or in connection with him.

What is known is that the earliest mentions of Ḥajjī Bektāsh date from 1295 and 1297, both of which imply that he was then already dead. There is some evidence that he did, in fact, come to Asia Minor from Khurāsān, had visited Mecca, and had built up a large following of dervishes, probably based around a village itself later named Ḥajjī Bektāsh. He appears to have been one of a number of Türkmen *baba*s, wandering mystics who combined in their teachings orthodox Islam with earlier Turkish beliefs and practices.

Under Bektāsh's successors, his order came to include elements from Christianity, Shiʿism, and, in particular, the 14th-century Ḥurūfī sect, with numerous secret rituals and teachings in which the Imām ʿALĪ came to form part of a Trinity with God and MUḤAMMAD. It is unlikely that many of these doctrines originated with Ḥajjī Bektāsh himself, although Birge has thought that he may have introduced some simple rituals [21: 50–51]. From the 15th century, the order developed close links with the Janissaries, the crack troops of the Ottomans. This and the general popularity of its practices as a form of folk Islam made the order a major feature of Turkish religious life in the Ottoman period, with Ḥajjī Bektāsh playing a leading role in popular piety. [21] (D.M.)

al-Ḥajj ʿUmar ibn Saʿīd al-Fūtī [XII] (*c.*1794–1864). Muslim missionary in West Africa. Born in Futa Toro in Senegal, ʿUmar went on pilgrimage to Mecca in about 1825. He was one of the West African founding members of the new Tijāniyya order of Ṣūfīs, and he became *Khalīfa* ('caliph') of the western Sudan for the order. He was a great expert at the holy war of the sword and the holy war of the word. He travelled widely in Bornu and Hausaland, along the Niger, in Futa Toro and Futa Jallon. He made many followers but also some powerful enemies. He established a base in what is now north-east Guinea and started training his students as soldiers. By 1855 he initiated a territorial expansion and started down the Senegal River, but soon he was confronted by excellent French guns and had to turn east, where he conquered Segu and Macina on the Niger in 1862. However, some of his new subjects rose against him, besieged him in Hamdullahi, south-west of the Niger, and when he broke out, killed him. His son Aḥmad ibn ʿUmar ruled his empire after him, until the French conquered it in 1891. Sulṭān

Aḥmad took refuge in Sokoto. The spiritual influence of al-Ḥajj ʿUmar remains strong to the present day. He spread the teaching of the Tijāniyya and its belief in the *awliyā'*, the saints whose special relationship with God makes them fit to be the leaders of Islam in times when atheism is threatening. [37; 86: III] (J.K.)

Hakon Sigurdarson [VIII] (10th century). Jarl of Hladir, the last ruler of Norway to support the pre-Christian religion enthusiastically. He was a devout follower of the gods, restoring shrines and keeping up sacrifices. He ruled northern Norway from about 963 to 995, and in alliance with HARALD GORMSSON of Denmark, extended his rule to western Norway, although he never took the title of king. He was especially devoted to the cult of a goddess known as Thorgerd, who was reputed to give him success in battle. Christian chroniclers are naturally hostile towards him, but the historian SNORRI STURLUSON admits his good qualities as a ruler. Some of the mythological poems of the *Poetic Edda* may have been composed at his court. He was finally overthrown by the Christian leader OLAF TRYGGVASON in 995, and is said to have been killed by a thrall while in hiding. [3: IV] (H.E.D.)

Hakuin Ekaku [IV] (1686–1769). Japanese Buddhist monk and reviver of the Rinzai Zen school. Hakuin showed an inclination for the religious life from the time he was a child and entered the Zen temple Shōin-ji at the age of 15. When he was 24 Hakuin experienced a 'Great Doubt', which was in turn shattered like the smashing of a sheet of ice or a jade tower. Driven by this enlightening experience, he visited the master Shōju Rōjin (1643–1721) at his hermitage of Shōju–an in Nagano. Further intense practice and struggling with kōans resulted in a deeper understanding of the Zen way. He travelled further and had many intense experiences of enlightenment, each revealing a new level of awareness. Hakuin also suffered from repeated bouts of psychosomatic disturbances, called 'Zen sickness', which were slowly cured after a visit to the hermit Hakuyū, who pointed out that these symptoms were based on Hakuin's extreme ascetic and meditational practices. This experience aided Hakuin in providing methods which he in turn used to help his disciples with regard to health problems. Hakuin finally returned to Shōin-ji in 1716, where he guided a growing number of disciples and his fame spread throughout Japan.

Hakuin's many writings include *Yasen kanna* ('Talks on a Boat in the Evening'); more famous is *Orategama* ('The Embossed Tea Kettle') in which he outlines his theories on health and long life. He is also famous for his bold and original calligraphy. Hakuin emphasized a strict regimen of meditation accompanied by active participation in daily chores in order to 'perceive one's (true) nature' (*kenshō*). He revitalized the Rinzai process of meditating on kōans, and his teachings became the central Rinzai tradition in Japan. All modern Rinzai masters in Japan trace their lineage to Hakuin. [262] (P.L.S.)

al-Ḥallāj, al-Ḥusayn ibn Manṣūr [XII] (*c*.858–922). Iranian Ṣūfī mystic, associated with a highly unorthodox sense of identification with the divinity. Al-Ḥallāj was born about 858 in the Iranian province of Fārs and spent most of his childhood and early youth in the Arab regions of Iraq and western Iran. From the ages of about 16 to 40 he associated closely with ascetics and mystics in the cities of Baṣra and Baghdad. His own increasingly radical interpretations of Ṣūfī doctrine eventually led to a breach between him and his teachers, notably ʿAmr al-Makkī and AL-JUNAYD, and in 897 he left Baghdad.

In the course of extensive travels to Khurāsān, northern India, and Turkistān, he preached a doctrine of extreme asceticism and absolute devotion to God. It is possible that, in his more distant journeys, he may have come under non-Islamic influences. Certainly, his opponents began to accuse him of fostering relations with dissident heretical groups such as the Carmathians.

In 908 he returned to Baghdad, following a residence of two years in Mecca. In the capital, he acquired large numbers of disciples. A combination of religious animus and political intrigue led to his arrest on the order of the chief vazir in 913. An eight-year imprisonment culminated in his execution on 26 March 922. His death subsequently became the supreme symbol of mystical love and self-sacrifice, and al-Ḥallāj himself the Ṣūfī martyr *par excellence*.

The most important surviving work of al-Ḥallāj is the *Kitāb al-ṭawāsīn*, a collection of mystical hymns and poems. Other fragments, including several letters and prayers, have also been preserved. His most famous *dictum* is the Arabic phrase *anā'l-ḥaqq*, variously translated as 'I am the (Absolute) Truth' or 'I am God', and often mistakenly interpreted as an expression of pantheism.

Ṣūfī poetry, particularly in Iran, makes frequent reference to the passion and sacrifice of al-Ḥallāj, who is often treated as an analogue of Jesus. [35: 'al-Hallādj'; 45; 87; 115: 62–77] (D.M.)

Hammurabi [II] (1728–1686BCE). During archaeological excavations at Susa in south-western Iran during 1901–2 there was found a large stone stela on which were recorded the laws enacted by Hammurabi, King of Babylon. It had apparently been captured from Babylon by some Elamite invader, probably at the beginning of the 12th century BCE, clearly not for its monetary value but perhaps for the numinous power it was supposed to have had for the Babylonians. It is the most comprehensive collection of prescriptions for the good ordering of society to have been discovered in the Middle East, and in its time was compared closely with biblical laws attributed to Moses. It can now be compared with earlier, less comprehensive collections of law as well as later more specifically formulated collections which have been discovered in Mesopotamia more recently.

The iconography on the stela shows the king receiving instruction from the sun-god Shamash, thus equating light with justice, an important religious concept throughout the Fertile Crescent. The first sentence of the inscription records that Hammurabi was chosen by Anum (the sky god) to spread justice, 'to rise like the sun over all mankind and shed light throughout the land', so that 'the weak will not be oppressed by the strong'. His devotion to religious duty and his attention to ameliorating the conditions of the citizens of many different localities are eulogized in line after line until the laws themselves are listed. It has become conventional for modern critical texts to divide them into 282 individual clauses, but in reality the boundaries between one section and another are not always easy to define.

It is generally agreed that this was not primarily an attempt to anticipate legal problems that might arise, but rather to record how such problems had been solved in the past. It represents, therefore, the cumulative wisdom of the age in matters of social justice, which explains why so many of the subjects are treated similarly in other collections of law. An important historiographic document which lists the achievements of Hammurabi year by year records that he 'established justice in the land' in his second year, but whether this refers to enacting formally this collection of laws, or more generally, to granting a general amnesty for offenders is disputed.

Hammurabi was the fifth of 11 kings who comprise the First Dynasty of Babylon, and is supposed to have reigned the longest. However, it is extremely uncertain whether they were native to Babylonia. Detailed study of the phonology of their names suggests that they belonged to families who had emigrated there from further west, a group known as Amorites or East Canaanites. This may explain why some religious traditions characteristic of later Mesopotamian society seem to have begun in the west. The biblical writers explained things differently by suggesting that the cultural movement was from east to west; this has been historicized in the story of Abraham's migration from Ur to Canaan.

Some have even concluded that the meaning of the name of Hammurabi, 'a widespread family', is sufficiently close to the traditional meaning of the name Abraham, 'father of a multitude', to suggest the names are the same. But since their biographies are so different it would be rash to build much on the idea. But more may be made of the fact that for the early Hebrews and for the early Babylonians there was a leader who was called by God at the dawn of history to establish justice in the land. [2] (M.R.)

Handel, George Frideric [VI.A] (1685–1759). English composer of German birth. He was born in Halle, Saxony, where he studied law at the university following an early education from the local organist. His success in Italy in the art of opera from 1706 led to his appointment as *Kapellmeister* at the court of Hanover in 1710, but his duties were interrupted by a stay in England from 1712. It was an embarrassment to him when the

Elector of Hanover became George I of England in 1714. Following the decline of opera in England in the late 1720s he turned to oratorio. His earlier attempts in this form, *Saul* and *Israel in Egypt* (1739), were not successful, but the first performance of *Messiah* in Dublin in 1742 was a great triumph, as were his later oratorios, especially *Samson* (1743) and *Judas Maccabaeus* (1747). [454; 703] (E.M.)

Handsome Lake [xx] (1735–1815). Seneca preacher and visionary, chief of the Turtle Clan. His teachings were directed at achieving peaceful coexistence between Indians and Whites, and represented an amalgamation of Shaker and traditional Amerindian beliefs and practices. During his youth Handsome Lake fought in the final wars with European settlers and witnessed the decline of his people's prestige and power. Later in his life he fell victim to alcohol and finally suffered a complete physical breakdown around 1800. His family and friends, thinking he was dead, prepared him for burial, dressing him in ceremonial robes. However, he regained consciousness, interpreting the resuscitation as a resurrection from the dead. This event marked his new vocation as a teacher and prophet. Over the next 15 years he was instructed by three messengers from God. These revelations formed the basis of his 130-section code. These were largely ethical directives, including total abstinence from liquor, the importance of obeying both traditional Indian authority and White men's laws, respect and support for the underprivileged, and the value of education. Despite his apparently conciliatory attitude toward religious and governmental authority, Handsome Lake was generally opposed by most Christian missionaries during his career. His vision of peaceful coexistence was commended by President Thomas Jefferson. Handsome Lake died at Onandaga on 10 August 1815. [15: 111, 115, 149–50, 186–7, 253–5, 239–318] (S.R.)

Han Hsiang-tzu. One of the EIGHT IMMORTALS of Taoism.

Harald Gormsson [VIII] [Harald Bluetooth] (10th century). The first Christian king of Denmark. He ruled from about 950 till 986, and the memorial he set up at Jelling with a long runic inscription claims that he won all Denmark and Norway and made the Danes Christian [4: iv]. He was a powerful king, responsible for the great mounds at Jelling and a large church standing between them on the site of the existing one, as well as the elaborate military centres set up at Trelleborg and elsewhere. He is believed to have moved his father Gorm, who was not a Christian, into a grave under the church, where skeletal remains were found in 1980 [6: IX]. Harald appears to have accepted Christianity about 960. According to the story first found in a popular German source, a missionary monk called Poppo offered to prove the power of Christ by carrying red-hot iron, and succeeded in convincing the Danes when he remained unburned. Poppo, presumably a German or Frisian, has not been satisfactorily identified, but his cult was established by the end of the 12th century, since pictures of the conversion are shown on gilded plates on the church door at Tamdrup. In 986 Harald was driven out by his son Svein, who took the kingdom; Harald took refuge with the Wends and died soon afterwards, to be buried at Roskilde. (H.E.D.)

Hardedef [VII] (26th century BCE). Prince Hardedef, son of King CHEOPS, is accredited with the Wisdom Instructions compiled for his own son, Au-ib-re [19: vol. 1: 58–9]. Probably written down *c.*2480 BCE, these are the earliest examples of wisdom maxims that have been found, although only the beginning of the text has survived. (A.R.D.)

Hargobind, Gurū [XXIII] (1595–1644). Sixth Gurū of the Sikhs. The period of Hargobind makes clear a change in the Sikh Panth which had already appeared under his father, GURŪ ARJAN. When he succeeded to the office as sixth Gurū in 1606 the hostility of the Mughal rulers of the Punjab was already evident and Hargobind had to spend some time imprisoned in Gwalior Fort. His following consisted by this time overwhelmingly of rural folk (particularly people belonging to the Jaṭ caste), and it was not inclined to bow before the threats of Mughal control.

Hargobind, by tradition, marked this change by a number of symbolic gestures. The first was that he wore two swords, one representing the spiritual authority which his predecessors had always possessed (*pīrī*) and the other the temporal power which he now assumed (*mīrī*). A second was that he had Akāl Takhat erected in Amritsar, a building signifying the same temporal power. A third was that he surrounded himself with armed men and preferred hunting to the peaceful pastimes of the first five Gurūs. Many of his Sikhs were disquieted by this, preferring to have a Gurū who stressed *nām simaraṇ* (remembrance of the divine Name) rather than the martial qualities emphasized by Hargobind.

Four skirmishes were fought with Mughal troops during his period, following which he retired with his armed retinue to Kīratpur at the edge of the Shivalik Hills. The direction of the Panth was now firmly fixed, with emphasis being laid on military defence as well as on remembrance of the divine Name. His eldest son had predeceased him and the eldest grandson was considered unsuitable. The succession was already firmly fixed in the male line of the Soḍhī Khatrīs and the actual candidate chosen to follow him as Gurū was his second grandson, HARI RĀI. No works were left by Gurū Hargobind. [3: IX] (W.H.M.)

Haribhadra [XIII] (*d.*529?). Śvetāmbara Jain scholar and teacher who is traditionally regarded as having died in 529 CE. There are two main accounts of his life, although the earlier does not seem to antedate the beginning of the 12th century. The first biography depicts the young Haribhadra as a Brahman who was so inordinately proud of his learning that he boasted that he would become the pupil of anyone who could utter an intellectual proposition which he, Haribhadra, could not explicate. However, he heard a Jain nun called Yākinī reciting a verse which he could not understand (in fact, it concerned Jain mythical history), and on being sent by her to her preceptor, he was given further instruction and subsequent monastic initiation. In remembrance of this, he took the title *Yākinīputra* ('Spiritual Son of Yākinī'). [8: VIII–IX]

According to the second biography, Haribhadra's nephews, who were also his students, left him, despite his forebodings, to study logic clandestinely in a Buddhist monastery. On being discovered, they fled, but one of the nephews was killed by the Buddhists. The other, having returned to Haribhadra and told him what had happened, died of grief for his brother. In fury, Haribhadra went to engage the Buddhists in philosophical debate and, after defeating them, compelled them as a penalty to leap into a vat of boiling oil. As a result of his anger and his grief for his nephews, both inappropriate to a Jain monk, he was required by his preceptor to undertake severe penance. Haribhadra then took the title *Virahāṅka* ('Having as signature/distinguishing characteristic separation [*viraha*]') to commemorate the loss of his nephews. It should be noted in passing that this story is similar in several respects to the biography of AKALAṄKA. [8: XIII–XVI]

The great 20th-century monk Jinavijaya seems to have been the first to point out that, since Haribhadra shows familiarity with the works of DHARMAKĪRTI, he must of necessity be dated at least after 650 CE, the approximate period when the Buddhist logician flourished. However, in line with Jain tradition, Jinavijaya was content to ascribe the many works attributed to Haribhadra to one author. Williams, on the other hand, has suggested that it would be more appropriate to accept the existence of two Haribhadras using the titles *Yākinīputra* and *Virahāṅka* respectively. The works of the former, Williams regards as being more archaic both in language and subject matter [31].

Leaving aside the question of identity and assuming for expediency's sake a body of work attributable to a single author (as mainstream Śvetāmbara Jainism has always done), we can see Haribhadra's significance as deriving firstly from his definitive establishment of Sanskrit rather than Prakrit as the language of intellectual discourse within Jainism, and also from his confident deployment of the techniques of brahmanical scholarship and learning which enabled Jainism to become fully integrated into the classical Indian thought-world. Although a staunch defender of his own religion, Haribhadra showed that respect for other religious traditions which has characterized Jainism to this day. Thus, in a celebrated verse, he stated that he did not judge philosophical doctrine on the grounds of religion or sect but on the grounds of conformity to logic.

Haribhadra is traditionally credited with authorship of around 1,400 works, but this is an artificially high number, and a figure in the region of 100 would probably be more accurate. While many of these are quite short and insignificant, others are among the greatest masterpieces of Jain literature. Among the most significant are: 'The Victory Banner of Relativism' (*Anekāntajayapatākā*) [6], an elaborate philosophical treatise which attempts to establish the Jain belief that, since only the enlightened and omniscient teacher can have a full and accurate grasp of reality, the non-enlightened should refrain from fixed and dogmatic judgements about ontology and should instead adhere to a multi-faceted relativism; 'The Rogues' Stories' (*Dhūrtākhyāna*) [7], a satire on Hinduism, in which a gathering of low-life characters compete against each other in the telling of increasingly outrageous lies, using the standard mythological accounts of the Hindu gods as their subject matter; 'The Fifties' (*Pañcāśaka*), a work of 19 sections of 50 verses in an archaic Prakrit dialect, which deals with ritual and spiritual aspects of Jainism; 'The Story of Samarāicca' (*Samarāiccakahā*) [8], a long prose romance which explores the workings of karma by describing how wrathful enmity causes one character to hound another through a series of existences; and the *Yogabindu*, in which Haribhadra places the Jain spiritual path in a wider Indian context [9].

Haribhadra's prestige has remained constant and it is no great exaggeration to say that 'Haribhadra', however many there may have been of this name, is one of the most important figures in Jainism after MAHĀVĪRA (P.D.)

Haridās, Svāmī [XI] (16th century). Devotee of Rādhā and Kṛṣṇa, author of a small corpus of Hindi verse, and inspiration behind a cult founded in his name. According to the hagiographies – effectively the only source for his biography – Haridās established in Vrindaban a 'self-manifest' (*svayambhū*) image of Kṛṣṇa; the temple of this 'Bāṅke Bihārī', and the 'Nidhiban' grove frequented by Haridās himself, now have an established place on Vaiṣṇava pilgrimage itineraries. A 17th-century schism divided the Haridāsī sect or *Sakhī sampradāy* into two branches, ascetic and householder, both of which are still active in uneasy tandem in Vrindaban (though the ascetic branch remains largely aloof in its own settlement). Haridās' devotional attitudes parallel those of his contemporary HIT HARIVAṂŚ – though it is to NIMBĀRKA that the foundation of his theology is traditionally ascribed. Haridās' *bhakti* is expressed in his eulogistic and descriptive *Kelimāl* ('Garland of Divine Sport'), in which the poet assumes the persona of a *sakhī* or attendant of Rādhā, while in the brief *Aṣṭādaś siddhānt* ('Eighteen Doctrinal Verses') the importance of devotion is stressed in a general way. Present-day devotees interpret Haridās's poetry from the perspective of successive generations of Haridāsī poets, among whom the late 16th-century Bihāriṇīdās holds pride of place as formalizer of sectarian doctrine. In the popular view, Haridās is revered as a fine singer who contributed to the development of the classical *dhrupad* genre, and also as teacher to AKBAR's court musician Tānsen. Whatever the historical facts may be, Haridās symbolizes the primacy of devotional song from the late medieval period to modern times; many would regard him as a kind of patron saint of the religious music of the Hindustani tradition. [40: 217–18; 45] (R.S.)

Hari Krishan, Gurū [XXIII] (1656–1664). Eighth Gurū of the Sikhs. He succeeded to the title of Gurū when only five years old. His elder brother, Rām Rāi, had offended his father, Gurū Hari Rāi, through his sycophantic dealings with the Mughals and was accordingly passed over in 1661. Hari Krishan was summoned from his home in the Shivalik Hills down to Delhi by the Mughal emperor Auraṅgzeb, and while there contracted smallpox. Before he died he indicated to his retinue that the next Gurū was to be his grandfather's half brother, TEGH BAHĀDUR. [40: 180–82] (W.H.M.)

Hari Rai, Gurū (1630–61), seventh Gurū of the Sikhs, was a younger grandson of the sixth GURŪ, HARGOBIND. His father had predeceased Hargobind and his elder brother was believed to be unsuitable as a successor. When Hargobind died in 1644, Gurū Hari Rai withdrew from Kiratpur back into the Shivalik Hills and settled, with a small retinue, at Nahan. From there he sometimes emerged onto the plains to preach and to visit his Sikhs. Before he died he bestowed the succession on his younger son, HARI KRISHNAN (then only five years old), preferring him to his elder son, Ram Rai. [40:178–81] (W.H.M.)

Harnack, Adolf von [IV.A] (1851–1930). German theologian and historian. He was born in Dorpat (Tartu) in Russian Livonia, the son of Theodosius Harnack, a professor of theology. He studied at Dorpat and then Leipzig, gaining his PhD in 1873 and being appointed Privatdozent in 1874. He was made Extraordinary Professor in 1876 and then a full professor at Giessen in 1879. He was professor at Marburg in 1886–9, and at Berlin from 1889 until his retirement in 1921. Thereafter he was Emeritus Professor until 1929. He was elected to the Prussian Academy of Sciences in 1890. He was founder and first president of the Evangelical Social Congress and from 1905 to 1921 was director of the Staatsbibliothek in Berlin. He was the first president of the Kaiser Wilhelm Gesellschaft (1811–30) and was ennobled by Kaiser Wilhelm II in 1914. A historian of the early church and early Christian doctrine, he was the author of a multi-volume *Lehrbuch der Dogmengeschichte* (1896–9; trans. as *History of Dogma*, 1902) and *Das Wesen Christentums* (1900; trans. as *What is Christianity?*, 1901) and hundreds of other works. [305; 346; 347; 882] (T.T.)

Harris, Charles [XXI] (1931–). President of Australia's largest Aboriginal organization, the Uniting Aboriginal and Islander Christian Congress, since its first national gathering in 1983. He was born in the sugar-cane district of Ingham, Queensland, his father of Torres Strait Island and Spanish descent, his mother an Aborigine with Malay ancestry. They belonged to a Pentecostal Christian tradition. Harris recalls wanting to be a minister while still on his mother's knee. His frustrations with the Aboriginal experience of White education and employment institutions made him an angry man; today he nurtures that anger but tries to prevent its lapse into bitterness or hate. Having worked in the sugar industry and with the railways, in his mid-20s he turned to theological training and served as a 'worker priest' with the Assemblies of God. He later continued his training at Nungalinya College and returned to a Brisbane Methodist church, from which he directed his ministry to the troubled Aboriginal people of that city. A very strong Aboriginal Christian revival emerged. He next moved to Townsville as a Uniting Church pastor. While at a conference in New Zealand (where he observed the aspirations of the Maori Church leaders) he conceived the idea of an Aboriginal Christian institution, freed from White Australian church structures. At the same time an Arnhem Land revival was developing; these two strands converged in the formation of the Congress [1]. An interim committee was first established in 1982. Harris, as chairman, travelled thoughout Aboriginal Australia to share the vision. Both his pride in Aboriginal traditions and anger at the maltreatment of Aborigines were reinforced during this period. His theology is always directed towards social justice and he is an outspoken critic of the church's historic role in Australia. At a wider level, he was the prime organizer of Australia's largest Aboriginal rally, the March for Justice, Freedom and Hope in which some 50,000 people protested against Australia's bicentennial celebrations. Harris believes Australia has a race history comparable with that of South Africa and the Jewish Holocaust, and he sees the church as having contributed to that oppression [21]. His vision is of a new, justice-oriented church sensitive not only to Aborigines but to indigenous people throughout the world. He sums up his life thus: 'Born in poverty, lived in anger, motivated by radical, revolutionary love and compassion.' (T.S.)

Harris, William Wadé [I.A] (*c.*1865–1929). West African prophet who carried out probably the most remarkable single evangelistic campaign Africa has ever known. A native Liberian of Grebo parents, Harris was originally educated at an American Methodist mission. Around 1885 he joined the Episcopal Church. He worked as a seaman, interpreter and for ten years as a schoolteacher. Either during a traditional sacrifice or while in prison in 1910 (sources are here in conflict) he experienced a personal conversion to Christianity. Famous for healings, mass conversions and baptisms in the southern Ivory Coast, and his ritual accoutrements (gourd rattle, gourd bowl, Bible and cross), he encouraged his converts (an estimated 120,000) to join an established Christian church. Forced by French authorities to return to Liberia in 1915, he was there spurned as a prophet. He died in poverty. Today several independent churches in the Côte d'Ivoire and Ghana recognize Harris as their spiritual founder. [15; 39] (R.H.)

Ḥasan al-Bannā' [XII] (1904–1949). Founder and ideologue of the Muslim Brotherhood (*al-ikhwān al-muslimūn*), a major Egyptian and international movement for the furtherment of radical Islam. Born in the Nile delta town of Muḥammadiyya, Ḥasan was the son of a religious teacher and prayer leader. Politicized by the growth of nationalism and secularism after the First World War, he established the Muslim Brotherhood as a youth club in 1928, stressing moral and social reform and engaging in religious propaganda. He himself had been much influenced by the conservative but radical Islamic journal *al-Manār*, edited by RASHĪD RIḌĀ, whose campaign for a renewal of religious life he continued in a more extreme fashion.

In 1933 Bannā' moved his headquarters to Cairo, and by 1940 his Brotherhood boasted 500 branches, each with a mosque, school and club. The aim was to prepare young Muslims for a *jihād* against foreign control of Egypt and ultimately the entire Islamic world. Cells – many of them secret – and other groupings were set up throughout the country and subsequently in other Arab states.

After the Second World War, the Brotherhood embarked on terrorist activities and was banned in 1948. They retaliated by assassinating the Prime Minister, in return for which Bannā' was himself assassinated by state agents in February 1949.

Bannā' was the first of the Islamic reformers consciously to organize his movement for change into a political party. Later members of the Brotherhood, such as SAYYID QUṬB, took Islam even further out of the mosque into the political arena, particularly by advocating direct action against the state. More than any of his predecessors, Bannā' influenced the long-term direction of radical Islamic politics for a generation disillusioned with nationalism. [35: 'al-Bannā', Ḥasan'] (D.M.)

Ḥasan ibn 'Alī [XII] (627/8–669). Eldest son of the Caliph (and Shiʿite Imam) ʿALĪ and MUḤAMMAD's daughter FĀṬIMA, brother of the Imām ḤUSAYN. Although Shiʿite legend exalts him, like his father and brother, to the rank of an Imām, even traditional accounts portray him in his youth as somewhat worldly. Following his mother's death, he became estranged from his father and brothers and became known for the ease and frequency with which he married, acquiring the soubriquet *al-miṭlāq* ('The Divorcer').

Following his father's assassination in 611, ʿAlid partisans in Iraq proclaimed Ḥasan Caliph, but he preferred to reach an accommodation with the Umayyad Caliph Muʿāwiya. A fee and pension having been agreed, Ḥasan publicly renounced all claim to the caliphate and retired to Medina, where he died of consumption. Shiʿite accounts attribute his death to poison administered on the orders of Muʿāwiya. [92: part II: I] (D.M.)

al-Ḥasan ibn al-Sabbāḥ [XII] (*d.*1124). Iranian founder of the Nizārī branch of the Ismāʿīlī sect within Shiʿite Islam (popularly known as Assassins; Arabic: *Hashshāshīn*). Born the son of a Twelver Shiʿite in Qumm, Ḥasan was educated in Rayy, where he converted to Ismaʿilism and pledged allegiance to the Fatimid Imām in Egypt. He soon came under suspicion as a political subversive and was forced to flee Rayy in 1076. Arriving in Cairo in 1078, he was received at court, but later clashed with the Fatimid military commander.

Returning to Iran in 1081, he travelled widely through the country, preaching the Ismāʿīlī cause and winning numerous converts in the northern provinces of Gīlān and Māzandarān. In 1090 he succeeded in taking control of the castle of Alamūt near Qazvīn, where he remained for the rest of his life.

From Alamūt, he organized a successful religious and military crusade against Iran's Seljuq rulers, capturing strongholds, converting large numbers and instigating widespread insurrection. His followers became famous for their use of selective assassination as a tool of political terror, notably in the celebrated murder of the Seljuq Grand Vizier, Niẓām al-Mulk in 1092.

In 1094, the Ismāʿīlīs of Iran split with the headquarters of the sect in Egypt over the issue of succession to the Fatimid Caliph al-Mustanṣir. The son whom they favoured, Nizār, had been murdered in prison, but Ḥasan brought his reputed grandson to Alamūt, to rule as the new Imām, thereby setting up a new line of Nizārī Imāms. In the

12th century the Nizārīs established a successful mission in Syria, where they played an important role at the time of the Crusades.

Although he is thought to have been a prolific author, all of Ḥasan's writings perished in the course of the Mongol destruction of Alamūt in 1256. [35: s.v.; 49] (D.M.)

Hastings, James [VI.A] (1852–1922). He received all his education in Aberdeen – grammar school, university and the Free Church Divinity College. He was ordained to the Presbyterian ministry in 1884 and served as pastor in the Free Church at Kinneff, Kincardineshire, from 1884. In 1897 he moved to Wilson Church, Dundee, and in 1901 to the United Free Church, St Cyrus, Kincardineshire. He retired to Aberdeen in 1911. He was editor of a number of encyclopaedias: *Dictionary of the Bible* (1898–1904); *Encyclopaedia of Religion and Ethics* (1908–21); *Dictionary of Christ and the Gospels* (1906–8); and *Dictionary of the Apostolic Church* (1915–18). (T.T.)

Hataria, Manekji Limji [XXVI]. The first agent sent by the Parsi Society for the Amelioration of the Condition of the Zoroastrians in Persia to their then desperately oppressed coreligionists in Iran. Manekji laboured from 1854 to 1890, his greatest achievement being to bring about, in 1882, the abolition of the poll-tax (*jizya*), an instrument of extortion and forced conversion. He founded schools, helped repair fire-temples and funerary towers, and gained a measure of justice and freedom of opportunity for the Zoroastrians. In all this he showed outstanding qualities of courage, tact, patience, honesty and resourcefulness, with unflagging devotion to his religion. [6; 42: 44–8] (M.B.)

Hayashi Razan [XIV] (1583–1657). Influential Chu Hsi neo-Confucian scholar and advisor to the Tokugawa shogunate in Japan. As a young man he entered a Rinzai Zen monastery, but refused to take the tonsure, returning home instead to study Chu Hsi and his interpretation of the *Analects*. In 1605 he lectured before Tokugawa Ieyasu, the Shogun, for the first time, impressing him with his encyclopaedic knowledge. In 1607 Razan took the tonsure, ostensibly becoming a Buddhist monk in order to serve as official advisor to the Shogun. This was ironic, since he was a strong opponent of Buddhism, which had dominated the shogunal courts for decades. In his capacity as advisor to the Shogun, Razan helped to draft laws and provide ideological support for shogunal policies.

Razan sought to realize Chu Hsi's goal of attaining 'great learning' (*po-hsüeh*); this is suggested by his writings, which cover law, diplomacy, medicine, military affairs, religion, philosophy and history. Many of these writings are characterized by a polemical tone: he attacked Christianity, Buddhism and other schools of Confucianism. In a series of works, including *Shunkanshō* (1629) and *Santokushō*, neo-Confucian teachings were presented in popular form. Razan also sought to legitimate the rise of the samurai class and to promote secular society and culture. In general, he promoted a form of secular humanism. Faced with the cultural prestige of Japanese 'mythistory' (myth-as-history), as found in the *Kojiki* [49] and the *Nihonshoki*, he attempted to reread these texts in rationalistic terms. The cosmogonic myth, for instance, was interpreted in an allegorical fashion by equating the *Kami* (deities) therein with Confucian categories. While Razan was essentially a rationalist thinker, his emphasis on the power of heaven, which governs all things through natural law, had a decidedly religious dimension. His teachings were influential in part because they corresponded to the real experience of people living under the absolute autocracy of the Tokugawa régime, while also offering ideological support for the status quo. Following Razan's death, the role of advisor to the Shogun became hereditary in his family. His major disciples include KAIBARA EKKEN and YAMAGA SOKŌ. [3; 18; 34: IV; 44; 45] (G.E.)

Hegel, Georg Wilhelm Friedrich [VI.A] (1770–1831). German idealist philosopher. He was born in Stuttgart and educated there. In 1788 he went to the Lutheran seminary in Tübingen where he first studied philosophy and then theology. He was a private tutor in Bern from 1793 to 1796 and in Frankfurt from 1797 to 1801, after which he went to Jena, where he successfully defended his thesis *De orbitis planetarum*. Success enabled him to qualify for the post of *Privatdozent*, in which he lectured on logic and metaphysics. He began work on his major work *Die Phänomenologie des*

Geistes (published 1807). The battle of Jena (October 1806) ended his university appointment. Thereafter he was employed as a newspaper editor and director of a Gymnasium. Following the publication of his *Wissenschaft der Logik* (1816) he became a professor at Heidelberg. In 1817 *Die Encyclopaedie der philosophischen Wissenschaften im Grundrisse* was published. He was professor in Berlin from 1818 until his death, by which time he had become rector of the university (1830). His lectures on the philosophy of religion were published posthumously. [251; 356; 776] (T.T.)

Hemacandra [xiii] (1089–1172). Śvetāmbara Jain monk and teacher whose polymathy led to him being referred to as 'The Omniscient One of the Current World Age' [4]. There is a disparate body of biographical material, not all of it consistent, relating to Hemacandra. The earliest source would appear to be the mid-13th-century Prabhācandra's 'The Deeds of the Exalters of the Doctrine' in which Hemacandra occurs as one of the more recent of a line of great teachers who have added to the fame of Jainism and served to promote it, while the 15th-century Merutuṅga's 'Wishing-Stone of Stories' portrays him in the context of a semi-legendary history of Gujarat. Other relevant sources are also at some distance from their subject matter, and should be judged as hagiography rather than as objective history. Nonetheless, they do enable us to delineate the broad contours of Hemacandra's career.

Hemacandra was born as Caṅgadeva in a village near what was to become Ahmedabad in Gujarat, his parents being Jains of the merchant caste. While still a young boy, he seems to have been handed over to a Jain teacher by his parents, and was initiated into the ascetic life, being given the name Somacandra. The sources say virtually nothing about their subject's life immediately after this, other than making clear that he followed a rigorous course of training in all the traditional branches of Indian learning. Then, in 1108, he was ordained as successor to his teacher and given the title *sūri*, that is, a teacher who was head of a group of monks and who had the right to expound and interpret the scriptures and appoint a successor. From this time he was known as Hemacandra.

The prime concern of the sources is the relationship between Hemacandra and the kings of the Caulukya family who ruled Gujarat at the time. Hemacandra's first patron was Jayasiṃha Siddharāja who ascended the throne in 1092, ruling until 1141. Warlike and aggressive towards his neighbours in the manner of most Indian kings, he turned his capital, Patan, into a city full of fine buildings and gardens. While evidently a worshipper of the Hindu god Śiva, Siddharāja seems nonetheless to have been curious about other religious paths, for he appointed Hemacandra as court scholar and historian, who, to this end, prepared new and authoritative grammars of Sanskrit and Prakrit (which are still in use amongst Śvetāmbara monks today) and also wrote a history of the Caulukya family. It is interesting that the sources decribe Hemacandra spectating at one of the greatest events in the history of Gujarati Jainism when, during a debate at Siddharāja's court, the Śvetāmbara logician Vādideva defeated the Digambara monk Kumudacandra, thus ensuring that the Śvetāmbara version of Jainism was dominant in Gujarat from then on.

For reasons about which the sources differ, Siddharāja fell out with his grand-nephew Kumārapāla, who was compelled to flee Gujarat and live incognito. Equally uncertain is how Kumārapāla came to establish a relationship with Hemacandra. At any rate, we are told that Hemacandra hid Kumārapāla from the wrath of Siddharāja before he left Gujarat, and on his return it was Hemacandra who validated him as successor to the deceased Siddharāja. Jain sources would naturally exaggerate, but there do seem to be grounds for believing them when they state that Hemacandra persuaded Kumārapāla to abstain from meat and alcohol and to issue edicts banning the killing of animals in his kingdom: in other words, to rule Gujarat in at least partial accord with Jain principles. Some accounts of Kumārapāla's enthusiasm do seem rather implausible, for example, the vast fine imposed upon a merchant for killing a louse. For all the Jain chroniclers' attempts to underplay the fact, Kumārapāla was almost certainly very strongly attached to the worship of Śiva. Hemacandra's efforts described by one writer to show Kumārapāla how the tenets of Jainism could be reconciled with those of orthodox Hinduism probably bear witness to this. Nonetheless, Hemacandra does seem to have provided, by his writings, preaching and performance of miracles, the motivation, if only on a temporary basis, for the emergence of the only Jain kingdom ever to have existed in India.

It does not imply criticism of Hemacandra to say that his surviving works are not profoundly original, for he would have seen his role as being that of a consolidator and synthesizer of the Jain literary and philosophical tradition which had come down to him. Of his many writings, two stand out as being of particular significance. 'The Deeds of the Sixty-three Illustrious Men' [10; 11] is the largest surviving example of the Jain literary genre which has come to be known as 'Universal History'. Here Hemacandra, drawing upon the versions of earlier Śvetāmbara writers and using in many respects the same material as the Digambara JINASENA, produced an encyclopaedic account of the *tīrthaṅkaras* (*see* MAHĀVĪRA), the universal emperors who accompany their appearance, and their previous lives and deeds, interspersing it with elaborate doctrinal disquisitions. Johnson's translation of this vast edifice is the best way for a Westerner to get to grips with Jainism. Hemacandra's other most important work has unfortunately not yet found an English translator. 'The Treatise on Yoga' deals with *yoga* in its broadest sense, namely, the activities of body, mind and speech. Supposedly written to instruct Kumārapāla in the proper duties of a Jain layman, it draws on a wide range of sources to provide a clear and concise summary of Hemacandra's view of Jainism. (P.D.)

Heracleon [IX] (2nd century). A student of VALENTINUS, he became a teacher of the western school of Valentinian Gnosticism and was active *c.*145–80. Extracts from his writings are preserved for us by CLEMENT OF ALEXANDRIA and ORIGEN. Heracleon seems to have been the first to write a commentary on a New Testament book. It is a highly allegorizing commentary on the fourth Gospel; e.g. he takes JESUS' going down to Capernaum (*John* 2: 12) as his descent into the material world to inaugurate the new dispensation. While acknowledging others, Heracleon claimed his own authority. He seems to have denigrated martyrdom, partly because the imitation of Christ involved is only imitation of what happened to the human Jesus. Rather he stressed that Christians should confess Christ 'in faith and conduct throughout their whole lives' [7: 97]. With Ptolemy, another of Valentinus' influential students who is best known from the moderate ethical stance he adopts in his *Letter to Flora* [6: 306–15], Heracleon taught that the church contained both spiritual and unspiritual elements; only the spiritual gnostics could bring the unspiritual to gnosis [2: 77–103; 7: 116]. (G.J.B.)

Heraclitus [X] (late 6th and early 5th centuries BCE). Philosopher of Ephesus, whose work survives in about 120 epigrams and paradoxes, a style he may have chosen in imitation of mystical writers in order to stimulate thought. His most influential doctrines are that Fire is the basic and ruling element, and, even more importantly, that the world is in a state of constant change ('everything is in flux'), which has influenced poets and thinkers from Plato to Gerard Manley Hopkins's 'That Nature is a Heraclitean Fire and of the comfort of the Resurrection'. [20: vol. 1; 24a; 48] (H.L.)

Herman of Alaska, St [VI.B] (1757–1837). A hermit from Valaam Monastery in Karelia from 1778, Herman joined the Valaam mission to Alaska (1794). They worked from Kodiak amongst the Inuit, Aleuts and Indians. Baranov, governor of the Russo-American company, objected to the monks' outspoken support of the exploited natives. He persecuted the monks and the natives but Herman remained to denounce his excesses. Befriended by a new governor, Herman spent his last years on Spruce Island, where he ran an orphanage, preaching among the natives till he died.

Herman's work was continued by Innokenty Veniaminov (1795–1879). Originally a missionary amongst the Siberian tribes, he was transferred to America in 1823. Innokenty translated or supervised the translations of numerous Christian texts into previously unwritten languages. He was consecrated Bishop of Kamchatka and the Kuriles and in 1868 he became Metropolitan of Moscow. Innokenty founded the Orthodox Missionary Society in 1870. [14; 39; 80; 81] (D.B.)

Hermes Trismegistus [XVII.A]. Thrice-great Hermes never existed. He was a name associated with a set of gnostic philosophical texts and magical treatises written in the 2nd and 3rd centuries CE, which until the late Renaissance were thought to have been written by a man contemporary with MOSES. He was thought to have been a sage of great wisdom, presaging the appearance of JESUS and PLATO. His esteem rose high in the Renaissance, for in 1463 a man at the Medici court, about to translate the works of Plato, published a translation of some texts that had arrived at the court in 1460 and which Cosimo de' Medici had asked him to complete before the Plato. These texts were the *Corpus Hermeticum*, nearly complete, the bulk of the writings attributed to Hermes Trismegistus. The translation and explanation of this work had a profound effect upon Renaissance intellectuals; some scholars have argued that the magical world-view was a necessary precursor to the scientific revolution, for the magical treatises were the first philosophical effort to describe man as the active centre of his world and not as the passive audience to God's creation. The varied writings address the search for revelation without a personal God. They speak of the creation by God, and the possibility of creation by man. Knowledge is gnosis, hidden insight revealed in moments of illumination or through careful study. Knowledge of the human is also knowledge of the universe, because the human contains as microcosm all elements of the universal macrocosm. The writings speak also of spells, charms, and astrology – they are direct and practical guides to magic. This combination was the inspiration of the complex Renaissance magical philosophy formulated by DEE, FLUDD, PARACELSUS and others.

The manuscripts were correctly dated by Isaac Casaubon in 1614, and their influence rapidly declined. [11; 25; 26; 28] (T.L.)

Herodotus of Halicarnassus [X] (*b*484 BCE). The 'father of history', whose *Historiai* or *Investigations* [53] present a complex theodicy in a subtle realization of historical *aitiē*, which is at once causation, responsibility and blame. He may be taken to represent the Archaic world-view in direct line with HOMER and HESIOD, and may stand in general for the religious values of Aeschylus, Sophocles, Pindar and Solon.

Herodotus' long account of Croesus embodies his own view of the moral order established by the jealous gods who have established the *dikē* (justice or righteousness) of the world order (*History* 2.52), and punish pride and excess (*hybris* and *koros*) which overpass the limits set for mortal men. They destroy the wrongdoer with retributive justice, and it was Croesus, says Herodotus, who first wronged the Greeks: 'The divinity permits no one but himself to think high thoughts.' (7.10); 'no unjust man shall fail to pay the penalty' (5.56). So doom is inevitable for the Lydian king Candaules (1.8), the Egyptian king Apries (2.161), the Athenian general Miltiades (6.135), the Persian princess Artaÿnte (9.109); and Greek tyrants such as Polycrates and Arcesilaus disastrously 'fulfil their own *moira*' (3.142; 4.164). The *peprōmenē moira* or 'fated portion' of Croesus cannot even be averted by great gifts to Delphic Apollo; for Apollo cannot turn aside the *Moirai* (1.191, the only mention of the personified Fates): 'For a god too it is impossible to evade the fated portion.'

Pessimism and quietism run deep in Solon's explanation to Croesus of human blessings. A moderate competence enjoyed throughout life may be better than great wealth and power temporarily possessed (1.30–33). For man's life is contingent: Herodotus knew this from his own experience (29.27–32). The wisdom of Artabanos to Xerxes fulfils a similar role: 'The divinity strikes with his thunderbolt what stands high.' (7.10). Solon employed the deliberately moderate language of Apolline morality: a genuinely blessed man enjoys *eutychiē* or good luck – this philosophy is not determinist – which keeps both *atē* and *epithumiē* (calamity and desire) from him. Such a man is sound of limb and eye, free from sickness, not afflicted by disasters, possessed of fine children, good to look upon (1.32). The virtues of the Athenian Tellus and the Argives Cleobis and Biton are thoroughly Greek: they spring from courage and physical prowess, are connected with the family and the city – moderate wealth, filial duty, piety – and win public honour (*timē*), even a public funeral. Indeed, it is clear elsewhere that the tyrant or despot or sole ruler – Greek or Persian or Lydian – is by the very nature of his power subject to arrogant pride and complacent excess, as the Persian Otanes argues when he condemns the *hybris* of Cambyses (Greek values put upon Persian lips), and praises the very word for the rule of the many, *isonomiē* (equality before the law) (3.80).

Croesus was complacent enough to deem Solon a fool; and so 'great retribution [*nemesis*] from the divinity took Croesus' (1.34). But his piety towards Apollo redeemed him for the pyre on which he was to be burned was quenched by the miraculous intervention of Apollo: 'in a clear and windless sky clouds gathered and a storm broke' (1.87). Moreover, Croesus had learned from his sufferings: 'There is a wheel [*kyklos*] in human affairs, and as it turns it does not permit the same men to enjoy good fortune continually' (1.207). No such factors redeemed Xerxes or his Persians, who were soft men living in a fat land, not the hardy highlanders whom Cyrus had led to freedom against the Mede; for the wheel had again turned (9.122). Xerxes was guilty of *megalophrosynē*, thinking high thoughts such as the gods do not permit to mortals (7.10, 24); haunted by dreams, he ignored the warnings of Artabanus (7.10–19). Here the deceptive dream sent by Zeus to Agamemnon may be the model in the mind of Herodotus. When his bridge across the Hellespont was shattered by the sea, he commanded that the Hellespont be lashed and insolent words addressed to it. When the Lydian Pythius asked that his eldest son be spared from the war, the anger and revenge of Xerxes were clearly excessive: the son was killed, his body cut in half and displayed on either side of the road by which the army marched (7.38–9). Later he ignored obvious portents of disaster (7.56–7) and the warning of the Spartan Demaratus that the Greeks would face the Persian host because their law was their master (*despotēs*). Just before the decisive Persian defeat at Salamis, Herodotus quotes an oracle of Bacis: *Dikē* shall quench mighty *Koros*, offspring of *Hybris* (8.77). In the words of Themistocles he condemns Xerxes for his presumptuous insolence and impiety (*anhosios* and *atasthalos*) (8.109). It was the gods and heroes of Hellas who had saved them, for they grudged that one man should become king over both Asia and Europe.

Herodotus' stated purpose was to record great deeds so that neither Greeks nor foreigners 'should lack glory'. Glory or fame (*kleos*) is in fact an epic virtue, and like Homer, Herodotus is evidence for the Greek view of the gods as human in nature (1.131). Indeed, he regards Homer as definitive (2.53), though he himself presents no divine family on Olympus, no epiphanies (except for local cult-heroes: 8.39) to intervene on behalf of favoured mortal offspring, but rather a collective entity: the divinity, the divine, the gods (*ho theos, to theion, hoi theoi* and sometimes *ho daimon, to daimonion, hoi daimones*). They communicate through dreams, portents and oracles, often riddling (1.66, 75), sometimes remarkably clear (8.77), and notably through the responses of Apollo's Delphic prophetess, the Pythia. He is fond too of oracles attributed to the Bacis.

Heracles he identifies as properly both a hero born to Amphitryon and Alcmene and a most ancient Egyptian (and Phoenician) god (2.43–44, 146), one of the Twelve. This is in the context of an extraordinary willingness to be a pan-Egyptianist and derive both gods and rites from the age-old wisdom of Egypt. Priests at Memphis, Thebes and Heliopolis had told him that Egyptians first 'used twelve names of gods', i.e. they created the distinctive identities or characters of the Twelve Gods, and also their altars, images and shrines. 'And that most of this had indeed happened thus they made clear to me' (2.4). A series of wooden figures of priest kings shown to him at Thebes stretched back over 11,000 years; before this gods had ruled Egypt, the last being Horus, son of Osiris. Horus he identifies with Apollo, Osiris with Dionysus (2.142–4). But in ancient Greece the aboriginal Pelasgians, inventors of the ithyphallic Herms, had sacrificed to 'unnamed' gods until the 'names' (identities) of the gods came to them from Egypt. This adoption was sanctioned by the oracle at Dodona (2.51–2), itself established from Egypt (2.54). As for ritual, both divination from sacrificial victims and the great festival gatherings and processions came to Hellas from Egypt (2.58), including rituals of Dionysus established by the seer Melampous (2.49) and the story and ritual of Demeter (2.171), i.e. Osiris and Isis. He is reticent about the Egyptian sacred *logoi* (stories) but does name the immortality and rebirth of the soul an Egyptian teaching (2.47, 65, 123). The descent of the gods from each other, their fully formed identities and honours (*timai*) had to wait for Hesiod and Homer to make clear, only about 400 years before his own time (2. 53).

His comment on Persian religion embodies both accurate detail and serious misinterpretation, some of which misinforms his presentation of the *hybris* of Xerxes. He in fact perpetrated a number of half-truths in the form of repeated literary *topoi*. Individual facts are important: the Iranians revered rivers, fire and trees (1.38; 3.16; 7.31). But this is not linked to the fundamentals of Zoroastrian theology (*see* ZOROASTER), the belief in two distinct creations, one good and one evil. Thus fire should not be called a 'god', but was venerated as part of the good creation; Xerxes' seven creations of Iranian ceremony were not a 'sacrifice' (7.55) but an offering to Mithra (who is seriously misidentified at 1. 131); the rebuke to the Hellespont, 'O bitter water, your lord [*despotes*] repays you', misunderstood as *hybris*, is nevertheless accurately recorded, so that one identifies the Iranian perception of impure waters, a part of the evil creation. Of great interest are his observations on the priestly tribe of the Magi (1.101, 107, 132, 140; 7.113, 191); on the *fravashis*, summoned as Greek heroes were; and on the invisible manifestation of Ahura Mazda (Zeus) in an empty chariot travelling with Xerxes' armies (7. 40, 43). The Persians thought Greek temples, altars and images foolish: 'I suppose this is because they do not consider gods to be human in nature as the Greeks do' (1.131). [6:28–63; 23; 25: 58–69; 29: 27–32; 33; 36; 40; 53] (J.P.K.)

Heschel, Abraham Joshua [xv] (1909–1972). Jewish philosopher and theologian. Born in Warsaw to a distinguished Ḥasidic family, he taught in Germany and, after his deportation by the Nazis in 1938, in Warsaw and London. In 1940 he went to the United States, teaching first at Hebrew Union College, Cincinnati, and from 1945 at the Jewish Theological Seminary, New York. His writings combined the traditional piety, mystical (especially Ḥasidic) thought and devotion to learning of Eastern European Jewry with modern Western attitudes, scientific scholarship and existentialist philosophy, presenting a modern theology founded on traditional sources. His social ethical teachings found a practical expression in his involvement with the civil rights movement (he marched with MARTIN LUTHER KING), his opposition to the Vietnam War and his active work in fostering the emergent Jewish–Christian dialogue.

According to Heschel, conceptual thinking must be complemented by situational thinking. God is the togetherness of all beings in holy otherness. The Bible, the source of certainty, relates not only man's search for God but also God's search for man; religion consists of God's questions and man's answers. God confronts the Jew with the commandments, requiring of him a 'leap of action'. Heschel develops a philosophy of human dignity, ascribing to Jewish law the concern with teaching man how to live with God at all times. [26]

His books, often poetic and aphoristic in style, include *The Sabbath* (conveying one of his major themes – the hallowing of time, expressed in Judaism especially in the Sabbath and festivals), *Man is not Alone, God in search of Man* and *The Prophets*. [66] (G.W.)

Hesiod [x] (*c.*700–650 BCE). The author to whom the Greeks attributed the *Theogony* ('Births of the Gods'), *Works* and *Days* [14; 54]. HERODOTUS [53] attributed the developed Greek picture of the births, relations, forms and honours of the gods to HOMER and Hesiod. In Hesiod nature-philosophy, nature-spirits, personified powers of human life and the anthropomorphic gods of cult – all found in unsystematic form in Homer – contribute to a systematized cosmogony and theogony which culminate in the wise and just order established by Zeus and the gods of Olympus. Out of Chasm, Earth and Tartarus – once Passion (Eros) activates their generative power – come all other divinities, which by definition endure for ever and cannot perish. Eros is a primal power, born *before* Aphrodite is generated from the severed genitals of Ouranos (castrated by Kronos). Much of the *Theogony* is catalogue poetry, mnemonic and oral in style; and it adapts an Ancient Near Eastern succession-myth. But the anthropomorphic Olympians of cult, the Greek heroes and Greek values constantly intrude upon Hesiod's mind as he presents the series of divine generations which are 'born'. So in the accounts of monstrous beasts derived from Near Eastern myths – for instance the Echidna (half lovely-cheeked girl, half serpent) and her offspring, Cerberus, the

Hydra of Lerna, the Chimaera – Hesiod cannot resist stating how Herakles, Bellerophon and Perseus slew them.

But it is Zeus who is the greatest monster-slayer, with his Homeric *aristeiai* against the Titans and Typhoeus. The divine power of Zeus combines with his wisdom to overthrow the older generation of Kronos and the Titans. He outwits Prometheus, and takes a subtle revenge on the fire-stealers by commanding Hephaestus to fashion Woman, a 'sheer inescapable snare for men'. The Hundredhands bow to his superior *prapides* (wits) and *noema* (sagacity). His power shakes the heavens and earth, as he continually wields scorching and blinding bolts of lightning against the enemy in 'the spirit of his might' (compare *Psalm* 97: 3–4) and overwhelms Typhoeus (compare *Psalm* 74: 12–14). It is Zeus who assigns honours (*timai*: ranks and spheres of authority) to the Olympians whom he rules (*see* HOMER). Then he takes as his brides Wisdom and Law, by whom his offspring are the *Horai* – Governance, Justice and Peace – and the *Moirai* or Fates, who dispense both life and death to men. Finally, from Zeus and the other Olympians the heroes are born. The *Works* presents the famous myths of Pandora (resembling *Theog.* 570ff.) and the Five Ages of Men, a decline from the Golden Age to Hesiod's own Age of Iron (the low point of a *recurring* cycle of ages). Into the Ancient Near Eastern myth Hesiod inserts the Greek age of Trojan heroes. He despairs of justice in his own time, and speaks of crooked untruths, evil envy, shameless power; but in the end Justice will win over *Hybris*, because it is blessed by Zeus. [14; 25: 32–6; 29: 38–68, 88–91; 38; 54] (J.P.K.)

Hildegarde of Bingen [VI.A] (1098–1179). German abbess and mystic. She was born of an aristocratic family and sent to an anchoress, Jutta, for education. In 1136 she became abbess of her own monastery at Bingen, Germany. In 1141 she had a prophetic vision and began to write her great theological work, *Scivias* ('Know the Ways'), completed in 1151, to be followed by two more volumes, *The Book of Life's Merits* and *On the Activity of God*. She also wrote a medical encyclopedia, *The Book of Simple Medicine*, supplemented by *Causes and Cures*, a handbook of diseases and their remedies. An artist, her theological books are richly illuminated by paintings of her visions. A musician, she composed a morality play with 82 melodies and a *Symphonia* comprising 77 song settings. She communicated with the Pope, BERNARD OF CLAIRVAUX, Barbarossa and many others; her letters extend to hundreds. She travelled widely and became a major influence in medieval spirituality. A feminist, she saw men and women as equal in their work for God. A true mystic, she saw God as 'creative greenness'; and 'moistness' the healing power of the Spirit. Her teaching celebrated the inherent divinity and beauty of all creation. [270; 271; 582] (A.B.)

Hillel [XV] (late 1st century BCE – early 1st century CE). Outstanding sage of the late Second Temple era. Born and educated in Babylonia, he went to Palestine (*c.*40 CE), where he pursued advanced studies, became a noted scholar and was eventually appointed *nasi* (patriarch, leader of the community). Few facts and many legends relate to his life. He was regarded as the paragon of many virtues – humility, patience, conciliation.

Hillel and his colleague Shammai founded two contrasting schools, between which over 300 controversies are recorded. In general, Hillel and his school took more lenient viewpoints than the rigid Shammai. This reflected social differences: Hillel was identified with the underprivileged and represented the common man; Shammai was the spokesman for the conservative and traditional elements, the affluent and the priests. As against a tradition which held that scholarship should be the preserve of the rich and aristocrats, Hillel felt that every man, regardless of economic or social standing, had the right to learning. Hillel's school was recognized as authoritative, and, with few exceptions, its decisions were accepted. One of Hillel's best known enactments was a formula, essentially a legal fiction, called *prosbul*, which enabled the needy to obtain loans immediately before the onset of a sabbatical year (when in the ordinary way all private loans are cancelled).

Hillel's basic outlook is illustrated by the story of a heathen who demanded that Hillel teach him Judaism while he stood on one leg. Hillel did not get angry but replied: 'What is hateful to you, do not to others. This is all the law; the rest is commentary. Now go and study.'

He was responsible for seven basic hermeneutical principles of biblical exegesis, subsequently expanded to 32 more detailed rules, which formed the basis for deriving Jewish law from the text of the Pentateuch. While the seven rules may not have been actually formulated by him, he was the first to apply them for the determination of religious law.

Hillel essentially established the foundation of normative Judaism. The affection with which he was regarded is reflected in the fact that down to the 5th century his descendants held the office of official leader (patriarch) of the Jewish community in Palestine. [31] (G.W.)

Hirata Atsutane [XIV] (1776–1843). Major figure in the Fukko Shintō (Restoration Shintō) movement. He urged a return to ancient and 'pure' Japanese ways and customs as preserved in the earliest Japanese texts, including the *Kojiki* [49] and *Nihonshoki*. In his writings he sought to purify Shintō of the 'corrupting' influence of both Buddhism and Confucianism, as well as to restore the centrality of the divine status of the imperial family. Although he had never met MOTOORI NORINAGA, Hirata Atsutane considered himself one of the latter's disciples.

While purporting to present a purified Shintō, Atsutane actually introduced a number of new concepts, some of which modern scholars suggest were influenced by the writings of Jesuits active in China, including MATTEO RICCI and Didacus de Pantoja. For instance, he promoted the *kami* Ame-no-minaka-nushi in the divine hierarchy to the position of creator god, above Amaterasu, the sun goddess, and the other heavenly deities. Borrowing from Taoist cosmology, Atsutane argued that the creator deity lived in the region of the Polar Star, that Japan was the land closest to this region and, thus, its inhabitants were the purest human beings. The Japanese, he felt, were innately pure and had no need for codified laws since they could lead moral lives by following their hearts. However, their nature had been defiled by foreign ideas, teachings and objects. This aspect of his teaching helped to feed the growing anti-foreign feeling in 19th century Japan. Eventually, however, Atsutane's vehement attacks on neo-Confucianism and Buddhism led to his being censured by the shogunate and confined in 1841 to his home province, where he died two years later. His thought, however, did help to pave the way for the Meiji Restoration and for the revitalization of the religio-political ideology of the divinity of the imperial family. [3; 34: 168–76; 39; 61] (G.E.)

Hīravijaya [XIII] (1527–1595). Celebrated Śvetāmbara Jain teacher. He belonged to the Tapā ascetic order founded by Jagaccandra in 1228, and is noteworthy for the close relationship which he formed with the great Moghul emperor AKBAR. [30] The latter seems to have had some kind of connection with Jain monks in his youth, and so great was the fame of Hīravijaya that in 1587 Akbar summoned him to his court in Agra. After hearing the Jain preach that the true religion was the one which involved compassion for all creatures, Akbar issued a decree ordering the freeing of all prisoners and caged birds and banned the slaughter of animals on the Jain festival of Paryuṣan. It would be going too far, however, to suggest, as some Jain writers have done, that Akbar in some way 'converted' to Jainism. Hīravijaya's successor as head of the Tapā order, Vijayasena, continued the Jain relationship with Akbar, but Jahangir, who succeeded his father as emperor, was much more erratic in his patronage of the Jain community.

Hīravijaya was cremated near Diu in Gujarat, with a funeral monument being erected in his memory. His significance lay in his charismatic preaching and the illustrious teachers who claimed descent as pupils from him, for no significant writings are attributed to him. (P.D.)

Hirsch, Samson Raphael [XV] (1808–1888). Orthodox Jewish leader in Germany. He served as rabbi in Oldenburg, Emden and Nikolsburg before moving to Frankfurt-on-Main in 1851. At that time Reform Judaism was sweeping Germany and Orthodox Jewry was widely looked upon as outdated. Hirsch showed that Orthodoxy was compatible with a modern outlook. The official Frankfurt Jewish community, like most others in Germany, was Reform, so he organized a separatist, autonomous Orthodox community which formed the pattern for others throughout Germany. His motto, 'Torah together with secular studies', came to characterize what became known as 'Neo-Orthodoxy'.

Already in 1836–8, he wrote his two basic books *Nineteen Letters of Ben Uzziel* and *Horeb*. The latter explains the traditional commandments systematically, with their inner moral and significance. He divided all the biblical laws into six categories: doctrines (i.e. the historically revealed principles of Jewish faith); the principles of justice *vis-à-vis* one's fellow-man; statutes (i.e. laws without apparent motivation enforcing justice to all creatures); symbolic observances, which enrich human life; and service (i.e. prayer, sacrifice and other forms of divine worship). Nothing matters but the Torah, which was given in the desert to show that nationhood does not depend on a particular land or soil but solely on the Torah. This is not intended to teach philosophical truths but the observance of religious law. It is this observance which is the essence of Judaism, and inculcates justice and morality to the Jew and, through him, to all mankind. The ideal man is the 'Man of Israel' (*Yisraelmensch*), i.e. the law-observing Jew. The Jewish mission can be accomplished in exile; the ideal condition is one of emancipation in which the Jewish message can also reach the non-Jew [81. vol. 3: IX]. On the practical level, Hirsch founded an educational network combining religious and secular studies, an innovation in the world of Orthodoxy.

His translation of the Pentateuch, *Psalms* and prayer book into German (accompanied by commentaries) shows great faithfulness to the original. [42: 161–78] (G.W.)

Hit Harivaṃś [XI] (*c*.1502–1552). Devotee of Kṛṣṇa and Rādhā as a joint entity. His life is told in increasingly elaborate sectarian hagiographies: a Gauḍ Brahman and son of a court astrologer, he followed a dream-instruction from Rādhā to leave his home near Saharanpur (in the northern part of modern Uttar Pradesh) and to establish in Vrindaban the worship of a Kṛṣṇa-image called Rādhāvallabh ('Lover of Rādhā'). The name 'Harivaṃś' allows his followers to regard him as an incarnation of the flute (*vaṃśī*) of Kṛṣṇa (Hari), a fact which reflects his high status as the 'founder' of the Rādhāvallabhan devotional tradition. His *bhakti* is expressed in two principal works: *Rādhāsudhānidhi*, a Sanskrit panegyric to Rādhā, and *Caurāsī-pad* or '*Hit-caurāsī*', a popular hymnal in Brajbhāṣā Hindi. Both texts look back to the allegorically sensual poetry of JAYADEVA, but are also in turn the basis of profuse imitation and commentary by subsequent generations of Rādhāvallabhan poets. Eschewing the broader Kṛṣṇa-narrative, Harivaṃś concentrates on the theme of amorous sporting in the bowers of a supernal Vrindaban; the divine lovers Rādhā and Kṛṣṇa are served by groups of adoring female attendants or *sakhīs*, whose vicarious pleasure in observing the divine couple provides a model attitude for poet and devotee. The elevated status given to Rādhā by Harivaṃśa must have been the subject of reciprocal influence with the first-generation followers of CAITANYA and HARIDĀS; but later Rādhāvallabhan poets emphasize their distinct sectarian conception of divine love, *hita*, as the basis for an autonomous theology incipient in the works ascribed to Harivaṃś (who himself developed no systematic theological system) and based on the worship of the eponymous deity Rādhāvallabha, whose temple in Vrindaban remains in the custodianship of descendants of Harivaṃś. [40: 199–200; 101; 114] (R.S.)

Hogg, Alfred George [VI.A] (1875–1954). He was born at Ramleh, Egypt, of a missionary family. He entered Edinburgh University in 1893 to study as a preparation for the ordained ministry of the United Free Church of Scotland and for missionary work. Having graduated in philosophy and begun the study of theology, he experienced a deep crisis of faith. He recovered but only by accepting a liberal stance in respect of religious belief. In 1902 he was sent to Madras to teach at the Christian College. From 1903 until 1915 he taught ethics and economics and later became professor of philosophy until he was made principal of the College in 1928. He married Mary M. Patterson in 1907. Among his students he counted PAUL DAVID DEVANANDAN and SARVEPALLI RADHAKRISHNAN, the Hindu Neo-Vendantist who became Spalding Professor of Eastern Religions at Oxford and later President of independent India. Hogg published *Karma and Redemption* (1909), *Redemption from This World* (1922) and, after retirement, *The Christian Message to the Hindu* (1947). He argued against HENDRIK KRAEMER at and after the Tambaram conference of the International

Missionary Council in 1938. He returned to Scotland in 1939 and took up ordinary parish work in various places until he retired to Elie, on the Fife coast, where he died. [727] (T.T.)

Ho Hsien-ku. One of the EIGHT IMMORTALS of Taoism.

Homer [x] (*c.*850 BCE). According to HERODOTUS, recognized as 'the poet' by the Greeks, who attributed to him the *Iliad, Odyssey* and *Hymns*, poems which must in fact be dated between *c.*750 BCE and 650 BCE. The saga poet of the *Iliad* sang of the baneful wrath of Achilles which fulfilled the will of Zeus; of god-equal half-gods (heroes) who had death as their portion (*moira*) and whose 'self' was the body, not the feeble surviving *eidōlon* (image) or *psychē* (soul). 'Not even mighty Heracles, who was dearest to Zeus, escaped death' (*Iliad* 18.115–21). The image of the gods offsets the 'recognizable oxymoron' of the hero – the immortals (*athanatoi*), 'who live for ever', 'who live at ease', 'who dwell in the halls of Olympus'. The heroic mortality of the *Iliad* values physical vigour, skill in combat and counsel. *Aretē* or excellence is the key term for 'virtue' in the hero's code, 'always to be best, and not to shame my fathers' seed' [29: 54–5]. *Dikē* – the right way to treat someone or to be treated – is structured by status; 'justice' is certainly not the same for all [19: 123–7; 25: 1–27], since the Olympians, notably Zeus, embody and maintain the code which grants different *timé* (honour) to different heroes and to different gods. 'Diomedes pursued Cypris (Aphrodite), knowing she was not powerful, not a god who lords it over men in war' (*Iliad* 5.330–7). Zeus is supremely powerful even among the gods, and threatens injury to other Olympians (*Iliad* 8.12–13; 15.17–19). But it is wrong to be unrelenting if due recompense is made for insult (*Iliad* 9.496–501; [25: 16]) and in the end Achilles relents, has pity as Apollo protests that he should (*Iliad* 24. 32–54) and grants the corpse of Hector to Priam.

The gods are at once closely linked and sharply contrasted with the heroes. They share their strong wills and passions, their anthropomorphic form and feelings, but not their fate; they repeatedly protect and uphold the *timé* of the particular hero with whom their own honour is linked, and yet can affirm that the heroes are like the leaves that fall from a tree. They delight in the *knisē* or 'savoury odour' of meat roasting for the feast, but eat only immortal foods and have *ichor*, not blood, in their veins. They rejoice in the harp of Apollo, the Muses' song, and sleep at day's end. Though their *aretē, timé, biē* (prowess, honour, might) are greater, they like the heroes can be turned by a gift (sacrifice) or entreaty (prayer); they feel affection and pity for the heroes, and look on with approval at the battle-triumphs of their favourites. In visible form or through a mysterious access of power they intervene and protect, or by dread *atē* (infatuation, blind folly) Zeus destroys. Otto's argument that the power of the Olympians is 'natural' or 'rational' as opposed to 'magical' is right [32: 9; 37: 81–2] and helps to explain the Doddsian 'overdetermination' whereby both the hero and the god are fully responsible for the event: 'When his heart bids him and a god rouses him . . .' (*Iliad* 9.702). The jars or scales of Zeus may settle the sufferings or fate of the hero [32: 263–86]. But Agamemnon's loss of control was his own fault (*Iliad* 9.119–20); also the will of Zeus (*Iliad* 1. 5), fulfilled by the Erinys; and it was bound to happen, his *moira*.

The *Odyssey* is not war-saga, but maintains the same heroic values as the *Iliad*. Odysseus, the embattled hero, again and again demonstrates his resourceful endurance and cunning intelligence as he struggles homeward from Troy aided by Athena but facing the wrath of Poseidon. There is a great emphasis on, and interest in, female characters in this extended set of folk-tales in which the sorceress too is a goddess. *Odyssey* 1.28–43 once more indicates dual responsibility – men blame the gods for their woes, but are also themselves responsible for pains 'beyond their lot'. It is clear too that the suitors to Penelope are the villains in a straightforward and simplified sense lacking from the *Iliad*: 'Doom from the gods [*moira theōn*] and their own reckless acts have destroyed these men' (*Odyssey* 22.413). Odysseus passes through an apparently magical world but employs no magical tricks or superhuman powers; it is sufficient that Athena helps him to a just revenge won through divine favour and his own resourcefulness. No male god is ever so close to a hero as in the scene where Odysseus and Athena are seated under the sacred olive; she loves him for his intelligence and endurance (*Odyssey* 13.287–310).

The *Hymns* again exhibit heroic values, but

have connections also with local cults, notably the *Hymn to Demeter* with the cult at Eleusis. This describes how the mysteries were established by the goddess (aetiology). The epiphany of Demeter demonstrates the power of 'Homeric' epic: 'The goddess walked to the threshold, and filled the doorway with a divine radiance . . . She altered her stature . . . beauty spread about her, a lovely fragrance came from her sweet-smelling robes and from her immortal body a light shone afar . . . the well-built palace was filled with brightness as with lightning.'

Scenes of religious activity involving priests or seers – oaths, sacrifices, prayers, omens – are frequent and important in Homer. The gods respond to sacrifice. Zeus hesitates over Hector's fate because 'he has burnt many fat thighs of oxen to me'. The insulted priest of Apollo prays for vengeance: 'If ever I roofed your shrine, if ever I burnt to you fat thighs of oxen . . . fulfil my prayer!' Homeric prayers show that the gods are all-powerful in a religious or psychological sense: they are able to perform the request if they will. [3: 119–25; 6: 1–27; 13; 17; 18; 19: 117–27; 25: 1–32; 29: 1–68; 31: 134–79; 32; 37; 55; 56; 57] (J.P.K.)

Hōnen [IV] [Genkū] (1133–1212). Japanese Buddhist priest, founder of the Jōdoshū (Pure Land Sect) and the representative figure of the new spirit of Kamakura era Buddhism. Hōnen was born in Mimasaka province (now Okayama prefecture) in the midst of the struggles for hegemony between the nobility and military clans. He was sent to a nearby Tendai monastery in 1141, after his father was killed in battle. In 1145 he started studying at the Tendai headquarters on Mt Hiei near Kyoto and was ordained a monk two years later at the age of 14. He soon gained the reputation of being a very dedicated monk, extremely well versed in the entire canon of Buddhist scriptures. GENSHIN's *Ōjōyōshū* made a deep impression on him and led him to discover the writings of the Chinese Pure Land master SHAN-TAO (613–681), whom he would later declare to be his only master. The reading of Shan-tao's words, 'Give yourself with undivided mind to the repetition of the Name of the Buddha of endless life (Amida)', made him take the decisive step. In 1775, at the age of 42, Hōnen left Mt Hiei to go and live in the outskirts of Kyoto, where he started preaching his Pure Land doctrine and gathering disciples around him. This is seen as the founding date of the Jōdoshū.

Devotion to Amida and the recitation of his Name (*nenbutsu*), with the belief that thereby one would be reborn in Amida's Pure Land, were an integral part of the many-sided Tendai practices, and had been propagated among the people since the 10th century. In monastic circles, however, the stress had been laid on meditative visualization of Amida and, among the people, the *nenbutsu* was often used as a magical formula to avert calamities. Hōnen's revolutionary step consisted in propagating the recitation of the *nenbutsu* with faith in Amida's saving activity (vows) as the *only* practice and path to liberation, bestowed by Amida himself and available to ordinary people in this degenerate age (*mappō*). He thereby stressed the superiority of simple recitation over all meditative practices and severed all links of the *nenbutsu* with magical practices. Thus, Hōnen came to found the first independent Pure Land Buddhist sect.

In the beginning of the 13th century a movement to have this new sect condemned as heresy developed among the Tendai and Nara sects, which led to Hōnen's banishment to the island of Skikoku in 1207. Allowed to return to Kyoto in 1211, he died there the next year. At the request of the regent Kanezane, Hōnen wrote down his doctrine in the *Senchaku hongan nenbutsu shū* ('Collection of Passages on the *Nenbutsu* Selected by the Primal Vow') in 1198. [41] (J.V.B.)

Hooker, Richard [VI.A] (1554–1600). Anglican theologian. He was born in Heavitree near Exeter, where he was educated at the Grammar School. In 1568 he entered Corpus Christi College, Oxford under the patronage of Bishop John Jewel of Salisbury and graduated in 1574. He became a fellow of the college and deputy professor of Hebrew. Ordained in 1581, he became rector of Drayton Beauchamp, near Aylesbury, in 1584. A few months later he became Master of the Temple in London. He was soon in dispute with Walter Travers, Reader in the Temple and a convinced Calvinistic Puritan. In 1588 he married Joan Churchman, his landlord's daughter. Hooker resigned from the Temple in 1591 and became rector of Boscombe near Salisbury but remained in London in the home of his in-laws. He later became rector of Bishopsbourne, near Canterbury, where he died. Most of his last years were devoted to writing *Of the Laws of Ecclesiastical Polity*. This work of apology is the single most important systematic work of its kind in the history of the Church of England. [362; 524; 574] (T.T.)

Horemheb [VII] (14th century BCE). King of Egypt of Dynasty 18, reigned 1335–1308 BCE. The successor of Kings Ay and TUTANKHAMUN, Horemheb was originally commander of the army under AKHENATEN (*c.*1355 BCE), and prepared a fine tomb at Saqqara. However, as king (1335–1308 BCE), he was responsible for restoring the traditional gods after the Amarna heresy, and was ultimately buried with other rulers in the Valley of the Kings at Thebes. (A.R.D.)

Hosea [XV] (8th century BCE). Israelite prophet, who prophesied in the northern kingdom of Israel during the reign of Jeroboam II. The only information concerning his life is contained in the biblical book of *Hosea*, and consists of a few meagre details. It states that in his first vision he was commanded by God to take a harlot as wife to symbolize Israel's faithlessness to God through its flirtation with Baal, the heathen god. Commentators sought to get round the literal meaning by interpreting the story as a parable. He married a woman called Gomer who was unfaithful to him; the prophet divorced her but they were later remarried. The concept of love is central to his thought: it is the basis of the God–Israel relationship: even if Israel's love becomes deflected to other gods, God's love for Israel is eternal and eventually Israel will return to its true love.

Hosea dwells at length on Israel's sins and punishment. God is angry at Israel's transgressions, which are both cultic (the turning to idolatry) and ethical (primarily in disobeying the Ten Commandments). Immoral acts are not expatiated merely by the offering of sacrifices and performance of the commandments. God will punish the people, abolishing all joyful festivals, destroying the land and removing its inhabitants. However, God's continuing love will culminate in his forgiveness, following the people's sincere repentance for its wicked ways. [38: 3]

Some scholars divide the book into *Hosea* 1–3, dating from the 9th century BCE and containing the biographical information about the prophet, and *Hosea* 4–14, dating from the mid-8th century BCE by an unnamed prophet. [4] (G.W.)

Hsien-yüan. *See* HUANG TI.

Hsüan-tsang [IV] (*c.*600–*c.*664). Famed Chinese scholar-monk, pilgrim to India, and translator of Buddhist texts. Born into an ancient aristocratic family whose lineage can be traced back to the Later Han dynasty, Hsüan-tsang is credited with the traditional virtues of quick intelligence and incisive insight. Finding the Yogācāra thought he encountered in China – probably that of PARAMĀRTHA's translations – difficult to understand, he resolved to journey to India in search of the true teaching. Undeterred by an imperial refusal to grant leave, he left China and reached India after an arduous journey. At one point he was captured by pirates and was about to be executed and his flesh offered to their goddess, when a series of prodigies consequent upon his entrance into deep concentration convinced them that they would be better served to spare his life. Arriving at the great monastic university of Nālandā, he learned Sanskrit and studied under Śīlabhadra, the disciple of DHARMAPĀLA. He returned to China in 645, bringing with him numerous Indian Buddhist texts. He recorded his journey in a detailed travelogue, the *Ta-t'ang hsi-yü-chi* ('Record of the Western Journey') [14]. He was accorded honour by the Emperor T'ai-tsung and appointed head of a vast translation project.

Unlike Paramārtha, who could never count on continued support because of the chaotic times in which he lived, Hsüan-tsang did have the good fortune to live in peaceful times and his efforts were well supported by the Imperial court. His many translations represented almost all the schools of Indian Buddhism he had encountered. His translations of Dharmapāla's Yogācāra commentaries established this lineage as the orthodox version of Yogācāra in China and Japan, known as the Fa-hsiang or Hossō school, studied even today in Buddhist universities and monasteries. [132]

His pilgrimage to India was taken as the model for the 16th-century Chinese folk novel *The Journey to the West* by Wu Ch'eng-en [263]. This famed novel weaves Taoist and Buddhist themes in presenting the adventures and misadventures of Hsüan-tsang and his band of half-animal, half-human protectors, the most central of which is 'Monkey', whose mischievous behaviour has entertained many a reader. [247] (J.K.)

Huai-hai. *See* PAI-CHANG HUAI-HAI.

Huang Ti [V] [Hsien-yüan]. The Yellow Emperor, who lived in mythical times and is credited with being ruler of the earliest Chinese 'empire'. He is a great culture hero, associated with such important inventions as the calendar, musical scales and the classical theories of medicine. For religion he is the First Ancestor of Taoism. He attained immortal transcendency and became the prototype of those adepts who ascended to heaven in broad daylight. The historian Ssu-ma Ch'ien (?145–?90 BCE) puts it thus:

> The Yellow Emperor took copper from Mt. Shou and smelted it . . . to make a bronze tripod (i.e., the first cauldron of the alchemical tradition). The tripod-vessel having been finished, a dragon let down its beard and came down to greet the Yellow Emperor. The latter mounted it together with more than seventy of his retinue. The petty servants, unable to get on, all held on to the dragon's beard and pulled at the Yellow Emperor's bow, causing them (beard and bow) to fall to the ground. The people gazed up at the sky and saw that the Yellow Emperor had already ascended. Then they held his bow and the dragon's beard in their arms and wailed . . .' [60: XXVIII]

Huang Ti played an important role during Han times (202 BCE–220 CE) in the Taoistic philosophy and religion called Huang-lao (thus associating LAO TZU and the Yellow Emperor). At that time he assumed the character of a Taoist divinity under the name Huang-Lao Chün (Lord Huang-Lao). Many of the Taoist texts are attributed to the Yellow Emperor, and under his personal name, Hsien-yüan, he is still alive in Chinese religion. [47; 42; 34] (L.T.)

Hubbard, L. Ron [XIX] [Lafayette Ronald Hubbard] (1911–1986). Founder of the religious philosophy of Scientology ® [19]. Born in Nebraska, Hubbard's early life is a subject of controversy [36: 693; 38: 128–30; 39], but in 1950 he published *Dianetics*, a book that was to change not only his life, but the lives of numerous others.

Dianetics ® is 'a system for the analysis, control and development of human thought which also provides techniques for increased ability, rationality, and freedom from the discovered single source of aberations and psychosomatic ills' [19: 6]. The technique employs an 'auditor' who asks questions, often using an 'E-meter', which gives readings that the auditor interprets as indications of a person's consciously or unconsciously recalling emotional experiences ('engrams') that have been recorded on to part of their minds during this or a previous life. A 'Clear', unobstructed by 'engrams', is 'the optimal individual'. [20: 421]

The Church of Scientology was founded in 1954. There has been some debate about whether it is a religion, but several courts have ruled that, for tax purposes, it is; in 1983, for example, the High Court in Australia ruled that it was because: 'The essence of Scientology is a belief in reincarnation and concern with the passage of the "thetan" or the spirit or soul of man through eight "dynamics" and the ultimate release of the "thetan" from the bondage of the body.' Hubbard himself always insisted upon the pragmatic nature of Scientology: he declared that the first principle of his philosophy was that wisdom is meant for anyone; the second principle was that it should be capable of being applied; and the third principle was that it is valuable only if it is true or if it works.

Hubbard gave thousands of lectures and wrote over 500 books, over 23 million copies of which are said to have been sold. Among the activities associated with Scientologists are the Alliance for the Preservation of Religious Liberty, a drug rehabilitation program (Narconon), New Era Publications and campaigns against, for example, psychiatric practices and the CIA.

Throughout his life Hubbard was surrounded by controversy. Scientologists claim that they have gained their spiritual freedom, been given new communication skills and learned ways of handling apparently intractable problems. Opponents claim that Scientologists are controlled by a vast bureaucracy that is interested only in their money, and that scientology can result in their breaking off previous relationships or ending up in life-long debts or signing billion-year contracts to work for the movement for next to no pay. Court cases have featured Scientologists as both plaintiffs and defendants. In 1979 Hubbard's wife was among the (then) top officials of the church convicted of theft of Government documents [36: 694]. From 1968 to 1980 restrictions were imposed on foreigners entering the United Kingdom to study or work for Scientology.

Since Hubbard's death both Dianetics and the Church of Scientology have continued to be controversial. They have, however, also succeeded in attracting increasing numbers of new converts, who are ready to testify to the remarkable contribution that Hubbard has made to their lives. (E.B.)

Hudson Taylor, James [VI.A] (1832–1905). English missionary. He was born in Barnsley, England into a Methodist family. As a youth he determined to be a missionary in China. At the age of 17 he underwent a conversion experience. As preparation for missionary work he studied medicine and surgery at Hull and London, and learned the Chinese language as well as Latin, Hebrew and Greek. In 1853 he went to China as a member of the Chinese Evangelization Society (CES). For four years he worked with difficulty in Shanghai and Ningpo and left the CES in 1857. He tried to support himself but his health broke and he returned to England in 1860. For the next six years he tried unsuccessfully to join other mission boards. In June 1865 he decided to form his own missionary organization and he formed the China Inland Mission (CIM). He and a group of young missionaries arrived in China in 1866 with no denominational or other form of support. By 1882 the mission had expanded to eight of the hitherto closed provinces of China. Eventually the CIM became the biggest Christian missionary organization in China and was the precursor of so-called 'faith-missions'. Hudson Taylor became famous as a missionary statesman and travelled throughout Europe and North America. In 1865 he published *China: Its Spiritual Needs and Claims*. From 1875 he edited *China's Millions*, a missionary magazine, in which he attacked the British government for its part in the opium trade. In 1881 he opened a school in Chefoo to which his missionaries were obliged to send their children for 12 years of education. Up until his death he led the CIM from its headquarters in China. [118; 654] (T.T.)

Hügel, (Baron) Friedrich von [VI.A] (1852–1925). Roman Catholic philosopher. He was born in Florence. His parents were Roman Catholic though his mother was born and raised a Scottish Presbyterian. They moved to England in 1867. Von Hügel was to a large extent self-taught. In 1870 he suffered an attack of typhus which left his health permanently damaged. Following a religious crisis he was restored to faith under the influence of a Dominican priest he met in Vienna in 1870. He was married in 1873 and spent the rest of his life in London. He was a friend of the Catholic 'modernists' ALFRED LOISY and GEORGE TYRRELL. He supported them when they were condemned by the Roman Catholic Church. He also wrote extensively on spirituality and mysticism. His chief work was *The Mystical Element of Religion as Studied in St Catherine of Genoa and her Friends* (1909). He also wrote works on the philosophy of religion, among them *Eternal Life* (1912) and *Essays and Addresses on the Philosophy of Religion* (1921). [48; 70; 753] (T.T.)

Hui-neng [IV] [Japanese: Eno] (638–713). The sixth patriarch in the Southern tradition of Ch'an Buddhism, a tradition which emphasized sudden awakening. Legend has it that Hui-neng was an illiterate disciple of Hung-jen (602–675), the fifth Ch'an patriarch. It is said that he bested the knowledgeable SHEN-HSIU (600–706) with a poem on the nature of awakening and secretly received the patriarchal robe signifying the spiritual succession of the Ch'an lineage. This story from the *Platform Sūtra of the Sixth Patriarch* is not accepted by scholars as historical. Rather it reflects the efforts of Hui-neng's disciple SHEN-HUI (648–758) and the success of the Southern School in eventually overshadowing the Northern School, which claimed Shen-hsiu as the true sixth patriarch. The Southern School emphasized the attainment of sudden and immediate awakening in contrast to the gradual approach advocated by the Northern School. The Southern School was also iconoclastic and rejected a reliance on written texts and formalities. The major significance of Hui-neng is as a representative of this shift, which came to characterize the mainstream of Ch'an Buddhism. [156; 261] (P.L.S.)

Ḥunain ibn Isḥāq [VI.A] (808–873). Nestorian Christian scholar. He was personal physician to Caliph al-Mutawakkil. When the Abbasid Caliph al-Ma'mun founded the Dar al Hikmah ('House of Wisdom') in 830, most of the professors were Nestorian Christians and a major translation enterprise was undertaken under the leadership of Hunain, who became head of the house. For every book translated, the Caliph paid him its weight in gold. Assisted by his son Ishaq, his nephew Hubaish ibn al-Hasan and by ʿIsa ibn Yahya, Hunain was responsible for the translation via Syriac into Arabic of an immense number of Greek works of medicine, mathematics, science and philosophy. In this way the Syriac-speaking Nestorian community became the transmission culture by which Greek learning was brought to the Muslim world. [5: XIV; 34] (D.J.M.)

Hung Hsiu-ch'üan [V] (1814–1864). Founder of the Religion of Complete Peace-and-Equality (*t'ai-p'ing tao*), from which developed the T'ai-p'ing revolutionary movement (1851–66) that shook the Manchu Ch'ing dynasty (1644–1911) to its foundations, and was certainly the most devastating civil war in pre-20th-century Chinese history. The military and political aspects of the T'ai-p'ing movement, its inspiration, its moral code and its social ideals derived entirely from the religious teachings of the founder.

Born into a poor Hakka peasant family (a Chinese ethnic group settled in south China), Hung Hsiu-ch'üan's ambitions to rise above this status were frustrated by repeated failures in the imperial examinations. At the same time he had two experiences that turned his later career towards religion. The first of these was hearing a missionary evangelist and acquiring some Christian pamphlets (1836). The second was a remarkable shamanic 'initiation' (1837). During more than a month of 'sickness', Hung undertook a trance-journey to Heaven, where his body was cut open and his inner organs replaced; he then received a seal of office and a demon-exorcizing sword. Thus far the experience is typical for shamans; the remarkable part is his later identification of the deities in Heaven as the Heavenly Father and the Heavenly Mother of Jesus and of Jesus as elder brother and of himself as younger brother. God the Father commissioned him with the title 'Sovereign Ch'üan, Celestial King of the Great Way of Complete Peace-and-Equality' (*t'ai-p'ing t'ien-wang ta-tao chün-wang Ch'üan*). It took some time for the meaning of these two experiences to become clear to Hung. After that awakening he was baptized – or, rather, baptized himself (1843). During 1847 Hung learned more about Christianity from the Southern Baptist missionary Issachar Roberts, and for the first time acquired a translation of the entire Bible. After this his confidence in his personal understanding and in his own religious mission became absolute, and he began his own evangelistic efforts in earnest. The first organization of converts was called the 'Society of God-Worshippers' (*pai shang-ti hui*) among a community of Hakka mountain people in Kuanghsi province.

The further history of the T'ai-p'ing movement is beyond the scope of this brief biography. During the course of its violent history Hung Hsiu-ch'üan became the pawn – or at least the victim – of various other leaders. However, his own charisma continued to be unique, and his teachings and edicts as the Celestial King (*t'ien wang*) had the force of sacred writ. His brand of Christianity, while hardly orthodox, incorporated such tenets as worship of a monotheistic God, a revised version of the Ten Commandments, equality of the sexes, monogamy for all but the top leaders and a puritanical moral code. The followers of the religion were fanatically devoted to their beliefs, dying heroically as imperial forces eventually overran the T'ai-p'ing capital at Nanking. By then Hung Hsiu-ch'üan had already committed suicide. [27; 36; 48] (L.T.)

Hus, Jan [VI.A] [John Huss] (1372/3–1415). Czech religious reformer. He was born in the village of Husinec in Southern Bohemia. He went to Prague University around 1390 and gained his master's degree in 1396. He joined the faculty of liberal arts in 1398 and became dean in 1401. Ordained priest in 1400, he began the study of theology but he never completed his doctorate. In 1402 he became the preacher at Bethlehem Church, Prague, where sermons were preached in Czech. He soon became involved in the national Czech reform movement. Influenced by the political and theological ideas of JOHN WYCLIFF, he began to apply them in Bethlehem Church and translated the work of Wycliff into Czech. At first he was supported by his bishop, who even appointed him preacher to the Prague synod in 1405. However, other clergy reacted negatively to Hus's attacks on clerical morals. He eventually lost the bishop's support and was forbidden to preach. He was excommunicated by the pope and eventually had to leave Prague. During exile he wrote his chief work, *De ecclesia*. He was brought before the Council of Constance in 1414, found guilty of heresy and burned at the stake. [706; 747; 748] (T.T.)

Ḥusayn ibn ʿAlī [XII] [Sayyid al-Shuhadāʾ, 'the Prince of Martyrs'] (626–680). Third Imām of Shiʿite Islam. The second son of ʿALĪ and FĀṬIMA (and thus a grandson of MUḤAMMAD), Ḥusayn was born in Medina, but later moved to Kūfa when his father established his capital there. Soon after ʿAlī's death in 661, Ḥusayn's elder brother ḤASAN abdicated his claim to the caliphate and returned to Medina, where he led a life of retirement for some eight years.

Ḥusayn remained with Ḥasan until the latter's death in 669, when he was recognized by ʿAlid partisans as the legitimate ruler of the Muslim community. But in spite of requests from his Iraqi followers to rebel against Muʿāwiya, the Umayyad caliph in Syria, he continued to adopt a politically quietist position similar to that of ʿAlī under the first three caliphs.

When Muʿāwiya died in 680, however, the caliphate passed directly to his son Yazīd, causing widespread outrage. Ḥusayn now acceded to Iraqi requests to rebel, and set off for Kūfa, where he had been promised massive support. A small party consisting of Ḥusayn, his family and over 70 men was intercepted by troops loyal to the Umayyad governor of Iraq; they were surrounded near Kūfa, at a site known as Karbalāʾ. On the 10th of Muḥarram (10 October) Ḥusayn and most of his supporters were massacred in the course of a brief engagement.

The events of Karbalāʾ and, in particular, the martyrdom of Ḥusayn proved a major turning-point for Shiʿism, and may be said to mark its beginning as a distinct religious movement. Shiʿites commemorate Ḥusayn's death annually during Muḥarram with passion plays, sermons and processions, often involving self-mutilation. A cultus has grown up round his self-sacrifice, which is understood as a redemptive act through which his followers are assured salvation. [19; 33: s.v.; 92] (D.M.)

Hussein, Sheikh [XII] (14th century?). Muslim missionary and saint of Bale, Ethiopia. He is regarded by many Muslims in Ethiopia, Northern Kenya and Somalia as their greatest saint, and his annual festival is an important religious and social event which draws huge crowds of pilgrims to his tomb in Arussi in Central Ethiopia. It has been established [12] that Sheikh Hussein lived 29 generations ago, that is at least 600 years. He was, according to the traditions of the local Galla-Oromo people, born in Anaadzina in Bale province where his father also lived, whose name was Sayyid Ibrahim al-Malkai, who claimed descent from ʿAqīl ibn Abī Ṭālib, a cousin of MUḤAMMAD. Sheikh Hussein was a teacher of Islam, especially of Islamic law in all its details. Numerous legends are told about him and the many miracles he is credited with. During celebrations, hymns are sung in his honour. His teachings demonstrate a spirit of gentleness, love and compassion. [12] (J.K.)

Hutchinson, Anne [VI.A] [née Marbury] (1591–1643). New England religious leader. She was born in Alford, Lincolnshire. She married William Hutchinson, a merchant, and raised a large family. She came under the influence of John Cotton, the vicar of a Boston, Lincolnshire parish around 1630, and in 1634 followed him with her family to Boston, Massachusetts. She advocated an extreme form of Cotton's teaching concerning the powerlessness of human endeavour in achieving the state of election. Not only should the elect bear witness to the presence of the Spirit but, she argued, the state of grace meant the actual indwelling of the Holy Spirit. She accused the Christian ministers of Massachusetts of preaching faith by works. The ensuing dispute brought condemnation at the hands of the General Court of the Boston congregation in 1637. She was excommunicated and had to flee to Rhode

Island. Dissension arose again and she left for New Netherland, where she and her children were massacred by Indians. [60; 553; 554] (T.T.)

Hwadam. *See* SŎ KYŎNGDŎK.

Hyakujō Ekai. *See* PAI-CHANG HUAI-HAI.

Hystaspes [XXVI] [Greek form of Vištāspa]. ZOROASTER's patron. He bore the hereditary title *kavi* (Middle Persian: *kay*), and his dynasty appears in FIRDAUSĪ's *Shāhnāma* as that of the Kayāniāns. In Vedic, *kavi* meant mantic seer; and according to Zoroastrian tradition Vištāspa ascended in spirit to Paradise, and saw the future happiness awaiting him there, before he accepted the faith. A Zoroastrian apocalyptic tradition became associated with him, and the *Oracles of Hystaspes*, a Greco-Persian work of probably the 3rd century BCE, are partly known through early Christian writings. The father of Darius the Great (*see* CYRUS AND HIS SUCCESSORS) was also called Hystaspes, probably after the eastern Iranian prince. [5: vol. 1: 187–8, 249, 279–81, vol. 3: XI] (M.B.)

I

Ibiam, Francis Akanu [VI.A] (1906–). Nigerian Christian figure. He was born in Unwana and educated at the Scottish mission's Hope Waddell Training Institution, Calabar. Unusually, he went on to qualify in medicine at St Andrew's University; he then received an unprecedented appointment as a medical missionary of the Church of Scotland in Nigeria. For 20 years he opened new and improved existing medical services. Knighted in 1950, the following year he became Principal of the Hope Waddell Institution. An impressive, forthright personality, he was by this time one of the few African lay Christians whose name was widely known beyond his country. He chaired the 1958 Ibadan conference which led to the formation of the All Africa Conference of Churches; he became in 1961 one of the six Presidents of the World Council of Churches. At Nigerian independence he became Governor of the Eastern Region. He continued to promote Christian enterprises; the emergence of a Nigerian Bible Society and a Christian medical fellowship owed much to him. In the Civil War he identified strongly with his 'Christian' region, renouncing his knighthood in protest at British support for the federal government. Retained as adviser to General Ojukwu, the Biafran leader, his international contacts were important in obtaining international sympathy and relief supplies for Biafra. After the war he again worked in the stricken hospitals of his home area, and settled there as a traditional ruler. [538: 159, 170] (A.F.W.)

Ibn ʿAbbās, ʿAbd Allāh [XII] (*d. c.*687). Cousin of MUḤAMMAD, prominent Muslim authority for interpretative material relating to the Qur'ān. Muslim tradition has ascribed to Ibn ʿAbbās the status of being the 'most knowledgeable' of the companions of Muḥammad in Qur'anic interpretation; his name is attached therefore to a vast number of reports on the topic. He is especially known for his authority in establishing the meaning of obscure words; thus, many of the texts which are ascribed to him relate to lexicographical matters: *Al-Lughāt fī'l-Qur'ān* ('The Dialects/languages of the Qur'ān'), *Gharīb al-Qur'ān* ('The Difficult Words of the Qur'ān') and *Masā'il Nāfiʿ ibn al-Azraq*, concerning words known only by the Arabian Bedouin tribes.

Ibn ʿAbbās appears to provide a symbol of the formative Muslim community, embodying those abilities and understandings most cherished by the later generations who cite him as their authority. Ibn ʿAbbās also acted as the person through whom those people conducted their arguments over legitimate procedures and legal deductions, especially during the ʿAbbasid period, when the ability to be able to call upon a name of a worthy ancestor was important. In that sense, Ibn ʿAbbās is mythic, in that his life is embellished with those elements which are important to those people creating the story. [40; 104: VIII] (A.R.)

Ibn ʿAbd al-Wahhāb, Muḥammad [XII] (1703–1787). Islamic theologian and eponym of the Wahhābiyya (also known as the Muwaḥḥidūn, the 'Unitarians'), the dominant strand of Islam in Saudi Arabia. Born in ʿUyayna in central Arabia, he studied in Medina and travelled and lived in Baṣra and eastern Arabia until he returned to his birthplace, where he worked on what has become his most famous book, *Kitāb al-tawḥīd* ('The Book of Divine Unity'). His doctrine was accepted by Muḥammad ibn Saʿūd, who became responsible for the political aspects of the foundation of the Wahhābī community. Ibn ʿAbd al-Wahhāb's doctrine follows the line of IBN ḤANBAL and IBN TAYMIYYA, especially with its rejection of saint worship and other popular practices, all of which are seen as impinging upon the worship of the one true God, making people guilty of the major Islamic sin of *shirk* ('polytheism'). [34: 'Wahhābīya'; 125: II] (A.R.)

Ibn (al-)ʿArabī, Muḥyī'l-dīn [XII] [al-Shaykh al-Akbar, 'the Greatest Master'] (1165–1240). The supreme theorist of philosophical mysticism in Islam. Of Arab stock, he was born in the Spanish town of Murcia. His father may have been chief minister to the local ruler, Ibn Mardanīsh. Following the latter's defeat by the Almohads in 1173, the family moved to Seville, where his father again rose to a prominent position.

Although he received a traditional education, Ibn al-ʿArabī embarked on mystical training at an early age and was formally inducted into a Ṣūfī order at the age of 20. His spiritual development was rapid, involving visions and, according to his own testimony, the transmission of knowledge from occult sources.

In the 1190s he travelled widely in Spain and North Africa, including Tunis (1194), and Fez (1195). A pilgrimage to Mecca (1202–4) proved a major turning-point. During a two-year sojourn there, he composed a number of works, including an important collection of mystical odes, the *Tarjumān al-ashwāq* ('The Interpreter of Desires'), addressed as love poems to a young Persian woman. It was at this period that he began his major work, the *Futūḥāt al-Makkiyya* ('The Meccan Revelations') and had a vision in which he believed himself confirmed as 'The Seal of Muḥammadan Sainthood' [55, p. 8].

Further travels took him to Mosul (1204–5), Cairo (1206), where his life was threatened by orthodox opponents, Konya in Anatolia (from 1210), where he formed important Ṣūfī contacts, Baghdad (1211), Aleppo (1213), Mecca again (1214), and Malatya in Anatolia (1215–*c.*1220) where he instructed a growing band of disciples.

From 1223 until his death in 1240, he took up residence in Damascus at the request of the governor. Here he completed the *Futūḥāt*, collected his poetry into a *Dīwān*, and wrote his single most influential work, the *Fuṣūṣ al-ḥikam* ('The Bezels of Wisdom'), a short synopsis of his teachings. On his death, he was buried in a mausoleum at the foot of Mount Qāsiyūn, which is still a place of pilgrimage.

Ibn al-ʿArabī has been described as 'the most prolific of all Sufi writers' [35: s.v.]; according to one estimate, he wrote some 400 works, although some of these are extremely short. Of the many surviving titles, few have been printed. The most important is the massive *Futūḥāt al-Makkiyya*, containing 560 chapters (2,500 pages in one edition) setting out his full mystical doctrine – 'a veritable compendium of the esoteric sciences in Islam' [96: 98]. More popular has been the *Fuṣūṣ al-ḥikam*, each of whose 27 chapters deals with the human and spiritual nature of a particular prophet, serving as a vehicle for a specific aspect of divine wisdom. At least 35 commentaries have been written on this short book. Other works include treatises on cosmology, practical aspects of the mystical life, Qur'anic sciences, Islamic law and Prophetic Traditions.

An important characteristic of Ibn al-ʿArabī's Ṣūfī writings is his claim to have composed them as a result of direct inspiration. Of the *Futūḥāt* he writes: 'God dictated to me everything that I have written through the angel of inspiration' [96: 98], while he claimed that the *Fuṣūṣ* had been revealed to him by the Prophet in a single dream.

Ibn al-ʿArabī's doctrine is highly complex and has long been the subject of involved debate. It is impossible to do it justice in a few words. His entire system is known as *waḥdat al-wujūd*, ('the singleness of being'), often misleadingly described as a form of pantheism, monism or 'existential monism'. According to this system, there is a single Reality, a 'seamless garment' of Being, of which all things are modes of expression. Within this schema, God (expressed as 'the Reality' – *al-ḥaqq*) is neither wholly transcendent nor wholly immanent, being both manifest in creation and hidden from it.

Creation is a process of self-manifestation (*tajallī*), whereby the Reality comes to see Itself in the mirror of contingent beings. Humanity, especially the Perfect Man (*al-insān al-kāmil*), is the link between the poles of Being, representing the Reality to the cosmos and the cosmos to the Reality. What distinguishes Ibn al-ʿArabī's system from others is the range of startling and original insights that emerge from his vision of absolute oneness, with profound consequences for theology, ethics, and mysticism. [5; 61: part 1; 115: 263–74] (D.M.)

Ibn Bābūya, Abū Jaʿfar Muḥammad [xii] [al-Shaykh al-Ṣadūq] (*c.*918–991). Outstanding Shiʿite scholar noted for his collection of religious traditions. Born in Qumm, a major Iranian centre of Shiʿite scholarship, he travelled widely in search of Imamite traditions. His famous collection of materials relating to the Imāms, *Man lā yahḍuruhu'l-faqīh*, came to be recognized as one of the 'Four Books' of Shiʿite tradition. Al-Ṣadūq's work in this field represents the apogee of the purely traditionalist approach in Shiʿism, soon to be qualified by the rationalism introduced by his pupil, AL-SHAYKH AL-MUFĪD. Al-Ṣadūq wrote altogether about 300 works, among which the *ʿIlal al-sharīʿa* and *ʿUyūn al-akhbār* are well known. [35: 'Ibn Bābawayh'; 89: IV] (D.M.)

Ibn Daud, Abraham [xv] (*c.*1110–1180). Spanish Jewish historian and philosopher. Born in Cordova, he lived his later years in Toledo, where he was martyred. The first Jewish Aristotelian philosopher, his attempt to harmonize Judaism and Aristotelianism is to be found in his *Emunah Ramah* ('Exalted Faith'). The work was motivated by a query concerning the apparent ambivalence of the Bible on the subject of human free-will. He found it necessary first to expound physics and metaphysics (in an Aristotelian spirit) so as to provide a foundation for the understanding of philosophy. However, the truths reached by philosophy with such difficulty have always been known to Judaism and there is no conflict between true philosophy and religion. Thus he discerns Aristotle's ten categories in *Psalm* 139. His theology, philosophy and psychology rely extensively on the works of IBN SĪNĀ (Avicenna). In his insistence on the freedom of human action, however, he diverges from the Arab Aristotelians. In asserting that events deriving from human freedom are not known beforehand to God he limits divine knowledge. From the Arab philosophers he derives the view of prophecy as the illumination of the human spirit by the Active Intellect but adds the qualification that prophecy is experienced only by Jews and only in the Holy Land. His work was soon overshadowed by the writings of MOSES MAIMONIDES [39: XII]

As a historian Ibn Daud is known for his *Sefer ha-Kabbalah* ('The Book of Tradition'). Like other works of medieval Jewish historiography, this had ulterior motivation. He wished to show the unbroken chain of tradition leading all the way from Moses to the rabbinical authorities of his own time, especially in Spain. This was directed against the Karaites who propounded a biblical fundamentalism which denied all later rabbinic interpretation and legislation. [19] (G.W.)

Ibn Ezra, Abraham [xv] (1093–1167). Spanish Jewish Bible commentator and philosopher. Born in Tudela, already in his youth he was a noted Hebrew poet and was proficient in many branches of learning. Much of his life was spent in wandering, and he is known to have spent time in North Africa, Italy, France and England. A prolific writer, he is said to have written 108 books although far fewer are extant. He is best known for his Bible commentary. He probably wrote on the entire Hebrew Bible but parts have been lost [18: X]. As an outstanding Hebrew grammarian, his exegesis expounds the literal meaning of the text, often considering philological problems. Possessed of an independent mind and a sharp critical sense, he was the first to hint that the book of *Isaiah* may have been the product of two authors and that MOSES may not have written the entire Pentateuch. His biblical commentary is also the main source for his Neoplatonic philosophy. He sees the universe as divided into three worlds: the highest is the eternal world soul of separate intelligences or angels; the intermediate world is also eternal and consists of nine spheres, including the seven planets; and the lowest contains the four elements and their various combinations and was created in time by the angels as agents of God. Man is the noblest of creatures, whose most important activity is knowledge of God [39: XI]. Ibn Ezra's commentary was widely regarded as second only to that of RASHI. He was also a versatile Hebrew poet. His poems range from the philosophical (on the nature of God, the soul, etc.) to the sacred (many entered the liturgy) and to the national and the secular (including a long poem on chess). [81: vol. 1: IX] (G.W.)

Ibn Gabirol, Solomon [XV] (*c.*1020–*c.*1057). Jewish poet and philosopher in Moorish Spain. He was of a melancholy disposition and his short life was tragic and lonely. He was a noted poet by the age of 16. Hundreds of his poems have survived. His secular poems are suffused with a strong sense of beauty, and include poems on nature, wine, ethics and love, as well as national verse in which he deplores the Jewish exile and expresses his longing for the messiah. In his sacred poems, he eulogizes God, before whose might man shrinks. He expresses the mystic longing to merge into God. The strength of his love for God is matched by his love for the Jewish people, of whose suffering he complains bitterly, begging God to redeem them. Many of his religious poems entered both the Sephardi and Ashkenazi prayerbooks, especially for the festivals; they include poems of devotion and penitence, both national and individual. The best known of his philosophical poems is the long work *Keter Malkhut* ('Royal Crown') which praises God's attributes and extols his creation – the universe, the soul, and man. [81: vol. 1: IX]

He was the first Jewish philosopher in Spain. His main philosophical work is *Mekor Ḥayyim* ('Fountain of Life'). Written in Arabic, it was translated into Hebrew and into Latin as *Fons vitae*, well known to the Christian scholastics. The Hebrew was lost and it was long thought that its author was an Arab called Avicebron. Only in the 19th century was this identified with Ibn Gabirol. The long attribution to an Arab shows the lack of Jewish specificity in the work, which presents a general system, largely – but not completely – Neoplatonic. Ibn Gabirol introduced the concept of the divine will (reminiscent of Philo's *logos*), which mediates between the transcendent God and the universe. The human soul, which is eternal, is an emanation of the world soul. [34: 2]

Ibn Gabirol also wrote an ethical tractate, *Tikkun Middot ha-Nefesh* ('Improvement of the Qualities of the Soul'), which relates personal virtues to the five senses and breaks new ground in a Jewish context by propounding an ethic not based on a religious system. [43: 45–54; 87: vol. 1: 33–64] (G.W.)

Ibn Ḥanbal, Aḥmad ibn Muḥammad al-Shaybānī [XII] (780–855). Muslim traditionist, theologian and jurist. His resistance to the Inquisition instituted by the ʿAbbasid caliph al-Maʾmūn gave him a fame that resounds through Islamic history. Aḥmad was born in Baghdad and, though fatherless, he grew up in relative ease, devoting himself to the established syllabus of religious studies: Arabic language, jurisprudence and traditions. The precise details of his education are muddled by inter-school rivalries which manipulate the biographical record: e.g. he was an assiduous attender of the classes of AL-SHĀFIʿĪ, or, possibly, hardly met him. His most influential teachers are shown to be Traditionists, not jurists. When the caliph al-Maʾmūn gave official support to the doctrinal beliefs of the Muʿtazilites, Aḥmad became the defender of orthodoxy and was particularly associated with the dogma of the uncreated Qurʾān. Though beaten and imprisoned on occasion, he spent most of this period in retirement and returned to teaching when the Inquisition ended in 232/847. He died and was buried in Baghdad amid popular emotion; his tomb became a place of pilgrimage.

Aḥmad's most famous work is a massive collection of Prophetic traditions, arranged under the names of their first transmitters; not a very practical arrangement. Its importance lies in its size – it contains many traditions not otherwise recorded – and its authority. Also attributed to him are two dogmatic treatises, which give a basic definition of orthodox views, a book of maxims on the ascetic life, and a handful of minor juristic responsa. Nearly all of these works were given their final form after his death. The Ḥanbalī school of law developed later; Aḥmad was the chief authority and was found to have opinions on all aspects of the law. On very many matters he had two opinions, a feature which ensured for the school a certain broadness and tolerance. Though reputed in some sources to be fanatical, the school exhibits in different times and places a wide spectrum of views. [35: 'Aḥmad ibn Ḥanbal'; 41: 209–14] (N.C.)

Ibn Ḥazm, Abū Muḥammad ʿAlī ibn Aḥmad [XII] (994–1064). Muslim jurist, theologian, philosopher and poet. He passed the whole of his life in Muslim Spain and became the chief exponent of the *Ẓāhirī* ('literalist') school of law, which did not long survive. Ibn Ḥazm came from a high-ranking family, part of the administrative hierarchy surrounding the Umayyad caliphs of Spain. During his lifetime caliphal power collapsed as Slavs, Berbers and Andalusians struggled for power and legitimacy. The last Umayyad caliph disappeared in 1031, and Spain was ruled by a number of independent dynasties in military and cultural competition. His education in Cordova covered all the disciplines of Islamic culture, at a time when Cordova was a pre-eminent cultural centre. Politically active in his youth (as soldier, vizier and prisoner), usually on behalf of the caliph, he abandoned politics after 1031 and devoted himself to writing and teaching. His early work relates to poetry and morals and includes the famous 'Dove's Necklace' on poetic diction and psychological truth. His theological writings are numerous, and notoriously sharp-tongued. In jurisprudence he was opposed to the Mālikī school, which prevailed in Muslim Spain, but instead adopted the principles of a minor school which derived from Dāwūd al-Ẓāhirī, a pupil of IBN ḤANBAL. Following him, Ibn Ḥazm abandoned the interpretative tradition which had grown up with the older schools, and insisted on a purely literal (*ẓāhirī*) reading of revealed texts. His *Kitāb al-Muḥallā* is a monument of juristic erudition and of intemperate criticism. In dogmatic and theological matters he attempted a similar literalist approach to revealed texts, and produced again an idiosyncratic synthesis opposed to both the Muʿtazilites and the Ashʿaris, the two major dogmatic schools of the time. His great work in this area is the 'Book of Sects' which demonstrates correct dogma by exhaustively analysing heretical deviation, including that of the Jews and Christians. He was a powerful intellectual in search of naive certainty. It is said that he has considerable appeal for modern Muslims. [42] (N.C.)

Ibn Isḥāq [XII] (704–767/8). Early Arab authority on the life of MUḤAMMAD and compiler of the first extant *Sīra* or biography of the latter. He was born in Medina with a family background of interest in early traditions, the sayings of the Prophet and the first Muslims, and spent his life in scholarly activities, travelling in search of knowledge from Egypt to northern Persia, dying in Baghdad. His *Sīra* was apparently preceded by works, now lost, on the specific topic of Muḥammad's raids when he was at Medina (i.e. 622–32), and there was clearly an atmosphere of great interest in Muḥammad's life; but no work compares in comprehensiveness, trustworthiness and in seeming regard for historical truth than Ibn Isḥāq's. Beginning with the semi-legendary history of the pre-Islamic kings of Yemen, Ibn Isḥāq passes to the Meccan background of Muḥammad's mission, then to the actual story of the mission (*mabʿath*) at Mecca, passing finally to his career in Medina after the *hijra* or migration thither in 622 and his role as leader of raids and expeditions (*maghāzī*). The pre-*hijra* section of the book demonstrates the uncertainty and hazy knowledge about Muḥammad's early life, even a century after his death, and the sparse historical information is filled out with legendary tales and miraculous details; popular stories (*qiṣaṣ*) clearly had an influence here. The post-*hijra* section, however, is amply documented by eye-witness accounts supported by chains of guarantors (*isnād*s) and giving an impression of reliability, one strengthened by the inclusion of items of information or views which indicate divergent or critical views of Muḥammad's actions and achievements by some of his Arabian contemporaries. Another feature of the narrative is the extensive citation of what is ostensibly contemporary poetry, shedding light, among other things, on the contemporary relations, at times strained, between the Meccan and the Medinan Muslims. Ibn Isḥāq's biography survives in what might be called a revised, edited version by the Egyptian philologist Ibn Hishām (*d.*828/33), who tried to excise weak sections in the opening parts of the work, gave explanatory glosses on difficult poems and generally endeavoured to make the *Sīra* more acceptable to the scholars of tradition from the influential Medinan school. Other sections of Ibn Isḥāq's work omitted by Ibn Hishām, including the *mubtada'* or opening section of the *Sīra* on biblical history, are quoted by other Islamic scholars, and a history of the caliphs by him is known fragmentarily; it therefore seems that Ibn Isḥāq had a distinct conception of composing a universal history, a conception developed to its peak a century and a half later by the greatest historian of medieval Islam, AL-ṬABARĪ. [31; 35: s.v.; 56; 85] (C.E.B.)

Ibn Khaldūn [xii] (1332–1406). Muslim historian and pioneer of the philosophy of history and sociology. His family had come from Muslim Spain, but he was born at Tunis and spent his earlier life in North Africa, moving to Egypt in 1382 and functioning there as a judge. He wrote an autobiography and a universal history on traditional lines, mainly valuable for its information on the Muslim West, but his masterpiece was his *Muqaddima* or 'Prolegomena', an introduction to his general historical work, setting forth the sciences and the techniques of knowledge necessary for the historian in the exercising of his craft. It emphasizes the social influences and institutions which contribute to the building-up of human civilization (*ʿumrān*) and the social psychology which lies behind human endeavour in this field. Human activity takes place in two principal milieus, the desert and the sedentary, agricultural and urban environment, and all society is held together, in greater or lesser degree, by group feeling or solidarity (*ʿaṣabiyya*); power is exercised by those most strongly motivated by *ʿaṣabiyya*; but such holders of power inevitably grow weaker socially and morally, so that in the cycle of historical evolution and change, a fresh ruling dynasty emerges. The place of religion in all this is not large, except that the leadership of a prophet or saint is regarded by Ibn Khaldūn as the only force which can unite essentially anarchic nomads into a mass movement that will change the course of history; the rise of Islam is an example of this, involving, however, a specific and unique act of divine intervention also in human affairs. Ibn Khaldūn is thus a highly original and atypical figure of medieval Muslim scholarship, and when discovered in the West in the early 19th century, he was rightly hailed as a figure of genius. [35: s.v.; 57; 60; 107] (C.E.B.)

Ibn Māja, Abū ʿAbd Allāh Muḥammad ibn Yazīd al-Qazwīnī [xii] (825–887). Muslim Traditionist and scholar of Qazwīn. His collection of Prophetic *ḥadīth* had at first a local fame which gradually increased until it was recognized as one of the six canonical collections, of which those of AL-BUKHĀRĪ and MUSLIM are the most admired. The scholar Abū ʿAmr ʿUthmān Ibn al-Ṣalāḥ al-Shahrazūrī (*d.*1245) affirmed the pre-eminent status of al-Bukhārī and Muslim, and mentioned five other authoritative collections. He does not know of a canonical six, and does not mention Ibn Māja at all. Nonetheless other writers had included Ibn Māja amongst the six more than a century previously. There was clearly differential development of the canon among different scholarly groups, gradually giving way to a consensus (from which there were dissenters even later). Ibn Māja's work, known as the *Sunan Ibn Māja*, is said to contain 4,000 *ḥadīth*, a conventional number; it probably contains fewer than this. Many of the *ḥadīth* are thought to be weak, i.e. the chain of transmitters is deemed in some way defective, and it is, as a collection, always deemed inferior to the other canonical collections, and was never accepted in North Africa. In addition to the usual legal material, it is particularly interesting and detailed on eschatological matters. [35: 'Ibn Mādja'; 41: 229–34] (N.C.)

Ibn Rushd, Abū 'l-Walīd Muḥammad ibn Aḥmad [xii] [Averroes] (1126–1198). Major Arabic-writing philosopher. He was born in Cordova into privileged circumstances. Both his father and grandfather had been prominent judges and it is as a jurist that he is remembered in medieval Arabic sources because of such works as *Bidāyat al-mujtahid*. His *al-Kulliyyāt* ('The Generalities'; the title of the Latin translation is *Colliget*), a medical encyclopaedia, was widely read by medieval Christian scholars. He is best known to the history of Islamic thought as the refuter of the great AL-GHAZĀLĪ, whose 'attack on the pretensions of rationalism', the book *Tahāfut al-falāsifa* ('Incoherence of the Philosophers'), was answered in Ibn Rushd's *Tahāfut al-tahāfut* ('The Incoherence of the Incoherence'). Among the ideas which al-Ghazālī abominated were those he ascribed to AL-FĀRĀBĪ and IBN SĪNĀ (who as a result became for him infidels): the eternity of the world, the disbelief in bodily resurrection, and the disbelief in a God who has knowledge of particulars. Ibn Rushd, a confirmed Aristotelian (he agreed with him that the world was round), argued in this work and elsewhere as a philosopher and a jurist, asking, for example, whether the religious law has anything to say about the study of philosophy. His conclusion was that the law commands the study of philosophy and, furthermore, that there were some topics about which it was permissible to hold wrong ideas because the Qur'ān itself was not sufficiently definite about them, although there were, to be sure, many things about which the Qur'ān was definite. Therefore one could not proclaim someone an infidel on the grounds of a merely erring interpretation of an unclear verse. Such was the nature of his defence. Ibn Rushd is seen as the 'last great Islamic philosopher' by many, though recently this view has been challenged by students of those philosophical developments in Islamic lands further east, where, as it happened, Ibn Rushd's influence was less marked and Ibn Sīnā's more strongly felt. [36: 107–28] (B.T.L.)

Ibn Saʿd [XII] (*c*.784–845). Muslim Traditionalist and compiler of the most important of early Arabic biographical dictionaries. Of Iraqi origin, he spent his life in search of traditions, i.e. the sayings of the early Muslims and of MUḤAMMAD, and in study before settling down in Baghdad, where he became secretary to the historian of Muḥammad's raids and campaigns (*maghāzī*) al-Wāqidī. Ibn Saʿd's *al-Ṭabaqāt al-kabir* ('Great Book of Classes'), for which al-Wāqidī's own *Book of Classes* (lost as a complete work) was almost certainly the prototype, was meant as an adjunct to the study of Islamic tradition, in that it gives biographical information on over 4,200 persons, including a good number of women, who from earliest Islam up to 845 had played a role as narrators or transmitters of traditions from or about Muḥammad. The information is arranged in 'classes', in the first place by region and then chronologically; the greatest space is naturally devoted to a biography of Muḥammad himself and then to his Companions, i.e. the first generation of Muslims, those born within the Prophet's own lifetime. Later biographical dictionaries of the Companions were on a more vast scale, but they bring little more material for the life of Muḥammad than Ibn Saʿd's pioneer work does, and in scope and arrangement are clearly grounded on his earlier efforts. [31; 35: s.v.] (C.E.B.)

Ibn Sīnā, Abū ʿAlī al-Ḥusayn ibn ʿAbd Allāh [XII] [Avicenna] (980–1037). Generally reckoned to be the greatest Islamic philosopher. He was born near Bukhārā, the Persian capital of the Samanid dynasty. His father was an Ismāʿīlī, but Ibn Sīnā apparently rejected his father's religion. From an early age he was an avid student and says that he had mastered all of human learning by the age of 18. When the Samanids fell in 999, Ibn Sīnā began his travels through Iran serving now one, now another petty prince. The last part of his life was spent as physician to ʿAlā' al-Dawla, the ruler of Isfahan. But he also maintained something of a private practice. He died in Hamadān while accompanying his patron on a military campaign.

His is a coherent, integrated philosophy which is Neoplatonic in form. While his earlier works repeat much of AL-FĀRĀBĪ's views, his later writings present marked developments. The strong distinction between essence and existence may be Ibn Sīnā's most influential philosophical discovery. His ontology depends upon One Whose Existence Is Necessary (e.g. the transcendent God of Qur'ān *sūra* 112, or the neoplatonic One) and Those Things Having Only Potential Existence (creation, including humanity). The latter may ultimately aspire to true existence through various processes. This important formulation influenced virtually all Muslim philosophers after him.

More than 100 of his works have survived: the mammoth *al-Shifā'* ('The Healing') is his major philosophical work. Apart from philosophical enquiries and commentaries on the Arabic translations of Greek philosophers, Ibn Sīnā is responsible for perhaps the single most important medical work of the Middle Ages. *Al-Qānūn fī'l-Ṭibb* ('The Canon of Medicine') was, in fact, the standard medical text at European universities until the late 17th century. His mysticism is found in his *Kitāb al-ishārāt wa'l-tanbīhāt* ('The Book of Directives and Remarks'), a work which was commented upon by the protean figure (KHWĀJA NAṢĪR AL-DĪN) AL-ṬŪSĪ. [33: 'Avicenna'; 36: 128–62; 78: part 1: V–VII; 96] (B.T.L.)

Ibn Taymiyya, Taqī al-Dīn Aḥmad [XII] (1263–1328). Muslim theologian and jurist of the Ḥanbalī school. He attacked innovation (*bidʿa*) and appealed against the intellectual tradition to the authority of the pious elders (*al-salaf*). Born in Syria, under the Mamlūk dynasty, he perceived in the intermittent Mongol advances into this area during his lifetime a token of the innovations and heresy which had grown up in Islam. He began early on a career of writing and debate which brought him regularly into conflict with the political and religious authorities of Mamlūk Egypt and Syria. In spite of occasional *rapprochements*, he was clearly seen as a nuisance: he was associated with sectarian demonstrations within the Islamic community and with inter-religious factionalism. He spent several periods of imprisonment in the citadels of Cairo and Damascus, and died in the latter, under orders, not for the first time, to refrain from publishing his opinions. His literary career was largely devoted to attacks on 'innovation', which he deemed to be a cause of division and weakness. To rectify this he proposed submission to the authority of the pious ancestors (*al-salaf*), and appeal to the literal words of Qur'ān and Traditions. He rejected the supple intellectual tradition of Islamic scholarship, condemning all major thinkers since the third Islamic century. He had two major themes: the theologians and the mystics (Ṣūfīs). He produced numerous versions of the Islamic creed, accompanied by vehement rejection of the intellectual speculations of philosophers like IBN SĪNĀ and of theologians like AL-ASHʿARĪ. IBN ḤANBAL, however, was a major figure of authority – and almost the last. Himself a moderate Ṣūfī, Ibn Taymiyya attacked the Ṣūfī practice of visiting tombs, the notion of the intercession of saints and the theological writings of IBN ʿARABĪ. His passionate conviction was less notable in the field of jurisprudence, where he produced a significant work of political theory. He is much admired by some modern Islamic thinkers (*see* MUḤAMMAD ʿABDUH). [77] (N.C.)

Ibn Ṭufayl [XII] (*c.*1102–1185). Philosopher and physician of Muslim Spain, celebrated as the author of a remarkable philosophical romance, *The Story of Ḥayy ibn Yaqẓān*. After filling various posts as a secretary and as a physician in his native Granada and in Morocco, he became court physician to the Berber Sultan of the Almohad dynasty of Morocco and Spain, Abū Yaʿqūb Yūsuf (1163–1184), retiring in 1182 and dying in Marrakesh. Not the least of his services to Islamic knowledge was his introduction of the great philosopher IBN RUSHD (Averroes) to the Almohad court. He was interested in medicine and astronomy, but it is *Ḥayy ibn Yaqẓān* (literally, 'Alive, the son of Wakeful'; the title was borrowed from an earlier work by IBN SĪNĀ) that has ensured his fame. It is the story of Ḥayy's spiritual and philosophical development in isolation on a desert island. Using his innate intelligence and through a combination of observation and reasoning, he succeeds over the years in attaining philosophical and metaphysical illumination to the highest level, involving the detachment of the intellect from the material world and a pure, mystical contemplation of God. The final message of the story is that the ultimate truths are indeed apprehendable through the exercise of pure reason by those of superior philosophical attainments, but that the less enlightened masses require the framework of the formal religious law, the *sharīʿa*, within which to practise the good life in conformity with God's requirements for Man. The book subsequently had a profound effect in the West, becoming known there as early as the 15th century; later, its theme was especially congenial to the advocates of natural religion in the late 17th and 18th centuries, while the framework of Ḥayy's life on an isolated desert island has been held to have influenced Defoe's *Robinson Crusoe*. [35: s.v.; 58] (C.E.B.)

Ibrāhīm [XII] (*c.*19th century BCE). The patriarch Abraham in the Islamic tradition. (For an account of the Jewish tradition, *see* ABRAHAM.) The Qur'ān pictures Abraham as a monotheist who was neither a Jew nor a Christian; he is termed a *ḥanīf*, someone who has 'submitted' to God, that is, become a Muslim. He is mentioned in 25 *sūras* of the Qur'ān, second only to MOSES (*see also* MŪSĀ), but his role in the scripture is generally seen to be more significant than the latter. He is pictured as a prophet in the Qur'anic mold: he receives revelation of scripture (called the 'leaves' of Abraham), is commissioned to take his message to his community, is frustrated to a large extent by the stubbornness of the people, but in the end his faith is personally victorious. A number of the elements of the Qur'anic recital are familiar from biblical and later sources; for example, Abraham attacks the idol worship of his father (called Āzar), and he is called upon to sacrifice his son (here unnamed, leading to the famous disputes in Islam over the identity of the boy). Abraham also plays some very specific Arabian-Qur'anic roles: for example, he builds the

Kaʿba in Mecca, with the help of Ishmael, as a centre of pilgrimage.

The outline of the life story of Abraham is elaborated in the traditional Muslim material called *qiṣaṣ al-anbiyā'* ('the stories of the prophets'); the story of Abraham's encounter with Nimrod is an especial favourite. Many of the details of these elaborations were borrowed from Jewish sources but others are simply invented edifying episodes, told to entertain and educate the audience. [73; 91; 130] (A.R.)

Ignatius Loyola [VI.A] [Iñigo López de Loyola] (*c.*1491–1556). Spanish theologian; founder of the Society of Jesus (Jesuits). The son of Basque parents, he was born in Loyola in northern Spain. From the age of 12 he was raised as a courtier and a gentleman in Arévalo in Castile. In 1517, following the death of his patron, he entered the service of the Duke of Nájera, Navarre. He was prominent in the defence of Pamplona against French attack in 1521. During the siege of the city he was badly injured by a cannon-ball and had to undergo horrific surgery then and later. During a long convalescence he read a life of Christ and a collection of saints' lives. The experience changed his life. In 1522 Ignatius set out on a pilgrimage to the Holy Land. He disposed of his servants and possessions and in the Benedictine monastery of Montserrat he laid up his sword, took on the clothes of a beggar and spent all-night vigils at the altar of the Blessed Virgin Mary. He moved to Manresa and lived by begging, devoting himself to long hours of prayer and devotional reading. He began to write his *Spiritual Exercises*, a manual for the organization of spiritual retreats. He reached Jerusalem in September 1523. He was not allowed to take up permanent residence in the city so he returned to Spain via Venice and settled for a time in Barcelona (1524–6). He studied philosophy in Alcalá (1525–7) and in Salamanca for a few months in 1527. He began to attract followers and the suspicion of the authorities. To escape the latter he went to the University of Paris in 1528, gained a master of arts in philosophy in 1534 and finished his studies there the following year. Ignatius attracted more followers and in August 1534, at a chapel in Montmartre, he and six companions took vows to observe poverty and, if possible, make a pilgrimage to Jerusalem. They travelled as far as Venice, where in June 1537 the group received ordination. Some time later the group decided to form the Society of Jesus. Pope Paul III approved a draft constitution in 1540. The aims of the order were evangelism, education and rooting out heresy. Ignatius was made superior general of the order. By the time of his death the number of members had reached nearly a thousand and he had founded the Gregorian University and the German College in Rome. Ignatius was canonized in 1622. [220; 301; 662] (T.T.)

Ignatius of Antioch [VI.A] (*c.*35–*c.*107). Bishop of Antioch. Very little is known of his life, except that he was arrested and taken under the escort of ten soldiers from Antioch to be executed in Rome. According to ORIGEN he was the second bishop of Antioch after PETER THE APOSTLE, but EUSEBIUS OF CAESAREA holds that Ignatius was the third bishop of Antioch after Peter and Euodius (*d* *c*69). It is conceivable that he may have met some of the first apostles, possibly PAUL, possibly JOHN. His extant writings consist of seven letters, authenticated by later scholarship, written during his journey to Rome, but he does not mention meeting any of the apostles. Four of the letters, to Ephesus, Magnesia, Tralles and Rome, were written from Smyrna, where he had been welcomed by Polycarp the bishop. The other three were written from Troas to Philadelphia, Smyrna and to Polycarp. He then travelled through Macedonia and Illyria to Dyrrhachium. From there he sailed to Rome. His martyrdom is chronicled by Origen and Polycarp. It is traditionally held that his death took place in the Colosseum. In his letters the main themes are his devotion to Christ, for whom he was ready to be martyred, and the catholicity and unity of the church under bishops and through the one eucharist. [484; 663: vol. 1: 63ff.; 700] (T.T.)

Ikeda Daisaku [IV] (1928–). The third president of Sōka Gakkai, a new NICHIREN Buddhist sect. At the age of 19 he became a disciple of Toda Jōsei (1900–1958), the second president of Sōka Gakkai. He succeeded Toda as president in 1960, bringing youthful energy, intellectual ability, and an understanding of the importance of the mass media to the job. He is perhaps best known for helping to create the Clean Government Party (Kōmeitō) in 1964, formalizing Sōka Gakkai's direct involvement in national politics. (The group had first run candidates for the national diet in 1956.) In 1970, under increasing pressure and experiencing criticism for this apparent mixing of religion and politics, Ikeda promulgated a policy of separating the two. Since this withdrawal from the political sphere he has devoted himself largely to scholarship, writing and lecturing on Buddhism, and the cause of world peace in many international forums. He retired as president of Sōka Gakkai in 1979. [104; 105] (G.E.)

Ikkyū Sōjun [IV] (1394–1481). Eccentric Japanese Zen master and noted poet and calligrapher who disdained worldly conventions and the Gozan ('five mountains') Zen establishment. Ikkyū was the son of Emperor Go-Komatsu (reigned 1382–1412), and was schooled from childhood at the Zen temple Ankoku-ji in Kyoto. He came to detest the sophisticated Zen establishment and left Ankoku-ji to practise with Ken'ō Sōi (*d.*1415) and then Kasō Sōdon (1352–1428), under whose strict tutelage he experienced *satori* ('enlightenment'). Ikkyū spent many years in Sakai, where he frequented the local taverns and brothels and exhibited a mad eccentricity, such as marching down the street waving a human skull. It is believed that Ikkyū accepted appointment in 1474 as abbot of Daitoku-ji, one of the central Gozan temples in Kyoto, and succeeded somewhat in its restoration from the ravages of the Ōnin war, but he soon left the post. His love affair late in life with the blind singer Mori is well known, and the subject of many of his poignant poems.

Ikkyū is also famed for his many striking poems in the classic Chinese style, and his dynamic calligraphy. His finest collection of poetry is the *Kyōunshō* ('Crazy Cloud Anthology'), containing over 1,000 poems. He is well known to the modern popular mind, due to his role as the hero of a Japanese cartoon, in which he is portrayed as an adolescent novice monk who betters his superiors through wit and clever antics. He also lives on in legend as an exemplar of the unconventional Zen monk whose eccentric behaviour exposes the vanity of worldly pretensions. [8; 188] (P.L.S.)

Imhotep [VII] (27th century BCE). Architect and vizier of King ZOSER (*c.*2660 BCE). Imhotep was also revered by later generations in Egypt as a great physician. He probably designed Zoser's unique pyramid complex at Saqqara; this provided the king with a series of buildings which would serve as a Royal Court in his afterlife. The central feature was the Step Pyramid, which is the world's first major stone building. This stepped structure was designed to mark the king's burial place and is probably a development of the earlier mastaba-style tomb. Many architectural innovations are used in this complex, and the craftsmen experimented with new building materials and techniques. The total concept of this complex was never repeated, although the pyramid form continued to be used for royal burials for hundreds of years.

However, the Egyptians particularly revered Imhotep as a healer and a physician, and later generations deified and worshipped him as a god of medicine. Deification of this kind was rare, although a few rulers and wise men were accorded divine cults. Imhotep's cult, however, survived for thousands of years, and he was ultimately identified by the Greeks (*c.*300 BCE) with Asklepios, their own god of medicine. Statues of Imhotep (all of a late date) show him as a man with a shaven head, holding a papyrus roll. Saqqara was his cult-centre, but his burial place has eluded discovery. (A.R.D.)

Indrabhūti [XIII]. First disciple of the Jain teacher MAHĀVĪRA, by whom, like the other ten disciples, he was enlightened. The construction of even a partial biography for Indrabhūti took several centuries. One of the oldest texts to refer to him, the *Bhagavatī*, the fifth book of the Śvetāmbara scriptural canon, knows him by the name of Gautama (signifying his clan) and presents him as an interlocutor of his master Mahāvīra, posing questions relating to cosmology, doctrine etc., each of which Mahāvīra is able to answer to his disciple's satisfaction [5]. The same text has Mahāvīra tell Indrabhūti that the two of them had been linked together during a large number of births, and that after their current existence, their final one, they will be equal [5: 209]. Also noteworthy is another canonical source which describes a debate between Indrabhūti and a follower of PĀRŚVA about the reason why the ascetics of Mahāvīra's order go naked [14: 119–29; 23]. According to tradition, he lived for 92 years before attaining salvation. (P.D.)

Innocent I [VI.A] (*d.*417). Pope, 401/2–17. Nothing of his life is known for certain before he became bishop of Rome in 401 or 402. He was held by JEROME to be the son of the previous bishop of Rome, Anastasius I. As bishop of Rome he made more substantial claims for the primacy of his see than any predecessor. He was pope at a time when Constantinople was challenging Rome as the leading city of Christianity and Alaric the Goth was threatening Rome itself. Innocent insisted that all matters ecclesiastical should be settled by his office. He forced his will in doctrinal and liturgical matters on the Western church. In a letter to Decentius, bishop of Gubbio, Innocent insisted that the church there should use the Roman liturgy. He also condemned the churches of Spain, Gaul, Sicily and Africa for not abiding by Roman usage. He intervened in the affairs of the Eastern churches, supporting the claims of John Chrysostom in Constantinople and Jerome in Jerusalem. He succeeded in bringing the churches in east Illyria which had been part of the Eastern Empire since 388 back under Western control. Innocent's statements concerning Roman supremacy were the basis for medieval claims about the power of the papacy. [383; 875] (T.T.)

Innocent III [VI.A] [Lotario de' Conti di Segni] (1160?–1216). Pope, 1198–1216. The son of a noble family of Campagna, he was first educated in Rome, possibly at the Schola Cantorum. He went to Paris to study theology and then to Bologna to study law. He entered papal service and rose quickly to cardinal (1190) and then to pope following the death of Celestine in 1198 before he was ordained priest. Before he became pope he had exercised considerable influence in the Roman Curia. While he was cardinal he wrote a number of tracts on the 'Misery of the Human Condition', 'Four Typologies of Marriage' and *De missarum misteriis* ('On the mysteries of the Mass'). When he became pope he used his power and the political situation of his time to promote the power of the papacy over secular as well as ecclesiastical affairs. The papacy assumed more powers than it had ever achieved or was to achieve again. He intervened in the succession to Emperor Henry VI, claiming that, while the electors had the right to elect the emperor, the pope had the right to examine the person elected and that the appointment of the emperor could occur only with the authority of the pope. He used his influence to secure the election of Henry's son, Frederick II, who paid him homage by giving him Sicily and appointing the pope as regent. He also intervened in other countries such as France and forced King John of England to recognize him as feudal lord. He ordered the prosecution of crusades, one of which was successful in recovering Constantinople. A European crusade wiped out the Albigensian heresy in Languedoc. He convened the Fourth Lateran Council in 1215 which set up the Inquisition. [641; 799] (T.T.)

Innokentii Veniaminov [VI.A] [John Popov] (1797–1879). Russian Orthodox missionary and priest. He was born in Anga, near Irkutsk (southern Siberia). His father was a church sacristan who gave his son his early education. In 1806 he entered the theological seminary in Irkutsk, where he adopted the name Veniaminov. He married and served as priest in Irkutsk. In 1823 he became a missionary to the Aleuts in Alaska. He learned Aleutian and created an alphabet for the language. His first major work was written in Aleutian, *A Guide to the Way to the Heavenly Kingdom*, which was translated into Russian. Although he also published work of a scientific and anthropological nature on the islands of Unalaska District he was mainly concerned with evangelism. In 1833 he went to Sitka in Alaska, where he worked for 14 years and then returned to Russia. He became a monk following the death of his wife and at that time took the name Innokentii. In 1840 he became bishop of the Diocese of North America and Kamchatka, returned as bishop to Sitka in 1841 and was made archbishop in 1850. Elected primate of the Russian church in 1868, he undertook many reforms and founded the Orthodox Missionary Society in 1870. He was canonized in 1977 and given the title Evangelizer of the Aleuts and Apostle to America. [5; 288] (T.T.)

Iolo Morganwg. *See* WILLIAMS, EDWARD.

Ippen [IV] (1239–1289). Founder of the Ji sect of Japanese Pure Land Buddhism, and known as an itinerant holy man (*hijiri*) who spread the practice of dancing while chanting the *nenbutsu* (name of the Buddha Amitābha; Japanese: Amida). Ippen first studied Tendai Buddhism on Mt Hiei but later went to Kyushu and became a disciple of Shōtatsu of the Seizan branch of Jōdo Pure Land Buddhism. He travelled widely, including pilgrimages to Zenkō-ji in Nagano, Shikoku, and Shitennō-ji in Osaka. During a pilgrimage to Kumano in 1274 he had a vision of Amida, who commanded Ippen to distribute *fuda* (talismans) on which were written *namu Amida-butsu* ('homage to the Buddha Amitābha'). These were to be distributed to all people, whether or not they had any faith or interest. Ippen devoted the rest of his life to travelling and preaching throughout the country. He began and popularized the practice of *odori-nenbutsu* ('dancing while chanting the *nenbutsu*') and attracted a large following. The dance served as a celebration of Ippen's belief that all beings are already saved through Amida's enlightenment. Though the Ji sect is now a minor school of Japanese Buddhism, *odori nenbutsu* is still a part of the folk religion of Japan and played a role in the development of Japanese theatre. Ippen's life and teachings are illustrated in the *Ippen Hijiri e*, a masterpiece in the genre of painted scrolls. The most reliable source of Ippen's teaching is the *Ippen Shōnin goroku* ('Record of Ippen'). [64; 96] (P.L.S.)

Ipuwer [VII]. He appears as the sage and prophet in the text known as *The Admonitions of a Prophet*. Set in a time of national crisis when Egypt is threatened by internal and external dangers, the text relates that the central government has collapsed and that the aged king in his palace is unaware of the calamity. Ipuwer (probably in his capacity as a Treasury official) arrives at the Court and addresses the king, describing graphically the terrible conditions that exist throughout the country and prophesying that the situation will deteriorate.

The text is preserved on Papyrus Leiden 344 which dates to Dynasty 19 (*c.*1300 BCE), but scholars originally considered that it described actual historical events and that it had been written by a man named Ipuwer; they dated it to the years stretching from the end of the Old Kingdom to the First Intermediate Period [12: 92–108]. However, more recent studies [19: vol. 1: 149–63] indicate that the *Admonitions* were a purely literary exercise, which developed the theme of 'national distress' but could not be equated with any specific historical period, and indeed may well have been composed during the late Middle Kingdom (*c.*1790 BCE) when Egypt enjoyed a time of peaceful prosperity. This text would appear to fall into the same category as the 'Prophecy of NEFERTI'. (A.R.D.)

Iqbal, Sir Muḥammad [XII] (1876–1938). Indian Muslim lawyer, statesman, poet and philosopher. Born in Sialkot, now in Pakistan, Iqbal was educated in Lahore and Munich and was knighted in 1922 for his contribution to Persian and Urdu poetry. He urged the establishment of a separate state for Muslims in north-west India as early as 1930. His major prose work, *The Reconstruction of Religious Thought in Islam*, lectures given in 1928 and published in 1934, embody his view of the need for a revival in Islam to take it out of its situation of decline. This he located in a return to the sources of Islam and away from the centuries of intellectualism which had obscured the true message. Islam would be able to provide the moral message which the modern world needed. His poetical works are deeply imbued with Ṣūfī thought influenced especially by RŪMĪ. His major books of poetry include the Persian *Jāvid-nāmah* ('Jāvid's Book') and the Urdu *Bāl-i Jibrīl* ('Gabriel's Wing'). [1: V; 6: VII, VIII; 114] (A.R.)

Irenaeus [VI.A] (*c.*130–*c.*200). Theologian. Nothing is known of his family, birth or place of origin. Irenaeus maintained that he had heard Polycarp, who was martyred *c.*155, as a young person, so it is suggested that he was possibly a native of Smyrna. He studied in the school of Justin in Rome and was present at a debate between Polycarp and Anicetus in Rome *c.*155. He was ordained a presbyter in Lyons sometime after 164. Irenaeus missed a persecution in Lyons and Vienne during which Pothinus, the bishop, was martyred because Pothinus had sent him with a letter to Pope Eleutherius pleading for toleration for the Montanists of Asia Minor. Irenaeus was made bishop of Lyons on his return. As bishop he intervened with Pope Victor on behalf of the Christians of Asia who had been excommunicated because they observed a different date for Easter, on the grounds that varieties of practice among the churches had never been a cause of breach of communion. Irenaeus did not accept the Apologists' approach to teaching and preaching. He based his teaching squarely on the Bible, especially in his attacks on the Gnostic heresy. His main work in this respect was his *Refutation and Overthrow of Knowledge* [Gnosis] *So-called*, more familiarly known as *Adversus omnes haereses*. His other main work, *The Demonstration of the Apostolic Preaching*, is an apologetic work heavily dependent on the Old Testament. [351; 387; 871] (T.T.)

Irene of Chrysobalanton, St [VI.A] (*d c*921). A Cappadocian originally destined for the 'bride show' of Emperor Michael III, Irene became abbess of the great Chrysobalanton convent in Constantinople. She was famous as a miracle worker and seer who levitated in prayer. Legend says St John the Apostle brought her golden apples from Paradise which healed those who tasted them. An important cult grew up around her. [73] (D.B.)

Irving, Edward [VI.A] (1792–1834). He was born in Annan, Dumfriesshire, and later educated in Edinburgh University. He served as a schoolmaster for a few years, in Haddington (1810) and Kirkcaldy (1812). He was licensed to preach in the Church of Scotland in 1815 and in 1819 became assistant pastor at St John's, Glasgow. In 1822 he went to London as pastor of the Caledonian chapel in Hatton Garden. His preaching attracted many hearers and a larger chapel had to be built in Regent Square in 1827. By this time Irving had been influenced by millenarian ideas, especially the work of a Spanish Jesuit, Manuel Lacunza, whose work he translated under the title *The Coming of Messiah in Glory and Majesty* (1827). He wrote two works: *The Doctrine of the Incarnation Opened* (1828) and *The Orthodox and Catholic Doctrine of Our Lord's Human Nature* (1830). The London Presbytery of the Church of Scotland brought charges of heresy against him, accusing him of teaching that Christ had a sinful nature. This he denied. Following the outbreak of revivalist phenomena in his church in 1831, he was deposed by the authorities in 1832 and excommunicated in 1833. Hundreds of his congregation founded the Catholic Apostolic Church while he became a roving preacher. When he returned to London they made him a deacon in the new church. He was buried in Glasgow Cathedral. [142; 603; 758] (T.T.)

ʿĪsā [XII] (*c*.7/6 BCE–*c*.30 CE). Jesus of Nazareth in the Islamic tradition. (For an account of the Christian tradition, *see* JESUS.) Jesus is mentioned in 15 *sūras* of the Qur'ān in a total of 93 verses. Some of the material is generally thought to have been drawn from the Apocryphal gospels, perhaps reflecting popular Christian beliefs from early Islamic times. He is called al-Masīḥ ('Messiah'), but this is considered to be his name and to have been given to him at birth; he is also named 'son of Mary', and the story of the annunciation and virgin birth is recounted. Other aspects of the life story include Jesus giving signs and performing miracles and his being crucified without dying (he was 'raised up' to God). Jesus is called the 'Word of God' and is spoken of as being 'fortified by the Holy Spirit'. The basically familiar Christian motifs are combined with a Qur'anic image of Jesus as a prophet – he brings the scripture called Injīl ('Gospel') to a disbelieving community – and the total denial of any sense of his divinity or status as the son of God.

For Muslims, the return of Jesus at the end of time is a widespread belief, although it is only hinted at in the Qur'ān. Elaborations of his life are found throughout the *qiṣaṣ al-anbiyā'* ('stories of the prophets') literature, and he is often seen in a mystic light, his life of elevation to existing alongside God being the model for the individual mystic. [35: 'ʿĪsā'; 73; 98; 141] (A.R.)

Isaac [XV] (*c*. 18th century BCE). Second of the Israelite patriarchs. Far less is related of him than of his father ABRAHAM or his son JACOB, and for the most part he plays a passive role in the events in which he figures and is the least colourful of the patriarchs. He was born to Abraham and Sarah in their old age, fulfilling a divine promise. As soon as he was weaned, Sarah insisted on the expulsion from the household of his half-brother, Ishmael, and her mother, Hagar, Sarah's maid, so as to prevent any questioning of Isaac's role as Abraham's legitimate heir. The traumatic event of Isaac's younger days was Abraham's unquestioning acceptance of the divine command to sacrifice his son on

Mount Moriah. Only at the last moment, with Isaac bound and Abraham prepared to slaughter him, was the sacrifice stayed by an angel, who explained that God was only testing Abraham's fidelity.

Abraham arranged Isaac's marriage to his cousin, Rebekah, who – after 20 years of barrenness – gave birth to twins, Esau and Jacob. Isaac lived in southern Canaan, where he was a successful agriculturist and cattle-raiser.

In his old age he lost his sight and fell victim to a plot hatched by Rebekah and Jacob whereby his birthright blessing was given to his younger son, Jacob, instead of to Esau, to whom it was rightfully due. Fearing Esau's wrath, Jacob fled to Mesopotamia to his mother's family.

Isaac lived to the age of 180 and was buried by Jacob and Esau (by now reconciled) in the family tomb at Machpelah in Hebron. [68: IX–XI].

The story of Isaac is related in *Genesis* 25–28, 35. (G.W.)

Isaac of Nineveh [VI.B] (*d c*700). Nestorian bishop and theologian. He came from the region of Qatar on the Persian Gulf. He became a monk and was consecrated bishop of Nineveh (near present day Mosul), but resigned after five months to become a hermit in the mountains of Khuzistan. He is said to have gone blind through study of scripture and to have died at the monastery of Rabban Shabur in Persia. His writings were translated from Syriac into Greek during the late 8th or early 9th century at the monastery of Mar Saba in Judaea. In this way the works of a Nestorian entered the Byzantine spiritual tradition; Arabic translations may have influenced Muslim writers also. [34; 62; 95] (K.P.)

Isaiah [XV] (late 8th century BCE). Israelite prophet whose prophecies are contained in the biblical book of that name. Scholars maintain that the book should be divided into two (or even three) parts, with the second part (chapters 40–66) written by another prophet (Deutero-Isaiah) in the Babylonian exile (6th century BCE).

The prophet Isaiah lived in the reign of four kings of Judah – Uzziah, Jotham, Ahaz and Hezekiah – at a period of great external pressure on the kingdom from Syria, the northern kingdom of Israel (735 BCE) and from the expanding Assyrian empire (701 BCE).

Isaiah came from a respected background and was familiar with both the royal court and the priestly leaders. His first vision (described in *Isaiah* 6) consisted of a call from God in which the prophet accepted the difficult mission with which he was entrusted. He was appalled at the rottenness and corruption in Israelite society and wished to save the nation from approaching catastrophe. He condemned the oppression and wickedness of the rulers, the decadence of the affluent and their pursuit of luxuries and pleasure, and foretold a terrible fate on the Day of the Lord.

During the reign of Ahaz, when Judah faced an Assyrian invasion under Tiglath-pileser, Isaiah confronted the king, demanding that he stand up to the Assyrians and diagnosing the danger not in the external threat but in the internal lack of trust in God. In the reign of Hezekiah he opposed the king's policy of joining an anti-Assyrian coalition, holding that only God could punish the proud Assyrians, and that if man should so try, the end would be calamity.

For Isaiah, God rules the world for moral ends and judges the nations of the world accordingly. Israel is God's people but they have forsaken him and will be punished unless they repent. A main theme of the prophet is the holiness of God, from which derives the holiness of his people and his temple. Another theme that he introduces is the End of Days. He spoke of future redemption, when a righteous remnant would be redeemed and Zion would be the spiritual centre of the world in an era of perfect peace and harmony. [38: 4]

In the second part of *Isaiah*, the main theme is the redemption of Israel to take place after the forthcoming fall of Babylonia at the hands of the Persian monarch CYRUS. This prophecy presupposes that the fall of Jerusalem (which occurred in 586 BCE) and the exile to Babylonia had taken place. It is a prophecy of consolation to the exiles and of love for destroyed, desolate Zion. A central motif is the Suffering Servant; the servant of the Lord through whose suffering salvation will come to the world. Interpreters of these passages disagree as to whether the references are to an individual or a collective. Christians early identified JESUS with the suffering servant; to

Jews it is Israel as whole, the ideal Israel, a righteous minority, the prophet himself, or a messianic figure.

According to Deutero-Isaiah, God does not coexist with other gods, but is totally unique; the implications of this are universalistic. However, God – who is responsible for history – will be especially merciful to persecuted Israel. Eventually Israel will be redeemed and the world purged of heathenism. All Israel will be righteous and the peoples of the world will acknowledge and worship the true God. [38: 8; 48]

Some scholars attribute chapters 56–66 to a third prophet (Trito-Isaiah) because the subject-matter seems to accord with that of the prophets Malachi and Zechariah after the return from exile to Zion. [24] (G.W.)

Ishida Baigan [XIV] (1685–1744). Founder of the Shingaku ('Heart Learning') movement. Born into a farm family in Tama province, he was apprenticed to a Kyōto merchant at the age of 11, thus entering the rising merchant class. He returned home, however, four years later, giving up any hope of a commercial career. He became interested in Shintō as a youth, perhaps influenced by the Ise priests active in organizing mass pilgrimages to the Ise Shrine. He returned to Kyōto at 23 and soon began preaching publicly, though with limited success. Nevertheless, he continued his studies of Shintō, neo-Confucianism and Buddhism, eventually under a master named Oguri Ryōun (1669–1729).

Devoting himself to the practice of contemplation (*kūfū* or *seiza*), Ishida had several experiences of awakening in which he is said to have overcome all distinction between his self and his nature. After the death of his teacher, Ishida opened his own lecture hall where he spoke each morning and every other evening before and after normal shop hours, teaching that the ultimate goal of spiritual devotions was to overcome one's selfish heart and to recover one's 'true heart' by realizing the Confucian virtues in all aspects of daily life. His central concepts of heart (*kokoro*) and nature (*sei*) were taken from MENG TZU (Mencius), but his teachings and practice incorporated aspects of Zen meditative techniques along with neo-Confucian ethics and values, including frugality and the dedication of oneself to humble occupations, as well as elements of Buddhism and Taoism. Ishida's school of neo-Confucianism, the Sekimon, became especially popular among small shopkeepers and other townsmen (*chōnin*). He did much to help overcome the stigma attached to economic activity by insisting that the merchant class had a legitimate and essential place within the sacred national community (*kokutai*), embodying the values of loyalty, selfless devotion, hard work, frugality, and so on. Ishida left only two published works – *Toimondo* ('City and Country Dialogues', 1740) and *Seikaron* ('Essay on Household Management', 1744). [3; 34: 155–60] (G.E.)

Isidore of Seville [VI.A] (560–636). Theologian and scholar. He was born in Seville, to which city his father had fled when Cartagena was destroyed by the Visigoths. After the death of his parents Isidore, under the guidance of his older brother Leander who was a monk, was educated at a monastery. This education gave him the basis of an encyclopaedic knowledge. He entered a monastery *c.*589 and continued his studies. His brother had become Archbishop of Seville, and when he died he was succeeded by Isidore. As such he presided over many councils, the most prominent being the Fourth Council of Toledo (633). He was involved in the process of turning the Visigoths away from Arianism to an orthodox faith and in the conversion of the Jews to Christianity. His writings included works on biblical studies, ecclesiastical and monastic rules, and spiritual guides; other, more secular writings include a history of Spain, a history of the world and works on education. [112; 187; 389] (T.T.)

Isserles, Moses [XV] [known by the acronym, Rema] (*c.*1525–1572). Rabbi and legal codifier in Poland. His father was a wealthy leader of the Jewish community in Cracow who built a synagogue which to this day is known as the Rema Synagogue and in whose adjacent cemetery Isserles is buried. Already in his youth he was a noted scholar. Thanks to his affluent circumstances he was able to build and maintain a talmudic academy which he headed throughout his life and which attracted students from near and far.

When his contemporary JOSEPH CARO wrote his codification of Jewish law, *Bet Yoseph*, Isserles wrote *Darkhei Moshe* ('The Ways of Moses') containing a critique of and commentary on Caro's work and expressing the views and decisions of the Ashkenazi rabbis, whom Caro had neglected. When Caro published his shorter code, *Shulḥan Arukh*, Isserles recognized its great merit but feared that it would prove so popular even among Ashkenazi communities that their own traditions would be overlooked or forgotten. He therefore wrote his *Mappah* ('tablecloth', i.e. to cover the *Shulḥan Arukh*, literally, 'Prepared Table'), in which he added Ashkenazi teaching and custom. The combined work became the standard Jewish code in all Ashkenazi communities.

Isserles wrote other works of Jewish law; his decisions were accepted as authoritative. He was especially lenient in cases involving financial hardship for the underprivileged. He was versed in philosophy, Kabbalah and natural sciences, which he expounded in his *Torah ha-Olah* ('Law of the Burnt-Offering'), but he always insisted on the primacy of religious law over mystic approaches and interpretations. [81: vol. 2: IV; 87: vol. 6: 29–40] (G.W.)

Isyllus [x] (end of 4th century BCE). Greek hymn-writer whose work has the important distinction of not having been shaped by the literary tradition but has survived in a long inscription. The *Hymn of Isyllus* supports *aretē* and *aidōs* (*see* HOMER), introduces a new law to establish a festival for Apollo and ASCLEPIUS, propagandizes for Epidaurus (not Tricca) as the aboriginal seat of Asclepius, and relates a personal encounter with Asclepius. [19: 249–52] (J.P.K.)

J

Jabavu, Davidson Don Tengo [VI.A] (1885–1959). South African Christian spokesman and writer. He was the eldest son of J. T. Jabavu (1859–1921), a Mfengu Methodist who edited South Africa's first independent African newspaper and attempted to influence national politics. Jabavu junior was educated at Lovedale Missionary Institution and then, unable to get admission where higher education was reserved to Whites, attended Colwyn Bay Institution in Wales and London University. In 1912 he became the first Black South African university graduate, and then studied education at Birmingham and in the United States. In 1915 he was appointed to the staff of the new South African Native College (later Fort Hare University), with a special concern for Bantu languages. He was a major figure in African education (for him this included health care, temperance and agriculture) and was active in promoting teachers' and farmers' organizations. A regular Black advocate and interpreter to government and the White community, he followed his father in seeking reform by liberalizing existing institutions. Abroad he became a regular 'voice of Africa' at conferences, including the International Missionary Council meetings at Jerusalem (1928) and Madras (1938). His books included *The Black Problem, The Segregation Fallacy, Disabilities in South Africa*, a life of his father and various works in Xhosa. [394] (A.F.W.)

Jacob [XV] (*c.* 18th century BCE). Third of the Israelite patriarchs; son of ISAAC and REBEKAH, younger twin of Esau; eponymous ancestor of the 12 tribes. He purchased from Esau the firstborn rights for a dish of lentils ('a mess of pottage' is the best-known translation) when Esau was fatigued. Subsequently he conspired with his mother to secure by stealth from Isaac the blessing of the firstborn. The rivalry between the brothers may reflect the tension between the hunter (Esau) and the husbandman (Jacob). Fearing his brother's wrath, Jacob left his home in the Land of Canaan and made his way to his mother's family in Paddan-Aram (Mesopotamia). *En route*, at Bethel, he had a vision in which God promised him a numerous progeny who would possess the Land of Canaan. Reaching his destination, he was welcomed by his uncle, Laban, whose daughters – LEAH and RACHEL – he married, working off the bride-price by minding his uncle's sheep for 14 years. Jacob's 12 sons and daughter were born from both wives, and from their maids, Bilhah and Zilpah. Through a stratagem Jacob became the owner of a large part of Laban's flock, which strained relations between them. Although they eventually made a covenant, Jacob set out with his family and possessions to return to Canaan. On the way, at the ford of Jabbok, he traditionally wrestled with an angel of God who changed Jacob's name to Israel (interpreted as 'you have struggled with God'). Esau came with a large troop of armed men to meet him, but Jacob's fears of the confrontation proved groundless and the brothers were reconciled.

When he arrived in Canaan, Jacob settled in Shechem but later moved to Bethel. Jacob's favouritism towards his son JOSEPH evoked deep jealousy among his other sons, culminating in their selling Joseph into slavery. Taken to Egypt, he eventually became the country's vizier and, in view of a famine in Canaan, Jacob and the rest of the family all eventually moved to the Land of Goshen in

Egypt. After blessing his 12 sons (an anticipation of the fate of the 12 tribes) Jacob died at the age of 147. His body was taken by Joseph and his brothers for burial in the Cave of Machpelah in Hebron beside his parents and grandparents.

The story of Jacob is contained in *Genesis* 30–35. [68: XI–XII] (G.W.)

Jacob Baradaeus [VI.B] [Yaqub al-Barda'i] (*b c*500). He became a monk and studied in Nisibis from 527 to 542/3. Empress Theodora had the imprisoned Coptic Patriarch Theodosius consecrate two bishops for the Christian Arab ruler al-Harith; Theodore as Bishop of Bostra, and Jacob as Bishop of Edessa. Justinian, however, was persecuting the Monophysite Church. Jacob escaped from Constantinople and travelled for years, dressed in rags, ordaining Monophysite bishops and priests throughout the East. He probably visited the court of the Persian King KHOSROW I at Seleucia in 559 and raised Bishop Ahudemmeh to the rank of 'Metropolitan of the East' or Maphrian. Jacob is venerated as the virtual founder of the Syrian Orthodox Church, called the Jacobite Church in his honour. [5: IX; 56: V; 60: 266ff.] (D.J.M.)

Jacob ben Asher [XV] [Ba'al ha-Turim] (*c*.1270–1340). Rabbinic codifier in Spain. Son of ASHER BEN JEHIEL, his knowledge – like that of his father – was almost exclusively rabbinic, and he had little familiarity with secular learning. He was born in Germany and emigrated with his father to Spain (1303), where he refused a rabbinical position so as to devote himself to study and writing. His Bible commentary, much influenced by that of MOSES NAḤMANIDES, concentrated on the literal meaning of the text but also made use of word-play and numerology. [81: vol. 2: II]

His father's code left room for a clear statement of the actual legal rulings. Jacob compiled his father's decisions and appended them to each tractate of the Talmud. On the basis of this he then wrote his classic code, *Sefer ha-Turim* ('Book of Rows', referring to the four rows of stones on the ancient breastplate of the high priest, used as oracles of judgment), from which he is widely known as Ba'al ha-Turim ('Master of the Rows'). Like his father, he omitted those laws no longer practised as a result of the destruction of the Temple and the exile from the Land of Israel. The work was divided into four parts: (1) *Oraḥ Ḥayyim* ('Way of Life'), dealing with the rituals of daily life, including blessings, prayers, synagogue regulations, Sabbath and festivals; (2) *Yoreh De'ah* ('Teacher of Knowledge') concerned mainly with dietary laws, ritual purity of women and ritual laws concerning mourning, vows and charity; (3) *Even ha-Ezer* ('Stone of Help', see 1 Samuel 3: 13) on personal status, family relations, such as marriage and divorce; (4) *Ḥoshen Mishpat* ('Breastplate of Judgment') on civil law and the dispensation of justice as applicable in the Diaspora.

Jacob succinctly states the law, usually without noting the source (unless there is a difference of opinion among his predecessors, in which case he quotes the differing views). His work was recognized as authoritative by most Jewish communities, and formed the basis of the ultimate code, the *Shulḥan Arukh* of JOSEPH CARO, which adopted the same quadripartite division. [81: vol. 2: IV] (G.W.)

Jaʿfar al-Ṣādiq [XII] (*c*.700–756). Sixth Imām of the Twelver Shiʿites. The son of the fifth Imam, Muḥammad al-Bāqir, Jaʿfar succeeded to the Imamate on his father's death around 735. This was a period of religious and political ferment, with a majority of Shiʿites supporting messianic revolutionary movements. Unlike other Shīʿī leaders of the time, however, Jaʿfar became famous for his learning, attracting large numbers of scholars, both Sunnī and Shiʿite, to his home in Medina.

In the early stages of the agitation leading to the ʿAbbasid rising, Jaʿfar was approached as a candidate for the role of 'Pretender', but declined. His quietist political stance reflected the attitude of the Imāmī Shīʿa from the time of the martyrdom of ḤUSAYN, and became a central feature of Shiʿite doctrine throughout the later period.

With the success of the ʿAbbasids, political victory for any extremist Shiʿite group became a virtual impossibility. Jaʿfar's response to this was to emphasize the non-political dimensions of the Imamate, portraying the Imām as a purely religious leader possessed of infallible knowledge and responsive to the spiritual rather than temporal needs of his followers.

Much of the later doctrine of the Imamate may be traced back to statements ascribed to Jaʿfar. He has also been considered an important influence on early Ṣufism. Several books on divination and related practices have been attributed to him, but their authenticity is doubtful.

Although Jaʿfar did not establish any organized legal system, modern Shiʿites refer to the 'Jaʿfarī' law-school, in token of his role as an authority on legal matters.

Jaʿfar died in Medina in 756 and was succeeded as Imām by his son Mūsā. A minority of his followers, however, retained their allegiance to another son, Ismāʿīl, who had predeceased him. These formed the nucleus of the important Ismāʿīlī sect. [64: X, XI; 92: II, V] (D.M.)

al-Jāḥiẓ, Abū ʿUthmān ʿAmr [XII] (*c*.776–868/9). An Arab (but actually with an admixture of Negro blood) writer and Islamic thinker of the period of the florescence of the ʿAbbasid caliphate in Iraq. Born in Baṣra of obscure parentage, he studied with the scholars of the Basran milieu, which was at that time in a state of intellectual ferment, acquiring a questioning mind and an immense range of interests, including obscure and intriguing topics that he was to use in his many literary works. Then he moved to the caliphal capitals of Baghdad and Samarra to work as a secretary and teacher, but returned to Baṣra for his last years. Al-Jāḥiẓ's religio-political polemics were firstly concerned with defence of the ʿAbbasid dynasty against its opponents of the Shīʿa, the partisans of the claims of ʿALĪ's descendants, and supporters of the memory of ʿUTHMĀN and of the previous Umayyad dynasty, regarding all of which he wrote several works on the nature of the imamate, i.e. the secular and spiritual leadership of the Muslim community. Second, he was a strong partisan of the Muʿtazilite movement in religion and philosophy, using the newly evolved weapons of *kalām*, dogmatic and argumentative theology, to write on (e.g.) the defence of Islam against Christianity, the createdness of the Qurʾān, the stripping of accretions from our conception of God (hence strongly attacking anthropomorphism) and the nature of our knowledge of God (that it is to be achieved only through experience and self-perfection). It is likely that he wrote on other characteristic doctrines of the Muʿtazilites, such as God's necessary justice, but the subsequent triumph of conservative orthodoxy over Muʿtazilism led to the destruction, or the failure to survive, of many Muʿtazilite works, almost certainly including some by al-Jāḥiẓ. [35: 'Djāḥiẓ'; 99] (C.E.B.)

Jaimal Siṅgh [XI] (1838–1903). The first guru of the Beas group of Radhasoamis. He was a Sikh from Gurdaspur in the Punjab who enlisted in the Indian army. When his regiment was posted to Agra in 1856, he came under the influence of the Radhasoami founder SHIV DAYAL SIṄGH, whose faithful disciple he remained until the latter's death in 1878. Jaimal Singh's background made him exceptional among the inner circle of the early Radhasoamis, most of whom were Hindus from Uttar Pradesh, and he came to see his special mission as carrying the message to the Punjab. On his retirement from the army he accordingly established his centre beside the river Beas, which became known as Dera Baba Jaimal Singh, or now in Radhasoami circles simply as 'Beas'. Jaimal Singh's loose ties with the parent body were severed when he refused to acknowledge the authority of BRAHMA SHANKAR MISRA. The Beas group he founded became the most important of the many Radhasoami sects under the long reign of his able successor Savan Singh (1858–1948), a Sikh military engineer whom he initiated in 1894, and it now has an extensive following both in the Punjab and overseas. The central Radhasoami doctrines of devotion to the living guru (*guru-bhakti*) and the practice of inner meditation (*surat-śabd-yoga*) are vigorously maintained by the Radhasoami Satsang Beas and its offshoot, the Ruhani Satsang in Delhi. The most notable difference from the Agra Radhasoamis is the emphasis laid on the line of spiritual succession supposed to link the Radhasoamis with the medieval Sants, more extreme theories even postulating direct links of discipleship between the last Sikh Guru, GOBIND SIṄGH, and Shiv Dayal's teacher Tulsi Sahib [83: 61]. [4: 71–90; 58: VII; 83: 52–69] (C.S.)

Jalaram [XI] [Jalabapa] (1799–1881). Lohana merchant from Saurashtra, famous for his miracles, for his charity and for his devotion to Lord Ram. Jalaram is widely revered by Gujaratis, but he is hardly known outside Gujarat. Although Jalaram is not considered to have been divine, he looks after his devotees and intercedes on their behalf with Lord Ram.

Jalaram's birthplace in Virpur in central Saurashtra is a centre of pilgrimage and is one of the four Annakshetras of Saurashtra, that is, places where food is available to all pilgrims, free of charge. There is no formal organization, nor rites nor gurus. The shrine contains the cult's sacred relics of a bag and staff. Lord Ram disguised as an old ascetic visited Jalaram, who gave him food and hospitality. The old man asked for a companion to help him on his journey and Jalaram sent his wife, who was always obedient to her husband. When they reached the river the old man gave Jalaram's wife his bag and stick. He vanished and Jalaram heard a voice which told him what had happened and instructed him to fetch his wife. The stick and the bag are on display in the shrine but no one is permitted to look in the bag.

The influence of Jalaram has been spread by migrant Gujaratis in East Africa and the United Kingdom among Jains, Hindu Panjabis and Sikhs. [77a; 89a] (R.M.J.D.)

Jāmāsp 'Velāyatī' [XXVI] (18th century). Learned Zoroastrian priest of Kerman, Iran, who in 1721 was invited by Parsis to Surat, Gujarat, to settle a ritual question. While there Jāmāsp 'Velāyatī' ('of the motherland') instructed three young priests further in the holy languages, Avesta and Pahlavi. Subsequently one of them, Dārāb Kumāna, translated the Avesta for Anquetil du Perron, who was able thus to acquaint Europe with the Zoroastrian scriptures. Through Jāmāsp's presence the Parsis became more aware of the difference of a month between their own and the Irani calendars, and some adopted the latter as the more ancient (*qadīm*). Thus the Parsi 'Kadmis' came into being, causing great dissension. [42: 62–4; 18: 444, 470–71; 9: 189–90] (M.B.)

Jāmī, Mawlānā Nūr al-Dīn ʿAbd al-Raḥmān [XII] (1414–1492). Famous poet of Afghanistan. Jāmiʿ was born in Kharjird in the district of Jām (hence his name) in the province of Herat in what was then the empire of Shāhrukh (1406–1447), the son of Tamerlane (Tīmūr Lang). Shāhrukh was known as a patron of the arts and sciences in his father's residence in Samarkand; he founded a famous library at Herat, where his successors Abū Saʿīd (1452–1469) and Ḥusayn Bayqara (1469–1506) resided and held court.

Jāmī led a busy life as a poet and religious leader of the great Ṣūfī order of the Naqshabandīs. He studied with the famous mystic teacher Saʿd al-Dīn Muḥammad al-Kāshgharī from Turkestan, the successor of the great BAHĀ' AL-DĪN NAQSHBANDĪ himself. He made the pilgrimage to Mecca and Medina, studied briefly in Baghdad and returned home via Tabrīz (1472).

Jāmī was the last great poet who used the Persian language in the great classical tradition of Saʿdī and Ḥāfiẓ. He wrote seven epic poems (*mathnavīs*), which he collected in a great work called *Haft Awrang* ('Seven Thrones'), and three books of lyrics. He also wrote scholarly works in prose, including a commentary on the Qur'ān and on *ḥadīth*. Jāmī's famous explanatory works on mysticism are *Nafaḥāt al-uns* ('Breaths of Divine Intimacy') and *Lawā'iḥ* ('Shafts of Divine Light'). [14; 115] (J.K.)

Jamsetji Jeejeebhoy. *See* JEEJEEBHOY, JAMSETJI.

Jassā Siṅgh Āhlūvālīā [XXIII] (1718–1783). Prominent Sikh military leader during the turbulent middle years of the 18th century. He was born in the village of Āhlū near Lahore. Gathering around himself a group of loyal followers, he made Kapūrthalā his headquarters and together with other Sikhs fought the Mughals and Afghāns for control of the Punjab. Other Sikh chieftains commanded similar groups and when they joined together to form a loose alliance Jassā Siṅgh Āhlūvālīā was recognized as supreme leader. He died issueless when the Sikhs were gaining mastery of the Punjab. [43: 24–44] (W.H.M.)

Javouhey, Anne-Marie [VI.A] (1779–1850). Pioneer of Catholic women's missions. She was born in Chamblanc, Burgundy, the daughter of a wealthy farmer. Under the French revolutionary regimes she sheltered priests and organized meetings. At 17 or 18 years of age she had the first of several visionary experiences; as a result she believed herself called to found a community for teaching and the care of the sick and to work with Black people. After some relationships with other orders, she formed a small community of her own, including several of her family, in 1807. This 'Association of St Joseph' made Cluny its headquarters. Early ventures in teaching, some disastrous, were financed or indemnified by her father. She adopted the Lancastrian educational method, despite its condemnation as 'Protestant'. Overseas work began in appalling conditions in colonial hospitals in Île de Bourbon (Réunion) in 1817 and Gorée (Senegal) in 1819. From 1822 to 1824 she worked not only in Senegal, but in the British hospitals in the Gambia and Sierra Leone, at the request of the crypto-Catholic Governor, Charles MacCarthy. Near Cayenne (French Guiana) she established a model Christian agricultural colony of freed slaves on the lines of the Paraguayan reductions, directing it in person between 1828 and 1843. She had long desired an order of missionary priests for Africans; on her return to France she met Jacob Francis Libermann, whose spiritual ideals she shared. The Sisters of St Joseph of Cluny were fused with the Libermann's Society of the Holy Spirit in 1848.

Mère Javouhey was frequently in controversy: with her father, with male ecclesiastics who sought control of her community (she was once ecclesiastically deprived of the sacraments for two years), and with slaveholders and commercial interests. Successive French governments wanted her efficient nursing and educational services for the colonies. In the 1848 Revolution she cared for the wounded, unmolested in Paris. She was early both in foreseeing the need for an African church led by Africans, and in organizing an overseas mission staffed by women. [529] (A.F.W.)

Jayadeva [XI] (12th century). Poet, author of the Sanskrit lyric poem *Gītagovinda*. The largely legendary biographies place his birth in Bihar, in Orissa, or in Bengal; he seems to have received the patronage of Lakṣmaṇasena in Bengal, and is particularly associated with the temple of Jagannāth at Puri in Orissa. The *Gītagovinda* is of lasting importance on three counts: by consolidating pre-existing mythic and poetic references it is the first text to establish Rādhā as a fully-fledged 'consort' for Kṛṣṇa; it establishes a mood of sublime eroticism which was to prove enormously influential on the later development of Kṛṣṇaism; and it is perhaps the only lyric poem of its kind to enjoy a pan-Indian popularity in traditions of song and dance. These factors establish Jayadeva as one of the most important literary-cum-religious figures of the medieval period. In the *Gītagovinda*, Kṛṣṇa is fully identified with Viṣṇu while yet being described as Rādhā's lover in the idealized context of the grove on the Yamuna riverbank. The secret love of Rādhā and Kṛṣṇa is in marked contrast to the open sporting of Kṛṣṇa with the *gopīs*; Jayadeva imbued well established conventions of erotic lyrical poetry with a newly symbolic import, and the *Gītagovinda*'s narrative interplay of separation and consummation was to provide a model for successive generations of Vaiṣṇava poets and theologians, whose debt to him is openly admitted. While capable of being read as a merely sensual lyric, Jayadeva's poem is thus typically interpreted from the perspective of late medieval Vaiṣṇavism, with Rādhā being drawn not merely as a poetic heroine but as the innate potency (*śakti*) of Kṛṣṇa. [78; 100] (R.S.)

Jeejeebhoy, Jamsetji [XXVI] (1783–1859). Leading Parsi merchant and the first Indian to receive a knighthood and baronetcy from the British Government. This was for his vast and general philanthropy. Within his own community he helped the poor, founded hospitals and endowed three fire-temples. Moving beyond such traditional Zoroastrian acts of charity, he created an education fund that supported 60 Parsi schools, with regular religious instruction. He also founded, in 1863, the Sir J. J. Zarthoshti Madressa (College) for priests' sons. Although socially progressive, allowing his wife and daughters to mix in society, he was staunchly traditionalist in matters of religion. [44; 1: 1–19; 42: 412–18; 53] (J.R.H.)

Jehu-Appiah, Jemisimiham [I.A.] (1892–1943). Founder and General Head Prophet and Leader of the Musama Disco Christo Church (MDCC), Ghana's earliest independent church. Of Fante origin, active politically as well as spiritually, he was an executive of the Aborigines Rights Protection Society. In 1919 he created the Faith Society within the Methodist Church. Dissatisfied, he founded the independent MDCC or Army of the Cross of Christ Church in 1922. First to found a pentecostal movement in West Africa, he worked to combine native culture and tradition with the Christian gospel. Upon his death church leadership was handed to his son, Mathapoly Moses Jehu-Appiah. [3] (R.H.)

Jenghiz Khan. *See* CHINGGIS KHAN.

Jeremiah [XV] (7th–6th centuries BCE). Israelite prophet. Born to a priestly family at Anathoth near Jerusalem, he began to prophesy at an early age during the reign of King Josiah (626 BCE). His initial message was directed against the apostasy and idolatry of the people and called for their repentance. Moving to Jerusalem, he was appalled at the sinfulness of the population, which he relentlessly denounced. Sometimes he resorted to symbolic actions which made him the butt of public mockery. His forecast that the Temple would be destroyed if the people did not change their ways brought on the anger of the priests and the masses. The priests sought his death, and as a precaution he began to dictate his prophecies to his scribe Baruch. When these were read to the king, Jehoiakim, he burned the scroll, which Jeremiah subsequently rewrote.

After the first exile to Babylon (597 BCE) Jeremiah advocated a policy of submitting to Babylon and called on those exiled to make the most of their captivity, and to continue to practise their religion as God is present in all lands. He saw the Babylonian ruler, Nebuchadnezzar, as the instrument of God; after a few generations the Babylonians would be punished but meanwhile they must be accepted. When King Zedekiah rebelled against Babylonian suzerainty, Jeremiah preached that resistance was futile. He was thrown into a cistern, from which he was rescued by an Ethiopian eunuch. After Jerusalem was destroyed (586 BCE), he foretold the return of the exiles after a period of 70 years. As a pro-Babylonian he was allowed by the conquerors to remain in Judah, but after the assassination of the Babylonian-appointed governor, the Jews remaining took fright and fled to Egypt, taking Jeremiah with them. He is last heard of warning the Jews in Egypt against the perils of idolatry.

Because the Book of *Lamentations* was (probably incorrectly) ascribed to him, Jeremiah became known as a lachrymose prophet, but his ultimate message is one of hope, forecasting the eventual return of the Jews to their land. Many of his main messages were already to be found in his prophetical predecessors – AMOS, HOSEA and ISAIAH. Among his special emphases were the unique and reciprocal nature of the covenant between God and Israel, the primacy of the ethical law, without which ritual is meaningless, expressed through truth and justice, and the eternity of Israel, despite all disasters [38: VI]. The writings of Jeremiah are contained in the biblical book named after him. [10] (G.W.)

Jerome [VI.A] [Eusebius Hieronymus] (*c*.347–420). Bible translator and Church Father. He was born in Stridon near Aquileia in Dalmatia. Sent to Rome to study under Aelius Donatus, a grammarian, he studied the principal Latin authors, some philosophy and rhetoric. He was later baptized, possibly in 366. The following year he went to study in Trier and was attracted by monasticism. In 374 he went on a pilgrimage to Antioch, studied Greek and began an intense study of the Bible. He spent a few years as a desert hermit at Chalcis, during which time he learned Hebrew. After returning to Antioch he was ordained priest by Paulinus. He returned to Rome by way of Constantinople, where he met GREGORY OF NYSSA and GREGORY OF NAZIANZUS, and from 382 to 385 was secretary to Pope Damasus. After the latter's death he returned to Antioch and thence to Egypt and Palestine. He settled in Bethlehem, where he was joined by two Roman women, Paula and Eustochium. Together they established two monasteries, one male and one female. For the rest of his life Jerome lived the life of a monk, spending time in translating the Bible from Hebrew and Greek into Latin, the Vulgate version, and translating the works of ORIGEN into Latin. His other works include polemics, letters and biblical studies. [400; 430; 575] (T.T.)

Jesus [VI.A] [Jesus of Nazareth; Jesus Christ] (*c*.7/6 BCE–*c*.30 CE). Deciding how much is known of the life of Jesus is a difficult scholarly problem. The basic documents concerning his life are 'The Gospels': *Matthew, Mark, Luke* and *John*. The first three, the so-called 'Synoptic Gospels', have much common material, though often with important discrepancies. The Fourth Gospel appears to belong to a rather different tradition. There is some material in documents written by Roman and Jewish writers which would merely confirm that Jesus was a historical person. There are those Christians who believe that the Gospels are an accurate biographical collection of stories concerning Jesus. Others believe that, while there is a significant amount of material of an authentic nature, much of the Gospel material is made up of early Christian legend and gloss on an originally small corpus of material. The latter group will vary in their acceptance of what is authentic from the very radical who claim that little of historical accuracy is known, to others who would claim that a fair amount of the Gospel material can be depended upon. Taking the minimal view would lead us to the conclusion that Jesus was a Galilean, whose parents were Joseph and MARY. He was a teacher who severely questioned the Jewish religion in which he was raised and a wonder-worker who attracted a number of followers. He was publicly executed near Jerusalem during the procuratorship of Pontius Pilate. Beyond that the problem is highlighted by the fact that the narrative in the Synoptic Gospels would suggest a public ministry of about one year, while the narrative in the Fourth Gospel would suggest about two or three years.

According to the traditions in the Gospels he was conceived miraculously and born of a virgin in the town of Bethlehem. At the age of 12 his parents took him with them from their home in Nazareth to Jerusalem where he showed wisdom beyond his years in his conversations with the temple intellectuals. He next appears publicly when he comes to JOHN THE BAPTIST at the river Jordan who was baptizing those who were repentant and desired renewal of life through a ritual cleansing. Jesus himself seeks baptism, which John is reluctant to give since he recognizes in Jesus someone who is greater than he. Following this episode Jesus retreats to the wilderness to ponder his vocation and to endure certain temptations; he resists these, thus confirming him as the one sent by God. He becomes an itinerant preacher and teacher using homely parables to present his message. The message is that the Reign of God is at hand so those who listen to him should repent and be ready to receive the Reign which was foretold by the Hebrew prophets.

Eventually his teaching and preaching, and possibly his popularity, led to opposition from the Jewish establishment in Jerusalem. It is not easy to decide what it was exactly that brought him to trial before Pontius Pilate. There is a suggestion of blasphemy in his claims about his relationship to God, but also that his ministry was a challenge to the state and subversive of state authority. Whatever the truth, tradition tells that there was a plot whereby one of his disciples, Judas Iscariot, was bribed to inform the authorities of his whereabouts so that Jesus was arrested away from the public eye, tried and found guilty of some crime which carried capital punishment. He was publicly crucified.

Thereafter his followers claimed that Jesus was 'raised from the dead', and his 'resurrection' is a key element in the structure of belief of his followers. There are stories in the tradition which tell of his followers actually meeting and speaking with him after his grave was found empty. There is also a tradition that some of his followers were present when Jesus 'ascended' into heaven. These stories are contained in the Gospels and in *The Acts of the Apostles*, which purports to carry the story on into the early history of the Christian church. Other documents, letters by early leaders to local churches or individuals, early apologetic material sometimes in simulated letter form and one document of an apocalyptic nature, make up the scriptures on which faith in Jesus as the saviour of the human race is based. Collectively these scriptures are referred to as the *New Testament*. Christians also reverence the scriptures of the Jews, giving them the title of *Old Testament*.

On these documents are based all belief in Jesus as the Christ (Hebrew: *Mashiah*), the Anointed of God, and all doctrine concerning his status as Son of God, the Second Person of the Holy Trinity, with the Father and the Holy Spirit. [75; 350; 551; 619; 708; 820] (For an account of Jesus in the Islamic tradition, *see* ʿISA.) (T.T.)

Jikaku Daishi. *See* ENNIN.

al-Jīlānī, ʿAbd al-Qādir [XII] (1077–1166). Supposed founder of the Qādirī Ṣūfī order and arguably the most popular saint of the Islamic world. He was born in the Iranian province of Jīlān (Gilan), to the south of the Caspian. At the age of 18 he was sent to Baghdad, where he studied religious law according to the Ḥanbalite school of Jurisprudence. On the completion of his legal studies, he received instruction in Ṣūfī mysticism from Abū'l-Khayr Muḥammad al-Dabbās. After this, he is thought to have spent some 25 years wandering as an ascetic in the desert regions of Iraq.

In 1127 he began to preach publicly in Baghdad, where he became head of the first Ḥanbalite college; but it is significant that his growing reputation was as a scholar, not a Ṣūfī shaykh. There is, in fact, no evidence that he claimed to act as a spiritual guide or to have established a separate Ṣūfī path. Only after his death did miracle stories, a body of mystical teachings, a liturgy and a distinct order attach themselves to him. His own extant writings are mainly sermons of a markedly orthodox bent.

In the course of time, the highly orthodox Ḥanbalī theologian and preacher was transformed into the prototype of Islamic saintliness throughout the Islamic world – a development for which no satisfactory explanation has yet been advanced [115: 247–8]. Cults centred around him have grown up everywhere, incorporating large numbers of sacred sites. His tomb in Baghdad is still a popular centre of pilgrimage. He is referred to as the *Ghawth-i aʿẓam* ('The Greatest Assistance'), the king of the saints, and the *quṭb* or spiritual axis of his age.

The Qādirī Ṣūfī order of which he is the supposed founder was never actually greatly popular, producing few eminent mystics and little Ṣūfī literature. [10; 34: 'ʿAbd al-Ḳādir al-Djīlī'; 65] (D.M.)

Jinasena [XIII] (9th century [29]). Digambara Jain author. He was a member of the Pañcastūpānvaya, later called the Sena Gaṇa, a Digambara monastic group which probably came originally from Benares and was later to develop connections with Śravaṇa Belgola, the centre of Jainism in south India. Although Jinasena was the author of an important commentary on one of the early Digambara scriptures, his real significance lies in his association with the 'Great Lorebook' (*Mahāpurāṇa*), perhaps the finest version of the 'Universal History', the account of the great teachers and kings of Jain legend. This genre of literature synthesizes a vast quantity of Jain and non-Jain literature and effectively provides a sectarian history of the world, of crucial importance for Jain religious identity.

Jinasena in fact did not live to finish the 'Great Lorebook' (it was completed by his pupil Guṇabhadra) but the large portion which he did write, the 'Lorebook of the Beginning' (*Ādipurāṇa*) provides a lucid and poetic account of the life of the first *tīrthaṅkara* (*see* MAHĀVIRA) Ṛṣabha who instructed humankind at the beginning of this world-era in all the social arts. It also contains a lengthy account of Bharata, the first universal emperor, and Bāhubali, his brother, who, after defeating Bharata in a battle for their father's kingdom, repented, became an ascetic and was, according to the Digambaras, the first being of this world-age to achieve spiritual salvation. It should be noted that the most famous Jain monument in India is the colossal monolithic image of Bāhubali at Śravaṇa Belgola, which was erected in 980 at the command of a victorious general Cāmuṇḍarāya.

Chapters 38 to 40 of the 'Lorebook of the Beginning' represent an attempt by Jinasena to legislate for the householder's way of life, providing, among other matters, Jain versions of Hindu life-cycle rituals which are still in use amongst Digambara Jains today. (P.D.)

Jineśvara [XIII] (11th century). Śvetāmbara Jain monk who was one of the founders of the reforming sect, the Kharatara Gaccha. One and a half millennia after the death of MAHĀVĪRA, many Jain monks in Gujarat and Rajasthan had taken to the temple-dwelling way of life. This practice involved the abandonment of the ascetic mendicancy prescribed in the scriptures and the adoption of a sedentary life in temples or monasteries built near temples, thus bringing about a loosening of the rigid rules about alms-begging and also, according to the critics of the temple-dwelling monks, the embezzlement of temple funds. Jineśvara was one of an apparently small group of monks centred around a teacher called Vardhamāna who resisted this heretical tendency and devoted themselves to its confutation.

Sources which are at least a century later relate how Jineśvara in 1024 defeated in debate a leading temple-dwelling monk named Sūra in front of the royal assembly of King Durlabha at his capital, Patan, in north Gujarat. As a result of this victory Jineśvara seems to have had the epithet '*Kharatara*' (meaning 'Fierce' or 'Quick-witted') bestowed upon him and the lineage of monks which succeeded him took this as the name of their sect (*gaccha*). Jineśvara's triumph was the first significant event in the history of the Kharatara Gaccha which subsequently succeeded in re-establishing the wandering mendicant life described in the scriptures.

Of Jineśvara's works (none of which has been translated into a Western language) perhaps the most interesting is a collection of stories in Prakrit, the *Kathākoṣaprakaraṇa*. (P.D.)

Jinshu. *See* SHEN-HSUI.

Jñānagarbha [IV] (8th century). Indian Buddhist philosopher within the Madhyamaka scholastic tradition, probably from Bengal. He is reputed to have been the teacher of ŚĀNTARAKṢITA, and his thought moves within the general ambit of that of BHĀVAVIVEKA. His most important work is a text whose title suggests that it explores the central Mādhyamika theme of the two truths (*Satyadvayavibhaṅga*, 'The Distinction Between the Two Truths' [59]), but which is actually a systematic exposition in a relatively short span of all the central systematic and soteriological ideas of late Indian Madhyamaka Buddhism. This work was translated into Tibetan at an early period, and has been much used as a teaching text ever since. [186: 67–71] (P.J.G.)

Jñāneśvar [XI] [Jñāneśvara; Jñānadeva] (1275–1296). The creator of almost the first and certainly the most venerated work of Marathi religious literature, usually called after him *Jñāneśvarī*, although its original and more descriptive title is *Bhāvārthadīpikā* ('The Lamp of Plain Meaning'). As with most early Indian writers, the accepted account of his life is taken from texts written centuries later, which for the Marathi 'poet saints' were finally fixed in the voluminous hagiographies of Mahipati (1715–1790). According to these traditions Jñāneśvar was the second son of a Brahman who was outcast by his fellows for having returned to domestic life, by his guru's order, after taking *sannyāsa*. Jñāneśvar's guru was his own elder brother Nivṛttināth, and he was born either at Apegaon, on the Godavari near Paithan, or at Alandi north-east of Poona, according to whichever tradition is preferred. In his short life he performed several miracles, went on pilgrimage round the northern holy places with NĀMDEV and finally returned to write his great work at Nevase on the Godavari again and take *samādhi* at Alandi. *Jñāneśvarī*, dated to 1290 in the colophons of some of the much later manuscripts, is an extended verse commentary on the *Bhagavad Gītā* in which Jñāneśvar expounds in vivid language and with a wealth of imagery the paths of action (*karma*), devotion (*bhakti*) and knowledge (*jñāna*). A good number of other shorter religious poems are ascribed to him, some of them acknowledged as spurious by even his most devoted adherents, and notably a work of purely vedantic teaching the *Anubhavāmṛta*, confusingly known also as *Amṛtānubhava*. In addition there are numerous *abhangas* – short devotional poems – addressed to the god Viṭṭhala of Pandharpur, the most important centre of pilgrimage in Maharashtra. In the last line of most of these he calls himself Nivṛttināth's Jñānabā, and so Jñāneśvar is regarded as having laid the foundations of the Vārkarī sect, the 'company of saints' who make regular pilgrimage to Pandharpur singing the devotional songs of all their saintly forebears. The discipleship of Nivṛttināth, implying a connection with the Śaiva Nāth sect, the sternly monistic teaching of the *Anubhavāmṛta*, the fact that there is no mention of Viṭṭhala in *Jñāneśvarī* but only a predilection towards *bhakti* that does no more than follow the *Gītā* itself, all this has given rise to innumerable controversies among scholars and to the postulation of several alternative Jñāneśvars. However, to the faithful of the Vārkarī sect and indeed to most Maharashtrians Jñānadev is one and unique and the author of everything to which his name is attached. He is worshipped as quasi-divine, especially in the temples of Alandi and Apegaon, and his *pālakhī* – the palanquin that carries his representative *pādukā* from Alandi to Pandharpur and back – is the most prestigious of the 30 or more that accompany each pilgrimage. [62; 109] (I.M.P.R.)

Joan of Arc [VI.A] [Jeanne d'Arc] (*c*.1412–1431). She was born and brought up in Domrémy in Champagne. She was known as the 'Maid of Orléans' and she called herself 'La Pucelle'. At the age of 13 she heard the 'voice of God' for the first time. The 'voice' instructed her to go to the Dauphin to advise him on driving the English out of France. She took a vow of perpetual virginity. The 'voices' increased in number and soon she was claiming to have heard the saints Catherine of Alexandria and Margaret of Antioch along with the archangel Michael. She pressed her claims to save France and was able eventually to persuade Charles VII to allow her to lead an expedition to Orléans. She was examined by theologians at Poitiers who cleared her of any taint of heresy and three women who examined her physically declared her a virgin. Her efforts succeeded in Orléans; other towns along the Loire were also captured. Her insistence on carrying on the fight led her into disobeying the king and to her capture by the English in May 1430 near Compiègne. The French authorities made no attempt to save her. The English handed her over to an episcopal court in Rouen for trial as a witch and heretic. Under pressure she briefly recanted but then stood by her stories of visions. The court found against her, declaring her visions 'false and diabolical'. She was burned at the stake on 31 May 1431. [53; 299; 664] (T.T.)

Johanan ben Zakkai [XV] (1st century). Rabbi and Jewish leader in the period immediately following the destruction of the Second Temple. The little biographical information available is a mixture of fact and legend. He apparently studied in Jerusalem and, after a period in Galilee, taught in Jerusalem, where he was involved in controversies with the Sadducees. Teaching was the focus of his life; he said that 'A Jew was born to study Torah.' He had many disciples to whom he taught law and homiletic exposition, ethics and esoteric lore. He is the first sage who is noted as having an involvement in the esoteric-mystical.

When the Jewish revolt against the Romans was at its height and Jerusalem was besieged, he decided to escape from the city to save Judaism from the liquidation which he foresaw might ensue from the destruction of the Temple. Various versions of his escape are recounted; the best known relates that he was concealed in a coffin carried out by his disciples. Brought before the Roman general Vespasian, Johanan correctly foretold that Vespasian would shortly be emperor (*compare* JOSEPHUS FLAVIUS). Asked by Vespasian what he wished in return, Johanan was granted the request that the small college at Jabneh, near the coast, should be spared, along with its scholars. The capture of Jerusalem, and the end of the last shreds of Jewish independence and sovereignty, together with the destruction of the Temple and its sacrificial system which was the focus of Jewish ritual, could well have meant the end of Judaism. However, Johanan built up in Jabneh an alternative religious centre, the seat of the Sanhedrin and of Jewish religious life, making key decisions regarding the calendar and the fate of ceremonies not previously conducted outside Jerusalem. To maintain the Torah without the Temple, Johanan reorganized religious life and worship (now exclusively synagogue-oriented) and re-established a national leadership around the Jabneh religious court. The rabbis were now undisputably the leaders of the people and Johanan worked to construct national unity. His parting words to his disciples (*c*.80 CE) were: 'May you fear God as much as you fear man.' It was due to his initiative that Judaism emerged from crushing blows and established new foundations for its future development. [59] (G.W.)

John XXIII [VI.B] [Baldassare Cossa] (*d*.1419). Antipope, reigned 1410–15. In 1309 Pope Clement V moved his court to Avignon. His successors, John XXII (1316–34), Benedict XII (1334–42), Clement VI (1342–52), Innocent VI (1352–70) and Urban V (1362–70) reigned in luxury there until CATHERINE OF SIENA persuaded Gregory XI to return to Rome (17 January 1377). On Gregory's death the Roman mob, fearing a French pope would return to Avignon, clamoured for the election of a Roman or at least an Italian pope. Archbishop Prignano of Bari was enthroned as Urban VI (18 April 1378): his arrogance, cruelty and irascibility showing him utterly unsuited for his office.

The cardinals withdrew to Anagni, declared Urban invalidly elected, and on 20 September 1378 elected Robert of Geneva as Clement VII. Clement failed to dethrone Urban, and in May 1379 moved to Avignon.

Rival popes now reigned, as Benedict XIII succeeded Clement in Avignon (1394), and Boniface IX (1389), Innocent VII (1404) and Gregory XII (1406) succeeded Urban VI.

In frustration cardinals of both lines summoned a council at Pisa which deposed Benedict XIII and Gregory XII and elected a third pope, Peter Philargos, Alexander V. On his death his cardinals elected John XXIII, Cardinal Baldassare Cossa, a former pirate and a libertine but a leading figure in the Council and a man of intelligence and ability. He convoked the Council of Constance, which accused him of terrible misdeeds. Failing to escape, he accepted deposition (29 May 1415). Gregory XII reconvoked the Council and abdicated (4 July 1415). Benedict XIII was declared deposed (26 July 1417) and Oddo Colonna was elected as Martin V (11 November 1417). Benedict's successor, Clement VIII, abdicated, his cardinals electing Martin (26 July 1429), thereby ending the schism.

When Angelo Roncalli, Pope John xxiii, was elected he was first proclaimed as John XXIV, thus indicating the uncertainty that had surrounded the status of John XXIII. [47; 89] (D.J.M.)

John XXIII [vi.a] [Angelo Giuseppe Roncalli] (1881–1963). Pope, 1958–63. He should not be confused with the antipope of the same name who died in 1419 (*see* preceding article). He was born in Sotto il Monte, near Bergamo, the son of a peasant family. He was educated at the local grammar school and was taught Latin by the local priest before entering a minor seminary at the age of 11. He received a scholarship to attend the Apollinaire seminary in Rome. He was ordained priest in 1904. In 1905 he received a doctorate in theology and was appointed secretary to the bishop of Bergamo. He and his bishop came under suspicion of heresy during Pope Pius X's attack on modernism. During the First World War he served in the medical corps and as a chaplain. In 1921 he was invited to Rome to take charge of the Society for the Propagation of the Faith, which funded foreign missions. He was made archbishop in 1925 and sent to Bulgaria to mediate between Rome and the Orthodox Church. In 1931 he became apostolic delegate and introduced Bulgarian into Catholic education and the liturgy. In 1934 with the titular archbishopric of Mesembria (Thrace) he was appointed apostolic delegate to Turkey. In 1944 he went to France as papal nuncio and helped reorganize the French church. He was made cardinal in 1953 and went to Venice as patriarch. In 1958 he was elected as a stop-gap pope but called an ecumenical council charged with the updating (*aggiornamento*) of the church and seeking unity between Christians and in the world. The documents of Vatican II, his two encyclicals, *Pacem in terris* and *Mater et magistra*, and his spiritual journal *Journey of a Soul* have been of lasting influence. [21; 404; 405] (T.T.)

John of Damascus [vi.b] (*c*.650–749). Syrian theologian. A civil servant in the Umayyad administration, he became a monk at Mar Saba in the Judean wilderness. His early writings defended the use of icons against the Byzantine emperors. Under Leo III (717–41) and his son Constantine V (741–75) iconoclasm triumphed in Byzantium. In 787 the Seventh Ecumenical Council met at Nicaea and restored the veneration of icons. A renewed outbreak of iconoclasm in the first half of the 9th century produced further iconophile writings, notably by Theodore Studites (759–826) and patriarch Nicephoros (806–815).

John composed many homilies and hymns. The *Octoēchos* of the Greek Church is attributed to him. But he is best known for *Pēgē gnōseōs* ('Fount of Knowledge') – a book in three parts, of which the last, 'On the Orthodox Faith', is perhaps the most important. In it John attempts to systematize the various theological strands within the Greek patristic tradition. It is encyclopaedic in form, and covers not only theology but aspects of natural science and medicine, showing that for John Christianity embraces every aspect of human knowledge. As he was a Chalcedonian living under Muslim rule and surrounded by Monophysites as well as Muslims, 'On the Orthodox Faith' may be seen as a manual for the propagation of Greek Christianity. [50; 64; 70; 77] (K.P.)

John of Ioannina [vi.b] (1508–1526). Martyr of the Orthodox Church. On his parents' death, John left Epirus for Istanbul. When his Turkish neighbours derided him for being a Christian and working as a tailor, John became convinced that he must prove the worth of his faith by martyrdom. At first his confessor tried to dissuade him, but at last gave his blessing. On Good Friday 1526 John made his last communion, and when again derided by his neighbours answered so forthrightly that he was denounced to the judge. Before the Cadi too he professed his faith in terms offensive to Muslim law and refused to convert. To avoid intercommunal strife the judge waited until after Easter before sentencing him to be burnt. He died, beheaded as he danced amidst the flames, singing the Easter hymn 'Christ is risen from the dead'.

The Ottomans generally exercised a remarkably liberal rule in religious matters but apostates from Islam, including former Christians reverting to Christianity, were automatically liable to the death penalty, as were persons condemned, like John, for insulting Islam. Conversion or reconversion to Islam was generally an effective way of avoiding the penalty. Several hundred 'new martyrs' of the Ottoman period are revered by the Orthodox churches. Some, like John, invited martyrdom out of religious zeal, some publicly renounced their conversion to Islam in order to expiate it by a martyr's death: their voluntary martyrdoms are respected in Eastern Christianity though contrary to Latin practice. A number were Turks like St Hasan of Epirus (1790–1814), a dervish who converted to Christianity. He was secretly baptized on Ithaca taking the name 'John'. His family were distressed to hear of his conversion, but left him in peace. An acquaintance eventually denounced him to the authorities as an apostate from Islam and he was executed. Another of the best known was St Ahmet, an architect who converted to Christianity after attending the Liturgy and who was also executed (1582). [65] (D.B.; D.J.M.)

John of Kronstadt, St [VI.B] (1829–1908). Russian Orthodox priest. John Sergiev came from Sora in North Russia. From 1851 he studied at St Petersburg Theological Academy, then married and became priest on Kronstadt Island (1855). He campaigned on behalf of the many homeless living in the port for housing and work. His success generated charitable institutions extending his work across Russia. Famous as a fiery preacher, he travelled widely, founding churches and monasteries, promoting liturgical reform. He held mass confessions and drew crowds to his celebration of the Liturgy. His spiritual autobiography *My Life in Christ*, based on a work by ST NICHOLAS CABASILAS, was very influential. [33: 346ff.; 40] (D.B.)

John of the Cross [IV.A] [Juan de Yepes y Álvarez] (1542–1591). The son of an impoverished noble family of Fontiveros, he was educated in the Jesuit college in Medina del Campo. In 1563 he entered the Carmelite monastery of Santa Ana and became Juan de Santo Matia. He studied theology at Salamanca from 1564 to 1567 and was ordained a priest in 1567. He came under the influence of TERESA OF ÁVILA, a Carmelite nun, who persuaded him not to become a Carthusian when he became disaffected with his own order. He took the name Juan de la Cruz and introduced the Reform of Teresa into his order. He became Master of the Carmelite College at Alcalá in 1570 and Confessor of the Convent of the Incarnation at Ávila in 1572. In 1577 he was imprisoned in the Carmelite monastery in Toledo by his superior for introducing the Teresian Reform. Nine months later he escaped to a lonely monastery in Calvario. By this time the Carmelites had split into two groups and John is regarded as the joint founder of the Discalced (sandal-wearing) Carmelites with Teresa. He became rector of the college at Baëza in 1579 but moved to Granada in 1581. In 1588 he was made prior at Segovia but again fell into dispute with his superiors. He was sent to one of the poorest monasteries in Ubeda and died there. He was canonized in 1726 and declared a Doctor of the Church in 1926. His mystical works include *The Ascent of Mount Carmel* and *The Dark Night of the Soul*. [401; 425; 637] (T.T.)

John Paul II [IV.A] [Karol Wojtyłal] (1920–). Pope, 1978–. He was born in Wadowice, near Kraków, Poland, and was educated in local schools until his family moved to Kraków in 1938 and he entered the Jagiellonian University to study Polish language and literature. During the German occupation the university was closed and he was made to work in a lime quarry and a chemical factory. He felt called to the priesthood and began to study theology clandestinely. After the war the university reopened and he graduated in theology in 1946. He was ordained priest in the same year. He went to Rome and gained a doctorate at the Pontifical University in 1948. From 1948 to 1951 he worked as a priest in Kraków parishes before returning to the Jagiellonian University to study philosophy. He also lectured on social ethics at Kraków seminary, and in 1956 he was appointed professor of ethics at Lublin University. In 1958 he became a bishop and in 1963 archbishop of Kraków. He became an international figure during the Second Vatican Council (1962–5). He was made a cardinal in 1967, and elected pope in 1978. He has travelled extensively as pope to Latin America (South and Central), the British Isles, South Korea, the Netherlands, southern Africa and Czechoslovakia (1990). He survived an assassination attempt in 1981. In social, political and theological matters he has been keen to reaffirm traditional values. [355; 491] (T.T.)

Johnson, James [VI.A] (*c.*1835?–1917). West African Anglican church leader. He was born to a poor Yoruba recaptive family near Benguema, Sierra Leone. He attended the Fourah Bay Institution and served as a teacher and catechist before ordination in 1863. From 1866 to 1874 he was a prominent Freetown minister, revealing the characteristics which marked his whole working life: deep Christian devotion (he was nicknamed 'Holy Johnson'), unswerving belief in African capabilities and destiny, and a gift for arousing controversy. Like E. W. BLYDEN he campaigned for the independence of the African church and for a West African university. In 1874 he went to the Yoruba mission, serving at Breadfruit Church, Lagos, until 1890, save for three years as superintendent of the inland stations. He was also a vigorous member of the colony's Legislative Council. He was equally uncompromising towards pre-Christian religious practices among African Christians and European attempts to dominate Africans, their church or their culture: 'Cannot God the Holy Ghost operate . . . for the Christianizing of the nations of Africa without their being denationalized?'

Johnson, the outstanding churchman in West Africa, was for long a bishop-in-waiting. The current in church and state was now strongly against African leadership, especially of such ability. But Johnson refused Blyden's appeal to form a new African church, even after young Europeans dismantled Bishop S. A. CROWTHER's Niger mission.

In 1890 Johnson agreed to become Assistant Bishop – a half bishop, he called it – of Western Equatorial Africa with responsibility for the Niger Delta (D. C. CROWTHER's Pastorate Church) and Benin. He itinerated incessantly. In later years his aggression was mostly directed into evangelism and against the liquor trade; and his end was clouded by the GARRICK BRAIDE controversy. He remains a crucial figure in the development of African consciousness. [33; 34; 696] (A.F.W.)

John the Baptist [IV.A, IX] (*fl.* 1st century). The son of Zacharias, a priest in the Temple in Jerusalem, and of Elizabeth, a cousin of MARY the mother of JESUS. His title derives from his self-adopted vocation of an apocalyptic preacher and ascetic who called upon people to repent of their sins and renew their spiritual life. The sign of this change in life was to be baptized in a remote place in the river Jordan. John had many followers including two men who became disciples of Jesus, PETER and ANDREW. The Gospel according to Mark begins with John's appearance in the wilderness and his baptism of Jesus. Jesus later acknowledges the importance of John as a forerunner preaching the coming of the Kingdom of God. John, in his preaching, condemned the king Herod Antipas, tetrarch of Galilee and Peraea, for divorcing his wife and marrying his half-brother's wife, Herodias. She took revenge on John by persuading her daughter Salome to require of Herod the head of John. John being already imprisoned, by tradition in the fortress of Machaerus by the Dead Sea, Herod ordered his beheading. John is honoured as a saint in the Christian tradition. [VI.A: 443a; 871a] (T.T.)

John the Baptist also features in several Gnostic traditions. IRENAEUS states that for some Gnostics John the Baptist is the son of Elizabeth of Ialdabaōth. Irenaeus also comments that according to Valentinian gnosticism John allegorized the 'boundary' (i.e. the cross) which is at the limits of the *plērōma* in his saying about the winnowing fork

(*Matthew* 3: 12, *Luke* 3: 17) [IX: 6: 288]. Logion 46 in the *Gospel of Thomas* is a version of *Matthew* 11: 11 and *Luke* 7: 28 [IX: 8: 123]; it heightens the esteem to be accorded John the Baptist, but implies that the gnostic 'child', not born of woman and so sexually undifferentiated, is superior even to John [IX: 1: 94–6].

John the Baptist is of special importance for the Mandeans, a gnostic group, partially indebted to MĀNĪ, which has survived from the late 4th century to the present. John is included among their prophets in the *Haran Gawaita* scroll [IX: 3: 2: 314]. He is described as the 'envoy of the king of light' and is opposed to and displaces Jesus, who perverted John's message [IX: 4: 39]; John also stands over against the Christian Holy Spirit, who in Mandean mythology is the demonic mother of the planets and the personification of evil. John is never depicted as the founder of the Mandean religion, but is called 'disciple' or 'priest'. Discourses which are attributed to John in the *Book of John*, a supplement to the Mandean *Ginza* ('Treasure'), are of no value for learning about the historical John the Baptist. The Mandean baptismal ceremony cannot be linked directly with the rite of John the Baptist and his followers but possibly with Jewish purificatory practice of the 1st century. The label 'John-Christians', given to Mandeans by 17th-century Christian missionaries, is of no historical significance. [IX: 9: 343–66] (G.J.B.)

John the Evangelist [VI.A]. The 'author' of the Fourth Gospel. Evidence for the clear identification of this figure is mixed. Tradition maintains that he is the person referred to in the Gospels as the brother of James, and son of Zebedee. With Simon PETER he belonged to the inner circle of the disciples of JESUS who were with him on significant occasions such as the Transfiguration of Jesus. The tradition maintains that they were known as 'the sons of thunder', a translation of the Aramaic 'Boanerges'. John also appears in *The Acts of the Apostles* as a companion of Peter and at the 'Council' of Jerusalem. Tradition further identifies John with the unnamed person in the Fourth Gospel 'whom Jesus loved'. Extra-scriptural tradition maintains that John went to Asia Minor and settled at Ephesus, that he was exiled to the island of Patmos under the Domitian persecution, where he wrote the *Apocalypse* (Book of Revelation). He is held to have returned later to Ephesus and that it was here, in old age, that he wrote the Fourth Gospel and the letters which bear his name. All these traditions are challenged for a variety of reasons, some scholars maintaining that the Gospel, Apocalypse and Letters are written by three different hands. Only in the *Apocalypse* is the author claimed to be named John. [181; 207; 414: 234–46; 450] (T.T.)

Jones, Eli Stanley [VI.A] (1884–1973). American missionary. He was born in Maryland, USA. While studying at Asbury College he felt called to be an evangelist and a missionary. He was ordained and sent to India in 1907. He worked in Lucknow, where he met his wife, Mabel Lossing, who was teaching in Isabella Thoburn College; she continued as an educational missionary until they both retired. They were married in Lucknow in 1911. Shortly thereafter they moved to Sitapur; it was during their long period there that he wrote his famous *Christ of the Indian Road* (1925). After completing it, he spent two years in America, during which period the book ran into many reprints. In England it ran to 15 editions within 18 months of publication. In 1928 he was elected a bishop by the General Conference of the Methodist Church in the United States. The morning after his election he resigned before consecration could take place, having determined to continue his work as an evangelist. By 1930 his title was 'Evangelist-at-large for India and the world'. By this time he was also an acquaintance of Mahatma GANDHI and RABINDRANATH TAGORE. Possibly under their influence, and certainly in order to work for the indigenization of Christianity in India, in 1930 Jones began an ashram in Sat Tal, initially as an annual seasonal event. In 1935 he instigated the formation of the Lucknow ashram. In 1938 he was hailed in *Time* magazine as 'the world's greatest missionary', and in 1964 he was awarded the Gandhi Peace Prize. He died in Bareilly, northern India. It was said of him that 'perhaps no Christian leader in America commands a wider popular following than he'. [406; 777] (T.T.)

Jones, Franklyn. *See* DA FREE JOHN.

Jones, James Warren [XIX] [Jim] (1931–1978). Leader of the ill-fated People's Temple, sometimes referred to as 'the suicide cult'. Jones was born into a poor family in Lynn, Indiana. His father, a disabled War Veteran, was a member of the Ku-Klux-Klan; his mother was rumoured to be a Cherokee. From an early age, Jones seems to have shown an unusual interest in religion. He dropped out of Indiana University in Bloomington and worked for a while as an orderly in a hospital, became the unordained minister of a church and ran a community centre for both Blacks and Whites. By 1956 he had opened the People's Temple. Married, with an adopted family of seven black, white and Asian children, he was frequently attacked in the local community as a 'nigger lover'; his healing services also became the object of intense suspicion [21: III]. In 1964 he became an ordained minister in the Christian Church, a branch of the Disciples of Christ; a year later he moved with his flock to Ukiah, California, where the People's Temple became a communal group, modelled along the lines of Father Divine's Peace Mission.

During the 1970s congregations of the People's Temple spread around the United States. Jones, preaching his message of socialism and racial equality, became an increasingly controversial figure in California. Some people saw him as a prophet and miracle-worker (he claimed to have raised several people from the dead); others saw him as a social reformer, alleviating the suffering of poor Blacks; yet others were becoming concerned as stories circulated about mistreatment of community members, child abuse, and violence being meted out to those who left his movement.

In 1977 Jones moved to 'Jonestown' in the Guyana jungle. In November of the following year Congressman Leo J. Ryan went to Jonestown to investigate the growing number of complaints. He and several of his accompanying party were shot dead, and a few hours later Jones and over 900 of his followers had committed suicide or been murdered. [21; 33; 48]

There is still considerable mystery surrounding Jones and the happenings at Jonestown [33; 48]. The incident continues to fuel public concern over 'cults', although the People's Temple had not been classified as such before the tragedy, and it differs in many important respects from the better known of the new religious movements. [4: VI] (E.B.)

José Gabriel Condorcanqui. *See* TUPAC AMARU II.

José Maria II [XXIV] (*fl.* 1912). Leader of the Contestado revolt, a Brazilian messianic rebellion of the years 1912 to 1916. José Maria II proclaimed himself the messiah and the brother of the self-appointed messiah João Maria, the legendary figure who reportedly wandered throughout Brazil during the 19th century. José Maria II was an army deserter who led groups that had been dispossessed of the lands expropriated for the railroad bed that ran from São Paulo to Uruguay. Many peasants from the states of Paraná and Santa Catarina joined the movement. In the face of overpowering force, José Maria retreated to a sacred mountain hideway to await the dawning of the messianic age, but he was eventually killed in a skirmish with government and private troops. His followers, who included bandits and railroad construction workers, maintained that he would return with an army of heavenly angels, and, in anticipation of that event, established a 'holy city'. In 1914 military forces attacked the communities of believers. More than 3,000 disciples were killed in the siege. [15; 18; 12; 16: 557] (L.S.)

Joseph [XV; VII] (*c.* 17th century BCE). Son of the patriarch JACOB and his wife Rachel; he rose to a high position in the Egyptian court. His story is told in *Genesis* 37–50.

As the firstborn son of his father's favourite wife, Joseph was spoiled by Jacob and received preferential treatment. This angered his ten older brothers. They sold him into slavery to a passing caravan of Ishmaelite traders, who took him to Egypt. The brothers took the many-striped garment (the 'coat of many colours') which Jacob had given to Joseph, stained it with animal blood and brought it to their father to prove Joseph's death. In Egypt Joseph was sold to Potiphar, captain of the Pharaoh's guard. When he spurned the attempt of Potiphar's wife to seduce him, she accused him of trying to rape her and he was imprisoned. In prison he won a reputation as a dream interpreter; when Pharaoh had a dream that could not be fathomed Joseph was brought before him.

Joseph's explanation was that the dream presaged seven years of plenty for the kingdom, followed by seven years of famine. Pharaoh was so impressed that he appointed Joseph vizier of the kingdom. In this capacity Joseph stockpiled corn over the next seven years so as to provide for the anticipated famine. This indeed materialized, extending also to Canaan, where Joseph's family was affected. His brothers went to Egypt to buy corn and encountered Joseph, whom they did not recognize. He knew them immediately, framing a charge against them which enabled him to detain one of them with the promise of release only if they brought back from Canaan his younger (full) brother, Benjamin. When this was done, Joseph revealed himself to his brothers, and told them to return once more to Canaan to bring their father, Jacob, and the rest of the family down to Egypt, where they settled in the Land of Goshen. Joseph's two sons, Ephraim and Manasseh, were blessed by Jacob; traditionally, from each of them was descended one of the twelve tribes. Joseph died in Egypt aged 110; centuries later, MOSES and the Israelites took his remains to Canaan, where they were buried in Shechem.

While some scholars have questioned the veracity of the story, others have been impressed by the authentication of many details, particularly by modern Egyptology. [68: XIII] (G.W.)

JOSEPHUS believed that the account of the sojourn in Egypt and the Exodus reflected the arrival of the Hyksos in Egypt and their subsequent expulsion by the Theban princes of Dynasty 17 (*c.*1580 BCE) [VII. 27]. However, there is no reference to these events in Egyptian records, and therefore no conclusive chronology can be established. Scholars have suggested that Joseph may have entered Egypt amongst the groups of Semitic-speaking peoples who took up residence there from the Old Kingdom (*c.*2340 BCE) down to the Hyksos period (*c.*1650 BCE), and settled in the Eastern Delta and also in Upper Egypt [VII. 26; 28]. There has also been an attempt [VII. 21] to identify Joseph with Yuya, the father-in-law of King Amenophis III. (A.R.D.)

Joseph of Volokalamsk, St [VI.B] (1439–1515). Russian Orthodox theologian. He urged monasteries to ensure that their monks lived a personally holy and ascetic life, but also that they as institutions should gather wealth in order to serve the church better. His followers were patrons of icon-painters, architects and church musicians, and followed him in vigorous action against heretics. Joseph was opposed by the followers of St Nil Sorsky who called the monasteries and the whole church to holy poverty and simplicity, treating heretics with gentle patience. The Council of 1551 canonized both teachers, but supported the doctrines of the Josephites. The wandering pilgrims, austere hermits, mystical teachers and 'holy fools' of orthodox tradition kept alive the spirit of St Nil.

Holy fools such as St Basil the Blessed (*d.*1552), to whom the cathedral in Red Square is dedicated, were a marked feature of Russian life, their crazy behaviour and feigned lunacy challenging current social values. The earliest holy fool (*salos/yurodivy* venerated by the church is St Simeon of Emesa: popular devotion to St Andrew the Scythian (*d c*911) spread this form of asceticism in Russia.

The old Believers were also in the spiritual tradition of St Nil. As Russian Church and Russian State drew closer together, the Old Believers drew apart from both into a spiritual and often apocalyptic vision of Christianity. [32; 49] (D.J.M.)

Josephus Flavius [XV] (*c.*37–100). Jewish historian and one-time military leader of the Galilean rebel forces in the uprising against Rome, which began in 66 CE. Josephus, who came from an upper class priestly family, spent some time practising asceticism in the desert as a member of an Essene-like sect, but in his mature religious outlook he was a Pharisee. His comments on the Bible cite teachings which have their parallels in Rabbinic literature. In his twenties he paid a visit to Rome as part of a Jewish delegation and was deeply impressed by Roman civilization. It seems he participated in the fight against Rome with considerable reluctance. When he found himself sheltering in a cave with one of the last remaining bands of Galilean rebels he contrived to be among the survivors of the suicide pact they undertook. Instead of killing himself Josephus gave himself up to the Romans. The Roman military commander, Vespasian, spared his life because he correctly predicted that Vespasian would become emperor (*compare* JOHANAN BEN ZAKKAI). Josephus henceforth adopted Vespasian's family name 'Flavius' and was used by the Romans to try and persuade the rebels in Jerusalem to surrender, without much success. After the revolt was crushed he spent the rest of his life in Rome writing works which were pro-Roman in character but which also explained Jewish history and beliefs to the Gentile world. His *Jewish War*, which is the main historical source for the events of the war against Rome, depicts the revolt as the work of a small band of zealots and not a popular uprising. He describes the fall of Jerusalem, drawing on official Roman documents and the reports of escapees, as well as the last days of the Jewish fort at Masada, where most of the defenders committed suicide. The various Jewish sects are characterized by Josephus as Greek philosophical schools for the benefit of his non-Jewish readers. Although his fellow Jews regarded him as a traitor, passing references to JESUS in his *Antiquities of the Jews*, now regarded as probably Christian interpolations, guaranteed the preservation of the Greek text of Josephus' works by the Christian Church. Josephus also wrote an autobiography defending his reputation and a reply to anti-Semitic attacks on Jews, *Against Apion*. His works preserve MANETHO's chronological list of Egyptian kings; he also comments on other Egyptian matters such as the possible relationship between the Hyksos, and JOSEPH, MOSES and the Exodus. [63a; 69a; 75a; 75b] (A.U.)

Josquin des Prez [VI.A] (1440–1521). Flemish composer. Of his early life little is known. He was born in the province of Hainaut but, like many other Flemish composers, moved to Italy in his youth. Members of the influential Sforza family became his patrons. For ten years he served at the papal chapel in Rome, and served Louis XII of France for a short while. He returned to Italy in 1503 to the employ of the Duke of Ferrara but after one year went into semi-retirement in the Netherlands. During his career he composed 18 masses and almost 100 motets. Luther described him as 'the master of the notes'. His music is remarkable for the way the religious text is emphasized and for the varied and unconventional treatment of the *cantus firmus*. [497; 610] (E.M.)

Juan Santos Atahualpa [XXIV] (*b* *c*1712). Peruvian religious leader of the mid-18th century. He was a Quechua speaker from the area of Cuzco, Peru, where, through his association with Jesuits there, he learned to read and write Spanish and some Latin. Apparently in his youth he had made a journey to Spain [8; 14: 1071]. At one point he was sought by Spanish authorities in connection with a murder in Guamanca. He claimed direct descent from the Inca emperor 'ATA WALLPA 'INKA, who had been murdered by Francisco Pizarro in 1533, and whose life had taken on legendary proportions in oral messianic traditions and folk theatre. In 1742 Juan Santos Atahualpa led native peoples, especially groups from the rain-forest areas of the eastern montane region of Peru (such as the Campa and Amuesha), in a religious rebellion. His aim was to restore the golden age of Inca rule. Beginning in the eastern jungles, the rebellion would spread to the Andean highlands by way of Jauja and Tarma (where his forces sacked 27 Franciscan missions) and end with his installation as emperor in Lima.

When Juan Santos began his rebellion in May 1742, he made a first dramatic appearance at Quisopango in the Gran Pajonal area of Peru. He styled himself a reluctant prophet, much as PAUL or the biblical prophet JEREMIAH. Wearing traditional native costume, he assumed the royal title of Apu Inka and announced that he was the reincarnation of the former emperors Atahualpa and Huayna Capac. He also named himself the messiah and the Son of God, come to lead his children (Indians, mestizos and African slaves) out of slavery to a kingdom wherein they would possess all the wealth of the Spaniards. In his new kingdom, devotee-citizens would perform ritual dances to honour Kesha, the cosmogonic hero who had rescued cosmic life from the flood. [20: 68]

Juan Santos portrayed himself as a prophet acting within the bounds of Catholicism. He sought a special papal dispensation so that Indian natives might be ordained to the priesthood. But he promised that native communities would no longer be forced to give personal service to missionaries or Spanish overlords. Spanish authorities mounted major military campaigns against Juan Santos in 1742, 1743, 1746 and 1750, but to no avail. His forces commanded the jungle terrain and Juan Santos always remained undefeated. Conflicting stories surround his death, variously put in 1755, 1756 and 1776. According to the accounts of the Campa people, Juan Santos will never die, for he ascended into heaven surrounded by clouds. For over 150 years his tomb was the centre of devotion and a new tunic, of the sort he wore on the day of his first dramatic appearance, was laid on his grave in the hope that he would return to wear his mantle once again. [7; 16: 568–70] (L.S.)

Judah ben Samuel he-Ḥasid of Regensburg [xv] (*d.*1217). German Jewish pietist and moralist. Little is known of his life, partly due to his extreme humility, which discouraged other people even from quoting him by name. He belonged to a family which gave leadership – both among his forebears and descendants – to the medieval pietist movement, the Ashkenazi Ḥasidim (i.e. the pious ones of Franco-Germany). About 1195, he left Speyer for Regensburg, where he established a rabbinical academy.

He is best known as the principal author of the classic work of the German Jewish pietists, *Sefer Ḥasidim* ('Book of the Pious'). This is apparently a composite work, other participants including Judah's father, Samuel, and his disciple, ELEAZAR BEN JUDAH OF WORMS. However, it bears the decisive imprint of Judah's teachings. Its object is to instruct in the pious life. The book contains many tales about people and events of its period, expositions of the Bible, especially on moral questions, and stories, real and fictitious, of pious individuals. It relates to man's conduct towards God (e.g. prayer, penitence) and his fellow-men, including marital life, relations with non-Jews, education and table manners, as well as treatment of animals. The basic themes are piety, humility and the fear of God. It incorporates much superstition, with a belief in the supernatural and stories of sorcerers, warnings against witchcraft and encounters with the dead. Its demons, such as vampires, stem more often from German than Jewish tradition. [72: 80–118]

The insistence on the love of all men is noteworthy, as the book was composed at a period when the Jews were subject to harsh persecutions. It became a popular practical guide among German Jewry and influenced later Jewish moralists. [46]

Other books by Judah, on mysticism, theology and a commentary on the prayer book, are known only from citations. One of these contains his criticism of the Jews of France and England for introducing liturgical changes. (G.W.)

Judah ha-Levi [xv] (*c.*1075–1141). Spanish Jewish poet and theologian. In his youth he lived in different parts of Spain, studying rabbinical and secular subjects. He settled in Toledo, where he worked as a doctor. The hapless situation of the Jews in Christian Spain induced him to move to Cordova in Moslem Spain, where he lived in wealth and respect. However, his yearning for Zion led him to leave Spain, his family, friends and pupils and set out for Jerusalem. He reached Egypt, where he remained for an extended period. A popular legend described his death at the hands of an Arab horseman when he was in sight of Jerusalem, but recent discoveries have shown that he died and was buried in Egypt without ever achieving his goal.

Judah ha-Levi and SOLOMON IBN GABIROL were the outstanding medieval Jewish poets. Judah was one of a group who introduced the forms and metres of Arabic poetry to Hebrew. His early verse followed the familiar topics of contemporary poetry: love and disappointment, friendship, nature, wine, wedding and mourning poems, riddles and eulogies of patrons. However, the tragic predicament of the Spanish Jewish community, caught in the midst of the Muslim–Christian struggle and suffering from the fanaticism of both sides, left its mark on his verse. He developed a negative attitude to philosophy and the pleasures of life and began to think deeply of the tragedy of Jewish exile. His deep religious faith brought him to messianism (and he tried to calculate the date of the end of the world through the book of *Daniel*). His later verse eschewed the secular and was devoted to religious and national themes. Deeply troubled by the contrast between the prophesied glory of the people of Israel and the terrible reality, he wrote a series of Songs of Zion ('Zionides') expressing his longing for the return of the Jewish people to its destroyed homeland. He contributed to all categories of Hebrew religious poetry and much of his religious verse entered the Jewish liturgy. [20; 87: vol. 1: 83–104]

His theological work *The Kuzari* (i.e. the Khazars) was written in Arabic. Its framework is the conversion to Judaism of the king of the Khazars (a Turkic tribe in the reaches of the lower Volga), traditionally after hearing a disputation between Christian, Jewish and Muslim representatives. The book, in dialogue form, conveys the Jewish argument, holding that Judaism is the sole source of religious life (as the other two faiths derived from Judaism, the original must enjoy greater authenticity) and the Jewish people constitute the heart of humanity. Judah ha-Levi belongs to no philosophical school and indeed maintains that Judaism is above rational truth. Philosophical certainty is impossible and the source of religious truth lies solely in biblical revelation. Attempts to reconcile religion and philosophy are useless. The Torah was given to the Jews because they are a special people, but this imposes on them special moral obligations. The sufferings of Israel's exile are seen as a process of purification in anticipation of its return to its own land. [39: X; 34: 120–33] (G.W.)

Judah Ha-Nasi [xv] [Judah the Patriarch] (late 2nd–early 3rd century). Jewish Patriarch and compiler of the Mishnah, the basic codification of Jewish law. Descended from HILLEL, he belonged to the outstanding family of the time and succeeded his father, the distinguished rabbi Simeon ben Gamaliel, in the Patriarchate. According to the rabbis, no other personality so successfully combined wealth, wisdom, statesmanship, learning and dignity. He headed an academy in Beth Shearim (near modern Haifa) and lived his later years in Sepphoris in Lower Galilee. During his 50 years in office, the country enjoyed comparative tranquillity, and he was able to work for the religious and economic welfare of the Jewish community. Many stories are told of his friendship and arguments with the Roman emperor 'Antoninus'; these are probably largely legendary, and it is unlikely that he had any such conversations with an emperor, though they reflect his close contacts with the Roman authorities. He himself enjoyed a quasi-princely status.

His lasting achievement was the redaction of the Mishnah. After the Roman persecutions in the first part of the 2nd century, intensive activity produced many collections in which the oral traditions were committed to writing by the rabbis for the use of their students and to ensure their survival. Judah sifted and combined all these works into a single compilation in order to produce an authoritative work for the study of the Oral Law and as a code for Jewish living. It is divided into six sections (called 'orders'), each subdivided into tractates. The sections are: (1) *Zera'im* ('seeds'), agricultural laws; (2) *Mo'ed* ('appointed time'), laws of the festivals; (3) *Nashim* ('women'), matrimonial law; (4) *Nezikin* ('damages'), civil law; (5) *Kodashim* ('holy things'), laws of sacrifices and consecrated objects; and (6) *Tohorot* ('purities'), laws of ceremonial purity. The Mishnah itself was the subject of discussions by the rabbis in Palestine and Babylonia over the following centuries. These were eventually codified in the Talmud, following the same six-part arrangement. [14: 179–244] (G.W.)

Judah Loew ben Bezalel [xv] [known by the acronym Maharal; also as Der Hohe Rabbi Loew] (*c.*1525–1609). Jewish scholar and thinker in Prague. After studying in Polish rabbinical academies, he served (1553–73) in Nikolsburg and eventually as head rabbi for all Moravia. In 1573 he moved to Prague where he founded and headed a talmudic academy. Apart from two periods in Posen, where he also served as head rabbi of Greater Poland, he remained in Prague and was its chief rabbi from 1598. Wherever he lived, he was involved in the efficient organization of the Jewish community.

As an educator, Judah reverted to the programme advocated by the earliest rabbis: 'Study Bible from the age of 5, Mishnah from the age of 10, Talmud from 15', and he was responsible for restoring the largely-neglected Mishnah (*see* JUDAH HA-NASI) to the curriculum. He stressed the study of Hebrew language and grammar and opposed the prevalent casuistic approach to the Talmud, preferring to concentrate on literal interpretations.

His writings on Judaism, notably on God and man, the fate of the Jews, exile and redemption, were often original, combining philosophical and mystical elements, with a preference for the latter. The study of Torah is the supreme good and the Torah mediates between man and God. His ethical book, *Netivot Olam* ('Paths of the World') was particularly influential.

Judah's involvement with mysticism led to the legend that he created a *golem* (an automaton) as his servant. When it went out of control, the rabbi destroyed it by removing the source of its animation, namely the divine name on its forehead. [76] (G.W.)

Judah the Maccabee [XV] (2nd century BCE). Jewish warrior. The Syrian Seleucid ruler Antiochus Epiphanes (ruled 175–164 BCE) issued a series of harsh edicts, forbidding the practice of Judaism, ordering the Jews to participate in idol-worship and declaring Jerusalem a pagan city with idol worship in its Temple. He won the support of an element of the Jewish population which had welcomed Hellenization. The standard of rebellion was raised in 167 BCE by the priest Mattathias of Modiin (near Lydda) and his five sons (the Hasmonean brothers), of whom Judah was the third. After his father's death (*c.*166 BCE), Judah (known as the Maccabee, a word of uncertain meaning) took over the leadership of the revolt. He was a brilliant military strategist who at first concentrated on guerilla tactics, avoiding direct contact with the superior enemy forces. His repeated ambushes sapped the Syrian morale. When he felt himself ready, he embarked on open battle, taking care to select suitable terrain, and achieved a series of successes culminating in the capture of Jerusalem (161 BCE). He cleansed the temple of its idols and restored the sacrificial service. In commemoration of this event, the festival of *Ḥanukkah* ('dedication', i.e. of the temple) entered the Jewish calendar. It lasts for eight days because of the traditional story that Judah found only enough oil to burn for one day in the Temple candelabra, but miraculously it lasted for eight days.

Eventually the Syrians sent a reinforced army, whose advance Judah failed to arrest. He was shut up in Jerusalem and saved only because internal disturbances in Syria compelled the withdrawal of its forces. The next army from Syria, under the general Nicanor, was defeated by Judah. The anniversary of the victory was observed as a festival ('Nicanor's Day') by Jews as long as the Temple stood. Judah then signed a treaty with the rising new power of Rome. However, he lost the battle with the next invading Syrian force and was killed. He was buried in the family mausoleum in Modiin. His brothers continued the struggle until complete independence was attained. [6]

The story of Judah the Maccabee is related in the Second Book of *Maccabees*. (G.W.)

Judson, Adoniram [VI.A] (1788–1850). American missionary. He was born in Malden, Mass. and educated at Brown University, Providence, Rhode Island, from 1804 to 1807. In 1808 he went to Andover Theological Seminary and two years later he visited England to confer with the London Missionary Society seeking collaboration with the American Board of Foreign Missions for missionary work in the East. He set out for India a Congregationalist and arrived a convinced Baptist. He resigned from the American Board. The East India Company refused him permission to work in its territory so he went to Burma after a brief visit to Mauritius. In Rangoon he evangelized and translated the Bible into Burmese. In 1824 he left Rangoon for Ava, the then capital, but was suspected of espionage in the Anglo-Burmese War and imprisoned for a year (1824–5). His wife, Ann Haseltine, nurtured him during the imprisonment, which severely damaged his health. She died in 1826. In 1829 he moved to Moulmein and worked further afield among the Karens. In 1849 he published a Burmese dictionary which had taken him seven years to write. [411; 844] (T.T.)

Julian of Norwich [VI.A] (1342–1416). English mystic. Little is known of her life except that she received a series of revelations, associated with a serious illness, when she was 30 years old (1373). These *Sixteen Revelations of Divine Love*, written in full 20 years later after further meditation, were visions of the Passion of JESUS Christ and of the Holy Trinity. It is thought that she took her name at a time when she lived the life of an anchoress in a cell outside St Julian's Church, Norwich. Although she claimed not to be very literate she had read the work of Dionysius the Areopagite (*c.*500) and from the life of ST BENEDICT in the *Dialogues* of GREGORY I. [159; 199; 705] (T.T.)

Julian the Apostate [XXII] [Flavius Claudius Iulianus] (332–363 CE). Roman emperor, 361–3, called 'the Apostate' because he reverted to paganism from the Christian faith in which he had been baptized and reared. This appellation indicates his primary significance in the history of religion: he attempted, but failed, to wrench the Roman world back to paganism from the Christianity into which CONSTANTINE and his sons had thus far steered it [7; 8].

Julian's father was Constantine's half-brother. At Constantine's death (337) he was murdered, with others of his family, to secure the succession for Constantine's sons. The child Julian was spared but was brought up thereafter in closely guarded, though comfortable, obscurity [7: III; 8: II–III]. Eventually, however, he was grudgingly brought into imperial power and administration by his cousin, the emperor Constantius, as the latter's sole surviving close relative. In 355 he was appointed Caesar (i.e. the emperor's junior colleague). He served in Gaul (modern France), fighting successfully against the barbarian tribes threatening it from across the Rhine [7: IV; 8: IV–V]. In 360 his army proclaimed him emperor (with little reluctance on his part), but Constantius died before battle could be joined, and so Julian acceded to the throne peacefully (361) [7: V–VI; 8: VI].

Julian's love of the old religion and his determination to restore it rested on profound intellectual conviction, acquired during his education, and on personal faith in its gods [1]. (Negatively, hatred of his murderous 'Christian' kindred, especially his cousin Constantius, also played its part.) Philosophically, he was attracted to the mystical and theurgical ('miracle-working') Neoplatonism expounded a generation earlier by Iamblichus, and his closest teachers and advisers (Aedesius, Maximus, Priscus, Oribasius, Salutius – the last probably the 'Sallustius' who wrote the important pagan theological treatise *On the Gods and the Universe* [1: 154–60; 7: 125]) were of that tradition. Julian was thus concerned not only with the public cults of the old official paganism but also with the mystery religions (he was an initiate of the cult of the solar deity Mithras) and with less focused theosophical and moral issues. He wrote extensively on religion, both polemically and in a more reflective vein. His 'Hymn to King Helios' (the sun god) and his 'Hymn to the Mother of the Gods' (i.e. *Orations* 4 and 5) exemplify well the arcane and somewhat fanciful quality of his Neoplatonic theology. In addition to his philosophical bent, the other pronounced quality of his religious life was his asceticism. His Christian opponents, replete with worldly success, he castigated as the new repositories of grossness and sensuality. Julian's ideal was the other great philosophical emperor, MARCUS AURELIUS, who was similarly fastidious by nature and ascetic in life-style.

As emperor, Julian tried to reinstate the old paganism by restoring and reforming the temples, the priesthoods and the rituals (especially blood sacrifice), which lay at its core [1; 7: viii; 8: ix]. He attempted, with little success, to introduce some of the practical charity which he rightly saw as one of Christianity's most attractive features (and paganism's great deficiency). He did little actively to suppress Christianity, both realizing that it was impractical to do so and in any case preferring conversion to coercion. He did, however, forbid Christians to teach the classics, considering them morally unfit as liberal educators. And, while deploring it, he did nothing to punish the lynch law of pagan mobs.

Julian ruled for a scant two years, dying from a wound inflicted in a skirmish in a failed invasion of Persia. The brevity of his reign ensured the failure too of his pagan counter-revolution – which was perhaps in any case inevitable, so vigorous were the institutions of Christianity at the time. As the last great standard-bearer of paganism, Julian has cut a romantic figure in history. Actually, he was an awkward and priggish person, but his conviction and bravery should still command respect. (R.B.)

al-Junayd, Abū 'l-Qāsim [XII] (*c*.840–910). Chief exponent of the 'sober' Ṣūfī school of Baghdad, regarded as 'the pivot in the history of early Ṣufism' [115: 57]. Born in Nihāvand in north-west Iran, he at first followed his father's trade of bottle merchant. At the age of 20, however, he went to Baghdad to study Shāfiʿī jurisprudence. His first instruction in Ṣufism came from an uncle, Sarīʿ al-Ṣaqaṭī (*d*.866), himself an outstanding figure in the early history of Ṣufism in Baghdad. Al-Ṣaqaṭī subsequently sent him to study further under al-Muḥāsibī, another Shāfiʿī theologian with a mystical vocation. Al-Ṣaqaṭī and al-Muḥāsibī impressed on al-Junayd the priority of the religious law over spiritual experience and the need to make Ṣufism conformable to orthodox sentiment and usage.

Al-Junayd's uneasiness with the ambiguity of the Ṣūfī position *vis-à-vis* the religious establishment is illustrated by his decision to break his ties with his fellow mystics around 880, in order to resume the role of a Shāfiʿī jurist. About the same time, however, he succeeded to the directorship of the Ṣūfī convent of Shuniz, a post in which he continued until his death.

His extant writings consist of private letters and short mystical treatises. They have survived in a unique but incomplete manuscript under the general title of *Rasā'il*. Their style is dense and cryptic, employing *ishārāt* or oblique allusions to the author's perceptions of mystical truth that preserve an outward conformity to orthodoxy.

During al-Junayd's lifetime, conflict between a sober Ṣufism seeking to ingratiate itself with mainstream theology and an antinomian mysticism passing the bounds of propriety became particularly fierce. He made a point of dissociating himself from the extremist doctrines and language of men like al-Bisṭāmī and al-Ḥallāj, although he was not directly involved in the public condemnation of the latter. [35: s.v.; 87: vol. 1: 75–8] (D.M.)

Justin Martyr [vi.a] (*c.*100–*c.*165). He was born in Flavia Neapolis (Nablus in Samaria). His family were not Semitic and he was uncircumcized and raised according to gentile culture. He studied with a series of teachers: a Stoic, an Aristotelian, a Pythagorean and a Platonist. Eventually he was converted to Christianity, *c.*130. He went to Ephesus, where he engaged in dialogue with Trypho, a Jew (*c.*135). He published this Dialogue about 20 years later. After moving to Rome he set up a Christian school. In Rome he wrote his best known works: the *First Apology*, addressed to the Emperor Antoninus Pius and his sons, Marcus Aurelius and Lucius Verus (*c.*155); the *Dialogue with Trypho* a little later; and his *Second Apology*, addressed to the Roman Senate shortly after Marcus Aurelius became emperor in 161. He was denounced and executed as a Christian along with some of his disciples. Justin was an Apologist who believed that all humans were recipients of the Seminal Logos (*logos spermatikos*) and as such had the gift of understanding the faith of Jesus, the incarnate Logos, who came to teach the truth. [96; 147; 413; 863] (T.T.)

K

Kaahumanu [XXI] (*c.*1772–1832). Hawaiian dowager queen and religious reformer. Born of noble parentage on Maui Island, she was married to the monarch Kamehameha I before Christianization of the islands. As his favourite queen, she became 'premier' to his successor, Liholiho Kamehameha II, in 1819. She initiated sweeping reforms to end many of the traditional tabus (*kapu*). After a feast in which she organized Liholiho to break an ancient *kapu* by eating with women, islanders went on the rampage destroying their effigies and temples. This was on the eve of the arrival of the New England missionaries (*see* BINGHAM, HIRAM). When Liholiho went to England, Kaahumanu became acting regent. Securing the dynastic line, she worked closely with the missionaries and was baptized a Christian in 1825. [17: 34–41; 30] (G.W.T.)

Kabīr [XI] (*c.*1398–*c.*1448). North Indian mystic and poet. He is associated with Benares, where he appears to have spent the greater part of his life. He was a weaver, belonging to the low weaver caste of Julāhās who had not long previously converted to Islam. He was, therefore, certainly a Muslim; he is thought to have married and had children; and it is claimed he was illiterate. Beyond this there is no firm historical evidence to support the many hagiographical accounts of his life, and certainly the claim that he was a disciple of Rāmānand is spurious [110: 27–8f.]. The poetry attributed to Kabīr is contained in three collections: the Sikh *Ādi Granth*, the Dādū-panthī *Pāñcvāṇīs* and the Kabīr-panthī *Bījak* [47]; of these the first contains the verses with the greatest likelihood of authenticity. Kabīr's poetry is couched in the forms and idiom of the Buddhist Sahajiyās and the Śaivite Nāths, that is, in *dohās* (couplets) and *padas* (hymns). Kabīr's tone is direct. He is scathing about all the externals of religion – idol-worship, pilgrimage, caste, ascetic practices, scriptures and the like are all targets for his scorn – and Hindu and Muslim divines fare equally badly. He calls for man to awake, to be aware of the inevitability of his own death, to transform inwardly and die to self, and to live in the awareness of God. His is the path of Love, which he depicts as being extremely difficult. His monotheistic religious stance, *nirguṇ bhakti*, or devotion to the Unqualified Absolute, is shared by all the other Sants of whom Kabīr was the first in North India. The sect that purports to follow his path, the Kabīr-panth, did not come into existence until two centuries after his death, and their Hinduized rituals and practices run counter to much that Kabīr stood for. The Kabīr-panth still flourishes in parts of India today, but Kabīr's verses are known to and appreciated by a far wider constituency. [110: 151–2] (S.C.R.W.)

Kagame, Alexis [VI.A] (1912–). Rwandan Catholic philosopher, poet and historian. He came from a leading Tutsi family closely allied to the traditional ruler. He was ordained to the priesthood and achieved prominence both as a poet (both in Kinyarwanda and French) and as an analyst and historian of Rwandan, and specifically Tutsi, culture. His *Le Poésie dynastique de Rwanda* (1951) and *Le Code des institutions politiques du Rwanda* (1952) glory in the indigenous courtly tradition. The Belgian colonial authorities seem to have found this threatening, and a long course in Rome was arranged for Kagame. There he produced as his Gregorian doctorate a major work *La Philosophie Bantu-*

rwandaise de l'être (1956), which gave more systematic form to ideas associated with PLACIED TEMPELS: namely that there is a specific African philosophy with categories of its own which are reflected in Bantu languages. Kagame presented the central idea of 'life force' with the categories *Muntu, Hantu, Kintu* and *Kuntu*, in terms comprehensible in classical Western philosophical discourse. There were clear theological implications, and Kagame was one of the group of African priests in Rome including MULAGO, who produced the manifesto *Des prêtres noirs s'interrogent* in 1956. His own essay was on Rwandan oral literature (he also contributed a poetic ode to the Virgin). Underlying all his work, including the later *La Philosophie Bantu comparée* (1976), is a plea for recognition of the basic harmony of Catholic religion and his own tradition. [353: 65, 119] (A.F.W.)

Kagawa Toyohiko [VI.A] (1888–1960). Japanese Christian leader. He was born a Buddhist. His parents died before he began his education, and he became a Christian through the influence of American missionaries while at school. He entered a Presbyterian theological seminary in Kobe in 1905 but spent the next year in hospital and in convalescence. He remained physically weak, suffering from glaucoma and tuberculosis. He left the seminary in 1908, was ordained in the Japanese Presbyterian church and was married. In 1914 he went to Princeton to study. He returned to Japan in 1917 and took up social work. In 1921 he founded a Labour Union and a Peasant Union. The National Anti-War League was founded by him in 1928 and the Kingdom of God Movement in 1930. By this time he was living in Tokyo. He visited the United States in 1941 and spoke out against militarism. On his return to Tokyo he was imprisoned as a pacifist but became a member of the cabinet formed to negotiate Japan's surrender at the end of the Second World War. He helped form the Socialist Party and in 1955 was nominated for the Nobel Peace Prize. He was a pastor in Tokyo until his death. His works included a novel *Across the Death Line, Christ and Japan* (English trans. 1934) and *Brotherhood Economics* (Rauschenbusch Lectures, 1937). [85; 416; 732] (T.T.)

Kāhn Singh Nābhā [XXIII] (1861–1938). Erudite Sikh scholar. His writings continue to be a major source for understanding Sikh history, theology, literature and rituals. Born to a learned family of Dhillon Jaṭs, he grew up to be a polyglot and a prolific writer. Although best known for writing a four-volume encyclopaedia of Sikh literature, first published in 1930, his most influential work is an 1897 tract: *Ham Hindū Nahīn* ('We are not Hindus'). First written to counter Aryā Samāj polemicists who claimed Sikhism to be a part of Hinduism, this widely read tract has become a charter of Sikh separatism. [64: 136] (H.S.O.)

Kaibara Ekken [XIV] (1630–1714). Outstanding neo-Confucian scholar of the early Tokugawa period. He was born into a samurai family in the Fukuoka domain. At the age of 19 he fell out of favour with a local *daimyō* and was forced to become a *rōnin* or masterless samurai. His career was resuscitated, however, in 1656, when the new feudal lord restored his former status and sent him to Edo to study neo-Confucianism and the use of medicinal herbs. During his lifetime he wrote more than 110 works in such varied fields as agriculture, medicine, botany, geography, mathematics, astronomy and philosophy.

Ekken came to know some of the most famous CHU HSI scholars of the time and was converted to this school of thought, although never slavishly or uncritically. Indeed, one of his most famous works, the *Tagiroku* ('Record of Grave Doubts'), published only posthumously, was a carefully reasoned critique of those aspects of Chu Hsi's thinking that he could not accept. Most especially, he faulted Chu Hsi and other Sung Chinese Confucian thinkers for those aspects of their thought that he felt were too influenced by Buddhism and Taoism. While quite critical of Buddhism – especially the *honji suijaku* theory that identified Shintō *kami* as manifestations of Buddhas and bodhisattvas – and Taoism, Ekken was favourably disposed towards Shintō, suggesting that Shintō and Confucianism form a unity. His nationalistic sentiments were shared by most neo-Confucian scholars of the time.

Ekken followed Lo Ch'in-shun in opposing the Sung Confucian view that *li* ('principle') and *ch'i* ('the principle of material force') are distinct. He held that the original reality of physical being is the nature of heaven-and-earth. Ekken also dismissed the doctrine of the immortality of the soul as a borrowing from Buddhism. His drive to acquire knowledge was based on the conviction that the object of learning is the rational exploration of principle at the heart of the nature of the universe and of human beings (*mono no ri*). His scholarship was not merely academic, but also emphasized experience and practical knowledge. In a simplified Japanese Ekken wrote a number of influential works intended for the education of the masses, including the widely read *Yōjōkun* ('Precepts for Healthy Living') and *Onna daigaku* ('The Great Learning for Women'), although modern scholarship has disputed the attribution of this last work. [3; 15; 29; 30; 34: 157–60; 39; 44] (G.E.)

Kamalaśīla [IV] (*c*.740–795). Indian Buddhist scholar-monk; the most important disciple of ŚĀNTARAKṢITA. Living towards the end of the period of Buddhism's flourishing in India, he was invited to Tibet to help continue the work of his master in establishing Buddhism in that country. Tibetan historians tell us that Kamalaśīla played a central rôle at the Council of Samye (*bsam-yas*), at which he debated and defeated a Chinese master's subitist interpretation of the Buddhist path. This was a key event in the establishment of Indian Buddhism as the dominant influence on nascent Tibetan Buddhism; with Kamalas'ī la's victory went the beginning of the end of Chinese influence upon the Buddhist schools of Tibet [50; 235].

In opposing the Chinese view that awakening may be realized suddenly, in the course of a single life, without necessarily having followed the complex aeons-long path to salvation that had been developed and systematized by Indian Buddhist scholars, Kamalaśīla gave a classic statement of the graduated 'stages of meditational practice' (*bhāvanākrama*) [235], in which that path essentially consists. Fundamental to his gradualistic view is the idea that tranquillity (*śamatha*) and insight (*vipaśyanā*) need to be developed in tandem and harmoniously interwoven before awakening can occur. This became the standard view in most of the Tibetan schools.

In addition to his works on meditational practice Kamalaśīla also wrote a large-scale systematic work of his own (*Madhyamakāloka*, not fully translated into any European language), and a large commentary upon his teacher's work, the *Tattvasaṅgraha* [110]. His importance for Buddhism lies largely in his historical and intellectual influence upon later Tibetan Buddhists, for whom he is a figure of paradigmatic importance [186: 93–9; 197: 231–5; 431–3]. (P.J.G.)

Kamo Mabuchi [XIV] [Kamo No Mabuchi] (1697–1769). Famous *kokugaku* (ancient Japanese literature) scholar and poet, best known for his studies and commentaries on the *Man'yōshū* [37], the late 8th-century anthology of Japanese poetry called *Ise monogatari* [21], and the *Genji monogatari* [52]. Like other *kokugaku* scholars, Mabuchi urged a return to pure Japanese values and virtues, values that were taken to predate the introduction of Buddhism and Confucianism to Japan. This involved an attempted rejection of all Chinese influence: Mabuchi suggested that the Japanese are distinguished from the Chinese by their unbroken line of sovereigns descended from Amaterasu, the sun goddess. The decline in general morality and social conditions were, he argued, due to the seduction of these sovereigns by Chinese luxuries and the passing of real political power into the hands of 'servants', i.e. the Fujiwara and others.

Early in his career Mabuchi studied the works of OGYŪ SORAI, but he rejected several of his basic positions. In the 1740s he became embroiled in a dispute with Kada Arimaro (1706–1751), a follower of Ogyū Sorai, who argued that poetry was insignificant in relation to the well-being of the state. Moreover, while affirming Ogyū's position that Confucianism is a humanly constructed way, Mabuchi went on to suggest that it is because of this that it is inferior to the authentic way found naturally expressed in ancient Japan. He attacked KAIBARA EKKEN and other neo-Confucians for their ignorance about the *Man'yōshū* age.

Mabuchi was thus very critical of Chinese learning, celebrating instead the wonder and sense of awe experienced in the face of nature and the world-as-given, something which cannot be expressed in rational language. Rational thought leads to an inevitable proliferation of (false) differences which in turn engender misunderstandings and disorder. Only pure (Japanese) poetry, on this view, can give expression to the immediate sincere feelings of human beings, which Mabuchi identified with the daily life of common folk. Mabuchi thus made the study of ancient Japanese poetry a decidedly political act. He eventually became the tutor to the son of the Shogun Tokugawa Yoshimune, but his longest lasting influence was through the development of the *kokugaku* movement, which has continued down to the present day. The important thinker MOTOORI NORINAGA was especially influenced by Mabuchi. [28; 34: 169–71] (G.E.)

Kamwana, Elliot [I.A]. Prophet who led the most important separatist movement in Central Africa. Born a Tumvuka in Nyasaland (now Malawi) during the late 1800s, he led large revivals and mass baptisms on behalf of the Church of Scotland in the early 1900s. Following the baptism of some 10,000 Tonga in 1908, his movement became more separatist in nature, and evolved into the Church of the Watchtower. His resulting millennialist movement was influenced by Watchtower ideas and literature. He was deported in 1909. Following his death the church has seen a steady decline. [32: 153–9] (R.H.)

Kanakadāsa [XI] (16th century). A low-caste contemporary of PURANDARADĀSA, devotee of the god Kṛṣṇa worshipped at Udupi, in coastal Karnataka. Tradition states that, barred from entry to the temple because of his lack of caste, Kanakadāsa prayed to the god for a *darśana*, a 'sight' of him. Kṛṣṇa turned himself around in his shrine, and caused an opening to appear on its western side through which, from the street outside, he could be seen by his devotees. Such a sight is possible, even today. Kanakadāsa is one of the great mystic poets in the Kannada lannguage to whom the name *Haridāsa*, 'slave of Kṛṣṇa', is applied. Much of their writing conveys the tender love, *Vātsalya*, that exists between a mother and her child. While the source for their episodes may be the *Bhāgavatapurāṇa*, a text of the 10th century, the Haridāsas invest their work with a compelling power, drawn both from their own convictions and their use of the Kannada language, a vernacular. [93] (J.R.M.)

Kaniṣka [IV]. King of the Kuṣāṇa dynasty in India, a supporter of Buddhism and of the Sarvāstivāda school in particular, who ruled over a large area of north-western India and central Asia. His dates are very uncertain; estimates vary from the 1st to the 3rd century CE, but the most common guess is somewhere in the late 1st or early 2nd century. A tradition extant in Chinese sources says that under his patronage a council was held, at which a Sanskrit version of the Buddhist Canon was written down (not simply recited, as in earlier councils); on this occasion also an important Sarvāstivādin commentary called the *Mahāvibhāṣā* was composed. Kaniṣka and this council thus hold a position in the Northern Buddhist tradition analogous to that of MOGGALLIPUTTA TISSA and AŚOKA in the Theravāda. [12: 60–61, 264] (S.C.)

Kānjī Svāmi [XIII] (1889–1980). Jain reformer. He was born in the Kathiāwār peninsula in Gujarat to Śvetāmbara Jain parents who belonged to the non-idolatrous Sthānakvāsi sect. Having a disposition towards religious activity and spiritual reflection from an early age, he was initiated as a Sthānakvāsi ascetic at the age of 22. By his own account, Kānjī tore his monastic robe while riding on a processional elephant during his initiation; this he took to be an inauspicious sign. Although fulfilling all his monastic obligations and earnestly studying the Śvetāmbara scriptures, he was not able to engage fully with the ascetic life. Eventually he came upon KUNDAKUNDA's *Samayasāra* [18] and the writings of the 18th-century scholar Ṭoḍar Mal (*see* BANĀRSĪDĀS) and came to regard them as true teachers of the way to liberation. In the face of great opposition from the Śvetāmbara community, he renounced his monastic state and proclaimed himself a Digambara layman at the town of Songaḍh in the Saurāṣṭra region of Gujarat, which remains the centre of the movement founded by him to this day.

Like Banārsīdās, Kānjī placed highest value on the inner, spiritual quest for a true understanding of the nature of the soul, in which, he claimed, lay the real significance of both the Jain path and human existence. Although not denigrating the monastic role, Kānjī Svāmi did not place any serious value on interaction with ascetics, and his movement has retained its lay character. While

Kānjī Svāmi maintained a prominent position through his preaching and extensive pilgrimages throughout India, it remains to be seen what his long-term significance will be. However, there can be no doubt that he made many people, both within the Jain community and outside it, take a greater interest in the spiritual traditions of Jainism. (P.D.)

Kant, Immanuel [VI.A] (1724–1804). German philosopher. He was born, lived and died in Königsberg in East Prussia. His parents were members of the prevailing Pietistic movement in the Lutheran church of the time. The same influence was present in the local school which he attended from 1732 to 1740. In that year he entered the University of Königsberg and graduated six years later, having studied science and philosophy. For some years he worked as a private tutor and worked for his master's degree, which he was awarded in 1755. He then became a *Privatdozent* at the university. In 1770 he became professor of logic and metaphysics. Most of his work was in strict philosophy as in his series of published critiques. He also wrote on religion, in particular *Religion within the Limits of Reason Alone* (1793). In 1792 Kant had been in difficulties with the Prussian government because of his religious beliefs. Religion for Kant was not orthodox Christianity. There was no need of a saviour, merely a moral ideal. To be religious was to be moral, and he referred to his view of religion as 'natural religion'. [146; 420; 845] (T.T.)

Kaplan, Mordecai [XV] (1881–1983). American rabbi and religious thinker; founder of the Reconstructionist movement. In 1909 he was appointed dean of the Teachers' Institute and professor of homiletics at the Jewish Theological Seminary in New York and played an important role in the development of the Conservative trend of Judaism. He initiated the concept of the Jewish Centre, which, combining worship and leisure activities, became a key factor in American Judaism. He also inaugurated the *Bat Mitzvah* confirmation ceremony for girls, corresponding to the boys' *Bar Mitzvah* which marks their religious adulthood. In 1922 he founded the Society for the Advancement of Judaism, out of which emerged the Reconstructionist movement. This sought to apply modern naturalism to Judaism and contended that Judaism is a dynamic civilization. Kaplan expounded his ideas in many books, the best known being *Judaism as a Civilization.* In 1941 he published his *New Haggadah* (Passover eve service), which emphasized the freedom symbolized by the Exodus rather than the traditional stress on the miracles. His *Sabbath Prayer Book*, more of an anthology than a fixed prayer service, enabling variety from week to week, led to his excommunication by extreme Orthodox rabbis in New York who publicly burned a copy. He subsequently published prayer books for the various festivals. Kaplan lived many of his latter years in Jerusalem.

He taught that Judaism to survive needed to be reconstructed and adapted to the modern world. Salvation is the ultimate purpose of life and he defined God as that power which makes for salvation. Religion is bound up with civilization and each people has its *sancta* – for Jews these include the Bible, the Day of Atonement, the festivals, Moses and Jerusalem. He rejected supernaturalism and its implications for the Jewish people, notably their chosenness. The past, he wrote, 'should have a vote but not a veto'. Zionism was basic to his thinking. The Land of Israel is vital to Jewish life and consciousness and Judaism must be enrooted there as a majority culture. [60: 253–80; 44: 175–216] (G.W.)

Kapūr Siṅgh [XXIII] (1697–1753). Prominent Sikh military leader during the early years of the struggle for supremacy against Muslim power in the Punjab. He first attained prominence when in 1733 the Mughal rulers, in an attempt to lessen Sikh opposition, offered the rank of Nawab to anyone chosen by the Khālsā and Kapūr Siṅgh was selected. During his lifetime the forces of the Khālsā were dispersed under different chieftains and Kapūr Siṅgh led his own group. He was, however, eventually recognized as the supreme leader of the Khālsā until, with advancing years, he stood aside in favour of JASSĀ SIṄGH ĀHLŪVĀLĪĀ. [43: 71–7] (W.H.M.)

Karma-pa [IV]. The Karma-pas, sometimes called 'Black Crowned' (*zhwa-nag*) for their distinctive ritual headgear, are considered to have been the first Tibetan Buddhist hierarchical succession of *sprul-sku-s*, a Tibetan institution whereby a child is recognized and raised as the rebirth of a recently deceased sage or ecclesiastical leader (*see also* DALAI LAMA; PAṆ-CHEN BLA-MA). The sect which they head, the Karma Bka'-brgyud, is a major branch of the larger Bka'-brgyud school traced back to the disciples of SGAM-PO-PA (1079–1153), among whom was the first Karma-pa, Dus-gsum-mkhyen-pa (1110–1193). He founded three monasteries, including Stod-lung Mtshur-phu, situated south-west of Lhasa, which became the sect's main seat. His successor Karma Pakshi (1204–1283) was much involved in affairs of the Mongol court in China, as was the third Karma-pa, Rang-byung rdo-rje (1284–1339); both the second and third Karma-pa also encouraged Bka'-brgyud syncretism with the Rnying-ma-pa school and excelled as doctrinal authors [11: 358–71; 56: Book 2, IV–V].

Connections with the Chinese court continued to be developed by Karma-pa IV Rol-pa'i rdo-rje (1340–1383) and Karma-pa V De-bzhin-gshegs-pa (1384–1415), whose influential role as guru of the Ming emperor Yong-le (reigned 1402–24) is well documented in Chinese sources [6: 280–9]. Under Karma-pa VI Mthong-ba don-ldan (1416–1453) the active function of imperial preceptor appears not to have been maintained. Karma-pa VII Chos-grags rgya-mtsho (1454–1506) is noted for his contributions as a philosophical writer, particularly in the field of Buddhist logic and epistemology, and so presaged his extraordinarily prolific and controversial successor, Karma-pa VIII Mi-bskyod rdo-rje (1507–54), whose attacks on the writings of TSONG-KHA-PA (1357–1419), the founder of the Dge-lugs-pa sect, occasioned considerable debate [254]. Karma-pa IX Dbang-phyug rdo-rje (1556–1603) is particularly renowned for his treatises on the Mahāmudrā system of meditation, and marks the end of the sect's pre-eminence in Central Tibetan political affairs: Karma-pa X Chos-kyi dbang-phyug (1604–1674) lived virtually as a mendicant during a period of civil war, and is popularly well-loved as the author of a delightful allegory, *The Buddha's Law among the Birds*, though the English translation is without attribution [45]. Karma-pa XI Ye-shes rdo-rje (1676–1702), Karma-pa XII Byang-chub rdo-rje (1703–1732) and Karma-pa XIII Bdud-'dul rdo-rje (1733–1797) witnessed the revival of their sect in the far-eastern Tibetan province of Khams, where Karma-pa XIV Theg-mchog rdo-rje (1798–1868) would become a leader of the 19th-century 'Universalist' or 'Eclectic' movement (*ris-med*), whose foremost exponent was his disciple KONG-SPRUL BLO-GROS MTHA'-YAS (1813–1899). The aims of the Eclectic movement continued to be promoted by Karma-pa XV Mkha'-khyab rdo-rje (1871–1922), an author of note. Karma-pa XVI Rang-byung rig-pa'i rdo-rje (1924–1981) presided over the hard task of relocating the sect's seat to exile in Rum-btegs, Sikkim, following the Tibetan diaspora of 1959. As an active and charismatic Buddhist missionary he travelled in Europe and North America, promoting the establishment of many Tibetan Buddhist meditation and study centres. At the time of writing (August 1989) a 17th Karma-pa has yet to be recognized publicly. [54; 114; 184: VIII]. (M.K.)

Kawate Bunjirō [XIV] [Konkō Daijin] (1814–1883). Founder of Konkōkyō, one of Japan's new religions. He was born into a farming family in Okayama province, and at 12 years of age he was adopted by a more prosperous but childless couple in a neighbouring village. He had an unremarkable (if difficult) early life until he fell seriously ill in his 42nd year (according to the oriental count), which popular belief holds to be an extremely dangerous time. In a traditional folk curing rite, Kawate's brother-in-law fell into a trance state of divine possession and announced that Kawate's illness was the result of a curse by the *kami* Konjin, a rather obscure deity associated with yin–yang beliefs. Kawate is said to have recovered after he swore obedience to this deity. By 1858 he was receiving direct verbal communications from Konjin; he retired from farming and on 21 October 1859 he was ordered by Konjin to found a new religion. This date is celebrated as the founding of Konkōkyō.

Kawate set aside a room in his house for counselling persons who came to him for *toritsugi* ('[divine] intercession'). Konkōkyō followers believe that the patriarch of the religion serves as a conduit of the will of the *kami*. Thus, the advice received is not merely a reasoned suggestion, but rather a direct revelation of the divine will. The main *kami* came to be known as Tenchi Kane no Kami, while Kawate's name was officially changed in 1868 to Konkō Daijin, recognizing him as a 'living *kami*' (*ikigami*). Konkō Daijin spent the rest of his life offering *toritsugi* for his followers. Subsequent patriarchs have continued to be selected from his immediate blood descendants. Konkōkyō has been characterized as a 'functional monotheism' since other Shintō *kami* are, if recognized at all, considered to be manifestations of Tenchi Kane no Kami. Konkōkyō claimed 469,153 members in 1984; while not among the largest of Japan's new religions, it continues to show respectable growth. [1: 372; 25; 26: 257–66; 34: 219–20; 35; 41: 97–122; 42: 15–17, 44–6; 48; 51] (G.E.)

Kay Khosrow Shahrokh. *See* SHAHROKH, KAY KHOSROW.

Keekhwei [XXIV] (*fl.* 1963). Prophetess who inspired the messianic uprising among the Ramkokámekra-Canela people in the state of Maranhão, Brazil, in 1963. During her sixth month of pregnancy Keekhwei claimed to be empowered by revelations received from the child in her womb. The child had exited the womb and appeared to the prophetess in the light of the full moon. The fetal girl, who said her name was Krââ-Kwei ('Dry Girl'), looked like a fully dressed prepubescent girl and predicted that her time of birth would be at sundown on 15 May 1963. She promised that by dawn on 16 May, she would already be fully grown and the Canela people would take over the villages of the Whites, fly their planes and drive their buses. The pregnant prophetess enjoined followers to return to traditional religious practices and, in particular, to perform liturgical dances and songs for Krâa ^-Kwei and her brother Auké (about whom there exists an elaborate messianic mythology). Young men and women formed choirs and dance troupes. Keekhwei prescribed songs and styles of dance attuned to specific days of the week. For the three days of the long weekend, Brazilian-style dances were proper (during which time sexual relations were prohibited). Now that the new age was dawning, Canela were free to take livestock from nearby ranchers. Whatever goods were given to the prophetess would be returned one hundredfold after the sacred child was born. When the messianic child – a boy – was born dead, the prophetess explained the delay in the dawning of the eschaton. She dismissed her husband, married the chief's son, and instigated a new symbolic order that included the breaking of sexual taboos between secondary relatives and in-laws. Ranchers attacked the village and, in spite of the prophetess's assurances of invulnerability, four residents were killed. Eventually Brazilians suppressed the movement and burned the village to the ground. Disillusioned, the Canela reckoned that her prophecies had been lies. [3; 2; 16: 583–4] (L.S.)

Kempe, Margery [VI.A] (*c.*1373–*c.*1440). English mystic. She was born in Lynn, Norfolk, the daughter of a five-times mayor of the town. She married John Kempe *c*1393, to whom she bore 14 children. At times she suffered hysterical fits and claimed to receive visions. She and her husband went on a pilgrimage to Canterbury. She became very critical of the pleasures of life. Because of her visions and uncontrollable writhings she barely escaped the accusation of heresy. In 1413 she and her husband took vows of chastity before the Bishop of Lincoln and soon went on a pilgrimage to the Holy Land. She made pilgrimages to almost every shrine in England, as well as Rome, Santiago de Compostela (1417), Norway and Danzig (1433). She recorded her experiences in *The Book of Margery Kempe*, dictated to a priest around 1438. It describes in detail her travels, her mystical experiences and her encounters with such people as the archbishops of Canterbury and York and JULIAN OF NORWICH. [8; 161] (T.T.)

Kendall, Thomas [VI.A] (1778–1832). He was among the first Church Missionary Society missionaries sent to New Zealand. After preparing the first grammar of the Maori language, he found that the Maoris had a religion of considerable profundity. Being unprepared for this he sometimes wondered if he himself was a Christian, a state of mind which induced a Calvinistic sense of guilt. SAMUEL MARSDEN condemned him for selling muskets to the Maori people, but he and his colleagues, William Hall and John King, had to support themselves as best they could, and, unlike the other two missionaries, he was a teacher, not a tradesman. Unhappily married, he was caught in attempting to understand Maori life by living with them and accepting their sexuality, in spite of sensing this as a vast sin. Dismissed from the New Zealand Mission, he was granted land in Australia, but was lost at sea during his journey there. [87; 287; 329] (J.I.)

Kenekuk [xx] [Kanakuk, literally, 'Putting His Foot Down'] (*c.*1785–1852). A Kickapoo prophet, chief of the northern branch of the Kickapoo tribe. In 1819 the Kickapoo ceded their lands and split into two bands. The group led by Kenekuk eventually settled along the Osage River and became known as pacifists. Kenekuk attributed his teachings to a vision in which he was told that his people should practise fasting and meditation as well as take up agriculture in place of their traditional nomadic, hunting ways. He preached coexistence with the whites and was successful for a time. He died of smallpox, having promised during his illness that he would return in three days. His followers dispersed shortly thereafter. [4: 133–4] (S.R.)

Kenyatta, Jomo [I.A] (*c.*1897–1978). Kenyatta is best known for his political roles as an anti-colonial activist and as Kenya's first president. He was also a great defender of traditional Kenyan culture and religion, as exemplified by his 1938 work *Facing Mount Kenya*, an emic ethnography of Kikuyu history, culture and religion [19]. Although dedicated to his own Kikuyu heritage, Kenyatta sought to stress the value of all Kenyan cultural heritages in the face of increasingly intrusive Western cultural norms. (R.H.)

Keret [II]. Of all the ports of the Eastern Mediterranean the port of Ugarit (just north of modern Lattakia in Syria) is the richest source for literature of the 2nd millennium BCE. It is from the ports that we expect to discover the literary relics of the Phoenicians, but the Ugaritic material is so rich that it is usually considered as a separate entity within Phoenician culture and a separate language within the Phoenician group. The archives from the temples there include a series of myths and legends in verse form, all of which are badly damaged and none of which can be adequately translated without considerable conjectural restoration and interpretation.

One of the better understood legends is about King Keret, who, apparently through no fault of his own, was placed in the unenviable position of having all his seven sons predecease him. While grieving bitterly alone on his bed the god El (cognate with Hebrew *'elōhîm* and Arabic *'allah*), described as the 'father of man' (i.e., *'adm*, cognate with Hebrew *'ādām*), instructs him first to sacrifice a lamb, a goat and a dove, and then, sitting astride a wall at the top of the temple tower, to invoke the aid of Baal. Afterwards he is to gather every citizen, able-bodied and disabled, and march for seven days to a city in the south where he will demand from the king of that city his beautiful daughter as his own wife.

When the girl is finally won and they are all back home Keret starts to rebuild his lost family. After seven years Keret has as many children as he had before the tragic accidents with which the story began. But there is a suggestion that Keret has not kept his part of some vow he made during his grief, which is probably why the joy of the great feast he calls to celebrate his new-found happiness is soon to fade. He becomes so ill that no remedy can be found to cure him despite the desperate efforts of his wife, his children and the gods.

The text at the end of the story is not easy to interpret. It seems to suggest that Keret is not in fact dying, but 'making a sacrifice', which calls for all kinds of music and feasts. What are apparently funeral customs are described as fertility rituals, in that they bring down the rain from Baal. The feast they prepare may be partly a wake and partly a celebration for the installation of Keret's son as the new king. The last preserved lines describe the new king castigating his father for having failed, and Keret replying from the grave that he should prepare himself for death.

The name 'Keret' can be identified with the island of Crete, and it has been suggested that the story reveals some popular belief at Ugarit that there was a time when Cretans were their kings. Such ideas must be extremely speculative though intriguing. But it is important to note that the three tablets on which this story is recorded were donated to the temple by one of the known kings of Ugarit called Niqmad. This was a port where much of the prosperity was derived from the trade with Egypt, and the well established Egyptian belief in the immortality of the soul could easily be spread.

Niqmad's literary gift seems to indicate that he, and probably the other kings of Ugarit, saw themselves as inheritors of all that Keret stood for: El would guarantee for them as he had for Keret support in adversity and even in death.

Moreover, Keret embodies the indestructible qualities of Baal, who seems to be dead during the seasonal drought but is seen to have overcome death during the rains which restore fertility on the earth. This belief was always central to Phoenician religion and popular in the hinterland. The Canaanites clearly attracted many to their rain-making ceremonies but their practices were severely condemned by the Hebrew theologians, as is shown by the story of ELIJAH and the prophets of Baal on Mount Carmel. But later the ideas survived and were transmitted to the west, especially through Greece. King Keret is the first identifiable adherent of Baalism. [3; 4] (M.R.)

Keshub Chunder Sen. *See* SEN, KESHUB CHUNDER.

Khadīja [XII] (*d.*619). The first wife of MUḤAMMAD and member of Asad, a leading clan of Mecca. Muḥammad is said to have entered her service as a young man, she being then a widow. He organized trading caravans for her as far as Syria and received a share of the profits for this work. Muḥammad is said to have acquired the sobriquet of 'The Faithful One', and it was doubtless this episode in his life which was to contribute to the favourable image of the merchant and his calling which Islam has retained ever since. Soon Muḥammad married her, she bore him several children, but none of the boys lived till adulthood. Marriage gave Muḥammad the stability which his earlier, unsettled life as an orphan had lacked; and Khadīja, together with her cousin Waraqa, seem to have encouraged the early development of his spiritual life and the beginnings of his prophethood. Muslim tradition makes the marriage a happy one, and certainly, it was not till after her death, shortly before the *hijra* or migration to Mecca, that Muḥammad took any further wives. [35: Khadīdja; 39: I; 82: XII, XXXI; 135: II] (C.E.B.)

Khama III [VI.A] [Kgama; Khame] (1837?–1923). Tswana Christian chief. He was a son of Sekgoma, Chief of the Ngwato, one of the major Tswana groupings. Sekgoma was consistently hostile to Christianity but after missionaries of the London Missionary Society settled with the Ngwato in 1862, Khama became a Christian. By refusing to take a second wife, he cut across Sekgoma's policy of alliances. Succession disputes among the Tswana were endemic; Khama briefly replaced Sekgoma in 1873 and returned to power in 1875.

Khama's long reign was crucial to the development of modern Botswana. He successively abolished initiation schools, rainmaking rituals, witchcraft trials and polygyny, and aimed at a godly commonwealth on the missionary model, with stress on education, protection of subject peoples, exclusion of alcohol and control over European traders. He accepted a British protectorate as the best way to preserve his autonomy and his godly commonwealth. In 1895 it was clear that the British government was preparing to hand over its protectorate to Cecil Rhodes's British South Africa Company. Khama and two other chiefs, with a missionary interpreter, came to London to protest to the Colonial Secretary in person. The Christian chief of the Ngwato who denounced the liquor trade and appealed to British honour to save his people attracted great public attention; the government gave way.

Khama was generous but rigid and autcratic. Family disputes continued; his relations with Sekgoma his son were as turbulent as those with Sekgoma his father. [559] (A.F.W.)

Kharshedji Rustamji Cama. *See* CAMA, KHARSHEDJI RUSTAMJI.

Khemā [IV] [Kṣemā] (5th century BCE). The chief female Arahat – those enlightened through the teaching of the BUDDHA. Before becoming a nun she was one of King Bimbisāra's queens, proud of her great beauty. Through the Buddha's teaching she saw the transience of the body and achieved Arahatship. Like Sāriputta (ŚĀRIPUTRA) among the monks, Khemā was the nun supreme in wisdom. She gave a celebrated teaching to King Pasenadi, answering his questions on what happens to Enlightened Ones after death; when he afterwards took the same questions to the Buddha himself, he received the same answers. The Buddha named Khemā, with UPPALAVAṆṆĀ, as the ideal Buddhist nun. [150: vol. 1: 727–8] (V.J.R.)

Khem Siṅgh Bedī [XXIII] (1832–1905). Fourteenth in lineal descent from GURŪ NĀNAK, Khem Siṅgh converted hundreds of people to Sikhism in the Potohar region of north-west Punjab. His illustrious genealogy, personal charisma and a fame for working miracles earned him much reverence among the Sikh masses [21: 15–18]. Many of his disciples uttered his name as a divine incantation. In 1873 Khem Siṅgh helped found the Amritsar Siṅgh Sabhā and in 1882 he became the President of the Khālsā Dīwān Amritsar [6: 29]. His deep conviction that there were no differences between Sikhs and Hindus made him suspect in the eyes of those Sikh reformers who were working towards establishing a separate Sikh identity. (H.S.O.)

Khety [VII] *The Instruction of Khety* (or *The Satire on Trades*) was a popular wisdom text which has been preserved on British Museum Papyrus Sallier II and Papyrus Anastasi VII. It was probably a Middle Kingdom composition (*c.*1900 BCE), and relates how Khety, a humble man, promotes to his son the virtues of education and of the scribal profession, against which all other careers are contrasted unfavourably. [12: 66–72; 16; 19: vol. 1: 184–92] (A.R.D.)

Khomeini, Ayatollah. *See* KHUMAYNĪ, ĀYAT ALLĀH RUḤ ALLĀH.

Khomiakov, Aleksei Stepanovich [VI.A] (1804–1860). He was born in Moscow. He studied literature and mathematics at the University of Moscow. He joined the army twice, in 1822 and 1828, but eventually took up the study of art. He married in 1836 and, being of independent means, devoted himself to the service of 'true Russia'. He was a founder of the Slavophile movement, which aimed to enhance the life of the Orthodox Church. Khomiakov wrote an essay titled *The One Church* (1850), in which he introduced the concept of *sobornost*, which stood for the freedom and catholicity of the Russian church as against the authoritarianism and catholicity of Rome and the licence and individualism of Protestantism. In the last years of his life he collaborated in the publication of *Rousskaia Beseda*, a journal which put forward Slavophile ideas. Under threat of censorship much of his work was published in French and only published in Russian after 1879. [88; 102; 152] (T.T.)

Khosrōw I Anōširavān [XXVI] (6th century). Sasanian king, reigned 531–79. As crown prince he had MAZDAK put to death, and because of the Mazdakite movement enacted stern measures to strengthen the state and Zoroastrian church, working closely with the *Mōbadān mōbad* (high priest). He sought also to prevent exploitation of the peasantry, and earned the byname 'the Just'. Since MUḤAMMAD was born in his reign, he received special attention from Muslim writers, and many stories are told of him. It appears to have been in his time that the writing down of the Avesta (*see* ZOROASTER) was completed after many centuries in oral transmission [3: 173; 9: 135; 14: 363–440]. The *Khwadāy Nāmag* (*see* FIRDAUSĪ) was also being composed then. (M.B.)

Khosrōw II Parvēz [XXVI] (6th–7th century). Sasanian king, reigned 591–628. His, the last long Sasanian reign, was famed for its splendour and luxury, supported by successful wars against Byzantium. Khosrōw made lavish benefactions to the Zoroastrian church, founded many fire-temples, and appointed many priests to pray at them. Other pious acts of his are recorded in FIRDAUSĪ's *Shāhnāma*. He was especially devoted to Ādur Gušnasp, the fire of 'warriors', hence kings, where he spent days in prayer. Embers from it were carried before his army into battle; and the extensive ruins of its temple [29] attest the power and wealth of Sasanian Zoroastrianism at this period, just before the Arab conquest. [9: 142–3] (M.B.)

Khri Srong-lde-btsan [IV] (755–797). A member of the line of Tibetan emperors, who reigned from 754. He performed great works in the establishment of Buddhism, especially in connection with the construction of the first monastery, Samyay (*bsam-yas*), and the ordination of the first Tibetan monks. He also set the course of Tibetan Buddhism along Indian rather than Chinese lines.

Khri Srong-lde-btsan at first acted with discretion in adopting Buddhism as a state religion, largely because of opposition from powerful state ministers associated with the older shamanic tradition (sometimes identified by the name Bön; see the entries on SHAR-RDZA BKRA-SHIS RGYAL-MTSHAN, SHES-RAB RGYAL-MTSHAN, GSHEN-RAB MI-BOCHE). Buddhist monks from China and Central Asia were already present in Tibet, but in order to construct a set of laws and a state-sponsored monastery he called upon the Indian Buddhist philosopher ŚĀNTARAKṢITA.

Śāntarakṣita was unsuccessful in the face of hostile indigenous deities who showed their displeasure with earthquakes and other natural disasters. He departed, advising the emperor to invite the tantric yogin PADMASAMBHAVA. This thaumaturge proceeded to the capital, subduing the local gods and demons along the way. When his work of subjugation had been completed he flew away (it is said to Sri Lanka). Then Śāntarakṣita returned to complete the establishment of Samyay (in 779).

Thereafter two factions arose among the Tibetan Buddhists – an 'Indian party' and a 'Chinese party'. The latter grew more popular under the leadership of a Ch'an monk captured in warfare and known as the *ho shang* (*ācārya*) Mahāyāna. In the Tibetan view of the conflict, the Ch'an party denied the importance of ethics and other elements of the gradual bodhisattva path in favour of an instantaneous awakening based upon the sudden cessation of conceptual thought. The Emperor sponsored a debate, taking place during the years 792–4 (a debate attested by Tibetan, Chinese and Sanskrit sources).

To present the Indian side of the dispute a disciple of Śāntarakṣita known as KAMALAŚĪLA was invited. From the texts it is clear that the Ch'an monk was no match for a trained Indian philosopher. For these, and perhaps for political reasons as well, the emperor determined to support the Indian version of Mahāyāna Buddhism, and since then the Ch'an master has appeared on the stage of Tibetan culture only as a clown in stage plays. [38: 259–81; 171: 186–95; 204; 238] (M.T.)

Khumaynī, Āyat Allāh Ruḥ Allāh [XII] [Imām Khomeini] (1902–1989). Modern Twelver Shiʿite leader and figurehead of the Islamic Revolution in Iran. Born in Khumayn near Iṣfahān to a clerical family, he commenced his theological studies under Shaykh ʿAbd al-Karīm Hā'irī Yazdī, first in Arāk (where he went at the age of 15 or 16) and from 1922 in Qumm, which began to develop after 1920 as a centre of religious learning under the latter's direction. After Hā'irī Yazdī's death, Khumaynī began to teach, specializing in jurisprudence, ethics, philosophy and mysticism. The popularity of his lectures on ethics led to government pressure for their closure.

His first important publication, *Kashf al-asrār* ('The Unveiling of Secrets'), appeared in 1944. In it, he condemned the Pahlavi regime and hinted for the first time at the possibility of clerical rule; he did not, however, attack the concept of monarchy as such. His political views remained muted during the lifetime of the leading *mujtahid* of that period, Āyat Allāh Burūjirdī (*d.*1961), who stressed a quietist policy.

After Burūjirdī's death, Khumaynī came out in open opposition to the rule of Muḥammad Riḍā Shāh, inheriting the mantle of the regime's chief clerical opponent, Āyat Allāh Abū'l-Qāsim Kāshānī (*d.*1962). In 1963 he began preaching anti-government sermons. Arrested during an attack on the Fayḍiyya theological college that March, he was released after a short detention. He continued to attack the regime, concentrating on supposed violations of the constitution, collaboration with America, and links with Israel.

In November 1964 he was again arrested and exiled to Ankara and Bursa in Turkey. He moved in the following year to the Shiʿite theological and shrine centre of Najaf in Iraq. There he engaged in lecturing, writing, and mobilizing opposition to the Iranian government. In 1970, in a series of lectures, he developed the concept of *vilāyat-i faqīh* ('government of the clergy'). Published as a book under that title, these lectures were to prove central to the debate about political activism in opposition to Pahlavi secularism. At the heart of Khumaynī's argument is the assumption that Islam is directly relevant to and has provisions for all areas of social, political, administrative and legal life, and that its restriction to 'religious' matters represents a fundamental distortion of its nature.

Khumaynī continued to lead the growing opposition to the Pahlavis, first from Najaf, then (after October 1978) from France. Following the flight of Muḥammad Riḍā Shāh, he returned to Iran in triumph on 1 February 1979, assuming the *de facto* position of leader of the revolution. In the Constitution of the following November, this position was formalized.

Despite reverses for the revolution, notably the losses sustained in the war against Iraq and the ignominy of his own decision to call a truce, Khumaynī's personal prestige suffered little during his ten-year rule. He continued to keep a tight rein on affairs of state almost to the end. One of his last actions, the issuance of a *fatwā* calling for the death of the British author Salman Rushdie, may yet prove to be his most enduring legacy to the international situation.

The Āyat Allāh's death left unresolved the crucial issue of how to institutionalize clerical leadership as a part of the state apparatus and, above all, the question of succession to the supreme office. There has, as yet, been no satisfactory clarification of the messianic overtones apparent in his leadership. [72; 131] (D.M.)

Khyung-po Rnal-'byor Tshul-khrims Mgon-po [IV] (11th–12th centuries). The 'yogin of the Garuḍa clan' was trained in the Tibetan Bön-po and Rnying-ma-pa traditions during his youth. He later travelled to Nepal and India, where he studied under the leading exponents of the Buddhist tantras. In particular, he is famed as the disciple of the mysterious yoginī Niguma, said to have been the sister or wife of the *mahāsiddha* NĀROPA. Returning to Tibet, he founded his seat at Zhang-zhong in the Shangs valley of Gtsang province, owing to which his tradition is called 'Shangs-pa bka'-brgyud', the 'Shangs valley lineage of the precepts'. Though this school enjoyed no temporal prominence, its systems of yoga became very widespread within the various sects of Tibetan Buddhism. Their leading 20th-century representative was Kalu Rinpoche (1903–1989; *see under* KONG-SPRUL BLO-GROS MTHA'-YAS). [6: 138–44; 11: 296–303; 184: IX; 195; 197: 499–504] (M.K.)

Kierkegaard, Søren Aaby [VI.A] (1813–1855). Danish existentialist philosopher. He was born in Copenhagen. His father, Michael Petersen, retired as a successful wool merchant at the age of 40 after the death of his first wife. Søren was the seventh child of the second marriage. His father was filled with guilt because of the death of his first wife and of most of the children of the second marriage. Søren was thus raised in a home full of pious gloom. In 1828 he went to Copenhagen university to study theology but studied philosophy and literature instead. He passed a theology examination in 1840, by which time his father had died leaving Søren a rich man, but was not ordained. In the following year he became engaged to Regine Olsen, a 17-year-old woman, but broke off the engagement very soon and caused a public scandal. In 1843 he published pseudonymously his first work, *Either/Or*. Over the next few years he published more works under different pseudonyms, including *Fear and Trembling* (1843), *Concluding Unscientific Postscript* (1846) and *The Sickness unto Death* (1849). He spent his time writing, publishing more than 20 books. His life-style and views were scurrilously attacked in 1846 by a periodical called *The Corsair*. Towards the end of his life Kierkegaard attacked the state church, accusing it of compromising the message of the New Testament. Except for three brief visits to Berlin, the first time to hear Schelling lecture on HEGEL, he never left Copenhagen. [160; 372; 513] (T.T.)

Kigozi, Blasio [VI.A] (1909–1936). East African revival leader. He was a Muganda from Kampala and attended a mission school there. Following an evangelical conversion in 1925, he wanted to emulate Apolo Kivebulaya as a missionary. He trained as a teacher and offered himself for distant service. He was appointed to the newly opened mission in Gahini, Rwanda, where he worked with the missionary J. E. Church. He was ordained in 1934, taking charge of the school for teacher evangelists. After a deep religious experience in 1935 Kigozi became the key figure in a movement which revitalized the mission in Gahini and spread far beyond it. The movement's teaching was in line with standard evangelical doctrine but was accompanied by open confession of sin and public testimony. It radicalized Christian commitment and attitudes to some aspects of local culture, and produced a new openness and freedom between Africans and missionaries. Kigozi, weakened by his exertions, died just as the Synod of the Church of Uganda was about to consider his call for revival in the church. The movement, continued by Church, WILLIAM NAGENDA and others, has subsequently deeply affected parts of Uganda, Rwanda, Burundi, Kenya, Tanzania and Sudan, and produced well known figures such as Archbishop JANANI LUWUM and Bishop Festo Kivengere. [154; 750] (A.F.W.)

Kimbangu, Simon [I.A] (1889–1951). One of Africa's greatest prophets and martyrs, through whom Jesus Christ became for the Congolese no longer the 'pale Christ of the Whites' but a living reality [4: 28]. A Kongo from Zaïre, Kimbangu was educated by the Baptist Missionary Society. He was baptized in 1915 and later served as a teacher. Between 1918 and 1921 he resisted a spiritual call until he healed a dying woman in April 1921. He then embarked upon a mission of healing and preaching. The movement grew rapidly in his home town of N'Kamba (which became known as New Jerusalem) and became a focus and outlet for anti-European sentiments. Although there was no uprising Kimbangu, seen by his followers as an African prophet of God (*ngunza wa Nzambi*) and messenger (*tunma*), was sentenced to death by the Belgian authorities in September 1921 but reprieved by the King of Belgium after direct appeal by British Baptist missionaries. Kimbangu died in captivity 30 years later. During his arrest and imprisonment in Elizabethville (now Lumbumbashi) Kimbangu sought to follow the example of Christ during his passion, thus adding power and legitimacy to his role as a martyr. After several decades of existence as an underground church under the leadership of Kimbangu's son DIANGIENDA the movement resurfaced in 1959. When independence was granted to Zaïre in 1960 the church, the Eglise de Jésus-Christ sur la Terre par le Prophète Simon Kimbangu (EJCSK), was elevated to the role of a national religion. Many view Kimbangu as a political martyr and father of the Congolese independence movement [36: 18]. The church was the first independent African church to become a full member of the World Council of Churches, and now claims over 3 million followers [17: 122–36; 20; 23]. (R.H.)

Kimḥi, David [XV] [Known by the acronym Radak] (*c.*1160–*c.*1235). Jewish Bible commentator and Hebrew grammarian, living in Narbonne (Provence). His father, Joseph, was an outstanding exegete and grammarian. David studied with his brother Moses, also noted for his scholarship in these subjects. David's classic philological work is *Mikhlol* ('Compendium'), a work on Hebrew grammar, the second part of which – *Sefer ha-Shorashim* ('Book of Roots') – was also published separately, giving all forms of Hebrew verbs and their derivatives. His grammatical works stimulated the scientific study of the Hebrew language. Based on the works of earlier grammarians (who wrote in Arabic), his was the first such work written in Hebrew.

Kimḥi wrote a commentary on much of the Bible – *Genesis*, all the prophetical books, *Psalms* and *Chronicles*. This is a lucid and popular exposition, usually concentrating on the literal meaning of the text (although sometimes bringing in homiletical views), frequently based on grammatical explanations. This commentary was printed in standard editions of the Hebrew Bible, along with those of RASHI and ABRAHAM IBN EZRA. Some of his comments, especially on the *Psalms*, attack Christological interpretations and contain anti-Christian polemics. However, his exegesis greatly influenced later Christian commentators and translators, especially in the period of the Reformation and Renaissance. [75] (G.W.)

King, George [XIX] (1919–). Founder and President of the Aetherius Society, 'An International Spiritual Brotherhood'. He is known as the Metropolitan Archbishop, His Eminence Sir George King, OSP, PhD, ThD, DD. Sir George was born in Shropshire; his father was a school teacher, his mother a practising spiritual healer. He became a London taxi driver and, a conscientious objector during the Second World War, he served as a section leader in the Fire Service. He practised yoga and studied a number of Eastern and New Age philosophies. In 1954, he claims to have received the command 'Prepare yourself! You are to become the voice of Interplanetary Parliament.' Sir George has since channelled numerous messages, especially from a Cosmic Master from Venus, known as Aetherius, and Master Jesus. [22]

The Aetherius Society was founded in 1955; it is registered as a Church, with its main branches in London and Los Angeles. Sir George is responsible for several inventions, such as Spiritual Energy Radiators and the Spiritual Energy Battery. [27; 4: app. 4] (E.B.)

King, Martin Luther, Jr [VI.A] (1929–1968). Black American Baptist leader. He was born in Atlanta, Georgia. He attended Morehouse College, where he studied sociology among other subjects. During this period he decided to become a minister of religion. He went to Crozier Theological Seminary to study divinity. He developed an awareness of the need for churches to engage in safeguarding social justice. He also became acquainted with the writings of Mahatma GANDHI. He went to Boston University School of Theology to do postgraduate studies. He was awarded a PhD. In Boston he met Coretta Scott, to whom he was married in 1953. In 1954 he became pastor of Dextor Avenue Baptist Church in Montgomery, Alabama. He was chosen to lead a boycott of the city's segregated buses in 1955 which led to such segregation laws being judged unconstitutional. King then founded the Southern Christian Leadership Conference to co-ordinate civil rights activities in 1957. This led to many campaigns against segregation in the 1960s. In 1964 he received the Nobel Peace Prize. Following Gandhi's example, King insisted on non-violent campaigning. He was assassinated in April 1968 in Memphis, Tennessee. [435; 436; 482] (T.T.)

Kingsford, Anna [XVII.A] (1846–1888). English occultist. She was born at Stratford, Essex, the daughter of a prosperous merchant. She became one of more prominent individuals in the 19th century who sought for traditional religion in untraditional ways. During the 1880s she came to articulate an individual theology drawn from Christianity, Renaissance Hermetic-kabbalistic magical philosophy, and late Victorian feminism. She was drawn to theosophy and in 1883–4 became the president of the London Lodge of the Theosophical Society (*see* BLAVATSKY, HELENA PETROVNA). She resigned because she disliked the emphasis upon Eastern ideas (and also because of internal friction) and in 1884 founded the Hermetic Society to promote Western esoteric knowledge, and particularly, an esoteric Christianity. She wrote of the feminine nature of the divine. Her views are contained within *The Perfect Way* (with E. Maitland, 1882), which argues that Christianity at its core incorporated the truths of esoteric paganism. Kingsford took her commitments seriously; she gained a medical degree in Paris in 1880 – no school in England was willing to accept her – in part because her training strengthened her arguments against vivisection. [5; 17; 20] (T.L.)

Kinjikitile Ngwale [I.A] [Bokero] (*d.*1905). Leader of an African millennialist movement known as the Maji-Maji rebellion. Little is known of Kinjikitile's early life. The first records regarding him concern his arrival in the central Tanzanian coastal area around 1902, at which time he was middle-aged. Drawing elements from the indigenous religions of the coastal peoples, he spread an apocalyptic message, promising that, through the observance of specific rituals, the Germans could be driven from the region. The locals believed him to be possessed by spirits, and gave him the name of 'Bokero', after a local high god. Kinjikitile's fame soon spread, and by 1904 he was attracting followers from the inland regions. Through the ritual drinking of *maji*, a sacred water collected from a special pool, followers were admitted to the movement and promised immunity from European bullets. Before an organized rebellion could be initiated under his command, groups of Kinjikitile's adherents began attacking the Germans in July 1905. Kinjikitile was soon captured and executed by the Germans. Thousands of lives were lost in the uprising which continued until 1907 and eventually spread over a large region, encompassing roughly one-third of present-day Tanzania. [11; 42: 244–5] (R.H.)

Kirdēr [XXVI] [Kartīr] (mid-3rd–early 4th century). Great Zoroastrian prelate who served seven Persian kings and is thought to have done much to give Sasanian Zoroastrianism its strongly authoritative and priest-dominated character. His activities are known from four rock inscriptions which he had carved, together with his portrait [11: 1209–13; 7: 10.3.3]. In these, the only ones in Persia made by a commoner, he recounts his career, rising from simple *hērbad* (a learned priest) under

ŠĀBUHR I to vastly more imposing titles and dignities in subsequent reigns. He was granted the rank of nobleman and the (doubtless lucrative) wardenships of two great fire-temples, and was given absolute authority over religious and judicial affairs throughout the empire. He must also have wielded considerable political influence. The detailed activities which he recounts are: overthrowing cult-images and founding instead sacred fires, a number at his own expense; seeing to the endowment deeds for such fires and for priestly colleges; increasing the prosperity of the priesthood; disciplining priests who did not serve the religion as he thought fit; increasing religious services; encouraging next-of-kin marriages; converting unbelievers to the faith; driving demon-worshippers from the land and 'assailing' Jews, Buddhists, Brahmans, Aramaic- and Greek-speaking Christians, Baptizers and Manichaeans – almost all at that time themselves proselytizers working against the state religion. Manichaean texts record that in the end he was responsible for MĀNĪ's being put to death. Further regulation of the Zoroastrian calendar took place during his term of high office [11: 807].

Kirdēr does not speak of doctrine, but since he served noted Zurvanite kings he was presumably himself of that persuasion. In two inscriptions he tells apparently of a vision in which, it seems, a girl, i.e. his *daēna* (*see* ZOROASTER), meets his spirit and leads it to blessedness, thus attesting the merit of what he has done [51]; but the texts here are badly mutilated and details are lacking. (M.B.)

Kisā-Gotamī [IV]. The subject of one of the most famous and best-loved Buddhist stories. Living at the time of the BUDDHA, she was married into a rich family, but badly treated by her relatives. She had a son, but he died while still small; maddened by grief, she carried his body about asking for medicine to cure him. Finally she sought the aid of the Buddha, who responded by telling her to bring him a mustard seed from a house which had not known death. She started to look for one, as if it were a medicine, but soon realized that no house was without knowledge of death, and that her suffering was shared by all humanity. She asked to become a nun, and soon afterwards reached enlightenment, and the end of all suffering. She wore coarse clothes as a form of asceticism, and the Buddha praised her as the foremost of his female disciples who undertook this practice. [150: vol. 1, 609–10] (S.C.)

Kitabatake Chikafusa [XIV] (1293–1354). Prominent political figure in the period of the rival northern and southern courts (1336–92). In 1325 he was appointed to the position of *dainagon* ('Great Counsellor'), but resigned five years later when the imperial prince under his tutelage suddenly died. His thought was influenced by the so-called 'Ise School' of Shintō, also known as Watarai Shintō or Deguchi Shintō, led by the Watari family of hereditary priests of the Outer Shrine at Ise. The Ise school was a movement which tried to systematize Shintō doctrine in order to free itself from heavy Buddhist influence and the influence of other powerful families. In 1333 the Emperor Go-Daigo (1288–1339) overthrew the Kamakura shogunate and attempted to reassert direct imperial rule. Only three years later, however, Ashikaga Takauji (1305–1358), the head of the main branch of the powerful Minamoto clan, gathered military forces and moved against Go-Daigo. Kitabatake advised Go-Daigo to take the imperial regalia and flee to the mountains of Yoshino. There they established a separate court in opposition to the northern one, where Takauji, now the new Shogun, placed another member of a different branch of the imperial family on the throne. This inaugurated the period of the northern and southern courts.

While Go-Daigo's supremacy was short-lived, the dream of Kitabatake and others of the restoration of direct imperial rule, legitimated by Shintō myth, did not die. Kitabatake is famous as the author of *Jinnō Shōtōki* ('The Chronicle of the Direct Descent of the Divine Sovereigns', 1339), an imperial history written to support the claims of the Go-Daigo faction, and *Engenshū*, another Shintō-inspired account of the origins of the Japanese nation. The former opens: 'Japan is the land of the *kami*. Our heavenly ancestor, the god Kunitokotachi, first laid the foundations for our country, and the sun goddess, Amaterasu, bequeathed the rule of our land to her descendants in perpetuity.' The *Jinnō Shōtōki* influenced many later scholars, including HAYASHI RAZAN and later imperial restorationists. Kitabatake wrote that the imperial regalia – a mirror, a *maga-tama* jewel, and a sword – symbolize the national virtues of truth, mercy and justice. He took note, however, of the contributions of Buddhism and neo-Confucianism to Japanese society, and did not vehemently attack them. [34: 101–2; 60: 273–82] (G.E.)

Kivebulaya, Apolo (1864?–1933). East African Christian missionary. Kivebulaya was a Ganda from a partly Muslim family. As a young man he fought in the civil wars of Buganda; in 1894 he was attached (perhaps as porter) to the British expedition to Toro. In 1895 he was baptized, taking the name Apolo, and offered to serve as an Anglican catechist. He was sent back to Toro, where he achieved great influence over the king. He was arrested and sent to the chain gang by a high handed British officer, although released without charges. He was ordained deacon in 1900 and priest in 1903 and made a canon in 1922, spending his life as a missionary in Toro. From 1897 to 1899, and especially from 1916, he worked to establish an effective church among the forest pygmy peoples across the border in Belgian Congo (Zaire). He never married. His simplicity, voluntary poverty and devotion were universally recognized. [498A; 649] (A.F.W.)

Kleanthes [x] (331–232 BCE). Greek philosopher and poet, born in Assos (in Troad, north-west Asia Minor, now Turkey), second head (in succession to Zeno) of the Stoic school in Athens. Stoicism offers a pantheistic explanation of the universe, in which everything is pervaded by the divine reason (*logos*), itself conceived as a material substance. In human beings, soul represents this divine *logos*: it is by no means unique, only a brighter 'spark of God' than informs other animate and inanimate beings. Even so, its freedom is severely curtailed within a rigidly deterministic universe subject totally to the dictates of providence and fate. Kleanthes gave religious expression to this view of the world in the only substantial text that survives from his pen, the 38 lines of the *Hymn to Zeus*, probably quoted by Paul (inaccurately) in his Athenian sermon recorded in *Acts* 17: 28. It begins (trans. G. Watt [27: LIV: 'I']):

Above all gods, most glorious, invoked by many a name, almighty evermore,
Who didst found the world and guidest all by law –
O Zeus, hail! for it is right that all mortals address thee.
We are thine offspring, alone of mortal things that live
and walk the earth moulded in image of the all;
therefore, thee will I hymn and sing thy might continually.

Stoicism provided an intellectual framework within which the traditional beliefs of classical paganism could be accommodated, as Cicero demonstrates for the Roman case [49: bk. 2].

The Stoic school was founded *c.*300 BCE, either shortly before or shortly after the school of Epicurus. Of the three parts into which, mirroring the Epicurean system, they divided philosophy – logic, physics, and ethics – their work in logic extended Aristotle's achievements very significantly.

In Stoic cosmogony, God transforms himself into a universe at recurrent intervals (in Stoic orthodoxy, every 30,000 years). Each cosmic cycle is an exact repetition of the last: God can never do things in less than the best possible way. There was no room for personal immortality (some said souls lived on after death to the end of each cycle before being reabsorbed into the cosmic fiery reason which is the essential nature of God). The Stoic ideal is the 'Wise Man', who lives in conformity to nature, understanding the *logos* and happily acquiescing in its grand design: this is virtue, the only true good, all normal human values being rejected as 'indifferent' and the emotions they arouse as being mistaken judgements.

Epictetus (*Manual* 53) quotes the following lines from another of Kleanthes' writings (trans. Long and Sedley [27: LXII: 'B']):

Lead me, Zeus and Destiny,
wherever you have ordained for me.
For I shall follow unflinching. But if I become bad
and am unwilling, I shall follow none the less.

[7; 26; 27; 35] (G.R.N.)

Klong-chen Rab-'byams-pa [iv] (1308–1363). Klong-chen-pa belongs to a critical period in Tibetan history, during which, in conjunction with the weakening and final collapse of Mongol power in China (1368), the Sa-skya-pa hegemony (1260–1350), which had successfully protected Tibet from outright Mongol invasion, grew feeble, with the result that Tibet was engulfed in a civil war from which the Phag-mo-gru-pa hierarchs eventually emerged victorious [190: 71–82]. The formative tendencies of the Rnying-ma-pa school now resurfaced as a powerful polemic upholding the spiritual and temporal magnificence of Tibet's imperial past. In this setting, Klong-chen-pa enjoyed a thorough Buddhist scholastic education, but in his mid-twenties he became disgusted with the pretensions of learning in the monastic colleges of Central Tibet, and decided to seek his enlightenment as a disciple of the wandering ascetic Kumārarāja (1266–1343), a saintly adept who specialized in the Rnying-ma-pa tradition of the Great Perfection. The inspiration derived from this teaching would motivate the entire course of Klong-chen-pa's later career, and the volume of his literary work devoted to it is enormous. He was not able to avoid political entanglement completely, and spent some years in exile in what is today Bhutan. The corpus of Klong-chen-pa's writings on the Great Perfection may be divided into two broad categories: his contribution, as final redactor, to the 11-volume collection of precepts, meditation texts and ritual manuals known as the 'Four-fold Innermost Spirituality' (*snying-thig ya-bzhi*); and his numerous independent treatises on the theory and practice of the Great Perfection, of which the best known are his 'Seven Treasuries' (*mdzod-bdun*) and 'Trilogy on Rest' (*ngal-gso skor-gsum*). His work is highly esteemed for its stylistic refinement, reflecting his early interest in poetry and poetics. Nonetheless, his influence on Tibetan Buddhist thought became extensive only after the 18th century, when 'Jigs-med gling-pa (1730–1798), a visionary inspired by Klong-chen-pa, initiated the widespread promulgation of his work. [56: book 2: IV; 80; 115; 196] (M.K.).

Knox, John [VI.A] (*c*.1514–1572). Scottish Protestant leader. He was born in Haddington, Lothian, and was probably educated in Glasgow and St Andrews. It is likely that he was ordained priest at about the age of 25, became an apostolic notary and in about 1544 became a private tutor. Soon afterwards he came under the influence of George Wishart and became a Protestant. He became a preacher in St Andrews in 1547 and was taken prisoner and made a galley slave by the French. His release in 1549 was arranged by the English and in 1551 he became a chaplain to Edward VI. He assisted in the revision of the Second Prayer Book. In 1554, following Mary's accession, he went to Frankfurt as pastor to English refugees but went on to Geneva following some dispute. He returned to Scotland briefly in 1555 but went back to Geneva the following year. In Geneva he published *The First Blast of the Trumpet against the Monstrous Regiment of Women*. He returned to Scotland in 1559 and became the leader of Scottish Protestantism. He had a hand in writing the Confession of Faith, the *First Book of Discipline* and *The Book of Common Order*. In 1560 he published a *Treatise on Predestination*. He preached against Queen Mary Stuart after 1561 and at the coronation of her successor James VI in 1567. His *History of the Reformation of Religion within the Realm of Scotland* was published posthumously. [244; 441; 442] (T.T.)

Kōbō Daishi. *See* KŪKAI.

Ko Hung [V] [Pao P'u Tzu] (283–343). Learned scholar, original and prolific thinker, and Taoist alchemist. All of these abilities are amply exhibited in his great work called after his sobriquet 'Pao P'u Tzu' ('The Master Who Holds in His Arms the Uncarved Block'), a reference to chapters 28 and 42 of the book of LAO TZU [58]. The 20 Inner Chapters (*nei p'ien*) of this work are devoted to the Taoist arts and techniques, while the 25 Outer Chapters (*wai p'ien*) are concerned with matters commonly associated with the Literati Tradition of classical scholarship, personal ethical cultivation and statesmanship. We are well informed about Ko Hung's life because he wrote an autobiography (chapter 50 of the Outer Chapters) and is the subject of a biography in the official history of the Chin dynasty (266–316), the Chin shu. Of most relevance to religion is his Taoist lineage as he himself gives it in the *Pao P'u Tzu*: the famous immortal transcendent Tso Tz'u or Tso Yüan-fang of Latter Han times (25–220) possessed certain scriptures or technical manuals which he passed along to Ko Hung's paternal uncle, Ko Hsüan; these the latter in turn gave to Cheng Yin who was Ko Hung's Taoist master. Ko Hung himself is said to have attained immortal transcendence in Mt Lo-fu, a famous Taoist retreat in the far south of China.

The *Pao P'u Tzu* is of basic importance in Taoist history because in it there are preserved detailed accounts of what were apparently every method or technique connected with the search for spiritual powers and immortal transcendency known to early Taoism. It also contains a long list of texts constituting the earliest extant bibliography of Taoism. Ko Hung is concerned, *inter alia*, with refuting sceptics who do not believe in immortal transcendence. In addition to his discussion of this matter in the *Pao P'u Tzu*, he compiled an anthology which he called 'Biographies of Spirits and Immortals' (*shen hsien chuan*), the earliest work of this genre. [37: 75–113; 43] (L.T.)

Kong-sprul Blo-gros mtha'-yas [IV] (1813–1899). Born in 1813 in far eastern Tibet to a family adhering to the Bön religion, Kong-sprul Blo-gros mtha'-yas was ordained by turns in the Rnying-ma-pa and Karma Bka'-brgyud sects of Tibetan Buddhism. Recognized as a prodigy, the administrative complications occasioned by his several sectarian affiliations filled him with a deep-seated distaste for sectarian exclusivity and triumphalism. Under the inspiration and guidance of a like-minded visionary and scholar, 'Jam-dbyangs Mkhyen-brtse'i dbang-po (1820–1892), Kong-sprul endeavoured to compile, preserve and transmit to future generations the accumulated Buddhist learning of Tibet, focusing in particular on those traditions of meditation and yoga that seemed most in danger of becoming lost. Because of the non-sectarian impartiality (*ris-med*) of his approach to this task, he is sometimes credited with founding a 'Universalist' or 'Eclectic' movement within Tibetan Buddhism, though there is no evidence that he wished this to supplant existing sectarian institutions. As an encyclopedist and author he produced 'Five Scriptural Treasuries' (*gsung-rab mdzod-lnga*), occupying more than 90 volumes altogether. Following his death in 1899 several rebirths were recognized, among whom the Ven. Kalu Rinpoche (1903–1989) became particularly active as a meditation teacher in Europe and North America, instituting in 1976 the first western centre for the practice of the traditional Tibetan three-year retreat in Toulon-sur-Arroux, France. [56: book 2: VI; 195] (M.K.)

Konkō Daijin. *See* KAWATE BUNJIRŌ.

Kook, Abraham Isaac [XV] [widely known as Rav (i.e. Rabbi) Kook] (1865–1935). Jewish religious thinker and leader. Born in north-western Russia, he was a child prodigy. He was a rabbi in Lithuania until 1904, when he moved to Palestine, becoming rabbi of Jaffa. During the First World War he was caught in Europe and served congregations in Switzerland and London until 1919, when he returned to Palestine. Two years later he was appointed the first Chief Rabbi (Ashkenazi) of Palestine.

The return of the Jewish people to the Land of Israel was of profound religious significance for Kook, who was an outstanding ideologist of religious Zionism. In the talmudic academy which he founded in Jerusalem, special attention was paid to the laws concerning agriculture and the temple service, which had been neglected in the Diaspora. Kook was extremely supportive of the motivations and achievements of the country's labour 'pioneers'; even though their outlook was secular, and sometimes even anti-religious, Kook felt they were helping to construct the 'Holy of Holies'. To him, every Jewish soul had a fundamentally religious nature. His views brought on charges of heresy from the extreme Orthodox.

His thinking is not systematic and is scattered through his works, many of which remain in manuscript. A student of the Kabbalah, his ideas were often mystically oriented. The world, he taught, possesses an indivisible harmony which comes from its divine origin. In what has been termed a 'mystical panentheism', Kook held that everything is penetrated by the divine unity which underlies the apparent chaos and multiplicity of the world. The truth can be grasped not by reason but through man's inner vision. Adam's sin, which separated the world from God, can be overcome only by 'repentant return', and everything must return to its divine source. Endorsing a Darwinian approach, he saw evolution as the ineluctable upward movement of man towards God. Evil is merely unrealized perfection and death is an imperfection of creation. [65: 219–38]

The Jewish people and the Jewish soul have a unique role. The Jew has a special gift for holiness, which is fully realizable only in the Land of Israel, where this holiness – impaired in exile – would be renewed. The Land of Israel differs metaphysically from the rest of the world and Jewish nationalism is a sacred phenomenon. [2; 9: VI]

Kook's son, Tzevi Yehuda Kook (1891–1982), who succeeded his father as head of the Rav Kook Academy in Jerusalem, further developed these ideas, and after 1967 was the spiritual inspiration of the extreme nationalist Gush Emunim movement, which insisted on Israel's spiritual right to sovereignty over the entire Land of Israel. (G.W.)

Kosmas Aetolos, St [VI.B] (1714–1779). Kosmas, an Athonite monk, worked from 1760 as an itinerant teacher and preacher combating the spread of Islam among the Greeks and Albanians, founding schools and distributing Bibles for daily reading. St Anthimos of Cephalonia (1727–1782) and several other monks conducted parallel missions to preserve Orthodoxy in the Balkans. Kosmas was killed at the orders of the Pasha of Berat in Albania. [21; 65: 201ff.] (D.B.)

Kotani Kimi [IV] (1901–1971). The co-founder and leader of Reiyūkai Kyōdan ('The Society of Friends of the Spirits'), a Japanese lay Buddhist organization. She received religious instruction from her brother-in-law Kubo Kakutarō (1892–1944), who had been heavily influenced first by Nichirenshugi, a nationalistic political interpretation of the teachings of NICHIREN, and later by Nishida Toshizō, who advocated a lay form of ancestral worship free of the priesthood. Kubo appropriated many of Nishida's teachings and practices, including the belief that natural disaster and social unrest are a result of failure to worship the ancestors properly. Kubo became convinced of the necessity of establishing a society of lay persons to address modern social ills through Buddhist ideals and practice, and he also emphasized the folk art of faith-healing. He was largely unsuccessful in gathering a following, however, until he gained Kotani Kimi as a convert; they founded Reiyūkai together in 1925.

Kotani was a charismatic figure with great organizational abilities and considerable fame as a faith-healer. While Kubo was the theorist, she carried his message that suffering and difficulties in one's life are the result of failure to worship ancestral spirits in a proper manner and of laxity in personal and public morality. This teaching, coupled with a traditional family-centred ethic, was acceptable to the authorities of State Shinto.

When Kubo died in 1944 Kotani succeeded him as head of Reiyūkai. She dropped nationalistic propaganda from Reiyūkai publications in the post-war period and substituted the theme of world peace. The ethical norms and values based on the extended family system, however, together with an opposition to 'individualism', have continued to be the core of Reiyūkai teachings. In Reiyūkai, the family is the locus of salvation; an authentic existence is only possible therein since the family is the proper site of ancestral worship. Family members, not priests working for pay, should conduct these rites. Kotani also continued to emphasize the concepts of karma – both personal and that transmitted by the ancestors – and repentance.

Kotani oversaw Reiyūkai's growth in the 1950s and 1960s into one of the largest of Japan's new religions. She also established close ties with the far right of the conservative Liberal Democratic Party, and especially with Ishihara Shintarō, a party leader. When Kotani died in 1971 she was succeeded by Kubo Kakutarō's son, Tsugunari. [126; 224: 109–16] (G.E.)

Ko Tha Byu [VI.A] (1778–1840). He was born in a jungle village near Bassein in Burma, a member of the Karen, a non-Buddhist people. He was bought out of slavery by a Burmese Christian and was converted under the influence of ADONIRAM JUDSON. He lived in Moulmein, where the fledgling church was reluctant to accept him into its community because of his reputation and because he was a Karen tribal. In 1828 he went with G. D. Boardman, a Western missionary, to help open a mission in Tavoy, south Burma, where Ko Tha was baptized by Boardman. His baptism was witnessed by other Karens who persuaded him to preach in their villages. He continued to evangelize among his own people for the remaining 12 years of his life. As a result a strong Karen church grew in Burma and constitutes about one-half of all Christians in Burma today. A Christian high school in Bassein is named after Ko Tha, the apostle to the Karen, and he is commemorated in the Karen church calendar. [687; 803] (T.T.)

Kraemer, Hendrik [VI.A] (1888–1965). Dutch missionary. He lost his parents at a young age and was raised in a Protestant orphanage where he experienced a religious conversion through reading the Bible. At the age of 16 he decided to become a missionary. Through the Dutch Bible Society he was enabled to take a doctorate in Eastern Languages and Religions. In 1919 he married Hyke van Gameren, who went with him to the Netherlands East Indies (Indonesia) in 1922. His work was to survey developing currents in Indonesian society, in indigenous religions, in Islam and in nationalism. He also worked as a translation consultant. During his time there he contributed greatly to missionary policy in his advocacy of early indigenization of the church in Java. In 1937 he returned to become professor of Comparative Religion at the University of Leiden. The following year he produced his major work, *The Christian Message in a Non-Christian World*, which was designed for discussion at the conference of the International Missionary Council at Tambaram, south India in 1938. His argument was that Christianity was the product of 'biblical realism', as against other religions which were the products of a human 'religious approach'. This argument caused much dissent especially among leading Indian Christians and some Western missionaries such as A. G. HOGG. During the Second World War he was interned in the Netherlands by the occupying Nazi power. In 1947 he became the first Director of the Ecumenical Institute at Bossey, near Geneva. He retired in 1955 and was a guest lecturer at Union Theological Seminary, New York from 1956 to 1957. [340; 444] (T.T.)

Krishnamurti, Jiddu [XI] (1895–1989). Indian religious figure. He was born in South India. When he was 13 his father, a theosophist, moved to Adyar to work in the International Headquarters of the Theosophical Society. There, one evening, Krishnamurti was picked out by Charles Edward Leadbeater to be the vehicle for the World Teacher, the Lord Maitreya (*see also* BESANT, ANNIE). He was sent to England for education, having undergone the Theosophical initiations. In August 1922 he had a three-day spiritual experience that transformed him and a 'process' began that affected him every day for about an hour in the evening and caused him great pain. This 'process', which he accepted as a necessary development of his consciousness, continued throughout his life. In 1929, having grown dubious about both his position and the Theosophical beliefs and practices he was exposed to, he dissolved the order of which he had been made the head, and resigned from the Society. Thereafter his life was one of travelling and giving talks to audiences around the world. This has produced a large published literature touching on a vast range of subjects. In essence, he sees man's state of sorrow and conflict arising from the fact that the mind is conditioned; for anything new to arise and for sorrow to end the mind has to be deconditioned. He knows that his own state is deconditioned, and bears witness to what that state is like, but he was himself puzzled by the mystery of his own state, and he never evolved a methodology whereby others might attain a similar state. He was to the end a witness to life at the unconditioned human level. Amongst his books are *The First and Last Freedom* (1954), *Commentaries on Living* (1956, 1959, 1960), *Krishnamurti's Notebook* (1976) and *Krishnamurti's Journal* (1982). [66] (S.C.R.W.)

Krishna Pillai [VI.A] [Henry Alfred] (1827–1900). He was born in the Tirunelveli district of South India of a high caste family. He had a good early education, especially in Tamil classical literature. Though strongly opposed to Christian proselytization, in 1853 he took a post as a teacher of Tamil at a Christian school in Sawyerpuram. A number of his friends were converted to Christianity but he still maintained a strong opposition. Eventually in 1858 he, too, was converted and baptized in Madras. Though he was given the Christian names Henry Alfred he never used them, and was always known by his original Hindu name. For 40 years he used his knowledge of Tamil to propagate the Christian faith. His most famous work, the *Rakshanya Yaatrikam* ('The Journey of Salvation'), takes its main theme from John Bunyan's *Pilgrim's Progress*. It was published in 1894 and was highly praised by Hindus as well as Christians. [20] (T.T.)

Kṣemā. *See* KHEMĀ.

K'uei-chi [IV] [Chi] (636–682). The main disciple of HSÜAN-TSANG (600–664), and a primary commentator on the translations of his master. He was also a systematizer of the Fa-hsiang school, one of the major philosophical schools of Chinese Buddhism. In addition to assisting Hsüan-tsang with his translations, K'uei-chi produced numerous commentaries on the works of the Yogācāra masters such as ASAṄGA and VASUBANDHU, the most important being his notes on the *Ch'eng wei-shih lun* (*Vijñaptimātratāsiddhiśāstra*), the massive commentary by DHARMAPĀLA on Vasubandhu's 'Thirty Verses' (*Triṃśikā-vijñaptimātratāsiddhi*). One of his original contributions to the development of Yogācāra thought is his analysis of the five-levelled contemplation of Vijñaptimātratā, an attempt to summarize the soteriological process at the core of Yogācāra Buddhism. Although the highly theoretical nature of the Fa-hsiang school prevented it from ever achieving a large popular following, it did have extensive influence on the development of Buddhist philosophical thought in East Asia. [200] (P.L.S.)

Kuei-feng Tsung-mi. *See* TSUNG-MI.

Kūkai [IV] [Kōbō Daishi] (774–835). Japanese Buddhist monk and transmitter of esoteric Buddhism from China to Japan. He was the founder of the Shingon school and, along with SAICHŌ, one of the two pre-eminent figures of Heian (794–1185) Japan.

Kūkai first entered a national college and studied Confucianism but converted to Buddhism and dropped out of school to wander around the country and to practise severe austerities in the mountains. In 804 he visited T'ang China (at the same time as Saichō) in search of training in esoteric Buddhism, and received initiation under Hui-ko (746–805), a disciple of AMOGHAVAJRA. Kūkai returned to Japan in 806 as a master of esoteric Buddhism, carrying with him an impressive and important collection of texts and ritual objects. He received the favour of Emperor Saga (reigned 809–23), established the headquarters of Shingon Buddhism on Mt Kōya, and was presented the important temple Tō-ji at the southern entrance of Kyoto. Kūkai travelled extensively, disseminating the teachings and practice of esoteric Buddhism, and was also concerned with works of social service such as the construction of wells and artificial lakes. Legends of Kūkai's presence and magical deeds abound in almost every corner of Japan. Kūkai 'entered *samādhi*' on Mt Kōya, and the faithful believe that he remains in a state of trance awaiting the arrival of Maitreya, the Buddha of the future.

The cult which has formed around the figure of Kūkai is still strong in Japan. Mt Kōya and Tōji are strong centres of pilgrimage and faith in Kōbō Daishi, Kūkai's posthumous title. The Shikoku pilgrimage of 88 temples, based on legends of Kūkai's exploits before his trip to China, is one of the major pilgrimage routes in Japan.

Kūkai's reputation as a philosopher and religious thinker is just as formidable. He perfected and systematized the esoteric Buddhist tradition, contributing profound treatises such as the *Jūjūshinron* ('Ten Stages of the Mind'), *Benkenmitsu nikyōron* ('On the Two Teachings, Esoteric and Exoteric'), and *Sokushin jōbutsu gi* ('Attaining Buddhahood in this Life').

Kūkai is also a well known figure in popular culture, famed as a master calligrapher, engineer, philosopher, saviour-figure and religious genius. He is also credited with inventing the Japanese *kana* syllabary, as well as the famous *i-ro-ha* poem, which expresses the Buddhist concept of impermanence through a single use of each of the sounds in the Japanese syllabary. [92; 121; 122: 39–51, 94–109] (P.L.S.)

al-Kulaynī, Thiqat al-Islām Muḥammad ibn Yaʿqūb [XII] (*d.*939/40). The first and most important of the systematizers of Shiʿite religious tradition, regarded as the *mujaddid* or 'renewer' of the Shiʿite faith for the 4th Islamic century. Born in the village of Kulayn near Rayy (to the south of modern Tehran), he became the leading Imamite scholar there and later in Qumm, the major centre of Shiʿite learning. This was the period of the 'Lesser Occultation' (874–941), when the last of the twelve Imāms (*see* MUḤAMMAD AL-MAHDĪ) was believed to have gone into hiding. Qumm was then dominated by a school of traditionalist scholars whose work continued that of earlier Shiʿite thinkers overshadowed by the presence of a living Imām. Like their counterparts in Sunnism, Shiʿite traditionists emphasized textual fidelity to authoritative religious utterances, engaging above all in the collection and classification of the sayings of the Imāms or reports about them.

Kulaynī's large collection of traditions from the Imāms, known as *al-Kāfī fī ʿilm al-dīn* ('The Sufficient Book concerning the Science of Religion') took 20 years to compile and represents the climax of Qumm traditionalism. As a source for Shiʿite doctrine, particularly with regard to the nature of the Imāms, it is unrivalled. Some writers have compared it to the Sunnī collection of traditions by AL-BUKHĀRĪ, but its religious status for Shiʿites is even higher.

Kulaynī left Qumm for Baghdad toward the end of the 9th century. With his departure Qumm began to decline in influence as a seat of learning, being replaced by Baghdad, which had already been the principal centre for Shiʿite activity for some time. Kulaynī's death coincided almost exactly with the end of the Lesser Occultation, leaving his compilation as one of the major influences on Shiʿite thought in the new era then about to begin. [35: s.v.; 89] (D.M.)

Kumārajīva [IV] (344–413). One of the greatest and most prolific translators of Buddhist texts into Chinese. He was born in Serindia, where he first studied Sarvāstivādin philosophy and other non-Buddhist subjects, but later converted to Mahāyāna and studied the Śūnyavāda tradition. He was taken captive by the Chinese army in 383 and brought to Liang-chou in north-western China, where, it is assumed, he learned Chinese. In 401 the Liang were conquered by the Later Ch'in, who welcomed Kumārajīva to their capital in Ch'ang-an, where he received the support to complete his voluminous and superb translations.

Kumārajīva's influential translations include that of the *Lotus Sūtra*, the major *Prajñāpāramitā Sūtras*, the *Vimalakīrti Sūtra*, and the *Amitābha Sūtra*; Nāgārjuna's *Ta chih tu lun, Po-lun* and *Mūlamadhyamakakārikā*; and the *Ch'eng shih lun (Satyasiddhiśāstra)*. He left very little of his own writings, one exception being the *Ta ch'eng ta i chang*, a collection of his correspondence with Hui-yüan (344–416), a disciple of TAO-AN and an early advocate of Pure Land practices. Kumārajīva's many eminent followers include SENG-CHAO (374–414) and Tao-sheng (4th century), who advocated the universality of the Buddha-nature and sudden enlightenment, both of which later became important aspects of the dominant Southern School of Ch'an and of Chinese Buddhism as a whole. Thus, not only did Kumārajīva introduce and establish Mādhyamika philosophy in China, but his translations became the authoritative and most widely read texts for much of East Asian Buddhism. [31: 81–5, 367–8; 234: 869–87; 267] (P.L.S.)

Kundakunda [XIII] (*c.*2nd century). The first and foremost teacher of Digambara Jainism who is regarded as being descended through teacher–pupil lineage from MAHĀVĪRA himself. The normative Digambara ascetic tradition, the 'Fundamental Community' (*Mūlasaṅgha*), claimed a particularly close association with Kundakunda as its progenitor.

Virtually nothing of historical value can be said about Kundakunda himself. Textual sources ascribe several alternative names to him. A consensus seems to have emerged among Indian scholars that he was originally named Padmanandin and that he came to be called Kundakunda after his home village of a similar name, which is to be located near the boundary between the current Indian states of Karnataka and Andhra Pradesh.

The traditional biographies of Kundakunda are late but of interest in that they give an insight into how the Digambara tradition came to view him. One recounts how Kundakunda was in his immediately preceding birth a cowherd boy who had come across in a burnt forest a copse of trees which had been miraculously preserved from the ravages of the fire. In fact, this copse had previously been the abode of a Jain ascetic, as proved by the copies of the scriptures which the cowherd boy found there and took home. A monk visited his master's home and, while his master gave food as alms, the boy bestowed the spiritually more efficacious gift of the scriptures. In his next birth he was born as his master's son, who, on renouncing the world, became a teacher (*ācārya*) at the age of

33 and lived for a further 52 years with the name of Kundakunda. The other main traditional story links Kundakunda with Sīmandhara, the *tīrthaṅkara* (*see* MAHĀVĪRA) who is currently living in the mythical continent of Mahāvideha. Kundakunda was magically transported to Mahāvideha either because (versions of the story differ) he had difficulties with understanding certain authoritative texts or because Sīmandhara had been told that he was the wisest man on earth. It was during his journey that Kundakunda lost his whisk of peacock feathers, one of the main distinguishing marks of a Digambara, so that he was forced to take an alternative one of vulture feathers, from which derives one of his most common alternative names, *Gṛdhrapiccha* ('Vulture Whisk'). The implication of this legendary stay of Kundakunda's in Mahāvideha is that he is the only figure in this world-age since Mahāvīra's disciples to have had direct and unmediated contact with a *tīrthaṅkara*.

Kundakunda is traditionally regarded as being the author of 84 texts known as *Pāhuḍa*, a designation which has been variously explained but probably means 'Treatise'. The number 84 is a fiction, and even when the texts attributed to Kundakunda is reduced to 16, these being the sole survivors, caution must still be exercised in attributing them in entirety to him. The group of writings known as the 'Eight Pāhuḍas', for example, can be viewed as of doubtful authenticity on the grounds of metrical and linguistic inconsistencies.

Kundakunda's most significant works and the ones which can be attributed to him with most certainty are all written in Prakrit: the *Niyamasāra* [15] ('The Essence of Restraint'); the *Pañcāstikāya* [16] ('The Five Constituent Elements of the Cosmos'), which gives the impression of being a loose anthology of verses that have been collected together; the *Pravacanasāra* [17] ('The Essence of the Scriptures'); and the *Samayasāra* [18] ('The Essence of the Doctrine'). The *Niyamasāra* deals in the main with the *āvaśyakas*, the ritual behaviour obligatory for the Jain lay and monastic communities, while the *Pañcāstikāya* gives an account of the basic elements which make up the universe. The *Pravacanasāra* is a manual dealing with ascetic behaviour and with spiritual practice and analysis, perhaps directed towards a young monk.

However, Kundakunda's overall soteriological standpoint is best exemplified in the *Samayasāra*, which is perhaps the single most important Digambara Jain scripture and which has maintained a high prestige to the current day. In this work, Kundakunda presents the soul as the ultimate and only significant reality which provides a 'certain/supreme standpoint' (*niścaya/paramārtha-naya*) with reference to which everything outside the soul can be judged. However, the soul as cognizer is, through the obscuring influence of karmic matter, ignorant about its true nature as pure bliss and omniscience. Kundakunda attempts to show how the individual as embodied soul can gain understanding of its innate nature and, to this end, he asserts that everything outside the soul, no matter how ostensibly pure and 'religious' (and this includes scripture, which Kundakunda regards as being unfamiliar with the true nature of the soul), has only an inferior transactional reality and should be approached from a 'worldly standpoint' (*vyavahāra-naya*). In what is perhaps the *Samayasāra*'s most striking example, Kundakunda asserts (verses 306–7) that various central practices of the Jain religion such as fasting, meditation and spiritual purification are a 'pot of poison' and that the 'pot of nectar' is in fact their opposites, namely non-fasting, non-meditation, etc. Kundakunda is here saying that the notion of moral and religious polarities, albeit apparently at the centre of Jainism, is no more than a feature of the transient world of *saṃsāra* in which the non-enlightened live, and should only be regarded as valid from the point of view of the worldly (*vyavahāra*). In reality the soul in its truest guise is free from conditioning by ordinary concerns such as good and bad. In the same way, the *Niyamasāra* demonstrates that the outward, ritual observances of Jainism are only of validity if approached in an 'inner' soul-oriented manner. It should be noted, however, that the pattern of two truths is not always consistent in Kundakunda's works (perhaps as a result of later interpolation), and it is often used in a non-mystical manner to point to doctrinal matters and the correctness of a specifically Jain philosophical analysis.

The *Samayasāra* was the subject of an important commentary by Amṛtacandra (?8th century). This proved to have great influence on the thought of important later

Digambaras such as *Banārsīdās* and KĀNJĪ SVĀMI. (P.D.)

Küng, Hans [VI.A] (1928–). Swiss Catholic theologian. He was born at Sursee, near Lucerne, into a Roman Catholic family. He was educated at a local *Gymnasium* and went to Rome to study at the Gregorian University and at the Collegium Germanicum in 1948. He earned Licentiates in Philosophy (1951) and Theology (1955), the latter for a thesis on the doctrine of justification of KARL BARTH. In 1955 he went to the Sorbonne and the Institut Catholique in Paris to prepare a doctoral thesis on Barth's work. In it he argued that Barth's doctrine of justification and the Council of Trent's were fundamentally the same. The publication of the thesis in 1957 caused a sensation in Protestant and Catholic circles. Küng, having been ordained priest, spent the next year and a half in pastoral work in Switzerland. In 1959 he taught at the University of Münster and in 1960 he went to the Catholic Theology Faculty in the University of Tübingen. From then on he was often in conflict with the Vatican over his studies on Catholic theology and the church. He was called to Rome to defend his book, *Structures of the Church* (1962). In 1963 he was banned from speaking in Catholic institutions in the United States by American bishops. His next books on the church and the infallibility of the pope were also censured by Rome. Following the publication of *Christ sein* (1974; English trans. as *On Being a Christian*, 1976) and *Does God Exist?* (1978) he was barred from being a Catholic theologian and from teaching in the Catholic Faculty in 1979. He became and continues to be professor of ecumenical theology and director of the Ecumenical Institute of the University of Tübingen. [337; 768; 769] (T.T.)

K'ung Tzu [V] [K'ung Fu-tzu; K'ung Ch'iu; Chung-ni; Confucius] (551–479 BCE). His latinized name, Confucius, was devised by Jesuit missionaries in the 17th century as a transliteration of K'ung Fu-tzu (Master K'ung). Master K'ung is most commonly rendered in Chinese as K'ung Tzu, the word 'Tzu' being added to the surnames of Chinese thinkers of ancient times. Modern Chinese scholars have usually regarded him not as a religious figure but rather as a philosopher and teacher, and as author *cum* editor of the ancient texts that have throughout history been considered the canon of the Literati (Confucian) tradition. Master K'ung was early referred to as the 'uncrowned king' (*su wang*), meaning that, although he was not technically qualified to become political sovereign, yet his writings made up a sort of 'constitution' for China. Later generations would associate him with LAO TZU and the BUDDHA as one of the founders of the three *chiao* – a term meaning teachings, body of doctrine, or great tradition. It is a fact that the spiritual descendants of the Master were opposed to deifying him, in spite of the fact that countless lesser persons were apotheosized in China. Nevertheless, ritual worship was given to his spirit throughout the ages by students and emperors, and the 'Confucian temple' (*wen miao*) was the most important centre of the state cult in every administrative capital.

Master K'ung did not attempt to found a religion. His driving purpose was to restore the legitimate authority of the reigning dynasty (Chou, *c.*1100–256 BCE), which by his times had been lost to the feudal states. He believed that restoration of the ancient social order would solve the problems of political chaos and immorality. Failing to obtain the ministerial office in any state that would have enabled him to launch such a restoration, Master K'ung in his old age devoted himself to teaching (he is the first person in China known to have taken in private students without regard to social class) and writing. His most important contribution was his unequivocal assertion of the moral law, something unprecedented in Chinese history. His ideal follower would be a moral paragon (*chün tzu*) whose example would influence the ruler to reform himself and to carry out good government. This ethical idealism struck a deeply resonant chord in the psyche of Chinese Literati throughout the ages, and the theory of government by moral example dominated – at least theoretically – Chinese political thinking.

Although Master K'ung did not express himself primarily in religious terms, his faith in the spirits to which sacrifices were offered in his times (such as the tutelary deities of territory and agriculture), and in the souls of the dead, is attested by many passages in the literature. He believed in a deity called Heaven, which he thought had given him his mission. And he was the great authority on rules of proper social deportment and ritual (*li*), many of which were concerned with such religious matters as funerals, burials and sacrifices. The religion of Master K'ung was no doubt a formal and ritualized one, and yet we have his own teaching that mere ceremonialism is no true sacrifice.

The texts associated with his name were adopted as the orthodox teachings of the state (mid-2nd century BCE), and from that time on constituted the central educational curriculum of all students. They soon became not mere teachings but unquestionable dicta, taking their place as scripture alongside the original sacred texts (*ching*) of antiquity. Because the social structure and ethics of Master K'ung were thus sanctified, he is the pivotal figure in the struggles of modern times between traditionalists and iconoclasts. [13; 14; 19; 45: 56–134; 49; 66] (L.T.)

Kurozumi Munetada [XIV] (1780–1850). Founder of Kurozumikyō, a Japanese new religion. He was the third son of a low-ranking priest of the Imamaura shrine in the Okayama domain, and underwent training for the hereditary priesthood. He studied the *Kojiki* [49], the *Man'yōshū* [37], the *Kokinshū* [50], some Confucian classics, the work of ISHIDA BAIGAN and the *kokugaku* ('national learning') scholars, divination and Chinese medicine.

In 1812 both of Kurozumi's parents died and he contracted tuberculosis. He had aspired to become a *kami* in this life, expressing the neo-Confucian goal of sagehood in a Shintō idiom, but believing that he would not survive, and despairing of his goal, he vowed to become a healing deity after death instead. In 1813 and early 1814 he worshipped the sun and miraculously recovered from his illness. On 19 November 1814, which was both his birthday and the date of the winter solstice, he experienced a transformative mystical union with Amaterasu, the sun goddess, which was to inspire him for the rest of his life.

Sun worship is at the heart of Kurozumikyō since Amaterasu is held to be the creatrix of the universe and the parent of all beings. Kurozumi taught that humankind participates in the divinity of Amaterasu, and that each individual life is a portion of the universal soul and its vital power. He also taught that the natural state of human beings is brightness and joy, but that lack of harmony with the deity has led to gloom, despair and illness. All of existence is, he believed, permeated by *yōki* ('yang essence'), which is the equivalent of *kami*-nature. By uniting the human and divine will one can realize one's own true *kami*-nature. Kurozumi stressed the this-worldly benefits of proper belief and practice, traditional ethical values, and reverence for the imperial family – but he did not identify Amaterasu exclusively as the ancestor of the imperial family.

Kurozumi also practised faith-healing without charge, transferring *yōki* by hand and breath while reciting the Shintō Great Purification Prayer. He taught that healing is the natural expression of unity with the deity, and he became famous as a healer. In 1843 he retired as priest of the Imamura shrine, turning this position over to his eldest son, and devoted himself to proselytizing. Kurozumi Kyōdan was established as an independent sect in 1846. Leadership of Kurozumikyō, which today has a membership of about 220,000, has continued to be passed down to direct male descendants of the founder. [19; 22; 26: 245–6; 34: 219–20; 53; 55; 59: 61–7] (G.E.)

L

Lal Ded [XI] [Lallā] (14th-century). Yogini and Kashmiri poetess, chiefly memorable for the unique quality of her mystical verse-saying (*vākh*). Around these and their author there later developed an increasingly exuberant hagiography, according to which she was born in a village near Srinagar into a Brahman family. Her marriage brought her under the control of a mother-in-law so cruel that she would serve her stones, thinly covered with rice to deceive any guests. Renouncing married life, she became the disciple of Siddha Śrīkaṇṭha, a Śaivite yogi, and is supposed simultaneously to have discarded her clothes and spent the rest of her life wandering about in the nude. Her name 'Granny Lal' is by some said to derive from the way in which her flabby lower belly (*lal*) hung over her pudenda [56: 12–13]. She is also said to have countered all criticisms of her nakedness by claiming she had yet to meet a real man among the Kashmiris. Only when she encountered Sayyid ʿAlī Hamadānī (*d.*1386), the Naqshbandī whose missionary efforts proved so successful in the Islamization of Kashmir, is she supposed to have run for cover, exclaiming 'I have seen a man.' [106: 9] The fantastic character of such anecdotes, important as they are for an understanding of popular attitudes to the complex religious history of Kashmir, is largely belied by the character of her *vākh*, numbering 109 in the standard edition [39]. Though many of these require a familiarity with the technical terminology of Śaivite yoga, their continuing status as the greatest religious classic of Kashmiri literature, appealing to the Muslim majority as well as the Kashmiri Pandits, has been ensured by their marvellous directness and their incorporation of such peculiarly local imagery as the symbolization of the coming of chaos by the simultaneous ripening of apples and apricots [106: 219]. [39; 56; 106] (C.S.)

Lallā. *See* LAL DED.

Lalou, Marie Dawono [I.A] (1892–1951). Prophetess who founded the Eglise Déimatiste (Church of Ashes of Purification), the largest of the new religions after the Harris Churches in the Côte d'Ivoire (*see* HARRIS, WILLIAM WADÉ). Of Bété origin and a former Roman Catholic, she had various mystical experiences before developing her own healing movement. She renounced marriage and claimed to replace Harris as well as the Bible, which was regarded as dangerously magical. She was succeeded as *papesse* (female pope) at her death by another woman, and her teachings have been developed into an official canon that has been translated into French. [28] (R.H.)

Landau, Ezekiel [XV] [widely known as Noda bi-Yehudah, after his most important book] (1713–1793). Jewish community leader and rabbinic scholar. Born to a distinguished Polish rabbinical family, he officiated as rabbi in Brody and Jampol, and from 1755 as rabbi of Prague and its region. The talmudic academy which he founded attracted thousands of students from many countries, drawn by his personality and his dialectic approach to talmudic study. He bitterly opposed the messianic movements of the followers of SHABBETAI TZEVI and of JACOB FRANK, and was also uncompromisingly hostile to the German Bible translation of MOSES MENDELSSOHN, in which he saw a new spirit that would threaten traditional Jewish life. Although attacking enlightenment, he was not opposed to secular knowledge, which he advocated as a useful adjunct to rabbinical study. He enjoyed a close relationship with the Austrian authorities which he used to benefit the Jewish community.

Landau's *Noda bi-Yehudah* ['Known in Judah') was the most important book of rabbinic *responsa* (answers to queries concerning Jewish religious law) of the 18th century. This contains 855 responses, systematically arranged, displaying broad erudition, great powers of analysis, a sharp mind and a willingness to make bold decisions in matters of law. It was long studied as a work of authority and was itself the subject of glosses and commentaries. Some of the rulings were overturned by later rabbis who regarded them as too lenient. [42: 77–98] (G.W.)

Lan Ts'ai-ho. One of the EIGHT IMMORTALS of Taoism.

Lao Tzu [v]. The central figure of Taoism. The text called by his name – commonly known also as the *Tao Te Ching* ('Scripture of the Tao and its Individuating Power') is the cornerstone of Taoist thought and – as interpreted esoterically – the fundamental scripture of all Taoist religion throughout history (among the better of the many English translations are [9; 56; 61; 67]). As is the case for most of the texts coming down from the age of the Warring States (403–221 BCE), almost nothing is known for sure about the author. His first biography was not produced until the 'Historical Records' (*shih chi*) [60] of Ssu-ma Ch'ien (?145–?90 BCE) was written, and this biographical essay is a hodge-podge of myth, legend and (perhaps) fact; the very existence of Lao Tzu is questionable.

According to the traditional belief Lao Tzu (i.e., 'the Old Master') was a somewhat older contemporary of K'UNG TZU (Confucius), and served as archivist at the court of the Chou king. K'ung Tzu is said (in Taoist sources) to have visited him and received a lecture on curbing his ambitions to reform the world, from which he emerged bewildered and in some awe of the Old Master. Eventually, goes the story, Lao Tzu was so disgusted with deteriorating conditions that he left China – the first of the Taoist transcendents to go 'no one knows where'. His book was written, it is said, at the request of the officer in charge of the Jade Gate, the pass from which travellers left China for the deserts of the western regions. A later embroidery on the story, which became a bone of contention between Taoists and Buddhists, is that Lao Tzu reached India where he became known as the BUDDHA.

The *Lao Tzu* text, in approximately 5,000 graphs, is sufficiently terse and ambiguous in some parts to lend itself to wildly divergent interpretations – especially when it was taken as a 'revealed' text whose cryptic meanings are decipherable only to the initiate. In this sense the *Chuang Tzu* (*see* CHUANG TZU), which in many places reads as a commentary on the *Lao Tzu*, is more of an exoteric interpretation.

Lao Tzu divinized is far more than merely the human author of a text, however important. As early as the Former Han (202 BCE–9 CE) he was paired with HUANG TI, the Yellow Emperor, as divine founder of Chinese culture, and with the passage of time his numinous character grew to the point that he was identified in Taoist religion as the Godhead – or, more accurately, in Chinese terms the Tao – in Three Persons (the supreme object of Taoist worship called the 'Three Pure Ones', *san ching*). Lao Tzu was reincarnated many times, descending to confer sacred texts and talismans upon favoured Taoists throughout history. As father of Taoist philosophy, and as the supreme deity of Taoist religion, Lao Tzu is a figure of unique importance to all Chinese, from antiquity to the present. [45: 186–254] (L.T.)

Las Casas, Bartolomé de [VI.A] (1474–1566). Spanish Dominican missionary. He was born and educated in Seville, Spain. His father sailed with Columbus. After ordination as a *doctrinero*, Bartolomé joined an expedition to Hispaniola (Dominican Republic and Haiti), where he acted as chaplain and lord of a large estate. As a priest in newly conquered Cuba, he was converted in 1514 to the cause of 'New World' Amerindians, and became a champion of their human rights, following the lead of Fray Antonio de Montesinos. Returning to Spain in 1515, he began to act as their chief advocate in higher circles. Early attempts to counteract colonial exploitation and to implement reform failed, as did his project to establish a peaceful settlement in what is now Venezuela. He became a Dominican friar and studied in a cloister in Hispaniola, 1522–6. Then he began his massive *History of the Indies* (1527–66) and *Apologetic History*. Insisting on evangelization by non-coercive means, he produced *De unico vocationis* ('The Only Method of Attracting All People to the True Faith') in 1537 and opposed violent incursions into Nicaragua and Peru. With papal backing for his missionary principles, he sought to evangelize Guatemala peacefully (1537–9). He persuaded Charles V of Spain to promulgate 'New Laws' against colonial corruption in 1542. In 1545 he became bishop of the impoverished diocese of Chiapas (southern Mexico). Thwarted by inhumane colonists at every turn, he returned to Spain, disillusioned, in 1547. This prepared the way for his epic court debate in Valladolid (1550–51) on the nature and rights of Amerindians: it was to 'establish the manner and the laws by which our Holy Catholic faith can be preached and promulgated in that New World' [278: 109; 655]. His political 'theology from below' [330: 202] denounced the scholastic rationalizing of the conquerors' spokesmen and won royal backing for several years. His *Very Brief Account of the Destruction of the Indies* (1552) had a dramatic morally sensitizing effect in Europe, and his impact was felt in missions and colonies as far afield as the Philippines. [278; 342; 578; 655] (A.C.S.)

Lassus, Orlande de [VI.A] (1532–1594). Flemish composer. He was born in the Franco-Flemish province of Hainaut. Little is known of his early life or education, but at the age of 12 it is recorded that he entered the service of Ferrante Gonzaga, with whom he travelled to Paris and various Italian cities. He worked in Naples and Rome, where in 1553 he became Maestro di Capella at St John Lateran. He left Rome for Antwerp in 1554, where the following year he began to publish a wide variety of music, both secular and sacred. His growing reputation led to his appointment in 1556 to the Duke Albrecht V of Bavaria in Munich, first as a member of the chapel choir, then as head of music at the court, a position he held until his death. His polyphonic musical output was prodigious, ranging from chansons and madrigals to approximately 60 masses (mostly based on the parody technique), four passions, over a hundred settings of the Magnificat and hundreds of motets. [692] (E.M.)

Laud, William [VI.A] (1573–1645). Archbishop of Canterbury, 1633–45. He was born in Reading and educated at St John's College, Oxford. In 1593 he became a fellow of the college. He was ordained in 1601 and in 1611 became president of the college. He was a strong opposer of Calvinism and sought the restoration of the pre-Reformation liturgy to the Church of England. In 1616 he became Dean of Gloucester Cathedral and provoked hostility by moving the communion table to the east end of the church. He became bishop of St David's, Wales, in 1621 and a year later was involved in controversy with a Jesuit maintaining that the Church of England and the Roman Catholic Church were both parts of the church catholic. Under Charles I he was made bishop of Bath and Wells in 1626 and of London in 1628. As Chancellor of the University of Oxford he carried out many reforms and donated many valuable manuscripts to the Bodleian Library. In 1633 he was made archbishop of Canterbury. In 1637 he tried to enforce liturgical changes on the church in Scotland and thenceforward his fortune changed. Impeached by the Long Parliament, he was imprisoned in the Tower of London in 1641. He was found guilty and executed after denying the charge of 'popery' and declaring his loyalty to the Protestant Church of England. [109; 460; 809] (T.T.)

Law, William [VI.A] (1686–1761). English Christian writer. He was born at Kings Cliffe, Northamptonshire and educated at Emmanuel College, Cambridge, becoming a fellow of the college in 1711. At the accession of George I in 1714 he refused the Oath of Allegiance and joined the Nonjurors. From 1727 to 1737 he was tutor to Edward Gibbon, father of the historian. In 1740 he retired to Kings Cliffe and engaged in organizing schools and almshouses. He is known for his spiritual writings, especially *On Christian Perfection* (1726) and *A Serious Call to a Devout and Holy Life* (1728). Later works such as *The Spirit of Prayer* (1749–50) and *The Spirit of Love* (1752 and 1754) show the influence of JAKOB BOEHME. [462; 614; 699] (T.T.)

Laws, Robert [VI.A] (1851–1934). Missionary in Malawi. He was born in Aberdeen, studied at Aberdeen University and the United Presbyterian Divinity Hall and qualified in medicine. In 1875 he went as an early member of the Free Church of Scotland mission in Central Africa to be called Livingstonia. He remained until 1927, setting his mark on an integrated complex of medical, industrial, agricultural, educational and religious work that did much to shape modern Malawi. [252; 457; 458; 488; 536; 571; 605] (A.F.W.)

Leah (*c.*18th century BCE): Jewish matriarch. The elder daughter of Laban, she was married to JACOB by deceit, when her father substituted her for her younger sister, RACHEL, whom Jacob had been promised. She is described as having 'weak eyes' and Jacob's love for her was much less than for Rachel, whom he later also married (*Genesis* 29:31–33). However, Leah was the more fertile, bearing seven of Jacob's 13 children. After the first four – Reuben, Simeon, Levi and Judah – she stopped becoming pregnant and gave her servant, Zilpah, to Jacob. After Zilpah had had two children, Leah again became fertile, giving birth to Issachar and Zebulun as well as Jacob's only daughter, Dinah. When Jacob quarrelled with Laban, she – like her sister – sided with her husband. She died, apparently in the Land of Canaan, before Jacob's journey to Egypt, and was buried in the family tomb, the Cave of Machpelah in Hebron. Despite her inferior role, she was the ancestor of the two key tribes: Levi, which provided the priests, and Judah, from which sprang the dynasty of DAVID. [68:XI–XII] (G.W.)

Lebbe, Vincent [VI.A] (1877–1940). Belgian Catholic priest, active in China. He was born at Ghent, Belgium. In 1895 he joined the Lazarists, the Congregation of the Mission, in Paris. While he trained with the Congregation he was exposed to modern critical, liturgical and Christian democratic ideas. In 1901 he was sent to China in the aftermath of the Boxer rebellion and was ordained priest. From 1906 to 1916 he worked in Tientsin and established links between Christianity and Chinese national renewal. He worked for what was later described as the indigenization of the church. He was opposed in his attempts and transferred to South China. In 1917 he wrote at length to his bishop arguing that the church should become more patriotic, that it should be free of Western domination, that local clergy should be given more responsibility including election as bishops. In 1920 he was sent to Europe as chaplain to Chinese students. By this time he had come to the attention of Cardinal Van Rossum, Prefect of Propaganda at Rome, who wished to put into practice the papal bull, *Maxima Illud*, of 1919. Lebbe was received by the pope and later a number of Chinese priests recommended by Lebbe were made bishops. He returned to China in 1927 and founded An-kwo, the 'Little Brothers of St John the Baptist' and the 'Theresian Sisters', to combine monastic life with missionary and social activity. During the Sino-Japanese war Lebbe served in a corps of voluntary stretcher-bearers organized by the Little Brothers. In 1938 the government gave him the task of creating a patriotic and cultural movement for the whole of China. He died at Chung King in June 1940 and was proclaimed a national hero, having become a naturalized citizen, with his Chinese name Lei Ming-yuan inscribed in the official annals of China. [465; 742] (T.T.)

Lee, Ann [VIB] [Mother Ann] (1736–1784). English prophetess and spiritual teacher. The Shakers or Shaking Quakers broke away from the Society of Friends in 1747 and set up their own meeting in Manchester, convinced the Second Coming of Christ was at hand. In 1758, Ann Lee, the illiterate daughter of a poor blacksmith, and already, at the age of 22, with 14 years experience of hard manual work, came to join the Shaker meeting. She was several times sentenced to imprisonment for her enthusiastic witnessing to the movement's message, and in 1770, when imprisoned in appalling conditions in Manchester Gaol, she underwent an intense religious experience in which Christ was so palpably present to her that she became a living vehicle of his presence, capable of sharing her certainty with those who heard and trusted her. On her release, her communication of her experience filled her community with the belief – a belief based on experience – that the Second Coming in Glory was a fact within and amongst them. The community was even more harshly persecuted, and in 1774 Mother Ann and eight companions left for America and established the Shaker Church there. The Shakers lived a common, disciplined, celibate life focussed on work and prayer. Their worship was distinctive and beautiful, involving dance and the receiving and sharing of spiritual gifts. Men and women lived in parallel, but separately. Shaker workmanship is famous for its functional beauty. [2; 16; 96; 519; 854] (D.J.M.)

Legge, James [VI.A] (1815–1897). He was born at Huntly, Aberdeenshire, Scotland. He was educated at King's College, Aberdeen University and graduated in 1835. He joined the London Missionary Society and after theological training at Highbury Theological College, London, he was ordained a Congregationalist minister. He arrived in Malacca in 1840 and took charge of the Anglo-Chinese College. After Hong Kong became a British possession in 1842 Legge moved the College there in 1843. As well as being head of the college he became minister of Union Church, Hong Kong, a post he held until 1873. He began to translate the Chinese classics into English and the first was published in 1861. By 1886 the five volumes were complete. Legge retired from Hong Kong in 1873 and in 1875 became a fellow of Corpus Christi College, Oxford. He became the first professor of Chinese at Oxford in 1876, a post he held until his death. [470] (T.T.)

Legs-ldan 'Byed-pa. *See* BHĀVAVIVEKA.

Lekganyane, Enginasi [I.A] [Ignatius] (*d c.* 1948). Founder of the Zion Christian Church, which was to become the largest of all the South African independent churches. A Pedi who was influenced by J. A. Dowie's Catholic Apostolic Church in Zion (based in Illinois) and Edward of Basutoland's Zionist Apostolic Faith Mission, he established his own church in 1925 in the Transvaal. It grew rapidly under his two sons and now has an impressive holy city and headquarters, known as Zion City Moriah, near Pietersburg, where more than a million pilgrims come from all over Southern Africa for the great Easter festival. (R.H.)

Lenshina [I.A.] [Alice Mulenga] (1924–1978). Prophetess and founder of the Lumpa (Visible Salvation Church) in Zambia. A Bemba woman, Lenshina (i.e., Regina or Queen) was raised as a Presbyterian. Following a revelation in 1953 she led a movement against witchcraft, gaining thousands of followers. In 1963 she was excommunicated by the Presbyterian Church and formed her own Lumpa ('that which excels') Church [15: 125]. The new movement clashed with the Zambian government over taxation in 1964, resulting in the deaths of some 700 persons. Following the conflict Lenshina was arrested and held for 11 years, while the church itself was banned. She died while still in detention. Despite such hardship, the church has remained alive as an underground movement. [5; 31] (R.H.)

Leo I [VI.A] [Leo the Great] (*d.*461). Pope, 440–61. He first appears as a deacon under pope Celestine I (422–32) and again under Sixtus III (430–40), and as an opponent of Pelagianism and Nestorianism. Nothing is known of his birth or upbringing. The *Liber pontificalis* claims that he was born in Tuscany at the turn of the 4th and 5th centuries. While he was on a mission to Gaul in 440 Sixtus III died and Leo returned to Rome to find himself elected pope. He intervened in ecclesiastical matters in Africa, Spain and Gaul. He secured jurisdiction over the Western provinces of the Empire. He became involved in the East in the dispute over EUTYCHES. In 449 he sent representatives to a synod at Ephesus with a copy of his *Tome* to enforce his theological views. The synod rejected the *Tome*, whereupon Leo dubbed the synod a *latrocinium*, the work of bandits, rather than a *concilium*. In 451 he prevailed at the Council of Chalcedon, with his *Tome* becoming the basis of the Chalcedonian Definition. This declared the two natures of Christ in one Person and effectively set conciliar orthodoxy on a Western basis thenceforward. Leo stands as one of the most important popes in advancing the Petrine basis (*Matthew* 16: 16–19) of the primacy of Rome in the Christian religion. [64; 396; 475; 875] (T.T.)

Leo XIII [VI.A] [Vincenzo Giocchino Pecci] (1810–1903). Pope 1878–1903. He was born in Carpineto in the Papal States. He was educated at the Jesuit college in Viterbo (1818–24), the Roman College (1825–32) and the Roman Academy of Noble Ecclesiastics (1832–7). He then entered the service of the pope. He was ordained priest in 1837, and was a papal delegate to a number of Italian provinces before becoming papal nuncio in

Brussels in 1843 with the rank of bishop. He became bishop of Perugia in 1846 and was made a cardinal in 1853. He opposed the secularization of Perugian law and anticlericalism after 1860. In 1878 Pecci was elected pope and immediately set about reconciling the Catholic church with the modern world. He succeeded in a rapprochement with Germany (*Kulturkampf*), Belgium and Britain, and in 1892 he sent an Apostolic Delegation to Washington. He arranged for Edward VII of Britain to visit the Vatican in 1903. His programme of modernization was based on Neo-Thomism, the reconciliation of natural law and theology, and an accommodation with modern democratic states. He issued a number of encyclicals: *Immortale Dei* on spiritual and temporal power; *Libertas Praestantissimum* on citizens' rights; *Graves de Communi* on Christian democracy; and *Rerum Novarum*, a condemnation of liberalism and socialism and a defence of workers' rights. In 1896 in *Apostolicae Curae* he declared the orders of Anglican priests invalid. (286; 741; 835] (T.T.)

Leonardo da Vinci [VI.A] (1452–1519). He was trained as a painter but is also famous as an anatomist, inventor and engineer. Among his early religious paintings is the *Adoration of the Kings* for the monks of St Donato a Scopeto, near Florence. Other important paintings are *Virgin of the Rocks*, *Madonna and Child with St Anne and St John* and his very late *St John*. The most famous, apart from the *Mona Lisa*, is the *Last Supper*, a mural in the refectory of Santa Maria delle Grazie, Milan; an experiment in oil on plaster rather than fresco, it was a technical disaster even before he finished it. It is the first painting to show the psychology of the scene and the tension of the announcement by Jesus that one of the disciples is about to betray him. [155] (T.T.)

Levi, Eliphas [XVII.A] [Alphonse Louis Constant] (1810–1875). French occultist. Born, Alphonse Louis Constant, the son of a poor cobbler, he received a free seminary education and eventually became a deacon. He relinquished his seminary career, however, and embarked upon a career as a philosopher and practitioner of magic, with the kabbala as his central concern. His major books, written under the pen-name Eliphas Levi, are *Dogme et rituel de la haute magie* (1855–6), *Histoire de la magie* (1860) and *La Clef des grandes mystères* (1861). The books gained him a certain degree of notoriety and had a significant impact upon later magical practitioners. Although the themes of specific volumes vary (indeed, he returned to Catholicism shortly before his death, and the books reflect this shift) they tend to share the same conception of a force, or medium, which is present in all objects. Magical power derives from the balanced use of these forces. Particularly in later life he asserted that the attainment of this power depended upon religious worship. This is a common theme in the annals of magical philosophy: that to wield power one must transcend one's own humanity and, indeed, one's own desire for power, and that ultimately, the magical quest for knowledge is a search for God. [9; 14] (T.L.)

Levi, Isaac, of Berdichev [XV] (*c.* 1740–1810). Ḥasidic rabbi. Descended from a family renowned for its scholarship, he spent his early years in study. In 1766 he became a disciple of the Ḥasidic master, Dov BER OF MEZHIRICH, and was the outstanding exponent of his teachings. He served as rabbi in a number of communities but had to leave because of his Ḥasidic leanings. From 1785 he lived in Berdichev, in the Ukraine, where he was communal rabbi and attracted a great following.

One of the best-loved figures in the Ḥasidic movement, he was known as 'The Defender of Israel'. Firmly convinced of the inherent goodness in man, he held every Jew to be holy and blameless. All creation exists only for Israel. On the Day of Atonement, he regarded himself as the advocate for the entire Jewish people before the heavenly throne. He was the subject of many legends. In a famous story, he summoned God to a religious court to account for his mistreatment of Israel ('You always make demands on your people; why not help them in their troubles?') but in the end submitted to the divine will [13: vol. 1: 203–34]. For him, God, the Torah and the Jewish people formed a mystic unity; and it was said of him that 'He loved God and he loved Judaism but his love for the Jewish people surpassed both.' [40: 115–21]

He wrote *Kedushat Levi* ('The Sanctity of Levi'), presenting his teachings in the form of a commentarv on the Pentateuch. A frequent theme is the virtue of humility. [53: 152–77] (G.W.)

Levi ben Gershom [XV] [also known as Gersonides, by the acronym, Ralbag, and as Leo Hebraeus] (1288–1344). Jewish polymath in southern France. Mastering the sciences of his time, he was a noted astronomer and mathematician as well as philosopher, Bible commentator and talmudist. By profession he was a physician, living in Perpignan and Avignon. Two important astronomical instruments – the staff of Jacob and the camera obscura – were invented or perfected by him and he propounded an original hypothesis for the movement of the stars.

His main philosophical composition is *Milḥamot Adonai* ('Wars of the Lord') which was greatly influenced by MAIMONIDES and by the Muslim philosopher IBN RUSHD (Averroes), although Levi takes issue with the latter on many aspects of his search for an original reconciliation of revelation and philosophical truth. The subject-matter of the book includes divine providence, the nature of the soul, miracles and prophecy. God, for him, is the supreme thought, and temporal creation emerges from God's will (rejecting the emanational theory largely prevalent in his time). The world was not created *ex nihilo* but out of eternal matter. The terrestrial world receives its forms from the active intellect (an immortal substance) which governs it. Levi believed firmly in astrology, holding that every event on earth depends on the heavenly world. God cannot know particulars and so divine providence relates to universals, but not to particulars.

He commented on most books of the Bible, presenting a threefold explanation: (1) grammatical and lexicographical; (2) interpretations of entire chapters; (3) summaries of the philosophical and ethical concepts contained in each section. He utilized symbolism and allegory to reconcile the Pentateuch with philosophy.

Levi's works aroused considerable controversy and were strongly criticized by ḤASDAI CRESCAS, who even found some of his ideas heretical. [39: XV; 34: 208–24] (G.W.)

Lewis, Clive Staples [VI.A] (1898–1963). British Christian author. He was born in Belfast, educated at Malvern College and later privately. At the age of 14, having read some Celtic and Norse mythology, he became convinced that the Christian religion was an inferior mythology and he became an atheist. He went to University College, Oxford, in 1917 but left after one term to join the army. He was wounded in battle in April 1918. He returned to Oxford in 1919 and was awarded degrees in classics, philosophy and English. From 1925 to 1954 he was Fellow of English Language and Literature at Magdalen College, Oxford. In 1955 he became Professor of Medieval and Renaissance Literature at Cambridge University. He married Joy Davidman Gresham in 1956. She died in 1960. His main academic work was *The Allegory of Love* (1936). Following his conversion to Christianity in 1931 he wrote many religious works which upheld a supernatural view of the Christian religion, including belief in the real existence of the Devil in *The Screwtape Letters* (1942). Other popular religious works were *Miracles* (1947) and *Mere Christianity* (1952). [316; 481; 838] (T.T.)

Libermann, [Jacob, Jägel] François Marie Paul (1802–52). Mission founder and spiritual leader. Jacob Libermann was born in Saverne, Alsace, the son of a rabbi, and received a Jewish education. Converted, like some members of his family to Christianity, he was baptized as François in 1826 and entered a seminary in Paris. Severe epilepsy barred him from the priesthood, but he was retained because of his spiritual example. Influenced by Fredéric Vavasseur, a creole from Ile de Bourbon (Réunion), he commenced a society for the succour and evangelization of slaves, and in 1840 submitted to Rome a short proposal for overseas missions. The proposal was approved and Libermann ordained priest. His society, the Missionaries of the Most Holy Heart of Mary, directed its work to slaves and abandoned people everywhere. He was particularly concerned for the people of Africa and the Caribbean. In 1848 his society joined the Congregation of the Holy Spirit, and he was elected Superior General. His remaining years gave the Congregation a new lease of life, and his cooperation with ANNE MARIE JAVOUHEY extended its work further.

Libermann's spirituality, which accompanied concrete and practical planning, has been influential; and is well reflected in

St Thérése de Lisieux. He was declared Venerable in 1910. [167a; 413b; 442a] (A.F.W.)

Lieh Tzu [v]. Like so many of the ancient Chinese teachers, Lieh Tzu is better known as putative author of a composite book than as an historical person. His name is found in several pre-Ch'in (pre-3rd century BCE) texts, including the *Chuang Tzu*, which speaks of his travelling by 'charioteering on the wind with light and wonderful skill', a description that applies to Taoist adepts who have attained immortal transcendence. The same work even has a chapter entitled 'Lie Yü-k'ou', presumably the personal name of Lieh Tzu. It is the opinion of many scholars that there was in fact a Lieh Tzu who lived before the time of CHUANG TZU (5th century BCE?), but that the book which goes under his name was not written by him [25]. It seems not to have appeared until as late as the Wei and Chin dynasties (202–419). Although its contents are in large part based on the *Chuang Tzu* and other early works, it has its own style and viewpoint, and it became the third of the trio of old Taoist texts to be 'canonized' (the other two being the *Lao Tzu* and the *Chuang Tzu*). (L.T.)

Lin Chao-en [v] (1517–1598). The founder of a Chinese religious cult. He was a native of Fuchien province, descended from a family numbering several distinguished scholars and officials. However, after taking his preliminary degree (*hsiu-ts'ai*) he refused to continue on the conventional path to an official career because he felt that the study of the canon of the Literati (Confucians) should be for personal character development rather than for the sake of worldly power and prestige. His sincerity in this matter was further exhibited by his openness to both Buddhism and Taoism, as well as to the Literati traditions. In the academy he established, the teachings of all of these three Chinese great traditions were expounded, and followers of all three ways were enrolled. For this reason he was called 'Teacher of the Three Traditions' (*san chiao hsien-sheng*). His credibility as a religious teacher was enhanced by his ability as a faith healer. Although his advocacy of Buddhism and Taoism as orthodox teachings made him suspect in the eyes of the authorities, who officially accepted only the Literati tradition according to the interpretations of the Ch'eng-Chu 'School of the Principle' (i.e., the interpretations developed by the Sung philosophers Ch'eng Yi and CHU HSI), he escaped persecution at least in part because of his admirable service to the state. Among other things, he had taken charge of burying thousands of victims of piratical incursions in 1561 and 1562. In addition, although he upheld the values of all three traditions, Lin was always careful to emphasize the primacy of orthodox behaviour in his school.

A 'Sect of the Three Traditions' remains alive in Fuchien and among overseas Chinese from that province. As is usual in such cases, the Master has long since been elevated to the status of a god. It should be emphasized that although Lin incorporated the teachings of Taoism and Buddhism, it was still the 'orthodox' teachings of K'UNG TZU and MENG TZU that were *primus inter pares*. This is a common feature of the 'ecumenical' new religions. [3; 18; 20; 21] (L.T.)

Lin-chi I-hsüan [IV] [Japanese: Rinzai Gigen] (9th century). Ch'an patriarch and protagonist of the *Lin-chi lu* ('Sayings of Lin-chi'), one of the classic works of Ch'an Buddhist literature. The biographical details of Lin-chi are largely unknown. He is said to have experienced 'Great Enlightenment' under the guidance of Huang-po Hsi-yün (*d.*850), who used drastic methods such as shouting to induce enlightenment. The *Lin-chi lu* contains discourses and sayings of Lin-chi, questions and answers on Ch'an Buddhism, and select biographical accounts on Lin-chi's enlightenment and life. It contains such classic Ch'an phrases as the 'true human of no rank' who is 'lively and dynamic' to express the Ch'an ideal of the free person who is not defined or limited by artificial social status. It also contains the famous admonition, 'If you meet the Buddha, kill the Buddha; if you meet the patriarch, kill the patriarch,' to express the ideal of freedom from all outward attachments.

Lin-chi and his sayings have served as a model of the Ch'an way for generations of Buddhists. The school which took his name and developed a tradition using often outrageous and paradoxical stories and riddles (*kōan*) as catalysts to spur the experience of enlightenment, grew to be one of the major streams of Ch'an Buddhism and, as Rinzai

Zen, one of the two dominant schools of Japanese Zen. [31: 357–61; 189] (P.L.S.)

Lini, Walter [XXI] (1942–). Anglican priest and Prime Minister of Vanuatu. From Raga or Pentecost Island, Lini trained for the ministry in New Zealand (1966–8), and worked as a Deacon at the Honiara Cathedral, the Solomon Islands. Pre-independence agitation drew him into politics. Dismayed at the unrepresentativeness of the Representative Assembly of the French–British Condominium of the New Hebrides in 1974, he and Father Gerard Lemang led the pro-independence Vanuaaku Party to victory in 1978. He followed Lemang as Prime Minister of the newly independent Vanuatu in 1980, after French efforts to forestall decolonization and back the rebellion of JIMMY STEVENS on Espiritu Santo.

Lini has taken a strong stance against the visit of nuclear-armed warships to Ni-Vanuatu waters. He has also provided strong support for the transnational political cause named the 'Melanesian Alliance', and showed remarkable equanimity during political trouble at Port Vila in 1988–9 (when traditional owners of Vila or the capital city area sought greater power, under his former ally Barak Sope). [25: 7–43, 51–5] (G.W.T.)

Li T'ieh-kuai. One of the EIGHT IMMORTALS of Taoism.

Livingstone, David [VI.A] (1813–1873). Scottish missionary. He was born in Blantyre, Lanarkshire, and was self-educated. As a young man he was employed in a cotton factory. He determined to become a foreign missionary and, after attending medical classes in Glasgow, joined the London Missionary Society in 1838. Although at first intending to go to China he landed in Africa in 1841 and spent the next ten years as a missionary in Bechuana. He then undertook exploration journeys through Africa. He returned to Britain in 1856, and in 1857 made a speech in Cambridge University which was instrumental in the formation of the Universities' Mission to Central Africa in 1861. In 1858 he published *Missionary Travels and Researches in South Africa.* He returned to Africa in 1858 but no longer with the missionary society. In 1859 he discovered lakes Shirwa and Nyasa. He was back in Britain in 1864–5, during which period he published *The Zambezi and its Tributaries.* He returned for more exploration work, was 'found' by H. M. Stanley in a state of exhaustion in Ujiji in November 1871, and died in the village of Ilala in May 1873. He was buried in Westminster Abbey. [487; 488; 721] (T.T.)

Llull, Ramon. *See* LULL, RAMÓN.

Lo Ch'ing [V] (1443–1527). An educated man from Shantung who obviously received training in Buddhism from unknown sources. According to his autobiographical statements, he spent some 13 years in personal religious cultivation at the conclusion of which he attained enlightenment and began preaching and writing for the salvation of others. It is known that his teachings were especially widely diffused among workers on the grain transport canals of eastern China, but eventually they spread more widely, even as far as Taiwan.

His writings, called by the inclusive description of 'Five Works in Six Volumes', indicate that his doctrine stresses gratitude for all those things and beings on which our life depends; identification of all men with the 'boundless emptiness' of the Infinite as the true *dharma*; the 'heresy' of all views and practices that depart from this emptiness – external rituals, prayers to supernaturals (including the *nien-Fo* to Amit'o [Amitābha/Amida] Buddha); Taoist practices intended to produce immortal transcendence; yogic concentration; occult techniques; escape from the sufferings of the samsaric world through true faith; strict vegetarianism – and so forth. Followers called Lo Ch'ing Ancestor Lo or Patriarch Lo (Lo tsu).

As time passed the religion diversified into several different sects, the most widely known of which are the Wu-wei Chiao ('Doctrine of Nonaction', a term taken from the text of the *Lao Tzu*); the Hsien-t'ien Chiao ('Doctrine of the Precosmos'); and the Lung-hua ('Dragon-flower Way'). The Hsien-t'ien sect follows the anti-ritualistic teaching of Lo Ch'ing, but the Lung-hua sect has become quite ritualistic. In these various guises the teachings of Lo Ch'ing have constituted the most successful and enduring new religion of modern times. [26: vol. 1: 176–241; 38; 39: 113–29] (L.T.)

Loisy, Alfred Firmin [VI.A] (1857–1940). French scholar and proponent of the Modernist Movement in the Roman Catholic Church. He was born in Ambrière, Lorraine and was educated in the seminary in Châlons-sur-Marne from 1874. He was ordained priest in 1879. He undertook further studies in the Institut Catholique, Paris from 1881. He also taught Hebrew and Old Testament there. Between 1882 and 1885 he attended the lectures of ERNEST RENAN and became attracted to pantheism. By 1886 his faith in traditional Catholicism was undermined, but he remained in the church with the intention of modernizing its teaching. He was appointed to the chair of Sacred Scripture in the Institut in 1889. His critical approach to the subject brought him into conflict with authority and he was allowed to teach only Assyrian and Hebrew. Following the publication of his critical theories he had to leave the Institut. From 1894 to 1899 he was chaplain to the Dominican nuns at Neuilly and in 1900 he began to teach at the École Pratique des Hautes Études. Following further publications and condemnation from the Archbishop of Paris in 1904 he resigned from the École. He gave up his priestly functions in 1906. In 1907 the pope issued the decree *Lamentabili* and the encyclical *Pascendi*, which condemned Modernist studies of revelation, Christ and the church. Loisy wrote *Simples Réflexions* as a commentary on these documents and *Les Évangiles synoptiques* in 1908. A few weeks later he was excommunicated. He was professor of the history of religions at the Collège de France from 1909 to 1930. He continued to publish Modernist works until 1933, the last of which was *Naissance du christianisme*, in which he summed up his teaching on the New Testament and described the Gospels not as historical documents but catechetical and cultural literature with a slight historical base. [489; 647; 825: 67–139] (T.T.)

Lonergan, Bernard [VI.A] (1904–1984). Canadian Catholic theologian. He was born in Buckingham, Quebec. He studied in local schools until he entered Loyola College, Montreal. In 1922 he became a Jesuit and studied Greek and Latin at Guelph, Ontario; philosophy at Heythrop College, London, gaining a degree of London University in 1930; and theology at the Gregorian University, Rome. He was ordained priest in Rome in 1936 and completed his doctoral work in 1940. He returned to Canada and taught theology at the Jesuit seminaries in Montreal and Toronto for 13 years before returning to the Gregorian University, where he taught for a further 12 years. In 1965 he underwent major surgery for cancer and had to take partial retirement. He continued writing and researching over the next ten years as a professor at Regis College, Toronto. In 1971–2 he was Stillman Professor at Harvard University. In 1975 he went to Boston College as a visiting professor. He finally retired to Canada in 1983. His main works were *Insight: A Study of Human Understanding* (1957) and *Method in Theology* (1972). His work consisted of creating a theological method based on the Roman Catholic doctrine of God as willing the salvation of all which he allied to modern disciplines in history, science, psychology and economics. His method also incorporates dialogue with religions other than Christianity. [177; 321; 490] (T.T.)

Loṅkā [XIII] (15th century). Svetāmbara Jain reformer. He was possibly a merchant who came from the city of Ahmedabad in Gujarat. On studying the Jain scriptures, he became convinced that they provided no authority for the universal practices of image-worship and the use of temples as cult centres. Although Loṅkā was mistaken in this (he may have been influenced by Islam), his discovery of scriptural prescriptions of a severe and upright mode of life for ascetics prompted him to denounce what he saw as various lax and corrupt practices which had become prevalent in Jainism. The sect which ultimately sprang from Loṅkā's reform, the Sthānakvāsis (literally 'Those who dwell in preaching halls'), while never a dominant force within the religion, has remained to this day an important element among the various modes of Jain practice. (P.D.)

Lopez, Gregorio. *See* LÔ WEN-TSAO.

Lô Wen-Tsao [VI.A] [Gregorio Lopez] (1611/17–1691). Chinese Catholic bishop. He was born in Fogan, Fukien. He was converted to Christianity in 1633 and baptized by a Spanish Franciscan. He went to Manila to study, became a Dominican and was ordained as the first Chinese priest in 1656. He was given the name Gregory Lopez by the

European priests. He was offered a bishopric and the position of vicar-apostolic of Nanking but he declined. In 1679 the offer was repeated, with the Dominicans insisting that he be given a European advisor. He again declined, this time on the grounds that an associate would inhibit his work. He was eventually consecrated bishop in Canton in 1685 by Bernardino della Chiesa, Italian Vicar Apostolic. He said Mass using a Chinese liturgy, but when he came to ordain Chinese priests it was done in Latin, possibly in order to avoid any suggestion of inferiority of priesthood. He was promoted to the see of Nanking but died six years later. [145; 459] (T.T.)

Loyola, Ignatius. *See* IGNATIUS LOYOLA, ST.

Lucaris, Cyril. *See* CYRIL I LUCARIS.

Luke the Evangelist [VI.A] The traditional author of the third Gospel. The same person is likely to be the author of the *Acts of the Apostles* since both have the same literary style, both documents are dedicated to a Theophilus and there is a reference in the latter work to a 'first book' which dealt with 'all that Jesus began to do and to teach until the day when he was taken up' (*Acts* 1:1,2). A person of the same name is mentioned three times in letters ascribed to Paul, only one of which is regarded indisputably from the hand of Paul, *Philemon.* In *Colossians* (4:14) arguably written by Paul, Luke is referred to as 'the beloved physician'. There are passages in the *Acts* (the so-called 'we' passages) where it would appear that the author was a travelling companion of Paul as far as Rome while the latter was under arrest (16: 10–17; 20: 5–15; 21: 1–18; 27: 1–27: 1–29). Later tradition (Eusebius, *Hist. eccl.* 3.4.6) maintains that Luke was a native of Antioch. Even less reliable tradition maintains that his relics were interred in the Church of the Apostles, Constantinople in 357. [265; 317; 414: 147–50, 174–85; 450] (T.T.)

Lull, Ramón [VI.A, XVII.C] [Ramon Llull; Raymond Lully] (1232/5–1316). Catalan philosopher. He was born in Palma de Mallorca, Majorca, and spent his youth as a courtier and troubadour. Around 1262 (or 1272 [XVII.C 10: 176]), on Mount Randa, Majorca, he had the mystical experience which became the foundation of the Lullian Art. He joined the Franciscan Order as a tertiary (lay follower) and devoted the rest of his life to the spreading of Christianity in the Islamic world, preparing himself by nine years' study of Arabic and philosophy. He taught at Paris, and made several missionary journeys to Asia and North Africa, where, according to one tradition, he was imprisoned and stoned to death at Bougie. Lull was an opponent of Averroism and he was himself influenced by Augustinianism, especially the work of BONAVENTURE. Though some of his teachings were condemned by Gregory XI in 1376 his movement was approved by Pius IX in 1847. [VI.A 105; 499; 638; XVII.C 5: 172–3; 8: 141–2]

Lull wrote mainly in Catalan, sometimes in Arabic, though most of his books survive only in Latin translations. The best known are those on his Art: *Ars magna* ('The Great Art'), *Ars generalis ultima* ('The Ultimate General Art') and *Arbor scientiae* ('The Tree of Knowledge'). [XVII.C 5: 174)

Lull saw nine attributes (or 'Dignities') of God as pervading creation; these were present, in appropriate form, on every level of existence: Goodness, Greatness, Eternity, Power, Wisdom, Will, Virtue, Truth and Glory. It was therefore possible to order all forms of knowledge on their pattern. The basic Lullian diagram was a wheel, with an A at the centre and the letters BCDEFGHIK, symbolizing the nine Dignities, around the rim. A series of such wheels could revolve concentrically, bringing together all possible combinations of ideas.

Lull's system could be used as a method of spiritual practice, like the letter and number meditations of Sufism and the Kabbala: no doubt he hoped that it would attract Muslims and Jews to Christianity. It functioned also as an 'Art of Memory', very different, however, from the Classical form of that Art, which worked by a technique of building up vivid mental pictures. Lull believed that his system was not artificial, but reflected the real nature of things [XVII.C 10: VIII].

The Lullian Art had a profound influence on Renaissance thought. In the 16th century a chair of Lullism was established at the Sorbonne [XVII.C 10: 193]. The Art was, however, perhaps less influential in its pure, abstract form than in combination with Kabbala or with occult forms of the Art of

Memory, as we find it in the works of GIORDANO BRUNO [XVII.C 10: 206–10]. In the 17th century it began to fall into disrepute, and was rejected by Bacon and Descartes on the ground that it enabled those without understanding to acquire a superficial appearance of knowledge. [XVII.C 10: 361] (V.J.R.; T.T.)

Luria, Isaac [XV] [known as the 'Ari', an acronym of the 'divine Rabbi Isaac' in Hebrew) (1534–1572). Kabbalist who founded a major school of Jewish mysticism. Many legends are told of his life but few facts are known from the period before he went to Safed, Palestine, in 1570. He was born in Jerusalem to a German family (he was known as Isaac Ashkenazi) but was raised and lived in Cairo, where he was a scholar and earned his livelihood as a merchant. In Safed he gathered a group of kabbalists who revered him as their master, but after two years there he died of a plague. Luria and his main disciple, Ḥayyim Vital, sought to keep his doctrines secret, but after his death they were published and became very influential from the end of the 16th century onwards.

Luria was an outstanding innovator, modifying the teachings of the *Zohar*, the basic work of the Kabbalah (*see* MOSES DE LEON) and concentrating on the striving of the soul for redemption. The Safed circle of mystics was permeated with expectations of the imminent advent of the messiah. Luria taught that the primordial act of creation consists in *tzimtzum* ('contraction'), a self-concentration of the Godhead enabling the constitution of empty space within which creation is possible. Light emanating from God entered this space and took the form of successive emanations. However, the vessels of emanation could not endure the inrush of the divine substance and they disintegrated. Their breaking produced chaos, along with evil. The mission of man is *tikkun* ('mending'), the repair of the broken vessels. Man can help by his behaviour (including the observance of the commandments), mystical meditations and ascetic practices which would eventually lead to messianic redemption. The human being has the capability to perfect his individual soul and participate in the improvement of the world. While this is the task of all mankind, the people of Israel were selected by God as his particular instrument. Every human deed has relevance in the striving for redemption. Luria linked this with his belief in the transmigration of souls.

Luria introduced various customs designed to hasten the coming of the messiah. He claimed to identify many graves in Galilee as those of the early rabbis of the Mishnah and Talmud and used to visit them on the eve of Sabbaths in order to unite with their souls. These identifications became widely accepted; pious Jews continue to make pilgrimages in order to prostrate themselves on these graves. A special liturgy emerged from Luria's teachings (including poems composed by Luria) which was adopted by the Ḥasidim, who were greatly influenced by Lurianic Kabbalah. [72: VII; 73: I] (G.W.)

Luther, Martin [VI.A] (1483–1546). German Protestant Reformer. He was born in Eisleben, Saxony but the family moved to Mansfeld, where he received his first education. He went to the cathedral school in Magdeburg in 1497, to Eisenach in 1498, and matriculated at the university of Erfurt in 1501. He received his master's degree in the liberal arts in 1505 and began a study of law. A short time later a shattering experience during a thunderstorm led him to take a vow to be a monk. In July 1505 he entered the monastery of the Eremites of St Augustine in Erfurt. The choice of order was dictated partly by his theological inclinations. In 1507 he was ordained priest and his sense of awe at his first celebration of the mass became a significant event in his life thereafter. Under the guidance of his superior, Johann von Staupitz, Luther began higher studies in theology, first in Erfurt, then in Wittenberg, where he was transferred by his order. He received his first degree in biblical studies in 1509 and transferred back to Erfurt. It was sometime later that he went to Rome on monastic business. His experience of the opulence of the city also became significant. He returned to Wittenberg and received his doctorate and began lecturing in biblical studies. His lectures covered the *Psalms*, Paul's letters to the *Romans* and *Galatians* and the letter to the *Hebrews*. In 1515 he was given charge of a number of monasteries in Saxony.

Within the next few years he underwent another significant religious experience, referred to as the 'Tower experience', when he became aware of 'the righteousness of God'

(*Romans* 1: 17) and of the sheer grace of God. Scholars cannot agree on the dating, considered to be either as early as 1514 or as late as 1518. The date is crucial for the events which led him to break with Rome for that break had to do with the substance of the experience. The key event was Luther's declaration of Ninety-five Theses in October 1517. (Recent scholarship is sceptical about the story of his pinning them to the door of Wittenberg Castle church.) The Theses raised questions concerning the theological validity of the current sale of indulgences, which gained for the purchaser a remission of time in purgatory, and could be understood as an attack on the pope. The Archbishop of Mainz, who was directly responsible for the sale of indulgences, initiated an examination of Luther's orthodoxy in Rome, which made the issue very public. Luther was summoned to Rome but the Elector of Saxony insisted that the examination took place in Augsburg. Examined by Cardinal CAJETAN Luther refused to recant and fled back to Wittenberg. His next confrontation was with JOHANN ECK in Leipzig in July 1519. Luther now questioned both the authority of general church councils and the authority of the church in relation to scripture. In June 1520 he was condemned in the papal Bull *Exsurge Domine*. Luther again refused to recant and burned the Bull publicly. In January 1521, through another Bull, *Decet Romanum Pontificem*, Luther was excommunicated. He was given another opportunity to make his case at the Diet of Worms in April 1521 but again he refused to recant. He and his followers were declared outlawed and his teachings condemned to be suppressed. For a time Luther had to hide in the castle of Wartburg but returned to Wittenberg in 1522 and laid out his view of ecclesiastical reform in a series of sermons. In June 1525 he married a former nun, Katharina von Bora. Over the next few years the foundations of the Protestant Reformation were made firm, though not without controversy among the reformers. Luther found himself at odds with ULRICH ZWINGLI over the interpretation of the meaning of the eucharist. Luther had rejected the doctrine of transubstantiation but would not adopt the radical view that Christ was only present in the eucharist in a symbolic as opposed to a real way. Luther's health was poor from this time onwards. He died near his birthplace mediating between the feuding counts of Mansfeld.

Luther's writings which are the basis for Lutheranism include his lectures on scripture, his 'table talk', hymns, catechisms and a number of treatises including: *To the Christian Nobility of the German Nation; On the Babylonish Captivity of the Church* and *Of the Liberty of a Christian Man.* Importantly, he gave the German-speaking peoples the Bible in German in a style which set the standard for literary German in the modern period. [40; 231; 439; 701] (T.T.)

Lutuli, Albert John Mvumbi [VI.A] [Luthuli] (1908?–1967). South African Black national leader. He was born near Bulawayo (now in Zimbabwe), the son of a Seventh Day Adventist evangelist from a Zulu chiefly family. Sent back to the ancestral home at Groutville, Natal, he gained a modest secondary education, and taught at Adams College. He was a Methodist lay preacher and committee member of the South African Christian Council. As a delegate to the International Missionary Council at Madras in 1938 he realized the social passivity of South African (by contrast with Asian) Christianity.

A 'progressive' chief, he concentrated at first on agricultural and social, rather than political development. He did not join the African National Congress until 1945. By 1952 he was President of the Natal branch, leading the non-violent civil disobedience campaigns. Soon afterwards he became President-General of the African National Congress. Several times banned, twice imprisoned, he was sent to trial for treason but discharged. In 1961 he received the Nobel Peace Prize. He died in what appeared to be an accident near his home.

Lutuli consistently ascribed to Christian conviction his non-violent resistance to oppression. Traditional African world-views influenced his thought ('I think as an African . . . and as an African I worship the God whose children we all are.'), and he denounced the 'distorted symbols' of white paternalist Christianity; but he sought no specifically African theology or church. He wanted the spread of the mutual cultural enrichment he associated with Christian schools such as Adams College. [502] (A.F.W.)

Lü Tung-pin [V]. One of the EIGHT IMMORTALS, he is said to have been an historical person of the T'ang period (618–907). An unsuccessful candidate for the highest degree in the imperial examinations, he was converted to Taoism by Chung-li Ch'üan (or, Han Chung-li), another of the Eight Immortals. While Lü was chatting with the latter in an inn, he dozed off, and during the time it took to cook a pot of millet, dreamed a whole lifetime of ups and downs in an official career. Astonished to learn that his companion knew what he had been dreaming, he realized that Chung-li was a Taoist master whose purpose was to bring him to understand the futility of worldly ambitions. Chung-li accepted him as a disciple and subjected him to ten tests of sincerity. Upon passing these tests, Lü was granted the teachings that enabled him to attain immortal transcendence.

Lü, whose Taoist appellation was 'Pure Yang' (*ch'un yang*), was enfoeffed as 'Trusted and Helpful Imperial Lord' (*fu yu ti-chün*) during the Yüan or Mongol period (1279–1368). He appears in the mortal world many times according to historical and quasi-historical accounts. Most importantly, he is considered the master of two disciples, one of whom founded the Northern, and the other the Southern, School of Taoism; hence he is the 'Ancestor' or patriarch of these sects. As one of the Eight Immortals he is identified by his chief attribute, a sword. Lü Tung-pin is the only one of these eight to be found as chief deity in Taoist temples today. In Taiwan there are over 50 such temples, the most famous of which is the Temple of Guidance (*chih-nan kung*) in a suburb of Taipei. The temple is so called because devotees spend the night there in order to receive a divinatory dream from Lü. [1; 16] (L.T.)

Luwum, Janani [VI.A] (1922–1977). Ugandan martyr. He was born in Mucwini, Acholi, the son of a Christian convert. He started school late and his early formal education was modest. A crucial experience in 1948 linked him with the *Balokole*, the East African revival movement, but he avoided its more extreme expressions. He received Anglican ordination in 1955, and had two periods of study in England. From 1965, as the Provincial Secretary, he was involved in reconciling inter-ethnic tensions in the Anglican church. He became Bishop of North Uganda, the first Acholi bishop, in 1969. Idi Amin's accession to power brought the Acholi massacres of 1972; Luwum and the Roman Catholic bishop were the natural spokesmen for their people. In 1974 Luwum was elected Archbishop of Uganda, Rwanda, Burundi and Boga-Zaire – a tribute to his gift for consensus but an exposed position for a northerner. The Ugandan church had no tradition of political criticism and a long one of Anglican–Catholic rivalry. As Amin's excesses, and his attacks on Christians, increased, Luwum attempted to protect victims and to co-ordinate protests with the Roman Catholic authorities. He was taken from a meeting of bishops and shot. He illustrates the place of the churches and their leaders in African nation states in providing national structures independent of central government. [353: 263] (A.F.W.)

Luzzatto, Moses Chaim [XV] (1707–1747). Jewish poet and mystic. Born in Padua to affluent parents, at a young age he was fascinated with Kabbalah and aged 15 ceased his regular education to establish a study circle of mysticism in his home. Later he devoted himself primarily to writing Hebrew poetry, including a biblical drama about Samson, 150 poems in the style of the Book of *Psalms* and *Migdal Oz* ('Mighty Tower'), an allegorical drama based on a parable in the *Zohar*, the classic work of Jewish mysticism. In his early twenties he again concentrated on mysticism, writing an imitation *Zohar*, called *Zohar Tinyana* ('Second Zohar'), and drawing up rules of conduct designed to hasten the advent of the messiah. When it became known that he attributed his teachings to a supernatural personality who spoke to him when he was awake, the rabbis – who suspected him of messianism (it was reported that he saw himself as a reincarnation of Moses) – forced him to undertake to abstain from kabbalistic studies and practices. When they banned his writings, he left Italy for Amsterdam, where he earned a living as a diamond polisher. There he wrote a further allegorical drama as well as his ethical work, *Mesillat Yesharim* ('Book of the Upright'). In 1743 he went to the Holy Land, living first in Safed, then in Acre, where he and his entire family died in a plague.

To many modern critics Luzzatto was the seminal figure in the birth of modern Hebrew literature. His dramas are secular works whose inspiration derives from aesthetics rather than the religious-legal values underlying earlier Jewish literature. The biblical style liberated Hebrew poetry from the artificial schemes of medieval poetry. A prolific author, he also wrote on philosophy, logic, rhetoric, polemics and talmudic dialectics.

Mesillat Yesharim was accepted as a classic moral work both among a general readership and in rabbinical academies. It lucidly expounded the social virtues (e.g. moderation, humility, piety) and served as a guide to moral conduct.

Luzzatto has been seen as a bridge between the traditional and modern periods of Judaism. His religious works were strictly orthodox but his dramas paved the way for secular Hebrew literature. [81: vol. 3: II; 87: vol. 6: 173–91] (G.W.)

Lycurgus [x] (7th century BCE?). Spartan law-giver, perhaps historical, of whom it was said that the Pythia at Delphi had revealed to him the constitution for Sparta determined by Apollo [53: 1.65], just as the Cretan one had been established by Zeus. [19: 184–5] (J.P.K.)

M

Maciel, Antonio [XXIV] [Antonio the Counsellor] (*c.*1842–1897). Central leader of the Canudos messianic uprising in Brazil in 1893–7. He was born in the town of Quixeramobim around the year 1842. An extreme ascetic of emaciated mien, he lived on alms and wandered widely, dedicating himself to the repair of churches and cemeteries. Popular accounts circulated concerning miraculous cures effected by this 'man without sin'. Multitudes accompanied him, singing hymns and carrying altars in processions when approaching towns. In the famine-ridden area of north-east Brazil Antonio preached that the end of the world was at hand. By 1896, he predicted, all distinctions would disappear: the line of the seashore would run through the interior of the continent of South America and the forests of the interior would circumscribe the coasts. By 1899 the waters of the world would turn to blood and the sun would crash into the sky. From the sea would emerge the glorious Dom Sebastian, the Portuguese king who had never died (but who had simply disappeared in the midst of a battle against the Moors). Antonio advocated chastity and the renunciation of marriage. He enjoined the faithful to abandon their possessions and prepare to face imminent final judgement.

When Emperor Don Pedro abdicated the throne in 1893 Antonio read the actions of the new republic as signs of Satan's work. His followers burned notices of taxation and skirmished with government troops. A long trek northward brought them to an abandoned farm near Bahia called Canudos. Here they built a fortified town. They passed the nights and days in prayer, singing hymns and reciting litanies. New followers streamed in and joined the crowds that attended the frequent sermons of the Counsellor. They sought to build a church large enough to accommodate the entire multitude of believers. In distant Rio de Janeiro, newspapers hinted that foreign money was being channelled through Canudos in order to mount a monarchist rebellion against the new republic. Three military expeditions failed to uproot the Canudos devotees, who zealously defended their sacred precinct. The fourth expedition of 10,000 troops, backed by replacements and heavy artillery, laid siege to Canudos for five months, from June to November 1897. Each night, after the bombardments and battles of the day, the government troops heard the sound of litanies and hymns. Although Antonio the Counsellor died, apparently of starvation due to his fasts, on 22 September 1897, his devotees refused to surrender. An estimated 20,000 of them died, so that by 5 November the entire population of the messianic city of Canudos had perished. [9; 14: 1099ff.; 16: 556, 562] (L.S.)

Mackay, Alexander [VI.A] (1849–1890). Scottish missionary in Uganda. He was born in Rhynie, Aberdeenshire. In 1876, as a Free Church of Scotland layman, he joined the (Anglican) Church Missionary Society's first party to Buganda. He proved the most durable of the party, and his many-sided skills, from translation to boat-building, were invaluable. After the slaughter of the Christian court pages by Kabaka Mwanga, Buganda became an outstanding example of rapid Christian expansion. Ganda Christians then brought much of the rest of modern Uganda within the same orbit. Mackay did much to determine the lines of Protestant development. [252; 332; 605; 649] (A.F.W.)

Mackenzie, Kenneth Robert Henderson [XVII.A] (1833–1886). English occultist. Born in Deptford, Kent, Mackenzie spent his childhood in Vienna, where his father held a medical appointment. He returned to England by 1851. He is primarily known for his esoteric freemasonry and for his involvement with the Golden Dawn, the late 19th-century magical and religious order from which much contemporary magical practical practice ultimately descends. Mackenzie visited the famous occultist ELIPHAS LEVI in Paris in 1861, and was initiated into freemasonry in 1870. During 1875–7 he published the *Royal Masonic Cyclopedia*, a work mostly ignored by conventional masons but notable for its rich collection of esoteric facts and theories. In 1872 he joined a 'Rosicrucian' masonic order, the Societas Rosicruciana in Anglia, where he may have met a founding member of the Golden Dawn, WILLIAM WYNN WESTCOTT. It has been suggested that Mackenzie was responsible for the supposedly foreign cipher manuscript used as the basis for the Golden Dawn, for his *Cyclopedia* listed Rosicrucian masonic grades that matched those of the manuscript precisely. The Golden Dawn actually came into being in 1888, after Mackenzie's death. [7; 8] (T.L.)

McPherson, Aimee Semple [VI.A] (1890–1944). American evangelist. She was born near Ingersoll, Ontario and was named Aimee Elizabeth Kennedy. Her family belonged to the Salvation Army but she was converted to Pentecostalism at an early age through the preaching of Robert James Semple. She married him in 1908 and they were missionaries in China until his death in 1910. Two further marriages ended in divorce. In 1917 she began an evangelistic and healing mission in the United States. She settled in Los Angeles in 1923 and built the Angelus Temple, a centre for worship and a welfare programme. She pioneered radio evangelism by launching in 1924 the first church-owned radio station (KFSG). By 1927 her organization had grown to include many churches and the International Church of the Foursquare Gospel was formed. She also founded a training institution called Lighthouse of International Foursquare Evangelism (LIFE) Bible College. Although she was often involved in scandalous events, when she died her church included 400 congregations in America, 200 foreign missions and over 22,000 members world-wide. Her writings include *This is That: Personal Experiences, Sermons and Writings* (1923), pamphlets, hymns and sacred operas. [540; 543] (T.T.)

Macuilxochitzin [XVIII] (*c*.1435). The daughter of Tlacaelel, the powerful counsellor of several Aztec rulers. She was a student of the *huehuetlatolli* (ancient words of the elders) and became a poet of some renown. Growing up during the florescence of Aztec culture, her poetry, at least on one occasion, depicted the manner in which warfare was conceived as sacred action carried out in an atmosphere created by the Aztec high god, Tloque Nahuaque (sometimes translated as 'Giver of Life'), Lord of the Near and Far.

She describes [5: 259–60] how the Tloque Nahuaque arms the warriors in order to receive the pleasure of successful warfare led by the Aztec ruler Axayacatl (ruled 1469–81). In the battle at Xiquipilco, the ruler was wounded by an Otomi warrior named Tlilatl, who was captured and brought before the king. Apparently at the moment of decision, a group of Otomi women intervened and persuaded the ruler to spare the warrior's life.

Macuilxochitzin's poetry depicts both the pervasiveness of sacred warfare among the Aztecs and introduces, in a rare instance, the image of women influencing a sacred ruler's decision to carry out human sacrifice. (D.C.)

Madhva [XI] (?1197–1276). Indian religious leader and philosopher. The information extant regarding his life is found in legendary and hagiographical works and thus lacks historical reliability. He is said to have been born in Udipi in South Kanara, the son of Madhyageha Bhaṭṭa. His teacher was Acyutaprekṣa. On initiation he was given the name of Pūrṇaprajña, and later he was also called Ānandatīrtha. His early training was in ŚAṄKARA's Advaita Vedānta, but he quickly revolted against it, regarding Śaṅkara as a reincarnation of a demon sent to confuse the world. In public disputation he slowly evolved his own system of faith, frankly dualistic, which owed much to the *Bhāgavata Purāṇa* [99]. It is said he travelled south and disputed with the Śankarites at Śṛṅgeri and then went to Rāmeśvaram where he worshipped Viṣṇu. He returned to Udipi as the founder of a new faith centred on the worship of Kṛṣṇa by means of *bhakti*, but sharply differentiating between man and God. He then went on a tour of North India again making many converts. The faith continued to grow, although not massively, and it is thought Madhva made a second pilgrimage to the North before his death at the age of 79 in 1276. Madva is credited with some 37 works, but probably the most significant are the *Bhāṣya* and the *Anuvyākhyāna* on the *Vedānta-sūtra*, and the *Bhāgavata-tātparya-nirṇaya* and the *Mahābhārata-tātparya-nirṇaya* which deal with the *Bhāgavata Purāṇa* and the *Mahābhārata* respectively. It is primarily as a philosopher and theologian that Madhva is remembered, although members of the sect are still to be found today. [22: vol. 4: 51–202; 99] (S.C.R.W.)

Ma-gcig Lab-sgron [IV] (1055?–1149?). The most eminent female Buddhist master in Tibetan history and the codifier of the important Gcod ('cutting') practice. Born in Lab-phyi, she was employed in her youth as a speed-reader of texts. She is said to have developed an early disregard for personal appearance and social convention, an attitude that she later prescribed for Gcod practitioners. Her principal teachers were Skyo-ston Bsod-nams Bla-ma and Grwa-pa Mngon-shes. When she took up with an Indian tantric yogin she was reviled as 'the nun who has repudiated her vows', and the couple moved to Kong-po. They had perhaps five children, after which she left her family and studied with Pha Dam-pa Sangs-rgyas, a famed Indian teacher of the Zhi-byed tradition. She retired to Mt Zangs-ri Mkhar-dmar, where she spent the rest of her life in retreat.

The Gcod meditational practice, concerning which she wrote a short treatise, draws on an ingenious mixture of indigenous pre-Buddhist ideas with the Prajñāpāramitā and Mahāmudrā doctrines she had studied with Pha Dam-pa: the meditator sets up a tent in a haunted area, contemplates emptiness, and in contrast with tantric practices performed for protection, offers (in visualization) her flesh and bones to local demons for their consumption, whereby she attains transcendence and power. Among her many disciples were the Nepalese yogin Pham-thing-pa, and her own offspring, especially her son (or grandson) Thod-smyon Bsam-grub, whom she cured of epilepsy and established as an accomplished meditator. An incident recalled with pride in the biographies is the visit of three 'fleet-footed' emissaries from Bodh Gaya, to whom she could preach in Sanskrit (remembered from her previous life as an Indian); Ma-gcig thereupon proclaimed herself to be the only Tibetan who transmitted the *dharma* to India. Gcod remains widely practised by Tibetans, both lay and monastic, of all sects, with Ma-gcig a visionary source of inspiration for new liturgies and lineages. [184: XIII; 85; 238: 87–92] (J.G.)

Mahādeva [IV]. An obscure figure associated with one of the most important events in Buddhist history: the first split in the monastic order, leading to a preliminary division into two schools, the *Mahāsāṅghika* or 'Great Community', and the *Theravāda* (*Sthaviravāda*), 'The Way of the Elders'. Subsequently, many more sub-schools arose (traditionally 18), sometimes because of differences over matters of discipline (*vinaya*), sometimes over doctrinal matters. Mahādeva seems to have been the author of one such dispute: the 'five theses' attributed to him concern the precise nature of the spiritual attainments of a Buddhist 'saint' (*arahant*). The division between the Mahāsāṅghika and Theravāda groups took place apparently, at least in part because of disagreements on this issue, at a meeting (sometimes called a council) held at Pātaliputra (modern Patna) in north-east India a little more than a century after the BUDDHA's death. It is difficult to date this precisely, not least because the date of the Buddha himself is still in dispute; if the traditional dates for the Buddha are accepted, this council would be between 367 and 346 BCE. The two groups seem also to have begun at this time to redact differing versions of the Canon. [136: 275–92] (S.C.)

Mahānāma [IV]. The name given to the author of the Buddhist historical poem written in Sri Lanka in the 5th century BCE, the *Mahāvaṃsa*, by the commentary on it (written probably in the 8th or 9th century CE). Although very little, if anything, is known about Mahānāma, his work is one of the most important sources available for the early history of Buddhism in India and Sri Lanka; apart from an earlier work, the

Dīpavaṃsa, which covers the same events but without the *Mahāvaṃsa*'s literary elegance and encomium on king Duṭṭhagāmaṇi, this text has been regarded as the earliest example of historiography proper to emerge from any South Asian culture. It is a national epic, and has been invoked by Sinhalese national sentiment ever since its composition, as it still is in modern times. [170: 117–18] (S.C.)

Mahāpajāpati [iv]. The younger sister and co-wife of the Buddha's mother queen Māyā. When the latter died immediately after the Buddha's birth, she nursed him as her son, giving her own son over to other nurses. Long afterwards, when her husband Suddhodana died, with 500 other women from the Śākya family whose husbands had become monks, she asked the Buddha's permission to be ordained as a nun. He demurred (without refusing outright), but Mahāpajāpati and her companions cut off their hair and put on yellow robes; she followed the Buddha and asked twice again, but again he demurred. When Ānanda saw her weeping, he asked why, and on being told went to the Buddha and persuaded him to give his permission, on the grounds that women were indeed capable of enlightenment just as men were. Mahāpajāpati was soon enlightened, and became a great preacher. She died at the age of 120. [150: vol. 2, 522–4] (S.C.)

Maharaji [xix] [Prem Pal Singh Rawat; Guru Maharaj Ji] (1957–). Founder of Elan Vital, the successor to the Divine Light Mission (DLM). Maharaji's father, Shri Hans Ji Maharaj, had formally organized the DLM in 1960, although he had been teaching the techniques since the death of his guru, Dada Guru, in the 1920s. [36: 901]

Born Prem Pal Singh Rawat, he is said to have started meditating when two, and given discourses at six. When Shri Hans died in 1966 his eight-year-old son is reported as having told the mourners 'O You have been illusioned by *maya*. Maharaj Ji [Shri Hans] is here, very much present amidst you. Recognize him, adore him, and obey him.' The boy thus became known as Guru Maharaj Ji, the Satguru, or Perfect Master.

In 1971 Maharaji made his first visit to England, where the media gave full coverage to the 13-year-old 'Boy Guru'. Soon afterwards, amid further publicity, he settled in the United States.

The Knowledge that Maharaji gives his followers is said to provide the key to self-understanding and self-realization. While the Knowledge is within each individual, it can only be revealed by Maharaji or one of his appointed initiators. The four techniques that comprise the Knowledge enable initiates to turn their senses within and to perceive what were described in the early 1970s as Divine Light, Music, Nectar and the 'primordial vibration' or 'Holy Name'. It is said that taking the Knowledge cannot be described – it can only be subjectively experienced, and initiates are asked not to reveal the techniques. [16]

The movement, which was run largely by Maharaj's mother Mata Ji, with the help of his older brother, grew quickly, attracting young people from the hippie culture, and by 1973 several tens of thousands of Westerners had become 'premies' (devotees). However, a financial crisis, followed by Maharaji's marrying his American secretary in 1974, precipitated a power struggle within his family, with Maharaji eventually taking sole control of the movement in the West.

Maharaji rejected many aspects of the movement associated with its Indian background and focused on the essence of his teaching [30]. The name Elan Vital was adopted in the early 1980s; Maharaji insisted that he was not to be worshipped as a god; the term 'premie' was dropped; and a low profile was adopted, although both Maharaji and his movement have become more visible in the late 1980s. [4: app. 4] (E.B.)

Maharishi Mahesh Yogi [xix] (Mahesh Prasad Varma] (1911/18–). Founder of the Transcendental Meditation (TM) movement. He was born as Mahesh Prasad Varma (or Warna) in Jubblepore (or Utter Kashi), the son of a local tax official (or forest ranger) of the Kshatriya (warrior) caste [38: 187). He graduated in physics from Allahabad University in 1940, then studied for 13 years with his spiritual master, Swami Brahmananda Saraswati Maharaj (1869–1953), who rediscovered the technique that is known as transcendental meditation.

After Saraswati's death, Maharishi spent two or three years in seclusion before starting teaching. In 1957 he founded Transcendental

Meditation. In the United States, the Sonorama Society, devoted to Saraswati, was formed in 1959 [36: 882]; and in India the International Academy of Meditation was established at Rishikesh. His followers grew slowly until 1967, when the Beatles and a number of other well known personalities took Transcendental Meditation lessons from Maharishi; the number of initiates increased dramatically until 1977, when they fell sharply [36: 890]. In recent years the numbers have increased in Asia and South America, and it is said that four million persons have now been taught TM.

In 1971 both the Science of Creative Intelligence and the Maharishi International University were founded. The World Plan Executive Council which consists of five task-oriented structures has its headquarters in Switzerland. Centres teaching Maharishi's courses can be found around the world, including one in Moscow.

The basic technique of Transcendental Meditation involves the use of a mantra while sitting in silence. Meditators are given their secret mantra at a short Hindu devotional ceremony (*puja*); they also attend some lectures and have personal instruction. The whole process of initiation takes less than ten hours, usually spread over a few days. It is claimed that regular meditation produces bodily changes that result in increased health, intelligence, achievement and happiness.

Meditators can proceed to Advanced TM-Sidhi courses to learn further techniques (such as the well-publicized ability to 'fly') and to study further the underlying philosophy of 'pure consciousness' [29]. The Science of Creative Intelligence is said to reveal 'the infinite organizing power of nature present in the field of pure knowledge, and equates the field of pure knowledge with the Veda'. Maharishi's thought is said to provide a means not only of enhancing the individual's life, but also of creating a heaven on earth, with ideal government, ideal education, world peace etc. It is claimed that where the square root of 1 per cent of the population is practising TM, crime rates and hospital admissions fall, and various other benefits accrue to the society – a phenomenon known as the 'Maharishi Effect'. Maharishi has encouraged the scientific testing of his claims, and many confirmatory studies have been made – and questioned. [49; 62; 38: 191] (E.B.)

Mahāvīra [xiii]. According to Jainism the twenty-fourth and final 'ford-maker' (*tīrthaṅkara*) of the current world-era. He is traditionally regarded as having lived from 599 BCE to about 527 BCE.

Jain mythical history holds that during the beginningless and endless motion of time there is a continual series of eras in each of which mankind, initially located in a state of bliss and contentment, over a period of millions of years gradually declines in stature and knowledge. During each one of these eras, which are repeated eternally, 24 ford-makers (also called Jinas, 'spiritual conquerors', from which word the Jain religion derives its name) appear. The function of these teachers is to reactivate the beginningless and uncreated Jain doctrine of Right Knowledge, Right Faith and Right Conduct and to found a community of ascetic and lay followers which will serve as a spiritual ford (*tīrtha*) for human beings over the ocean of rebirth.

Physically, the ford-makers are identical in the possession of bodies of a particularly hard and adamantine structure to enable them to withstand the rigours of intense ascetic practice, although Jain texts stipulate that, at the beginning of each chronological era, they are, in common with other human beings, massive in size and live for millions of years, with a gradual decline setting in so that the last ford-maker is of normal height and life-span. Each of them preaches in a dialect known as Ardhamāgadhī in an assembly hall built by the gods in the presence of humans, gods and animals.

Of the 24 ford-makers of this current era, only the last two, Pārśva and Mahāvīra, are historically verifiable, although many Jains would deny that the previous 22 are figures existing only in legend. Mahāvīra's biography, like that of the Buddha, is best treated as a composite put together on the basis of a cluster of doubtless partially remembered facts and a good deal of legend.

The most important early sources for Mahāvīra's life are to be found in the scriptural canon of the Svetāmbara sect, a body of material rejected by the Digambaras who have their own traditions which differ in certain respects, e.g. they deny that Mahāvīra was married before his renunciation. The oldest of these accounts would appear to be the eighth chapter of the first book of the *Ācārāngasūtra*, a fairly short poetic account of the hardships endured by Mahāvīra in the course of his mendicant wandering and the fasts and austerities which he practised before his attainment of enlightenment [13: 79–87]. Since the canonical texts were redacted for the final time as late as the 5th century CE, this material can be dated only relatively and vaguely on the basis of language and metre, but it is not unreasonable to assume that it contains some accurate historical reminiscences. Another source difficult to date, but clearly in origin an independent text, is the fifteenth chapter of the *Bhagavatī Sūtra*, the huge fifth book of the canon, where is found a fascinating account of the relationship between Mahāvīra and Makkhali Gosala, the leader of the Ājīvaka sect, along with numerous and often highly comical descriptions of the latter's enmity towards the ford-maker [2: 39–79; 5: 214–20]. The *Bhagavatī Sūtra* is also an important source for Mahāvīra's doctrinal teachings which are usually couched in the form of a dialogue with his chief disciple Indrabhūti Gautama [5].

The earliest text to attempt to give a full biography is the *Kalpasūtra* which can be dated approximately to the 2nd or 1st century BCE [13: 218–70]. Here Mahāvīra's life is not treated in isolation but is linked with accounts of the first and twenty-third ford-makers Ṛṣabha and Nemi, his immediate predecessor Pārśva, as well as the other ford-makers who are described briefly. The *Kalpasūtra* can be viewed as representing the first stage in the expansion of Mahāvīra's biography.

It is with the voluminous commentary literature on the Śvetāmbara scriptures dating from about the 3rd century CE that we find a massive development of Mahāvīra's biography. Previous births are produced for him, as well as a fully worked-out account of his mendicant itinerary and career and an elaborate version of the preaching by which he converted his chief disciples. All these sources, canonical and post-canonical, were drawn together by Hemacandra in 'The Deeds of Mahāvīra', the tenth book of his version of Jain legendary history [11], which provides a full and consistent biography of Mahāvīra, with which Śvetāmbara Jains seem to have been familiar since about the 10th century. [23]

Hemacandra's biography describes how Mahāvīra experienced 26 existences in this chronological era, gaining the right belief which provided the necessary impetus to further spiritual development in his first birth, when as a village overseer he helped a Jain monk who had lost his way in the forest. After a succession of births he completed his life as a god in heaven before his final birth as a human ford-maker. Originally arising in the womb of a Brahman woman, Devānandā, he was subsequently transferred by the general of Indra's divine army to the womb of Queen Trisalā, a woman of the warrior class and wife of King Siddhattha. After his birth-consecration by Indra, which was carried out at Mount Meru, the axis of the universe, he was given the name Vardhamāna ('The Increasing One') by his parents since his family's prosperity increased from the time of his appearance in his mother's womb. After leading a blameless childhood, during which occasional signs of his greatness manifested themselves, he married (this is denied by the Digambara sect) and led the life of a householder. However, having convinced himself of the worthlessness of worldly existence, he resolved to renounce after his parents' death. His initiation took place at the age of 30 with Indra and the other gods in attendance. From that moment he was Mahāvīra ('The Great Hero').

There followed a period of 12 years wandering within and occasionally outside the area of the Ganges basin, during which Mahāvīra practised the meditation and austerities necessary to burn away the karma which had become attached to his soul. Initially clad in a robe given to him by Indra, he subsequently rejected all garments and spent the rest of his career naked. The biography stresses the harshness of Mahāvīra's life at this time, the hostility of villagers and the attacks of demons and other creatures, all of which he endured with equanimity. During the course of his wandering, Mahāvīra was joined by another ascetic, Makkhali Gosāla, who had decided of his own volition to become his disciple. Gosāla is portrayed as a foolish mischief-maker, jealous of Mahāvīra's spiritual attainments and attached to the false doctrine of the all-powerful efficacy of the principle of fate, who eventually leaves the ford-maker in disgust at his complete forbearance. Later, after Mahāvīra's attainment of enlightenment, Gosāla is defeated in attempting a duel with his former teacher (a blast of ascetic heat emitted from his body rebounds upon him) and dies in agony, admitting to the genuineness of Mahāvīra's achievements.

In the thirteenth year after his renunciation, Mahāvīra attained omniscience, whereby he was aware of the state of every creature in the universe in past, present and future. After this he set about the formation of the *tīrtha*, the community of ascetics and lay followers which forms the bridge to salvation. To this end, he first converted 11 brahmans, among whom was INDRABHŪTI Gautama. These brahman converts were to be the 11 *gaṇadharas*, the heads of the male ascetic order (the nun Candanā was head of the female order), who structured the scriptural canon on the basis of Mahāvīra's preaching in the Ardhamāgadhī language.

Finally, after a period of almost 30 years of preaching as an omniscient ford-maker, Mahāvīra eradicated his karma completely, and having risen through the various stages of meditation died at the town of Pāvā, which is located in the present-day Indian state of Bihar. His body was cremated with Indra in attendance, the gods taking his bones to heaven and his ashes being distributed among the various clans of the Ganges basin.

Some historical facts can with plausibility be distilled from this legendary biography [12]. Mahāvīra was an ascetic teacher who lived at the same time and operated in the same area as the BUDDHA, although it would appear that the two never met. Probably drawing on a tradition going back to PĀRŚVA, he claimed enlightenment, taught a doctrine relating to the gaining of spiritual salvation through the pursuit of radical non-violence and attracted a community of followers. It seems likely that Mahāvīra was a reformer of an already existing monastic code of practice, making it more rigorous through the promulgation of five ascetic vows rather than the four with which both Jain and Buddhist texts associate Pārśva's followers.

It would be rash to state categorically what Mahāvīra's teachings were, since the Jain scriptures contain a great deal of disparate material owing to their being in a state of evolution until well into the Christian era [25]. However, the central tenets of Jainism are clear enough and can doubtless be linked to Mahāvīra, if not to Pārśva. All creatures in the universe have a soul: humans, gods, hell-beings, animals. Plants are composed of clusters of entities with souls, while there are souls in earth, water, air and fire. As a consequence of the omnipresence of souls, every action, witting or unwitting, must of necessity cause injury to them. Moreover, each action performed by a creature with a soul (for Jainism, this effectively means human beings and, to a lesser extent, animals) sets up a vibration which attracts karma, regarded as a substance, commensurate with the intensity of the particular action involved, which clogs up the soul and obstructs its natural omniscience and state of bliss. This karmic obstruction can be burnt off the soul by the generation of heat (*tapas*) through the performance of austerity. The only environment in which this austerity can be practised is that of the mendicant renouncer who has left behind the world of social action and relations and leads a life of rigorous mental and physical discipline, subsisting on alms and ceasing from the wandering life only during the four months of the monsoon period. If the various spiritual practices of Jainism are followed correctly, then the soul will become free from karma and enlightened, whereupon it will leave the confines of its body and, travelling instantaneously to the top of the universe, dwell there with the other liberated souls.

Mahāvīra is one of India's greatest religious teachers. Like the Buddha, he rejected the world of Brahman ideology, while at the same time recasting some of its central tenets into a soteriological framework which still has meaning 2,500 years after his death. (P.D.)

al-Mahdī. *See* MUḤAMMAD AḤMAD IBN ʿABD ALLĀH.

Mahinda [IV] (*c*.282–222 BCE). The son of Emperor AŚOKA, he became enlightened on the day of his ordination as a Buddhist monk. He led the mission sent by Aśoka to Sri Lanka, where he preached to the island's king Devānampiyatissa and converted him. Remaining in Sri Lanka for the rest of his life, he helped found the Mahāvihāra, the great monastery at the capital Anurādhapura, organized a recitation of the scriptures there (parts of the later tradition call this the Fourth Council), and arranged for relics to be brought from India. One of these was a branch of the Bodhi tree, said to have been brought to the island by his sister, the nun Saṅghamittā. The tree which grew from this is held to be that which survives in Anurādhapura to this day, from which branches have been taken all over the Buddhist world in South and South-east Asia. [150: vol. 2: 583–85] (S.C.)

Ma Hua-Lung [XII] (*d.*1871). Chinese Islamic leader. Leader of the second Islamic rebellion, 1862–1878, in the province of Gansu, Ma Hua-Lung had his headquarters in Chi'in-Chi-P'u just north-west of Yümen on the caravan road to Hami (Kumul) and a centre of Muslim activity. He appears to have commanded several major battles against the Chinese army, which was trying to crush Muslim rebellion in the area; however, he was ultimately defeated and executed. He was responsible for the promulgation in Ch'in-Chi-P'u of the Muslim 'New Teaching', a neo-orthodox movement which was started in the mid-18th century by MA MING-HSIN. He discouraged Muslims from building mosques, arguing that prayer indoors or in the open air was equally valid. He wanted no Islamic hierarchy and desired a return to the values of pristine Islam. He became a saintly martyred figure for Chinese Muslims after his death. [35: s.v.] (J.K.)

Maimonides, Moses [XV] [Moses ben Maimon; known by the acronym Rambam] (1135–1204). Jewish jurist, philosopher and physician; the outstanding Jewish medieval intellectual personality. Born in Cordova, Spain, to a distinguished rabbinical family, he was 13 when the fanatical Almohades captured Cordova. In 1158/9 he and his family fled to Morocco, living in Fez until 1165. He then went briefly to the Holy Land and proceeded to Egypt, where he settled in Fostat (Old Cairo). There he practised medicine and was court physician to Saladin's vizier. He was the leader of Egyptian Jewry, an office that remained hereditary in his family for many generations. He was buried in Tiberias in Palestine where his grave is still visited.

His first work, written at the age of 16, was a treatise on logical terminology. As a jurist, he systematized Jewish jurisprudence and formulated legal categories within which he organized the traditional legislation. He also sought to demonstrate the rationality of all the laws. His commentary on the Mishnah (the basic rabbinic code) deduced the underlying principles and the main legal teachings of each traditional law. His commentary on the Mishnah tractate, *Avot* ('The Sayings of the Fathers') was circulated independently and became a classic of Jewish ethics. In the framework of his Mishnah commentary, he made the first formulation of Jewish dogma (previously scattered unsystematically through Jewish teachings). These 'Thirteen Principles of Faith' consisted of: (1) God's existence; (2) His unity, (3) incorporeality and (4) eternity; (5) God alone is to be worshipped; (6) Prophecy and (7) MOSES' primacy as prophet; (8) The divine origin of the Mosaic laws and (9) their immutability; (10) God's omniscience; (11) Reward and punishment; (12) the coming of the messiah; (13) Resurrection of the dead. This statement entered both the Sephardi and Ashkenazi liturgies and in a poetic version (*Yigdal*) became one of the best known Jewish hymns.

Maimonides' *Sefer ha-Mitzvot* ('Book of the Commandments', written in Arabic) summarized all Jewish law under the headings of the traditional 613 commandments derived from the Pentateuch. However, this did not satisfy him and he went on to write a magisterial synthesis of all Jewish law in his monumental Hebrew code *Mishneh Torah* ('Repetition of the Law'; also known as *Yad ha-Ḥazakah*, 'The Strong Hand' because the numerical value of the word *Yad* = hand is 14, corresponding to the 14 sections into which the book is divided). This covered the entire Mosaic legislation – both that still practised and that not relevant in view of the destruction of the Temple (such as the sacrificial code) and the exile from Israel (such as the agricultural laws). This was a pioneering achievement which systematized all previous legislation, including the entire Talmud, and determined the final legal decision extracted from the long and complicated discussions in the sources. Although criticized for its failure to identify the sources of its decisions (*see* CARO, JOSEPH), it became a standard work of Jewish law.

Maimonides' other major contribution was in philosophy in his *Moreh Nevukhim* ('Guide of the Perplexed', written in Arabic), the most important and influential work in medieval Jewish philosophy, which was predominantly an attempt to reconcile Aristotelianism with Jewish tradition. For Maimonides, reason was pre-eminent; should it appear to clash with the Bible, the Bible required allegorical interpretation. The book contains philosophical proofs of the existence of God (using Aristotelian terminology), a discussion of divine attributes (of which man can only affirm the negative, knowing what God is not but not what he is), the nature of prophecy, good and evil, divine providence and a characterization of the ideal man. The omnipotent creator, he held, determined the laws of nature and could also make exceptions, as expressed through miracles or prophecy. The prophet, who is the ideal religious type, received his inspiration through mediation, namely in visions, but true revelation occurred only at Sinai where Moses' prophecy emanated directly from God. Maimonides differed from Aristotle in his account of creation, maintaining that it occurred *ex nihilo* and rejecting the theory of the eternity of matter. Man bears responsibility for his deeds as he enjoys free will and ethical choice, despite God's omniscience. The commandments are the outcome of divine wisdom and are ordered for the good of man, both physical and spiritual. They have a rational basis but are meant to be kept even if not comprehended. [39: XIII; 34: 152–82]

Already in his lifetime his views aroused widespread dissension in orthodox circles. He was accused of excessive reliance on reason and even of heresy. Throughout the subsequent centuries Jewry was divided by the controversy between the Maimonists and the anti-Maimonists but eventually his writings won universal acceptance. [67]

His medical writings were widely disseminated. Written in Arabic, they were translated into Hebrew and Latin and were highly regarded, especially in Muslim circles. His philosophical works were influential among Christian scholastics and were quoted by THOMAS AQUINAS, Meister ECKHARDT and DUNS SCOTUS. [35; 37] (G.W.)

Maitrīpa [iv] (*c.*1007–1085). The name used by Tibetans for the philosopher and tantric yogin of the late period of Buddhism in India [221]. This name renders the Indic Maitrīpāda ('the good Maitrī'). His full name as a Buddhist monk was Maitrīgupta; as a tantric yogin it was Advayavajra; and he is sometimes called Avadhūtipāda, a generic designation for someone who performs the yoga of winds and channels.

Born a Brahman under the Pāla dynasty, probably in present-day Bengal, Maitrīgupta was well educated and became a Brahmanical renunciate. Converted to Buddhism by the scholar NĀROPA after a debate, he subsequently became a monk and studied at the monastic universities of Vikramaśīla and Vikramapura.

Visions of the compassionate deities Tārā and Avalokiteśvara inspired him to quit monastic life and embark upon a spiritual quest. According to a Tibetan historical tradition that is hostile to Maitrīgupta and his legacy, he was expelled after being discovered with liquor and a woman in his room. According to a favourable tradition he outgrew monastic discipline to practise higher tantra with a '*vajra* female yogin' (*vajrayoginī*).

In any case, Maitrīgupta departs to seek a tantric *guru* known as Śabari ('the mountain man'). This Śabari, born into an itinerant theatrical family, has retired to an area of aboriginals around Mount Glory (*śrīparvata*) in the south-east. The region is probably Dhānyakaṭaka, upriver from the Kṛṣṇa delta. Maitrīgupta's journey there is a spiritual quest in which disorientation prepares him for a new kind of endeavour. Frustrated by the long barren search, he has reached the point of slitting his own throat when the mountain man appears.

This appearance is characterized as a vision. The *guru* Śabari is probably to be dated many decades earlier. He belongs to the line of tantric adepts (*siddha*) characterized by the composition of mystic songs (the *doha* line; *see* SARAHA). Maitrīgupta meets his 'rainbow body'.

Śabari has two companions, female yogins Padmāvalī and Jñānāvalī, who may also be sisters. These three *gurus* appear to Maitrīgupta in the guise of aboriginals and hunters. The killing and sexual licence of their way of life are made into further lessons for Maitrīgupta, punctuated with songs that point to the non-duality of mind and reality, subject and object, bondage and liberation. But Maitrīgupta's doubts obstruct his awakening. He is initiated into various tantric cycles, and sent back to the north to publish the philosophy in the academic world. On the way, he awakens one morning to find that all the teachings have been forgotten. He despairs, but Śabari reappears to ask him what it means to have forgotten doctrines that are empty from the beginning. With that Maitrīgupta reaches the first stage of comprehension.

Back in the north Maitrīgupta composes treatises, engages in philosophic controversy, founds a hermitage at the Cool Grove (śītavana) charnel ground, and marries the king of Malabar's daughter.

Maitrīgupta is known for works on tantric theory and method, and for a set of works expounding the more exoteric system known as 'not directing the mind' (*amanasikāra*), a form of Great Symbol (*mahāmudrā*) [22]. His philosophy is that of the middle (*madhyamaka*), and several of his works deal with comparative philosophy. Maitrīgupta had 21 Indian disciples, but because of the interruption to Buddhism in India his legacy must be assessed by developments in Tibet. Although his reputation and influence do not compare with those of Nāropa he is still an important figure. (M.T.)

Majlisī, Muḥammad Bāqir [XII] (1628–1699/1700). Leading Shiʿite scholar of the late Safavid period in Iran and 'one of the most powerful and influential Shīʿī *ʿulamāʾ* of all time' whose 'policies and actions reorientated Twelver Shiʿism in the direction that it was to develop from this day on'. The son of Muḥammad Taqī Majlisī, himself a prominent religious figure, he studied under several important scholars, including Mullā Muḥsin Fayḍ Kāshānī and Shaykh Muḥammad al-Ḥurr al-ʿĀmilī.

Apart from his scholarship, which was prolific and important, Majlisī was particularly active in three areas: the suppression of Ṣufism and mystical philosophy; the propagation of a dogmatic and legalistic form of Shiʿism; and the suppression of Sunnīs and other religious minorities. He exercised a powerful influence over the last two Safavid monarchs, Shāh Sulaymān (reigned 1666–94) and Shāh Sulṭān Ḥusayn (reigned 1694–1722). His own appointment (1687) as Shaykh al-Islām of the capital, Iṣfahān, signalled the coming to power of a new Shiʿite hierocracy.

Up to Majlisī's time, Ṣufism (in both its popular and élitist forms) had been an important aspect of Iranian Shiʿism. Many leading clerics, such as MULLĀ ṢADR, combined it with mystical philosophy to create an intellectualized form of the faith. Majlisī – whose own father had been a leading Ṣūfī – was successful in enlisting the power of the state to enforce his decree condemning Ṣufism as heresy, and neither it nor its philosophical counterpart have been serious rivals of Shiʿite orthodoxy since then.

More broadly, by writing extensively in Persian (rather than Arabic) on a wide variety of topics (including theology, history and ritual), Majlisī was able to encourage popular support for his version of Shiʿism. His best-known work is the encyclopaedic collection of Shiʿite traditions known as the *Biḥār al-anwār* ('Ocean of Lights', published in 110 volumes), which provided an important basis for the extension of Shīʿī law in the ensuing period. It has been claimed that 'there is hardly a feature of contemporary Shiʿism that is not either fully depicted or at least presaged in his writings'. Other well-known works include *ʿAyn al-Ḥayāt, Ḥaqq al-yaqīn* and *Zād al-maʿād*.

Apart from his writing Majlisī also had a marked influence on popular religion, first by encouraging a cult of the Imāms as intercessors, and second by fostering the development of ritual practices, including the celebration of festivals (such as mourning for the Imām ḤUSAYN) and pilgrimages to shrines.

Paradoxically, Majlisī's persecution of Sunnīs was itself a factor precipitating the Afghan invasion of 1722, which almost succeeded in destroying Shiʿism as the state religion in Iran. But it is a measure of the popularity of the new synthesis promoted by him that it endured until the re-establishment of a centralized Shiʿite state under the Qājārs in 1785. This in itself was a development much encouraged by the triumph of Uṣūlī Shiʿism under BIHBIHĀNĪ, whose father, Muḥammad Akmal, was a student of Majlisī. [16; 89] (D.M.)

Makiguchi Tsunesaburō [IV] (1871–1944). Together with Toda Jōsei (1900–1958), the founder of the religious organization now known as Sōka Gakkai. Both were school teachers who converted to NICHIREN Shōshū Buddhism in 1928. Makiguchi was born in Niigate Prefecture, but moved to Hokkaido after primary school. There he later attended the Sapporo Normal School. As a teacher and school administrator in Tokyo during the first two decades of the 20th century he developed his philosophy of 'value creation'. In 1921 Toda was assigned to Makiguchi's school, where he became his disciple. Makiguchi published his four-volume work *Sōka kyōikugaku taikei* ('A System of Value-Creation Education') between 1930 and 1934, blending his religious beliefs with educational theory. Sōka Gakkai dates its founding from 1930, which was the date of the publication of the first volume of that work.

In 1937 Makiguchi founded the Sōka Kyōiku Gakkai ('Value Creation Educational Institute'), with about 60 members. Although ostensibly dedicated to the study of pedagogical issues, the society sought to promulgate the Nichiren Shōshū faith through aggressive proselytization and a monthly publication, *Kachi Sōzō* ('The Creation of Value'), which presented Makiguchi's philosophy. Makiguchi believed that this-worldly values, beauty and goodness should be the goals of education. Engaging the Kantian position that the goals of life are the good, the true and the beautiful, Makiguchi argued that the true, which can only be known through experience, can generate both happiness and unhappiness and, thus, is in itself unworthy of being designated an ultimate value. Rather, he argued, the pursuit of happiness is the ultimate goal of life, and this includes the good, the beautiful and the profitable. Thus, it is the quality of one's everyday life which is important, and material comforts are not to be disparaged as antithetical to the religious life.

In 1943 the government attempted forcibly to consolidate all Nichiren sects under its control, but this was widely resisted by Nichiren priests as well as by Makiguchi and Toda. In addition, both Makiguchi and Toda refused to pay homage to the imperial shrine at Ise, and they were jailed. Makiguchi died in prison of malnutrition on 18 November 1944. Toda reconstituted the society under its present name, Sōka Gakkai, after his release from prison in 1945. He built this lay Buddhist society into one of the fastest growing and most powerful of the 'new religions' in the post-war period. [61: 69–110; 149; 158] (G.E.)

Malcolm, Arthur [xxi] (1934–). Australia's first Aboriginal bishop, serving as assistant bishop in the Anglican diocese of North Queensland with special responsibility to Aborigines. His father was of the Koko-Bera people and his mother a Koku-Gundjun; they were forcibly brought by police to the Yarrabah mission reserve, where Malcolm was born. As was mission policy, he was confined to a dormitory from the age of 10 until 16, when he was extensively schooled and trained in Christian thought and practice. After schooling he continued his education so that he could train for the Anglican Church Army and was commissioned in 1959. His subsequent ministry to Aborigines covered a diverse range, from remote New South Wales to Redfern, Sydney, and Lake Tyers in Victoria. In 1974 he returned to Yarrabah, was ordained a deacon and a priest in the following year, and in 1985 became the first Aboriginal bishop. He has been instrumental in building the Aboriginal ministry in this region and the training of 14 priests thus far. Since his return, Yarrabah has been noted for visionary experiences, a tradition going back to his uncle James Noble (the first Aboriginal deacon) but recently becoming widely spread in the community. The visions include images of JESUS and others in children's 'butterfly' painting, cloud formations, tree shapes and the scorch marks of irons on paper. Malcolm's own ordination was associated with a vision of a mynah bird being attacked, interpreted as the Bishop John Lewis being set upon by White clergy for supporting an Aboriginal bishopric. Malcolm also makes strong use of 'deliverance' prayers, sometimes accompanied by glossalalia, and performed a widely publicized 'exorcism' in a prison in which several Aborigines had committed suicide [23: 250–57]. Malcolm is concerned more with advocating a biblical life for Aborigines than in developing a specifically Aboriginal theology, though he supports traditional beliefs not in conflict with Christian principles [26]. While conscious that the church has often failed Aborigines, he feels the need to remain within recognized church structures to achieve his goals. (T.S.)

Malcolm X [xii] (1925–1965). First Plenipotentiary of the Nation of Islam. Born Malcolm Little in Omaha, Nebraska, he was a petty criminal for many years before converting to the Nation of Islam in 1947. Prominent as an organizer and speaker, Malcolm X came to symbolize the essence of the civil rights movement and Black power in the United States of the 1950s and 1960s. He was chosen by ELIJAH MUHAMMAD to be 'national representative' of the Nation of Islam, second in command in the organization. In 1964 Malcolm X left the Nation of Islam after a period of controversy within the movement and, while on pilgrimage to Mecca, converted to orthodox Sunnī Islam and adopted the name el-Hajj Malik el-Shabbaz. The emphasis in his beliefs then turned to general human rights, de-emphasizing racial issues. This was a trend which was ultimately embraced and continued with the Nation of Islam under the leadership of Wallace Deen Muhammad after Malcolm/Malik's assassination in 1965 and the death of Elijah Muhammad in 1975. [81; 84] (A.R.)

Mālik ibn Anas, Abū ʿAbd Allāh [XII] *d. c.*795). Muslim jurist of the city of Medina, and eponymous patron of the Mālikī school of law. Mālik functioned as repository of local norms, and was consulted by political authorities as well as by the public on religious and judicial affairs. His independence of ruling officials is represented in many stories which illustrate both his exemplary opposition to governors and his shrewd statesmanlike approach to them as adviser and representative of Prophetic knowledge. Three ʿAbbasid caliphs are said to have visited him while on pilgrimage to the Prophet's city. Some political problems and a public whipping, though historically difficult to pin down, naturally enhanced his reputation. Three qualities may be singled out as prefiguring those of his school. (1) His respect for Prophetic Traditions: his fear of transmitting inauthentic material neatly accounts for the relatively small number of Prophetic Traditions in his work *al-Muwaṭṭa'*. (2) His acknowledgement of local practice in Medina, MUḤAMMAD's city, as a source of the law. (3) His distaste for an excessively intellectual approach to the law: he disliked the cultivated hypothetical exploration of the law evident amongst the followers of ABŪ ḤANĪFA, and looked upon the answer 'I don't know' as an essential component of wisdom. His death was associated with numerous visions confirming the high place reserved for him in Paradise. His lawbook, *al-Muwaṭṭa'*, became available in a number of editions of which two survive, along with fragments of others. It is one of the earliest Muslim legal texts and represents the aspiration to bring the whole of life, even the most humble activities, into the sphere of divine interest. Its structure is designed to foreground Prophetic traditions, but it contains rather more non-Prophetic traditions, and much discursive material in Mālik's name. Its small size and great authority made it an outstanding basis for commentary and it accordingly dominates the Mālikī school tradition in a way which has no parallels in the other Muslim schools of law. [35: s.v.; 41: 198–209] (N.C.)

Ma Ming-Hsin [XII] (*d.*1781). Chinese Islamic leader. Ma Ming-Hsin led a Turkic-speaking people known as the Salars and proclaimed himself a 'preacher of the true faith' of the 'New Teaching' neo-orthodox movement. He made the pilgrimage to Mecca around 1760 and was initiated into the Naqshbandī order of Sufism. On his return to China he started preaching the reform of Islam in the Salar area of north-west China in a manner influenced by Ṣūfī practices: vigorous movement during prayer, loud chanting of scripture and belief in miracles and visions. It was a continuation of this movement which MA HUA-LUNG promulgated in the 19th century. Conflict with fellow Muslims of the more traditional kind eventually led to fighting and the suppression of the movement by the Chinese authorities. Ma Ming-Hsin was apparently executed in Lanchow, but he survived as a saint among the people of the area. [35: s.v.] (J.K.)

Manco Capac. *See* MANQO QHAPAC.

Manetho [VII]An Egyptian priest, Manetho probably lived at the Temple of Sebennytos in the Delta in the 3rd century BCE. He is accredited with the authorship of eight literary works, the most important being the *Aegyptiaca* ('History of Egypt') [20]. This divides the history of ancient Egypt into 31 dynasties of royal rulers, from NARMER (*c.*3100 BCE) to Alexander the Great's conquest in 332 BCE. This is accepted and used by modern scholars as the basic structure of Egypt's history. Manetho also includes the semi-divine rulers who preceded Narmer. His writings are only partially preserved in the works of Sextus Julius Africanus (early 3rd century CE), Eusebius (early 4th century

CE), JOSEPHUS (1st century CE), and George called Syncellus (*c*.800 CE). (A.R.D.)

Māni [IX] (216–*c*.277). Founder of a gnostic world religion, Māni was born on 14 April 216 near the Parthian capital of Ctesiphon. His father, who came originally from Hamadan, had earlier joined a baptizing sect in southern Babylonia which appears to have acknowledged the Jewish–Christian teacher Elchasaios as its founder. Māni was reared in that sect from age four until 24, when he broke away from it over the question of ritual ablution. He founded his own sect based on teaching which he claimed to have received from his Divine Twin (Syzygos).

The main theme of his teaching is a cosmic conflict between the primordial powers of Light and Darkness, Good and Evil, which results in the creation of the universe. The material world is seen as the procreation of the powers of Darkness who had swallowed in them Particles of Light. The ethics and cultic practices of the sect focus therefore on the liberation of Light from its captivity by Matter. This involves the abstention from meat-eating, harvesting and sexual intercourse for the Elect members of the sect, who had their dietary needs attended to by Hearers. The latter were not subject to the same strict regulations. Māni styled himself as the Apostle of JESUS Christ and his system clearly owes much to the teachings of MARCION and Bardaisan. Its debt to Zoroastrianism is much less clear, although the religion was propagated at a time of Zoroastrian revival under the Sasanians.

On leaving the sect Māni travelled to Media but found no significant support for his new religion. The same was true of a short spell of missionary journeys he undertook in India. The decisive breakthrough came when Pērōz, the brother of ŠĀBUHR I, was won over to the new religion and Māni was granted an audience with the Shāhanshāh. Šābuhr gave Māni permission to propagate his religion within his domain. The military success of the early Sasanians in Central Asia and against the Romans was a major factor in the successful diffusion of Manichaeism outside Iran. According to Manichaean historical texts, Manichaean missionaries were active in Palmyra, Egypt, Armenia and the lands east of the Amu Darya before the mid-3rd century.

The exact details of Māni's middle years are little known and the scanty evidence we possess indicates that he spent much of his time teaching in Ctesiphon. His privileged position was threatened by the rise of KIRDĒR as the Chief Mobed, and it was mainly at his instigation that Māni was tortured and executed by the Shāhanashāh Bahrām II at Bet Lapat (Bishapur) some time between 276 and 277. His death was viewed by his followers as a form of crucifixion and was commemorated by the Feast of the Bema, one of the most important dates in the liturgical calendar of the sect.

The Manichaeans preserved a canon of seven works, which probably included many original writings by Māni. In the Islamic period Māni was also remembered as a great painter. The sect was severely persecuted in Iran after Māni's death. Many of his followers escaped westwards into the Roman Empire and eastwards into Central Asia. Among the most famous non-Iranian converts to Manichaeism was AUGUSTINE OF HIPPO, who was a Hearer in his native North Africa for almost nine years. The sect was prohibited in the Roman Empire from the time of Valentinian onwards and was virtually extinguished by persecutions under Justinian. The title of the Sect was used as a term of opprobrium in the Middle Ages by the Catholic and Orthodox churches against the Paulicians, Bogomils and Cathars. In the East, Manichaeism won the patronage of the Uighur (Turkish) Khaghan in the 9th century, and under his patronage the religion was established first in Inner Mongolia and later in the Turfan Basin. Manichaean missionaries were also active in China, and the religion survived the persecution against foreign cults in the 9th century and re-emerged as a secret society in South China. Even as late as the 16th century it still retained written records of its Mesopotamian origins.

Bibliography *Sources*: The main sources of Māni's life are the *Fihrist of al-Nadim*, trans. B. Dodge (New York, 1970), vol. 2, pp. 773–94, and the *Cologne Mani Codex*, ed. L. Koenen and K. Römer, *Der Kölner Mani-Kodex: Kritische Edition*, Abhandlungen der Rheinische Westfälische Akademie der Wissenschaften, Sonderreihe Papyrologica Coloniensia, vol. 14. Fragments of Manichaean missionary history are collected in A. Böhlig and J. P. Asmussen, *Die Gnosis*

III: Der Manichäismus (Zurich and Munich, 1980), pp. 75–102 and W. Sundermann, *Mitteliranische manichäische Texte kirchengeshichtlichen Inhalts* (Berlin, 1981). *Studies*: There is no up-to-date biography of Māni in English. See, however, S. N. C. Lieu, *Manichaeism in the Later Roman Empire and Medieval China* (Manchester, 1985), pp. 25–80. The best and most up-to-date single volume study of Manichaeism is M. Tardieu, *Le Manichéisme* (Paris, 1981). The main critical studies of Māni's life and the history of the Manichaean sect are in German: see especially W. Sundermann, 'Studien, zur kirchengeschicht-lichen Literatur der iranischen Manichäer', *Altorientalische Forschungen*, 13/1 (1983), pp. 40–92; 13/2 (1986), pp. 239–317; 14/1 (1987), pp. 41–107. See also M. Hutter, *Mani und die Sasaniden: Der iranisch-gnostische Synkretismus einer Weltreligion* (Innsbruck, 1988). (S.N.C.L.)

Māṇikkavācakar [XI]. The author of *Tiruvācakam* and *Tirukkovaiyār*, which together make up *Tirumuṟai* VIII. Interestingly, he does not appear in the hagiography *Pěriya purāṇam* which marks the culmination of the NĀYAṈMĀR tradition. One is therefore entitled to presume him to have been later, and he perhaps dates from the 8th or 9th century, prior to the compilation by Nampiyāṇṭār nampi of the *Tirumuṟai*. However, an extensive tradition concerning Māṇikkavācakar is embodied in the *sthalapurāṇas* of the Śiva and Mīnākṣī temple at Madurai, Tamil Nadu. These legends are related in two Tamil texts, of the 14th and 16th centuries, and a Sanskrit work of uncertain date. Māṇikkavācakar was born in Vātavūr of a ministerial Brahman family. He is said to have embezzled funds provided him by the Pāṇṭiya king of Madurai for the purchase of horses and cavalry: the saint used this money for renovating Śiva temples. The god saved his devotee by turning a pack of jackals into horses, thus appeasing the king. However, this made Māṇikkavācakar complacent, so Śiva turned them back into jackals. The king imprisoned his minister. He was released only when the god threatened the city of Madurai with a flood. Both Māṇikkavācakar's poems are mystical, concerning loving devotion to Śiva, who is very much his personal god. *Tiruvācakam* includes a poem in the same form as the *Tiruppāvai* of ĀṆṬĀL, wherein Śiva this time is addressed as 'My sole Idol'. The poem is differentiated by being called *Tiruvěmpāvai*, and is of 20 verses. *Tirukkovaiyār*, the other text, is a love poem frequently erotic in tone, addressed to Śiva worshipped at Chidambaram by a maiden (the devotee) deeply in love with the god. [73; 118] (J.R.M.)

Manī Siṅgh [XXIII] (1673–1734). Sikh martyr. Born in a village near Paṭiālā, he attached himself to GURŪ GOBIND SIṄGH, and after the evacuation of Anandpur in 1704 he escorted two of the Gurū's wives to Delhi. Returning to join the Gurū in Damdamā Sāhib, he is said to have written a copy of the *Ādi Granth* at the Gurū's dictation. He is also said to have gathered together the various works which now form the *Dasam Granth* (the second Sikh scripture). In 1721 he was placed in charge of the Harimandir Sāhib in Amritsar. He was executed by the Mughal governor of Lahore on a spurious charge of failing to pay tribute. [40: 386–9] (W.H.M.)

Manning, Henry Edward [VI.A] (1808–1892). English Roman Catholic cardinal. He was educated at Harrow School and Balliol College, Oxford. His early ambition was to follow his father into politics but he had to settle for a clerk's job in the Colonial Office. He became a fellow of Merton College, Oxford in 1832 and was ordained deacon. In 1833 he married and became rector of Lavington. His wife died in 1837. He became Archdeacon of Chichester in 1841. Though an Evangelical he became attracted to the High Church and wrote *Tract 78* of the Oxford Movement's *Tracts for the Times*, though, as a critic of *Tract 90*, which interpreted the Thirty-Nine Articles of Religion of the Church of England in a Catholic way, he remained for a time anti-papal. In 1851, following the Gorham judgment, Manning became a convert to Rome. He was soon ordained priest and went to Rome for two years' study. In 1857 he was made provost of the Westminster Metropolitan Chapter and founded the Oblates of St Charles Borromeo. He became Archbishop of Westminster in 1865. He was ultramontane in his loyalty to the pope and papal infallibility. He was made cardinal in 1875. In 1889 he successfully mediated between employers and workers in a dock strike in London. He was buried in

Kensal Green Cemetery but his body was later reburied in Westminster Cathedral, which he had founded. [515; 535; 759: 3–115] (T.T.)

Manqo Qhapaq [XXIV] (Manco Capac). Legendary founder of the Inca royal dynasty who ruled at a time difficult to chronicle in exact historical terms. He and his successors are known only through the Spanish chronicles of the 16th century, since no pre-Columbian documents exist to recount religious life in the Andes. Genealogically speaking, Manqo Qhapaq lived nine generations before the rule of Pachakuti 'Inka Yupanki (1438–71). Many of Manqo Qhapaq's movements became paradigms for royal ritual and official calendrical cult in the Inca empire, which, by the early 16th century, stretched nearly 3,000 miles along the Pacific coast of South America. With his three brothers and four sisters, Manqo Qhapaq (referred to in Spanish as Manco Capac) emerged from a sacred place of origin at Paqariq-tampu in the valley of Cuzco, high in the Peruvian Andes. The *paqarina* (the Quechua word for the sacred place of origin) was an important shrine where rites were held; it served as a model structure for other sacred precincts. The royal family wandered for years in search of a proper settlement before taking up residence in Cuzco. They often sacralized the landscape where they passed and where they were subsequently memorialized. In the course of the ancestral migrations, Manqo Qhapaq managed to rid himself of his brothers and to father a child (Zinchi Roq'a; Spanish: Sinchi Roca) by his sister Mama Ocllo. The marriage of the emperor to his royal sister became the norm for Inca rulers after Thupa 'Inka Yupanki (1471–93) and was modelled on the marriage of the moon goddess Mama-Kilya to the sun god Inti, from whom all Inca rulers reckoned their descent. [13; 16; 19; 22] (L.S.)

Manson, Charles Miles [XIX] (1934–). Founder and leader of the 'Manson Family'. He was the illegitimate child of a 16-year old girl, and spent much of his life in foster homes, remand centres and prison. In 1967, he formed a 'paramilitary mystical sect'. The ideological lawlessness with which he ran his commune in Death Valley, California, was matched only by the authoritarian control exerted over his 'Family' by Manson, who called himself both Jesus Christ and the Devil. He is currently serving a life-sentence for masterminding the ritual murder in 1969 of a number of people, including the film star, Sharon Tate. [3; 8] (E.B.)

Manuščihr [XXVI] (9th century). Hereditary high priest of the Zoroastrians of Fars and Kerman in the latter part of the 9th century. When he held office Zoroastrianism was under heavy pressure from Islam, and his *Dādestān ī dīnīg* ('Religious Judgments') was written to answer questions from perplexed or harassed coreligionists on matters of doctrine, ritual and practice. Their increasing poverty is apparent and the difficulty of finding enough priests. Manuščihr instructs, adjudicates and urges faithfulness to tradition. Three letters of his survive, written in an elaborate, difficult style, to his brother ZĀDSPRAM and his congregation. These again stress the need to maintain ancient observances exactly [55; 11: vol. 4: 546–50]. (M.B.)

Maranke, Johane [I.A.] (1912–1963). Founder of the African Apostolic Church of John Maranke (AACJM). Maranke, a Manyika-Shona born in Rhodesia (Zimbabwe), was educated and raised a Methodist. He reported having visions as early as age six. At age 32, while working as a labourer, he experienced a divine revelation and returned to his homeland in south-west Rhodesia to begin his religious work. Here he set up his own church, the AACJM or Vapostori (Apostles), and filled the church hierarchy with members of his own family. Through works such as healings, exorcisms, prophetism and teaching, Maranke's fame spread quickly. The church had over 100 branches by 1940, and in 1967 it claimed some 50,000 followers in Rhodesia alone, with Maranke's travels in such neighbouring countries as Botswana, Zambia, Malawi and South Africa having gained him still more adherents. Following his death in 1963 a small schism resulted. [18] (R.H.)

Marcion [VI.A] (*d. c.*160). Founder of the Marcionite sect. He was a native of Sinope in Pontus and a wealthy shipowner. He left his home after being excommunicated from the church. He arrived in Rome, following rejection by churches in Asia Minor, *c.*140. In

Rome he donated a large sum of money and was accepted but soon his views were again rejected. His money was returned to him and he was excommunicated. In 144 he founded his own church, which spread throughout the Roman empire with its own clergy, forms of worship and scriptures. Most of the leading apologists for the Christian religion felt obliged to attack him and refute his views. His teaching was based on a strong belief in the grace and love of God, therefore anything that might challenge this view of God, such as God as judge, was rejected. He rejected the Hebrew scriptures; for him Christ was unique and not connected with Hebrew prophesy. While rejecting the Hebrew scriptures he also edited the Christian documents, for instance he edited out the infancy narratives and genealogies in Luke's Gospel. He accepted only ten Pauline letters, excluding 1 and 2 *Timothy* and *Titus*. He was the first to establish a canon of scriptures. He was a serious threat to the church in the 2nd century, and much of what is now considered orthodox, including the canon of scripture, was established through opposition to Marcionite views. [92; 347; 368] (*see also* entries on Gnosticism [IX] (T.T.)

Marcus Aurelius [XXII] (121–180). Roman emperor from 161 to his death [5]. Marcus' significance as a religious figure lies not in his public office or achievements (though these were distinguished: the last of the 'five good emperors', he was a conscientious administrator and an effective, if reluctant, soldier, who preserved the increasingly beleaguered Roman world in the face of both external foes and internal tensions) but rather in his authorship of a remarkable spiritual diary, entitled *To Himself*, usually known as the *Meditations* [14: 197–200; 32: 172–7; 33]. He is thus one of the very few ancients whose interior life – or as much of it as he has chosen to reveal and edit – is perennially accessible (*compare* AELIUS ARISTIDES).

As with many other Greeks and Romans, the outlet for Marcus' deep religious sensibilities lay not through the worship of the gods in the formalities of public cult, but through the theory and practice of philosophy. Marcus was an adherent of the Stoic school (*compare* EPICTETUS, whom Marcus greatly admired), and the *Meditations* record his attempts to lead the life of a good Stoic amid the corrupting hurly-burly of high office. Stoicism, in its Roman form, reinforced his sense of duty and determination to do his allotted part in the world, however uncongenial, and it taught him also – a hard lesson for a naturally fastidious and withdrawn temperament – to recognize his fellow humans (and imperial subjects) as rational co-workers in the rational Stoic cosmos and to associate with them accordingly. Militating against these schooled attitudes were Marcus' more instinctive pessimism, a feeling of the randomness and futility of existence, a certain 'hatred of the flesh', and a mistrust of the world of matter and the senses. The *Meditations* are the intimate record of these tensions. (R.B.)

Maritain, Jacques [VI.A] (1882–1973). He was born in Paris into a Protestant family, though from an early age he regarded himself as an unbeliever. He studied at the Sorbonne from 1901 to 1906 but found the positivistic and rationalist emphasis in philosophy unacceptable. He came under the influence of Henri Bergson, whose lectures at the Collège de France encouraged his return to metaphysics. Maritain converted to Catholicism in 1906 along with his Russian Jewish wife, whom he had married two years earlier. He then spent two years studying in Heidelberg. When he returned to France he began to study the *Summa theologiae* of THOMAS AQUINAS. Thereafter his philosophy was based on Thomist principles. He held professorships in philosophy at the Institut Catholique de Paris (1914–33), the Institute of Medieval Studies, Toronto (1933–45) and Princeton University (1948–52). From 1945 to 1948 he was French ambassador to the Vatican. His wife died in 1960, and in 1961 he retired to France to the monastery of the Little Brothers of Jesus, a Dominican order. He joined the order in 1969. Among his works are *True Humanism* (1936, English trans., 1938), *Man and the State* (1951), *Approaches to God* (1954) and *On the Church of Christ* (1970). He held to the traditional teaching of the Church while adapting it to modern demands. [282; 432; 521] (T.T.)

Mark Eugenicus, St [VI.B] (1392–1444). A Constantinople noble, Mark studied under Plethon and other leading scholars. He became a monk at the Mangana Monastery after living as a hermit on Principo Island. He was consecrated Metropolitan of Ephesus (1437) to represent the Patriarchates of Antioch and Jerusalem at the Council of Ferrara-Florence (1438–9). He consistently opposed Union with Rome. After a period in Ephesus and Athos, he was imprisoned on Lemnos for ten years. Still active in the Orthodox cause, he died in Constantinople. [75; 76: 104ff; 87] (D.B.)

Mark the Evangelist [VI.A]. The traditional author of the second Gospel. He was not one of the disciples of Jesus. A person by the name of John Mark is mentioned a number of times in the New Testament (*Acts* 12:12,25; 15:37,39), or simply as Mark (*Colossians* 4:10; *2 Timothy* 4:11; *Philemon* 24; *1 Peter* 5:13). He is referred to as the cousin of Barnabas who accompanied Paul on missions until they quarrelled, and also as a fellow worker of Paul. There are those who consider that the person so named is the author of the Gospel. Although the association of a person of this name with Paul is well established in tradition, his identification with the Gospel is not in the earliest traditions. A late tradition holds that Mark was the first to preach in Egypt, that he was martyred in Alexandria in the time of Nero and that his remains were moved to Venice at a later date. His symbol, a lion, is the emblem of Venice. [414: 95–8; 450; 589; 778: 1–8] (T.T.]

Marsden, Samuel [VI.A] (1764–1838). Chaplain to the New South Wales colony, Australia, founder of the New Zealand Mission (to the Maoris) and gentleman farmer. Influenced by Methodism, Marsden was of Evangelical persuasion when he became an Anglican priest in 1793, the year he set sail for Australia. He was for some years the only establishment clergyman on the mainland. Stationed at Parramatta, he took to farming. His efforts to evangelize the convicts and the aborigines bore little fruit, although he established an orphanage and a school, and had greater success in training and sending out missionaries to New Zealand. Between 1814 and 1837 he made seven journeys to New Zealand. These were disturbing years, in which he had to discipline the missionary THOMAS KENDALL and face criticism for defending Governor Bligh against the rebellious Rum Corps. (354; 523) (G.W.T.)

Martineau, James [VI.A] (1805–1900). English Unitarian theologian. He was born in Norwich and educated in Norwich Grammar School. In 1822 he entered Manchester College, York. He worked as a Unitarian minister in Dublin and Liverpool between 1831 and 1857. During his pastorate at Liverpool he was made professor of philosophy at Manchester New College, and in 1869 he became principal. In 1848–9 he spent time in Germany, where he came further under the influence of radical biblical criticism having previously given up belief in the evidential value of miracles. He stood against the growing anti-supernaturalism among Unitarians, maintaining a strong theistic position and adapting the argument from design for the existence of God on the basis of Darwinian evolution. He tried to remove the name 'Unitarian' from his church, preferring the name 'Presbyterian' or a new 'Free Christian' name. In this he did not succeed and made many enemies, though in great old age he was revered by most for his erudition. His works include *Types of Ethical Theory* (2 vols., 1885) and *A Study of Religion* (2 vols., 1888), in which he proposed grounds for belief in the existence of a moral consciousness and of laws of nature. He also composed many hymns and prayers. (143; 530] (T.T.)

Mary [VI.A] (*fl.* 1st century). The mother of JESUS. She is referred to as such in the first two chapters of the Gospels of MATTHEW and LUKE. According to these accounts she conceived the child Jesus in a mysterious way, 'of the Holy Spirit' or by the Holy Spirit 'coming upon her', before she and her husband Joseph 'came together'. Thus it is believed that Mary was a virgin when Jesus was born. Later Christian teaching maintains the 'perpetual virginity' of Mary, though the Gospels record the existence of 'his brothers' (*Mark* 3:31 and parallels), there is a view, however, that the word translated as brothers *adelphoi* can mean 'next of kin'. The virginal conception and birth are not referred to in the gospels of *Mark* and *John*, nor in any other New Testament document. PAUL refers to Jesus being 'born of woman, born under the law, to redeem those who were under the law, so that we might receive adoption as sons'. Mary is mentioned in *Acts* 1:14 as present with the disciples after the ascension of Jesus. In John's Gospel all references are to 'the mother of Jesus', and she is recorded as present at the wedding in Cana of Galilee along with his brothers (*John* 2:2–4, 12), and at the foot of the cross (*John* 19:25–27). Various doctrines have developed around the figure of Mary besides her perpetual virginity. These include: her own immaculate conception, formulated in the Middle Ages and defined officially in 1854; her title *theotokos*, Mother of God, confirmed at the councils of Ephesus (431) and Chalcedon (451); her bodily assumption to heaven, formally defined in 1950. It is also believed that Mary as mother of God plays a role in the Redemption. Some Catholics believe that she is co-redemptrix with Christ, but this is not a Roman Catholic doctrine. In Orthodox churches deep piety is shown towards Mary and the title *theotokos* is acknowledged in the tradition, but other doctrines are not recognized as they are in Roman Catholicism. Orthodox churches have reacted against modern Roman definitions. In Protestantism piety and doctrines exist in a variety of ways: these range from high church Anglicans who differ only in degree from Rome to the more Protestant sections where Mary receives no particular reverence or attention. In those areas of Christianity which revere her a number of festivals commemorate the Annunciation (by an angel of the birth of Jesus), her Purification (following his birth according to Jewish religious law) – the biblical events – while in addition there are the more legendary events – the Immaculate Conception, Nativity and Dormition. Many other forms of devotion to Mary exist in some parts of the religion. [123; 415; 841] (T.T.)

Massaja, Guglielmo (Lorenzo) [VI.A] (1809–1889). Italian Roman Catholic missionary. He was born in Piedmont and entered the Capuchin order. After teaching theology and acting as a royal chaplain, he was sent to Ethiopia as first Vicar Apostolic of Galla in 1846. Unable to reach his appointed destination until 1852, he worked in Egypt and Sudan. In Ethiopia he developed medical missions and an indigenous clergy. He had excellent relations with Menelik, but Yohannes IV imprisoned and expelled him in 1879. He was made Cardinal in 1884. Massaja wrote a vast record of his '35 years in upper Ethiopia' (1885–95). One of the most publicly successful Catholic missionaries of his century, he was a popular hero in Italy. [189] (A.F.W.)

Mathers, Samuel Liddell MacGregor [XVII] (1854–1918). English occultist. His father was a commercial clerk who died young, and Mathers lived with his widowed mother in Bournemouth for many years, during which time he was initiated into freemasonry in 1877. He became involved with a masonic society primarily devoted to esoteric ends, the Societas Rosicruciana in Anglia, and became deeply immersed in arcane kabbalistic studies, which he is said to have pursued all day, every day, in the British library. W. B. YEATS said of him that he had 'much learning, but little scholarship, much imagination and imperfect taste'. Mathers claimed Jacobite ancestry and called himself Comte de Glenstrae. He published a number of translations and interpretations of early magical works, including *The Kabbalah Unveiled* (1887), *The Key of Solomon the King: Clavicula Salomonis* (1889) and *The Book of the Sacred Magic of Abramelin the Mage* (2nd edn, 1900). In 1888 he became one of the three chiefs and founders of the Hermetic Order of the Golden Dawn (*see also* WESTCOTT, WILLIAM WYNN), a masonic-style magical order that spoke of magic, mysticism and intense spirituality, and relied upon a complex mixture of Renaissance Hermetic-kabbalistic magical philosophy and Egyptian mythology. Mathers was responsible for many of these rituals and seems himself to have been a flamboyant, dramatic man whom one historian has compared to Frederick Rolfe, Baron Corvo. He died in Paris. [7; 8] (T.L.)

Matthew the Evangelist [VI.A]. The traditional author of the first Gospel. The name Matthew occurs in each list of the disciples of JESUS (*Matthew* 10:3; *Mark* 3:18; *Luke* 6:15; *Acts* 1:13). According to the first Gospel Jesus called Matthew to be a disciple when he was collecting taxes in his office. In the list in the first Gospel he is referred to as 'Matthew the tax collector'. In two other Gospels a tax collector is also called by Jesus but his name is Levi (*Mark* 2:13–14; *Luke* 5:27–8). The authorship of the first Gospel by this disciple is severely questioned by critical scholarship on the grounds that there is no evidence that the author was an eye-witness, that he has depended on Mark's Gospel, written in Greek as opposed to Matthew's own language, Aramaic, for much of the material, and that the evidence points to the Gospel being written at a date too late to be the work of a disciple. [41: 119–21; 450; 542: XXX–XXXII] (T.T.)

al-Māturīdī, Abū Manṣūr Muḥammad ibn Muḥammad [XII] (*d.*944). Muslim theologian whose influence was significant in the emergence of Sunnī Islam. Living in Transoxiana, he attacked the doctrines of the Muʿtazila and set down the foundations of his theological system. Like AL-ASHʿARĪ, al-Māturīdī followed a middle path between Traditionalism and rationalism, forging an Islam which saw the written sources of the faith dominate but which found a place for the activities of the human mind.

Only a few texts have come down to us from al-Māturīdī and his school but one of the most important, his *Kitāb al-tawḥīd* ('The Book of Divine Unity'), is extant. The work commences by declaring that unconditional following of the teaching of another person is not valid: God has given humanity intelligence so that all may think and that gift must be used. This is a doctrine held in common with the Muʿtazila. Reason leads to knowledge, as do the senses and transmissions from the past, either from authoritative sources or from prophets. Reason must be used to judge the information provided by the other sources of knowledge. Reason also allowed knowledge of God before prophets were sent, a position contrary to al-Ashʿarī, who held that prophets were necessary and thus belief not incumbent upon those who had not been reached by God's messengers.

The matter of God's attributes is dealt with by al-Māturīdī such that what the text of the Qur'an says about God must be believed, although we cannot know 'how' God is to be conceived of as 'sitting' on His throne, for example; this suggests a greater tendency towards interpretation of such matters than that found in al-Ashʿarī. Al-Māturīdī supports the idea of the free will of humanity, although God is, in fact, the only creator and He creates the actions of His creation; using the same notion as al-Ashʿarī of individuals 'acquiring' their actions, al-Māturīdī suggests that this acquisition is connected to the choice or intention which precedes an act. This is to be distinguished from al-Ashʿarī's sense of acquisition being the contemporaneous coming into the possession of the capacity to act at the time of the action. Evil deeds, while predetermined by God, are the actions of the individual as a consequence of the choice and intention to do such acts.

For a century after the death of al-Māturīdī, his teaching does not seem to have been of much importance, not drawing the attention of even Ashʿarite opponents for some 150 years. The reason for this neglect undoubtedly lies in the fact of al-Māturīdī's residency in Samarqand and thus being well away from the centre of Islamic intellectual activity. The position of al-Māturīdī is generally presented as being a development of ABŪ ḤANĪFA's stance, which had already spread to Samarqand by al-Māturīdī's time. Abū Ḥanīfa's position as eponym of the Ḥanifite legal school allowed al-Māturīdī's later followers to argue for the acceptance of their theological stance in areas outside Samarqand which were already dominated by the Ḥanifite legal school; they argued this on the basis of this previous relationship between the two schools of thought. The spread and the eventual success of the school was a result of the conversion of Turks in Central Asia to Islam of this Ḥanafite-Maturidite persuasion. The theological position of later Maturidism is represented for example in the *ʿaqīda* or creed of al-Nasafī (*d.*1142), which has proven popular throughout the Muslim world, attracting many commentaries and elaborations even from Ashʿarites. [32; 88; 105: V] (A.R.)

Maudgalyāyana. *See* MOGALLĀNA.

Maurice, Frederick Denison [VI.A] (1805–1872). English Anglican clergyman and social reformer. He was born at Normanstone, near Lowestoft into a Unitarian family. His mother and three older sisters left Unitarianism for a form of Calvinism. He went to Trinity College, Cambridge, in 1823 and in 1825 to Trinity Hall. He was unable to graduate because he refused to subscribe to the Thirty-Nine Articles of Religion of the Church of England. Following a deep conversion experience which began in 1828, in 1830 he was baptized in the Church of England and went to Exeter College, Oxford. He was ordained in 1834. He served a curacy in

Warwickshire where he wrote *Subscription No Bondage* (1835). In 1836 he became chaplain of Guy's Hospital, London and published *The Kingdom of Christ* (1838). The book roused some hostility. In 1840 he became professor of English literature and history at King's College, London and in 1846 chaplain of Lincoln's Inn and professor of divinity. In 1848 he was one of the founders of the Christian Socialist movement. In 1853 he published *Theological Essays*, which stirred up even more hostility. He attacked the notions of eternal punishment and that eternity meant endless time. He was forced to resign. After founding a Working Men's College in 1854 and being chaplain of St Peter's, Vere Street, he became professor of Moral Philosophy at Cambridge and in 1870 incumbent of St Edward's, Cambridge. His other works include writings on the New Testament and on moral theology. [533; 534; 668; 824] (T.T.)

Mawdūdī, Mawlānā Sayyid Abū'l-aʿlā [XII] (1903–1979). Founder of the Jamāʿat-i Islāmī in India (1941) and a major religio-political leader in Pakistan. Educated in both modern and traditional sciences, Mawdūdī spent the initial period of his working life as a journalist and later became editor of the leading Indian Muslim newspaper, *al-Jamʿiyyat*. He resigned from this position in 1928 in order to devote himself to writing, taking up the editorship of the monthly religious magazine *Tarjumān al-Qur'ān* in 1933. This magazine became a major vehicle for the promulgation of his views.

A return to the Qur'ān and *ḥadīth* was the essence of his call in order to revitalize Islam, the true vision of which had been obscured through the ages. Opposed to all nationalism as non-Islamic, he resisted the formation of a Muslim state in India, but when faced with its creation in 1947 he moved to Pakistan and attempted to use political means to put his ideas into practice in the formation of a truly Muslim state. Socio-political issues became the focus of his attentions and he and his party became major forces in the political opposition in the country, denouncing the government for its failure to institute the Islamic *sharīʿa*. He was a prolific writer; one bibliography (8: I] lists 138 works, many of which have been translated into several languages. One of his most famous works is *Rasā'il-i Dīniyāt* ('Towards Understanding Islam', 1933), written in Urdu and translated into at least 14 languages, which argues for the rationality of the belief in God and the finality and superiority of Islam. He is also well known for his Urdu translation and commentary of the Qur'ān, *Tafhīm al-Qur'ān* (1949–72). [1: VI; 4; 6: XII] (A.R.)

Maximus the Confessor [VI.B] (*c*.580–662). The outstanding Greek theologian of the 7th century, defended Chalcedonian orthodoxy during the Monothelite controversy. After 25 years in North Africa he was arrested in 653 by order of Constans II (642–68) and taken to Constantinople to be tried for treason. He died in 662 after undergoing mutilation for his persistent criticism of Monotheletism. Hence his title 'confessor'. His writings hold in tension the two doctrines of 'deification' and 'apophaticism' of the Greek patristic tradition. Taking the relationship of the divine and the human in Christ as paradigm, he shows the interdependence of the spiritual and the material, not only in the individual but in all of creation. His cosmic vision of Christian salvation is apparent in his *Mystagogia*, an exposition of the symbolism of the liturgy. [9; 12; 86] (K.P.)

Māyā, Queen [IV] [Mahāmāya]. Wife of king Suddhodana, mother of the BUDDHA and elder sister of MAHĀPAJĀPATI. She is said to have been between 40 and 50 years of age when the Buddha was born. Some texts suggest that the Buddha's conception took place without sexual intercourse. On the day of conception she dreamt that she was transported to the Himalayas, where the Buddha entered her side in the form of a white elephant. The child was born in Lumbinī (in modern Nepal) while Māyā was travelling to her home town; she gave birth standing up and holding on to a Sal tree (*shorea robusta*), a scene often represented in Buddhist art. She died a week later, and was reborn in a heaven as the god Mahādevaputta; the Buddha later went there and preached the third and last portion of the scriptures, the *Abhidharma* (Pali: *Abhidhamma*). [150: vol. 2: 608–18] (S.C.)

Mazdak [XXVI] (6th century). Iranian prophet, regarded as a Zoroastrian heretic. He apparently refounded a religion taught earlier by Zardušt Khurragān, a Zoroastrian priest who, it seems, claimed new insight into ZOROASTER's teachings by finding inner meanings in the Avesta. In the early 6th century Iran was weakened by wars and heavy taxation, which bore crushingly on the peasantry; Mazdak, a charismatic figure, developed Zardušt's essentially ethical and soteriological teachings into a militant movement which seriously threatened traditional society and religion. Knowledge of this movement comes from external sources, which concentrate on its social aspects. Mazdak, it appears, sought to abolish class distinctions, redistribute wealth, free women from the harems of the rich, and care for the needy. He is also said to have demanded the closure of many fire-temples. His moral philosophy was that people are corrupted by the demons Envy, Wrath, Vengeance, Need and Greed. Equality of rank and possessions would defeat these and enable all to be righteous. Doctrinally Mazdakism was a gnostic faith, with typical admixture of Zurvanite Zoroastrian with Semitic and Greek elements. There was belief in a remote supreme Being, and two 'managers' of this world, one good, one evil, born of the mingling of water, fire and earth. On the side of good are four Powers, seven viziers and twelve spiritual forces. When all these enter a man he becomes godly and freed from religious obligations. The supreme Being rules by power of the supreme Name, and those who learn the letters of which this is composed have the key to the Great Secret and will be saved. Mazdak succeeded in converting king Kavād, but was put to death by KHOSROW I, who persecuted his adherents ruthlessly. The movement survived secretly and contributed to the formation of certain extreme Shiʿite Islamic groups. [11: vol. 3: 991–1024] (M.B.)

Meher Baba [XIX] [Merwan Shehiar Irani] (1894–1969). Indian guru who built up a following of 'Baba Lovers' in India and the West. He was born in Poona as Merwan Shehiar Irani to Zoroastrian parents (*see* ZOROASTER), who had immigrated from Persia. He was educated at a Christian high school, then Deccan College, until he 'was given God-Realization' by Hazrat Babajan, 'an ancient Mohammedan woman and one of the five Perfect Masters of the Age' [31: 365]. This experience left him in a semi-conscious state for nine months, during which, it is claimed, he did not eat. He then began to travel, meeting other spiritual teachers. Upasni Maharaj, a Hindu Perfect Master, gave Merwan 'Gnosis' or Divine Knowledge over a seven-year period and, in 1921, pronounced him a Satguru. Merwan then established an ashram in Bombay where his followers gave him the name Meher Baba (Compassionate Father). The group included Muslims, Hindus and Zoroastrians, who would attend places of worship of their own faith as well as joining in daily meditation at the ashram. Meher Baba's teachings were, they felt, compatible with and transcendent of their own particular paths. [37: 176]

In 1924, after a period of travel with his disciples, Meher Baba established Meherabad, a colony near Ahmednagar with shelters for the poor, a free school, hospital and dispensary. Disciples were trained in moral discipline, love for God, spiritual understanding and selfless service.

In 1925 Meher Baba announced that he would observe Silence; in 1927 he ceased writing and used an alphabet board to dictate his messages and main works [34; 35]; in 1954 he reduced all communication to gestures.

The period 1936–49 was devoted to finding and bringing together in ashrams the 'masts' or 'God-intoxicated' throughout India, thus creating accumulators of spiritual energy to help humanity through the war years.

Meher Baba travelled to the West on several occasions. His United States disciples established the Meher Spiritual Center at Myrtle Beach, South Carolina; other centres have continued to be formed since his death.

Baba Lovers accept Meher Baba's claim to be the Avatar of the Age [31: 365]. His message was the metaphysical unity of all persons, and that by loving him, Baba Lovers could learn to love others. In the highest state of love, Divine Love, the distinction between the lover and the beloved ceases and one attains union with God. [37: 177; 34; 35] (E.B.)

Meherjī Rānā [XXVI] (*d.*1592). Learned Zoroastrian priest of Navsari, Gujarat. When in 1573 the Mogul emperor AKBAR questioned Parsis in Surat about their beliefs, Meherjī was fetched to expound these. In 1578 he was summoned to Akbar's court to join in a discussion between adherents of different religions. Akbar, impressed by

Meherjī's contribution, is said to have adopted certain Zoroastrian observances, and to have kept a sacred fire burning continually thereafter at his court. He abolished the poll-tax (*jizya*) for Parsis; and in Navsari the title 'Great Dastūr' was conferred in gratitude on Meherjī. This is still held by his descendants. [9: 182; 34: vol. 2: 3–4] (M.B.)

Meir of Rothenburg [XV] [known by the acronym, Maharam] (*c.*1215–1293). German Jewish talmudic scholar, codifier and liturgical poet. He came from a family of noted scholars and studied in talmudic academies in France and Germany. He officiated as a rabbi in various German communities, eventually in Rothenburg, where he remained for over 40 years, and his authority was widely recognized. In 1286 he was imprisoned by Emperor Rudolf I and an enormous sum was demanded for his release. As the emperor regarded this as payment of tax and the Jews were not prepared to recognize his right to tax them, the sum was not paid and Meir remained in prison, where he continued to write and study for seven years until his death. His body was returned to the community only 13 years later, when it was redeemed for a large payment. It was buried in the cemetery in Worms where the grave is still visited.

Meir was the author of comments on the Talmud, elucidating difficult issues. About a thousand of his *responsa* (answers to religious legal queries) are known, dealing with many subjects including the regulations for blessings, ritual slaughter and the laws of mourning. His presentation is clear and logical, and he was steeped in the writings of his predecessors. His endorsement was the source of the standardization of many customs in the home and synagogue. His writings on Jewish law proved highly influential, especially through his pupil ASHER BEN JEHIEL.

Meir also wrote religious poetry; many of his poems were incorporated in the Ashkenazi liturgy, including that of the Day of Atonement. [1] (G.W.)

Melanchthon, Philipp [VI.A] [Philipp Schwartzerd] (1497–1560). German scholar and leading figure of the Lutheran Reformation. He was born in Bretten, Germany and after receiving private tuition entered Heidelberg University at the age of 12. He was awarded the BA in 1511 but was barred from studying for an MA because he was deemed too young. He was awarded an MA in Tübingen in 1514. He published translations of classical literature and his own *Rudiments of the Greek Language* in 1518. He began to teach Greek at Wittenberg University in 1518 and came under the influence of MARTIN LUTHER. He studied theology while he taught and gained another bachelor's degree in 1519. Thereafter he taught the classics and theology. He married Katherine Krapp in 1530. In 1521 he published his *Loci communes rerum theologicarum* the first systematic statement of Protestant theology and followed this with translations and commentaries on the Bible. He participated in the Diet of Speyer and the Marburg Colloquy, where he opposed ULRICH ZWINGLI's eucharistic doctrine, in 1529. He was the leading figure at the Diet of Augsburg in 1530 and the author of the *Augsburg Confession* and the *Apology for the Augsburg Confession* (1531). He was responsible for the reform of German universities and schools and wrote many textbooks. He sought reconciliation between disputing Protestants and was irenic towards Rome, but to no avail. [516; 628; 693] (T.T.)

Melville, Andrew [VI.A] (1545–1622). Scottish religious reformer. He was born in Baldovie, near Montrose, and was educated at St Andrews University. He went to Paris in 1564 to study oriental languages and in 1566 to Poitiers to study civil law. Owing to the political situation in France he went to Geneva, where he became professor of humanity in the Academy. He returned to Scotland in 1574 and became principal of Glasgow University. He instituted many reforms and established chairs in languages, science, philosophy and theology. In 1572 he took leadership in the Church of Scotland. He drew up the *Second Book of Discipline*, largely inspired by the Genevan model. He became principal of St Mary's College, St Andrews in 1580, and a year later he led the General Assembly of the Church of Scotland to give full authority to the prebyteries as ecclesiastical courts and to ratify the *Second Book of Discipline*. This and other activity as Moderator of the Church in 1582 brought him into conflict with James VI of Scotland. He was charged with treason in Edinburgh in 1584 but fled to England. He returned the following year and was made Moderator again in 1587. He became Rector of St Andrews in 1590. Further conflict with the King led to the loss of this post, but he was made Dean of the Theology Faculty in St Andrews in 1599. After James's accession to the English throne he was summoned to London in 1606, charged before the Privy Council and confined to the Tower of London in 1607. He was released in 1611 to take up the chair of biblical theology in Sedan, France, at that time a Huguenot centre, and remained there for the rest of his life. [537; 881: 37–48] (T.T.)

Menander. *See* MILINDA.

Mencius. *See* MENG TZU.

Mendelssohn, Moses [xv] (1729–1786). German Jewish philosopher, enlightenment pioneer, communal leader and Bible translator. His own career foreshadowed the historical trend which he came to symbolize – the movement of the Jews out of the ghetto and into the world of European culture.

Born in Dessau, at the age of 14 he followed his rabbi-teacher to Berlin, where he continued his religious studies along with a general education. He earned his living as a merchant. Entering the city's intellectual élite (he was the first Jew to publish in German), in 1763 he received first prize for a paper in metaphysics from the Berlin Academy of Science (the other competitors included Kant). He became lionized by Berlin society, where he was known as 'the German Socrates'. His friend, the dramatist Gotthold Ephraim Lessing, based the title character in his play *Nathan the Wise* on Mendelssohn.

Until he was 40, Mendelssohn's prime interest was the dissemination of German culture. In 1769 a Swiss clergyman, Johann Caspar Lavatar, challenged him to prove the superiority of Judaism over Christianity. One effect of the ensuing controversy was that for the rest of his life Mendelssohn devoted himself primarily to Jewish matters and to the challenge of Jewish enlightenment and emancipation. He wished to prepare the Jews in German lands to enter the life about them. To do this he sought to familiarize them with the German language. He therefore translated the Pentateuch into German, publishing it in Hebrew letters so that the Jewish masses could read it. Together with like-minded colleagues he added a Hebrew commentary (*Be'ur*), written in a rationalist spirit. He fostered the foundation, in Berlin, of the first modern Jewish school in Germany and was the spiritual leader of Jewish emancipation.

His general philosophical work, *Phaedon*, was one of the most widely read and translated books of its day. Following the format of Plato's dialogues, it sought to prove human immortality, with arguments based solely on logic and reason. His only philosophical treatise on Judaism was entitled *Jerusalem, or On Religious Power and Judaism.* In its first part he pleaded for the separation of church and state. The state is charged with regulating social relationships, while the domain of religion is man's relationship with God. In the second part he addressed his critics, denying any conflict between his philosophical rationalism and his fidelity to Judaism. Judaism is in essence a rational non-doctrinal faith, directed towards the instruction of conscience. It is not a revealed religion but revealed legislation.

The trends ushered in by Mendelssohn were not without their dangers. As Jews entered German society and culture, many – including nearly all Mendelssohn's descendants (among them, the composer Felix Mendelssohn-Bartholdy) – chose to break all bonds with Judaism and embrace Christianity. Nevertheless, Mendelssohn exemplified the symbiosis of European culture with faithful adherence to Jewish tradition, which was to characterize the modern era of Jewish history. [3] (G.W.)

Menes. *See* NARMER.

Meng Tzu [v] [Mencius] (*c*.390–305 BCE). One of the earliest and most important systematic or quasi-systematic thinkers to take up K'UNG TZU's legacy. Born in the small principality of Tsou, a dependency of Lu (in present-day Shantung province), he was sponsored and supported by king Hsüan of Ch'i, and also gained a hearing from king Hui of Liang. Neither, though, seems to have taken Meng Tzu very seriously. The Chinese historian Ssu-ma Ch'ien (?145–?90 BCE) says of him that 'he never secured a sympathetic hearing no matter where he went'. [45: 258]

The literary work preserved under Meng Tzu's name [33] must, as it now stands, be a compilation produced by his disciples, just as is that preserved under K'ung Tzu's name. But Meng's work differs from his predecessors' in that it contains not just aphorisms but also extended dialogues and sustained discussions of theoretical matters. He presents the tradition of the Literati (Confucians) as the proper middle path between the extremes of Mo Tzu's (*c.*480–390 BCE) logic-chopping and Yang Chu's (*c.*395–335 BCE) egoism [24], and emphasizes the innate capacity (*hsing*) of human beings for proper action without regard for the short-term benefits of such action. Meng's importance for the later Literati lies in the rich resources found in his work for the systematic development of this theme. (P.J.G.)

Menno Simons. *See* SIMONS, MENNO.

Mercier, Désiré Joseph [VI.A] (1851–1926). Belgian Catholic cardinal and scholar. He was born at Braine-l'Alleud, near Waterloo, Belgium. He studied philosophy and theology at Malines, was ordained priest in 1874 and gained a licentiate in theology at Louvain University in 1877. The same year he became professor of philosophy at the Petit Séminaire at Malines and in 1882 the first professor of Thomist philosophy at Louvain following the revival of Thomism as a result of the papal encyclical *Aeterni Patris* of 1879. In 1889, with papal approval, he set up the Institut Supérieur de Philosophie in Louvain. In 1906 he was made Archbishop of Malines and a cardinal in 1907. A critic of Modernism, he published a Lenten Pastoral in 1908 in which he denounced GEORGE TYRRELL. During the First World War he defended the rights of his people against the German invaders. After the war he took a lead in encouraging ecumenical action with the Orthodox churches and was responsible on the Roman Catholic side for the Malines Conversations (1921, 1923, 1925) with representatives of the Church of England, a movement which ended upon his death. His published works include *Psychologie* (1892), *Logique* (1894), *Métaphysique* (1894) and *Critériologie* (1899). He founded the *Revue néo-scolastique de philosophie* in 1894. [281; 546; 547] (T.T.)

Merton, Thomas [VI.A] (1915–1968). American Trappist monk. He was born in Prades, France, of artist parents. The family moved to New York City to avoid the First World War. He was educated there and in Bermuda, France and England before entering Clare College, Cambridge and later Columbia University, New York. He converted to Roman Catholicism in 1938. In 1939 he was awarded an MA in literature at Columbia. He began research on the English Jesuit poet Gerald Manley Hopkins and taught English at Saint Bonaventure University in New York State until he entered the abbey of Gethsemani, Kentucky, and the Cistercian Order of Strict Observance in 1941. Later he took a public stance on political and social matters, such as opposition to American participation in the Vietnam war, opposition to nuclear arms and support for American Black civil rights. Towards the end of his life he became interested in Hindu and Buddhist spirituality, especially Zen Buddhism with its emphasis on experience rather than dogma. He died in Bangkok through accidental electrocution. His works include many volumes of poetry, works on mysticism and *Seven Storey Mountain*, an autobiography. [568; 616] (T.T.)

Mgijima, Enoch [I.A] (1858–1928). Founder of the 'Israelites' in South Africa in 1912, one of the few examples of movements which regard themselves as African Jews. From 1918 Mgijima's anti-colonial message and forceful personality attracted a number of followers to the Bulhoek location (near Queenstown). There he founded an 'Israelite' colony, of which he became the 'Bishop, Prophet and Watchman'. He advocated the keeping of the Sabbath, an annual Passover festival at Bulhoek, and taught that the New Testament was a European fabrication. The Israelites looked forward, as God's chosen people, to their deliverance from white bondage. In 1921 military forces dismantled some 300 unlicensed dwellings, but Mgijima had told his people that the bullets of the white man would turn to water. The tragic outcome was the death of well over 100 of the prophet's 500 Israelites. The Bulhoek incident served to harden government suspicions about the potential political subversion of the independent churches in South Africa. The Israelites still existed in the 1950s, and wore small photographs of Ngijima on their clothes, acknowledging him as their founder. [34: 72–3; 42: 61–3] (R.H.)

Micah [XV] (8th century BCE). Israelite prophet. He came from the southern coastal plain of the Land of Israel and at least one of his prophecies was directed to this region (see *Micah* 1: 10–16). The major part of his utterances was spoken in Jerusalem during the reigns of the kings of Judah, Jotham, Ahaz and Hezekiah, and were addressed to both the southern and northern kingdoms. This was a period which saw the expansion of the Assyrian empire and the decline in the fortunes of the northern kingdom of Israel, whose downfall was foreseen by the prophet. According to the prophet Jeremiah (*Jeremiah* 26: 18–19), Micah also prophesied the destruction of Jerusalem but this was averted by King Hezekiah's repentance.

Micah was a contemporary of the prophet ISAIAH, and there are similarities in their messages as well as differences. Micah condemns the nation's sins; its leaders in particular are castigated for their social transgressions, especially for the oppression of the poor and the perversion of justice. His teaching is summarized in his statement that the Lord requires 'only to do justice, to love mercy and to walk humbly with your God' (*Micah* 6: 8). He does not become involved in political aspects, such as objecting to foreign alliances, while idolatry and sexual misdemeanours figure only marginally in his denunciations. Micah stresses God's role in history, expressing his confidence in divine salvation and the redemption of Israel from the exile he foresaw. [38: V]

Micah's prophecies are contained in the biblical book bearing his name. (G.W.)

Michelangelo Buonarroti [VI.A] (1475–1564). Italian sculptor and painter. He was born in Caprese, Italy. Soon after his birth his family moved to Florence. In 1488 he was apprenticed to Domenico Ghirlandaio for three years though he only stayed a few months. He went on to a school in the Medici Garden under the patronage of Lorenzo de' Medici ('the Magnificent'), and supervised by Bertoldo. In 1496 he went to Rome and sculpted his first well known piece, the *Pietà* now in St Peter's. In 1501 he returned to Florence and was there for four years, during which time he completed *David*, the *Bruges Madonna* and the unfinished *St Matthew*. He was called back to Rome by Pope Julius II to build his tomb. The first grand design gave way to smaller designs but eventually only *Moses* was installed on the finished tomb, with two completed *Slaves* and a number of unfinished ones left of the original design. Between 1508 and 1512 he painted the ceiling of the Sistine Chapel. In 1513 he was back in Florence and in 1520 he began the design of the Medici funerary chapel attached to the church of San Lorenzo but the work did not begin until 1524, at which time he also designed the Laurentian Library. In 1534 he went back to Rome and was there for the rest of his life, working on the *Last Judgement* in the Sistine Chapel from 1536 to 1541. Other important religious works are the two *Pietàs*, one in Florence Cathedral and the *Pietà Rondanini*, on which he was working a few days before his death. [349; 804] (T.T.)

Míguez Bonino, José [VI.A] (1924–). Argentinian liberation theologist. He was born in Santa Fe, Argentina and studied in Buenos Aires and the United States. Ordained a Methodist minister in 1948, he carried out pastoral duties in Bolivia and Argentina until 1954, since when he has been lecturer and professor of systematic theology in Buenos Aires and abroad. An observer at the Second Vatican Council (1962–5) and long-standing member of the Presidium of the World Council of Churches, he has been a bold campaigner for human rights – 'for life and against death' – through many hard years in his native land. His *Doing Theology in a Revolutionary Situation* (1975) was a leading Protestant contribution to the development of liberation theology. He has devoted considerable attention, in a wide variety of writings, to the capitalism–socialism debate and Christian–Marxist dialogue. Further important works from Latin America's foremost ethicist of Protestant liberation include *Towards a Christian Political Ethics* (1983). [260: 39–41; 297: 313–14; 551] (A.C.S.)

Mihr-narseh [XXVI] (4th–5th century). Chief minister of the Sasanian kings Yazdegird I, Vahrām V and Yazdegird II (reigned 399–457). He was an enlightened and cultured man, and a devout Zoroastrian of the Zurvanite persuasion. An inscription on a bridge built by him near Firuzabad in Fars asks a blessing for himself and his sons from those crossing it. All three sons also held high office, and Mihr-Narseh endowed fire-temples in four villages for his and their souls' sake. A letter by him to the Armenians (then converted to Christianity), seeking to win them back to Zoroastrianism, is an important document for knowledge of Zurvanite beliefs. [9: 121–2; 14: 277–8; 48: 75–6, 106, 108–12, 113; 57: 39–47] (M.B.)

Miki Tokuchika [XIV] (1900–). The son and successor of MIKI TOKUHARU. After the Second World War and his release from prison Miki Tokuchika re-established Hito-no-michi and P[erfect] L[iberty] Kyōdan. He taught that all activities – housekeeping, working in a factory, farming etc. – could be forms of art, and that 'living life as art' is the highest goal. Known to his followers as Oshieoya ('Teaching Parent'), he organized Perfect Liberty Kyodan into an effective *oyako* ('parent-child') hierarchical organization. This religion continues to follow the 21 precepts revealed by Kanada Tokumitsu (known as the 'hidden founder') and Miki Tokuharu, whose tomb is a principal Perfect Liberty Kyōdan shrine. These precepts include: the individual is a manifestation of deity; the true self is revealed when one's ego is effaced; there is one way for men and another for women; the environment is the mirror of the mind; one should attain the perfect harmonious state of mind and matter; one should live in perfect liberty.

Miki Tokuchika led Perfect Liberty Kyōdan followers in efforts to realize the full value of the first precept that 'Life is art'. He taught that true happiness is achieved through the expression of one's own authentic true nature. Whether one is a teacher, a housewife, or a painter, the expression of oneself can transform the mundane into art and spirit. Perfect Liberty Kyōdan sponsors nationally ranked high school sports teams, hospitals and medical research facilities, and is a major patron of the arts. [2; 12: 178–205; 34: 319–21; 41: 123–44; 59: 183–98] (G.E.)

Miki Tokuharu [XIV] (1871–1938). Founder of Hito-no-michi, one of the many Japanese new religions to begin in the early 20th century. Originally an Ōbaku Zen priest, he joined Tokumitsukyō, founded by Kanada Tokumitsu (1863–1919), which was itself affiliated with the mountain sect Mitakekyō. Kanada believed that the phenomenal world is a manifestation of the one deity, symbolized by the sun and known as Dainichi Nyorai in Shingon Buddhism and Amaterasu in Shintō. All people share the nature of this deity and so are equal. After Kanada's death, Miki claimed to be his spiritual heir. Following his master's deathbed instructions, Miki planted a memorial tree and worshipped there daily for the next five years. He had three mystical experiences; these led him to found his own group, which he announced as the successor to Tokumitsukyō. In 1931 he renamed it Hito-no-michi ('The Way of Man'); its name was then changed to P[erfect] L[iberty] Kyōdan ('The Religion of Perfect Liberty') after the Second World War.

Miki incorporated many of Kanada's beliefs and practices, including *ofurikae*, a practice through which members transfer their sufferings to the founder, Miki, who then, like a bodhisattva, takes them upon himself. Miki emphasized harmonious relations within the traditional family structure, industriousness and the material rewards of virtue. Initially his teachings were attractive to merchants in Osaka. Miki suggested that though the Chinese characters for 'virtue' and 'profit' are different, the fact that they are homonyms (both are read *toku*) indicates their essential identity. He also inaugurated the practice of morning gatherings (*asamairi*), where a sermon, liturgy and testimonials were offered, and a free communal meal served. In the 1930s Miki sought accommodation with the government and with State Shintō, recognizing Amaterasu as the supreme deity and accepting the state's interpretation of the *Kojiki* [49] imperial myths, as well as the Imperial Rescript on Education. Nevertheless, the government was not appeased and took legal action against Hito-no-michi in 1936. Although Miki stepped down as head of the movement, turning control over to his son MIKI TOKUCHIKA, he was arrested two days later and died in 1938 while on bail from prison. He is venerated by his posthumous *kami*-name Amamizu-umihi-arawaru-hiko-no-mikoto. [2; 12: 178–205; 34: 319–21; 41: 123–44; 59: 183–98] (G.E.)

Mi-la Ras-pa. *See* MILAREPA.

Milarepa [IV] [Mila; Mi-la Ras-pa]

(1040–1123). The best known and best loved of Tibetan Buddhist saints. According to the standard Tibetan biography of Milarepa, compiled almost 400 years after his death [140], while Milarepa was still young, his father died and his family was dispossessed of its wealth and reduced to begging. As a young man, Mila sought to destroy those who had wronged him and eventually brought about the deaths of many people through sorcery. Realizing the enormity of his deed, Mila wanted to redeem himself through Buddhism, and so searched out and studied under a master named Marpa, a Tibetan who had made several trips to India and was in possession of the Vajrayāna teachings of the *siddhas* (tantric Buddhist adepts) TILOPA and NĀROPA. After many years of strenuous discipleship under the demanding and wrathful Marpa, Mila finally received the teachings he ardently desired, and was recognized as chief disciple by Marpa. The latter, in accord with his tradition, encouraged Milarepa to meditate in strict retreat. Milarepa embraced the contemplative life and, walling himself up in caves for months and even years at a time, spent most of the rest of his long life meditating, eventually being recognized as an enlightened master. In spite of his seclusion, many disciples, both lay and monastic, were attracted to him, and he encouraged many of these to enter upon the anchoritic life.

Milarepa is regarded as one of the founding fathers of the Kagyu school of Tibetan Buddhism, a school which emphasizes meditation and strict retreat. He is also of pan-Tibetan importance since he represents the paradigmatic Tibetan Buddhist anchorite, an example to all, of whatever station and background, of humility, devotion to the guru, and ardent meditation. Two collections of songs of realization are attributed to him, one found in the *Hundred Thousand Songs of Milarepa* [34], and the other in *Drinking by the Mountain Stream* [128] and *Miraculous Journey* [129]. His lineage of meditating yogins survives in contemporary times in the person of cotton-clad hermits living in the Himalayas who continue to express their realization and to teach through the singing of songs of realization. (R.R.)

Milinda [IV] [Menander] (mid-2nd century BCE). A Greek ruler of Bactria (modern Afghanistan). He is known through coins and the writings of Greek historians, and also as a character in the Buddhist text *Milindapañha* ('The Questions of Milinda') [99], composed from the 1st century CE on. This text is a dialogue between the king and a Buddhist monk called Nāgasena, about whom nothing else is known; it deals with a number of important doctrinal issues, and is frequently cited in modern Theravādin writings. The text is extant in Pali and Chinese, but it seems to have been composed in India, and may have been originally in Sanskrit or Prakrit; it also shows signs of Sarvāstivāda influence. The king is said in the text to have been converted to Buddhism; archaeological evidence from the area shows that it was normal for kings there, as in India, to support a number of different traditions. [136: 419–26] (S.C.)

Milton, John [VI.A] (1608–1674). English poet. He was born in London and educated at St Paul's School, London and Christ's College, Cambridge. His first important poem, *Ode on the Morning of Christ's Nativity*, was written in 1629. From 1632 to 1638 he lived on his father's estate in Horton, Buckinghamshire. He turned against the established church and its clergy and expressed his criticism in *Lycidas* (1637). He travelled in Italy in 1638 and when he returned settled in London and became involved in ecclesiastical and political controversy. In 1641 he joined the Presbyterians and a little later he wrote *The Reason of Church Government Urged against Prelacy*. He married in 1643 but his wife soon left him. This event led to *The Doctrine and Discipline of Divorce* in which he argued that the sacramental character of marriage was a clerical invention. The publication was discussed in Parliament and Milton wrote *Areopagitica* as a defence of the freedom of the press. In 1645, reconciled to his wife, he published his first book of *Poems*. After 1649 he was employed by the Commonwealth government and defended it in his writings. Following the restoration of the monarchy he left public life and turned again to poetry. Between 1658 and 1665 he wrote *Paradise Lost*; in 1671 its sequel *Paradise Regained* was published as well as *Samson Agonistes*, a poignant work in view of Milton's own blindness since 1651. [193; 556; 557] (T.T.)

Mindon Min [IV] (1814–1878). King of

Burma, 1853–78. His reign was notable for its social reforms and as a golden age of Burmese cultural and religious life. It was also of critical importance for the modern social organization of the Buddhist monastic order in Burma.

Like MONGKUT in Thailand, Mindon spent time in monasteries before he became king, and it is reported that he met the SHWEGYIN SAYADAW while he was a monk. Mindon became king after the Second Anglo-Burmese War in 1852 and he was forced to accept British annexation of lower Burma (Pegu). Subsequently many of Mindon's actions as king were meant to prevent further inroads into his kingdom by the British, but he was also significantly involved with religious affairs.

Mindon built a new capital at Mandalay and sought to make it a centre of Buddhist learning. Perhaps because of his own background as a monk, Mindon showed great interest in monastic reform. In part, reforms were necessary because of the dislocations suffered by the Burmese *saṅgha* at the beginning of the colonial period. But, in addition, monastic reform was an important way of constituting proper kingship in the Theravādin tradition. In 1871 Mindon convened his 'Fifth' Buddhist Council, with the purpose of purifying the text of the Pali canon; the revised text was inscribed on stone at Mandalay. Mindon was often directly involved in monastic affairs, and not above playing off sides in monastic disputes. He established the independent status of the Shwegyin sect in the Burmese *saṅgha*. Mindon's acceptance of sectarian movements with the Buddhist monastic order allowed the *saṅgha* to develop a new social organization which, in turn, enabled it to survive the cultural disruptions of the colonial period that followed the overthrow of Mindon's son, Thibaw, in 1885. [157: II] (C.H.)

Mīrābāī [XI] (late 16th–early 17th century). Poetess and Kṛṣṇa-devotee. The popularity of this 'poet-saint' grows with the passing centuries: but as with so many of her Vaiṣṇava contemporaries, her historical biography is obscured by the accretions of legend. Apparently a Rajput princess from Merta, she became a fervent devotee of Kṛṣṇa, expressing in her lyric poems the turbulent emotions of an intensely personal devotional love; the directness, urgency and plangency of her poetic voice distinguishes her from the more moderate attitudes of contemporary *bhakti* poets such as SŪRDĀS, for whom a female yearning for the male deity had to be contrived by assuming the identity of a *gopī*. Mīrā was, according to legend, married off to a prince from a Rajput dynasty allied to her own family; but she preferred the company of pious folk to the ties of domestic relationships, and so incurred the displeasure of her in-laws, who tried to poison her. The seeds of such stories lie in cryptic references in the poems themselves, and may allude to a merely symbolic dissociation from worldly things, but they are elaborately developed as literal narrative by the hagiographers. Mīrā's songs, directed to Kṛṣṇa as 'Holder of Govardhan mountain', are widely sung throughout Northern India, and make her the archetypal devotee in the popular imagination. Though her songs primarily celebrate the beauty and charm of Kṛṣṇa's physical attributes, they show too some traces of a familiarity with the terminology, at least, of the *nirguṇ* mode of 'non-qualified' devotionalism favoured by such figures as KABĪR. Great uncertainty surrounds the history of poems attributed to Mīrā, which have been transmitted and expanded variously in Rajasthani, in Gujarati and in Brajbhāṣā Hindi; but the tone of an impassioned longing for union, flying in the face of worldly values, pervades and typifies the popular corpus. [2; 38; 77: 80–81] (R.S.)

Mīrzā Ghulām Aḥmad Qādiyānī [XII] (*c.*1835–1908). Eponymous founder of the Aḥmadiyya sect within Islam. Born the son of a courtier and landowner in the Punjab, he received a traditional education intended to prepare him for the law or government service under the British. His early life appears to have been devoted to legal affairs and the administration of his family estates, combined with much prayer and meditation. By 1877, however, Aḥmad gave up involvement in secular matters to devote himself entirely to Islamic propaganda.

In 1880 he began publication of his *magnum opus*, the *Barāhīn-i Aḥmadiyya*, a four-volume work composed in Urdu, the aim of which was to revitalize Islam. As early as 1882 he claimed to have received divine appointment as the *mujaddid* or renewer of Islam, and in

1889 publicly announced the establishment of a brotherhood whose members pledged personal allegiance to him. Two years later he proclaimed himself the promised Messiah (*masīḥ maw'ūd*) and Mahdī, thereby stirring up serious opposition within the Muslim community. At a later stage he claimed to be an *avatar* of Krishna, Jesus (*see also* 'ĪSĀ) returned to earth, and the manifestation (*burūz*) of MUḤAMMAD.

Whether he actually claimed to be a prophet (*nabī*) and, if so, what he meant by the term, continues to be a matter for dispute between the two branches into which the Aḥmadī movement divided after his death. The majority based at Qādiyān regard him as a full prophet after Muḥammad, whereas the minority faction centred on Lahore consider him simply a reformer and see their position as closer to that of Sunnī orthodoxy.

Ghulām Aḥmad taught a number of novel doctrines, including the belief that Jesus did not die on the cross but was resuscitated and travelled to Kashmir, where he finally died and was buried at the age of 120. [9; 11] (D.M.)

Moctezuma I [XVIII] [Moctezuma Ilhuicamina] (15th century). Fifth ruler of Tenochtitlan (reigned 1440–69). He was the cousin of his predecessor Itzcoatl. Moctezuma Ilhuicamina ('Angry Lord who Shoots into the Sky') presided over three types of expansions in Aztec history: the expansion of the empire into new territories, the enlargement of the Great Temple of Tenochtitlan and the increase in human sacrifices in the ceremonial cycles of the empire. Along with TLACAELEL, who assisted in the revisioning of a world-view dedicated to war and sacrifice, he led the establishment of the Flowery Wars, periodic battlefield confrontations during peacetime in order to obtain sacrificial victims and re-establish political and territorial balances of power. [1] (D.C.)

Modi, Sir Jamshedji Jivanji [XXVI] (1854–1933). Parsi scholar and hereditary priest-in-charge (*panthaki*) of a Bombay fire-temple. He received a Western-type schooling, and then studied Avestan and Pahlavi at the Sir J. JEEJEEBHOY Madressa. For 38 years secretary of the Parsi Panchayat, he wrote many books and articles, in Gujarati and English, on Zoroastrian rituals, customs, history, beliefs and folklore. He travelled and lectured widely, received much recognition from foreign learned societies, and a knighthood and the title Shams-ul-Ulema from the British Government. His major work is *The Religious Ceremonies and Customs of the Parsees* (1922; 2nd edn 1937; reprinted 1979). [1: 454–74] (M.B.)

Moffat, Robert [VI.A] (1795–1883). Scottish missionary in Southern Africa. He was born in Ormiston, East Lothian, and worked as a gardener. He was accepted by the London Missionary Society in 1817, and began his service with Khoikhoi in Namaqualand. He then moved to the Northern Cape, and his station at Kuruman (1821) became both a showpiece and an important base for activities northwards, not least by his son-in-law DAVID LIVINGSTONE. Moffat first made Setswana a written language and made a Setswan translation of the Bible. He visited the Ndebele in 1829 and thereafter in their migration to modern Zimbabwe, maintaining a friendship with Mzilikazi over many years. His book, *Missionary Labours and Scenes in South Africa* (1842), was one of the early missionary bestsellers. [252; 560; 593; 707; 836] (A.F.W.)

Moggallāna [IV] [Maudgalyāyana]. The second of the BUDDHA's two chief disciples, after SĀRIPUTTA, represented iconographically as standing at the Buddha's left side. The two were friends from childhood, and both decided to renounce the world after seeing a mime show. At first they were pupils of a teacher called Sañjaya, but later agreed to join whatever teacher could bring them Release. Sāriputta was the first to join the Buddha's community, and Moggallāna followed suit, becoming enlightened a week later. He was renowned for his magical powers, which allowed him to visit heavens at will, defeat demons and perform numerous wonders in the service of the Buddha's teaching. Despite all this, he is said to have died a violent death as a result of a bad deed in a former life: he had murdered his parents, and as a result was brutally done to death by bandits. [150: vol. 2; 541–7] (S.C.)

Moggalliputta Tissa [IV] (*c.*322–342 BCE). Renowned in the Theravada Buddhist tradition as an enlightened monk at the time of the

Emperor Aśoka. He is alleged to have presided over a Third Council, at which the last section of the Buddhist Canon, the *Abhidhamma*, was finally closed when he composed an account of the various doctrinal controversies of the time, the *Kathāvatthu*, known in its English translation as 'Points of Controversy' [9]. (This is accepted as the 'Word of the Buddha' by the device of having the Buddha announce in advance – by means of his foreknowledge – the text's section-headings, which Moggaliputta Tissa then filled in.) It was at his instigation that Aśoka's two children, Mahinda and Saṅghamitta, were ordained; he was Mahinda's preceptor-teacher (*uppajjhāya*). Only the Pali tradition knows of him and the Third Council, however, and modern scholars have expressed scepticism about the full historicity of the accounts of them. [150: vol. 2, 644–6; 136: 204–5, 295–9] (S.C.)

Moghila, Peter [vi.a] (1596–1646). Moldavian Orthodox theologian. He was born in Moldavia and educated at the Orthodox school in Lwów. It is possible that he also studied at the University of Paris. He became abbot of the monastery of Caves in Kiev in 1627 and was made Metropolitan of Kiev in 1633. Many Orthodox Christians in the Ukraine of his time chose to submit to Rome. He was open to considering union with Rome, but meanwhile strengthened the position of the Orthodox church through education and doctrine. He introduced Western ideas through the medium of Latin in the college he opened in Kiev. Western influence was seen in his liturgical reforms and in the *Orthodox Confession of Faith* for which he was largely responsible and which he wrote in 1639–40. He employed the term 'transubstantiation' and maintained that the moment of the consecration of the bread and wine in the liturgy occurred at the words of institution, the words of Christ at the last supper, rather than at the epiclesis of the Holy Spirit, a prayer for the descent of the Holy Spirit on the bread and wine. He also adopted the Roman teaching on Purgatory. The *Confession* had to be radically altered before it was given the approval of the Eastern patriarchs in 1643. Moghila resented these changes and maintained his teaching in a *Little Catechism* published in 1645. In other ways he was a traditional Orthodox, especially with regard to the *filioque* clause and papal primacy. [385; 514; 613] (T.T.)

Mohan Siṅgh Vaid [xxiii] (1881–1936). A distinguished medical practitioner, Mohan Siṅgh first became famous within Sikh circles at the turn of the century when he wrote several tracts in support of the Tat Khālsā initiative to transform Sikh life-cycle rituals, redraw sacred boundaries and separate Sikhs from Hindus [6: 27]. An early identification with Sikh religious causes made him a leading activist of the Siṅgh Sabhā movement, the Chief Khālsā Dīwān and later on the Akālī movement. To promote the ideologies of these movements and more specifically to advance social reform, education and Punjabi language among the Sikhs, Mohan Siṅgh wrote hundreds of books and tracts. (H.S.O.)

Möhler, Johann Adam [vi.a] (1796–1838). German Catholic church historian. He was born in Igersheim, Germany, and educated in Ellwangen seminary, which was incorporated into Tübingen University in 1817. He was ordained priest in 1819. After a year in a parish he returned to Tübingen to study philology but was persuaded to study church history with a view to teaching the subject in the seminary. In 1823 he began to teach church history, patristics and canon law. His first major work appeared in 1825, *Einheit in der Kirche*, in which he argued that the Romantic urge for unity originated in the church of the first three centuries. He also argued that the outward forms of the church are changeable. Although he is regarded by some as the precursor of Catholic Modernism he criticized such scholars as Schleiermacher, especially in his *Athanasius der Grosse*. In 1828 he became professor of church history at Tübingen. In 1832 he published the first edition of *Symbolik, oder Darstellung der dogmatischen Gegensätze der Katholiken und Protestanten*, a discussion of the credal basis of the church. It led to confrontation with the Protestant f. c. Baur. In 1835 Möhler moved to Munich. [505; 506] (T.T.)

Momis, John [xxi] (1942–). Melanesian Catholic priest, theologian and prominent politician. Born in Salamaua (Morobe, New Guinea), Momis was the son of a Buin from Bougainville, and came under the influence of the Marist missionaries. He trained for the priesthood at Bomana Seminary (then at Madang), was priested in 1972 and taught in a Marist school. He began writing on the bases for a Melanesian Christian society, and responded to pressures to put his ideals into practice through politics (from 1972). A gifted man, he was appointed as Deputy Speaker of the pre-Independence House of Assembly of Papua New Guinea. Fearing the threat of centralization at independence, after his chairmanship of the Constitutional Planning Committee he was among the leaders of the secessionist movement on Bougainville, which was backed by a ground-swell of Catholic sentiment, including the indigenous Bishop Gregory Singkai (1975) [18: 209–17]. Eventually compromising, he accepted the portfolio of Decentralization in the parliament of independent PNG (1977–82), and became the early architect of the country's provincial government. As Head of the Melanesian Alliance Party, he has served as Deputy Prime Minister under Michael Somare (1985), is now Minister for Provincial Affairs, and is the author of important articles on a just society. [28; 31; 35] (G.W.T.)

Mongkut [IV] [Rama IV] (1804–1868). The most important religious reformer in Thailand during the 19th century, first as a monk, and then as King Rama IV. Mongkut became a Buddhist monk shortly before the death of his father, Rama II, and remained in the *saṅgha* when he was passed over to succeed to the throne. Mongkut's monastic career was wide-ranging, beginning with an emphasis on ascetic practice and meditation, and moving to a serious study of the Pali language and authoritative Buddhist literature. The more that Mongkut learned of the Theravāda tradition, the more dissatisfied he became with the state of Thai Buddhism. He eventually became convinced that the Mon tradition of the Theravāda was purer than the Thai monastic fraternities. He and a number of followers were reordained in the Mon monastic lineage. Mongkut then began a reform of the daily practice, rituals, preaching and even the Pali pronunciation of his followers, who stood out as a group since they wore their monks' robes in the Mon fashion with both shoulders covered rather than just one. Mongkut's group was invited by the king to move to Wat Bowonniwet, a public acknowledgement of Mongkut's reformist order. This group Mongkut called *Thammayut* (*Dhammayuttika* – 'Adhering to Truth'). His reforms were in practice directed at upgrading monastic discipline, but they had a doctrinal side which permitted an openness to rationalism and science which had been introduced from Europe. The most dramatic instance of Mongkut's doctrinal reforms was his rejection of the traditional Theravādin cosmology on the grounds that it was not confirmed by empirical observation.

Mongkut became king of Thailand in 1851. He initiated a variety of social, economic and political reforms in an effort to modernize Thai society. As king, he provided patronage to the older *Mahanikai* monastic lineage, which he had broken away from as a monk, but he also supported and encouraged the activities of the *Thammayut* followers. He continued to look for ways to upgrade monastic discipline.

As both monk and king Mongkut set in motion the gradual but pervasive process of modernist reform that has shaped the character of contemporary Thai Buddhism. [258: XI] (C.H.)

Montanus [VI.A] (2nd century). A prophetic figure who gave his name to a charismatic and apocalyptic movement which existed from the second half of the 2nd century and lasted until the 4th or 5th centuries. Montanus began to prophesy in either 157–7 or 172, claiming that the Heavenly Jerusalem was about to descend on Pepuza in Phrygia. There were two women, Prisca and Maximilia, associated with him. Little is known of the details of his life and his teaching is known only from opponents of a later period, his own contemporaries' writings having been lost. In North Africa *c.*260 his movement had the support of TERTULLIAN, mainly for its attempts to return to the purity of the early pre-institutionalized church. Montanists wished to recapture glossolalia, the gift of prophecy and a restoration of ethical standards, including disallowing second marriages in expectation of an early second coming of Christ. Reports of him claim that he was a recent convert to Christianity when he began to prophesy and that he had been a priest at a pagan altar before then. Though he was a schismatic there is no real evidence that he was heretical. [448; 450: V, XVI–XVII] (T.T.)

Moody, Dwight Lyman [VI.A] (1837–1899). American evangelist. He was born in Northfield, Massachusetts. He left home in 1854 to work in Boston. He was received into the Congregational church in 1856, after which he moved to Chicago, again to work in boot and shoe salesmanship. He left business in 1860 to devote more time to religious work in his Sunday school. Between 1861 and 1865, the period of the Civil and Spanish wars, he worked with the YMCA, evangelizing among the wounded. He returned to Chicago in 1865 and began to organize state and international Sunday school teachers' conventions. Moody visited England in 1867. He met Ira Sankey, singer and musician, with whom he joined for evangelistic work in 1870, and they conducted an evangelistic tour of Britain from 1872 to 1875. In 1873 they published the *Sankey and Moody Hymn Book*. They conducted similar campaigns in Brooklyn, Philadelphia and New York in the winter of 1875–6 and in Boston in 1877. Moody returned to his home town and in 1879 founded the Northfield Seminary for Young Women and the Mount Hermon School for Young Men in 1881. Later he founded the Moody Bible Institute for the training of evangelists in Chicago. He travelled to England again in 1891–2 and in 1893 organized a mission at the World Trade Fair in Chicago. [262; 541] (T.T.)

Moon, Sun Myung [XIX] (1920–). Founder of the Unification Church, whose members are popularly known as 'Moonies'. He was born in a rural area of what is now North Korea. When he was 10 years old, his family converted to Christianity. On Easter Day 1936 Moon claims that JESUS appeared and told him that God had chosen him for a special task. For the next nine years, he is said to have discovered through prayer and spiritual communications with other religious leaders (such as MOSES and BUDDHA) and with God himself, revelations that were later to form the basis of Unification theology. [25: 1–2; 41: preface]

Moon studied electrical engineering in Japan, then worked as an electrician in Korea. After the end of the Second World War he started his own Church; but, always a controversial figure, he found himself arrested on several occasions, and spent a period in a labour camp under the communists. Many stories are told about the suffering and persecution that he endured. The Holy Spirit Association for the Unification of World Christianity was established in 1954.

In the *Divine Principle*, Moon teaches that the Fall was the result of Eve's having had a spiritual sexual relationship with Lucifer, then a physical sexual relationship with Adam. Their children were, consequently, born with 'fallen natures' [25: II]. History is interpreted as God's efforts to realize His original plan with the help of key individuals. Because Jesus was murdered before he had a chance to marry, he was able to offer only spiritual, not physical salvation to the world. [25: III, VII, XIII]

Moon's interpretation of the Bible reveals that the Messiah will have been born in Korea some time between 1917 and 1930 [25: 207]. In this role, Moon is believed to have laid the foundation for the restoration of God's kingdom by his marriage to his present wife in 1960 [25: 207]. Through the Holy Wine ceremony at which Moon officiates before mass wedding ceremonies, the participants are said to have their 'blood lineage' purified so that their children will be born without fallen nature. [42: 37–54]

Moon first visited the West in the late 1960s, when he delivered lectures transcribed as 'Master Speaks . . .' (later speeches have been entitled 'Reverend Sun Myung Moon Speaks on . . .'). Some of his teachings to his followers have been published (e.g. [24; 41; 42]). In the early 1970s he established his base in the United States. His movement came under the scrutiny of the Committee on International Relations of the House of Representatives with the Investigation of Korean–American Relations in 1978. No charges resulted from the investigation.

Moon has been the object of more suspicion and enmity than almost any other contemporary religious leader. He has been attacked for his theology, which has been described as blasphemy; his political beliefs, which are strongly anti-communist; his business empire, which is now immense, and in 1984 he went to prison for tax evasion. Among the numerous projects for which he and his movement are responsible are the Korean Folk Ballet, the Unification Theological Seminary, the Washington Institute, the *Washington Times*, the International Religious Foundation, the Collegiate Association for the Research of Principles (CARP), CAUSA, and a projected international highway that includes a tunnel between Japan and Korea.

The Unification Church has frequently appeared in the courts as both defendant and plaintiff. While the London *Daily Mail* successfully defended a libel case in which it had claimed that the movement brainwashed its members and split up families, the movement accuses its opponents of misrepresentation and discrimination, and it has gained the support of a number of non-members (especially among anti-communists and members of the Black churches) who admire Moon, his leadership and his accomplishments. (E.B.)

Morrison, Robert [VI.A] (1782–1834). English missionary and translator. He was born in Morpeth, Northumberland. He went to school in Newcastle-upon-Tyne and was apprenticed to his father as a boot-last maker. He joined the Church of Scotland in 1798 and went to Hoxton Academy, London, in 1803. He joined the London Missionary Society in 1804 and went to the Missionary Academy at Gosport, where he began to study Chinese. He was ordained in 1807 and left for China via America. He was not able to evangelize and was forced to go to Portuguese Macao. There in 1809 he married an English woman and was employed by the East India Company as a translator. He proceeded to translate the Bible into Chinese using an earlier Jesuit version. His was the first version produced by a Protestant. By 1814 he had published the whole New Testament and by 1823 the whole Bible. He also produced a Chinese grammar and the three-volume Chinese–English dictionary (1815–23). His first convert was baptized in 1814 and after 25 years only ten had been converted. In 1818 he founded the Anglo-Chinese College in Malacca. His wife died in China in 1822 and he returned to England in 1824. In 1826 he returned to China with his second wife and remained there until his death. [565; 682; 807] (T.T.)

Moses [VII; XV] (*c.*13th century BCE). Leader, prophet and lawgiver; seminal personality in the emergence of Judaism and the Israelite nation. (For an account of Moses in the Islamic tradition, *see* MŪSĀ.) The story of his life is to be found in the last four books of the Pentateuch. According to this account, his parents were of the tribe of Levi, enslaved with the rest of the Children of Israel in Egypt. When the Pharaoh ordered the drowning in the Nile of all their male children, Moses was hidden by his mother on the river's bank, where he was later discovered by an Egyptian princess, who adopted him and brought him up at court. However, after killing an Egyptian taskmaster whom he found maltreating a Hebrew slave, he fled to Midian. There he tended the flocks of the Midianite priest Jethro, whose daughter Zipporah he married. At the foot of Mount Horeb (identified with Mount Sinai), he experienced a theophany in which God spoke to him out of a bush which burned but was not consumed by the fire. Moses was instructed to return to Egypt to lead the Hebrews out of slavery. His reluctance to appear as a leader, because of his stammer, was overcome when God agreed that his brother AARON act as his spokesman.

The two appeared before Pharaoh, who refused to accede to the demand to release his Hebrew slaves. Only after the Egyptians had been afflicted by ten miraculous plagues, brought down at the instigation of Moses and Aaron, did Pharaoh eventually consent. Following the last plague, in which all the Egyptian firstborn males were killed, Pharaoh agreed to the departure of the slaves (who, according to the Bible, numbered 600,000) but after they had left changed his mind and pursued them. When the fugitives reached the banks of the Red Sea (in Hebrew, the Sea of Reeds, whose exact location is disputed) the sea – at Moses' command – parted to allow the Hebrews to cross; but when the Egyptian army pursued them it was drowned as the waters came together again. These events, known as the Exodus from Egypt, played a basic role in the formation of the Jewish national and religious consciousness. Moses' song of praise on the occasion is regularly recited in the Jewish liturgy.

A few weeks later, when the Hebrews reached Mount Sinai, a second traumatic event occurred. While the people remained at the foot of the mount, Moses went to its top on his own and remained there for 40 days and nights. He received the two tablets of stone on which were inscribed the Ten Commandments and was instructed by God in the entire legislation recorded in the Pentateuch (the Written Law). According to rabbinic tradition, Moses also received supplementary traditions which were committed to writing only some 15 centuries later (the Oral Law). At Sinai, God made a covenant with the Israelites, who voluntarily bound themselves to the One God while he undertook unfailingly to watch over Israel.

After Moses came down from the mountain he found that the people's faith had wavered in his absence; in his anger he broke the stones containing the Decalogue. However, he interceded with God to avert collective punishment of the people and once again ascended the mount to receive a second copy of the Ten Commandments. He then instructed the craftsman Bezalel in the building of a portable sanctuary. Its central feature was an ark in which were placed the two tablets of stone containing the Decalogue. This was henceforward the focus of the Israelite cult and was eventually placed in the temple built in Jerusalem by SOLOMON. Moses consecrated his brother Aaron as high priest, and he, together with his family, conducted the daily sacrificial ritual, according to the regulations laid down by Moses.

Moses proceeded to lead the people throughout the period of their wanderings in the Sinai desert. This lasted for 40 years, but for 38 of these they were quartered at Kadesh-Barnea. He had to cope with various waves of dissatisfaction and challenges to his leadership. He died at the age of 120 on Mount Nebo on the edge of the Promised Land, which he was not allowed to enter because he had disobeyed the Lord at Marah, where he had struck a rock instead of only speaking to it, as divinely instructed, in order to produce water. Before his death he assembled the people and presented them with a recapitulation of the Sinaitic legislation (contained in *Deuteronomy*, a word which means literally 'second law'), as well as his final blessing. He passed the leadership on to his devoted associate, Joshua. [xv: 45: 212–44].

Moses founded the nation, impressed on it the teaching of monotheism and developed the covenant, previously between God and the individual patriarchs, into one between God and the nation as a whole. As the people's great lawgiver, he lay down the legal code which formed the basis of Judaism. This comprehensive document not only incorporated details of the cult and sacrificial system but also a humanistic ethic whose influence was to extend far beyond the immediate confines of the Jewish people. He organized the judiciary, according to tradition with the initial advice of his father-in-law, Jethro. To the Jews the Mosaic-code as God-given was immutable, and although in the course of time new interpretations were introduced, the laws themselves, in the Orthodox tradition, cannot be changed. The same applied to the accepted text of the Pentateuch, which was regarded as of unique sanctity in the belief that it was all written by Moses under divine inspiration. In Jewish tradition Moses was considered the greatest of the prophets, thanks to the immediacy and intimacy of his knowledge of God. This was expressed by MAIMONIDES in his principles of faith which include the affirmation that 'the prophecy of Moses our master was true and that he was the greatest of all the prophets – both of those who preceded and those who followed him'. [xv: 12] (G.W.)

Although Moses was regarded by the Jews as a great spiritual leader and teacher and the Exodus as a milestone in their religious and political history, there is no known reference to these events in Egyptian sources. This is not surprising since the Egyptians would not have wished to record a successful and, for them, relatively unimportant uprising of their work-force. From the Egyptian sources, it is therefore impossible to establish a firm date for the Exodus. JOSEPHUS identified it with the expulsion of the Hyksos (*c*.1580 BCE), but most modern scholars would accept a date in Dynasty 19 (*c*.1200 BCE) [VII: 26].

The working conditions of the Hebrews which are described in the Bible (*Exodus* 1) appear to reflect conditions of life in the New Kingdom. By now the Hebrews were probably part of a group of itinerant labourers (the Apiru) who had lived in the eastern Delta for centuries, being engaged on various building projects. By Dynasty 19 they would have been employed to make bricks for the Delta cities of Avaris and Pi-Ramses.

Originally, scholars believed that Merenptah (1224–1214 BCE) was the Pharaoh of the Exodus, but in 1896 the Israel Stela was discovered. Merenptah had usurped this from Amenophis III and had it inscribed with a text which is a major source for Egypt's Libyan War. More importantly, however, it provides the only reference to Israel in an Egyptian inscription, and, according to this, Israel is already an established geographical entity by the middle of

Merenptah's reign. Therefore his predecessor, RAMESSES II, is more appropriately identified as the Pharaoh of the Exodus. (A.R.D.)

Moses ben Maimon. *See* MAIMONIDES, MOSES.

Moses de Leon [xv] (*c.*1240–1305). Spanish Jewish mystic; probable author of the *Zohar*, the classic work of Jewish mysticism. Much of his early life was spent wandering in Castile, where he studied with various kabbalists. Eventually he settled in Avila. He was the author of pseudepigraphical mystical works, written in both Hebrew and Aramaic. The *Zohar* is attributed to the second century rabbi Simeon bar Yoḥai, and Moses during his lifetime claimed to possess the ancient original of this work. After his death his widow denied the existence of any such manuscript, and already by then it was suspected that Moses was the author. Modern scholars, notably Gershom Scholem, have unequivocally concluded on the basis of its literary style, language and ideas, and on a comparison with Moses' other works, that Moses de Leon wrote the *Zohar*, except perhaps for a small amount of supplementary material. The main part was apparently written after 1270 but before 1300 as it forecasts the advent of redemption for the latter date. Traditional kabbalists adhere to the ascription to Simeon bar Yoḥai as the basic source. [72: 5]

The *Zohar* (literally 'splendour'), most of which purports to be based on the discussions of second century rabbis, is in fact a collection of works. The main section is a commentary on the Pentateuch arranged according to the weekly synagogue readings. Written in Aramaic, it encompasses theology and mysticism, legend and myth. The divine, according to the *Zohar*, manifests itself in the creative process through a series of emanations. A dualistic conception contrasts the 'right side' and the 'left side' of the divine and the created worlds. The lower world corresponds to the upper world and an action below has its impact above, and therefore the deeds and prayers of man have cosmic significance. The key to this process is contained in the Torah.

After the Bible and Talmud, the *Zohar* was the most influential work of Jewish literature and is regarded as of special sanctity. It made an especial impact following the expulsion of the Jews from Spain in 1492, when the Jews in their sufferings found solace in its pages. Many later works were based on it and it is still venerated by many Jews, especially in Ḥasidic circles and among communities originating from Muslim lands. It has had a strong influence on Jewish folklore and customs. [71: 213–43] (G.W.)

Moshoeshoe [VI.A] [Moshesh; Moshweshwe; Msheshwe] (*c.*1786–1870). Founder of Lesotho. He was the son of a minor headman at Menkhoaheng in the north of modern Lesotho. Between 1824 and the mid-1830s he built up the nation of the Basotho from a base at Thaba Bosiu, incorporating various detached and displaced groups. By military prowess, conciliation and diplomacy he kept at bay the forces, European and African, threatening his kingdom. In 1868 he chose British colonial rule as the least evil option available, thus averting incorporation into South Africa.

Religion was central to Moshoeshoe's policy of adaptation. In youth he was influenced by a religious reformer, Mohlomi. In 1833 he brought in Protestant missionaries from the Paris Mission, using them, but also listening to them. Late in life he admitted Catholic missionaries also. His career was a dialogue with Christian teaching. In his day the significance of Molimo, the Supreme God, identified with the God of the Bible, increased within the ancestor-dominated Sotho world-view; the encouragement of Christian burial led in the same direction. Moshoeshoe would not allow the killing of witch-suspects and undermined the prestige of diviners. For a time he even closed the traditional initiation ceremonies; several of his sons never were circumcised. There were many conversions in his family, especially between 1839 and a relapse in 1847, but he avoided actions likely to split or undermine the nation. (Polygyny, for instance, was essential to his alliance system.) Though illiterate, he knew much of the Bible. At the time of his death he was listening to Catholic missionaries, though his Protestant baptism was imminently expected.

Moshoeshoe represents transitional religion in Africa as primal and Christian worlds met. Today Lesotho's leading independent church, the Kereke ea Moshoeshoe, claims to perpetuate his legacy. [793] (A.F.W.)

Motoori Norinaga [XIV] (1730–1801). One of the most famous scholars of the 'national learning' (*kokugaku*). A disciple of KAMO MABUCHI (1697–1769), the famous *kokugaku* scholar, Motoori is best known for his philological and interpretive studies of the *Kojiki* [49] and the *Man'yōshū* [37]. He participated in the *fukko* ('Return to Antiquity') movement in Shintō circles. He rejected all philosophies and religions other than Shintō as foreign and false, urging instead a return to the primal truths revealed in the *Kojiki*. He also attacked the syncretistic Shintō sects that had developed an accommodation with Buddhism in the medieval period. Only by returning to the path of the *Kojiki*, he felt, can people be fully human and experience authentic *mono no aware*, a deep and immediate sensitivity to the things and activities of everyday life. Because Japan is the land which gave birth to the Sun (Nippon, 'Origin of the Sun'), Japan and its people are superior to all other lands and peoples. Moreover, since each Japanese sovereign is a direct descendant of Amaterasu, the mind and heart of each is in perfect harmony with the deity's. Consequently, in Japan the age of the gods and the present age are one and the same.

Motoori argued that to understand the world human beings need revelation, especially that contained in the *Kojiki*. However, he did not propose a return to a golden age; neither did he urge his contemporaries to copy the language and style of the ancients. Rather, he took the poetry of the *Man'yōshū* to be the expression of pure intention (*magokoro*) based upon sincerity. He urged a return to the nativist tradition in which he perceived a unity of practice in mundane life and the content of expression unmediated by inappropriate forms.

Others, including Kamo Mabuchi, had earlier turned to the *Man'yōshū* as a repository of the 'spirit of ancient Japan', but Motoori was largely responsible for drawing the *Kojiki* out of the shadows of the *Nihonshoki*, and rescuing it from scholarly neglect. He promoted the *Kojiki* as the primary scripture of Shintō rather than as an imperial history; the goal of his (largely philological) method was to make it evident that although the *Kojiki* was written in Chinese it was intended to be read in Japanese. Thus, he asserted, a proper philology can recover the original meaning and intention of words direct from the age of the gods – it can move beyond a literal reading to immediate encounter with the words of the *kami*. In Japan, the argument runs, although people know naturally what they are intended to do because they have been divinely created, in this present age they need to study the *Man'yōshū* and the *Kojiki* in order to recover this proper way of acting and performing, i.e. to reappropriate *kami no michi* or Shintō. Motoori's thought remains extremely influential up to the present day. [34: 169–70; 40; 62; 66] (G.E.)

Mott, John Raleigh [VI.A] (1865–1955). American Methodist layman. He studied at Upper Iowa and Cornell universities. In 1888 he became student secretary of the American–Canadian Intercollegiate YMCA movement. In the same year he was made first chairman of the Student Volunteer Movement for Foreign Missions, a post he held for 30 years. In 1895 he became secretary of the World Student Christian Federation, an organization he had done much to found. In 1901 he became assistant general secretary of the world-wide YMCA. The Volunteer Movement adopted the motto 'The Evangelization of the World in this Generation', which gave Mott the title of one of his works published in 1900. He was prominent in the Ecumenical Missionary Conference organized in New York in 1900 and was the chairman of the committee which called the first International Missionary Conference in Edinburgh in 1910. In 1912–13 he convened and presided over 21 conferences in Asia, meetings which led eventually to the formation of National Christian Councils in Japan, Korea, China and India after he had become chairman of the International Missionary Council in 1921. His other works are *The Present-day Summons to the World Mission of Christianity* (1932) and *Addresses and Papers* (6 vols. 1946–7). [531; 566; 567] (T.T.)

Mozart, (Johann Chrysostom) Wolfgang Amadeus [VI.A] (1756–1791). Austrian composer. He was born in Salzburg. He received little or no formal education. At the age of six, he and his sister travelled with their father, Leopold, to Munich and Vienna, demonstrating their formidable musical skills. The success led a year later to a tour of the principal German cities, Paris and London. Three formative visits to Italy followed while

Mozart was in his teens. His appointments to the Archbishop of Salzburg as *Konzertmeister* in 1772 and organist in 1778 were frustrating to him as he was torn by the lack of opportunities at home when he had exciting prospects elsewhere. Most of his sacred music, including the two great *Vespers*, *Coronation Mass* (1779) and *Missa solemnis* (1780), dates from these years. The final break came in 1781, when he was removed from the Archbishop's presence. This left him free to try his fortunes in Vienna, where his artistic renown in all genres, especially opera, did not guarantee security, domestic or financial. Two notable works were composed after his move from Salzburg: the profound but incomplete Mass in C minor (1782), composed as an offering to his bride, Constanze; and the legendary *Requiem*, on which he was working when he died in poverty. [56; 237; 453] (E.M.)

Mpadi, Simon-Pierre [I.A] (*c.*1905–). A legendary figure in the history of Congolese religious dissent and one of the longest-serving African prophets with an extensive history of suffering, persecution and imprisonment. Founder of the Eglise des Noirs (Church of the Blacks), Mpadi was a Ntandu-Kongo born in the Congo (now Zaïre). He served as an evangelist for the Salvation Army, 1934–7, and studied at the Salvation Army theological school, 1938–9. In 1939 he broke away to found his own church which reputedly revived many of the millennialist aspects of Kimbanguism (*see* KIMBANGU, SIMON). Imprisoned by the Belgian authorities in 1944, he was not released until the granting of independence in 1960, when the church grew rapidly. His endless stream of writings –myths, rituals, autobiography – have given him an international reputation. [17: 136–40] (R.H.)

Msheshwe. *See* MOSHOESHOE.

al-Mufīd, al-Shaykh Muḥammad ibn Muḥammad al-Baghdādī [XII] (948/50–1022). Leading scholar of the Imāmī Shiʿites in the early period after the Imāms. Born in ʿUkbarā in Iraq, he came at an early age to Baghdad, then the major centre of Shiʿite activity and thought. Under the protection of the nominally Shiʿite dynasty of the Būyids, then in control of Iraq, Shiʿite scholarship underwent a rapid development during al-Mufīd's lifetime. His own teachers included prominent Shiʿite traditionists such as IBN BĀBŪYA, whose work continued that of AL-KULAYNĪ. Traditionalism, which had reached its apogee in Qumm, the Iranian centre of Shiʿite learning at that period, dominated Shiʿite thought.

Al-Mufīd's work, however, took Shiʿite learning in a more rationalist direction, following a pattern already established within Shiʿism. His successful establishment of a rationalist school was crucial to the intellectual development of the Shiʿite community, deprived of charismatic leadership in the absence of an Imām or an acknowledged representative for him. This rationalist school rapidly displaced that of the traditionists, chiefly through al-Mufīd's personal influence as the leading Shiʿite scholar of his day.

His pupils represented a new generation of Shiʿite thinkers, including men like the immensely influential AL-ṬŪSĪ and Sharīf al-Murtaḍā ʿAlam al-Hudā. His own literary output was considerable, amounting to some 200 titles, including the *Kitāb al-irshād*, a full-length account of the lives of the Imāms. The *Irshād* serves as a symbolic marker of the transition from the Imām-dominated period of Twelver Shiʿism, which ended shortly before al-Mufīd's birth, and that of the independent Shiʿite scholars, which still continues. Not only does al-Mufīd provide a sense of historical completeness, but he takes the doctrine of the Imām's superhuman attributes to its greatest orthodox lengths. [83; 92] (D.M.)

Muḥammad Aḥmad ibn ʿAbd Allāh [XII] [known as al-Mahdī, 'He whom God guides'] (*c.*1840–1885). Sudanese religious leader and rebel. Born in Dongola, Sudan, Muḥammad Aḥmad had from childhood been deeply religious; he studied with several teachers and was initiated in a Ṣūfī order. For a time he lived at Abbā, an island in the White Nile where he acquired a reputation for holiness and magic powers. He was attended by a small company of devout men and many followers. When he turned 40, Muḥammad Aḥmad, like the prophet MUḤAMMAD himself at that age, decided that he must fulfil the mission which God had entrusted to him. He wished to cleanse the House of Islam by removing faults and accretions, to re-establish the Faith and the Custom (*al-*

īmān wa'l-sunna) of the Islam of Muḥammad, and then to prepare the Path of the Lord, i.e. make the world ready for Resurrection (*qiyāma*) and the Day of Reckoning (*yawm al-ḥisāb*). It was from Abbā that in June 1881 Muḥammad Aḥmad dispatched letters to all the leaders of the Sudan informing them that he was the expected Mahdī. It is believed that before Doomsday God will send the prophet Muḥammad back to earth in human form as al-Mahdī, who will with God's guidance re-establish the rule of righteousness by destroying the power of the wicked, the atheists and all non-Muslims. Muḥammad Aḥmad called his followers the *anṣār* ('Helpers'), just as the prophet Muḥammad had done when he settled in Medina in 622 CE.

In August 1881 the government of the Sudan sent an army against Abbā, which was miraculously defeated, so that many now believed that Muḥammad Aḥmad was indeed sent by God. A second, third and fourth attempt by the government to defeat the Mahdī also failed, so that thousands now believed he was protected by God. El Obeid, the capital of Kordofan province, capitulated in January 1883. In November an Egyptian army under the Arab governor and a British officer, W. Hicks, was annihilated, including Hicks and all his officers. This ended Turco-Egyptian rule in the Sudan. Darfur, Baḥr al-Ghazāl and other provinces rallied to the Mahdī as their saviour from foreign rule. In January 1885 the Mahdists stormed Khartoum and overwhelmed the garrison. General Charles Gordon was killed. Then, at the height of his glory, the Mahdī died in June 1885 in Omdurman. [50; 51] (J.K.)

Muḥammad al-Mahdī [XII] (*b* 869?). Twelfth and last Imām of the Twelver Shīʿa, reputed to be continuously alive in a supernatural realm. His return to this world as the Mahdī is awaited as one of the events of the Last Day. His father, Ḥasan al-ʿAskarī (845–874), the eleventh Imām, spent the last six years of his life in seclusion in the city of Samarra, near the ʿAbbasid capital of Baghdad. Like his predecessors following the death of Ḥusayn, Ḥasan adopted a quietist policy *vis-à-vis* the caliphal government, but he and his followers continued to be viewed in some circles as a threat to the state. Shīʿī sources allege that, when he died, Ḥasan had a son of some four or five years, whom he had not publicly acknowledged for fear of ʿAbbasid reprisals. A group among Ḥasan's followers maintained that such a child existed, was named Muḥammad, and was the rightful Imām, but that he could at present only be contacted through an intermediary (variously named his 'gate', 'vicegerent', or 'ambassador').

A succession of four men, all resident in Baghdad, claimed vicegerency over a prolonged period (874–941), but at no time did anyone appear to lay claim to the imamate itself. This period of almost 70 years came to be known as the Imām's 'Lesser Occultation'. At some point not long after the death of the last of the vicegerents, a large section of the Shīʿa agreed that the Imām had now passed into a state of 'Greater Occultation', from which he would return in due course as the rightful ruler of humanity.

Since the 10th century a small number of individuals have claimed to be the return of the twelfth Imam, the most recent and best known of whom was Sayyid ʿAlī Muḥammad, THE BĀB. [92: II, X, XI; 110] (D.M.)

Muḥammad ibn ʿAbd Allāh [XII] (570–632). Founder and prophet of Islam. The date of Muḥammad's birth is open to question; the date 570 is fixed by a tradition which records that the 'Expedition of the Elephant' – the expedition by the ruler of south Arabia, Abraha, into the homeland of Muḥammad, the Ḥijāz – was in the same year. The evidence for the date of the expedition being 570 is undermined by inscriptional material found in south Arabia, which makes it more likely to have been at the end of the 540s. The significance of the date in the Muslim context is that it serves to establish Muḥammad's age as 40 when he started to receive revelations, seizing on the symbolic spiritual significance of that number.

The outline of the traditional accounts of the life of Muḥammad is as follows. Muḥammad was born into the family of Banū Hāshim in the tribe of Quraysh. He was orphaned at an early age, and lived a meagre existence until he married KHADĪJA, an older woman with substantial financial involvement with the camel-caravan trade. At the age of 40 he is said to have gone on a solitary retreat in the hills near Mecca, following a religious practice of the time, at which point the angel Gabriel came to him to inform him of his commission as a prophet of the one God, Allāh. Stories of self-doubt are connected with this call to prophethood, but eventually Muḥammad followed his orders and preached the message of the Qur'ān. He had little success to begin with, perhaps converting some of the lower-class members of his society, along with his wife Khadīja and his cousin ʿALĪ.

As Muḥammad hardened his attack on the polytheistic society of Mecca the inhabitants became more resentful of his presence, especially since he attacked the institutions of Meccan society, including the town's connection to the religious shrine, the Kaʿba. Persecution of the members of the new religion increased substantially, and a group of believers emigrated to Abyssinia, perhaps going there to find asylum among the Christians or to attempt to make more converts among an audience who may have been thought to be sympathetic to the message of the movement. Meanwhile, Muḥammad made efforts to find a new place to live in Arabia, and was invited to Yathrib (later to be called Medina) some 400 kilometres northeast of Mecca. Communities of Jews were living in Yathrib, and these people are thought to have been part of the attraction of the location, for a sympathetic audience for the message of Muḥammad was anticipated among these 'people of the book'.

The move to Yathrib is referred to as the *hijra* ('emigration' or 'flight') and the year in which it happened (622 CE) serves as the focal point of the Muslim calendar. It was in Yathrib/Medina that Muḥammad emerged as a forceful religious and political leader, leading the Medinan community under the terms of a type of treaty, the so-called 'Constitution of Medina', within which his authority is ultimately said to derive from God: the ideal religio-political aspects of Muslim community life are embodied here. The actual conversion of the inhabitants of Medina to Islam was not immediate and the Jewish communities were accused of treachery and eventually all were either removed or attacked.

Muḥammad's strategy in Medina was to return to Mecca. This aim was pursued through an attempt to curtail the trade of Mecca by random attacks on the camel caravans, producing unstable conditions for the reliable conduct of business as well as bringing the profits of such raids into Medinan hands, thus producing power and prestige for the community in the eyes of the Arabian tribes. The results of this strategy were successful and the power of the Medinan community grew by great strides in Arabia, such that by the year 630 Muḥammad was able to attack and take over Mecca with little resistance. The final two years of Muḥammad's life were spent in Medina, with him attempting to consolidate his position in Arabia by means of alliances, and at least nominal conversion to Islam, of the nomadic Bedouin of Arabia.

Muḥammad's biography is provided in many texts, which start to emerge some 150 years after his death; his scripture, traditionally believed by Muslims to be the literal Word of God and not a product of Muḥammad himself, contains a negligible amount of biographical material. The earliest complete extant text stems from a version edited by Ibn Hishām (*d.*833) of the biography (*Sīra*) of Muḥammad by IBN ISḤĀQ (*d.*767). This may be supplemented by other fairly early texts such as those by al-Wāqidī (*d.*823) and IBN SAʿD (*d.*845). In broad outline, all these sources present the same story but matters of chronology and detail are always problematic. The reasons for the emergence of this elaborated, detailed picture of Muḥammad are complex and at the same time vital to the enterprise of Islam itself. The significance for Muslims of the person himself does not lie particularly in the historical narrative of his life at all. Rather, it is the anecdotes about his life and the more generalized aspects of what that behaviour represents that concerns the community most of all: this is the *sunna*, the 'example' provided by the life of Muḥammad, which every Muslim attempts to emulate.

Muḥammad, as is implied in the basis of the entire concept of the *sunna*, is the 'perfect man'. He is the most liberal, the best, the bravest. Most of all, Muḥammad is considered to have lived his life in a state of sinlessness (*ʿiṣma*); with such a doctrine, everything Muḥammad did is considered to be the perfect embodiment of the will of God – nothing at any point of his life would have been in contravention of that will. This is a doctrine which took a number of centuries to become firmly established in Islam, as evidenced by some early, divergent material, which seems to present Muḥammad as capable of making mistakes, even on very basic religious issues. The doctrine, however, has clearly influenced, if not provided, the basic impulse for the writing of the biographical material which is available to us today. [26; 56; 105: III; 113] (A.R.)

al-Muḥāsibī, al-Ḥārith ibn Asad [XII] (*c*.781–857). Early Islamic theologian and ascetic, noted for his rational and orthodox presentation of Ṣūfī doctrine. Born in Baṣra, he left at an early age to study in Baghdad. His father was apparently a heretic; although he died leaving a large fortune to his son, al- Muḥāsibī preferred a life of poverty to accepting his inheritance.

He became a leading representative of the Shāfiʿī school of canon law, having studied under AL-SHĀFIʿĪ himself. His theological work is particularly noted for its emphasis on the use of reason and for the way in which al- Muḥāsibī employs the dialectical methods of the Muʿtazilite school to refute their doctrinal positions. Unfortunately his identification with rationalism combined with his acknowledged position as 'chief of the Ṣūfī Shaykhs of Baghdad' led to his being forbidden to teach following the accession of the Caliph al-Mutawakkil (847–61), who proscribed all theological speculation.

Banished for a period to Kūfa on the insistence of the strict legist AḤMAD IBN ḤANBAL, al-Muḥāsibī eventually returned to Baghdad but was forced to spend his last years there in retirement.

A prolific writer (some sources ascribe 200 titles to him), al-Muḥāsibī is best known for his *Kitāb al-riʿāya li-ḥuqūq Allāh* ('The Book of Observance of that which is owed to God'), a book of spiritual counsel. Here and in other works, he stresses the importance of self- examination (Arabic: *muḥāsaba*, hence his name), a process involving more than mere physical asceticism, demanding as it does an ongoing psychological analysis of one's thoughts.

Al-Muḥāsibī's work did much to enhance the religious and intellectual standing of Ṣufism, and his own writings are the first to provide Islamic mystical thought with an adequate technical vocabulary. His influence was considerable, notably on the thought of the great synthesiser of orthodox Ṣufism, AL- GHAZĀLI. [34: s.v.; 121] (D.M.)

Muktananda, Paramahansa [XIX] [Baba] (1908–1982). Founder of the SYDA Foundation. He was born to a wealthy Hindu family in Mangalore, India. He left home at the age of 15 and began a 25-year quest for spiritual enlightenment, spending some time learning Sanskrit, yoga and Vedanta with Siddharudha Swami. In 1947 he met Bhagwan Sri Nityananda, a master of the Siddha tradition, at Ganeshpuri. After a further nine (often difficult) years of visiting Nityananda he reached the state of self-realization [45]. Muktananda then worked with Nityananda until the latter's death in 1961, when Muktananda took over Ganeshpuri, renaming it Shree Gurudev Ashram in honour of Nityananda.

Muktananda was revered by his followers as a Perfected Being, capable of imparting *Shaktipat* – 'the full grace of the supreme guru' [45: 47] – the power to awaken the *kundalini*, the serpent-like power in each individual [37: 187; 47: 210]. He claimed that he was the head of an ancient lineage of Siddha Yoga Masters which traces its genesis to Lord Shiva. [7: 49] A true *siddha*, he wrote, is one who 'through spiritual practices is able to annihilate his ego and achieve unity with the Lord'. [43; 44: vol. 1: 176]

A number of Westerners, including Franklyn Jones (DA FREE JOHN) and Richard Alpert (Baba Ram Dass), were influenced by Muktananda, and in 1970 Muktananda made the first of three world tours. During the 1970s the SYDA Foundation was established as a world-wide organization and, at the time of Muktananda's death, there were more than 100 centres (Siddha Yoga Dhams) in the United States. [37: 187] (E.B.)

Mulago, gwa Cikala Musharhamina [VI.A] [Vincent Mulago] (1928?–). Zairian Catholic theologian. He was born in Bukavu, then in the Belgian Congo. He entered the priesthood and received his doctorate from the University of the Propaganda Fide in 1955. In Rome he was, with ALEXIS KAGAME, among the most outstanding of a group of African priests. In 1956 these with others published *Des prêtres noirs s'interrogent*, which challenged much Catholic missionary thought and practice. The Second Vatican Council gave their aspirations better scope, and Mulago, with his concern for 'Christianity with an African face', became a representative African voice in Catholic theology. He became professor in the theological faculty of Lovanium University, Kinshasa, the most academically developed theological centre in Africa. His method uses traditional Catholic sources, categories and terminology in new directions, to explore the encounter of 'the Christian mystery' with 'the centre of gravity of a people's religion'. In the Bantu case, the latter is the divinely given 'vital union' (a point anticipated by PLACIED TEMPELS), which corresponds to and illuminates the 'ecclesiastical unity' of the divine life in Christ. [69: IX; 353: 119, 170] (A.F.W.)

Mulla Feroze bin Mulla Kaus Jalal [XXVI] (1758–1830). Zoroastrian religious teacher who studied in Iran. He became high priest of Qadmi Zoroastrians (Indian followers of the Iranian calendar, not the traditional Parsi, or Shenshai calendar) in 1794 at the Dadiseth Ataš Bahram, Bombay. In 1768, then known as Peshotan, he had set out with his father, Kaus Jalal, to Iran to seek clarification of calendar disputes. The journey was both long (taking three and a half months) and hazardous for these lone Zoroastrian travellers. Peshotan, was left in Yazd to study Avesta. After staying there over three years they moved to Isfahan, where Peshotan studied Persian and Arabic and came out top, ahead of the Muslim students, earning the title 'Feroze (= Victorious) Mulla'. After a three year stay they moved to Yazd where the father negotiated relief for the local Zoroastrians from the *jizya* tax on non-Muslims (*see also* HATARIA, MANECKJI LIMJI). They travelled next to Baghdad, where Peshotan studied Turkish. Father and son both impressed the Caliph and were given the honorific title 'Mulla'; from then Peshotan was known as 'Mulla Feroze'. When they returned to Bombay via Surat in 1779 Mulla Feroze became a widely respected source for information on Zoroastrianism, not only within his community but also among a number of Western writers on Iran, India and Zoroastrian (e.g. Sir John Malcolm and Maria Graham). The account of the travels of father and son were written in Persian. Unfortunately many of the books they brought back were lost in a storm at sea. Their teachers under whom they had studied were venerated by the Parsis, and the tradition grew that Mulla Feroze 'heard voices from afar'. Mulla Feroze was influential in giving temporary credibility to the *Desātir* and *Dabīstān*, two works which claimed to be ancient hitherto lost Zoroastrian mystical texts, studied avidly by some of the great Orientalists of the day such as Sir William Jones, but which on further investigation turned out to be modern productions (although they are referred to by some of the followers of Ilm-i Khshnoom, *see* SHROFF BEHRAMSHAH NAOROJI). Mulla Feroze was active in the very early days of the spread of Western education among the Parsi community. [26a; 49] (J.R.H.)

Mullā Ṣadr al-Dīn Muḥammad ibn Ibrāhīm Shīrāzī [XII] [Mullā Ṣadrā] (1571–1640). Chief representative of the Ishrāqī school of Shiʿite philosophical gnosis in Iran during the Safavid period and 'one of the most profoundly original and influential thinkers in the history of Islamic philosophy'. Born the son of a governor of Fārs province, Ṣadrā was educated in his home town of Shīrāz. At an unspecified date, he left for the Safavid capital of Iṣfahān, which had become an outstanding centre of Shiʿite theology and philosophy, where he studied under eminent teachers, including Shaykh Bahā' al-Dīn ʿĀmilī (Shaykh Bahā'ī) and Mīr Dāmād.

Ṣadrā's adult life coincided broadly with the reign of Shāh ʿAbbās I (1588–1629), which marks the culmination of the establishment of Shiʿism as the state religion of Iran. During this period, an important split developed within the ranks of the Shiʿite clergy, between a professionalized hierocracy and exponents of gnostic Shiʿism, with Ṣadrā as the chief representative of the latter. Clashes with the orthodox clergy led to his excommunication (*takfīr*) and a period of self-imposed retreat of seven to fifteen years in a village near Qumm.

At the request of Shāh ʿAbbās, Ṣadrā finally returned to Shīrāz, where he taught in a mosque school built for him. He died in Baṣra on the way back from his seventh pilgrimage to Mecca and was buried there.

Ṣadrā's literary output was substantial, being concentrated mainly in the latter period of his life, when he was teaching at Shīrāz. His best known works include *al-Hikma al-ʿarshiyya* ('The Wisdom of the Throne'), *al-Shawāhid al-rubūbiyya* ('The Divine Witnesses'), *al-Ḥikma al-mutaʿāliyya fi'l-asfār al-*

ʿaqliyya al-arbaʿa (or simply, *al-Asfār*, 'The Journeys'), and the *Kitāb al-mashāʿir* ('Book of Metaphysical Penetrations'). In these works, a complex philosophical system is worked out, centred around the underlying concept of spiritual transcendence. [90; 93; 95; 101] (D.M.)

Mun, Acharn [IV] [Ācān Man Phūritatta; Bhūridatto Thera] (1870/71–1949). He is regarded in Thailand today as having been a great meditation master and exemplary monk. During his lifetime he developed a wide reputation among Thai Buddhists, both monastic and lay, because of his strict ascetic life. At the time of his death, many believed Acharn Mun to be an enlightened saint (*arhat*), while many more respected him as the holiest man in modern times.

Born as Man Kāēnkāēo in north-eastern Thailand, Mun followed the usual Thai custom of taking temporary ordination as a novice when he was a teenager. At the age of 21 he again entered the monastic order, taking the name of Bhūridatto Thera, although he was generally known as Phra Mun. Immediately after ordination, Mun took up the path of a *dhutaṅga* monk, a course of practice which emphasized renunciation, asceticism and meditation; apparently this choice was unusual for the times, since the role of the *dhutaṅga* monk was not greatly respected or practised when Acharn Mun began his monastic career. As a wandering monk, Acharn Mun travelled to many places in northern and north-eastern Thailand, as well as Laos, mainly in search of forest hermitages suitable for his meditation. In his old age he returned to north-eastern Thailand, settling in a remote monastery where he lived to the end of his life.

Acharn Mun gained the title of teacher (*ācān*, from Sanskrit *ācārya*) not from his learning or didactic instruction, but because of his example. During his lifetime he attracted a number of followers who as monks sought to lead a similar ascetic life. Indeed, Acharn Mun's main legacy is the revitalization of the ascetic ideal in Thai Buddhism through his own exemplary life and the lives of his famous disciples. Another of Acharn Mun's legacies, although clearly secondary to his ascetic example, centres on the continuing career of his bodily relics, which are widely reputed to have miraculous powers. [215: VI–VIII] (C.H.)

Muncherji Merwanjee Bhownagree. *See* BHOWNAGREE, MUNCHERJI MERWANJEE.

Münzer, Thomas [VI.A] (*c.*1490–1525). German Protestant reformer. He was born in Stolberg, Saxony. He went to Leipzig University in 1506 and to Frankfurt an der Oder University in 1512. He completed his studies in 1516 with an MA. He was ordained, possibly in 1513. Between 1516 and 1520 he was an itinerant priest and for a time confessor to a community of nuns in Thuringia. About this time he may have met MARTIN LUTHER. Under the influence of JAN HUS he became a Protestant. In 1520, following a recommendation from Luther, he became a Protestant preacher at Zwickau. He became involved in the political and social problems of the town and led a radical group known as the Zwickau Prophets awaiting the end of the world. In 1521 he was dismissed and went to Prague. Here again he ran into trouble and had to leave. In 1523 he married and took a pastorate in Allstedt. Here he claimed to be under the power of the Holy Spirit. He created a new church order and a German evangelical mass. He attacked the church in Wittenberg in revolutionary tracts and called himself a 'new Daniel'. He left Allstedt because of the opposition of the authorities and went to Mühlhausen in Thuringia, where he became chaplain to the peasants in their revolt. By this time he had lost Luther's support. In May 1525 the peasants were defeated, Münzer fled but was captured, tortured and beheaded. Luther claimed that it was a 'just and terrible judgement of God'. [238; 276; 324] (T.T.)

Murray, Margaret [VIII] (1863–1963). British scholar and writer on pre-Christian religion. She was born in India, spending some time in Germany at the age of ten, and studied Egyptology at University College, London. She did fieldwork under Flinders Petrie and afterwards conducted excavations in Egypt and elsewhere in the Mediterranean area. In 1899 she became a lecturer at the College; she published books and articles and finally received her doctorate and a fellowship, retiring in 1935. It was fairly late in her career that she began to study the history of witchcraft and particularly the Scottish witch-trials. In 1921 she published *The Witch-Cult in Western Europe*, in which she claimed that the witches of the 17th century belonged to a secret 'Dianic' cult, which continued as an underground religion from pre-Christian times. In *The God of the Witches* (1933) she went still further, declaring that many Anglo-Saxon and medieval kings up to Stuart times died violent deaths as sacrificial victims of this secret cult. Dr Murray had a trained and lively mind, and there is valuable material in her first witchcraft book, but she became increasingly selective in use of evidence and obsessed by theories which have no firm foundation. Her writings have encouraged modern practitioners of witchcraft to believe that they can trace back their organizations from remote times; she could never have anticipated the influence that her ideas have had on those with little historical knowledge. (H.E.D.)

Mūsā [XII] (*c.*13th century BCE). The prophet Moses in the Islamic tradition. (For an account of the Jewish tradition, *see* MOSES.) Referred to 502 times in the Qur'ān, more than any other prophet, Moses has a certain prominence but yet remains simply a prophet within the view of the Muslim scripture. The recounting of his story echoes much of the biblical account: Pharaoh and the miracles in Egypt, Sinai and the burning bush, the revelation of the Torah (*tawrāt*), the presence of Aaron (Hārūn). Most significant from the perspective of the Qur'ān are the analogies between the life of Moses and the life of MUḤAMMAD – their forced emigration, their persecution and their formation of a community; Moses' life is the model for that of Muḥammad and *vice versa*.

The life story of Moses is expanded and filled in for and by later Muslims in the *qiṣaṣ al-anbiyā'* ('stories of the prophets') literature. Moses plays a significant role in the elaborations of Muḥammad's ascension into heaven; it is Moses who keeps making Muḥammad return to God after the initial imposition of 50 prayers a day for all Muslims, until the requirement is reduced to five. [25; 73; 130] (A.R.)

Mūsā, Mansa [XII] (14th century). Emperor of Mali, 1307–32, and spreader of Islam. Mansa ('King') Mūsā's empire was extended, partly by his own campaigns, from Senegal in the west, Walata in the north and Gao in the east, to Futa Jallon in the south-west. He sent ambassadors to the rulers of Morocco and caravans from Cyrenaica and Egypt visited his kingdom regularly to trade. When he made the pilgrimage to Mecca, travelling via Egypt, he astounded the locals by his wealth, even though at that time Egypt itself flourished as never before or since. He brought 500 slaves and over 1,000 kilograms of gold which he distributed among the scholars, the preachers and the poor as *ṣadaqa* ('charity'). The empire slowly disintegrated after his death. Although he was not the first Muslim ruler of Mali, he brought home from Egypt prominent scholars, who raised the level of Islam. One of them, al-Sāhilī, introduced the use of baked brick in Mali and built the first mosque at Timbuktu, thus laying the foundation for its reputation for piety and learning. [47: II] (J.K.)

Muslim ibn al-Ḥajjāj al-Qushayrī [XII] (817/21–875). Muslim Traditionist and scholar. His collection of Prophetic *ḥadīth* is generally recognized as second only to that of AL-BUKHĀRĪ. Muslim was born in Nīshāpūr and, like the other great Traditionists, travelled through Iran, Iraq, Egypt, Syria and Arabia in order to hear reports of the words and deeds of the Prophet MUḤAMMAD. He is said to have studied under all the great Traditionists of the age, including IBN ḤANBAL and al-Bukhārī. Reports emphasize the quantity of *ḥadīth* known to him (300,000 being the usual number) and the selective nature of his great collection, known, like that of al-Bukhārī, as the *Ṣaḥīḥ*, or valid collection. It is suggested that there are 4,000 *ḥadīth* in this work, excluding repetitions, but this is a conventional number and there are in fact fewer. His work and that of al-Bukhārī were the first to achieve undoubted pre-eminence amongst the numerous *ḥadīth* collections of the 3rd and 4th Muslim centuries. The popularity of Muslim's work was greater in North Africa and Spain, where it was sometimes preferred to that of al-Bukhārī, but the dominant view is reflected in a late biographical detail with a clear polemical purpose: on meeting al-Bukhārī, Muslim said: 'Let me kiss your feet, O Master of Masters, Prince of Traditionists, Doctor of *ḥadīth* and their ailments'. Later Shāfiʿī writers sometimes prefer AL-NASĀ'I to Muslim. The canonical *ḥadīth* collections were recognized as sources of authority for juristic and theological problems, and disputes about the relative merits of Traditionists are affected by their integration into a particular school of juristic or theological thought. Muslim's *Ṣaḥīḥ* contains 52 books covering all the topics of Islamic law, prophetic biography, community history, theology, eschatology and Qur'anic exegesis. The first book, entitled *Kitāb al-Īmān* ('Book of Faith'), is particularly valuable for the early history of Muslim theology. Also attributed to Muslim are a number of works on the biographies of *ḥadīth*-transmitters and on juristic questions. [34: q.v.; 41: 226–9] (N.C.)

Musō Soseki [IV] [Musō Kokushi] (1275–1351). Japanese Buddhist monk of the Rinzai Zen school. Musō first studied esoteric Tendai and Shingon Buddhism before studying Zen under the Chinese master I-shan I-ning (1244–1317) and then under Kōhō Kennichi (1241–1316) in Kamakura. He spent many years wandering and meditating in the mountains. Eventually he was invited to be abbot of Nanzen-ji, one of the major Gozan ('five mountains') temples in Kyoto. Musō himself played a central role in the establishment of the Gozan system. He headed a number of major Zen temples and trained many disciples, and was an influential figure in the political world of his day, ushering the Gozan monasteries to a leading role in the culture and life of medieval Japan.

Musō taught a traditional Rinzai combination of seated meditation and kōan study, as well as incorporating elements of esoteric Buddhism. His many works include *Muchū mondō* ('Dialogue in a Dream'), in which he explains Zen Buddhism in response to questions raised by the Shogun Ashikaga Tadayoshi. His *Rinsen kakun* contains strict rules for the community of Zen monks.

Musō was also a designer of gardens, the most famous being the 'moss garden' at Saiho-ji. [42; 127] (P.L.S.)

N

Nabonidus [II] (555–539 BCE). The Assyrians controlled the political affairs of Western Asia for several centuries until they were defeated at the Battle of Nineveh (612 BCE) by the Babylonians assisted by the Medes. The new political leaders were known as Chaldaeans, and under them Babylon flourished as a centre of art, science and philosophy. The early kings (Nabopolassar and Nebuchadnezzar) were brilliant leaders and duly received adulation for their religious devotion from the contemporary historical documents.

These documents, most if not all of which were written by scribes from the temple, begin to tell a very different story about the last king of the dynasty, Nabu-na'id, usually known by the Greek form of his name, Nabonidus. This is the king who allowed Cyrus to capture Babylon in the name of the Persians without a struggle, and thus to mark the end of Semitic domination of the Fertile Crescent. They blamed him for the loss of Babylonian power in a tragic verse lament because he had offended the protective spirit of his god by introducing into the temple complex an image of a lunar deity together with images representing the Storm, the Dragon and the Wild Bull. Then he abandoned the city to the care of his son and built a new Babylon in the Arabian desert at Tema.

Thus he achieved what he had desired,
but an achievement which was to deceive.
His building was a sin and an abomination.
Then at the beginning of the third year
he left the place to his first-born son
and called up his troops from all over the land . . .

He set out on a long expedition on a narrow track
He arrived in Tema, and there killed the prince in battle.
He slaughtered the flocks, the men in the fields and in the city.
He made Tema the residence for himself and for the army of Akkad.
He made the town beautiful like Babylon and built walls all round it.

Rather confusingly this appears to be the same king referred to in the Bible as King Belshazzar, who saw God's hand writing cryptically on the wall during his marvellous feast, and was able to understand the ominous judgement that he had been 'weighed in the balances and found wanting', through the mediation of Daniel. It was important for the Jewish writer of this story to show to later generations how God had clearly judged the magnificent but sinful might of Babylon. But because of the geographical and historical divide between the composition of the Nabonidus material and the book of Daniel the actual historical details have become blurred.

What does clearly unite the Bible and Babylonian tradition is the record of the welcome Cyrus the Great received from the priestly establishment in Babylon, so disillusioned were they with the desultory behaviour of their own king. A clay cylinder, designed to be read aloud formally as it was ceremonially rotated, describes how the god of Babylon, Marduk, gave him the authority to rule in stead of Nabonidus.

> He brought him on the road to Babylon walking beside him as his companion. He had a vast number of troops, who marched along like the rolling river without any

weapons on display. He brought him into Babylon and gave it to him without a battle, without trouble. He handed over Nabonidus, the king who would not worship him, into his custody. The faces of the inhabitants of Babylon and those of the whole country of Sumer and Akkad, including the princes and the provincial governors, shone radiantly, happy that he had received the kingship, and they came and kissed his feet.

So ended the greatness that was Babylon; henceforth it was to be a Persian province, and hardly a good word was to be said about its last king. [8; 9] (M.R.)

Nāgārjuna [IV] (2nd century?). The foundational thinker of the Mādhyamaka school of Buddhism in India. Almost nothing is known of his life with any degree of certainty, though it is probable that he was active in South India at approximately the same time as the reign of the Kuṣāna king KANIṢKA. There are many later legendary and quasi-legendary accounts of Nāgārjuna's life, including, most famously, one supposed to have been translated into Chinese by KUMĀRAJĪVA. According to this, Nāgārjuna was born into a Brahmanical family in South India, was trained in traditional Brahmanical lore, and then converted to Buddhism. He then mastered the entire corpus of Buddhist literature, defeated Hindu and Buddhist opponents in debate, and composed many subtle and innovative philosophical works of his own [182: 21–3; 186: 4–6].

A large number of works have been attributed to Nāgārjuna by the Buddhist traditions in Tibet, China and Japan. It is almost certain that many of these cannot be by Nāgārjuna, and contemporary scholarly orthodoxy is moving towards an acceptance of 12 works as probably genuine [142; 143]. Among these the most important are the *Mūlamadhyamakakārikā* ('Basic Verses on the Middle Way') [106; 112; 207] and the *Vigrahavyāvartanī* ('Removal of Disputation') [18]. Both of these are polemical treatises aimed at the systematic refutation of all substantive philosophical views (*dṛṣṭi*) through the application of dialectical method. Nāgārjuna's claim for himself is, notoriously, that he has no substantive philosophical view, no standpoint, of his own, but is interested only in deconstructing those put forth by others – both Buddhist and non-Buddhist. This approach later came to be called that of the *prāsaṅgika*: a philosophical method designed to demonstrate the absurdity of another's position by drawing out the contradictions inherent in it.

Nāgārjuna's interests were not merely intellectual. His understanding of the key Buddhist concepts of emptiness (*śūnyatā*) and dependent co-origination (*pratītyasamutpāda*) was one which saw in the proper appropriation of these ideas the key to attaining *nirvāṇa*. Such an attainment is blocked, on the other hand, by persistent conceptual and cognitive errors, errors which Nāgārjuna's method is designed to correct. Nāgārjuna's importance for the Buddhist tradition can hardly be overstated: he is one of the truly numinous figures of Buddhist history, and his thought has prompted more commentarial and exegetical effort by Buddhists than that of any other single figure. His influence extends beyond the bounds of the Buddhist tradition: he has been paid a great deal of attention both by classical Hindu thinkers and contemporary Western philosophers. (P.J.G.)

Nagenda, William [VI.A] (1912–1973). East African Revival leader. He came from an important Ganda family; his father, Manyangenda, was a regent chief when the Kabaka of Buganda was unable to act. William was educated at King's School, Budo, and Makerere College, and became a government clerk. As a young man he underwent an experience of evangelical conversion through Simeon Nsibambi, brother of BLASIO KIGOZI. In 1936, when Kigozi's death threatened the revival movement in Rwanda, Nagenda came to Gahini and became leader of the revival there. He was much involved with preaching teams of revival Christians who travelled widely in East Africa, calling nominal Christians to repentance and commitment. In 1940 he entered Mukono Theological College, with education, gifts and experience well beyond the usual, to prepare for the Anglican ministry. The revival, however, had split the college; Nagenda and 25 other revival students were expelled. He spent his life thereafter as an itinerant lay evangelist, but never broke from the Church of Uganda, resisting separatist movements and new formulations of doctrine. Besides traversing East Africa, Nagenda became internationally known, taking the message of the East African Revival to Europe, America and Asia. From 1964 Parkinson's disease restricted him, but he continued to preach in partnership with his wife, Sala. [154; 750] (A.F.W.)

Naḥmanides, Moses [xv] [Moses ben Naḥman, known by the acronym Ramban] (1194–1270). Spanish Jewish communal leader, Bible commentator, talmudist and kabbalist. Born in Gerona, he was a noted talmudic scholar while still a youth. He served as rabbi in Gerona, and in the course of time was recognized by all Spanish Jewry as its spiritual authority. He earned his livelihood as a physician. In 1263 a Jewish convert to Christianity challenged him to a public disputation over the respective messianic beliefs of the two faiths. This was held in Barcelona in the presence of King James I of Aragon and his court. The king was impressed by Naḥmanides' presentation, and even rewarded him. However, his success aroused the anger of the Dominicans and Naḥmanides had, for his safety, to leave Spain [5: vol. 1: IV]. He made his way to Palestine, where he revived Jewish life in Jerusalem after its destruction by the Crusaders, and lived his last days in Acre. Both he and his Christian opponent published accounts of the Barcelona disputation, which concentrated on the questions whether the messiah had already appeared and was he God incarnate or a human being.

He enhanced the importance of talmudic study among Spanish Jewry and was a pioneer in the field of *novellae* (the derivation of fresh ideas from talmudic and rabbinic writings in order to throw light on religious law) which became a major branch of rabbinic literature. His own *novellae*, covering much of the Talmud, were distinguished by keen dialectic analysis. [70: VII]

His commentary on the Pentateuch is based on a literal interpretation of the text combined with homiletic, philosophic and mystical explanations. Naḥmanides gives expositions of many subjects, displaying historic and psychological insights. He seeks to show the reason for each commandment. For him the Bible and Talmud were the ultimate authorities. [18: XII]

His philosophy is embedded in these writings. While utilizing philosophical concepts, he rejected an overarching philosophical rationalism, especially as expressed through Aristotelianism. The Pentateuch, which derived from a supernatural source and could not be challenged by human intellect, is a more rewarding subject of study than philosophy. Moreover, much of his orientation is kabbalistic, although he felt that mystical enquiry should be limited to the privileged few. (G.W.)

Naḥman of Bratslav [xv] (1772–1812). Ḥasidic rabbi. The great-grandson of the founder of Ḥasidism, the BA'AL SHEM TOV, he was early influenced by the kabbalistic system of ISAAC LURIA, which brought him to indulge in ascetic practices, often fasting for a whole week at a time. In 1798 he made a pilgrimage to Palestine that made a profound impact on him and which became clothed with mystical significance for him and his followers. He held that all holiness comes by way of the Holy Land and stated: 'Wherever I go, I am going to the Land of Israel.' In 1802 he settled in Bratslav, Podolia, and lived his last three years in Uman, in the Ukraine.

His approach to Ḥasidism was individual. Putting aside his books and Kabbalah, he found God in nature, as had his great-grandfather. God is present in everything and all creation is one living body, yearning for God. He was opposed to philosophy, which fosters doubt, and regarded prayer as the greatest expression of devotion, but insisted that this must emanate from the heart and not consist in mechanical repetition. At the same time, all life and action must be permeated with joy, and the concept of joy – including dance – played a large role in his teachings. He also stressed the moral life, emphasizing charity, hospitality and honesty.

He attributed the decline in Ḥasidism in his day to its leaders, whom he attacked sharply as liars and hypocrites. However, he himself became boastful (despite his advocacy of the virtue of humility) and saw himself as the conqueror of the spiritual world. He discerned four great teachers in the history of the Jewish Diaspora – Simeon bar Yoḥai (traditional author of the mystical classic, the *Zohar*, *see* MOSES DE LEON), ISAAC LURIA, BA'AL SHEM TOV and himself. [53: 230–72]

His personality made a great impact and he built up a large body of followers, telling them they would have no need to find a successor after his death as he would continue to lead them. To this day his followers continue to make pilgrimages to his grave in Uman and dance around it on the anniversary of his death.

A gifted storyteller, Naḥman is best known for his tales. Considered classics of Yiddish literature, they convey his teachings and became very popular. [87: vol. 9: 140–68] (G.W.)

Nakayama Miki [XIV] (1798–1887). Founder of Tenrikyō, one of the largest of Japan's new religions. She was brought up as a devotee of the Buddha Amida in present-day Nara Prefecture. She married, and as a housewife had a largely undistinguished religious life until her middle age. It is reported that she suffered under an oppressive mother-in-law, while her husband blocked her desire to engage in certain forms of religious practice. Then, at the age of 40, she fell seriously ill and began to exhibit bizarre behaviour. A Shugendō *yamabushi* or mountain priest was called to perform an exorcism or healing rite; during the performance of this rite Miki became possessed by a *kami* who identified himself as Tenri-O-no-mikoto ('the Lord of Heaven'). This *kami* demanded that the Nakayama family dedicate itself and its material wealth to him for the benefit of mankind. The family resisted, but Miki fell more seriously ill and they relented somewhat.

This initiated a series of divine possessions with a patterned scenario – the *kami*, through Miki, demanding sacrifices from the family, and the family resisting but finally acceding. Miki began to give away all of the furniture, family heirlooms, and so on, and the family thought her mad. Meanwhile, the *kami* at one point demanded that a new addition to the family home be dismantled. Finally, Miki won approval to devote herself to the service of this deity, but by the time her husband died the family fortune had disappeared. Thereafter she continued to have visions and revelations.

Miki, like many other founders of new religions, initially gained fame as a faith-healer. She incorporated folk beliefs and practices, shamanic elements, and visions into Tenrikyō. Her message was a utopian and eschatological one: she preached that the corrupt world was about to end and that a new age was dawning. While promulgating belief in Tenri-O-no-mikoto, she argued that greed and avarice have poisoned the human heart and led to the corruption of the world. She urged the purification of the heart, restoring the original purity of the human condition which is oneness with the *kami*. Physical and mental illnesses are also ascribed to the impurity of the mind. Gradually Miki began to write down her revelations, often in 31-syllable *waka* verses. These and other divinely-inspired writings became the scriptures of Tenrikyō.

Some aspects of the development of Tenrikyō recall other revitalization movements. For instance, Miki had a vision in which the primordial site of the creation was revealed. Called the Kanro-dai ('Nectar Platform') by Miki, it became the central pilgrimage site of Tenrikyō. The sacred site includes a pillar, which functions as an *axis mundi*, with a bowl on the top which collects the nectar of heaven. The faithful who make the pilgrimage there return to the sacred centre and to sacred time. Miki also introduced a form of sacred dance to be performed at the centre, a form which blended the folk *kagura* dance tradition with the religious impulse behind the mass pilgrimages and ecstatic dances known as *ee ja nai ka*. Like other leaders of new religions, Miki was persecuted for her criticism of the government and of social ills. Tenrikyō is one of the oldest surviving new religions, and has continued its phenomenal growth in the post-war period. [4; 11; 12; 14; 26: 267–86; 34: 220–21; 43; 54; 58; 59: 33–60] (G.E.)

Nāmdev [XI] [Nāmadeva] (1270–1350?). Marathi saint poet whose life and dates are more than usually nebulous. All accounts agree that he was of the Shimpī (tailor) caste and a devotee of Viṭṭhala. He is supposed to have been a contemporary of JÑĀNEŚVAR and to have accompanied him on pilgrimage to the shrines of the north. He witnessed his *samādhi* and wrote his biography in a series of short poems (*abhanga*). Afterwards he is said to have gone north to the Panjab, and there are certainly verses by a Nāmdev included in the Sikh *Ādi Granth*. Out of the 2,000 or so Marathi *abhangas* attributed to Nāmdev some are quite certainly by the much later 16th-century poet Viṣṇudās Nāma; many Marathi scholars have argued that even the original Nāmdev must have lived a good century after Jñāneśvar. Altogether one would have no difficulty in postulating at least three Nāmdevs, but the Vārkarī sect venerate him as the second major saint of their tradition and he lies buried beneath the main steps of the great temple at Pandharpur so that he may for ever feel the touch of the feet of the faithful. He is described always as being surrounded by a cluster of minor poets such as Janī his maidservant, Sena the barber and COKHĀMELĀ the Mahār, from which he is known as *kuṭumba kavi* – the family poet. Some of his *abhangas* are among the best known and best loved of those sung by the pilgrims to Pandharpur. [68] (I.M.P.R.)

Nammāḻvār [XI] One of the twelve ĀḺVĀR. He was born in Āḻvārtirunakari, Tirunĕlveli District, of a Veḷḷāḷa family. He is also known as Māṟaṉ or Caṭakopaṉ, and is the author of sections 5 to 7 of the third thousand of *Nālāyira ppirapantam* (*see* ĀḺVĀR), and of the whole of the fourth thousand entitled *Tiruvāymŏḻi*. He is thus the second most prolific author included in this collection of Tamil devotionalism. An inscription of the Chola king Rājarāja I, dated 998, at Ukkal, makes it clear that Nammāḻvār lived before that date, as Viṣṇu is referred to therein as Tiruvāymŏḻideva, alluding to this text. [17; 43; 118] (J.R.M.)

Nānak, Gurū [XXIII] (1469–1539). First Gurū of the Sikhs. All Sikhs date the foundation of their community (the Panth) from his career of preaching. Although there exist profuse accounts of his life in traditional biographies known as *janam-sākhīs*, little of the information that they provide can be accepted as proven or indeed as possible [53: XIV]. The *janam-sākhīs* have, however, been widely accepted within the Panth, and the traditional account which they offer can be summarized as follows.

Nānak was born, the son of Kālū Bedī, in a village of Central Punjab in 1469. This much seems to be universally accepted, and likewise the date of his death, which is accepted by most authorities as 1539. Also accepted is the fact that Nānak had one sister, that he was married to Sulakhaṇī, and that two sons (Lakhmī Dās and Sirī Chand) were born to them. Many stories are recounted in the *janam-sākhīs* concerning the marvels associated with the child Nānak. [58: 3–18]

As a young man Nānak was despatched to Sultānpur to find work with his brother-in-law's employer, Nawab Daulat Khān. There he received a mystical call from Ākal Purakh (God) to surrender himself to a life of preaching the one means of liberation, the divine Name (the *nām*). The *janam-sākhīs* diverge at this point, many members of the modern Panth accepting the pattern of the *Purātan janam-sākhīs*. These take Nānak on a series of travels, dividing them into four major and one minor missionary journeys. One journey took him to the east of India; a southern one took him as far as Srī Laṅkā; a trip to the north led him up Mount Sumeru (interpreted as Mount Kailash); and in the west he travelled as far as Mecca. Finally there was the short journey to destinations within the Punjab. Nānak then settled down on land given to him by a wealthy follower, founding the village of Kartārpur on the right bank of the Rāvī river several miles north-east of Lahore. In Karta¯rpur he died in 1539, having attracted a following which was the nucleus of the Panth and having appointed GURŪ AṄGAD as his successor. [55: III]

This is the traditional account which is found in the *janam-sākhīs*. Only a small amount of it stands up to historical analysis. [55: IV]

The many hymns by Gurū Nānak are incorporated in the *Ādi Granth*, the scripture compiled by the fifth Gurū, ARJAN, in 1603–4. In these Nānak holds up the *nām* or divine Name as the sole and sufficient means of liberation. All are subject to transmigration in accordance with their past deeds, but by devoutly meditating on the divine Name they can overcome all their evil impulses and attain liberation from the transmigratory round. The divine Name comprises all that is around one and all that is within, functioning in accordance with the order of Akāl Purakh or God.

Akāl Purakh utters the *śabad* or Word; and the Word, if heard, illumines all that constitutes the divine Name. Meditate on this and you shall find liberation progressively revealed. Ascending to higher and yet higher levels of mystical experience the devout practitioner of *nām simaraṇ* (remembrance of the Name) finds opening out before him or her a developing sense of peace and joy. Eventually the level of *sach khaṇḍ* is reached, the 'abode of truth' in which the believer passes into a condition which is in perfect and absolute accord with Akāl Purakh. This condition cannot be described, only those who have experienced its transcending wonders ever comprehending it. They are the sants and they alone have found liberation. [55: V]

Although Nānak was born a Hindu, the way of *nām simaraṇ* was open to anyone of any faith, specifically Muslim as well as Hindu. In practice, however, a substantial majority of Sikhs were from Hindu backgrounds and at a later date the establishment of the Khālsā order by the tenth Gurū, GOBIND SIṄGH, required those who joined the order to observe outward symbols which proclaimed their identity. This led to the conviction that the Sikhs (at least the Sikhs of the Khālsā) were distinctively different, and there developed the conviction that they were a completely separate community. (W.H.M.)

Nand Lāl [XXIII] [Goyā] (1633–1715). Sikh poet born in Ghaznī. From there he travelled as a young man via Multān (where he married a Sikh wife) to Delhi. He worked as the servant of Prince Muazzam (later Bahādur Shāh), but his real skill lay in composing Persian poetry. In 1689 he moved to Anandpur where he entered the service of GURŪ GOBIND SIṄGH, and it is as a Sikh poet that his reputation was securely established. Two of his collections of Persian poems merit special attention. These are his *Dīvān* and the *Zindagī-nāmā*. After the death of the Gurū he retired to Multān and died there in 1715. [40: 379–86; 56: 94–5] (W.H.M.)

Naorozji Feerdoonji [XXVI] (1817–1885). Leading Parsi lay reformist who strove tirelessly to increase knowledge in his community. He was chiefly responsible for establishing the first Parsi girls' school, lending library, literary society and political and law associations. In 1851 he founded, with DADABHAI NAOROJI, the *Rāhnumāi Mazdayasnān Sabha*, known in English as the Zoroastrian Reform Society, 'to fight orthodoxy, yet with no rancour or malice, . . . to break through the 1,001 religious prejudices that tend to retard the progress and civilization of the community'. This society concerned itself largely with examining, and often rejecting, ceremonials and customs, some of which derived from Hindu usages. [1: 32–44; 42: 459–62] (M.B.)

Naqshbandī, Bahā' al-Dīn [XII] (1317–1389). Regarded by many as the patron saint of Bukhārā in Uzbekistan. Born in Turkestan, Naqshbandī founded a Ṣūfī order, still called the Naqshbandiyya, the influence of which is still great in Islamic Central Asia, Afghanistan, Chinese Hsin Kiang and especially the Indian subcontinent. He taught a special form of mysticism characterized by interiorization of the mystic awareness and extreme caution in dealing with the outside world. The mystic, he taught, is alone in the crowd, is conscious of every step, of every breath taken. The mystic constantly concentrates on God at all times so that the mystic journey takes place within. Later scholars have found traces of shamanism in this thinking.

Naqshbandī and his successors had great influence at the court of Tamerlane (Tīmūr Lang: 1379–1405) in Samarkand and on his son Shāhrukh (*d.*1447) and nephew Abū Sa'īd (1452–69); they not only virtually dominated the religious affairs but also had close relations with the merchants and the guilds of the crafts workers. Their religious influence lasts to the present day in Afghanistan and further east. [115: 363–7] (J.K.)

Narmer [VII] [Menes] (*c.*3100–3040 BCE). According to mythology, Narmer received his kingship from a line of semi-divine rulers. With his conquest of the northern region, this southern ruler united the kingdoms of Upper and Lower Egypt and became the symbolic unifier of the Two Lands. [11: 38–49] (A.R.D.)

Narokobi, Bernard [XXI] (1945–). Melanesian philosopher, legal reformer and theologian. From among the Arapesh, a Sepik culture of New Guinea, the talented Narokobi was educated at school in New Britain and Queensland, and in Law at the University of Sydney (during the days when Australia governed the Territories of Papua and New Guinea). Graduating as a lawyer in 1971, he emerged as a popular philosopher and lay Catholic theologian, advocating 'the Melanesian Way' as a unification of the best indigenous and Christian values [32]. Foundation Chairman of the Law Reform

Commission, constitutional planner and active human rights agitator, Narokobi eventually entered Parliament in 1986. Under Rabbie Namaliu's new government in 1988 he became Minister for Justice. [35] (G.W.T.)

Nāropa [IV] (1016–1100). One of the Indian '84 *siddhas*' or tantric Buddhist saints. Nāropa is revered in Tibet as second member of the Kagyu lineage, whose founder was Nāropa's guru, the *siddha* TILOPA. According to Nāropa's principal biography [82], he was born to a north Indian Brahman family and, after a brief marriage, entered the Buddhist monastic order, excelling as a scholar and eventually attaining a high post at the monastic university of Nālandā. One day, in a vision, an old hag (*ḍākinī*) revealed the fraudulence of Nāropa's Buddhism: he was a great academic master but had no genuine experiential realization. The *ḍākinī* sent him into the jungle, enjoining him to seek wisdom at the feet of Tilopa. After an extended search for Tilopa, during which Nāropa comes across the master repeatedly but fails to recognize him, the young scholar and would-be yogin, driven to despair by his fruitless quest, finally meets Tilopa and presents himself as disciple to guru.

In the ensuing years Tilopa puts Nāropa through a most severe tutelage, subjecting him to 12 terrible ordeals during which Nāropa must abandon his life again and again. In the course of these ordeals Tilopa passes on to Nāropa his principal teachings – primarily yogic practices – and recognizes him as his spiritual son. Later Nāropa grants these in turn to his own main disciples, including the Tibetan Marpa, who in turn teaches them to his disciple MILAREPA. Along with his guru Tilopa, his disciple Marpa, and the latter's disciple Milarepa, Nāropa is considered a founding father of the Tibetan Kagyu lineage, which emphasizes yogic practices and meditation in strict retreat. In addition to Nāropa's activity of consolidating Tilopa's teachings and working to establish his lineage, a number of texts in the Tibetan Buddhist canon are attributed to Nāropa, including several tantric liturgies, two collections of songs of realization (*vajragīti*), and a number of commentaries on Vajrayāna topics. (R.R.)

Narsī Mehtā [XI] [Narasiṃha Mahetā] (1414–1480, or perhaps a century later). The great *bhakti* poet of Gujarati. Traditionally born in a Nāgar Brahman family near Junagadh in Saurashtra, he neglected all the affairs of worldly life – in spite of having a short-lived wife and two children – for the composing and singing of devotional songs addressed to Kṛṣṇa, especially Dwārkanāth, the Kṛṣṇa of the temple at Dwārka. The details of Narsī's life are little more than a series of anecdotes, which nonetheless play a big part in later Gujarati literature, in which Kṛṣṇa comes to his aid in various personal crises. Among the hundreds of *padas* attributed to him some are in that highly erotic genre in which the poet imagines himself as Kṛṣṇa's lover, as Rādhā or some other *gopi*, and suffers either the pangs of separation or the physical and emotional bliss of union, employing language in which only the eye of faith can perceive a spiritual rather than a sexual meaning. These verses now tend either to be dismissed as spurious or put down to the bad influence of the VALLABHA sect to which Narsī probably belonged. Other verses, those *padas* of knowledge and devotion (*jñāna-bhaktīna pado*) which are sung by countless Gujarati Hindus as their morning prayers, are filled with a profound awareness of the immanence of the divine. *Vaiṣṇava jana*, Narsī's description of the ideal Hindu, is well known to have been one of GANDHI's favourite 'hymns'; and Narsī first used the term *harijana* – people of Hari (that is Viṣṇu) – that was taken up by Gandhi and forced on his fellow Hindus as a name for the outcastes of their society. [70; 71] (I.M.P.R.)

al-Nasā'ī, Abū ʿAbd al-Raḥmān Aḥmad ibn Shuʿayb [XII] (*d*.915). Muslim Traditionist and scholar. His collection of Prophetic *ḥadīth* came to be recognized as one of the canonical six collections, the most important of which are those of AL-BUKHĀRĪ and MUSLIM. Al-Nasā'ī, like all Traditionists, travelled extensively in order to receive *ḥadīth* orally from the masters of the age. He settled in Egypt, moved later to Damascus, and died either there or in some other part of Syria, as a result, it is said, of ill-treatment at the hands of the sectarian Kharijites. This story may be a result of his writing a book on the qualities of ʿALĪ, which was explained as representing, not a Shīʿite affiliation, but an orthodox response to those who preferred Muʿāwiya to ʿAlī. He is described as a pious man, much given to prayer, fasting and other modes of worship. He enjoyed lawful sexual activity often, having four wives, and slave-girls too. His collection is more narrowly focused than those of al-Bukhārī and Muslim, having an almost exclusively juristic application. It is composed of 51 books, divided into chapters, covering all aspects of Muslim jurisprudence. It is distinguished by the detail it provides on subtle and rare legal points. Being slightly later than the other major Traditionists, his work did not emerge clearly as superior to other collections for some time. Ibn Ṣalāḥ al-Shahrazūrī (*d.*1245) lists him as a major Traditionist in a group which includes Abū Bakr ibn Khuzayma and Abū 'l-Ḥasan al-Dāraquṭnī, neither of whom was elevated to the canonical six. The Shāfiʿī juristic tradition recognized him as belonging to their school of law and preserve much characteristic praise for his work; e.g. that al-Nasāʾī was superior to all his contemporaries in the science of *ḥadīth* and that the conditions he laid down for criticism of transmitters were more stringent than those of al-Bukhārī and Muslim. There is a distinct tendency amongst some Shāfiʿīs to prefer his work to that of Muslim. In addition to his collection, known as the *Sunan al-Nasāʾī*, and his work in praise of ʿAlī, he wrote on the biography of *ḥadīth*-transmitters. [34: s.v.; 41: 229–34] (N.C.)

Nātamuni [XI] [Nāthamuni] (10th century). The compiler of the Vaiṣṇava hymnology called *Nālāyira ppirapantam* ('Four Thousand Compositions'), which is the extant work of the 12 ĀḺVĀR and of two other Vaiṣṇava Ācāryas. He was a Brahman in charge of the temple ritual of Rājagopāla in Vīranārāyaṇapuram in the Naṭunāṭu, and the grandfather of YĀMUNA. There are several hagiographical accounts of how he came to compile the hymnology, but nothing definite is known of his life. He did not arrange the authors chronologically, and Vaiṣṇava *bhakti* antedates them considerably. The position of the Āḻvār in Vaiṣṇava ritual and worship was firmly established by Nātamuṇi's anthology. [17; 43; 118] (J.R.M.)

Natochí [XXIV] [Evaristo Ausencio] (*fl.* 1933). Shaman in the Toba community of Argentina who, during the devastating drought of 1933, declared himself the son of God and lord of thunder. He gathered followers when he predicted the destruction of oppression, the imminent end of the world and the dawn of a new age of prosperity. He enjoined followers to reject the Christian religion of Whites and to cease all mundane routines. Supernatural powers of a past age had returned to the world, he warned, in the form of batons, the traditional ceremonial wands of Toba shamans. Natochí sold these batons to his followers as 'admission tickets' to the spectacle of the new age. Under the prophet's direction a cult formed whose main activities were collective liturgical dances and songs in honour of the morning star and supernatural mountain beings. Armed police forcibly put down the movement and arrested many native leaders, but Natochí himself escaped, some say by causing a violent electrical storm or by flying into heaven, from which he will one day return. [16: 554, 602] (L.S.)

Naudé, (Christiaan Frederick) Beyers [VI.A] (1915–). Afrikaner churchman and opponent of apartheid. He studied at Stellenbosch and was ordained in the Dutch Reformed Church (NGK) in 1939. He was a member of the Afrikaner secret society, the Broederbond. In the 1950s he came to question the theology and practice of his church on race matters. In 1960 he supported the declaration of the Cottesloe Conference (convened by the World Council of Churches) that no one should be excluded from church, land or participation in government on grounds of race. His church rejected it. By 1963 Naudé was editor of the journal *Pro Veritate*, which articulated theological opposition to apartheid, and Director of the Christian Institute of Southern Africa. The latter was formed to unite Christians across racial, linguistic and denominational barriers and to make Christians a force for positive change in society. Naudé was deprived of his ministerial status. The Institute, always small, published research on the effects of official policy and mobilized Christian opposition to apartheid. It also helped links between Catholics and Protestants and between the historic and the African Independent churches. Naudé was a committed pacifist, but a government commission declared the organization violent.

Naudé refused to testify to the commission, and was tried and convicted in 1975. The Institute, long harassed, was banned, and attention turned to the South African Council of Churches. The theological and practical critique begun by the Institute was maintained. [353: 145ff.; 384] (A.F.W.)

Nauroji, Dadabhai [XXVI] (1825–1917). A Parsi popularly known as 'the Grand Old Man of India' because of his leading role in the Indian National Congress and his work as the first Indian Member of the British Parliament in Westminster (a Liberal for Central Finsbury, 1892–5) (*see also* BHOWNAGREE, MUNCHERJI MERWANJEE; SAKLATVALA, SHAPURJI). In 1854 he was the first Indian to become a university professor (of mathematics). Until 1855 his energies were spent mainly in social reform, above all female education, seeking to remove the bans on infant marriage and on the remarriage of widows. In 1855 he went into business in Britain with KHARSHEDJI RUSTAMJI CAMA. In 1861 he was a leading member of a small group which founded the first South Asian religious group in Britain, the Religious Funds of the Zoroastrians of Europe. He was first Trustee, then President, until his final return to India in 1906.

His political work merits only brief reference in this context: he was a founder member of the Bombay Presidency Association (1885), an active, indeed the leading, campaigner on behalf of India in London, where he founded the London Indian Association (1861) and the East India Association (1866), through which he sought to inform MPs likely to be sympathetic to the cause of Indian political reform. While in Parliament Nauroji founded the Indian Parliamentary Party, which acted as a forum for MPs interested in India. He started, or was active in, two newspapers dedicated to the same end, the *Rast Goftar* ('Truth Teller') in 1851, which was dedicated to social reform, and *The Voice of India*, which provided English translations and accounts of articles in the Indian vernacular press. It was not until 1904 that he argued for the removal, not simply the reform, of British rule. Politically he was important for the establishment of the 'drain theory', which showed that despite the investment Britain put into India it drained more away in the form of taxes [37: 173–82, 217–24; 41].

In terms of religion he was important because of the respectability he brought to the reform movement among Indian Zoroastrians, together with Cama. He helped found the Zoroastrian religious reform movement in Bombay, the Rahnumae Mazdyiasnian Sabha (Guide to the Worshippers of One God), which continues to function. While in Britain he lectured to the Liverpool Philosophical Society and other bodies on Zoroastrianism. Although his account was proclaimed to be impartial, his picture of the orthodox and reform movements of the community inclines towards the reform wing, referring disparagingly to 'the later priest-made literature and ceremonial' and seeks above all to present an image of the religion that would command the respect of his English audience. He repudiated the label 'fire worshippers', stressed the pure monotheism of the religion, and explained the purity laws in terms of modern understandings of hygiene. He emphasized in his writings that much of the 'superstition' evident in the modern Parsi community was due to the adoption of Hindu and Muslim ways. He was also concerned for Iranian Zoroastrians. He kept in contact with MANEKJI LIMJI HATARIA, was active in raising funds for his oppressed coreligionists and led a deputation to the Shah during his royal visits, to London in 1889 and 1902. Thus his deep involvement in Indian and British political life did not undermine his sense of Zoroastrian identity or commitment. His emphasis on a Westernised interpretation of the religion gave the reform movement, led by figures like Cama and M. N. DHALLA, great respectability, coming as it did from one who stood so high in popular and international esteem. [26; 41] (J.R.H.)

Nāyaṉmār [XI]. The title bestowed on 63 saints of Tamil Śaivism (singular: *nāyaṉār*, 'lord', 'leader'). Their hagiographies are included in the *Pĕriya purāṇam* of Cekkiḻār, a work of the 12th century, with which a sculptured frieze of the same period in the Tārācuram, Tanjavur District, Śiva temple is clearly linked. *Pĕriya purāṇam* built upon and vastly expanded earlier enumerations of these saints' names by SUNTARAR and Nampiyāṇṭār Nampi, compiler of the *Tirumuṟai*. This work, misleadingly called by some writers the 'Śaiva canon', consists of a hymnology of 11 books, to which *Pĕriya purāṇam* was added to form the twelfth. (*Tirumuṟai* means 'sacred order or system'.) The poetry of six Nāyaṉmār and 20 other Śaiva saints figures in the *Tirumuṟai*. Three Nāyaṉmār – TIRUÑĀṈACAMPANTAR, APPAR and Suntarar – are authors of *Tirumuṟai* I–III, IV–VI and VII respectively. These seven books are known collectively as the 'Garland of God', *Tevāram*. The other three Nāyaṉmār's writings are in *Tirumuṟai* XI, which is also notable for the inclusion of *Tirumuruk'āṟṟuppaṭai*, which praises the six *paṭaivīṭu*, the Armoury-shrines of the war-god Murukaṉ or Skanda. It perhaps stems from a much earlier epoch; as it is included in the anthology of early court poetry called *Pattuppaṭṭu* ('Ten Songs'). *Tirumuṟai* VIII represents the work of a most important devotee, MĀṆIKKAVĀCAKAR. [28; 73; 118] (J.R.M.)

al-Naẓẓām, Ibrāhīm ibn Sayyār ibn Ḥāni' ibn Isḥāq [XII] (*d.* between 835–845). Formative Muslim Muʿtazilite theologian. Raised in Baṣra, al-Naẓẓām spent most of his life in Baghdad teaching and writing concerning theology. His influence has lasted indirectly throughout Muslim history, for he isolated and developed several of the core doctrinal stances of Islam, influencing such people as AL-MĀTURĪDĪ; he especially came to the defence of Islam from Manichaean influences (*see* MĀNĪ), and this led to the characteristic Muʿtazilite emphases on the unity of God – the divinity is to be described only in negative terms and He can only do what is best for His creation. None of al-Naẓẓām's works are still in existence but extracts of his writings are perhaps to be found in other works, especially those of his pupils (e.g. AL-JĀḤIẒ) and his adversaries. [34: s.v.] (A.R.)

Neferti [VII]. In the *Prophecies of Neferti* (preserved on Papyrus Leningrad 1116B, Dynasty 18, *c.*1450 BCE, and on several writing boards and ostraca), Neferti appears as a sage summoned to the Court of the Old Kingdom ruler Sneferu (*c.*2600 BCE). Asked to entertain the king, he prophesies civil strife which will ultimately be defeated only by the accession of a strong king, AMENEMMES I (1991–1962 BCE). However, this 'prophecy' is regarded as a piece of political propaganda, probably composed during the reign of Amenemmes I, and designed to glorify the king [12: 110–15; 15; 19: vol. 1: 139–45]. It also enables the theme of social unrest to be considered and the traditional solution – centralized rulership under a strong king – to be promoted. (A.R.D.)

Nefertiti [VII] (14th century BCE). The queen of AKHENATEN (1367–1350 BCE), Nefertiti is well known from her famous sculptured head, now in Berlin. However, little is known of her background, though she was probably not of royal birth.

The discovery at Karnak and Luxor of thousands of blocks of stone, carved with reliefs and inscriptions, provided new information relating to Akhenaten's Aten temples built at Thebes during the early years of his reign. Using a computer, the Akhenaten Temple Project has extracted sufficient information from these reliefs and inscriptions to reconstruct the original content of the wall scenes in these temples, and they indicate that Nefertiti played a cultic role of unparalleled importance for a queen in the Aten rituals, holding an equal status with her husband. [25] (A.R.D.)

Nehemiah [XV] (5th century BCE). Jewish governor of Judah and rebuilder of the walls of Jerusalem. He was cupbearer of the Persian king, Artaxerxes I (464–424 BCE), who appointed him governor of Judah, then part of the Persian Empire, in 444 BCE. The only source for his history is the biblical book of *Nehemiah*: this gives no information concerning his early life, how and why he was appointed or about most of his activities in Jerusalem.

When news reached Babylonia of the dilapidation of the walls of Jerusalem and the burning of its gates, apparently in 445 BCE, he received permission to go there for a limited time to reconstruct the city, but remained for 12 years. He travelled to Jerusalem with army officers and cavalry and took with him timber for the rebuilding. His first activity was the restoration of the walls of Jerusalem, in which all the populace of Judah participated. This work was opposed by a group of enemies centred around Samaria, who even threatened war. To counter this Nehemiah armed the builders of the wall, who finished the work in 52 days. This achievement buoyed the spirits of the Judahites and lowered the morale of their enemies. Nehemiah took advantage of the new spirit among the people to introduce social edicts, such as the cancellation of the debts of the poor who had mortgaged their land and the transfer of part of the rural population to Jerusalem. He participated in the ceremony of the reading of the Pentateuch by EZRA and was the first to sign the covenant renewing the people's religious commitment. He organized the ceremony of the dedication of the wall, on which occasion further edicts were issued supporting the temple cult and obliging the removal of foreign wives.

After he returned to Babylon, the situation in Judah again deteriorated, with a continuation of mixed marriages, the neglect of the Temple and the desecration of the Sabbath. Nehemiah returned to Jerusalem and took appropriate steps to rectify these manifestations, including a purge of the priesthood and the imposition of punishments for Sabbath violation. He was an inspiring, godfearing leader whose activities were marked by organizational skills, energy and determination. [55] (G.W.)

Nektarios, St [VI.B] (1846–1920). Bishop of Pentapolis. A Thracian from Silivria, Nektarios Kephalas became a monk at the Nea Moni on Chios (1873), was sent to study in Athens and then Alexandria, where he was consecrated bishop of Libyan Pentapolis (1889). From 1891 he was rector of Rizarion Theological Academy in Athens. He died in the Aegina Holy Trinity convent: almost immediately his tomb became a place of pilgrimage. He was the author of over 20 books. He founded an important convent on Aegina (1905) and revived the female diaconate, though his example was not followed. With St Savas of Kimolos (1862–1948), his Thracian companion, Nektarios was the reviver of female monasticism in Greece. [20] (D.B.)

Neolin [XX] (1725–1775). Prophet and religious leader among the Ohio Delaware Indians in the 1760s. An early opponent of European expansion and its displacement of Amerindian peoples, Neolin began his preaching after having claimed to have made a spirit journey to the dwelling place of the Great Spirit (or Master of Life). A sacred map recorded his vision; it depicted at the centre of the cosmos the home of the Great Spirit, the ultimate place of repose for the faithful after their death. To the east were the lands that had belonged to the Delaware, but were now in the possession of Whites, a development permitted by the Great Spirit as punishment for the tribe's wickedness. The way to salvation and the regaining of their lands lay in a strict code of morality (avoiding alcohol, sexual promiscuity, and inter-tribal warfare) and a return to traditional ways. According to Neolin's teachings the Delaware's fate was to be seen as a death through which they could pass to rebirth if faithful to the vision revealed by the Great Spirit. Neolin, also known as 'The Enlightened One', successfully convinced the Ottawa chief Pontiac of his vision, and the latter attempted to forge a confederation of frontier tribes to resist White expansion. [4: 73–4] (S.R.)

Nerses of Cla [VI.A] (1101–1173). Catholicos of the Armenian Church, 1166–73. He was born in the province of Tlouk' in Cilician Armenia. His guardian, the Catholicos Grigor II Vekayaser, sent him to the Monastery of Shoughri, where he studied under Stepanos Manouk. He was ordained priest in 1118 and was made bishop in 1136. He became an important figure in Cilician Armenia, securing the peace of the region. He worked for the reconciliation of the Greek and Armenian churches. He succeeded his brother as Catholicos of the Armenian Church in 1166. He was buried in Hromcla. His works include a commentary on *Matthew*, a prayer, *Havatov Khosdovaneem*, and writings on theology, philosophy and pastoral theology. He fought for the independence of the Armenian church and for its freedom from Chalcedonian orthodoxy. [870] (T.T.)

Nerses the Great [VI.A] (*d. c.*373). Catholicos of the Armenian Church. He was raised and educated at Caesarea in Cappadocia. He served as chamberlain in the court of King Arshak II of Armenia. After the death of his wife he became an ecclesiastic, and as a descendant of Gregory the Illuminator he was elected Catholicos (*c.*363) and returned to Caesarea to be consecrated by the metropolitan bishop. He occupied the see of Ashtishat and called a council of bishops there. He instituted a number of reforms through the council, including the banning of marriages between relations and rules governing fasting. He was instrumental in founding schools, hospitals and orphanages. He criticized King Arshak III for his immoral ways and was deposed. He was restored in the reign of King Pap, *c.*370, but again he found royal morals reprehensible. There is a tradition that he was poisoned by the king but it is likely that he died of natural causes. [456; 608] (T.T.)

Neryōsang Dhaval [XXVI] (*fl.* late 11th or early 12th century). Learned Parsi priest of Sanjan, Gujarat. He initiated the translation of the Zoroastrian holy book, the Avesta, into Sanskrit, of which he had a good knowledge. His rendering is carefully literal, with special Zoroastrian terms retained. He also translated some Middle Persian texts, and was the first to transcribe Middle Persian works from the difficult Pahlavi script, with its Aramaic ideograms, into the Avestan alphabet. This usage, known as Pazand, sheds light on pronunciation in his day. His work marks a peak in Parsi scholarship. [9: 168–9] (M.B.)

Nestorius [VI.A] (*c.*381–*c.*451). Bishop of Constantinople whose teachings gave rise to Nestorianism. He was born in Germanica in Cilicia, a Roman province in Asia Minor. He entered a monastery in Antioch, where he came under the influence of Antiochene theology with its stress on the humanity of JESUS the Christ. He became famous for his preaching and for his ascetic life. In 428 there was disagreement over the election of a new patriarch, so Emperor Theodosius II appointed Nestorius. As bishop he vigorously attacked the Arian (*see* ARIUS) and Novatian heresies. Trouble began when he supported his assistant Anastasius, who preached against *Theotokos* as a title for Mary the mother of Jesus as tending to Apollinarianism. Nestorius himself preferred the title *Christotokos*. Since *Theotokos* had become a mark of orthodoxy it was an opportunity for CYRIL OF ALEXANDRIA to attack Nestorius. At a council in Rome in 430 Cyril persuaded Pope Celestine to condemn Nestorius; Cyril was appointed to carry out the sentence of deposition in a document containing 12 anathemas. At the council of Ephesus in 431 the Emperor was also persuaded of Nestorius' lack of orthodoxy. Nestorius was deposed and went back to his monastery. In 435 his books were condemned and he was banished to Upper Egypt, where he lived at least until the year of the Council of Chalcedon, at which council he thought he had been vindicated though he was never rehabilitated. [212; 492; 660: 247–307; 723: 107–257] (T.T.)

Newman, John Henry [VI.A] (1801–1890). English Catholic cardinal. He was born in London. At the age of 15 he underwent an evangelical religious experience. In the same year (1816) he entered Trinity College, Oxford, and was elected fellow of Oriel College in 1822. He was ordained priest in the Church of England in 1825 and became vicar of the University Church, St Mary the Virgin, in 1828. In 1833 he became one of the leaders of the high church Oxford Movement. In the same year he began editing the *Tracts for the Times*. He wrote 24 tracts himself. Tract no. 90 (1841), an interpretation of the Thirty-Nine Articles of Religion along Tridentine lines, caused serious controversy. Meanwhile his sermons at the University Church (*Parochial and Plain Sermons*, 1834–42) were extremely popular. Other published works of the period included *The Arians of the Fourth Century* (1833) and *Lectures on the Doctrine of Justification* (1838). Tract no. 90 marked a watershed. He retired to Littlemore outside Oxford in 1842, resigned as vicar of the University Church in 1843 and in 1845 his Oriel fellowship. The same year he converted to Roman Catholicism, went to study in Rome and published *An Essay of the Development of Christian Doctrine*, written before his conversion 'by one who in the middle of his days, is beginning life again'. Following ordination in Rome he returned to found the Oratory in Birmingham. From 1854 to 1858 he was rector of Dublin University. In 1859 he became editor of *The Rambler*, which led to controversy with Cardinal MANNING. In 1864 he wrote *Apologia pro vita sua* and the following year the poem *Dream of Gerontius*. He was made a cardinal in 1879. His many other works include a book on university education. [93; 583; 808] (T.T.)

Nezahualcoyotl [XVIII] [Fasting Coyote] (1402–1472). Ruler of the Aztec city-state of Texcoco, renowned for his cultural achievements in poetry, engineering, law and libraries. He was the son of Ixtlixochitl I, who was slain by the Tepanec king of Atzcapotzalco, Tezozomoc. Forced into exile, he apparently organized his recovery of the throne of

Texcoco by participating in the revolt against Atzcapotzalco (1423–26) and the establishment of a new governmental system called the Triple Alliance, consisting of the city states of Tenochtitlan, Texcoco and Tlacopan.

As ruler of Texcoco, he reorganized the legal system, collected the pictorial manuscripts into a corpus and assisted in the planning of the political capital of Tenochtitlan. He was primarily responsible for the construction of the great dike in the lake of Texcoco which protected the sweet water chinampa system, vital for the agricultural production of the developing empire. During his rule, he was consulted by neighbouring rulers, nobles, and engineers. [1: 389–90]

Nezahualcoyotl was an influential poet and theological visionary, who according to some scholars developed an approach to truth on earth which deviated from the mystico-military vision of the Aztec rulers [4, 5]. More than 30 of his poems have survived and have been translated into a number of languages. His poetic vision was based, in part, on the Nahuatl conception of change, *cahuitl* ('that which leaves us'). All of life on earth is transitory, passing, brittle, 'only a little while here'. Humans are like paintings to be erased, like flowers to dry up. This earthly condition led him to ask if there was any permanent reality *can avac micohua* ('where death does not exist'). His discovery was that in true art and symbolism, or what the Aztecs called 'flower and song' (*in xochitl, in cuicatl*) there was an everlasting, true reality. The ritual responsibility for the human is to discover this eternal truth by an internal composition of poetry, art and insight which draws one near to the true deity, Tloque Nahuaque, the Lord of the Near and Close. This conception of the invisible god who dwelled in all things but was above all things, was developed by Nezahualcoyotl into a complex theological notion which invited reflection by a number of poets, artists and *tlamatinime* (wise men, 'knowers of things'). A number of composers sought ways of invoking and paying homage to the 'Giver of Life', the great god who is the mystery of divinity. (D.C.)

Nezahualpilli [XVIII] (1460–1515). Ruler of the Aztec city-state of Texcoco. The successor of his father, Nezahualcoyotl, he developed the city into the cultural centre of the Valley of Mexico. His own religious interests focused on astronomy and astrology, i.e. the patterns of celestial bodies which served as the basis, in part, for his reign and the leadership he expressed. He used the palace as an observatory and was consulted by other rulers as to the astronomical influences on political and ritual events. In some accounts, Moctezuma II consulted him concerning difficulties in the kingdom. [1: 163, 346, 478] (D.C.)

Ngundeng [I.A] (*d.*1906). The most important of a series of prophets among the Nuer and Dinka of the Sudan who led their communities' resistance to Anglo-Egyptian colonial rule. Through various types of ascetic practices he would become possessed by a spirit called *deng*. He constructed a small pyramid in Nuer country that became a major pilgrimage site for the Nuer and introduced a series of new rituals within his community. His focus on *deng*, a spirit of Dinka origin, was an important conduit for the introduction of Dinka concepts of lesser spiritual beings into Nuer religion, as well as new sources of religious power to assist the Nuer in their frequent revolts against Arab or British intruders. At his death in 1906 his son Gwek inherited Ngundeng's spiritual authority and continued his prophetic role until he was killed by the British. [7] (R.M.B.)

Nichiren [IV] (1222–1282). Japanese Buddhist monk and founder of the Nichiren (or Hokke/Lotus) sect. He was born in Kominato, a small seaside village in modern Chiba prefecture. He entered Kiyosumi-dera, a neighbouring Tendai temple, at the age of 12 and studied Tendai, Pure Land and esoteric Buddhism. After a few years in Kamakura he continued his studies on Mt Hiei, Mt Kōya and Nara. In 1253 Nichiren returned home to Kiyosumi-dera, where he proclaimed his faith in the *Lotus Sūtra* and rejected all other forms of Buddhism, proposing instead the chanting of the *daimoku*, *namu myōhōrengekyō* ('homage to the *Lotus Sūtra*'). His message was not well received and Nichiren went to Kamakura, where he presented his *Risshō ankoku ron* ('Treatise on Establishing Orthodoxy to Bring Peace to the Country') to Hōjō Tokiyori (1227–1263), the *de facto* ruler of Japan. Nichiren blamed other Buddhist (especially Pure Land) schools for various disasters and predicted further troubles including foreign invasion if the government did not accept the 'true' Buddhism of the *Lotus Sūtra*. Instead, Nichiren was exiled to Izu.

After being released from exile in 1263, Nichiren travelled widely, continued his provocative preaching which was buoyed by the Mongol invasions which fulfilled his prophesies, escaped assassination and execution, and finally faced exile again in 1271, this time to Sado Island in the Japan Sea. Here he wrote *Kaimokusho* ('Opening the Eyes'), in which he claimed to be a reincarnation of Jōgyō Bosatsu, the figure presented in the *Lotus Sūtra* as one who will appear in later times to preach and uphold this sūtra. He also composed a distinctive maṇḍala as a representation of all living beings and Buddhas surrounding the *daimoku* in the centre. Another text composed at this time was the *Kanjin honzon sho* ('Contemplating the Object of Worship'), perhaps his most important work, in which Nichiren expands on the Tendai concept of *ichinen sanzen* ('all of reality in a single thought') and the ideal of setting up a Buddha land in this world.

Nichiren was released from Sado in 1274 and returned briefly to Kamakura but settled at Minobu. He gathered many disciples and wrote numerous letters, revealing a sensitivity which belies his reputation as an acerbic fanatic. He died in 1282 after a long period of illness.

Nichiren is famous for his fierce denunciation of other schools: '*Nenbutsu* leads to hell, Zen followers are devils, Shingon ruins the country, and members of the Ritsu school are traitors.' He summed up the true Lotus faith in three parts: (1) *honzon*, Śākyamuni, the personification of truth, as the object of worship; (2) *kaidan*, the ordination platform as a religious centre; and (3) *daimoku*, the chanting of homage to the *Lotus Sūtra*.

Nichiren still commands a large following among Buddhists in Japan, and many of the new religious movements stem from the Nichiren tradition. [5; 183] (P.L.S.)

Nicholas Cabasilas, St [VI.A] (1322–1391). Lay mystic and theologian of the Orthodox Church. A nephew of Archbishop Nilus Cabasilas, he was a close associate of ST GREGORY PALAMAS and for a time minister to Emperor John Cantacuzene. In 1353 he was one of the three elected candidates for the Patriarchal throne. He wrote a celebrated commentary on the liturgy and *The Life in Christ*, a masterpiece of sacramental theology. [17; 18] (D.B.)

Nicholas of Cusa [VI.A] (1401–1464). German scholar and cardinal. He was born in Kues on the Moselle. He studied at Heidelberg (1416), Padua (1417) and at the university of Cologne from 1425 emerging a doctor of canon law. Ordained priest in 1430, he became Dean of St Florin's church in Koblenz. He exercised his legal training in a dispute over the archiepiscopal see of Trier at the Council of Basel in 1433. He advocated reform of church and empire and the power of conciliar authority in his *De concordantia catholica* (1433), in which year he worked for the reconciliation of the Hussites (*see* HUS, JAN). He became a defender of the papacy, and in 1437 represented the Pope in Constantinople in an attempt at reconciliation with the Eastern church. In 1450 he was made bishop of Brixen in the Tyrol and papal legate for the Germanic countries. Conflict with Duke Sigismund from 1459 onwards eventually forced him to return to Rome, where he spent the rest of his life as Camerarius of the Sacred College. He wrote original philosophy, including *De docta ignorantia* (1440), and adopted an ecumenical attitude towards other religions, especially Islam after the fall of Constantinople, in *De pace fidei* (1453) and *Cribratio Alcoran* (1461). [373; 584] (T.T.)

Nicholls, Sir Douglas Ralph [XXI] (1906–1988). Aboriginal Church of Christ pastor, highly influential in many domains. He was born at Cumeroogunga, an Aboriginal station, his mother of Wimmera ancestry and his father of Yota Yota descent. His reputation began as an athlete; he was a prize-winning runner, travelled with a boxing troupe and represented Victoria in Australian Rules football. He came from a strong Christian family, but it was not until 1932 that he 'confessed Christ' in a Melbourne Church of Christ. His religious convictions began to focus on social justice when his relative William Cooper moved to Melbourne and founded the Australian Aborigines' League, the first all-Aboriginal organization established to fight for citizenship and other rights. Nicholls was seen as the League's main liaison with Whites. He was further involved in protesting against the 150th Australian Day celebrations and in creating both the Aboriginal 'Day of Mourning' (1938) and the first Aboriginal strike at Cumeroogunga (1939). Both were symptomatic of the frustration of Aborigines with oppressive regimes. Nicholls was instrumental in securing legal aid for convicted Melbourne Aborigines and in 1944 negotiated the establishment of the Churches of Christ Aborigines Mission. He strongly protested at the explosion of atomic weapons near Aboriginal homelands in 1957, and travelled to witness the appalling consequences of the Maralinga tests. As a partial result of these visits he became a full-time field-officer with the newly formed Aborigines Advancement League, and later became its director (1969–74). In 1958 he opened a hostel providing shelter to Aboriginal girls. He was the first Aborigine to receive an OBE (1957) and a Knighthood (1972). He was accorded the honour of Father of the Year in Victoria, 1962, and in 1976 was appointed Governor of South Australia. Ill health forced his early retirement the following year. Sir Douglas lived to see many of the battles he helped fight at least partially won: citizenship rights, land rights, the establishment of the Department of Aboriginal Affairs, rising Aboriginal population, and improvements in health and education services. A new generation of Aboriginal activists has been critical of his comfortable associations with White institutes and honorific titles, and he himself at times realized he was judging fellow Aborigines by White standards. He was aware of his failings but was nevertheless proud of his heritage, believing he came from a people traditionally 'really close to God'. [6; 7] (T.S.)

Nicolar, Joseph [xx] (1827–1894). A Penobscot holy man, author and tribal leader. He was born 15 February 1827, a descendant of a long line of Penobscot leaders. With the benefit of a relatively extensive education, at least for the time, Nicolar was able to realize his long-standing ambition of recording the myths, legends and history of the Penobscot people. He contributed articles on Amerindian history, crafts and arts to Maine newspapers; his reputation earned him the distinction of serving as the Penobscot tribal representative to the Maine Legislature. He also was Governor of the Penobscot Tribe from 1889 to 1894. His major work, *The Life and Traditions of the Red Man* (1893), claimed to be a pure and complete record of Penobscot myth and history, yet it shows clear signs of Christian influence. Central to Nicolar's narrative are the exploits of Klose-kur-beh (or Gluskabe/Glooscap), the creator/culture-hero who prepares the universe for the appearance of human beings. This account is completed by a history of the Penobscots. Nicolar's passionate commitment to the preservation of the Penobscot religious and cultural heritage gained him a reputation as a holy man as well as a man of letters. [12: IX–XVI] (S.R.)

Nicoll, Henry Maurice Dunlop [xvii.d] (1884–1953). Author and teacher of the Gurdjieff system. He was the son of Sir William Robertson Nicoll, a distinguished literary figure and editor of *The British Review*. He was educated at Cambridge and St Bartholomew's Hospital, London, qualifying in medicine in 1910. He then studied psychological medicine in Vienna and Zurich, being very close to Jung. After serving as a doctor in the army during the First World War, he returned to England in 1917. Three books belong to this period, *Dream Psychology*, *In Mesopotamia* and *The Blue Gem*. He resumed his practice in Harley Street, and, in 1920, married Catherine Champion Jones. In 1922 he went to meetings given by Ouspensky, who had just arrived in England, and was greatly impressed. Gurdjieff himself arrived in London, and it was decided to set up Gurdjieff's Institute for the Harmonious Development of Man in Paris. Nicoll gave up his lucrative practice and in November 1922 went to the Institute, where he worked intensively with Gurdjieff until the latter dissolved the Institute in the autumn of 1923. He never saw Gurdjieff again. Nicoll returned to London and resumed his practice, continuing to work on the system with Ouspensky, until, in 1931, Ouspensky told him to go away and establish and teach his own group. This he did, teaching in London and at a house in the Essex countryside built by his newly established group. The Second World War led to Nicoll and some members of the group living in Gloucestershire, but after the war they returned to new premises near London. Besides the system, Nicoll had a particular interest in what he termed 'esoteric Christianity', which is in fact what Gurdjieff used to claim his system was, and his thoughts on this were published as *The New Man* (1950), and also in *The Mark*, which appeared posthumously. His major publication, however, is the five-volume *Psychological Commentaries on The Teaching of Gurdjieff and Ouspensky* (1952), which remains one of the clearest expositions of the system [5]. There is no material available on his own personal inner life, but he was clearly an excellent teacher and is spoken of with much affection and gratitude in the accounts of his various pupils and helpers. The portrait of Nicoll by his secretary and pupil Beryl Pogson is the closest that one can come to him. [6] (S.C.R.W.)

Niebuhr, Reinhold [VI.A] (1892–1971). American theologian. He was born in Wright City, Missouri. He was educated at Elmhurst College (1910), Eden Theological Seminary and Yale Divinity School. He graduated from Yale in 1914 (BD), was awarded an MA in 1915 and ordained in the same year, entering on a pastorate at Bethel Evangelical Church, Detroit. He ministered there until 1928, when he was appointed Professor of Applied Christianity at Union Theological Seminary, New York. He married Ursula Keppel-Compton in 1931. Apart from his pastoral and professorial duties Niebuhr was always involved with preaching and social and political action. For many years he was a socialist and a pacifist. His main works were *Moral Man and Immoral Society* (1932) and the Gifford Lectures of 1939, *The Nature and Destiny of Man* (2 vols. 1941–3). [272; 429; 756] (T.T.)

Niemöller, Martin [VI.A] (1892–1984). German Protestant pastor. He was born in Westphalia, the son of a Lutheran pastor. In the First World War he served as U-boat commander. He became a pastor of the Protestant church in Westphalia in 1924 and in Berlin-Dahlem in 1931. He was an early supporter of National Socialism but turned against it on account of the pagan element he detected in it, and gave his support to the Confessing Church. He was arrested for his anti-Nazi stance in 1937 and sent to Sachsenhausen concentration camp. Although offered release on certain conditions he refused and remained a prisoner until May 1945. He later became the head of the Foreign Relations Department of the Evangelical Church and Vice-Chairman of its council until 1949. In 1947 he became the first Kirchenpräsident of the newly formed Evangelical church of Hesse-Nassau and remained in that post until 1964. He was a president of the World Council of Churches from 1961 to 1968. [586; 711] (T.T.)

Nijima, Jo [VI.A] [Joseph Hardy Neeshima] (1843–1890). Japanese Christian. He was born in Yedo (Tokyo), the son of a *samurai*, and a subject of the feudal lord Annaka Clan. His family were devout Confucianists and he was trained in the martial arts and Chinese classics, but also studied English and Dutch. He acquired a copy of the Bible in Chinese which he read clandestinely. Soon he decided to defy the law and escape to America. He arrived in Boston in 1864. He was befriended by Alpheus Hardy, the owner of the ship which brought him. Hardy, a merchant and member of the American Board of Commissioners for Foreign Missions, supported Nijima's education at Amherst College and Andover Seminary. When a Japanese government mission visited the United States and Europe in 1871 Nijima served as interpreter, and was granted official pardon and permission to teach Christianity on his return to Japan in 1874. He was supported in his aim to found a college by the American Board and was accorded the status of a missionary. He visited his aged parents at Annaka and began to preach the gospel there. This activity led to the formation of the first church in the interior. He established a college in Kyoto. He received official permission to open Doshisha College. Christianity was to be taught as Moral Science and Bible teaching had to be extra-curricular. The college was organized as a Japanese institution and in time became the largest Christian college and the only one to attain university status by 1890, the year Nijima died. [144; 194; 345; 790] (T.T.)

Nikodemos of the Holy Mountain, St [VI.B] (1749–1809). Born on Naxos, he studied under Chrysanthos, brother of ST KOSMAS AETOLOS, then in Smyrna, becoming an Athonite monk at the age of 26. He wrote, edited or translated over 27 books. With St Makarios Notaras, Archbishop of Corinth, he compiled the *Philokalia*, an anthology of spiritual writings (published at Venice, 1782) famous throughout the Orthodox world. PAISSY VELICHKOVSKY published a Slavonic translation, the *Dobrotolubye*, in 1793. [22; 23] (D.B.)

Nikolai Kasatkin, St [VI.B] [Ivan Dmitrovich Kasatkin] (1836–1912). Russian orthodox missionary and Archbishop of Japan. Nikolai went to Japan as chaplain to the Russian Embassy, but also devoted himself to missionary work among the Japanese, ordaining Japanese priests and translating service books. In 1880 he was consecrated Archbishop of the church he had founded. His translations are remarkable examples of Meiji Japanese. During the Russo-Japanese war (1904–5) he refused to compromise his spiritual work and gave his wholehearted support to the Japanese cause. [29; 80] (D.B.)

Nikon [VI.A] [Nikita Minin] (1605–1681). Patriarch of Moscow, 1652–8. He received a monastic education, married and served as a parish priest in Moscow for ten years until the early 1630s, when his three children died. By agreement his wife entered a convent and he a monastery at Solovietski on the White Sea. From 1634 to 1643 he lived a solitary life. After a disagreement with his fellow monks he left for the Kojeozerski hermitage, where he was elected abbot. During a visit to Moscow in 1646 the Tsar made him the archimandrite of the Novospaski monastery. Three years later he was made Metropolitan of Novgorod. In 1652 he was made Patriarch of Moscow. He instituted changes, including changes to the Russian liturgy. He sought to bring it in line with Greek usage, which he considered universal, and also changed certain rituals in the same way. He alienated the revivalists or Old Believers and the split was never healed. After his election as Patriarch he strengthened the power of his office and offended the Tsar. By 1658 he was out of imperial favour. He resigned his office and retired to the 'New Jerusalem' monastery which he had founded. He tried to be restored but in 1667 the Council of Moscow finally deposed and banished him, though his liturgical reforms were accepted. After 14 years of imprisonment the new tsar Feodor II rehabilitated him and invited him back to Moscow. He died before he got there. [618; 624; 888] (T.T.)

Niles, Daniel Thambyrajah [VI.A] (1908–1970). Born near Jaffna, Ceylon (Sri Lanka) into a Methodist family, he studied for the ministry at Bangalore, at what is now the United Theological College. He graduated in 1933, and in that year attended the Quadrennial of the Student Christian Movement for India, Burma and Ceylon. In 1938 he attended the conference of the International Missionary Council in Madras. In 1948 he delivered the keynote address at the first Assembly of the World Council of Churches (WCC) in Amsterdam. He was awarded a doctorate by the University of London and was General Secretary of the National Christian Council of Ceylon and the first Chairman of the WCC Youth Department. From 1953 he was executive secretary of the WCC Department of Evangelism, principal of Jaffna Central College, pastor of St Peter's Church, Jaffna, and Chairman of the World Student Christian Federation. In Uppsala in 1968 he replaced the assassinated MARTIN LUTHER KING in an address to the Assembly of the WCC. By this time he was Executive Secretary of the East Asia Christian Council, whose *Hymnal* he edited in 1963, President of the Methodist Church of Ceylon and one of the presidents of the WCC. For a time he was Harry Emerson Fosdick Visiting Professor at Union Theological Seminary, New York City. A few of his published works were originally lectures: *Preaching the Gospel of the Resurrection* (Bevan Memorial Lectures, Adelaide, Australia, 1952; published 1953); *The Preacher's Calling to be a Servant* (Warreck Lectures, Scotland, 1959; published 1959); and *The Preacher's Task and the Stone of Stumbling* (Lyman Beecher Lectures, Yale, 1957; published 1958). [280; 587; 588] (T.T.)

Niʿmat Allāh Valī, Shāh [VI.A] (1329–1431). Eponymous founder of the Niʿmatallāhī Ṣūfī order of Iran, one of the very few Shiʿite orders in existence. Born in Aleppo, he came to Iraq at an early age. After a formal education, he embarked on a mystical quest that took him through Iran to Egypt and, finally, Arabia. Arriving in Mecca at the age of 24, he spent the next seven years there as one of the chief disciples of Shaykh ʿAbd Allāh al-Yāfiʿī (*d.*1366).

After a period in Transoxiana (Samarkand, Herat), he returned to Iran, moving from place to place until finally settling in the village of Māhān, near Kerman, where he spent the last 25 years of his life. A magnificent shrine now marks the site of his grave there.

Niʿmat Allāh enjoyed excellent relations with a number of rulers in the course of his travels, and several of his descendants later married into the Safavid royal family. After his death, leadership of the Niʿmatallāhī order moved to India, although members of his family and disciples remained in Iran. The order underwent an important revival in Iraq and Iran in the 18th and 19th centuries, becoming the focus for violent persecution by the Shiʿite clergy.

Niʿmat Allāh's literary output was considerable. He is credited with some 500 Ṣūfī treatises, but is better celebrated for his *Dīwān* of mystical poetry, which, though of inferior quality, is widely known. [18] (D.M.)

Nimbārka [XI] [Nimbāditya; Niyamānanda] (12th–13th century). Brahman from Andhra, regarded as the founder of the Kṛṣṇaite Nimbārka or Sanakādi sect, which constitutes one of the four principal Vaiṣṇava *samprada ̄yas*. His dates are highly contentious and range widely from source to source, especially, it would seem, *vis-à-vis* those of RĀMA ̄NUJA (and even VALLABHA). Nimbārka, whose name is traditionally connected to a story in which the beams of the setting sun (*arka*) were made to hang in a neem (*nimba*) tree in order to accommodate a vow of not eating after nightfall, promotes the philosophy of *dvaitādvaita*, 'dualistic non-dualism'. His equating of Brahman with Kṛṣṇa, and his emphasis on *prapatti* or submission as the only approach to divine grace, form an essential component in the make-up of late medieval Vaiṣṇavism; his importance thus extends well beyond the confines of sectarian institutions. The modern Nimbārka sect, based in Salemabad near Jaipur, follows the same mythological and theological Rādhā-Kṛṣṇa constructs as the parallel traditions of Vallabha and CAITANYA, while remaining indebted (in principle at least) to the *dvaitādvaita* philosophy. Though many of the early sectarian teachers were Brahmans from the Braj city of Mathura, the traditional claims that Nimba ̄rka himself lived at Mathura and Govardhan remain unsubstantiated, and perhaps represent little more than an attempt to antedate the establishment of the mode of devotionalism practised in the modern era. [31; 22: vol. 3: XXI] (R.S.)

Nino, St [VI.B] (*d. c.*340). Enlightener of the Georgians. According to Rufinus (*d. c.*403) she was a slave whose saintly life drew her Georgian owners to Christianity. Orthodox tradition says she preached throughout Georgia, baptizing King Mirian and his family, thus laying the foundations of the Georgian Orthodox Church. [60: 103ff.] (D.B.)

Ninomiya Sontoku [XIV] (1787–1856). Japanese agriculturalist, philosopher and the founder of the Hōtoku movement. He urged farmers to adopt new agricultural techniques and farming methods as a means of increasing their production. By doing so, he argued, they would also contribute to the government treasury and thus fulfil their duty to support the nation. This ideal was known as *hōtoku* ('repaying virtue'), and is virtually synonymous with *hōon* ('repaying blessings'). Ninomiya combined natural science, carefully calculating fertilizer and irrigation needs for individual farm plots, with neo-Confucian ethics and Buddhist ideals, and presented them in the form of practical and simple teachings.

Ninomiya presented the traditional family system and filial piety as expressions of the ideal of *hōtoku*, for one's body is a result of the labours and frugality of one's ancestors. He portrayed the farmer's life and work as central to the establishment and maintenance of a universal society of peace and prosperity. In his view, labour itself has an essential sacrality. In pursuing the Way, one improves not only one's own lot but also that of one's neighbours and the nation and one's descendants. He rejected Confucian ideas of historical cycles and all Buddhist theories of transmigration and degenerative cosmic cycles, arguing that through the cultivation of diligence and economy one could assure one-way continuous progress. Other expressions of Ninomiya's blending of religion and economic rationalization are his urging the establishment of village credit unions, called Hōtoku Societies, which made interest-free loans for capital improvements, and the principal of *bundo*, accumulating more in a year than one would use in the next, with the surplus saved for emergencies or capital investments. As a result of the missionary zeal of his followers, Ninomiya became a paradigmatic figure in the 19th and 20th centuries, and statues of him were (and in many areas still are) found on the grounds of most elementary schools. [34: 160] (G.E.)

Niveditā, Sister [XI] [Margaret Noble] (1867–1911). Hindu nun and Indian nationalist. She was born in a Methodist family in Dungannon, Co. Tyrone, Ireland, and became a teacher in England, starting her own school at Wimbledon in 1892. In 1895–6 she became attracted to VIVEKANANDA's ideas, and in 1898 she went to India to join his movement, was initiated as a *brahmacāriṇī* (celibate student) in the RAMAKRISHNA order, and was given the name Niveditā ('given', 'dedicated') by Vivekananda. She revisited the West in 1899–1900 (partly with Vivekananda), 1900–1902, 1907–9, and 1910–11. She died in Darjeeling in 1911. Her work for the Ramakrishna movement included education, fund-raising, plague relief and writing. She left the order formally in 1902, while remaining its supporter, to free herself for political work. In 1902–4 she toured India giving public lectures attacking British policies. From 1905, when Curzon's partition of Bengal aroused an upsurge of Bengali nationalism, she worked with Bepin Chandra Pal, AUROBINDO and other Bengali leaders; she supported the Swadeshi movement (promoting the manufacture and use of Indian products to replace British imports). When Aurobindo left Calcutta in 1910, she took over his paper *Karmayogin*. Her political activities were inspired by the belief, shared with Vivekananda, that the key to India's problems was spiritual. Her work on education, art and science aimed to show that India was capable of independence in these fields, and her work on religion extolled popular Hinduism as well as Vedanta. [82; 95] (D.H.K.)

Niwano Nikkyō [IV] (1906–). Co-founder with Naganuma Myōkō (1889–1957) of the Dai Nippon Risshō Kōseikai ('The Great Society to Establish Righteousness and Foster Fellowship') in 1938. Born in Niigata prefecture, Niwano went to Tokyo in his youth and there became a member of a divination society. After he was drafted and had served three years in the navy, he married and opened a pickle shop. When a daughter fell seriously ill he was converted to the teachings of Reiyūkai. He closed his shop and became a milkman in order to support his family while proselytizing. One of his early converts to Reiyūkai was Naganuma, who, after they left the parent group, quickly became the co-leader of Risshō Kōseikai. By 1945 the group had more than 3,000 members, and by 1955 more than a million.

Like Reiyukai, Risshō Kōseikai holds the *Lotus Sūtra* to be the key to universal salvation; recitation of the *daimoku* is a central practice and NICHIREN is held to be the pivotal figure in the history of Buddhism. However, in contradistinction to the teachings of Reiyūkai, Niwano taught that recitation of the *daimoku* does not lead to the accrual of any spiritual merit, but is rather an affirmation of one's faith in the *Lotus Sūtra*. This doctrinal difference was a major cause of the split between these two groups. Risshō Kōseikai remains loosely affiliated with other Nichiren groups, but is not as militant in its advocacy of the *Lotus Sūtra* as Sōka Gakkai, for instance (*see* MAKIGUCHI TSUNESABURŌ; IKEDA DAISAKU). This lay Buddhist movement's practice includes the veneration of ancestral spirits, divination, group counselling sessions and rites for dealing with negative karmic factors in one's life. During his career Niwano was an active public speaker and writer, and was deeply involved in the international peace movement. [168; 169; 161: 158–63; 198: 231–48] (G.E.)

Nobili, Roberto de [VI.A] (1577–1656). Italian Jesuit missionary. He was born in Tuscany, and joined the Society of Jesus in 1597. In 1604 he was sent to the mission in India, where he arrived in 1605. After a period learning the Tamil language he was sent to Madurai. He distanced himself from the Portuguese mission already existing there and adopted an Indian style of living. He patterned his life on the highest, Brahman, caste and decided that those who were converted would not be required to abandon caste apart from practices considered idolatrous. He also learned Sanskrit, the language of Brahman scholars, and conducted his mission through public discussions on religious topics. He persuaded some high-caste Hindus to accept baptism. Other missionaries objected to his work and he had to defend himself before his bishop in Goa in a 'reply to objections' in 1610. His work generally received the approval of Rome in a Bull issued by Gregory XV, *Romanae Sedis Antistes* (1623). He later extended his mission to Trichinopoly and Salem, and brought many of the lower castes into the church. In 1645 he was withdrawn from the Madurai mission and spent the rest of his years at Mylapore, near Madras, poor and almost totally blind. [171; 591] (T.T.)

Nongqause [I.A] (*c.*1840–*c.*1900). A major figure in the great Xhosa cattle sacrifice/killings of 1856–7 in South Africa. Early in 1856 Nongqause reported a vision to her uncle, Mhlakaza, himself an established prophet. In her vision, Xhosa ancestors promised a millennium of freedom from European intrusion in return for the sacrifice of material wealth and spiritual purification. This message was communicated to Sarili, the Gcaleka Xhosa leader, who worked to support its implementation. In the following ten months some 150,000 cattle and great amounts of crops and grain reserves were destroyed by the Gcaleka Xhosa and some of the neighbouring peoples. When the forecast millennium failed to arrive, famine and destitution fell upon the region, in which tens of thousands are reported to have perished. Many Xhosa migrated to the Cape Colony in search of food and work. To escape persecution, Nongqause fled and was later placed in 'protective custody' by the British colonial authorities, unlike her uncle, who was killed soon after the prophecies proved incorrect. Nongqause was later released, and lived out the remainder of her life in obscurity. [30; 42: 239–41] (R.H.)

Ntsikana [VI.A] (*d.*1821). Xhosa prophet. He was a mature man, head of a family and a councillor when, in or about 1815, he had a call-vision. He was certainly aware of VANDERKEMP's preaching, but the precise degree of acquaintance with missionary teaching is unclear. His vision took place at the gateway to the cattle byre, a place sacred to the ancestors, one of several features pointing to continuity with Xhosa tradition; but he attributed it not to the ancestors but to God, and it led him to break with some cherished traditions. In response, he washed off his red ochre and began to pray and to preach. He denounced the prophet Nxele, who was calling for reinforcement of old ways, and called for turning to God and moral purification. His later preaching became more explicitly Christian. His independence, however, led him to reconceive Xhosa traditional terms and give them new meaning. He is thus an early pioneer of African theology. His followers became absorbed in Xhosa Christianity, the father of TIYO SOGA providing a link. Ntsikana's Xhosa *Great Hymn* is in regular use. [365; 366] (A.F.W.)

Numa Pompilius [XXII] (*fl. c.*700 BCE). The second of the kings who were said to have ruled Rome in its infancy (traditional dates of reign, 715–673 BCE). Following the ancient practice of ascribing a state's institutions to heroic and semi-legendary early founders, much of Rome's official religious apparatus (i.e. the priesthoods, certain temples, and especially the calendar with its cycle of festivals [2: I–V; 12; 16: I–XIII; 31: 157–236]) was ascribed to Numa, just as its political establishment was ascribed to the first king, Romulus. Stories record that Numa acquired the wisdom for his initiatives from two sources, his mistress, the local goddess Egeria, and the Greek sage Pythagoras. The first is obviously mythical, the second chronologically impossible. What elements of public Roman religion were actually established by an historical king called Numa is finally undiscoverable – one suspects not many. An enjoyable biography, clearly fictional for the most part, exists in the series of *Parallel Lives* (Greek and Roman) written by Plutarch in the early 2nd century CE [28], where Numa is paired with the Spartan founder Lycurgus. (R.B.)

O

Oberá [XXIV] (16th century). Leader of a messianic revolt against Spanish overlordship, on behalf of the Guaraní people of Paraguay, in the latter 16th century. Oberá proclaimed himself the son of God, born of a virgin, and demanded adoration and offerings of his followers. He promised his disciples a return to traditional Guaraní lifeways. As proof of his heavenly origins and election the messiah kept in a ritual gourd container the great comet that had recently been seen in the west. In due time, he assured, he would bring it out to scorch the earth and destroy the Christians. Oberá called himself the 'radiant splendour of God'. He ordered his followers to cease sowing and harvesting. Instead, they should perform liturgical dances and songs without cease. Oberá gave his son Guiraró ('Dry Branch') a cross to carry and commissioned him to baptize disciples and give them new names. Another son was named emperor and given police powers to punish wayward followers. Oberá menaced Spanish authorities in Paraguay. Indians came from far and wide to join him, his influence extending as far as Asunción. Juan de Garay, governor of the province, set out with a squad of 120 soldiers to disperse the faithful and capture the prophet. Several thousand followers, led by a disciple named Guayraca, took refuge in trenches protected by a stockade. The messiah instructed one of the Guaraní chiefs to sacrifice a calf and scatter its ashes in the wind. Contrary to the prophet's prediction, this rite failed to disperse the enemy troops. Demoralized by Oberá's powerlessness, the Guaraní attempted to flee the stockade but were massacred by the soldiers. The messiah escaped without a trace. [8: 23–7] (L.S.)

Obu, Olumba Olumba [I.A] (1918–). Founder and Sole Spiritual Head of the Brotherhood of the Cross and Star, a Nigerian independent Christian movement. Within a period of just over 30 years Obu has overseen the development of his movement from healing home to international evangelistic organization. He was born in Biakpan, in the Cross River State of eastern Nigeria. His birth and early childhood are surrounded by legends. In 1934 he moved to the city of Calabar as a petty trader and started holding prayer meetings in his home. Obu had very little formal or religious education. He founded his movement in 1956 in Calabar based upon 'practical Christianity' and perfectionist moral teaching. His followers revere his exceptional spiritual and healing powers and his ascetic way of life; he has become increasingly divinized over the years. He is popularly known as 'Holy Father' and later Brotherhood publications are entitled *His Deity is Revealed* and *The Supreme Being*. His birthplace is known as Bethlehem or the New Jerusalem and the waters of the local river are believed to have curative powers. Brotherhood members regularly go on overseas missions and also congregate three times yearly in Calabar to adulate their leader. Obu is renowned for speaking out on issues of national importance. His sermons are published regularly by the movement's own prolific publishing house. [12: 186–92; 38] (R.H.)

Ockham, William of. *See* WILLIAM OF OCKHAM.

Ogyū Sorai [XIV] (1666–1728). One of the most famous Tokugawa Confucian scholars. He advocated a return to the way of the ancient sages before Confucius (*see* K'UNG TZU) in order to learn how to cultivate one's nature and the regulation of the emotions by composing in classical literary styles and by rehearsing ancient ritual etiquette. He looked primarily to the Six Classics, including especially the *Shih ching* ('Book of Odes') [64], *Shu ching* ('Book of History') [32], *Li chi* ('Book of Rites') [36] and *Yüeh ching* ('Book of Music'), as the repository of the ancient way, recording the deeds and achievements of the sages and kings following the will of heaven. His study of ancient literary styles was a form of neoclassical philology indebted to the (Chinese) Ming critics Li P'am-lung (1514–1570) and Wang Shih-chen (1526–1590). In his writings he attacked Ch'eng-chu scholars for what he took to be misreadings of the classics, as well as for adopting modern prose styles. He was also influenced by Itō Jensei's dualistic ontology.

Ogyū attacked the notion of mind in Ch'eng-chu orthodoxy, a notion popularized by Fujiwara Seika (1561–1619), Nakae Tōju and the disciples of YAMAZAKI ANSAI; he did this first by denying the existence of the transcendental, and second by claiming that there are only individual minds devoid of any moral endowment. For Ogyū the potential chaos of the relativism promised by the existence of an infinite number of particular minds was checked by the final moral standard reflected in the Six Classics. What his contemporaries called 'principle' was, he argued, mere subjective theory, not an authentic universal principle. If men cannot hope to know the active material force in heaven, spirits and natural phenomena, they can, Ogyū believed, know the concrete things, particularly the institutions and practices of classical China, through the study of the Six Classics. In contrast to YAMAGA SOKŌ and others, who were chiefly interested in cultivating morality, Ogyū felt that human nature is not naturally good and that self-cultivation is not sufficient for establishing a just society; this requires legal and institutional controls as well. He accepted the then new cosmological conception that change, not stasis, is the normal condition of the cosmos and human beings. Yet he argued that classical Chinese civilization is timeless and changeless, writing that: 'In the teachings [of the ancient sages] there is neither past nor present. The Way has neither past nor present.' In *A Proposal for the Great Peace* and *A Discourse on Government* he maintained that the inadequacies of present-day institutions are due to their having evolved over time without proper attention to history and human emotions. In many ways, however, Ogyū was a realist. Surveying the socio-economic situation of Japan, he argued that the samurai had become self-sufficient in order to overcome their dire financial straits, and he suggested that the sale of land should be legalized. [3; 34: 159–67; 38: 7; 65; 66] (G.E.)

Okada Mokichi [XIV] (1882–1955). Founder of Sekai Kyūseikyō ('The Church of World Messianity'). After suffering from a variety of illnesses as a child, he lost the family business in the Tokyo earthquake of 1923. Shortly thereafter he was introduced to the teachings and faith healing practices of Ōmotokyō, becoming an active member and quickly rising in its leadership ranks. In 1926, in a state of divine possession, the creator god revealed to Okada that he was the messiah of the present age. In 1934 Okada left Ōmotokyō to found the Dai Nihon Kannonkai ('Great Japan Kannon [Avalokiteśvara] Association'), which was renamed Sekai Kyūseikyō in 1950.

Okada enjoyed fame as a faith-healer. He taught that illness can be cured through purifying one's spirit, while medicines are harmful. The central ritual practice in Sekai Kyūseikyō is called *jorei*, channelling the divine light through cupped raised hands to parts of the body; this is supposed to purify the body. Okada taught that an earthly paradise can be realized through the elimination of the three evils of sickness, poverty and strife. These evils can be dissipated, like dark clouds, by divine light, which is transmitted by the teachers of Sekai Kyūseikyō. Okada also advocated organic farming and natural methods of cultivation. During his lifetime, Okada distributed more than 600,000 pieces of paper on which he had written the Chinese character for 'light': these were said to have curative powers. After his death the leadership of the group passed first to his wife and then to a daughter. [12: 111–46; 34: 314–16; 46; 59: 173–82] (G.E.)

Olaf the Holy [VI.A] [Olaf Haraldsön; Olaf II] (995–1030). King of Norway, *c.*1016–28. He became a Viking at an early age and attacked shipping in the Baltic Sea and off the coast of England. He fought for the Duke of

Normandy against the Danes. Following a dream in which it was revealed that he should be king of Norway he returned there via Rouen, where he stayed the winter of 1013–14. While he was there he was baptized. He arrived in Norway in 1015, defeated Earl Sweyn at the battle of Nesje in 1016 and became king. For some years he carried out the elimination of the old religion and the forceful conversion of his people. The Norwegian chieftains eventually revolted and in alliance with the Danish king Canute forced Olaf to flee to Russia. As the result of another dream he tried to recover his throne but was killed at the battle of Stiklestad. His people ousted their new Danish rulers and restored the throne to his son Magnus; Olaf was sanctified and became Norway's patron saint. His shrine at Nidaros (Trondhjem) was a famous pilgrimage centre in the Middle Ages. [328; 370] (T.T.)

Olaf Tryggvason [VIII] [Olaf I] (*c.*968–*c.*1000). King of Norway, 995–1000, who established Christianity there. Olaf was the son of a minor king in southern Norway; his father died when he was very young, and his mother had to escape with him to Russia. According to tradition, they were captured and sold as slaves on the way, but Olaf finally reached Russia and was brought up in the court of Vladimir of Kiev. He became a ruthless Viking leader, plundering in the British Isles, but was received into the Christian church there in 991 or 994. He became a fanatical convert, determined to spread the new faith and force the Norwegians to accept it. In 995 he defeated Jarl Hakon, who supported the old religion, and ruled for five years until he was killed in a sea battle when the Danes attacked him with a fleet supported by many Swedes and Norwegians. For a long while he was believed to have escaped to the Holy Land, and men expected his return. Olaf was a charismatic leader, with great strength and courage, and for five years he held Norway with a strong fleet and the money won by raiding. He was credited in sagas and legends with the conversion of Norway, Iceland, Greenland, the Faroes and the Shetlands, but seems to have done little more than set up the church in Norway and crushed opposition, while he sent missionaries to Iceland. [5: II] The Scandinavians established him as a great Christian hero, and the first Latin account of his life, written about 1190 by the Icelandic monk Odd Snorrason, represented him as a miracle-worker, possessed of magical powers against the heathen, but gave few facts about his career. When SNORRI STURLUSON wrote a long saga about him in *Heimskringla*, his great history of the Norwegian kings (*c.*1230), he found it hard to obtain much information and had to improvise a splendid setting for a few bald facts. Olaf figures in many popular legends as a Christian champion against wizards, trolls and the ancient gods, who try unsuccessfully to overthrow him, and as the protector of his men against the forces of evil. [4: IV] (H.E.D.)

Olcott, Henry Steel [IV] (1832–1907). American author, attorney and co-founder of the Theosophical Society. Olcott's early life story is one of worldly success and achievement; by his mid-twenties he was a successful writer and educator on agricultural topics. During the American Civil War, he was a special commissioner in the US War and Navy Departments, and was given the rank of Colonel, a title he used throughout his life. After the Civil War he became a prominent lawyer in New York.

During his early adulthood, Olcott became interested in spiritualism, an indigenous American religious movement, and more generally in the occult. His acquaintance with HELENA PETROVNA BLAVATSKY led to the founding of the Theosophical Society in 1875, with Olcott as its first president. He visited India with Blavatsky in 1878 and in 1882 established the Society's permanent headquarters in Adyar, India. He edited the Society's journal, *The Theosophist*, from 1888 to 1907.

In 1880 Olcott visited Sri Lanka, then Ceylon, with Blavatsky, and played an instrumental role in the modern revival of Buddhism in that country. He was welcomed by Sinhala Buddhists, who appreciated his organizational skills and perceived him as an ally in their opposition to the influence of Christian missionaries in Sinhala society. Olcott repeatedly visited Sri Lanka between 1880 and 1907 and helped to establish numerous Buddhist educational institutions there, including Ananda College in Colombo. Olcott was also the author of a *Buddhist Catechism*, which he self-consciously wrote as a contribution to the Buddhist revival in Sri Lanka. For all his efforts Olcott is still warmly remembered by Sinhala Buddhists, especially of the 'Protestant Buddhist' stripe. [29; 152: VI–VII] (C.H.)

Oldham, Joseph Houldsworth [VI.A] (1874–1969). Scottish layman prominent in missionary activities. He was born in Bombay, India. He was educated at Edinburgh Academy until 1892 and then Trinity College, Oxford. There he was converted at a meeting addressed by DWIGHT L. MOODY. In 1896 he became the first full-time Secretary of the Student Christian Movement, but a year later he left for Lahore (then in India), to work under the Scottish YMCA among students and young civil servants. He married Mary Fraser in Lahore Cathedral in 1898. In 1901 both contracted typhoid and had to be invalided home to Scotland. He entered New College, Edinburgh, to study for the ministry of the United Free Church of Scotland. Along with his biblical studies he learned German, and after graduation went to Germany and studied at Halle University. He was never ordained, though he held an assistantship at Free St George's Church, Edinburgh. He worked for a time with the Student Christian Movement and as organizer of mission study in Scottish churches. In 1910 he was Secretary of the World Missionary Conference held at Edinburgh, after which he was appointed Secretary of the Continuation Committee. From 1912 until 1927 he edited *The International Review of Missions*. At the outbreak of the First World War Oldham transferred to the Conference of British Missionary Societies. In 1921, with the formation of the International Missionary Council, he was appointed its Secretary. In this post he did much to advance the cause of Blacks in Africa, and in 1924 wrote *Christianity and the Race Problem*. He organized the Oxford Conference on Church, Community and State in 1937 and edited the *Christian News Letter* from 1939 to 1945. In 1952 he retired to the YMCA college at Dunford in Sussex and continued writing until his death in a nursing home in St Leonards on Sea. [599; 600; 601] (T.T.)

Onyioha, K.O.K. [I.A] Founder and High Chief Priest of Godianism, a neo-traditional movement in Nigeria. Known first as the National Church of Nigeria, the movement was formed in 1948–50 by a group of well educated Igbo. They were associated with the radical wing of the National Council of Nigeria and the Cameroons which fought under Azikiwe for independence in the 1940s and 50s. Under Onyioha's leadership they sought to rekindle interest in traditional African forms of religion, rather than the 'foreign' religions of Christianity and Islam. The movement merged with the Edo National Church or Holy Aruosa, founded by Oba Akenzua II, the king of Benin, to form Godianism. Onyioha has attempted to transcend ethnic and even national boundaries, drawing elements from a variety of Nigerian and other African religious sources to expand the movement's appeal. In the mid-1970s he was instrumental in forming an Organization of Traditional Religions in Africa. He has published and lectured widely, including an address to the United Nations in 1978. [26] (R.H.)

Oppong, Sampson [VI.A] [Opon; Oppon] (*c.*1890?–1965). Christian prophet in Ghana. He was the son of a slave in Brong Ahafo, Gold Coast. The chronology of his early life is uncertain. His contacts with mission Christianity seem to have been episodic and superficial. A wandering labourer, he was imprisoned for embezzlement while working on the Ivory Coast railway. While in gaol a vision first called him to radical reform and a preaching mission. On release, however, he ignored it, and became a practising sorcerer and a successful swindler. A further vision brought him to repentance, and, in or about 1917, to become a travelling prophet calling for total abandonment of fetish and turning to God. In 1920 a Methodist minister in Aśante brought him into the work of the mission. In three years Methodist work in Aśante was transformed; 20,000 people came into the church through Oppong's preaching. In the mid-1920s Oppong was excluded from the church after drinking heavily and a conviction in the native court. He dropped into obscurity but in later life returned to the church and preached in his home area.

Although Oppong was illiterate, he knew the Bible well, and was a spellbinding preacher who related his radical message to Aśante life and history. He is one of several African prophets of the time – W. W. HARRIS is the best known – who led mass movements to Christianity; with no hostility to the missions, but claiming a divine commission independent of them. [55: 188ff.; 197: 310–11] (A.F.W.)

Origen [VI.A] [Oregenes Adamantius] (*c.*185–*c.*254). Greek theologian and scholar. He was the eldest of seven children of a Christian family in Alexandria. He was taught Greek literature and the Bible by his father, Leonides. In 202 Leonides was martyred and Origen opened a school of rhetoric to support his family. Later he changed to teaching Christian doctrine exclusively. He studied philosophy and Hebrew: these studies became the basis of his theology for intellectuals and his exegesis of the Old Testament. Through the patronage of a wealthy Christian whom he converted from Valentinianism (*see* VALENTINUS), Origen was able to produce theological and mystical literature. (Much of this is lost and the rest extant mainly in Latin translation.) He travelled extensively, to Rome, Antioch and Caesarea. Though a theologian he remained for a large part of his life a layman. He was ordained priest while on a visit to Caesarea, an act which angered his home bishop in Alexandria. A synod of Egyptian bishops and priests ordered him to leave Egypt and another synod of bishops declared him not to be a priest. Bishops of other provinces ignored this condemnation. He settled in Caesarea, where he opened another school; his patron followed him there with his publishing resources. He was imprisoned and tortured during the Decian persecution but survived the death of Decius, dying not long after, following a period of broken health.

Origen's teaching enjoys mixed favour. His teaching on the pre-existence of human souls is condemned as heretical. According to the biography recorded by Eusebius, Origen castrated himself in his zeal to fulfil the prophecy in *Matthew* 19:11 that some would become eunuchs for the sake of the Kingdom of Heaven. He also helped to prepare his own disciples to achieve martyrdom. [147; 176; 191; 607] (T.T.)

Orimolade, Moses [I.A] [Tunolase] (*c.*1879–1933). Supreme founder of the Cherubim and Seraphim Society, one of Nigeria's earliest independent, prayer-healing (*Aladura*) churches. His birth and childhood in Ikare, western Nigeria, were surrounded by legends. Following his conversion to Christianity in 1916 and a paralyzing illness of seven years he began evangelizing, though he was illiterate. He lived an ascetic life as an itinerant preacher, 1916–24, before settling in Lagos, where he became known as 'Baba Aladura' ('Praying Father'), because of his emphasis upon prayer and faith-healing. As a result of his association with CHRISTIANAH ABIODUN, he was instrumental in the formation of the Seraphim Society, later to become the Cherubim and Seraphim Society and eventually the Eternal Sacred Order of the Cherubim and Seraphim. Despite the departure of his close followers, Orimolade remained the father of the Society, seeking to reunite the dissident groups. The place of his death, Ojokoro, has become a sacred place to church members. Prayers are said to the 'God of Moses Orimolade' by every section of the Society and he has been canonized by the Advisory Board of the church. [25: 25–39] (R.H.)

Oschoffa, Samuel Bileou J. [I.A] (1909–1985). Founder of the Celestial Church of Christ in the Republic of Benin (formerly Dahomey) in 1947, which has developed into an African independent church with an international outreach. The only son of a Gun father and Yoruba mother, Oschoffa was educated in several mission schools before becoming a carpenter. For three months in 1947 he was marooned in the forest while searching for ebony. During an eclipse of the sun he received a vision which commissioned him to found a new church for Africans. On returning home he began healing people. Gradually his nucleus of followers developed into an organization known as 'le Christianisme Céleste' or the Celestial Church of Christ. Oschoffa never claimed messianic status, but he provided a strong charismatic focus, always emphasizing the spiritual and African nature of his church. The church later expanded into Nigeria, where the headquarters are now situated, as well as into neighbouring West African countries and Europe and North America. Oschoffa became a well known figure because of his purported ability to raise people from the dead and also for his many wives and children. Pastor Founder Oschoffa, or Papa, as he was affectionately known by his followers, died in Lagos on 10 September 1985 as the result of a road accident. Following a funeral which assumed national proportions, he was buried at Imeko, Ogun State, where a centre of pilgrimage – Celestial City – is springing up. [13: 161, 167–9, 176–7] (R.H.)

Oshitelu, Josiah Olunowo [I.A] (1902–1966). Founder of one of West Africa's most renowned independent churches, the Church of the Lord (Aladura). A Nigerian of Ijebu-Yoruba origin and Anglican upbringing, he served as a teacher within the mission school and a catechist within the church. In 1930 he founded the Church of the Lord (Aladura) and soon won many followers through his charismatic personality and many revelations (notably his revealed script) and writings, which included yearly prophecies about Nigeria. Oshitelu resembled other Aladura prophets in his condemnation of traditional medicine and charms and his encouragement of healing through prayer, fasting and holy water, prophecy and ecstatic signs. Oshitelu remained administrative and spiritual head of the church until his death in 1966, despite his inability to keep up with the rapid social change occurring in Nigeria at the time. [37] (R.H.)

Ostanes [XXVI] (5th century BCE). Zoroastrian magus who accompanied the Persian expedition that invaded Greece in 480 BCE. He was supposed to have been the teacher of several Greek intellectuals of the time, especially Democritus. On the basis of this reputation much arcane Greek learning was falsely attributed to him by the ancients [1:553–64; 2.I: 165–212, II: 265–356; 3: vii]. The elder Pliny (1st century CE) describes him as the primary agent for the introduction of magic among the Greeks and the founder of necromancy in particular (*Natural History*, 30.2.8, 28.2.5–6). He was also reputed, just as implausibly, to have studied and taught alchemy in Egypt as one of the early practitioners and theoreticians of that art. Very few fragments of his alleged works survive. He is important not as an historical figure or even as a pseudonymous author but as an ideal construct of the oriental sage who imparted exotic wisdom of a vaguely religious nature to Greek culture (compare ZOROASTER's similar reputation). [4; Beck, R.L., 'Thus Spake Not Zarathustra: Zoroastrian Pseudepigrapha of the Graeco-Roman World', in 5: vol. 3; Lindsay, J., *The Origins of Alchemy in Graeco-Roman Egypt*, London, Muller, 1970] (R.B.)

Ouspensky, Pyotr Demianovich [XVII.D] (1878–1947). Searcher and teacher. He was born in Moscow into a talented and artistic family. From an early age, he became deeply interested in the natural sciences, in dreams and psychology, and in mathematics where he was fascinated by the idea of the fourth dimension. He began to travel from 1896. In 1905 he wrote a novel, which was published in Russian in 1915 and in English in 1947 under the title *The Strange Life of Ivan Osokin*. In 1907 he began to investigate the esoteric and the occult, and in 1909 moved to St Petersburg, where he lectured and published several books, including *Tertium organum*. He went to Egypt, Ceylon and India in 1913–14 and lectured on his travels and searches in 1915.

It was in the spring of 1915 that he first met GURDJIEFF who was to transform his life and understanding. The account of his time with Gurdjieff from 1915 to 1917, the nature of the teaching, and the techniques and their effect on Ouspensky, are all recorded in his *In Search of the Miraculous* [5]. By the summer of 1918 he felt he no longer understood Gurdjieff, although being totally convinced of the validity of his system. He remained in the Caucasus until 1919, when he left Russia for good. He went to Istanbul, where he met up again with Gurdjieff, but, as before, felt unable to work with him. Making his way to London, he began to lecture and work with people there in 1921. He helped Gurdjieff establish his work in France, but broke with him finally in 1924.

In 1931 Ouspensky published the English translation of *A New Model of the Universe*, which he had written between 1911 and 1914, before his meeting with Gurdjieff. 1934 saw a major expansion of Ouspensky's work: a farm and country house were bought in Surrey, and in 1938 a larger house was acquired in London. The typescripts of Ouspensky's meetings from 1921 to 1947 are preserved in Yale University Library, and a selection of some of these was published after his death with the title *The Fourth Way*. In 1941 Ouspensky went to America, and held meetings in New York up to 1946; practical work was organized by Madame Ouspensky at Franklin Farms, New Jersey, just as she had done in England. In 1947 Ouspensky, already ill, returned to London and in a series of six meetings 'set free' his followers to follow their own lines of work. He died in 1947 at Lyne Place in Surrey. It was only after his death that *In Search of the Miraculous*, *The Fourth Way*, and a small collection of lectures entitled *The Psychology of Man's Possible Evolution* were published.

Ouspensky is rightly acclaimed as a leading exponent of Gurdjieff's system, which he brought to many through his writings and groups, yet he became increasingly convinced that there was something crucial missing as he had been given it, and this problem he never resolved. A man of great personal integrity and honesty, he helped many to struggle with themselves and with the system, displaying throughout his characteristic clarity, humour and great kindness. [8] (S.C.R.W.)

P

Pacal [XVIII] [Lord Shield] (6th century). Ruler of the Classic Maya city of Palenque, 615–83. His life and death left an indelible mark on the public and private representation of cosmology in art [10: VII]. His reign and that of his son Chan Bahlum display the Maya commitment to royal ancestor worship to a vivid degree.

Pacal was born in 603, ascended to throne at the age of 12 in 615 and ruled for 68 years. During his lifetime he utilized religious and political strategies to transform Palenque into a powerful Maya city. *c.*675 he began the construction of his funerary temple, which is considered one of the masterpieces of Meso-American temple art, representing many of the major religious ideas of the Classic Maya. Lodged beneath the majestic Temple of the Inscriptions, Pacal's tomb contains a huge sarcophagus of creamy white limestone covered with an image of the Maya cosmos and Pacal descending down the World Tree into the underworld of Xibalba [10: 282]. Pacal chose to depict the three levels of the Maya cosmos in elaborate detail with stylized serpents, mirrors, corn, gods, jewels and other items representing the Overworld, Middleworld and Underworld. Variations of this theme of the cosmic tree at the centre of the world appear in different locations at Palenque. As he descends into the ordeal of Xibalba, Pacal is depicted as a god who is prepared to defeat death and be reborn as both agricultural power and as the solar disk.

Pacal's eldest son, Chan-Bahlum, reigned from 684 until 702, when his younger brother Kan-Xul came to the throne and erected another temple to hold the dangerous forces which had accumulated in the ceremonial temples of Palanque during his brother's reign. This illustrates the religious character of Maya temple architecture and the role of dynastic power, which was deeply rooted in supernatural authority. [3: 180–81] (D.C.)

Pachakuti 'Inka Yupanki [XXIV] (15th century). Ninth Inca emperor, 1438–71. Spanish chronicles called him Pachacuti Inca Yupanqui, although he was named Kusi 'Inka Yupanki by his father WIRAQOCHA 'INKA, whom he succeeded after capturing the capital throne in a civil war. To overcome his father's forces, Pachakuti 'Inka Yupanki negotiated a tenuous alliance with the Chancas, an ethnic group from Hancavelica which wielded considerable political power in the area west of the Inca domain. After having his brother, Capac Yupanqui, killed for disobeying orders, Pachakuti 'Inka Yupanki and his sons rapidly expanded the Inca empire so that it extended from the Titicaca Basin of Bolivia in the south to Quito, Ecuador, in the north. Pachakuti restructured religious practice and belief in the Inca empire and in Cuzco, the capital. Forced resettlement policies went hand in hand with a highly regulated ritual system into which all conquered peoples were absorbed. The space of the conquered land and its resettled peoples were factored into groups and each group became a carefully calibrated cog in a complicated religious calendar of ritual and economic activities. More than any other Inca ruler, Pachakuti 'Inka Yupanki was responsible for the formation of an imperial religion founded on devotion to Viracocha, a creator deity. While under siege by the Chancas, Pachakuti had a dream sent to him as a divine message from Viracocha. In the dream Viracocha revealed himself to be the divine patron of the emperor. In thanksgiving for his victory over the

Chancas, Pachakuti constructed a temple to Viracocha in Cuzco and installed in it a gold figure of the god. The worship of Viracocha was spread throughout the empire as an official cult centred on Cuzco. Its centrifugal force was governed by an official priesthood who were masters of ceremonies performed at local temples. Apparently, the imperial cult was an overlay of all-absorbing religious importance. Although it left local religious beliefs largely intact, it relativized them by subordinating them to Inca gods of greater stature in the hierarchical pantheon. Local people need not give up their beliefs, but they did have to worship the more powerful Inca gods in addition to their own. [4; 13; 22] (L.S.)

Pachomius [VI.A] (293?–346). As the originator of the coenobitic form of monasticism he has been subject to many hagiographical legends which have obscured the facts of his life. He appears to have been born of pagan parents in Upper Egypt and served in the army. While on military duty in modern Isna he was impressed by the local Christian community and was converted. After three years' discipleship he started his own monastery in Tabennis. Previously the hermit type of monasticism had been popular. Pachomius' monastery was organized on community lines, hence coenobitic. He was responsible for founding nine monasteries and two convents. He became the hegumen of the monastery in Pebu, which replaced Tabennis as the central monastery. He wrote the rules for his community in Coptic: these survive in a Latin translation of the Greek version. Monasticism in the West was largely influenced by his rules, which are still observed by the monks of Mount Athos. [26; 72: 109ff.; 615] (T.T.)

Padmasambhava [IV] (8th century). An Indian Buddhist master reported to have visited Tibet during the reign (which ended in 797) of KHRI SRONG-LDE-BTSAN, Padmasambhava is revered as the 'precious guru' of the Rnying-ma-pa school of Tibetan Buddhism, and is the object of a widespread cult among Tibetan Buddhists generally. It is not at present possible to determine exactly the historical facts underlying the elaborate legends about Padmasambhava, many of which portray him as a miraculously born immortal [6: 45–52]. Most accounts agree, however, that he was raised in a royal family in north-western India, and abandoned this to become a Buddhist tantric adept. During a period of prolonged retreat in Nepal, he gained mastery of the exorcistic rites associated with the *kīla*, or ritual spike, this being asserted even in the oldest extant references to Padmasambhava, found among the pre-11th century documents discovered at Dunhuang [146: 11–28]. His reputation as an exorcist led to his invitation, at the suggestion of the Indian monk and scholar ŚĀNTARAKṢITA, to travel to Tibet to dispel the resistance of indigenous deities to the construction of Tibet's first Buddhist monastery, Bsam-yas. His devotees maintain that after accomplishing this task he remained for some years in Tibet as the principal religious preceptor of King Khri Srong-lde-btsan and his court, his teachings being recorded by his Tibetan consort Ye-shes mtsho-rgyal. For the most part these were concealed for the edification of future generations, to be revealed as 'treasures' (*gter ma*) by a succession of masters specially graced by Padmasambhava, who continues to live in the terrestrial paradise of the 'Glorious Copper-coloured Mountain' (*zangs-mdog dpal-ri*), whence he is always accessible to his disciples' devotions [225]. The cult of Padmasambhava was promoted from the 12th century onwards through the revelation of his treasures, several of which include detailed hagiographies of him. Though some Tibetan Buddhist sectarian leaders condemned these developments, and occasionally sought the suppression of the cult, popular acceptance always seems to have been widespread and was effectively given the highest official sanction by the fifth DALAI LAMA, Ngag-dbang blo-bzang rgya-mtsho (1617–1682), himself a leading 'treasure-revealer' (*gter-ston/-bton*). [53; 56: book 2, II, III, VI; 62: 105–92; 115; 146: 29–126; 197: V; 238: I] (M.K.)

Pa Hsien. *See* EIGHT IMMORTALS.

Pai-chang Huai-hai [IV] [Japanese: Hyakujō Ekai] (720–814). Compiler and definer of the *Pai-chang Rules* (*Pai-chang-ch'ing-kuei*) for the Ch'an Buddhist monastic order in China. The *Pai-chang Rules* defined the moral code for Ch'an monks as well as dealing in detail with such matters as offices, Ch'an ceremonies, hierarchical ranks, temple buildings, and so forth. The incorporation of a special monk's hall, where the monk would eat and sleep as well as meditate during special times of ascetic practice, as part of the Buddhist monastery was an innovation of Pai-chang.

Pai-chang emphasized the importance of work, and is famous for his dictum, 'A day without work means a day without food.' He followed this rule throughout his life, and even in his old age when his disciples took away his garden tools out of concern for his weak health, he refused to eat until his tools were returned.

The *Rules* of Pai-chang became definitive for Ch'an and Zen monasteries, providing a disciplined structure within which to practise meditation and the Buddhist way. (P.L.S.)

Paissy Velichkovsky, St [VI.B] (1722–1792). He came to Kiev from Poltava and eventually entered the Monastery of the Caves then travelled through Romania to Athos (1746). At St Elijah Skete he and his disciples collected, edited and translated patristic texts on the spiritual life, many of them texts that ST NIKODEMOS and St Makarios were to include in the *Philokalia*. In 1763 Paissy returned to Romania, but fled when Austria annexed the Sekoul area. In 1779 he refounded the Moldavian monastery of Neamts and translated the *Philokalia* into Slavonic.

The *Philokalia* was translated into Russian by the spiritual teacher and missionary Ignaty Bryanchaninov (1807–1867), bishop of the Caucasus from 1857 until his retirement into a monastery in 1861.

A second, enlarged Russian version of the *Philokalia* was made by St Theophan the Recluse (1815–1894), who had directed Olonets Seminary and then St Petersburg Theological Academy and for seven years worked in Turkey (1847–54) before becoming bishop of Tambov (1859) and Vladimir. In 1866 he became a hermit at Vyshensk and in 1872 a recluse. He wrote major works on the spiritual life in which the influence of St Tikhon of Zadonsk (*d.*1783) is visible. [14; 59] (D.B.)

Palamas, St Gregory. *See* GREGORY PALAMAS, ST.

Palestrina, Giovanni Pierluigi da [VI.A] (1525–1594). Italian composer. He was born in the town whose name he took. Most of his work consists of sacred music, which reflects his career in various ecclesiastical situations, none further than a few miles from his birthplace. He studied music while he was a chorister in Rome, returning to Palestrina Cathedral in 1544. His bishop became Pope Julius III, which probably accounts for his return to Rome to become first chorister at the Julian chapel of St Peter's and later composer at the Papal Chapel. This patronage ended with the death of the Pope in 1555. A period of uncertainty followed, caused partly by the reforms of the Council of Trent. In the same year, however, he succeeded LASSUS as choirmaster at St John Lateran. Later he worked at Santa Maria Maggiore, where he had been a chorister, and then at the newly established Roman Seminary. In 1568 he began a successful association with the Duke of Mantua, returning some time later to his post at the Julian chapel. His musical style, in which the rich counterpoint is never allowed to obscure the text, remained influential for generations. [399; 671; 691] (E.M.)

Paliau Maloat [XXI] (1915–). Founder of the Melanesian Independent Church. Born on Mouk, off Baluan Island in the Manus or Admiralty Island group, New Guinea, Paliau rejected his culture and entered the Whites' world. Rising by 1940 to the rank of sergeant in the Australian Colonial Government's Native Constabulary at Rabaul, New Britain, he kept sending money home to establish a local fund to pay the colonial head-tax. He was credited with a vision of JESUS during the Pacific War; but, because he had retained his office under the Japanese, the victorious Allies sent him back to Baluan in 1946. He was acclaimed by his fellow islanders as hero and new spiritual guide, and became founder of the Baluan Native United Christian Church, Melanesia's first independent church [37]. With his following, the augmented fund and rising popular expectations that he knew the secret source to the Whites' Cargo, he went on to engage in political and religious activities of significance for Papua New Guinea's emergent nationhood (independent in 1975). [33; 44; 47: 59–60]

Paliau's publications include an autobiographical lecture and a short rewriting of the

Bible as a platform for his newest politico-religious organization called Makasol. [34] (G.W.T.)

Paṇ-chen Bla-ma [IV]. The first Paṇ-chen Bla-ma, the distinguished scholar Blo-bzang chos-kyi rgyal-mtshan (1567–1662), rose to prominence as a tutor of the fourth DALAI LAMA, Yon-tan rgya-mtsho (1589–1617), and of the fifth, Ngag-dbang blo-bzang rgya-mtsho (1617–82). Thereafter his successive rebirths were recognized at his monastery, Bkra-shis lhun-po in Gzhis-ka-rtse (Shigatse), West Tibet, where they often wielded considerable political power, officially second in rank to, but sometimes actually rivalling, the Dalai Bla-mas themselves. His immediate successor was Paṇ-chen II Blo-bzang ye-shes dpal-bzang-po (1663–1737), tutor of the ill-fated sixth Dalai Bla-ma, Tshangs-dbyangs rgya-mtsho (1683–1706). Paṇ-chen III Blo-bzang dpal-ldan ye-shes (1737–80) was the most highly regarded Tibetan political leader of his day, and skilfully forged Tibet's first official relationship with a European power, the East India Company's administration in Bengal under the Governor-Generalship of Warren Hastings, whose emissary to Tibet, George Bogle, left an affecting record of his friendship with the Paṇ-chen Bla-ma [47: 119–20; 147: 113–14]. Paṇ-chen IV Blo-bzang bstan-pa'i nyi-ma (1781–1854) was tutor of several of the short-lived Dalai Bla-mas of the 19th century and became the administrator of Lhasa in 1844–5. He was succeeded by Paṇ-chen V Chos-kyi grags-pa bstan-pa'i dbang-phyug (1854–1882), whose successor, Paṇ-chen VI Chos-kyi nyi-ma (1883–1937), became (perhaps against his own will) the leader supported by Tibetan factions opposing the government of the 13th Dalai Bla-ma (1876–1933). After 1925 he lived as an exile in China, his followers allying themselves with the Guomintang. Paṇ-chen VII Bskal-bzang tshe-brtan (1938–1989) similarly became the temporary representative of Chinese Communist opposition to the Dalai Bla-ma's leadership. His objections to the Party's harsh policies in Tibet, however, led to his being purged, followed by his arrest and imprisonment in 1964. In 1978 he was released from prison, rehabilitated and permitted to assume a leadership role in the liberalization of Buddhist religious life in the People's Republic of China during the decade which followed. His death in Shigatse in early 1989 occasioned the intensification of enmities between the Chinese government and the people of the Tibet Autonomous Region, the former wishing to honour him as a purely political leader, the latter for his traditional role in Tibetan religious life. [10; 47: V; 190] (M.K.)

Pannikar, Raimundo [VI.A] (1918–). He was born in Barcelona, of a Hindu father and Spanish Catholic mother. During his early years he studied the Hindu *Veda* alongside the Christian Bible. He studied in Spain, Germany and Italy, and was awarded a PhD (Philosophy) in 1945, a DSc (Chemistry) in 1958 and a DD (Theology) in 1961. He was ordained a priest in 1946. From 1960 onwards he worked in the University of Mysore, India and later in Benares, where he lectured on Hindu philosophy and engaged in Hindu–Christian encounter and dialogue. In 1968 he published *The Unknown Christ of Hinduism*, in which he argued that certain Hindu concepts could be used to interpret Christ in India and that the faithful Hindu achieves salvation through the Hindu sacraments. In the revised edition of this work (1981) he no longer accepts the superiority of Christianity over other religions nor does he accept that Hinduism, for instance, is fulfilled in Christianity. He has held joint posts in Benares and the University of California in Santa Barbara. (413a; 619a; 619b] (T.T.)

Panṣūrī, Ḥamza [XII] (*d. c.*1607). First scholar to write down Islamic religious and mystic ideas in Malay. Perhaps born in Panṣūr on the coast of northern Sumatra, Panṣūrī was responsible, to a large extent, for the creation of the Malay vocabulary necessary to discuss religious concepts in that language. He visited Mecca and Medina and came in contact with the mysticism of MUḤYI'L-DĪN IBN ʿARABĪ, of which he became a devout follower. He left four major works: *al-Muntahī* ('The Adept'), *Asrār al-ʿĀrifīn* ('The Secrets of Those Who Know'), *Sharāb al-ʿĀshiqīn* ('The Lovers' Potion') and a collection of poems. [35: 'Ḥamza Fansūrī'; 104: XII] (J.K.)

Pao P'u Tzu. *See* KO HUNG.

Papoonan [XX] (18th century). A Delaware prophet and visionary who combined elements of Quakerism and traditional Amerindian beliefs. According to his own testimony, while victim to alcoholism, and sorrowed by the death of his father, he was granted a vision of the true nature of things. He glimpsed the Great Spirit, creator of all, and saw for the first time, the imperfection of this earthly world. At first Papoonan felt himself unworthy of the Great Spirit and set out on a vision quest. The effort resulted in his acceptance by the Creator and his embarking upon a preaching career in 1758. His teachings included a strong code of moral conduct, known as 'The Way'; this led those who followed it to the 'Place of Happiness'. His town, located on the upper Susquehanna River, was governed according to his teachings. Eventually Papoonan's colleagues, previously opposed to Christian influences, rejected him in favour of David Zeisberger, a Moravian missionary whose message they found more appealing. [14: 350–52] (S.R.)

Paracelsus [XVII.A] [Theophrastus Bombastus (Baumastus) von Hohenheim] (1493–1541). Swiss alchemist and physician. Born in Einsiedeln, Switzerland, the son of a physician, he himself studied medicine and travelled extensively throughout Europe. His medical studies are alchemical and kabbalistic in nature, and draw heavily upon the Neoplatonic Hermetic-kabbalistic philosophy which had such prominence in the Renaissance. Man as microcosm is the reflection of the macrocosmic universe, and one of the physician's tasks is to determine more precisely the nature of the symbol-determined correspondences. Paracelsus' major works include: *Archidoxis* (*c.*1524), the treatises on syphilis (*c.*1529), *Opus paragranum* (*c.*1529), *Philosophia sagax* (*c.*1536) and *Labyrinthus medicorum* (1538) [19; 21; 24: vol. 5: XIX, XXIX; 25; 27] (T.L.)

Parākramabāhu I [IV] [Parakkamabahu; Pärakumba] (12th century). King of Sri Lanka, whose reign, 1153–86, marked the beginning of a golden age in the cultural and religious history of that island. 'There is no name in all the annals of Sinhalese history which commands the veneration of the people in such measure as that of this prince of the "mighty arm" Parākramabāhu.' [151: 175] Parākramabāhu I unified the island politically, ending the civil wars that followed Vijayabāhu I's reign, during which Sinhala rule over Sri Lanka was restored. Soon after he was secure on his throne as overlord, Parākramabāhu turned to religious affairs, and especially to the restoration of Buddhist institutions which had suffered during the Cōḷa invasions. He convened a Buddhist council, presided over by Mahākassapa, which succeeded in unifying the Buddhist monastic order in Sri Lanka. Parākramabāhu's favour at this council gave a lasting pre-eminence to the Mahāvihāra monastic lineage in Sinhala Buddhism. In the traditional manner of Buddhist kings, Parākramabāhu restored or built numerous monasteries and shrines throughout Sri Lanka, but especially in his capital Polonnaruva. [151: IX] (C.H.)

Paramārtha [IV] (499–569). Indian Buddhist monk scholar who spent the latter part of his life in China as a missionary and translator of Sanskrit texts. He was born into the Brahman class in Ujjain, India, but apparently moved to Funan (modern Kampuchea), from where he made his way into southern China in 546. Not much is known of his life before his arrival in China. Social and political conditions were chaotic throughout Paramārtha's years in China. He did bring many Buddhist writings with him and was well received by EMPEROR WU of the Liang dynasty in the capital of Chien-k'ang (Nanking). But the promise of imperial support for his translation project soon evaporated with the rebellion of Hou-ching in 549. Paramārtha was forced to flee the chaotic situation, finding temporary patronage with Lu Yüan-che, the local governor of Fu-Ch'un. But Hou-ching, who had executed his erstwhile imperial patron, Emperor Wu, set himself up as the new emperor and called Paramārtha back to the capital. Hou-ching himself, however, was overthrown after only 120 days in power. Under the reign of Emperor Yüan, Paramārtha settled for a time at monasteries in Chien-k'ang and in Yüchang, but social and political chaos forced him to move a number of times. A wanderer in a foreign land, Paramārtha grew melancholic and longed to return to his Indian homeland. He did set out in a small ship from Liang-nan, but storm winds blew his ship back to Canton. Resigned to spend his remaining days in China, he continued his translation efforts with a number of Chinese disciples. He died in Canton at 71 years of age.

His many translations were very influential in the development of Chinese Buddhist doctrine. In particular his translation of VASUBANDHU's *Mahāyānasaṃgrahabhāṣya* (Chinese: *She-lun chu*) became the foundational doctrine of the Chinese version of Yogācāra philosophy called the She-lun school. Paramārtha was fond of the Tathāgatagarbha theme of the originally pure Buddha nature and at times interpolated this doctrine into Vasubandhu's text. It was this She-lun school that was later eclipsed by the DHARMAPĀLA Fa-hsiang lineage of Yogācāra thought introduced into China by HSÜAN-TSANG. Yet Paramārtha's many translations did exert profound influence on later Chinese notions of the Buddha nature, especially in the T'ien-t'ai thought of CHIH-I and the Hua-yen doctrine of FA-TSANG. [175; 77] (J.K.)

Parker, Quannah [xx] (1845–1911). Comanche leader. Born May 1845, among the Kwahadi band, near Wichita Falls, Texas, the son of a white woman (Preloch) and Chief Petu Nocona, Parker was a noted warrior in his youth, especially against buffalo hunters encroaching on traditional reserves. After the defeat of Indian forces at Adobe Walls in 1875 Quannah Parker was forced to live on a reservation in south-western Oklahoma. While a young man, he claimed to have been cured of a serious illness by a *curandera* (a medicine woman) who used a psychedelic cactus. Impressed by the power of the plant, Parker introduced peyote ritual to the Comanche. Throughout the balance of his life he preached peaceful coexistence with the Whites, urging education and agriculture on his people, but affirming the importance of traditional religious observances along with the peyote cult. Quannah Parker died on 21 February 1911. [8] (S.R.)

Parmenides [x] (*c*.515–after 450 BCE). Philosopher of Elea, who developed the doctrine of XENOPHANES that the world is one and unchanging. Of special interest are his denial of the reliability of sense-perception (hinted at by Xenophanes); his appeal solely to logical argument, even though he puts his doctrine into the mouth of a goddess; and his denial of the existence of the void or of non-being, even as a coherent possibility. [20: vol. 2; 48] (H.L.)

Pārśva [XIII]. According to Jainism the twenty-third of the 24 ford-makers (*tīrthaṅkara*) of the current world-era (*see* MAHĀVĪRA). While the first 22 ford-makers can scarcely be assigned any historical reality, there seems little doubt that Pārśva is not a figure of legend, but a real teacher who lived and preached in the Ganges basin. If we accept the traditional Jain dating for him, and there is no other material to draw on, he can be situated at about 800 BCE.

The earliest biographical account of Pārśva can be found in the text of the Śvetāmbara Jain scriptural canon, the *Kalpasūtra* (*c*.2nd–1st century BCE) [12: 271–5]. According to this source, Pārśva descended from heaven, where he had lived as a god, to the womb of Queen Vāmā, wife of Aśvasena, who is described as being the king of Benares. After living as a householder for 30 years, the gods prompt Pārśva to renounce the world and live the life of an ascetic in accordance with his destiny as a future ford-maker. After following the obligatory path of mendicancy, austerities and meditation, Pārśva attained that state of omniscience which for the Jains characterizes enlightenment. The *Kalpasūtra* tells us that Pārśva lived for 70 years as an ascetic teacher, establishing a community of 16,000 male ascetics and 38,000 female ascetics. Finally, after fasting for a month and destroying the accretions of karma which still clung to him, he died on Mount Sammeta in what is now the state of Bihar.

A great deal of this material is stereotyped, being probably modelled on the developing biography of Mahāvīra. The source of Pārśva's popularity as an object of devotion among the Jain community to this day can be seen in the legend which came to be associated with him in the early centuries of the Christian era [3]. According to this, Pārśva from his first existence in this world-age becomes linked through a series of rebirths with a bitter enemy who refuses to accept the validity of the Jain religion. In his pre-ford-maker birth, Pārśva rescues a snake which is being burnt in the sacrificial fire of his enemy, who has been reborn as the Brahman ascetic Kamaṭha. Kamaṭha's enmity continues into Pārśva's final birth, where, as a terrible demon, his enemy attacks him as he sits in meditation, raining down hail and fire upon him. However, the snake rescued by Pārśva in his previous birth is reborn as a great serpent prince (*nāga*) and shields Pārśva with his hood. Iconographically, Pārśva is always depicted with cobra's hoods above his head; because of his rescue of the burning snake he is widely regarded by the Jain community as a form of saviour figure.

Very little can be said of Pārśva from a strictly historical point of view and scholarship has focused upon the extent to which Mahāvīra can be regarded as a reformer or adapter of Pārśva's teachings. Buddhist sources which are aware of Mahāvīra, whom they call Nigaṇṭha Nātaputta and which must present a reasonably accurate picture, refer to Jain monks following the fourfold restraint (abstinence from violence, lying, taking what has not been given, and possessions) which Jainism associates with Pārśva, while Mahāvīra is by all sources linked with the promulgation of a fivefold ascetic vow, adding chastity to Pārśva's list. A well-known passage in the Śvetāmbara scriptures attempts to explain this difference by suggesting that there had been a decline in morals amongst Jain ascetics after Pārśva's time, which Mahāvīra rectified by introducing a vow of sexual abstinence [14: 119–29]. However, it does seem unlikely that Pārśva's monastic followers were not subject to a vow of celibacy and it has been argued that the fourfold restraint in fact has reference to the four modalities of mind, body, speech and senses, and that Mahāvīra tried to make the particular moral areas involved more specific.

Mahāvīra undoubtedly drew on some of Pārśva's ideas, particularly his views on cosmology, but in general the Śvetāmbara scriptures portray his followers as requiring conversion to the true Jainism preached by Mahāvīra, and later writers associate them, long after their disappearance, with the performance of dubious practices such as magic. (P.D.)

Patrick [VI.A] (*c.*390–*c.*460). Apostle to the Irish. He was born into a Christian family in Roman Britain, the son of Calpurnius, a Roman citizen and a local administrative official. Details of his life are dependent on his *Confessions* and a letter addressed to the 'Soldiers of Coroticus'. When he was about 16 years old he was captured by marauding Irish tribesmen and enslaved by them in Ireland for about six years. He managed to escape and return to his family in Britain. It would seem that he then spent some years in a British monastery and possibly some time in Gaul. He received a vision in which his former captors called him back to minister to them. Around 431 he was sent by the British bishops to assist Palladius in Ireland. It is assumed that he had learned to speak Irish while he was a slave. His own language was British and he spoke some coarse Latin. Palladius died soon after Patrick's arrival in Ireland so Patrick was made a bishop in 432 and thereafter carried on a mission to the inhabitants of Ireland, with his headquarters probably in Armagh, the centre of the local kingdom. He was not an intellectual but a hard working missionary and pastor, and a good organizing bishop. At this time the leadership of the church was still in the hands of local bishops with no diocesan structure. Many legends grew up around him which suggest that he was a charismatic figure who carried on his ministry for about 30 years. [84; 130; 344] (T.T.)

Paul VI [VI.A] [Giovanni Battista Montini] (1897–1978). Pope, 1963–78. He was born in Concesio, near Breschia in Italy. He was raised for high office in the church by his family, and through his seminary career he made contacts which fitted him for the future. He was ordained in 1920. He occupied a number of posts in the Vatican Secretariat of State for over 25 years until Pius XII made him archbishop of Milan in 1954. He was made a cardinal by JOHN XXIII in 1958 and elected Pope in 1963. He presided over the remaining sessions of the Second Vatican Council called by his predecessor. Although he continued the process of reforming the church he was conservative in many ways. His reforms included the introduction of regular episcopal synods, a more collegiate leadership for the church and reform of the Curia Romana. He was the first pope to engage in world travel, visiting Jerusalem, India, Uganda, the Philippines, the United Nations in New York and the World Council of Churches in Geneva. He encouraged formal ecumenical contacts with other Christian churches and set up a secretariat for relations with other religions. He was concerned for the poor and for social justice, as evidenced by his letter *Populorum Progressio* in 1967. On the traditional side he stood against the abandonment of celibacy for the clergy in *Sacerdotalis Caelibatus* in 1967 and against the liberalization of sexual behaviour by refusing in *Humanae Vitae* (1968) to accept his own commission's advice on the introduction of birth control. [17; 821; 839] (T.T.)

Paul the Apostle [VI.A] [Saul] (*d. c.*62). He was a Jew, born and raised in the Hellenistic environment of the Diaspora and a native of Tarsus. The sources for his life consist of two autobiographical passages from his own letters (*Galatians* 1:12–2:14; *Philippians* 3:3–6), further autobiographical references scattered in other letters, especially *2 Corinthians* 11:22–9 and in the major portion of *The Acts of the Apostles*. In spite of so much material, constructing a life of Paul presents many problems. Traditionalists have depended heavily on *The Acts of the Apostles* in spite of inconsistencies between its narrative of events and that of Paul himself. Recent scholarship has turned more positively to Paul's own record of events along with a radical re-appraisal of the authorship of letters ascribed to him. Scholars accept the authenticity of *Romans*, *1 & 2 Corinthians* (edited), *Galatians*, *Philippians*, *Philemon*, *1 Thessalonians* and possibly *2 Thessalonians*. More conservative scholars would include *Ephesians* and *Colossians*, but there is broader unanimity that the so-called *Pastoral Epistles*, *1 & 2 Timothy* and *Titus* are not Pauline. Very conservative Christians accept *Hebrews* as Pauline, being thus identified in the Authorized Version of the Bible. More recent versions have dropped the ascription. Many recent scholars see Paul as a well educated man, of Hellenistic Jewish stock, trained as a tent-maker in the family business, a trade which made him self-supporting, a charismatic, apocalyptic, mystical figure who invited controversy by his anti-establishment views; they reject the picture of the conventional, conservative figure and systematic theologian who conforms to the social mores of his time.

Paul admits that at one time he persecuted the followers of JESUS and as such built himself a reputation among his own people. Following an experience which bears the marks of a theophany he turned from persecution to being a follower of Jesus. This event took place near Damascus, calculated by some scholars as in the year 34. He then spent some time in Arabia before returning to Damascus. It is likely that he was baptized then, not immediately after his 'Damascus road' experience as recorded in *Acts*. Three years later he went to Jerusalem where he met PETER THE APOSTLE and James the brother of Jesus. For the next 14 years he was engaged in initiating or helping to initiate new communities of those who believed in Jesus, consisting of Jews and Gentiles in Syria, Cilicia and Greece. His work, often among those who knew of him as a former persecutor of their sect, was often the occasion for opposition and violent reaction from those who believed strongly that the communities were a continuation of the Jewish tradition. At the end of this period he visited Jerusalem, probably in the year 51. This visit brought the issue of Jewish-Christian and Gentile converts to a head. Were the communities that were initiated to be a new form of Judaism adhering to the Torah or were they to be radically new, with new adherents admitted without the obligations to the Torah, more specifically without having to accept circumcision? It would appear that Paul was able to persuade the Jerusalem community that, on the evidence of the success he and his colleagues had enjoyed, Gentiles should not be required to submit to the demands of the Torah. An agreement was reached that Paul should carry on his work among the Gentiles, while Peter should concentrate on work among Jews. Later Paul had to engage in a serious confrontation with Peter in Antioch because the latter was exhibiting ambivalence towards the agreement reached in Jerusalem.

Paul's interpretation of the message of the death and resurrection of Jesus brought so much opposition from Jews or 'Judaizers' within the Christian communities that he was eventually arraigned before the Roman secular authorities. Before then he had planned to visit Jerusalem once more to take a financial donation collected from the primarily Gentile churches, especially from the church at Corinth. After that he planned a visit to Rome in preparation for a mission to Spain. The visit to Jerusalem took place probably in the year 57. Paul and his Gentile companions were given a mixed reception. The old problem of the demands of the Torah was raised again. Paul tried to compromise but was arrested by the Romans on the accusations of the Judaizers. He scarcely avoided assassination before reaching Caesarea. At his pre-trial Paul demanded that as a Roman citizen he plead his case in Rome. After a hazardous journey he arrived under arrest in Rome, probably in the year 60. Two years later, under the Emperor Nero, he was executed.

Much of Paul's teaching was developed through his letters as he responded to the needs and problems of the churches with which he was associated. The message which has received most attention in succeeding centuries was the one which emerged from the internal controversies, namely that salvation did not result from following the demands of Torah but rather that 'a man is not justified by works of the law but through faith in Jesus Christ . . . I have been crucified with Christ; it is no longer I who live, but Christ who lives in me; and the life I now live in the flesh I live by faith in the Son of God, who loved me and gave himself for me.' *Galatians* 2: 16, 20) [403; 426; 720] (T.T.)

Pelagius [VI.A] (*d*.418?). British monk who first appeared in Rome towards the end of the 4th century. There he was occupied with teaching moral and spiritual values to Roman society. He was an ascetic and was offended by Christians who did not exhibit the perfection which he thought was achieved through baptism. He was influenced by those who earlier stressed the importance of the moral life, of the discipline of the will and the expression of faith through righteous deeds. Pelagius thought that such a life was demanded of all Christians, and not just of ascetics. He attacked AUGUSTINE OF HIPPO's statement in his *Confessions*, 'Give what you command and command what you will', for undermining human moral responsibility by transferring it to God. His teachings met with success, but when he travelled to Africa and Palestine after 410 he met with opposition from Augustine of Hippo and JEROME. He was accused of exalting the power of the human will to the detriment of divine grace. He was also attacked for maintaining that sinless human beings had lived before Christ. He was accepted by Eastern bishops and acquitted in councils in Palestine in 415. Under the influence of Augustine's attacks Pelagius was condemned in Africa in 416 and by Pope Innocent in 417. He was vindicated for a time but finally condemned by the Pope, at the Council of Carthage in 418, and came under imperial ban. Little of his writings have survived, his most important, *De natura* and *De libero arbitrio*, only in fragments in the writings of Augustine. [249; 650] (T.T.)

Penn, William [VI.A] (1644–1718). English Quaker leader. He became a student at Christ Church, Oxford, but was expelled in 1661 for refusing to conform after the re-establishment of the Church of England. He spent some time at a Protestant academy in Saumur, France, and in 1665 was admitted to Lincoln's Inn, London. In the same year he came under Quaker influence and began to write in defence of his new faith. In 1668 he was imprisoned following the publication of *The Sandy Foundations Shaken*, in which he attacked widely held doctrines such as the Trinity, the Atonement and justification by faith. While in prison he wrote *No Cross, No Crown* (1669), a classical exposition of the Quaker faith. He was acquitted in 1670 and proceeded to plan the foundation of an American colony in which liberty of conscience would be safeguarded for its inhabitants. The result was Pennsylvania, for which he obtained letters patent in 1682. Its constitution was based on belief in monotheism, and worship and religious liberty consonant with such belief. He sailed to America the same year but returned to England in 1684 as a supporter of James II. After the Revolution of 1688 he lost prominence and was deprived of the governorship of Pennsylvania in 1692. He carried out a ministry as an apologist for Quaker principles, expressed in his book *Primitive Christianity*. In 1699 he returned to Pennsylvania but in 1701 left again when the province was converted to a Crown Colony. [77; 225; 243] (T.T.)

Peregrinus [XXII] [nicknamed Proteus (after the shape-changing demigod) from his erratic career] (2nd century CE). Peregrinus travelled widely as a moral and religious teacher in the Roman empire of the mid-2nd century CE [11: 59–63; 14: 184]. Philosophically, he was a Cynic, and the radical and 'outsider' attitudes of that school suited him well. Wherever he went (Palestine, Egypt, Italy, Greece) he tended to fall foul of the authorities. Like ALEXANDER OF ABONUTEICHOS, he was the target of the satirical essayist Lucian, and the latter's *On the Death of Peregrinus* provides most of the extant information concerning him. Certainly, he was both a trouble-maker and a deeply troubled individual (he lived much of his life under suspicion of parricide), but scattered attestations elsewhere speak highly of him and he seems to have engendered both respect and loyalty. For a time, in Palestine, he was a Christian, achieving a local leadership position as *prophētēs*. He was put in prison for his pains, where he lived not uncomfortably, Lucian suggests, on the charity of his gullible coreligionists. His end was literally spectacular: he committed suicide, with considerable advance publicity, by casting himself on a pyre at the Olympic games of 165 CE. Whatever his motives – and they can only be guessed at – the consequences were that he achieved semi-divine status, for a cult, albeit an ephemeral one, was formed in his honour. (R.B.)

Peter Lampadarios [VI.B] [Petros Peloponnesios] (1730–1777). Greek composer. He studied in Smyrna and then Constantinople, where he studied Byzantine chant with John of Trebizond, succeeding him as director of the patriarchal choir. As Lampadarios, Succentor of the Patriarchal Church, he worked with the Protopsaltes Daniel, whose exquisitely lyrical style contrasts with the serene, sober beauty of Peter's liturgical chant. Peter wrote the classic version of the *Anastasimatarion*, the music for the Sunday offices in all eight modes. He was also an accomplished performer and teacher of music in the Arabo-Persian style of Ottoman music, performing for Sultans Hamid I and Selim III. He died of plague in 1777. With the Patriarch's permission, dervishes from all Istambul sang their traditional funeral hymns in the church after the Christian funeral and followed his body to the grave. (D.J.M.)

Peter Lombard [VI.A] [Pierre Lombard; Petrus Lombardus] (*c*.1100–1160). Italian theologian. He was born in Lumellogno, Novarre in Lombardy but little else is known about his early years. He appears to have studied at Bologna before going to France where he continued his studies at Reims and Paris (*c*.1134). Apart from one possible visit to Rome in 1154 he spent the rest of his life in France, especially Paris where he taught in the Cathedral School of Notre Dame. In the middle 1140s he became a canon of Notre Dame and was influential as a teacher. In 1147 and 1148, at the Council of Reims, he was engaged in an examination of the orthodoxy of Gilbert of Poitiers. He was appointed archdeacon of Paris in 1156 and consecrated bishop of Paris in 1159. Peter was known as a biblical expositor and as a teacher of doctrine. Most significant was his *Sententiarum libri quatuor*, completed in 1157–8, a systematic study of doctrine. The *Sentences* covers all the major doctrines and the sacraments and draws on a wide range of sources, prominent among them being AUGUSTINE OF HIPPO. The work was not without its critics, and attempts were made to have it censured at the Fourth Lateran Council in 1215. Having survived this attack it became the standard work in the medieval curriculum, and Peter was given the title 'Master of Sentences'. [114; 642; 643] (T.T.)

Peter the Apostle [VI.A] (*d*.64?). According to the tradition in the Gospels, he was one of the first men called to be a disciple by JESUS. He and his brother ANDREW were fishermen. The New Testament documents and later traditions are variously evaluated as sources of information on the life and status of Peter. The problem is how much is authentic and how much has been written back into the record as a result of later tradition. The two epistles in the New Testament which bear his name are regarded as pseudepigraphal, as of course are the numerous extra-biblical documents which bear his name. Peter is spoken of twice by PAUL, during his lifetime, as someone whom he knew. (*Galatians* 1:13; 2:11–14; *1 Corinthians* 15:5). The implications of these references are that Peter was a leading, if not the leading, figure in Jerusalem and in the wider church at the time. According to the Gospels Peter was prominent among the twelve and stood out on various occasions: on the one hand he recognized Jesus as the Christ, (*Matthew* 16:16), but Jesus rebuked him when he remonstrated against his teaching that he was destined to suffer and be put to death. Before Jesus' betrayal Peter protested that he would never lose faith in him, but within hours denied that he was one of his followers (*Matthew* 26:69–75). Peter was also prominent in the primitive church. His addresses to the public are given prominence in *The Acts of the Apostles* (2:14–36; 3:12–26). It is recorded also that he worked miracles. In the references by Paul, Peter is involved in the controversy over the imposition of Torah obligations on converts to the Christian movement. Peter is said to have agreed with Paul's view and to have agreed to be the apostle to the Jews, leaving the Gentiles to Paul. Later Paul criticized Peter for not abiding strictly by the agreement on Torah obligations. It is likely that Peter ministered to the wider church: his name is associated with Antioch, where he met Paul, with Corinth (*1 Corinthians* 1:12) and Rome. Further tradition maintains that he was martyred in Rome; there is early evidence of his grave being a place of reverence. Such a grave has been excavated under St Peter's Basilica. The prominence given to Peter in the Gospels and *Acts* develops into a tradition that he was the first pope of Rome and that Jesus gave him apostolic authority over his whole church (based on *Matthew* 16:17–19). [122; 180; 550] (T.T.)

'Phags-pa [IV] ['Phags-pa Blo-gros-rgyal-mtshan] (1235–1280?). Is numbered as one of the 'five greats' of the Sa-skya order of Tibetan Buddhism. (The other four are Kundga'-snying-po, Bsod-nams-rtse-mo, Rje-btsun Grags-pa-rgyal-mtshan and SA-SKYA PAṆḌITA.) 'Phags-pa was a distinguished scholar and prolific author who wrote on all of the major topics of Tibetan Buddhism, from Mādhyamika philosophy to tantric liturgy. However, his fame beyond the confines of Buddhist scholarship derives from his position in the Mongol court of the Yüan emperor Qubilai Khan. When 'Phags-pa's uncle, Sa-skya Paṇḍita, was summoned to the court of the Mongol prince Godan in 1244 he took his young nephew with him. As a result of Sa-skya Paṇḍita's influence the head lamas of the Sa-skya order were given political rule over Tibet with Mongol patronage. With the founding of the Yüan Dynasty, the new emperor of China, Qubilai Khan, wished to keep an important member of the Sa-skya hierarchy at his court to insure Tibet's continued submission to Mongol rule. 'Phags-pa thus went to the Chinese court as a hostage. He soon so impressed the emperor with his learning and magical powers that he was asked to bestow tantric initiation on the emperor and his consort and later converted the members of the court to Tibetan Buddhism. Their interest seems to have been based less on an appreciation of Buddhist doctrine than on the fact that Tibetan medicine and magic proved more efficacious than that of the court shamans. Qubilai Khan appointed 'Phags-pa as Teacher to the Emperor (*Ti-shih*) and Teacher to the State (*Kuo-shih*), making him in the process the vassal-ruler (*in absentia*) of Tibet. Their relationship provided the model for the subsequent relationship between Tibet and China, at least as perceived by the Tibetans. In this relationship, known as 'Patron and Priest' (*yon mchod*) the leading lama of Tibet (in subsequent centuries, this role was played by the Dalai Lama) was seen as spiritual advisor and chief priest to the emperor, who acted as patron and protector of the lama and, by extension, of Tibet. 'Phags-pa is also credited with creating a script for the Mongolian language. [98] (D.L.)

Philip, John [VI.A] (1775–1851). Scottish missionary in South Africa. He was born in Kirkcaldy, Fife. Successively a mill manager (he resigned over the conditions of child workers), trader and Congregational minister, he went to South Africa in 1819 as an inspector for the London Missionary Society. He stayed for a generation as superintendent, constantly in conflict with settlers and government (and sometimes colleagues), especially over the oppression of Khoikhoi by colonists, but also over aspects of frontier policy. He was a regular source of information for T. F. BUXTON and the Aborigines Committee, and assisted American, German and French missions in the establishment of their work in South Africa. [252; 496; 695] (A.F.W.)

Philo [XV] (*c.*25 BCE–50 CE). Jewish philosopher and Bible commentator in Alexandria, Egypt. Few details are known of his life. He came from a wealthy family. His brother, a high official in the Roman administration in Egypt, donated the silver and gold plating for the gates in the Jerusalem Temple. The only incident known concerning him is that in 40 CE he headed a Jewish delegation to Rome to plead for the cancellation of Caligula's edict ordering the worship of statues of the emperor as a divinity, which the Jews could not accept and which had led to anti-Jewish riots in Alexandria. The problem was solved by the death of Caligula and the accession of Claudius (with whom Philo's brother was friendly). Philo, who sought to reconcile Judaism and Platonism, was the first thinker endeavouring to synthesize the doctrines of a faith based on supernatural revelation with the results of philosophical thinking. The concepts of God as transcendent Being and the personal God, close to man, were united through the *logos*, the divine mediator embracing God's word and wisdom, which is God's manifestation in the world. [32]

Philo expounded his ideas chiefly in the form of commentaries on the Pentateuch. The outstanding representative of Hellenistic Jewish thought, he wrote in Greek and his comments were based on the Greek translation of the Bible. He wrote different groups of works directed to the Jews and the non-Jews. For the latter his object was to demonstrate the superiority of the Jewish Bible as both revealing God's will and containing philosophical truths. For the Jews, he expounded Platonism, which he harmonized with Scripture by means of far-reaching allegorization. He was convinced that Judaism provided the answer to all problems. His writings display a strain of mysticism and were influential in religious contemplative writings.

His work was soon forgotten in Jewish circles, where even his name was unknown until rediscovered in the 16th century. However, he made a deep impression on Christian theologians, notably the Church Fathers, who were influenced by his doctrine of the *logos* and by his allegoristic approach. [86] (G.W.)

Photius the Great, St [VI.B] (*c*.810–*c*.895). Patriarch of Constantinople, 858–67, 877–86. A noble lay scholar, courtier, civil servant and diplomat, Photius was a major figure in Byzantine intellectual life even before he became Patriarch. His *Bibliothēkē* contains a critical summary of over 700 books, many lost.

He was appointed Patriarch of Constantinople on the deposition of Ignatius Nicetas in 858. Ignatius, and the monastic zealots who supported him (powerful because of their leadership in the triumph over iconoclasm) refused to accept his deposition. Photius and Emperor Michael III asked Pope Nicholas I to help settle the dispute. Papal legates took part in a synod which confirmed Ignatius' deposition (861). The Pope, however, annulled his legates' acts, formally recognized Ignatius and declared Photius deposed.

A dispute between Rome and Byzantium over missionary work in Bulgaria led Photius to hold a council, which in 867 condemned the Pope and declared him deposed. In 867 Michael III was murdered, and the new emperor, his killer, Basil I, reinstated Ignatius. Councils in Rome (869) and Constantinople, the latter later accounted the Eighth Oecumenical by Rome, condemned Photius and asserted papal authority. The researches of F. Dvornik have shown that this council was overturned by a later one (879), held after Ignatius's death, and that the decisions of this later council, which included a much more moderate statement of papal authority, were both affirmed by the papal legates present and confirmed by the Pope. The reconciliation was, however, more formal than real and the relations between Papacy and Patriarchate were to remain strained. The mutual excommunications in 1054 by the papal legate Humbert of Silva and Patriarch Michael Caerularius set a seal on this mutual estrangement.

Photius was deposed by the Emperor Leo VI (886) and retired from public life. He had formulated the basic grounds of the Orthodox critique of the Roman view of the Papacy, and had made the Latin use of the *filioque* clause a main ground of his condemnation of Rome, accusing the West of unorthodoxy. The conversion of the Slavs took place in this atmosphere of hostility between East and West. At the Council of 879, however, he had accepted an agreement which could still have a role in Catholic–Orthodox relations. [31; 45: 69–90; 68: 210ff.] (D.J.M.)

Phra Mun. *See* MUN, ACHARN.

Pico Della Mirandola, Count Giovanni [XVII.A] (1463–1494). Italian humanist philosopher. He was born in Mirandola, near Modena, a younger son in a family of feudal lords. He was primarily responsible for the use of kabbalistic philosophy and symbology in the Renaissance, for he grafted kabbalistic thought on to the Neoplatonic philosophy of the *Corpus Hermeticum* and Ficino's natural magic. He argued that the Kabbala actually demonstrated the truth of Christian teaching and, moreover, that kabbalistic magic was far stronger than natural or Hermetic magic because with the Kabbala, one invoked the names of God. These arguments are found in his *Conclusiones* (1486) and in the *Apologia* (1487). Pico is primarily famous, however, for his doctrine of the dignity of man. The early humanists praised man and his dignity; Ficino went farther to place him in the middle of the universal hierarchy, the line between the corporeal and non-corporeal world; Pico went farther still, asserting man's freedom to occupy any place within the hierarchy. The dignity of man lies in his freedom. *De hominis dignitate, heptaplus, de entre et uno, e scritti vari* (1492) may be the most widely known document of early Renaissance thought. [13; 24: vol. 2: LIX, LXI; 25; 26] (T.L.)

Pius IX [VI.A] [Giovanni Maria Mastai-Ferretti] (1792–1878). Pope, 1846–78. He was born of a leading family in the Papal States, and was ordained in Rome in 1815. Between 1823 and 1825 he served as an assistant to the papal mission to Chile. He became successively bishop of Spoleto (1827) and Imola (1831). In 1840 he was made a cardinal and in 1846 he was elected pope. Hopes of a liberal regime and a reform of the Papal States soon vanished. Having refused to become involved in the war with Austria, he was besieged in the Quirinal and had to escape to Gaeta with the help of French forces. From 1850 onwards, the date of his return to Rome, Pius IX discarded any liberal intentions. A period of reaction led to the occupation of Romagna and Umbria and the Marches in 1859–60 by Cavour, prime minister of Piedmont, who desired a united Italy. In 1870 Rome was seized by Victor Emmanuel. The Pope was isolated and virtually deprived of all temporal power. He is known for vigour in advancing the cause of the church through missionary work and the restoration of the hierarchy to England (1850) and Holland (1853), and his attack on Modernist theology by the publication of the encyclical *Quanta cura*, to which the famous *Syllabus errorum* was attached. He also defined the Immaculate Conception of the Blessed Virgin Mary in 1854 and the Vatican Council of 1869–70 defined the Infallibility of the Pope under his leadership. [29; 518; 528] (T.T.)

Plato [X] (*c*.429–347 BCE). Athenian philosopher. Although Plato deliberately refrained from giving a complete exposition of his ideas anywhere in his work, his mature religious thought is best studied initially in the *Timaeus* [69; 70], provided one remembers that Plato explicitly says that he is providing a myth or 'likely story', an image of the truth rather than pure truth itself. The *Timaeus* asserts that since the physical world consists of things that come into being and have a cause, it must itself have a cause or Creator. Since the world is good, its Creator must be good: the alternative is 'not right' to consider, presumably because not to recognize such goodness (admittedly imperfect) as there is in the world would cut one off from any understanding of goodness at all. Hence Plato calls the Creator of the world 'the Divine Craftsman'. Since the time of ARISTOTLE it has been disputed whether this is to be interpreted literally or metaphorically. The Craftsman was 'not envious' (*phthoneros*) – Plato here rejects the traditional Greek idea that the gods are jealous – and so wished the world to be as good as possible. He therefore fashioned it on the model of the Forms [69: 28–31].

Plato's theory of Forms is a theory that reality consists of universal principles corresponding to all the kinds of things that exist in the physical world, whether moral qualities, such as Justice or Courage, mathematical principles, such as Threeness or Triangularity, or natural kinds such as Horse, Oak or Fire. The existence of Forms is inferred from the fact that everything physical can be observed to be an imperfect instance of its kind and also to be continually changing – Plato learnt this from HERACLITUS – and yet is recognizable as having certain properties and belonging to a certain class, which can be accounted for only if it is an 'imitation' of an unchanging, perfect principle. Since Plato assumes that order is good and disorder bad, he regards the Form of the Good as the supreme Form, in which all other Forms participate.

So the world was constructed as a physical and temporal 'copy' of a set of eternal and non-physical perfect principles. But its Creator had to fashion it out of pre-existing formless and chaotic matter: he did not create out of nothing. Consequently, the world is imperfect: the Creator could not altogether overcome the deficiencies of his material, or eliminate change and decay. So there is evil in the world, but it arises from the inevitably imperfect nature of matter, and not from any independently existing evil principle or any ill-will on the Creator's part.

But the world contains Soul as well as Body; indeed Soul (i.e. life and intelligence) precedes body. Soul has a kind of existence intermediate between Forms and physical things, eternal but still subject to change. It is diffused through the world, but also present in particular beings within it. The most superior of these, and the only ones directly created by the Craftsman, are the gods. The only gods we know about, for Plato, are the heavenly bodies, which he believed to be divine. Other gods exist, can help us and should be worshipped, but we have no real knowledge about them: Plato suggests ironically that it is not for us to question those who claim to be descended from them and tell us about their ancestors [69: 41].

Although Plato seems to be a monotheist – there is only one Creator – he never suggests that the Craftsman should be worshipped; but instead worships these created things. Moreover, although he was very critical in the *Republic* [67: bk. 3] and *Laws* [63] of the morally unsavoury parts of Greek mythology, in both dialogues he regards the setting up of a cult and a mythology as the responsibility of the state, as if the form it takes, provided it is morally edifying, is unimportant. Possibly he regarded all mythologies and cults as metaphorical expressions of religious truth, necessary for the non-philosophical majority to make contact with the divine, so that it does not matter which one a particular society adopts. There is, however, a surprisingly authoritarian strain in the *Laws*: Plato there advocates the outlawing of three 'heresies' – that the gods do not exist, that they take no interest in human behaviour or in rewarding or punishing it, and that they can be bribed with sacrifices – and the eventual putting to death of those who cannot be educated out of them [63: bk. 10].

But in the *Timaeus* Plato represents the gods as creating human beings. The human soul has three parts: the immortal intellect and the two mortal parts, the sense of honour or 'spirit' and the physical desires, which die with the body. There are as many souls as stars; and if one lives well and resists the temptations – desire and fear – that are inseparable from being physical, one will return to one's star, i.e. perhaps, escape from the 'wheel' of reincarnation. Otherwise, one's intellect will survive in a corrupt form, being re-born as a woman (this suggestion is to Plato's shame), and then as animal, bird, or, at the lowest level, fish [69: 69–73; 89–92].

However, the most important and influential part of Plato's religious thought does not lie in these metaphysical ideas, though an account of them is essential for an understanding of his philosophy. Rather, it is to be found in the accounts in books 5–7 of the *Republic* [67], in the *Symposium* [68], and to some extent in the *Phaedo* [62], of how a person, an individual soul, can ascend intellectually and emotionally from the world of sense-perception to an understanding of the principles on which it is based, and ultimately to an intuition of the Forms themselves which is simultaneously mystical and, since it is an intuition of order, supremely rational. It is this that influenced not only Platonism and Neo-Platonism but also the mystical traditions of Christianity, Judaism and Islam. (*See also* DIOTIMA; PLOTINUS; SOCRATES) [20: vols. 4–5; 27a; 59–70] (H.L.)

Plotinus [x] (*c*.205–*c*.270). Neoplatonist philosopher. Nothing is known of his parents, family or ethnic origin. He studied at Alexandria for 11 years with the mysterious Ammonius Sakkas, about whose teaching very little is known, though a great deal has been written, mostly on insufficient evidence. It is generally assumed that Plotinus came from Egypt, though this is not certain and would not necessarily tell us anything about his origins. His writings clearly show that his education was entirely Greek. After an abortive attempt to visit the East he finally settled at Rome and remained there till his death. In the last 16 years of his life he wrote a number of works, in difficult but often splendid Greek, which were faithfully and accurately edited by his disciple Porphyry, but somewhat oddly and fantastically arranged by him for publication in six *Enneads* or sets of nine treatises, and it is on these that his lasting fame and wide influence depends.

Plotinus was in essentials a late Greek philosopher: that is, he was an independent person, with a deep devotion and loyalty to the founder of the tradition he adopted (in his case PLATO) and to his personal teacher, teaching on his own authority to whom he pleased, without institutional affiliations or academic status. He is generally regarded, and rightly, as the founder of Neoplatonism, but he felt free to disagree with earlier Platonists, and later Neoplatonists disagreed with him, often strongly and on points of importance. He deserves his place in this volume for two reasons. First, he was a great 'mystic'. He would not have liked, and does not use in its usual context, the word. But he had a vision of eternal reality, on which the world of everyday experience intimately depends like a shadow or reflection, and beyond it a vision, which might sometimes pass into a union, of its source which is beyond thought or speech but is called in the Platonic tradition the One or the Good, and expressed this in language of unequalled power and beauty. The second is the width and depth of his influence. His thought influenced Judaism, Christianity and Islam in both orthodox and unorthodox forms, often indirectly, and through works attributed to others. And it extended far beyond formal philosophy and theology, into the fields of poetry and the visual arts. Most of what is called Platonism in European cultural and religious history in fact derives from Plotinus. Within the Christian tradition he represents an independent way of non-Abrahamic thought and piety which may be capable of further development. This is all the more important nowadays because of its indubitable likeness to some aspects of Indian thought, though it is better to be agnostic about any actual influence. Contact between Greeks and Indians was perfectly possible in the Alexandria of his time, but there is no good evidence of strong philosophical or religious influence. [34a; 39; 71] (A.H.A.)

Pope [xx] (*d.*1690). A San Juan Tewa medicine man and political leader who led a nearly successful attempt to expel the Spanish from the territory now known as New Mexico in the 1680s. His date of birth is unknown. First mention of Pope is in 1675, when he was arrested by the Spanish governor and flogged for witchcraft. The experience seems to have hardened his resolve, for shortly thereafter he began preaching independence for the Pueblo peoples and calling upon them to return to traditional ways. His religio-political message culminated in a plan for the Great Pueblo Revolt of 1680. During the action, 400–500 Spanish were slain and the Pueblo tribes, under Pope's direction, quickly moved to extirpate all evidence of Christianity in the region. 'Anti-baptisms' were visited upon Christian converts and traditional Indian ceremonials were restored. The *kachinas* (the masked spirit protectors) were believed to be responsible for Pope's success. His rule, despotic at times, led to a brief period during which he was replaced by Luis Tupatu, though he was restored to power in 1688. [4: 219–20] (S.R.)

Potter, Philip Alford [VI.A] (1921–). Third General Secretary of the World Council of Churches. He was born in Dominica, West Indies, and worked in law offices until entering the Methodist ministry via the United Theological College of the West Indies and Richmond College. As a student he addressed the first Assembly of the World Council of Churches in 1948; after five years as a minister in Haiti he was serving in the Council's Youth Department. In 1961 the British Methodist Missionary Society appointed him secretary for West Africa and the Caribbean. In this period the International Missionary Council was controversially integrated into the World Council of Churches. Potter's next task was, as Director of the Commission on World Mission and Evangelism, the accomplishment of that merger, where he had to bring some coherence to widely diverse understandings of the nature of mission. In 1972 he became the Council's General Secretary. He was responsible for the assemblies of Nairobi, 1975 and Vancouver, 1983. His reports there emphasize the confession of Christ, the Scriptures, the common vocation of the churches and the Trinitarian basis of mission. The Council's Programme to Combat Racism earned him much abuse; the lifelong pacifist was accused of fomenting violence. During his service with the World Council Potter edited successively the *International Review of Mission* and the *Ecumenical Review*. Since leaving the Council in 1984 he has been teaching at the University of the West Indies. There is a bibliography of his writings: A J van der Bent, *The Whole Oikumene* (Geneva, 1980). (A.F.W.)

Prabhupada [XIX] [Abhay Charan De; His Divine Grace A. C. Bhaktivedanta Swami Prabhupada] (1896–1977). Founder-Acarya of the International Society for Krishna Consciousness (ISKCON). Born Abhay Charan De, he graduated from the University of Calcutta in English, philosophy and economics and then worked as the manager of a pharmaceutical firm. In 1922 he first met His Divine Grace Bhaktisiddhanta Thakura of the Gaudiya Vaishnava Mission, and was formally initiated in 1933, and then entrusted with the task of carrying Krishna Consciousness to the West. Married, with a family, he produced English-language material for the mission and undertook a considerable amount of translation, but it was not until he had retired and taken *sannyasin* in 1959 that he seriously set himself the task that his spiritual master had given him over 20 years earlier. [17; 45: foreword]

In 1965, at the age of 69, Prabhupada sailed to Boston with little more than $7, a trunk of books and a few clothes. By late 1966 he had accepted a small number of disciples in New York, and ISKCON had been established [18]. In 1967 he moved to California and there attracted an enthusiastic following from among the members of the hippie counterculture. Unlike many contemporary gurus from India, Prabhupada insisted that his disciples should not think of him as God, but as someone who was '*trying* to be a servant of God'. Krishna devotees soon became visible on the streets of most major cities throughout North America and Europe, dancing and singing the Hare Krishna mantra to the accompaniment of ancient Indian instruments, the women in brightly coloured saris, the men in white or saffron robes, heads shaved, save for the *sikha* or 'top-knot', with the clay marking or *tilaka* on their forehead and nose.

Prabhupada's philosophy was not a new one; it was in the Vaishnavite devotional tradition of the Bengali saint Chaitanya (1486–1534?). [45; 17; 18] The most important form of devotional service that Prabhupada taught is the repetition of the mantra: *Hare Krishna, Hare Krishna; Krishna Krishna, Hare Hare; Hare Rama, Hare Rama; Rama Rama, Hare.Hare.* Prabhupada expected his disciples to lead an ascetic life-style, abstaining from drugs, alcohol, meat and sex (except, within marriage, for the procreation of children).

Prabhupada taught his disciples that, through sincere devotional practices, it is possible to reach a state of blissful consciousness in this lifetime; that we are not our bodies, but eternal spiritual souls that are themselves an integral part of Krishna, the eternal, all-knowing, omnipresent Godhead, the sustaining energy of the entire cosmic creation. Prabhupada also taught that, while all the great scriptures contain the Absolute Truth, it is the *Bhagavad-Gītā* which is the literal record of God's words, and his translation and commentary [52] is the most widely studied book by ISKCON devotees. Prabhupada was a prolific writer and translator and the Bhaktivedanta Book Trust has published over 60 volumes of his work.

Prabhupada continued to lead ISKCON until his death. He had, however, established an administrative body, the Governing Body Commission (GBC), and 11 gurus who were to be empowered to initiate new devotees. After his death the movement underwent a number of difficulties, with half the gurus either leaving or being expelled from ISKCON; several splinter groups broke away from the main body. Since the mid-1980s there have been strenuous efforts to overcome its problems, and ISKCON continues to attract not only Western devotees, but also provides tens of thousands from the Asian community in the West with the rituals and temples that they need to worship according to their own traditions. (E.B.)

Prester John [VI.A]. The earliest literary reference to this legendary figure is in the Chronicle of Otto of Freising, 1145. A somewhat later letter, purportedly from Prester John to Christian rulers, was widely copied. In both sources Prester John is a powerful Christian prince (and priest, hence 'Prester') living eastward of the Muslims with whom the Crusaders were fighting. His military aid can be expected. The letter makes him guardian of the tomb of ST THOMAS THE APOSTLE at Mylapur. Stories continue until the 17th century. Some link Prester John with the Mongols (in one story CHINGGIS KHAN is his son, in another the conqueror of his kingdom). William of Rubruck thinks him a Chinese prince, John of Montecorvino a Turkish one. For others he is the heir of the Three Wise Men. All these stories may derive from knowledge of Nestorian Christianity. There is a recurrent stream of tradition, however, linking Prester John with the

Christian kingdom of Ethiopia, which could be thought of vaguely as in 'the Indies'. Certainly Pope Alexander III in 1177 wrote a letter to 'The King of the Indies, most holy priest'. [595; 678] (A.F.W.)

Prokopovich, Feofan [VI.A] (1681–1736). Russian Orthodox theologian. He was raised by his uncle and studied in Jesuit colleges in the Polish Ukraine and in Rome. In Rome he was converted to Uniate Roman Catholicism. He returned to Russia and reconverted to the Orthodox Church in Kiev, where he was made rector of the Theological Academy in 1711. He became bishop of Pskov in 1718 and archbishop of Novgorod in 1720. He collaborated with Peter the Great in bringing the administration of the church under lay authority through the establishment of the Ecclesiastical Regulation, which Prokopovich wrote and which was promulgated in January 1721. The patriarchate of Moscow was abolished and the church was ruled by an Ecclesiastical College, later known as the Holy Synod, whose members did not have to profess the Christian faith. At least one president was an avowed rationalist. The clergy were subject to police authority and were forced to reveal the secrets of the confessional or be prosecuted. The measure proved to be contentious until 1905, when it effectively came to an end. Prokopovich supported the German Anna Ivanova of Kurland who ruled Russia from 1730 to 1740. However, he soon found himself having to defend the hierarchical organization of the church and its apostolic succession against the ruler. His *Words and Speeches* appeared posthumously in 1765. [169; 184; 573] (T.T.)

Prophet, Elizabeth Clare [XIX] [née Wulf; Guru Ma] (1940–). Leader of The Summit Lighthouse since the death of the founder, the second of her four husbands, Mark L. Prophet (1918–1973). In 1974 Mrs Prophet, known to her students (followers) as 'Guru Ma', 'responded to the call from Jesus to found his Church', and The Summit Lighthouse incorporated Church Universal and Triumphant.

Elizabeth Clare Wulf was born in Red Bank, New Jersey. She says that while still a child she recollected past lives, and by the age of nine she had attended the synagogue and all the local churches without finding answers to her questions. From nine to 18 she attended Christian Science meetings, then she opened a book on the Ascended Masters and 'realized that Saint Germain was the one she had to find'. This, she says, was the turning point in her life.

She studied in Switzerland and at Antioch College before receiving a BA in political science at Boston University. In 1961, while still a student, she met Mark Prophet, 'the messenger for the Ascended Masters'. Within six weeks, the Ascended Master El Morya appeared to her and told her to be trained by Mark. Three years later she received Saint Germain's anointing to be the messenger of the Great White Brotherhood. Mark and Elizabeth Clare were married in 1963 and together they published many of the Masters' teachings (e.g. [55; 56]).

Since Mark's death, Mrs Prophet has travelled widely, taught thousands of students and established centres around the world. She has written numerous books (e.g. [54]) and produces a weekly letter, *Pearls of Wisdom*, from the Ascended Masters. The teaching is in the tradition of Madame BLAVATSKY and Guy Ballard, with the Church seeing itself as the true church of both JESUS Christ *and* Gautama BUDDHA; it also venerates the Virgin MARY. [38: 137; 54; 55; 56]

Recently, Elizabeth Clare Prophet (now Mrs Francis) and her organization, especially its headquarters in Montana, have been the subject of controversy, with accusations being made about 'exploitation' and illegal arms purchases by a member of the community. Her followers vehemently deny that Guru Ma has done anything wrong. (E.B.)

Ptah-hotep [VII] (24th century BCE). The vizier of King Isesi of Dynasty 5. The most extensive extant early Wisdom Instructions are attributed to him. Such instructions were usually set out as advice given by a sage to his son, but attribution to a particular wise man may not be genuine, and these maxims may have been compiled as late as Dynasty 6 (*c.*2200 BCE). Papyrus Prisse (a later, Middle Kingdom copy, *c.*1900 BCE), now in the Bibliothèque Nationale in Paris, preserves the only known complete version.

The Instructions in Wisdom comprised a major genre of Egyptian literature. Originating in the Old Kingdom (*c.*2686–

2113 BCE), when Egypt enjoyed a stable, orderly and hierarchical society, the Instructions were copied frequently in later periods and 'books' by new authors were added.

The Old Kingdom maxims embodied the pragmatic wisdom of the aristocracy, but by the New Kingdom (*c.*1575–1087 BCE), they tended instead to reflect middle-class values and to emphasize religious and ethical standards. The Old Kingdom Instructions, however, concentrated on teaching a code of behaviour to young courtiers and civil servants which would advance their careers. Not only did the Instructions provide training in wisdom and good manners, extolling the virtues of self-control and moderation, obedience to superiors, tact and discretion, the ability to remain silent, kindness, justice and generosity to subordinates, truthfulness, humility, and good manners in the presence of others; they were also written as literary examples which would enable generations of students to acquire the ability to express themselves effectively in the language [12: 54–66].

The Instructions of Ptah-hotep contain a prologue, an epilogue and 37 maxims, and provide a vivid insight into the 'ideal man' of the Old Kingdom – courteous, discreet and serene [19: vol. 1: 61–80; 30].

In general, the Wisdom Texts supply information, unobtainable elsewhere, which relates to the ethics and morals of an early and complex society. (A.R.D.)

Ptolemies, the [vii]. Following the conquest of Egypt by Alexander the Great (332 BCE), the country was governed by a dynasty of Macedonian rulers, descendants of Ptolemy I, Alexander's friend and army commander whom he left in charge of the country. This line ended with the reign of Cleopatra VII when Egypt passed under Roman rule in 30 BCE.

Under the Ptolemies many Greeks entered Egypt, and the ancient traditions and customs underwent a profound change. However, some religious ideas relating to the afterlife and the practice of mummification were adopted by some of the Greeks, and the Ptolemies continued to build Egyptian temples for their own political reasons. [3] (A.R.D.)

Pu-k'ung Chin-kang. *See* AMOGHAVAJRA.

Purandaradāsa [xi] (1480–1564). Poet and devotee of Kṛṣṇa. He was born in what is now Pune (Poona) District in Maharashtra, and was named Kṛṣṇappa Nāyaka. He inherited a prosperous moneylending business, and had also a learned upbringing. The story runs that Kṛṣṇappa grew more and more rich and miserly. One day a pauper was turned away from his door. In pity, Kṛṣṇappa's wife gave him her nose-jewel which, in due course, the poor man brought to sell at Kṛṣṇappa's counter. (A motif with several parallels in India and Central Asia!) Enraged, the miser locked him up and hurried to punish his wife. In despair, she prepared poison for herself. She was about to drink it when in the vessel she saw her jewel. She took it out and showed it to her husband. He was redeemed by this miracle: the jewel and the pauper both vanished. Kṛṣṇappa renounced the banking business, went to Pandharpur, and became a devotee of Kṛṣṇa there. With his existing interest in music, it was natural for Kṛṣṇappa to follow in the path of *kīrtana*-singing already established in the Deccan by Tallapākam Aṇṇamācārya, traceable to such Viṣṇu-devotees as CAITANYA. He adopted the name of Purandaradāsa, and commenced the lyrical compositions called *Devaranāma* that have made him famous. Only the *libretti* are original: the melodies are the work of later musicians. If only by reason of his date, Purandaradāsa is regarded as the 'Founding Father' of Karnatic or South Indian classical music [93]. (J.R.M.)

Pythagoras [x] (6th century BCE). Philosopher, mathematician and seer. There are many legends but few reliable facts about the life and teaching of Pythagoras; but a fair amount is known about the doctrines of his followers, particularly in the 4th century BCE. The Pythagorean Brotherhood (which included both women and men) was both a religious and a political community, which flourished in the Greek colonies of southern Italy, and sometimes obtained political dominance in particular cities (Plato's *Republic* [67] may possibly express their political ideals). It lasted from the 6th to the 4th century BCE; but the doctrines were revived as part of 'Neopythagoreanism' in the 1st century BCE. The Pythagorean way of life involved a strict code of morality (for example, marital fidelity was required of men as well as women); self-discipline to the point of asceticism; a number of ritual requirements (the most famous being the prohibition of eating beans), the significance of which is unknown, but which were probably either symbolic or served to promote group identity; and the pursuit of wisdom, the very word 'philosopher', or 'lover of wisdom', being, according to tradition, coined by Pythagoras because only God could be called wise.

The Pythagorean doctrines were believed by the Greeks to come from Egypt, but are much closer to Indian thought than to anything the ancient Egyptians are known to have held: the doctrines were for a long time kept secret from outsiders and probably revealed in stages to disciples as they advanced in knowledge. The most famous of their beliefs was the reincarnation of the soul, each new incarnation being determined by the degree of intelligence and virtue exercised in the previous one, and transmigration between human and animal being a frequent occurrence: because of this kinship between humans and animals, the Pythagoreans objected both to meat-eating and to animal sacrifice. They also regarded the desires and fears of the physical body as an obstacle to the cultivation of the soul, i.e. of virtue and intelligence; hence their emphasis on asceticism.

The other pillar of Pythagoreanism was the belief that the world is to be understood mathematically – that it is the proportions of its components to each other that make everything what it is: and that there are ideal ratios, so that the nearer the proportions of a thing approach to the ideal the better and more beautiful it is. This was applied not only to such things as music (Pythagoras was credited with discovering the relation between length of string and pitch) and astronomy; but also to psychology, moral goodness involving inner harmony and balance of the soul. Wisdom is the understanding of these ideal ratios: it is thus, to use a modern distinction, simultaneously mystical and rational, since, for the Pythagoreans, to intuit the real nature of things was also to discover how perfectly things are ordered and proportioned rationally. These ideas have greatly influenced Western thought, but mainly via Plato and Platonism. [2; 4; 20: vol. 1; 48; 52]. (H.L.)

Q

Quṭb, Sayyid [XII] (1906–1966). Intellectual spokesperson for the Egyptian Muslim Brotherhood. Having spent a period in the United States at the end of the 1940s, Quṭb became involved with the Muslim Brotherhood in the 1950s, triumphing a return to 'pure Islam' and away from the materialism of the Western culture which he perceived as contaminating Islam. Intellectually he followed in the line of IBN TAYMIYYA. He was politically active in the movement while declaring his political independence from everything but Islam; all else was declared *jāhiliyya*, existing in a state of 'ignorance' of Islam. His major work *Fī Ẓilāl al-Qur'ān* ('In the Shade of the Qur'ān') was written mainly in the period 1954–64 while he was in gaol; it provides a meditation on the Qur'ān in the modern context. Quṭb was executed in 1966 for conspiring to kill Egyptian president Abdel Nasser; this made him a symbol for many Muslim fundamentalists thereafter.

Islam is a 'simple' way of life according to Quṭb and it provides a perfect social system for all of humanity, one which cures all the ills of the modern world. What is needed is the establishment of a truly Islamic state, an enactment of the period of MUḤAMMAD; this will bring Islam back into its own and all of life will fall into place as a result. No borrowing from the West is needed; Islam is self-sufficient. [100; 120] (A.R.)

R

Rabīʿa al-ʿAdawiyya [xii] (713/17–801). Famous female Ṣūfī mystic. Born in Baṣra to a poor family, she was sold into slavery as a child but later freed by her master, reputedly on account of her piety. Adopting a life of celibacy (unusual for Ṣūfīs and difficult for a woman in Arab society), she lived for a time as a hermit in the desert before returning to Baṣra. Here, large numbers of disciples and fellow mystics gathered round her.

Her life is unusually obscured by a mass of legends, including many that link her name improbably to those of other early ascetics, such as al-Ḥasan al-Baṣrī (*d.*728). More plausible are her links with Sufyān al-Thawrī, Shaqīq Balkhī and Mālik ibn Dīnār. What is clear is that Rabīʿa was highly regarded within the circles of early Irāqī Ṣufism, and that her influence extended to both men and women.

Accounts of her asceticism and constant devotions figure largely in the biographical literature. Numerous reports speak of her frailty and ill health, particularly in her later years. She died and was buried in Baṣra. Her tomb there became an important place of pilgrimage.

Rabīʿa's outstanding quality was that of absolute devotion, as a result of which she is generally regarded as the pioneer of the notion of selfless love in early Islamic mysticism. Within a context of extreme asceticism and an emphasis on divine transcendence, she spoke of love for God and the possibility of the beatific vision, laying a basis for genuine mysticism in Islam.

Although Rabīʿa left no writings, many of her prayers and sayings were reported by later writers and have attained considerable popularity. Above all, she demonstrated the possibility of a role for women within Ṣufism, even if she herself remains the supreme example of the female mystic in Islam. [34: s.v.; 123] (D.M.)

Rachel (*c.*18th century BCE): Jewish matriarch. The younger daughter of Jacob's uncle, Laban, Jacob met her by a well and wanted to marry her. Laban made this conditional on Jacob first working for him for seven years. However, when this had been accomplished and the time arrived for the marriage, Laban substituted Rachel's elder sister Leah, on the grounds that the elder had to be wed before the younger. His condition for Jacob marrying Rachel was now a further seven years' service, to which Jacob agreed. Rachel was Jacob's preferred wife and the Bible comments on her beauty.

When Jacob and Laban quarrelled, both Laban's daughters sided with Jacob, and Rachel by a strategem obtained her father's household goods (*teraphim*) to take with them on the journey back to Canaan. When on the journey news was received of the approach of Esau and his followers, Jacob, fearing his brother's vengeance, placed Rachel and her son, Joseph, in the most protected position at the very back of his caravan.

When they reached the Land of Canaan, Rachel gave birth to a second son, Benjamin, but she died in childbirth. Her burial place has been traditionally identified with a site outside Bethlehem, still the scene of pilgrimage (the 'Tomb of Rachel'), especially by barren women coming to supplicate her intervention in view of her own history of barrenness before eventually becoming pregnant. According to the Bible, even after her death she continued to be concerned with the fate of her descendants (Jeremiah 31:15). [68:XI–XII] (G.W)

Radhakrishnan, Sarvepalli [XI] (1888–1975). Philosopher and President of the Indian Republic. He was born in South India and was educated at the Lutheran Mission High School in Tirupati, Voorhees College, Vellore, and Madras Christian College. He became Professor of Philosophy in the Presidency College, Madras, and then in the University of Mysore. As Upton Lecturer in Comparative Religion at Oxford, he delivered the Hibbert Lectures in 1929–30. He was Professor of Philosophy at Calcutta University, 1921–39, and Vice-Chancellor of Benares Hindu University, 1939–48. He was the first Spalding Professor of Eastern Religion and Ethics at Oxford from 1936 to 1952. He was involved in a number of international cultural organizations and served as India's ambassador in various posts, including the Soviet Union. He was Vice-President of India from 1952 to 1962, and President from 1962 to 1967 when he retired. Among his books are: *Indian Philosophy*, *The Hindu View of Life*, *An Idealist View of Life*, *The Reign of Religion in Contemporary Philosophy*, *Eastern Religions and Western Thought*, *Bhagavad Gita* and *The Principal Upanishads*. A lucid expositor, his own position was a blend of Advaita Vedanta and Absolute Idealism. His contribution is clearly considerable, although as yet not adequately assessed, and it has been said of him that he did for Indian religious philosophy what VIVEKANANDA did for Indian spirituality. [76] (S.C.R.W.)

Radhasoami [Rādhāsvāmī]. *See* SHIV DAYAL SINGH.

Raël [XIX] [Claude Vorilhon] (1946–). Leader of the Raëlian Movement. Raëlians claim that an extraterrestrial appeared to Claude Vorilhon in France in 1973 and invited him to step into his craft. He explained that long ago, on a distant planet, a 'humanity' had reached a scientific and technological level equal to one we shall reach in years to come. We are told that the Elohim (our fathers from space) renamed Vorilhon as 'Raël', the messenger of those who come from the sky. The messages tell of impending dangers and how to prepare for the coming of the Elohim [68]. Raël also teaches his followers 'sensual meditation' [67]. (E.B.)

Rahner, Karl [VI.A] (1904–1984). German Jesuit priest and theologian. He was born and grew up in Freiburg im Breisgau, Germany. He joined the Society of Jesus in 1922. From 1924 to 1927 he studied philosophy and from 1929 to 1933 theology. He was ordained priest in 1932 and in 1933–4 he spent a year in pastoral and ascetic studies. From 1934 he was engaged in doctoral research in Freiburg. When his supervisor rejected his thesis on the grounds that it lacked the traditional approach he left for Innsbruck, where he soon completed his thesis and began to teach theology in 1937. He moved to Vienna in 1938 when the Nazis closed the Innsbruck faculty and taught at the Pastoral Institute until 1944. Between 1945 and 1948 he taught at Pullach bei München and returned to Innsbruck in 1949. In his teaching he attempted to correlate the historical with the transcendental, and later to see the history of salvation as coextensive with the history of the world. Because of his popularity his works were collected and published as *Schriften zur Theologie* from 1954 onwards, the sixteenth and final volume appeared in 1984. He became co-editor of *Lexicon für Theologie und Kirche* from 1957. He began to publish works on pastoral theology and spirituality. He was not popular with the traditionalists, who tried to obstruct his appointment as one of the consultants preparing for the Second Vatican Council. He became professor at the University of Munich in 1964 and at Münster in 1967. He retired to Munich in 1971. He continued writing and lecturing, always criticized by the traditionalists, until his final retirement to Innsbruck in 1984. [597; 665; 832] (T.T.)

Raidās. *See* RAVIDĀS.

Rai Saligram [XI] (1829–1898). The second guru of the Radhasoamis. He was born in Agra into a family of Kayasths, the professional caste of northern India. After a brilliant student career, he joined the postal department, where his administrative abilities eventually led to his appointment as Postmaster General of the North-Western Provinces, and the title Rai Bahadur. These official duties were combined with an extreme devotion to SHIV DAYAL SIṄGH, whom he first met in 1858 and whom he succeeded in 1878 as guru of the Radhasoamis, by whom he is given the honorific title Huzur Maharaj. His rich hagiography dwells on the perfection of his *guru-bhakti*, which made him defy caste and social prejudice by carrying his Khatri guru on his shoulders when himself a senior official, and on his own miracles, which included the power to ensure that devotees who forgot their official duties in the bliss of his *satsang* would return to their offices to find their allotted tasks accomplished and themselves marked present in the attendance register [74: 58]. Rai Saligram's prolific Hindi writings include the prose *Prem patra* ('Letters of Love') and the verse *Prem bāṇī* ('Words of Love'), beside the short English guide *Radhasoami mat prakash* (1896). These reveal 'a vigorous and orderly mind' [32: 164], whose systematic elaboration of Radhasoami theology neatly sets out the descending divisions of creation, namely spiritual, spiritual-material, and material-spiritual, their subdivisions, and the way to spiritual ascent through them by the practice of *surat-śabd-yoga* [49; 74: V]. Rai Saligram is equally remarkable for the success of his practical leadership of a growing community. The Radhasoami Satsang was to be open to members of all religions, provided only that they recognized these were but imperfect manifestations of the higher reality, and were willing to accept simple dietary rules, e.g. the avoidance of meat and intoxicants. At the same time the ties of the *satsang* to the *santsatguru* were strengthened through such institutions as *ārtī*, defined as inner meditation while listening to hymns in the guru's presence, the special celebrations prescribed for past gurus' death-anniversaries (*bhaṇḍārā*), and the injunction to perform pilgrimage to their mausolea (*samādhi*). Rai Saligram's own *samādhi* in Agra continues to be a focus of Radhasoami devotion. [32: 163–7; 49; 74: IV–V] (C.S.)

Rājacandra, Śrīmad [XIII] (1867–1901). Jain mystic and reformer. He was born in the Saurāṣṭra region of Gujarat as Rāychandbhai Mehta (later to be called Śrīmad Rājacandra) [19]. Although his mother was a Jain, Rājacandra's family seem to have been oriented towards a Hindu style of worship, as is not uncommon in Gujarat and Rajasthan. Later in life he claimed that, as a boy, he had experienced memory of his previous births, a sign of great spiritual attainment, and it is said that at the age of 20 he gave proof of his phenomenal mnemonic powers to a public gathering in Bombay. Although Rājacandra regarded his social role as a married householder (he was a jeweller by profession) to be a necessary feature of his life owing to the karma he had acquired in previous existences, as he grew older and studied texts of the Digambara sect of Jainism more intensely, he came to view himself as a spiritually enlightened person, going so far as to claim omniscience and the intention to propagate true religion. Rājacandra was particularly vexed by what he saw as the sectarianism and obscurantism of contemporary Jainism, and his writings castigate his co-religionists for their lack of familiarity with doctrine and excessive interest in ritual. He saw his mission to be one of persuading the world to focus exclusively upon the soul as the eternal agent and experiencer and repository of enlightenment, expressing his ideas in Jain terminology, but also showing the influence of Hindu Vedānta theology. According to Rājacandra, the goal of true religious practice is the attainment of that pure and pristine state of the soul which lies beyond the phenomenal world and which is to be achieved through the direct path of meditation based on the study of scriptural texts, with no sectarian allegiance involved. It was not necessary to renounce the world and become a full-time ascetic to enter this path. Rājacandra argued that the householder's life was the more appropriate for the religious quest precisely because of the inherent difficulties which it posed.

A noteworthy aspect of Rājacandra's life was his relationship with GANDHI, who, while not a Jain, was unquestionably influenced by Rājacandra in the gradual formation of his views about non-violence. Three letters survive in which Rājacandra instructs the young Gandhi about Jain precepts and the cultivation of certain Jain principles such as compassion for living creatures. In addition, and significantly for Gandhi's later views about society, Rājacandra advised him that he should not deviate from the rules prescribed by the social group to which he belonged.

The climax of Rājacandra's career took place on a hill outside Īdār in north Gujarat, where, after a period of fasting meditation and study, he proclaimed himself as a liberated soul to some of his followers. He died at Rajkot in 1901, perhaps worn out by the practice of austerities.

Rājacandra's approach to Jainism and its scriptural literature was selective. His most important work is 'The Attainment of the Soul' (*Ātmasiddhi*) [22], which, in its stress on the inner, spiritual aspects of Jainism, can be seen to be in a direct line of descent from KUNDAKUNDA and BANĀRSĪDĀS. There is a small but growing number of Rājacandra temples, with two outside India, in Mombasa and Leicester respectively. It is likely that, as the number of Jains outside India with little or no access to the ascetic interpretation of the religion increases, so will the influence of Rājacandra's brand of Jainism. [20] (P.D.)

Rajneesh, Bhagwan Shree [XIX] (1931–1990). His followers have been known as Rajneeshees, Sannyasins, Neo-Sannyasins, the Orange People or, simply, followers of Bhagwan. He was born as Mohan Chandra Rajneesh in a small town in India, one of 12 children of a Jain cloth merchant. According to a number of reports, he was a difficult, independently minded child. [64: 13]

During his youth, Rajneesh studied both political ideologies and the main religious traditions. He claimed that he became enlightened while still a student, on 21 March 1953. He obtained a Master's degree in philosophy and then began a career as an academic, but he resigned from his post at the University of Jabalpur in 1966, and took on the role of a full-time spiritual teacher.

At first he taught from an apartment in Bombay, gathering around him a small band of followers; then in 1974 he moved to Poona, where he rapidly became one of the best-known and most controversial of contemporary gurus. Visitors flocked from around the world to hear him and to take part in the activities organized at the ashram – these included a wide variety of therapies, meditations and 'experiences'. The meditations advocated by Rajneesh (especially the 'Dynamic' and Kundalini meditations), far from being of a contemplative nature, often involve violent physical exercises, followed by relaxation. For some, Poona was an enlightening experience that opened new avenues and brought enlightenment. Others reported frenzied sexual activity, drug trafficking, and mental and physical injuries resulting from some of the more experimental programmes that were on offer. [40: VII, X]

Followers who 'took *sannyas*' were expected to feel a desire to surrender to Bhagwan and to become his disciple, to be as honest and open as possible, and to enjoy life and to learn to love themselves. The outward signs were to wear orange (usually a shade of pink or purple), and a mala with Bhagwan's picture, and to accept a new name.

In the summer of 1981 Rajneesh suddenly disappeared from Poona, only to turn up several weeks later at a large ranch in Oregon, which came to be known as Rajneeshpuram. Here a vast city was planned; Rajneesh's followers laboured ('worshipped') to build it under the direction of Rajneesh's personal secretary, Ma Anand Sheela – Rajneesh himself having taken a vow of silence from 1981 to 1984.

Perhaps the most striking characteristic of Rajneesh's philosophy is that, while drawing from numerous traditions, it denies any tradition – and revels in contradiction [57; 58; 59]. It rejects social conditioning and advocates 'doing one's own thing'. But while many undoubtedly benefited, and felt spiritually, psychologically and socially liberated by the free sex and uninhibited self-exploration that Rajneesh and his followers extolled, life at Rajneeshpuram became increasingly controlled and authoritarian [40: XIV; 64]. By 1985 the situation had become critical. Sheela absconded (she was later imprisoned for a number of offences) and, a few weeks afterwards, Rajneesh was arrested while trying to leave the United States. He was convicted on immigration charges and expelled from the country. After trying to get permission to stay in a number of other countries, he returned to Poona, whence his movement reorganized itself, and where he adopted the name 'Osho'. His followers were no longer expected to wear their malas, or 'orange' all the time (white was advocated for meditation by oneself or in Osho's presence). Another sign that circumstances had changed since the Poona of the 1970s was that those who wished to enter the precincts had to produce an AIDS-free certificate – a requirement that continues to be rigidly enforced by Osho's followers, who have continued to offer courses and to publicize his philosophy of life since their Master's death. (E.B.)

Ral-pa-can [IV] [Khri Gtsug-lde-btsan] (805–838). Penultimate in the line of ancient

Tibetan emperors (*btsan po*), he reigned from 815. His proper name was Khri Gtsug-lde-btsan; the name Ral-pa-can derived from his long hair, like a lion's mane. He was such a fanatical Buddhist, it is reported, that he allowed monks at court to sit on the ends of his braids, extended by ribbons, signifying the ultimate establishment of Buddhism as state religion. There is, however, evidence that the shamanic state cult held equal place: a peace treaty with China of the year 821, demarcating the borders, was consecrated not only with a Buddhist ritual, but also with animal sacrifice in the manner of Bön.

Ral-pa-can's strong devotion to Buddhism is also well attested. Many temples were constructed during his reign, and he instituted taxation of seven households to support each monk. More importantly for the future pattern of theocracy in Tibet, monks became ministers and were even ennobled with land grants. A scandal involving one such monk-minister and the queen led to the downfall of this emperor, who was assassinated by anti-Buddhist ministers. They placed his brother Glang-dar-ma on the throne, and consequent persecutions put an end to the early period of Buddhism in Tibet.

The religious language was standardized during Ral-pa-can's reign. In a lexicographical project sponsored by the state, a committee of translators composed Sanskrit–Tibetan lexicons, along with explanations of translation methodology, and brought existing translations up to date. [171: 196–7; 197: 404–29; 238: 239, 250] (M.T.)

Ramabai, Pandita [VI.A] (1858–1922). Indian Christian. She was born, the youngest of six children, into a Hindu Brahman family in a forest ashram in Mangalore District in the present state of Karnataka, India. Her father and mother were progressive in their ideas on female emancipation, expressed primarily in the education of women. Ramabai was taught Sanskrit and the Indian classics at an early age. Following the death of her parents in 1874 she was given the title 'Pandita' in Calcutta in 1878 for her knowledge of Sanskrit. She married in 1880 and bore a daughter the following year, but a year later her husband died. In 1882 she arrived in Pune (Poona), Maharashtra, and her work centred on this city and Bombay until a plague and famine forced her to set up a centre called Mukti Sadan in Khedgaon, Maharashtra, in 1898. Early on she was associated with reforming and devotional Hindu movements. She journeyed to Britain in 1883, and was baptized in Wantage, the home of the Community of St Mary the Virgin, an Anglican order of nuns. In 1886 she moved on to America, returning to India in 1888. While she was on these visits she spent much time participating in and studying the education of women. In 1889 she founded a secular school for Hindu girls in Bombay, with financial support from America, but moved the institution to Pune the following year. Gradually the school became more Christian. Although baptized under the influence of high church Anglicans, she remained independent of denominational influence, and consciously following the example of the Welsh revival of 1905 the Mukti Mission became heavily evangelical and remained so. She published a number of works, mainly on the status of women, in Sanskrit, Marathi and English. [4; 510] (T.T.)

Ramakrishna [XI] [Rāmakṛṣṇa; also called Ramakrishna Paramahaṃsa (title of the highest grade of Hindu ascetics)] (1836–1886). Hindu spiritual leader. He was born in Kamarpukur, Hughli District, Bengal, and named Gadadhar Chatterji. His father, a poor Brahman, died in 1843, leaving him to be brought up by his elder brother Ramkumar. In 1852 he moved to Calcutta, where he worked as a *purohit*, conducting household rituals. In 1855 he became priest at a new temple of Kālī at Dakshineshwar, four miles north of Calcutta, where he remained for most of his life, except for periods spent in his home village; it was here that he began to be called Ramakrishna. In 1859 he married the five-year-old Sarada Devi; she later became his disciple and spiritual consort, known to his followers as Holy Mother. After some years of Tantric practice (1861–3), he was initiated as a *sannyāsī* by a wandering teacher of Advaita Vedanta named Tota Puri. He also showed characteristics of Vaiṣṇava devotion, seeing himself as a lovesick cowherd girl. He lived for a time like a Muslim, and later devoted himself to JESUS; each of these experiences culminated in mystical ecstasy. While the Ramakrishna Mission, founded in his name by VIVEKANANDA, regards him as essentially an Advaita Vedantin, he cannot be placed in a particular intellectual tradition. Though literate in Bengali and having some knowledge of Sanskrit, he was not a systematic thinker. His sayings (90; 24: vol. 2, 85–94], taken down by others, are earthy, practical and sometimes coarse, using stories and examples from rustic and modern life. Besides his remarkable personality, his importance lies in the fact that his message, nourished by oral tradition, was communicated to highly literate contemporaries and thence to the world. KESHUB CHUNDER SEN, DAYANAND SARASVATI, DEBENDRANATH TAGORE, Bankin Chandra Chatterji and, above all, Vivekananda met him, and through him became aware of the popular traditions of Bengal [64; 32: 188–200). (D.H.K.)

Ramana Maharshi [XI] (1879–1950). Hindu spiritual leader. He was born in the village of Tirucculi in South India. His full name was Venkataraman Aiyer, and the family were Brahmans. On the death of his father, the family moved to Madurai to be looked after by his uncle. When he was 16 years old in 1896 he first heard the name Arunachala which awoke in him a great fascination. He also began to read the lives of the Tamil saints. In 1896 he had his first spiritual experience, brought on by a sudden fear of death, in which he saw that his 'I' was immortal. A few weeks later he ran away from home determined to renounce the world. He went to Tiruvannamalai to the Arunachalesvara temple, where he experienced ecstatic joy. He then began a life of total renunciation and austerity and never moved from Tiruvannamalai for the rest of his life. There can be no doubt that he evolved inwardly and people came to be with him from all over the world including a number of prominent Westerners like Jung, Somerset Maugham and Zimmer. He gave counsel rather than teaching, urging the pursuit of the question 'Who am I?', and his basic position was that of Advaita Vedanta. His writings are very small in number, and were only written to meet the needs of specific disciples. [85] (S.C.R.W.)

Rāmānuja [XI] (traditionally 1017–1137, but 1077–1157 is a more recent and reasonable hypothesis [15: II]). Theologian, philosopher and the third leader (*ācārya*) of the Śrī Vaiṣṇava community after NĀTAMUNI and YĀMUNA. He is primarily renowned for his influential theistic interpretation of Vedānta, Viśiṣṭādvaita, in opposition to the monistic position of ŚAṄKARA.

There are biographies in both Sanskrit and Tamil, but it is unlikely that any of them was written less than a century after Rāmānuja. He was born in Śrī Perumbūdūr, a town not far from modern Madras, to Āsuri Keśava Perumāḷ and his wife Bhūmi, who was the sister of one of Yāmuna's most prominent disciples. The family were Brahmans of the Vaḍama subcaste, probably Smārtas with Vaiṣṇava leanings, and upholders of the traditions of Vedic scholarship. It is recorded that Rāmānuja studied scriptures with his father, was married, and moved from home to study with Yādava Prakāśa, who was an Advaitin, although of what precise persuasion is not known. Rāmānuja's disagreements with his teacher over the interpretation of the Upaniṣads became so extreme that it is even said that Yādava Prakāśa tried to have him murdered. Finally Rāmānuja broke with his teacher and it is recorded that Yāmuna, the leader of the Śrī Vaiṣṇava community, who was terminally ill at the time, on hearing the news sent a disciple to bring Rāmānuja to him, but unfortunately by the time Rāmānuja arrived Yāmuna was dead. There are, however, difficulties with the chronology for this element of the biography.

The disciples of Yāmuna decided to prepare Rāmānuja to succeed as leader of the Śrī Vaiṣṇavas and accordingly he was initiated and began to receive instruction. Rāmānuja then became an ascetic and established a monastic house near the temple in Kāñcīpuram, but the Śrī Vaiṣṇavas at Śrīraṅgam begged him to go there. This he did and gradually brought about changes in the organization and personnel at the Śrīraṅgam temple, thereby upsetting a number of the previous functionaries. In addition to being the general manager of the temple, Rāmānuja was also the leader of the community; it is related that he received the secret doctrine of the community from five of the disciples of Yāmuna.

The next stage of Rāmānuja's life was as a peripatetic debater, and he certainly travelled round South India, and the North too, as far as Kashmir, but it is not clear how successful he was in theological debate. Certainly he won converts, and he was also able in places to introduce more Vaiṣṇava rituals in the temples, but the biographies are ambiguous on the question of his skills as a polemicist, choosing to emphasize rather the strength of his devotion to Viṣṇu. It seems that Rāmānuja was obliged to spend a great part of his later life in the Hoysala kingdom, in what is now Mysore state, owing to the persecution of the Cola king Kulottunga, who was a fanatical Śaivite. It is also said that when the king finally died, Rāmānuja was able to return to Śrīraṅgam, where he lived out his days surrounded by an increasingly large body of disciples.

Of Rāmānuja's works, the most renowned and influential is undoubtedly the *Śrībhāṣya*, his major commentary on the *Vedānta Sūtras*. Two other commentaries on the *Vedānta Sūtras* are also attributed to him, the *Vedāntadīpa* and the *Vedāntasāra*, although the authenticity of the latter has been questioned. His earliest work is probably the *Vedārthasaṃgraha*, which is not a commentary, but a philosophical statement of his position on a restricted range of topics. More devotional than philosophical is his commentary on the *Bhagavad Gītā*, the *Bhagavadgītābhāṣya*, which is his second longest work and was probably written after the *Śrībhāṣya*. The four other works attributed to Rāmānuja are three prose works, the *Śaraṇāgatigadya*, the *Śrīraṅgagadya*, and the *Vaikuṇṭhagadya*, all highly devotional in tone, and a manual of daily worship entitled *Nityagrantha*. There is some uncertainty as to the authenticity of these last four works, but the first three have played an important part in the history of the Śrī Vaiṣṇava sect. Rāmānuja is highly regarded for his Viśiṣṭādvaita, qualified non-dualism, which opened up Vedānta to theism, and for his emphasis on divine grace (*anugraha*) and the need for surrender (*prapatti*) on the part of the devotees, but he also helped complete the reconciliation begun by his predecessors between the Sanskitic traditions and Tamil devotionalism, and he led the Śrī Vaiṣṇava community at a critical period in its evolution. Rāmānuja's contribution may have been not so much original as articulative, but he was clearly a truly great *ācārya* and his influence is still felt to this day. [15; 22: vol. 3] (S.C.R.W.)

Rām Dās Gurū [XXIII] (1534–1581). Fourth Gurū of the Sikhs. He was born in Lahore, a member of the Soḍhī subcaste of the Khatrīs. Known as Jeṭhā until he became a Sikh, he was married in 1554 to Bhānī, the daughter of GURŪ AMAR DĀS. Before Amar Dās died in 1574 at the advanced age of 95 his choice as Gurū fell upon Rām Dās.

Sources for the life of Gurū Rām Dās are sparse (as they are for all Gurūs from the second to the eighth) and although it is clear that he should undoubtedly be associated with the founding of Amritsar it is not certain whether he did so on his own initiative or in response to instructions from Gurū Amar Dās. Amritsar was nevertheless established by Gurū Rām Dās, known first as Chak Gurū and then as Rāmdāspur. The first act of the Gurū was to excavate the pool which ultimately gave the site its name of Amritsar.

Gurū Rām Dās is credited with having established the *masands*, vicars who would act for the Gurū in his absence. Evidently they replaced the *mañjīs* appointed by Amar Dās. During their early years the *masands* apparently performed their duties faithfully, but by the time of the tenth Gurū they had become corrupt and independent. GOBIND SIṄGH therefore abolished the order.

Composing hymns was a particular skill of Gurū Rām Dās and many of his works have been recorded in the *Ādi Granth* (the primary Sikh scripture). In the early Panth the singing of hymns in praise of the divine Name was the dominant activity, an emphasis which continues to the present day. As a contributor to this tradition Gurū Rām Dās made a very important contribution. To succeed him as the fifth Gurū of the Sikhs Rām Dās chose his youngest son, ARJAN. Thereafter all the Sikh Gurūs were his direct male descendants in the Soḍhī subcaste. [68: XIII] (W.H.M.)

Rāmdās [XI] [Rāmadāsa] (1608–1681). Hindu religious leader. He was born at Jamb in Parbhani District and following the usual path of holy men, wandered all over India in his youth before settling at Chaphal south of Satara in Maharashtra in 1644. During his travels he had become a devotee of Rām and so assumed the name by which he is always known. He was an inspiring leader and organizer, founding a whole series of temples to Rām, Lakṣman and Hanumān, and later to the goddess Bhavānī. He also established a chain of monasteries (*maṭha*) all over the South Maratha country, each with one of his many disciples at its head. His period corresponds closely with that of the rise of Śivājī and the founding of the Maratha kingdom, so that his teaching exhibits the characteristics of a kind of militant Hinduism, considerably different from the quietistic *bhakti* of the other poet-saints of Marathi. Among his many literary works the *Dāsabodha* is a huge poem which apparently was composed in stages over the last 20 years of Rāmdās's life. As well as teaching on religious matters, it contains numerous homilies on right action in the world, for kings as well as their subjects, and clearly reflects the socio-political state of Maharashtra at the time. There is controversy over the date at which Rāmdās and Śivājī first met, but they undoubtedly did meet towards the end of Śivājī's life (he died in 1680), possibly several times, and Śivājī granted Rāmdās the fort of Sajjangad near Satara as his last residence. The argument over dates is now mixed up with Marathi politics because upon it hinges the degree to which the spiritual advice and teaching of Rāmdās (a Brahman) may have guided Śivājī (a Maratha) in the early days of his rule. Rāmdās has become the preferred saint of the Brahman minority in Maharashtra and the high-caste schoolchildren of Poona recite his *Manāce śloka* ('Verses Invoking the Mind') at their morning prayers. [27] (I.M.P.R.)

Ramesses II [VII] [Ramesses the Great; Ramses II] (13th century BCE). King of Egypt of Dynasty 19, reigned 1290–1224 BCE. The son of SETHOS I, Ramesses was one of Egypt's most powerful rulers. His mummy has been the subject of intensive scientific investigation [1]. As a great warrior, Ramesses fought against the Hittites, and recorded his military and other exploits in a bombastic style on the temple walls. During his reign an extensive building programme was carried out at various temples, including Luxor, Karnak, the Ramesseum, the temples at Abydos and at Abu Simbel. Here, in recent years, the rock-cut temples to glorify Ramesses and his favourite wife, Nefertari, were moved to new locations following the construction of the High Dam at Aswan [18]. Although no record of the event has been found in Egyptian sources, Ramesses II was probably the Pharaoh who attempted to stop MOSES and the Hebrews from leaving Egypt. (A.R.D.)

Rammohun Roy [XI] [Ram Mohan Roy] (1772?–1833). Hindu thinker and founder of the Brahmo Samaj ('Theistic Society'). He was born in Radhanagar, Bengal, in a Vaiṣṇava Brahmin family. He worked in different parts of Bengal between 1803 and 1815 with officials of the East India Company, becoming familiar with Western ideas. From 1815 to 1830 he lived in Calcutta, and produced the bulk of his writings in English, Bengali and Sanskrit, besides editing weekly papers in Bengali and Persian. In 1830 he sailed to England, partly as envoy of the Mughal Emperor Akbar II, who conferred on him the title of Raja, but also to have closer contact with British and European thinkers, with many of whom he had corresponded. He died in Bristol in 1833. While he remained formally a Hindu, wearing the sacred thread until his death, he was strongly influenced by Western rational theism, and was closely linked with the Unitarians; the Brahmo Samaj, which he founded in 1828, was sometimes called Hindu Unitarianism. He upheld Advaita Vedanta, but interpreted it in a rationalistic way, identifying knowledge of Brahman with the rational contemplation of God as revealed in nature. Believing that this knowledge is available to all, he denied that images and mythological beings were necessary aids to worship, unless for debased people. While he constantly cited Hindu texts (particularly the Upaniṣads, Purāṇas and Tantras) when addressing Hindus, he did not regard these as ultimate authorities, but as guides to a general revelation available to all in the natural world. He similarly used the Bible in arguing with Christian opponents. His *Precepts of Jesus*, a compilation from the Gospels, presented JESUS' moral teachings as the essential Christian message, rejecting Trinitarian Christology, and led him into controversy with the Baptist missionary Joshua Marshman. Rammohun's tracts against *suttee* (the burning of widows) sought to show that this practice was not authorized by the ancient texts. He addressed many other public issues, being an ardent liberal in politics. [18; 24: vol. 2, 19–35; 37; 59] (D.H.K.)

Ramon Medina Silva [XVIII] (1925–1971). Renowned Huichol *mara'akame* (shaman-priest) from the Sierra Madre Occidental of Mexico. Among the many divining, healing and ritual activities which *mara'kames* like Ramon Medina Silva carry out, the most outstanding is the annual peyote pilgrimage to Wirikuta, the sacred lands of the ancestors in order to collect peyote (*hikuri*), experience visions and Huichol solidarity. The ritual process of the peyote hunt was revealed to Barbara Myerhoff [7: 112–89], who wrote a detailed report and interpretation of the cult. Her report reveals a complex rite of passage in which the *peyoteros* or *hikuritamete* become transformed into the first peyote pilgrims in mythical times and re-enact the primordial union. This rite of passage involves the taking of divine names, the symbolic burning of one's human identity, ritual reversals, purifications, a journey to the sacred lands, hunting the peyote, eating the peyote and experiencing fantastic visions. Ramon Medina Silva was apparently an unusually talented musician, artist, and communicator of the mythology, rituals and meaning of the peyote journey. He was killed in a village quarrel in 1971. The sacred journeys of the Huichol continue today. [7] (D.C.)

Rām Siṅgh [XXIII] (1816–1885). The second and most influential Gurū of the Kūkā or Nāmdhārī sect of the Sikhs. The Kūkās believe that the line of Gurūs did not end with GOBIND SIṄGH, but that he passed it on to Balak Siṅgh and he in turn to Rām Siṅgh. Under Rām Siṅgh the Kūkās became a predominantly rural sect with their centre in Ludhiānā District. In 1871–2 there was serious trouble with the British authorities, as a result of which Rām Siṅgh was deported to Rangoon, to die there in 1885. The Kūkās are recognized by their white homespun clothing and turbans tied horizontally across the forehead. [67: 27–35] (W.H.M.)

Ranade, Mahādev Govind [XI] (1842–1901). Maharashtrian Brahman born at Niphad near Nasik. He studied law at the University of Bombay and served as magistrate, then subordinate judge in various towns of Maharashtra and finally became a High Court Judge at Bombay in 1893. He was an active proponent of the moderate party and a tireless campaigner for a reformed brand of Hinduism in all the *causes célèbres* of the late 19th century, notably in relation to the Age of Consent Bill and the Hindu widow's right to remarry. Almost a founder member of the Prarthana Samaj, the Bombay equivalent of the Brahmo Samaj (*see* RAMMOHUN ROY), he supported a Hinduism which distanced itself from the worship of specific deities, strove to lower the barriers between castes and conducted weekly prayer meetings (hence the name *prārthanā*) which were considerably influenced by Christian forms of worship. The devotional verses of TUKĀRĀM were increasingly used by this society more or less like hymns. Ranade occupied an uncomfortable position between his British employers and his own countrymen, who tended to be more extreme than him either in politics or in social reform. He was briefly transferred to Dhulia in 1879 owing to government mistrust of him at the time of a small local revolt. On the other hand, when his first wife died he allowed himself to be pushed into an orthodox Hindu second marriage with a girl of 12, for which he was much mocked. Nevertheless, he never totally lost his position of influence with all parties and he was a member, often chairman, of nearly every worthy society in Bombay and Poona during the last quarter of the 19th century. Furthermore, he made sure that his second wife became well educated, so much so that her reminiscences of their life together is one of the most celebrated biographies in Marathi. His own copious writing included history (*The Rise of the Maratha Power*, 1900), literary criticism and articles on religion and economics, as well as countless speeches and addresses to conferences of one kind and another. Most of these appeared originally in journals such as that of the Poona Sarvajanik Sabha – another institution of which he was nearly a founder member – and were published in book form only after his death. [57; 107] (I.M.P.R.)

Ranīrī, Shaykh Nūr al-Dīn ibn ʿAlī [XII] (*d.* after 1664). Islamic Malay writer. He was born in Ranīr, a port town in Gujerat where merchants from Iran, Siam, Burma, Arabia and Malaya came and went. He made the pilgrimage to Mecca in 1621. He lived most of his life at the court of Sultan Iskandar Muda in Pahang, now a part of the Malaysian Federation. When the Sultan died Ranīrī moved to Acheh in 1636. In 1628 he completed the work which would make him famous and one which is still popular in Malay literature, *Ṣirāṭ al-mustaqīm* ('The Straight Path'), an extended exposition of the duties of the Muslim. He also translated from Arabic into Malay a work on the same subject as well as a work on Islamic doctrine by al-Taftazānī of Samarkand. Ranīrī's most important work is the *Būstān al-Salāṭīn* ('The Kings' Garden'), which discusses the prophets and rulers of the past, foolish and disloyal counsellors, heroes in battle, pious men and saints, physiognomy and medicine. In 1642 he completed a work on the 'Creation of Light', a common theme in mystical literature, and the creation of the souls of Muḥammad, Adam and Eve, and death. It ends with the last day and the resurrection. In the same year he completed another work entitled *Jawāhir al-ʿulūm fī kashf al-maʿlūm* ('The Jewels of the Sciences concerning the Revelation of that which is known [to God]'). Ranīrī owes his popularity not only to his fine, pure Malay but also to the fact that he extols the true orthodoxy of Islam against the mystic philosophers of his time. (75; 140] (J.K.)

Rañjīt Siṅgh [xxiii] ['Lion of the Punjab'] (1780–1839). Remembered with affection and respect by the Sikhs as their greatest ruler. When he was born control of the Punjab was disputed between several masters, among them Sikh chieftains known as *misldārs*. One of the leading *misls* was the Shukerchakīā, and Rañjīt Siṅgh was the son of its leader. In 1792 his father died and Rañjīt Siṅgh inherited his position at the head of the Shukerchakīā *misl*. By this time power in the Punjab was flowing strongly towards some of the Sikh *misls*; Rañjīt Siṅgh's task was to pick off his rivals. This he achieved through marriages, alliances and open wars. By 1799 he had captured Lahore and in 1801 he assumed the title of Mahārājā of the Punjab.

During the next two decades Rañjīt Siṅgh enlarged the scope of his dominions, capturing Multān, Peshawar and Kashmir. The only direction in which his ambitions were frustrated was the south-east, where the advancing British compelled him to recognize the Satluj river as his boundary. Greatly interested in the army, Rañjīt Siṅgh brought in several Europeans to train it according to European patterns. Unfortunately he did not possess the same skill with regard to economics, with the result that the finances of the kingdom were never put on a thoroughly sound footing. The same must also be said for his training of a successor. When he died the kingdom rapidly descended into a murderous quest for power. After two wars were fought with the British, in 1849 the Punjab was annexed to British India. [4: III–V; 29: I–III] (W.H.M.)

Rashi [xv] [acronym of Rabbi Shlomo Yitzḥaki] (1040–1105). French Jewish commentator on Bible and Talmud. Born in Troyes, Champagne, he studied in Worms and Mainz, and at the age of 25 returned to Troyes, where he devoted himself to teaching and writing while earning his livelihood as a vintner. Little is known of his life, although he was the subject of many legends. [74]

Rashi's commentaries on the Bible and the Babylonian Talmud became the indispensable key for their understanding. Eschewing the esoteric, polemic or mystical, and minimizing the homiletic, he elucidates the text rationally and logically, explaining the main literal meaning, utilizing his profound knowledge of the sources and his understanding and clear use of the Hebrew language. Often he gives the Old French equivalent to explain a word, and as these are written in Hebrew letters, they have provided invaluable evidence of the contemporary pronunciation of Old French. Unlike other medieval Jewish Bible commentators, Rashi does not digress into lengthy excursuses, but concisely addresses himself to explaining the unfamiliar word or the puzzling context. The text is sacrosanct; Rashi would not contemplate emendations. His comments opened the Bible to the Jewish reader and, through Christian scholars, influenced the classic European translations.

Rashi's Talmud commentary is a remarkable achievement as the complexities of the text – both its Aramaic language and its often convoluted argumentation – threatened to close it to the masses. Rashi unravels the complexities; his commentary is the first such work to provide a key to the elucidation of the text. Thanks to Rashi, the Babylonian Talmud, on which he commented, became the accepted authority in Jewish life, while the Jerusalem Talmud, lacking such a key, remained neglected and largely unstudied.

Rashi's commentaries on both Bible and Talmud reflect his broad general interests. His views on Jewish laws and customs are pragmatic and undogmatic. Most printed texts of both works contain his comments, and are still widely used in Jewish studies. [61]

His pupils and descendants constituted a successor school of talmudic commentators known as the tosafists (from the Hebrew *tosafot*, 'additions'), so called because they added to Rashi's explanations. This school lasted for some two centuries and its super-commentaries appear in most Talmud editions alongside those of Rashi. (G.W.)

Rashīd Riḍā [XII] (1865–1935). Chief disciple and interpreter of the modern Islamic thinker, MUḤAMMAD ʿABDUH. Born in Tripoli (then in Syria, now Lebanon), he was inspired by the reformist journal *al-ʿUrwa al-wuthqā*, published by ʿAbduh and JAMĀL AL-DĪN AL-AFGHĀNĪ. In Egypt he became a close collaborator of ʿAbduh, whom he first met in 1894, and on his death devoted himself to the perpetuation of his ideas. Between 1908 and 1931 he produced a biography and collected works of his mentor, while continuing his influential but incomplete Qur'ān commentary.

His own principal contribution to modern Islamic thought came through the pages of *al-Manār* ('The Lighthouse'), a journal edited by him from 1898 to 1935. Here and in other works he expressed a deepening conservatism on religious issues, defending Islam from the impact both of Western secularism and internal reductionism. Although eager to purge Islam of what were seen as medieval accretions and to find a way back to its original purity, he was concerned to preach unyielding commitment to ideals such as the infallibility of the Prophet and the Qur'ān, or the need for uncompromising adherence to Islamic law.

In 1920 he was elected President of the Syrian National Congress, and three years later published his views on Islamic government in his book entitled *al-Khilāfa* ('The Caliphate'). This work established him as 'the founding theoretician of the Islamic state in its modern sense' [46: 56], arguing for a Constitution based on the Qur'ān, the sacred Traditions, and the example of the first caliphs. In Riḍā's theory, the head of the state must be a caliph possessed of the ability to exercise autonomous reasoning in religious matters. He also outlines a leading role for the Islamic clergy.

Although himself politically quietist, Riḍā had a powerful influence on later exponents of Islamic radicalism, notably ḤASAN AL-BANNĀ'. [52: IX; 103] (D.M.)

Ratana, Tahupotiki Wiremu [XXI] (1873–1939). Founder of the Ratana Church of New Zealand. In 1907 his aunt began a mission to lead people away from superstition. In one announcement under trance, she spoke of a time when 'a boy child will come to take action directly and strongly'. He would have 'no favourites and be more than a man in his attributes'. She said that it would be one of her nephews. Ratana had been noted for being wild and moody, but had given himself to God when seeking the healing of one of his children. Following a series of dreams and visions and seeing two great whales cast on the shore near his farm, he felt God had confirmed special powers in him, despite his lack of confidence and education. Shortly after this in 1918 he found he had a gift for healing. When Maori people came to him he insisted that they must give up all reliance on *tapu* proceedings and not to depend on ancestral relics, but to be faithful to God. The orthodox churches welcomed him until the Anglican Church noted how he added to the Trinitarian formula in the Benediction the phrase 'and all His Holy Angels'. This was considered schismatic and the Anglicans withdrew their approval. Ratana now formed his own church, ordaining Bishops, Apostles and Leaders of Worship. He gave a special task to women. In each area there were *Neehi* (nurses) whose tasks were to share with the sick and by prayer and exhortation help them find health.

He established his headquarters in the village of Ratana that had been founded by his grandfather. Here a temple was built. He considered his ministry to have two modes: he spoke of *te taha wairua me te taha ture* (the spiritual side and the physical side). The *Taha ture* meant to secure that the government would accept the Treaty of Waitangi between Whites and Maoris (signed in 1840 but never subscribed to by the Queen). In the latter part of his ministry he encouraged young men to stand for Parliament to capture the four Maori seats. This they eventually did.

In the Ratana Church, the ministry is not paid. In worship the Benediction formula remains idiosyncratic (as above). Many of the hymns refer to the 'mouthpiece of God', alluding to his claim that God had called him as such. Thus Ratana has tended to replace Christ in the minds of many in the congregations. Today there are about 20,000 members of the Ratana Church. [9: 167–71; 22; 27; 43]. (J.I.)

Ratan Siṅgh Bhaṅgū [XXIII] (*d*.1846). Sikh historian. He was the grandson of Matāb Siṅgh, who had fought prominently for the Sikhs during the 18th-century struggle for the Punjab. In 1809 he was invited to relate the story of the Sikhs to Captain Murray in Ludhiana; he eventually issued his account in 1841 under the title of *Panth Prakāś*. Although he retained the same emphasis on destiny and struggle of earlier writers the focus is strongly on the Khālsā order founded by GURŪ GOBIND SIṄGH in 1699. The Khālsā was created to rule; all who acknowledge its discipline must be prepared to assert that right. [59: 12, 71–3] (W.H.M.)

Ratnakīrti [IV] (11th century). Indian Buddhist scholar-monk active at the University of Vikramaśīla towards the end of the period of Buddhist intellectual life in India. He was a disciple of Jñānaśrīmitra, and, like his master, was a systematizer of the Yogācāra-Vijñānavāda school of Buddhist philosophical thought, using the logical and epistemological tools developed by DIGNĀGA and DHARMAKĪRTI. He is best known for a rigorous attempt to demonstrate, logically, the truth of the thesis that impermanence is a necessary concomitant of existence, and for attempts to connect this thesis with a nonreferential theory of language [154]. As with all Buddhist intellectuals, Ratnakīrti's interests were not merely theoretical: realization and appropriation of the truth of the theses he argues for are of central importance for the liberation of the individual. (P.J.G.)

Rauschenbusch, Walter [VI.A] (1861–1919). Prominent figure of the American Social Gospel movement. He was born in Rochester, New York had his early education there and graduated from Rochester Theological Seminary, where his father, a Lutheran-turned-Baptist, taught German-speaking students, in 1886. In 1886 Walter Rauschenbusch became the pastor of the Second German Baptist Church on the edge of the 'Hell's Kitchen' area of New York City. The experience led him to turn to the 'Social Gospel'. For the next 11 years, while remaining an evangelical, he studied and wrote on social problems, participated in the Brotherhood of the Kingdom, which held an annual meeting for prominent members of the Social Gospel movement, and drew inspiration from British and European Christian socialists. In 1897 he became professor of New Testament in Rochester Theological Seminary and professor of church history in 1902 until his death. Among his works are *Christianity and the Social Crisis* (1907), *The Social Principles of Jesus* (1916) and *A Theology for the Social Gospel* (1917). [341; 377; 725] (T.T.)

Rav [XV] [Abba bar Aivu, or Abba Arikha, i.e. Abba the tall] (*c*.175–247). Rabbi in Babylonia. Born in Babylonia of a distinguished family, he went to study in Palestine at the academy of JUDAH HA-NASI, who ordained him to teach. He achieved considerable recognition before returning to Babylonia. In 219 he founded his own academy in Sura, which for centuries was an outstanding centre of rabbinic learning and authority. In Rav's time it had 1,200 permanent students and many others coming for limited periods. Babylonian Jewry regarded him as their most notable teacher and therefore called him merely 'Rav' (i.e. the teacher *par excellence*). His closest colleague was Samuel, head of the academy in the town of Nehardea, and their discussions and arguments feature prominently in the Babylonian Talmud, of which they are considered the founders. Where they differed, Rav's views were generally followed in matters of ritual law and Samuel's in civil law. Their joint influence helped to establish the authority of the Babylonian academies in the Jewish world as a whole.

Rav regarded the study of the Torah as a Jew's most important occupation. He also devoted himself to ethics and many of his homilies dealt with ethical questions. He strongly opposed asceticism, saying 'Every individual will be called to account in the hereafter for every enjoyment in this world he declined without sufficient cause'. [58: vol. 1] (G.W.)

Ravidās [XI] [Raidās] (*c*.1500). Poet-saint of the medieval Sant tradition of northern India.

He is particularly venerated as the patron of the Chamars, the great untouchable caste of leather-workers and cobblers. Little can be gleaned of his life from the hagiographic sources, many of which set out in the usual Brahmanical fashion to explain away his Chamar birth, but he was apparently born in or near Benares where he was a younger contemporary of KABĪR, with whom he is said to have been a co-disciple of Rāmānand, although this is open to question. The hagiographies also persistently portray his later spiritual prestige as having attracted the homage of royal ladies from Rajasthan, particularly Queen Jhālī of Chitaur and the poetess MĪRĀBĀĪ [7:I–II]. The best known of Ravidās's hymns, also extensively preserved in the Dādūpanthī scriptures, are the 40 included in the Sikh *Ādi Granth* (*see* NĀNAK, GURŪ) [67:321–42]. These are less remarkable for any doctrinal novelty than for the lyrical directness with which they combine the characteristic devotional idiom of *nirguṇ bhakti* with repeated reference to Ravidās's low caste-status, e.g. 'This cobbler cannot mend, yet shoes to me they send. No awl have I for holes, nor scraping-knife for soles. Folk fix and fix but still are lost: not fixing, I have safely crossed. Raidās repeats His holy Name, and Death on me has no more claim' [*Ādi Granth*: 659]. In the 20th century the cult of Ravidās, traditional amongst the Chamars, has been given a new focus and organization by the general contemporary movement of Indian untouchables to challenge the abysmal conditions to which they have traditionally been assigned, and to realize the utopian vision of his beautiful hymn [67:322] depicting life in the Sorrowless City (*begamapurā*). The Ravidāsī movement of the Punjabi Chamars has proved particularly successful, and is vigorously represented in the diaspora community in the United Kingdom [52: 223–57]. [20; 52; 67] (C.S.)

al-Rāzī, Fakhr al-Dīn Abū ʿAbd Allāh Muḥammad ibn ʿUmar [XII] (1149–1209). Famous Islamic theologian and religious philosopher. Born in Rayy in Iran, he was a major scholar in the schools of AL-SHĀFIʿĪ and AL-ASHʿARĪ. He spent a great deal of time combating the rationalist Muʿtazilite doctrines, especially as found at his time in parts of Central Asia. He is significant for his attempt to reconcile religious traditionalism and philosophical thought as witnessed in his commentary on works of IBN SĪNĀ. His most famous work is his commentary on the Qur'ān, *Mafātiḥ al-ghayb* ('The Keys to the Unseen'), in which he expounds his philosophical ideas while arguing against the Muʿtazilite stance especially of AL-ZAMAKHSHARĪ. He also wrote works on law, astrology and rhetoric. [34: s.v.] (A.R.)

Rebekah (alternative English spelling; *c.*18th century BCE): Jewish matriarch. A niece of Abraham, she was born and brought up in Mesopotamia. Abraham sent his servant to visit his family and select a wife for his son, ISAAC, the servant was divinely guided to select Rebekah when she came out of the city of Haran to draw water from the well. The sign was to be that on being asked for water, she would offer it not only to the servant but also to his camels. The servant gave her the gifts he had brought with him and received her agreement and the consent of her family to the match.

After marrying Isaac, she was barren for twenty years but in answer to Isaac's prayer, she became pregnant and delivered twins, Esau and JACOB. Before the birth she experienced a divine oracle foretelling that each child would become the father of a nation and that the older would serve the younger.

The Bible relates that when Isaac was in Gerar the king, attracted by Rebekah's beauty, sought her for himself, believing that she was Isaac's sister. This is a repetition of an identical story about SARAH and has been seen as a doublet.

Rebekah is depicted as a strong-minded woman, devoted to her younger son, Jacob, and to ensure his precedence over Esau, she resorted to a deceitful plot. Esau, as the elder, should have received the birthright, but Rebekah showed Jacob how to trick his blind father by posing as Esau. After this was accomplished she advised Jacob to flee to her brother Laban in view both of Esau's intense anger and in order that he should find a wife among her family. She died before Jacob returned and was buried in the Cave of Machpelah in Hebron. [68: IX–XI] (G.W.)

Reichelt, Karl Ludvig [VI.A] (1877–1952). Norwegian missionary to China. He was born in the parish of Barbu, near Arendal, Norway. He underwent teacher's training at the

Notodden Teachers' Training College; after graduation he taught for a brief period in a school in Telemark and also did some lay preaching. In 1897 he attended the college of the Norwegian Missionary Society at Stavanger. He was ordained in 1903 and went to China. His fiancée, Anna Dorothea Gerhardsen, joined him and they married in 1905. After one year of studying Chinese he was sent to Ninghsiang in Hunan. There he met Buddhist monks at Weishan Monastery and this led him to a deep study of Far Eastern religions. In 1911 he returned to Norway and gave a series of six lectures at Oslo university which were later published under the title *Religion in Chinese Garment* (English trans. 1951). He returned to China in 1913 to teach at the Lutheran Theological Seminary in Shekow near Hankow. In 1920 he was back in Norway and gave lectures later published as *Truth and Tradition in Chinese Buddhism* (1930). His home mission board was unhappy with his concentration on work among Buddhist monks so in 1927 he formed the Christian Buddhist Mission. Political unrest in China forced him to move to Hong Kong, where he established Tao Fong Shan, the Mountain of the Logos Wind. In 1930–31 he returned to Scandinavia to raise support for this institution. He was interred in Hong Kong during the Second World War and wrote his three-volume *Men of Religion in the Far East*. He was back in Oslo in 1947 but returned to Tao Fong Shan in 1951, where he died and was buried. [371; 673; 785] (T.T.)

Reimarus, Hermann Samuel [VI.A] (1694–1768). German philosopher. He was born in Hamburg. He studied under J. A. Fabricius, who taught ethics and rhetoric in Hamburg. Later he studied theology, classical philology and philosophy in Jena. After graduation he became a *Privatdozent* in Wittenberg and later rector of the *Hochschule* at Wismar. From 1727 until his death he was professor of Oriental languages at Hamburg. His main claim to fame is his insistence that the Christian revelation is only true in so far as it agrees with reason. In a number of fragments published by G. E. Lessing between 1774 and 1778 Reimarus rejected miracles and revelation and declared such revelations as the resurrection of Jesus to be false on the grounds of contradictions in the text. He also drew a distinction between the message of Jesus and its developments in the early church. The fragments were part of a manuscript entitled *Apology for, or Defence of, the Rational Worshipper of God*. He influenced a number of other scholars including DAVID F. STRAUSS and ALBERT SCHWEITZER. [500; 718: 13–26; 770] (T.T.)

Renan, Joseph Ernest [VI.A] (1823–1892). French scholar. He was born in Tréguier, Brittany and entered the seminary of St-Nicholas-du-Chardonnet in 1838. Later he went to the seminary of St-Sulpice. His study of science, along with German theology and Semitic languages, led him to question Christian orthodoxy; he left the seminary and the church in 1845. He complained that the church restricted his freedom to study science. Three years later he wrote *L'Avenir de la science*, a positivist view of science, which remained unpublished until 1890. In 1848 he won a prize for an essay on Semitic languages and in 1852 he became an assistant keeper of Eastern manuscripts at the Bibliothèque Nationale, Paris. Around this time he published his doctoral thesis, *Averoès et l'averroïsme*. In 1860 he went on an archaeological expedition to Syria. While in Palestine he wrote the first of the seven volumes of *Histoire des origines du christianisme* (1863–81), *Vie de Jésus*. Though highly controversial and rejected by the orthodox it became enormously popular in the original language and in European translations. The *Life* was written from the standpoint of historical criticism of the Gospels and the background of Middle Eastern religions. In 1862 he was appointed professor of the history of religions at the Collège de France, but was removed in 1864 following the controversy over the publication of the *Life*. In 1870 he was reappointed, and in 1878 he was elected to the Académie Française. A five-volume supplement to the earlier volumes of history, *Histoire du peuple d'Israël*, appeared between 1887 and 1893. [247; 674; 675] (T.T.)

Rennyo [IV] (1415–1499). Eighth *hossu* (head priest) of the Honganji branch (later to split into Higashi [east] and Nishi [west]) of the Jōdo Shinshū, originated by SHINRAN. Rennyo is considered the 'second founder' of the sect since, by his organizational talent and powerful missionary activity, he made Hongan-ji into the centre of Shinshū and one of the strongest religious organizations in Japan. Succeeding his father Zonnyo as *hossu* in 1457, his success soon attracted the enmity of the warrior-monks of Mt Hiei, who burnt down his head temple in 1465. From then on he moved his headquarters to several places, especially Yoshizaki in Hokuriku (1471–1475) and Yamashina near Kyoto (from 1483). Historians tend to see in him not so much a religious man as a clever politician, organizer and propagandist. In Shinshū itself, however, his pastoral letters (*gobunsho* or *ofumi*), wherein he teaches the Pure Land doctrine in a popular way, have long been the most quoted sources of their doctrine. Some would argue, however, that he compromised the purity of Shinran's religiosity by bringing it into line with the requirements of the 'Japanese spirit' by enjoining the faithful to respect all Buddhas and all *kami*, and to be obedient to civil authorities in the same way as to the Buddha. [185; 260] (J.V.B.)

Ricci, Matteo [VI.A] (1552–1610). Italian Jesuit missionary to China. He was born in Macerata in the Papal States. He studied scientific subjects and law in the Roman College from 1571 and became a Jesuit novice. Having volunteered for missionary work he was sent to Portugal in 1577 and from there to the Portuguese colony of Goa, India, in 1578. He completed his theological training there and in 1580 he was ordained in Cochin further south on the Malabar coast. In 1582 he went to Macao where he studied Chinese language and culture. He and a colleague went to Chao-ch'ing in China in 1583 and remained there until expelled in 1589, whereupon he went to Shao-chou (Kwangtung). Later he and colleagues went to Nanchang and from there to Peking in 1598, to Nanking in 1599 and finally to Peking in 1601. He was welcomed by officials, less as a priest and more as a scientist, because of his possession of clocks and his publication of a world map, a revised edition of which was published in 1600. He adopted Chinese dress and manners and believed that converts to the Christian religion could continue using certain Chinese rituals. Ricci was buried outside the walls of Peking, where his grave has been desecrated twice but was restored to its present state in 1980. His views on the behaviour of converts caused controversy and were eventually condemned by popes in 1704 and 1742. [275; 677] (T.T.)

Richard, Timothy [VI.A] (1845–1919). Welsh missionary to China. He was born in a village in Carmarthenshire, of a Baptist family. He was employed initially as a schoolteacher and later studied at a theological college in Haverfordwest. He joined the Baptist Missionary Society and was sent to China in 1870. In 1876 to 1879, while working in a famine, he decided that China's leaders needed introduction to modern civilization. He began to give lectures and scientific demonstrations in Tai Yuan which were attended by crowds of government officials and students. In 1889 he edited a Chinese newspaper, *The Times*, writing on contemporary issues including the need for reforms. This brought him to the attention of a wide range of Chinese society, including the emperor himself. In 1891 he became secretary of the Christian Literature Society. Following the defeat of China by Japan in 1895 Richard translated a *History of the Nineteenth Century* into Chinese. It was widely read and students petitioned the emperor for reforms. In 1896 the Prime Minister called on Richard to discuss reforms and in 1898 he was invited to become one of the Emperor's advisers. Before he could have any influence the Empress Dowager seized power, executed reform leaders, and began the reaction which ended in the Boxer troubles of 1900. Richard succeeded in establishing a university in Tai Yuan. The many Christian and pro-Christian Chinese who were leaders in the 1911 revolution and in the resultant republic owed much to Richard's influence. He received honorary doctorates from the University of Wales and two in the USA, and two of the highest honours of the Chinese empire. He returned to Britain in 1911 owing to illness, and died in London. [672; 679; 743] (T.T.)

Rin-chen bzang-po [IV] (958–1055). A prolific and masterful translator (*lotsāva*) of Buddhist texts from Sanskrit into Tibetan, he was instrumental in the revival (the 'later spread') of Buddhism in Tibet, and in the reform of Tantric practices. He made three visits to Kashmir, being sent initially to learn Sanskrit and Buddhism by the king of Guge (western Tibet), Ye-shes 'od.

He transmitted to Tibet the later stages of syncretistic Mahāyāna, including esoteric Tantrism – notably a form of the Buddha Vairocana – but reserving the higher tantras for those advanced in practice and emphasizing the classical bodhisattva path of ethics and philosophy as a bedrock. In this way, according to the lama historians, he (and ATIŚA) reversed the tendency of Buddhism in Tibet to degenerate into primitive magic and exorcism.

Rin-chen bzang-po's translation work spans the range of Indian Buddhist literature; he is credited with 158 translations [237: 40–49). But among the 75 masters that he brought with him from Kashmir, according to his biography, were also many craftsmen, and he is known for the construction of temples (108 according to Tibetan sources), some of which survive in areas of Indian Ladakh. These *lha khang* bear, as Tucci puts it, 'evident traces of the Kashmiri craftsmen's work: bronzes and wooden portals sculpted with a soft suppleness and a plastic relief' [239: 273]. Recent studies of these buildings and the images that populate them have recovered an entire era of Indian art and the spiritual practices that inspired it; these had been almost entirely lost. These works, at least as much as Rin-chen bzang-po's literary productions, furthered the spread of Buddhism in Tibet and had much influence upon its modern forms. (M.T.)

Rinzai Gigen. *See* LIN-CHI I-HSÜAN.

Ritschl, Albrecht [VI.A] (1822–1889). German Lutheran theologian. He was born in Berlin but grew up in Stettin. His father was a pastor in the Evangelical Church. He studied at a number of German universities from 1839 to 1846: Bonn, Halle (where he was awarded his PhD in 1843), Heidelberg and Tübingen. He taught in Bonn from 1846, becoming professor of Theology in 1859. In 1864 he moved to Göttingen as professor of Dogmatics or Systematic Theology and remained in the post until his death. His first two publications, *Das Evangelium Marcions und das kanonische Evangelium des Lukas* (1846) and *Die Entstehung der altkatholischen Kirche* ('The Rise of the Early Catholic Church', 1851) showed the influence of the Tübingen school and of F. C. BAUR, his teacher at Tübingen. Ritschl later, in the second edition of the 1851 publication, rejected the thesis of conflict between the 'Petrine' and 'Paulinist' factions in the early church. In his systematic theology Ritschl taught the importance of 'justification' and 'reconciliation' as set forth in the New Testament, and of the community as the receiver of divine revelation and of the ethical response of the community to the revelation. He argued against many developments within Protestantism including intellectualism (neo-scholasticism), rationalism, mysticism and pietism. He exercised considerable influence on later German theologians, including HARNACK and TROELTSCH, and some of his followers constituted a 'Ritschlian school'. [494; 685; 686] (T.T.)

Romero, Oscar Arnulfo [VI.A] (1917–1980). Archbishop of El Salvador, 1977–80. He was born into rural poverty in Cuidad Barrios, El Salvador. He studied theology in Rome (1937–1943). After 24 years as a hard-working priest in his homeland, he rose in approved fashion to become bishop of the remote diocese of Santiago de Maria in 1974. As a 'safe' cleric who appeared most unlikely to disturb the republic's oligarchy and *status quo*, he was chosen to be El Salvador's archbishop in February 1977. The murder then of Rutilio Grande, a respected radical priest and personal friend, incensed him and led to his 'conversion'. Given his awareness of the peasants' plight at the hands of the armed forces, he decided to guide the national Church to put itself 'at the disposition of the poor' who needed assistance in their effort to defend their basic human rights. He radicalized quickly as violence escalated throughout the country and supported popular reform organizations. His bold declarations and pointed pastoral letters enraged the right-wing military regime, with the result that he was daringly assassinated on 24 March 1980. The Monseñor was martyred for being a champion of the poor and oppressed. Since then, he has been venerated as Central America's outstanding episcopal 'voice of the voiceless' as a modern LAS CASAS. [76: 119–154] (A.C.S.)

Rosenzweig, Franz [XV] (1886–1929). German Jewish existentialist philosopher. He was seriously contemplating conversion to Christianity in 1913 when a Day of Atonement visit to a small Orthodox congregation left him a changed person and he felt that he had found what he was seeking. God, he concluded, needs no mediation and Judaism is not a religion but a living faith. Serving with the German army in the Balkans in the First World War, he wrote the draft of his most famous book, *Der Stern des Erlösung* ('The Star of Redemption') on postcards mailed from the front to his parents for safe keeping. After the war he founded in Frankfurt-on-Main a new type of Jewish educational institution, the *Freies Jüdisches Lehrhaus*, a college of adult Jewish education where outstanding Jewish thinkers and scholars taught hundreds of students. From 1922 he was progressively paralysed, and could eventually only communicate through giving signals. However, even at this stage, he translated poems of JUDAH HA-LEVI and began a translation of the Bible into German with MARTIN BUBER.

Rosenzweig's philosophy starts from the human being. The three elements of total existence are God, the universe and man, which are interconnected through creation, where God places himself in a relationship with the universe and, through revelation, with man. Creation points to revelation, and revelation, which is a continuing process of God, to redemption. By converting his love for God into love for his fellow man, man helps to bring the universe towards redemption. Judaism gives redemption a symbolic representation through the ritual and liturgy, Sabbath and festivals.

Rosenzweig pioneered the construction of a relationship between Judaism and Christianity without polemic, considering Christianity to be a possible way to the truth. He was the first Jewish theologian to view Christianity as possessing equal legitimacy with Judaism, both originating in the divine. Each possesses only part of the truth and the full truth is only with God. He proposed the doctrine of the 'two covenants', which in a mysterious way stand united before God. Through their covenant, the Jews are already with God. The vocation of Christianity is to bring the nations of the world to the covenant. Both faiths are true, both are required in the divine economy, but the wall between them will be broken only at the end of time, when, he felt, Christianity would become Jewish. [30; 52] (G.W.)

Roy, Rammohun. *See* RAMMOHUN ROY.

Rūmī, Jalāl al-Dīn ⌊VI.A⌋ [Mawlānā; Mevlānā] (1207–1273). Persian Ṣūfī poet and founder of the Mevlevi brotherhood (the 'Whirling Dervishes'), author of the *Mathnavī-yi maʿnavī*. He was born in Balkh in Central Asia, into a family connected by marriage to the royal house of Khwārazm. His father, Bahā' al-Dīn Walad, was a preacher in the city. When Jalāl al-Dīn was about five years old, however, his father was forced to leave Balkh following a dispute with the Khwārazmshāh. After lengthy journeys, he and his family settled about 1226 or 1227 in Konya in Anatolia, where he came under the protection of the Seljuk ruler ʿAlā'l-Dīn Kayqubād.

On his father's death in 1271 Jalāl al-Dīn succeeded him as a teacher, but his interest moved increasingly to mystical matters. In 1244 he met for the first time the remarkable figure known as Shams-i Tabrīzī, a wandering dervish who exercised a profound spiritual influence on Rūmī over a 15-month period. This influence became so great, however, that the latter's own disciples forced him to leave Konya. Eventually, however, Rūmī had him brought back from Syria, after which a group of his followers then conspired to murder him, accomplishing their aim at the end of 1247. In the course of his search for Shams, which took both a physical and spiritual form, Rūmī found his inspiration as a poet and mystic. He began to compose mystical verse, and founded a Ṣūfī order in which dance and music, normally proscribed in Islam, played a prominent role.

Rūmī remained in Konya until his death on 17 December 1273. The Mevlevi order was subsequently organized and its rituals elaborated by his son Sulṭān Walad (*d.*1312). A hereditary order, ruled by lineal descendants of Rūmī, the Mevleviyya became a major force in Turkish society, particularly in the Ottoman period, when it attracted a large number of the aristocracy. The centre of the order, and the residence of its head, the Celebi, is still in Konya, but its activities have been much curtailed in the modern period.

Jalāl al-Dīn is best remembered for his prodigious literary output, principally in Persian, of which the best known works are the *Dīvān-i Shams-i Tabrīz*, a lengthy collection of lyric poems, and the *Mathnavī*. This last is a vast mystical poem extending over six volumes. It explores a wide range of themes and employs materials from an unusually broad spectrum, from love symbolism to obscene stories. The poet Jāmī referred to it as 'the Qur'ān in Persian', and it has more recently been described as containing 'almost every inconceivable mystical theory known in the thirteenth century' [115: 316]. In spite of its unquestioned importance, the *Mathnavī* is a difficult work to read, lacking as it does any coherent pattern or internal order. It has been widely commented upon in Persian and Turkish.

Rūmī's influence, both spiritual and cultural, has been considerable throughout the central Islamic regions, notably Turkey, Iran, and India. Much of his poetry has been translated into European languages, principally German and English, and his ideas have been widely known in the West since the 18th century. [15; 97; 108; 109; 116] (D.M.)

Rūpa Gosvāmī [XI] (early 16th-century). Poet, dramatist and theologian of the CAITANYA or Gauḍīya sect. He was born in Bengal, where with his brother Sanātana he had served under Husain Shah at the court of Gauḍ. According to sectarian hagiologies, Rūpa encountered Caitanya at Allahabad and was converted to his form of emotional devotionalism, becoming one of the so-called 'six Gosvāmīs' who constituted the core of Caitanya's following. He was sent by Caitanya to Vrindaban in 1517, where he ultimately established a temple for the 'self-manifest' Kṛṣṇa image of Govind Dev. In Vrindaban he began the process of codifying the sectarian doctrine whose initial inspiration was Caitanya's own mystical experience of Kṛṣṇa, and which had previously been expressed mainly through the Bengali congregational songs called *kīrtana*. Having had a traditional Sanskrit-based education at Nabadvip in Bengal, Rūpa brought to his theological task a wide learning both of scriptural texts and of dramatic and aesthetic theory. He first composed a number of literary works, subsequently extrapolating a theory of devotionalism which was to have an enormous influence not only on his own sect but also on the broader field of Vaiṣṇavism. Rūpa's system harnessed the concepts and terminology of classical aesthetic theory, according to which a particular *bhāva* or sentiment, portrayed through the artificial medium of art (especially drama), is experienced by the audience as *rasa*, or unconditioned aesthetic delight. Rūpa interpreted *bhāva* as the various possible attitudes or modes of relationship open to the devotee in his connection with Kṛṣṇa (who was to be adored variously as son, master, friend or – and especially – lover); the various characters in the Kṛṣṇa story provided models for the devotee to imitate in vicariously achieving these attitudes and in relishing the joy of devotion as *rasa*. Though consummately intellectual, Rūpa's system is wholly consistent with the emotional priorities of popular devotionalism, and its basic terminology at least has been widely adopted. [23; 42] (R.S.)

Russell, Charles Taze [VI.A] (1852–1916). Founder of the Jehovah's Witness movement. He was raised as a Congregationalist in Pittsburg, Pennsylvania. He became a draper. As a youngster he decided that he did not agree with the doctrine of eternal punishment. Following an intense period of study of the Bible he came to the conclusion that the Second Coming of Christ would happen secretly in 1874. He also calculated that the end of the world would occur in 1914. He published his views in *The Object and Manner of Our Lord's Return*. The book brought him wide publicity and a following. In 1878 he became the minister of an independent church in Pittsburg and became known as Pastor Russell. The publication of *The Watchtower* magazine was started in 1879 and this led to a further following, including one in Europe. His main work, *Food for Thinking Christians*, was published in 1881 and republished in 1886 under the title *Millennial Dawn*. There followed the Watch Tower Bible and Tract Society in 1884 as a successful publishing venture; he also engaged in other business ventures. In 1909 his wife divorced him on the grounds of immoral conduct with some of his followers and he travelled abroad for some time. The outbreak of the First World War in 1914, though not the forecast end of the world, nevertheless brought him more publicity and his movement grew. His movement was originally known as International Bible Students but later was renamed Jehovah's Witnesses. [158; 204; 240] (T.T.)

Rustam [XXVI]. Son of Zāl, ancient hero of the Saka (Scythian) people. His legend was probably brought into Iran by Saka invaders in the 2nd century BCE. They settled in the south-east, embraced Zoroastrianism, and intermarried with the Zoroastrian Parthians. Stories about Rustam became blended with those of the Kayāniāns (*see* HYSTASPES), and he came to overshadow Spentōdāta (Persian: Isfandiyār), Vištāspa's elder son, as champion of the faith. He was celebrated in the Middle Persian *Book of Kings*, and even more splendidly by FIRDAUSĪ, who drew on additional local sources. He is still regarded by Zoroastrians as a great warrior who fought for their religion. [11: vol. 3: 373–7, 453–7] (M.B.)

Ruth [xv]. Moabite ancestress of King DAVID; central figure in the biblical book of *Ruth*. The book relates the story of Elimelech and Naomi of Bethlehem, who move to Moab to escape a famine. While there, their two sons marry Moabite wives; Elimelech and his two sons both die in Moab. When Naomi decides to return to Bethlehem, one daughter-in-law agrees to remain in Moab, but the other, Ruth, insists on accompanying her mother-in-law, stating: 'Your people shall be my people and your God, my God.' [*Ruth* 1:16] While gleaning barley in the fields along with the other poor, Ruth meets the landowner Boaz, a kinsman of her husband, whom she marries. Their son Obed was the father of Jesse, father of David. Through this genealogy, Ruth is mentioned in *Matthew* 1:5 as an ancestress of JESUS.

The book has been assigned to various dates, but recent scholarship, basing itself on language and style, suggests the early period of the Israelite Kingdom. Because of its association with the barley harvest, it is read on the festival of Pentecost – also the traditional anniversary of the death of David. In Jewish tradition Ruth was regarded as the archetypal proselyte; female converts to Judaism have frequently adopted the name of Ruth. [16] (G.W.)

Ryōkan [IV] (1758–1831). Japanese Zen monk of the Sōtō school and renowned poet and calligrapher. He was born the eldest son of a village elder and Shinto priest. He was expected to succeed his father, but Ryōkan entered a Zen temple at the age of 17. He took his vows under Kokusen, at whose temple, Entsūji, Ryōkan underwent severe practices for over ten years. After his master's death Ryōkan wandered around the country for a number of years and finally settled in a simple retreat near his home village. He lived a simple and frugal existence, writing poetry on the joys of a simple life and stressing the unity of all Buddhist teachings. In his later years Ryōkan developed a strong relationship with the nun Teishin, a widow 40 years his junior. They exchanged a series of poems which were collected by Teishin, along with other poems by Ryōkan, into *Hachisu no tsuyu* ('Dew on the Lotus'). Ryōkan left no immediate disciples, but his poetry in a variety of styles has been widely read and admired, especially in recent years. [206; 249; 264] (P.L.S.)

S

Sa'adiah Ga'on [xv] (882–942). Jewish scholar and communal leader in Babylonia. Little is known of his early life. He was born in a village in Upper Egypt. At the age of 20 he completed his Hebrew dictionary and rhyming lexicon and had begun to write polemics against the Karaites, the sect which based itself on the Bible and denied rabbinic authority. He left Egypt in 915 and eventually settled in the Babylonian town of Sura, where he taught in its famed academy. In 928 he was appointed its head (which carried the title *ga'on*). Two years later he quarrelled with the lay head of the Babylonian community, the exilarch David ben Zakkai, who deposed Sa'adiah from office and each put the other under a ban. Sa'adiah then lived for six years in Baghdad, engaged in study and writing, before the two were reconciled and he returned to head the Sura academy.

Sa'adiah made important pioneering contributions to all branches of Jewish study, many of them designed to counter the challenges of the Karaites on the one hand and the inroads of Greco-Arab philosophy on the other. The Jews of the time lacked the tools to respond and Sa'adiah set out to create them. As well as his dictionary he wrote on Hebrew grammar; he also laid the foundations of Hebrew philology, translated the Bible into Arabic and added a commentary, and was a talmudic expert whose legal decisions were accepted as authoritative. His edition of the prayer book provided the complete text of the services together with the relevant laws and customs. He was also the first thinker to evolve a systematic philosophy of Judaism, giving answers to the questions agitating his contemporaries. This he accomplished in the book *Sefer Emunot ve-De'ot* ('Book of Doctrines and Belief'), in which he presents an interpretation of Judaism in the light of reason. His basic premise is that Judaism teaches nothing contrary to reason, and intellectual speculation only confirms the truths of the Jewish faith. No contradiction is possible between the postulates of reason and those handed down by tradition. The Torah provides the person who has not studied philosophy with a rational system. Sa'adiah teaches that creation was *ex nihilo* and inside time, and from creation can be derived irrefutable evidence of God's existence. God is incorporeal; any indications otherwise found in the Bible are concessions to the limitations of human understanding. The goal of creation was to bring happiness to everything created and above all to man, who realizes himself through accepting the commandments. The Torah is revealed reason and was given to all mankind; those who do not accept its ritual prescriptions are still bound by its moral injunctions. [49; 39: III] (G.W.)

Šābuhr I [xxvi] (3rd century). Sasanian king, reigned *c.*240–*c.*270; son of ARDAŠĪR. His chief priest was KIRDĒR, to whom he gave authority over all his Zoroastrian subjects. He was famed for intellectual curiosity and ordered to be brought to Iran Greek and Indian scientific and philosophical works to be 'collated with the Avesta' [7: 10.3.4.4]. This influx of foreign learning can be traced in the Middle Persian commentaries on the holy texts. He was benevolent to MĀNĪ, who dedicated to him the *Šābuhragān*. In a great inscription Šābuhr recorded founding fire-temples and making pious endowments for the souls of relatives and courtiers from wealth gained in his Roman wars. [7: 10.3.2; 14: 179–82, 218–26] (M.B.)

Šābuhr II [xxvi] (4th century). Sasanian king, reigned 309–79. There were dogmatic disputations during his reign, and Ādurbād ī Mahraspandān, the Zoroastrian high priest, surviving an ordeal by molten metal, upheld the 'true religion', i.e. the Zurvanite form of Zoroastrianism [7: 10.3.4.5; 9: 118–19; 14: 304]. This Šābuhr thereafter zealously maintained. In his reign Christianity became virtually the state religion of the Roman empire, Persia's enemy. Zoroastrians in the eastern Roman provinces were persecuted, and in 322 Šābuhr began persecuting Christians in his domains, and also Manichaeans, who likewise were active proselytizers. Syriac martyrologies [10; 28], though biased, shed valuable light on Zoroastrianism at this period. (M.B.)

Sāhib Singh Bedī [xxiii] (1756–1834). He was in the direct male line from GURŪ NĀNAK, and as such was greatly venerated by the Sikhs. While still a young man he acquired Ūnā in Hoshiarpur district as a gift. He developed a considerable reputation as a Sikh preacher, and being in Nānak's lineage he gathered a large following of admiring chieftains and peasantry in central Punjab. Amongst these RAÑJĪT SINGH figured conspicuously, and in 1801 Sāhib Singh Bedī conducted his coronation ceremonies in Lahore. [47: 195–200] (W.H.M.)

Sai Baba of Shirdi [xi] (1856?–1918). A guru who had an enormous, all-India following in his later years. He appeared, apparently aged about 16, in 1872 at the village of Shirdi in the Ahmadnagar district of what is now Maharashtra, and took up residence in a little mosque where he remained for the rest of his life. He was directed towards a mosque rather than to a Hindu temple because the village people considered he was dressed more like a Muslim fakir than a Hindu mendicant, but he claimed to have been the disciple of a Hindu guru as well as of a Muslim teacher in his earlier life and was careful never to identify himself exclusively with either religion. His philosophy was couched in the form of peremptory and often irascible pronouncements, and it is likely that he was illiterate, but the example of his asceticism gradually spread his fame throughout India and vast crowds eventually came on pilgrimage to Shirdi in order to hear his words, to participate in his holiness and, especially, to be cured of their ills. Towards the end he allowed himself to be treated as a deity and his effigy in the large modern temple at Shirdi now receives the traditional Hindu daily worship. The temple trust is one of the richest in Maharashtra. The current SATHYA SAI BABA built his reputation on a claim to be his reincarnation, and both are believed by their followers to be avatars of Dattātreya. [85a]. (I.M.P.R.)

Sai Baba, Sathya [xix] [Sathyanarayana Raju] (1926–). Possibly the best known of India's 'miracle-workers', with an estimated 50 million devotees around the world [6: 345]. Sathyanarayana Raju was born at Puttaparthi, Andhra Pradesh, South India. Stories are told of omens around the time of his birth and how a cobra was found in the baby's cot. [6: 212; 7: 19; 46: V]

At the age of 13 he collapsed and was unconscious for several days [6: 341; 7: 21]. Three months later he announced that he was SAI BABA OF SHIRDI [37: 245–6; 46: VI; 61]. (Later he claimed to be Krishna incarnate.) He then left school and started his religious vocation with the name Sathya Sai Baba. He soon became known for the miracles that he performed, 'materializing' objects (frequently sacred ash, but also Swiss watches) out of the air, healing people of incurable diseases, raising the dead and, it is claimed, transcending the dimensions of space and time to bless seekers and sufferers in far-off places. [7: I–III; 32]

Sai Baba stresses the importance of leading a pure life and of surrender, the guru–disciple relationship being of central importance [61]. His miracles are, he insists, only a means toward the end of spreading *dharma* [47: 53]. Devotees from around the world flock to attend Sai Baba's *darshan* at his ashram, Prashanthi Nilayam, just outside Puttaparthi, which has now become a place of pilgrimage with lodging for several thousand resident followers. [32; 46; 47: 51–8] (E.B.)

Saichō [iv] [Dengyō Daishi] (767–822). Japanese Buddhist monk. He was the founder and transmitter of the Tendai school and, along with KŪKAI, one of the two pre-eminent Buddhist figures of Heian (794–1185) Japan.

Saichō was born in Omi near Lake Biwa and at the age of 12 entered a nearby temple, where he studied under Gyōhyō (722–797). Shortly after he was ordained Saichō forsook the established Buddhist temples for a simple retreat on Mt Hiei. His *Ganmon* (vows) written at this time reveal an idealistic and fervently dedicated personality.

Saichō travelled to China in 804 to study T'ien-t'ai Buddhism. While in China he also received initiations in Ox-head Ch'an, the *Fan-wang* Mahāyāna precepts, and esoteric Buddhism. After returning to Japan Saichō founded the Tendai school on Mt Hiei on the basis of these four pillars (esoteric Buddhism, Zen, the Mahāyāna precepts, and T'ien-t'ai proper). The new Tendai school was recognized by the court in 806 through the approval of two annual ordinands, one to major in Tendai and one to major in esoteric Buddhism.

Saichō spent the rest of his life defending and building up his new school. He sought to establish an independent official ordination platform based on the *Fan-wang* Mahāyāna precepts in order to prevent his disciples from defecting to the established Nara schools. His petitions submitted to the court concerning annual ordinands (*Rokujōshiki* and so forth) were written at this time. Saichō also carried on a long debate with Tokuitsu (780?–842?) of the Hosso school over the respective worth of their schools' teachings, with Saichō supporting the idea of the universal attainment of Buddhahood in works such as the *Shugo kokkaishō* ('Essays on Protecting the Nation') and *Hokke shūku* ('Elegant Words on the *Lotus Sūtra*'). Saichō also sought to incorporate esoteric Buddhism under the rubric of Tendai Buddhism, but in this area he was overshadowed by Kūkai, and the completion of Tendai esoteric Buddhism (*taimitsu*) was accomplished by Saichō's disciples Ennin and Enchin.

Saichō was outshone by Kūkai during his lifetime, but the Tendai school he founded grew to be the largest and most influential school of Buddhism during much of Japanese history. Tendai .Buddhism, with its headquarters at Enryaku-ji on Mt Hiei, was the womb from which sprang the 'new' schools of Kamakura Buddhism, and nurtured such major figures as Eisai, Dōgen, Hōnen, Shinran, Ippen and Nichiren. Saichō's doctrinal position of universal Buddhahood became the accepted norm of Japanese Buddhism, and his Mahāyāna ideals have had incalculable influence throughout Japanese history. [78] (P.L.S.)

Saigyō [iv] (1118–1190). Japanese Buddhist priest of the Shingon school and renowned poet. Saigyō became a priest at the age of 22. His poems are included in numerous imperial anthologies, such as the *Shin kokinshū*, reflecting his popularity throughout the years. Collections of his work include the *Sankashū* ('Mountain Hermitage'), collected and arranged by Saigyō himself. Saigyō is known as an accomplished poet who wandered around the country while maintaining strong ties to the court. His strongly autobiographical poems concern the beauty of nature and the sadness of this impermanent world. His poetry is marked by a tension between an attraction to the beauty of this world and human feelings, and his Buddhist ideal of detachment from worldly things. [133] (P.L.S.)

Saklatvala, Shapurji [xxvi] (1874–1936). He was a nephew of the Parsi industrial giant J. N. Tata, for whom he worked. Personal tensions arose with the younger Tata, and Saklatvala was sent to the company 'backwater', England. Because of ill-health he 'took the waters' at the Derbyshire spa town of Matlock; there he met and married an English lady (1907). Because of this marriage out of the community, and for his political allegiance (first a member of the Independent Labour Party (1909) and later of the Communist Party), he was not actively included in many of the London Zoroastrian activities organized by his Tory opponent Muncherjee Bhownagree. He was elected Independent Labour Member of Parliament for Battersea North in 1923, and after the split between the Labour and Communist parties he held the seat as a Communist until 1929. Although as a pupil at a Catholic school in Bombay he had undergone the rite of Christian baptism he resolutely affirmed throughout his life that he had done this merely to see what it was like, that no certificate of baptism had been issued and that he always remained a Zoroastrian. His children were initiated into the Zoroastrian religion at Caxton Hall, London, in 1927 with the agreement of the Zoroastrian Association, and his ashes were buried at the

Association's Brookwood cemetery. [26; 37: 228–31] (J.R.H.)

Śākyamuni. *See* BUDDHA.

Salanter, Israel [XV] [Israel Lipkin] (1810–1883). Lithuanian rabbi. A boy prodigy, by the age of ten he was delivering casuistic discourses before scholars. When he was 12 years old he was sent to study in the academy of Salant (whence his name), where he remained for 18 years. He headed talmudic academies at Vilna (Wilnius, 1840–47) and Kovno (Kaunas, 1849–57). He then moved to Prussia, living in Halberstadt, Königsberg and Memel, and in 1880–82 in Paris. He refused to accept rabbinical office and concentrated on teaching.

One of the most influential Orthodox rabbis of his period, his original contribution was the foundation of the *Musar* (the religious ethics of Judaism) movement, initially in the Lithuanian academies and later further afield. Up to his time rabbinic studies concentrated on legal and ritual subjects, but Salanter introduced the study of ethics, based on the classics of Jewish moral literature, and attracted large audiences to his own homilies, which stressed themes such as repentance. A famous episode in his life occurred during a cholera outbreak, when on the solemn fast of the Day of Atonement he ordered the congregation to eat; he himself set the example from the reader's platform. He left no writings but his disciples published his teachings. Distinguished pupils of Salanter founded large academies in which the teaching of ethics was stressed. [29: 145–94; 42:197–211] (G.W.)

Salazar, Domingo de [VI.A] (1512–1594). Bishop of Manila, 1579–94. He was born in Spain and having become a Dominican friar he was sent to Mexico as a missionary to the Indians. He was made vice-provincial of his order. In 1579 King Philip II of Spain nominated him for the newly created see of Manila. Salazar arrived in the Philippines in 1581. He set to work to establish the diocese with a cathedral, a college and a hospital, and generally work for the welfare of the Filipinos. The brutality of the *conquistadores* was condemned at a synod which he convened shortly after his arrival. He fought to bring the work of the missionary orders under the jurisdiction of the diocesan bishop. He was up against the *omnimodo* faculties granted by Pope Adrian VI. He successfully petitioned Pope Gregory XIV in 1591 to establish episcopal authority over all the missionaries in his diocese. In 1592 Salazar returned to Spain to plead with the King the cause of the maltreated Filipinos. The King responded by introducing reforms. Three new dioceses were created in the Philippines, and Manila was made a metropolitan see, though Salazar died before he could receive the Bull of his appointment as archbishop. [261; 581: XII, 259] (T.T.)

Salvado, Rosendo [VI.A] (1814–1900). Spanish Benedictine bishop who founded the New Norcia mission in Western Australia in 1847. His memoirs are autobiographical and contain valuable ethnographic notes on the Aborigines he sought to convert and civilize [704]. He portrays himself (and today is eulogized by many) as a compassionate man, determined to care humbly for and instruct Aborigines and fight the prejudices of the day. These images, partially true, must be weighed against the views of his critics, who emphasize that he was a shrewd political manoeuvrer who amassed one million acres of land, whipped Aborigines who left his employment, and forcibly separated Aborigines from their families. [751] (T.S.)

Samuel [XV] (11th century BCE). Israelite prophet and judge. His mother, Hannah, was barren for many years and vowed that if she were blessed with children, her firstborn would be consecrated as a Nazirite in the service of God. Accordingly, when Samuel was a child he was taken to the sanctuary at Shiloh to be raised by the chief priest, Eli. While Samuel was still a youth, he experienced a vision of God who foretold the end of the line of Eli.

In the course of time Samuel became the outstanding figure among the people of Israel – a wonder-working man of God, central personality of the cult, judge, seer, prophet and even military leader. He headed a group of prophets devoted to the maintenance of the traditional Israelite religion. As a prophet he strengthened the morale of the people in crises, and when Shiloh was destroyed he activated other cult centres, including those at Bethel, Gilgal and Mizpeh. He was the last of the judges who ruled the people and made moral demands on them.

When the people urged, in the interests of national unity, the appointment of a king, Samuel at first objected, seeing the step as a rejection of the kingship of God, but he later reluctantly acceded. As his own sons had proved corrupt, he had to look elsewhere, and selected Saul of the tribe of Benjamin, a choice endorsed by the people.

Samuel anointed Saul but over the years the relations between the two deteriorated. Eventually Samuel decided that Saul would not be permitted to found a dynasty and clandestinely anointed DAVID as Saul's successor. The Bible relates that after Samuel's death his spirit was raised by the 'witch of Endor' and prophesied the final defeat and death of Saul.

The rabbis placed Samuel on a par with MOSES and AARON, and attributed to him authorship of the books of *Judges* and *Ruth*. His story is given in the biblical book called by his name (later split into two parts), notably in 1 *Samuel* 1–16. [47] (G.W.)

Sanjana, Edal [XXVI] (19th century). First high priest (*dastūr*) of the Wadia Ātash Bahrām (founded in 1830) in Bombay. Traditionally learned and reclusive, he was forced in old age into an unwelcome prominence as chief spokesman for the orthodox group of Parsis when a Christian missionary, J. Wilson, attacked Zoroastrianism, in particular for its dualism. His defence is valuable as calmly stating traditional belief in Ahriman as an independent malign being directly opposed to Ohrmazd. This was just before Parsi reformists, shaken by Wilson's polemic, adopted a monotheistic interpretation of ZOROASTER's teachings, and while occultism was gaining strength through the publication of the *Desātīr* by MULLA FEROZE. [9: 193, 196–9; 42: 66; 56: 106ff.] (M.B.)

Śaṅkara [XI] [Śaṅkarācārya] (traditional dates 788–820, but some argue for an earlier birth date). Indian philosopher and metaphysician. Considered by many to be the greatest philosopher of India, he is certainly the most influential, since his Advaita Vedānta is to this day the most widely held philosophical position among Hindus. The hagiographical accounts of his life are all late and therefore unreliable, but they are all there is. From the oldest of these, the picture that emerges, accurate or not, is as follows [65]. Śaṅkara was born into a pious Brahman family in Kālati in Kerala. He was a very precocious child, excelling in his studies, and became a *sannyāsī* at the age of seven. His teacher was Govindanātha, a pupil of Gauḍapāda. He was sent by his teacher to Benares, where he acquired his first pupil, Sanandana, later to be called Padmapāda. Śaṅkara is then said to have moved to Badrīnāth in the Himalayas, where, aged 12, he wrote his famous *Brahma sūtra bhāṣya*, and later the other works discussed below. He is said to have spent the rest of his life as a peripatetic engaged in philosophical disputations in defence of his Advaita Vedānta. There is also a tradition that he established a network of monasteries and teachers to propagate Advaita Vedānta, with either four or five major *maṭhs* being established at Badrīnāth in the North, Dvārakā in the West, Purī in the East, and Śṛṅgerī in the South, with, possibly, one further one in Kāñcīpuram. The ascetics belonging to these monasteries were called the Daśanāmīs. Modern scholarship has greatly reduced the number of works attributed to Śaṅkara, leaving the *Brahma sūtra bhāṣyā*, commentaries on the *Bṛhadāraṇyaka*, *Taittirīya*, *Chāndogya*, *Aitareya*, *Īśa*, *Kaṭha*, *Kena*, *Muṇḍaka* and *Praśna Upaniṣads* and the *Māṇḍūkya Upaniṣad* with the *Gauḍapādiyakārikā*, the commentary on the *Bhagavad Gītā* and the *Upadeśasāhasrī* [75]. This reduced corpus excludes the devotional verses that have been attributed to him. There are two traditions about where he died: Mādhava claims Kedāranāth, while Anantānandagiri claims Kāñcīpuram. Though Western scholars regret that so little is really known about such a towering and influential figure, Hindu scholars are unconcerned, pointing to his works and the endurance of Advaita Vedānta as the true measure of this remarkable man. [22; 65; 75; 87] (S.C.R.W.)

Śaṅkaradeva [XI] (traditionally 1449–1569). Hindu religious leader who established Vaiṣṇavism in Assam. He is thought to have been a Śūdra by caste, although there are alternative theories, and was born to a Bhuya family in Alipukhari, a village approximately 16 miles from the town of Nowga on the southern bank of the Brahmaputra. He was educated in the Sanskritic tradition and became a scholar at the age of 22. He married Sūryavatī, a Kayasth girl, but she died four years later having given birth to a daughter. Śaṅkaradeva is said to have set out in 1541 on a pilgrimage to most of the holy sites of India and to have come in contact with the leaders of various Vaiṣṇava sects. The influence of these religious leaders can be seen in the Vaiṣṇava movement he subsequently established in Assam. Śaṅkaradeva propagated *nāmadharma* as the practical method of *bhakti*. It comprised chanting the name of Hari by everyone irrespective of age, caste, time or place. He was not a philosopher, and the philosophical basis of his religion was essentially the *bhakti* movement of North India. In one important aspect, however, he differed from his North Indian contemporaries: he established an institutional Vaiṣṇavism in Assam. The two main institutions were the *satras* and the *nāmagharas*. The *satras*, similar to ancient monasteries, are huge highly complex structures with numerous departments and activities. *Nāmagharas* were originally set up as the central religious institutions of the villages but later they came to co-ordinate the social, economic and religious life of the Assamese, serving as *pancayat* halls, where villagers gather to discuss and solve their problems. Women also have had a role in the running of the *Nāmagharas*. Assam had a very diverse racial and tribal population, with any number of cults, both tribal and Tantric. It was Śaṅkaradeva's great contribution that he brought such a diverse population within the fold of his Vaiṣṇava faith by incorporating within it various aspects of the social and cultural life of the tribal peoples such as community life, congregational gatherings, the eating of meat and fish, and art forms, music and dance. Śaṅkaradeva received considerable support in propagating his faith and institutions from the Kock King of Western Assam and West Bengal. Śaṅkaradeva composed a number of works to assist in the celebration of his faith, all devotional, and all in Assamese, including hymns, dramas and poems on various Kṛṣṇaite themes, of which the *Kīrttana Ghoṣā* is regarded by some as the greatest [54]. This was of course the 'golden age' of Vaiṣṇava *bhakti*, but few of the great devotees of the time can claim to have had such a profound effect as did Śaṅkaradeva on the religious and social life of an entire region. [5; 54] (T.M.)

Śāntarakṣita [IV] (*d.*788). The teacher of KAMALAŚĪLA and one of the most influential systematic thinkers of late Indian Buddhism. He was probably born in Bengal. He was active in several of the great monastic universities of the time, and instrumental in the transmission of Indian Buddhist scholasticism to Tibet. He visited Tibet (from Nepal) for the first time in 763, and was the abbot of the first Buddhist monastery in Tibet at Samye (bsam-yas), where he lived from 775 to his death in 788 [186: 88–9]. The influence of his thought on Tibetan Buddhism has been enormous; Tibetan doxographers classify his position as a synthesis of Yogācāra and Mādhyamaka, and his systematic works, mediated through the commentaries of his disciple Kamalaśīla, have been extensively commented upon and expounded in the Tibetan schools.

Śāntarakṣita's most important work is the *Tattvasaṅgraha* ('Compendium of Truth') [110], a critical survey and analysis of the doctrinal systems of all the main schools of Indian philosophical thought, Buddhist and non-Buddhist. This text, extant both in its original Sanskrit and in Tibetan translation, together with its commentary by Kamalaśīla, is the most important single source for our understanding of late Indian Buddhist systematic thinking. In addition to this work Śāntarakṣita wrote a short treatise entitled *Madhyamakālaṅkāra* ('Ornament of the Middle'), in which he gives a detailed presentation of Yogācāra doctrines and subjects them to a Mādhyamika critique. (P.J.G.)

Santokh Siṅgh [XXIII] (1788–1844). The supreme Sikh hagiographer. Employed first by the ruler of Paṭiālā, he produced in 1823 his *Gur Nānak Prakāś*. He then transferred to the service of the ruler of Kaithal and in 1844, shortly before his death, followed it with his account of the other nine Gurūs entitled *Gur Pratāp Suray* (popularly known as *Sūraj Prakāś*). Santokh Siṅgh wrote in poetry, his language being a mixture of Punjabi and Braj. To this day his accounts of the Gurūs are widely believed. [59: 12, 29–30] (W.H.M.)

al-Sanūsī, Sīdī Muḥammad ibn ʿAlī [XII] (1791–1859). Founder of the militant Ṣūfi brotherhood of the Sanūsīs (Senusis). Born in

Algeria, al-Sanūsī studied religious sciences there and in Fez, where he gravitated towards Ṣufism. In the course of a pilgrimage to Mecca (1828–30), he was initiated into several North African orders, and while living there (1830–40) came under the tutelage of the influential Ṣūfī master, Aḥmad ibn Idrīs al-Fāsī (1760–1837). After al-Fāsī's death, al-Sanūsī founded a convent for his own order.

Forced to leave Mecca, in 1843 he founded a *zāwiya* in Cyrenaica, from which he sent out emissaries to establish branches of his order throughout North Africa. During a second residence in Mecca he was able to direct the growth of his order by meeting followers annually at the time of the pilgrimage. Returning to Cyrenaica, in 1855 he transferred his headquarters to Jaghbūb in the Libyan desert. Here and in other centres, his followers (who came to comprise most of the Bedouin tribes of the region) established self-sufficient theocratic and military communes free of Ottoman control.

After al-Sanūsī's death in 1859, his order continued to grow under the direction of his son Sayyid al-Mahdī (1844–1902), winning adherents in central Sudan, Chad, Senegal, and elsewhere. The order played a leading role in Libyan politics well into the 20th century.

Like other Ṣūfī leaders of the period, al-Sanūsī believed himself in direct communion with MUḤAMMAD, teaching that all existing lines of Ṣūfī initiation converged in his own person. Under the influence of Ibn Idrīs, he called for the unity of all Muslims through a return to the Qur'ān and traditions, rejecting later legal and theological innovations. He wrote a number of works, of which the best known is *Al-salsabīl al-ma'īn*, a derivative account of the rites of 40 earlier orders. [142] (D.M.)

Sarah (*c*.19th century BCE): Jewish matriarch. Her original name was Sarai but this was changed to Sarah (meaning 'princess') at the same time that Abram was changed to ABRAHAM. She came from Ur of the Chaldees and was married to Abraham, who was apparently her half-brother (*Gen.* 12:13; 20:12), and travelled with him to Canaan. She is described as beautiful (*Gen.* 12:11) and the Dead Sea Scrolls contain a legendary portrayal of her beauty. The impression made on the kings of Egypt and Gerar was such that each sought to take her as their wife. She was restored to Abraham after God had informed the king of Gerar that she was in fact Abraham's wife, and not his sister, as she had been presented (*Gen.* 12:10–20; 20).

Barren for many years, she eventually gave Abraham her maidservant, Hagar, and from their union, ISHMAEL was born. However, fourteen years later, divine messengers informed Abraham that Sarah would become pregnant, at which Sarah – who was eavesdropping – could not restrain her laughter (she was now 90). Nevertheless, she did indeed conceive and gave birth to ISAAC. Now she became jealous of Ishmael, and fearing that he might receive the birthright destined for Isaac, drove Hagar and Ishmael out into the desert where they were miraculously saved.

The Bible relates that she died at the age of 127, to which the rabbis added that this occurred on receiving news that Abraham intended to sacrifice Isaac. She died in Hebron, where Abraham purchased the Cave of Machpelah for her burial. [68: IV–X] (G.W.)

Saraha [IV] Little is known of the life or date of this Indian master of tantric Buddhism, though hagiographical anecdotes about him are plentiful. He is generally portrayed as a Brahman of eastern India by birth ('Great Brahman' is one of his epithets) who became a learned Buddhist monk. Abandoning the monastery in favour of the life of a wandering yogin, he realized the enlightenment of the 'Great Seal' (*Mahāmudrā*) following an encounter with an outcaste girl who made arrows, whose symbolic instruction to him pierced through all mundane conceptions. Hence his name, which means 'Pierce-arrow'. Saraha wrote many fine songs (*dohā-s*), which remain popular among Newari and Tibetan Buddhists. Several of these survive in an eastern Apabhraṁśa dialect, and so are of considerable importance for the early history of the modern languages and literatures of Bengal, Assam and Orissa. [44: 224–39; 55; 83; 184: 41–3] (M.K.)

Saraṇaṁkara, Välivițē [IV] (*c*.1698–1779). Buddhist monk who played a central role in the revival of Buddhism in Sri Lanka during the 18th century. He was born in the

Kandyan kingdom at a time when this region preserved a precarious cultural and political independence while the low-country areas of Sri Lanka were under colonial control. He was ordained at 16, in a reformist monastic lineage which had recently been introduced to Sri Lanka from Burma. Monastic discipline and learning was at a low ebb in Sri Lanka at this time and it was necessary for Saraṇaṁkara to teach himself Pali because he could find no competent monastic teacher. Saraṇaṁkara finally sought out a layman who knew Pali, but had been exiled to a remote area by the king. While Saraṇaṁkara lived near him, he returned to a strict observance of Buddhist monastic discipline (*vinaya*). He was joined by a number of companions, and together they became known as the *Silvat Samagama* ('the fraternity of the virtuous'). Saraṇaṁkara and his group attracted the attention of the king, who was impressed by their ascetic discipline and learning, and extended his patronage to them. Saraṇaṁkara became a very capable author and wrote a number of books to facilitate the study of Pali, as well as various commentaries and doctrinal manuals in Sinhala. At Saraṇaṁkara's request, King Vijaya Rājasiṁha (reigned 1739–47) took steps to reintroduce a pure ordination lineage in Sri Lanka, and in 1741 five of Saraṇaṁkara's pupils went to Thailand for reordination. In 1753 he was appointed *saṅgharāja* ('king of the monastic order') by King Kīrti Śrī Rājasiṁha.

Saraṇaṁkara's efforts always aimed at the revitalization of Buddhism in Sri Lanka. He largely accomplished this, but his efforts also resulted in the growth of a strong and centralized religious 'establishment'. However, this new social organization of the monastic order did not survive long during the subsequent colonial period when all of Sri Lanka came under British control. [151: XIII; 152: I] (C.H.)

Sargon [II] (2371–2316 BCE). The earliest settlers in ancient Iraq who could write were the Sumerians. Where they came from or why they came is uncertain, but they were responsible for building some of the earliest large temples in mud brick and writing down the first religious liturgies and mythologies on clay tablets. The native inhabitants soon learned the complicated script used by the foreign Sumerians and adapted it to write down their own Semitic language, Akkadian. As a result of archaeological excavations during the later part of the 19th and the early part of the 20th centuries hundreds of religious texts in Sumerian and Akkadian from many different religious centres in southern Mesopotamia have been discovered.

From the historical texts of this period we learn that the first king to unite the land politically was a Semite called Sharru-kin, a name which means 'The King shall endure for ever', and which has been anglicized as Sargon. However great his political achievements might have been in his day he became venerated as a hero many centuries later.

In the British Museum, London, are copies of a poem in which Sargon describes the mystery of the circumstances of his birth. His mother was a priestess but his father an anonymous man from the hill country. Having been born in secret his mother left him in a bitumen-coated reed basket to float to his fate down the river. It was thus that he came to be found in an irrigation canal by a peasant farmer and brought up by him under the protection of the beautiful goddess Ishtar. The text is badly damaged but the poem seems mainly to eulogize the famous victories and superhuman achievements of this famous ancient king.

Since the document we have is so much later than the events it describes it is better to infer from it the attitude of a later generation to Sargon rather than to reconstruct from it the historical circumstances of his birth. It was probably written about the time of Sargon II, the King of Assyria from 721 BCE, who almost certainly chose his royal name in conscious emulation of his illustrious predecessor. The fact that this motif of the miraculous preservation of an abandoned baby in a river is seen also in the story of the discovery of MOSES by the Egyptian princess has been of considerable interest to biblical scholars, who are inclined to believe that the biography of Moses could well have been written first around the time of Sargon II.

A later tablet, from the late Babylonian period, credits Sargon with having conquered virtually the whole of the Middle East:

> He crossed the Eastern Sea and conquered
> all the Western lands in his eleventh year
> and made them speak one language.

But then it suggests that even this great hero was not without sin against Marduk, the chief god of Babylon. Towards the end of his reign there was a great famine in the land. This is blamed on Sargon's decision to remove soil from the foundations of Babylon in order to build a new Babylon in his own town of Akkad.

> It was through this sin that he committed that Marduk, the Noble Lord, became angry and destroyed his people by famine.

So for two millennia the name of this ancient king was venerated. That later generations should have seen fit to record his sin is clearly an attempt to explain national disasters as a consequence of some moral turpitude of contemporary leaders, an important element in Biblical theology. [10; 7; 11: 92ff.; 13] (M.R.)

Śāriputra [IV] [Sāriputta]. The leader (*mahāsvāmi*) of the Buddhist monastic order in Sri Lanka during the second half of the 12th century and one of the greatest exegetes of the Theravāda Buddhist tradition. Very little is known about Śāriputra's life before his appointment as *mahāsvāmi*. He tells us in his own works that he was a disciple of Mahākassapa, who presided over the Buddhist council convened by PARĀKRAMABĀHU, but it is not clear that he belonged to Kassapa's 'forest-dwelling' (*vanavāsī*) monastic fraternity. Śāriputra probably participated in that Council, since Parākramabāhu built a luxurious monastery for him at the Jetavana Vihāra in Polonnaruva. Traditionally, Śāriputra is said to be the author of at least five subcommentaries (*ṭīkā*) on the various commentaries of the Pali Canon. His *magnum opus* is his *ṭīkā* on BUDDHAGHOSA's *Vinaya* commentary, the *Sāratthadīpanī*. He was also the author of a Sinhala commentary on Anuruddha's *Abhidhammatthasaṅgaha*; this commentary was translated into Pali by Śāriputra's disciple, Sumangala, and that work has become one of the most popular texts in Theravādin scholasticism. Śāriputra also wrote some synthetic works on monastic discipline and meditation subjects, as well as a Sanskrit grammar. While it is possible that Śāriputra was not the direct author of all these works, and only supervised their composition, for just his *Vinaya-ṭīkā* he is worthy of the title accorded him by later tradition: *sāgaramati* – like an ocean in wisdom. Śāriputra's exegetical style was doctrinally inclusive and eclectic. It appears that he was striving to create a commentarial tradition that would be acceptable to various factions within the Sri Lankan monastic order of his day. [151: IX–X] (C.H.)

Sāriputta [IV] [Śāriputra]. The chief disciple of the BUDDHA, represented as standing at his right hand (*see also* MOGGALLĀNA). His three brothers and three sisters all joined the Buddhist order, but his mother resented the loss of her children and did not become a Buddhist lay-supporter until the end of her life. Sāriputta was declared the foremost of the Buddha's disciples in wisdom, and is recorded in the scriptures as having delivered a number of sermons and other texts gathered in the *Sutta-piṭaka*; he was also especially concerned with the *Abhidhamma* (*Abhidharma*), which the Buddha taught to him at the same time as to the gods of the Tavatiṃsa heaven (*see* QUEEN MĀYĀ). His severity in doctrinal and disciplinary matters is blended in Pali texts with affection and compassion for his fellow monks and nuns, particularly for the Buddha and his son Rāhula. In Mahāyāna texts he often appears as the archetype of the over-scholastic monk, too concerned with doctrinal minutiae to comprehend the deeper truths of Emptiness. [150: vol. 2: 1108–18] (S.C.)

Sarkar, Prabhat Rainjan. *See* ANANDAMURTI, SHRII SHRII.

Sa-skya Paṇḍita [IV] (1182–1251). The honorific title, often abbreviated as Sa-pan, of Kun-dga'-rgyal-mtshan, traditionally regarded (along with the 14th-century figures KLONG-CHEN RAB-'BYAMS-PA and TSONG-KHA-PA) as one of the three greatest scholars in the history of Tibetan Buddhism. He also played a key role in defining Tibet's relation with the Mongols. He was one of the last Tibetans to study extensively with scholars from the great Buddhist universities of India. His collaboration with such scholars as Śākyaśrībhadra resulted in his becoming the first Tibetan to be recognized as a *paṇḍita*. He was a renowned scholar of Buddhist logic and epistemology (*pramāṇa*); his major work on the subject, the *Tshad ma rigs gter* ('Treasury of

Reasoning on Valid Knowledge'), was translated into Sanskrit and circulated in India. His other major works include the *Mkhas 'jugs* ('Entrance for the Wise'), which deals with methods of philosophical inquiry, including debate; the *Sdom gsum rab dbye* (Discrimination of the Three Vows'), which discusses the Hīnayāna, Mahāyāna, and Vajrayāna ethical systems; the *Thub pa'i dgongs gsal* ('Illumination of the Sage's Intention'), an overview of Mahāyāna theory and practice; and finally a collection of verse aphorisms. In 1244 Sa-skya Paṇḍita was selected to respond to the summons to the court of the Mongol prince Godan, who had sent raiding parties into Tibet in 1239. He impressed the Mongols with his magical powers as much as with his learning and offered submission to Godan on behalf of Tibet in return for freedom from military attack and occupation. He remained at Godan's court as regent, sending orders to officials in Tibet. For roughly the next century, the head lamas of the Sa-skya sect exercised political control over Tibet with Mongol support. Sa-skya Paṇḍita's nephew, 'PHAGS-PA, became the religious teacher of Qubilai Khan. [107; 238: 126–7] (D.L.)

Savonarola, Girolamo [VI.A] (1452–1498). Italian preacher and reformer. He was born in Ferrara, Italy, was educated in religious and liberal studies and later in medicine. In 1475 he entered the Dominican Order of Preachers at Bologna. He completed his novitiate there and studied at the Dominican Studium Generale. In 1482 he went to the Dominican priory of San Marco in Florence. A study of his sermon notes and other writings shows him developing his reforming ideas on morality and asceticism. Through a study of scripture and of the social environment in Florence he began to preach an apocalyptic type of sermon. The Lenten sermons he preached in the Collegiate Church in San Gimignano in 1485 and 1486 are good examples. In 1487 he went to Bologna as *magister studiorum* and built up his reputation as a preacher. In 1490 he was called back to San Marco by Lorenzo de' Medici, who was unofficial ruler of Florence. Savonarola constantly preached against the corruption of those in authority and began to claim visions and to warn of trouble to come. In 1490 Charles VIII invaded Italy, the people of Florence revolted against Piero de' Medici and Savonarola became the popular ruler. He ruled with severity but lacked the actual support of Charles. He was summoned to Rome and when he refused to go he was excommunicated. Resistance to his rule came from a Franciscan who challenged him to a test by fire. When Savonarola failed to meet the challenge he and two other friars were taken by a Florentine mob, interrogated, tortured and finally hanged and burned in the Piazza della Signoria. [684; 848] (T.T.)

Sawyerr, Harry Alphonso Ebun [VI.A] (1909–1987). Sierra Leone theologian. The son of a Krio Anglican Church worker (eventually ordained) in Boma Sakrim, he was educated at Fourah Bay College. Ordained in 1934, he became tutor at the college. After studying theology at Durham University from 1945 to 1948 he returned to Fourah Bay, where he spent most of the rest of his working life, assisting the transformation of a small mission institution into an independent university college and the nucleus of a national university system. He was Professor of Theology from 1962, Principal from 1968, Vice Chancellor from 1972 to 1974. A Canon of St George's Cathedral from 1962, he taught in Codrington College, Barbados and headed the Sierra Leone Divinity Hall after his university retirement. As head of the Fourah Bay Theology Department in the 1950s, Sawyerr was probably Africa's senior academic theologian. Though engaged in biblical scholarship on the Western model, he was an early advocate of indigenous, but church-related, African theology. He especially stressed the Christian significance of sacrifice and the ancestor concept. (His main works are listed in a festschrift, M. E. Glasswell and E. W. Fasholé-Luke, eds, *New Testament Christianity for Africa and the World*, London, 1974.) In Sierra Leone he was a national figure, affirming the cultural traditions of both Krio Freetown and of Mendeland where he grew up. He attended the seminal Manchester Pan African Conference of 1945, and well represents the generation that established the independent states of Africa. [353: 165, 231] (A.F.W.)

Schechter, Solomon [XV] (1847–1915). Jewish scholar and leader of Conservative Judaism. Born in Rumania, he studied in Vienna and Berlin, and in 1882 moved to

England. In 1890 he was appointed lecturer (later, reader) in rabbinics at Cambridge University. While there he was informed of a trove of old Jewish documents that had been discovered in Cairo. He immediately made his way there and was shown a roomful of manuscripts in a synagogue storeroom. He brought back 100,000 fragments dating from the Middle Ages to Cambridge, where they are still being studied. Schechter identified various lost treasures of Jewish literature including the long-lost Hebrew original of *Ecclesiasticus*. After a period as professor of Hebrew at London University he moved to New York to become principal of the Jewish Theological Seminary of America, the Conservative rabbinical college. He built up the Seminary into a major institution, attracting a distinguished faculty, developing an outstanding library and a teachers' seminary. He also founded the United Synagogue of America, the lay arm of the Conservative movement.

He formulated the principles which served as the ideological basis of Conservative Judaism. Judaism, while including immutable doctrines, was a living organism, developing from age to age. However, it was not to be adapted to every passing whim, and only that reform was acceptable which accorded with the 'catholic conscience of Israel', a concept which determined what to retain and what could be altered without endangering the structure. The guidelines must be based in tradition. Schechter was in sympathy with the Zionist movement, holding that Jews could revive their national life only in the Land of Israel, and that Jewish nationalism must be seen as an essential part of Judaism. [8]

His writings include scholarly editions of ancient texts as well as essays on Judaism characterized by a lucid and attractive English style. (G.W.)

Schleiermacher, Friedrich Daniel Ernst [VI.A] (1768–1834). German Protestant theologian. He was born in Breslau, Silesia. His father was a pastor and army chaplain who was converted to the Moravian church. The son followed in 1783. Friedrich was sent to the Moravian Brethren's school at Niesky (1783–5) and attended their seminary in Barby from 1785 to 1787. This pietistic influence remained with him although he found Moravian studies too restricting. He went to Halle University in 1787 and sat, successfully, his theological examinations. He was made a tutor to a noble family in West Prussia in 1790 and went as assistant pastor to Landsberg in 1794. In 1796 he became Reformed chaplain at the Charité Hospital, Berlin. It was here that he wrote his first famous work, *Über die Religion* (1799). His appeal is based on the romanticism then prevalent in Berlin; religion is defined as 'a sense and taste of the infinite'. His next work, *Monologen* (1800), outlined the ethics of his new understanding of religion. In 1804 he became professor of theology at Halle but left for Berlin in 1807 following the city's capture by Napoleon. In 1810 he became Dean of the Theology Faculty of the new university, having held posts as a civil servant and a pastor. He was involved in many projects, both academic and ecclesiastical, including the union of the Reformed and Lutheran churches. In 1821–2 he published *Der christliche Glaube*, a systematic treatment of Protestant theology based on his lectures in dogmatics. He amplifies his teaching that religion is based on experience in human self-consciousness. Religion is to be understood as 'the feeling of absolute dependence', monotheism is the highest form and Christianity the purest form of religion. Schleiermacher was the most influential single Protestant theologian of the 19th century. [668; 709; 710] (T.T.)

Scholarios, Georgios. *See* GENNADIOS SCHOLARIOS.

Schweitzer, Albert [VI.A] (1875–1965). German theologian and mission doctor. He was born in Kaisersberg and raised in Günsbach, both in Alsace. He studied in the university of Strasbourg, gaining a doctorate in philosophy in 1899, becoming a pastor in the same year, and a doctorate in theology in 1900. In 1901 he published *Das Messianitäts- und Leidensgeheimnis* (English trans., *The Mystery of the Kingdom of God*, 1925). In this work he first expounded his view that Jesus' teaching centred on his belief in the imminent end of the world. In 1902 he became a lecturer in the University of Strasbourg and principal of a theological college. In 1906 he published *Von Reimarus zu Wrede* (English trans., *The Quest of the Historical Jesus*, 1910). The work is partly a review of earlier attempts to interpret the life of Jesus, hence the German title, but more significantly it is a severe criticism of the failure of his predecessors to take the lack of historical evidence for Jesus seriously. He suggests that Jesus was a purely apocalyptic figure who, when the apocalyptic vision failed, tried to initiate the end by his own suffering. Though not universally accepted, this work left its mark on all future studies of Jesus. While he was engaged in this work he was also working on the music of J. S. BACH. Later, when he was engaged in medical missionary work in Africa, he raised funds for this work by public performances of organ music in Europe. By 1913 he had studied and graduated in medicine. He and his wife, Hélène Bresslau, went to Lambaréné in Gabon and set up a hospital in which he served for the next 50 years, working out his 'reverence for life', a personal philosophy which came to him in a kind of mystical experience in 1915. He made a reputation as a stern humanitarian and was awarded the Nobel Peace Prize in 1952. [113; 410; 718; 722] (T.T.)

Segundo, Juan Luis [VI.A] (1925–). Pioneer liberation theologian of Latin America. He was born in Uruguay and spent most of his life ministering there. A Jesuit priest, ordained in 1955, he completed his philosophical studies in Argentina and then theological studies at Leuven, Belgium, in 1956. He received the degree of Doctor of Letters from the Sorbonne, Paris, in 1963 for two theses on the philosophy of religion. He founded the Peter Faber Pastoral Centre in Montevideo, his home city, and served as its director until it closed in 1975. In collaboration with others, he authored a major course in theology for adult lay people from grassroots communities, publishing it in a five-volume series entitled *A Theology for Artisans of a New Humanity* (1973–4). At present chaplain to various groups in Uruguay, he has taught at Harvard and at universities in Chicago, Toronto, Montreal, Birmingham and São Paulo.

He is one of the most prolific writers among Latin American liberation theologians, having produced more than 20 books and scores of journal articles since 1948. Among his celebrated works, translated from Spanish into English, are: *The Liberation of Theology* (1976), *The Hidden Motives of Pastoral Action* (1978), *Faith and Ideologies* (1984) and the monumental five-volume series entitled *Jesus of Nazareth Yesterday and Today* (1984–9). For a useful introduction to his thought until 1978, see Alfred T. Hennelly, *Theologies in Conflict: The Challenge of Juan Luis Segundo* (1979). [297: 22–7] (A.C.S.)

Sen, Keshub Chunder [XI] [Keshab Chandra Sen] (1838–1884). Leader of the Brahmo Samaj (*see* RAMMOHUN ROY). He was born in Calcutta in a prominent Vaiṣṇava family, and educated, like DEBENDRANATH TAGORE, at the Hindu College; his intellectual background was Western. He joined the Brahmo Samaj in 1857, becoming a protégé of Debendranath and a leading figure in the movement, noted for his public lectures in English. He formed an inner group within the Samaj, the Sanghat Sabha, committed to his own ideas of social reform, particularly widow remarriage, intercaste marriage, and the abolition of caste privileges, and to spreading Brahmoism, hitherto a Calcutta movement, into other parts of India. He advocated a freer social life for Hindu women and an education for girls, though this was only to prepare them for a domestic role. In 1861 he became the first non-Brahman Acarya or minister in the Samaj. Differences between him and Debendranath Tagore on social questions led him to separate and form the Brahmo Samaj of India, which embraced the majority of the former Samaj. In his lecture 'Jesus Christ: Europe and Asia' (1866) he declared his love of JESUS, suggesting that Indians, as fellow-Asiatics, were better able than the British to understand Jesus' message. However, he did not regard Jesus as a unique manifestation of God, and became increasingly interested in the CAITANYA tradition. In 1870 he visited England, making a good impression as a public speaker and social reformer. In 1878 he arranged a marriage between his daughter and the heir to the Hindu kingdom of Cooch Behar, which many regarded as a compromise with idolatry and backwardness, and a mark of Keshub's increasing autocracy. Most members of the Samaj joined a new and more democratic movement, the Sadharan Brahmo Samaj, while Keshub, believing himself to be under divine guidance, formed his remaining followers into an eclectic sect, the 'Church of the New Dispensation'. [9; 19; 21: 78–101; 24: vol. 2: 63–75; 32: 41–69; 98] (D.H.K.)

Seng-chao [IV] (374–414). One of the pre-eminent disciples of KUMĀRAJĪVA and an early interpreter of Mādhyamika Buddhism in China. Seng-chao converted to Buddhism upon reading the *Vimalakīrtinirdeśasūtra*, and as Kumārajīva's disciple assisted him in his translation work. Seng-chao's composition entitled '*Prajñā* is not Knowledge' was well received and praised highly by Kumārajīva. He later composed essays on *śūnyatā* ('The Emptiness of the Unreal'), on time ('The Immutability of Things'), on the unnameability of *nirvāṇa*, a commentary to the *Vimalakīrtinirdeśasūtra*, various introductions to Buddhist texts, and Kumārajīva's obituary. He attempted to clarify the Mādhyamika concepts of the two truths and emptiness, and explained a middle path which synthesized the Chinese concepts of essence (*t'i*) and function (*yung*). Seng-chao was known for his profound understanding of emptiness; his short but insightful essays have been studied and admired as classics of Buddhist reflection which synthesized Buddhist and traditional Chinese thought. (234: 380–98; 182: 123–60; 31: 86–8] (P.L.S.)

Senghor, Léopold Sédar [I.B](1906–). He was born in Joal, Senegal, son of a Christian convert, one of a tiny but powerful minority. In 1928 he went to France for an education, and became the first black African to qualify to teach at secondary level. He began to write poetry, and throughout the 1930s and 1940s was prolific. With friends he helped form the Négritude Movement, which had political, literary and spiritual aspects. In 1948 he entered politics and became the first President of Senegal when the country gained independence. While wishing to reconcile the cultures of France and Senegal, the colonizer and the colonized, he argues for the uniqueness, yet universality, of the black experience. A modern griot, together with Aimé Césaire and Louis Damas of Martinique he worked out a programme for Négritude: to tell black history, vindicate black culture and prepare for the future. All poets, thinkers and politicians should be close, for the word is magical, and relates the individual to the universe. He insisted that communion with the ancestors, as the classic African view, must be maintained, for the dead are the principal force controlling the living. His great despair was the appropriation of Christianity by the bourgeoisie. While the power of Négritude in Africa became literary and cultural, its impact on the diaspora has been diffuse yet powerful, underlying many later movements of black self-awareness and pride. [15; 17; 19] (K.W.)

Seraphim of Sarov, St [VI.B] (1759–1833). Russian *starets*. A builder's son from Kursk, he entered Sarov monastery in 1793, becoming a hermit in the forests around Sarov. In 1804 he was attacked by bandits, an event that made him re-examine his whole life. Emulating the stylites, he knelt for 1,000 days praying on a high, exposed rock. In 1810 poor health forced him back to the monastery, where he lived as a recluse till 1825. He then began to receive visitors and offer spiritual counsel. Famous as a mystic and prophet, he drew disciples from all walks of life. [33: 242ff.; 98; 99] (D.B.)

Sergii [VI.A] [Ivan Nikolaevich Stragorodskii] (1867–1944). Russian Orthodox theologian and an advocate of church reform in tsarist Russia. He was a signatory to the Declaration of Loyalty in 1927 in which the USSR was acknowledged as the motherland of the Orthodox Church. Further aims of the Declaration were to express loyalty to the Soviet regime, to exclude churchmen who were deemed undesirable both in the USSR and abroad, and to formalize the relationship of the church to the regime through state organs. The Declaration caused a schism in the church and many bishops and their lay followers refused to accept it. The Declaration did not save the church from numerous persecutions, which only abated when Stalin saw the advantages of involving the church in saving the Soviet Union in the face of German invasion from 1941 onwards. In 1942 Sergii published *The Truth about Religion in Russia*, in which he denied that the church had been persecuted by the regime. The following year Stalin invited him to restore the patriarchal administration and he was made patriarch. The church was partially restored on both sides of the war front and seminaries were reopened. Most of the estranged bishops recognized Sergii's primacy before he died. [182; 266; 657] (T.T.)

Sergii of Radonezh [VI.A] [Bartholomew] (1314–1392). Russian Orthodox monk. He was born in Rostov, Russia, but while still a child his family moved to Radonezh. What is known of him comes down through hagiographical material and medieval chronicles. His brother Stephen was a monk and Sergii persuaded him to join him in a forest hermitage. They built a wooden chapel and called it Trinity Church. The asceticism of this existence was too much for Stephen so for two or three years (*c.*1345–8) Sergii spent his time in solitude. Other monks were attracted to him so a monastery of the Holy Trinity was set up, of which, having become a priest, he became first abbot. It was the first of about 30 such monasteries set up in Sergii's lifetime. He attracted state attention and became an important political cleric. He inspired Prince Dimitri to successful resistance against the Tartars in 1380. However, he refused to be made bishop or metropolitan. He claimed a number of visions, including one of the Mother of God, who promised protection for his monastery. Following his death the monastery was renamed Trinity-Saint Sergii Monastery. His relics have remained in the monastery church in what is now Zagorsk. He is regarded as the virtual patron saint of Russia. [258; 438] (T.T.)

Serra, Junipero [VI.A] (1713–1784). Spanish Franciscan monk and missionary. He was born in Mallorca, and was educated at the Royal and Pontifical University of Palma. He became professor of philosophy at the university but in 1749 he decided to go to Mexico as a missionary. He worked among the Pamé Indians, first in Sierra Gorda (1750–58) and then in Baja California. Following Spain's annexation of Alta California (1769) he established the first mission in San Diego, to which in time he added another eight. He intervened with the Spanish viceroy to initiate the development of the territory from San Diego to San Francisco. This resulted in the Reglamento Echeveste (1773), which became the law of the State of California. He was also given rights to introduce transportation to import goods and settlers. In 1776 over 200 people arrived at Mission San Gabriel from Arizona. Later four towns, including San Francisco and Los Angeles, were founded. Serra limited the settlers to married couples, and organized occupations for each mission with artisans apportioned to each settlement. These developments were funded from the Pious Fund of the expelled Jesuits. In 1931 the State of California erected a statue of Serra in Washington DC [289; 795] (T.T.)

Servetus, Michael [VI.A] [Miguel Serveto] (1511–1553). Spanish theologian and physician. He was born in Villanueva, Spain. He studied law at Saragossa and Toulouse and travelled in Italy and Germany, where he met MELANCHTHON and BUCER. He turned to theology, and on the basis of his reading of the Bible wrote *De Trinitas erroribus*, in which he argued the case for a modalistic Trinity, i.e. that the Divine is expressed in different modes or appearances in the Trinity rather than as equal 'persons'. He offended both Protestants and Catholics, and initially escaped the Inquisition by adopting the name Michel de Villeneuve. Still under his assumed name, he took up the study of medicine in 1538 and, having qualified, became physician to the Archbishop of Vienne. In 1546 he wrote *Christianismi restitutio*, a clearer statement of his earlier anti-trinitarian views. The work was published anonymously in 1553. A copy was brought to the attention of the Inquisition and Servetus, having been identified as the author, was arrested together with the printer. Servetus escaped and fled to Geneva, where he was tried under CALVIN, found guilty of heresy and burned at the stake at Champel near Geneva. As a physician he made an important contribution to studies on the circulation of the blood. [41; 83; 724] (T.T.)

Sethos I [VII] (14th–13th century BCE). As one of the most powerful kings of Egypt of Dynasty 19 (1309–1291 BCE), Sethos I built a magnificent tomb in the Valley of the Kings, and mortuary temples at Qurna and Abydos. The latter, dedicated to six gods, has the best preserved wall reliefs and inscriptions relating to the daily temple rituals. [6] (A.R.D.)

Seton, Elizabeth Ann [VI.A] [née Bayley] (1774–1821). American Roman Catholic founder of the Sisters of Charity. She was probably born in New York. Little is known of her early years except that she went to school and learned to play the piano and to speak French. She married William Magee Seton of New York in 1794, with whom she had five children. In 1797 she helped form a society to aid destitute widows. Under the influence of an assistant priest at Trinity (Episcopal) Church in New York City in 1800 she began to lead a new spiritual life. Her husband died while they were visiting Italy in 1803 and Elizabeth became friendly with two Italian Roman Catholic families who sought to convert her to their faith. She was under pressure for a time from Anglican and Catholic friends and relatives. In 1805 she became a Roman Catholic. She was invited to Baltimore in 1808 to found a school for Catholic girls. She taught there for a time and founded the Sisters of Charity of Saint Joseph, before the school was moved to Emmitsburg, Maryland. The fees of the wealthier pupils helped pay for the education of needier girls. The community of Sisters expanded their work to include care of the sick, orphans and the poor. New houses were founded in Philadelphia (1814), New York (1817) and Baltimore (1821). Two miracles performed by her were validated in 1961. She was beatified in 1963 and proclaimed Saint Elizabeth Ann Seton in 1975. [206; 545] (T.T.)

Severus of Antioch [VI.A] (*c.*465–538). Greek monk and theologian. He was born in Apollonia, Thrace. He studied philosophy in Alexandria and rhetoric in Berytus (modern Beirut). He was baptized in 488 and became a monk in a monastery in Maiouma, near Gaza. Later he founded his own monastery there, was ordained and became an archimandrite. In 508 he went to Constantinople to plead the cause of the Monophysite monks. There he gained the favour of Emperor Anastasius I. Severus spent his time in Constantinople writing against Chalcedonian orthodoxy. In 512 he went to Antioch, where he was elected patriarch. Following the death of Anastasius in 518 and the proclamation as emperor of Justin I, a pro-Chalcedonian, Severus was deposed and expelled from Antioch. He took refuge in the monastery of Annaton in Egypt. While supporting and encouraging a form of Monophysitism he attacked the extreme Monophysitism of Julian of Halicarnassus. Emperor Justinian invited Severus to Constantinople in 535, where he worked with Patriarch Anthimus to restore Monophysitism. They were opposed, and when Anthimus was deposed Severus had to flee to Egypt again. He lived in Alexandria and continued to write until his death. He is venerated as a saint by the Copts and by Jacobite Syrians. [165; 464] (T.T.)

Sgam-po-pa Bsod-nams rin-chen [IV] [also known as Dwags-po Lha-rje, 'the physician from Dwags-po'] (1079–1153). A leading disciple of the poet-sage MILAREPA (1040–1123) and a key figure in the early formation of the Bka'-brgyud schools of Tibetan Buddhism. The most prominent of them are referred to collectively as the Dwags-po Bka'-brgyud ('the lineage of the precepts of Dwags-po'). A lay physician by training, he renounced worldly life in his 20th year, following the tragedy of his wife's early death. Studying initially in the Bka'-gdams-pa tradition stemming from ATIŚA (*d.*1054), he later employed the Mahāyāna teachings of this school as the basis for his expositions of the 'Great Seal' (*Mahāmudrā*) precepts of Marpa (1012–1096) and Milarepa. For this reason, his unique approach to Buddhist thought and practice is described as 'the unification of the two streams'. His leading disciples gave rise to the four main subsects of the Bka'-brgyud school, including that of the KARMA-PA, and from his disciple Phag-mo gru-pa (1110–1170) eight further subsects arose. Sgam-po-pa's *thar-pa rin-po-che'i rgyan* ('Jewel Ornament of Liberation') remains the foremost Mahāyāna textbook of the Bka'-brgyud traditions, and, like his many shorter writings, is treasured for its clarity, erudition and gentle wit. [34: XLI; 81; 184: 451ff.; 238: 63–4] (M.K.)

Shabbazi, Shalem [XV] (1619–after 1680). Jewish religious poet in Yemen. The only information on his life is deduced from his poems. He was apparently a weaver by trade and lived in poverty. Shabbazi wandered around Yemen, frequenting homes of patrons and keeping in touch with scholars and other poets. In 1679/80, he was exiled to Mawza, on the southern shore of the Red Sea, together with the rest of the Jewish community of Yemen, and nothing more is known of him. His reputed grave is in Taiz, to which both Jews and Arabs, who regarded him as a wonder-worker, made pilgrimages.

His poems reflect his wide knowledge of the Talmud and later rabbinic writings, of Jewish mysticism and philosophy, as well as of astronomy and astrology. He was also familiar with Muslim literature and wrote in Arabic, besides Hebrew and Aramaic. Over 500 of his poems and hymns are known, most of them are on sacred themes (such as hymns for Sabbaths and festivals or poems for wedding and circumcision ceremonies), even though only a few were intended for liturgical use. Frequent themes include the Jewish people, Torah, the world to come and, especially, redemption. He reflected the sufferings of Yemenite Jewry and their yearnings in time of persecution. His clear and simple language derived from earlier verse, especially in Spain and Yemen, and he in turn greatly influenced later Yemenite Jewish poetry, although he only became known to the outside world from the mid-19th century. [87: vol. 4: 107–16] (G.W.)

Shabbetai Tzevi [xv] (1626–1676). Jewish pseudo-messiah. Born in Smyrna (Izmir), he immersed himself in mystical writings while still a youth. Already then he manifested symptoms of the manic-depression which characterized his career. After the massacres of the Jews in Poland in 1648–9 he claimed to have experienced a heavenly voice informing him that he was destined to be the Jewish redeemer. He symbolized his messianic mission in various ways, such as pronouncing the ineffable name of God and cancelling fast-days. This led to his expulsion by the local rabbis and move to Salonika (*c.*1651), where he declared his messiahship in a ceremony in which he 'wedded' the Torah. Moving through Greece and Turkey, he shocked the Jewish establishment with his claims, but his sermons and messianism attracted a large popular following. In 1662 he went to Egypt, where he married a Marrano girl of doubtful reputation who had announced that she would only be betrothed to the messiah. He continued to the Holy Land and in Gaza encountered the kabbalist Nathan of Gaza, who declared himself Shabbetai Tzevi's prophet and crowned him king-messiah. The result of this action was his excommunication by the rabbis of Jerusalem. Nathan informed the Jewish world that Shabbetai Tzevi would depose the Sultan of Turkey and gather in the scattered exiles of Jewry to the Land of Israel. They travelled back to Turkey, everywhere being greeted royally by the Jewish masses. The messianic ferment had by now spread throughout Europe. Jews from as far away as Italy, Poland, Holland and England began to make preparations for the return to the Holy Land and the advent of the messiah. The rabbis were divided, some endorsing the claims of Shabbetai Tzevi, others branding him a heretic. When he reached Smyrna, he cancelled the commandments and performed a series of acts forbidden by Jewish law. A date was set for redemption (18 June 1666), and fast-days were converted into festivals. He sailed to Constantinople in order to depose the Sultan, but on arrival was arrested and imprisoned in a fortress in Gallipoli. With the aid of bribery he was allowed complete freedom in gaol, where he continued to preach to multitudes. His regal and arrogant behaviour angered the Turkish authorities, who gave him a choice between death or conversion to Islam. He chose the latter and underwent a conversion ceremony in the presence of the Sultan. Most Jews were aghast, but Shabbetai Tzevi and his immediate followers found kabbalistic justification for his action, following the belief of ISAAC LURIA that the righteous must descend to the depths of evil prior to redemption and that the sufferings of the messiah will atone for Israel. They also quoted the doctrine of the kabbalistic classic the *Zohar* that the messiah will be perfect internally but evil externally. In 1672 Shabbetai Tzevi was transferred to a fortress close to the Albanian border where he remained in touch with his followers until his death.

After he died his believers maintained that his disappearance was temporary, and that he would reappear as redeemer. Various sects believing in his divinity continued to exist, the best-known being the Dönmeh (Turkish: 'apostates'), which had communities in Turkey well into the 20th century. They maintained a 'Jewish' identity, rejecting intermarriage with Muslims, but repudiated many traditional Jewish laws. [73] (G.W.)

al-Shāfiʿī, Abū ʿAbd Allāh Muḥammad ibn Idrīs [XII] (767–820). Muslim jurist, eponymous patron of the Shāfiʿī school of law. The biographical sources give an idealized vision of his life, and many details are merely extensions of school polemics. It is said that he was born in 767, on the day that ABŪ ḤANĪFA (also founder of a law school) died, a useful symbolic coincidence, but there is no unanimity about the day nor the year. Being poor, he had to struggle for his education which took place mostly in Mecca. He was a member of the Quraysh family, and thus related both to MUḤAMMAD and to the first two ruling dynasties of Islam. This relationship was exploited to bolster his authority. After an early education devoted to Arabic language, poetry and tribal lore, he was converted to divine law by a vision, featuring, some say, Muḥammad. His training as a jurist was dominated by the personality of MĀLIK, who taught him in Medina, and whose school, broadly, he followed. Some trouble in politics brought him to the court of Hārūn al-Rashīd where, it is said, his fluent tongue alone saved him from execution. His juristic skills were further sharpened by attention to the works and person of AL-SHAYBĀNĪ, whom he defeated in many debates – according to the Shāfiʿī tradition. From 188 hijrī till his death in 204 he resided either in Baghdad or Egypt, both of which areas preserved his opinions and writings, leading to a double corpus of Iraqi and Egyptian works. He died and was buried in Egypt, where his grave became and still is a centre of pilgrimage and veneration.

Al-Shāfiʿī's jurisprudence is described as having every appropriate quality, even contradictory ones. Many anecdotes relate that he never debated merely to win, but rather to establish the truth; but we see him debating with al-Shaybānī, and taking up successively, and winning, both sides of a question. His real importance (or that of his school) lies in his absolute commitment to Prophetic traditions and the Qur'ān as the only valid bases for juristic argument; and in his elaboration of a methodology for interpreting revealed texts. His *Risāla* is the earliest and still one of the most brilliant works on the hermeneutic disciplines. Other schools accommodated themselves over time to his views. His other major work, now called the *Umm* ('Guidance'), is a huge compendium of Islamic law, incorporating some methodological treatises. The recensions that have survived are very late and seem to include divergent Egyptian and Iraqi elements, a feature which has ensured flexibility within the school tradition. Parallel strategies for a multiplication of views may be found in other schools. [112] (N.C.)

Shahrokh, Kay Khosrow [XXVI] (*d.*1940). Distinguished Zoroastrian layman from Kerman. As a boy he was sent by HATARIA to study in Bombay, and returned eager to serve his country and community. In 1909 he was elected the first Zoroastrian deputy to the Majles (Parliament), and served there for over 30 years. Largely through him, Zoroastrian month names were adopted in the new national calendar; and he persuaded most of his coreligionists to observe the *faṣlī* calendar (*see* CAMA, KHARSHEDJI RUSTAMJI). He wrote two books, *Āyīn-ī Mazdēsnān* and *Furūgh-ī Mazdēsnān*, introducing Parsi reformist ideas to the Irani Zoroastrians, i.e. he maintained that ZOROASTER taught a simple monotheism, high morality and virtually no observances. [20: vol. 2: 93–5] (M.B.)

Shan-tao [IV] (613–681). Patriarch of Chinese Pure Land Buddhism. Shan-tao is usually considered one of a group of three illustrious Chinese Pure Land masters. The first, T'an-luan (476–542) is known for his spirituality and his efforts to disseminate the teachings and practices of Pure Land Buddhism in all areas of Chinese society. T'an-luan was an important influence on SHINRAN, the Japanese founder of the Shin ('true') Pure Land school. The second, Tao-cho (562–645), wrote the *An-lo chi* ('Essays on the Land of Bliss'), which advocated the practice of *nien-fo* (meditating on or reciting the name of the Buddha) to be reborn in the Buddha's Pure Land, in light of the belief that his age had entered the 'latter days' of the corrupt *dharma*.

Tao-cho and Shan-tao are considered the major founders of the Chinese Pure Land tradition. Shan-tao's most important work is his commentary on the *Sūtra on Contemplating Amitābha*. In this text Shan-tao outlines five 'correct' practices for attaining rebirth in Amitābha's Pure Land in the west: chanting the sūtras, meditating on the features of the Pure Land, offering worship to Amitābha, chanting the name of Amitābha, and offering praises to Amitābha. Chanting the name is considered the primary practice. This text also contains the famous parable of the 'white road between two rivers', in which a man travelling to the west comes upon a narrow path threatened by a river of fire to the south and a river of raging water to the north. The man is pursued from behind by bandits. Just when all seems hopeless, a figure at the other side of the path beckons and encourages him to proceed upon the path. Upon doing so the man is saved and joins his good friends on the western side. The figure, of course, is Amitābha, who encourages all people to follow the pure and narrow path of faith to escape this world of sorrow and tribulation and experience rebirth in the Pure Land. [31: 346–7; 67] (P.L.S.)

Shapurji Saklatvala. *See* SAKLATVALA, SHAPURJI.

Sharīʿatī, ʿAlī [XII] (1933–1977). Leading lay theorist of modern revolutionary Shiʿism. Born the son of a cleric in Eastern Iran, he received a traditional religious education combined with secular instruction at a secondary school and a teacher training college in Mashhad. By his late teens he had become active in nationalist politics, and in 1957, while working as a schoolmaster, he was arrested along with his father and imprisoned for an unspecified period.

Between 1960 and 1964 Sharīʿatī carried out doctoral studies in Paris; his dissertation is popularly supposed to have been in sociology, but was, in fact, in medieval Iranian philology. Much legend attaches to this period, with rumours of close associations with prominent French intellectuals such as Sartre and FANON. What is certain is that he became sensitized to Third World issues, contributing to an Algerian nationalist newspaper and organizing Iranian student opposition to the Pahlavis.

Returning to Iran, he was again imprisoned for six months, but soon secured a post at Mashhad University, where he introduced a popular course on the sociology of Islam. Soon dismissed, he came to Tehran about 1965 and began to teach at the newly-established Ḥusayniyya Irshād, a Shiʿite establishment where much of the intellectual foundation for the Islamic Revolution was laid. In 1973 the government closed the institution and arrested Sharīʿatī. Released after two years, he spent a further two in internal exile before travelling to London, where he died of heart failure.

His published lectures gave new political force to traditional religious concepts and had a powerful impact on large numbers of young Iranians. More than anyone, he was responsible for the idea that Shiʿism had degenerated from a movement of active social protest into mere pietism and that it had to be revived as a political force against Western influence. [117; 118; 119] (D.M.)

Shar-rdza Bkra-shis rgyal-mtshan [XXV] (1859–1935). Monk from Shar-rdza, 'Eastern Rdza', a district in east Tibet (Khams). He was an adherent of the Bön religion (*see* GSHEN-RAB MI-BO-CHE), the religious tradition which, while heavily influenced by Buddhism in matters of doctrine and practice, has nevertheless maintained a separate identity through its claim to represent the true, pre-Buddhist religion of Tibet.

Although his loyalty to Bön never wavered, Shar-rdza Bkra-shis rgyal-mtshan is in fact known as a major figure within the so-called Eclectic (*ris-med*) Movement which was particularly active in east Tibet in the 19th century. This movement was characterized by its disregard of the sectarian divisions between the various schools of Tibetan Buddhism, as well as between Buddhism and Bön. To a considerable extent the Eclectic Movement was inspired by the Great Perfection (*rdzogs-chen*) school of meditation, which emphasized spontaneous enlightenment and propagated a monistic philosophy, ignoring sectarian and doctrinal differences. As far as Bön is concerned, the Eclectic Movement was to some extent identified with the so-called 'New Bön' (*bon-gsar*), which, starting perhaps in the 13th century, strove to provide a historical and philosophical basis for a *rapprochement* between Bön and Buddhism. Shar-rdza Bkra-shis rgyal-mtshan is counted among the masters of New Bön, although he is venerated by all adherents of Bön.

Shar-rdza Bkra-shis rgyal-mtshan was a prolific and learned author; his complete works comprise some 18 volumes. His major work is the five-volume *Mdzod-lnga* ('Five Treasuries'), which includes the *Dbyings-rig mdzod* ('The Treasury of the Knowledge of Infinite Space'), a detailed exposition of the Great Perfection, and the *Legs-bshad mdzod* ('The Treasury of Good Sayings'), a comprehensive history of the Bön religion. The central portion of the latter has been translated into English [2].

Shar-rdza Bkra-shis rgyal-mtshan travelled widely in east and north-east Tibet. He is highly venerated today by all adherents of Bön, and his memory is particularly honoured in the important Rtogs-ldan Monastery in Rnga-ba (Amdo), as well as in numerous lesser monasteries. In the same way as other adepts of the Great Perfection, he is believed to have transformed himself into a 'rainbow-body' (*'ja'-lus*) at death, i.e. having left no physical remains behind.

There exists a biography, written by his disciple Bskal-bzang bstan-pa'i rgyal-mtshan in 1949. [2: 15–16] (P.K.)

al-Shaybānī, Muḥammad ibn Ḥasan [XII] (749–805). Muslim jurist of Kūfa, pupil to ABŪ ḤANĪFA and ABŪ YŪSUF. He moved to Baghdad in middle life, where, it is said, he gained the notice of Hārūn al-Rashīd. He may have been appointed judge at Raqqa, but accounts are vague and may represent a tendentious elevation of an authority who was deemed to merit both rank and office. Biographical sources, which are largely extensions of school polemic, depict him as a person of outstanding intellect and debating skill, a position confirmed in the mouths of rival authorities. AL-SHĀFIʿĪ had never seen anyone so physically fat, so mentally agile; nor ever debated with anyone who did not pall at the prospect, save al-Shaybānī. IBN ḤANBAL, asked where he had acquired his subtlety in jurisprudence, replied that he had learned it from the books of al-Shaybānī. A considerable number of books are attributed to al-Shaybānī, notable among them the monument *al Kitāb al-Aṣl* ('The Source'), a compendium of what were probably originally separate treatises, combined in such a way as to catch all aspects of religious and social life in the network of the Law. His most characteristic work is *al-Jāmiʿ al-kabīr* ('The Great Collection'). Depicting the quality of this work to a non-expert is not easy, but it has been attempted: 'Al-Shaybānī in his "Great Collection" is like a man who builds a building. As he builds it higher he builds a stairway by which he ascends, to raise the height of the building; until he completes it. Then he descends, destroys the stairway, and, turning to the people, he says, Now get to the top.' The work is a primer for advanced students, containing only the knottiest of problems, few of them of common or likely occurrence. It represents the fact that concern for the law was not merely a matter of practical life (though it was that) but also an exploration of concepts and ideas, articulated through hypothetical cases. [34: 'Shaibānī'] (N.C.)

Shembe, Isaiah [I.A] (1870–1935). Founder of the Nazirite Baptist Church or AmaNazaretha, one of South Africa's largest independent churches; he is widely revered as a black Messiah. A South African Zulu who was never formally educated, Shembe was baptized into the African Native Baptist Church. In 1911 he founded his own Nazirite Baptist Church (amaNazaretha). He claimed to be the king of his people and adopted many traditional Zulu leadership patterns and customs into the new church. A messianic figure whom many believed to have the power of healing and to be a hymn writer of genius, he established the holy village of Ekuphakameni near Durban in 1916. In the same year, he was inspired by a vision to go to the Nhlangakazi mountain in Natal, which has since become an important annual festival centre for the Nazirites. Shembe was later imprisoned by state authorities, and died in captivity in 1935. He was buried with great honours at Ekuphakameni; Nazirites consider the mausoleum constructed there to be holy and flock there in great numbers every July. His status as a Black Christ is in part legitimated by the belief that he wrote several hymns following his resurrection [34: 286]. Church leadership was passed down to his son, Johannes Galilee Shembe (*d.*1976), the same year that a major split in the movement occurred. [27; 33: 161–205, 326–9; 34: 196–7, 281–9, 328–30] (R.H.)

Shen-hsiu [IV] [Japanese: Jinshu] (606?–706). The major figure in the Northern school of early Chinese Ch'an Buddhism. An innovator in Ch'an doctrine, Shen-hsiu's historical accomplishments contrast with the largely negative image of him found in HUI-NENG's *Platform Sūtra* [261] and subsequent orthodox Ch'an texts.

Shen-hsiu was born to an aristocratic family during the early years of the 7th century. As a youth he travelled around central and south-eastern China studying Buddhist doctrine and monastic discipline.

Beginning in 651 he practised meditation for a few years at Huang-mei in modern Hunan province under Hung-jen (601–674), who is remembered as the fifth patriarch of Ch'an. During the early 660s Shen-hsiu was active under the name Wei-hsiu in Ch'ang-an, where he acted along with the biographer and Vinaya specialist Tao-hsüan in support of the independence of the Buddhist *saṅgha*.

Shen-hsiu's most productive period of teaching (675–700) took place at Yü-ch'üan ssu, a former residence of the great T'ien-t'ai CHIH-I. Shen-hsiu began to teach after Hung-jen's death, and left in 701 to return to Ch'ang-an. Arriving at the invitation of the EMPRESS WU CHAO, who did obeisance to him as her personal teacher, Shen-hsiu lectured in the palace and generated great interest in his interpretation of Buddhism as an exhortation to vigorous meditational practice.

Although he wrote only one text, the *Kuan-hsin lun* ('Treatise on the Contemplation of Mind'), Shen-hsiu was widely associated with the use of 'expedient means' (*upāya*; *fang-pien*). In textual terms this refers to the radical reinterpretation of conventional Buddhist doctrinal formulations as metaphors for the 'contemplation of mind'. In practical terms it refers to the spontaneous interaction between teacher and student, and thus constitutes the foundation of subsequent Ch'an 'encounter dialogue' practice. [135: 94–102, 158–9; 156] (J.M.)

Shen-hui [IV] (684–758). An important figure in early Chinese Ch'an Buddhism. Probably initially a student of SHEN-HSIU of the so-called Northern school, Shen-hui is known primarily as a disciple of HUI-NENG.

In 730 Shen-hui began a series of public lectures denouncing the Northern school (a pejorative label of his devising) as unorthodox and inferior. Branding it gradualist in spiritual training and dualistic in doctrine, he campaigned vigorously on behalf of Hui-neng's acceptance as sixth patriarch of Ch'an. This campaign was continued after his move to Lo-yang in 745, and in 753 Shen-hui was banished, perhaps because of pressure by Northern school proponents, for attracting excessive crowds. In 757, however, he returned to imperial favour by collecting money for the government forces, which had been weakened by the An Lu-shan rebellion of 755, by selling ordination certificates.

Shen-hui is unique among early Ch'an figures in having extant texts from different periods of his life: the *Platform Sermon* contains his early teachings, the *Definition of the Truth of the Southern School of Bodhidharma* is an edited rendition of a polemical sermon, and the *Miscellaneous Dialogues* contains later material. There also exist teachings set in the form of popular songs.

Shen-hui's most important idea was that awakening occurs suddenly and is followed by gradual self-improvement, rather than vice versa. He was an excellent storyteller, and this and his sharp criticisms combined to turn Ch'an masters to the use of exemplary anecdote rather than logical formulation. Although largely forgotten by the orthodox tradition, Shen-hui's ideas and functionalist campaign had a major impact on the *Platform Sūtra*, which was first compiled about 780. In modern times his works were discovered by the historian Hu Shih (1891–1962), and have been instrumental in the reassessment of early Ch'an Buddhism. [31: 353–4; 136: 1–11, 145–7; 156] (J.M.)

Shes-rab rgyal-mtshan [XXV] (1356–1415). Monk from Rgya-mo-rong in the extreme east of Tibet. He is regarded as the most important ecclesiastical figure within the Bön religion, second only to the Enlightened Teacher of Bön, GSHEN-RAB MI-BO-CHE, hence his common titles Mnyam-med ('the Incomparable'), and Rgyal-ba gnyis-pa ('the Second Conqueror', i.e. Enlightened One).

He pursued extensive studies in logic and metaphysics under various Buddhist masters in central Tibet, and gradually became famous as a great scholar and teacher. In 1405 he founded the monastery of Sman-ri in Gtsang in central Tibet. This monastery has remained the spiritual centre of the Bön religion, and its abbots (the present one, the 33rd, currently lives in exile in India) are regarded as the heads of Bön. Sman-ri has remained famous for its strict monastic discipline and intensive spiritual practice.

Shes-rab rgyal-mtshan played a crucial role in the history of the Bön religion, similar to that played by the great TSONG-KHA-PA (whom he is reported to have met) in Tibetan Buddhism. Both lived in a formative period of Tibetan history during which religious life was further institutionalized within the bounds of rapidly expanding monasteries.

Shes-rab rgyal-mtshan organized monastic life according to a pattern which a large number of Bön monasteries, perhaps the majority, have followed until today, and set a standard of scholastic excellence which was rarely if ever to be surpassed. [2: 140–45] (P.K.)

Shin Arahan [IV]. Legendary monk in the history of Buddhism in Burma, said to have lived in the 11th century. Shin Arahan collaborated with King Anawrahta (Aniruddha) (reigned 1044–77) in the restoration of Buddhist orthodoxy in Burma and in a purification of the Burmese monastic order. In Burmese tradition the establishment of a pure Theravāda in Burma is traced to the actions of these two.

What we know of Shin Arahan's life is sketchy and complicated by conflicting accounts in various Burmese monastic chronicles. He is said to be from Thaton in lower Burma, the son of a Brahman and trained in the Vedas. His monastic name after ordination was Dhammadassī and he was an ascetical forest monk. The biography of Shin Arahan often serves as a founding charter for various monastic factions in Burma, and his ordination lineage is traced variously through Sri Lanka, the forest monks of Upper Burma, or the missionaries that are said to have been sent to Burma by King Aśoka. The *Sāsanavaṃsa* says that although there are different accounts of Shin Arahan: 'the fact that the Elder Arahanta (Shin Arahan) came to Arimaddana (Pagan) and established the religion there is alone sufficient here. It should not be undervalued.' [138: 67]

Shin Arahan converted Anawrahta, and the two of them purified the Burmese *saṅgha* of an unorthodox group of monks known as the Ari, whom Shin Arahan regarded as 'sham ascetics'. On Shin Arahan's advice, Anawrahta brought a set of Pali scriptures from Thaton. The paradigm of a pure textual tradition combined with a purified monastic order effected by the collaboration of a strong king and a great monk, represented in ideal fashion by Shin Arahan and Anawrahta, became a persistent theme in Burmese Buddhist history. [138: VI; 157: I] (C.H.)

Shinran [IV] (1173–1262). Founder of the *Jōdo Shinshū* (True Pure Land Sect) of Japanese Buddhism. Shinran lived as a Tendai *dōsō* (menial monk) on Mt Hiei outside Kyoto from 1181 till 1201. This life of various Buddhist practices brought him to the conviction that he could not reach liberation by his own efforts. In 1201 he left Mt Hiei to join the community of Hōnen in Kyoto and 'abandoned the difficult practices and took refuge in the Primal Vow' of Amida. In 1207 he was sent into exile to Echigo province (present Niigata prefecture), where he married and started a family of seven or eight children, declaring himself to be 'neither monk nor lay'. Life among the common people of the provinces put a deep mark on his spirituality. Pardoned, he migrated to the Kantō region in 1214, to propagate his Pure Land doctrine. Around 1235 he returned to Kyoto and lived there quietly until his death, forever emending his *magnum opus*, the *Kyōgyōshinshō* ('True Teaching, Practice and Realization of the Pure Land Way'), a reasoned anthology of passages on the Pure Land Way found in the sūtras and the writings of the 'patriarchs' of Pure Land Buddhism, plus many short treatises and hymns in the vernacular (*wasan*) for the instruction of the common people. After his death one of his disciples, Yuienbō, collected some of his sayings into the *Tannishō* ('Treatise Lamenting Dissensions'), possibly the most popular religious booklet in Japan.

Like Hōnen, of whom he considered himself the loyal disciple, Shinran carried on the Indo-Chinese Pure Land tradition. At the same time, however, he radicalized it by way of a very personal reinterpretation of the transmitted texts. Thereby his doctrine came to show a marked originality over against that of his master. While Hōnen felt the need to stress the independence of the Pure Land Way over against the 'Path of the Sages' (self-power Mahāyāna) by rejecting many of its notions (e.g., original awakening, *bodhicitta* and, in general, the wisdom tradition), Shinran tends to reinterpret these same notions so as to reconcile them with the basic tenets of the Pure Land Way. While Hōnen found his inspiration mainly in the *Meditation Sūtra* and Shan-tao (631–681), Shinran sees the *Larger Pure Land Sūtra* as *the* true doctrine and relied much on the other Chinese patriarch, Tanluan (476–542).

Shinran rids the Pure Land Way of all lingering traces of self-reliance. All activity of salvation is exclusively Amida's doing and the role of sentient beings is one of pure receptivity. Thus, transference of merits (*ekō*) does not occur among sentient beings but only from Amida to us; the *nenbutsu* is no longer seen as a work we perform as a condition for salvation, but as a spontaneous echo in us of the mutual *nenbutsu* of the Buddhas (17th Vow); and faith itself is the working of Amida without any contribution on our part. Shinran also redirects the future-oriented (toward the moment of death and the Pure Land after death) Pure Land religiosity towards the present by centring everything on the 'one moment of faith' in this life. [20; 21; 209; 241; 259] (J.V.B.)

Shiv Dayal Singh [XI] (1818–1878). The first guru of the Radhasoamis. He was born in Agra into a Khatri banking family of Punjabi origin. He soon abandoned a career as a Persian teacher to devote himself to the service of the family guru, one Tulsi Sahib of the nearby town of Hathras. In the fashion typical of so many Indian religious movements, the extent of Shiv Dayal's indebtedness to this somewhat shadowy figure is less evident than the degree to which the subsequent appeal of Radhasoami ideas has derived from their systematic formulation by his successor RAI SALIGRAM. It was, indeed, only on the latter's urging that Shiv Dayal was induced to proclaim in 1861 the formal existence of a Radhasoami Satsang embracing his followers. Shiv Dayal's teachings are contained in two unsystematic collections of Hindi prose and verse, both entitled *Sār bacan* ('Essential Utterances'). Much speculation has been devoted to his description of God as Radhasoami, i.e. Rādhā plus *svāmī* ('Lord'), a seemingly original coinage whose apparent Vaiṣṇava connotations are belied by the uncompromisingly impersonal character of his theology. Further confusions have arisen from Rai Saligram's application of 'Radhasoamiji' as an honorific to Shiv Dayal himself as the incarnation of the Supreme Being, or from his more usual title of Soamiji, inappropriately suggesting a Radha-role for his wife Naraini Devi [74: 25–9]. Vaiṣṇava devotionalism has in fact no place in Shiv Dayal's teachings, which reject all idol-worship and ritual in favour of the *nirguṇ* path of loving devotion to an impersonal God. This is to be successfully accomplished only through *guru-bhakti*, the devotion of the company of the faithful (*satsang*) to the one true guru (*santsatguru*), since he alone can guide the devotee in the inner spiritual discipline called *surat-śabd-yoga*, through which the divine spirit in man (*surat*) can be liberated through establishing contact with the eternal sound-current (*śabd*). [32: 163–7; 74: III] (C.S.)

Shneour Zalman of Lyady [XV] (1745–1813). Ḥasidic rabbi. A child prodigy, he was encouraged by his teacher, DOV BER OF MEZHIRICH, to compile a reworking of the authoritative code of JOSEPH CARO, the *Shulḥan Arukh*, as a guide for Ḥasidim, and also to show that they faithfully observed the traditional commandments.

When ELIJAH BEN SOLOMON ZALMAN, the Vilna Ga'on, launched a bitter campaign against the Ḥasidim, Shneour Zalman tried to see him to make peace but Elijah refused to have him admitted and increased their persecution. Shneour Zalman, who was regarded as the leader of the Ḥasidim in Belorussia, attracting thousands of followers, took the lead in rebutting the attacks of the Vilna Ga'on. In 1799 a hostile informer accused him of treachery and blasphemy. He was arrested by the Russian authorities and imprisoned in St Petersburg. After investigation he was set free; the anniversary of his release was observed annually as a day of celebration by his followers. The following year he was again slandered and arrested for a brief period. His imprisonments became the subject of many legends. In 1804 he settled in Lyady, Belorussia, where he taught and wrote. With the approach of Napoleon, he forecast the Russian victory and fled to the Russian interior, dying on the journey. [42: 51–75]

Shneour Zalman founded a new stream of Ḥasidism founded on reason, rather than the emotional approach of the other Ḥasidic trends. Called *Ḥabad* (acronym of the Hebrew for 'wisdom, understanding, knowledge'), it became highly influential, and the Lubavich dynasty which he established (today centred in Brooklyn, New York) remains one of the most widespread of Ḥasidic groups, with extensive educational programs in many parts of the world. According to Shneour Zalman, the Ḥasidic leader is a spiritual guide rather than a wonder-worker or mediator with the divine, as taught by other Ḥasidic leaders. His classic work was *Likkutei*

Amarim ('Collected Sayings'; better known as *Tanya*, 'It is taught') which presents both an exposition of Ḥasidism and a commentary on the basic Jewish creed, the *Shema* ('Hear O Israel the Lord your God, the Lord is one': *Deuteronomy* 6:4). He combined a passionate and intellectual approach to Judaism, teaching that the commandments must be kept as a result of knowledge, with study of the Torah as the supreme value. [40: 122–33; 53: 178–204] (G.W.)

Shoghi Effendi [III] [Rabbānī] (1897–1957). Head of the Bahā'ī religion from 1921 to 1957. A great-grandson of the movement's founder, BAHĀ' ALLĀH, Shoghi Effendi was born into the Bahā'ī exile community at Acre in Palestine. He moved to Haifa as a child and was educated there and at the Syrian Protestant College (later the American University) in Beirut. He also studied briefly at Oxford, but was forced to abandon his studies there on the death of his grandfather, 'ABD AL-BAHĀ', who designated him in his will as 'Guardian of the Cause of God' (*valī-yi amr Allāh*) and his successor as head of the faith.

Shoghi Effendi's appointment proved exceptionally astute. An intelligent and dedicated man, he combined a traditional upbringing with a western education, and under his leadership Bahā'īsm underwent radical transitions that laid the basis for its subsequent international spread and internal reorganization. There already existed small convert communities in Europe and North America, and it was to these rather than the larger but more conservative Bahā'ī communities of the Middle East that he directed his attention.

A natural if somewhat autocratic organizer, he encouraged western communities to systematize their affairs under an increasingly bureaucratic administrative system based on elected local and national assemblies and incorporating western methods of business management. From 1937 he inaugurated a series of national and international plans designed to expand the Bahā'ī organization and widen the field of proselytization.

He himself remained in Palestine, where he displayed much energy and creativity in establishing the buildings and gardens that were to form the basis for the Bahā'ī World Centre. He never visited Bahā'ī communities abroad or permitted any form of cult based on his own personality.

His own letters to individuals, communities and, from the 1950s, to 'the Bahā'ī World', were important sources of inspiration and instruction for his growing international community. More significantly, his original writings (notably a historical work entitled *God Passes By*) and his English translations of works by Bahā' Allāh proved landmarks in the systematization of Bahā'ī historical theory and doctrine.

His English letters have been collected in several volumes, among which the best known are *The Advent of Divine Justice*, *The Promised Day is Come*, and *The World Order of Baha'u'llah*. Although their style is heavily rhetorical and archaic, these are nonetheless forceful presentations of the world view he sought to inculcate, and remain to the present day central non-scriptural texts within the Bahā'ī canon.

Shoghi Effendi died on 4 November 1957 and was buried in London, where his grave is now a site of pilgrimage. Since he died childless and had by then excommunicated almost all his own family, a direct succession was in doubt. His grandfather's will had intended him to be the first of a line of guardians; but following the election of a body known as the 'Universal House of Justice' in 1963, it was decreed that no successor could be found or appointed. Shoghi thus ceased to be the 'first Guardian' and became 'the Guardian' *par excellence*. [14; 17; 19; 21; 22; 23] (D.M.)

Shōmu, Emperor [IV] (701–756). Emperor of Japan (45th in the traditional list, reigned 724–749; an early patron of Buddhism.) Emperor Shōmu was a devout believer of Buddhism, and his support allowed the relatively new schools of Buddhism to gain a strong following in Japan. Shōmu instituted the establishment of national temples (Kokubun-ji) throughout the country, in imitation of the Ta-yün ('great cloud') temples of the Chinese Empress WU CHAO. He planned and built the Great Buddha (*daibutsu*), a huge image of Mahāvairocana at Tōdai-ji in Nara, to symbolize national unity and the central role of the Emperor. GYŌGI was asked to assist in raising funds to pay for this project. Emperor Shōmu was the first Japanese Emperor to declare himself a servant of the three treasures (Buddha, *dharma*, *saṅgha*) of Buddhism. [120: 42–4] (P.L.S.)

Shōtoku Taishi [IV] (574–622). Prince regent during the reign of Empress Suiko (reigned 593–628) and early supporter and interpreter of Buddhism. Prince Shōtoku was a distinguished statesman and devout follower of Buddhism who contributed greatly both to the political development of Japan and the early progress of Buddhism in Japan. He sent embassies to China which opened the way for Chinese Buddhism and culture to enter and flourish in Japan. In 604 he promulgated the so-called 'Seventeen-Article Constitution', more a set of moral injunctions than a set of laws, which included the admonition to 'revere the three treasures (Buddha, *dharma*, *saṅgha*) . . .' He also supported the building of temples such as Asukadera, Shittenō-ji, and Hōryū-ji.

Shōtoku is credited with composing commentaries on three major Mahāyāna texts, the *Lotus Sūtra*, *Vimalakīrti Sūtra* and *Śrīmālādevī Sūtra*, all of which have proven to be important texts for Japanese Buddhism. Shōtoku's last testament to his wife, that 'the world is an illusion; only the Buddha is real' reveals, for his time, an uncommon insight with regard to Buddhist teachings.

Shōtoku was revered by many Buddhists throughout Japanese history, including major personalities such as SAICHŌ, and he remains a figure much admired for his political accomplishments and religious devotion. [20: 24–34] (P.L.S.)

Shroff, Behramshah Naoroji [XXVI] (1858–1927). Parsi religious teacher whose message started a movement known as 'Ilm-i Khshnoom', popularly interpreted as 'Science of (Spiritual) Satisfaction'. He was brought up in Surat and lacked any substantial education. When he was 18 years old he left home after a disagreement with his mother and travelled north. Near Peshawar he is said to have come into contact with a caravan of secret Zoroastrians, who led him to a colony of Zoroastrian spiritual masters living in a hidden place in Mount Demavend in Iran. There the material and spiritual treasures from pre-Islamic Zoroastrian Iran are preserved. He stayed in this Paradise (Firdaus) for three years. Before he entered Firdaus he is said to have stuttered and to have been illiterate; he left it a powerful orator, an interpreter of ancient texts and the possessor of occult powers. The only other persons thought to have entered Firdaus are an Iranian astrologer, Rustom Nazoomie, concerning whom nothing is known and Revd Dr Otoman Zardusht, who started the Mazdyasnan Society in Oregon. From 1881 to 1891 Shroff travelled around India meeting other spiritual masters. Until 1907 he remained silent, thereafter his teaching mission began, first in Surat then in Bombay [39]. His teaching is essentially a Zoroastrianized form of theosophy (*see* BLAVATSKY, HELENA PETROVNA), accepting the idea of reincarnation, vegetarianism, the belief in occult powers, a commitment to the mystical powers of traditional rites and prayers in the ancient language which are thought to produce powerful vibrations which may harm the uninitiated but benefit the initiated.

His teachings have been followed by numerous Zoroastrians, though since no separate ritual practice or centre is required, and no formal membership is involved, numbers cannot be estimated. His early exponents were two pairs of brothers, F. S. and J. S. Chiniwalla [13] and F. S. and D. S. Masani [40], but his appeal stretched to include many of the leading contemporary Zoroastrian writers, notably KHARSHEDJI RUSTAMJI CAMA and the scholarly Secretary of the Bombay Parsi Punchayet, Sir JAMSHEDJI JIVANJI MODI. The claim of direct mystical insight and affirmation of the value of the traditional religion and homeland was, presumably, an inspiration compared to what seemed the arid nature of scholarly writing. In the 1980s there were two different interpreters of Shroff, (Mrs) Meher Master Moos, who asserts that she has access to hitherto unknown manuscripts of Shroff's writing [46], and K. Dastoor, who is a respected figure among many orthodox Parsis [15]. The followers of another interpreter of Shroff, Minocher Pundol (1908–1975), believe that he too entered the Firdaus. They emphasize the importance of purity laws and pilgrimages to important holy sites, and have opened a temple close by the most revered of all temples, that in the village of Udwada, where the fire still burns that was consecrated soon after the Parsi arrival in India in the 10th century.

This act and his teaching concerning the effects of some pilgrimages are considered heretical by many orthodox Parsis. (J.R.H.)

Shwegyin Sayadaw [IV] (1822–1893). Founder of a reformist sect within the Buddhist monastic order in Burma during the reign of MINDON MIN; this sect now bears his name. Sayadaw is a title of respect for a Buddhist monk in Burma; in the case of the Shwegyin Sayadaw, the title is used with the name of his birthplace, Shwegyin, near Shwebo in upper Burma. He was ordained as a monk there with the monastic name Jagara. Quite early in his monastic career, the Shwegyin Sayadaw developed a reputation as a Buddhist scholar, especially in the code of monastic discipline (*Vinaya*). He also had associations with the reformist and ascetic forest monk movement centering on the Shangegyun Sayadaw.

The Shwegyin Sayadaw was invited to the new capital Mandalay in 1861 by Mindon, who built a monastery for him there and made him a royal tutor. The Shwegyin either insulted or was insulted by – accounts of the event differ – the head of the Burmese monastic order, and he asked Mindon's permission to leave the capital and return to a forest hermitage. Mindon decided that the Shwegyin and his reformist followers were no longer to be subject to the authority of the central leadership of the monastic order. The existence of the Shwegyin sect within the Burmese monkhood can be traced to this decision.

Mindon continued to give royal patronage to the Shwegyin's group and honours to the Shwegyin Sayadaw, helping the sect to prosper. But the Shwegyin Sayadaw was able to keep his independence from the king as well. He did not take part in Mindon's Buddhist Council, and spent increasing amounts of time in British-controlled lower Burma, or at forest retreats. He visited the holy places of Sri Lanka even though Mindon refused him permission to go.

When Thibaw became king in 1878 the Shwegyin Sayadaw was appointed one of the two heads of the monastic order, although he did not assume any leadership role. He was not recognized by the British as a monastic leader after they overthrew Thibaw in 1885, but his fame continued to grow, extending to Sri Lanka and Thailand, up to his death in 1893.

In his actions and teachings, the Shwegyin Sayadaw emphasized the ascetic ideals of Buddhist monasticism as a response to cultural change. His life has continued to serve as an inspiring and unifying example for Burmese reformers within the Buddhist monastic order. [157: II; 215: V] (C.H.)

Siddhasena Divākara [XIII] Jain logician who can very tentatively be located in the fourth century of the Christian era [27]. Although probably a member of the Śvetāmbara sect, some of his writings show close links with Digambara works. The celebrated Indian Jainologist A. N. Upadhye argued on the basis of this and later inscriptional evidence that Siddhasena was a member of the Yāpanīya sect, which seems to have incorporated both Śvetāmbara and Digambara elements into its monastic practice and doctrinal tenets. [26: XV–XVI]

The general features of Siddhasena's biography are of a legendary nature. After synthesizing this material, which mostly dates from the medieval period, it is possible to identify the incidents in his life which Jain tradition was to find particularly significant. It should be emphasized, however, that the bulk of this biographical material is more interested in Siddhasena's exercising of supernormal powers which he had attained through mastery of a book of magic than with any serious consideration of his intellectual career.

Siddhasena was originally a Brahman who was converted to Jainism after being defeated in debate by the logician Vṛddhavādin. Siddhasena's learning subsequently led to him becoming associated with the court of the legendary King Vikramāditya of Ujjain; such was his fame there that he was given the epithet 'Sun' (*divākara*). Indeed, one of the biographies states that Siddhasena became so attached to the honour that was bestowed upon him that Vṛddhavādin had to warn him of its possible evil consequences. One of the most interesting episodes connected with him is his supposed banishment from the monastic community for 12 years for proposing that the scriptures of the Śvetāmbara canon be translated from their original Prakrit into Sanskrit so that they might become more widely disseminated. During this period of exile, he miraculously caused a phallic emblem (*liṅga*) of the Hindu god Śiva to split asunder and reveal an image of the *tīrthaṅkara* PĀRŚVA within.

Siddhasena's real significance for Jainism lies in his development of a purely Jain logic, with his 'Descent of Logic' (*Nyāyāvatāra*) being the earliest Jain work solely devoted to the subject [27]. However, it is his Prakrit 'Examination of the True Doctrine' (*Sanmatitarka*) that is his most significant work, especially the second chapter, which contains a highly important account of epistemology [28]. Siddhasena is here concerned with the structure of omniscience, the enlightenment which provides the central authority for all the tenets of the Jain faith. The Śvetāmbara scriptures had divided omniscience into two elements, general cognition (*jñāna*) and specific cognition (*darśana*), and had stated that these occurred in succession in the enlightened person. Siddhasena attacked this notion, arguing that the two types of cognition took place simultaneously and were, in effect, identical. This dispute was the only major disagreement about a point of metaphysics that took place in the history of Jainism.

Another work of Siddhasena's is 'The Thirty-twos' (*Dvātriṃśika*), 21 verse treatises, nearly all of which contain 32 verses. Written in highly poetical Sanskrit, they are of a mainly devotional or philosophical nature (although treatise 11 is a eulogy of an unknown king, possibly Siddhasena's patron) and show a close familiarity with the Brahmanical metaphysical systems. Also worthy of note is the *Kalyāṇamandirastotra*, a devotional poem to Pārśva, still in use today, which is ascribed to Siddhasena, although it is unlikely that he did compose it. (P.D.)

Silouan, St [VI.B] [Silouan Antenov] (1866–1938). Russian Orthodox *starets.* A peasant from Tambov province, on finishing his military service in 1892 he went to Mt Athos. At the Monastery of St Panteleimon, Silouan became famous as a *starets.* His disciple, Archimandrite Sophrony, founded the Monastery of Tolleshunt Knights in Essex. [82; 83] (D.B.)

Simeon Stylites, St [VI.B] (390–459). The son of a shepherd from Cilicia, Simeon lived in various Syrian monasteries and hermitages before moving in 423 to Telanissus and living on a high pillar to avoid the crowds who came to see him. Others who followed his example include Daniel (409–493), Simeon the Younger (*d.*592) and Alypius the Cionite (*d.*640). Vast ruins remain of the massive church and pilgrimage centre that were built around the saint's pillar. [56: V; 92] (D.B.)

Simeon the New Theologian, St *See* SYMEON THE NEW THEOLOGIAN, ST.

Simon Magus [IX] (1st century). The Simonians, a gnostic sect of the 2nd and 3rd centuries, were supposed to have originated with Simon Magus, though some scholars suggest that JUSTIN MARTYR has confused Simon Magus with another Simon, of Gitta, who may rather have been a 2nd-century Gnostic. According to *Acts* 8:9–24 Simon Magus was known as 'the power of God which is called Great' and practised magic in Samaria. After believing the preaching of Philip, he was baptized. Subsequently he tried to acquire spiritual gifts for money and was rebuked by PETER THE APOSTLE. Hippolytus records other clashes with Peter in Rome, where Simon died when his magic failed him. Justin Martyr says that Simon came to Rome in the reign of Claudius (41–54 CE), was honoured by his disciples as a god, and that he taught a gnostic doctrine. IRENAEUS called him the 'father of all heresies' and describes Simon's position as basically emulating Isis and Zeus; Simon descends to this world order to rescue his companion Helen who, as Thought, has generated the angels and powers by whom this world was made and who has been entrapped by them in a series of incarnations [9: 294–8]. The Christian elements play a relatively small part; some scholars conclude that Simon was never a Christian but only ever taught a rival message [4: IV] (G.J.B.)

Simons, Menno [VI.A] (1496–1561). Dutch Anabaptist leader. He was born in Witmarsum, Friesland, The Netherlands. He was educated in his early days in a monastic school. It seems likely that he belonged to the Order of Premonstratensian Canons, and that he was trained in the Order, since he was placed as priest in the parishes of Pingjum (1524) and Witmarsum (1531) by the Order. Not long after ordination he began to have doubts about the doctrine of the Real Presence in the Mass and about infant baptism. He was concerned that the Protestant Reformers had not addressed the second of these issues. By 1528 he had become known as an 'evangelical preacher' and by 1536, his views having become known abroad, he felt he had to go into hiding. A year later he was invited to minister to scattered groups of Dutch Anabaptists. He received adult baptism and a second ordination. He also married a woman named Gertrude, of whom no more is known. In 1536 he published *The Spiritual Resurrection*, in which he wrote of 'The New Birth', the title of his next work published in 1537. He also wrote of the nature of the church, 'the bride of Christ', the true church being a pure church, sinless. This thinking led him to adopt ever-stricter criteria about membership of such a church, with increasing emphasis on excommunication. He also taught that both natures of Christ came down directly from God. He was severely persecuted and a price was put on his head. He journeyed through Germany as far as Danzig and eventually settled in Holstein. Those who followed him eventually formed the Mennonite communities and church. [108; 374; 851] (T.T.)

Siovili of Eva [XXI] ['Joe Gimlet'] (*c*.1810–1842). An early Samoan convert to Christianity. As a young man from the northern coast of Upolu island, he travelled as a seaman and became familiar with many of the 'marvels' of the science during the mid-19th century. In Tahiti he came across the Mamaia movement and was attracted to the idea of the basic millenarian promise of 'good things to come'.

Siovili was said to have been subject to trances, visions and spiritual possession (very similar to RATANA, but Ratana was able to work towards the attainment of the ideals through political achievement). When he returned to Samoa he had a series of visions giving him several rites and practices, which he began to teach to those who gathered around him; at the same time he held out the promise that European goods would come to them. He drew around a number of folk who believed they were Christian – they worshipped Jehovah and JESUS and they believed both spoke to them through Siovili. The Samoans believed that their own material culture was devised by the gods and given to them by the gods. Thus when they came to learn of Christianity they naturally concluded that Jehovah gave to these white men all their riches and cleverness. In fact it is fairly clear from missionary writings that they often emphasized that the spiritual and the material blessings of European culture go together, and that they looked to the coming of abundance from heaven as a kind of second Advent. [10: 194–5]

The Siovili cult only lasted a couple of decades. The adherents would gather together in lonely bush places to pray, particularly in a dark hut where there was a tattered remnant of a Bible. Siovili claimed to be able to read this, which greatly increased the people's sense of his *mana*. One of his followers, an old lady, believed herself to be possessed by Christ and announced that he was about to return to earth and the dead would rise from the graves. The group continued together despite this unfulfilled prediction [4: 22–31; 10; 14; 20]. (J.I.)

Siri Maṅgala [IV]. Buddhist scholar-monk and commentator who wrote during the renascence of Buddhist culture which took place in northern Thailand (Lanna) in the late 15th and early 16th centuries. His most famous work, the *Maṅgalatthadīpanī* ('Illustration of Good Omens') became a foundation of Pali learning throughout South-east Asia, and continues to be a major component of monastic education in modern Thailand. The *Maṅgalatthadīpanī* is also an inspirational source for the fundamentalist Dhammakāya movement currently active in Thailand.

As is often the case with Theravādin scholar-monks, we have very little certain information about the life of Siri Maṅgala. The epilogue of the *Maṅgalatthadīpanī* says that it was written in 1524, during the reign of King Müang Keao, a great patron of the Sīhaḷa (Sri Lankan) sect of the Buddhist monastic order in northern Thailand. During his reign a number of classics of Thai Buddhist literature, in addition to the *Maṅgalatthadīpanī*, were written. The same epilogue says that Siri Maṅgala was the student of Buddhavira, which would make him a member of this Sīhaḷa fraternity. Some traditions say that Siri Maṅgala was the monastic tutor of King Müang Keao. Siri Maṅgala wrote a number of other works, but none have had a continuing influence comparable to the *Mangalatthadīpanī*, the appeal of which seems to be due to his skill as a story-teller. [187: I–II] (C.H.)

Siri Sanga Bō [IV] [Siri Sangha Bodhi] (3rd century). King of Sri Lanka who ruled for only two years, *c.*251–3, but whose life came to be perceived as an exemplary model of the ideal Buddhist king. The *Mahāvaṃsa*, the most important of the Sri Lankan monastic chronicles, says that Siri Sanga Bō ruled keeping the five precepts of Buddhist ethical practice, and it portrays him as being able to end drought and pestilence by virtue of his compassion and his 'power of *dhamma*' ('salvific truth'). Siri Sanga Bō's reign was cut short because he was hounded into exile by a friend-turned-usurper. While a fugitive, he took his own life so that a timid peasant might collect a bounty that the usurper had offered.

In medieval Sri Lanka, alternating kings took Siri Sanga Bō's name as one of their throne titles, thus associating themselves with his virtuous example. During the same period, the life of Siri Sanga Bō became the subject of an extensive body of hagiographic literature paralleled only by that portraying the deeds of DUṬṬHAGĀMAṆI. In these hagiographies Siri Sanga Bō is explicitly identified as a future Buddha (*bodhisattva*). His life story came to serve as a contested illustration in debates about the true nature of Buddhist kingship. [69: XXXVI] (C.H.)

Sir Sayyid. *See* AḤMAD KHĀN.

Sivananda [XI] (1887–1963). Holy man and founder of The Divine Life Mission. He was originally Kuppuswami Iyer, a Brahman and descendant of the 16th-century scholar-saint Appayya Diksita. Born in Pattamadai in Tamil Nadu, he was educated at the Tanjore Medical School. He obtained the MB at the age of 20 and practised in Trichy for six years. In 1913 he left for Singapore and practised in Malaya for ten years. In 1923, having given away most of his possessions, he returned to India to a life of renunciation. He was initiated by Swami Visvananda at Rishikesh in 1924 as a *sannyāsī* with the name of Sivananda Saraswati. After 12 years of intense asceticism and pilgrimage he returned to Rishikesh and *paramahansa*-hood in 1936. In 1936 Sivananda founded the Sivananda ashram, which became the headquarters for the society he founded in the same year, The Divine Life Society This is now a world-wide organization, having some 300 branches inside and outside India. Divine Life claims to represent a synthesis of the fundamentals of all religions, and to be non-sectarian, but its essential position is that of Advaita Vedanta. Sivananda wrote a great deal on a wide range of subjects, advocating a life of yoga, of service and of moral purity. Sivananda died in 1963, but the Divine Life Society continues his work, maintaining the ashram, running a hospital and selling Ayurvedic medicines, as well as publishing works of a spiritually and morally improving nature. [63] (S.C.R.W.)

Slocum, John [XX] (1840–1898). A Skokomish prophet and religious leader. As part of the Puget Sound Shaker movement, he and his wife Mary founded the Indian Shaker Church in the early 1880s. Slocum's prophetic mission had its origin in an experience in 1881 in which he claimed to have died and been resurrected in a fit of shaking and incomprehensible speech, an event witnessed by his family and fellow tribesmen. Before his conversion John Slocum worked infrequently as a logger and admitted to having fallen victim to gambling and alcoholism. Following some contact with Shaker missionaries, he blended features of that denomination with aspects of traditional Amerindian religion. His return from the dead was interpreted as a divine directive to lead others to salvation through Christ's teachings. His own shamanic transformation lent credence to his preaching. A distinctive feature of Slocum's church was the ritual confession of sins, although the prophet himself rang a bell during the recitation in order not to hear the penitent's faults. Even after his conversion, John Slocum occasionally fell prey to his earlier vices, and, on one occasion, likely as a consequence of his excesses, he became deathly ill and was brought back to life only through the miraculous curing efforts of his wife. Slocum's Indian Shaker Church was spread by missionary activity throughout the Pacific Northwest, including into British Columbia and Northern California. After his death in 1898, the church continued; followers may still be found to the present time. [3] (S.R.)

Smith, Joseph [VI.A] (1805–1844). American founder of the Church of Jesus Christ of

Latter-day Saints (Mormons). He was born in Sharon, Vermont, one of nine children. He grew up in a religious Christian family though not in a main-line denomination. In 1816 the family moved to Palmyra on the bank of the Erie Canal, in western New York State. In 1820 Joseph Smith claimed to experience visions and in 1827 revelations which led to the discovery of a text printed on golden plates under a hill on his parents' farm. In 1829 he received a divine call to be the priest of this new church and in 1830 he published the translation of the text as the *Book of Mormon* and organized the first Mormon church in Fayette, New York State. He claimed that the text was the sacred history of earlier inhabitants of America, some of whom were the ancestors of the American Indians. It was also claimed that Christ had appeared to these people after his ascension in order to establish his church in the New World. Smith led his group to Kirtland, Ohio, where he first published the *Book of Commandments* (1833), which later became *Doctrine and Covenants* (1835). Settlements were also established in Missouri, but the Mormons, or the Saints of the Church of Jesus Christ of Latter-day, were driven out of that state in 1839. Smith's first major establishment occurred in Nauvoo on the Mississippi River, the largest city in Illinois at the time, which was completely ruled over by Smith. Following the introduction of such rituals as baptism for the dead and the institution of multiple marriage severe divisions arose among the Saints during Smith's lifetime. The Saints also drew antagonism from outside the movement; opponents organized a mob which killed Joseph and his brother Hyrum. [119; 737; 738] (T.T.)

Smith, William Robertson [VI.A] (1846–1894). Scottish biblical scholar. Smith, raised in the Free Church of Scotland, had his earlier education in Aberdeen and entered New College, Edinburgh, in 1866. He also visited Germany and studied at Bonn and Göttingen. In Edinburgh he was a research student in the Old Testament. On his graduation in 1870 he became professor of oriental languages and Old Testament exegesis at the Free Church College, Aberdeen. Having accepted German biblical critical methods he proceeded to use them in his entries on the Bible in the ninth edition of the *Encyclopaedia Britannica*, of which he later became editor-in-chief. These writings were brought to the attention of the General Assembly of the Free Church. His 'trial' lasted five years and ended with his dismissal from his chair in 1881. In 1883 he went to Cambridge, where he was made a fellow of Christ's College in 1885. He later became professor of Arabic. He taught, wrote and researched on Old Testament and Islamic topics. His seminal work was *Lectures on the Religion of the Semites* (1889). He travelled extensively in the Near East and published *Kinship and Marriage in Early Arabia* (1885). The sociologist of religion Émile Durkheim acknowledged his indebtedness to Smith's sociological insights. [71; 90; 91] (T.T.)

Smohalla [XX] [Shmoquala ('The Prophet')] (*c.*1818–1907). Chief of the Sokulk tribe of the Middle Columbia River in the State of Washington. Despite a humpback, Smohalla became a respected warrior before his religious conversion. As a young man he attended Roman Catholic services and later was to incorporate some ritual and doctrinal elements of that tradition into his own movement. Smohalla witnessed the decline of the Plateau tribes in the face of westward expansion by the Whites. His reputation as a warrior sparked a conflict with Chief Moses of the Sinkiuse-Columbia; in the ensuing fight, Smohalla was severely wounded and left for dead. He recovered and secretly left the region, travelling for several years as far south as Mexico. When he returned to his people in 1850 he claimed to have been to the land of the spirits, where he had received a revelation. Indian peoples, he taught, must return to their traditional ways of life. They should avoid contact with the Whites and follow fully the 'dreams' and instructions of The Prophet. Consequently, Smohalla's followers became known as the 'Dreamers'. He quickly gained a reputation as a visionary and medicine man. His teachings echoed the beliefs of the Ghost Dance movement, including a belief in an imminent destruction and renewal of the world. The distinctive dances performed by Smohalla's followers were believed to imitate those done by the dead, and were thus a prefigurement of things to come. He was married ten times. His movement continued after his death and claims some adherents even today. [4: 274–5] (S.R.)

Snorri Sturluson [VIII] (1179–1241). An Icelandic chieftain from a powerful family who took a leading part in politics at a time when the Norwegian king was seeking to impose direct rule over Iceland. Snorri was Lawspeaker of Iceland for some years, took part in many bitter family feuds, and was finally assassinated as a result of a dispute with the Norwegian King Hakon [7: V]. But he was more than a politician: he grew up at Oddi, the centre of secular learning in Iceland, and was a gifted antiquarian, historian, poet and story-teller, writing brilliant Icelandic prose. He produced *Heimskringla*, a massive and entertaining history of the kings of Norway from early times, and is thought to have written *Egils Saga*, one of the outstanding sagas of Iceland, based on the life of the great poet who was a member of Snorri's family. Snorri left an account of the gods and myths of earlier times in *Ynglinga Saga*, the first section of *Heimskringla*, and in the *Prose Edda*, a handbook for poets to enable them to understand the rich mythological imagery of their predecessors. In this he describes the world of the gods, its creation and destruction, as presented in early poetry; he retells many myths of gods and tales of heroes, and finally deals in detail with poetic metres. He has quotations from many sources now lost, and includes some folklore [3: I]. Some scholars have claimed that so late a work written in the early 13th century, long after the adoption of Christianity, cannot be trustworthy, but Snorri is unlikely deliberately to invent, although he might misinterpret early sources or use ingenious speculation to clear up obscure material. He had a strong sense of intellectual integrity, and is unusual among medieval scholars in being a non-churchman, and free of bias against paganism. A great part of our knowledge of the pre-Christian religion of Scandinavia is due to this gifted writer. (H.E.D.)

Sobrino, Jon [VI.A] (1938–). Spanish Jesuit missionary. Born in Barcelona and brought up as a Basque, he took on El Salvadorean nationality and has become the country's most prominent liberation theologian. He earned degrees in philosophy and engineering in St Louis, Missouri, by 1965 and a doctorate in theology at Hochschulen St Georgen, Frankfurt, Germany, in 1975. An honorary degree from the Catholic University of Louvain, Belgium, followed in 1985. As Professor of Philosophy and Theology at the Centre for Theological Reflection in the University of José Simeon Canas, San Salvador, he gained international attention for writing *Christology at the Crossroads: A Latin American Approach* (1978) and the follow-up, *Jesus in Latin America* (1987). Since the assassination of Archbishop ROMERO in 1980, and of six Jesuit faculty colleagues in 1989, he has been particularly courageous as a champion of the rights of the ravaged poor who seek liberation by peaceful means. Dedicated to keeping Romero's memory alive and operative, he and his fellow priests established a 'pastoral centre' to advance the salvific cause espoused by basic Christian communities: namely to dispel untruth, to unmask idolatrous systems of exploitation, and to establish the just rule of God in society. His overriding concern is to make Christ come alive in the context of Latin American oppression [297: 41–4]. Significant publications of his, translated from Spanish, include *The True Church and the Poor* (1984), *Theology of Christian Solidarity*, with J. H. Pico (1985), and *Spirituality of Liberation: Toward Political Holiness* (1988). (A.C.S.)

Socinus, Faustus. *See* SOZZINI, FAUSTO PAVOLO.

Socrates [x] (469–399 BCE). Athenian philosopher. Because he wrote nothing and gave no formal expositions of his ideas, claiming he had no ideas to expound, and because PLATO [60; 61; 62], Xenophon [74] and Aristophanes [45] give such different portraits of him, it is not easy to describe Socrates' religious thought. He was executed in 399 on charges summarized in the *Apology* [62] and elsewhere as 'not acknowledging the gods of the state, introducing new gods, and corrupting the young'; and this is how he appears in Aristophanes' comedy, the *Clouds* [45]. A truer picture is provided by Plato and Xenophon, from which he appears to have been a man of deep and more or less orthodox piety, but convinced that to take conventional religious and moral ideas uncritically and on trust was neither practically wise nor in accordance with human dignity, and that unexamined and unjustified beliefs, even if true, did not deserve the name of knowledge. Accordingly, he came to see the examining of moral and political beliefs as a pious and religious act (he had no interest in scientific or metaphysical theories), and his mission as that of 'stinging' his fellow citizens into the hard task of rational self-examination and moral inquiry; or at the very least beginning the task by convincing them of their lack of real knowledge by demonstrating radical inconsistencies in their views: he interpreted the statement of the Delphic oracle that no one was wiser than Socrates as meaning that he alone knew his own ignorance. This work, seen by Socrates as a divine mission (he even experienced a 'divine sign', which prevented him doing a number of things, notably going into political life, and also took oracles and dreams very seriously), was variously interpreted: for Xenophon it deepened and endorsed his commitment to traditional morality and religion, for Plato it stimulated philosophical enquiry, but for Socrates' accusers it was essentially morally and politically subversive. Posterity has on the whole agreed with Plato and Xenophon, and Socrates' commitment to finding out the truth for oneself, together with the uprightness of his life and dignity of his death, have made him a figure comparable to JESUS or MUḤAMMAD for those who are drawn to religion but not to any particular organized religion.

Socrates' method of inquiry and of giving advice may be studied in Xenophon's *Conversations of Socrates* [74] and in Plato's early dialogues, especially the *Apology*, and *Crito* [62], *Gorgias* [61] and *Protagoras* [66]. The *Symposium* [68] gives a vivid picture of his personality, and the *Phaedo* [62] of the calmness and dignity of his end; but the ideas put into his mouth in these dialogues are almost certainly largely Plato's own. There is a fine imaginative reconstruction in Mary Renault's novel *The Last of the Wine*, and an interesting discussion of his trial by I. F. Stone [37a]. [20: vol. 3; 37a; 45; 59; 60; 61; 62; 66; 68; 73] (H.L.)

Söderblom, Nathan [VI.A] [Lars Olaf Johnathan Söderblom] (1866–1931). Swedish Lutheran archbishop and scholar. He was born in Trönö, near Söderhamn in Hälsingland Province, Sweden, the son of a Lutheran pastor. He entered Uppsala university to study classical and Oriental languages but changed to the study of divinity. He found the study at Uppsala too conservative, and when he turned to German criticism he had difficulties adapting to it at first. Under the influence of RITSCHL he adopted a liberal position and spent much time studying the concept of revelation. He was ordained in 1893 and served as a chaplain at a hospital. The following year he went to Paris as pastor to the Swedish legation. There he met scholars in the history of religions and spent time studying Zoroastrianism. He published two books on the subject. In 1901 he was made professor of theology at Uppsala but concentrated on the history of religions. He also held the chair of the history of religions at Leipzig University from 1912. He wrote *The Nature of Revelation* (1903; English trans., 1933) and *Natürliche Theologie und allgemeine Religionsgeschichte* (1913). In 1914 he was made archbishop of Sweden and developed his interest in the ecumenical movement which had begun during his membership of the Student Missionary Society. The work led to the agreement between Swedish Lutherans and Anglicans in 1922. He was the leading figure of the Stockholm Conference on Life and Work in 1925. He was awarded the Nobel Peace Prize in 1930 for his efforts at reconciliation during the First World War and for his work for Christian unity. His last published work was *The Living God* (posthumously in 1933), the text of the Gifford Lectures of 1931, which were not completed because of his death. [14; 183; 740a] (T.T.)

Soga, Tiyo [VI.A] (1829–1871). Xhosa Christian minister. He was born in the Ngqika lands of the Eastern Cape, the son of a leading chiefly counsellor who had partly broken with traditional rites. He was educated at Lovedale Missionary Institution and in Scotland, serving as a teacher for the Glasgow Missionary Society from 1848 to 1851. He then studied for the ministry, again in Scotland. In 1857 he returned ordained, with a Scottish wife, and worked as a missionary to his own Xhosa people until his death from tuberculosis. He translated Bunyan's *Pilgrim's Progress*, helped revise the Xhosa Bible and composed hymns (he used NTSIKANA's hymns in services). In English he wrote confidently of the God-given dignity and high destiny of Africa. One of his children became a medical missionary, one a minister and anthropological writer, one South Africa's first veterinary surgeon. [150; 865; 866] (A.F.W.)

Sŏ Kyŏngdŏk [XVI] [better known by his honorific name Hwadam] (1489–1546). He is generally considered one of the three outstanding neo-Confucian thinkers of Korea's Chosŏn dynasty (1392–1910), the others being YI HWANG (T'oegye) and YI I (Yulgok). Korea is renowned for its fidelity to the complex system of thought of CHU HSI, the mainline or orthodox school in China. The thought of Yi Hwang and Yi i developed divergent emphases latent in Chu Hsi's dualistic system of *li* and *ch'i* ('principle' and 'material force'). But Sŏ, the earliest of the three, was less inclined to stay at all within the boundaries of Chu Hsi's thought; rather he proclaimed his independence and developed a system of thought that is basically a monism of material force, principle (*li*) being reduced to the status of the pattern or order inherent in material force, which is the stuff of all existence. In its original form he refers to material force as the Supreme Vacuity, an empty or formless condition from which the diversely formed phenomenal world emerges by a kind of process of condensation. Having emerged from the Supreme Vacuity, the stuff of our being returns to it at death and continues in the endless process of transformation. Thus he argued that in the strict sense there is no such thing as death, only transformation.

Sŏ Kyŏngdŏk took pride in intellectual independence, but many of his ideas are very similar to those of the early Chinese neo-Confucian thinker Chang Tsai (1020–1077). Nonetheless, in the Korean context, which saw a divergence of schools emphasizing either principle or material force in their interpretation of Chu Hsi's dualism, his thought has stood through the centuries as definitively marking out a polar position. [1; 4] (M.Kal.)

Solomon [XV] (*c*.986–*c*.930 BCE). Israelite monarch. Son of DAVID and Bathsheba, the story of his accession is the final episode in the court history of David. After the death of David's eldest son, Absalom, next in line was Adonijah, but a court intrigue engineered by Bathsheba, together with the prophet Nathan and the military commander Benaiah, succeeded in having Solomon crowned in David's lifetime. After David's death Solomon had Adonijah and the veteran commander Joab killed, according to the Bible, following his father's deathbed behests.

Solomon reigned for 40 years. Unlike his predecessors the Bible brings little information concerning his personal life. It concentrates on the first half of his reign, which was particularly magnificent, characterized by wealth and prosperity, flourishing foreign trade and extensive building. The great achievement was the construction of the temple in Jerusalem, a stone building standing within the royal compound and made of the finest materials, which thereafter was the focus of the Jewish cult. In its construction, which lasted seven years, Solomon enjoyed the assistance of Hiram, king of Tyre, who provided workmen, timber and gold. In return, Solomon ceded considerable territory to Hiram. The two kings also co-operated in running a fleet of ships for foreign trade out of the Red Sea, Solomon supplying the boats and Hiram the sailors. Solomon also built strong fortified cities, notably Hazor, Megiddo and Gezer. To maintain this programme, every Israelite had to spend a third of the year in the king's service and to pay heavy taxation; the dissatisfaction which built up showed itself in the rebellion of Jeroboam, which proved unsuccessful in Solomon's lifetime but led to a split in the kingdom after his death.

Solomon lived in great luxury and reportedly had a harem of 700 wives and 300 concubines. The most important of his wives – and an indication of his international reputation – was the pharaoh's daughter, an unusual gesture by an Egyptian ruler. Traditionally Solomon was noted for his wisdom and was the father of Israelite wisdom and wisdom literature. The Bible gives examples of his sagacity and suggests that the state visit of the queen of Sheba was a result of his fame for wisdom, although it may well have been for political and economic reasons [77]. Because of his reputation, the Bible ascribed to Solomon the authorship of the books of *Proverbs* and the *Song of Songs*, and the rabbis identified him with the 'preacher' who wrote *Ecclesiastes*. He was the subject of many legends.

The story of his reign is told in 1 *Kings* 1–11. [28: vol. 4: V] (G.W.)

Soloveichik, Joseph Ber [XV] (1903–). Jewish Orthodox religious thinker in the United

States. Born into a family with an outstanding reputation for scholarship, he lived his early years in Belorussia, devoted to the study of Jewish law. He then attended the University of Berlin, where he specialized in philosophy. From 1932 he lived in the United States, first as a rabbi in Boston, where he founded a Hebrew day school, and then in 1941 succeeding his father as professor of Talmud at the Rabbi Isaac Elchanan Theological Seminary (later part of Yeshiva University, where he also taught Jewish philosophy). The spiritual mentor of the mainstream of 'modern Orthodoxy', he devoted his time to teaching; apart from a few essays, he did not publish. His pupils committed his teachings to writing.

Soloveichik's thinking revolves around the *halakhah*, the comprehensive rabbinic system of jurisprudence based on laws traditionally revealed at Mount Sinai. His object is to develop a halakhic-oriented world outlook for the modern Jew. He offers an original interaction of *halakhah* and philosophy, the latter largely influenced by neo-Kantianism and existentialism. The key to the human personality is loneliness (one of his best known essays is entitled 'The Lonely Man of Faith'). Religious life is a process of spiritual self-awareness. At the acme of religious experience man both issues a call to God and answers God's call to him. However, the 'repentant man' (a significant concept) will not attain salvation in solitude but only as part of the community of Israel. [62]

God's will is fulfilled through the *halakhah*, by which God and man are drawn into a covenantal community. Through *halakhah*, man – who is at the centre of Soloveichik's religious thought – confronts God, orders his life accordingly and witnesses to God in all his deeds. The intellectual approach is fundamental to his system; God is the great teacher and study a *sine qua non* of religious observance.

Soloveichik laid down guidelines for Jewish–Christian dialogue, which have been adopted by mainstream Orthodoxy. His basic premise is that it is impossible for faith communities to communicate with each other except on secular grounds. Since each faith believes that its own values are for the ultimate good, it must be unyielding and cannot equate them with those of another community. At the same time there is no contradiction in co-ordinating cultural activity (e.g. speaking as historians or sociologists of religion) but not theology. [60: 280–97] (G.W.)

Sonni Ali [XII] (15th century). King of Niger, 1462–92. The Sonni ('king') dynasty began in Songhay in what is now western Niger, during the last quarter of the 13th century. Its most famous scion was Sonni Ali, who took Timbuktu from the Twaregs in 1468 and Jenne in 1473. Although nominally he was a Muslim ruler, he has been vilified by the orthodox Muslim chroniclers of West Africa as a heathen, because he still worshipped his ancestors, and even practised magic. The scholars of Timbuktu especially felt that being ruled by a half-Muslim degraded them. Yet his pagan practices may well have been inspired by the political need to stay on good terms with the numerous non-Muslims in his empire. Syncretism was and is extremely common in West Africa. Sonni Ali was succeeded by a Muslim general, Muḥammad Ture, who took the title of Askiya ('marshal'). [47: II; 54] (J.K.)

Sozzini, Fausto Pavolo [VI.A] [Faustus Socinus] (1539–1604). Italian Unitarian theologian, whose teaching formed the basis of Socinianism. He was born in Siena. He inherited the theological ideas of his uncle Lelio Francesco Maria Sozzini, also Sienese, who had espoused Protestant ideas, and had met many of the leading Reformers. Fausto fled Italy when his uncle was threatened by the Inquisition. On his uncle's death in 1562 Fausto acquired the former's manuscripts; these influenced his own thinking. While he lived in Zurich and Basel he wrote a work on St John's Gospel in which he denied the essential divinity of Christ. In 1563 Fausto returned to Italy to serve in the court of the Duke of Florence. The Duke soon died and Fausto returned to Switzerland, where he continued his study of theology. In 1578 he published *De Jesu Christo Servatore* in which he argued that Christ was saviour merely by example and teaching. He went to Transylvania to persuade Dávid Ferenc to give up his opposition to prayer to Christ. When his mission failed he journeyed on to Cracow, Poland, where he arrived in 1579. He allied himself with the Polish Brethren and defended their anti-trinitarian stance in many works. In 1586 he married but his wife soon died. His life was threatened in Cracow so he moved to Luclawice in 1589; there he held colloquies in 1601 and 1602. His teaching was the basis for the Unitarianism which spread to other countries, sometimes under the name Socinianism. It was also the basis for the *Racovian Catechism* of the Polish Brethren. [740; 867; 868] (T.T.)

Spartas, Reuben S.S. Makasa [I.A] (1899–1982). Founder and Vicar-General of the African Greek Orthodox Church. A Ganda Ugandan, who was well educated and an accomplished sportsman, Spartas (hence his nickname) left the Anglican Church in 1929 to found the African Orthodox Church. He was very keen to assert African ecclesiastical autonomy. In 1946 his church was admitted to the Greek Orthodox communion. Politically active, Spartas was imprisoned from 1949 to 1953, and later served in the Ugandan parliament. Conflict with the Greek church in 1957, over such topics as external support, led to a severing of ties. He has authored both a history of the church and an autobiography. [15: 33–4] (R.H.)

Spener, Philipp Jakob [VI.A] (1636–1705). German theologian, a leading proponent of Pietism. He was born in Rappoltsweiler, Alsace, into a devout Lutheran family. He studied history, theology and philosophy at the University of Strasbourg from 1651 to 1653. His professor of theology, J. K. Dannhauer, influenced him, especially in his study of MARTIN LUTHER. Spener travelled to Basel where he studied Hebrew, and Geneva, where he came under the influence of Jean de Labadie, a French Pietist. He also visited Tübingen, where he began to turn to Pietism himself. He returned to Strasbourg, completed a doctoral degree and married Susanne Ehrhardt. He became pastor successively at Strasbourg (1663) and Frankfurt (1666). He concentrated on raising the devotional life of his flocks by holding house meetings and spending much time in catechizing. His efforts were met with criticism by other ministers so he left for Dresden, where he became chaplain to the court of Saxony. Again he met with hostility from the theology faculty in Leipzig. He became rector of Nikolaikirche in Berlin and found favour with the Elector of Brandenburg, later King Frederick I of Prussia. Pietism was firmly established by this time in spite of the general opposition of many Lutheran clergy. The University of Halle was founded in 1694 largely under Spener's influence. He was charged with heresy but cleared. In 1689 he withdrew to the quiet of pastoral work but the Pietism he fostered remained a potent force in German Protestantism. [82; 745; 837] (T.T.)

Spurgeon, Charles Haddon [VI.A] (1834–1892). English Baptist minister. He was born in Kelvedon, Essex, the son and grandson of Congregational ministers. In 1850 he underwent a conversion experience in a Primitive Methodist church and the following year became a Baptist. He soon preached his first sermon and in 1852 he was appointed minister of a Baptist church in Waterbeach, Cambridgeshire. In 1854 he was called to Southwark, London, and drew such large congregations that the large Metropolitan Tabernacle in Newington Causeway was built for him. Here he ministered until his death. He was responsible for other works such as the building of an orphanage, a college for preachers and an association for the distribution of religious literature. More than 3,000 of his sermons were published weekly and read by more than a million readers. The sermons amounted to 63 volumes, *New Park Street Pulpit* (1855–60), *Metropolitan Tabernacle Pulpit* (1861–1917), and were translated into 23 languages. He edited a monthly magazine, *The Sword and the Trowel*, for 27 years. He was strictly Calvinistic in his theology and caused controversy over his opposition to baptismal regeneration, which led him to withdraw from the Evangelical Alliance in 1864, and his opposition to higher criticism and liberal theology, which led him to leave the Baptist Union in 1887. He remained an independent Baptist. [648; 749] (T.T.)

Srong-btsan Sgam-po [IV] (618?–649). The emperor credited with establishing Buddhism in Tibet. For world history his greater importance was that he completed the process of uniting the tribes of central Tibet and marched into Central Asia with military force. He was thus largely responsible for containing Chinese influence in that region throughout the period of the T'ang dynasty.

In the process of military expansion under Srong-btsan Sgam-po (enthroned at age 13), the Tibetans found the world, in almost all directions, to be Buddhist. So it is no accident that Tibet adopted Buddhism, though it is perhaps more surprising that Tibetans managed to preserve the tradition into the middle of the 20th century, long after it had decayed or disappeared all around them.

The extent of Srong-btsan Sgam-po's personal interest in Buddhism is questioned by contemporary historians, although the traditional lama historians of Tibet strongly affirm it. That he constructed temples 'as far as the borders with China', as the latter affirm, is doubtful. However, it is clear that at least one important temple was built – the Ramoche temple that still stands in Lhasa – by his consort Wen-cheng, a princess of the T'ang. Also likely to be dated from his reign is the Jo-khang temple, the 'cathedral of Lhasa' whose building is attributed to another consort, the Nepalese princess Bhṛkuti. So the establishment of Buddhism is really to be credited to junior queens (these are two among six, the senior queens being Tibetan) who came from abroad and built temples to house family images – of Śākyamuni the historical BUDDHA, and of the tantric Buddha Akṣobhya.

Along with princess Wen-cheng came many elements of Chinese culture. But to devise a script for writing the emperor sent a minister to India. This decision to look to India for a higher culture was the greatest single determining factor in Tibetan cultural history. The minister Thon-mi Sambhoṭa developed a script based upon a Gupta dynasty form of writing, and a literary grammar based upon Sanskrit. With this new system of writing, not only religious texts but also many other kinds of Indian texts – on medicine, for example – were translated into Tibetan.

The emperor and his two foreign queens are believed to have been absorbed, upon death, into the statue of thousand-armed Avalokiteśvara, the bodhisattva of compassion, which stood in the Jo-khang temple. That image was smashed during the Cultural Revolution, but Tibetans smuggled some limbs of it out of Tibet to the DALAI LAMA, who is considered the spiritual heir of the ancient emperors, including Srong-btsan Sgam-po, through Avalokiteśvara. [171: 183–5; 197: 414–21; 238: 222–49] (M.T.)

Ssu-ma Ch'eng-chen [V] (647–735). The twelfth patriarch of the Taoist sect called 'Highest Clarity' (*shang ch'ing*) who, although leading an eremitic life on several mountains, was well known and respected at the T'ang court. He is said to have been the spiritual mentor of the emperor posthumously called 'Mysterious Ancestor' (*hsüan tsung*, reigned 713–56), who had a temple complex built for him on top of Mt Wang-wu in Shansi province. Ssu-ma Ch'eng-chen left some influential writings, including two pieces on meditation, and some poems. He was on friendly terms with such literary lights as Li Pai (or Po, 701–762). It is said that the Shang-ch'ing sect became the leading Taoist school of T'ang times primarily because of the existence of Ssu-ma Ch'eng-chen. [28; 29; 30; 41] (L.T.)

Starhawk [XVII.A] [Miriam Simos] (1951–). Starhawk is the pseudonym, and possibly the religious name, for Miriam Simos, probably the most prominent of contemporary witchcraft priestesses. She was born in St Paul, Minnesota, the daughter of social workers (her mother was also a writer). Her primary work lies in feminist politics and spirituality, projects she sees as one. She describes her practice as 'a rebirth of the ancient religion of the Great Goddess', and as a polytheistic nature religion which draws upon the images of Greek, Egyptian and Celtic religions. Starhawk's version of this newly emerging religion is feminist and political: feminist, in that Goddess worship is often interpreted as a particularly female spirituality, a religion that can express and evoke the nature of woman as Christianity cannot, and political in that religious spirituality is interpreted also as a way of political action within the world. Starhawk's best-known book is *The Spiral Dance* (1979), which is essentially a guide to the magical practice of the religion. Beautifully written, it may in itself have spawned many practising covens. [1; 16] (T.L.)

Steiner, Rudolph [XVII.B] (1861–1925). Founder of the religious and philosophical system Anthroposophy (wisdom of humanity). Steiner, a former Roman Catholic, born in Hungary, combined occultism and clairvoyance with a scholarly knowledge of the works of Goethe, and used scientific thinking to convey his revelations in a language of the times. His experiences of spiritual knowledge were backed up by many years of systematic exercises and training. With his own rather individualistic approach he rose to General Secretary of the Theosophical Society in Germany (*see* BLAVATSKY, HELENA PETROVNA). By 1913 he had broken with the declining Theosophical Society, proclaiming himself herald of Anthroposophy, and took with him most of the Society in Germany.

Anthroposophy shares the basic tenets of theosophy (wisdom of God), but emphasizes the central place of humanity in the 'spiritual science' – serious students are not simply content with their own spiritual development. It is a method of attaining knowledge of higher worlds by occult powers latent within man, and through mental, physical and spiritual exercises of meditation and concentration; the aim is to develop a state of clear vision and a subtler sense of perception.

Unlike Theosophy, which considers there to be a number of avatars (deities that have descended to earth), Steiner's system assigned a central place to Christ, the great solar being who rescued the world from ruin. The Anthroposophical Society organized itself into Christian Fellowships, the first of these being in Stuttgart in 1922, and the celebration of the sacrament is the central act in these fellowships.

Anthroposophists have used Steiner's ideas as a basis for experimental work in agriculture. Steiner also founded the Waldolf Schools and various schools of curative education for the disabled. [3; 10] (K.M.)

Stevens, Jimmy [XXI] (*c*.1920–). Pacific Islander founder of an independent church and advocate of regional separation. Of mixed Tongan, Melanesian and settler descent, Stevens campaigned against the alienation of land on the New Hebrides by white *colons*. At first an unrealistic visionary, Stevens established a powerful land reform movement, called NaGriamel, but waning influence before Vanuatu's independence led him to betray his original biblical ideals of keeping just boundaries to pro-French interests and the Phoenix Foundation of the USA [46]. At the very time the British and French military left the New Hebrides to make independence possible, Papua New Guinea troops arrived on Espiritu Santo to begin the assault on Stevens' headquarters (1980). This successful operation, in which modern armed forces were used to put down an Independent Church, is known as the Coconut War. Stevens has been in prison at Vila ever since. [42; 47: 63–5] (G.W.T.)

Ston-pa Gshen-rab. *See* GSHEN-RAB MI-BO-CHE.

Strauss, David Friedrich [VI.A] (1808–1874). German Protestant theologian and philosopher. He was born in Ludwigsburg, Württemberg and entered the seminary in Blauberen as a pupil of F. C. BAUR in 1821. In 1825 he entered the Tübingen Stift where he was influenced by the work of SCHLEIERMACHER and HEGEL. After studying in Berlin he became a teacher at the Stift in 1832 and later lectured on Hegelian philosophy at Tübingen university. In 1835–6 he published *Das Leben Jesu* (English trans. by George Eliot, *Life of Jesus*, 1846), in which all supernatural elements of the Gospel were explained away as myth. He was dismissed from Tübingen. In a later work, *Die christliche Glaubenslehre* (1840–41), the history of Christianity is seen as dissolving into Hegelian philosophy. In 1839 he tried to become professor at Zürich but failed. He wrote on politics and biography. He attacked Schleiermacher's attempt to combine the 'Jesus of history' with the 'Christ of faith' in *Der Christus des Glaubens und der Jesus der Geschichte* (1865). Lastly, he tried to negate the claims of Christianity in favour of scientific materialism in *Der alte und der neue Glaube* (1872; English trans., *The Old Faith and the New*, 1873). [348; 718: 68–120; 734: vol. 1: 215–60; 883] (T.T.)

Strehlow, Carl Friedrich Theodor [VI.A] (1870–1922). German missionary. Having collaborated on the first translation of the New Testament into an Australian Aboriginal language (Dieri), he was appointed to take over the Lutheran Hermannsburg mission in 1894. He was a strict disciplinarian with outstanding linguistic skills. The latter led him to contest the data of the ethnographer W. Baldwin Spencer and to publish a valuable five-volume study of Loritja and Aranda beliefs [761]. Spencer, with some justification, was in turn outspoken against the inefficiency and authoritarianism of the mission. Strehlow died tragically, believing his own Mission Board had refused him assistance to reach medical care. [762] (T.S.)

Suarez, Francisco de [VI.A] (1548–1617). Spanish theologian and philosopher. He was born in Granada. He went to study canon law at the University of Salamanca; later, after his entry into the Society of Jesus in 1564, he studied philosophy and, from 1566–70, theology. One of the main influences of the time was THOMAS AQUINAS. In 1571 he was sent to Segovia to teach philosophy. A year later he was ordained priest. For some years he taught in a number of Jesuit colleges in Castile, including Valladolid, lecturing on Aquinas' *Summa theologiae*. In 1580 he went to the Roman College in Rome and continued his lectures on the *Summa*. Owing to ill health he returned to Spain in 1585 and taught the remainder of his lectures on the *Summa* in Alcalá. In 1592 he moved to Salamanca and in 1597 to Coimbra in Portugal, at that time under the Spanish crown, where he taught until 1616. The following year he died in Lisbon. He published many works on the Incarnation, the divine right of kings and, in 1597, *Disputationes metaphysicae*. Though he was ostensibly a Thomist, some of what he taught was at odds with Aquinas. His *Omnia opera* were published in 1747 and again in 1856. His influence continues among non-Thomist Roman Catholic theologians. [359; 719] (T.T.)

Ṣubḥ-i Azal, Mīrzā Yaḥyā Nūrī [III] (*c.*1830–1912). Founder of the Azalī branch of the Bābī religion, now a small minority largely confined to Iran and adhering to the original doctrines of the movement. The son of a government functionary, Ṣubḥ-i Azal was converted to Babism about 1844. In the last years of THE BĀB's life (*c.*1848–50), he was designated his successor. After the Bāb's execution the majority of his followers recognized him as such.

From 1853 to 1863 he lived in Baghdad, where an exile community had grown up after a Bābī attempt on Nāṣir al-Dīn Shāh's life in August 1852. Although generally recognized as head of the sect, he lived in seclusion. During this period, numerous other individuals claimed some form of divine inspiration, several achieving a limited recognition. More seriously, Azal left most of his affairs in the hands of representatives, of whom the most important was his older brother, BAHĀ' ALLĀH, who became *de facto* leader.

About 1866, while exiled in Turkey, a permanent breach occurred between the two brothers, leading to the formation of Azalī and Bahā'ī factions of Babism. For modern Bahā'īs, Azal is an Antichrist, condemned for refusing to recognize the superior station of his brother.

In 1868 the Ottoman authorities exiled Ṣubḥ-i Azal together with his family and a small group of followers to Cyprus. He remained there until his death on 29 April 1912, writing extensively in elucidation of Bābī doctrine and support of his own claims. Only a few of his works have subsequently been published in Iran; none has been translated. Azalī Babism, unlike its Bahā'ī rival, retained a traditional Bābī outlook and never grew to any size. Nevertheless, several members of the sect became famous as exponents of political and social reform in late 19th-century and early 20th-century Iran. [12: s.v.] (D.M.)

Subuh, Pak. *See* SUMOHADIWIJOJO, MUHAMMAD SUBUH.

Suhrawardī, Shihāb al-Dīn Yaḥyā [XII] [Shaykh al-Ishrāq] (1155–1191). Founder and chief exponent of the school of Ishrāqī or Illuminationist philosophy in Iranian Shiʿism (not to be confused with two famous Ṣūfīs, Abū Ḥafṣ ʿUmar al-Suhrawardī and ʿAbd al-Qāhir Suhrawardī). Born in 1155 in northwestern Iran, he completed his early studies at Marāgha and Iṣfahān. This was followed by a peripatetic existence, during which he frequented Ṣūfī communities in Iran and Anatolia. After a number of years in Diyarbakr, he travelled to Aleppo, where he enjoyed cordial relations with the Ayyubid ruler, al-Malik al-Ẓāhir, who was favourably disposed towards Ṣūfīs. Before long, however, Suhrawardī's outspoken espousal of unusual metaphysical doctrines led to his formal condemnation for heresy by the orthodox religious establishment. Al-Malik al-Ẓāhir's protests having been overridden by his father,

Saladin, Suhrawardī was placed in prison, where he died on 29 July 1191.

In spite of the brevity of his life, Suhrawardī produced some 50 works in which he expounded his philosophy of illumination (*ishrāq*). These works, of which the best known is the *Ḥikmat al-ishrāq* ('Philosophy of Illumination'), range from conventional discussions of peripatetic philosophy in Islam to elaborate mystical narratives employing a complex and striking symbolism. The most original feature of Suhrawardī's work is the manner in which he combines Islamic philosophy with elements from Iranian (Zoroastrian), Hellenistic and Hermetic sources into a coherent system. In this system, the Orient stands for a world of pure illumination to which man, exiled in the Occident (a realm of darkness and matter), seeks to return. After Suhrawardī, a school of Illuminationist philosophers (Ishrāqiyyūn) continued to be active in Iran; in the Safavid period Ishrāqīs like MULLĀ ṢADR came to dominate Shiʿite philosophy. Suhrawardī's influence also extended to India, where it was felt, not only in Muslim mystical circles, but also among Parsis. [28: vol. 2; 96; 126; 127; 128; 129] (D.M.)

Sumedha [IV]. The name of the BUDDHA (Śākyamuni) in a former life [6]. He had been a rich Brahman who renounced the world to live as an ascetic in the Himālayas. When the Buddha of that time, Dīpaṅkara, was visiting the town of Ramma, Sumedha helped with the preparation of the road on which he was to walk; when Dīpaṅkara arrived before Sumedha's section was finished, he lay down on the ground and invited the Buddha to walk over him, then made a vow not to join the monkhood to strive for *nirvāṇa* there and then, but to fulfil all the Perfections during countless lives in order to become a Buddha himself. In the sequence of lives between Sumedha and Śākyamuni (*see* BUDDHA), stories of which are recorded in many Buddhist texts, he is known as the *Bodhisatta* (*Bodhisattva*), usually translated as 'Being (bound for) Enlightenment'. (This is essentially the '*Bodhisattva* vow' made in Mahāyāna Buddhism, where such an aspiration is said to be appropriate for every Buddhist.) [109] (S.C.)

Sumohadiwidjojo, Muhammad Subuh [XVII.D] [Pak Subuh; Bapak] (1901–1987). The founder and spiritual guide of the spiritual brotherhood of Subud. He was born near Semarang in central Java, Indonesia, on 22 June 1901. Although claiming descent from the sultans of Central Java, Muhammad Subuh was brought up in quite humble circumstances, and as a young man became an accountant for the municipality of Semarang. A devout Muslim, he sought out various religious teachers for guidance, and they all told him he had a special role. One evening in 1925 he had a spiritual experience which was accompanied by strong vibrations throughout his body, and he found himself making the involuntary movements which characterize what is now known as the *latihan kejiwaan*, the spiritual exercise of Subud. This was the first of a series of unsought spiritual experiences which continued for several years and caused a profound transformation in his inner being. In 1933 he was given to understand that what he had received was the contact with the power of God which was for the benefit of all mankind. He gave up his job and began to share the contact with a few followers in Java, who also began to experience involuntary movements and an inner transformation when they surrendered themselves to the *latihan kejiwaan*. In 1947 he gave the name Subud to the spiritual brotherhood he had founded – Subud being a contraction of the three Sanskrit words *suśīla*, *buddhi* and *dharma*, which he interpreted as meaning 'right living, with all one's parts awakened, according to the Will of God'. In 1950 the first Westerner joined Subud, and in 1957 Pak Subuh was invited to London, where several thousand people received the contact and began to experience strongly the *latihan kejiwaan*. From then on Subud spread rapidly world-wide and Pak Subuh subsequently travelled the world more than 17 times. Wherever he went he gave talks to Subud members and shared with them in their worship through the *latihan kejiwaan*. He died in Jakarta on 23 June 1987. Since the Spiritual Brotherhood of Subud is a democratically self-governing association of men and women of different religions in about 70 countries who follow the form of worship or *latihan kejiwaan* which Pak Subuh was the first to receive, he has no spiritual successor. In addition to his talks and enormous correspondence, Pak Subuh wrote several books, the most important being *Susila Budhi Dharma*, a long poem in High Javanese, which was published in 1952 [9]. Subud members await with interest his spiritual autobiography, which is only to be published three years after his death, but all who met him were convinced they were in the presence of someone charged with a high spiritual mission who was totally surrendered to the Will of God [10]. (S.C.R.W.)

Sunan Bonang, Ibrāhīm ibn Raḥmatallāh Nyakrawātī [XII] (*d. c.*1525). Disseminator of Islam in Java; it is uncertain that he was ever *sunan* ('sovereign'). He seems to have referred to himself as Pangéran Bonang, 'prince' of Bonang. He was the son of Sunan Ngampel (=Ampel) and Nyai ('Lady') Ageng Manila, daughter of Arya Téja of Tuban on East Java. Bonang lies further west, also on the north coast, near Semarang, downstream from Demak, where Sunan Bonang was *imām* for a time, and where he built the mosque which is still there. The date of his birth is not known, but he was active in Tuban between *c.*1475–1500. He studied in Malacca, which was then, before the Portuguese destroyed it in 1511, a great centre of Islamic scholarship. Legend relates that Sunan Bonang was one of the nine saints of Java responsible for the Islamization of that large island. Legend relates further that Sunan Bonang died in Bonang, his father's town, his body was shipped to Ampel near Surabaya to be buried near his father's, but a storm pushed the ship ashore near Tuban, where he now lies, because God willed it so. Many miracles are told of him. He was a student of al-Bārī, a Persian scholar from Nīshāpūr. Sunan Bonang taught orthodox Islamic dogma in Java, which (at least along its northern coast) had accepted a form of Islam which was too mystic to be strictly doctrinaire. He refuted the Hindu-influenced pantheism and insisted that God was separate from this world: He was not a featureless being, but a person with will and the power to create material beings (*makhlūqāt*) without being material himself. Indeed, Allāh is incomparable, undivided, unique, distinguished from His *ṣifāt* or qualities: 'He lives without body, He knows without brain, He works without limbs or tools, sees without eyes, speaks without lips or voice, hears without ears, kills without weapons.' No one else gives life, strength or knowledge, food or intelligence. There is and never was any primeval substance from which we were created. God is pure and alone. It is impossible to say, 'The soul merges [*fanā'*] with God' in the mystic union, since God is not mixed with anything. [35: III, 1218–19] (J.K.)

Sundar Singh, Sadhu [VI.A] (1889–*c.*1929). Indian Anglican layman. He was born in Rampur, Patiala (Panjab), India, into a Sikh family. As such he was encouraged to read not only the holy book of the Sikhs, the *Guru Granth Sahib* (*see* ARJAN, GURŪ) but also the Hindu *Bhagavad Gītā* and *Upanishads* and the Muslim *Qur'an*, all of this by the age of 16. He was introduced to the Bible in the Presbyterian mission school in his home village. In December 1904 following an experience of a vision of JESUS he was converted to the Christian religion. He was baptized in the Church of England at Simla in September 1905. As a Christian he decided to adopt the traditional role of an Indian holy man or *sadhu*. For two years he wandered through north-west India, teaching and preaching. In 1908 he went on a mission to Tibet. The next two years were spent as a student in a Christian college in Lahore, while continuing in the role of *sadhu*. Here he read some of the classics of Christian spirituality, including the life of FRANCIS OF ASSISI. He decided against ordination in the Church of England. He visited Europe and America in 1920 and 1922. He returned to further work in Tibet. He was last heard of in 1929. The place and date of his death are unknown. [358; 760] (T.T.)

Sunjata [XII] (13th century). Prince of Mali. Sunjata or Soundjata was a prince of the Kaita (Keita or Keta) dynasty which ruled Mali or Manding, which was then only part of the present Republic of Mali on the Niger Bend. It was during the 13th century that Sunjata succeeded in liberating his people from the domination of the Susu ruler Sumanguru, and set up an independent kingdom, in which he united all the branches of the Mali or Manding nation: Malinke, Bambara, Mande and others as well. His son Mansa ('king') Ulli made the pilgrimage to Mecca and forged diplomatic and cultural ties with early Mamluk Egypt (*c.*1260). Sunjata himself was probably, like SONNI ALI, a Muslim who saw the political necessity of maintaining ties with the non-Muslim groups in his empire by ancestor-worship. He has remained famous ever since he freed his people from foreign bonds, thanks to the epic songs of the *griots* (bards) who immortalize him in Manding to this day. [59] (J.K.)

Sun Ssu-mo [v] [Sun Ssu-miao] (7th century). He is thought of as a Taoist, although he has also been characterized as at least partly Buddhist. His Taoist *persona* comes from the claim that he was a recluse in the Great White Mountains (*t'ai pai shan*), where he learned Taoist arts. He was said to be fond of the philosophy of the Old Master (LAO TZU) and that of Master Chuang (CHUANG TZU), the Taoist forefathers. His historical career is hazy, to say the least, but one fact is prominent, namely that he was a famous physician. Indeed, legend has made him one of the most famous physicians in Chinese history. This too connects him with Taoism, for medicine and Taoist arts are intimately related, both having the intention of prolonging life and both being based on the same theories. Sun is the author of a well known medical-pharmaceutical text entitled 'Prescriptions Worth a Thousand [Pieces of Gold]' (*ch'ien chin yao fang*), and putative author of some other works. [50] (L.T.)

Suntarar [xi] [proper name, Nampiyārūrar] (7th–8th century). One of the NĀYAṈMAR. He was born into a Brahman family at Tirunāvalūr. In a sense the whole tradition concerning the Nāyaṉmār originates from him, for, in poem 39 in his *Tirumuṟai* VII, he praises all 62 Nāyaṉmār that preceded or were contemporary with him. The 10th century compiler of the *Tirumuṟai*, Nampiyāṇṭār Nampi, included his own poems in the last book (XI) thereof, of which six poems are on TIRUÑĀṈACAMPANTAR, one on APPAR and one that closely follows and expatiates on Suntarar's list of Nāyaṉmār, adding as the 63rd devotee the name of Suntarar himself. In his *Pĕriya purāṇam* (*see* NĀYAṈMĀR), Cekkiḻār embedded in the story of Suntarar's life the tales of the other 62 saints. The first portion on the *purāṇam* describes Suntarar's celestial life in Śiva's abode, the last narrates Suntarar's earthly life that was a fulfilment of the former wherein he had made a pact with the god. He was promised marriage on earth to two maidens, incarnations of two he had desired in his previous birth, provided he would praise Śiva on earth. He agreed, but, reborn, forgot his vow and was about to be married. Śiva appeared and angrily stopped the ceremony. Straightway, the contrite Suntarar rushed to the local temple at Tiruvĕṇṇĕynallūr and commenced his *Tevāram* (*see* NĀYAṈMĀR) referring to the irate god: 'O Madman with the moon in your tresses.' In due course he married Paravaiyār and Caṅkiliyār, the reincarnations of his two heavenly loves. He became close friends with a royal Nāyaṉār, Ceramāṉ Pĕrumāḷ, was blind in his old age, and died around 730 CE, leaving the 1026 hymns that form *Tirumuṟai* VII. [28; 73; 118] (J.R.M.)

Sūrdās [xi] (*c*.1478?). The most popular of all Kṛṣṇa-poets in the Hindi area. A voluminous anthology of lyric poems on a wide range of Kṛṣṇaite themes is ascribed to him under the title *Sūr-sāgar*; and a detailed hagiography portrays him as a devout Brahman poet, blind from birth, converted to the Vallabhan sectarian attitude through an alleged encounter with VALLABHA himself. But the history of the manuscripts and the formulaic contents of the hagiography – Sūr's high caste status, his meeting with the Mughal emperor AKBAR, the magical completion of a textual corpus through divine intervention – indicate that the received text and the traditional biography are mutually supportive constructions representing a (successful) attempt by the Vallabhan tradition to assimilate the prestige of an already popular devotional poet. Despite the prolix hagiologies, and the reverence paid to his verses, which are used liturgically in Vallabhan temples, the historical Sūrdās remains an obscure figure whose traditional biography must be regarded as largely legendary. The oldest poems in the *Sūr-sāgar* are probably those on the themes of humble supplication (*vinay*) and the lovesick pangs (*virah*) of the anguished *gopīs* deserted by Kṛṣṇa – both well-established conventional items from the devotional repertoire; the famous 'child-Kṛṣṇa' poems which represent Sūr's hallmark in the popular view, and which reflect an important aspect of Vallabhan theology, seem to be largely a later addition to the text. Such observations, born of the coldly analytical techniques of objective research, are unlikely to dent the popular appraisal of Sūrdās as the devotional poet *par excellence*: the poems of the expanded *Sūr-sāgar*

– in which the transcendence of God is juxtaposed with the familiar domestic experiences of worldly life – remain for the Vaiṣṇava devotee an unparalleled celebration of Kṛṣṇa's sublime epiphany. [6; 13; 44; 111] (R.S.)

al-Suyūṭī, Jalāl al-Dīn [XII] (1445–1505). Egyptian writer of the Mamlūk period, a prolific scholar on almost every topic – theology, law, history, *belles-lettres* – whose works have been estimated to exceed 500; of course, much plagiarism and repetition of earlier authorities lies behind this prodigious output. He stemmed from Asyuṭ in Middle Egypt. In the course of his career he filled various legal and teaching posts in Cairo. His many works in the theological field include collections of traditions and on the special privileges (*khaṣā'iṣ*) of MUḤAMMAD; a compendious work on the various sciences used in study of the Qur'ān, *al-Itqān fī ʿulūm al-Qur'ān*, much used by the pioneer modern authority on the composition of the Holy Book, Theodor Nöldeke, for information on the Muslim exegetical tradition; and the completion of a Qur'ān commentary begun by his teacher Jalāl al-Dīn al-Maḥallī (*d.*1460), so that the completed work became known as *Tafsīr al-Jalālayn* ('The Commentary of the Two Jalāl al-Dīns'). This last work was early used in manuscript by pioneer Western orientalists, and is extensively cited, for instance, by George Sale in the explanatory notes to his English translation of the Qur'ān of 1734. [34: s.v.; 111] (C.E.B.)

Suzuki, Daisetz Teitarō [IV] (1870–1966). Japanese Zen Buddhist layman who, by his writings and lectures, 'single-handedly' made Zen a household word in the West. Born in Kanazawa, where his lifelong friendship with Nishida Kitarō (1870–1945), Japan's pre-eminent modern philosopher, began, he underwent Zen training under Shaku Sōen Rōshi in Kamakura while studying in Tokyo. He lived in the United States of America for two longer periods: from 1897 till 1908 as a collaborator of the Orientalist Paul Carus, and again from 1949 lecturing in various universities. In Japan he held the chair of Buddhist philosophy at Ōtani University (from 1921). His American wife, Beatrice Lane, whom he married in 1921, was his faithful collaborator until her death in 1939. Among his voluminous literary output (32 volumes in Japanese and almost 30 in English) his introductions to Zen are best known in the West: *Essays in Zen Buddhism* [211], *An Introduction to Zen Buddhism* [210], *Zen and Japanese Culture* [212], and so forth. He also contributed to the present flowering of Buddhist studies in Japan as well as in the West by his many translations of and introductions to Buddhist sūtras and śāstras. (J.V.B.)

Svaminarayan [XI] [Svāmīnārāyaṇa; Sahajānanda] (1781–1830). The founder of the reformist Hindu sect now called after him and in which he now has quasi-divine status as an avatar of Parabrahma. Born in North India near Ayodhya, he is said to have left home at the age of 11 to begin the traditional Hindu pilgrimage round the sacred places of India. In 1800 he arrived in Saurashtra and became the favourite disciple of an established *sadhu*, Rāmānand, whom he succeeded as head of his 'fellowship of virtue' (*satsanga*) – the descriptive name most favoured within the sect. He travelled widely in Saurashtra and mainland Gujarat with an ever-growing band of followers, teaching a conventional form of Vaiṣṇava devotionalism and a strict morality which was a conscious reaction against the hedonistic excesses of the Vallabhite sect which had dominated Gujarati Vaiṣṇavism before his time. Bishop Heber met him on his travels and has left an account of their debate, a little cameo of mutual incomprehension between Christian bishop and Hindu *ācārya*. After Svaminarayan's death of fever in 1830 the sect continued to grow and prosper, subsequently splitting into several sub-sects, as is the way with most religious movements. What are generally considered the two senior branches are at Ahmadabad and Vadatal, between Nadiad and Anand, but there is now a grand Svaminarayan temple in almost every town and large village in Gujarat. Outside India, wherever Gujarati people have established themselves in any number, there are followers of one or other branch of the *satsanga* and temples such as those in London and New York. Svaminarayan's teaching is preserved in the *Vacanāmṛta* and the *Śikṣāpatrī*, collections of his sayings (*vacana*) and his teachings (*śikṣā*) which were compiled by his followers after his death. The latter was first translated by the Sanskritist Monier-Williams in 1882, but the *Vacanāmṛta* still has to be translated adequately. [115] (I.M.P.R.)

Sveinbjorn Beinteinsson [VIII] (20th century). An Icelandic farmer and poet who, with the help of a journalist, Dagur Thorleifsson, attempted to revive the pre-Christian religion in Iceland under the name *Ásatrúarmenn* (believers in the Æsir, the northern gods). It was recognized as an official religious sect in 1973, and the first midsummer sacrificial feast was held on Sveinbjörn's farm in Borgarfjord in that year, but was not a success owing to appalling weather conditions and disruption by drunken 'hippies'. The cult advocated a return to folk beliefs with a vague background of theosophy, but there was no strong religious content in what was offered, and apart from celebrating a few marriages the movement now does little and is on the decline. (H.E.D.)

Swedenborg, Emanuel [VI.A] [Emanuel Svedberg] (1688–1772). Swedish scientist, philosopher, theologian and mystic. His father, a Lutheran, was professor of theology at Uppsala and Bishop of Skara. Emanuel studied at the University of Uppsala. After travel to England he was appointed to the Royal College of Mines by Charles XII in 1715, a post he held until 1747. He published works on mathematical and scientific subjects until 1734, when, following a religious crisis, he turned to religious questions. His study of geology and palaeontology led to his theories on creation, which were published in *Principia rerum naturalium* (1734) and *De infinito et causa finali creationis* (1734). He studied physiology and anatomy and published *Oeconomia regni animalis* (1740–41) and *Regnum animale* (1744–5), in which he speculated on the relationship between soul and body. His religious writings include *Arcana caelestia* (eight volumes, 1749–56) in which he gave interpretations of *Genesis* and *Exodus*. His religious views rejected traditional Christian views of redemption, Christ being merely the highest manifestation of humanity. He published many works on religion; his religious views were summed up in *The Christian Religion* (1771). He died in London and was buried there until his remains were removed to Stockholm in 1908. The New Church, which he founded as a movement alongside the traditional churches, not as a separate sect, has buildings and groups in Europe, the United States and in Australia. [409; 731] (T.T.)

Symeon the New Theologian [VI.B] (949–1022). Byzantine monk and mystic. He entered the Studios monastery in Constantinople in his late twenties. He became abbot of the monastery of St Mamas in 980, but the monks rebelled against his austere regime. The example of his spiritual father, Symeon the Pious, is central to his view of the religious life. He stresses individual spiritual experience and believes all Christians capable of knowing God directly. This may be seen as a reaction against the rigid formalism of Byzantine Christianity in his time. His hymns and discourses refer repeatedly to the divine light that transfigures the true believer. [19; 51; 88] (K.P.)

Synesius of Cyrene [VI.B] (*b c.* 375). A pagan aristocrat, Synesius studied in Alexandria under Hypatia, a pagan Neo-platonist philosopher later killed by a Christian mob. Elected Bishop of Ptolemais though not baptized and not a believing Christian, he accepted the office provided he could live openly with his wife (celibate bishops were usual) and accept as symbolic and mythical many Christian beliefs such as the resurrection of the body and the virgin birth of Christ. As bishop he was an eminent defender of his flock. He wrote widely, including devotional hymns. Synesius is the antithesis of Hypatia: she is an outpost of pagan philosophy in a world turned Christian; he, a pagan intellectual who becomes Christian as the only way to contribute fully to the cultural and social life of his world. [13] (D.J.M.)

T

al-Ṭabarī, Abū Ja ʿfar Muḥammad ibn Jarīr [XII] (839–923). Islamic religious scholar and historian. A Persian who spent most of his life in Baghdad, al-Ṭabarī devoted himself to scholarly activities, collecting Muslim traditions from the preceding generations. He attempted to form his own legal school, following to a great extent the position of AL-SHĀFIʿĪ, but it quickly fell into obscurity after his death.

Al-Ṭabarī wrote on many subjects including poetry, lexicography, grammar, ethics, law, mathematics and medicine, but he is most famous for two very extensive works, one on history, the other on the interpretation of the Qur'ān. His world history, *Ta'rīkh al-rusul wa'l-mulūk* ('The History of the Prophets and the Kings'), commences with the Biblical patriarchs, details some early rulers and then moves on to Sasanian history. The text is far more detailed when covering the history after this point and is organized year by year for the life of MUḤAMMAD, the first four caliphs of Islam (ABŪ BAKR; ʿUMAR; ʿUTHMĀN; ʿALĪ), the Umayyad dynasty and the ʿAbbasid rulers up until the year 915. The work compiles records from a variety of sources, often presenting unreconciled variant accounts. Regional and partisan accounts, reflecting al-Ṭabarī's own views, can be noted.

Al-Ṭabarī's *Jamīʿ al-bayān ʿan ta'wīl āy al-Qur'ān* ('The Gathering of the Explanation of the Interpretation of the Qur'ān') is another massive work bringing together a vast amount of traditional material relating to the interpretation of the Qur'ān. There is once again a significant amount of duplication in the reports which are collated in the work, presenting many different opinions on topics of grammar, lexicography, theology and basic interpretational issues. Here al-Ṭabarī frequently interjects his own opinions, not necessarily supported by the reports which he cites.

The value of al-Ṭabarī's works is enormous to modern scholarship. His works are among the most extensive and the earliest available on both history and Qur'ānic interpretation. The voluminous nature of both works, however, meant that their circulation was limited until the 20th century; in fact, for much of the 19th century, the complete version of al-Ṭabarī's Qur'ān commentary was considered to have been lost. [27; 130] (A.R.)

Tagore, Debendranath [XI] (1817–1905). Bengali Hindu thinker. The eldest son of a wealthy Calcutta businessman, Dwarkanath Tagore, he was educated at a school founded by RAMMOHUN ROY, who led him to renounce idolatry, and then at the Hindu College, a school which fostered Western learning. Unlike his ancestors, who were much influenced by Mughal culture, and his father, who looked Westwards and travelled twice to England, Debendranath retained an allegiance to Hindu traditions while remaining open to Western intellectual influence. In 1843 he reorganized Rammohun's Brahmo Samaj, giving it for the first time a definite membership, committed to the daily worship of the one formless God, and to the renunciation of idolatry. At this period he believed that the Brahmanical tradition, if properly studied, would provide a basis for his theistic views; however, criticism of that tradition from the Christian standpoint forced him to change his position, first dissociating himself from Advaita Vedanta (the interpretation of the Upaniṣads which insists that Brahman is the sole reality) and then, in 1850, abandoning the authority of the Vedas in favour of 'the pure heart, filled with the light of intuitive knowledge' [102: 161]. He was partly influenced by a similar change of position in Unitarianism, led by JAMES MARTINEAU and Theodore Parker. In the 1860s he became increasingly identified with the conservative, Hinduizing faction in the Brahmo Samaj; the opposite faction led by KESHUB CHUNDER SEN separated in 1866, leaving Debendranath's minority group to survive as the Adi ('original') Brahmo Samaj. Much of his thought was devoted to the development of Brahmo rituals to replace traditional Hindu rituals, which he rejected as idolatrous. He established his own place of retreat, Śāntiniketan, which was developed further by his son RABINDRANATH TAGORE. In 1898 he published an autobiography which reveals his contemplative personality. [21: 62–77; 24: vol. 2: 52–63; 102] (D.H.K.)

Tagore, Rabindranath [XI] (1861–1941). Bengali poet. He was born in Calcutta, and brought up in the Brahmo tradition of his father DEBENDRANATH TAGORE. He had little formal education, but read prodigiously in Bengali and English. He composed Bengali poetry [104] from his childhood to his deathbed, as well as novels, plays and essays, and holds a unique position in Bengali literature; he also composed music, and in 1925 took up painting. The reputation he acquired in the English-speaking world was anomalous, and something of an embarrassment: on his third visit to England, in 1912, he brought with him a book of English versions of some of his poems, which attracted the admiration of English critics who knew nothing of Bengali and little of India, and led to his receiving the Nobel Prize for Literature, the first Indian to do so. The English versions in this collection, *Gitanjali*, and others by himself and his associates, were but dim reflections of the originals. Though he became secretary of the Adi Brahmo Samaj in 1884, he was never a religious leader; his influence spread through his writings and through personal friendships. In the 1890s he associated himself with the growing nationalist movement, and in 1905 he opposed the partition of Bengal, but in 1907 he withdrew from politics, rejecting nationalism for internationalism. From 1921 he publicly opposed GANDHI's non-cooperation movement, being reconciled with Gandhi only in 1933. In 1921 he founded Visvabharati University at Śāntiniketan, his father's rural retreat, promoting the study of agriculture and the arts. His Hibbert Lectures in Oxford in 1930 [103] exemplify some recurrent themes of his religious thought: his love of the Upaniṣads inherited from his father; his dislike of constraints and boundaries; his identification of God with the human spirit; his faith in aesthetic experience as a source of truth; and his sense of affinity with the Bāuls, the wandering devotional poets of Bengal. [61] (D.H.K.)

Ṭāhira Qurrat al-ʿAyn [III] [Ṭāhirih] (1813?–1852). An outstanding female exponent of the Bābī movement, and author of a small but important collection of Persian and Arabic poetry. Born in Qazvīn, Iran, into a family of Shiʿite clerics, she was well educated and achieved a reputation as a woman cleric (*ʿālima*). In the 1830s, after converting to the Shaykhī school, she lived in Iraq, studying under the school's leader, Sayyid Kāẓim Rashtī (who named her Qurrat al-ʿAyn, 'Solace of the Eyes'). When a radical group of younger Shaykhīs initiated the Bābī movement in 1844 she was among the first to join them, and by 1845 had become the movement's chief exponent in Iraq. She and her followers espoused radically antinomian views, splitting with more conservative Bābīs. Reports that she appeared unveiled in public and encouraged others to defy Islamic custom led to her arrest and confinement.

Expelled from Iraq in 1847, she returned to Qazvīn, but was soon forced to flee, following an accusation of involvement in the murder of her uncle, an anti-Bābī cleric. In the summer of 1848 she played a central part in a gathering where Islamic law was formally abrogated and the Resurrection announced. During the Bābī-state struggles from late 1848, she remained in hiding, but in 1850 was arrested and confined in Tehran. Most of her poetry was written during this period. Following an attempt on Nāṣir al-Dīn Shāh's life in August 1852, she was among some 50 Bābīs put to death in retribution.

Ṭāhira became famous in European literary circles. A play and numerous poems were written about her, in which she figures as a champion of women's rights against the forces of Islamic obscurantism. Modern Bahāʾīs regard her as the first suffragette martyr, but none of her own extant writings give any support to this. [13: 'Ḳurrat al'Ayn'; 18] (D.M.)

T'ai-hsü [IV] (1889–1947). Modern-day reformer of Chinese Buddhism. T'ai-hsü was a monk who worked from within the Buddhist community for reform in the midst of modern decadence and an anti-Buddhist social milieu. He aimed to renew and reform the monastic community, use Buddhist property to benefit the people at large, and revive the study of Buddhist doctrines, a programme outlined in his work on *The Reorganization of the Buddhist Community* published in 1915. He organized the Chinese Buddhist Society in 1929, which grew to include millions of members. He encouraged Buddhist scholarship by founding a number of institutes, the most famous being the Wu-ch'ang Buddhist Institute founded in 1922, which, along with the Institute of Inner Learning founded by Ou-yang Chien in Nanking, the Buddhist Institute of Southern Fukien in Amoy, and the Institute of the Three Times in Peking (all founded at around the same time), contributed to the development of new Buddhist leaders. Another result of these efforts was the publication of various texts from the Buddhist canon. T'ai-hsü also contributed to Buddhist periodicals, especially the *Hai-ch'ao-yin* ('Sound of the Ocean Tide'), which was edited and published under the auspices of the Wu-ch'ang Buddhist Institute. He was also actively involved in the revival of Fa-hsiang scholarship inspired by the reintroduction from Japan of K'UEI-CHI's commentary on the *Ch'eng wei-shih lun*. T'ai-hsü's collected works were published in 64 volumes. [31: 456-8; 252: 51–7] (P.L.S.)

Takuan Sōhō [IV] (1573–1645). Japanese Buddhist monk of the Rinzai Zen school and noted scholar, calligrapher, and painter. He was affiliated with Daitoku-ji, the most important temple of the Gozan ('five mountains') system and a centre of Zen culture. Appointed abbot of Daitoku-ji at the young age of 35, he made important contributions to the Zen arts of tea, swordsmanship, calligraphy, poetry and painting. He was spiritual advisor to the Shogun Tokugawa Iemitsu, and his relationship with Iemitsu's sword master Yagyū Munenori is especially well known. Takuan also wrote extensively on Zen theory and was well acquainted with Confucian studies. His *Ri-ki sabetsu ron* ('The Difference between *ri* and *ki*') is a study of Confucianism from the perspective of Zen Buddhism. (P.L.S.)

Tallis, Thomas [VI.A] (*c.*1505–1585). English composer. He was organist at Waltham Abbey from 1538 until its dissolution two years later. He then became a lay clerk at Canterbury Cathedral. In 1541 he was appointed as Gentleman of the Chapel Royal; this marked the beginning of an association with the royal family which continued for the rest of his life. In 1575 he and his younger colleague WILLIAM BYRD were granted a monopoly of music printing. His works include large-scale liturgical settings in Latin (including works in Latin produced after the accession of Elizabeth I) and anthems for Anglican services. His music reflects pre- and post-Reformation traditions. His works include *Lamentations of Jeremiah* for five voices and *Spem in alium nunquam habui* for 40 voices. [208] (E.M.)

Tam, Jacob ben Meir [XV] [also known as Rabbenu Tam = 'our perfect rabbi'] (*c.*1100–1171). Rabbinical authority in France. He was born in Ramerupt, eastern France, and was a grandson of RASHI. He studied with members of his family, including his two brothers, both outstanding talmudists. Jacob headed an academy in his home town which attracted great scholars from near and far, and to which Jewish communities from many lands referred their queries on matters of Jewish law. In 1147 his home was destroyed by passing Crusaders, during the Second Crusade, and he himself narrowly escaped death. After this he moved to Troyes, where he convened a rabbinical synod which issued decrees binding on Jews throughout northern France to meet contemporary exigencies and strengthen religious observance.

He was a member of the school of Tosafists which developed Rashi's comments on the Talmud. His own best known work was *Sefer ha-Yashar* ('Book of the Righteous'), which contains many of his expositions and *novellae* and also seeks to determine the correct text of the Talmud. He was the first French rabbinical scholar to exhibit interest in the work of his Spanish counterparts. He also wrote on Hebrew grammar and the Bible, as well as composing religious verse and hymns. [87: vol. 2: 18–21] (G.W.)

Taniguchi Masaharu [xiv] (1893–1985). Founder of Seichō no ie ('The Household of Growth'), a Japanese new religion. Born near Kobe, he was adopted by a maternal aunt at the age of four. She sponsored his education at Waseda University where he studied English literature. He left the university, however, after an affair with a 17-year-old. In his twenties and thirties Taniguchi was active in Ōmotokyō, where his journalistic skills were recognized. He styled himself 'St. Francis of Ōmoto'.

In 1929 he had a series of revelations which led him to start publishing a magazine, *Seichō no ie*, in which he offered advice on how to resolve various problems in the lives of his readers. He also published numerous other magazines and books, including one entitled *Seimei no jissō* ('The Truth of Life') [57], a collection of his magazine pieces which sold more than 750,000 copies up to 1935. This became a serial publication, with over 40 volumes appearing. From Ōmoto he took the idea that sin and divine punishment are unreal. He taught that the material world is only the shadow of the mind, and that the only fundamental reality (*jissō*) is the mind and the original nature of man. According to his religious anthropology, humankind is the child of the deity and, thus, original human nature is pure. The corruption of the world is a reflection of the corruption of mind, most importantly through the lack of gratitude.

Taniguchi taught that all religions are essentially the same and thus worthy of respect, although Seichō no ie alone has disclosed the fundamental reality that informs them all. His world-view was eclectic, incorporating elements from Buddhism, Christianity and Christian Science, as well as Freudian psychology and aspects of philosophers such as HEGEL and Bergson. A nationalist (or, according to some, an opportunist), he supported the war effort and promoted worship of the emperor. He also registered his organization as a publishing concern and then later as a religious organization as socio-political conditions altered. In the post-war period he favoured a return to what he held to be traditional Shintō beliefs and proper morality, while professing universalism and nationalism in so far as he sought to reveal the essential truth in the authentic Japanese way of life preserved in the *Kojiki* [49], *Nihonshiki*, *Norito*, and other literary classics. Taniguchi was a tireless writer, producing more than 300 books and thousands of articles [5; 12: 147–77; 34: 223–4, 313–14; 41: 145–72; 56; 59: 153–72] (G.E.)

Tansar [xxvi] [Tosar] (3rd century). The first great prelate of Sasanian times. He was chief priest (*hērbad*) under ARDAŠĪR, and, as is shown by a letter from him (surviving through various redactions), acted as a persuasive propagandist for that king at the outset of his reign [7: 10.3.1]. Tansar is described in a Pahlavi text as 'the spiritual leader, eloquent, truthful, just', to be hearkened to as exponent of ZOROASTER's faith [9: 103]. On his advice, Ardašīr had all extant Avestan texts (still in oral transmission) collected, and Tansar 'selected those which were trustworthy and left the rest out of the canon' [7: 10.3.4.3] (*compare* VALAKHŠ). He was, it seems, directly succeeded by KIRDĒR. (M.B.)

Tao-an [iv] (312–385). Eminent Chinese Buddhist monk and scholar. Tao-an studied Buddhist texts on *prajñā* wisdom and *dhyāna* practice under Fo-t'u-teng (232–348), a master of spiritual powers from Central Asia, and produced a series of commentaries on texts translated by An Shih-kai (2nd century). At this time it was common to translate Buddhist texts using the *ke-yi* ('matching terms') method of using indigenous Chinese philosophical terms to translate Buddhist concepts. Tao-an criticized this method, arguing that the practice ultimately contributed to misunderstanding, and he provided new translations and commentaries on Buddhist texts such as the *Prajñāpāramitā Sūtras*. His efforts to communicate the Buddhist *dharma* included the compilation of a pioneering catalogue of Buddhist texts, the *Tsung-li chung-ching mu-lu*, more commonly known as the *Tao-an lu*. He identified many texts as spurious sūtras, providing scholars and monks with convenient data on the origin and identification of texts, and laid the groundwork for a whole genre of Buddhist scholarship, the textual catalogues.

Tao-an also developed his own rules for the monastic community, since the complete *vinaya* was not available in China at that time, initiated the practice of adding the 'Shih' prefix (for Śākyamuni – *see* BUDDHA) to monks' names instead of their family names, and organized a cult to Maitreya, the Buddha of the future. His disciples include Hui-yüan (334–416), who founded the centre for Pure Land practices at Lu-shan and carried on a famous correspondence with KUMĀRAJĪVA. [234: 553–99, 655–753; 31: 94–103] (P.L.S.)

T'ao Hung-ching [v] (456–536). In effect the founder of the Taoist Sect of Highest Clarity (*shang ch'ing*) based on the mountain of the Three Mao Brothers (*mao shan*) in Kiangsi province. A broadly educated scholar, T'ao came upon the manuscripts of spirit-writing dictated to the medium YANG HSI between 364 and 370, and was profoundly impressed by their contents. He devoted much of his considerable talents to putting these revelations in order and commenting on them, the result being the establishment of the Shang Ch'ing scriptural corpus. Especially interesting in this connection is what T'ao called the 'Declarations of the Perfected' (*chen kao*). T'ao was also an alchemical adept in both the exterior elixir (*wai tan*) and the interior elixir (*nei tan*) forms. The former involves concoction of the elixir from substances, while the latter is a kind of meditative concoction of the elixir. The Sect of Highest Clarity, thanks to T'ao Hung-ching's efforts, became one of the most important Taoist movements, its scriptures constituting one of the three major divisions of the canon (*tao tsang*). [51; 52] (L.T.)

Tārā Siṅgh, Master [XXIII] (1885–1967). Sikh political and religious leader. A Hindu Khatri by birth, Tārā Siṅgh embraced Sikhism at the age of 17. On graduating from Khalsa College in 1908 he was appointed headmaster of a school, hence the prefix 'Master' to his name. His active role in the Akālī movement in the 1920s propelled him to a leadership position both in Sikh politics and religious affairs [45: 65–6]. After leading Sikhs through the traumatic experience of India's partition in 1947, Tārā Siṅgh vigorously pushed for the establishment of Punjabi Sūbā, a Sikh majority state in independent India [1: 3; 65: 7]. Although several of his campaigns for securing Punjabi Sūbā backfired and considerably diminished his leadership, eventually his aspirations were fulfilled with the creation of a Sikh majority

state in 1966. Tārā Siṅgh is an excellent examplar of the Sikh idea that religion and politics are not to be separated. (H.S.O.)

Tasan. *See* CHŎNG YAGYONG.

Teacher of Righteousness [XV]. The prophet of the Dead Sea sect, whose name and date of activity are unknown. The documents of the sect were first discovered at Qumran, on the shores of the Dead Sea, in 1947 and have given rise to intense speculation concerning the identity of the community and of the persons mentioned in its scrolls. The most widely accepted theory is that they belonged to a branch of the Essenes, an ascetic group that existed in the last centuries of the Second Temple period.

The scrolls state that 'God raised a teacher of righteousness to guide them' and that 'God made known to him all the mysteries of the words of his servants, the prophets'. The teacher was apparently either the founder or re-founder of the community, which regarded his words as divinely inspired. He forecast the forthcoming end of the world. His fate is described in apocryphal terms which have been interpreted in various ways. He was opposed by 'the man of lies' and had to flee to exile in 'the land of Damascus' (probably not to be taken literally), and even in exile was persecuted by 'the wicked priest'. Many identifications have been proposed for these individuals. Most of the suggestions concerning the teacher of righteousness (or 'righteous teacher') relate to individuals who lived between the 2nd century BCE and the 1st century CE. The authors of the scrolls held that faith in the teacher's mission was essential for salvation, and that the teacher would return at the end of days. The community's belief in their election as members of a 'New Covenant' and their adoption of a calendar that differed from the standard Jewish one brought them into sharp conflict with the Jewish mainstream of their day. [11; 15] (G.W.)

Tecayehuatzin [XVIII] (late 15th century). Famous Nahuatl sage who lived in the Aztec community of Huexotzinco, where he was the ruler for a period. Not only was he a renowned poet whose compositions explored the cosmological powers of Tloque Nahuaque, Lord of the Everywhere and Giver of Life, but he also organized a festival of poetry in which the leading sages and poets from neighbouring cities participated in a dialogue on the nature of symbolism, truth, God and artistic creation. Around 1490 in the gardens of his palace he fed his guests chocolate and tobacco and initiated a discourse on the nature of reality on earth and the role of *in xochitl, in cuicatl* ('flowers and songs', i.e. poetry and art) in achieving true knowledge of the divine. [4: 175]

His own exploration of the human–divine relationship included the designation of God as 'the inventor of himself', whom humans should 'gladden' with their poems, rites, sacred architecture and music. For in the moment when these words, actions, places and sounds are truly expressed with hearts which are inspired, then 'the Giver of Life . . . adorns himself in the place of the drums', i.e. is alive within these expressions.

This statement of cosmovision initiated the discourse with poetic responses from Prince Ayocuan, the noble Aquiauhtzin, the noble Motenehuatzin, Prince Xayacamach and others. Of particular note is the view of Ayocuan, who emphasized the distance between humans and gods and the tendency of poets actually to spoil the songs, insights and truths which come from heaven, for 'our inventiveness makes them lose their fragrance' [5: 257–8]. Yet in spite of this human frailty, the truth of flowers and songs will endure in the highest region of heaven.

These poets and their world-view were long remembered and repeated, even after the conquest of 1521. (D.C.)

Tecumseh [xx] (*d.*1813). Shawnee war chief and brother of Tenskwataya, 'The Prophet'. He was one of the greatest Amerindian leaders, drawing in later life upon the religious visions of his brother to promote his message of unity among native peoples. Tecumseh is known principally for his belief in a separate political state for Amerindians in which they might pursue their traditional religion and ways of life. A staunch opponent of land sales to the Whites, he often expressed the view that one could no more sell the land than the sea or the air one breathed. His message of tribal unity was carried personally from the Great Lakes region to the Gulf of Mexico and gained acceptance among the Winnebagos, Ojibwas and Potawatomis. The westward White expansion resulted in inevitable conflicts, and Tecumseh engaged in occasional conflicts with the settlers and emigrants. During the war of 1812 he fought on the side of the British in the expectation that they would permit the independent Indian state he dreamed of. Tecumseh was killed on 5 October 1813, at the Thames River, Southern Canada. [5] (S.R.)

Tegh Bahādur, Gurū [xxiii] (1621–1675). Ninth Gurū of the Sikhs. He was a younger son of the sixth Gurū, Hargobind. Tradition regards him as a withdrawn person, a view which receives some support from his works, which were later added to the *Ādi Granth*. Most of his life before becoming Gurū was spent in the village of Bakālā, near Amritsar. Tradition also records that he became the ninth Gurū when his predecessor, Hari Krishan, uttered the words 'Bābā Bakāle' ('The Bābā who is in Bakālā') just before his death in 1664.

After being refused entry to Amritsar by a rival who was in possession of the town, Gurū Tegh Bahādur moved to Kīratpur at the edge of the Shivalik Hills, and from there to the neighbouring village of Makhovāl, where the new centre of Chak Nānakī (later Anandpur) was developed. In 1665 he departed on an extended journey to the east of India where in Paṭnā his only son, Gobind Rāi (later Gobind Siṅgh), was born in December 1666.

Returning to Chak Nānakī he spent time touring on the plains, visiting those Sikhs who had remained faithful to him. This was the period of rival Gurūs and there was marked hostility from other contenders to the title. In 1675 he was arrested in circumstances which are disputed. According to Muslim sources he was taken as a brigand. Sikh sources, however, vigorously resist this interpretation. The dominant view attributes it to the Gurū's intercession on behalf of a group of Kashmiri Brahmans threatened with conversion to Islam. A minority interpretation maintains that the reason was a request put to the Mughal authorities by one of the Gurū's rivals, Dhīr Mal. Later in the same year Gurū Tegh Bahādur, having refused the choice of Islam, was beheaded in Delhi. [17: II–VII; 37: II–VII] (W.H.M.)

Teilhard de Chardin, Pierre [vi.a] (1881–1955). French philosopher and palaeontologist. He was born near Clermont-Ferrand, France into a farming family. He entered the Society of Jesus in 1899 and from 1905 to 1908 taught at the Jesuit school in Cairo. It was during this period that he began to take an interest in geology and palaeontology. He was ordained priest in 1911 and then studied for a doctorate in geology and palaeontology at the Sorbonne, Paris. In 1914, at the outbreak of the First World War, he became a stretcher-bearer. After the war he continued his doctoral studies and completed them in 1922. In the same year he was appointed professor of geology at the Institut Catholique in Paris. He was removed from this post by his superior in the order on account of a paper he wrote on the relation of evolution to original sin. He was sent to China, where he remained for 20 years, continuing his palaeontological researches in excavations near Tientsin and Peking. He was involved in the discovery of the 200,000-year-old 'Peking Man'. He returned to France in 1946 and became director of research at the Centre Nationale de la Recherche Scientifique. In 1948 he sought permission from the order to apply for the chair of palaeontology at the Collège de France. Permission was refused, as were his attempts to publish his papers on evolution. In 1951 he moved to New York and died there. During his life he wrote three books and many essays on evolution and the Christian religion, none of which was published until after his death, when with the publication of *The Phenomenon of Man* (1959) and *The Divine Milieu* (1960), he immediately became posthumously famous. [179; 311; 562] (T.T.)

Tejā Siṅgh Bhasauṛ [XXIII] (1866–1933). Born into a respected family of Sidhu Jaṭs, Tejā Siṅgh grew up to be the most controversial of modern Sikh religious leaders. A civil-engineer by profession, Tejā Siṅgh founded a branch of the Siṅgh Sabhā in his native village of Bhasaur in 1893 and very rapidly turned it into a powerful vehicle to advance Sikhism [6: 26–7]. He gained wide recognition for his success in administering *Khālsā pāhul* to hundreds of people, particularly women. His ceaseless efforts to transform Sikh doctrines, rituals and code of conduct prompted considerable debate and opposition. In 1928 Tejā Siṅgh was excommunicated for garbling and altering the order of writings in the *Ādi Granth*, the Sikh scripture. (H.S.O.)

Tekakwitha, Kateri [VI.A] (*c*.1656–1680). Amerindian Christian. She was born in Gandahouhaguen, in Iroquoian territory, near present-day Fonda, New York. Her father was Mohawk and her mother Algonquin. When she was four years old Tekakwitha's family died of smallpox. She also caught the disease but survived, though the illness badly affected her eyesight. In 1667 she first met Jesuit missionaries and began to adopt Christian ways. Her Indian neighbours urged her to remain within her own culture. Eventually she was baptized on Easter Day 1676. Her own people objected to her conversion so she left her native region and settled in a community of Catholic Indians near the St Lawrence river in Canada. She eventually lived in Caughnawaga, or Le Prairie de la Madeleine, a village of Christian Indians bound by their religious allegiance rather than by tribal affiliation. She adopted a life of chastity and self-denial. In 1678 she founded a community on the lines of the Hospital Sisters of Montreal. Her life of renunciation led to her grave becoming a shrine for Indian and French Catholics. She was nominated for sainthood in 1932 and was pronounced blessed in 1980. [126; 468] (T.T.)

Te Kooti Rikirangi Te Turuki [XXI] (1830–1883). Founder of a quasi-Christian sect that became a church. He was exiled to Chatham Island as a rebel in the Hauhau movement, and developed tuberculosis. His delivery from its effects he ascribed to God, and subsequently gave much attention to the Bible, particularly *Joshua* and *Judges* and many of the *Psalms*. He used *Joshua* and *Judges* to explain what had happened to him: his home was New Zealand, with the Chathams as the place of bondage. He told his fellow prisoners that God would deliver them; as the Israelites found solace in the songs of Zion so the prisoners were taught to find comfort in the *Psalms*.

In 1868, after two years of imprisonment, Te Kooti engineered an escape by capturing a schooner. Arriving in New Zealand, he sought to avoid arrest by saying he wanted peace. Armed forces attempted to capture him but failed. In reprisal he massacred some hamlets in Poverty Bay where those who had helped deport him still lived. He then escaped and lived for some years in the hills of the Urewera. Ultimately the Maori King Tawhiao gave him refuge for several years, during which time he put together prayers, hymns and scriptural readings.

Eventually he was granted a pardon, and returned to an area near Opotiki. He spent time visiting the developing number of his followers, instructing them in the prayers, hymns and readings he had devised. These are still memorized and said aloud in independent church services. He trained ministers (*tohunga* or experts), especially for the task of caring for the sick, and ensured that correct prayers were said. Today there are about 5,000 members of his church, spread mainly in rural areas. When young people leave to go to cities they have the church's *tapu* removed from them. [9: 139–45; 19; 36] (J.I.)

Tempels, Placied [VI.A] [Placide Tempels] (1906–1977). Belgian Roman Catholic missionary and religious interpreter. He was born in Limburg, Belgium, and entered the Franciscan order in 1924. He was ordained in 1930 and sent to Katanga, Belgian Congo (Zaire), in 1933. Tempels divided his African career into three phases. In the first ten years he was a conventional 'Bush Father' engaged in the colonial *mission civilisatrice*, assuming it a Christian duty to destroy the pre-Christian past. From about 1943, however, he began to listen attentively to his parishioners, discover the depth of African thinking, and to adapt, both in his teaching and personal life. One product was a book which appeared first in articles in Flemish and then in 1946 as *La Philosophie bantoue*, arguing the existence of a rich indigenous African philosophy with 'vital force' as its foundation. The book was enthusiastically greeted by the rising exponents of Negritude; Alioune Diop wrote a preface for a new edition by Présence Africaine, and a new generation of African theologians such as KAGAME and MULAGO took the ideas into Catholic theology. The hierarchy, however, disapproved, and Tempels was kept away from Congo for three years. In Belgium his third phase began, with a critical religious experience which caused him to see Christian faith in interpersonal terms, easily correlated with the 'desire for full, total, intense life . . . for union with others' which marked 'Bantu philosophy' as he had met it. Allowed to return to Congo in 1949, he began to apply these principles in his teaching about union with Christ, union of priest and people, union of husband and wife, unity of the Christian community. There was a warm response, one aspect of which was the formation of the lay movement Jamaa ('family') within the Catholic Church. The movement disturbed the Church authorities, and Tempels was inhibited by his order in 1963. He was cleared of heterodoxy and improper behaviour by a Vatican examination but not permitted to return to Zaire. Jamaa had its own dynamic, and remains an important factor in the religious life of Katanga. [170; 250] (A.F.W.)

Temple, William [VI.A] (1881–1944). Archbishop of Canterbury, 1942–4. He was born when his father, Frederick Temple, later Archbishop of Canterbury (1896–1902), was Bishop of Exeter, England. William studied at Balliol College, Oxford, from 1900 and in 1904 became a fellow of Queen's College, Oxford. He became headmaster of Repton, an English public school, in 1910 before becoming rector of St James's, Piccadilly, London in 1914. He was made a Canon of Westminster in 1919 and then became Bishop of Manchester (1921), Archbishop of York (1929) and Archbishop of Canterbury in 1942. He was closely associated with the Workers' Educational Association, of which he was president from 1908 to 1924 and also with the Student Christian Movement. He was prominent as a theologian, philosopher and social thinker in the Church of England. He also devoted time to the ecumenical movement and was president of the putative World Council of Churches (formally inaugurated in 1948) from 1943. Among his main works are *Mens Creatrix* (1917), *Christus Veritas* (1924) and *Nature, Man and God* (Gifford Lectures for 1932–3 and 1933–4, published in 1934). [386; 668; 781] (T.T.)

Tenskwataya [XX] [Tenskwatawa] (1768–*c.*1836). A Shawnee prophet and brother of TECUMSEH. He was born in Chillicothe, Ohio, in March 1768 and embarked upon his prophetic career at the age of 37, achieving fame early by successfully predicting an eclipse. Tenskwataya preached the necessity of returning to traditional ways and of avoiding the evils of alcoholism and intermarriage with Whites. His religious vision merged with the political strategy of his brother, Tecumseh, and led to significant clashes with Whites, though at first both tried to avoid such conflicts. His prestige declined markedly after 1811, when the federation of tribes he and his brother had attempted to forge was broken. After living for a time in Canada he returned to Kansas, where he died. [5] (S.R.)

Tenzin Gyatso. *See* DALAI LAMA.

Teresa, Mother [VI.A] [Agnes Gouxha Bojaxhiu] (1910–). Roman Catholic founder of the Congregation of the Missionaries of Charity. She was born in Skopje, Yugoslavia, of Albanian parents. She attended the local state school and joined a Catholic association for children known as the Sodality of Mary. She read of the work of Yugoslav Jesuit missionaries in Calcutta. In 1928 Agnes offered herself to the Congregation of Loreto nuns who had work in Bengal. Before entering on her novitiate in Darjeeling she was sent to Loreto Abbey in Rathfarnham, Dublin, to learn English. For a time she taught in the Loreto Convent School in Darjeeling and then took her first vows in 1931, taking the name Teresa. For 17 years she taught in a high school in Calcutta run by her order, during which time she took her final vows (1937). In 1946 she felt called to respond to the poverty around her. She had a brief medical training and in 1948 she started her new work. The following year she was joined by her first postulant and in 1950 the Pope approved the Congregation of the Missionaries of Charity. The order has a number of houses in Calcutta and elsewhere in the world, over 60 in 1980, for missionary sisters and brothers, where they minister to the sick, the dying, leprosy patients and the hungry. Mother Teresa planned to retire as superior of the order in April 1990 but was dissuaded. She was awarded the Nobel Peace Prize in 1979. [746] (T.T.)

Teresa of Ávila. [VI.A] [Teresa de Cepeda y Ahumeda] (1515–1582). Spanish Carmelite nun and mystic. She was born in Ávila, Castile, Spain, of a wealthy family which had recently converted from Judaism. She was a spiritual child fond of reading the legends of the Holy Grail. At the age of 16 she was sent to the Augustinian convent school of Our Lady of Grace in Ávila but had to return home because of illness after a year and a half. In 1536 she entered the Carmelite Convent of the Incarnation in Ávila and became a nun a year later. The regime at the convent was relaxed, even fashionable. She was afflicted with some illness again in 1538. At about the age of 40 she underwent a religious experience while praying before a statue of the flagellation of Christ. This experience was deepened by reading AUGUSTINE's *Confessions*. She adopted as her confessor St Peter of Alcantara and soon after experienced the first of her ecstasies. Thereafter she followed a more rigorous life and found convent life insufficiently demanding. Under the influence of visions she established in 1562 a reformed discalced Carmelite convent in Ávila dedicated to St Joseph. She adopted the name Teresa of Jesus. Over the next 15 years she established a new convent each year in Spain and wrote many spiritual works, including her *Life*, *Foundations* and *The Interior Castle*. She was associated with JOHN OF THE CROSS in the establishment of monasteries for friars from 1568. While returning to Ávila from Burgos where she had established her fifteenth convent she fell ill in Alba de Tormes, died and was buried there. She was canonized in 1622 and declared a doctor of the church in 1970. The nuns of the Incarnation convent themselves became discalced in 1940. [156; 313; 639] (T.T.)

Tertullian [VI.A] [Quintus Septimius Florens Tertullianus] (160?–225?). Christian theologian. A native of Carthage in North Africa, he received a pagan education in the classics and possibly in law. There is disagreement over whether he actually practised law in Rome. He was converted to Christianity some time between 193 and 195. According to JEROME he was a priest but this information is also contested in recent scholarship, the argument being that he identifies himself in his writings as a member of the laity. Tertullian identified himself with the Montanist sect, an apocalyptic and ascetic movement. Much of his writing reflects the rigour of the movement. He advocated a clear separation for Christians between correct and pagan practices. He believed Christians should not try to escape martyrdom, 'a second baptism', though he showed the futility of state persecution in his *Apology*. The saying 'The blood of the martyrs is the seed of the church' is an adaptation of Tertullian's words. He advocated a preference for celibacy, for a single marriage, fasting and the wearing of veils by virgins. Though he wrote an apology, unlike the so-called Apologists he spurned philosophy as part of his argument. In doctrine he was a forerunner of AUGUSTINE OF HIPPO, arguing strongly the case for original sin and, refuting modalism as a defence of the relations within the godhead, the first theologian to use the term 'Trinity'. [49; 783; 784] (T.T.)

Thang-stong Rgyal-po [IV] (*c.*1361–1485). Tibetan visionary yogin and Treasure (*gter-ma*) discoverer. He was also a folk hero, renowned for his exceptionally long life and his virtually unique career as a civic engineer who built iron chain suspension bridges throughout Tibet. He is remembered as the founder of the theatrical A-lce Lha-mo tradition as well. Born in Lha-rtse, he showed precocity and received novice vows at Byang Ngam-ring, seat of the Phag-mo Gru-pas. He became known as a mad eccentric. He received full ordination from Bka'-lnga-pa Dpal-'byor Shes-rab, and studied Bka'-brgyud and Rnying-ma meditative traditions. A series of retreats followed, and he may have toured India and Nepal. During this period he had a number of revelatory visions which inspired his composition of a cycle of teachings of the Indian yoginī Niguma; a short and still popular visualization treatise on his patron the bodhisattva Avalokiteśvara; a widely practised 'long-life empowerment'; and a version of MA-GCIG LAB-SGRON's Gcod. A group of Ḍākinīs named him in jest Thang-stong rgyal-po, or 'King of the Empty Plain'. In middle age he travelled extensively. At the age of 69, after being refused passage on a ferry because of his unkempt appearance, he began building bridges. Receiving the support of local officials, he mined iron in south-eastern Tibet, employed monks and blacksmiths, and completed perhaps 58 bridges, some of which still stand. He built the first temple of Sde-dge Lhun-grub, and established monastic centres at Ri-bo-che and Chu-bo-ri. He is also said to have converted the cannibals of Klo and a king of Kāmata to Buddhism. In the 19th and 20th centuries Thang-stong became an inspiration and model for the eclectic Ris-med movement. Images of him are kept by monasteries of virtually every sect; he is portrayed as a corpulent dark-skinned yogin holding a long-life vessel and an iron chain. He has been praised by the Chinese Communist regime for his public works, and an outdoor statue of him, uncommon in Tibet, has recently been erected on the Potala hill in Lhasa. [7; 56; 86; 84; 203] (J.G.)

Theodore of Mopsuestia [VI.A] (350–428). Syrian theologian. He was born in Antioch and studied rhetoric under Libanius. In 369 he entered the Asketerion, the school of Diodore in a monastery near Antioch. He remained at this school for ten years, as befitted the son of a noble family. In 392 he was made bishop of Mopsuestia, which post he held for the rest of his life. He occasionally taught at his old school and gained a reputation as a biblical exegete and theologian. He wrote against APOLLINARIS' *On the Incarnation of Christ*, adopting what may be seen as an extreme form of the two nature theory. He believed that MARY could be called the mother of God only in a nominal way. He also taught a strong humanist view of redemption which undermined the concept of original sin. As such he may be seen as a fore-runner of PELAGIUS and NESTORIUS. As a result of holding these views Theodore was condemned at the councils of Ephesus (431) and Constantinople (553). [767; 786] (T.T.)

Theodotus [IX] (mid-2nd century). A disciple of VALENTINUS and a teacher of the Egyptian school of Valentinian Gnosticism. He is known from the fragments of his writings preserved by CLEMENT OF ALEXANDRIA in his *Excerpta ex Theodoto*. Among these fragments, which describe an elaborate christology [2: 257–67], are three sayings of JESUS which do not appear in the canonical Gospels; one is like *John* 2:16 and another, 'Save thyself and thy life', echoes the story of Lot's flight from Sodom (*Genesis* 19:17), which Jesus applied eschatologically more than once (*Matthew* 10:15, 11:23, *Luke* 17:28–32). The third, 'There shall be death as long as women bear children', corresponds with the overall theme in the *Excerpta* that, although the creator God is both male and female [7: 56–7], in the *plērōma* maleness denotes angelic wholeness and the female is subjected to and transformed into the male [1: IV]. According to Theodotus salvation for Valentinians could only come about through the unification of male and female into a male syzygy, which implies a reversal of the creation story of *Genesis* 2. (G.J.B.)

Thomas, Madathiparampil Mammen [VI.A] (1916–). He was born in Panavila, Kerala, India. He entered college at Trivandrum in 1931 to study chemistry. In 1935, having experienced an evangelical religious experience, he joined the Mar Thoma Ashram in Perumpavoor after graduation. In 1937 he joined the Christavashram in Allepey and the following year left to undertake social work among homeless boys in Trivandrum. The same year he helped form the Kerala Youth Christian Council of Action and became its secretary. He engaged in social work and studies of social and political issues and was for a time youth secretary of the Mar Thoma Orthodox Church which had refused him ordination. He married Pennamma Elizabeth in 1945. In 1947 he went to Geneva to be a secretary of the World's Student Christian Federation and later an officer until 1953. In that year he went to America and studied at the Union Theological Seminary, New York, under PAUL TILLICH and REINHOLD NIEBUHR. In 1956 the Christian Institute for the Study of Religion and Society was founded in Bangalore with PAUL DEVANANDAN as Director and Thomas as associate. When Devanandan died in 1962 he succeeded him as Director until his retirement in 1976. His wife died in 1969, a year after he had been elected Chairman of the Central Committee of the World Council of Churches. He is the author of many books on Christian approaches to social and political issues and on theological issues of mission and inter-religious encounter. Among his best known works are *Christian Response to the Asian Revolution* (Duff Missionary Lectures, Edinburgh, 1966) and *Acknowledged Christ of the Indian Renaissance* (1970). In retirement he has gone back to Kerala and continues to write, mainly in the Malayalam language. [787; 788; 789] (T.T.)

Thomas à Kempis [VI.A] [Thomas Hemerken] (1379/80–1471). Theologian born in Kempen, near Cologne. He entered a school of the Brethren of the Common Life in Deventer, Holland at the age of 14. He was ordained priest in 1413 and entered an Augustinian monastery in Zwolle, Holland, where he remained until his death. Although he wrote many works he is primarily known as the author of *Imitation of Christ*. Although his authorship is not indubitably established, the balance of scholarly opinion is in his favour. The work, on the experience of the spirit of Christ, gained popularity in the face of late medieval intellectualism. [380; 434] (T.T.)

Thomas Aquinas [VI.A] (1225–1274). Italian Dominican theologian. He was born in the family castle of Roccasecca, near Aquino, Italy. At the age of five he was sent to the nearby monastery of Monte Casino to be educated. He studied the Latin psalter, reading, writing and mathematics. In 1239 he had to leave the monastery and went to the newly established University of Naples, where he remained until 1244 studying, among other subjects, the philosophy of Aristotle. While he was in Naples he was attracted by the Dominican Order of Preachers and joined them at the age of 19. Fearing family interference the order sent him first to Rome and then to Paris. *En route* he was abducted by his mother's servants and held at home against his will for over one year. His mother eventually relented and he made his way to Paris in the summer of 1245. After three years studying under Albertus Magnus in Paris Thomas accompanied him to Cologne. He was sent back to Paris in 1252 to train to be a professor. He studied and lectured on PETER LOMBARD'S *Sentences*. He wrote a commentary on the *Sentences* and a treatise entitled *Principles of Nature*. Although technically under age he was granted a licence to teach in 1256 and went on to lecture on the Bible. He began to write *Summa contra gentiles* as an aid to Dominican missionaries in Spain and North Africa. In 1259 he returned to Italy and taught at Naples, Orvieto, Rome and Viterbo until 1268. In Rome he conceived his *Summa theologiae*. The first part was completed in 1268 when he was ordered back to Paris. There he had to defend the mendicant orders against secular clergy besides preaching, teaching and continuing his work on the *Summa*, completing the second part by 1272. He returned to Naples in the same year to begin a new Dominican school. He worked intensely there and suffered some kind of nervous breakdown. The Pope insisted on his attending the Council of Lyons due to begin in May 1274 and to bring with him his treatise *Against the Errors of the Greeks* (i.e. the Greek Orthodox churches). On the journey he suffered an accident near Maenza and was taken to the Cistercian monastery of Fossanova, where he died a few days later. Though buried there, his remains were later removed to the Dominican priory in Toulouse in 1369. His *Summa theologiae*, with the third part begun, remained unfinished. [791; 792; 849] (T.T.)

Thomas the Apostle [VI.A]. St Thomas has long been associated with the establishment of Christianity in India, but, although he appears several times in St John's Gospel, his name does not occur in the Synoptic Gospels. In the Syriac tradition, his name is given as Judas Thomas or Judas the Twin, which is of interest, as in the apocryphal *Acts of St Thomas*, which contains the most elaborate account of his mission to India, he appears as Judas Thomas. These *Acts* exist in Syriac, Greek, Latin, Armenian, Ethiopic and Arabic versions; that in Syriac is considered to be the earliest, and is attributed to Bardesana of Edessa and placed in the 2nd century. They state that Thomas was sold into slavery by a merchant, Habbān, so that he might go to India, where he was engaged as a carpenter by King Gūdnaphar. This ruler is generally identified with Gondophares of Taxila, whose accession, according to the Takht-i Bāhī inscription, occurred in 21 CE. The *Acts*, however, do not readily support the tradition, specific to the 'Syrian' Christians of Kerala who claim descent from St Thomas's converts, that connects him with South India. But tradition there also makes mention of Knāyil Thomma (Thomas of Cana), who arrived in Kerala from Edessa in 345 to found the Christian settlement of Maha¯devapat.t.an.am. Mahādeva is a name of Śiva, and this might be linked with further traditions that connect the saint with Mylapore, a famous Śiva site at Madras, where he is said to have been martyred. Tangible evidence for early Christian settlements in both Kerala and Madras is afforded by the Nestorian-type foliated crosses, some bearing Pahlavi and Syriac inscriptions, which have been excavated at St Thomas' Mount, Madras and at Koṭṭayam and Cranganore in Kerala; a fifth was found in Sri Lanka. In the light of these, it is difficult not to connect Christianity in South India with Nestorians from southern Persia from the 4th century onwards, and to restrict the Apostle's mission to Gandhāra, in present-day Pakistan. Conflating the two would appear then to be a medieval confusion, but one already well established when Marco Polo went to India in 1290 [522] (J.R.M.)

Thomson, James [VI.A] [Diego Thomson] (1788–1854). He was born in Creetown, Kircudbrightshire, Scotland. As a young man he served as co-pastor of Leigh Walk Tabernacle, Edinburgh. Later he trained at the British and Foreign Bible Society (BFBS) school at Borough Road, London. In 1818 he went on his own initiative to Buenos Aires, where he set up schools and distributed the Bible. He worked in Chile from 1821 and was made director of elementary education. Both countries granted him honorary citizenship. He went to Peru in 1822 and organized public education there while arranging for the translation of the New Testament into the Quechua language. In 1825 he went to Bogotá and persuaded politicians and the Roman Catholic clergy to organize the Bible Society of Colombia. The society did not last long. He returned to Britain and got married and then spent the next 15 years as official agent for the BFBS in Mexico (1827–30), the Antilles (1831–8) and Canada (1838–42). He also studied medicine at McGill University, and graduated in 1842. For two years he was in Britain speaking on behalf of the Bible Society and then went to Spain, where he succeeded George Borrow as the Society's agent. Thomson's wife died there in 1848. In 1849 he left the Society but carried on Protestant work in Portugal and Spain. [819] (T.T.)

Thorgeir Thorkelsson [VIII] (10th century). The Lawspeaker of Iceland for 15 years before the acceptance of Christianity in *c.*1000. A number of chieftains had already adopted Christianity, and wanted a new code of laws, and their leader, Hall, requested the non-Christian, Thorgeir, to act as arbiter. After a day and night in darkness and silence, the traditional way in which seers sought inspiration, he gave his decision that Iceland must have one faith and one law only, to avoid discord, and this should be the Christian one.

Those unwilling to adopt the new faith should be permitted to continue eating horseflesh and exposing unwanted children, and might practise sacrifice to the gods in private. Thus the Christian church in Iceland began without martyrs on either side. An unusually detailed account of this decision was left by Ari Thorgilsson the Wise, a gifted and reliable scholar, who included it in his *Book of the Icelanders*, written about 1125. His information was handed down from those present at the time when Christianity became the official religion of Iceland. [5: I] (H.E.D.)

Tikhon [VI.A] [Vasili Ivanovich Belavin] (1865–1925). Patriarch of the Russian Orthodox Church, 1917–25. He was the son of a village priest in Russia. He studied at the church seminary in St Petersburg. In 1897 he was made Bishop of Lublin and the following year Bishop of the Aleutians and North America. He moved to the see of Yaroslav in 1907 and then to Vilna in 1914. In 1917, shortly after the deposition of the Tsar, he was elected Metropolitan of Moscow and then, days after the Bolshevik coup, he was elected Patriarch of Russia, the first for 200 years, by the Great Sobor. There followed a violent struggle with the communist regime. The attack of the Bolsheviks on the church, its property and its personnel, was met by Tikhon with an encyclical calling for an end to the terror and excommunicating all who collaborated in it. The state responded viciously by depriving the church of its legal status and its property. It aided the setting up of the schismatic Living Church and arrested Tikhon. By 1922 the Living Church had been allowed to seize the patriarchal palace and its administration. Though some church leaders were tried and executed, Tikhon was not. The Soviet regime realized that it could not go that far. Tikhon had ordered his clergy and laity not to engage in anti-state behaviour. In 1923 he agreed to issue an encyclical declaring his personal loyalty to the state. The regime withdrew its support for the Living Church; Tikhon was released from prison but had to remain in the Donsskoi monastery in Moscow, where he eventually died. [182; 185; 657] (T.T.)

Tilak, Bala Gangadhara [XI] [Ṭiḷaka] (1856–1920). Maharashtrian politician, whose implacable opposition to British rule earned him the title of 'father of Indian unrest'. A Chitpavan Brahman born in the Konkan, he was educated at Deccan College, Poona, and Elphinstone College, Bombay, one of the young men who came under the influence of the first nationalist Marathi writer Viṣṇuśāstrī Cipaḷūṇkar. With others he was a founder member of the New English School in Poona, where for a time in the late 1880s he taught, but his main influence was exerted as editor of the Marathi newspaper *Kesarī*, in which he constantly put forward the view that freedom must come before social reform. Tilak became the acknowledged leader of the extremists, as opposed to the moderates who were headed by his old friend Āgarkar and GANDHI's mentor, Gokhale. He was imprisoned three times: first for libel, then for incitement to disaffection and finally for sedition. On the last occasion in 1908 he was deported to Mandalay for six years; when he returned he had lost his dominating position but was still very much beloved of the people, as is expressed by his popular title 'Lokamānya'. He can be called a religious leader only in that he turned the Gaṇeś festival, traditionally celebrated by Hindus on a domestic scale only, into a sustained cultural manifesto. In a similar way he used the figure of the Maratha hero Śivājī to make statements about Hindu valour and fitness to rule. Apart from his letters and speeches and his voluminous journalism published in Marathi by the Kesari press, his only books in English are *The Orion* (1895) and its sequel *The Arctic Home in the Vedas* (1903), a gallimaufry of theories about the origin of the Aryans, and *Gītārahasya*, a long and turgid exposition of his interpretation of the *Bhagavad Gītā*, written in exile in Burma and first published in Marathi in 1915. It was translated into English in 1935. [16; 105; 117] (I.M.P.R.)

Tilak, Narayan Vaman [VI.A] (1862–1919). Indian Presbyterian minister and poet. He was born in Karazgaon, in the district of Dapoli, Ratnagiri, south of Bombay, in a family of Chitpavan Brahmans. He had an unhappy childhood and left home at the age of 11, on the death of his mother, because of the treatment he received from his father. He went to Nasik, Maharashtra, and entered school there and later college. At the age of 18 he married Lakshmi, also a Brahman, who was aged 11. They had three sons, only one of whom survived. He moved from town to town, changing jobs, teaching, printing, editing a magazine, but all the time writing Marathi poetry and acting in Marathi plays. In 1893, on the way to yet another job, he was given a copy of the New Testament in a chance encounter in a railway carriage. He had already formulated religious beliefs which were contrary to some parts of Hinduism and akin to Christianity. Reading the Sermon on the Mount brought him to a crisis which was finally resolved when he was baptized in Bombay in 1895 by an Indian minister in the American Marathi Mission, a Congregationalist organization. Later he was a Presbyterian minister for a time. He was an early advocate of the indigenization of Christianity in India. He continued to live the unattached life of a poet. Although his conversion to Christianity was a notorious affair in Hindu society, in 1915 he was, nevertheless, made president of the *Natyasammelan*, a high literary honour in Maharashtra. Apart from his secular poetry he composed hundreds of hymns in Marathi in vernacular metres which became very popular among all denominations in Maharashtra. [395; 796] (T.T.)

Tile, Nehemiah [I.A] (19th century). Considered by many to be the founder of the African independent church movement in South Africa. Tile was a prominent African leader within the Wesleyan Church who broke away in 1882 because of his strong Tembu-nationalistic sympathies. By 1884 he had founded his own 'Tembu Church', with a paramount chief as leader. The cause of this important secession was not only opposition to European control, but also a positive desire to adapt the message of the Church to the heritage of the Tembu people. He wrote the first hymnal ever produced by an African for an independent church. [34: 38] (R.H.)

Tillich, Paul [VI.A] (1886–1965). American theologian of German birth. He was born in Starzeddel, Brandenburg, the son of a Lutheran pastor. He had his early education in Königsberg and Berlin. Between 1904 and 1909 he studied philosophy and theology at the universities of Berlin, Tübingen and Halle. In 1910 he received a doctorate from the University of Breslau. In 1912 he was ordained and worked as an assistant pastor for two years in Berlin. During the First World War he was an army chaplain and spent time at the front. From 1919 to 1924 he was a *Privatdozent* in the University of Berlin. In 1924 he married his second wife, Hannah. From 1924 he was professor of philosophy and theology in the University of Marburg, the Dresden Institute of Technology and the University of Leipzig, and from 1929 the University of Frankfurt. In 1933 he was removed from his chair by the Nazis. He had been a critic of National Socialism, especially in *The Socialist Decision*, published in 1932. He had also been active in campaigning for the rights of Jews. He was invited to New York and was visiting professor at Columbia University and the Union Theological Seminary, where he remained until his retirement as full professor in 1955. In 1955 he became University Professor at Harvard University and in 1962 Nuveen Professor of Theology at the Divinity School, Chicago University. He was still in this post when he died. His main work is *Systematic Theology* (3 vols., 1951–63). His most popular works are *The Courage to Be* (1952), two volumes of sermons, *The Shaking of the Foundations* (1948), *The Eternal Now* (1963), and *Christianity and the Encounter of the World Religions* (1963). As a systematic theologian Tillich attempted to answer the questions posed by human existence with the eternal answers found in the Christian message. [3; 175; 797; 798] (T.T.)

Tilopa [IV] (988–1069). One of the '84 *siddhas*' or 'realized ones' of Indian Tantric Buddhism. Tilopa is venerated in Tibet as the human founder of the Kagyupa lineage of Tibetan Buddhism, via his Indian disciple NĀROPA, this latter's Tibetan disciple Marpa, and subsequent Tibetan teachers of that lineage (MILAREPA, SGAM-PO-PA BSOD-NAMS RIN-CHEN, the KARMA-PA incarnations and so forth).

Tilopa, according to his biography by Pemakarpo (16th–17th century), was born a Brahman in north India. At a young age he met the great *siddha* Nāgārjuna (not the same person as the philosopher NĀGĀRJUNA), who recognized his spiritual precocity and gave him teachings. Tilopa subsequently became a Buddhist monk and, later, a wandering yogin, studying with various Vajrayāna masters. Like other *siddhas*, Tilopa often travelled and practised incognito, as when, for 12 years, he crushed sesame seeds by day while acting as servant for a prostitute at night.

In spite of attaining some degree of realization Tilopa remained unsatisfied and, eventually, repaired to a grass hut on the banks of the Ganges, where he sat motionless in meditation. At this time he met the celestial Buddha Vajradhara, the embodiment of reality itself, face to face. After this meeting Tilopa declared his realization, accepted disciples, taught widely, composed texts, and acted in other ways to establish his lineage. Among his most important teachings are four 'special transmissions' (*bka'-babs*), yogic practices particularly characteristic of the Kagyupa lineage. Works attributed to Tilopa in the Tibetan canon include a collection of tantric songs, several commentaries on Vajrayāna topics, and some tantric liturgical texts. [97: 140–45; 180] (R.R.)

Timothy, Ailuros [VI.A] (*d.*477). The first patriarch of the Coptic Church in Alexandria. Little is known of his early years. His second name, meaning 'weasel', was given to him by his opponents because of his stature and alleged behaviour. He was on the side of those who opposed the decree of the Council of Chalcedon in 451. That council appointed an 'orthodox', Proterios, as patriarch of Alexandria. He was lynched by a mob. Timothy was elected in 457 by the local bishops. He was soon banished by Emperor Leo I in 460. During his exile he wrote in support of Monophysitism, although he condemned EUTYCHES for holding that Christ's body was not of the same substance as other humans. A change of emperor, for whom he wrote an encyclical which attempted to impose Monophysitism on the whole church, saw Timothy reinstated in 475, but he died two years later. [800] (T.T.)

al-Tirmidhī, Abū ʿĪsā Muḥammad ibn ʿĪsā ibn Sawra [XII] (*d.* between 883–892). Muslim Traditionist, scholar and ascetic, his collection of Prophetic *ḥadīth* is recognized as one of the six canonical collections, of which those of AL-BUKHĀRĪ and MUSLIM are the most important. Al-Tirmidhī, conforming to pattern, travelled through the Islamic Middle East in search of *ḥadīth*, meeting *inter alios* IBN ḤANBAL, al-Bukhārī and ABŪ DĀWŪD. He died in Tirmidh, where, apparently, he spent most of his working life. His collection of *ḥadīth* was in competition with others, a fact reflected in biographical anecdote: he is said to have reported from al-Bukhārī that the latter had not benefited more from al-Tirmidhī, than al-Tirmidhī had from him – a somewhat oblique claim to parity. Al-Tirmidhī is also reported to have said that he showed his book to all the scholars of Arabia, Iraq and Khurasān, and they were pleased with it. His collection includes sections on all the major divisions of Islamic law, on theology, eschatology, devotion, manners and hagiology (*manāqib*). It is remarkable for its critical remarks on individual *ḥadīth*, which seem to represent a sustained effort to classify *ḥadīth* and to elaborate a technique for doing so. It seems, however, that the manuscripts are not consistent in reporting his remarks, and the principles behind his classification are not clear. He also gives information about the relationship of a *ḥadīth* to legal rulings in the major schools, thus representing an early source for our knowledge of juristic *ikhtilāf*, i.e. divergence of opinion amongst the juristic schools. In addition to his *ḥadīth* collection, he wrote works on the character of the Prophet (*al-Shamāʾil*), on asceticism, on biographical history and on juristic topics. [34: s.v.; 41: 229–34] (N.C.)

Tirumaṅkai Āḻvār [XI] (8th century). One of the most celebrated of the Viṣṇu devotee-poets collectively termed ĀḺVĀR, and the most prolific contributor to the 'Four Thousand Compositions', *Nālāyira ppirapantam*. Tirumaṅkai was a petty chieftain ruling on what is now Tanjavur District, Tamil Nadu. He was also known as Parakālaṉ. His was a somewhat dubious reput tion as a thief: he abducted the daughter of a Śrī Vaiṣṇava doctor of higher caste, and for her sake changed his religious adherence. He also stole from a Buddhist *vihāra* at Nākapaṭṭaṉam a gold image to defray the cost of renovating the Śrīraṅkam temple. As he refers to the Pallava king Nandivarmaṉ II (731–796) as his contemporary, we know that Tirumaṅkai belonged to the 8th century. His voluminous writings in *Nālāyira ppirapantam* are all three sections in the second Thousand, entitled *Pĕriya tirumŏḻi*, and sections 8 to 10 of the third Thousand. His warlike nature is reflected in his being regarded as an incarnation of Viṣṇu's bow, *Sāraṅga*. Tirumaṅkai's poetry, especially in *Pĕriya tirumŏḻi*, embodies much pilgrims' devotion to the various shrines of the god he visited. It also uses a good deal of secular love-imagery traceable back to the courtly love poetry of *Akattiṇai*, belonging to a much earlier epoch of Tamil literature. [17; 43; 118] (J.R.M.)

Tiruñāṉacampantar [XI] (7th century). One of the NĀYAṈMĀR. He was born in Cīrkāḻi (in modern Tanjavur District) and is stated to have died on his wedding day at the age of 16, around 650. The names Āḷuṭaiyapiḷḷaiyār – conferred on him by Nampiyāṇṭār Nampi (*see* NĀYAṈMĀR; SUNTARAR) – and Drāviḍaśiśu which ŚAṄKARA called him, testify to his youthfulness. His father was the temple priest at Cīrkāḻi, and *Pĕriya purāṇam* relates how he left the baby saint on the temple-tank's steps while he went in to pray. The child, hungry, called out 'Mother! Father!' Straightway beside him the god Śiva and his consort Pārvatī appeared; she took milk from her breast and gave it to the baby in a golden cup. Replete with the Milk of Wisdom, *Ñāṉappāl*, the child burst forth into his first *Tevāram* hymn, calling the Lord the One with the ear-rings of man and woman, as embodying in himself both male and female. The child's father returned and, seeing milk dribbling from the baby's mouth, was furious that he had been fed by a stranger. He started to beat the child who, dancing with joy as he sang his hymn, pointed up to the sky where the god and goddess could still be discerned receding heavenwards. Thus was Tiruñāṉacampantar's father pacified. Tiruñāṉacampantar's poems, forming *Tirumuṟai* I–III, are more prosaic than those of APPAR or SUNTARAR, and are more iconically descriptive of the forms of god and goddess he witnessed at the various shrines to which, like the other saints, he made pilgrimage. Moreover, in virtually every hymn, he makes insulting references to Buddhists and Jains. Each *patikam*, as such hymns are termed, ends with the poet's own 'signature' (*mudrā*) in the manner of much medieval poetry in India and elsewhere. [28; 73; 118] (J.R.M.)

Tiruvaḷḷuvar [XI]. The author of *Tirukkuṟaḷ*. Controversy both as to his date and his religious persuasion has raged for more than a century since missionary figures such as Caldwell and Pope, impressed by *Tirukkuṟaḷ*'s ethical, non-sectarian value, became interested in it. To them, it embodied 'natural religion' and provided a *point de départ* for Christian teaching. Its opening invocation, for instance, to 'The Lord who is foremost in the Universe just as the letter *A* is foremost among letters', would put one in mind of ' "I am Alpha and Omega" saith the Lord' (*Revelation* 1:8). Little is known of Tiruvaḷḷuvar's life, though a cycle of legends is preserved in a late text, *Tiruvaḷḷuva mālai*. *Tirukkuṟaḷ*, which is in a form of the early *Vĕṇpā*-metre, is included among 18 works of a didactic nature usually assigned to the 1st to the 7th centuries. The author may have lived in Mylapore – now part of Madras – and because of the 'non-denominational' nature of his work, he has been described as a Jain or a Christian! One story even suggested that he was in touch with ST THOMAS at Mylapore. *Tirkkuṟāḷ* is so called from the couplets, *kuṟaḷ vĕṇpās*, that it is composed in. It is of 133 chapters of ten couplets each, and is divided into *Aṟam* (*dharma*), right conduct, *Pŏruḷ* (*artha*), wealth and *Iṉpam* (*kāma*), pleasure. Such an arrangement shows indebtedness to the four *puruṣārthas*, aims of man, in Sanskrit treatises, but there is a lack of the specifics of the Sanskrit, particularly with reference to *Iṉpam*, and the whole should perhaps be regarded as an abridgement or abstract of Sanskrit *Sūtra*-literature rather than an embodiment of any one work or tradition thereof. *Tirukkuṟaḷ*'s moralistic and ethical tone led to its early translation into English, such as that by the Rev. G. U. Pope, and it has been translated into more Indian and non-Indian languages than any other Tamil text. [86; 118] (J.R.M.)

Tlacaelel [XVIII] (*d.*1480). The unusually powerful *cihuacoatl* or counsellor to several Aztec kings, including Itzcoatl and MOCTEZUMA I. According to the sacred genealogies of Aztec Tenochtitlan, Tlacaelel was born at sunrise on the same day as the ruler Moctezuma Ilhuicamina and shared his nobility and destiny. As a young warrior, he was renowned for having spurred the Aztec rulers into revolt against the Azcapotzalcan empire (1423–6).

He became the intellectual and to some extent the theological power behind the Aztec throne during the period of its enormous expansions beyond the Valley of Mexico. He managed to outline a mystico-militaristic world-view of the Aztec government, which resulted in part in the Flowery Wars, a tradition of ritual warfare with enemy states dedicated to obtaining sacrificial victims but also used to redraw geo-political boundaries. [5]

Tlacaelel's contribution to Aztec religion derives primarily from his role as the architect of ideology. He laid the basis for a military aristocracy and compared the capture of warriors on the battlefield to a market-place where men provided tortillas for the gods. These markets were the communities of Tlaxcala, Huexotzinco, Cholula and others. He developed a theological basis for Aztec expansion over enemy territories and organized the plan for a new social organization in the Aztec capital. It also appears that he organized the burning of pictorial manuscripts which presented competing genealogies and theologies to the new social order [4]. In their place, he restructured the sacred traditions so that Aztec religion and ideology could be traced to the Toltec royal line. However, the dominant religious vision which emerged was based on warfare, sacrifice and the nurturance of the gods through 'debt payment' with red and precious liquid provided in the sacrifice of humans. In this way he appears partially responsible for the rise of the god Huitzilopochtli to the position of supreme war god of the Aztec state. [8] (D.C.)

T'oegye. *See* Yi hwang.

Tŏṇṭaraṭippŏṭi Āḻvār [xi]. The author of Sections 7 and 8 of the first Thousand of *Nālāyira ppirapantam* (*see* Āḻvār). He was a Brahman from Tanjavur District, and worshipped the god Viṣṇu at Śrīraṅkam. His title-name is of great self-abasement, meaning 'The Āḻvār who is the dust on the feet of devotees'. He is regarded as the incarnation, *amśa*, of the god's flower garland. Tŏṇṭaraṭippŏṭi's best poem is, perhaps, *Tiruppaḷḷiy ĕḻucci*, the Awakening hymn (Section 8 mentioned above). In this, the god is ceremonially aroused from his sacred couch. The poet's work is characterized not only by self-abasement, but by a puritan streak of devotion that eschews the love-imagery that figures in so much Śrī Vaiṣṇava poetry both within *Nālāyira ppirapantam* and elsewhere. [17; 43; 118] (J.R.M.)

Topiltzin Quetzalcoatl [xviii] (late 10th century). Enlightened ruler and legendary founder of the Toltec Kingdom (950–1150), whose creative genius became an example for rulers, priests and artists in post-Toltec central Meso-America. Also known as Ce Acatl Topiltzin Quetzalcoatl (One Reed, Our Young Prince, the Feathered Serpent) he appears in several sources as the son of the Chichimec ruler Mixcoatl (Cloud Serpent) [6]. The legendary biography of his life can be divided into seven phases, based on a compilation of all the sources: his miraculous birth, his orphaned status, his ritual training, his priestly discoveries, his kingship, downfall, death and promise to return [2: II]. It is widely accepted that he was an historical figure who ruled Tollan near the end of the tenth century.

The 'teachings' or patterns of meanings associated with Topiltzin Quetzalcoatl derive largely from his life experience, from which 'the priests took their manner of conduct' [9: III]. Outstanding themes in his life-legend are: ritual training, the image of the abundant sacred city [2: II] and the quest for true knowledge.

Topiltzin Quetzalcoatl's life is referred to in over 50 sources, including pictorial manuscripts, 16th-century ethnohistorical accounts, songs, sagas and liturgical texts. Following his miraculous birth, where in one account his mother swallows a precious stone which impregnates her, he grows and undergoes seven years of rigorous ritual training, practising 'autosacrifice', the bleeding of oneself through insertion of spines or other ritual implements into parts of one's body. These techniques were considered at once offerings to the gods and 'openings' in the human body designed to enhance direct communication with deities. At a later stage in his ritual career, he had a direct encounter with Ometeotl, the Creative Heavenly Pair who dwelt in the innermost part of heaven at the top of the celestial levels [4: 111]. He combined ritual temple construction, fasting, bathing in freezing waters and prayer to achieve direct knowledge of the deity.

Controversy highlights Topiltzin's Quetzalcoatl's career as a warrior and sacrificer. It is possible that he changed his attitude toward war and ritual sacrifice during his lifetime. It is also possible that this controversy reflects the achievements of more than one historical person called Quetzalcoatl or Topiltzin Quetzalcoatl or Ce Acatl. While one tradition tells that he carried out sacrifices of enemies at mountain shrines, another states that he forbade human sacrifice as part of a ritual reformation during his reign in Tollan. Instead of sacrificing humans he offered snakes, birds and butterflies. This ritual strategy led to his downfall at the hands of a competing cult under the inspiration of Tezcatlipoca (Lord of the Smoking Mirror) [9: III], who later became the protean deity of the Aztecs. Whatever the historical fact, by Aztec times the high priests of the main temple communities who carried out some of the crucial heart sacrifices were called Quetzalcoatl priests in reference to the Toltec leader.

One of the most creative elements of Topiltzin Quetzalcoatl's life was the great ceremonial centre associated with his reign. It was recalled in oral and pictorial traditions as a site of wonderful ritual buildings facing cardinal directions, excellent technological achievement, agricultural abundance and cosmo-magical discoveries, i.e. astronomical patterns, theological positions, ritual innovations.

When the Spaniards arrived they heard numerous accounts of Topiltzin Quetzalcoatl, who was identified as the founder of temple architecture, fasting, ritual asceticism, music in ceremony and sacrifice. In fact, his presence in the folklore and oral tradition was strong enough that one theme, i.e. his promise to return one day, was identified with the coming of the Spaniards who were grafted on to this belief. [2: IV] (D.C.)

Torquemada, Tomás de [VI.A] (1420–1498). He was born in Valladolid, Spain, the nephew of Juan de Torquemada (1388–1448), a distinguished theologian, cardinal, and papal politician who belonged to the Dominican Order. The nephew, though not as distinguished as his uncle, is notorious as the Grand Inquisitor. Like his uncle, Tomás entered the Dominican Order in his youth and was prior of the convent of Santa Cruz in Segovia for 22 years. In 1474 he became confessor to Isabella I of Castile and later of Ferdinand V of Aragon. In 1482 Tomás became an assistant inquisitor and a year and a half later grand inquisitor, first for Castile and León and then Catalonia, Aragon, Valencia and Majorca. He established tribunals in Seville and other cities, including Toledo. His inquisatorial methods were listed in 54 articles of *Instrucciones de la santa Inquisición*, published in 1576 as a handbook for succeeding inquisitors. His inquisition, the first example in history of official anti-Semitism, harassed Marranos (Jews who practised their faith subversively) and Moriscos (Muslims who behaved similarly). He was chiefly responsible in 1492 for the eviction from Spain of all Jews who refused baptism. He was responsible for possibly 2,000 deaths and the torture and deprivation of property and rights of thousands more. [463; 812] (T.T.)

Torres, Camilo [VI.A] (1929–1966). He was born in Bogotá, Colombia. His father was a consul to Berlin in the early 1930s, and Camilo attended a German school in Bogotá until 1941. He then studied law at a Catholic school. He later joined the Dominican Order and attended the local diocesan seminary. From there he went to Louvain. He studied modern Catholic scholars and Marxism. He returned to the National University, Bogotá, to lecture and be university chaplain. He began to organize students as social workers and set up a farm and schools. He tried to organize facilities for training shoe-makers and tailors and to establish a medical clinic. The authorities, state and church, objected to his social activities. In June 1965 he was given leave to revert to lay status. Frustrated in his attempts at social reform he joined an armed guerrilla group. In early 1966 he was killed in action against government forces. Though he had become a layman he regarded himself as still a priest. In August 1965 he wrote: 'When my neighbour no longer has anything against me, and when the revolution has been completed, then I will offer Mass again, if God so wills it. I believe that in this way I am following Christ's injunction.' [283; 295] (T.T.)

Toṭagamuvē Śrī Rāhula [IV] (15th century). Sri Lankan Buddhist monk and author. He was perhaps the most distinguished monk and the foremost scholar of his day. His poems, especially *Kāvyaśekhara* and *Sälalihiṇisandeśa*, are considered classics of Sinhala literature. In modern times, however, Śrī Rāhula is not thought of highly as a monk, owing to a perception of a laxity on his part with respect to Buddhist monastic discipline (*vinaya*).

Śrī Rahula was the step-son of King Parākramabāhu VI and he enjoyed royal patronage throughout his monastic career. He was a *gāmavāsī* ('town-dwelling') monk, and followed the *granthadhura* ('scholarly') course of monastic practice. His scholarly career led him to become head of the monastic college at Toṭagamuva in south-west Sri Lanka.

In addition to his poetry, Śrī Rāhula wrote a number of grammatical works, where he displayed his extensive knowledge of Indian literature. For works such as these he received the title 'Master of Six Languages'. In religious practice he appears to have been tolerant, if not actually syncretic; his writings indicate an openness to practices more commonly associated with the Hindu and Mahāyāna Buddhist traditions. A good example of this openness is his devotion to Nātha, or the bodhisattva Avalokiteśvara as he was acculturated in Sri Lanka.

Śrī Rāhula is an excellent example of an urbane and cosmopolitan monk, a monastic type which is rarely acknowledged to have been encouraged in the Theravāda tradition. [151: XII; 253: VIII–IX] (C.H.)

Trithemius, Johannes [XVII.C] [Johann Tritheim] (1462–1516). Abbot of Sponheim and the author of the *Steganographia*, an influential text on magic, which circulated in manuscript in his lifetime, though it was not published until 1606 [10: 86]. While purporting to be concerned with secret codes, the *Steganographia* contains much kabbalistic material on angels believed to rule planets, parts of the world, and hours of the day and night: it gives instructions for using these rulerships, by means of talismans and invocations, for such purposes as sending telepathic messages and learning what is happening at a distance [12: 145; 10: 87–8]. Many of his contemporaries thought such practices highly dangerous, and some believed that the beings invoked by them might in fact be demons: Trithemius, however, insisted that what he was doing was virtuous and right [10: 89–90]. Despite the suspicions, Trithemius strongly influenced the occult thought of the Renaissance, through his own writings and those of his friend and pupil, AGRIPPA VON NETTESHEIM [12: 145]. (V.J.R.)

Troeltsch, Ernst [VI.A] (1865–1923). German theologian. He was born in Haunstetten, Bavaria, and grew up and was educated in nearby Augsburg. He went to a preparatory school in Augsburg (1883) and then to Erlangen (1884) to study Protestant theology and a wide range of subjects in the humanities. In 1885 he transferred to Berlin and thence to Göttingen in 1886. There he studied under ALBRECHT RITSCHL and was considerably influenced by him. However, he differed from Ritschl in arguing that theology should be studied in a historical rather than a dogmatic way. As such he was one of the members of the religious-historical school which influenced early 20th-century study of theology. Following a short period as a lecturer in Bonn he was offered the chair of systematic theology at Heidelberg in 1894. For a time he represented the university in the parliament of the Duchy of Baden. In 1915 he moved to Berlin as professor of 'religious, social, and historical philosophy and the history of the Christian religion'. He remained in the post until his death. Among his most important works are: *The Absoluteness of Christianity and the History of Religions* (1902) and *The Social Doctrines of Christian Churches and Groups* (1912; English trans., *The Social Teaching of the Christian Churches*, 1931). In the latter work he presented his typology of church and sect which still exercises some influence. He was one of the major influences on PAUL TILLICH. [309; 698; 734: vol. 3, 305–32] (T.T.)

Trungpa, Chögyam [IV] [Chos-rgyam Drung-pa] (1939–1987). Chögyam Trungpa, Rinpoche ('precious master'), was born in Kham, East Tibet, in 1939. He was recognized and enthroned at 18 months as the 11th incarnation of the line of Trungpa 'Tulkus' (incarnate lamas), who ruled the Surmang group of Kagyu monasteries in East Tibet and had particularly close ties to the Nyingma sect. Trungpa received novitiate and full ordinations in 1948 and 1958 respectively. As a youth he trained in the contemplative, scholastic and liturgical traditions of the Kagyupa and, to a lesser extent, Nyingma traditions under various teachers, both Kagyu and Nyingma. Foremost among his gurus was his principal teacher, the Nyingma Jamgon Kongtruel of Sechen.

In 1959 Trungpa fled to India from Chinese-occupied Tibet, where, under the DALAI LAMA's appointment, he was made spiritual advisor to a school for young lamas. In 1963 he travelled to Oxford, England, to study comparative religion, philosophy and fine arts at Oxford University and, in 1967, founded Samyeling Meditation Center in Scotland. In 1969 he relinquished his monastic vows and in 1970 married and moved to North America, where for 17 years he propagated the Tibetan traditions of Buddhist meditation through lectures and publications, and through the inauguration of several religious and secular organizations. He also hosted the visits of many important Tibetan lamas, particularly of the Nyingma and Kagyu schools, to North America, and facilitated their teaching.

The most important organizations founded by Trungpa include the Vajradhātu Association of Buddhist Churches, comprising several contemplative centres in Colorado, Vermont and Nova Scotia, and regional centres in some 100 cities and towns in North America and Europe; the Nāropa Institute, an upper divisional accredited college in Boulder, Colorado; Shambhala Training, a non-sectarian training programme in meditation (Boulder); and the Nalanda Translation Committee (Halifax, Nova Scotia; Boulder). His own works include the autobiographical *Born in Tibet* [228]; *Meditation in Action* [231], *Cutting Through Spiritual Materialism* [229] and *Myth of Freedom* [232] on the meditative path in Buddhism; *Journey Without Goal* [230] on Tibetan tantric Buddhism; and *Shambhala: The Sacred Path of the Warrior* [233]. In addition he produced several other works of poetry, philosophy and drama, some 25 articles, 25 unpublished volumes of Buddhist teachings, six plays, several films and a number of art exhibitions (photography, flower arranging).

Trungpa's immediate significance lies in the transition he was able to make from the 'medieval' culture of Tibet to that of the modern West, coupled with his ability to render Tibetan Buddhism and its meditative traditions accessible to modern Westerners within their own cultural context. His long-term significance will depend considerably upon history's judgement of his various works and, even more, of the long-range success of his disciples and various projects in effectively propagating authentic Buddhism in the West. (R.R.)

Ts'ao Kuo-chiu. One of the EIGHT IMMORTALS of Taoism.

Tsizehena, John [VI.A] (1840–1912). Malagasy Christian preacher. He was a product of the short-lived presence of the Church Missionary Society in Madagascar. He was 25 years of age when baptized in 1865 in Vohemor. Recovery from a critical illness convinced him he should preach to the Antankarana and Sakalava, northern peoples little touched by Christianity. He had no training and no resources but the Malagasy Bible, and his work, begun in 1885, was unsupported by the official Anglican church. Nevertheless a sizeable northern church arose from his work, quite isolated from the mission-related bodies further south. It used the Anglican formularies that Tsizehena had known in Vohemor and claimed to be the diocese of the North, or Northern Church of Madagascar. The official church delayed recognition and Tsizehena was eventually consecrated 'Lord Bishop of the North, DD' by his followers. Shortly before his death the Anglican bishop visited Tsizehena, and the Northern Church, of entirely indigenous origin, was absorbed into the Anglican Church. [50: 180; 437] (A.F.W.)

Tsong-kha-pa [IV] (1357–1419). The common appellation of Blo-bzang-grags-pa, the most famous of Tibetan Buddhist thinkers. He was born in the Kokonor region of north-eastern Tibet and was soon recognized as a prodigy. He began his studies under a teacher of the Bka'-gdams-pa sect. In 1372 he was sent to central Tibet, where he continued his studies, distinguishing himself in all fields of Buddhist learning and practice. He became the disciple of the noted Sa-skya scholar Red-mda'-ba but went on to study under the major scholars of the day, without regard to sectarian affiliation. According to the traditional biographies, Tsong-kha-pa experienced visions of Indian masters such as NĀGĀRJUNA and Buddhapālita, who clarified difficult points of doctrine. He is said to have had a special relationship with the bodhisattva of wisdom, Mañjuśrī, who appeared to him throughout his later life to offer instruction and advice.

The biographies speak of Tsong-kha-pa's four major deeds. The first was his refurbishing of an image of the future Buddha Maitreya in 1399. The second was the 1403 assembly of monks of all orders for a council on the monastic discipline (*vinaya*). The third was the inauguration of the Great Prayer Festival (*smon lam chen mo*) in Lhasa in 1409, an event which became the grandest celebration of the Tibetan calendar, drawing pilgrims from all over Tibet and Central Asia. Finally, he founded the monastery of Dga '-ldan outside of Lhasa, completed in 1410. His followers were subsequently known as 'those of the system of Dga'-ldan' (Dga '-lugs-pa), a term that eventually evolved into the current Dge-lugs-pa.

Tsong-kha-pa was a prolific writer, his collected works filling over 17 volumes. He was a brilliant and original scholar who saw reason as a fundamental element in the path to enlightenment. He therefore sought to determine a systematic consistency in all of the myriad subjects on which he wrote. Three of his major works include the *Lam rim chen mo* ('Great Exposition of the Stages of the Path'), the *Snags rim chen mo* ('Great Exposition of the Stages of Mantra'), and *Drang nges legs bshad snying po* ('Essence of Good Explanation on the Definitive and Interpretable'). Tsong-kha-pa's fame and influence after his death were enhanced greatly by the political power gained by his followers, the Dge-lugs-pas, with the establishment of the institution of the Dalai lama. [218; 226; 227; 250] (D.L.)

Tsung-mi [iv] [Kuei-feng Tsung-mi] (780–841). Chinese Buddhist Ch'an and Hua-yan scholar. He was born in the Kuo Prefecture in Szechwan Province, and in 804, after extensive training in the Confucian classics, he adopted Ch'an Buddhism and became a monk in 808. He was later drawn to the scholastic study of Hua-yen, and after 816 began to compose his own commentaries and systematic works. Tsung-mi succeeded in giving traditional Hua-yen metaphysics a largely new direction, and in developing a hermeneutical theory through which the wide variety of Chinese Buddhist (and non-Buddhist) positions could be properly related to one another and arranged in a hierarchical structure. He was one of the great systematic thinkers of Chinese Buddhism. [23; 73; 266] (P.J.G.)

Tukārām [xi] [Tukārāma] (1598–1649). The last and greatest of the Marathi saint-poets. He was born at Dehu, near Poona. He was of the Kunbi caste, theoretically peasant farmers, but he made his living from a small shop. According to legend he turned to god – that is of course Viṭṭhala of Pandharpur – after his child and first wife died in a famine. Ever after he is depicted as spending all his time, to the detriment of his trade and to the fury of his second nagging wife, in pilgrimage, in dancing in ecstasy and in singing *kīrtaṇs* on the sands of the river Bhima at Pandharpur. An almost certainly apocryphal story has him meeting the great Śivājī towards the end of his life. A total of 4,600 *abhanga*s is credited to Tukārām, but no sustained attempt has been made to sort the wheat from the chaff on linguistic or any other grounds. Many of his short pungent poems have a bite that is rivalled only by Kabīr, and more than any other Marathi saint-poet he rejects forms and ceremonies, the worship of the image in the temple, and instead dwells on the internalization of god's name and form and on the joy of association with the company of the saints – the devoted pilgrims of all castes who regularly journey to Pandharpur. Christian missionaries and to some extent Prarthanasamajists like Rānade saw in Tukārām a *mens naturaliter christiana*. His *abhanga*s were sung like hymns by the Prarthana Samaj and he must be the most translated of all Marathi poets because of the attention of the missionaries. Yet it is hard to see in his *abhanga*s more than a supreme representation of that personal, aching devotionalism that is called *bhakti* and Tukārām himself is for Maharashtra the archetypal *bhakta*. Tukārām's powerful verse which constantly experiences the divine even in the dust of the road to Pandharpur, lies at the heart of the Marathi mysticism industry, exemplified in R. D. Ranade's *Mysticism in Maharashtra* and its derivatives. An alternative view sees Tukārām as a champion of the rights of man, claiming equality for people of all castes in the sight of God. The mysticism is inherent in the world view of all Hindus, and the democracy has been much exaggerated. [25; 69; 81] (I.M.P.R.)

Tu Kuang-T'ing [v] (850–953). Prolific Taoist scholar and liturgist. Unlike many other eminent Taoists, who preferred the reclusive life, Tu spent more than four decades in the service of the emperors of the late T'ang and the succeeding kingdom of Shu (modern Szechwan), and was the recipient of many honours. He was also an intimate of many of the most prominent Literati (Confucians) of the age. Tu wrote about the lives of immortal transcendents, accounts of Taoist 'religious geography' (in particular the famous mountains and 'grotto-heavens' associated with the religion), and produced systematizations of the liturgical traditions from their origins by the 'Masters Designated by the Heavens' (*t'ien shih*) to his own times. His name is connected with some 28 texts in the Taoist canon. Although very broadly versed in Taoist (and non-Taoist) learning, Tu is known as an adherent of the Sect of Highest Clarity (*shang ch'ing*) based on Mt Mao in Kiangsi province. He retired in old age to the Taoist centre called Blue-Walled Mountain (*ch'ing-ch'eng shan*) and, having predicted his death, underwent 'transformation' in the manner customarily attributed to Taoist (and Buddhist) masters, sitting in the lotus position. [2; 4] (L.T.)

Tulsī Dās [xɪ] (1543?–1623). Hindī devotional poet, probably born in 1543, although this is disputed, at either Rājāpur in the Banda district, or at Ayodhyā. He was certainly born into a Brahman family, but nothing more is known of his parentage except that he was abandoned at an early age, presumably for being born at an astrologically inauspicious time. It can be inferred that he was taken in by some Vaiṣṇava holy men, under whose tutelage he studied many of the scriptures and developed his love for Rām. There is a tradition that he was unhappily married, but there is no historical evidence to support this. By his 21st year he was already an expert singer and poet, and had visited Benares. His earliest dated poem is *Rāmājñā-praśn* (1564), to which year also belongs the *Jñānadīpikā*. Stylistically the *Rāmalalā Nahchū* also belongs to this period. In 1574 he was in Ayodhyā beginning what was to be his most renowned work, the *Rāmcaritmānas*, or the Holy Lake of the Acts of Rām [48]. To an earlier period belong two lesser works, the *Jānakī Maṅgal* and the *Vairāgya Sandīpinī*. It is thought he completed his masterpiece in 1576. In 1585 he compiled a *Satsaī* and in 1586 *Pārvatī Maṅgal*. The next years saw works designed mainly to be sung, the *Gītāvalī*, the *Kṛṣṇa Gītāvalī* and the *Vinay-Patrikā* [1]. His final years were marked by the plague that broke out in Benares first in 1612 and again in 1616, when his health began to deteriorate. The works of these years are the *Kavitāvalī*, the *Dohāvalī*, and the *Hanumān Bāhuk*. He died in 1623 in Benares. In the above corpus of works there is much outstanding devotional poetry, but it is the *Rāmcaritmānas* that established his reputation and which has become very widely known and loved. Telling the story of Rām in a Puranic format, it is marked by an emphatic orthodox piety and an intense devotion to Rām and his Name. It has been aptly described as the Bible of North India. [1; 48] (S.C.R.W.)

Tupac Amaru II [xxɪv] [José Gabriel Condorcanqui] (1740–1781). Leader of the most important social movement of Peru's colonial history. Born José Gabriel Condorcanqui in the town of Surimana, he was privately tutored by Antonio López, a local priest, before studying under the Jesuits in Cuzco. José Gabriel was inspired by the chronicle, *Comentarios reales*, compiled by Inca Garcilaso de la Vega. This historical work painted a highly sympathetic portrait of the Inca past, including a prophecy that the empire would one day be restored to its former glory. After interceding in Lima on behalf of native groups pressed into labour by Spanish overlords, José Gabriel sought to initiate change more directly and on a larger scale. In Cuzco on 4 November 1780 he captured the abusive corregidor Antonio de Arriaga, had him publicly hanged, and assumed the title Tupac Amaru ('Royal Serpent'), the name of the last reigning Inca emperor, who had been beheaded by the Spanish in 1572. The rebellion quickly became a mass movement among both Quechua- and Ayemara-speaking groups of the Andean highlands. Tupac Amaru II was a charismatic leader, skilful in his oral and written communications with other leaders. He used biblical imagery to strong effect, declaring that the cries of the just natives had finally reached heaven so that God was moved to send a saving leader. Native Peruvians were like the Israelites suffering servitude in Egypt. Tupac Amaru was like DAVID or MOSES, sent to free people but also to restructure the world. Although the Catholic religion would triumph, Spanish rule would crumble in favour of Inca rule over a multi-ethnic society. Tupac Amaru styled his life and his hopes for reform around the messianic prophecies surrounding the return of the mythic Inkarrí (Inca-King), who would arrive at the end of time. In 1781, after being forced to watch his wife of 21 years die by painful execution, he was tortured, mutilated and then drawn and quartered in a public square. His trial and condemnation became an occasion for the proclamation of decrees that eradicated the use of Inca names, clothing, musical instruments, religious practices, dramaturgy, public symbols and the Quechua language itself. [5; 16: 600–602; 17] (L.S.)

al-Ṭūsī, Abū Jaʿfar Muḥammad ibn Ḥasan Shaykh al-Ṭāʾifa [XII] [al-Shaykh] (955–1067). The leading Shiʿite scholar in the second generation after the final occultation of the twelfth Imām. After early studies at his home town of Ṭūs in Iran's Khurāsān province, he travelled to Baghdad, where he studied under several important scholars, including AL-MUFĪD and al-Sharīf al-Murtaḍā. In common with these teachers, al-Ṭūsī emphasized the role of rationalism in theology. He is, however, best known for his contribution to the development of Shiʿite law, in which he also favoured analytical and rational methods. His *Kitāb al-nihāya* became the most authoritative Shiʿite legal text for two centuries, and the school founded by him dominated legal scholarship for some 300 years. In spite of this emphasis on rationalism, al-Ṭūsī is also well known for his collections of Shiʿite religious traditions, the *Tahdhīb al-aḥkām* and *al-Istibṣār*, both of which are counted among the 'Four Books' of Shīʿī tradition. Three other works of his are also famous: the *Kitāb al-ghayba* on the occultation of the twelfth Imām, and the *Kitāb al-rijāl* and *Kitāb al-fihrist*, important sources for Shiʿite biography and bibliography. Following the burning of his library during anti-Shiʿite riots in 1056, he moved to al-Najaf, where he died 11 years later. [34: s.v.; 89: IV] (D.M.)

al-Ṭūsī, Khwāja Naṣīr al-Dīn [XII] [al-Muḥaqqiq al-Ṭūsī] (1201–1274). Leading medieval Shiʿite theologian, philosopher, and scientist. Born in Ṭūs in the eastern Iranian province of Khurāsān, he studied theology and philosophy in his youth. At an early age he entered the service of the Ismāʿīlī ruler of the neighbouring province of Qūhistān, later moving to the northern Ismāʿīlī stronghold of Alamūt. The exact nature of his relations with the Ismāʿīlī sect is unclear, but over a period of more than 30 years in their service, he wrote several works in accordance with their doctrines, and is, in consequence, regarded by them as one of their foremost authorities.

After the fall of Alamūt and other Ismāʿīlī strongholds to the Mongol Hulāgū Khān in 1256, al-Ṭūsī entered the conqueror's service as an astrologer. Owing to his intervention, many important manuscripts in Alamūt and Baghdad were preserved from Mongol depredations. Following the capture of Baghdad in 1258, he became involved in the construction of an astronomical observatory at Marāgha.

Al-Ṭūsī was a polymath who wrote with equal facility on astronomy, cosmology, mathematics, logic, ethics, medicine, geography, poetry and history; in the theological field, he was responsible for incorporating philosophical concepts into orthodox Shiʿite thought. In Nasr's opinion, 'He may . . . be considered in many ways as the greatest of the Shiʿite theologians'. His best known work is probably the *Akhlāq-i Nāṣirī*, written in 1235, regarded as 'the principal treatise in Persian on ethics, economics, and politics' [139]. Al-Ṭūsī's own ethical position has often been a subject of controversy. He is said to have advised the Ismāʿīlī commander of Alamūt to surrender to the Mongols, and later to have recommended that Hulāgū put the ʿAbbasid caliph in Baghdad to death. His willingness to serve the strongest party, whatever his own convictions, has sometimes led to disapproval. [94] (D.M.)

Tutankhamun [VII] (14th century BCE). King of Egypt of Dynasty 18, reigned 1347–1339 BCE. He succeeded Smenkhkare as king when he was a nine-year-old child. Probably the son of Amenophis III by a secondary wife, and half-brother of the heretic king, AKHENATEN, Tutankhamun was married to Ankhesenamun (Ankhesenpaaten), the third daughter of Akhenaten. During Tutankhamun's brief reign, Egypt began to return to the worship of the multitude of traditional gods, eliminated by his predecessor, Akhenaten, and notably to Amen-Re, the supreme state-god. However, Tutankhamun is best known for his tomb which was discovered in the Valley of the Kings in 1922 by Howard Carter and his patron, Lord Carnarvon [4]. The tomb contents were found virtually intact, and included the king's mummy, coffins and treasure. (A.R.D.)

Tutu, Desmond Mpilo [VI.A] (1931–). South African Christian leader. He was born in Klerksdorp, Transvaal, the son of a Mfengu schoolteacher. He trained as a teacher at Pretoria Bantu Normal College, and while teaching took an external degree. He entered the Anglican ministry (ordained priest 1961) and studied at Kings College, London. He taught at the South African Federal Seminary (1967–9) and the University of Botswana, Lesotho and Swaziland (1970–72) before becoming Assistant Director (with special responsibilities for Africa) of the Theological Education Fund of the World Council of Churches. In 1975 he became Dean of Johannesburg (an appointment previously always held by a White) but chose to live in Soweto African township rather than the deanery. The following year he became Bishop of Lesotho, but in 1978 returned to South Africa as General Secretary of the South African Council of Churches. In 1986 he was elected Archbishop of Cape Town; Black leadership of the Anglican church was unprecedented.

As General Secretary and as Archbishop, Tutu became, both inside and outside South Africa, the most visible spokesman of Black South Africans. By this time the churches represented in the Council provided almost the only significant and organized legal opposition to the government. Tutu asserted Black dignity and called for common citizenship, a common educational system, an end to compulsory population removals and to the pass laws, and the freeing of Nelson Mandela and other prisoners. He led clergy and other church people in symbolic breaking of unjust laws, in acts of civil disobedience and identification with oppressed groups. His positions were grounded in Christian confessional orthodoxy (humanity as the image of God, the scope of Christ's redemption) and traditional Christian ethics, set in a context of Christian prayer and worship and the exercise of pastoral duty; he consistently pleaded against violence by any party. In 1984 he was awarded the Nobel Peace Prize. Significantly, Nelson Mandela's public presentation on his release in 1990 was made in the gardens of Bishopscourt. [213] (A.F.W.)

Twitchell, John Paul [XIX] (1908/9/12/22?–1971). Founder of ECKANKAR. The story of his childhood, and, indeed, much of the rest of his life, has been critically questioned [26: 10–11]. It is, however, known that he had been a journalist and a student of Kirpal Singh (1894–1974), the founder of Ruhani Satsang and teacher of the Divine Science of the Soul [37: 262–4]. Twitchell was also one of the first to achieve the state of a 'Clear' in L. RON HUBBARD's Dianetics. In 1965 Twitchell declared himself to be the living ECK Master, and founded his first public ECK group. [36: 899]

ECKANKAR, the Ancient Science of Soul Travel, is considered to be an advanced form of *surat shabda* Yoga. The student (*chela*) concentrates on physical techniques and spiritual exercises that enable the soul to travel beyond the physical limitations of the body to the higher spiritual realms of 'Sugmad', defined as the formless, All-embracing, impersonal and infinite, the Ocean of Love and Mercy, from which flows all of life, the equivalent of God in theistic religions [38: 148; 65; 66]. The teachings are said to have been handed down through an unbroken line of ECK Masters, Twitchell having been the 971st. (E.B.)

Tyāgarāja [XI] (1767–1847). One of the great trinity of South Indian classical music composers who were contemporaries towards the end of the 18th century. All were born in Tiruvārūr, east of Tanjavur (Tanjore). The other two are Muttusvāmi Dīkṣitar (1775–1835) and Śyāmā Śāstri (1762–1821), a devotee of the goddess Kāmākṣī at Kāñcīpuram. Originally named Tyāgabrahmam, Tyāgarāja, whose popular name echoes that of the form of Śiva worshipped at Tiruvārūr, hailed from a Telugu-speaking

Brahman family. A number of such families, seeking the protection of the Mahratha Hindu rulers at Tanjavur established there since 1674, had drifted southwards thither during the 18th century. Tyāgarāja learnt from his father both Telugu and Sanskrit, and accompanied him to Tanjore, to the court of Tulaja II, when he went there to recite the *Rāmāyaṇa* during the Rāmanavāmī festival. His father died when Tyāgarāja was 20, and the young man was turned out of their house by a vicious elder brother. He went to Tiruvaiyāṟu, where he dwelt for the rest of his life and died. He made journeys and pilgrimages to a number of places in South India, and many of his songs were uttered spontaneously at such places. He resisted all invitations to become a musician at court. He had in early life become a devotee of the god Viṣṇu in his incarnation as Rāma, hero of the epic *Rāmāyaṇa*, and most of his compositions are to that deity. These songs, largely composed *extempore*, are frequently in head-rhymed prose, and bear the author's 'signature', *mudrā*. For their texts and melodies we are indebted to Tyāgarāja's disciples, who copied them out. The two principal sets of such manuscripts are the Umaiyāḷpuram and Wālājapet collections, and these are the *ur*-texts of his work. In addition to discontinuous devotional songs, termed *Kīrtana*, Tyāgarāja composed two musical dramas. One, *Naukā caritramu*, tells of a boating trip on the Jumna by Kṛṣṇa and the *gopīs*, the other, *Prahlāda bhakti vijayamu*, tells of the final vindication of the Viṣṇu-devotee, Prahlāda. [97] (J.R.M.)

Tyrrell, George [VI.A] (1861–1909). Irish-born Jesuit priest. He was born in Dublin, Ireland and educated at Rathmines School. He entered Trinity College in 1878 but soon moved to London. In 1879, previously having been under Anglican high church influence, he was received into the Roman Catholic Church and the following year joined the Society of Jesus. He was priested in 1880 and studied at a Roman Catholic seminary. While at seminary he was introduced to the notions of modernization in THOMAS AQUINAS and history in NEWMAN. Both notions raised questions about the dogmatism of scholastic theology. In 1894 he became a lecturer in ethics at the Jesuit Stonyhurst College in Lancashire. His attitude to Catholic theology caused his removal to parish work in London. Here he met VON HÜGEL, who introduced him to the work of a wider circle of modernists such as LOISY. An article on hell entitled 'A Perverted Devotion' began an increasing alienation from his order and the church. In 1905 he sought laicization but was refused. The following year, after the publication of a 'Letter to a Professor', in which he contrasted a living faith with a dead theology, he was expelled from the order. In 1907 two letters to *The Times* of London attacking the Pope's encyclical *Pascendi*, which itself attacked Catholic modernism, led to his excommunication. A posthumous work, *Christianity at the Cross-Roads* (1909), questioned the finality of the Christian revelation. He was refused a Roman burial and was buried in an Anglican churchyard in Storrington, Sussex. [714; 815; 816] (T.T.)

U

Uchimura, Kanzō [VI.A] (1861–1930). Japanese Christian leader. He was the son of a Japanese samurai civil servant. He studied at an agricultural college and became a Christian there under the influence of American Calvinist teachers. He graduated in 1881 and worked briefly as a government fisheries scientist. He went to the United States and studied at Amherst College. Following graduation in 1887 he returned to Japan and worked as administrator of a school with American missionaries. He and the American missionaries disagreed over evangelistic methods, Uchimura wanting to stress Japanese virtues alongside the Christian. He left to work in a government school. When asked to bow before the signature of the Emperor he hesitated; this cost him any further state employment. He became the editor of a large newspaper but in 1903, before the start of the Russo-Japanese war, he declared himself a pacifist and again lost his post. He maintained himself by editing a Bible Study magazine and became the leader of the 'No-church' movement. He believed that the churches were too identified with Western history and values. The 'No-church' movement eschewed church organization and was held together merely by a common discipline of Bible study and the leadership of Uchimura. [563; 817] (T.T.)

Ŭichŏn [IV] (1055–1101). The founder of the Korean Buddhist Ch'ŏn-t'ae (Chinese: T'ien-t'ai) school. He was the son of a king of the Koryŏ dynasty, and one of the greatest Buddhist scholars ever to flourish in Korea. Ŭichŏn criticized the sectarian divisions between the scholastic Hwaŏm (Chinese: Hua-yen) and the experiential Sŏn (Chinese: Ch'an) of his time, and attempted to resolve the tension by proposing a method of practice evenly balanced between the theoretical and the meditative. Ŭichŏn visited China in 1085 and transmitted from there the T'ien-t'ai lineage to Korea, so establishing the Ch'ŏnt'ae as an independent school. One of his greatest achievements was the formation and cataloguing of a collection of Chinese Buddhist texts, a collection of greater scope than any previously made in Korea. [25] (P.J.G.)

Ŭisang [IV] (625–702). The founder of the Korean Buddhist Hwaŏm (Chinese: Hua-yen) school. He was ordained as a monk at the age of 29, and left Korea for China shortly thereafter. He stayed in China, studying under Chih-yen (602–668), the second patriarch of the Hua-yen school, until 668, when he returned to Korea and was instrumental in forestalling a planned Chinese invasion of Korea. He spent the remainder of his life at Pusŏk monastery on Mount T'aebaek, becoming the most famous Buddhist teacher of his time in Korea. Ŭisang was not a prolific writer; his most influential work was a short poem expounding the *Avataṃsakasūtra*, written while he was still in China [172]. But his intellectual influence has been out of proportion to the volume of his written works, extending even to some of the more famous Hua-yen thinkers in China itself. [26; 139] (P.J.G.)

ʿUmar ibn al-Khaṭṭāb [XII] (*c.*592–644). Companion of MUḤAMMAD and the second Caliph or successor to Muḥammad over the Muslim community. He came from the Meccan clan of ʿAdī and became a convert four years before the *hijra* or migration from Mecca to Medina (hence in 618). Once the new faith became established at the latter place he threw himself into its consolidation and its strengthening militarily, working in close concert with ABŪ BAKR. Like the latter also, ʿUmar himself became Muḥammad's father-in-law through his daughter Ḥafṣa's marriage to the Prophet. Succeeding as Caliph in 634 on Abū Bakr's death, ʿUmar directed the expansion of the new Muslim state into Syria, Iraq, Egypt and western and southern Persia, showing remarkable talent as an administrator and placing the caliphate on a firm financial basis, above all through his tax system and his *dīwān*, or system of official stipends for the Arab warriors. In later centuries ʿUmar also became regarded as the ruler who fixed the relationship between the Muslim state and the so-called 'Protected Peoples' – Jews, Christians and Zoroastrians – through his famed 'Covenant' with them. (In fact, this is a composite document reflecting conditions which evolved over the two centuries after ʿUmar's death.) Popular tradition makes of him a stern authoritarian figure, dispensing justice with a whip, but also setting for himself high standards of self-control and self-denial. Sunnī Islamic modernists and conservatives alike have frequently looked back on his caliphate as a golden age for puritanical, uncomplicated Islam, although the Shīʿa have regarded ʿUmar with hatred as the person who thwarted ʿALĪ's claims to leadership of the Muslim community. Finally, one should note that widespread Muslim traditions attribute to ʿUmar a role in the first collecting together of the Qur'ān, although this work seems rather to have fallen within the reign of his successor ʿUTHMĀN. [34: "ʿOmar b. al-Khaṭṭāb'; 70; 133: III] (C.E.B.)

Umāsvāti [XIII] Author of the important Jain work *Tattvārthādhigamasūtra* ('The Mnemonic Statements relating to the Understanding of the Meaning of the Truth' usually known as the *Tattvārthasūtra*), who can very tentatively be dated to the 5th century CE [21: 135–40]. Nothing can be said of Umāsvāti's life, although his name suggests that he may have converted to Jainism from Śaiva Hinduism. There has been considerable debate about his sectarian allegiance, but the most likely conclusion is that he wrote before the monastic disputes concerning whether ascetics should or should not wear clothes had led to the emergence of the fully formed Śvetāmbara and Digambara sects. While tradition attributes 400 works to Umāsvāti, only a handful can realistically be attributed to him, with the *Tattvārthasūtra* (and what might well be an auto-commentary) being his only work of real importance.

The *Tattvārthasūtra* is, in essence, a summary of the Śvetāmbara Jain scriptural canon, without slavishly following it. It is clearly designed to emulate the mnemonic statements (*sūtra*) which the Hindu philosophical schools produced to sum up their basic teachings. The work has ten chapters dealing with the following subjects: cognition, the nature of the soul, hells and their inhabitants, gods, the fundamental entities, the causes of spiritual bondage, vows and morality, the nature of karma, the ways of putting a stop to karma, enlightenment and spiritual deliverance [24].

The Digambara sect produced three very important commentaries on the *Tattvārthasūtra* by Pūjyapada, AKALAṄKA and Vidyānandin. (P.D.)

Unas [VII] (24th century BCE). The last king of Egypt of Dynasty 5 (*c.*2330 BCE). He built his pyramid and mortuary temple at Saqqara. His pyramid provides some interesting innovations and includes, on the inner walls of the corridor, carved scenes showing a wide range of agricultural and other activities that Unas wished to be magically perpetuated in the next world. However, the most important feature is the Pyramid Texts which appear for the first time in this pyramid, carved on the walls of the chambers and corridors. These texts were compiled from considerably older works and comprise the oldest body of inscribed religious literature yet found in Egypt. They consist of magical spells, intended to secure a desirable afterlife for the king, and may have been recited at the funeral. [10: 170–74] (A.R.D.)

Underhill, Evelyn [VI.A] (1875–1941). She was born in Wolverhampton, England. After secondary education she studied for a time at King's College, London. In 1907 she married and underwent a deep spiritual experience which led to her increasing interest in mysticism. She was influenced by many mystical writers and philosophers, including Henri Bergson and RABINDRANATH TAGORE. In 1911 she published her highly successful work

Mysticism. She also met VON HÜGEL and was influenced by him. The first edition of *Mysticism* was partly historical and comparative. In a revised edition of 1930 the comparative element is played down and the distinctiveness of the Christian experience is stressed; such was the influence of people like von Hügel. She became more and more 'orthodox' and was in demand as a retreat conductor. Her other major work, *Worship* (1936), is a study of Christian worship and the centrality of the eucharist. In later years she was a keen pacifist. [22; 46] (T.T.)

U Nu [IV] (1907–). Burmese nationalist and prime minister of Burma, 1948–58 and 1960–62. He is well known for his idea of 'Buddhist socialism', which he made the foundation of his political agenda.

U Nu came to prominence in the Burmese independence movement in 1936, when he was expelled by the British colonial authorities from the University of Rangoon. He was jailed in 1940 for sedition, and became the leading nationalist leader after the assassination of Aung San. At independence he became the first prime minister of Burma.

Throughout his term of office, U Nu, himself deeply pious, made religious affairs a central concern of his government. In 1951 he declared that apathy to religion was responsible for 80 per cent of the disorders in Burma, and that to overcome them it was necessary to bring about a religious revival. Among other actions to bring about this end, he established a Buddha Sāsana Council to facilitate state support for Buddhism, convened the Sixth Buddhist Council in 1954, and made Buddhism the state religion in 1960. U Nu's government was overthrown in a *coup* led by Ne Win in 1962, and he was imprisoned until 1969. U Nu then lived in exile until 1980, when he returned to Rangoon to be ordained as a Buddhist monk.

U Nu's state patronage of religion recalled the traditional patterns of cooperation between king and *saṅgha* in Burmese Buddhism. His advocacy of Buddhist socialism, which attempted to apply Buddhist values to public life, was in many ways typical of modernist trends in contemporary Buddhism. His political failure is a sobering example of the difficulties that face the communal expression of Buddhism in the modern world. [157: V; 194] (C.H.)

Upagupta [IV]. An important figure, often the narrator, in the *avadāna* literature of Sanskrit Buddhism (and thence translated into other Northern Buddhist languages). He is held to have been a master of the *Sarvāstivāda* school. He is known particularly as an associate of AŚOKA in the 3rd century BCE: he tells him many stories and acts as his guide on a pilgrimage tour of Buddhist holy places. He is also known for having defeated the Buddhist 'devil' Māra. Although he is widely known in South-east Asia as a figure in Buddhist rituals, where he is associated with rain and fertility, he is curiously absent from the Pali literate tradition (with one exception, itself dependent on previous Sanskrit sources), and seems to be unknown in Sri Lanka. [136] (S.C.)

Uppalavaṇṇā [IV] [Utpalavarṇā] (5th century BCE). With KHEMĀ, one of the two chief female Arahats, enlightened through the teaching of the BUDDHA. The beautiful daughter of a wealthy family, Uppalavaṇṇā chose not to marry and became a nun. Shortly afterwards, when sweeping the meeting-hall by lamplight, she focused her attention on the flame and, through meditation, achieved Arahatship. Once, when living in a forest, she was raped by a former suitor. When some suggested that she could not therefore be free from desire, the Buddha declared that, as an Arahat, she was free of all defilements. (The attacker, it is said, was swallowed up by the earth, so great was his crime.) Uppalavaṇṇā was the female counterpart of MOGGALLĀNA, supreme in psychic power. The Buddha named her, with Khemā, as the ideal nun. (150: vol. 1: 418–21] (V.J.R.)

Urabe Kanetomo [XIV] (1435–1511). Member of a traditional family of Shintō priests and diviners associated with the Japanese imperial court. He is best known as the founder of Yuiitsu Shintō (or Yoshida or Urabe Shintō), a syncretistic movement incorporating esoteric Shingon and Tendai Buddhist concepts as well as Chinese cosmology and divinatory practices. Urabe based his theology on texts he claimed were direct revelations from the *kami*, although scholars date them only from the 14th century or ascribe them to his own hand. He called his school of thought and practice Gempon Sōgen ('Fundamental') Shintō or Yuiitsu ('Unique' or 'One and Only') Shintō. In a work entitled *Yuitsu Shintōmōhō yōshū* ('The Teachings of Unique Shintō), he delineated three traditions within Shintō history: the ancient teachings and practices handed down by shrines (Honjaku Engi Shintō); Buddhist Shintō (Ryōbu Shintō); and that unique form transmitted through his own family. His goal was to unite all of Shintō under the control of the Urabe family; he did suceed in gaining control of the court shrine, as well as of the exclusive right to grant ordination to priests and to authorize new shrines. Yuit su Shintō divided Shintō into esoteric and exoteric realms; like Shingon, it gave primacy to the exoteric and ritual practices. [24](G.E.)

Urhobo, Gideon Meriodere [I.A] (1903–1952]. Founder of the God's Kingdom Society in Nigeria, one of the few examples in Africa of a Hebraist movement. An Urhobo, from Oghareki in mid-Western Nigeria, he converted to Roman Catholicism in his youth, before becoming interested in the Watchtower Society. In 1934 he left the Jehovah's Witnesses and began to attack them publicly, as well as Christians and Muslims in general. His own movement, the God's Kingdom Society, closely resembled the Jehovah's Witnesses. Urhobo's growing interest in politics was stimulated in 1937 by an encounter with MARCUS GARVEY, founder of the Universal Negro Improvement Association. Until his death in 1952, Urhobo was involved in Nigerian nationalist politics. The God's Kingdom Society has enjoyed some expansion since 1970 and Urhobo is still regarded by members of the Society as a saint. [16] (R.H.)

ʿUthmān ibn ʿAffān [XII] (*d.*656). The third Caliph or successor to MUḤAMMAD over the Muslim community. He came from one of the leading Meccan clans, Umayya, which was for long especially hostile to Muḥammad's cause, but ʿUthmān was an early convert, and thus an indication of the new faith's ability to attract adherents from the highest as well as the lowest strata of Meccan society. His closeness to Muḥammad was seen by his successive marriages to the latter's daughters Ruqayya and Umm Kulthūm, thereby becoming Muḥammad's son-in-law. Though he had played little part in public affairs, when in 644 ʿUMAR was assassinated, a small *shūrā* or consultative committee chose ʿUthmān as a compromise candidate for the caliphate when other contenders proved mutually hostile. ʿUmar had firmly established the Islamic state on a secure financial and military basis, and ʿUthmān sensibly continued his policies; but his own advanced age and his lack of personal prestige and forcefulness allowed opposition to grow, and in 656 he was murdered by malcontent troops. Later Sunnī Muslim tradition built up ʿUthmān into a martyr figure, opposing him to ʿALĪ and his supporters of the Shīʿa, especially as ʿAlī had stood passively by when ʿUthmān was killed; a party of ʿUthmāniyya, partisans of the martyr Caliph, was still in existence two centuries later. One of the strands of opposition to ʿUthmān in his lifetime had been that of pious religious elements, stirred up by ʿUthmān's action in establishing a standard, canonical text of the Qur'ān between 650 and 656, which brought the Holy Book into the form we know now, but whose process of collection inevitably entailed the suppression of variant textual versions which had been circulating in the provinces of the caliphate and to which local interests were understandably attached. We may, however, rcgard this collecting of the Qur'ān as the supreme achievement of ʿUthmān. [34: "ʿOthmān b. ʿAffān'; 70: III; 133: III] (C.E.B.)

ʿUthmān ibn Muḥammad ibn ʿUthmān ibn Ṣāliḥ ibn Fūdī [XII] (1754/5–1817). Muslim reformer, poet and warrior. Known among the Hausas as Shehu Usumanu dan Fodio ('son of Fodio'), ʿUthmān was born into the Muslim Fulani family of the Fodiawa, scholars in the kingdom of Gobir. Gobir was a small kingdom in Hausa-speaking lands. In those days the Hausas, like many African peoples of the Niger lands, were lukewarm Muslims whose Islam was mixed with idolatry, or so the later historians of Islam lead us to believe. Usumanu was educated as a scholar with a good command of Arabic, and a fluent knowledge of both Hausa and Fulani or Fulfulde, his mother tongue. He wrote poetry in all three languages, as did his younger brother, ʿAbd Allāh ibn Muḥammad, who was an even greater scholar and poet than Usumanu. From 1774 till 1804 Usumanu and ʿAbd Allāh conducted a revivalist campaign in Gobir, Katsina, and surrounding regions as *mujaddid*s, rejuvenators of Islam. They used to recite or sing their long poems of warning and admonition to remind the people of the day of judgment and the punishments of hell, and of the need to repent, reform and pray. When in 1804 Yunfa, the king of Gobir, fearful of Usumanu's influence on the people, started plotting against him, Usumanu fled to Gudu with his followers, who rallied round him in such numbers that he was in a position to counter-attack. One night the famous saint ʿABD AL-QĀDIR AL-JĪLĀNĪ appeared in a dream to Usumanu, and handed him the *sayf al-ḥaqq*, the 'Sword of Truth', God's weapon against the infidel and idolaters. Usumanu now preached the *jihād*, and in four years of fierce battles conquered the kingdom of Gobir (1804–8). This sparked off others in neighbouring Hausa states, where Fulani leaders rose as rebels and when successful, were recognized by Usumanu as emirs, while he himself, by 1812, was hailed as Caliph 'emperor', with his residence in Sokoto, while ʿAbd Allāh ruled in Gwandu. Their successors ruled until the British took over in 1902. Usumanu died in 1817. His pious poems are still sung by the people. [44; 48; 86: I] (J.K.)

Utpalavarṇā. *See* UPPALAVAṆṆA.

Uways, Shaykh [XII] [Uways ibn Muḥammad al-Barāwī] (1847–1909). East African Muslim missionary. Called in Somali Awisu and in Swahili Shehe Uwesi, he was responsible for a wave of Islamic expansionism that rippled from southern Somalia through Kenya and Tanganyika into Zaire (then still the Belgian Congo), into Ethiopia and Malawi, after 1880. Uways ibn Muḥammad al-Barāwī was born in Barāwa, which was then still a Swahili-speaking town (before it became part of Somalia in 1922). In those days Barāwa was a famous centre of learning and Swahili religious poetry. There young Uways was educated, in Shāfiʿī law, Arabic grammar and the principles of Sufism. At an early age he retreated to an old minaret, from which he expelled many *jinn* with his ardent prayers, for the benefit of the local fishermen, whose boats were often blown on the rocks by these evil spirits. After 1870 Uways travelled to Baghdad (via Mecca, where he performed the *ḥajj*). In Baghdad, where AL-JĪLĀNĪ had lived most of his life, Uways studied the Qādiriyya philosophy and was sent home as a fully authorized spiritual leader. He returned to Barāwa *c.*1880, having received the blessing of many saints at their tombs on his way home. There Uways became the leader of the Qādiriyya order, and this community became known as the Uwaysiyya, who made many converts to Islam. He was murdered in 1909 by members of the rival Ṣāliḥiyya order. Uways was a good organizer, starting farms along the middle Juba river. He was also a poet in Somali, and some of his poems are still recited. Shortly after 1880 Uways went to Zanzibar, which he made the centre of his East African operations. From there he visited Dar es Salaam to set up another branch of his Qādiriyya, which in turn extended to Lindi, Bagamoya, Pangani, Uzaramo, Mikindani, Uyao, Uhehe, Ujiji, Tabora, Unyamwezi and even along the Lualaba-Congo River in Maniema, Kindu, Kasongo and Kisangani, which is still a centre of the Qādiriyya sect. Poems and hymns in Arabic, Somali and Swahili by and about Sheikh Uways are still sung at all vigils of the Qādiriyya. [76; 86: VI] (J.K.)

V

Vajirañāṇavarorasa [IV] [Wachirayan Warorot] (1860–1921). The most significant Thai Buddhist reformer of the early 20th century, continuing the process of social and religious modernization begun by his father, King MONGKUT. Vajirañāṇa's autobiography, the first of that genre in Thai literature, portrays his life in a classic pattern stemming from the life of the BUDDHA himself. His youth was one of luxury, which he left behind in 1879 to be ordained in the Thammayut order, the reformist and ascetic fraternity of monks founded by his father. He distinguished himself in Pali studies and became abbot of the main Thammayut monastery in 1892. He subsequently devoted himself to an expansion and reform of that movement. He collaborated with his half-brother, King Chulalongkorn (Rama V), in the promotion of basic education throughout Thailand. In 1910 Vajirañāṇa was appointed patriarch (*sangharāja*) of the entire monastic community in Thailand, and with strong royal support, he began a thorough reorganization and reform of Thai Buddhism. A significant result of his efforts was the institutional unification and homogenization of the Thai *saṅgha*. [179] (C.H.)

Valakhš [XXVI] [Vologeses]. One of several Arsacid kings who bore that name in the first and second centuries CE. Although their dynasty ruled the Parthian empire from *c.*139 BCE to *c.*224 CE, only he is honoured in Zoroastrian tradition as it was transmitted by their adversaries and successors, the Sasanians. He gained this distinction by seeking to preserve throughout his domains 'whatever had survived in purity of the Avesta and Zand' (i.e. the holy texts and their exegesis), after the havoc wrought by Alexander and the Seleucids [7: 10.3.4.2]. This laudable action appears to have inspired TANSAR to the further step of establishing the Avestan canon. (M.B.)

Valentinus [IX] (2nd century). A native of Egypt, Valentinus was an influential Gnostic, though some scholars describe him as simply an imaginative Platonist theologian (2: 57–74; 5: 75–102]. His disciples seem to have claimed that Valentinus stood in the tradition of PAUL THE APOSTLE because he had been taught by Theudas, one of Paul's pupils. He lived in Rome from *c.*136 to *c.*165 and may have had hopes of being made bishop on account of his intellectual prowess [7: 36–9]. The place and circumstances of his death are unknown.

Valentinus was a prolific author, but little has survived of his writings [6: II]. He wrote a *Gospel of Truth* which may be the work of that name recovered in a Coptic version from Nag Hammadi [8: 37–49]; it is a speculative work on the gnostic JESUS. Overall his teaching was based on the Platonic notion of the parallelism between the world of ideas (the *plērōma*) and the world of phenomena (*kenōma*). From the Monad or Father there is a succession of pairs of aeons (worlds or ages) whose ultimate offspring, brought about by the abortive generation of Sophia (wisdom), one of the lowest aeons, was the Demiurge or God of the Jews who created the visible world. Redemption was brought about by the aeon Christ, who united himself to the human Jesus at his baptism to bring gnosis [4: VIII; 9: 320–22]. Just as he held a tripartite anthropology of spirit, soul and body, so Valentinus divided humanity into three, the pneumatics, i.e., the Valentinians who through gnosis enter into the *plērōma*, the psychics, Christians who attain the realm of the Demiurge, and the hylics, the rest of mankind who remain trapped in the material world.

Unlike some Gnostics, particularly MARCION, Valentinus and his followers did not reject allegory, and so had no need to depreciate the whole Hebrew Bible; rather, they distinguished between parts inspired by God, parts inserted by MOSES, and unauthoritative parts made up by Jewish elders. Valentinus is correctly regarded as the most influential of the Gnostics [5: 103–353]; some of his disciples such as THEODOTUS and HERACLEON founded schools of their own, and several tractates amongst the Nag Hammadi library are suitably labelled Valentinian. [8: 435–42; 9: 319] (G.J.B.)

Välivițē Saraṇaṁkara. *See* SARAṆAṀKARA, VĀLIVIṬĒ.

Vallabha [XI] [Vallabhācārya] (1478–1530). Vaiṣṇava theologian and founder of the Vallabha sect or *Puṣṭi Mārg*. He was born near Raichur in Madhya Pradesh while his parents were on a journey from Benares to their home in Andhra (though births which take place during journeys are a commonplace and therefore perhaps formulaic feature of Hindu hagiology). His childhood was spent in Benares, where at a young age he attained a prodigious mastery of Hindu learning: he allegedly preached widely on the Vaiṣṇava *Purāṇas*, defending them against the rival theological precepts of the Śaṅkarite *advaita* monists. Later in life, Vallabha came to live in Adail, near modern Allahabad, as a householder-devotee. Like his contemporary CAITANYA, he was instrumental in developing the sectarian worship of Kṛṣṇa, and in translating the Puranic Kṛṣṇa-mythology into geographical reality in the 'actual' locations of Kṛṣṇa's divine sports played out in the environs of Mathura and Vrindaban. The hagiographers describe how his conventional Brahmanical training was followed by the development of an individual philosophy, *Śuddhādvaita*, which maintains that the whole world is real and that the individual soul is one with Brahman. God is characterized as Kṛṣṇa, who creates the world through his own will. The sectarian teaching emphasizes the efficacy of worshipping Kṛṣṇa as divine child, *vātsalya* or 'parental fondness' being the preferred devotional mode; also stressed is the role of *puṣṭi*, here interpreted as 'divine grace', in which the guru or 'Maharaj' enjoys a central rôle as intermediary between devotee and deity.

Vallabha's devotion was directed primarily towards the deity Śrīnāthjī, installed in a temple on Govardhan hill (where it had allegedly manifested itself on the day of Vallabha's birth), originally under the custodianship of priests from the sect of Caitanya; later, in a period of intolerant Muslim rule under Auranzeb, Śrīnāthjī had to be removed to Rajasthan, where it was to form the focus of the modern sect at Nathdwara. After Vallabha's death, the development of the sect was supervised by his son and successor Viṭṭhalnāth (1516–1586), who elaborated the temple ritual into a complex sequence of eight daily sacraments (*aṣṭayāma*); a group of eight poets, the *Aṣṭachāp*, was allegedly convened by Viṭṭhalnāth – though many such episodes represent pious invention rather than historical fact. Viṭṭhalnāth distributed seven further Kṛṣṇa-images amongst his seven sons, to be installed in different parts of Rajasthan and Gujarat. With its emphasis on the householder mode of life, the Vallabha sect has always had a large following among the mercantile classes of these areas and the diaspora. [6; 7; 72; 94] (R.S.)

Vanderkemp, Johannes Theodorus [VI.A] (1747–1811). Missionary in South Africa. He was born in Rotterdam, the son of a professor of theology. A conversion experience led him to prepare for missionary service. He was one of the founders of the Netherlands Missionary Society in 1797; two years later he arrived in Cape Town. He worked with slaves and Khoikhoi, from 1803 at a settlement at Bethelsdorp intended for agricultural and industrial progress. His identification with Khoikhoi (even in life-style) made him unpopular with the Dutch and British, the more so after his marriage in 1807 to a Malagasy slave girl. The Xhosa feared Bethelsdorp and suspected his intentions, though his interaction, however slight, with NTSIKANA proved fruitful. Always controversial, he represents many of the contradictions in South African Christian history. [244] (A.F.W.)

Varro [XXII] Marcus Terentius Varro (116–27 BCE). Roman scholar and author. Though active politically (he backed the losing, Republican, cause in the civil wars, but was pardoned successively by Julius Caesar, who put him in charge of founding the state library, and by AUGUSTUS), Varro's fame was as a man of learning [6; 30: 96–7]. He wrote on virtually every subject of liberal study. Among his most important works were the 16 volumes on Roman religion, the *Divine Antiquities* (10; 30: 312–16]. The work is unfortunately lost, but it was extensively cited by AUGUSTINE OF HIPPO, who uses it as the definitive authority on the pagan religion which he challenged in the *City of God*. Varro approached his task from an institutional (and somewhat antiquarian) perspective: religion is treated as the creation of *human* societies, not of divine revelation. Thus, although the gods are discussed and exhaustively catalogued (but only in the fifth and final triad of volumes), Varro's focus is rather on the public religious institutions of Rome and Italy, the priesthoods, the various types of sacred space, the calendar of festivals, and the actual rituals. A more philosophical treatment of religion and the gods was given by Varro's contemporary, the Neopythagorean mystic and astrologer, Nigidius Figulus. [30: 94, 309–12] (R.B.)

Vasubandhu [IV] (4th–5th century?). According to PARAMĀRTHA's life of Vasubandhu (the only surviving early source) [214], he was the half-brother of ASAṄGA, associated, like his sibling, with the foundation and systematization of the Yogācāra school of Buddhist philosophy. According to the legend, Vasubandhu was a noted Indian Buddhist scholar-monk who began his career by defeating a prominent non-Buddhist philosopher in public debate, and who then went on to compose the single most influential non-Mahāyāna text of Buddhist metaphysics in Indian history – the *Abhidharmakośa* ('The Treasury of Metaphysics') [131]. He was granted patronage by Gupta kings, was converted to the Mahāyāna by Asaṅga, wrote exegetical and commentarial works in the Yogācāra tradition, as well as two very influential brief works *The Twenty Verses* and *The Thirty Verses* [2; 123], summarizing Yogācāra metaphysics, and died at the age of 80 in Ayodhya.

Western scholars have devoted a large amount of attention to the variant historical and quasi-historical accounts of Vasubandhu's life preserved in Indic languages, Tibetan and Chinese. No consensus has been reached. Some would split the corpus of works attributed to Vasubandhu, dividing it between two figures (both called Vasubandhu), and placing one in the 4th century and one in the 5th [66]. Others try to stay closer to the traditional account [108]. The available information does not permit such debates to be finally resolved. Vasubandhu's importance for the Buddhist tradition is as a systematic metaphysician and as a paradigm of the scholar-monk. His magnum opus, *The Treasury of Metaphysics*, is still used as a teaching text among Tibetan Buddhists, and his formulations of the 'three aspect' (*trisvabhāva*) theory of consciousness and the arguments in favour of a 'mind-only' (*cittamātra*) metaphysic are still prompting commentary in Japan and, more recently, Europe and the United States. (P.J.G.)

Veleda [VIII] (1st century). A seeress of the Bructeri, a Germanic tribe of the Rhineland mentioned in Book IV of Tacitus' *Histories* and briefly by other writers. She appears to be one of a number of such women held to possess special gifts and particularly that of prophecy. Others mentioned by name are Ganna, said by Cassius Dio to be Veleda's successor, and Albruna, referred to in *Germania* 8. Veleda's name is from *veles* (seer), and may have been a professional title. She enjoyed extensive authority in her tribe, and was one of the arbiters chosen when an agreement was made with the people of Cologne, while the Roman general Cerialis appealed directly to her to persuade her people to end their resistance. When consulted she is said to have remained in a high tower while one of her kindred took questions to her and returned with her replies. She is said to have foretold the destruction of the Roman legions in 69 CE. After the fighting of 77–8 she was taken to Rome, but whether against her will or not is unknown. A Greek inscription found in the temple of Ardea in Rome in 1926 (now lost) was thought by some scholars to be a mocking reference to Veleda serving in the temple, but this is doubtful [1]. The religious influence of such women, who according to Tacitus were treated almost as goddesses, was evidently considerable, but we know little of their organization or techniques. (H.E.D.)

Venancio Christo [XXIV] (19th century). Leader of the 1858 millenial movement among the Baniwa people of the Vaupés River region in the north-west Amazonian region of Brazil. Following shamanic precedent, Christo made ecstatic journeys to the highest heavens. He predicted the imminent end of the world through a cosmic fire that would end all suffering and clear the world for an era of happiness. The Baniwa followers of Venancio Christo were to hasten the arrival of the end of time through intense ritual dancing and singing. In order to purify themselves for their task, the self-proclaimed messiah urged his followers to reject industrial trade goods as well as ideas imported from White culture. [16: 555–6; 21] (L.S.)

Veniaminov, Innokentii. *See* INNOKENTII VENIAMINOV, ST.

Venn, Henry (1796–1873). A missionary director, born in Clapham, near London. His father, an associate of WILLIAM WILBERFORCE, was a founder of the Church Missionary Society; his grandfather, a pioneer of the Evangelical movement in the Church of England. Venn became a Fellow of Queens' College, Cambridge and a clergyman in Yorkshire and London. From 1841 he was part-time, and from 1846 full-time, Clerical Secretary of the Church Missionary Society. He never took a salary and served until the year before his death.

Venn was the outstanding missionary theorist and administrator of the 19th century. He declared the missionary objective as the creation of 'self-governing, self-supporting, self-propagating churches', which he envisaged as parallel to the various 'national' churches of Europe. He expected and welcomed a variety of cultural ('national' was his term) expressions of Christianity. He pressed for indigenous church leadership to supersede missionary control. He secured 'native churches' in Sierra Leone and Lagos and the advancement of the African bishop SAMUEL ADJAI CROWTHER. His policies aimed at an Africa economically self-reliant and free from slavery. He saw missionary societies as essentially voluntary lay organizations outside Church structures – a position often resulting in friction with overseas bishops.

A later imperially conscious generation, while never formally repudiating Venn's objectives, heavily qualified his stress on indigenous leadership. [439A; 728A; 841A; 881A] (A.F.W)

Vessantara [IV]. The name of the BUDDHA in his previous life as a human being before that of Siddhartha Gautama, during which he fulfilled the last of the Perfections, that of Giving (*dāna*). His story is the longest of the collection of *Jātaka* stories in the Pali canon; it is found in many different versions in vernacular languages, and is also a very frequent subject of temple paintings. He was a prince in the kingdom of Sivi, who gave away a magical rain-producing elephant to some Brahmans from a neighbouring kingdom during a drought. The citizens of Sivi were angry and demanded that he be exiled; he went, accompanied by his wife, son and daughter, after having held a large almsgiving ceremony. On his journey to life as a forest hermit, he gave away his horses and carriage and refused the offer of kingship in a neighbouring country ruled by his uncle. Once in the forest, he gave away his children to a cruel Brahman, and then his wife to the king of the gods, who had come in disguise. His wife was immediately returned to him, as were his children shortly after; eventually he returned to take the throne in his home country. [43] (S.C.)

Victoria, Tomás Luis de [VI.A] (1548?–1611). Spanish composer. Nothing is known of his birth and childhood except that he was a choirboy at Avila Cathedral. In 1565 he went to Rome and entered a Jesuit college. It is possible that he was an ordained priest. It is also possible that he studied under PALESTRINA at this time. He held various posts in Rome, including that of choirmaster at his college, and he published several volumes of sacred music. To this period belong his two settings of the Passion and nine Lamentation lessons contained in his *Holy Week Office* (1585). He returned to Spain and became chaplain to Philip II's sister Maria. His *Requiem*, composed at her death in 1603 and published in 1605, is one of his finest works. He remained organist at a convent in Madrid until his death. His musical ability is often compared to that of Palestrina but is generally recognized to betray his nationality in its expressiveness and dramatic content. [754] (E.M.)

Vidyāpati [xi] (14th–15th century). Maithili poet, remembered above all for his songs on Rādhā-Kṛṣṇa themes. An orthodox Śaiva Brahman, Vidyāpati lived in the Hindu kingdom of Tirhut or Mithila – an important centre of Hindu learning – in what is now northern Bihar, and he composed his best-known verse in the Maithili language. His contemporary status was such that he was granted a gift of land by his patron, Śiv Siṃha, who acceded to the Mithila throne in 1412. As Mithila lies on the borders of the Hindi and Bengali linguistic areas (whose centres lie to the West and East respectively), its language shows characteristics of both; Vidyāpati is consequently claimed as belonging to both the Hindi and the Bengali traditions in addition to being acknowledged as a Sanskrit scholar and Apabhramsha poet. Vidyāpati's verse largely follows the conventions of court poetry in its descriptions of hero and heroine in the various amorous situations so elaborately distinguished by literary rhetoric; but at the same time, his use of a popular idiom, and a directness and vividness of description which modern conventions might recognize as 'realism', make his songs accessible to an audience much wider than the small élite circle of literary aesthetes. A commonplace tendency to view Vidyāpati's poetry retrospectively, i.e. in terms of *bhakti* norms which were not to be fully established until a century or so after his death, makes it easy for his love poetry to be seen as primarily devotional in character; a truer assessment would see his use of Kṛṣṇaite themes as an exploitation of convenient literary conventions, in which devotionalism played a vital but not necessarily dominant part. Vidyāpati represents an important step in the development of vernacular literatures in Northern India, inhabiting as he does an intermediate position between on the one hand his great forebear the Sanskrit poet JAYADEVA, with whom he is so frequently compared, and on the other the vernacular *bhakti* poets who were to come to prominence in the 16th century under the inspiration of such sectarian figures as VALLABHA and CAITANYA. (8; 77: 29–30] (R.S.)

Vincent de Paul [VI.A] (*c.*1580–1660). French founder of the Priests of the Mission (Lazarists). He was born in Ranquine, Landes, in south-west France. He was ordained priest in 1600. He was captured by Moorish pirates and taken to Tunis, but escaped and returned to France. In Paris he began to engage in works of charity. From 1610 to 1612 he was chaplain to Marguerite de Valois, wife of Henry IV of France. In 1613 he became a tutor in the household of Count de Gondi, general of the galleys; again he engaged in charitable works among the convicts. He organized confraternities of charity for men and women and in 1625 founded the Priests of the Mission or Lazarists (so-named after the Convent of St Lazare where they were located). In 1633 he established with Louise de Marillac the Daughters of Charity or Little Sisters of the Poor. He also founded hospices for the old and the poor (La Salpêtrière) and sent missionaries abroad. In 1643 he was made a member of Louis XVI's Council of Conscience. He was a campaigning opponent of Jansenism. He was canonized in 1737. A lay organization, the Society of St Vincent de Paul, was founded in 1833 to defend Catholic truth. (167; 476) (T.T.)

Vinoba Bhave [xi] (1895–1982). Social and religious reformer and co-worker with GANDHI. He was born in 1895 in Gogode in Baroda to a family of Brahmans. He was deeply influenced in his childhood by his extremely devout mother and his progressive and religious grandfather. At the age of ten he took a vow of celibacy and of service to his country. Educated in Baroda, he proved a brilliant student, but abandoned his studies in 1916 to work further on Sanskrit in Benares.

Here Vinoba Bhave heard about Gandhi and left to join him in the Kochrab ashram in Ahmedabad. His life in the ashram was spent in spinning, at which he became adept, in weaving, cooking, labouring and teaching. In 1921 he was sent by Gandhi to establish an ashram at Wardha which he ran with rigour and discipline. In 1923 he spent his first term of two months in jail for joining the 'flag' *satyāgraha*. In 1924 Gandhi sent him to Travancore to lead the *satyāgraha* there against the banning of Harijans (untouchables) from a temple, which was eventually successful. Returning to Wardha, Vinoba resumed his work in the ashram experimenting with Gandhian ideas and working for rural and village development. He launched a scheme encompassing 300 villages and worked at every task himself. In 1931 he was jailed again, this time for six months. In 1932 Gandhi sent him to a Harijan village called Nalwadi, where he worked for five years at eliminating untouchability and at village development. In 1938 he was sent by Gandhi to Pavnar, where he established an ashram. His health was bad at this period and he became somewhat withdrawn, but he learnt Arabic and translated parts of the Qur'ān to help with Hindu–Muslim unity. In 1939 Gandhi selected him to be the first individual *satyāgrahi* in order to launch the non-cooperation movement in response to the Viceroy having declared war against Hitler on India's behalf. With occasional breaks Vinoba spent until 1944 in jail, writing, studying scriptures, teaching and learning the South Indian languages. On the death of Gandhi, Vinoba was instrumental in launching the *sarvodaya* (welfare of all) movement. In 1951 he began his famous *pad-yātrā*, huge journeys on foot through the villages in many parts of India, urging people to donate land so that it could be redistributed. This became known as the *bhūdān* movement which later developed into *grāmdān*, that is, the gift of villages. Vinoba continued as a major figure in these movements until he retired to Pavnar in 1970. He died in 1982.

Throughout his life Vinoba Bhave was extremely austere, hardworking and deeply religious, although he 'sought not God in the Himalayas, but in society'. He worked tirelessly to try to bring about *rām-rāj* in the villages. Although in much of what he tried to accomplish he was unsuccessful, he came to be regarded as a saint. This was not so much on account of his spiritual state, but because of his manifest goodness, and because he was the living embodiment of Gandhian values. [80] (S.C.R.W.)

Vipassī [IV] [Vipaśvin]. The name of the 19th in the list of 24 Buddhas who prophesied the future Buddhahood of the BUDDHA (Śākyamuni) [9: 886–7; 18: 199–221]. He is said to have lived 91 world-ages ago, to have been 80 cubits tall and to have lived for 80,000 years. The earliest version of the story, which later became part of the legend of Śākyamuni, is told of Vipassī: how he was provided with a life of unimaginable luxury by his royal father, but on seeing, during trips outside his palace, an old man, a sick man and a corpse, he discovered the great problems of life and death. Seeing also an ascetic holy man, he renounced the world likewise and later reached enlightenment. In the case of Vipassī the tale is told in a 'realistic' manner; in most later versions of this story told about Śākyamuni, the 'four sights' are in fact gods in disguise. [150: vol. 2: 886–7; 248: 199–221] (S.C.)

Viracocha Inca. *See* WIRAQOCHA 'INKA.

Vīrāz [XXVI] His soul is among those blessed in the ancient *Farvardīn Yašt*, i.e. he lived in the early days of Zoroastrianism. His story, transmitted orally, survives in a final written version of the 9th century CE. Because he was perfectly just, the lot fell to Vīrāz (known as 'the just') to undertake in spirit the dangerous journey to the other world to confirm the truth of ZOROASTER's teachings. His spirit was gone for seven days. On its return to the body he recounted all that he had seen in heaven and hell. The influence of this story is traceable in the Jewish *Second Book of Enoch* and Dante's *Divine Comedy*. [5: vol. 3: XI; 7: 6.3; 21] (M.B.)

Virgil [XXII] [Vergil; Publius Vergilius Maro] (70–19 BCE). The greatest of the Roman poets and the one who expressed most fully the moral and spiritual values of Roman society as renewed – ideally, at least – under his patron, the emperor AUGUSTUS [3; 16: XVIII; 17; 19; 22]. Virgil's major creation was the *Aeneid*, rightly and immediately hailed as Rome's national epic. Through its mythic narrative (the story of the hero Aeneas' flight from Troy to a new home in Italy), Virgil expounds Rome's god-given destiny of empire, the values that achieve and exemplify it (especially that 'piety' which consists in the scrupulous honouring of one's various obligations to the gods and one's fellow men), and the human costs of its realization. Virgil's seriousness of purpose, his sense of the numinous, and his profound humanity eventually commended him, above all pagan writers, to the Christians, and the fourth poem in his *Eclogues*, foretelling the birth of a mysterious child saviour, was read by them as a prophecy of the Nativity. His suitability as a guide to the underworld in the *Divine Comedy* of DANTE rests on the sixth book of his *Aeneid*, though Virgil dispatched his hero to the underworld not so much to view the torments of the dead and damned as to meet the as yet unborn heroes of Roman history. (R.B.)

Vīr Siṅgh [XXIII] (1872–1957). Leading intellectual of the Siṅgh Sabhā movement who played a key role in both formulating and disseminating modern Sikhism. He experimented with a wide variety of literary genres – novel, epic, poetry, biography – to represent his views on Sikh doctrines, rituals and identity. In addition he wrote hundreds of pamphlets and newspaper articles to advance the cause of social reform and communal consciousness among the Sikhs [34: III]. In 1899 Vīr Siṅgh launched a Punjabi newspaper, the *Khālsā Samāchār*. This was to become one of the most influential Sikh newspapers in the 20th century. His works of exegesis and critical editions of Sikh classics like the *Sūraj Prakāś* still remain a major source for understanding Sikh scriptures, theology and history [34: VII]. (H.S.O.)

Visser 't Hooft, Willem Adolph [VI.A] (1900–). Dutch General Secretary of the World Council of Churches, 1948–66. He was born in Haarlem, Netherlands, and received his primary and secondary education there. His parents were members of the Arminian or Remonstrant Church. At secondary school he was introduced to ancient and modern European languages and joined the Dutch Student Christian Movement. In 1918 he went to the University of Leiden to study theology and law. He spent a few weeks at a Quaker centre in Birmingham in 1920 and on a return visit two years later he met his future wife, Jetty Boddaert, also Dutch. Between 1921 and 1923 he was involved in the World's Student Christian Federation and their relief programme for Europe. In 1923 he graduated in theology and in 1924 he was married and went to Geneva to work for the YMCA in their Boys' Work programme. In 1925 he attended the Stockholm Conference on 'Life and Work' as a representative of the YMCA. In 1928 he published his doctoral thesis awarded by the University of Leiden, *The Background of the Social Gospel in America*. He joined the staff of the World's Student Christian Federation in Geneva in 1928, and was General Secretary from 1932. From 1929 to 1939 he was editor of *The Student World*. He was ordained as a minister of the National Protestant Church in Geneva in 1936. In 1938 he became the General Secretary of the putative World Council of Churches. The post was confirmed after the Amsterdam Assembly of 1948. He remained General Secretary until 1966. His wife died in 1968. In the same year he was elected an Honorary President of the World Council of Churches. [579; 827; 828] (T.T.)

Vivekananda, Swami [XI] [Narendranath Dutt] (1863–1902). Hindu religious leader. He was born in Calcutta, the son of a lawyer, and received a good English education. Shortly after taking a BA in law at Calcutta University in 1884, he became a disciple of RAMAKRISHNA. In 1886, after Ramakrishna's death, he became a *sannyāsī*, though he did not take the name Vivekananda until 1883. In 1893, after six years of study and travel in India, he sailed to the United States, where he was an impressive figure at the Parliament of Religions held that year in Chicago. He attracted followers in the USA and England, founding the Vedanta Society of New York in 1896. After his return to India in 1897, marked by a triumphal lecture tour [113: vol. 3: 103–361], he organized the Ramakrishna Mission to carry on his work, and the Ramakrishna Order, an order of *sannyāsīs* with a strict programme of training and a centralized organization. After a second visit to London and the USA in 1899–1900, he returned to Belur Math, the headquarters of the Order near Calcutta, where he died. In all his work he claimed to be carrying out the teachings of Ramakrishna, though his methods and ideas were far more structured and sophisticated than those of his master. While rejecting as false such features of Hinduism as caste restrictions and rules of purity, he identified the true Hinduism as Advaita Vedanta. All other religious doctrines, whether Hindu or non-Hindu, he regarded as imperfect representations of the truth. He found an affinity between Advaita Vedanta and Western thought, particularly as represented by Herbert Spencer. His works [113] consist largely of talks in English, addressed to Western audiences and English-educated

Hindus; they show great rhetorical skill and facility, particularly in explaining traditional ideas in modern terms. He presented Hinduism as an intellectually respectable religion with a place in the modern world, and his legacy is found in AUROBINDO, RADHAKRISHNAN and many others. [24: vol. 2: 95–107; 30; 32: 200–205] (D.H.K.)

Vladimir I [VI.A] [St Vladimir] (956–1015). A pagan prince of Kiev until he married Anna, the daughter of the Byzantine emperor, in *c.*987. In 978 he had ousted his elder brother from Kiev and conquered Polotsk and much of White Russia. Following his marriage he was baptized and he invited Greek clergy to baptize his people in the river Dnieper in 988. He may have been influenced in his conversion by the fact that his grandmother Olga had been baptized following the death of her husband, a former ruler of Kiev, or by the prospects of military and political alliance with Byzantium. The legends in the *Primary Chronicle* tell of a devout Christian ruler who introduced Christian virtues and eliminated pagan deities from among his people. In fact he was quite brutal with those of his subjects who refused baptism. He introduced Slavonic into the liturgy using the language developed by CYRIL AND METHODIUS. His rule was marred by insurrections mounted by the sons of his former pagan wives between 1015 and 1036. He was canonized and is regarded as the founder of the Russian Orthodox church with the liturgical title 'equal to the apostles'. [63; 174; 230] (T.T.)

von Hügel, Friedrich. *See* HÜGEL, FRIEDRICH VON.

W

Wachirayan Warorot. *See* VAJIRAÑĀṆA-NARORASA.

Waite, Arthur Edward [XVII.B] (1857–1942). Major figure in the events leading to the break-up of the Order of the Golden Dawn and a prolific writer and translator of occult and mystical texts. Born in New York, he was brought up in London by his Catholic mother. His writing career spanned some 60 years and covers a wide range of subjects: from poetry and fairy tales to standard translations of ELIPHAS LÉVI and major studies of alchemy. An early publication attacks previous occult studies as being unscholarly and grossly inaccurate.

Waite was a theosophist for a short while and in 1891 first joined the Golden Dawn (*see* WESTCOTT, WILLIAM WYNN). There are many negative comments on record of his impressions of the magicians' incompetence. He rejoined in 1896, and by 1903 he had successfully turned a large part of the membership away from magic toward mysticism. This period coincides with more editing and translation of mystical texts. He also became a freemason at this time, and wrote for the Masonic Press at least one important work on the obscure history of English freemasonry. He had become committed to the belief that all mystical and hermetic traditions contained within them a true path to be followed in the quest for mystical unity with God. His views of mysticism are expressed in his writings, but are best conveyed through the Golden Dawn-influenced rituals he developed for his own organization, the Fellowship of the Rosy Cross. He founded this in 1915, by which time the Golden Dawn had completely collapsed. The rituals employed were aimed to be more religious than magical, and in dramatic form led towards the attainment of mystical union. The main interest throughout his life remained Rosicrucianism.

He had one of the more significant influences on literature during the era of the 'occult revival' at the turn of the last century, Charles Williams, Arthur Machin and Evelyn Underhill all being strongly affected by Waite. As a scholar in the esoteric field his translations are well respected by other specialists, the Jewish scholar Gershom Scholem for instance. [4] (K.M.)

Walī Allāh, Shāh [XII] (1703–1762). The greatest Islamic theologian of 18th-century India. He was born into a family of Delhi *ʿulamā* with Sufi affiliations, particularly to the Naqshbandī order. Apart from a year of pilgrimage and study in Arabia, most of his life was spent in Delhi as an influential teacher and prolific writer, chiefly in Arabic, his most famous treatise being the *Ḥujjat Allāh al-bāligha*. The notorious difficulty of his elliptical style results from his urgent preoccupation with producing an integration of all the rational, traditional and esoteric branches of the Islamic sciences which would serve to safeguard a faith that had been severely shaken in India by the chaos ensuing from the collapse of Mughal authority in the early 18th century. This endeavour was based on a rejection of blind traditionalism (*taqlīd*) and the productive use of reasoning (*ijtihād*) to support the validity of the *sharīʿah*, with whose values the esoteric teachings of Ṣufism were integrated in a fashion similar to that of his Naqshbandī predecessor Shaykh AḤMAD SIRHINDĪ. In this regard Shāh Walī Allāh's emphasis on a commonsense approach to the study of Ḥadīth [19a: XI) is noteworthy, while the creativeness of his thinking is remarkably demonstrated in the socio-economic ideas implied in his concept of *irtifāqāt* [19a: XV]. His overwhelming concern with putting the Muslims of India in touch with the basic realities of Islam found practical expression in his revolutionary Persian translation of the Qur'ān. This was followed by a translation into Urdu by his son Shāh ʿAbd al-ʿAzīz, whose disciple Sayyid Aḥmad Barelvī (*d.*1831) was inspired by Shāh Walī Allāh's teachings to instigate a *jihād* which would restore the purity of Islam in India [7: 209–17]. Shāh Walī Allāh is thus both the spiritual ancestor of South Asian Wahhābism and the intellectual precursor of the rationalism of Sayyid AḤMAD KHĀN [7: IX; 19a; 92a: 277–82] (C.S.)

Wang Che [v] (1112–1170). He is considered the ancestor of the so-called northern school of Taoism. His Taoist appellation is Ch'ung-yang Chen-ren ('Redoubled Yang True Man'). He was a native of Shensi province and, originally a student of military arts. At the age of 47 he encountered two of the EIGHT IMMORTALS, Chung-li Ch'üan and LÜ TUNG-PIN, who converted him to Taoism. This did not mean that he forsook Literati (Confucian) and Buddhist doctrines, however, because it was common in his time to hold all three Great Traditions in esteem. Wang mastered the secret teachings of the Golden Elixir, and so changed his personal name to Che, written with the graph for 'lucky' repeated thrice. He had seven major disciples who formed the original Northern School, which was dubbed the Perfection of Truth (*ch'üan chen*). This is one of the two major Taoist schools still in existence. Its headquarters are at the White Cloud monastery (*pai-yün kuan*) in Peking. [31; 57: 13–15] (L.T.)

Wangomend [xx] (*c.*1750–*c.*1795). Delaware Indian preacher. He rose to prominence among the Ohio bands in the 1790s after the collapse of the tribal confederation in the wake of the Pontiac wars. Wangomend's religious career began in 1766 with the claim that he had been selected by the Great Spirit to show to all Indian peoples the true path of salvation. His teachings included a strong distrust of all Whites and an emphasis on the importance of traditional Indian ways. In 1775, fearing a threat to his power by those whom he identified as witches, he proposed a general hunt to rid himself of his enemies. The general Council of the Delaware did not support this effort. Wangomend was one of many such prophetic figures to arise among the Delaware as their political and cultural influence began to erode. [7: 293–5] (S.R.)

Wang Po-an. *See* WANG YANG-MING.

Wang Shou-jen. *See* WANG YANG-MING.

Wang Yang-ming [v] [Wang Shou-jen; Wang Po-an] (1472–1529). After CHU HSI, the most important scholar and systematizer of the renascent Literati (Confucian) tradition in China. He lived during the Ming dynasty (1368–1644), at the time when that dynasty reached the peak of its prosperity and cultural creativity. While he came from a distinguished Literati family, he was also interested from an early age in the contemplative methods developed by Taoists and Buddhists. He was a writer, philosopher, statesman, and successful military campaigner; his life and thought are marked by a tension between activity and silence, between a desire for worldly achievement and aspiration towards the Literati ideal of sagehood.

Wang Yang-ming's thought is complex and subtle. Central to it is the idea of the 'unity of knowing and acting' (*chih-hsing ho-i*), and this complex idea, when fully understood, goes a good way towards resolving the tension mentioned above [12; 55]. Like most Literati after Chu Hsi, Yang-ming regarded the perfectibility of the human individual – the attainment of sagehood – as possible through effortful self-cultivation. His many works explore the proper methods for doing this [7; 11]. Yang-ming's thoughts and writings were influential long after his death and far beyond the bounds of China: they were taken up and used by Literati in both Japan and Korea. (P.J.G.)

Washakie [xx] (*c.*1804–1900). Shoshone chief and religious leader, who grew up in eastern Utah and southern Wyoming. He came to lead the eastern band of his tribe and was known for his emphasis on peaceful coexistence with Whites. Washakie (literally, 'Gourd Rattle') was a fierce warrior, especially against the Blackfeet and the Crows, but accorded safe passage, and even assistance, to emigrants passing through his territory. He was converted to Episcopalianism later in his life and was buried with full honours at the fort in Wyoming that bears his name. [6] (S.R.)

Weil, Simone [VI.A] (1909–1943). French mystic and philosopher. She was born in Paris into a non-practising Jewish family. She was a brilliant student at the École Normale, where she studied until 1931. She suffered in health owing to nervous debility and under-nourishment. She was also politically active on behalf of unemployed or striking workers. From 1931 to 1934 she taught in a number of schools in different French towns. She took work herself in a factory for a brief period and was attracted by Marxism. In 1936 she went to Spain and served in the Loyalist army as a front-line cook. But soon she withdrew from this activity too. From 1937 onwards, following a number of visions of Christ, she became a Christian and wrote mainly on religious topics. Her thoughts have come down in a journal and essays she published. She wrote no complete book. She was inclined towards the Roman Catholic church but declined baptism on the grounds that the church accepted the Old Testament, which, with its tales of war and tribalism, was deficient in universality to be Catholic. She went to England during the Second World War and died there from what is believed to be anorexia nervosa. [360; 858] (T.T.)

Wei Pai-yang [V] [Wei Po-yang] (*fl.* 2nd century). The putative author of the first extant Taoist treatise on alchemy, the *Chou Yi Ts'an T'ung Ch'i*, a title whose connotations are difficult to compress but which may for convenience be rendered 'Alchemical Correspondences' in connection with the 'Scripture of Change' (*Yi Ching*, or, as here, *Chou Yi*). The 'Alchemical Correspondences', so challenging to scholars of later times, is by general agreement a text with multi-layered meanings. It occupies a place of special honour in the Taoist tradition of esoteric techniques. About its author there are no firm historical facts, but by way of making up for this there are various legends. The most interesting of these stories has Wei testing his disciples by taking a pill of his elixir, apparently dropping dead, and later reviving, to find that only one man had had sufficient faith to eat the pill that had apparently killed his master. Thereupon Wei and the faithful disciple (together with a white dog that was their companion) 'grew feathers' and ascended to the numinous realm as immortal transcendents.

Although the text of the 'Alchemical Correspondences' is opaque, it is sufficiently clear that it depends on the 'classical' Taoist thought of LAO TZU:

Induce and nurture the congenital nature!
The 'spontaneity' of the Yellow Emperor and the Old Master
Contains within it all the abundance of the determinants (*te*).
The return to the Root, the reversion to the Origin,
Is as near my own heart [mind], And is not something apart from my own body.
Cherishing the One without abandoning it,
I can long be preserved.
Compounding the pill for ingestion.
Male and female are properly arranged.

[23: 67–8; 37: 50–75] (L.T.)

Wesley, John [VI.A] (1703–1791). English founder of the Methodist movement. He was born at Epworth, Lincolnshire, in his father's parsonage. Educated at Charterhouse School, London and Christ Church, Oxford, he was ordained priest in 1725 and elected Fellow of Lincoln College, Oxford in 1726. He served for two years as his father's curate until 1729, when he returned to Lincoln College. There he became the leader of a group begun by his brother Charles (1708–1788), which met for the purpose of systematically deepening personal Christian devotion. Groups multiplied and became known as 'The Holy Club' or 'Methodists'. In 1735 both brothers set out for the colony of Georgia under the Society for the Propagation of the Gospel. John returned two years later, totally frustrated by his lack of personal assurance of salvation. Through Moravian influence he sought this assurance and on 24 May 1738 he experienced Christ in a way that convinced him. He proceeded to organize bands of people who sought his spiritual leadership to share their spiritual experiences. His activity led to the Church of England increasingly closing its doors to him. He began his 'field preaching'. He covered the whole of Great

Britain between 1739 and 1751. He engaged lay preachers to help in the ministry. All this activity increasingly alienated him from the Church of England, although he desired to keep his group within the church. He collaborated with GEORGE WHITEFIELD for a time but split with him in 1741, having opted for Arminian rather than Calvinist teaching. In 1744 he called a conference of his colleagues, and in 1748 this conference was legally established as the governing body of what became the Methodist church. He ordained THOMAS COKE and sent him to America to oversee the church there. His *Sermons* and *Journals* became popular reading for Christians of all shades of opinion.

Charles Wesley became the hymn writer of the movement, writing over 5,500 hymns which are among the most loved in the English language and include 'Hark, the herald angels sing'. He did not work closely with John. He experienced conversion a few days before John and was also an itinerant preacher until 1756. In 1771 he settled in London and preached regularly at City Road Chapel. He remained closer to the Church of England and was unhappy with John's acts of ordination. [42; 43; 314; 612] (T.T.)

Westcott, William Wynn [XVII.A] (1848–1925). He was the initial impulse behind a late 19th-century society of the Hermetic Order of the Golden Dawn, and was one of its three founding 'chiefs' (*see also* MATHERS, SAMUEL LIDDELL MACGREGOR). Born in Leamington, Warwickshire, the son of a surgeon, he himself studied medicine and became Coroner for north-east London during the 1890s. He claimed that in 1887 he acquired and deciphered an encoded manuscript containing esoteric initiatory rituals and the name and address of a German 'adept'. Westcott wrote to the adept and was given the authority to found the Isis–Urania temple of the Golden Dawn. The manuscript may have been a forgery, and may have come from within a 'Rosicrucian' masonic society with much interest in the esoteric: the suggested author is KENNETH MACKENZIE. In any event the Golden Dawn was founded as a scientific exploration of the spiritual. The elaborate rituals were rich with masonic, Greek and particularly Egyptian and Renaissance Hermetic-kabbalistic imagery, and the practitioners claimed to use the imagination scientifically, to contact the psychical world and work with it as a form of technology to produce spiritual effects. By the time internal dissension split the group in 1903 there had been perhaps 400 initiates, most of them from the upper and middle classes and many from the literary and artistic world (W. B. YEATS, who was heavily involved, and even ran the Order for a year, is its most famous literary member). Much contemporary magical practice stems ultimately from this source. [7; 8] (T.L.)

White, Ellen Gould [VI.A] [née Harmon] (1826–1915). American co-founder of the Seventh-Day Adventist Church. She was born near Gorham, Maine, to a Methodist family. Her family soon moved to Portland. As a consequence of a severe childhood accident she had very little education but studied for a time at Westbrook Seminary and Female College. In 1840 she joined a millenarian sect, the Millerites. When Christ failed to appear on 22 October 1844 as predicted by William Miller, in December the young Miss Harmon went into a trance and claimed that she received a vision that the beginning of heavenly judgement had occurred on 22 October. In 1846 she received another vision which led her to observance of the Sabbath on the seventh day. In the same year she married James White. He joined with her in itinerant preaching of the sabbatarian adventist message. When her children were born she left them with friends. In 1852 the couple settled in Rochester, New York, where her husband set up a printing press. Three years later they moved to Battle Creek, Michigan, and formally set up the Seventh-Day Adventist Church some 3,500 strong. Ellen's health was always indifferent owing to the childhood accident. In 1863 she received a vision that Adventists should avoid drugs, even medical drugs, smoking, alcohol and meat. She began to set up health sanatoria built on these principles. The Whites preached on the West Coast during the 1870s. James died in 1881. Ellen undertook missions to Europe (1885–7) and Australia and New Zealand (1891–1900). In 1900 she settled in California. She never became the formal leader of the organization but her influence as a prophetess was, and continues to be, great. Her writings are regarded as inspired by the members of the church. [855; 856; 857] (T.T.)

Whitefield, George [VI.A] (1714–1770). English Calvinistic Methodist leader. He was born in Gloucester, England and was educated at Christ Church, Oxford. There he came under the influence of the Wesley brothers, being a student of JOHN WESLEY. He graduated and was ordained deacon in 1736. In 1737 he journeyed to Georgia in the American colonies on the first of seven voyages. He returned less than a year later and was ordained priest. By this time he was showing his 'enthusiasm' by preaching in the open air in the mode of the Wesleys. As with them, the Church of England began to close its doors to him. Much of this 'enthusiasm' was recorded in his published journals. On his second visit to Georgia (1739–41) he preached extensively and founded the Bethesda orphanage on land donated by the colony's trustees. He particularly appealed to congregations of Calvinist hue. In 1741 he published an attack on John Wesley for his Arminianism and their relationship was broken. Whitefield still enjoyed success throughout Britain, especially in uniting the Calvinistic Methodists. In America he was associated with Princeton University and with Dartmouth School. In 1770 he went again to America, where he died in Newburyport, Massachusetts. He is buried beneath the pulpit in the town's Presbyterian church. [361; 859] (T.T.)

Wierwille, Victor Paul [XIX] (1916–1985). Founder of The Way organization. He was born into a fundamentalist home on a 147-acre farm outside New Knoxville, Ohio, which became the headquarters of The Way International. He studied at Mission House College, the University of Chicago Divinity School and the Moody Bible Institute; he obtained a Master's degree from Princeton Seminary and an honorary doctorate from Pike's Peak Bible Seminary in 1948. In 1941 he was ordained a minister of the Evangelical and Reformed Church. In 1944 he started Vesper Chimes, a radio station in Lima, Ohio; this eventually developed into The Chimes Hour Youth Caravan, which was chartered as The Way Inc. in 1955. In 1957 he resigned from his Church to devote himself to biblical study and teaching. [71]

In 1953 Wierwille started giving classes entitled 'Power for Abundant Living' (PFAL) [70], based on his interpretation of the Bible, particularly the promise: 'I came that they might have life, and might have it abundantly.' (*John* 10:10) This developed into a 33-hour course on film. After a slow beginning, Wierwille began to attract growing numbers as part of the 'Jesus movement' that flourished in the late 1960s. It is claimed that, by 1983, 100,000 had participated in PFAL. In 1970 'The Way Corps', a leadership training programme, was started, and 'Word Over the World Ambassadors' were dispatched in 1971 to teach Wierwille's version of the scriptures. An annual festival, 'Rock of Ages', was inaugurated – over 17,000 attended the 1983 Festival. In 1978 the LEAD (Leadership, Education, Adventure, Direction) Outdoor Academy and The University of Life, a home-study correspondence school, opened. In 1982 Wierwille transferred the presidency of The Way to L. Craig Martindale (1948–).

Wierwille's theology rejects the view of the Trinity adopted by most main-line churches – it accepts that JESUS is the Son of God, but not God the Son [69]. It teaches that the Bible is to be seen as a progressive dispensation, and that a further dispensation began after Easter with the New Testament Church; as there is only one baptism – that of the Holy Spirit (*Ephesians* 4: 5–6) – water baptism is rejected.

The Way has come under attack from its opponents on account of its theological position, and there have been accusations that undue pressure is put on converts to join and stay in the movement. (E.B.)

William of Ockham [VI.A] (1280/85?–1349?). English philosopher. He was born in Ockham, Surrey. He became a Franciscan and studied at the Franciscan house in Oxford. He did not receive a master's degree, but remained an inceptor, the *Venerabilis Inceptor*. It may be that he was denied the higher qualification because the chancellor of the university, John Lutterell, objected to his philosophical and theological views. Following a series of lectures on PETER LOMBARD's *Sentences* he was summoned, in 1324, by the Pope to Avignon to face a charge of heresy. In 1326 51 of his propositions were pronounced heretical. He was held there for a time and became engaged in the dispute which divided Franciscans concerning poverty. He sided with the 'Spirituals', the stricter section of the order, against the Pope. He was forced to flee in 1328 to Bavaria, where he was sheltered by Ludwig, the German emperor, who was also in dispute with the Pope. Apart from his Franciscan views William was the founder of nominalist philosophy. He held that knowledge of particulars was not obtained by local inference from the nature of things and their causal and other relations, but from observation. In this sense, while remaining a realist, he was an empiricist. For Ockham religious belief was based on revelation: thus, rather than seeking the unification of theology and philosophy sought by Scholastics, he separated them. After his dispute with the Pope this authority was understood as Scripture not the church. His teaching displaced the old scholasticism although out of favour officially. MARTIN LUTHER was one leader who adopted Ockham's teaching. [61; 101; 469] (T.T.)

Williams, Edward [VIII] [Iolo Morganwg] (1746–1826). Welsh reviver of the druidic religion. He was the son of a poor stonemason at Panon, Glamorganshire, too frail to attend school and educated by his gifted mother. He was trained in the traditions of the local bards, and walked long distances in search of early manuscripts. When his mother died in 1770 he went to London and mixed with Unitarians, reformers and revolutionaries, joining a group of Welshmen which included some of Stukeley's disciples. Williams became obsessed with their belief that the bardic tradition could be traced back to the druids, and set out to prove it, producing what are now considered skilled forgeries of early documents. He adopted the bardic title Iolo Morganwg (Iolo of Glamorgan). About 1791 he held his first druidic ceremony, the Gorsedd of the Bards of the Isle of Britain, on Primrose Hill in London. His revolutionary ideas at first made the movement unpopular, but in 1791 he linked the druidic ritual he had organized with an Eisteddford at Carmarthen. Such gatherings originated with assemblies of bards and musicians in the Middle Ages, but were developing into folk festivals with competitions and awards. Williams introduced the bardic script, the bardic calendar, and other seemingly archaic features mostly invented by himself and his supporters. Only at the close of the 19th century was doubt thrown on the antiquity of the Gorsedd, which still formed part of Eisteddford ritual. Williams was a man of great gifts, a self-taught scholar and fine poet, and an able organizer; in spite of attacks from academics, many continued to defend the druidic rites which he created with undiminished enthusiasm. [9: IV] (H.E.D.)

Williams, John [VI.A] (1796–1839). English missionary in the Pacific islands. He was born in Tottenham, London into an evangelical family. He had little formal education and was apprenticed at the age of 14 to a London ironmonger. In 1814 he underwent an experience of religious conversion. This was a time of success for Christian missions in the South Seas. Knowledge of this and his reading of accounts of Captain James Cook's voyages led him to be a missionary. In 1816 he was ordained to the Congregational ministry and joined the London Missionary Society. He and his wife sailed the same year for Tahiti. King Pomare of Tahiti had recently been baptized and Christianity had taken root there. In 1818 Williams moved to Raiatea and won the confidence of King Tamatoa. He taught secular arts and science subjects as well as evangelizing. He helped the king to draw up a code of laws for the island. The Christian community grew rapidly and other islands were also evangelized by the new converts. From 1823 until his death he sailed among the island groups, to the Hervey Islands (Cook Islands), Samoa, Tonga and the New Hebrides, evangelizing, educating and training indigenous teachers to continue the work. He was murdered by islanders while he was on his way to the island of Erromanga. He translated the New Testament into Raratongan. His *Narrative of Missionary Enterprises in the South Sea Islands* (1837) is a classic of exploration. His name has been given to a succession of boats which have been used for Christian work among the islands. (532; 594; 661] (T.T.)

Willibrord [VI.A] (658–739). Anglo-Saxon bishop and missionary. He was born in Northumbria, England and was educated at the monastery in Ripon under Wilfrid, Bishop of York. Willibrord went to Ireland in 678, to the abbey of Rathmelsigi, and was ordained priest there in 688. In 690 he went to Friesland in what is now the Netherlands to begin missionary work. Pepin of Herstal offered him protection and gave him land near Utrecht. Willibrord made two visits to Rome, first in

693 to secure the Pope's support for his mission, and a second visit when he was consecrated archbishop by Pope Sergius I. He built his cathedral on the donated land near Utrecht. In 698 he founded a monastery in Echternach in Luxembourg which was the springboard for further missionary work. An invasion by the Franks drove him out between 715 and 719 but he was able to carry on his missionary work into Denmark and possibly Heligoland and Thuringia. He collaborated with BONIFACE in organizing *chorepiscopi*, 'country bishops', to help them with their work in Western Europe. [323; 480: 1–69; 772] (T.T.)

Wiraqocha 'Inka [XXIV] [Viracocha Inca] (15th century). Eighth emperor of the Inca empire, whose exact ruling dates are unknown. He launched the expansionist Inca conquest of the early 15th century. Known as Viracocha Inca to Spanish chroniclers, his reign marked the first establishment of permanent rule over ethnic groups conquered by the Incas. Permanent overlordship, in contrast to the sporadic raiding carried on by his predecessors, involved the imposition not only of military garrisons under the able direction of the emperor's two uncles, Wika-k'iraw (Spanish: Vicaquirao) and 'Apu Mayta (Apo Mayta), but also of religious installations and practices associated chiefly with overlord groups and lineages. [13; 19; 22] (L.S.)

Wise, Isaac Mayer [XV] (1814–1900). American Reform rabbi. He studied in his native Bohemia and in 1846 went to the United States, where he was appointed rabbi in Albany. From 1854 he served in Cincinnati. In his early years in America he moved cautiously in introducing reforms, saying he would not go against traditional law, but eventually he proposed drastic revisions in Jewish practice. These included the introduction of a mixed choir in his temple (the Reform name for their synagogues), the use of an organ in Sabbath services, the abolition of the observance of second days of pilgrim festivals and of the covering of the head during prayer, and a reduction in the amount of Hebrew employed at prayer in favour of the vernacular. He introduced a prayer rite based on moderate reform, which he hoped would win universal acceptance. Theologically he accepted the Pentateuch as the source of authoritative law, but even there only the Decalogue was to be seen as obligatory; the remainder was open to interpretation. Legislation introduced by the rabbis was not necessarily binding.

Primarily a man of action, he helped to establish the Reform rabbinical seminary, Hebrew Union College (of which he was the first president) in 1875 and the Reform rabbinical association, the Central Conference of American Rabbis, in 1889. [36] (G.W.)

Wobokieshiek [XX] (*c.*1794–*c.*1841). A Winnebago prophet and medicine man who came to prominence during the Black Hawk wars of the 1830s. Born of Winnebago and Sauk parents, Wobokieshiek (literally, 'The Light' or 'The White Cloud') received a vision that foretold the eventual victory of Indian forces over Whites through the leadership of Black Hawk. His fierce ways and his cruelty toward Whites were widely known. After the defeat of his peoples at Bad Axe in 1832, Wobokieshiek was imprisoned briefly and lived in obscurity till his death. In common with many other prophets of that era, a time when Amerindian power was on the wane, Wobokieshiek sought to shift the emphasis of traditional religion in the direction of a more explicit code of behaviour. [4: 298] (S.R.)

Wodzuwab [XX] [Wodziwob ('The Grey-Haired One'); Tavibo] (*d.*1869). Northern Paiute visionary and prophet who received visions in the late 1860s and early spread the Ghost Dance religion among his peoples. In common with many other Ghost Dance prophets who arose between 1855 and the early 1890s, Wodzuwab taught that Indian land would be restored, White settlers expelled, and dead tribesmen resurrected if Amerindians would engage in a series of dances and chants based upon a vision of the other world. [13: 256–8; 10: 5] (S.R.)

Wŏnhyo [IV] (617–686). The founder of the Pŏpsŏng ('Dharma Nature') school of Korean Buddhism, and a close friend of ŬISANG, the founder of the Hwaŏm school. Wŏnhyo twice planned to visit China: on the first occasion he was arrested by border guards as a spy; and on the second, in 661, he attained awakening, a direct experiential penetration to the truth of the Buddhist doctrinal position that the universe is a product of the mind, and so gave up his trip as unnecessary.

Wŏnhyo spent most of his life as an itinerant teacher in Korea. He was instrumental – perhaps the most important single individual – in establishing Buddhism as the national religion of Korea, and was a very prolific writer, producing more than 100 philosophical and exegetical works. He is especially notable for having attempted to reconcile the divergent intellectual approaches of the Yogācāra and Madhyamaka schools, and for having written commentaries on a very wide range of Buddhist texts. Syncretism is the hallmark of Wŏnhyo's thought, and this approach to Buddhism had an indelible effect on the development of Korean Buddhism after Wŏnhyo's time. [118; 27] (P.J.G.)

Wovenu, C. K. N. [I.A] (1918–). Founder and Spiritual Head of the Apostles Revelation Society who has had a prominent role in reforming the life of his nation, Ghana. Wovenu was born of Ewe parents in 1918, and received educational instruction only to the elementary level. Combining charisma and organizational ability, Wovenu founded the Apostles Revelation Society (Apostolowo Fe Dedefia Habobo) in 1939 [36: 184]. Of great influence in Ghana, the society has constructed several schools and hospitals and has even carried on mission work and opened branches in Great Britain, the United States and within other African states. (R.H.)

Wowoka [XX] [Wanekia; also known as Jack Wilson] (*c*.1856–1932). Paiute Indian visionary and prophet. He was born in the Mason Valley of western Nevada. After his father's death, he went to live with the David Wilson family, for whom he worked for many years and from whom he took the name Jack Wilson. In 1887 Wowoka claimed to have had a vision in which he was taken up to the other world to meet God. There he was given a new code of human conduct, one that directed Indians to live in peace with the Whites, to work hard and to refrain from lying, stealing and former war practices. The benefit of such living, Wowoka taught, would be not only the improvement of conditions here and now, but the promise of joining all those friends and relatives who had died and were now living in that place where there is no sickness, old age or death. He brought back from his visionary trip dances, costumes and songs that prefigured this transformed existence. The dances were to be performed at intervals for five consecutive days and would hasten the onset of the new order of things. The credibility of Wowoka's vision was enhanced by the fact that a solar eclipse coincided with his being stricken by a fever and his falling into a deep trance. His recovery was seen as evidence of the prophet's power over the weather and natural elements. Wowoka's vision and teaching inspired the Ghost Dance movement that spread, with regional variations, among neighbouring tribes and as far distant as the Plains peoples. The gatherings of Ghost Dancers were frequently misinterpreted by White authorities, who viewed them as challenges to their authority. The most disastrous confrontation was the massacre of nearly 300 Sioux at Wounded Knee in 1891. Wowoka, though greatly depressed by the unfortunate consequences of his teachings, never recanted his vision. He died at Schura, on the Walker River Reservation in Nevada, on 20 September 1932. [1: passim] [10: 1–18] (S.R.)

Wu, Emperor [IV] (5th–6th century). Chinese Emperor (reigned 502–549) and patron of the Buddhist community during one of the 'golden eras' of Chinese Buddhism. Emperor Wu, the founder of the Liang dynasty, converted to Buddhism in 504 and devoutly supported it throughout his reign. He abandoned Taoist rituals, insisted on vegetarian meals at the court, supported the construction of many temples, invited Buddhist monks to serve as his advisers, and wrote commentaries and introductions to Buddhist texts. A famous legend has it that BODHIDHARMA came to the capital and met Emperor Wu, but was unimpressed by the many favours bestowed on the Buddhist religion.

More than once Emperor Wu 'donated' himself to a temple, which forced the state to pay for his release with large donations. The emperor also established 'Inexhaustible Treasuries' to manage donations and benefit the Buddhist community. His devout faith, however, contributed to his fall and the end of the Liang dynasty at the hands of the rebel Hou Ching. (P.L.S.)

Wu Chao, Empress [IV] (7th–8th century). Chinese Empress (reigned 690–705), founder and only ruler of the Chou dynasty, and patron of Buddhism. Empress Wu Chao was raised among Buddhist influences, and her support of the religion is best reflected in the vast cave carvings at Lung-men, built with her encouragement and carried on by popular support. The Empress took over the administration of the government in 683 after the death of Emperor Kao-tsung. Since Confucian tradition did not allow her to assume the throne, she sought justification in the Buddhist *Ta-yün ching* ('Great Cloud Sūtra'), which contained a prophecy that 700 years after the Buddha's death a woman would be chosen king to rule the entire world. Buddhist monks at the court utilized such passages to declare that Empress Wu Chao was the incarnation of Maitreya. The Empress circulated copies of the sūtra throughout the country and established numerous temples, leading to a popular flourishing of Buddhism, especially the Maitreya cult. The Empress declared herself the founder of a new dynasty (the Chou) in 690, and eventually the official policy of the court was overturned to give priority to Buddhism over Taoism. When her health failed, however, the T'ang dynasty was restored. (P.L.S.)

Wyclif, John [VI.A] (1330?–1384). English theologian and church reformer. He was born at Wycliffe-on-Tees near Richmond, Yorkshire. Not much else is known of his early life. He was a student at Balliol College, Oxford, and from about 1360 a regent master of the college, a post held for a fixed period after graduation. Sometime around this date he was ordained. Later he went to the Queen's College, where he graduated with a Bachelor of Divinity degree in 1369 and Doctor of Divinity in 1372. From 1361 he held the living of the parish of Fillingham in Lincolnshire, and the following year he received the prebendary of Aust in the collegiate church of Westbury-on-Trym, near Bristol. In 1368 he exchanged Fillingham for Ludgershall in Buckinghamshire. He was made vicar of Lutterworth in 1374, a post he held until his death. Between 1376 and 1379 he published a series of treatises in which he challenged the right of the church to hold temporal possessions. These publications brought him into the political affairs of the time. John of Gaunt tried to use Wyclif's teaching to his own ends. He was summoned in 1377 to answer for his views by the English bishops; later the Pope denounced many propositions from his writings. The result was a ban on Wyclif's preaching. He continued to write on such subjects as the authority of scripture and the need to translate it into the vernacular. He also attacked the eucharistic doctrine of transubstantiation. In 1382 Archbishop Courtenay of Canterbury brought charges against Wyclif; although some of Wyclif's propositions were found heretical and the rest erroneous no action was taken against him before his death. Wyclif strongly influenced HUS and the writings of both men were condemned at the Council of Constance in 1415. [794; 872; 879] (T.T.)

X

Xavier, Francis [VI.A] [Francisco de Jassu y Xavier] (1506–1552). Spanish Jesuit missionary. He was born in the family castle in Navarre, northern Spain. He was initially educated at home and by local priests. He went to the University of Paris in 1525, where he studied philosophy (graduated 1530) and theology (graduated 1536). He also taught philosophy there from 1530 to 1534. During this period Xavier came under the influence of IGNATIUS LOYOLA. On 15 August 1534 the two of them with five other students vowed to live lives of poverty, to bring salvation to others, to go on pilgrimage to Jerusalem and to serve at the Pope's discretion. A year later, with additional students, they renewed their vows and effectively founded the Society of Jesus. Reaching Venice in 1537, Xavier along with others was ordained priest. He never reached Palestine but went to Rome instead, taking part in the discussions which led to the formal foundation of the Society. In 1540 he answered a call to mission from the King of Portugal. He sailed for the East in April 1541 and landed in Goa, India, in May 1542. For three years he worked in the southern tip of India and Sri Lanka, reportedly converting over 10,000 people in Travancore in one month. In 1545 he sailed from Madras to Malacca, the Moluccas and the Moro Islands. He returned to Goa in 1548. The following year he sailed for Japan, where he made over 2,000 converts, and returned again to Goa. In 1552 he sailed for China but was refused entry and died on the island of Sancian (near Canton). His body was returned to Goa, where it is still venerated in the Church of Bom Jesu. He was canonized in 1622 and named 'Patron of Foreign Missions' in 1927. [716] (T.T.)

Xenophanes [X] (*c.*580–*c.*480 BCE). Greek philosopher, poet and satirist. Although his work survives only in a few fragments and in summaries by later philosophers, he is important in the history of religious thought for two reasons. First, he was the first recorded person in the West to put forward the doctrine of pantheism, that the universe is identical with God, and is therefore One, divine and eternal. Second, he was also the first to criticize popular religion, including the poets HOMER and HESIOD, for attributing morally disgraceful acts, such as 'theft and adultery', to the gods, and for its anthropomorphism, which he ridiculed by saying 'if . . . horses . . . had hands, . . . then horses would draw the forms of gods like horses', which may be compared with Yeats' poem – 'The Indian upon God'. [20: vol. 1; 48] (H.L.)

Xoc, Lady [XVIII] (*c.*660–*c.*720). The ritual partner of the Maya ruler Shield Jaguar of the ceremonial city of Yaxchilan. While only limited information of her biography is available, what we do know illustrates, in part, one of the historical roles royal women played in Maya religion. Her ritual action appears on two magnificently carved lintels, which are today in the British Museum [10: 186–188]. In one she appears kneeling, alongside a standing Shield Jaguar, who is dressed in a sacrificial costume. Lady Xoc, dressed in a *huipil* with cosmological and astronomical signs, is drawing a thorn-lined rope through her mutilated tongue. The rope falls into a woven basket where blood-spotted paper and a sting-ray spine receives the blood.

The second lintel shows Lady Xoc, this time apparently in 681 CE, in a ritually induced hallucinatory vision which takes the shape of a huge rearing serpent. Lady Xoc is crouched, holding plates containing bloody paper and lancets, while gazing upward at the apparition, which emerges from another plate on the floor containing blooded paper lancets and a rope. An enormous serpent twists and rears upward displaying a body of jade disks, feather and blood fans. Out of its mouth emerges an armed warrior.

While these scenes have not been fully deciphered, what is clear is that royal Maya women such as Lady Xoc played a crucial historical ritual role during the ascension, reign and warfare of male rulers. This role combines the practice of autosacrifice (i.e. the bleeding of oneself) [10: 175–209] and the experience of visions, within temple precincts, which link rulers and ancestors, the king and divinities, the mythic past, present and future. Maya sculpture reveals that other royal women such as Lady Balam-Ix and Lady 6-Tun among many others played powerful ritual roles, often including bloodletting to mark important ritual/historical events among the Classic Maya. (D.C.)

Y

Yali Singina [xxi] (*c.*1912–1975). Melanesian cargo cult leader. From Sor village in the Rai coast hinterland culture of Ngaing, Madang, New Guinea, Yali was a hero from the Second World War who was acclaimed by most Madang peoples as the key to the Whites' goods. After working as labourer, village health officer and constable, Yali was trained by the Australian Army as a coastwatcher, at a time when Australian colonial interests in New Guinea were threatened by Japanese invasion. Making an astounding escape from a war theatre near Hollandia (now Djayapura), Yali survived the long walk back to New Guinea. In 1945 he received government sponsorship to establish the Rai Coast Rehabilitation Scheme, believing that the Australian Army would act upon its pre-war promises to bring a radical betterment of living conditions among the Madangs. Popular local idealization of him as the 'way to the Cargo', however, as well as his disillusionment with the missions and Australian Administration (which accused him of fomenting trouble and confusion), forced Yali into religio-political separation. He organized a network of 'lieutenants' and 'law bosses' along the Madang coast, and supervised 'table ritual' designed to multiply money and thus gain access to the Cargo [24: 179–221; 29: 39–43].

Various imprisonments failed to stem Yali's influence. By his death *wok bilong Yali* ('Yali's movement' in Pidgin) had the makings of an independent church. If the Whites acclaimed Jesus, Yali's Madang followers upheld him as their equivalent figure. Although he did not write anything, his sayings were collected together in an exercise book to form a kind of New Testament, with an anthropological work on Madang cargo cults by Peter Lawrence becoming the Old Testament. [45; 47: 67–8] (G.W.T.)

Yaliwan, Matias [xxi] (*c.*1929–). Melanesian cargo cult leader and apocalypticist. Together with Daniel Hawina (a man of more managerial style), Yaliwan stirred up over 200,000 people in the East Sepik Province of Papua New Guinea in opposition to White desecration of Mt Hurun. On 7 July 1971 a human chain gang took down US geodesic markers from the summit to Hurun's base, amidst talk that great wealth, including a flood of European-style goods, would come to the participants' clans. [11: 39–77]

After this flashpoint, Yaliwan and Hawina worked to hold their following into a membership group, with ritual acts to create money and a succession of manoeuvres to secure prosperity in the region [12]. The vacuum left by Yaliwan's rejection of the Catholic Church was eventually filled by the New Apostolic Canadian missionaries in 1979 [5]. Although the Canadians have been debarred from continuous operations in the Hurun area, Yaliwan and Hawina run an independent church along lines their work suggested. [47: 66–7] (G.W.T.)

Yamaga Sokō [xiv] (1622–1685). Famous *kogaku* ('ancient studies') Japanese Confucian scholar and military tactician who first studied in Edo under Hayashi Razan. A samurai himself, Sokō rejected first the Chu Hsi school of neo-Confucianism, then the orthodox ideological support of the shogunate, arguing that it had been developed under a socio-political system very different from that of Tokugawa Japan, and thus largely irrelevant to the contemporary situation. He recommended the practical ethics of Confucianism as more appropriate for everyday life. He also contributed to the development of a Confucian philosophy which was to be known as *bushidō*, the way of the samurai; this blended a sacrificial samurai ethic with the ideal of *kokutai*, or the nation as a corporate body.

Sokō argued that even in times of peace a samurai could continue to serve the nation by being a paragon of Confucian virtue, sacrificing selfish desires for material goods and comforts to a complete and unselfish loyalty to his superiors. Samurai should cultivate not only physical and martial skills but also mind and character; for the basis of moral life is the achievement of serenity, sincerity, and magnanimity, coupled with courage, discernment and firmness of purpose. The samurai's central ethical norm is *giri*, the sense of duty or obligation to one's master. In *bushidō*, maintaining one's own or one's master's honour is more important than life itself. In this regard it is useful to remember that Sokō is also remembered as the teacher of Ōishi Kuranosuke, the leader of the famous 'forty-seven *rōnin*' or masterless samurai immortalized in the *bunraku* puppet play by Chikamatsu [33], later on the Kabuki stage and in the modern cinema; this story was the inspiration behind the ritual suicides of General Nogi and others in this century.

In 1665 Sokō published a work entitled *Seikyō Yōroku*, which challenged the Chu Hsi teachings used to support the shogunate. This book was soon banned, and Sokō exiled from the capital. Later he turned to the study and explication of classical Japanese literature, becoming a founder of the *kogaku* tradition of study. Sokō was one of the first major intellectual figures to proclaim the superiority of Japanese culture and ethical values over those of China. [7; 34: 159–60; 39; 63] (G.E.)

Yamazaki Ansai [XIV] (1618–1682). Famous neo-Confucian thinker, as well as the founder of Suiga (or Suika) Shintō, a syncretic mix of Isa and Urabe (Yoshida) Shintō (*see* URABE KANETOMO) with CHU HSI neo-Confucianism. His father was a samurai who left his master to become an acupuncturist in Kyoto. As a youngster Ansai studied for the priesthood at Enryjaku-ji, the headquarters of the Tendai Buddhist sect on Mt Hiei outside Kyoto. Later he studied at a Rinzai Zen temple and then went to Tosa domain, where he studied neo-Confucianism with Tani Jichu and Nonaka Kenzen, the chief retainer of the Tosa domain. According to his autobiography, at the age of 23 Yamazaki abandoned Buddhism after hearing a lecture by Tani. Shortly thereafter he also took up the study of Shintō.

In 1646 he left the priesthood and returned to secular life. The following year he published *Hekii* ('The Refutation of Heresies'), in which he attacked Buddhism and advocated Chu Hsi neo-Confucianism. He was to argue that Chu Hsi's thought represents the true transmission of Confucianism. In 1655 he began to lecture on Chu Hsi in Kyoto, founding the Kimon school. He emphasized self-restraint and loyalty to one's lord, and he valued sincerity above righteousness or wisdom. He also advocated *shinju kengaku*, the simultaneous study of Shintō and neo-Confucianism. He was instructed in Shintō by both Watarai Nobuyoshi and Yoshikawa Koretaru. The form of Shintō Yamazaki developed, Suiga Shintō, incorporated esoteric elements he had absorbed while studying Tendai Buddhism in a neo-Confucian structure, a structure which Urabe or Yoshida Shintō had earlier used in creating a systematic Shintō theology. Thus 'neo-Confucianism' and 'Shintō' began to lose their meaning as doctrinally distinct entities. Like Fujiwara Seika (1561–1619) and HAYASHI RAZAN, Ansai helped to mediate between the interests of the new ruling class and the culturally available symbolic systems. His syncretism, however, was not always appreciated, and several of his followers deserted him when he began moving in this direction. Ansai's teachings survive largely through some of his study notes and in the lecture notes of his students. From 1665–72 he served Hoshina Masayuki, the fourth Tokugawa Shogun, who was very interested in both neo-Confucianism and Yoshida Shintō.

Ansai read the traditional Japanese cosmogonic myth as a metaphor for the transition from a formless state to the phenomenal world through the transformation of yin and yang, which were equated with the creator *kami*-couple Izanagi and Izanami. He said that, as a divine creation, human beings have both a religious and a filial obligation to obey the *kami* and to be reverent in action. In the last ten years of his life he came to claim that Shintō was superior to all other Ways, while maintaining the Five Confucian Relationships and Five Virtues as the bases of the Way. Aspects of Ansai's thought continued to be influential down through the Meiji Restoration as a result of the efforts of many disciples and members of the Kimon school. [47] (G.E.)

Yāmuna [XI] [Āḷavandār] (?918–1038). One of the early *ācāryas* of the Śrī-Vaiṣṇava community in South India. Very little of any certainty is known about his life. He was the son of Īśvaramuni, grandson of NĀTAMUNI, and was probably born in 918. His teacher was Rāma Miśra and it is said that already by the age of 12 he had great debating skills. He apparently became a king and had two sons, Vararaṅga and Śoṭṭhapūṛṇa. His teacher interrupted his comfortable life by teaching him the *Bhāgavad Gītā*, which had such an effect on him that he renounced everything and went to Śrīraṅgam, where he made over his kingdom to the service of Raṅganātha, the presiding deity there. He was instructed by Rāma Miśra to go and learn the *aṣṭāṅga-yoga* from Kurukānātha, who had been entrusted with it by Nātamuni, but, tradition has it, he was so preoccupied with his visit to the Ananta Padmanābha temple in Trivandrum that he was late for the appointment and Kurukānāth died before they could meet. Yāmuna had a number of disciples whom he invested with the Vaiṣṇava *sanskāras*, amongst whom were the Cola king and queen. Yāmuna wrote six works: *Stotra-ratnam*, *Catuḥ śloki*, *Siddhi-traya*, *Gītārtha-saṅgraha*, *Āgama-prāmāṇya* and *Maha -puruṣa-nirṇaya*. In these works lie the beginnings of what was later to become modern Vaiṣṇavism and the foundations of Viśiṣṭādvaita, the theistic philosophy which RĀMĀNUJA was to elaborate so effectively. It is said that Yāmuna sought to meet Rāmānuja, but died in 1038 before Rāmānuja arrived. [22: vol. 3] (S.C.R.W.)

Yang Hsi [V] (350–?386). The most gifted and prolific amanuensis in the history of Chinese spirit-writing. Employed by the official Hsü Mi (303–373), Yang wrote down records of his numerous visitations by many different supernaturals at Mt Mao (in Kiangsi province) during the years 364–70. These texts became the scriptures of a new Taoist school, the Sect of Highest Clarity (*shang ch'ing*), as well as one of the major divisions of the Taoist canon. 'Highest Clarity' refers to the Taoist heaven from which Yang's informants descended. The writings of Yang Hsi, as dictated by these supernaturals, were collected, systematized and commented on over a century later by the great Taoist adept and scholar T'AO HUNG-CHING. According to the latter's testimony Yang was not only a supremely talented medium, but a calligrapher scarcely inferior to the eminent Wang Hsi-chih (321–379) and his equally renowned son, Wang Hsien-chih (344–388). It is rumoured that Yang Hsi, who had been promised a high position in the ranks of the celestial immortals, ingested what he must have known was a poisonous 'elixir' in order to hasten his release from mortal trammels and his elevation to divinity. [52] (L.T.)

Yaśodharā [IV]. One of the names of the wife of the BUDDHA, perhaps the most widely used in the West. It appears in Sanskrit texts; in early Pali texts, she is normally called simply Rāhulamātā, 'the mother of Rāhula' (the Buddha's only son), while a number of other names, including the Pali form Yasodharā, are found in later materials. They had been husband and wife in many previous births; in their final life they were born on the same day and married at the age of 16; Rāhula was born 13 years later. When the Buddha renounced the world she is said to have adopted a life of religious austerity, although she remained at home. After Rāhula had been ordained as a monk by SĀRIPUTTA, and an order of nuns had been started, she became a nun under MAHĀPAJĀPATI, and subsequently became enlightened. [150: vol. 2: 737–40] (S.C.)

Yaśovijaya [XIII] (1624–1688). Jain logician and reformer. He was born in Gujarat and took monastic ordination in the Tapā sect of Śvetāmbara Jainism, tracing his lineage back to the great HĪRAVIJAYA. While still a young monk, Yaśovijaya travelled to Benares, the centre of Hindu scholarship, and studied the various branches of Brahmanical learning with a special emphasis on logic [27: 214–19]. It was doubtless at this time that he attained his formidable mastery of the techniques of 'New Logic' (*Navyanyāya*) which was to characterize his later writings. He also seems to have spent some time at Agra, where he familiarized himself with the Śvetāmbaras, heretical doctrines of BANĀRSĪDĀS and the Adhyātma movement.

Yaśovijaya is perhaps the last great intellectual figure in the Jain tradition. The author of many difficult works on logic, he seems late in life to have been influenced by the mystical tendencies of Jainism and produced works such as 'The Essence of Knowledge' (*Jñānasāra*) [32], in which he dwells on the inner, soul-oriented aspects of the religion. He also wrote a series of doctrinal poems in Gujarati. As a reformer, Yaśovijaya set himself the task of breaking down the barriers between Śvetāmbara Jain sects. However, he cannot be judged to have been entirely successful in this. (P.D.)

Yeats, William Butler [XVII.B] (1865–1939). Poet, playwright and one of the few members of the Order of the Golden Dawn (*see* WESTCOTT, WILLIAM WYNN) to leave any literature of any note inspired by this work. Yeats explored from an early age the close connection he saw between magic and poetry. Yeats's commitment to occult studies is generally underestimated, his notebooks preserve volumes of notes and comments on his practical investigations.

In 1883 he met George Russell, an artist who combined esoteric reading and the painting of visions. Together they joined a group in 1885 to study magic and mysticism. A few years later Yeats joined the Dublin Lodge of the Theosophical Society, and shortly afterwards was admitted to the Esoteric Theosophists at the invitation of its head, Madame BLAVATSKY. Within a year he was at odds with her as he became more involved with the Order of the Golden Dawn and his relationship with SAMUEL LIDDELL MACGREGOR MATHERS was growing. Mathers was to be the biggest influence of his life; Yeats respected him primarily for his knowledge of ritual.

By 1900 the Golden Dawn was in considerable turmoil, and Yeats found himself, unwillingly it seems, as the strategist for the rebels. Yeats was finally the one responsible for suspending Mathers from the Order and took over the leadership in order to restore an atmosphere of work, although by then the seeds of ruin were already sown. His main contribution during this period was to try to reaffirm the emphasis the Golden Dawn placed on Christian doctrine.

Yeats's poetry and plays contain innumerable references to occult practices and is rich in the use of mythical imagery. His essays explain the use of occult symbols to contact 'the great mind' – a notion, not unlike Jung's collective unconscious, of a vehicle that produces correspondences in many minds across time and space.

Celtic mythology affected the Anglo-Irish Yeats from his youth. Throughout his life he attempted to determine the place of Ireland, its folklore, mythologies and politics in his poetry and life. His work in the occult traditions showed him how he might use the Celtic imagery to achieve his great vision, to unify the culture and people of Ireland. [5; 11] (K.M.)

Yeboa-Korie, Yaw Charles [I.A] (1938–). Founder of the Eden Revival Church (later the Feden Church) in Ghana. A Presbyterian teacher whose ill health disappeared after prayer, fasting, visions and Bible study, Yeboa-Korie founded his church in 1963. The church, with its emphasis on music, education and large-scale evangelization, spread widely and was the first independent church to join the Ghanaian Council of Churches in 1970. Influenced by American evangelicalism, Yeboa-Korie is a powerful preacher and renowned charismatic healer who has worked to unite the spiritual churches in Ghana and improve theological training for the clergy. He resisted political involvement with Nkrumah, and as a modern prophet-healer is an important mediator between the older and the independent churches. (R.H.)

Yen-shou. *See* YUNG-MING YEN-SHOU.

Yi Hwang [XVI] [T'oegye; Yi T'oegye] (1501–1570). The outstanding symbol of Korea's neo-Confucian tradition, rivalled in Korean neo-Confucian thought only by YI I (Yulgok). Korea's Chosŏn dynasty (1392–1910) was founded under neo-Confucian auspices, and the orthodox school of thought stemming from the synthesizing genius of CHU HSI was pursued with even more fervour on the peninsula. There it came to full maturity with the thought of T'oegye, whose balanced and integral grasp of this complex system of thought became a major reference point for all subsequent Korean thinkers. In particular he was able to ground fully the intense ascetical practice of self-cultivation in its complex framework of psychological and metaphysical theory, establishing a secure place for it in the mainstream of Korean society.

T'oegye is most famous for an important development in the metaphysically grounded psychological theory that is the essential counterpart of practical self-cultivation in neo-Confucian thought. He broke new ground by explicitly distinguishing the basis for the function of distinctively human feelings from that of feelings more related to our physically based needs and urges. His making this distinction in terms of *li* ('principle') and *ki* (Chinese: *ch'i*, 'material force'), the two basic components of Chu Hsi's dualistic metaphysics, became a focus of controversy and set a distinctive intellectual agenda that has shaped Korean neo-Confucian thought down to this day. There was no similar development in China, where the question instead gave rise to the radically divergent school of WANG YANG-MING. T'oegye's thought is now seen as offering a new perspective on potentials in Chu Hsi's thought overlooked in China and in China-centred Western scholarship. [1: 223–82] (M.Kal.)

Yi I [XVI] [Yi Yulgok; more commonly known as Yulgok] (1536–1584). Together with YI HWANG (T'oegye), the outstanding neo-Confucian thinker of Korea's Chosŏn dynasty (1392–1910). Korean intellectual history for the remainder of the dynasty is generally framed in terms of schools standing in the line of either Yi Hwang or Yulgok. Yulgok is especially famous for his penetrating critique of Yi Hwang's differentiation of the basis of certain kinds of feelings in terms of a distinctive relationship to *li* ('principle') and *ki* (Chinese: *ch'i*, 'material force') respectively, the two components of the dualistic metaphysics of the CHU HSI school of neo-Confucian thought. In contrast to Yi Hwang's granting the most distinctively human feelings a special relationship to principle, Yulgok insisted on an interpretation that emphasized the absolute and consistent interdependence of *li* and *ki* in the constitution or function of any concrete being. Thus, in contrast to Yi Hwang's emphasis on *li*, Yulgok's school is often described as emphasizing *ki*.

Yulgok's mother was Sin Saimdang, who is famed as pre-modern Korea's finest female poet and painter. After her death, when he was just 16 years of age, Yulgok entered a Buddhist monastery. After several years he left, however, and committed himself to Confucian studies. He entered government service after passing first in nine consecutive levels of the intensely competitive civil service examinations, an unprecedented feat. He became one of the king's most trusted advisors, and his writings include numerous proposals and plans relating to administrative reform and military and economic organization, as well as philosophical treatises. Thus, in addition to his fame as a philosophical thinker, he is looked upon as the precursor of the later *sirhak* ('practical learning') movement which made such concerns the focus of scholarly attention. [1: 303–48] (M.Kal.)

Yōmyō Enju. *See* YUNG-MING YEN-SHOU.

Yōsai. *See* EISAI.

Young, Brigham [VI.A] (1801–1877). American Mormon leader. He was raised in a devout New England Methodist family which had to move to western New York State owing to poverty. As a Methodist he had insisted on baptism by immersion. He was trained as a painter, carpenter and glazier. His family were converted to Mormonism soon after the publication of the Book of Mormon in 1830. Brigham, however, waited two years before he was convinced and joined the Church of the Latter Day Saints himself. He accepted all the beliefs of the church, including plural marriage and baptism for the dead. After engaging in a mission in the eastern United States he went to Ohio and helped to build the Kirtland Temple. He was in the expedition, the Zion's Camp, which tried to rescue isolated, persecuted saints who lived in Missouri. He was elected to the Quorum of the Twelve, the ruling council of the church in

1835 and became president in 1841. He helped administer the movement of the whole organization from Missouri to Nauvoo, Illinois, in 1839 and established a Mormon mission in England in the early 1840s. After the death of JOSEPH SMITH in 1844 Young became the leader of the faction which wanted to maintain particular beliefs such as plural marriages and led them from Illinois to Salt Lake Valley in 1847. He assumed complete leadership and, as such, the federal government made him state governor in 1849. The title was later taken from him on the grounds of his practice of polygamy. He was survived by 27 wives and 56 children. [25; 164; 402] (T.T.)

Yui, David Z. T. [VI.A] [Yu Jih-Chang] (1882–1936). The son of a Christian minister from Hupeh Province, China, he studied at Boone and St John's Universities. He then studied at Harvard University, where he was awarded an MA. Following his return to China he worked for the YMCA, of which he was National Secretary for 16 years. He represented Chinese people's organizations at the Washington Disarmament Conference in 1921, and in 1932 he travelled abroad to arouse support for China in her struggle against Japan. He was active in the Institute of Pacific Relations, and a prominent member of the Chinese delegation at the Jerusalem Conference of the International Missionary Council in 1928. He became Chairman of the National Christian Council of China, a post which he held for ten years until his death. [107] (T.T.)

Yulgok. *See* YI I.

Yun, (Baron) Tchi-ho [VI.A] (1865–1945). The offspring of an influential Korean family, in 1883 he became the interpreter for the first American diplomatic mission to Korea. In 1885 a political coup led to his family being displaced so he sought refuge in Shanghai. Through contact with the Anglo-Chinese College he became a Christian in 1887. The following year he went to the United States to study and attended the universities of Emory and Vanderbilt until 1893. While in America he urged the Southern Methodists to begin work in Korea. This they did in 1896. From 1895 to 1906 Yun served Korea as a diplomat, spokesman for reform and vice-minister of education. When Korea became a Japanese protectorate in 1905 he turned to religious work from 1906 to 1920. He was principal of the Anglo-Korean School from 1906 to 1911, a delegate to the Edinburgh Missionary Conference in 1910 and General Secretary of the Korean YMCA from 1915 to 1920. From 1911 to 1915 he was imprisoned for alleged independence activity. In 1930 he was engaged in the negotiations that united northern and southern Methodist mission work in the autonomous Methodist Church of Korea. He was the first Korean president of Chosen Christian College (later Yonsei University) from 1941 to 1944. [702: 14–34] (T.T.)

Yün-chi Chu-hung. *See* CHU-HUNG.

Yung-ming Yen-shou [IV] [Japanese: Yōmyō Enju] (904–975). Ch'an Buddhist master, representative of Sung Buddhism and most influential advocate of the synthesis of the Ch'an and Pure Land schools. A disciple of the Ch'an and T'ien-t'ai master Te-shao (891–971), Yung-ming compiled the comprehensive *Tsung-ching lu* ('Record of the Mirrors') in 100 volumes, quoting over 300 past Buddhist masters of India and China to buttress his syncretistic teachings, especially the unity of Ch'an and Pure Land practices. His *Wan-hsi t'ung-kuei chi* ('All Things Return to the Same Place') was also influential in promoting Ch'an–Pure Land syncretism. He taught that reciting and meditating on Amitābha should include not only focusing the mind on the name of the Buddha, but also contemplating on the reality behind the name, hence merging the practice and teachings of both Ch'an and Pure Land traditions, as well as the T'ien-t'ai tradition. (P.L.S.)

Yūsuf of Makassar, Sheikh [XII] [Yūsuf of Bantam] (*d.*1699). Founder of Islam in South Africa. He was a scion from the ruling Islamic dynasty of Makassar in what is now Indonesia. After his return from a pilgrimage to Mecca he settled in Bantam where he married the daughter of Sultan Ageng, *c.*1650. When the Sultan died, Yūsuf claimed the throne, so his opponents invoked the authority of the Dutch governor at Batavia. The latter found against Yūsuf, but Yūsuf could not agree, so that an armed conflict ensued. This ended only in 1683 with the surrender of Yūsuf and his followers. He was taken to Batavia, but there the people revered him as a saint, so the authorities took him to Ceylon (then a Dutch 'sphere of influence', now the republic of Sri Lanka), and finally in 1694 to Cape Town, where he was honourably treated, and allowed to settle with his retinue of relatives and scholars. When he died in 1699 his prestige had established Islam as the religion of the Malays in Cape Town, though his relatives returned to Makassar. [30] (J.K.)

Z

Zādspram [xxvi] (9th century). Younger brother of MANUŠCHIHR, and himself a fully qualified Zoroastrian priest (*mōbad*). His attempt to simplify the main purification ritual evoked a rebuke from Manušchihr, but he is shown to be otherwise traditionalist by his *Wizīdagīhā* ('Selections'). These are taken from the Middle Persian translation of the Avesta, with its commentaries, and treat of cosmogony and cosmology; the legendary life of ZOROASTER; man's physiology and the human condition; and eschatology. Some sections show how in Sasanian times Zoroastrian scholastics had sought to reconcile Greek science (*see* ŠĀBUHR I) with their own ancient myths and traditional learning. There is no trace of any impact by Islam. [2; 11: vol. 3: 1190–3] (M.B.)

Zäkaryas [VI.A] (*c*.1845–1920). Ethiopian Muslim and Christian prophet. He was born in an Amhara Muslim family in Nägälla, Bägémder Province, Ethiopia, and received a Qur'anic education. In 1892 came the first of a series of visions. These made him first a Muslim reformer, though one who stressed the common features of Qur'ān, Torah and Gospel. By 1895 his preaching was causing alarm and divisions in Muslim communities. Zäkaryas had an Arabic Bible, obtained through the Swedish Mission, and was preaching the divinity of Jesus. He still spoke as a Muslim expounding the Qur'ān (though he identified 'satanic' elements in it), but he believed it to point to Christ, and he expounded the Christian Scriptures also. He had a substantial following among Tigrenna and Amhara Muslims. His teaching (still justified by his visions) survived a full imperial investigation in 1907.

In 1910 Zäkaryas was baptized in the Orthodox Church; 3,000 other Muslims joined him. He seems to have ceased preaching and become an Ethiopian dignitary, with imperial grant, armed followers and duties of taxing and judging. However, the conversion movement from Islam continued. There are signs of tension between the Orthodox Church and Zäkaryas and the other new Christians. In some respects the movement foreshadows the evangelical 'New Churches Movement' a generation after the prophet's death. [178] (A.F.W.)

al-Zamakhsharī, Abū'l-qāsim Maḥmūd ibn ʿUmar [XII] (1075–1144). Muslim philologist and Qur'ān commentator. Born in northern Persia, he studied in Mecca but spent most of his life working in his native Khwārizm. A native speaker of Persian, he excelled at Arabic and believed strongly in the superiority of the Arabic language. He wrote some 50 works, most of which deal with the Qur'ān or Arabic language in general. Al-Zamakhsharī's major work is his Qur'ān commentary, *al-Kashshāf ʿan ḥaqā'iq ghawāmid al-tanzīl* ('The Unveiler of the Realities of the Sciences of Revelation'). This book covers the Qur'ān phrase by phrase, providing philosophical and philological commentary in a concise and somewhat difficult style. Among the major traits of the work are the concern with the rhetorical beauty of the text of scripture and the rationalist theological position which is maintained throughout the commentary. Ideas of the free will of humanity, the 'created' Qur'ān and the need for de-anthropomorphization are prominent. Despite this theological argumentation, which had already lost much of its support before al-Zamakhsharī's time, the work has proved popular throughout the Muslim world and has been subject to much super-commentary, to distillations minus the objectionable theological elements (e.g. by AL-BAYḌĀWĪ) and partial refutations (e.g. by FAKHR AL-DĪN AL-RĀZĪ). For the rationalists of Islam, however, this work represents the peak of intellectual achievement in Qur'ān commentary. [29; 34: s.v.] (A.R.)

Zeno of Citium [x] (334–262 BCE). Founder of Stoicism, and teacher of KLEANTHES (q.v. for details about the school). This Zeno is to be distinguished from Zeno of Elea (southern Italy), the pupil of Parmenides from the 5th century BCE famous for the paradox of Achilles and the tortoise and other arguments aiming at disproving plurality and motion. [7; 26; 27; 35] (G.R.N.)

Ziegenbalg, Bartholomäus [VI.A] (1682–1719). German Protestant missionary. He was born in Pulsnitz, Saxony. He was attracted to Pietism so he went to the university of Halle. When the king of Denmark wished to send missionaries to his Indian colony in Tranquebar he contacted A. H. Francke in Halle; Francke chose Ziegenbalg along with Henry Plütschau. They both went to Copenhagen and were ordained. Towards the end of 1705 they sailed for India and arrived in Tranquebar in July 1706, the first Protestant missionaries to India. In 1707 he secured the first converts, but the following year he was imprisoned for four months by the Danish governor, who opposed his missionary work. In 1715 he set up a printing press and by the following year the whole of the New Testament had been printed in Tamil translation. As well as learning Tamil he made a study of Hinduism, a work which did not meet with the approval of his Danish superiors. His manuscript of *The Genealogy of the Malabar Gods* was not published until 1867. He started schools, orphanages and a seminary for the training of teachers and later pastors. For two years (1714–16) he toured Europe raising funds for the mission and met the King of Denmark and the Archbishop of Canterbury. He died in Tranquebar. [81; 263: 127–134; 471] (T.T.)

Zoroaster [XXVI]. The name used by Western writers for the prophet of the ancient Iranians, Zarathuštra (later Zardušt). The two dates assigned to him in antiquity (5,000 years before the Trojan War, 258 years before Alexander) were both invented by Greeks [36], and the only reliable information about him has to be deduced from the Avesta, the collection of Zoroastrian holy texts. These are in two stages of an otherwise unknown Iranian language. 'Young Avestan' texts are attributed to *c*.800–600 BCE, 'Old Avestan' ones (which are linguistically very close to the Hindu *Rigveda*) to several centuries earlier [35: 12–13]. The latter include the *Gāthās*, 17 hymns composed by Zoroaster, who thus lived perhaps *c*.1200 BCE or earlier. The Iranians then dwelt on the Inner Asian steppes, thereafter moving south into the land named after them, Iran. In the 'Young Avesta' Zoroaster's homeland is called Airyanem Vaējah ('the Iranian expanse'), apparently a region of the steppes [8: I, II; 22: IV].

The *Gāthās* are very difficult texts, composed in a richly allusive, intricate style, with many unknown words. They attract philologists as well as students of religion, and translations differ greatly [30; 31; 35; 47]. They were orally transmitted as part of the main Zoroastrian liturgical text, the *yasna*, and are cited accordingly as *Y(asna)* 28–34, 43–51, 53. Despite their obscurities, they show Zoroaster to have been a priest, poet, mantic seer and thinker who made huge innovations in religious thought. Brought up in a polytheism, he came to believe that there is one eternal uncreated Being, Ahura Mazdā, wholly wise, just and good, who evoked all other beneficent divine beings from his own selfhood. With them he created this world, which is essentially good. Opposed to him, and likewise original and self-existent, is Angra Mainyu, the Evil Spirit, with a host of evil forces. Life is a struggle between their powers, and humanity has the duty to engage in this on its Creator's side. At death each soul is judged by the weighing of its thoughts, words and acts. If the good are heavier, it crosses a bridge up to heaven, if the bad, it falls from this down to hell. When goodness finally triumphs and Angra Mainyu is destroyed, souls will be brought from heaven and hell and joined to their resurrected bodies for the last judgment by fiery ordeal. In this sinners will perish [38: 29ff.; 5: vol. 1: 242–3], the blessed be saved to live for ever in Mazdā's kingdom to come on this earth, made wholly good again as it was at creation.

Profound thought clearly underlies this doctrinal system, in which elements from the old Iranian religion are developed with striking coherence and ethical force; but Zoroaster became convinced of its truth through visions in which he believed that he saw and spoke with Mazdā. He failed to gain a hearing from his own community (*Y.*46.1), but after leaving it converted Vištāspa (*see* HYSTASPES), prince of another tribe, and his wife Hutaosā, who brought their people to adopt his religion. He married, had children (*Y.*53.3) and according to tradition lived long. This agrees with the fact that he was able to establish his faith, linking doctrine to ritual and observance in ways which, with its moral and spiritual values, have enabled it to endure to the present day.

Little more that is factual is known of the prophet. In the Young Avesta his spirit, *fravaši*, is revered; and the legend developed that at his birth his *fravaši* and *khvarenah*, divinely given glory, were sent down from heaven to be miraculously united with his bodily nature in his mother's womb [5: vol. 1: 277–8; 45: 15–23]. He was said to be the only infant to laugh at birth. Wicked priests tried to kill him, but repeatedly he was saved. On reaching manhood he left his parents' house to wander, eventually receiving enlightenment on a river bank at dawn. He met hostility at Vištāspa's court from priests of the old religion, suffered harsh imprisonment, but won freedom and the king's favour through a series of miracles [24: 94ff.; 32: 26ff.; 45: 20ff.]. He had received the gift of all-wisdom from Ahura Mazdā, and was held to be a fountain-head of later Zoroastrian mantic prophecy. Probably well before the 6th century BCE the myth evolved that the future World Saviour, the Saošyant, to come at the end of time, will be born of a virgin from Zoroaster's seed, miraculously preserved in the depths of a lake [5: vol. 1: 282–5].

His religion enters recorded history with its adoption by the Achaemenians (*see* CYRUS AND HIS SUCCESSORS). Zoroaster's name thus became familiar to peoples throughout their vast empire and on its borders. His dualistic teachings were known to PLATO and ARISTOTLE, and in Hellenistic times Greeks regarded him as a great astronomer and 'magician' (since the magi of western Iran were the best known Zoroastrian priests). PYTHAGORAS was said to have studied with him in Babylon, and his name was given to a mass of Greek pseudepigrapha [5: vol. 3: excursus]. Jews and Christians, who appear to have absorbed much Zoroastrian doctrine, identified him with various Old Testament figures: Nimrod, Balaam, Baruch, EZEKIEL [4: vol. 1: 41–50].

In Iran rival claims came to be made, notably in Azarbaijan and Balkh, that this or that region had been Zoroaster's homeland. The motive appears to have been mainly to attract pilgrims. After the Arab conquest in the 7th century CE Zoroastrianism ceased to be Iran's state religion, but was upheld by what came in time to be a tiny persecuted minority, which attained toleration only in the late 19th century (*see* HATARIA). A small group sought religious freedom in western India in the 10th century, where their descendants still flourish as the Parsis (i.e. 'Persians'). From the 19th century idealized portraits of Zoroaster have been painted, which hang in many fire-temples and private homes, and are garlanded by Parsis on holy days [24: 97]. By long tradition, one day each year is solemnized as the anniversary of his death, with communal gatherings at fire-temples. He is venerated with the fixed epithet *ašo* (from *ašavan*; 'just', 'righteous') and is held to have possessed all wisdom and virtues. (M.B.)

Zoser [VII] (27th century BCE). King of Egypt of Dynasty 3. He was the founder of a new epoch, the first king of the Old Kingdom. His architect, IMHOTEP, designed the unique royal burial complex at Saqqara, which incorporated the Step Pyramid (the world's first great stone building), and featured many architectural innovations [10: 34–57]. His reputation as a wise and enlightened ruler lasted for many centuries. (A.R.D.)

Zumárraga, Juan de [VI.A] [Zummarraga; Cummaraga] (*c.*1468–1548). He was born in Basque Spain. After entering the Franciscan order he embarked for Mexico in 1528 as its first bishop-elect. He was consecrated in 1533 and became archbishop in 1546. Appointed as 'protector and defender of the Indians', he also acted as a zealous, iconoclastic Apostolic Inquisitor until 1543. He energetically organized structures of church life there and greatly encouraged missionary friars in evangelizing the Amerindian peoples; vernacular catechisms were published and churches, convents, hospitals and schools were built. Although his sincere attempt to train an indigenous clergy at the College of Tlatelolco failed, he stands out as the dominant figure in Mexico's early church history. [512; 581: XIV, 1137–38] (A.C.S.)

Zunz, Leopold [xv] (1794–1886). Jewish scholar. He studied at the University of Berlin where, in 1819, he was among the founders of the Society for the Culture and Science of the Jews and, in 1823, he became editor of the *Zeitschrift für die Wissenschaft des Judentums* ('Journal for the Science of Judaism'), in which he published important studies including a life of RASHI. The *Wissenschaft des Judentums* ('Science of Judaism') movement, in which Zunz was a pivotal figure, applied modern critical methods to the study of Jewish history and culture. Its proponents felt that objective research into Judaism in its broadest context would help to make it attractive to Jews who had enjoyed a secular, scientific education, with the hope of stemming the tide of assimilation and apostasy that was especially strong among the Jews of Germany. From 1841 Zunz directed the newly founded Berlin Jewish Teachers' seminary.

He was the author of many studies, shaping a methodology and research tools which guided generations of Jewish scholars. His first outstanding work, *Die gottesdienstlichen Vorträge der Juden* ('Sermons of the Jews', 1832), which traced the Jewish homiletic tradition, was written as an answer to the Prussian law forbidding the introduction of sermons in Jewish services. Zunz demonstrated the antiquity not only of preaching but preaching in the vernacular. When another law forbade Jews to use German first names, Zunz wrote a history of Jewish names to show that the use of foreign first names was an ancient Jewish practice. He wrote a comprehensive work on Jewish sacred poetry, covering a period of 1,000 years, identifying 6,000 poems and over 1,000 poets. He was known as the father of Jewish studies in the 19th century. [80; 81: vol. 3: X] (G.W.)

Zwemer, Samuel Marinus [vi.a] (1867–1952). American missionary. He was born in Vriesland, Michigan, the son of a Dutch Reformed minister. He had his early education at Hope College. In 1887 he entered the New Brunswick Theological Seminary of the Reformed Church with the intention of being ordained and becoming a missionary. While he was a student there he studied medicine and assisted in a clinic in New York City. He and a colleague, James Cantine, decided that they would be missionaries in the Arab world and formed the Arabian Mission. Zwemer graduated in 1889 and was ordained in 1890 before leaving for Beirut. He studied Arabic there but soon moved to Cairo and from there to Aden. In 1891 he visited the city of Sanʿa, normally closed to foreigners. He worked for a time with the British and Foreign Bible Society in Basra and in 1892 he arrived in Bahrain. In 1894 the Arabian Mission was adopted by the Reformed Church. In 1896 he married an Australian missionary, Amy Wilkes. He began to write books on the Christian mission to Islam. In 1905 the Zwemers went to New York and he took up work as field secretary of the Reformed Board of Foreign Missions and as an officer of the Student Volunteer Movement. Following his work in connection with the Edinburgh Missionary Conference of 1910 he became editor of the new quarterly *The Moslem World* which he edited for 37 years. In 1912 he returned to work in North Africa. He also visited South Africa, the Dutch East Indies, Iran, India and China, always advising on the Christian mission to Islam. In the late 1920s he became professor of History of Religion and Christian Missions at Princeton University. His wife died in 1937 and he retired a year later. In 1949 he visited Bahrain for the 60th anniversary of the Arabian Mission. He died in New York State. [153; 885; 886] (T.T.)

Zwingli, Ulrich [vi.a] (1484–1531). Leading figure of the Swiss Protestant Reformation. He was born in Wildhaus, canton of St Gall. He was educated at Berne, Vienna and Basel between 1498 and 1506, in which year he was ordained priest. From 1506 to 1516 he served in Glarus. He took up humanistic studies, taught himself Greek and read the New Testament and the Fathers. Twice, in 1513 and 1515, he served as a military chaplain to mercenaries in papal service. In 1516 he went to serve in Einsiedeln, where there was a famous shrine in the Benedictine monastery that drew pilgrims. This and the earlier military experience provoked his first criticisms of political and ecclesiastical life. He denounced both the mercenary system and the superstitions surrounding pilgrimage. In 1518 he was elected minister at the Great Minster in Zürich. The following year his lectures on the New Testament signalled the first stirring of reform in Switzerland. He attacked the doctrine of purgatory, the invocation of saints and monasticism. Soon he was contesting the authority of popes and bishops. The city council gave him their support and the minster chapter was reconstituted outside episcopal control. In 1524 he publicly married Anna Meyer in the minster. He took steps to abolish the mass, and succeeded in doing so in 1525. Images and pictures were removed from churches. He attacked any interpretation of the presence of Christ in the eucharist other than the purely symbolic. This brought him into conflict with LUTHER, a disagreement which they failed to resolve in the Colloquy of Marburg in 1529. In 1531 war broke out between those cantons that supported Zwingli and those that did not. Zwingli who as their chaplain carried his forces' banner, died in battle at Cappel on 11 October 1531. [338; 658; 887] (T.T.)

Bibliography

[I] African Religions

[I.A] Traditional Religions and New Religious Movements
Compiled by Rosalind Hackett

Note Extensive use has been made of 'Who's Who of African Independent Church Leaders' in *Risk*, ed. D. B. Barrett, and the *Dictionary of African Historical Biography*, ed. M. R. Lipschutz and R. K. Rasmussen (made available, together with other publications, by Dr Harold W. Turner and the Centre for New Religious Movements, Selly Oak Colleges, Birmingham, to whom the author wishes to record sincere gratitude).

1. Augé, M., *et al. Prophétisme et Thérapeutique: Albert Atcho et la Communauté de Bregbo*. Paris: Hermann, 1975.
2. Ayandele, E. A. *A Visionary of the African Church, Mojola Agbebi (1860–1917)*. Religion in Africa, no. 1. Nairobi: East African Publishing House, 1971.
3. Baëta, C. G. *Prophetism in Ghana*. London: SCM Press, 1962.
4. Barrett, D. B. 'Who's Who of African Independent Church Leaders', *Risk* (Geneva), 7,3 (1971), pp. 23–34.
5. Bond, G. C. 'A Prophecy that Failed: The Lumpa Church of Uyombe, Zambia'. In *African Christianity: Patterns of Continuity*, ed. G. Bond *et al*. New York: Academic Press, 1979. pp. 137–60.
6. *Dictionary of African Historical Biography*, ed. M. R. Lipschutz and R. K. Rasmussen. London: Heinemann, 1978.
7. Evans-Pritchard, E. E. *Nuer Religion*. London: Oxford University Press, 1956.
8. Fu-Kiau, K. Kia Bunseki. *Self Healing Power and Therapy: Old Teachings from Africa*. New York: Vantage Press, 1990.
9. Fu-Kiau, K. Kia Bunseki. *Le Mukongo et le monde qui l'entourait: N'Kongo Ye Nza Yakun' Zungidila*. Kinshasa: Office National de la Recherche et de Developpement, 1969.
10. Girard, J. *Genèse du pouvoir charismatique en Basse Casamance (Sénégal)*. Dakar: IFAN, 1969.
11. Gwassa, G. C. K. 'Kinjikitile and the Ideology of Maji Maji'. In *The Historical Study of African Religion*, ed. T. O. Ranger and I. N. Kimambo. Berkeley: University of California Press, 1972. pp. 202–17.
12. Hackett, R. I. J. *Religion in Calabar: The Religious Life and History of a Nigerian Town*. Berlin: Mouton de Gruyter, 1989.
13. Hackett, R. I. J., ed. *New Religious Movements in Nigeria*. Lewiston, NY: Edwin Mellen Press, 1987.
14. Haliburton, G. M. *The Prophet Harris*. London: Longman, 1971.
15. Hastings, A. *A History of African Christianity*. Cambridge: Cambridge University Press, 1979.
16. Ilega, D. I. 'The God's Kingdom Society in Nigeria'. In [13: 141–60].
17. Janzen, J. M., and MacGaffey, W. *An Anthology of Kongo Religion: Primary Texts from Lower Zaïre*. University of Kansas Publications in Anthropology, no. 5. Lawrence, Kansas: University of Kansas, 1974.
18. Jules-Rosette, B. *African Apostles: Aspects of Ritual and Conversion in the Church of John Maranke*. Ithaca: Cornell University Press, 1975.
19. Kenyatta, J. *Facing Mount Kenya: The Tribal Life of the Gikuyu*. London: Speck & Warburg, 1938.

20. MacGaffey, W. *Religion and Society in Central Africa*. Chicago, University of Chicago Press, 1986.
21. MacGaffey, W. *Modern Kongo Prophets*. Bloomington: Indiana University Press, 1983.
22. *Le Kimbanguisme a 50 ans/The 50th Anniversary of Kimbanguism*. Kinshasa/Paris: Continent, 1971.
23. Martin, M.-L. *Kimbangu: An African Prophet and his Church*. Oxford: Blackwell, 1975.
24. Martin, M.-L. 'The Mai Chaza Church in Rhodesia'. In *African Initiatives in Religion*, ed. D. B. Barrett. Nairobi: African Publishing House, 1971.
25. Omoyajowo, J. A. *Cherubim and Seraphim: The History of an African Independent Church*. New York: Nok, 1982.
26. Onyioha, K. O. K. *Godianism: A Series of Papers Presented to the Conference of Traditional Religions of Nigeria, May 22, 1975*. n.p., n.d.
27. Oosthuizen, G. C. *The Theology of a South African Messiah*. Leiden: E. J. Brill, 1967.
28. Paulme, D. 'Une Religion Syncrétique en Côte d'Ivoire'. *Cahiers d'Etudes Africaines*, I (1962), pp. 5–90.
29. Peel, J. D. Y. *Aládura: A Religious Movement among the Yoruba*. London: Oxford University Press, 1968.
30. Peires, J. B. *The Dead Will Arrive: Nogqawuse and the Great Cattle-Killing Movement of 1856–7*. Bloomington: Indiana University Press, 1989.
31. Roberts, A. 'The Lumpa Church of Alice Lenshina'. In *Protest and Power in Black Africa*, ed. R. I. Rotberg and A. A. Mazrui. New York: Oxford University Press, 1970.
32. Shepperson, G., and Price, T. *Independent African: John Chilembwe and the Origins, Setting and Significance of the Nyasaland Native Rising of 1915*. Edinburgh: Edinburgh University Press, 1958.
33. Sundkler, B. G. M. *Zulu Zion*. London: Oxford University Press, 1976.
34. Sundkler, B. G. M. *Bantu Prophets in South Africa*. 2nd edn. Oxford: University Press for International African Institute, 1961.
35. Tasie, G. O. M. 'The Prophetic Calling, Garrick Sokari Braide of Bakana'. In *Varieties of Christian Experience in Nigeria*, ed. E. Isichei. London: Macmillan, 1982. pp. 99–115.
36. Turner, H. W. *Religious Innovation in Africa*. Boston: G. K. Hall, 1979.
37. Turner, H. W. *African Independent Church*. 2 vols. Oxford: Clarendon Press, 1967.
38. Umoh, J. U., and Ekanem, A. *Olumba Olumba Obu, the Mystery Man of Biakpan*. Vol. 1: *Brotherhood of the Cross and Star: Facts you Must Know*. Calabar: Brotherhood Press, 1979.
39. Walker, S. S. *The Religious Revolution in the Ivory Coast*. Chapel Hill, NC: University of North Carolina Press, 1983.
40. Webster, J. B. *The African Churches Among the Yoruba, 1888–1922*. Oxford: Clarendon Press, 1964.
41. Welbourn, F., and Ogot, B. A. *A Place to Feel at Home: A Study of Two Independent Churches in Western Kenya*. London: Oxford University Press, 1966.
42. Wilson, B. R. *Magic and the Millennium*. London: Heinemann, 1973.

[I.B] Afro-Caribbean Diaspora
Compiled by Katherine Williams

1. Burkett, Randall K. *Black Redemption: Churchmen Speak for the Garvey Movement*. Philadelphia: Temple, 1978.
2. Burkett, Randall K. *Garveyism as a Religious Movement: The Institutionalization of a Black Civil Religion*. Metuchen, NJ: Scarecrow, 1978.
3. Clarke, J. H., and Garvey, Amy Jacques (eds). *Marcus Garvey and the Vision of Africa*. New York: Random House, 1974.
4. Cronon, E. David. *Black Moses*. Madison: University of Wisconsin Press, 1955.
5. Fanon, Franz. *Black Skin, White Mask*. New York: Grove, 1967.
6. Fanon, Franz. *A Dying Colonization*. New York: Grove, 1967.
7. Fanon, Franz. *Towards the African Revolution*. New York: Grove, 1968.
8. Fanon, Franz. *The Wretched of the Earth*. New York: Grove, 1966.
9. Garvey, Jacques. *Garvey and Garveyism*. New York: Collier, 1967.
10. Gendzier, Irene. *Franz Fanon*. London: Wildwood House, 1973.
11. Haile Selassie. *My Life and Ethiopia's Progress*. London: Oxford University Press, 1976.
12. Hill, Robert, and Barr, B., eds. *Marcus Garvey: Life and Lessons*. Berkeley: California University Press, 1987.

13. Lockot, R. *The Life, Reign and Character of Haile Selassie*. London: Hurst, 1989.
14. Morsley, Leonard. *Haile Selassie: The Conquering Lion*. London: Weidenfeld & Nicholson, 1964.
15. Reed, J., and Wake, C., eds. *Senghor: Poetry and Prose*. London: Heinemann, 1965.
16. Sandford, L. *The Lion of Judah hath Prevailed*. New York: Greenwood, 1972.
17. Senghor, Léopold Sédar. *Poèmes*. Paris: du Seuil, 1972.
18. Ullendorf, Edward. *The Ethiopians*. London: Oxford University Press, 1973.
19. Wauthier, Claude. *The Literature and Thought of Modern Africa*. London: Heinemann, 1987.

[II] Ancient Near Eastern Religions

Compiled by Mervyn Richardson

1. Aitken, K. *The Arquat Narrative*. Journal of Semitic Studies Monograph, no. 13. Manchester, 1990.
2. Driver, G. R., and Miles, J. C. *The Laws of Hammurabi*. Oxford: Clarendon Press, 1959.
3. Gibson, J. C. L. *Canaanite Myths and Legends*. Edinburgh: T. & T. Clark, 1982.
4. Gray, J. *The Legend of King Krt*. Leiden: E. J. Brill, 1970.
5. Heidel, A. *The Epic of Gilgamesh and Old Testament Parallels*.
6. Oppenheim, A. L. 'The Sumerian King List'. In [10: 265–6].
7. Oppenheim, A. L. 'The Sargon Chronicle'. In [10: 266).
8. Oppenheim, A. L. 'Nabonidus'. In [10: 308ff.].
9. Oppenheim, A. L. 'Cyrus'. In [10: 316–17].
10. Prichard, J. B. *Ancient Near Eastern Texts Relating to the Old Testament*. Princeton, NJ: Princeton University Press, 1969.
11. Saggs, H. W. F. *The Might that was Assyria*. London: Sidgwick & Jackson, 1984.
12. Sanders, N. A. *The Epic of Gilgamesh*. Harmondsworth: Penguin, 1967.
13. Speiser, E. A: 'The Legend of Sargon'. In [10: 119].

[III] Bahā'ī

Compiled by Dennis McEoin

1. ʿAbd al-Bahā'. *The Secret of Divine Civilization*, trans. Marzieh Gail. Wilmette, Ill: Bahá'í Publishing Trust, 1957.
2. ʿAbd al-Bahā'. *Selections from the Writings of ʿAbdu'l-Baha*, trans. Marzieh Gail. Haifa: Bahá'í World Centre, 1978.
3. ʿAbd al-Bahā'. *A traveller's Narrative Written to Illustrate the Episode of the Bab*, trans. E. G. Browne. 2 vols. Cambridge: Cambridge University Press, 1891. Repr., Amsterdam: Philo Press, 1975.
4. Bāb. *Le Béyân persan*, trans. A. L. M. Nicolas. 4 vols. Paris: Geuthner, 1911–14.
5. Bāb. *Selections from the Writings of the Bab*, trans. M. Taherzadeh. Haifa: Bahá'í World Centre, 1976.
6. Bahá'u'lláh. *Gleanings from the Writings of Bahá'u'lláh*, ed. and trans. Shoghi Effendi. Rev. edn. Willmette, Ill.: Bahá'í Publishing Trust, 1976.
7. Bahá'u'lláh. *The Hidden Words of Bahá'u-'lláh*, trans. Shoghi Effendi. London: Bahá'í Publishing Trust, 1929, 1975.
8. Bahá'u'lláh. *Kitáb-i-Íqán: The Book of Certitude*, trans. Shoghi Effendi. London: Bahá'í Publishing Trust, 1946, 1982.
9. Balyuzi, H. M. *ʿAbdu'l-Baha: The Centre of the Covenant of Baha'u'llah*. London: George Ronald, 1971.
10. Balyuzi, H. M. *The Bab*. Oxford: George Ronald, 1973.
11. Balyuzi, H. M. *Bahá'u'lláh: The King of Glory*. Oxford: George Ronald, 1980.
12. *Encyclopaedia Iranica*. London: Routledge, 1985–.
13. *Encyclopaedia of Islam*. New edition. Leiden: E. J. Brill, 1960–.
14. Giachery, Ugo. *Shoghi Effendi*. Oxford: George Ronald, 1973.
15. MacEoin, D. *Early Babi Doctrine and History*. Los Angeles: Kalimat Press, forthcoming.
16. Momen, M., *The Babi and Baha'i Religions, 1844–1944: Some Contemporary Western Accounts*. Oxford: George Ronald, 1981.
17. Rabbani, Ruhiyyih. *The Priceless Pearl*. London: Bahá'í Publishing Trust, 1969.
18. Root, Martha L. *Tāhirih the Pure: Iran's Greatest Woman*. Karachi, 1938. Repr. Los Angeles: Kalimat Press, 1981.
19. Shoghi Effendi. *The Advent of Divine Justice*. Rev. edn. Wilmette, Ill.: Bahá'í Publishing Committee, 1984.
20. Shoghi Effendi, trans. and ed. *The Dawn-Breakers: Nabil's Narrative of the Early*

Days of the Bahá'í Revelation. New York: Bahá'í Publishing Committee, 1932.
21. Shoghi Effendi. *God Passes By*. Rev. edn. Wilmette, Ill.: Bahá'í Publishing Committee, 1974.
22. Shoghi Effendi. *The Promised Day is Come*. Rev. edn. Wilmette, Ill.: Bahá'í Publishing Committee, 1980.
23. Shoghi Effendi. *The World Order of Bahā'u'llāh*. Rev. edn. Wilmette, Ill.: Bahá'í Publishing Committee, 1955.
24. Taherzadeh, Abid. *The Revelation of Bahá'u'lláh*. Vols. 1 and 2. Oxford: George Ronald, 1974, 1977.
25. Ward, A. L. *239 days: ʿAbdu'l-Baha's Journey in America*. Wilmette, Ill.: Bahá'í Publishing Trust, 1979.

[IV] Buddhism

Compiled by Paul Griffiths

1. Ambedkar, B. R. *The Buddha and his Dhamma*. Bombay: Siddarth College Publications, 1957.
2. Anacker, Stefan. *Seven Works of Vasubandhu the Buddhist Psychological Doctor*. Delhi: Motilal Banarsidass, 1984.
3. Anagārika Dharmapāla. *Return to Righteousness*, ed. A. Guruge. Colombo: Government Press, 1965.
4. Andrews, Allan. *The Teachings Essential for Rebirth: A Study of Genshin's Ōjōyōshū*. Tokyo: Sophia University, 1973.
5. Anesaki Masaharu. *Nichiren, the Buddhist Prophet*. Cambridge, Mass.: Harvard University Press, 1916.
6. Aris, Michael, and Aung San Suu Kyi, eds. *Tibetan Studies in Honour of Hugh Richardson*. Warminster: Aris & Phillips, 1980.
7. Aris, Michael. *Bhutan: The Early History of a Tibetan Kingdom*. Warminster: Aris & Phillips, 1979.
8. Arntzen, Sonja. *Ikkyū and the Crazy Cloud Anthology*. Tokyo: University of Tokyo Press, 1986.
9. Aung, Shwe Zan, and Rhys-Davids, C. A. F., trans. *Points of Controversy, or Subjects of Discourse*. London: Pali Text Society, 1979.
10. Avedon, John F. *In Exile from the Land of Snows*. New York: Knopf, 1984.
11. Aziz, Barbara Nimri, and Kapstein, Matthew, eds. *Soundings in Tibetan Civilization*. New Delhi: Manohar, 1985.
12. Basham, A. L. *The Wonder that was India*. New York: Grove Press, 1959.
13. Basham, Arthur L. 'Aśoka'. In *The Encyclopedia of Religion*, ed. Mircea Eliade. New York: Macmillan, 1987.
14. Beal, Samuel, trans. *Buddhist Records of the Western World*. 2 vols. London: Trübner, 1906.
15. Beyer, Stephan V. *The Cult of Tārā*. Berkeley: University of California Press, 1973.
16. Bhattacharya, Benoytosh, ed. *Niṣpannayogāvalī*. Baroda: Oriental Institute, 1972.
17. Bhattacharya, D. C. 'Vajrāvalī-nāma-maṇḍalopāyika'. In *Tantric and Taoist Studies Dedicated to R. A. Stein*, ed. M. Strickmann. Brussels: Institut Belge des Hautes Études Chinoises, 1981.
18. Bhattacharya, Kalidasa, trans. *The Dialectical Method of Nāgārjuna*. Delhi: Motilal Banarsidass, 1978.
19. Bielefeldt, Carl. *Dōgen's Manuals of Zen Meditation*. Berkeley: University of California Press, 1988.
20. Bloom, Alfred. *Shinran's Gospel of Pure Grace*. Tucson: University of Arizona Press, 1965.
21. Bloom, Alfred. *The Life of Shinran Shōnin: The Journey to Self-Acceptance*. Leiden: E. J. Brill, 1968.
22. Broido, Michael. 'Sa-skya Paṇḍita, the White Panacea and the Hva-Shang Doctrine'. *Journal of the International Association of Buddhist Studies*, 10/2 (1987), pp. 27–68.
23. Broughton, Jeffrey L. *Kuei-feng Tsung-mi: The Convergence of Ch'an and the Teachings*. PhD diss., Columbia University, 1975.
24. Buddhadāsa. *Me and Mine*, ed. Donald K. Swearer. Albany: State University of New York Press, 1989.
25. Buswell, Robert E. 'Ŭich'ŏn'. In *The Encyclopedia of Religion*, ed. Mircea Eliade. New York: Macmillan, 1987.
26. Buswell, Robert E. 'Ŭisang'. In *The Encyclopedia of Religion*, ed. Mircea Eliade. New York: Macmillan, 1987.
27. Buswell, Robert E. 'Wŏnhyo'. In *The Encyclopedia of Religion*, ed. Mircea Eliade. New York: Macmillan, 1987.
28. Buswell, Robert E. *The Korean Approach to Zen: The Collected Works of Chinul*. Honolulu: University of Hawaii Press, 1983.
29. Campbell, B. F. *Ancient Wisdom Revived: A*

history of the Theosophical Movement. Berkeley: University of California Press, 1980.

30. Carrithers, Michael. *The Buddha*. Oxford: Oxford University Press, 1983.
31. Ch'en, Kenneth. *Buddhism in China: A Historical Survey*. Princeton, NJ: Princeton University Press, 1964.
32. Chan, Wing-tsit, ed. *A Source Book in Chinese Philosophy*. New York: Columbia University Press, 1963.
33. Chang, Garma G. C. *The Buddhist Teaching of Totality: The Philosophy of Hua-yen Buddhism*. University Park. Pa.: Pennsylvania State University Press, 1971.
34. Chang, Garma G. C. *The Hundred Thousand Songs of Milarepa*. 2 vols. New York: Oxford University Press, 1962.
35. Chappell, David W., ed. *Buddhist and Taoist Practice in Medieval Chinese Society*. Honolulu: University of Hawaii Press, 1987.
36. Chappell, David W., *et al.*, trans. *T'ien-t'ai Buddhism: An Outline of the Fourfold Teachings*. Tokyo: Daiichi Shōbō, 1984.
37. Chattopadhyaya, Alaka. *Atīśa and Tibet*. Calcutta: Indian Studies, 1967.
38. Chimpa [Lama] and Chattopadhyaya, Debiprasad, trans. *Tāranātha's History of Buddhism in India*. Atlantic Highlands, NJ: Humanities Press, 1980.
39. Cleary, Thomas, trans. *Entry into the Inconceivable: An Introduction to Hua-yen Buddhism*. Honolulu: University of Hawaii Press, 1983.
40. Cleary, Thomas, trans. *Shōbōgenzō: Zen Essays by Dōgen*. Honolulu: University of Hawaii Press, 1986.
41. Coates, H. H., and Ishizuka, Ryūgaku. *Hōnen the Buddhist Saint: His Life and Thought*. 5 vols. Kyoto: Sekai Seiten Kankōkai, 1949.
42. Collcutt, Martin. *Five Mountains: The Rinzai Zen Monastic Institution in Medieval Japan*. Cambridge, Mass.: Harvard University Press, 1981.
43. Cone, Margaret E., and Gombrich, Richard F. *The Perfect Generosity of Prince Vessantara*. Oxford: Oxford University Press, 1977.
44. Conze, Edward, *et al. Buddhist Texts Through the Ages*. New York: Harper & Row, 1964. First published 1954.
45. Conze, Edward. *The Buddha's Law among the Birds*. Oxford: Bruno Cassirer, 1955.
46. Cook, Francis. *Hua-yen Buddhism: The Jewel Net of Indra*. University Park, Pa.: Pennsylvania State University Press, 1977.
47. Das, Sarat Chandra. *Contributions on the Religion and History of Tibet*. New Delhi: Mañjuśrī, 1970.
48. De Visser, M. W. *Ancient Buddhism in Japan*. 2 vols. Leiden: E. J. Brill, 1928, 1935.
49. de Bary, Wm. Theodore, ed. *Self and Society in Ming Thought*. New York: Columbia University Press, 1970.
50. Demiéville, Paul. *Le Concile de Lhasa: une controverse sur le quiétisme entre bouddhistes de l'Inde et de la Chine au VIIIe siècle de l'ère chrétienne*. Collège de France: Institut des Hautes Études Chinoises, 1987. First published Paris, 1952.
51. Dhammapāla. *The Discourse on the All-Embracing Net of Views: The Brahmajāla Sutta and its Commentarial Exegesis*, trans. Bhikkhu Bodhi. Kandy: Buddhist Publication Society, 1978.
52. Donner, Neal A. *The Great Calming and Contemplation of Chih-i: Chapter One, the Synopsis*. PhD diss., University of British Columbia, 1977.
53. Douglas, Kenneth, and Bays, Gwendolyn, trans. *The Life and Liberation of Padmasambhava*. 2 vols. Emeryville, Cal.: Dharma Publications, 1978.
54. Douglas, Nik, and White, Meryl. *Karmapa: The Black Hat Lama of Tibet*. London: Luzac, 1976.
55. Dowman, Keith. *Masters of Mahāmudrā*. Albany: State University of New York Press, 1986.
56. Dudjom Rinpoche. *The Nyingma School of Tibetan Buddhism: Its Fundamentals and History*, trans. Gyurme Dorje and Matthew Kapstein. London: Wisdom Publications, 1990.
57. Dumoulin, Heinrich. *Zen Buddhism: A History*. Vol. 2: *Japan and Tibet*. New York: Macmillan, 1989.
58. Eckel, Malcolm David. *A Question of Nihilism: Bhāvaviveka's Response to the Fundamental Problems of Mādhyamika Philosophy*. PhD diss., Harvard University, 1980.
59. Eckel, Malcom David. *Jñānagarbha's Commentary on the Distinction Between the Two Truths*. Albany: State University of New York Press, 1987.
60. Eliot, Charles. *Japanese Buddhism*. New York: Barnes & Noble, 1960.
61. Ellwood, Robert S., Jr. *The Eagle and the*

Rising Sun: Americans and the New Religions of Japan. Philadelphia: Westminster Press, 1974.

62. Evans-Wentz, W. Y. ed. *The Tibetan Book of the Great Liberation*. London: Oxford University Press, 1954.
63. Faure, Bernard. 'Bodhidharma'. In *The Encyclopedia of Religion*, ed. Mircea Eliade. New York: Macmillan, 1987.
64. Foard, James H. *Ippen and Popular Buddhism in Kamakura Japan*. PhD diss., Stanford University, 1977.
65. Frauwallner, Erich. 'Dignāga, sein Werke und seine Entwicklung'. *Wiener Zeitschrift für die Kunde Süd- und Ostasiens*, 3 (1959); pp. 33–164.
66. Frauwallner, Erich. *On the Date of the Buddhist Master of the Law, Vasubandhu*. Rome: Istituto Italiano per il Medeo ed Estremo Oriente, 1951.
67. Fujiwara Ryōsetsu. *The Way to Nirvāṇa: The Concept of the Nembutsu in Shan-tao's Pure Land*. Tokyo: Kyoiku Shinchosha, 1974.
68. Gabaude, L. *Une Herméneutique bouddhique contemporaine de Thaïlande: Buddhadāsa Bhikkhu*. Paris: École Française d'Extrême-Orient, 1988.
69. Geiger, Wilhelm, trans. *The Mahāvaṃsa, or The Great Chronicle of Ceylon*. London: Pali Text Society, 1912.
70. Gimello, R. M., and Gregory, Peter N., eds. *Studies in Ch'an and Hua-yen*. Honolulu: University of Hawaii Press, 1983.
71. Gombrich, Richard F., and Obeyesekere, G. *Buddhism Transformed: Religious Change in Sri Lanka*. Princeton, NJ: Princeton University Press, 1988.
72. Gray, J., ed. and trans. *Buddhaghosupatti*. London: Luzac, 1982.
73. Gregory, Peter N. *Tsung-mi's 'Inquiry Into The Origin of Man': A Study of Chinese Buddhist Hermeneutics*. PhD diss., Harvard University, 1981.
74. Gregory, Peter N., ed. *Sudden and Gradual Approaches to Enlightenment in Chinese Thought*. Honolulu: University of Hawaii Press, 1987.
75. Gregory, Peter N., ed. *Traditions of Meditation in Chinese Buddhism*. Honolulu: University of Hawaii Press, 1986.
76. Griffiths, Paul J. *Indian Buddhist Meditation-Theory: History, Development, and Systematization*. PhD diss., University of Wisconsin-Madison, 1983.
77. Griffiths, Paul J., Hakamaya Noriaki, and Keenan, John P. *The Realm of Awakening: A Translation and Study of the Tenth Chapter of the Mahāyānasaṅgraha, with its Commentaries*. New York: Oxford University Press, 1989.
78. Groner, Paul. *Saichō: The Establishment of the Japanese Tendai School*. Berkeley: Asian Humanities Press, 1984.
79. Grousset, René. *The Empire of the Steppes: A History of Central Asia*. New Brunswick, NJ: Rutgers University Press, 1970.
80. Guenther, Herbert V. *Kindly Bent to Ease us*. 3 vols. Emeryville, Cal.: Dharma Publications, 1975–6.
81. Guenther, Herbert V. *The Jewel Ornament of Liberation by Sgam.po.pa*. Berkeley: Shambhala, 1971.
82. Guenther, Herbert V. *The Life and Teaching of Nāropa*. New York: Oxford University Press, 1963.
83. Guenther, Herbert V. *The Royal Song of Saraha*. Berkeley: Shambhala, 1973.
84. Gyatso, Janet. 'Thang-stong rGyal-po, Father of the Tibetan Drama Tradition: The Bodhisattva as Artist'. In *Zlos-gar: Performing Traditions of Tibet*, ed. Jamyang Norbu. Dharamsala: Library of Tibetan Works and Archives, 1986, pp. 91–104.
85. Gyatso, Janet. 'The Development of the Good Tradition'. In *Soundings in Tibetan Civilization*, ed. Barbara Nimri Aziz and Matthew Kapstein. Delhi: Manohar, 1985, pp. 320–41.
86. Gyatso, Janet. *The Literary Transmission of the Traditions of Thang-stong rgyal-po: A Study of Visionary Buddhism in Tibet*. PhD diss., University of California at Berkeley, 1981.
87. Gyatso, Tenzin [the XIVth Dalai Lama]. *Kindness, Clarity, and Insight*, trans. and ed. Jeffrey Hopkins; co-editor Elizabeth Napper. Ithaca, NY: Snow Lion, 1984.
88. Gyatso, Tenzin [the XIVth Dalai Lama]. *My Land and My People: Memoirs of the Dalai Lama of Tibet*. New York: Potala, 1977. First published 1962.
89. Gyatso, Tenzin [the XIVth Dalai Lama]. *The Bodhgaya Interviews*, ed. José Ignacio Cabezón. Ithaca, NY: Snow Lion, 1988.
90. Hahn, Michael. *Joy for the World*. Emeryville, Cal.: Dharma Publishing, 1987.
91. Hakeda Yoshito, trans. *The Awakening of Faith*. New York: Columbia University

Press, 1967.

92. Hakeda Yoshito. *Kūkai: Major Works*. New York: Columbia University Press, 1972.
93. Hattori Masaaki. *Dignāga on Perception, Being the Pratyakṣapariccheda of Dignāga's Pramāṇasamuccaya*. Cambridge, Mass.: Harvard University Press, 1968.
94. Hayes, Richard. *Dignāga on the Interpretation of Signs*. Studies of Classical India, vol. 9. Dordrecht: Kluwer Academic Publishers, 1988.
95. Heissig, Walther. *The Religions of Mongolia*. Berkeley: University of California Press, 1980.
96. Hirota, Dennis. *No Abode: The Record of Ippen*. Kyoto: Ryukoku University 1986.
97. Hoffmann, Helmut. *The Religions of Tibet*. New York: Macmillan, 1961.
98. Hoog, Constance, trans. *Prince Jin-gim's Textbook of Tibetan Buddhism: The Ses-bya rab-gsal (Jñeya-prakāśa)*. Leiden: E. J. Brill, 1983.
99. Horner, I. B., trans. *Milinda's Questions*. 2 vols. London: Pali Text Society, 1969.
100. Hurvitz, Leon. *Chih-i (538–597): An Introduction to the Life and Ideas of a Chinese Buddhist Monk*. Brussels: Institut Belgie des Hautes Études Chinoises, 1980.
101. I-hang Chou. 'Tantrism in China'. *Harvard Journal of Asiatic Studies*, 8 (1945); pp. 241–332.
102. Ichirō Hori. *Folk Religion in Japan*, ed. and trans. Joseph M. Kitagawa and Alan L. Miller. Chicago: University of Chicago Press, 1968.
103. Iida Shotaro. *Reason and Emptiness: A Study in Logic and Mysticism*. Tokyo: Hokuseido Press, 1980.
104. Ikeda Daisaku. *A Lasting Peace: Collected Addresses of Daisaku Ikeda*. New York: Weatherhill, 1981.
105. Ikeda Daisaku. *Proposals for the 21st Century*. Tokyo: Soka University Student Union, 1987.
106. Inada, Kenneth K., trans. *Nāgārjuna: A Translation of his Mūlamadhyamakakārikā with an Introductory Essay*. Tokyo: Hokuseido Press, 1970.
107. Jackson, David Paul, trans. *The Entrance Gate for the Wise (Section III): Sa-skyapaṇḍita on Indian and Tibetan Traditions of Pramāṇa and Philosophical Debate*. Vienna: Arbeitskreis für Tibetische und Buddhistische Studien, 1987.
108. Jaini, Padmanabh S. 'On the Theory of the Two Vasubandhus'. *Bulletin of the School for Oriental and African Studies*, 21 (1958); pp. 48–53.
109. Jayawickrama, N. A. *The Story of Gotama Buddha*. London: Pali Text Society, 1990.
110. Jha, Ganganatha, trans. *The Tattvasaṃgraha of Śāntarakshita with the Commentary of Kamalashīla*. 2 vols. New Delhi: Munshiram Manoharlal, 1986. First published 1937–9.
111. Johnston, E. H., ed. and trans. *The Buddhacarita, or Acts of the Buddha*. Delhi: Motilal Banarsidass, 1972. First published Lahore, 1936.
112. Kalupahana, David J. *Nāgārjuna: The Philosophy of the Middle Way*. Albany: State University of New York Press, 1986.
113. Karma Gyatsho. 'Dudjom Rinpoche'. *The Tibet Journal*, 12/3 (1987); pp. 79–81.
114. Karma Thinley. *The History of the Sixteen Karmapas of Tibet*. Boulder: Shambhala, 1978.
115. Karmay, Samten G. *Origins and Early Development of the Tibetan Religious Traditions of the Great Perfection*. Leiden: E. J. Brill, 1988.
116. Keel, Hee-sung. *Chinul: Founder of the Korean Sŏn Tradition*. Berkeley: Asian Humanities Press, 1984.
117. Keenan, John P. *A Study of the Buddhabhūmyupadeśa: The Doctrinal Development of the Notion of Wisdom in Yogacara Thought*. PhD diss., University of Wisconsin-Madison, 1980.
118. Ki-yong, Rhi. 'Wŏnhyo and His Thought'. *Korea Journal*, 11 (1971); pp. 4–9.
119. King, Winston. *Death was his Koan*. Berkeley: Asian Humanities Press, 1986.
120. Kitagawa, Joseph. *Religion in Japanese History*. New York: Columbia University Press, 1966.
121. Kiyota, Minoru. *Shingon Buddhism: Theory and Practice*. Los Angeles: Buddhist Books International, 1978.
122. Kiyota, Minoru. *Tantric Concept of Bodhicitta: A Buddhist Experiential Philosophy*. Madison: University of Wisconsin South Asian Area Center, 1982.
123: Kochumuttom, Thomas P. *A Buddhist Doctrine of Experience: A New Translation and Interpretation of the Works of Vasubandhu the Yogācārin*. Delhi: Motilal Banarsidass, 1982.
124. Kodera, Takashi James. *Dōgen's Forma-*

tive Years in China. Boulder: Prajñā Press, 1980.

125. Koseki, Aaron K. 'The Concept of Practice in San Lun Thought: Chi-tsang and the "Concurrent Insight" of the Two Truths'. *Philosophy East and West*, 31 (1981); pp. 449–66.

126. Kotani Kimi. *A Guide to Reiyu-kai*. Tokyo: Reiyūkai Kyōdan, 1958.

127. Kraft, Kenneth L. 'Musō Kokushi's Dialogues in a Dream'. *Eastern Buddhist*, 14 (Spring 1981): pp. 75–93.

128. Kunga, L., and Cutillo, B. *Drinking the Mountain Stream*. New York: Lotsawa, 1978.

129. Kunga, L., and Cutillo, B. *Miraculous Journey*. New York: Lotsawa, 1986.

130. La Vallée Poussin, Louis de. 'Bhāvaviveka'. *Mélanges chinoise et bouddhiques*, 2 (1933): pp. 60–67.

131. La Vallée Poussin, Louis de. *Abhidharmakośabhāṣyam*. English trans. (of La Vallée Poussin's French original) by Leo M. Pruden. 4 vols. Berkeley: Asian Humanities Press, 1988–9.

132. La Vallée Poussin, Louis de. *Vijñaptimātratāsiddhi: la siddhi de Hiuan Tsang*. Paris: Geuthner, 1928–48.

133. Lafleur, William, trans. *Mirror for the Moon: A Selection of Poems by Saigyō*. New York: New Directions, 1977.

134. Lafleur, William. *Dōgen Studies*. Honolulu: University of Hawaii Press, 1985.

135. Lai, Whalen, and Lancaster, Lewis R., eds. *Early Ch'an in China and Tibet*. Berkeley Buddhist Studies, vol. 5. Berkeley: Asian Humanities Press, 1983.

136. Lamotte, Etienne. *History of Indian Buddhism*, trans. Sara Webb-Boin. Louvain: Peeters Press, 1988.

137. Lamotte, Etienne. *La Somme du grand véhicule d'Asaṅga (Mahāyāna-Saṃgraha)*. 2 vols. Louvain-la-neuve: Institut Orientaliste, 1973.

138. Law, B. C. *The History of the Buddha's Religion (Sāsanavaṃsa)*. London: Pali Text Society, 1962.

139. Lee, Peter H. 'Fa-tsang and Ŭisang'. *Journal of the American Oriental Society*, 82 (1962): pp. 56–62.

140. Lhalungpa, L. *The Life of Milarepa*. New York: Dutton, 1977.

141. Liebenthal, Walter. *Chao Lun: The Treatises of Seng-Chao*. 2nd edn. Hong Kong: Hong Kong University Press, 1968.

142. Lindtner, Chr. *Master of Wisdom: Writings of the Buddhist Master Nāgārjuna*. Oakland, Cal.: Dharma Press, 1986.

143. Lindtner, Chr. *Nāgārjuniana: Studies in the Writings and Philosophy of Nāgārjuna*. Delhi: Motilal Banarsidass, 1987. First published 1982.

144. Ling, Trevor O. *Buddhist Revival in India*. New York: St Martin's Press, 1980.

145. Lopez, Donald S., Jr. 'The Dalai Lama of Tibet'. In *The Christ and the Bodhisattva*, ed. Donald S. Lopez, Jr., and Steven C. Rockefeller. Albany: State University of New York Press, 1987, pp. 209–16.

146. Macdonald, Ariane, ed. *Etudes tibétaines dédiées à la mémoire de Marcelle Lalou*. Paris: Maisonneuve, 1971.

147. Macgregor, John. *Tibet: A Chronicle of Exploration*. London: Routledge & Kegan Paul, 1970.

148. Magnin, Paul. *La Vie et l'oeuvre de Huisi (515–577)*. Paris: École Française d'Extrême-Orient, 1964.

149. Makiguchi Tsunesaburō. *The Philosophy of Value*. Tokyo: Seikyo Press, 1964.

150. Malalasekara, G. P. *Dictionary of Pali Proper Names*. 2 vols. London: Pali Text Society, 1938.

151. Malalasekara, G. P. *The Pali Literature of Ceylon*. Colombo: M. D. Gunasena, 1958.

152. Malalgoda, Kitsiri. *Buddhism in Sinhalese Society, 1750–1900*. Berkeley: University of California Press, 1976.

153. Matsunaga, Daigan, and Matsunaga, Alicia. *Foundations of Japanese Buddhism*. 2 vols. Los Angeles: Buddhist Books International, 1974.

154. McDermott, A. C. Senape, ed. and trans. *An Eleventh Century Buddhist Logic of 'Exists'*. Dordrecht: Reidel, 1970.

155. McFarland, Horace Neill. *Daruma: The Founder of Zen in Japanese Art and Popular Culture*. Tokyo: Kodansha, 1987.

156. McRae, John R. *The Northern School and the Formation of Early Ch'an Buddhism*. Honolulu: University of Hawaii Press, 1986.

157. Mendelson, E. M. *Sangha and State in Burma*, ed. John P. Ferguson. Ithaca, NY: Cornell University Press, 1975.

158. Mori Koichi. *Study of Makiguchi Tsunesaburō: The Founder of Sōka Gakkai*. ThD thesis, Graduate Theological Union, 1977.

159. Morrell, Robert E. *Early Kamakura Buddhism: A Minority Report*. Berkeley: University of California Press, 1987.

160. Morrell, Robert E., trans. *Sand and Pebbles (Shasekishū): The Tales of Mujū Ichien, a Voice for Pluralism in Kamakura Buddhism.* Albany: State University of New York Press, 1985.
161. Murakami Shigeyoshi. *Japanese Religion in the Modern Century*, trans. H. Byron Earhart. Tokyo: University of Tokyo Press, 1980.
162. Nakamura, Kyoko Motomichi. *Miraculous Stories from the Japanese Buddhist Tradition.* Cambridge, Mass.: Harvard University Press, 1973.
163. Nanamoli [Thera], trans. *The Path of Purification.* 2 vols. 3rd edn. Kandy: Buddhist Publication Society, 1975.
164. Nanamoli [Thera]. *A Thinker's Notebook.* Kandy: Buddhist Publication Society, n.d.
165. Nanamoli [Thera]. *The Life of the Buddha.* Kandy: Buddhist Publication Society, 1972.
166. Naquin, Susan. *Millenarian Rebellion in China: The Eight Trigrams Uprising of 1813.* New Haven: Yale University Press, 1976.
167. Nikam, N. A., and McKeon, R. *The Edicts of Aśoka.* Chicago: University of Chicago Press, 1959.
168. Niwano Nikkyō. *Buddhism for Today: A Modern Interpretation of the Lotus Sūtra.* Tokyo: Rissho Kōseikai, 1976.
169. Niwano Nikkyō. *Travel to Infinity: An Autobiography of the President of an Organization of Buddhist Laymen in Japan*, trans. Chido Takeda and Wilhelm Schiffer. Tokyo: Risshō Kōseikai, 1968.
170. Norman, K. R. *Pali Literature.* Wiesbaden: Harrassowitz, 1983.
171. Obermiller, E., trans. *The History of Buddhism in India and Tibet by Bu-ston.* Delhi: Sri Satguru, 1986. First published 1932.
172. Odin, Steve. *Process Metaphysics and Hua-yen Buddhism.* Albany: State University of New York Press, 1982.
173. Overmyer, Daniel L. *Folk Buddhist Religion.* Cambridge, Mass.: Harvard University Press, 1976.
174. Park, Sung Bae. *Buddhist Faith and Sudden Enlightenment.* Albany: State University of New York Press, 1983.
175. Paul, Diana Y. *Philosophy of Mind in Sixth-Century China: Paramārtha's 'Evolution of Consciousness'.* Stanford, Cal.: Stanford University Press, 1984.
176. Powell, William F., trans. *The Record of Tung-shan.* Honolulu: University of Hawaii Press, 1986.
177. Reischauer, Edwin O. *Ennin's Diary: The Record of a Pilgrimage to China in Search of the Law.* New York: Ronald Press, 1955.
178. Reischauer, Edwin O. *Ennin's Travels in T'ang China.* New York: Ronald Press, 1955.
179. Reynolds, C. *Autobiography: The Life of Prince-Patriarch Vajirañāṇa of Siam, 1860–1921.* Athens, Ohio: Ohio University Press, 1979.
180. Robinson, James B. *Buddha's Lions.* Emeryville, Cal.: Dharma Publications, 1979.
181. Robinson, Richard H. *Chinese Buddhist Verse.* London: J. Murray, 1954.
182. Robinson, Richard R. *Early Mādhyamika in India and China.* Madison: University of Wisconsin Press, 1967.
183. Rodd, Laurel Rasplica. *Nichiren: Selected Writings.* Honolulu: University of Hawaii Press, 1980.
184. Roerich, George, trans. *The Blue Annals.* 2nd edn. Delhi: Motilal Banarsidass, 1976. First published 1953.
185. Rogers, Minor L. 'The Shin Faith of Rennyo'. *Eastern Buddhist*, 15 (Spring 1982); pp. 56–73.
186. Ruegg, David Seyfort. *The Literature of the Madhyamaka School of Philosophy in India.* Wiesbaden: Harrassowitz, 1981.
187. Saksri, Y. *The 'Maṅgalatthadīpanī': Chapters I and II.* PhD diss., University of Pennsylvania, 1971.
188. Sanford, James H. *Zen Man Ikkyū.* Chico, Cal.: Scholar's Press, 1981.
189. Sasaki, Ruth Fuller, trans. *The Recorded Sayings of Ch'an Master Lin-chi Hui-chao of Chen Prefecture.* Kyoto: Institute for Zen Studies, 1975.
190. Shakabpa, Tsepon W. D. *Tibet: A Political History.* New Haven: Yale University Press, 1973.
191. Shastri, H. P., ed. *Advayavajrasaṃgraha.* Baroda: Oriental Institute, 1927.
192. Sherburne, Richard S. J., trans. *A Lamp for the Path and Commentary.* London: Allen & Unwin, 1983.
193. Smith, B., ed. *Religion and the Legitimation of Power in Sri Lanka.* Chambersburg, Penn.: Anima Books, 1978.
194. Smith, D. E. *Religion and Politics in Burma.* Princeton; NJ: Princeton University Press, 1965.
195. Smith, E. Gene. Introduction to

Kongtrul's Encyclopedia of Indo-Tibetan Culture. Delhi: International Academy of Indian Culture, 1970.

196. Smith, E. Gene. *Introduction to Śaṅs-pa gser-' phreṅ*. Leh, Ladakh: Smanrtsis Sungrab Spendzod, 1970.

197. Snellgrove, David. *Indo-Tibetan Buddhism: Indian Buddhists and their Tibetan Successors*. 2 vols. Boston: Shambhala, 1987.

198. Spae, Joseph J. *Japanese Religiosity*. Tokyo: Oriens Institute for Religious Research, 1971.

199. Sponberg, Alan, and Hardacre, Helen, eds. *Maitreya, the Future Buddha*. Cambridge: Cambridge University Press, 1988.

200. Sponberg, Alan. *The Vijñaptimātratā Buddhism of the Chinese Monk K'uei-chi*. PhD diss., University of British Columbia, 1980.

201. Sprung, Mervyn, trans. *Lucid Exposition of the Middle Way: The Essential Chapters from the Prasannapadā of Candrakīrti*. London: Routledge & Kegan Paul, 1979.

202. Stcherbatsky, Th. *Buddhist Logic*. 2 vols. New York: Dover Publications, 1962. First published 1930–32.

203. Stearns, Cyrus. *The Life and Teachings of the Tibetan Saint Thang-stong rgyal-po, 'King of The Empty Plain'*. Master's diss., University of Washington, 1980.

204. Stein, R. A. *Tibetan Civilization*. Stanford, Cal.: Stanford University Press, 1972.

205. Steinkellner, Ernst. *Dharmakīrtis Pramāṇaviniścayaḥ: Zweites Kapitel, Svārthānumānam*. Teil I and II. Sitzungsberichte der Osterrreichische Akademie der Wissenschaften, Band 358, Heft 15. Vienna: Böhlaus, 1973, 1979.

206. Stevens, John. *One Robe, One Bowl: The Zen Poetry of Ryōkan*. Tokyo: Weatherhill, 1977.

207. Streng, Frederick J. *Emptiness: A Study in Religious Meaning*. Nashville: Abingdon Press, 1967.

208. Strong, J. S. *The Legend of King Aśoka*. Princeton, NJ: Princeton University Press, 1983.

209. Suzuki Daisetz Teitarō, trans. *The Kyōgyōshinshō*. Kyoto: Shinshu Otaniha, 1973.

210. Suzuki, Daisetz Teitarō. *An Introduction to Zen Buddhism*. New York: Grove Press, 1964. First published 1934.

211. Suzuki, Daisetz Teitarō. *Essays in Zen Buddhism*. 3 vols. New York: Weiser, 1971–5. First published 1927–34.

212. Suzuki, Daisetz Teitarō. *Zen and Japanese Culture*. New York: Pantheon Books, 1959. First published 1938.

213. Swanson, Paul L. *Foundations of T'ien-t' ai Philosophy: The Flowering of The Two Truths Theory in Chinese Buddhism*. Berkeley: Asian Humanities Press, 1989.

214. Takakusu Junjirō, trans. 'The Life of Vasubandhu'. *T'oung Pao* (1904), pp. 269–96.

215. Tambiah, Stanley J. *The Buddhist Saints of the Forest and the Cult of Amulets*. Cambridge: Cambridge University Press, 1984.

216. Tambiah, Stanley J. *World Conqueror, World Renouncer*. Cambridge: Cambridge University Press, 1976.

217. Tanabe, George, and Tanabe, Willa Jane. *The Lotus Sūtra in Japanese Culture*. Honolulu: University of Hawaii Press, 1989.

218. Tatz, Mark, trans. *Asaṅga's Chapter on ethics with the Commentary of Tsong-Kha-Pa*. Lewiston, NY: Edwin Mellen Press, 1986.

219. Tatz, Mark. 'On the Date of Candragomin'. In *Buddhism and Jainism*. Part 1. Cuttack: Institute of Oriental and Orissan Studies, 1976, pp. 281–97.

220. Tatz, Mark. 'The Life of Candragomin in Tibetan Historical tradition'. *Tibet Journal*, 7/3 (1982); pp. 3–22.

221. Tatz, Mark. 'The Life of the Siddha-Philosopher Maitrīgupta'. *Journal of the American Oriental Society*, 107/4 (1987); pp. 695–711.

222. Tatz, Mark. *Difficult Beginnings: Three Works by Candragomin on the Bodhisattva Path*. Boston: Shambhala, 1985.

223. Thomas, E. J. *The Life of Buddha as Legend and History*. London: Routledge & Kegan Paul, 1975. First published 1927.

224. Thomsen, Harry. *The New Religions of Japan*. Rutland, Vermont: Tuttle, 1963.

225. Thondup Tulku. *Hidden Teachings of Tibet*. London: Wisdom Publications, 1986.

226. Thurman, Robert A. F., ed., and Sherpa Tulku, trans. *The Life and Teachings of Tsong-khapa*. Dharamsala: Library of Tibetan Works & Archives, 1982.

227. Thurman, Robert A. F., trans. *Tsong Khapa's Speech of Gold in the Essence of True Eloquence: Reason and Enlightenment in the Central Philosophy of Tibet*. Princeton, NJ: Princeton University Press, 1984.

228. Trungpa, Chögyam. *Born in Tibet*. Boulder: Shambhala Publications, 1977.

229. Trungpa, Chögyam. *Cutting Through Spiritual Materialism*. Boulder: Shambhala Publications, 1973.
230. Trungpa, Chögyam. *Journey Without Goal*. Boulder: Shambhala Publications, 1981.
231. Trungpa, Chögyam. *Meditation in Action*. Boulder: Shambhala Publications, 1969.
232. Trungpa, Chögyam. *Myth of Freedom*. Boulder: Shambhala Publications, 1976.
233. Trungpa, Chögyam. *Shambhala: Sacred Path of the Warrior*. Boulder: Shambhala Publications, 1984.
234. Tsukamoto Zenryu. *A History of Early Chinese Buddhism from its Introduction to the Death of Hui-yüan*, trans. Leon Hurvitz. 2 vols. Tokyo: Kodansha, 1985.
235. Tucci, Giuseppe. *Minor Buddhist Texts*. 3 parts. Rome: Istituto Italiano per il Medeo ed Estremo Oriente, 1956–1971.
236. Tucci, Giuseppe. *On Some Aspects of the Doctrines of Maitreya(nātha) and Asaṅga*. Calcutta: University of Calcutta Press, 1930.
237. Tucci, Giuseppe. *Rin-chen-bzaṅ-po and the Renaissance of Buddhism in Tibet around the Millennium*, trans. Nancy Kipp Smith. New Delhi: Aditya Prakashan, 1988. First published (in Italian) 1932.
238. Tucci, Giuseppe. *The Religions of Tibet*. Berkeley: University of California Press, 1980.
239. Tucci, Giuseppe. *Tibetan Painted Scrolls*. Rome: Istituto Italiano per il Medeo ed Estremo Oriente, 1949.
240. Ueda Yoshifumi. 'Two Main Streams of Thought in Yogācāra Philosophy'. *Philosophy East and West*, 17 (1967); pp. 155–65.
241. Ueda, Y., and Hirota, Dennis. *Shinran: An Introduction to his Thought*. Kyoto, 1989.
242. Ueda, Y., ed. *Shin Buddhism Translation Series*. 9 vols. Kyoto, 1978–87.
243. Unno, T., trans. *Tannishō: A Shin Buddhist Classic*. Honolulu: University of Hawaii Press, 1984.
244. Vetter, T. *Dharmakīrtis Pramāṇaviniścayaḥ: Pratyakṣam*. Sitzungsberichte der Osterrreichische Akademie der Wissenschaften, 250, Band 3. Vienna: Böhlaus, 1966.
245. Vetter, T. *Erkenntnisprobleme bei Dharmakīrti*. Sitzungsberichte der Osterrreichische Akademie der Wissenschaften, 245, Band 2. Vienna: Böhlaus, 1964.
246. Waddell, Norman. *The Unborn: The Life and Teaching of Zen Master Bankei*. San Francisco: North Point Press, 1984.
247. Waley, Arthur, trans. *Monkey*. New York: Grove Press, 1958.
248. Walshe, Maurice. *Thus Have I Heard*. London: Wisdom, 1987.
249. Watson, Burton, trans. *Ryōkan: Zen Monk/Poet of Japan*. New York: Columbia University Press, 1977.
250. Wayman, Alex, trans. *Calming the Mind and Discerning the Real: Buddhist Meditation and the Middle View*. New York: Columbia University Press, 1978.
251. Weinstein, Stanley. *Buddhism Under the T'ang*. Cambridge: Cambridge University Press, 1987.
252. Welch, Holmes. *The Buddhist Revival in China*. Cambridge, Mass.: Harvard University Press, 1968.
253. Wickramasinghe, M. *Landmarks of Sinhalese Literature*. Colombo: M. D. Gunasena, 1963.
254. Williams, Paul M. 'A Note on Some Aspects of Mi Bskyod Rdo Rje's Critique of Dge Lugs Pa Madhyamaka'. *Journal of Indian Philosophy*, 11 (1983); pp. 125–45.
255. Williams, Paul M. *Mahāyāna Buddhism*. New York: Routledge, 1989.
256. Willis, Janice Dean, trans. *On Knowing Reality: The Tattvārtha Chapter of Asaṅga's Bodhisattvabhūmi*. New York: Columbia University Press, 1979.
257. Wright, Arthur F. *Buddhism in Chinese History*. Stanford, Cal.: Stanford University Press, 1959.
258. Wyatt, D. K. *Thailand: A Short History*. New Haven: Yale University Press, 1984.
259. Yamamoto Kōshō, ed. *Private Letters of Shinran Shōnin*. Tokyo: Okazakiya Shoten, 1956.
260. Yamamoto Kōshō, trans. *The Words of St Rennyo*. Ube, Japan: Karinbunko, 1968.
261. Yampolsky, Philip, trans. *The Platform Sūtra of the Sixth Patriarch*. New York: Columbia University Press, 1967.
262. Yampolsky, Philip, trans. *The Zen Master Hakuin: Selected Writings*. New York: Columbia University Press, 1977.
263: Yu, Anthony C., trans. *The Journey to the West*. 4 vols. Chicago: University of Chicago Press, 1977–1983.
264. Yuasa Nobuyuki, trans. *The Zen Poems of Ryōkan*. Princeton, NJ: Princeton University Press, 1981.

265. Yü-Chün-fang. *The Renewal of Buddhism in China: Chu-hung and the Late Ming Synthesis*. New York: Columbia University Press, 1980.
266. Yün-hua, Jan. 'Tsung-mi: His Analysis of Ch'an Buddhism'. *T'oung-pao*, 58 (1972), pp. 1–53.
267. Zürcher, Erich. *The Buddhist Conquest of China*. 2 vols. Leiden: E. J. Brill, 1959.

[V] Chinese Religions, excluding Buddhism

Compiled by Laurence Thompson

1. Baldrian-Hussein, Farzeen. 'Lü Tung-pin in Northern Sung Literature'. *Cahiers d'Extrême-asie* (Kyoto), 2 (1986), pp. 133–69.
2. Bell, Catherine. 'Tu Kuang-t'ing'. In *The Encyclopedia of Religion*, ed. Mircea Eliade. New York: Macmillan, 1987.
3. Berling, Judith A. *The Syncretic Religion of Lin Chao-en*. New York: Columbia University Press, 1980.
4. Cahill, Suzanne. 'Reflections of a Metal Mother: Tu Kuang-t'ing's Biography of Hsi Wang Mu'. *Journal of Chinese Religions*, 13/14 (1985–6), pp. 127–42.
5. Ch'ien, Edward T. 'The Neo-Confucian Confrontation with Buddhism'. *Journal of Chinese Philosophy*, 9 (1982), pp. 307–28.
6. Chan, Wing-tsit, ed. *Chu Hsi and Neo-Confucianism*. Honolulu: University of Hawaii Press, 1986.
7. Chan, Wing-tsit, trans. *Instructions for Practical Living and Other Neo-Confucian Writings by Wang Yang-ming*. New York: Columbia University Press, 1963.
8. Chan, Wing-tsit, trans. *Reflections on Things at Hand: The Neo-Confucian Anthology Compiled by Chu Hsi and Lü Tsu-ch'ien*. New York: Columbia University Press, 1967.
9. Chan, Wing-tsit, trans. *The Way of Lao Tzu*. Indianapolis: Bobbs-Merrill, 1963.
10. Chan, Wing-tsit. *A Source Book in Chinese Philosophy*. Princeton, NJ: Princeton University Press, 1963.
11. Ching, Julia, trans. *The Philosophical Letters of Wang Yang-ming*. Canberra: Australian National University Press, 1972.
12. Ching, Julia. *To Acquire Wisdom: The Way of Wang Yang-Ming*. New York: Columbia University Press, 1976.
13. Creel, Herbert G. *Confucius: The Man and the Myth*. New York: John Day, 1949.
14. Crow, Carl. *Master Kung*. New York: Harper's, 1938.
15. de Bary, Wm. Theodore. *Neo-Confucian Orthodoxy and the Learning of the Mind-and-Heart*. New York: Columbia University Press, 1981.
16. *Echo Magazine* (Taipei), 5/2–3 (1975).
17. Eichhorn, Werner. 'Bemerkungen zum Aufstand des Chang Chio und zum Staate des Chang Lu'. *Mitteilungen des Instituts für Orientforschung*, 3 (1955), pp. 291–327.
18. Fange, Lienche Tu. 'Lin Chao-en'. In *Dictionary of Ming Biography*, ed. L. Carrington Goodrich and Chaoying Fang. New York: Columbia University Press, 1976.
19. Fingarette, Herbert. *Confucius: The Secular as Sacred*. New York: Harper & Row, 1972.
20. Franke, Wolfgang. 'Some Remarks on Lin Chao-en'. *Oriens extremus*, 20 (1973), pp. 161–74.
21. Franke, Wolfgang. 'Some Remarks on the "Three-in-One" Doctrine'. *Oriens extremus*, 19 (1972), pp. 121–30.
22. Fu, Charles Wei-hsun. 'Chu Hsi on Buddhism'. In *Chu Hsi and Neo-Confucianism*, ed. Wing-tsit Chan. Honolulu: University of Hawaii Press, 1986, pp. 377–407.
23. Giles, Lionel. *A Gallery of Chinese Immortals*. London: John Murray, 1948.
24. Graham, A. C. 'The Background of the Mencian Theory of Human Nature'. *Tsing Hua Journal of Chinese Studies*, 1/2 (1967), pp. 215–71.
25. Graham, A. C., trans. *The Book of Lieh-tzu*. London: John Murray, 1960.
26. Groot, J. J. M. de. *Sectarianism and Religious Persecution in China*. Taipei: Literature House, 1963. First published Leiden, 1901.
27. Jen, Yu-wen. *The Taiping Revolutionary Movement*. New Haven: Yale University Press, 1973.
28. Kohn, Livia. 'The Teaching of T'ien-Yin-Tzu'. *Journal of Chinese Religions*, 15 (1987), pp. 1–28.
29. Kroll, Paul. 'Notes on Three Taoist Figures of the T'ang Dynasty'. *Society for the Study of Chinese Religions Bulletin*, 9 (1981), pp. 19–22.
30. Kroll, Paul. 'Szu-ma Ch'eng-chen in T'ang Verse'. *Society for the Study of Chinese Religions Bulletin*, 6 (1978), pp. 16–30.
31. Kubo Noritada. 'Wang Che', trans. (from Japanese) James C. Dobbins. In *The*

Encyclopedia of Religion, ed. Mircea Eliade. New York: Macmillan, 1987.

32. Lagerwey, John. 'The Taoist Religious Community'. In *The Encyclopedia of Religion*, ed. Mircea Eliade. New York: Macmillan, 1987.
33. Lau, D. C., trans. *Mencius*. Harmondsworth: Penguin, 1970.
34. Le Blanc, Charles. 'A Re-examination of the Myth of Huang-ti'. *Journal of Chinese Religions*, 13/14 (1985–6), pp. 45–63.
35. Merton, Thomas. *The Way of Chuang Tzu*. New York: New Directions, 1965.
36. Michael, Franz, with Chung-li Chang. *The Taiping Rebellion*. Vol. 1: *History*. Seattle: University of Washington Press, 1966.
37. Needham, Joseph. *Science and Civilization in China*. Vol. 5.2. Cambridge: Cambridge University Press, 1976.
38. Overmyer, Daniel L. 'Values in Chinese Sectarian Literature: Ming and Ch'ing Pao-chüan'. In *Popular Culture in Late Imperial China*, ed. David Johnson *et al*. Berkeley: University of California Press, 1985, pp. 219–54.
39. Overmyer, Daniel L. *Folk Buddhist Religion*. Cambridge, Mass.: Harvard University Press, 1976.
40. Robinet, Isabelle. 'Chang Lu'. In *The Encyclopedia of Religion*, ed. Mircea Eliade. New York: Macmillan, 1987.
41. Robinet, Isabelle. 'Ssu-ma Ch'eng-chen'. In *The Encyclopedia of Religion*, ed. Mircea Eliade. New York: Macmillan, 1987.
42. Roth, Harold D. 'Huang-lao Chün'. In *The Encyclopedia of Religion*, ed. Mircea Eliade. New York: Macmillan, 1987.
43. Sailey, Jay, trans. *The Master who Embraces Simplicity*. San Francisco: Chinese Materials Center, 1978.
44. Saso, Michael, and Chappell, David W., eds. *Buddhist and Taoist Studies*. Honolulu: University of Hawaii Press, 1977.
45. Schwartz, Benjamin I. *The World of Thought in Ancient China*. Cambridge, Mass.: Belknap Press, 1985.
46. Seidel, Anna. 'A Taoist Immortal of the Ming Dynasty: Chang San-feng'. In *Self and Society in Ming Thought*, ed. Wm. Theodore de Bary. New York: Columbia University Press, 1970, pp. 483–531.
47. Seidel, Anna. 'Huang-ti'. In *The Encyclopedia of Religion*, ed. Mircea Eliade. New York: Macmillan, 1987.
48. Shih, Vincent Y. C. *The Taiping Ideology*. Seattle: University of Washington Press, 1967.
49. Shryock, John K. *The Origin and Development of the State Cult of Confucius*. New York: Century, 1932.
50. Sivin, Nathan. *Chinese Alchemy: Preliminary Studies*. Cambridge, Mass.: Harvard University Press, 1968.
51. Strickmann, Michel. 'On the Alchemy of T'ao Hung-ching'. In *Facets of Taoism*, ed. Holmes Welch and Anna Seidel. New Haven: Yale University Press, 1979, pp. 123–92.
52. Strickmann, Michel. *Le Taoïsme du Mao Chan: chronique d'une révélation*. Paris: Collège de France, 1981.
53. Tu Wei-ming. *Confucian Thought: Selfhood as Creative Transformation*. Albany: State University of New York Press, 1985.
54. Tu Wei-ming. *Humanity and Self-Cultivation: Essays in Confucian Thought*. Berkeley: Asian Humanities Press, 1979.
55. Tu Wei-ming. *Neo-Confucian Thought in Action: Wang Yang-ming's Youth (1472–1509)*. Berkeley: University of California Press, 1976.
56. Waley, Arthur, trans. *The Way and its Power: A Study of the Tao Te Ching and its Place in Chinese Thought*. London: Allen & Unwin, 1934.
57. Waley, Arthur. *The Travels of an Alchemist: The Journey of the Taoist Ch'ang-ch'un from China to the Hindukush at the Summons of Chinghiz Khan*. London: Routledge, 1931.
58. Ware, James R., trans. *Alchemy, Medicine, and Religion in the China of A.D. 320: The Nei P'ien of Ko Hung*. Cambridge, Mass.: MIT Press, 1966.
59. Watson, Burton, trans. *The Complete Works of Chuang Tzu*. New York: Columbia University Press, 1968.
60. Watson, Burton, trans. *Records of the Grand Historian of China: Translated from the 'Shih Chih' of Ssu-ma Ch'ien*. 2 vols. New York.
61. Wei, Henry, trans. *The Guiding Light of Lao Tzu*. Wheaton, Ill.: Theosophical Publishing House, 1982.
62. Welch, Holmes, and Seidel, Anna, eds. *Facets of Taoism*. New Haven: Yale University Press, 1979.
63. Welch, Holmes. 'The Chang T'ien-shih and Taoism in China'. *Journal of Oriental Studies* (Hong Kong), 4 (1957–8), pp. 188–212.

64. Welch, Holmes. *Taoism: The Parting of the Way*. Boston: Beacon Press, 1957.
65. Werner, E. T. C. *A Dictionary of Chinese Mythology*. New York: Julian Press, 1961.
66. Wilhelm, Richard. *Confucius and Confucianism*, trans. (from German) George H. and Annina P. Danton. New York: Harcourt, Brace, Jovanovich, 1931.
67. Wu, John C. H., trans. *Lao Tzu/Tao Teh Ching*. New York: St John's University Press, 1961.
68. Yang, Richard F. S. 'A Study in the Origin of the Legend of the Eight Immortals'. *Oriens extremus*, 5/1 (1958), pp. 1–22.

[VI] Christianity

[VI.A]

Compiled by Terence Thomas; Christopher Smith (Latin America); G. Trompfe (Pacific); Andrew Walls (Africa) *et al*

1. Achu'tegui, P. S. de, and Bernad, M. A. *Religious Revolution in the Philippines*. 3 vols. Manila, 1960–.
2. Acosta, J. de. *Obras*. Bibliotecade Autores Españoles, vol. 73. Madrid, 1954.
3. Adams, J. L., *et al. The Thought of Paul Tillich*. San Francisco, 1985.
4. Adhav, S. M. *Pandita Ramabai*. Madras, 1979.
5. Afonsky, G. *A History of the Orthodox Church in Alaska, 1794–1917*. Kodiak, Alaska, 1977.
6. Ajayi, J. F. A. *Christian Mission in Nigeria, 1841–1891: The Making of a New Elite*. London, 1965.
7. Allen, G. W. *Waldo Emerson*. New York, 1981.
8. Allen, H. E., and Meech, S. B., eds. *The Book of Margery Kempe*. London, 1940.
9. Allen, R. *The Life Experience and Gospel Labors of the Rt. Rev. Richard Allen*. New York, 1960.
10. Allen, W. *A Brief History of the Glorious Martyrdom of twelve Reverend Priests, Father E. Campion and his Companions*. London, 1908.
11. Alves, R. 'The Seed of the Future: The Community of Hope', *International Review of Missions*, 63 (1974), pp. 551–69.
12. Ambrose. In *Patrologia Latina*, ed. J.-P. Migne. Vols. 14–15. Paris, 1845.
13. Ambrose. *Some of the Principal Works of Ambrose*. The Nicene and Post-Nicene Fathers, 2nd series, vol. 10 (1896). Repr. Grand Rapids, Mich., 1955.
14. Andrae, T. *Nathan Söderblom*. Uppsala, 1932.
15. Andrews, C. F. *What I Owe to Christ*. London, 1932.
16. Andrews, E. D. *The People Called Shakers*. New edn. New York, 1963.
17. Andrews, J. F., ed. *Paul VI: Critical Appraisals*. New York, 1970.
18. Animananda, B. *Life and Work of Brahmabhandab Upadhyaya*. Calcutta, n.d.
19. Anstey, R. *Anti-slavery, Religion and Reform: Essays in Memory of Roger Anstey*. Folkestone, 1980.
20. Appasamy, A. J. *Tamil Christian Poet*. London, 1966.
21. Aradi, Z., *et al. Pope John XXIII: An Authoritative Biography*. New York, 1959.
22. Armstrong, C. J. R. *Evelyn Underhill (1875–1941): An Introduction to her Life and Writings*. Grand Rapids, Mich., 1976.
23. Armstrong, R. J., and Brady, I., eds. *Francis and Clare: The Complete Works*. New York, 1982.
24. Arnot, F. S. *Garanganze, or Seven Years Pioneer Mission Work in Central Africa*. London, 1889.
25. Arrington, L. J. *Brigham Young: American Moses*. New York, 1985.
26. Athanassakis, A. N., trans. *The Life of Pachomius: Vita Prima Graeca*. Missoula, Mont., 1975.
27. Athenagoras. In *Patrologia Graeca*, ed. J. P. Migne. Vol. 6, pp. 887–1024.
28. Atlas, A. W., ed. *Papers read at the Dufay Quincentenary Conference, Brooklyn College, Dec. 6–7, 1974*. New York, 1976.
29. Aubert, R. *Le pontificat de Pie IX, 1846–1878*. 2nd edn. Histoire de l'église depuis les origines jusqu'à nos jours, ed. A. Fliche and V. Martin, vol. 21. Paris, 1962.
30. Augé, M., *et al. Prophétisme et Thérapeutique, Albert Atcho et la Communauté de Bregbo*. Paris, 1975.
31. Augustine of Hippo. In *Patrologia Latina*, ed. J.-P. Migne. Vols. 32–47. Paris, 1841–1842.
32. Aulén, G. E. H. *Reformation and Catholicity*, trans. Eric H. Wahlstrom. Edinburgh, 1962.
33. Ayandele, E. A. *The Missionary Impact on Modern Nigeria, 1842–1914*. London, 1966.
34. Ayandele, E. A. *A Visionary of the African Church, Mojola Agbebi (1860–1917)*. Religion in Africa, no. 1. Nairobi, 1971.

35. Ayandele, E. A. *Holy Johnson: Pioneer of African Nationalism, 1836–1917*. London, 1917.
36. Azariah, V. S. *Christian Giving*. London, 1954.
37. Baëta, C. G. *Prophetism in Ghana*. London, 1962.
38. Baillie, J., *et al.*, *The Library of Christian Classics*. Vols. 6–8. Philadelphia, 1953–1958.
39. Bainton, R. H. *Erasmus of Christendom*. New York, 1969.
40. Bainton, R. H. *Here I Stand: A Life of Martin Luther*. Nashville, 1955.
41. Bainton, R. H. *Hunted Heretic: The Life and Death of Michael Servetus, 1511–1553*. Boston, 1953.
42. Baker, F. *From Wesley to Asbury: Studies in Early American Methodism*. Durham, 1976. Ch. 9.
43. Baker, F., ed. *The Works of John Wesley*. Oxford, 1975–1983; Nashville, 1984–.
44. Bangs, C. *Arminius: A Study in the Dutch Reformation*. 2nd edn. Grand Rapids, Mich., 1985.
45. Bardy, G. *Clément d'Alexandrie*. Paris, 1926.
46. Barkway, L., and Menzies, L. *An Anthology of the Love of God*. 1953. Repr. Wilton, Conn., 1976.
47. Barlow, F. *Thomas Becket*. London, 1986.
48. Barmann, L. F. *Baron Friedrich von Hügel and the Modernist Crisis in England*. Cambridge, 1972.
49. Barnes, T. D. *Tertullian: A Historical and Literary Study*. Oxford, 1971.
50. Barrett, D. B. *Schism and Renewal in Africa: An Analysis of Six Thousand Contemporary Religious Movements*. Nairobi, 1968.
51. Barrett, D. B. 'Who's Who of African Independent Church Leaders'. *Risk* (Geneva) 7:3 (1971), pp. 23–34.
52. Barrett, D. B., ed. *World Christian Encyclopedia*. Nairobi, 1982.
53. Barstow, A. Ll. *Joan of Arc: Heretic, Mystic, Shaman*. Lewiston, NY, 1985.
54. Barsukov, I. P. *Innokentii Mitropolit i Kolomenskii, Tvoreniia* (Writings) and *Pis'ma* (Letters). 7 vols. Moscow, 1883–8; Saint Petersburg, 1897–1901.
55. Bartels, F. L. *The Roots of Ghana Methodism*. Cambridge, 1965.
56. Barth, K. *Wolfgang Amadeus Mozart*. Michigan, 1986.
57. Barth, K. *Church Dogmatics*, ed. Geoffrey W. Bromiley and Thomas F. Torrance. 4 vols. Edinburgh, 1956–69.
58. Basil of Caesarea. In *Patrologia Graeca*, ed. J.-P. Migne. Vols. 29–32. Paris, 1857, 1886.
59. Basil of Caesarea. *Letters and Selected Works*, trans. Blomfield Jackson. Select Library of Nicene and Post-Nicene Fathers, 2nd series, vol. 8. 1886. Repr. Edinburgh, 1978–9.
60. Battis, E. J. *Saints and Sectaries: Anne Hutchinson and the Antinominan Controversy in the Massachusetts Bay Colony*. Chapel Hill, NC, 1962.
61. Baudry, L. *Guillaume d'Occam*. Paris, 1949.
62. Baum, J. W., *et al.*, eds. *Ioannis Calvini opera quae supersunt omnia*. 59 vols. Braunschweig, 1863–1900.
63. Baumgarten, N. de. *Saint Vladimir et la conversion de la Russie*. Rome, 1932.
64. Baus, K., *et al. The Imperial Church from Constantine to the Early Middle Ages*. History of the Church, vol. 2. New York, 1980. pp. 264–9.
65. Bazin, R. *Charles de Foucault: Hermit and Explorer*. London, 1923.
66. Beals, C. *John Eliot*. New York, 1957.
67. Bede. *Corpus Christianorum, series latina*. Vols. 118–22. Turnhout, Belgium, 1955–69.
68. Bede. *Ecclesiastical History of the English People*, ed. Bertram Colgrave and R. A. B. Mynors. Oxford, 1969.
69. Bediako, K. *Theology and Identity in the Second Century and Modern Africa*. Oxford, 1990.
70. Bedoyère, M. de la. *The Life of Baron von Hügel*. London, 1951.
71. Beidelman, T. O. *W. Robertson Smith and the Sociological Study of Religion*. Chicago, 1974.
72. Bell, H. I. *Egypt from Alexander the Great to the Arab Conquest*. Oxford, 1948.
73. Benesch, O. *German Painting from Dürer to Holbein*, trans. H. S. B. Harrison. Geneva, 1966.
74. Benoit, A. *Saint Grégoire de Nazianze: Sa vie, ses ouvres, son époque*. 1884. Repr. New York, 1973.
75. Berkey, R. F., and Edwards, S. A., eds. *Christological Perspectives*. New York, 1982.
76. Berryman, P. *The Religious Roots of Rebellion: Christians in the Central American Revolutions*. London, 1984.

77. Besse, J. *A Collection of the Works of William Penn, to which is Prefixed a Journal of His Life.* London, 1726.
78. Besse, L. *Father Beschi of the Society of Jesus: His Times and his Writings.* Trichinopoly, 1918.
79. Bessières, A. *Le nouveau François-Xavier, St. Jean de Britto.* Toulouse, 1947.
80. Bethge, E. *Dietrich Bonhoeffer: Theologian, Christian, Contemporary.* 3rd. abr. edn. New York, 1970.
81. Beyreuther, E. *Bartholomaeus Ziegenbalg.* Madras, 1955.
82. Beyreuther, E. *Philipp Jakob Spener Schriften.* Hildesheim, 1979–.
83. *Bibliotheca Dissidentium.* Vol. 10, ed. Gordon Kinder. Baden-Baden, 1989.
84. Bieler, L. *The Works of Saint Patrick by Saint Secundinus.* Westminster, Md., 1953.
85. Bikle Jr., G. *The New Jerusalem: Aspects of Utopianism in the Thought of Kagawa Toyohiko.* Tucson, 1976.
86. Biko, S. *I Write what I Like: A Selection of his Writings, with a Personal Memoir,* ed. Aelred Stubbs. London, 1978.
87. Binney, J. *A Legacy of Guilt.* Auckland, 1968.
88. Birbeck, W. J. *Russia and the English Church during the Last Fifty Years: Containing a Correspondence between Mr. William Palmer Fellow of Magdalen College, Oxford and M. Khomiakoff, in the Years 1844–1854.* 1895. Repr. Farnborough, 1969.
89. Birtwhistle, A. *Thomas Birch Freeman: West African Pioneer.* London, 1950.
90. Black, J. S., and Chrystal, G., eds. *Lectures and Essays of William Robertson Smith.* London, 1912.
91. Black, J. S., and Chrystal, G. *The Life of William Robertson Smith.* London, 1912.
92. Blackman, E. C. *Marcion and His Influence.* London, 1948.
93. Blehl, V. F. *John Henry Newman: A Bibliographical Catalogue of His Writings.* Charlottesville, Va., 1978.
94. Bligny, B. *Saint Bruno, le premier chartreux.* Rennes, *c.*1984.
95. Bligny, B. *La Grande Chartreuse par un Chartreux.* Rennes, 1984.
96. Blunt, A. F. W. *Apologies.* Cambridge, 1911.
97. Blyden, E. W. *Christianity, Islam and the Negro Race,* ed. C. Fyfe. Edinburgh, 1967.
98. Boase, T. S. R. *Boniface VIII.* London, 1933.
99. Boebe, L. *Hans Egede: Colonizer and Missionary of Greenland.* Copenhagen, 1952.
100. Boehme, Jakob. *Sämmtliche Schriften.* ed. Will-Erich Peuckert. 10 vols. Stuttgart, 1955–60.
101. Boehner, P. *Collected Articles on Ockham.* ed. Eligius Buytaert. New York, 1958.
102. Bol'shakov, S. *The Doctrine of the Unity of the Church in the Works of Khomyakov and Moehler.* London, 1946.
103. Bonaventure. *Works,* ed. Franciscans of Quaracchi. 10 vols. *Ad Claras Aquas,* 1882–1902; trans. J. de Vinck. 5 vols. 1960–1970.
104. Bond, G. C. 'A Prophecy that Failed, the Lumpa Church of Uyombe, Zambia'. In *African Christianity: Patterns of Christianity,* ed. G. Bond. *et al.* New York, 1979. pp. 137–60.
105. Bonner, A. *Selected Works of Ramon Lull.* Princeton, 1985.
106. Bonner, G. *Famulus Christi: Essays in Commemoration of the Thirteenth Centenary of the Birth of the Venerable Bede.* London, 1976.
107. Boorman, H. L. *Biographical Dictionary of Republican China.* New York, 1967.
108. Bornhäuser, C. *Leben und Lehre Menno Simons.* Neukirchen, 1973.
109. Bourne, E. C. E. *The Anglicanism of William Laud.* London, 1947.
110. Bowen, E. G. *The Settlements of the Celtic Saints in Wales.* 2nd edn. Cardiff, 1956. pp. 50–65.
111. Boyd, R. H. S. *An Introduction to Indian Christian Theology.* Madras, 1969.
112. Bréhaut, E. *An Encyclopaedist of the Dark Ages: Isidore of Seville.* New York, 1912.
113. Brabazon, J. *Albert Schweitzer.* New York, 1975.
114. Brady, I. 'Pierre Lombard'. In *Dictionnaire de spiritualité.* Paris, 1985.
115. Braithwaite, W. C. *The Beginnings of Quakerism.* Rev. edn. Cambridge, 1955.
116. Brockman, J. R. *Romero: A Life.* Maryknoll, NY, 1989.
117. Brooks, P. *Thomas Cranmer's Doctrine of the Eucharist: An Essay in Historical Development.* London, 1965.
118. Broomhall, A. J. *Hudson Taylor and China's Open Century.* 3 vols. London, 1981–2.
119. Brosie, F. M. *No Man Knows My History: The Life of Joseph Smith, the Mormon Prophet.* 2nd edn. New York, 1971.
120. Broucker, J. de. *Dom Helder Camara: The*

Conversions of a Bishop. London, 1977.
121. Brown, J. *John Bunyan, 1628–1688: His Life, Times, and Work*, rev. Frank Mott Harrison. London, 1928.
122. Brown, R., *et al. Peter in the New Testament*. Minneapolis, 1973.
123. Brown, R. E., *et al.*, eds. *Mary in the New Testament: A Collaborative Assessment by Protestant and Roman Catholic Scholars*. Philadelphia, 1978.
124. Brown, R. McA. *Gustavo Gutiérrez*. Atlanta, 1980.
124a. Brown, R. McA. *Gustavo Gutiérrez: An Introduction to Liberation Theology*. Maryknoll, NY, 1990.
125. Bruno. In *Patrologia Latina*, ed. J.-P. Migne. Vols. 152–3. Paris, 1853.
126. Buehrle, M. E. *Kateri of the Mohawks*. Milwaukee, 1954.
127. Bultmann, R., *et al. Kerygma and Myth*, ed. Hans W. Bartsch. New York, 1961.
128. Burkholder, R. E., and Myerson, J. *Critical Essays on Ralph Waldo Emerson*. Boston, 1983.
129. Burns, I. *Memoirs of the Rev. Wm. C. Burns*. New edn. London, 1885.
130. Bury, J. B. *The Life of Saint Patrick and His Place in History*. New York, 1905.
131. Busch, E. *Karl Barth: His Life from Letters and Autobiographical Texts*. London, 1976.
132. Buxton, C. *Memoirs of Sir Thomas Fowell Buxton, Bart*. London, 1847.
133. Buxton, T. F. *The African Slave Trade and its Remedy*. London, 1841. Intro. G. E. Metcalf. London, 1968.
134. Buytaert, E. M., ed. *Petri Abelardi opera theologica*. Corpus Christianorum Continuatio Mediaevalis, vols. 11–12. Turnhout, Belgium, 1969.
135. Buytaert, E. M. *Peter Abelard*. Louvain, 1974.
136. Cadorette, C. *From the Heart of the People: The Theology of Gustavo Gutiérrez*. Oak Park, Ill., 1988.
137. Calienes, R. F. 'Bibliography of the Writings of Orlando E. Costas'. *Missiology: An International Review*, 17 (1989), pp. 87–105.
138. Calvin, J. *Institutes of the Christian Religion*, ed. J. T. McNeill, trans. F. L. Battles. Philadelphia, 1960.
139. Campbell, A. *The Christian System*. 4th edn. 1866. Repr. New York, 1969.
140. Campion, E. *Decem Rationes* (1581), *English Recusant Literature* (1558–1640), ed. and trans. D. M. Rogers. 1971.
141. Carey, S. *William Carey*. London, 1925.
142. Carlyle, G. *The Collected Writings of Edward Irving*. 5 vols. London, 1864–5.
143. Carpenter, J. E. *James Martineau, Theologian and Teacher: A Study of His Life and Thought*. London, 1905.
144. Cary, O. *History of Christianity in Japan*. Vol. 2. New York, 1909.
145. Cary-Elwes, C. *China and the Cross: A Survey of Missionary History*. London, 1957.
146. Cassirer, E. *Kant's Life and Thought*, trans. James Haden. New Haven, 1981.
147. Chadwick, H. *Early Christian Thought and the Classsical Traditions: Studies in Justin, Clement and Origen*. New York, 1966.
148. Chalmers, J. *Work and Adventure in New Guinea*. London, 1885.
149. Chalmers, J. *Pioneering in New Guinea*. London, 1887.
150. Chalmers, J. A. *Tiyo Soga: A Page of South African Mission Work*. Edinburgh, 1877.
151. Chatterton, P. *Day that I have Loved*. Sydney, 1980.
152. Christoff, P. K. *An Introduction to Nineteenth-Century Russian Slavophilism: A Study in Ideas*. Vol. 1: *A. S. Xomjakov*. The Hague, 1961.
153. Christy, Sr., W. J. *Apostle to Islam*. Grand Rapids, Mich., 1953.
154. Church, J. E. *Quest for the Highest: An Autobiographical Account of the East African Revival*. Exeter, 1981.
155. Clarke, K. M. *Leonardo da Vinci*. Rev. edn. Baltimore, 1967.
156. Cohen, J. M., trans. *The Life of Saint Teresa*. Harmondsworth, 1957.
157. Coillard, F. *On the Threshold of Central Africa*. London, 1897.
158. Cole, M. *Jehovah's Witnesses*. London, 1956.
159. Colledge, E., and Walsh, J. *Juliana, Anchoret, 1343–1443: A Book of Showings to the Anchoress Julian of Norwich*. 2 vols. Toronto, 1978.
160. Collins, J. D. *The Mind of Kierkegaard*. Chicago, 1953.
161. Collis, L. *Memoirs of a Medieval Woman: The Life and Times of Margery Kempe*. New York, 1964. Alternative title, *The Apprentice Saint*. London, 1964.
162. Conzemius, V. *Ignaz von Döllinger: Briefwechsel 1820–1890*. 3 vols. Munich, 1963–71.
163. Cook, G. *The Expectation of the Poor: Latin*

American Basic Ecclesial Communities in Protestant Perspective. Maryknoll, NY, 1985.

164. Cooley, E. L. *Diary of Brigham Young*. Salt Lake City, 1980.

165. *Corpus scriptorum Christianorum Orientalum, Scriptores Syri*. Vols. 4–7, 68–9, 104–5, 124–7, 136–7. Paris, 1929–71.

166. Costas, O. E. 'The Missiological Thought of Emilio Castro', *International Review of Missions*, 73 (1984), pp. 86–123.

167. Coste, P. *Le Grand Saint du Grand Siècle*. 3 vols. Paris, 1932. Eng. trans. 3 vols. 1934–5.

167A. Coulon, P., Brasseur, P. A., and others. *Libermann 1802–1852: Une pensée et une mystique missionnaires*. Paris: Ed du Cerf, 1988.

168. Cox, H. *The Silencing of Leonardo Boff: The Vatican and the Future of World Christianity*. Oak Park, Ill., 1988.

169. Cracraft, J. *The Church Reform of Peter the Great*. Stanford, Cal., 1971.

170. Craemer, W. de. *The Jamaa and the Church: A Bantu Catholic Movement in Zaire*. Oxford, 1977.

171. Cronin, V. *A Pearl to India: The Life of Robert de Nobili*. London, 1959.

172. Cross, F. L. *The Study of St Athanasius*. Oxford, 1945.

173. Cross, F. L. *St Cyril of Jerusalem's Lectures on the Christian Sacraments: The Procatechesis and the Five Mystagogical Catecheses*. London, 1951.

174. Cross, S. H., and Sherbowitz-Wetzor, O. P. *Primary Chronicle*. Medieval Academy of America, no. 60. Cambridge, Mass., 1953.

175. Crossman, R. C. *Paul Tillich: A Comprehensive Bibliography and Keyword Index of Primary and Secondary Writings in English*. London, 1983.

176. Crouzel, H. *Bibliographie critique d'Origène*. The Hague, 1971.

177. Crowe, F. E. *Son of God, Holy Spirit, and World Religions: Bernard Lonergan's Contribution to the Wider Ecumenism*. Toronto, 1984.

178. Crummey, D. 'Shaikh Zäkaryas: an Ethiopian Prophet'. *Journal of Ethiopian Studies*, 10 (1972), pp. 55–66.

179. Cuénot, C. *Teilhard de Chardin*. Baltimore, 1965.

180. Cullmann, O. *Peter, Disciple, Apostle, Martyr: A Historical and Theological Study*. Philadelphia, 1953.

181. Culpepper, A. *The Anatomy of the Fourth Gospel*. Philadelphia, 1983.

182. Cunningham, J. W. *Vanquished Hope: The Church in Russia on the Eve of the Revolution*. New York, 1981.

183. Curtis, C. J. *Nathan Söderblom: Theologian of Revelation*. Chicago, 1966.

184. Curtiss, J. S., ed. *Essays in Russian and Soviet History in Honor of Geroid Tanquary Robinson*. New York, 1963.

185. Curtiss, J. S. *The Russian Church and the Soviet State, 1917–1950*. Boston, 1953.

186. Cyril of Alexandria. In *Patrologia Graeca*, ed. J.-P. Migne. Vols. 68–77. Paris, 1859.

187. Díaz y Díaz, M. C., ed. *Isidoriana*. León, 1961.

188. Dakin, E. F. *Mrs. Eddy: The Biography of a Virginal Mind*. New York, 1929.

189. Dalbesio, A. *Guglielmo Massaja, Bibliografia-Iconografia, 1846–1967*. Turin, 1973.

190. Daniélou, J. *Platonisme et théologie mystique*. Paris, 1944.

191. Daniélou, J. *Origen*. New York, 1955.

192. Dante Alighieri. *Inferno*, trans. Dorothy L. Sayers. Harmondsworth, 1947. *Purgatorio*. Harmondsworth, 1955.

193. Darbisher, H. *The Early Lives of Milton*. London, 1932.

194. Davis, J. D. *A Sketch of the Life of Joseph Hardy Neeshima*. New York, 1894.

195. Day, D. *The Long Loneliness*. New York, 1952.

196. Deansely, M. *Augustine of Canterbury*. London, 1964.

197. Debrunner, H. *A History of Christianity in Ghana*. Accra, 1967.

198. Dehqani-Tafti, H. *Design of my World*. London, 1959.

199. Del Mastro, M. L. *Revelation of Divine Love by Juliana of Norwich*. Garden City, NY, 1977.

200. Devanandan, P. D. *The Concept of Maya*. London, 1950.

201. Devanandan, P. D. *The Gospel and Renascent Hinduism*. London, 1959.

202. Devreese, R. *Essai sur Théodore de Mopsueste*. Vatican City, 1947.

203. *Dicconario Historico y Biografico del Peru: Siglos XV–XX*. 12 vols. Lima, 1986.

204. *Dictionary of American Biography*. Vol. 16. New York, 1935.

205. Digard, G. A. L. *Philippe le Bel et le saint siège de 1295 à 1304*. Paris, 1936.

206. Dirvin, J. I. *Mrs. Seton, Foundress of the American Sisters of Charity*. New York, 1962.

207. Dodd, C. H. *The Interpretation of the Fourth*

Gospel. Cambridge, 1953.
208. Doe, P. *Tallis*. London, 1976.
209. Doering, H. *Johannes de Brito*. Freiburg im Breisgau, 1920.
210. Drake, S. *Galileo at Work*. Chicago, 1978.
211. Drake, S. *Galileo*. New York, 1980.
212. Driver, G. R., and Hodgson, L. *Nestorius: The Bazaar of Heraclides*. Oxford, 1925.
213. Du Boulay, S. *Tutu: Voice of the Voiceless*. London, 1988.
214. Du Plessis, J. *The Life of Andrew Murray of South Africa*. London, 1919.
215. Dubb, A. A. *Community of the Saved: An African Revivalist Church in the East Cape*. Johannesburg, 1976.
216. Dubois, J. A. *Hindu Manners, Customs and Ceremonies*. 3rd edn. repr. London, 1959.
217. Dubois, J. A. *Letters on the State of Christianity in India*. London, 1823. Repr. 1977.
218. Duckett, E. S. *Anglo-Saxon Saints and Scholars*. New York, 1947.
219. Dudden, F. H. *The Life and Times of Saint Ambrose*. Oxford, 1935.
220. Dudon, P. *St Ignatius of Loyola*. Milwaukee, 1949.
221. Duff, A. *India and its Evangelization*. London, 1851.
222. Duff, A. *India and Indian Missions*. Edinburgh, 1839.
223. Dumas, A. *Dietrich Bonhoeffer: Theologian of Reality*. New York, 1971.
224. Duncan, S., ed. *John Knox: A Quatercentenary Reappraisal*. Edinburgh, 1975.
225. Dunn, M. M., and Dunn, R. S. *The Papers of William Penn*. Vol. 1: *1644–1679*; vol. 2: *1680–1684*. Philadelphia, 1981–2.
226. Duren, W. L. *Francis Asbury*. New York, 1928.
227. Duthilleul, P. *L'Évangélisation des Slaves: Cyrille et Méthode*. Tournai, 1963.
228. Dvornik, F. *The Idea of Apostolicity and the Legend of the Apostle Andrew*. Cambridge, Mass., 1958.
229. Dvornik, F., *Byzantine Missions among the Slavs: SS Constantine-Cyril and Methodius*. New Brunswick, NJ, 1970.
230. Dvornik, F. *The Slavs: Their Early History and Civilization*. Boston, 1956.
231. Eck, J. *Enchiridion locorum communium adversus Lutherum et alios hostes ecclesiae, 1525–1543*, ed. Pierre Frankael. Münster, 1982.
232. Eckhart, J. *Die lateinischen Werke*. Stuttgart, 1956–64.
233. Eckhart, J. *Die deutschen Werke*. Stuttgart, 1958–.
234. Eddy, M. B. *Prose Works*. Boston, 1920.
235. Edgecombe, R. *Bringing Forth Light: Five Tracts on Bishop Colenso's Zulu Mission*. Pietermaritzburg, 1982.
236. Eells, H. *Martin Bucer*. 1931. Repr. New York, 1971.
237. Einstein, A. *Mozart: His Character, His Work*. 4th edn. New York, 1960.
238. Elliger, W. *Thomas Müntzer*. Göttingen, 1975.
239. Ellsberg, R. *By Little and Little: The Selected Writings of Dorothy Day*. New York, 1983.
240. Ellverson, A.-S. *The Dual Nature of Man: A Study in the Theological Anthropology of Gregory of Nazianzus*. Uppsala, 1981.
241. Ellwood, T., ed. *Journal of George Fox*. Repr. Richmond, Ind., 1983.
242. Emerson, E. W. *The Complete Works of Ralph Waldo Emerson*. 12 vols. *The Journals and Miscellaneous Notebooks of Ralph Waldo Emerson*. 14 vols., Cambridge, Mass., 1960–78.
243. Endy, M. B. *William Penn and Early Quakerism*. Princeton, 1973.
244. Enklaar, I. H. *Life and Work of Dr. J. Th. Van Der Kemp, 1747–1811*. Cape Town, 1988.
245. Erasmus. *Collected Works*. 40–45 vols. projected. Toronto, 1974–.
246. Ervine, St. J. *God's Soldier: General William Booth*. 2 vols. New York, 1935.
247. Espinasse, F. *The Life of Ernest Renan*. 1895. Repr. Boston, 1980.
248. Evans, G. *The Mind of Saint Bernard of Clairvaux*. Oxford, 1983.
249. Evans, R. F. *Pelagius: Inquiries and Reappraisals*. New York, 1968.
250. Fabian, J. *Jamaa: A Charismatic Movement in Katanga*. Evanston, Ill., 1971.
251. Fackenheim, E. L. *The Religious Dimension in Hegel's Thought*. Bloomington, Ind., 1967.
252. Fage, J. D., and Oliver, R., eds. *The Cambridge History of Africa*. Vols. 4–8. Cambridge, 1975–84.
253. Fahey, M. A., *Cyprian and the Bible: A Study in Third-Century Exegesis*. Tübingen, 1971.
254. Fallows, D. *Guillaume Dufay*. London, 1982.
255. Farquhar, J. N. *The Approach of Christ to Modern India*. Calcutta, 1913.
256. Farquhar, J. N. *An Outline of the Religious*

Literature of India. London, 1920.
257. Farrow, J. V. *Damien the Leper*. London, 1937.
258. Fedotov, G. P. *The Russian Religious Mind*. Vol. 2: *The Middle Ages: The Thirteenth to the Fifteenth Centuries*, ed. John Meyendorff, (1966). Belmont, Mass., 1975, ch. 6.
259. Fedwick, P. J., ed. *Basil of Caesarea: Christian, Humanist, Ascetic; A Sixteen-Hundredth Anniversary Symposium*. 2 vols. Toronto, 1981.
260. Ferm, D. W. *Third World Liberation Theologies: an Introductory Survey*. Maryknoll, NY, 1986.
261. Ferrando, J. *Historia de los PP. Dominicos en las Islas Filipinas*. Vol. 1. Madrid, 1870.
262. Findlay, J. F. *Dwight L. Moody, American Evangelist, 1837–1899*. Chicago, 1969.
263. Firth, C. B. *An Introduction to Indian Church History*. Madras, 1961.
264. Fitzer, J. *Moehler and Baur in Controversy, 1832–1838: Romantic-Idealist Assessment of the Reformation and Counter-Reformation*. Tallahassee, 1974.
265. Fitzmeyer, J. A., trans. and ed. *The Gospel According to Luke, I-IX. Anchor Bible*, vol. 28. New York, 1981.
266. Fletcher, W. C. *A Study in Survival: The Church in Russia, 1927–1943*. New York, 1965.
267. Forbes, A. P., ed. *Kalendars of the Scottish Saints*. Edinburgh, 1872.
268. Ford, J. M. 'Was Montanism a Jewish-Christian Heresy?'. *Journal of Ecclesiastical History*, 17 (1966), pp. 145–58.
269. Forrest, J., and Greaves, R. L. *John Bunyan: A Reference Guide*. Boston, 1982.
270. Fox, G. *The Works of George Fox*. 8 vols. Philadelphia, 1831.
271. Fox, M. ed., *Hildegarde of Bingen's Book of Divine Works*. New Mexico, 1987.
272. Fox, M. *Illuminations of Hildegarde of Bingen*. New Mexico, 1985.
273. Fox, R. W. *Reinhold Niebuhr: A Biography*. New York, 1985.
274. Franceschini, L. *Mons. Daniele Comboni (1831–1881 Bibliografica)*. Rome, 1984.
275. Franke, W. 'Ricci'. In *Dictionary of Ming Biography, 1369–1644*. Vol. 2. New York, 1976.
276. Franz, G., and Kirn, P. *Thomas Müntzer: Kritische Gesamtausgabe*. Gütersloh, 1968.
277. Frend, W. H. C. *The Rise of the Monophysite Movement*. Cambridge, 1979.
278. Friede, J., and Keen, B., eds. *Bartolomé de las Casas: Toward an Understanding of the Man and his Work*. DeKalb, Ill., 1971.
279. Fulton, A. *Through Earthquake, Wind and Fire: Church and Mission in Manchuria, 1867–1950*. Edinburgh 1967, ch. 2.
280. Furtado, C. L. *The Contribution of Dr. D. T. Niles to the Church Universal and Local*. Madras, 1978.
281. Gade, J. A. *The Life of Cardinal Mercier*. New York, 1934.
282. Gallagher, D., and Gallagher, I. *The Achievement of Jacques and Raïsa Maritain: A Bibliography, 1906–1961*. New York, 1962.
283. Garcia, J. A., and Calle, C. R. *Camilo Torres: Priest and Revolutionary. Political Programme and Messages to the Colombian People*, trans. Virginia M. O'Grady. London, 1968.
284. Gardner, C. E. *Life of Father Goreh*. London, 1900.
285. Gardy, F. L. *Bibliographie des oeuvres théologiques, littéraires, historiques et juridiques de Théodore de Bèze*. Geneva, 1960.
286. Gargan, E. T., ed. *Leo XIII and the Modern World*. New York, 1961.
287. Garrett, J. *To Live among the Stars*. Geneva, 1982.
288. Garrett, P. D. *Saint Innocent, Apostle To America*. Crestwood, NY, 1979.
289. Geiger, M. *The Life and Times of Fray Junipero Serra*. 2 vols. Washington, DC, 1959.
290. Geiger, W. *Spekulation und Kritik: Die Geschichtstheologie Ferdinand Christian Baurs*. Munich, 1964.
291. Geiringer, K. *Johann Sebastian Bach: The Culmination of an Era*. London, 1966.
292. Geisendorf, P. F. *Théodore de Bèze*. Geneva, 1967.
293. Gellinek, C. *Pax optima rerum: Friedensessais zu Grotius und Goethe*. New York, 1984.
294. George, C. V. R. *Segregated Sabbaths: Richard Allen and the Emergence of Independent Black Churches*. New York, 1973.
295. Gerassi, J. *Revolutionary Priest: The Complete Writings and Messages of Camilo Torres*. London, 1971.
296. Germann, W. *Missionar C. F. Schwartz*. Erlangen, 1870.
297. Gibellini, R., ed. *Frontiers of Theology in Latin America*. Maryknoll, NY, 1979.
298. Gibellini, R. *The Liberation Theology Debate*. London, 1987.

299. Gies, F. *Joan of Arc: The Legend and the Reality*. New York, 1981.
300. Gill, J. *Personalities of the Council of Florence and Other Essays*. Oxford, 1964.
301. Gilmont, J.-F., and Daman, P. *Bibliographie ignatienne (1894–1957)*. Paris, 1958.
302. Gilson, E. *History of Christian Philosophy in the Middle Ages*. New York, 1955.
303. Gilson, E. *The Philosophy of St Bonaventure*, trans. Dom Illtyd Trethowan. London, 1938.
304. Giotto. *The Complete Paintings of Giotto*, intro. Andrew Martindale, notes & catalogue by Edi Baccheschi. London, 1969.
305. Glick, G. W. *The Reality of Christianity: A Study of Adolf von Harnack as Historian and Theologian*. New York, 1967.
306. Gogarten, F. *Christ the Crisis*, trans. R. A. Williams. London, 1970.
307. Goizueta, R. S. *Liberation, Method, and Dialogue: Enrique Dússel and North American Theological Discourse*. Atlanta, 1988.
308. Goodall, N. *A History of the London Missionary Society, 1895–1945*. London, 1954.
309. Graf, F. W., and Ruddies, H. *Ernst Troeltsch Bibliographie*. Tübingen, 1982.
310. Grant, R. M. *Eusebius as Church Historian*. Oxford, 1980.
311. Gray, D. P. *The One and the Many*. New York, 1969.
312. Green, C. J. 'Bonhoeffer Bibliography: English Language Sources'. *Union Seminary Quarterly Review*, 31 (1976), pp. 227–60.
313. Green, D. *Gold in the Crucible: Teresa of Avila and the Western Mystical Tradition*. Longmead, Shaftesbury, Dorset, 1989.
314. Green, H. H. *John Wesley*. 1964.
315. Green, N. 'The Cry for Justice and Equality'. In *Aboriginal Australians and Christian Missions*, ed. T. Swain and D. B. Rose. Adelaide, 1988. pp. 156–73.
316. Green, R. L., and Hooper, W. *C. S. Lewis*. London, 1974.
317. Green-Armytage, A. H. N. *Portrait of St Luke*. London, 1955.
318. Gregory of Nazianzus. In *Patrologia Graeca*, ed. J.-P. Migne. Vols. 35–8. Paris, 1857–62.
319. Gregory of Nyssa. *Works: Contra Eunomium*, ed. W. Jaeger. 2 vols. Berlin 1921. *Epistulae*, ed. G. Pasquali. Berlin, 1925. *Opera Ascetica*, ed. W. Jaeger *et al*. Part 1. Leiden, 1925. Other titles up to 1960.
320. Gregory Palamas. In *Gregorius Palamas: Opera Omnia*. In *Patrologia Graeca*, ed. J.-P. migne. Vol. 150: pp. 771ff.; vol. 151: pp. 1–550. Paris, 1865.
321. Gregson, V. J. *Lonergan, Spirituality, and the Meeting of Religions*. Lanham, NY, 1985.
322. Gribble, J. B. *Dark Deeds in a Sunny Country*. Perth, 1886.
323. Grieve, A. J. *Willibrord, Missionary in the Netherlands, 691–737*. Westminster, 1923.
324. Gritsch, E. W. *Reformer without a Church*. Philadelphia, 1967.
325. Groner, J. F. *Kardinal Cajetan*. Louvain, 1951.
326. Grubb, N. P. *C. T. Studd*. London, 1933.
327. Guilday, P. K. *The Life and Times of John Carroll*. 1922. Repr. Westminster, Md., 1954.
328. Gunnes, E. *Rikssamling og Kristning, 800–1177*, Norges Historie, vol. 2, ed. Knut Mykland. Oslo, 1976.
329. Gunson, N. *Messengers of Grace*. Melbourne, 1978.
330. Gutiérrez, G. *The Power of the Poor in History*. London, 1983.
331. Guy, J. *The Heretic: A Study of the Life of John William Colenso*. Johannesburg, 1983.
332. H., J. W. *A. M. Mackay, Pioneer Missionary of the Church Missionary Society to Uganda*. London, 1898.
333. Habig, M. A., ed. *St. Francis of Assisi: Writings and Early Biographies: English Omnibus of the Sources*. Chicago, 1973.
334. Hackett, R. I. J. *Religion in Calabar: The Religious Life and History of a Nigerian Town*. Berlin, 1989.
335. Hackett, R. I. J., ed. *New Religious Movements in Nigeria*. Lewiston, NY, 1987.
336. Haliburton, G. M. *The Prophet Harris*. London, 1971.
337. Häring, H., and Kuschel, K-J. *Hans Küng: His Work and His Way*. London, 1979.
338. Hadidian, D., ed. *Huldrich Zwingli Writings*. 2 vols. Allison Park, Pa., 1984.
339. Hall, M. *A Quest for the Liberated Christian*. Frankfurt, 1978.
340. Hallencreutz, C. F. *Kraemer Towards Tambaram*. Uppsala, 1966.
341. Handy, R. T., ed. *The Social Gospel in America, 1870–1920*. New York, 1966.
342. Hanke, L. *Bartolomé de las Casas, Historian*. Gainesville, Fla., 1952.
343. Hanley, T. O'B. *The John Carroll Papers*. 3 vols. Notre Dame, Ind., 1976.
344. Hanson, R. P. C. *Saint Patrick: His Origins and Career*. Oxford, 1968.
345. Hardy, A. S. *Life and Letters of Joseph*

Hardy Neeshima. Boston, 1891.
346. Harnack, A. von. *Reden und Aufsätze*. 7 vols. Giessen, 1904–30.
347. Harnack, A. von. *Marcion: Das Evangelium vom Fremden Gott; Eine Monographie zur Geschichte der Grundlegung der katholischen Kirche*. Leipzig, 1921.
348. Harris, H. *David Friedrich Strauss and his Theology*. Cambridge, 1973.
349. Hartt, F. *Michelangelo*. 3 vols. London, 1965–71.
350. Harvey, A. E. *Jesus and the Constraints of History*. London, 1982.
351. Harvey, W. W., ed. *Sancti Irenaei libros quinque adversus haereses*. 2 vols. Cambridge, 1857.
352. Hasbrouck, J. *The Rule of Saint Benedict: A Doctrinal and Spiritual Commentary*. Kalamazoo, Mich., 1983.
353. Hastings, A. *A History of African Christianity, 1950–1975*. Cambridge, 1979.
354. Havard-Williams, P. *Marsden and the New Zealand Mission*. Dunedin, 1961.
355. Hebblethwaite, P. *Introducing John Paul II*. London, 1982.
356. Hegel, G. W. F. *Werke*, ed. E. Moldenhauer and K. M. Michel. 19 vols. Frankfurt, 1969.
357. Heikel, I. A., *et al. Eusebius Werke: Die griechischen christlichen Schriftsteller der ersten drei Jahrhunderte*. Berlin, 1902–75.
358. Heiler, F. *The Gospel of Sadhu Sundar Singh*. London, 1927.
359. Hellin, J. *La analogia del ser y el conocimiento de Dios en Suárez*. Madrid, 1947.
360. Hellman, J. *Simone Weil*. Atlantic Highlands, NJ, 1982.
361. Henry, S. C. *George Whitefield: Wayfaring Witness*. New York, 1957.
362. Hill, W. S., ed. *The Folger Library Edition of the Works of Richard Hooker*. Cambridge, Mass., 1977–.
363. Hinchcliff, P. *Cyprian of Carthage and the Unity of the Christian Church*. London, 1974.
364. Hinchliff, P. *John William Colenso, Bishop of Natal*. London, 1964.
365. Hodgson, J. *The God of the Xhosa*. Cape Town, 1982.
366. Hodgson, J. *Ntsikana's 'Great Hymn': A Xhosa Expression of Christianity in the Early 19th Century Cape*. Cape Town, 1980.
367. Hodgson, P. C. *The Formation of Historical Theology: A Study of Ferdinand Christian Baur*. New York, 1966.
368. Hoffman, R. J. *Marcion and the Restitution of Christianity*. Chico, Cal., 1984.
369. Hogg, W. R. *Ecumenical Foundations: A History of the International Missionary Council and its Background*. New York, 1952.
370. Hollander, L. M. *Heimskringla: History of the Kings of Norway by Snorri Sturluson*. Austin, 1964.
371. Holth, S. 'Karl Ludvig Reichelt, 1877–1952'. *International Review of Missions*, 41 (1952), pp. 444–51.
372. Hong, H. V., and Hong, E. H., eds. and trans., with Malantschuk, G. *Søren Kierkegaard's Journals and Papers*. 7 vols. Bloomington, Ind., 1967–78.
373. Hopkins, J. *Nicholas of Cusa on Learned Ignorance: A Translation and Appraisal of De Doctor Ignorantia*. Minneapolis, 1981.
374. Horst, I. B. *A Bibliography of Menno Simons*. The Hague, 1962.
375. Hough, J. *A Reply to the Letters of the Abbé Dubois on the State of Christianity in India*. London, 1824.
376. Howorth, H. H. *Saint Augustine of Canterbury*. London, 1913.
377. Hudson, W. S. *Walter Rauschenbusch: Selected Writings*. Mahwah, NJ, 1984.
378. Huntingford, G. W. B. 'The Lives of Saint Takla Haymanot'. *Journal of Ethiopian Studies*, 4 (1966), pp. 35–40.
379. Hutton, W. H. *Thomas Becket, Archbishop of Canterbury*. Rev. edn. Cambridge, 1926.
380. Hyma, A. *The Brethren of the Common Life*. Grand Rapids, Mich., 1950.
381. Ilega, D. I. 'The God's Kingdom Society in Nigeria'. In [335: 141–60].
382. Imkamp, W. *Das Kirchenbild Innocenz' III, 1198–1216*. Päpste und Papsttum, vol. 22. Stuttgart, 1983.
383. Innocent I. In *Patrologia Latina*, ed. J.-P. Migne. Vol. 20: *Epistolae et decreta*. Paris, 1845. Cols. 457–637.
384. International Commission of Jurists. *The Trial of Beyers Naudé: Christian Witness and the Rule of Law*. London, 1975.
385. Ionesco, T. *La Vie et l'oeuvre de Pierre Movila, métropolite de Kiev*. Paris, 1944.
386. Iremonger, F. A. *William Temple*. London, 1948.
387. Irenaeus. *Against Heresies*. In *The Ante-Nicene Fathers*, vol. 1, ed. and trans. Alexander Roberts and James Donaldson. 1867. Repr. Grand Rapids, Mich., 1975.
388. Iserloh, E. *Die Eucharistie in der Darstellung des Johannes Eck*. Münster, 1950.
389. Isidore of Seville. In *Patrologia Latina*,

ed. J.-P. Migne. Vols. 81–4. Paris, 1844.
390. Jäschke, E. *Bruno Guttman: Afrikaner-Europäer in nächstenschaftlicher Entsprechung*. Stuttgart, 1966.
391. Jäschke, E. 'Bruno Guttman's Legacy'. *Occasional Bulletin of Missionary Research*, 4 (1980), pp. 165–9.
392. Jäschke, E. *Gemeindeaufbau in Afrika: Die Bedeutung Bruno Guttmans für das afrikanische Christentum*. Stuttgart, 1981.
393. Jörgensen, J. *St Bridget of Sweden*, trans. Ingeborg Lund. 2 vols. London, 1954.
394. Jabavu, D. D. T. *The Black Problem: Papers and Addresses on Various Native Problems*. Lovedale, SA, 1921.
395. Jacob, P. S. *The Experiential Response of N. V. Tilak*. Bangalore, 1979.
396. Jaffé, P. *Regesta pontificum Romanorum*. Vol. 1. 2nd edn. Leipzig, 1885.
397. James, J. W., ed. *Rhygyfarch's Life of St David*. Cardiff, 1967.
398. Janzen, J. M., and MacGaffey, W. *An Anthology of Kongo Religion: Primary Texts from Lower Zaïre*. University of Kansas Publications in Anthropology, no. 5. Lawrence, Kansas, 1974.
399. Jeppesen, K. K. *The Style of Palestrina and the Dissonance*. New York, 1970.
400. Jerome. In *Patrologia Latina*, ed. J.-P. Migne. Vols. 22–30. Paris, 1844.
401. Jesús, Crisógono de. *The Life of Saint John of the Cross*, trans. Kathlene Pond. New York, 1958.
402. Jesse, D. C. *Letters of Brigham Young to his Sons*. Salt Lake City, 1974.
403. Jewett, R. *A Chronology of Paul's Life*. Philadelphia, 1979.
404. John XXIII. *Journal of a Soul*, trans. Dorothy White. New York, 1965.
405. John XXIII. *Discorsi, messagi, colloqui del Santo Padre Giovanni XXIII*. 5 vols. Vatican City, 1961–4.
406. Jones, E. S. *Christ at the Round Table*. London, 1928.
407. Jones, T. J. *Education in Africa*. New York, 1922.
408. Jones, T. J. *Education in East Africa*. New York and London, 1925.
409. Jonsson, I. *Emanuel Swedenborg*. New York, 1971.
410. Joy, C. R. *Albert Schweitzer: An Anthology*. Boston, 1965.
411. Judson, E. *Adoniram Judson, . . . his Life and Labours*. London, 1883.
412. Jules-Rosette, B. *African Apostles: Aspects of Ritual and Conversion in the Church of John Maranke*. Ithaca, 1975.
413. Justin Martyr. In *Patrologia Graeca*, ed. J.-P. Migne. Vol. 6. Paris, 1857.
413a. Knitter, Paul F. *No Other Name?* Maryknoll, NY, 1985.
413b. Kamm, A. L. van. *A Light to the Gentiles*. Milwaukee: Dimension Books, 1962.
414. Kümmel, W. G. *Introduction to the New Testament*. Nashville, 1975.
415. Küng, H, and Moltmann, J., eds. *Mary in the Churches*. In *Concilium* 168. New York, 1983.
416. Kagawa, T. *Kagawa Toyohiko zenshu*. 24 vols. Tokyo, 1962–4.
417. Kannengiesser, C. *Athanase d'Alexandrie: Éveque et écrivain*. Paris, 1983.
418. Kannengiesser, C. *Holy Scripture and Hellenistic Hermeneutics in Alexandrian Christology: The Arian Crisis*. Berkeley, 1982.
419. Kannengiesser, C. 'Arius and the Arians'. *Theological Studies*, 44 (1983), pp. 456–75.
420. Kant, E. *Religion within the Limits of Reason Alone*, trans. Theodore M. Greene and Hoyt H. Hudson. LaSalle, Ill., 1960.
421. Kaplan, S. 'Ezana's conversion reconsidered'. *Journal of Religion in Africa*, 13 (1982), pp. 101–9.
422. Kates, F. W. *Charles Henry Brent*. London, 1948.
423. Kaunda, K. D. *Zambia shall be Free: An Autobiography*. London, 1962.
424. Kaunda, K. D. *A Humanist in Africa: Letters to Colin M. Morris from Kenneth D. Kaunda*. London, 1966.
425. Kavanaugh, K., and Rodriguez, O., trans. *The Collected Works of Saint John of the Cross*. Washington, DC, 1979.
426. Keck, L. E. *Paul and his Letters*. Philadelphia, 1979.
427. Kegley, C. W. *The Theology of Emil Brunner*. New York, 1962.
428. Kegley, C. W. *The Theology of Rudolf Bultmann*. New York, 1966.
429. Kegley, C. W., and Bretall, R. W., eds. *Reinhold Niebuhr: His Religious, Social, and Political Thought*. Rev. edn. New York, 1982.
430. Kelly, J. N. D. *Jerome: His Life, Writings, and Controversies*. London, 1975.
431. Keogh, D. *Romero: El Salvador's Martyr*. Dublin, 1981.
432. Kernan, J. *Our Friend, Jacques Maritain: A Personal Memoir*. Garden City, NY, 1975.
433. Kerrigan, A. *Saint Cyril of Alexandria,*

Interpreter of the Old Testament. Rome, 1952.
434. Kettlewell, S. *Thomas à Kempis and the Brothers of the Common Life*. 2 vols. London, 1882.
435. King, M. L., Jr. *Stride Towards Freedom: The Montgomery Story*. New York, 1958.
436. King, M. L., Jr. *Where Do We Go From Here: Chaos or Community?* New York, 1967.
437. King, G. L. *A Self-made Bishop: The Story of John Tsizehena, 'Bishop of the North, D.D.'*. London, 1933.
438. Klimenko, M. *The 'Vita' of St Sergii of Radonezh*. Houston, 1980.
439. Knaake, J. K., *et al. D. Martin Luthers Werke: Kritische Gesammtausgabe*. Weimar, 1883–1974.
439a. Knight, W. *Memoir of the Rev. H. Venn. The missionary secretariat of Henry Venn*. London: Longman, 1880.
440. Knight, W. S. M. *The Life and Works of Hugo Grotius*. London, 1925.
441. Knox, J. *History of the Reformation in Scotland*, ed. W. C. Dickinson. 2 vols. London, 1949.
442. Knox, J. *The Works of John Knox*, ed. D. Laing. 6 vols. Edinburgh, 1846–64.
442a. Koren, H. J. *To the ends of the earth. A general history of the Congregation of the Holy Ghost*. Pittsburgh: Duquesne University Press, 1983.
443. Koyré, A. *La Philosophe de Jacob Boehme*. 1929. Repr. New York, 1968.
443a. Kraeling, C. H. *John the Baptist*. New York, 1951.
444. Kraemer, H. *Religion and the Christian Faith*. London, 1956.
445. Krapf, J. L. *Travels, Researches and Missionary Labours during an Eighteen Years' Residence in Eastern Africa*. 1860. 2nd edn, intro. R. C. Bridges. London, 1968.
446. Kysar, R. *The Fourth Evangelist and His Gospel: An Examination of Contemporary Scholarship*. Minneapolis, 1975.
447. Lösch, S. *Döllinger und Frankreich*. Munich, 1955.
448. Labriolle, P. de. *Les Sources de l'histoire du montanisme*. Paris, 1913.
449. Lacey, R. 'Boismenu, Alain Marie Guynot de'. In *Encyclopaedia of Papua and New Guinea*, ed. P. Ryan. Melbourne, 1972.
450. Lake, K., Lawlor, H. J., and Oulton, J. E. L. *Eusebius' Ecclesiastical History*. 2 vols. Loeb Classical Library. London, 1927–8.
451. Landon, H. C. R., *Haydn*. London, 1972.
452. Landon, H. C. R. *Haydn: Chronicle and Works*. London, 1976.
453. Landon, H. C. R. and Mitchell, D., eds. *The Mozart Companion*. London, 1956.
454. Lang, P. H. *George Fridric Handel*. London, 1967.
455. Langford, J. J. *Galileo, Science and the Church*. Ann Arbor, 1971.
456. Langlois, V. *Collections des historiens anciens et modernes de 'Arménie*. Paris, 1868.
457. Langworthy, H. W. 'Charles Domingo, Seventh Day Baptists and Independency'. *Journal of Religion in Africa*, 15 (1985), pp. 96–121.
458. Langworthy, H. W. 'Joseph Booth, Prophet of Radical Change in Central and South Africa, 1891–1915'. *Journal of Religion in Africa*, 16 (1986), pp. 22–43.
459. Latourette, K. S. *A History of Christian Missions in China*. London, 1929.
460. Laud, W. *The Works of the Most Reverend Father in God William Laud*, ed. W. Scott and J. Bliss. 7 vols. Library of Anglo-Catholic Theology. Oxford, 1847–60.
461. Launay, A. *Histoire des missions de l'Inde*. 3 vols. Paris, 1898.
462. Law, W. *The Works of the Reverend William Law M.A.* 1762. Repr., 9 vols. in 3, London, 1892–3.
463. Lea, H. C. *A History of the Inquisition in Spain*. 1907. Repr. New York, 1966.
464. Lebon, J. *Le Monophysisme sévérien*. Louvain, 1909.
465. Leclercq, J. *Thunder in the Distance: The Life of P. Lebbe*. New York, 1964.
466. Leclercq, J., Talbot, C. H., and Rochais, H. M. *Sancti Bernardi Opera*. 8 vols. Rome, 1957–77.
467. Leclercq, J., ed. *Saint Bernard théologien*. Rome, 1953.
468. Lecompte, E. *An Iroquois Virgin: Catherine Tekakwitha*. New York, 1932.
469. Leff, G. *William of Ockham: The Metamorphosis of Scholastic Discourse*. Manchester, 1975.
470. Legge, H. E. *James Legge*. London, 1905.
471. Lehmann, E. A. *It Began at Tranquebar*. Madras, 1955.
472. Lehner, F. C. *Saint Dominic: Biographical Documents*. Washington, D.C., 1964.
473. Leitzmann, H., ed. *Apollinaris von Laodicea und seine Schule*. 1904. Repr. Tübingen, 1970.
474. *Le Kimbanguisme a 50 ans/The 50th Anniversary of Kimbanguism*. Kinshasa, 1971.
475. Leo I. *The Letters and Sermons of Leo the*

Great, trans. Charles Lett Feltoe. A Select Library of Nicene and Post-Nicene Fathers, 2nd series, vol. 12. Oxford, 1890.
476. Leonard, J., trans. *The Conferences of St. Vincent de Paul to the Sisters of Charity*. 4 vols. London, 1938–40.
477. Lesser, M. X. *Jonathan Edwards: A Reference Guide*. Boston, 1981.
478. Levasti, A. *My Servant, Catherine*, trans. D. M. White. Westminster, Md., 1954.
479. Levin, D. *Jonathan Edwards: A Profile*. New York, 1969.
480. Levison, W. *England and the Continent in the Eighth Century*. Oxford, 1946.
481. Lewis, C. S. *Surprised by Joy: The Shape of my Early Life*. London, 1955.
482. Lewis, D. L. *King: A Biography*. 2nd edn. Urbana, Ill., 1978.
483. Liébaert, J. *La Doctrine christologique de saint Cyrille d'Alexandrie avant la Querelle Nestorienne*. Lille, 1951.
484. Lightfoot, J. B., ed. and trans. *The Apostolic Fathers*. 1956. Repr. Grand Rapids, Mich., 1973.
485. Lilla, S. R. C. *Clement of Alexandria: A Study in Christian Platonism and Gnosticism*. Oxford, 1971.
486. Lindley, D. R. *Apostle of Freedom*. St Louis, 1957.
487. Livingstone, D. *Last Journals in Central Africa from 1865 to his death*, ed. H. Waller. 2 vols. London, 1874.
488. Livingstone, W. P. *Laws of Livingstonia*. London, n.d.
489. Loisy, A. F. *Mémoires pour servir à l'histoire religieuse de notre temps*. Paris, 1930–31.
490. Lonergan, B. *Philosophy of God, and Theology*. Philadelphia, 1973.
491. Longford, Lord. *Pope John Paul II: an Authorized Biography*. London, 1982.
492. Loofs, F. *Nestoriana: Die Fragmente des Nestorius*. Halle, 1905.
493. Lopetegui, L. *El Padre José de Acosta, S.J. y las Misiones, Especialmente Americanas, del Siglo XVI*. Madrid, 1942.
494. Lotz, D. W. *Ritschl and Luther: A Fresh Perspective on Albrecht Ritschl's Theology in the Light of His Luther Study*. Nashville, 1974.
495. Lovett, R. *James Chalmers. His Autobiography and Letters*. London, 1902.
496. Lovett, R. *The History of the London Missionary Society, 1795–1895*. London, 1899.
497. Lowinsky, E. E. *Josquin des Prez*. London, 1976.
498. Luciani, S., and Taddia, I. *Fonti Combo-niane per la storia dell' Africa nord-orientale*. Bologna, 1986.
498a. Luck, *African Saint. The story of Apolo Kivebulaya*. London: Collins, 1963.
499. Lull, R. *Obres: Edición original*. 20 vols. Palma de Mallorca, 1906–36.
500. Lundsteen, A. C. *Hermann Samuel Reimarus und die Anfänge der Leben-Jesu Forschung*. Copenhagen, 1939.
501. Luscombe, D. E. *Peter Abelard*. London, 1979.
502. Luthuli, A. *Let my People Go: An Autobiography*. London, 1962.
503. Lynch, H. R. *Edward Wilmot Blyden, Pan-Negro Patriot, 1832–1912*. London, 1967.
504. Lynch, H. R., ed. *Black Spokesman. Selected Published Writings of Edward Wilmot Blyden*. London, 1971.
505. Möhler, J. A. *Die Einheit in der Kirche, oder Das Prinzip des Katholizismus*, ed. J. R. Geiselmann. Cologne, 1957.
506. Möhler, J. A. *Symbolik*, ed. J. R. Geiselmann. 2 vols. Cologne, 1960–61.
507. MacGaffey, W., *Religion and Society in Central Africa*. Chicago, 1986.
508. MacGaffey, W. *Modern Kongo Prophets*. Bloomington, Ind., 1983.
508a. Mackenzie, P. R. *Inter-religious encounters in West Africa. Samuel Ajayi Crowther's attitude to traditional religion and Islam*. Leicester Studies in Religion, 1976.
509. Mackintosh, C. W. *Coillard of the Zambezi*. London, 1907.
510. Macnicol, N. *Pandita Ramabai*. Calcutta, 1926.
511. Macquarrie, J. *The Scope of Demythologizing: Bultmann and His Critics*. New York, 1961.
512. Magner, J. A. 'Fray Juan de Zummárraga – His Social Contributions', *The Americas*, 5 (1959), pp. 264–74.
513. Malantschuk, G. *Kierkegaard's Thought*. Princeton, NJ, 1971.
514. Malvy, A., and Viller, M. *La Confession Orthodoxe de Pierre Moghila métropolite de Kiev, 1633–1646*. Orientalia Christiana, vol. 10. Rome, 1927.
515. Manning, H. E. *England and Christendom*. London, 1867.
516. Manschreck, C. L. *Melanchthon: The Quiet Reformer*. New York, 1958.
517. Mantzaridis, G. *The Deification of Man*. Crestwood, NY, 1984.
518. Marcone, Abbé. *La parole de Pie IX*. 2nd edn. Paris, 1868.

519. Marini, S. A. *Radical Sects of Revolutionary New England*. Cambridge, Mass., 1982.
520. Maritain, J., *et al. Étienne Gilson: Philosophe de la Chrétienté*. Paris, 1949.
521. Maritain, J. *Distinguish to Unite, or the Degrees of Knowledge*, trans. Gerald B. Phelen. New York, 1959.
522. Marr, J. R. 'Some Thoughts upon the Traditions concerning St Thomas in India'. In *Paritimāṟ kalaiñar nūṟṟāṇṭuvilā malar*, ed. Cupramanyam. Madurai, 1970. pp. 207–13.
523. Marsden, J. B. *Life and Work of Samuel Marsden*, ed. J. Drummond. Christchurch, 1913.
524. Marshall, J. S. *Hooker and the Anglican Tradition: An Historical and Theological Study of Hooker's Ecclesiastical Polity*. Sewanee, Tenn., 1963.
525. Marshman, J. C. *The Life and Times of Carey, Marshman and Ward*. 2 vols. London, 1859.
526. Martin, M.-L. *Kimbangu: An African Prophet and his Church*. Oxford, 1975.
527. Martin, M.-L. 'The Mai Chaza Church in Rhodesia'. In *African Initiatives in Religion*, ed. D. B. Barrett. Nairobi, 1971.
528. Martina, G. *Pio Nono*. Rome, 1974–.
529. Martindale, G. C. *Life of Mère Anne-Marie Jahouvey*. London, 1953.
530. Martineau, J. *Essays, Reviews, and Addresses*. 4 vols. London, 1890–91.
531. Mathews, B. *John R. Mott: World Citizen*. London, 1934.
532. Matthews, B. *Williams the Shipbuilder*. London, 1915.
533. Maurice, F. D. *The Kingdom of Christ*. 2 vols. London, 1958.
534. Maurice, F. *The Life of Frederick Denison Maurice Chiefly told in His Own Letters*. London, 1884.
535. McClelland, V. A. *Cardinal Manning: His Public Life and Influence, 1865–1892*. London, 1962.
536. McCracken, J. *Politics and Christianity in Malawi, 1875–1940: The Impact of the Livingstonia Mission in the Northern Province*. Cambridge, 1977.
537. McCrie, T.. *The Life of Andrew Melville*. 2nd edn. Edinburgh, 1824.
538. McFarlan, D. M. *Calabar: The Church of Scotland Mission, Founded 1846*. 2nd edn. London, 1957.
539. McGrath, M. *Étienne Gilson: A Bibliography*. Toronto, 1982.
540. McLoughlin, W. G. 'Aimee Semple McPherson: Your Sister in the King's Glad Service'. *Journal of Popular Culture*, 1 (Winter 1968), pp. 193–217.
541. McLoughlin, W. G. *Revivalism: Charles Grandison Finney to Billy Graham*. New York, 1959.
542. McNeile, A. H. *The Gospel According to St Matthew*. London, 1915.
543. McPherson, A. S. *This Is That: Personal Experiences, Sermons, and Writings*. Los Angeles, 1923.
544. McVeigh, M. J. *God in Africa. Conceptions of God in African Traditional Religion and Christianity*. Cape Cod, Mass., 1974.
545. Melville, A. M. *Elizabeth Bayley Seton, 1774–1821*. 1951. Repr. New York, 1976.
546. Mercier, D. J. *Cours de Philosophie*. 4 vols. Louvain, 1894–9.
547. *Mercier, le cardinal, 1851–1926*. Brussels, 1927.
548. Meulen, J. ter, and Diermanse, P. J. J. *Bibliographie des écrits imprimés de Hugo Grotius*. The Hague, 1950.
549. Meyendorff, J. *A Study of Gregory Palamas*. London, 1964.
550. Meyendorff, J., *et al. The Primacy of Peter*. London, 1963.
551. Miguez Bonino, J., ed. *Faces of Jesus: Latin American Christologies*. Maryknoll, NY, 1984.
552. Miller, P., and Smith, J. E. *The Works of Jonathan Edwards*. New Haven, 1957–.
553. Miller, P. *The New England Mind: The Seventeenth Century*. New York, 1939.
554. Miller, P. *Orthodoxy in Massachusetts, 1630–1650*. 1933. Repr. Gloucester, Mass., 1965.
555. Miller, W. D. *Dorothy Day*. New York, 1982.
556. Milton, J. *Paradise Lost*, ed. Tillyard, E. M. W. Bks. 1–2: London, 1956. Bks. 9–10: London, 1960.
557. Milton, J. *The Poetical Works of John Milton*, ed. Helen Darbishire. 2 vols. Oxford, 1952.
558. Mobley, H. W. *The Ghanaian's Image of the Missionary*. Leiden, 1970.
559. Mockford, J. *Khama: King of the Bamangwato*. London, 1931.
560. Moffat, R. *Missionary Labours and Scenes in Southern Africa*. London, 1842.
561. Mohn, G. *Roland Allen: Sein Leben und Werk*. Gütersloh, 1970.
562. Mooney, C. F. *Teilhard de Chardin and the*

Mystery of Christ. New York, 1966.
563. Moore, R. A. *Culture and Religion in Japanese–American Relations: Essays on Uchimura Kanzo, 1861–1930*. Ann Arbor, 1981.
564. Moorman, J. R. H. *St Francis of Assisi*. London, 1976.
565. Morrison, E., ed. *Memoirs of the Life and Labours of Robert Morrison*. London, 1839.
566. Mott, J. R. *The Evangelization of the World in this Generation*. New York, 1900.
567. Mott, J. R. *Addresses and Papers*. New York, 1946–7.
568. Mott, M. *The Seven Mountains of Thomas Merton*. Boston, 1984.
569. Mottesi, O. L. *An Historically-Mediated 'Pastoral' of Liberation: Gustavo Gutiérrez's Pilgrimage Towards Socialism*. PhD diss., Emory University, Atlanta, 1985.
570. Moule, C. F. D. *The Origin of Christology*. Cambridge, 1977.
571. Mufuka, K. N. *Missions and Politics in Malawi*. Kingstown, Ontario, 1977.
572. Mulholland, J. F. *Hawaii's Religions*. Rutland, 1970.
573. Muller, A. V., ed. *The Spiritual Regulation of Peter the Great*. Seattle, 1972.
574. Munz, P. *The Place of Hooker in the History of Thought*. London, 1949.
575. Murphy, F. X., ed. *A Monument to Saint Jerome: Essays on some Aspects of His Life, Works, and Influence*. New York, 1952.
576. Myklebust, O. G., ed. *Hans Egede, 1686–1758*. Oslo, 1958.
577. Nassau, R. H. *Fetichism in West Africa. Fifty Years' Observation of Native Customs and Superstitions*. London, 1904.
578. Neill, S. C. *Colonialism and Christian Missions*. London, 1966.
579. Nelson, J. R. *No Man is Alien: Essays on the Unity of Mankind*. Leiden, 1971.
580. Neuner, P. *Döllinger als Theologie der Ökumene*. Paderborn, 1979.
581. *New Catholic Encyclopedia*. New York, 1967.
582. Newman, B. *Sister of Wisdom: St. Hildegarde's Theology of the Feminine*. California, 1987.
583. Newman-Studien. *Internationales Cardinal-Newman-Kuratorium*. Nuremberg, 1948–.
585. Nicholas of Cusa. *Opera omnia*. Leipzig and Hamburg, 1932–.
585. Nichols, J., and Bagnall, W. R. *The Works of James Arminius*. 3 vols. 1853. Repr. Grand Rapids, Mich., 1956.
586. Niemöller, M. *Pastor Niemöller and his Creed*, trans. Margaret Blunt. London, 1939.
587. Niles, D. T. *Buddhism and the Claims of Christ*. Richmond, Va., 1967.
588. Niles, D. T. *Upon the Earth*. New York, 1962.
589. Nineham, D. E. *St. Mark*. Harmondsworth, 1963.
590. Ninomiya, T. *Pastorale Missiologie: Die Protestantische Theologie in Latinamerika am Beispiel Emilio Castros*. Frankfurt, 1980.
591. Nobili, R. de. *Première Apologie* [Latin text with French trans. by P. Dahmen]. Paris, 1931.
592. Norberg, D. *S. Gregorii Magni registrum epistularum*. Corpus Christianorum, Seria Latina, vols. 140, 140A. Turnhout, Belgium, 1982.
593. Northcott, C. *Robert Moffat, Pioneer in Africa, 1817–1870*. London, 1961.
594. Northcott, C. *John Williams Sails On*. London, 1939.
595. Nowell, C. E. 'The Historical Prester John'. *Speculum*, 28 (1953), pp. 345–455.
596. O'Connor, D. *The Testimony of C. F. Andrews*. Bangalore, 1974.
597. O'Donovan, L. J., ed. *A World of Grace: An Introduction to the Themes and Foundation of Karl Rahner's Theology*. New York, 1980.
598. O'Meara, T. F. 'An Eckhart Bibliography'. *The Thomist*, 42 (April, 1978), pp. 313–36.
599. Oldham, J. H. *Real Life is Meeting*. London, 1942.
600. Oldham, J. H. *The Christian Message in the Modern World*. London, 1932.
601. Oldham, J. H. *New Hope in Africa*. London, 1955.
602. Olin, J. C., ed. *Christian Humanism and the Reformation: Selected Writings of Erasmus with the Life of Erasmus by Beatus Rhenanus*. Rev. edn. New York, 1975.
603. Oliphant, M. *The Life of Edward Irving*. 2 vols. London, 1862.
604. Oliver, R., *et al.*, eds. *History of East Africa*. Oxford, 1963–76.
605. Omoyajowo, J. A. *Cherubim and Seraphim: the History of an African Independent Church*. New York, 1982.
606. Oosthuizen, G. C. *The Theology of a South African Messiah*. Leiden, 1967.
607. Origen. *The Anti-Nicene Fathers*. Vol. 4, ed. Alexander Roberts and James

Donaldson. Edinburgh, 1965.

608. Ormanian, M. *The Church of Armenia*. 2nd edn. London, 1955.

609. Orme, W. *The Practical Works of . . . Richard Baxter*. 23 vols. London, 1830.

610. Osthoff, H. *Josquin Desprez*. 2 vols. Tutzing, 1962–5.

611. Oussoren, A. H. *William Carey: Especially his Missionary Principles*. London, 1945.

612. Outler, A. C. *John Wesley*. New York, 1964.

613. Overbeck, J. J., and Robertson, J. N. W. B., eds. *The Orthodox Confession of the Catholic and Apostolic Eastern Church*. London, 1898.

614. Overton, J. H. *William Law: Conjuror and Mystic*. London, 1881.

615. Pachomius. *Sancti Pachomii vitae Graecae*, ed. François Halkin. Subsidia Hagiographica, vol. 19. Brussels, 1932.

616. Padovano, A. *The Human Journey: Thomas Merton, Symbol of a Century*. New York, 1982.

617. Padwick, C. E. *Temple Gairdner of Cairo*. London, 1929.

617a. Page, J. *The Black Bishop. Samuel Adjai Crowther*. London: Hodder and Stoughton, 1908.

618. Palmer, W. *The Patriarch and the Tsar*. 6 vols. London, 1871–6.

619. Pannenberg, W. *Jesus, God and Man*. 2nd edn. Philadelphia, 1977.

619a. Pannikar, Raimundo. *The Vedic Experience*. Berkeley, Cal., 1977.

619b. Pannikar, Raimundo. *The Trinity and the Religious Experience of Man*. Maryknoll, NY, 1973.

620. Panofsky, E. *Albrecht Dürer*. 2 vols. 3rd edn. Princeton, NJ, 1948.

621. Paradkar, B. A. M. *The Theology of Goreh*. Bangalore, 1969.

622. Parker, T. H. L. *John Calvin*. Philadelphia, 1960.

623. Pascal, P. *La Vie de l'archiprêtre Avvakum écrite par lui-même*. 2nd edn. Paris, 1960.

624. Pascal, P. *Avvakum et les débuts du Raskol: La crise religieuse au dix-septième siècle en Russie*. 2nd edn. Paris, 1963.

625. Paton, D. M. *Reform of the Ministry: A Study in the Work of Roland Allen*. London, 1968.

626. Paton, D. M., and Long, C. H., eds. *The Compulsion of the Spirit*. Grand Rapids, Mich., 1983.

627. Paton, W. *Alexander Duff*. London, 1923.

628. Pauck, W. *Melanchthon and Bucer*. Philadelphia, 1969.

629. Paul, R. D. *Chosen Vessels*. Madras, 1961.

630. Paulin, A. *Saint Cyrille de Jerusalem Catechète*. Paris, 1959.

631. Paulme, D. 'Une Religion Syncrétique en Côte d'Ivoire.' *Cahiers d'Etudes Africaines*, 1 (1962), pp. 5–90.

632. Pearson, A. F. S. *Thomas Cartwright and Elizabethan Puritanism, 1535–1603*. Cambridge, 1925.

633. Pearson, H. *Memoirs of the Life and Correspondence of the Reverend Christian Frederick Schwartz*. 2 vols., London, 1835.

634. Peel, A., and Carlson, L. H., ed. *Cartwrightiana, Elizabethan Nonconformist Texts*. Vol. 1. London, 1951.

635. Peel, J. D. Y. *Aladura: A Religious Movement among the Yoruba*. London, 1968.

636. Peel, R. *Mary Baker Eddy: The Years of Discovery; The Years of Trial; The Years of Authority*. New York, 1966–77.

637. Peers, E. A. *The Complete Works of Saint John of the Cross, Doctor of the Church*. 3 vols. London, 1953.

638. Peers, E. A. *Ramon Lull: A Biography*. London, 1929.

639. Peers, E. A., ed. and trans. *The Complete Works of Saint Teresa of Jesus*. 3 vols. London, 1946.

640. Pennington, E. L. *The Reverend Thomas Bray*. Philadelphia, 1934.

641. Pennington, K. *Pope and Bishops: the Papal Monarchy in the Twelfth and Thirteenth Centuries*. Philadelphia, 1984.

642. Peter Lombard. In *Patrologia Latina*, ed. J.-P. Migne. Vols. 191–2. 1879–89. Repr. Turnhout, Belgium, 1975.

643. Peter Lombard. *Sententiae in IV libris distinctae*. 3rd edn. Rome, 1971.

644. Peterson, P. M. *Andrew, Brother of Simon Peter. His History and his Legends*. Supplements to Novum Testamentum, vol. 1. Leiden, 1958.

645. Petit, L., Siderides, X. A., and Jugie, M., eds. *Works of Gennadios [Georgios] Scholarios*. 8 vols. Paris and Athens, 1928–36.

646. Petitot, H. *St Bernadette*. Cork, 1949.

647. Petre, M. D. *Alfred Loisy: His Religious Significance*. Cambridge, 1944.

648. Pike, G. H. *The Life and Work of Charles Haddon Spurgeon*. 6 vols. London, 1894.

649. Pirouet, M. L. *Black Evangelists: The Spread of Christianity in Uganda, 1891–1914*. London, 1978.

650. Plinval, G. de. *Pelage: Ses écrits, sa vie et sa*

reforme. Lausanne, 1943.

651. Pobee, J. S., ed. *Religion in a Pluralistic Society*. Leiden, 1976.

652. Pollock, J. *Billy Graham: The Authorized Biography*. New York, 1966. Updated edn. Minneapolis, 1969.

653. Pollock, J. *Billy Graham Evangelist to the World*. San Francisco, 1979.

654. Pollock, J. *Hudson Taylor and Maria: Pioneers in China*. New York, 1962.

655. Poole, S., ed. *In Defense of the Indians*. DeKalb, Ill., 1974.

656. Pope-Hennessy, J. *Fra Angelico*. London, 1952.

657. Pospielovsky, D. *The Russian Church under the Soviet Regime, 1917–1982*. 2 vols. Crestwood, NY, 1984.

658. Potter, G. R. *Zwingli*. New York, 1976.

659. Powicke, F. J. *A Life of the Reverend Richard Baxter, 1615–1691*. London, 1924.

660. Prestige, G. L. *Fathers and Heretics*. London, 1940.

661. Prout, E. *Memoirs of the Life of the Rev. John Williams*. London, 1843.

662. Puhl, L. J., ed. *The Spiritual Exercises of St. Ignatius*. Westminster, Md., 1952.

663. Quasten, J. *Patrology*. Utrecht, 1950.

664. Quicherat, J. *Procès de condamnation et de réhabilitation de Jeanne d'Arc*. New York, 1960.

665. Rahner, K. *Theological Investigations*. 20 vols. New York, 1961–.

666. Raven, C. E. *Apollinarianism*. Cambridge, 1923.

667. Raymond of Capua. *The Life of Catherine of Siena*, trans. Conleath Kearns. Wilmington, Del., 1980.

668. Reckitt, M. B. *Maurice to Temple: A Century of the Social Movement in the Church of England*. London, 1947.

669. Redeker, M. *Schleiermacher: Life and Thought*. Philadelphia, 1973.

670. Redpath, H. M. D. *God's Ambassadress: St. Bridget of Sweden*. Milwaukee, 1947.

671. Reese, G. *Music in the Renaissance*. New York, 1959.

672. Reeve, B. *Timothy Richard*. London, 1912.

673. Reichelt, K. L. 'Buddhism in China at the Present Time and the New Challenge to the Christian Church'. *International Review of Missions*, 26 (1937).

674. Renan, E. *Oeuvres complètes*, ed. Henriette Psichari, 10 vols. Paris, 1947–61.

675. Renan, E. *The Memoirs of Ernest Renan*. London, 1935.

676. Reyes, I. de los, ed. *Catedra de la Iglesia Filipina Independente*. Manila, 1932.

677. Ricci, M. *China in the Sixteenth Century: The Journals of Matteo Ricci, 1583–1610*, trans. Louis Gallagher. New York, 1953.

678. Richard, J. 'L'Extrême-Orient au Moyen Age'. *Annales d'Ethiopie*, 2 (1957), pp. 225–44.

679. Richard, T. *Forty-five Years in China*. London, 1916.

680. Richards, J. *Consul of God: The Life and Times of Gregory the Great*. London, 1980.

681. Richardson, R. *Memoirs of Alexander Campbell*. 2 vols. Philadelphia, 1868–70.

682. Ride, L. *Robert Morrison: The Scholar and the Man*. Hong Kong, 1957.

683. Ridley, J. *Thomas Cranmer*. Oxford, 1962.

684. Ridolfi, R. *The Life of Girolamo Savonarola*, trans. Cecil Grayson. New York, 1959.

685. Ritschl, A. *Gesammelte Aufsätze*, ed. Otto Ritschl. 2 vols. Freiburg im Breisgau, 1893–6.

686. Ritschl, O. *Albrecht Ritschls Leben*. 2 vols. Freiburg im Breisgau, 1893–6.

687. Robbins, J. *Boardman of Burma*. Philadelphia, 1940.

688. Roberts, A. 'The Lumpa Church of Alice Lenshina'. In *Protest and Power in Black Africa*, ed. R. I. Rotberg and A. A. Mazrui. New York, 1970.

689. Robertson, A., ed. *Select Works and Letters of Athanasius*. A Select Library of Nicene and Post-Nicene Fathers of the Christian church, 2nd series, vol. 4. New York, 1892.

690. Robertson, J. C., and Sheppard, J. B. *Materials for the History of Thomas Becket*. 7 vols. Rolls Series. 1875–85.

691. Roche, J. *Palestrina*. London, 1971.

692. Roche, J. *Lassus*. London, 1982.

693. Rogness, M. *Philip Melanchthon: Reformer with Honour*. Minneapolis, 1969.

694. Rosen, E., ed. and trans. *Three Copernican Treatises: The Commentariolus of Copernicus, The Letter against Werner, The Narratio prima of Rheticus*. New York, 1971.

695. Ross, A. C. *John Philip (1775–1851): Missions, Race and Politics in South Africa*. Aberdeen, 1986.

696. Rotberg, R. I. *Christian Missionaries and the Creation of Northern Rhodesia, 1880–1924*. Princeton, NJ, 1965.

697. Rotberg, R. I. 'Plymouth Brethren and the Occupation of Katanga, 1886–1907'. *Journal of African History*, 5 (1964), pp. 285–97.

698. Rubanowice, R. J. *Crisis in Consciousness: The Thought of Ernst Troeltsch*. Tallahassee, 1982.
699. Rudolph, E. P. *William Law*. Boston, 1980.
700. Ruis-Camps, J. *The Four Authentic Letters of Ignatius, the Martyr*. Orientalia Christina Analecta, no. 123. Rome, 1980.
701. Rupp, E. G., and Drewery, B., eds. *Martin Luther*. New York, 1970.
702. Ryang, J. S., ed. *Southern Methodism in Korea*. Seoul, 1927. pp. 14–34.
703. Sadie, S. *Handel*. London, 1962.
704. Salvado, R. *The Salvado Memoirs*, trans. E. J. Stormon. Perth, 1977.
705. Sayer, F. D. *Julian and her Norwich: Commemorative Essays and Handbook to the Exhibition 'Revelations of Divine Love'*. Norwich, 1973.
706. Schaff, D. S., ed. *De Ecclesia: The Church, by John Hus*. 1915. Repr. Westport, Conn., 1974.
707. Schapera, T., ed. *Apprenticeship at Kumana, being the Journals and Letters of Robert and Mary Moffat, 1820–1828*. London, 1951.
708. Schillebeeckx, E. *Jesus*. New York, 1981.
709. Schleiermacher, F. D. E. *On Religion: Speeches to its Cultured Despisers*, trans. John Oman. New York, 1958.
710. Schleiermacher, F. D. E. *The Christian Faith*, ed. H. R. Mackintosh and J. S. Stewart. Edinburgh, 1968.
711. Schmidt, D. *Pastor Niemöller*, trans. Lawrence Wilson. London, 1959.
712. Schmitt, F. S. *S. Anselmi opera omnia*. 5 vols. Seckau, 1938–42. Repr. plus vol. 6. Edinburgh, 1946–61.
713. Schoedel, W. R. *Legatio and De Resurrectione*. Oxford, 1972.
714. Schultenover, D. G. *George Tyrrell: In Search of Catholicism*. Shepherdstown, W. Va., 1981.
715. Schurhammer, G., and Wicki, J. *Epistolae S. Francisci Xaverii aliaque eius scripta*. Monumenta historica Societatis Iesu, vols. 67–80. Rome, 1944–5.
716. Schurhammer, G. *Francis Xavier: His Life, His Times.*. 4 vols. Rome, 1973–82.
717. Schwartz, E. *Der Prozess des Eutyches*. Munich, 1929.
718. Schweitzer, A. *The Quest for the Historical Jesus*. London, 1911.
719. Scorraille, R. de. *François Suarez de la compagnie de Jésus*. 2 vols. Paris, 1912–13.
720. Scroggs, R. *Paul for a New Day*. Philadelphia, 1977.
721. Seaver, G. *David Livingstone: His Life and Letters*. London, 1957.
722. Seaver, G. *Albert Schweitzer: The Man and His Mind*. 6th edn. New York, 1969.
723. Sellers, R. V. *Two Ancient Christologies*. London, 1940.
724. Servetus, M. *The Two Treatises of Servetus on the Trinity*, trans. Earl Morse Wilbur. Harvard Theological Studies, no. 16. 1932. Repr. New York, 1969.
725. Sharpe, D. R. *Walter Rauschenbusch*. New York, 1942.
726. Sharpe, E. J. *J. N. Farquhar: A Memoir*. Calcutta, 1963.
727. Sharpe, E. J. *The Theology of A. G. Hogg*. Bangalore, 1971.
727a Sharpe, E. J. *Nathan Söderblom and the Study of Religion*. University of North Carolina Press, 1990.
728. Sharrock, R. *The Miscellaneous Works of John Bunyan*. Oxford, 1976–.
728a. Shenk, W. R. *Henry Venn – Missionary Statesman*. Maryknoll, NY: Orbis, 1983.
729. Shepperson, G., and Price, T. *Independent African: John Chilembwe and the Origins, Setting and Significance of the Nyasaland Native Rising of 1915*. Edinburgh, 1958.
730. Shook, L. K. *Étienne Gilson*. Toronto, 1984.
731. Sigstedt, C. S. *The Swedenborg Epic*. New York, 1952.
732. Simon, C. M. *A Seed Shall Serve: The Story of Toyohiko Kagawa, Spiritual Leader of Modern Japan*. New York, 1958.
733. Slade, C. *Approaches to Teaching Dante's Divine Comedy*. New York, 1982.
734. Smart, N., *et al.*, eds. *Nineteenth Century Religious Thought in the West*. 3 vols. Cambridge, 1985.
735. Smith, A. C. *The Essentials of Missiology from the Evangelical Perspective of the Fraternidad Teológica Latinoamericana*. PhD diss., Southern Baptist Theological Seminary, Louisville, 1983.
736. Smith, E. W. *Aggrey of Africa: A Study in Black and White*. London, 1929.
737. Smith, Jr, J. *History of the Church of Jesus Christ of Latter-Day Saints*. 6 vols. 2nd edn, rev. B. H. Roberts. Salt Lake City, 1950.
738. Smith, L. M. *Biographical Sketches of Joseph Smith the Prophet*. 1853. Repr. New York, 1969.
739. Smith, W. T. *Augustine: His Life and*

Thought. Atlanta, 1980.
740. *Socini opera*. Bibliotheca Fratrum Polonorum quos Unitarios vocant, vols. 1–2. Amsterdam, 1656.
741. Soderini, E. *The Pontificate of Leo XIII*. 2 vols. London, 1934–5.
742. Sohier, A., ed. *Lettres du P. Lebbe*. Tournai, 1960.
743. Soothill, W. E. *Timothy Richard of China*. London, 1924.
744. Southern, R. W. *Saint Anselm and his Biographer: A Study of Monastic Life and Thought, 1059–1130*. Cambridge, 1963.
745. Spener, P. J. *Theologische Bedencken*. 4 vols. in 2. Halle, 1700–1702. *Letzte theologische Bedencken*, ed. Karl Hildebrand von Canstein. 3 vols. Halle, 1711.
746. Spink, K. *For the Brotherhood of Man under the Fatherhood of God*. New Malden, 1981.
747. Spinka, M. *John Hus: A Biography*. Princeton, NJ, 1968.
748. Spinka, M. *John Hus at the Council of Constance*. New York, 1965.
749. Spurgeon, C. H. *Autobiography*. Vol. 1: *The Early Years, 1834–1859*. London, 1962. Vol. 2: *The Full Harvest, 1860–1892*. Edinburgh, 1973.
750. St.John, P. *Breath of Life*. London, 1971.
751. Stannage, T. 'Bishop Salvado: A Review of the Memoirs'. In *European-Aboriginal Relations in Western Australian History*, ed. B. Reece and T. Stannage. Perth, 1984. pp. 33–55.
752. Steere, D. V. *God's Irregular: Arthur Shearley Cripps*. London, 1973.
753. Steere, D. V., ed. *Spiritual Counsels and Letters of Baron Friedrich von Hügel*. London, 1964.
754. Stevenson, R. *Spanish Cathedral Music in the Golden Age*. Berkeley, 1961.
755. Stiller, G. *Johann Sebastian Bach and Liturgical Life in Leipzig*. St Louis, 1948.
756. Stone, R. H. *Reinhold Niebuhr: Prophet to Politicians*. Nashville, 1972.
757. Stoudt, J. J. *Sunrise to Eternity*. Philadelphia, 1957.
758. Strachan, C. G. *The Pentecostal Theology of Edward Irving*. London, 1973.
759. Strachey, L. *Eminent Victorians*. London, 1918.
760. Streeter, B. H., and Appasamy, A. J. *The Sadhu*. London, 1921.
761. Strehlow, C. *Die Aranda- und Loritjastamme in Zentral-Australien*. 5 vols. Frankfurt, 1907.
762. Strehlow, T. G. H. *Journey to Horseshoe Bend*. Sydney, 1969.
763. Stupperich, R. *Martin Bucers deutsche Schriften*. 6 vols. Gütersloh, 1960–.
764. Stupperich, R. *Bibliographia Bucerana*. Gütersloh, 1952.
765. Sundkler, B. G. M. *Zulu Zion*. London, 1976.
766. Sundkler, B. G. M. *Bantu Prophets in South Africa*. 2nd edn. Oxford, 1961.
767. Swete, H. B. *Theodore of Mopsuestia on the Minor Epistles of S. Paul*. 2 vols. Cambridge, 1880–82.
768. Swidler, L. *Küng in Conflict*. New York, 1981.
769. Swidler, L., ed. *Consensus in Theology? A Dialogue with Hans Küng and Edward Schillebeeckx*. Philadelphia, 1980.
770. Talbert, C. H., ed. *Reimarus: Fragments*, trans. Ralph S. Fraser. London, 1971.
771. Talbot, C. H., ed. and trans. *The Anglo-Saxon Missionaries in Germany*. New York, 1954.
772. Talbot, C. H. *The Anglo-Saxon Missionaries in Germany*. New York, 1954.
773. Tangl, M., ed. *Bonifacius: Die Briefe des heiligen Bonifacius und Lullus*. Vol. 1. Berlin, 1916.
774. Tasie, G. O. M. 'The Prophetic Calling, Garrick Sokari Braide of Bakana'. In *Varieties of Christian Experience in Nigeria*, ed. E. Isichei. London, 1982. pp. 99–115.
774a. Tasie, G. O. M. *Christian Missionary Enterprise in the Niger Delta 1864–1918*. Leiden: Brill, 1977.
775. Tavard, G. H. *Transiency and Permanence: The Nature of Theology According to St Bonaventure*. New York, 1954.
776. Taylor, C. *Hegel*. New York, 1975.
777. Taylor, R. W. *The Contribution of E. Stanley Jones*. Madras, 1973.
778. Taylor, V. *The Gospel According to Mark*. London, 1952.
779. Taylor, W. *The Story of My Life*. New York, 1896.
780. Telfer, W. *Cyril of Jerusalem and Nemesius of Emesu*. London, 1955.
781. Temple, F. S., ed. *Some Lambeth Letters, 1942–1944*. London, 1963.
782. Terry, C. S. *Bach's Biography*. London, 1928.
783. Tertullian. *Corpus Christianorum*. Series Latina, vols. 1–2. Turnhout, Belgium, 1954.
784. Tertullian. *The Ante-Nicene Fathers*. Vols.

3–4. Grand Rapids, Mich., 1956.
785. Thelle, N. N. *Karl Ludvig Reichelt*. Oslo, 1959.
786. Theodore of Mopsuestia. In *Patrologia Graeca*, ed. J.-P. Migne. Vol. 66. Paris, 1860.
787. Thomas, M. M. *Man and the Universe of Faiths*. Bangalore, 1975.
788. Thomas, M. M. *The Acknowledged Christ of the Indian Renaissance*. Madras, 1970.
789. Thomas, M. M. *Some Theological Dialogues*. Bangalore, 1977.
790. Thomas, W. T. *Protestant Beginnings in Japan, 1859–1889*. Tokyo, 1959.
791. Thomas Aquinas. *Opera omnia*. 48 vols. Vatican City, 1882–.
792. Thomas Aquinas. *On the Truth of the Catholic Faith*, ed. and trans. Anton C. Pegis. 4 vols. in 5. New York, 1955–7.
793. Thompson, L. *Survival in Two Worlds: Moshoeshoe of Lesotho, 1786–1870*. Oxford, 1975.
794. Thomson, S. H., and Thomson, W. R. *The Latin Writings of John Wyclif: An Annotated Catalog*. Toronto, 1983.
795. Tibesar, A., ed. *The writings of Junipero Serra*. 4 vols. Washington, DC, 1955–66.
796. Tilak, L. *I Follow After*, trans. E. J. Inkster. Delhi, 1900. Abridged edn as *From Brahma to Christ*. London, 1956.
797. Tillich, P. *On the Boundary*. London, 1967.
798. Tillich, P. *Main Works/Hauptwerke*. Vol. 4: *Writings in the Philosophy of Religion*, ed. John Clayton. Berlin, 1987. Vol. 5: *Writings on Religion*, ed. Robert Scharlemann. Berlin, 1988.
799. Tillmann, H. *Pope Innocent III*, trans. Walter Sax. New York, 1980.
800. Timothy Ailuros. *Patrologia Graeca*, ed. J.-P. Migne. Vol. 86, pt. 1. Paris, 1860.
801. Tinker, H. *The Ordeal of Love: C. F. Andrews and India*. London, 1980.
802. Tintori, L., and Borsook, E. *Giotto: The Peruzzi Chapel*. New York, 1965.
803. Tobert, R. *Venture of Faith*. Philadelphia, 1955.
804. Tolnay, C. de. *Michelangelo*. 2nd edn. 5 vols. Princeton, NJ, 1969–71.
805. Tommaseo, N., ed. and trans. *Le Lettere di S. Caterina da Siena*, rev. Piero Misciattelli. 1860. Repr. Florence, 1940.
806. Torrance, T. F. *Karl Barth: An Introduction to his Early Theology, 1910–1931*. London, 1962.
807. Townsend, W. *Robert Morrison, the Pioneer of Chinese Missions*. London, 1888.
808. Trevor, M. *Newman: Light in Winter*. 2 vols. New York, 1962.
809. Trevor-Roper, H. R. *Archbishop Laud, 1573–1645*. London, 1940.
810. Trochu, F. *Saint Bernadette Soubirous, 1844–1879*, trans. John Joyce. London, 1957.
811. Trompf, G. W., with Aerts, T. 'The Catholic Missions'. In G. W. Trompf, *Melanesian Religion*. Cambridge, 1990.
812. Turberville, A. S. *The Spanish Inquisition*. 1931. Repr. London, 1949.
813. Turner, H. W. *Religious Innovation in Africa: Collected Essays on New Religious Movements*. Boston, 1979.
814. Turner, H. W. *African Independent Church*. 2 vols. Oxford, 1967.
815. Tyrrell, G. *The Faith of the Millions*. 2 vols. New York, 1901.
816. Tyrrell, G. *Through Scylla and Charybdis*. London, 1907.
817. *Uchimura Kanzo zenshu*. 38 vols. Tokyo, 1981–84.
818. Umoh, J. U., and Ekanem, A. *Olumba Olumba Obu, the Mystery Man of Biakpan*. Vol. 1: Brotherhood of the Cross and Star, Facts you Must Know. Calabar, 1979.
819. Varetto, J. C. *Diego Thomson*. Buenos Aires, 1918.
820. Vermès, G. *Jesus the Jew: A Historian's Reading of the Gospels*. London, 1976.
821. Vian, N. *Anni e opere di Paolo VI*. Rome, 1978.
822. Vicaire, M.-H. *Saint Dominic and his Times*, trans. Kathleen Pond. London, 1964.
823. Vickers, J. A. *Thomas Coke, Apostle of Methodism*. Nashville, 1969.
824. Vidler, A. *The Theology of F. D. Maurice*. London, 1948.
825. Vidler, A. R. *The Modernist Movement in the Roman Church*. Cambridge, 1934.
826. Villa-Vicencio, C., and De Gruchy, J. W., eds. *Resistance and Hope: South African Essays in Honour of Beyers Naudé*. Grand Rapids, Mich., 1985.
827. Visser't Hooft, W. A. *Memoirs*. London, 1973.
828. Visser't Hooft, W. A. *No Other Name*. London, 1963.
829. Vivès, L., ed. *John Duns Scotus: Opera omnia*. Paris, 1891–5.
830. Vogüé, A. de. *Dialogues: Grégoire le Grand*. In Sources chrétiennes, vols. 251,

260, 265. Paris, 1978–80.
831. Vogüé, A. de. *Le Règle de Saint Benoît*. 7 vols. Paris, 1971–7.
832. Vorgrimler, H. *Karl Rahner: His Life, Thought and Works*. London, 1966.
833. Walker, S. S. *The Religious Revolution in the Ivory Coast*. Chapel Hill, NC, 1983.
834. Walker, W. *Ten New England Leaders*. Chicago, 1901.
835. Wallace, L. P. *Leo XIII and the Rise of Socialism*. Durham, NC, 1966.
836. Wallis, J. P. R., ed. *The Matabele Journals of Robert Moffat, 1829–1860*. London, 1945.
837. Wallmann, J. *Philipp Jakob Spener und die Anfänge des Pietismus*. Tübingen, 1970.
838. Walsh, C. *The Literary Legacy of C. S. Lewis*. London, 1979.
839. Walsh, J. *The Mind of Paul VI on the Church and the World*. Milwaukee, 1964.
840. Ward, W. E. F. *Fraser of Trinity and Achimota*. Accra, 1965.
841. Warner, M. *Alone of All Her Sex: The Myth and Cult of the Virgin Mary*. New York, 1976.
841a. Warren, M. (ed). *To Apply the Gospel. Selections from the writings of Henry Venn* Grand Rapids: Eerdmans, 1971.
842. Watt, P. M. *Nicolaus Cusanus: A Fifteenth-Century Vision of Man*. Leiden, 1982.
843. Waugh, E. *Edmund Campion*. 1935. 3rd edn. London, 1961.
844. Wayland, F. *A Memoir of the Life and Labours of the Rev. A. Judson*. 2 vols. London, 1853.
845. Webb, C. C. *Kant's Philosophy of Religion*. Oxford, 1926.
846. Weber, R., *et al. Sancti Cypriani episcopi opera*. 2 vols. Corpus Christianorum, Seria Latina, 3, 3A. Turnhout, Belgium, 1972–6.
847. Webster, J. B. *The African Churches among the Yoruba, 1888–1922*. Oxford, 1964.
848. Weinstein, D. *Savonarola and Florence: Prophecy and Patriotism in the Renaissance*. Princeton, NJ, 1970.
849. Weisheipl, J. A. *Friar Thomas d'Aquino: His Life, Thought and Works*. 1974. Repr. Washington, DC, 1983.
850. Welbourn, F., and Ogot, B. A. *A Place to Feel at Home: A Study of Two Independent Churches in Western Kenya*. London, 1966.
851. Wenger, J. C., ed. *The Complete Writings of Menno Simons, c.1496–1561*. Scottdale, Pa., 1956.
852. Wesley, C. *Richard Allen, Apostle of Freedom*. 2nd edn. Washington, DC, 1969.
853. Westman, R. S. *The Copernican Achievement*. Berkeley, 1975.
854. White, A., and Taylor, L. S. *Shakerism: Its Meaning and Message*. Columbus, Ohio, 1904.
855. White, A. L. *Ellen G. White*. Projected 6 vols. Vol. 5: *1900–1905*. Washington, DC, 1981–.
856. White, E. G. *Life Sketches of Ellen G. White*. Mountain View, Cal., 1915.
857. *White, Ellen G., Comprehensive Index to the Writings of*. Mountain View, Cal., 1962–3.
858. White, G. A. *Simone Weil: Interpretations of a Life*. Amherst, Mass., 1981.
859. Whitefield, G. *Journals*. London, 1960.
860. Whittemore, L. B. *Struggle for Freedom*. Greenwich, Conn., 1961.
861. Wiedemann, T. *Dr. Johann Eck, Professor der Theologie an der Universität Ingolstadt*. Regensburg, 1865.
862. Wietzke, J. *Theologie im modernen Indien: P. D. Devanandan*. Bern, 1973.
863. Williams, A. L. *Dialogue with Trypho*. London, 1930.
864. Williams, C. *The Figure of Beatrice*. London, 1958.
865. Williams, D. *Ufumdisi: A Biography of Tiyo Soga, 1829–1871*. Lovedale, SA, 1978.
866. Williams, D. *The Journal and Selected Writings of the Reverend Tiyo Soga*. Cape Town, 1983.
867. Williams, G. H. *The Radical Reformation*. Philadelphia, 1962.
868. Williams, G. H. 'The Christological Issues between Francis Dávid and Faustus Socinus during the Disputation on the Invocation of Christ, 1578–1579'. In *Antitrinitarianism in the Second Half of the Sixteenth Century*, ed. R. Dán and A. Pirnát. Leiden, 1982. pp. 287–321.
869. Wilson, B. R. *Magic and the Millennium*. London, 1973.
870. Wingate, J. S. *Jesus Son*. New York, 1947.
871. Wingren, G. *Man and the Incarnation: A Study in the Biblical Theology of Irenaeus*, trans. Ross Mackenzie. Edinburgh, 1959.
871a. Wink, W. *John the Baptist in the Gospel Tradition*. Cambridge, 1968.
872. Winn, H. E. *Wyclif: Select English Writings*. Oxford, 1929.
873. Winslow, O. E. *John Eliot, 'Apostle to the Indians'*. Boston, 1968.
874. Winter, D. *Hope in Captivity: The Prophetic Church in Latin America*. London, 1977.
875. Wojtowytsch, M. *Papsttum und Konzile*

von den Anfängen bis zu Leo I, 440–461: Studien zur Entstehung der Überordnung des Papstes über Konzile. Stuttgart, 1981.

876. Wolter, A. B. *Duns Scotus on the Will and Morality*. Washington, DC, 1986.
877. Wolter, A. B. *Duns Scotus: Philosophical Writings*. Edinburgh, 1962.
878. Wood, C. T. *Philip the Fair and Boniface VIII*. 2nd edn. London, 1971.
879. Workman, H. B. *John Wyclif: A Study of the English Medieval Church*. 2 vols. Oxford, 1926.
880. Wright, M. *German Missions in Tanganyika, 1891–1941*. Oxford, 1971.
881. Wright, R. S., ed. *Fathers of the Kirk*. London, 1960. pp. 37–48.

881a. Yates, T. E. *Venn and Victorian Bishops Abroad*. London: SPCK, 1978.

882. Zahn-Harnack, A. von. *Adolf von Harnack*. 2nd edn. Berlin, 1951.
883. Zeller, E., ed. *Gesammelete Schriften von David Friedrich Strauss*. 12 vols. Bonn, 1876–8.
884. Zissis, T. *Gennadios II Scholarios: Bios, sungrammata, didaskalia*. Thessalonica, 1980.
885. Zwemer, S. M. *Studies in Popular Islam*. New York, 1939.
886. Zwemer, S. M. *The Cross above the Crescent*. Grand Rapids, Mich., 1940.
887. Zwingli, U. *Huldreich Zwingli Sämtliche Werke*, 14 vols. Corpus Reformatorum, vols. 88–101. Berlin, Leipzig, Zurich, 1905–59.
888. Zyzykin, M. V. *Patriarkh Nikon: Ego gosudarstvennye i kanonicheskie idei*. Warsaw, 1931–8.

[VI.B]
Compiled by D. Melling

1. Allen, J. L., ed. *An Orthodox Synthesis*. New York: SVS, 1981.
2. Andrews, E. D. *The People Called Shakers*. New York: Dover, 1963.
3. Anon. *The Church of Ethiopia*. Addis Ababa: Ethiopian Orthodox Church, 1970.
4. Athanasius, St. *Life of Antony-Letter to Marcellus*. London: SPCK, 1987.
5. Atiya, A. S. *A History of Eastern Christianity*. London: Methuen, 1968.
6. Atkinson, C. W. *Mystic and Pilgrim: The Book and World of Margery Kempe*. London, 1983.
7. Aubert, R. *Le Pontificat de Pie IX, 1846–1875*. Histoire de l'Eglise, ed. Fliche and Martin, vol. 21. Paris, 1952.
8. Ayad, B. 'Currents in Coptic Church Studies'. *Coptic Church Review*, 9 (1988).
9. Balthasar, U. von. *Kosmische Liturgie, Das Weltbild Maximus des Bekenners*. 2nd edn. Einsiedeln, 1961.
10. Bamberger, J. E., trans. *The Praktikos: Chapters on Prayer* (Evagrius). Spencer, Mass.: Cistercian Publications, 1970.
11. Basilli, M. and A. *Pope Kirellous VI*. London: St Mark, 1986.
12. Berthold, G. *Maximos Confessor: Selected Writings*. London, 1985.
13. Bregman, J. *Synesius of Cyrene*. Berkeley: University of California Press, 1982.
14. Brianchaninov, I. *On The Prayer of Jesus*, trans. Father Lazarus. Shaftesbury, Dorset: Element Books, 1987.
15. Brock, S. *St. Ephrem the Syrian: Hymns on Paradise*. New York, 1990.
16. Brock, S. *The Luminous Eye: The Spiritual World Vision of St Ephrem*. Rome, 1985.
17. Cabasilas, N. *Commentary on the Divine Liturgy*, trans. J. M. Hussey and P. A. McNulty. London: SPCK, 1960.
18. Cabasilas, N. *The Life in Christ*, trans. C. J. de Catanzaro. New York: Saint Vladimir Seminary (SVS), 1974.
19. Catanzaro, J. de. *Symeon the New Theologian: The Discourses*. London, 1982.
20. Cavarnos, C. *St Nectarios of Aegina*. Mass.: Institute of Byzantine and Modern Greek Studies, (IBMGS), 1988.
21. Cavarnos, C. *St Cosmas Aetolos*. Mass.: IBMGS, 1971.
22. Cavarnos, C. *St Nicodemos the Hagiorite*. Mass.: IBMGS, 1973.
23. Cavarnos, C. *St Macarios of Corinth*. Mass.: IBMGS, 1972.
24. Cooper, D. J. C. 'Eastern Churches and the Reformation in the Sixteenth and Seventeenth Centuries'. *Scottish Journal of Theology*, 31/5 (1978).
25. Davey, C. 'Anglicans and Eastern Christendom'. *Sobornost*, 7/2 (1985).
26. Dawes, E., and Baynes, N. *Three Byzantine Saints*. London: Mowbrays, 1977.
27. De Beausobre, I. *Russian letters of Direction, 1834–1860, Marcarius, Starets of Optino*. New York: SVS, 1975.
28. Dillon, J. *The Middle Platonists*. London: Duckworth, 1977.
29. Drummond, R. H. *History of Christianity in Japan*. Michigan, 1971.

30. Dunlop, J. B. *Staretz Amvrosy*. London: Mowbrays, 1972.
31. Dvornik, F. *The Photian Schism*. Cambridge, 1948.
32. Fedotov, G. P. *The Russian Religious Mind*. Vol. 2. Cambridge, Mass., 1962.
33. Fedotov, G. P. *A Treasury of Russian Spirituality*. Sheed & Ward, 1950.
34. Fleming, S. 'Islamic Science in Baghdad: A Greek Inheritance'. *Archeology*, 38/4 (1985).
35. Frend, W. H. C. *The Rise of the Monophysite Movement*. Cambridge, 1972.
36. Gill, J. *The Council of Florence*. Cambridge, 1959.
37. Gill, J. *Personalities of the Council of Florence*. Oxford: Blackwell, 1964.
38. Gingras, G. E. *Egeria: Diary of a Pilgrimage*. New York, 1970.
39. Golder, F. A. *Father Herman, Alaska's Saint*. Platina, Cal., 1968.
40. Grisbrook, W. Jardine. *The Spiritual Counsels of Father John of Kronstadt*. New York: SVS, 1981.
42. Guillaumont, A. *Les 'Kephalaia Gnostica d'Evagre le Pontique et l'Histoire de l'Origenisme chez les Syriens*. Paris, 1962.
43. Hansbury, M. *St. Isaac of Nineveh: On Ascetical Life*. New York, 1990.
44. Herrin, J. *The Formation of Christendom*. Oxford: Blackwell, 1987.
45. Hussey, J. M. *The Orthodox Church in the Byzantine Empire*. London: Oxford University Press, 1986.
46. Johnson, W. *The Mysticism of the Cloud of Unknowing*. Wheathampstead, 1978.
47. Kelly, J. N. D. *The Oxford Dictionary of the Popes*. London: Oxford University Press, 1986.
48. Kontzevich, I. M. *Optina Monastery and its Era*. Platina, Cal., 1970.
49. Kontzevich, I. M. *The Northern Thebaid*. Platina, Cal., 1975.
50. Kotter, B., ed. *Die Schriften des Johannes von Damaskos*. Berlin, 1969.
51. Krivocheine, B. *In the Light of Christ: St Simeon the New Theologian*. New York, 1986.
52. Lagorio, V. M., and Bradley, R. *The Fourteenth Century English Mystics: A Comprehensive Annotated Bibliography*. London, 1981.
53. Long, A. A., and Seedley, D. N. *The Hellenistic Philosophers*. 2 vols. Cambridge, 1987.
54. Lough, A. *Denys the Aeropagite*. London: Geoffrey Chapman, 1989.
55. Markus, R., and John, E. *Papacy and Hierarchy*. London: Sheed and Ward, 1969.
56. McCullough, W. S. *A Short History of Syriac Christianity to the Rise of Islam*. Chico, Cal.: Scholars Press, 1982.
57. McKitterick, R. *The Frankish Kingdoms under the Carolingians, 751–989*. London, 1983.
58. McVey, K. E. *Ephrem the Syrian: Hymns*. London, 1989.
59. Metrophanes (Schemamonk). *Paisius Velichkovsky*. Platina, Cal., 1976.
60. Meyendorff, J. *The Church in History*. Vol. 2: *Imperial Unity and Christian Divisions*. New York: St Vladimir's Seminary Press, 1989.
61. Meyendorff, J. *The Byzantine Legacy in the Orthodox Church*. New York: SVS, 1982.
62. Miller, D. *Ascetical Homilies of St Isaac of Nineveh*. Boston, 1984.
63. Mitchell, R. J. *The Laurels and the Tiara*. London: Harvill, 1962.
64. Nasrallah, J. *Saint Jean de Damas, son époque, sa vie, son oeuvre*. Harissa, 1950.
65. Nikodemus, St. *Neon Martyrologion*. Athens: Astir, 1961.
66. Obolensky, D. *Six Byzantine Portraits*. London: Oxford University Press, 1988.
67. Origen. *Origen contra celsum*, trans. and ed. H. Chadwick. Corrected edn. Cambridge, 1965.
68. Ostrogorsky, G. *History of the Byzantine State*. Oxford: Blackwell, 1968.
69. Palmer, G. E. H., Sherrard, P., and Ware, K., trans. *Philokalia*. Vol. 1. London: Faber & Faber, 1979.
70. Parry, K. 'Theodore Studites and the Patriarch Nicephoros on Image-Making as a Christian Imperative'. *Byzantion*, 59 (1989).
71. Richards, J. *The Popes and the Papacy in the Early Middle Ages*. London: Routledge & Kegan Paul, 1979.
72. Rist, J. M. *Stoic Philosophy*. Cambridge, 1969.
73. Rosenquist, J. O. *The Life of St Irene, Abbess of Chrysobalanton*. Uppsala, 1986.
74. Runciman, S. *The Eastern Schism: A Study of the Papacy and the Eastern Churches during the XIth and XII Centuries*. Cambridge, 1955.
75. Runciman, S. *The Fall of Constantinople, 1453*. Cambridge, 1965.
76. Runciman, S. *The Great Church in Captivity*. Cambridge, 1968.
77. Sahas, J. *John of Damascus on Islam: The Heresy of the Ishmaelites*. Leiden, 1972.

78. Segal, J. B. *Edessa 'The Blessed City'*. Oxford, 1970.
79. Sigmund, P. E. 'The Catholic Tradition and Modern Democracy'. *Review of Politics* (1987).
80. Smirnoff, E. *Russian Orthodox Missions*. Welshpool: Stylite, 1986.
81. Smith, B. S. *Orthodoxy and Native Americans: The Alaskan Mission*. New York: SVS, 1980.
82. Sofrony, Archimandrite. *The Undistorted Image*, trans. R. Edmonds. London: Faith Press, 1958.
83. Sophrony, Arch. *Wisdom from Mount Athos*. New York: SVS, 1974.
84. Sophrony, Arch. *The Monk of Mount Athos: Staretz Silouan*. New York: SVS, 1973.
85. Stuart, J. *Ikons*. London: Faber & Faber, 1975.
86. Thunberg, L. *Man and the Cosmos: the Vision of St Maximus the Confessor*. New York, 1985.
87. Tsirpanlis, C. N. *Mark Eugenicus and the Council of Florence*. Center for Byzantine Studies, 1979.
88. Turner, H. J. M. *St. Symeon the New Theologian and Spiritual Fatherhood*. Leiden, 1990.
89. Ullmann, W. *The Growth of Papal Government in the Middle Ages*. 3rd edn. London, 1970.
90. Velimirovich, N. *The Life of St Sava*. New York: SVS, 1989.
91. Vogt, J. *Constantin der Grosse und sein Jahrhundert*. Munich, 1960.
92. Voobus, A. *History of Asceticism in the Syrian Orient*. Vol. 2: *Early Monasticism in Mesopotamia and Syria*. CSCO, 184, subsid. 14. Louvain, 1958.
93. Voobus, A. *History of the School of Nisibis*. CSCO 266, subsid. 26. Louvain, 1960.
94. Voobus, A. *Literary, Critical and Historical Studies in Ephrem the Syrian*. PETSE 10. Stockholm, 1958.
95. Wensinck, A. J. *Mystic Treatises by Isaac of Nineveh*. Wiesbaden, 1969.
96. Whitson, R. E. *The Shakers*. London: SPCK, 1983.
97. Wilson, N. G. *Scholars of Byzantium*. London: Duckworth, 1983.
98. Zander, V. *St Seraphim of Sarov*. London: SPCK, 1975.
99. Zander, V. *The Pilgrimage to St. Seraphim's Monasteries*. Walsingham: St Seraphim, 1988.
100. Ziese, J. *Wibert von Ravenna: der Gegenpapst Clemens III (1084–1100)*. Stuttgart: Hiersemann, 1982.

[VII] Egyptian Religion, Ancient

Compiled by A. Rosalie David

1. Balout, L., and Roubet, C., ed. *La Momie de Ramsès II*. Paris, 1985.
2. *The Bible*. Book 1: *Genesis*; Book 2: *Exodus*.
3. Bowman, A. K. *Egypt after the Pharaohs*. London, 1986.
4. Carter, H. *The Tomb of Tutankhamun*. 3 vols. London, 1923–33.
5. Černý, J. *A Community of Workmen at Thebes in the Ramesside Period*. Cairo, 1973.
6. David, A. R. *A Guide to Religious Ritual at Abydos*. Warminster, 1981.
7. Davies, N. de G. *The Rock Tombs of El-Amarna*. 6 vols. London, 1903–8.
8. Diodorus of Sicily, *The Library of History*. 12 vols. Loeb Classical Library. London and Cambridge.
9. Drioton, É. 'Sur la Sagesse d'Aménémopé'. In *Mélanges Bibliques rédigés en l'honneur de André Robert*, ed. H. Cazelles. Paris, 1957. pp. 254–80.
10. Edwards, I. E. S. *The Pyramids of Egypt*. Harmondsworth, 1985.
11. Emery, W. B. *Archaic Egypt*. Harmondsworth, 1972.
12. Erman, A. *The Ancient Egyptians: A Sourcebook of their Writings*. Introduction W. K. Simpson. New York, 1966.
13. Glanville, S. R. K. *Catalogue of Demotic Papyri in the British Museum*. Vol. 2: *The Instructions of Onchsheshonqy (British Museum Papyrus 10508)*. London, 1955.
14. Griffiths, J. G. *Plutarch: De Iside et Osiride*. Cardiff, 1970.
15. Helck, W. *Die Prophezeiung des Nfr.tj*. Wiesbaden, 1970.
16. Helck, W. *Die Lehre des Dw3-Ḫtjj*. Wiesbaden, 1970.
17. Herodotus. *The Histories*, trans. A. de Sélincourt. Harmondsworth, 1961.
18. Kitchen, K. A. *Pharaoh Triumphant: The Life and Times of Ramesses II*. Warminster, 1987.
19. Lichtheim, M. *Ancient Egyptian Literature*. 3 vols. Los Angeles, 1975–80.
20. *Manetho*, trans. W. G. Waddell. Loeb Classical Library. London, 1940.
21. Osman, A. *Stranger in the Valley of the Kings*.

London, 1987.
22. Otto, E. *Egyptian Art and the Cults of Osiris and Amun.* London, 1966.
23. Pendlebury, J. D. S. *Tell el Amarna.* London, 1935.
24. Simpson, D. C. 'The Hebrew Book of Proverbs and the Teaching of Amenophes'. *Journal of Egyptian Archaeology*, 12 (1926), pp. 232–41.
25. Smith, R. W., and Redford, D. B. *The Akhenaten Temple Project. Vol. 1 Initial Discoveries.* Warminster, 1976.
26. Rowley, H. H. *From Joseph to Joshua.* London, 1950.
27. Van Seters, J. *The Hyksos.* New Haven, 1966.
28. Vergote, J. *Joseph en Egypte.* Louvain, 1959.
29. Williams, R. J. 'The Alleged Semitic Original of the Wisdom of Amenemope'. *Journal of Egyptian Archaeology*, 47 (1961), pp. 100–106.
30. Zaba, Z. *Les Maximes de Ptahhotep.* Prague, 1956.

[VIII] European Religions, Ancient
Compiled by H. Ellis Davidson

1. Walser, G. 'Veleda'. In *Realencyclopädie der classicschen Altertums-wissenschaft*, ed. Paulys. 2nd edn. Stuttgart, 1955.
2. Cathasaigh, D. O. 'The Cult of Brigid'. In *Mother Worship*, ed. J. J. Preston. University of N. Carolina Press, 1982.
3. Turville-Petre, E. O. G. *Myth and Religion of the North.* London, 1964.
4. Jones, G. *History of the Vikings.* 2nd edn. London: Oxford University Press, 1984.
5. Strömbäck, D. *The Conversion of Iceland*, trans. P. Foote. London: Viking Society, University College, 1975.
6. Roesdahl, E. *Viking Age Denmark.* London: British Museum, 1982.
7. Johannesson, J. *History of the Old Icelandic Commonwealth*, trans. H. Bessason. University of Manitoba, 1974.
8. Robinson, C. H. *Anskar, Apostle of the North.* London, 1921.
9. Piggott, S. *The Druids.* London, 1968.

[IX] Gnosticism
Compiled by George Brooke

See also entries for Marcion and Montanus under Christianity and the separate entry for Mani.

1. Buckley, J. J. *Female Fault and Fulfilment in Gnosticism.* Chapel Hill: University of North Carolina Press, 1986.
2. Faye, E. De. *Gnostiques et Gnosticisme.* Rev. edn. Paris: P. Geuthner, 1925.
3. Foerster, W. *Gnosis.* 2 vols. Oxford: Clarendon Press, 1972–4.
4. Jonas, H. *The Gnostic Religion.* Enlarged edn. Boston: Beacon Press, 1963.
5. Layton, B., ed. *The Rediscovery of Gnosticism.* Vol. 1: *The School of Valentinus.* Leiden: E. J. Brill, 1980.
6. Layton, B. *The Gnostic Scriptures.* Garden City, NY: Doubleday, 1987.
7. Pagels, E. *The Gnostic Gospels.* New York: Random House, 1979.
8. Robinson, J. M., ed. *The Nag Hammadi Library in English.* 3rd edn. Leiden: E. J. Brill, 1988.
9. Rudolph, K. *Gnosis: The Nature and History of an Ancient Religion.* San Francisco: Harper & Row, 1983.
10. Wilson, R. McL. *The Gnostic Problem.* London: Mowbray, 1958.

[X] Greek Religion, Ancient
Compiled by John P. Kane

The first part of this bibliography lists modern scholarly works on Greek religion and on the individuals discussed. The second part, from item 42, lists translations of the ancient texts themselves. The *Penguin Classics* paperback translations are especially recommended. Sometimes more than one translation of the same work has been listed: particularly in the case of the *Iliad* it is useful to use both the older one (Rieu) and the newer (Hammond).

1. Bailey, C. *The Greek Atomists and Epicurus.* Oxford, 1928.
2. Burkert, W. *Lore and Science in Ancient Pythagoreanism.* Cambridge, Mass., 1972.
3. Burkert, W. *Greek Religion.* Oxford: Blackwell, 1985.
4. Burkert, W. 'Craft Versus Sect: The Problem of Orphics and Pythagoreans'. In *Jewish and Christian Self-Definition*, vol. 3, ed. B. F. Meyer and E. B. Sanders. Philadel-

phia: Fortress Press, 1982.
5. Demoulin, H. *Epimenide de Crete*. Repr. New York: Arno, 1979.
6. Dodds, E. R. *The Greeks and the Irrational*. Repr. Berkeley: University of California Press, 1959.
7. Dragona-Monachou, M. *Stoic Arguments for the Existence and the Providence of the Gods*. Athens, 1976.
8. Edelstein, E. J. and L. *Asclepius*. 2 vols. Baltimore: Johns Hopkins University Press, 1945.
9. Eliade, M. *Zalmoxis: the Vanishing God*. Chicago: University of Chicago Press, 1972.
10. Evans, J. D. G. *Aristotle*. New York: St. Martin's Press, 1987.
11. Festugière, A.-J. *Personal Religion among the Greeks*. Berkeley: University of California Press, 1954.
12. Festugière, A.-J. *Epicurus and his Gods*. Oxford: Blackwell, 1955: rev. French edn, 1968.
13. Finley, M. I. *The World of Odysseus*. 2nd edn. London: Chatto & Windus, 1977.
14. Frazer, R. M. *The Poems of Hesiod*. Norman, University of Oklahoma Press, 1983.
15. Gernet, L., and Boulanger, A. *Le Génie grec dans la religion*. Paris, 1932. Repr. with new bibliography, 1970.
16. Grant, M. *Myths of the Greeks and Romans*. 2nd edn. New York, 1987.
17. Griffin, J. *Homer on Life and Death*. Oxford: Clarendon Press, 1980.
18. Griffin, J. *Homer: the Odyssey*. Cambridge: Cambridge University Press, 1987.
19. Guthrie, W. K. C. *The Greeks and their Gods*. London: Methuen, 1950.
20. Guthrie, W. K. C. *A History of Greek Philosophy*. 6 vols. Cambridge: Cambridge University Press, 1962–.
21. Halliday, W. R. *Greek Divination*. London, 1913.
22. Hamilton, M. *Incubation and the Cure of Disease in Pagan Temples and Christian Churches*. St Andrews: Henderson, 1906.
23. Hart, J. *Herodotus and Greek History*. London: Croom Helm, 1982.
24. Herzog, R.. *Die Wunderheilungen von Epidauros*. Leipzig: Dieterich, 1931.
24a. Kahn, C. H. *The Art and Thought of Heraclitus*. Cambridge, 1979.
25. Lloyd-Jones, H. *The Justice of Zeus*. Berkeley: University of California Press, 1971.
26. Long, A. A. *Hellenistic Philosophy*. London: Duckworth, 1974.
27. Long, A. A., and Sedley, D. N. *Hellenistic Philosophers*. Cambridge: Cambridge University Press, 1987, 2 vols.
27a. Melling, D. J. *Understanding Plato*. Oxford, 1988.
28. Mikalson, J. D. *Athenian Popular Religion*. Chapel Hill: University of Carolina Press, 1983.
29. Murray, O. *Early Greece*. Hassocks: Harvester Press, 1980.
30. Nilsson, M. P. *Geschichte der griechischen Religion*. Vol. 1. 3rd edn. München: Beck, 1967.
31. Nilsson, M. P. *A History of Greek Religion*. Oxford: Clarendon Press, 1949.
32. Otto, W. *The Homeric Gods: The Spiritual Significance of Greek Religion*. London: Thames & Hudson, 1954.
33. Race, W. H. *Pindar*. Boston: Twayne Publishing, 1986.
34. Rist, J. M. *Epicurus, an Introduction*. Cambridge, 1972.
34a. Rist, J. M. *Plotinus: the Road to Reality*. Cambridge, 1967.
35. Sandbach, F. H. *The Stoics*. London: Chatto & Windus, 1975.
36. Segal, E. *Oxford Readings in Greek Tragedy*. London: Oxford University Press, 1983.
37. Silk, M. *Homer: the Iliad*. Cambridge: Cambridge University Press, 1987.
37a. Stone, I. F. *The Trial of Socrates*. Picador, 1988.
38. Walcot, P. *Greek Peasants Ancient and Modern: A Comparison of Social and Moral Values*. Manchester: Manchester University Press, 1970.
39. Wallis, R. T. *Neoplatonism*. London: Blackwell, 1972.
40. Winnington-Ingram, R. P. *Studies in Aeschylus*. Cambridge: Cambridge University Press, 1983.
41. Wright, M. R. *Empedocles: the Extant Fragments*. New Haven, 1981.
42. Aeschylus. *The Oresteia*, trans. Fagles. Harmondsworth: Penguin.
43. Aeschylus. *The Oresteian Trilogy*. Harmondsworth: Penguin.
44. Aeschylus. *Prometheus Bound*, etc. Harmondsworth: Penguin.
45. Aristophanes. *Lysistrata, Acharnians, Clouds*. Harmondsworth: Penguin.
46. Aristotle. *Complete Works: the Revised Oxford Translation*, ed. J. Barnes. 2 vols. Oxford, 1984.

47. Aristotle. *Ethics*. Harmondsworth: Penguin.
48. Barnes, J., trans. and ed. *Early Greek Philosophy*. Harmondsworth: Penguin. [A translation of the surviving fragments of the Pre-Socratic philosophers, with commentary.]
49. Cicero. *Nature of the Gods*. Harmondsworth: Penguin.
50. Euripides. *Alcestis, Iphigenia in Tauris, Hippolytus*. Harmondsworth: Penguin.
51. Euripides. *Bacchae*, etc. Harmondsworth: Penguin.
52. Guthrie, K. S. *The Pythagorean Sourcebook and Library*. Phanes Press, 1987.
53. Herodotus. *Histories*. Harmondsworth: Penguin.
54. Hesiod and Theognis. *Theogony, Works and Days, Elegies*. Harmondsworth: Penguin.
55. Homer. *Iliad*, trans. Hammond. Harmondsworth: Penguin, 1987.
56. Homer. *Iliad*, trans. Rieu. Harmondsworth: Penguin.
57. Homer. *Odyssey*. Harmondsworth, Penguin.
58. Lucretius. *On the Nature of the Universe*. Harmondsworth: Penguin.
58a. Pindar. *Odes*. Harmondsworth: Penguin.
59. Plato. *Collected Works*, ed. Huntingdon and Cairns. Princeton, NJ, 1961.
60. Plato. *Early Socratic Dialogues*. Harmondsworth: Penguin.
61. Plato. *Gorgias*. Harmondsworth: Penguin.
62. Plato. *Last Days of Socrates (Euthyphro, Apology, Crito, Phaedo)*. Harmondsworth: Penguin.
63. Plato. *Laws*. Harmondsworth: Penguin.
64. Plato. *Phaedrus and Letters VII and VIII*. Harmondsworth: Penguin.
65. Plato. *Philebus*. Harmondsworth: Penguin.
66. Plato. *Protagoras* and *Meno*. Harmondsworth: Penguin.
67. Plato. *Republic*. Harmondsworth: Penguin.
68. Plato. *Symposium*. Harmondsworth: Penguin.
69. Plato. *Timaeus and Critias*. Harmondsworth: Penguin.
70. *Plato's Cosmology* (Timaeus), trans. Cornford, with commentary. London: Routledge, 1977.
71. Plotinus. *Enneads*. Loeb text and translation.
72. Sophocles. *Theban Plays*, trans. Fagles. Harmondsworth: Penguin.
73. Sophocles. *Theban Plays*, trans. Watling. Harmondsworth: Penguin.
74. Xenophon. *Conversations of Socrates*. Harmondsworth: Penguin.

[XI] Hinduism

Compiled by Simon Weightman

1. Allchin, F. R. *The Petition to Rām*. London: George Allen & Unwin, 1966.
2. Alston, A. J. *The Devotional Poems of Mīrābāī*. Delhi: Motilal Banarsidass, 1980.
3. Arya, K. S., and Shastri, P. D. *Swami Dayanand Saraswati: A Study of his Life and Works*. Delhi: Manohar, 1987.
4. Ashby, P. H. *Modern Trends in Hinduism*. New York: Columbia University Press, 1974.
5. Barua, B. K. *Śankaradeva Vaiṣṇava Saint of Assam*. Calcutta: Association Press, 1960.
6. Barz, R. *The Bhakti Sect of Vallabhācārya*. Faridabad: Thompson Press, 1976.
7. Bhandarkar, R. G. *Vaiṣṇavism, Shaivism, and Minor Religious Systems*. Varanasi: Indological Book House, 1965.
8. Bhattacharya, D. *Love Songs of Vidyāpati*, ed. with introduction by W. G. Archer. London: George Allen & Unwin, 1963.
9. Borthwick, M. *Keshub Chander Sen: A Search for Cultural Synthesis*. Calcutta: Minerva, 1977.
10. Briggs, G. W. *Gorakhnāth and the Kānphaṭa Yogīs*. Calcutta: YMCA publishing house, 1938.
11. Brown, J. *Gandhi's Rise to Power, 1915–1922*. London: Cambridge University Press, 1972.
12. Brown, J. *Gandhi and Civil Disobedience, 1928–1934*. London: Cambridge University Press, 1977.
13. Bryant, K. E. *Poems to the Child-God: Structures and Strategies in the Poetry of Sūrdās*. Berkeley: University of California Press, 1978.
14. Callewaert, W. M. *The Hindī Biography of Dādū Dayāl*. Delhi: Motilal Banarsidass, 1988.
15. Carman, J. B. *The Theology of Rāmānuja*. New Haven: Yale University Press, 1974.
16. Cashman, R. I. *The Myth of the Lokamānya: Tilak and Mass Politics in Maharashtra*.

Berkeley: University of California, 1975.

17. Champakalakshmi, R. *Vaiṣṇava Iconography in the Tamil Country*. New Delhi: Orient Longman, 1981.
18. Collet, S. D. *The Life and Letters of Raja Rammohun Roy*. 3rd edn, ed. D. K. Biswas and P. C. Ganguli. Calcutta: Sadharan Brahmo Samaj, 1962.
19. Damen, F. L. *Crisis and Renewal in the Brahmo Samaj*. Leuven: Department Oriëntalistiek, Katholieke Universiteit, 1983.
20. Darshan Singh. *A Study of Bhakta Ravidāsa*. Patiala: Punjabi University, 1981.
21. Das, S. K. *The Shadow of the Cross: Christianity and Hinduism in a Colonial Situation*. Delhi: Munshiram Manoharlal, 1973.
22. Dasgupta, S. N. *A History of Indian Philosophy*. 5 vols. Cambridge, 1920–49. Repr. Delhi: Motilal Banarsidass, 1975.
23. De, S. K. *Early History of the Vaisnava Faith and Movement in Bengal*. 2nd edn. Calcutta: Firma K. L. Mukhopadhyay, 1961.
24. De Bary, W. T. *Sources of Indian Tradition*. 2nd edn. 2 vols. New York: Columbia University Press, 1967.
25. Deleury, G. A. *Toukaram: Psaumes du Pèlerin*. Paris: Gallimard, 1956.
26. Deming, W. S. *Eknāth a Maratha bhakta*. Bombay: Karnatak Printing Press, 1933.
27. Deming, W. S. *Rāmdās and the Rāmdāsīs*. Calcutta: Association Press, 1928.
28. Dehejia, Vidya. *Slaves of the Lord*. Delhi: Munshiram Manoharlal, 1988.
29. Desai, P. B. *Basaveśvara and his Times*. Kannada: Kannada Research Institute, 1968.
30. Dhar, S. N. *A Comprehensive Biography of Swami Vivekananda*. 2 vols. Madras: Vivekananda Prakashan Kendra, 1975–6.
31. Entwistle, A. W. *Braj: Centre of Krishna Pilgrimage*. Groningen: Egbert Forsten, 1987.
32. Farquhar, J. N. *Modern Religious Movements of India*. Oxford, 1914. Repr. Delhi: Munshiram Manoharlal, 1967.
33. Filliozat, J. *Le Tiruppavai d'Āṇṭāḷ*. Pondicherry: Institut Français d'Indologie, 1972.
34. Gandhi, M. K. *An Autobiography, or The Story of my Experiments with Truth*. Ahmedabad: Navajivan Trust, 1927.
35. Gargi, B. *Nirankari Baba*. Delhi: Thomson Press, 1973.
36. Ghose, A. *Sri Aurobindo Birth Centenary Library*. 30 vols. Pondicherry: Sri Aurobindo Ashram, 1970–72.
37. Ghose, J. C., and Bose, E. C., ed. *The English works of Rammohun Roy*. Allahabad: Panini Office, 1906. Repr. New York: AMS Press, 1978.
38. Goetz, H. *Mira Bai: Her Life and Times*. Bombay: Bharatiya Vidya Bhavan, 1966.
39. Grierson, G. A., and Barnett, L. D., eds. *Lallā vākyāni, or the Wise Sayings of Lal Ded*. London: Royal Asiatic Society, 1920.
40. Growse, F. S. *Mathurá: A District Memoir*. Allahabad: North Western Provinces and Oudh Government Press, 1882.
41. Gupta, K. C. *Sri Garib Das, Haryana's Saint of Humanity*. New Delhi: Impex, 1976.
42. Haberman, D. *Acting as a Way of Salvation: A Study of Rāgānugā bhakti sādhana*. New York: Oxford University Press, 1988.
43. Hardy, Friedhelm. *Viraha-bhakti. The Early History of Kṛṣṇa Devotion in South India*. Delhi: Oxford University Press, 1983.
44. Hawley, J. S. *Sūr Dās: Poet, Singer, Saint*. Seattle: University of Washington Press, 1984.
45. Haynes, R. D. *Swāmī Haridās and the Haridāsī Sampradāy*. PhD diss., University of Pennsylvania, 1974.
46. Hein, Norvin. 'Caitanya's Ecstasies and the Theology of the Name'. In *Hinduism: New Essays in the History of Religion*, ed. L. Bardwell Smith. Leiden: E. J. Brill, 1976.
47. Hess, L., and Singh, S. *The Bījak of Kabīr*. San Francisco: North Point Press, 1983.
48. Hill, W. P. D. *The Holy Lake of the Acts of Rāma*. Oxford: Oxford University Press, 1971.
49. Johnson, J. *The Path of the Masters: The Science of Surat Shabda Yoga*. Beas: Sawan Service League, 1939.
50. Jones, K. W. *Arya dharma: Hindu consciousness in 19th-century Punjab*. Berkeley: University of California Press, 1976.
51. Jordens, J. T. F. *Dayānanda Sarasvatī, his Life and Ideas*. Delhi: Oxford University Press, 1978.
52. Juergensmeyer, M. *Religion as a Social Vision: The Movement against Untouchability in 20th-century Punjab*. Berkeley: University of California Press, 1982.
53. Kakati, B. K. *Aspects of Early Assamese Literature*. Gauhati University, 1953.
54. Kanal, P. V. *Bhagwan Dev Atma*. Lahore: Dev Samaj Book Depot, 1942.

55. Kanal, S. P. *An Introduction to Dev Dharma*. Moga: Dev Samaj, 1965.
56. Kaul, J. L. *Lal Ded*. New Delhi: Sahitya Akademi, 1973.
57. Kellock, James. *Mahadev Govind Ranade*. Calcutta: Association Press, 1926.
58. Khushwant Singh, ed. *Gurus, Godmen and Good People*. Bombay: Orient Longman, 1975.
59. Killingley, D. H. *The Only True God: Works on Religion by Rammohun Roy*. Newcastle upon Tyne: Grevatt & Grevatt, 1982.
60. Klaiman, M. H. *Singing the Glory of Lord Krishna: The Śrikṛṣṇakīrtana*. Chico, Cal.: Scholars Press, 1984.
61. Kripalani, K. *Rabindranath Tagore: A Biography*. London: Oxford University Press, 1962.
62. Kripananda, Swami. *Jnaneshwar's Gita, a Rendering of the Jnaneshwari by Swami Kripananda*. Rev. version of the translation by Pradhan and Lambert. Albany: Suny Press, 1989.
63. Krishnananda, Swami. *The Divine Life Society*. Sivanandanagar: The Yoga-Vedanta Forest Academy Press, 1967.
64. *The Life of Sri Ramakrishna Compiled from Various Authentic Sources*. Calcutta: Advaita Ashrama, 1928.
65. Lorenzen, D. N. 'The Life of Śaṅkarācārya'. In *The Biographical Process*, ed. F. E. Reynolds and P. Copps. The Hague, 1976.
66. Lutyens, Mary. *Krishnamurti*. 2 vols. London: John Murray, 1983.
67. Macauliffe, M. A. *The Sikh Religion*. Vol. 6. Oxford: Clarendon Press, 1909.
68. Machwe, P. *Namdev*. Patiala: Panjabi University, 1968.
69. Machwe, P. *Tukaram's poems*. Calcutta: United Writers, 1977.
70. Mahadevananda, Swami. *Devotional Songs of Narsī Mehtā*. Delhi: Motilal Banarsidas, 1985.
71. Mallison, Françoise. *Au point du jour: les prabhātiyāṃ de Narasiṃha Mahetā*. Paris: E ́cole Française d'Extrême Orient, 1986.
72. Marfatia, M. I. *The Philosophy of Vallabhācārya*. · Delhi: Munshiram Manoharlal, 1967.
73. Marr, J. R. 'The Periya *purāṇam* Frieze at Tārācuram: Episodes in the Lives of the Tamil Śaiva Saints'. *Bulletin of the School of Oriental and African Studies*, London (BSOAS), 42/2 (1979).
74. Mathur, A. P. *Radhasoami Faith, a Historical Study*. Delhi: Vikas, 1974.
75. Mayeda Sengaha. *A Thousand Teachings: The Upadeśasāhasrī of Śaṅkara*. Tokyo, 1979.
76. McDermott, R. A. *Radhakrishnan: Selected Writings on Philosophy, Religion and Culture*. New York: E. P. Dutton, 1970.
77. McGregor, R. S. *Hindi Literature from its Beginnings to the Nineteenth Century*. Wiesbaden: Harrossowitz, 1984.
77a. Michaelson, M. 'Domestic Hinduism in a Gujerat Trading Caste'. In *Hinduism in Great Britain*, ed. R. Burghart. London: Tavistock, 1987.
78. Miller, B. S. *Love Song of the Dark Lord: Jayadeva's Gītagovinda*. New York: Columbia University Press, 1977.
79. Munshi, K. M. *Gujarat and its Literature from Early Times to 1852*. 2nd edn. Bombay: Bharatiya Vidya Bhavan, 1954.
80. Narayan, Shriman. *Vinoba, His life and Work*. Bombay: Popular Prakashan, 1970.
81. Nelson-Fraser, J. *The Poems of Tukārām, translated*. 3 vols. London: Christian Literature Society, 1909–15.
82. Nivedita. *The Complete Works of Sister Nivedita*. 4 vols. Calcutta: Sister Nivedita Girls' School, 1967.
83. O'Connell, J. T., *et al*., eds. *Sikh History and Religion in the Twentieth Century*. University of Toronto Press, 1988.
84. Orr, W. G. *A Sixteenth Century Indian Mystic*. London: Lutterworth Press, 1947.
85. Osborne, A. *Ramana Maharshi*. London: Rider, 1954.
85a. Osborne, A. *The Incredible Saibaba*. London: Rider, 1958.
86. Pope, G. U. *The Sacred Kural of Tiruvalluvar-Nayanar*. London: Oxford University Press, 1886.
87. Potter, K. H., ed. *Advaita Vedānta up to Śaṅkara and His Pupils*. The Encyclopedia of Indian Philosophies, vol. 3. Delhi, 1981.
88. Purani, A. B. *Life of Sri Aurobindo*. Pondicherry: Sri Aurobindo Ashram, 1964.
89. Pyarelal, N. *Mahatma*. 2 vols. Ahmedabad: Navajivan Press, 1956, 1965.
89a. Rajdev, S. M. *Bhakta Shri Jaralam*. Rajkot, 1966.
90. Ramakrishna. *Sayings of Sri Ramakrishna*. Madras: Sri Ramakrishna Math, 1971.
91. Ramanujan, A. K. *Speaking of Śiva*. Harmondsworth: Penguin, 1973.
92. Rangaramanuja Ayyangar. *History of South Indian (Carnatic) Music*. Madras, 1972.

93. Ranade, R. D. *Pathway to God in Kannada Literature*. Bombay: Bharatiya Vidya Bhavan, 1960.
94. Redington, J. D. *Vallabhācārya and the Love Games of Kṛṣṇa*. Delhi: Motilal Banarsidass, 1983.
95. Reymond, L. *The Dedicated: A Biography of Sister Nivedita*. New York: J. Day, 1953.
96. Richards, G. *A Source Book of Modern Hinduism*. London: Curzon Press, 1985.
97. Sambamoorthy, P. *Great Composers*. Book 2: *Tyagaraja*. Madras: Indian Music Publishing House, 1954.
98. Scott, David C., ed. *Keshub Chunder Sen: A Selection*. Bangalore: Christian Literature Society, 1979.
99. Siauve, S. *La Doctrine de Madhva: Dvaita Vedānta*. Pondicherry: Institut Français d'Indologie, 1968.
100. Siegel, L. *Sacred and Profane Dimensions of Love in Indian Traditions as Exemplified in the Gītagovinda of Jayadeva*. Delhi: Oxford University Press, 1978.
101. Snell, R. *The Eighty-four Hymns of Hita Harivaṃśa*. Delhi: Motilal Banarsidass, forthcoming.
102. Tagore, D. *Autobiography of Maharshi Debendranath Tagore*, trans. S. Tagore and I. Devi. London: Macmillan, 1914.
103. Tagore, R. *The Religion of Man*. London: George Allen & Unwin, 1931.
104. Tagore, R. *Selected Poems*, trans. W. Radice. Harmondsworth: Penguin, 1985.
105. Tahmankar, D. V. *Lokamanya Tilak*. London: John Murray, 1956.
106. Temple, R. C. *The Word of Lalla the Prophetess, being the Saying of Lal Ded or Lal Diddi of Kashmir (Granny Lal), Known also as Laleshwari, Lalla Yogiswari and Lalishri, between 1300 and 1400 A.D.* Cambridge: Cambridge University Press, 1934.
107. Tucker, R. P. *Ranade and the Roots of Indian Nationalism*. Chicago: University of Chicago Press, 1976.
108. Tulpule, S. G. *Classical Marathi Literature*. A History of Indian Literature, vol. 9.4. Wiesbaden: Harrassowitz, 1979.
109. Vaudeville, C. *L'Invocation: le Haripāṭh de Dñyāndev*. Paris: École Française d'Extrême Orient, 1969.
110. Vaudeville, C. *Kabīr*. Vol. 1. Oxford: Oxford University Press, 1974.
111. Vaudeville, C. *Pastorales par Soûr-Dâs*. Paris: Gallimard, 1971.
112. Vaudeville, C. 'Cokhāmeḷā, an Untouchable Saint of Maharashtra'. *South Asian Digest of Regional Writing*, 6 (1977), pp. 60–79.
113. Vivekananda. *The Complete Works of Swami Vivekananda*. 8 vols. Calcutta: Advaita Ashram, 1964–70.
114. White, C. *The Caurāsī Pad of Śrī Hit Harivaṃś*. Honolulu: Hawaii University Press, 1977.
115. Williams, R. B. *A New Face of Hinduism: The Swāmīnārāyaṇ Religion*. Cambridge: Cambridge University Press, 1984.
116. Wilson, F., trans. *The Bilvamaṅgalastava*. Leiden: E. J. Brill, 1973.
117. Wolpert, S. A. *Tilak and Gokhale*. Berkeley: University of California Press, 1962.
118. Zvelebil, Kamil. *The Smile of Murugan: On Tamil Literature of South India*. Leiden: E. J. Brill, 1973.

[XII] Islam

Compiled by Andrew Rippin

1. Abbott, Freeland. *Islam and Pakistan*. Ithaca: Cornell University Press, 1968.
2. Abbott, Nabia. *Aishah, the Beloved of Mohammad*. Chicago: University of Chicago Press, 1942. Repr. London: Al-Saqi Books, 1985.
3. Abun-Nasr, Jamil. *The Tijaniyya: A Sufi Order in the Modern World*. London: Oxford University Press, 1965.
4. Adams, Charles J. 'The Ideology of Mawlana Mawdudi'. In *South Asian Politics and Religion*, ed. Donald Eugene Smith. Princeton, NJ: Princeton University Press, 1966. pp. 371–97.
5. Affifi, A. A. *The Mystical Philosophy of Muhid Din Ibnul Arabi*. Cambridge: Cambridge University Press, 1936.
6. Ahmad, Aziz. *Islamic Modernism in India and Pakistan, 1857–1964*. London: Oxford University Press, 1967.
7. Ahmad, Aziz. *Studies in Islamic Culture in the Indian environment*. Oxford: Clarendon Press, 1964.
8. Ahmad, Khurshid and Ansari, Zafar Ishaq. *Islamic Perspectives: Studies in Honour of Mawlānā Sayyid Abul Aʿlā Mawdūdī*. Leicester: Islamic Foundation, 1979.
9. Ahmad, Mirza Ghulam. *Barāhīn-i-Aḥmadiyya*, trans. Masum Beg. Lahore: Ahmadiyya Anjuman Isha'at-i-Islam,

1955.
10. Aïnî, M. A. *Un Grand Saint de l'Islam, Abd-al-Kadir Guilânî*. Paris: Paul Geuthner, 1938.
11. Ali, Muhammad. *The Founder of the Ahmadiyya Movement*. Lahore: Ahmadiyyah Anjuman Isha'at-i-Islam, n.d.
12. Andrzejewski, B. W. 'A Genealogical note relevant to the Dating of Sheikh Hussein of Bale'. *BSOAS*, 38 (1975), pp. 139–40.
13. Andrzejewski, B. W. 'The Veneration of Sufi Saints and its Impact on the Oral Literature of the Somali People and on their Literature in Arabic'. *African Language Studies*, 15 (1974), pp. 15–53.
14. Arberry, A. J. *Classical Persian Literature*. London: George Allen & Unwin, 1958.
15. Arberry, A. J. *Mystical Poems of Rumi*. Chicago: University of Chicago Press, 1968.
16. Arjomand, Said Amir. *The Shadow of God and the Hidden Imam*. Chicago: Chicago University Press, 1984.
17. al-Ashʿarī. *The Theology of al-Ashʿarī: The Arabic Texts of al-Ashʿarī's Kitāb al-Lumaʿ and Risālat Istiḥsān al-Khaw fī ʿilm al-Kalām*, trans. R. J. McCarthy. Beirut: Imprimerie Catholique, 1953.
18. Aubin, Jean. *Matériaux pour la biographie de Shah Niʿmatullāh Walī Kermānī*. Tehran: Institut Franco-iranien, 1956.
19. Ayoub, M. *Redemptive Suffering in Islam*. The Hague: Mouton, 1978.
19a. Baljon, J. M. S. *The Reforms and Religious Ideas of Sir Sayyid Ahmad Khan*. 3rd edn. Lahore: Sh. Muhammad Ashraf, 1964.
20. Beeston, A. F. L. *Bayḍāwī's Commentary on Sūrah 12 of the Qur'ān*. London: Oxford University Press, 1963.
21. Birge, J. K. *The Bektashi Order of Dervishes*. London: Luzac, 1937. Repr. New York: AMS Press, 1982.
22. al-Bīrūnī. *Alberuni's India*, trans. Edward C. Sachau. London: 1888. Repr. Delhi: S. Chand, 1964.
23. al-Bīrūnī. *In den Garten der Wissenschaft*, trans. Gotthard Strohmaier. Leipzig: Reclam, 1988.
24. Bovill, E. W. *The Golden Trade of the Moors*. 2nd edn. London: Oxford University Press, 1968.
25. Causse, Maurice. 'Théologie de rupture et théologie de la communauté. Etude sur la vocation prophétique de Moïse d'après le Coran'. *RHPR*, 44 (1964), pp. 60–82.
26. Cook, Michael. *Muhammad*. London: Oxford University Press, 1983.
27. Cooper, J. *The Commentary on the Qur'ān by Abū Jaʿfar Muḥammad b. Jarīr al-Ṭabarī, Volume 1*, London: Oxford University Press, 1988.
28. Corbin, Henry. *En Islam iranien*. Paris: Gallimard, 1971.
29. Cragg, Kenneth. *The Mind of the Qur'ān: Chapters in Reflection*. London: George Allen & Unwin, 1973.
30. Damann, Ernst. 'Der Islam in Süd Afrika'. *Zeitschrift für Missionswissenschaft und Religionswissenschaft*. 4 (1980), pp. 179–292.
31. Duri, A. A. *The Rise of Historical Writing among the Arabs*, ed. and trans. Lawrence I. Conrad. Princeton, NJ: Princeton University Press, 1983.
32. Elder, E. E. *A Commentary on the Creed of Islam: Saʿīd ad-din al-Taftazānī on the Creed of Naim al-din al-Nasafi*. New York: Columbia University Press, 1950.
33. *Encyclopedia Iranica*. London: Routledge, 1985–.
34. *Encyclopaedia of Islam*. Leiden: E. J. Brill, 1913–36. Repr. 1987.
35. *Encyclopedia of Islam*. New edn. Leiden: E. J. Brill, 1960–.
36. Fakhry, Majid. *A History of Islamic Philosophy*. New York: Columbia University Press, 1983.
36a. Friedmann, Y. *Shaykh Aḥmad Sirhindī, an Outline of his Thought and a Study of his Image in the Eyes of Posterity*. Montreal: McGill-Queen's University Press, 1971.
37. Gaden, Henri. *La Vie d'El Hady Omar, Qacida en Poular par Mohammadou Aliou Tyam*. Paris: Institut d'Ethnologie, 1935.
38. Gairdner, W. H. T. *Al-Ghazālī's Mishkāt al-Anwār (The Niche for Lights)*. London: Royal Asiatic Society, 1924.
39. Gaudefroy-Demombynes, M. *Mahomet*. 2nd edn. Paris: Albin Michel, 1969.
40. Gilliot, Cl. 'Portrait "mythique" d'Ibn ʿAbbās'. *Arabica*, 32 (1985), pp. 127–83.
41. Goldziher, Ignaz. *Muslim Studies*. Vol. 2, ed. S. M. Stern. London: George Allen & Unwin, 1971.
42. Goldziher, Ignaz. *The Ẓāhirīs: Their Doctrine and their History*, trans. W. Behn. Leiden: E. J. Brill, 1971.
43. Grunebaum, Gustave E. von. *A Tenth-Century Document of Arab Literary Theory and*

Criticism: The Sections on Poetry of al-Bâqillânî's Iʿjâz al-Qur'ân. Chicago: University of Chicago Press, 1950.
44. Haafkens, J. *Chants Musulmans en Peul*. Leiden: E. J. Brill, 1983.
45. al-Ḥallāj, Ḥusayn ibn Manṣūr. *Kitāb aṭ-ṭawāsīn, texte arabe . . . avec la version persane d'al-Baqlī*, ed. and trans. L Massignon. Paris: Paul Geuthner, 1913.
45a. Hasrat, B. K. *Dārā Shikūh, Life and Works*. Santiniketan: Visvabharati, 1953.
46. Hiro, Dilip. *Islamic Fundamentalism*. London: Grafton Books, 1988.
47. Hiskett, Mervyn. *The Development of Islam in West Africa*. London: Longman, 1984.
48. Hiskett, Mervyn. *The Sword of Truth: The Life and Times of the Shehu Usuman Dan Fodio*. New York: Oxford University Press, 1973.
49. Hodgson, M. G. *The Order of Assassins: The Struggle of the Early Nizārī Ismāʿīlīs against the Islamic World*. The Hague: Mouton, 1955.
50. Holt, P. M. *The Mahdist State in the Sudan 1881–1898*. Rev. edn. London: Oxford University Press, 1970.
51. Holt, P. M. *A Modern History of the Sudan from the Funj Sultanate to the Present Day*. London: Weidenfeld & Nicolson, 1961.
52. Hourani, Albert. *Arabic Thought in the Liberal Age, 1798–1939*. London: Oxford University Press, 1962.
53. Hourani, George. *Islamic Rationalism: The Ethics of ʿAbd al-Jabbār*. London: Oxford University Press, 1971.
54. Hunwick, John O. 'Religion and State in the Songhay Empire'. In *Islam in Tropical Africa*, ed. I. M. Lewis. London: Oxford University Press, 1966. pp. 296–317.
55. Ibn al-ʿArabī. *The Bezels of Wisdom*, trans. R. W. J. Austin. London: SPCK, 1980.
56. Ibn Isḥāq. *The Life of Muhammad*, trans. A. Guillaume. London: Oxford University Press, 1955.
57. Ibn Khaldūn. *The Muqaddimah, an Introduction to History*, trans. Franz Rosenthal. New York: Pantheon Books, 1958.
58. Ibn Ṭufayl. *Hayy ibn Yaqzān, a Philosophical Tale*, trans. Lenn Evan Goodman. Boston: Twayne, 1970. Repr. Los Angeles. Gee Tee Bee, 1983.
59. Innes, Gordon. *Sunjata: Three Mandinka versions*. London: School of Oriental and African Studies, 1974.
60. Issawi, Charles. *An Arab Philosophy of History*. London: John Murray, 1950.
61. Izutsu, Toshihiko. *Sufism and Taoism: A Comparative Study of Key Philosophical Concepts*. Berkeley: University of California Press, 1983.
62. Jabre, F. *La Notion de certitude selon Ghazali*. Paris: J. Vrin, 1958.
63. Jabre, F. *La notion de la maʿrifa chez Ghazali*. Beirut: Editions les Lettres Orientales, 1958.
64. Jafri, S. H. M. *The Origins and Early Development of Shiʿa Islam*. London: Longman, 1979.
65. al-Jīlānī, ʿAbd al-Qādir. *Futūḥ al-ghayb*, trans. M. Aftab ud-Din Ahmad. Lahores, n.d.
66. Kamili, S. A. *Al-Ghazālī's Tahāfut al-Falāsifah, or Incoherence of the Philosophers*. Lahore: Pakistani Philosophical Congress, 1958.
67. Kattani, Sulayman. *Imām ʿAlī*, trans. I. K. A. Howard. London: Routledge & Kegan Paul, 1983.
68. Keddie, N. *Sayyid Jamāl ad-Dīn 'al-Afghānī': A Political Biography*. Berkeley: University of California Press, 1972.
69. Kedourie, E. *Afghani and ʿAbduh: An Essay on Religious Unbelief and Political Activism in Modern Islam*. London: F. Cass, 1966.
70. Kennedy, Hugh. *The Prophet and the Age of the Caliphates: The Islamic Near East from the Sixth to the Eleventh Century*. London: Longman, 1986.
71. Kerr, M. H. *Islamic Reform: The Political and Legal Theories of Muhammad ʿAbduh and Rashīd Riḍā*. Berkeley: University of California Press, 1966.
72. Khomeini, Imam. *Islam and Revolution: Writings and Declarations*, trans. and annotated Hamid Algar. London: Routledge & Kegan Paul, 1985 [contains translation of *Vilāyat-i faqīh*].
73. al-Kisāʾī. *The Tales of the Prophets of al-Kisa'i*, trans. W. M. Thackston, Jr. Boston: Twayne, 1978.
74. Klein, Walter C. *Abu 'l-Ḥasan ʿAlī Ibn Ismāʿīl al-Asʿarī's al-Ibānah ʿan uṣūl ad-diyānah (The Elucidation of Islām's Foundation): A Translation with introduction and notes*. New Haven: American Oriental Society, 1940.
75. Knappert, Jan. *Malay Myths and Legends*. Singapore: Heinemann, 1980.
76. Knappert, Jan. 'A Swahili Islamic Prayer from Zaire'. *Orientalia Lovanensia Periodica*, 4 (1973), pp. 197–207.
77. Laoust, Henri. *Essai sur les doctrines sociales*

et politiques de Taki-d-din Ahmad B. Taimiya. Cairo: Institut Français d'Archaeologie Orientale, 1939.
78. Lerner, Ralph, and Mahdi, Muhsin, eds. *Medieval Political Philosophy: A Sourcebook.* New York. Free Press of Glencoe, 1963.
79. Lewis, Bernard. *The Emergence of Modern Turkey.* London. Oxford University Press, 1961.
80. Lewis, Geoffrey. *Turkey.* 3rd edn. London: Benn, 1965.
81. Lincoln, C. Eric. *The Black Muslims in America.* Boston: Beacon Press, 1963.
82. Lings, Martin. *Muhammad, his Life Based on the Earliest Sources.* London: George Allen & Unwin, 1983.
83. MacDermott, M. J. *The Theology of al-Shaikh al-Mufīd.* Beirut: Dar al-Machreq Editeurs, 1978.
83a. Mahfuz-ul-Haq, M., *Majma'-ul-baḥrain, or The Mingling of the Two Oceans by Prince Dāra Śikūh.* Calcutta: Asiatic Society of Bengal, 1929.
84. Mamiya, Lawrence H. 'Minister Louis Farrakhan and the Final Call: Schism in the Muslim Movement'. In *The Muslim Community in North America,* ed. Earle H. Waugh, Baha Abu-Laban, Regula B. Qureshi. Edmonton: University of Alberta Press, 1983.
85. Margoliouth, D. S. *Lectures on Arabic Historians.* Calcutta: University of Calcutta, 1930.
86. Martin, Bradford, G. *Muslim Brotherhoods in 19th-Century Africa.* Cambridge: Cambridge University Press, 1976.
87. Massignon, L. *The Passion of al-Hallaj, Mystic and Martyr of Islam,* trans. Herbert Mason. Princeton, NJ: Princeton University Press, 1982.
88. al-Māturīdī. *Kitāb al-Tawḥīd,* ed. (with English summary) Fathalla Kholeif. Beirut: Dar el-Machreq, 1970.
89. Momen, Moojan. *An Introduction to Shi'i Islam.* Oxford: George Ronald, 1985.
90. Morris, J. W. *The Wisdom of the Throne by Mullā Ṣadrā.* Princeton, NJ: Princeton University Press, 1981.
91. Moubarac, Y. *Abraham dans le Coran: L'histoire d'Abraham dans le Coran et de la naissance de l'Islam.* Paris: Librairie philosophique J. Vrin, 1958.
92. al-Mufīd, al-Shaykh. *Kitab al-Irshad. The Book of Guidance,* trans. I. K. A. Howard. Horsham: Balagha Books, 1981.
92a. Mujeeb, M. *The Indian Muslims.* London: George Allen & Unwin, 1967.
93. Mullā Ṣadrā Shīrāzī. *Livre des pénétrations metaphysiques (Kitāb al-mashā'ir),* ed. and trans. H. Corbin. Paris: Maisonneuve, 1964.
94. Nasr, Seyyed H. *Ideals and Realities of Islam.* London: George Allen & Unwin, 1966.
95. Nasr, Seyyed H. *Ṣadr al-Dīn Shīrāzī and his Transcendent Theosophy.* Tehran: Imperial Academy of Philosophy, 1978.
96. Nasr, Seyyed H. *Three Muslim Sages.* Cambridge, Mass.: Harvard University Press, 1963.
97. Nicholson, R. A. *Rumi: Poet and Mystic.* London: George Allen & Unwin, 1950.
98. Parrinder, Geoffrey. *Jesus in the Qur'an.* London: Faber & Faber, 1965.
99. Pellat, Charles. *The Life and Works of Jahiz: Translations of Selected Texts.* London: Routledge & Kegan Paul, 1969.
100. Quṭb, Sayyid. *In the Shade of the Qur'ān.* Vol. 30, trans. M. Adil Salahi and Ashur A. Shamis. London: MWH London Publishers, 1979.
101. Rahman, F. *The Philosophy of Mullā Ṣadrā.* Albany: State University of New York Press, 1975.
102. Rescher, Nicholas. *Al-Farabi: An Annotated Bibliography.* Pittsburg: University of Pittsburg Press, 1962.
103. Riḍā, Rashīd. *Le Califat dans la Doctrine de Rashid Rida,* trans. H. Laoust (of *al-Khilāfa*). Beirut: Publication Institut Français de Damas, 1938.
104. Rippin, Andrew, ed. *Approaches to the History of the Interpretation of the Qur'ān.* London: Oxford University Press, 1988.
105. Rippin, Andrew. *Muslims, their Religious Beliefs and Practices.* Vol. 1: *The Formative Period.* London: Routledge, 1990.
105a. Rippin, Andrew, and Knappert, Jan. *Textual Sources for the Study of Islam.* Manchester: Manchester University Press, 1986.
106. Rizvi, S. A. A. *Religious and Intellectual History of the Muslims in Akbar's Reign, with Special Reference to Abu'l Fazl (1556–1605).* Delhi: Munshiram Manoharlal, 1975.
107. Rosenthal, Erwin I. J. *Political Thought in Mediaeval Islam, an Introductory Outline.* Cambridge: Cambridge University Press, 1968.
108. Rūmī, Maulānā Jalāladdīn. *Mathnawī-i ma'nawī,* ed. and trans. R. A. Nicholson. London: Gibb Memorial Series, 1925–40.

109. Rūmī, Maulānā Jalāladdīn. *Selected Poems from the 'Divan-i Shams-i Tabriz'*, trans. R. A. Nicholson. Cambridge: Cambridge University Press, 1961.
110. Sachedina, A. A. *Islamic Messianism: The Idea of the Mahdi in Twelver Shiʿism*. Albany: State University of New York Press, 1981.
111. Sartain, Elizabeth M. *Jalāl al-dīn al-Suyūṭī*. Cambridge: Cambridge University Press, 1975.
112. Schacht, Joseph. *The Origins of Muhammadan Jurisprudence*. Oxford: Clarendon Press, 1950.
113. Schimmel, A. M. *And Muhammad is His Messenger: The Veneration of the Prophet in Islamic Piety*. Chapel Hill: University of North Carolina Press, 1985.
114. Schimmel, A. M. *Gabriel's Wing: A Study into the Religious Ideas of Sir Muhammad Iqbal*. Leiden: E. J. Brill, 1963.
115. Schimmel, A. M. *Mystical Dimensions of Islam*. Chapel Hill: University of North Carolina Press, 1975.
116. Schimmel, A. M. *The Triumphal Sun: A Study of the Works of Jalaloddin Rumi*. Boston: Shambhala, 1978.
117. Shariati, ʿAli. *The Islamic View of Man*, trans. A. A. Rasti. Bedford, Ohio: Free Islamic Literature, 1978.
118. Shariati, ʿAli. *Marxism and Other Western Fallacies: An Islamic Critique*, trans. R. Campbell. Berkeley: Mizan Press, 1980.
119. Shariati, ʿAli. *On the Sociology of Islam*, trans. H. Algar. Berkeley: Mizan Press, 1979.
120. Sivan, Emmanuel. *Radical Islam: Medieval Theology and Modern Politics*. New Haven: Yale University Press, 1985.
121. Smith, Margaret. *An Early Mystic of Baghdad: A Study of the Life and Teaching of Ḥārith b. Asad al-Muḥāsibī*. London: Sheldon, 1935.
122. Smith, Margaret. *Al-Ghazali, the Mystic*. London: Luzac, 1944.
123. Smith, Margaret. *Rābiʿa the Mystic and Her Fellow-saints in Islam*. Cambridge: Cambridge University Press, 1928.
124. Smith, Vincent A. *Akbar, the Great Mogul, 1542–1605*. London: 2nd edn. Oxford University Press, 1919.
125. Smith, Wilfred Cantwell. *Islam in Modern History*. Princeton, NJ: Princeton University Press, 1957.
126. Sohravardî, Shihâboddîn Yahyâ. *L'Archange Empourpré: Quinze traités et récits mystiques*, trans. H. Corbin. Paris: Fayard, 1976.
127. Sohravardî, Shihâboddîn Yahyâ. *Oeuvres philosophiques et mystiques*. Vol. 1, ed. H. Corbin. Tehran: Institut Franco-iranien, 1952 [contains *Ḥikmat al-ishrāq*].
128. Sohravardî, Shihâboddîn Yahyâ. *Oeuvres Philosophiques et mystiques*. Vol. 2, ed. Seyyed Hossein Nasr. Tehran. Institut Franco-iranien, 1979.
129. Sohravardî, Shihâboddîn Yahyâ. *Opera metaphysica et mystica*. Vol. 1, ed. H. Corbin. Istanbul. Maarif Matbaasi, 1945.
130. al-Ṭabarī, Abū Jaʿfar. *The History of al-Ṭabarī. Vol. 2: Prophets and Patriarchs*, trans. William M. Brinner. Albany: State University of New York Press, 1987.
131. Taheri, Amir. *The Spirit of Allah: Khomeini and the Islamic Revolution*. London: Hutchinson, 1985.
131a. Troll, C. W. *Sayyid Ahmad Khan: A Reinterpretation of Muslim Theology*. New Delhi: Vikas, 1978.
132. Waltzer, Richard. *Greek into Arabic*. London: Oxford University Press, 1962.
133. Watt, W. Montgomery. *Bell's Introduction to the Qur'an*. Edinburgh: Edinburgh University Press, 1970.
134. Watt, W. Montgomery. *The Faith and Practice of al-Ghazali*. London: George Allen and Unwin, 1951 [translation of the *Munqidh min al-ḍalāl* and *Bidāyat al-Hidāya*].
135. Watt, W. Montgomery. *Muhammad at Mecca*. Oxford: Clarendon Press, 1953.
136. Watt, W. Montgomery. *Muslim Intellectual: A Study of al-Ghazali*. Edinburgh: Edinburgh University Press, 1963.
137. Wensinck, A. J. *The Muslim Creed: Its Genesis and Historical Development*. Cambridge: Cambridge University Press, 1932.
138. Wensinck, A. J. *La Pensée de Ghazzali*. Paris: Adrien-Maisonneuve, 1940.
139. Wickens, G. M., trans. *The Nasirean Ethics (Akhlāq-i Nāṣirī)*, Persian Heritage Series. London: Routledge & Kegan Paul, 1964.
140. Winstedt, Richard. *A History of Classical Malay Literature*. London: Oxford University Press, 1969.
141. Wismer, Don. *The Islamic Jesus: An Annotated Bibliography of Sources in English and French*. New York: Garland Publishing, 1977.
142. Ziadeh, Nicola A. *Sanūsīyah: A Study of a Revivalist Movement in Islam*. Leiden: E. J. Brill, 1958.

[XIII] Jainism

Compiled by Paul Dundas

1. Banārsīdās. *The Ardhakathānaka*, trans. introduced and annotated by Măkund Lath, Rajasthan Prakrit Bharati Sansthan. Jaipur, 1981.
2. Basham, A. L. *History and Doctrine of the Ajivikas*. London: Luzac, 1951.
3. Bloomfield, Maurice. *The Life and Stories of the Jaina Savior Pārśvanātha*. Baltimore: University of Maryland Press, 1919.
4. Buhler, Georg. *Life of Hemacandra*. Shantiketan, 1936.
5. Deleu, Jozef. *Viyāhapannati (Bhagavaī): The Fifth Aṅga of the Jaina Canon: Introduction, Critical Analysis, Commentary and Indexes*. Bruges: Rijksuniversiteit te Gent, 1970.
6. Haribhadra. *Anekāntajayapatākā*, ed. H. R. Kapadia. 2 vols. Gaekwad's Oriental Series, nos. 88, 105. Baroda, 1940–47.
7. Haribhadra. *Dhūrtākhyāna*, ed. A. N. Upadhye. Singhi Jain Series 19. Bombay: 1944.
8. Haribhadra. *Samarāiccakahā*, ed. Hermann Jacobi. Calcutta, 1921.
9. Haribhadra. *Yogabindu*, ed. and trans. K. K. Dixit. Lalbhai Dalpatbhai Series, no. 19. Ahmedabad, 1968.
10. Hemacandra. *Triśaṣṭiśalākāpuruṣacarita*, trans. Helen M. Johnson. Gaekwad's Oriental Series 51, 77, 108, 125, 139. Baroda, 1931–62.
11. Hemacandra. *Triśaṣṭiśalākāpuruṣacarita*. Vol. 6. Gaekwad's Oriental Series, no. 140. Baroda, 1962.
12. Jain, Kailash Chand. *Lord Mahavira and his Times*. Delhi: Varanasi, 1974.
13. *Jaina Sūtras*. Part 1: *The Ācārāṅga Sūtra and the Kalpa Sūtra*, trans. Hermann Jacobi. Sacred Books of the East, vol. 22. Oxford, 1884.
14. *Jaina Sūtras*. Part 2: *The Uttarādhyayana Sūtra and the Sūtrakṛtānga Sūtra*, trans. Hermann Jacobi. Sacred Books of the East, vol. 45. Oxford, 1895.
15. Kundakunda. *Niyamasāra*, trans. Uggar Sain. Lucknow, 1931.
16. Kundakunda. *Pañcāstikāyasāra*, trans. A. Chakravarti. Arrah, 1920.
17. Kundakunda. *Pravacanasāra*, trans. B. Faddegon. Cambridge, 1935.
18. Kundakunda. *Samayasāra*, trans. Rai Bahadur J. L. Jaini. Lucknow, 1931.
19. Mehta, Saryu R., and Seth, Bhogilal G. *Shrimad Rajacandra: A Great Seer*. Agas, 1971.
20. Nathmal, Muni. *Acharya Bhiksu: The Man and his Philosophy*. Churu, 1968.
21. Ohira, Suzuko. *A Study of Tattvārthasūtra with Bhāṣya*. Lalbhai Dalpatbhai Series, no. 86. Ahmedabad, 1982.
22. Rājacandra, Shrimad. *Ātma-siddhi (Self-Realisation)*, trans. D. C. Mehta. Bombay, Bharatiya Vidya Bhavan, 1976.
23. Ratnaprabhavijaya. *Sramaṇa Bhagavān Mahāvīra*. Vol. 1, parts 1–2: vol. 2, part 1. Ahmedabad, 1948. Vol. 2, part 2. Ahmedabad, 1951.
24. Sanghvi, Sukhlal. *Pt. Sukhlalji's Commentary on Tattvartha Sūtra of Vācaka Umāsvāti*. Lalbhai Dalpatbhai Series, no. 44. Ahmedabad, 1974.
25. Schubring, Walther. *Worte Mahaviras*. Göttingen, 1926.
26. Shah, Nagin J. *Alalaṅka's Criticism of Dharmakīrti's Philosophy*. Lalbhai Dalpatbhai Series, no. 11. Ahmedabad, 1967.
27. Siddhasena Divākara. *Nyāyāvatāra and Other Works*, ed. A. N. Upadhye. Bombay, 1971.
28. Siddhasena Divākara. *Sanmatiprakaraṇa*, trans. S. Sanghavi and B. J. Doshi. Bombay, 1939.
29. Upadhye, A. N. *Jinasena and his Works*. Mélanges d'Indianism à la Mémoire de Louis Renou. Paris: l'Institut de Civilisation Indienne, 1968.
30. Vidyavijaya. *A Monk and a Monarch*. Ujjain, 1942.
31. Williams, R. W. 'Haribhadra'. *Bulletin of the School of Oriental and African Studies*, 28 (1965).
32. Yaśovijaya. *Jñānasāra*, trans. Amritlal S. Gopani. Bombay, 1986.
33. Zydenbos, Robert J. 'Bhadrabāhu and the Sravanabelgola Ksetra'. In *Gommatesvara Commemoration Volume*, ed. T. G. Kalghatgi. Shravanabelgola, 1981.

[XIV] Japanese Religions, excluding Buddhism

Compiled by Paul J. Griffiths

1. Anesaki Masaharu. *History of Japanese Religion*. London: Kegan Paul, Trench, Trübner, 1930.
2. Bach, Marcus. *The Power of Perfect Liberty*.

Englewood Cliffs, NJ: Prentice-Hall, 1971.

3. Bellah, Robert N. *Tokugawa Religion: The Values of Pre-industrial Japan.* Glencoe, Ill.: Free Press, 1957.
4. Chinnery, Thora E. *Religious Conflict and Compromise in a Japanese Village: A First-Hand Observation of the Tenrikyō Church.* Vancouver, BC: Department of Asian Studies, University of British Columbia, 1971.
5. Davis, Roy Eugene. *Miracle Man of Japan: The Life and Work of Masaharu Taniguchi, One of the Most Influential Spiritual Leaders of our Times.* Lakemont, Ga: CSA Press, 1970.
6. de Bary, Wm. Theodore, and Bloom, Irene, eds. *Principle and Practicality: Essays in Neo-Confucianism and Practical Learning.* New York: Columbia University Press, 1979.
7. de Bary, Wm. Theodore. 'Sagehood as a Secular and Spiritual Ideal in Tokugawa Neo-Confucianism'. In *Principle and Practicality: Essays in Neo-Confucianism and Practical Learning*, ed. Wm. Theodore de Bary and Irene Bloom. New York: Columbia University Press, 1979. pp. 127–88.
8. Deguchi Nao. *Ofudesaki: The Holy Scriptures of Oomoto*, trans. Hino P. Iwao. Kameoka: Oomoto Central Office, 1974.
9. Deguchi Onasiburō. *A Guide to God's Way: Extracts from the Scripture 'Miti no Siori' Written in 1925*, trans. Teruo Nakamura. Kameoka: Oomoto Central Office, 1957.
10. Earhart, H. Byron. *The New Religions of Japan: A Bibliography of Western-Language Materials.* Ann Arbor: Center for Japanese Studies, 1983.
11. Ellwood, Robert S. *Tenrikyō: A Pilgrimage Faith.* Tenri: Tenrikyō Central See, 1982.
12. Ellwood, Robert S. *The Eagle and The Rising Sun: Americans and the New Religions of Japan.* Philadelphia: Westminster Press, 1974.
13. Franck, Frederick. *An Encounter with Oomoto, 'The Great Origin': A Faith Rooted in the Ancient Mysticism and the Traditional Arts of Japan.* West Nyack, NY: Cross Currents, 1975.
14. Fukaya Tadamasa. *Fundamental Doctrines of Tenrikyō.* Tenri: Tenrikyō Central See, 1972.
15. Graf, Olaf. *Kaibara Ekken.* Leiden: E. J. Brill, 1942.
16. Haga Noboru. 'Ishida Baigan'. In *The Encyclopedia of Religion*, ed. Mircea Eliade. New York: Macmillan, 1987.
17. Haga Noboru. 'Kamo no Mabuchi'. In *The Encyclopedia of Religion*, ed. Mircea Eliade. New York: Macmillan, 1987.
18. Hall, John Whitney. 'The Confucian Teacher in Tokugawa Japan'. In *Confucianism in Action*, ed. David S. Nivison and Arthur F. Wright. Stanford: Stanford University Press, 1959. pp. 268–301.
19. Hardacre, Helen. *Kurozumikyō and the New Religions of Japan.* Princeton, NJ: Princeton University Press, 1986.
20. Hardacre, Helen. *Lay Buddhism in Contemporary Japan: Reiyūkai Kyōdan.* Princeton, NJ: Princeton University Press, 1984.
21. Harris, H. Jay, trans. *Tales of Ise.* Tokyo: Tuttle, 1972.
22. Hepner, Charles William. *The Kurozumi Sect of Shintō.* Tokyo: Meiji Japan Society, 1935.
23. Hino, Iwao P., ed. *The Outline of Oomoto.* Kameoka: Oomoto Central Office, 1970.
24. Hirai Naofusa. 'Shintō', trans. Helen Hardacre. In *The Encyclopedia of Religion*, ed. Mircea Eliade. New York: Macmillan, 1987.
25. Holtom, Daniel C. 'Konkō Kyō – A Modern Japanese Monotheism'. *Journal of Religion*, 13 (1933), pp. 279–300.
26. Holtom, Daniel C. *The National Faith of Japan.* London: Kegan Paul, Trench, Trübner, 1938.
27. Hori Ichirō. *Folk Religion in Japan*, ed. and trans. Joseph M. Kitagawa and Alan L. Miller. Chicago: University of Chicago Press, 1968.
28. Ishida Ichirō. 'Kokugaku'. In *The Encyclopedia of Religion*, ed. Mircea Eliade. New York: Macmillan, 1987.
29. Kaibara Ekken. *The Way of Contentment*, trans. Ken Yoshino. New York: Dutton, 1913.
30. Kaibara Ekken. *Women and Wisdom of Japan*, trans. Shingaro Takaishi. London: J. Murray, 1905.
31. Kamstra, J. H. 'En no Gyōja'. In *The Encyclopedia of Religion*, ed. Mircea Eliade. New York: Macmillan, 1987.
32. Karlgren, Bernhard, trans. 'The Book of Documents'. *Bulletin of the Museum of Far Eastern Antiquities* (Stockholm), 22 (1950).
33. Keene, Donald, trans. *Major Plays of Chikamatsu.* New York: Columbia Uni-

versity Press, 1961.
34. Kitagawa, Joseph. *Religion in Japanese History*. New York: Columbia University Press, 1966.
35. Konkō Churches of America. *Konkō Daijin: A Biography*. San Francisco: Konkōkyō, 1981.
36. Legge, James, trans. *The Li Ki*. Sacred Books of the East, vols. 27–8. Oxford: Clarendon Press, 1885.
37. Levy, Ian Hideo, trans. *The Ten Thousand Leaves: A Translation of the 'Man'yōshū', Japan's Premier Anthology of Classical Poetry*. Vol. 1. Princeton, NJ: Princeton University Press, 1981.
38. Lidin, Olof. G. *The Life of Ogyū Sorai, a Tokugawa Confucian Philosopher*. Lund: Studentlitt, 1973.
39. Maruyama Masao. *Studies in the Intellectual History of Tokugawa Japan*, trans. Mikiso Hane. Princeton, NJ: Princeton University Press, 1975.
40. Matsumoto Shigeru. *Motoori Norinaga, 1730–1801*. Cambridge, Mass.: Harvard University Press, 1970.
41. McFarland, Horace Neill. *The Rush Hour of the Gods: A Study of New Religious Movements in Japan*. New York: Macmillan, 1967.
42. Murakami Shigeyoshi. *Japanese Religion in the Modern Century*, trans. H. Byron Earhart. Tokyo: University of Tokyo Press, 1980.
43. Nakayama Shozen. *Anecdotes on the Foundress and her Disciples*, trans. Michio Nishidai. Tenri: Tenrikyo Central See, 1964.
44. Nosco, Peter, ed. *Confucianism and Tokugawa Culture*. Princeton, NJ: Princeton University Press, 1984.
45. Nosco, Peter. 'Confucianism in Japan'. In *The Encyclopedia of Religion*, ed. Mircea Eliade. New York: Macmillan, 1987.
46. Okada Mokichi. *Excerpts from the Teachings of Meishusama*. Los Angeles: Church of World Messianity, 1947.
47. Okada Takehiko. 'Yamazaki Ansai'. In *Principle and Practicality: Essays in Neo-Confucianism and Practical Learning*, ed. Wm. Theodore de Bary and Irene Bloom. New York: Columbia University Press, 1979.
48. Okamoto Masayuki. *The Life of the Founder*, trans. Yutaka Yokoyama. Konkō: Konkō Kyotosha Foundation, 1962.
49. Philippi, Donald L., trans. *Kojiki*. Tokyo: University of Tokyo Press, 1968.
50. Rodd, Laura Rasplica, and Henkenius, Mary Catherine, trans. *Kokinshū: A Collection of Poems Ancient and Modern*. Princeton, NJ: Princeton University Press, 1984.
51. Schneider, Delwin B. *Konkōkyō: A Japanese Religion*. Tokyo: Institute for the Study of Religion Press, 1962.
52. Seidensticker, Edward, trans. *The Tale of Genji*. 2 vols. New York: Knopf, 1976.
53. Stoesz, Willis, ed. *Kurozumi Shintō*. Chambersburg, Pa: Anima Books, 1988.
54. Straelen, Henry. *The Religion of Divine Wisdom: Japan's Most Powerful Religious Movement*. Kyoto: Veritas Shoin, 1957.
55. Tanaka Goro. *The Brief Outline of the Kurozumi-kyō, the Most Genuine Japanese Religious Faith*. Okayama: Nisshinsha, 1956 [text in Japanese and English].
56. Taniguchi Masaharu. *Divine Education and Spiritual Training of Mankind*. Tokyo: Seicho-no-ie Foundation, 1956.
57. Taniguchi Masaharu. *The Truth of Life*. 7 vols. Various translators. Tokyo: Seicho-no-ie Foundation, 1961–77.
58. Tenrikyō. *The Divine Model: The Life of the Foundress of Tenrikyō*. Tenri: Tenrikyō Central See, 1958.
59. Thomsen, Harry. *The New Religions of Japan*. Tokyo: Tuttle, 1964.
60. Tsunoda, Ryusaku, de Bary, Wm. Theodore, and Keene, Donald, eds. *Sources of Japanese Tradition*. 2 vols. New York: Columbia University Press, 1958.
61. Ueda Kenji. 'Hirata Atsutane'. In *The Encyclopedia of Religion*, ed. Mircea Eliade. New York: Macmillan, 1987.
62. Ueda Kenji. 'Motoori Norinaga'. In *The Encyclopedia of Religion*, ed. Mircea Eliade. New York: Macmillan, 1987.
63. Uenaka Shuzo. 'Last Testament in Exile: Yamaga Sokō's Haisho Sampitsu'. *Monumenta Nipponica*, 32 (1977), pp. 125–52.
64. Waley, Arthur, trans. *The Book of Songs*. New York: Grove Press, 1960.
65. Yamashita, Samuel H. 'Nature and Artifice in the Writings of Ogyū Sorai, 1666–1728'. In *Confucianism and Tokugawa Culture*, ed. Peter Nosco. Princeton, NJ: Princeton University Press, 1984, pp. 65–138.
66. Yoshikawa Kojiro. *Jinsai, Sorai, Norinaga: Three Classical Philologists of Mid-Tokugawa Japan*. Tokyo: Toho Gakkai, 1983.

[XV] Judaism

Compiled by Geoffrey Wigoder

1. Agus, Irving Abraham. *Rabbi Meir of Rothenburg*. 2 vols. New York: Ktav Publishing House, 1947.
2. Agus, Jacob. *High Priest of Rebirth: The Life, Times and Thought of Abraham Isaac Kuk*. New York: Bloch Publishing, 1972.
3. Altmann, Alexander. *Moses Mendelssohn*. London: Routledge & Kegan Paul, 1973.
4. Anderson, Francis I. and Freedman, David Noel. *Hosea*. Anchor Bible. New York: Doubleday, 1980.
5. Baer, Yitzhak. *A History of the Jews in Christian Spain*. 2 vols. Philadelphia: Jewish Publication Society of America, 1961.
6. Bar-Kochva, Bezalel. *Judas Maccabeus*. Cambridge: Cambridge University Press, 1989.
7. Baron, Salo Wittmayer. *A Social and Religious History of the Jews*. 18 vols. New York: Columbia University Press, 1952–83.
8. Bentwich, Norman. *Solomon Schechter*. Cambridge: Cambridge University Press, 1938.
9. Bergman, Samuel Hugo. *Faith and Reason*. Washington: B'nai B'rith Hillel Foundations, 1961.
10. Bright, John. *Jeremiah*. Anchor Bible. New York: Doubleday, 1965.
11. Bruce, Frederick Fyvie. *The Teacher of Righteousness in the Qumran Text*. London: Tyndale Press, 1957.
12. Buber, Martin. *Moses*. London: East and West Library, 1947.
13. Buber, Martin. *Tales of the Hasidim*. 2 vols. New York: Schocken Books, 1961.
14. Buechler, Adolf. *Studies in Jewish History*. London: Jews' College Publications, 1956.
15. Burrows, Millar. *The Dead Sea Scrolls* (1955) and *More Light on the Dead Sea Scrolls* (1958). New York: Viking Press.
16. Campbell, Edward F., Jr. *Ruth*. Anchor Bible. New York: Doubleday, 1975.
17. Carlson, Rolf August. *David the Chosen King*. Stockholm: Almqvist & Wiksell, 1964.
18. Casper, Bernard M. *An Introduction to Jewish Bible Commentary*. New York: Thomas Yoseloff, 1960.
19. Cohen, Gerson D. *Sefer ha-Qabbalah: The Book of Tradition*. Philadelphia: Jewish Publication Society of America, 1967.
20. Efros, Israel. *Judah Halevi as Poet and Thinker*. New York: Histadruth Ivrith of America, 1941.
21. Epstein, Isidore. *The Responsa of Rabbi Solomon ben Adreth of Barcelona*. New York: Ktav Publishing House, 1968.
22. Finkelstein, Louis. *Akiva, Scholar, Saint and Martyr*. Philadelphia: Jewish Publication Society of America, 1962.
23. Freehof, Solomon B. *The Book of Ezekiel*. New York: Union of American Hebrew Congregations, 1978.
24. Freehof, Solomon B. *The Book of Isaiah*. New York: Union of American Hebrew Congregations, 1972.
25. Friedlander, Albert. *Leo Baeck, Martyr of Theresienstadt*. London: Routledge & Kegan Paul, 1973.
26. Friedman, Maurice. *Abraham Joshua Heschel and Elie Wiesel*. New York: Farrar, Straus, Giroux, 1987.
27. Friedman, Maurice. *Martin Buber's Life and Work*. 3 vols. New York: E. P. Dutton, 1981–3.
28. Ginzberg, Louis. *The Legends of the Jews*. 7 vols. Philadelphia: Jewish Publication Society of America, 1942.
29. Ginzberg, Louis. *Students, Scholars and Saints*. Philadelphia: Jewish Publication Society of America, 1958.
30. Glatzer, Nahum Norbert. *Franz Rosenzweig, His Life and Thought*. New York: Schocken Books, 1967.
31. Glatzer, Nahum Norbert. *Hillel the Elder: The Emergence of Classical Judaism*. Washington: B'nai B'rith Hillel Foundations, 1959.
32. Goodenough, Erwin Ramsdell. *Introduction to Philo Judaeus*. London: Oxford University Press, 1962.
33. Greenberg, Moshe. *Ezekiel 1–20*. Anchor Bible. New York: Doubleday, 1983.
34. Guttman, Julius. *The Philosophies of Judaism*. New York: Holt, Rinehart & Winston, 1964.
35. Hartman, David. *Maimonides: Torah and Philosophic Quest*. Philadelphia: Jewish Publication Society of America, 1976.
36. Heller, James Gutheim. *Isaac Mayer Wise*. New York: Union of American Hebrew Congregations, 1965.
37. Heschel, Abraham Joshua. *Maimonides*. New York: Farrar, Straus, Giroux, 1982.
38. Heschel, Abraham Joshua. *The Prophets*. New York: Harper & Row, 1962.
39. Husik, Isaac. *A History of Medieval Jewish*

Philosophy. Philadelphia: Jewish Publication Society of America, 1944.
40. Jacobs, Louis. *Hasidic Thought*. New York: Behrman House, 1976.
41. Jacobs, Louis. *The Palmtree of Deborah*. London: Vallentine Mitchell, 1960.
42. Jung, Leo, ed. *Jewish Leaders*. New York: Bloch Publishing Co., 1953.
43. Katz, Steven S., ed. *Jewish Philosophers*. New York: Bloch Publishing, 1975.
44. Kaufman, William E. *Contemporary Jewish Philosophies*. New York: Behrman House, 1970.
45. Kaufmann, Yehezkel. *The Religion of Israel*. London: George Allen & Unwin, 1960.
46. Kramer, Simon Gad. *God and Man in the Sefer Hasidim*. New York: Bloch Publishing, 1966.
47. McCarter, Kyle, Jr. *I Samuel*. Anchor Bible. New York: Doubleday, 1980.
48. McKenzie, John L. *Second Isaiah*. Anchor Bible. New York: Doubleday, 1968.
49. Malter, Henry. *Saadia Gaon, His Life and Works*. Philadelphia: Jewish Publication Society of America, 1970.
50. Mansoor, Menahem. *The Book of Direction to the Duties of the Heart*. London: Routledge & Kegan Paul, 1973.
51. Marx, Alexander. *Essays in Jewish Biography*. Philadelphia: Jewish Publication Society of America, 1947.
52. Mendes-Flohr, Paul. *The Philosophy of Franz Rosenzweig*. Waltham, Mass.: Brandeis University Press, 1988.
53. Minkin, Jacob S. *The Romance of Hassidism*. New York: Macmillan, 1935.
54. Moore, Carey A. *Esther*. Anchor Bible. New York: Doubleday, 1971.
55. Myers, Jacob M. *Ezra-Nehemiah*. Anchor Bible. New York: Doubleday, 1965.
56. Netanyahu, Benzion. *Don Isaac Abravanel*. Philadelphia: Jewish Publication Society of America, 1968.
57. Nemoy, Leon. *A Karaite Anthology*. New Haven: Yale University Press, 1952.
58. Neusner, Jacob. *A History of the Jews in Babylonia*. 5 vols. Leiden: Brill, 1965–70.
59. Neusner, Jacob. *A Life of Johanan ben Zakkai*. Leiden: Brill, 1970.
60. Noveck, Simon, ed. *Great Jewish Thinkers of the 20th Century*. Washington: B'nai B'rith Department of Adult Education, 1963.
61. Pearl, Chaim. *Rashi*. London: Peter Halban, 1988.
62. Peli, Pinhas. *On Repentance in the Thought and Oral Discourses of Rabbi Joseph B. Soloveitchik*. Jerusalem: Oroth Publishing House, 1980.
63. Rabinowicz, Harry. *A Guide to Hassidism*. New York: Thomas Yoseloff, 1960.
63a. Rajak, T. *Josephus: The Historian and his Society*. London: Duckworth, 1983.
64. Ringren, Helmer. *The Messiah in the Old Testament*. London: SCM Press, 1956.
65. Rotenstreich, Nathan. *Jewish Philosophy in Modern Times*. New York: Holt, Rinehart and Winston, 1968.
66. Rothschild, Fritz A. *Between God and Man: An interpretation of Judaism from the writings of Abraham J. Heschel*. New York: Harper, 1959.
67. Sarachek, Joseph. *Faith and Reason: The Conflict over the Rationalism of Maimonides*. New York: Hermon Press, 1970.
68. Sarna, Nahum M. *Understanding Genesis*. New York: McGraw Hill, 1966.
69. Sassoon, David Solomon. *History of the Jews in Baghdad*. Letchworth: Sassoon, 1949.
69a. Schay, J. D. Cohen. *Josephus in Galilee and Rome: His Vita and Development as a Historian*. Leiden: Brill, 1979.
70. Schechter, Solomon. *Studies in Judaism*. First series. Philadelphia: Jewish Publication Society of America, 1938.
71. Scholem, Gershom. *Kabbalah*. Jerusalem: Keter Publishing, 1974.
72. Scholem, Gershom. *Major Trends in Jewish Mysticism*. New York: Schocken Books, 1946.
73. Scholem, Gershom. *Sabbatai Ṣevi*. London: Routledge & Kegan Paul, 1973.
74. Shereshevsky, Esra. *Rashi: The Man and his World*. New York: Sepher-Hermon Press, 1982.
75. Talmage, Frank Ephraim. *David Kimhi: The Man and his Commentaries*. Cambridge, Mass.: Harvard University Press, 1975.
75a. Thackeray, H. St John, *et al*. *Josephus*. 9 vols. Loeb Library. London: Heinemann, 1926.
75b. Thackeray, H. St John. *Josephus: The Man and the Historian*. New York: Ktav, 1967.
76. Thieberger, Frederick. *The Great Rabbi Loew of Prague*. London: East and West Library, 1954.
77. Thieberger, Frederick. *King Solomon*. London: East and West Library, 1947.

78. Twersky, Isadore. *Rabad of Posquières*. Cambridge, Mass.: Harvard University Press, 1962.
79. Vermes, Pamela. *Buber*. London: Peter Halban, 1988.
80. Wallach, Luitpold. *Liberty and Letters: The Thoughts of Leopold Zunz*. London: East and West Library, 1959.
81. Waxman, Meyer. *A History of Jewish Literature*. 5 vols. New York: Yoseloff, 1960.
82. Werblowsky, Raphael Juda Zwi. *Joseph Caro, Lawyer and Mystic*. London: Oxford University Press, 1962.
83. Wiener, Aharon. *The Prophet Elijah in the Development of Judaism*. London: Routledge & Kegan Paul, 1978.
84. Wiener, Max. *Abraham Geiger and Liberal Judaism*. Philadelphia: Jewish Publication Society of America, 1962.
85. Wolfson, Harry Austryn. *Crescas' Critique of Aristotle*. Cambridge, Mass.: Harvard University Press, 1929.
86. Wolfson, Harry Austryn. *Philo: Foundations of Religious Philosophy in Judaism, Christianity, and Islam*. 2 vols. Cambridge, Mass.: Harvard University Press, 1947.
87. Zinberg, Israel. *A History of Jewish Literature*. 12 vols. Cleveland: Case Western Reserve University Press, 1972–8.

[XVI] Korean Religions, excluding Buddhism

Compiled by Michael Kalton

1. de Bary, Wm. Theodore, and Haboush, JaHyun Kim, eds. *The Rise of Neo-Confucianism in Korea*. New York: Columbia University Press, 1985.
2. Henderson, Gregory. 'Ch'ŏng Ta-san: A Study in Korea's Intellectual History'. *Journal of Asian Studies*, 16 (1957), pp. 377–86.
3. Kalton, Michael C. 'Ch'ŏng Tasan's Philosophy of Man: A Radical Critique of the Neo-Confucian World View'. *Journal of Korean Studies*, 3 (1981), pp. 3–38.
4. Lee, Ki-baik. *A New History of Korea*, trans. Edward W. Wagner and Edward J. Schultz. Cambridge, Mass.: Harvard University Press, 1984.

[XVII] Magic and the Occult

[XVII.A]

Compiled by Tanya Luhrman

1. Adler, M. *Drawing Down the Moon*. Boston: Beacon, 1986.
2. Barrett, F. *The Magus*, with introduction by T. D'Arch Smith. Secaucus, NJ: 1967.
3. Besterman, T. *Mrs Annie Besant*. London: Kegan Paul, Trench, Trubner, 1934.
4. Brandon, R. *The Spiritualists*. London: Weidenfeld & Nicholson, 1983.
5. Campbell, B. *Ancient Wisdom Revived*. Berkeley: University of California Press, 1980.
6. French, P. *John Dee*. London: Routledge & Kegan Paul, 1972.
7. Howe, E. *The Magicians of the Golden Dawn*. London: Routledge & Kegan Paul, 1972.
8. Gilbert, R. *Golden Dawn*. Wellingborough: Aquarian, 1983.
9. King, F., and Sutherland, I. *The Rebirth of Magic*. London: Corgi, 1982.
10. Kristeller, P. O. *The Philosophy of Marsilio Ficino*. New York, 1943.
11. Kristeller, P. O. *Renaissance Thought II*. New York: Harper and Row, 1965.
12. Kristeller, P. O. 'Marsilio Ficino'. *Encyclopedia of Philosophy*, ed. P. Edwards. London: Collier, 1967.
13. Kristeller, P. O. 'Count Giovanni Pico Della Mirandola'. *Encyclopedia of Philosophy*, ed. P. Edwards. London: Collier, 1967.
14. Levi, E. *The History of Magic*, with introduction by A. E. Waite. London: Rider, 1913.
15. Luhrmann, T. M. 'An Interpretation of the *Fama Fraternitatis* with Respect to Dee's *Monsa Hieroglyphica*'. *Ambix*, 33/1 (March 1986).
16. Luhrmann, T. M. *Persuasions of the Witch's Craft*. Oxford: Basil Blackwell, 1989.
17. Maitland, E. *Anna Kingsford*. London: Watkins, 1913. 2 vols.
18. Murray, M. *Witchcult in Western Europe*. Oxford, 1921.
19. Norden, L. van. 'Paracelsus'. *Encyclopedia of Philosophy*, ed. P. Edwards. London: Collier, 1967.
20. Oppenheim, J. *The Other World*. Cambridge, 1985.
21. Pagel, W. *Paracelsus*. New York: S. Karger, 1958.
22. Passmore, J. 'Robert Fludd'. *Encyclopedia of Philosophy*, ed. E. Edwards. London: Collier, 1967.

23. Richardson, A. *Priestess.* Wellingborough: Aquarian, 1987.
24. Thorndike, L. *A History of Magic and Experimental Science.* 8 vols. New York: Columbia, 1923–58.
25. Walker, D. P. *Spiritual and Demonic Magic.* Notre Dame, 1958.
26. Yates, F. A. *Giordano Bruno and the Hermetic Tradition.* London: Routledge & Kegan Paul, 1964.
27. Yates, F. A. *The Rosicrucian Enlightenment.* Frogmore, Herts: Paladin, 1975.
28. Yates, F. A. *The Occult Philosophy in the Elizabethan Age.* London: Arkana, 1979.

[XVII.B]
Compiled by Keith Munnings

1. Castaneda, C. *Journey to Ixthlan.* London: Bodley Head, 1973.
2. Castaneda, C. *The Teachings of Don Juan.* London: Bodley Head, 1968.
3. Easton, S. C. *Man and World in the Light of Anthroposophy.* New York: Anthroposophic Press, 1975.
4. Gilbert, R. *A. E. Waite: A Bibliography.* Wellingborough: Aquarian Press, 1983.
5. Harper, G. M. *Yeats's Golden Dawn.* Wellingborough: Aquarian Press, 1974.
6. Van Engen, J., (Ed), *Devotio Moderna – Basic Writings,* Classics of Western Spirituality. New York: Pan List Press, 1988.
7. Hyma, A. *The Christian Renaissance: A History of the Devotio Moderna.* 2nd ed. Archon Books, 1965.
8. Kempis, T. à. *The Imitation of Christ,* trans. Betty Knott. London: Collins, 1963.
9. Kettlewell, S. *Thomas à Kempis and the Brothers of the Common Life.* London: Kegan Paul & French, 1885.
10. Wachsmuth, G. *Life and Work of Rudolph Steiner.* New York: Whittier Books, 1955.
11. Wade, A. *Bibliography of the Writings of W. B. Yeats.* London: Rupert Hart-Davis, 1958.

[XVII.C]
Compiled by Valerie Roebuck

1. Aquilecchia, G. *Giordano Bruno.* Rome: Instituto della Enciclopedia Italiana, 1971.
2. Boulting, W. *Giordano Bruno: His Life, Thought and Martyrdom.* London: Kegan Paul, Trench, Trubner, 1914.
3. Bruno, G. *Dialoghi Italiani: Dialoghi Metafisici e Dialoghi Morali,* ed. G. Gentile and G. Aquilecchia. Florence: Sansoni, 1957.
4. Campanella, T. *La Città del Sole,* ed. B. Widmar. Milan: Rizzoli, 1964.
5. Coplestone, F. C. *A History of Medieval Philosophy.* London: Methuen, 1972.
6. Jaki, S. L., trans. *Giordano Bruno: The Ash Wednesday Supper: La Cena de le Ceneri.* The Hague: Mouton, 1975.
7. Namer, E. *Giordano Bruno: ou L'Univers infini comme fondement de la philosophie moderne.* Paris: Seghers, 1966.
8. Vignaux, P. *Philosophy in the Middle Ages.* London: Burns and Oats, 1959.
9. Walker, D. P. *Spiritual and Demonic Magic from Ficino to Campanella.* London: Notre Dame, 1969.
10. Yates, F. A. *The Art of Memory.* London: Routledge & Kegan Paul, 1966.
11. Yates, F. A. *Giordano Bruno and the Hermetic Tradition.* London: Routledge & Kegan Paul, 1964.

[XVII.D]
Compiled by Simon Weightman

1. Bennett, J. G. *Witness.* London: Turnstone Books, 1975.
2. Bennett, J. G. *The Dramatic Universe.* 4 vols. London: Hodder & Stoughton, 1966.
3. Ouspensky, P. D. *In Search of the Miraculous: Fragments of an Unknown Teaching.* London: Routledge & Kegan Paul, 1950.
4. Bennett, J. G. *Gurdjieff: Making a New World.* New York: Harper & Row, 1973.
5. Nicoll, Maurice. *Psychological Commentaries on the Teaching of G. I. Gurdjieff and P. D. Ouspensky.* London: Vincent Stuart, 1952.
6. Pogson, Beryl. *Maurice Nicoll, A. Portrait.* London: Vincent Stuart, 1961.
7. Ouspensky, P. D. *In Search of the Miraculous: Fragments of an Unknown Teaching.* London: Routledge & Kegan Paul, 1950.
8. *Remembering Pyotr Demianovich Ouspensky.* New Haven: Yale University Library, 1978.
9. Sumohadiwidjojo, M. S. *Susila Budhi Dharma.* Tunbridge Wells: SPI, 1975.
10. Lyle, R. *A Way through the World.* Bristol: Altamira, 1985.

[XVIII] Meso-American Religions

Compiled by David Carrasco

1. Boone, Elizabeth Hill. *The Aztec Templo Mayor*. Washington, DC: Dumbarton Oaks Research Library and Collection, 1987.
2. Carrasco, David. *Quetzalcoatl and the Irony of Empire*. Chicago: University of Chicago Press, 1982.
3. Henderson, John S. *The World of the Ancient Maya*. Ithaca: Cornell University Press, 1981.
4. Leon Portilla, Miguel. *Aztec Thought and Culture*. University of Oklahoma Press, 1963.
5. Leon Portilla, Miguel. *Native Mesoamerican Spirituality*. New York: Paulist Press, 1980.
6. Lopez Austin, Alfredo. *Hombre-Dios, Religion y Politica en el Mundo Nahuatl*. Universidad Nacional Autonoma de Mexico, Imprenta Universitaria, 1973.
7. Myerhoff, Barbara. *The Peyote Hunt*. Ithaca, NY: Cornell University Press, 1974.
8. Nicholson, H. B. 'Religion in Pre-Hispanic Central Mexico'. In *Handbook of Middle American Indians*. Austin: University of Texas Press, 1976. Vol. 10, pp. 395–445.
9. Sahagun, Bernardino de. *The Florentin Codex: General History of the Things of New Spain*, ed. Arthur J. O. Anderson and Charles Dibble. 12 vols. Santa Fe, NM, 1950–69.
10. Schele, Linda, and Miller, Mary. *The Blood of Kings: Dynasty and Ritual in Maya Art*. Fort Worth: Kimball Art Museum, 1986.

[XIX] New Religious Movements in the West

Compiled by Eileen Barker

1. Anandamurti, S. S. *16 Points for Individual and Social Development*. London: Ananda Marga Publications, n.d.
2. Anandamurti, S. S. *The Chorus of Humanity: Discourses by Shrii Shrii Anandamurti*. London: Ananda Marga Publications, n.d.
3. Atkins, S., with B. Slosser. *Child of Satan, Child of God*. London: Hodder & Stoughton, 1978.
4. Barker, E. V. *New Religious Movements: A Practical Introduction*. Norwich: HMSO, 1989.
5. Bhajan, Yogi. *The Teachings of Yogi Bhajan: The Power of the Spoken Word*. Pomona, Cal.: Arcline Publications, 1977.
6. Bowen, D. *The Sai Baba Community in Bradford: Its Origin and Development, Religious Beliefs and Practices*. Leeds: Department of Theology and Religious Studies, University of Leeds, 1988.
7. Brooke, R. T. *Riders of the Cosmic Circuit*. Tring, Herts.: Lion, 1986.
8. Bugliosi, V., with Curt Gentry. *Helter Skelter: The Manson Murders*. Harmondsworth: Penguin, 1977.
9. Chinmoy, S. *A Sri Chinmoy Primer*. Forest Hills, NY: Vishma Press, 1972.
10. Chinmoy, S. *Awake! Awake!*. New York: Frederick Fell, 1972.
11. Creme, B. *Messages from Maitreya*. Vol. 1: messages 1–100. London: Tara Press, 1977–80. Vol. 2: messages 101–140. London: Tara Press, 1980–2.
12. Da Free John. *The God in Every Body Book: Talks and Essays on God-Realization*. Clearlake, Cal.: Dawn Horse Press, 1983.
13. Da Love Ananda. *The Holy Jumping-Off Place*. 2nd edn. San Rafael, Cal.: Dawn Horse Press, 1987.
14. David, M. *The Basic Mo Letters*. Geneva: The Children of God, 1976.
15. Davis, D. *The Children of God*. Basingstokc: Marshalls, 1985.
16. Downton, J. V. *Sacred Journeys: The Conversion of Young Americans to Divine Light Mission*. New York: Columbia University Press, 1979.
17. Goswami, S. D. *Prabhupada: He Built a House in Which the Whole World Can Live*. Los Angeles: Bhaktivedanta Book Trust, 1983.
18. Goswami, S. D. *Planting the Seed – New York City 1965–1966: A Biography*. Los Angeles: Bhaktivedanta Book Trust, 1980.
19. Hubbard, L. R. *Scientology: The Fundamentals of Thought*. Los Angeles: The Church of Scientology in America, 1956.
20. Hubbard, L. R. *Dianetics: The Modern Science of Mental Health*. Copenhagen: New Era Publications, 1950.
21. Kilduff, M., and Javers, R. *The Suicide Cult: The Inside Story of the Peoples Temple and the Massacre in Guyana*. New York: Bantam, 1978.
22. King, G. *You are Responsible*. London: Aetherius Society, 1961.
23. Kundalini Research Institute. *Sadhana Guidelines: For Kundalini Daily Practice*.

Pomona, Cal.: Arcline Publications, 1978.

24. Kwak, C. H. *The Tradition.* Book 1. New York: Holy Spirit Association for the Unification of World Christianity, 1985.
25. Kwak, C. H. *Outline of The Principle: Level 4.* New York: Holy Spirit Association for the Unification of World Christianity, 1980.
26. Lane, D. C. *The Making of a Spiritual Movement: The Untold Story of Paul Twitchell and Eckankar.* Del Mar, Cal.: Del Mar Press, 1983.
27. Lawrence, R. *The Theology of Aetherius.* London: Aetherius Society, 1987.
28. Madhuri [Nancy Elizabeth Sands]. *The Life of Sri Chinmoy.* Jamaica, NY: Sri Chinmoy Lighthouse, 1972.
29. Maharishi Mahesh Yoga. *The Science of Being and Art of Living.* 4th ed. London: SRM Publications, 1967.
30. Maharaj Ji, Guru. *The Living Master.* Denver, Col.: Divine Light Mission, 1978.
31. Mani [Manija Sheriar Irani]. *82 Family Letters to the Western Family of Lovers and Followers of Meher Baba.* North Myrtle Beach, SC: Sheriar Press, 1969.
32. Marwah, A. *. . . and the Greatest is LOVE: My experiences with Bhagwan Sri Sathya Sai Baba.* New Delhi: Annemarie Marwah, 1985.
33. McCoy, A. *The Guyana Murders.* San Francisco: Highland Press, 1988.
34. Meher Baba. *God Speaks.* Dodd: Mead, 1955, 1973.
35. Meher Baba. *Listen, Humanity,* narrated and ed. D. E. Stevens. San Francisco: Harper & Row, 1957.
36. Melton, J. G. *The Encyclopedia of American Religions.* 3rd edn. Detroit: Gale Research, 1989.
37. Melton, J. G. *Biographical Dictionary of American Cult and Sect Leaders.* New York: Garland, 1986.
38. Melton, J. G. *Encyclopedic Handbook of Cults in America.* New York: Garland, 1986.
39. Miller, R. *Bare-Faced Messiah: The True Story of L. Ron Hubbard.* London: Michael Joseph, 1987.
40. Milne, H. *Bhagwan: The God That Failed.* London: Caliban, 1986.
41. Moon, S. M. *New Hope: 12 talks.* Washington, DC.: Holy Spirit Association for the Unification of World Christianity, 1973.
42. Moon, S. M. *God's Will and the World.* New York: Holy Spirit Association for the Unification of World Christianity, 1985.
43. Muktananda, S. *Muktananda: Selected Essays,* ed. Paul Zweig. San Francisco: Harper & Row, 1976.
44. Muktananda, S. *Satsang with Baba.* 3 vols. South Fallsburg: SYDA Foundation, 1974–.
45. Muktananda, S. *Play of Consciousness.* San Francisco: Harper & Row, 1974.
46. Murphet, H. *Sai Baba: Man of Miracles.* London: Vrindavanum Books, 1971.
47. Murray, M. *Seeking the Master: A Guide to the Ashrams of India.* St Helier, Jersey: Neville Spearman, 1980.
48. Naipaul, S. *Black and White.* London: Hamish Hamilton, 1980.
49. Orme-Johnson, D. W., and Farrow, J. T., eds. *Scientific Research on the Transcendental Meditation Program: Collected Papers.* 2nd edn. West Germany: Maharishi European Research University Press, 1977.
50. P. R. Sarkar Defense Committee. *The Persecution of Ananda Marga in India.* London: Ananda Marga Publications, n.d.
51. Prabhupada, A. C. B., trans. and ed. *Bhagavad-Gita As It Is.* Los Angeles: Bhaktivedanta Book Trust, 1983.
52. Prabhupada, A. C. B. *The Science of Self-Realization.* London: International Society for Krishna Consciousness, 1977.
53. Prasad, A. R. *Prout-Giita.* New Delhi: Proutist Universal, 1978.
54. Prophet, E. C. *The Great White Brotherhood in the Culture, History and Religion of America.* Livingston MT: Summit University Press, 1976.
55. Prophet, M. L. and E. C. *The Lost Teachings of Jesus* (2 Volumes). Livingston, Mont.: Summit University Press, 1986.
56. Prophet, M. L. and E. C. *Climb the Highest Mountain: The Path of the Higher Self.* Livingston, Mont.: Summit University Press, 1972.
57. Rajneesh, B. S. *Tantra Spirituality and Sex.* Rajneeshpuram: Rajneesh Foundation International, 1983.
58. Rajneesh, B. S. *The Orange Book: The Meditation Techniques of Bhagwan Shree Rajneesh.* Rajneeshpuram: Rajneesh Foundation International, 1983.
59. Rajneesh, B. S. *I am the Gate.* New York: Harper and Row, 1977.
60. Sai Baba. *Sathya Sai Speaks,* ed. N. Kasturi. 10 vols. Bombay: Sri Sathya Sai

Education and Publication Foundation, 1977–.

61. Sahukar, M. *Sai Baba: The Saint of Shirdi*. San Francisco: Dawn Horse Press, 1952.
62. Scott, R. D. *Transcendental Misconceptions*. San Diego: Beta Books, 1978.
63. Sontag, F. *Sun Myung Moon and the Unification Church*. Nashville: Abingdon, 1977.
64. Thompson, J., and Heelas, P. *The Way of the Heart: The Rajneesh Movement*. Wellingborough: Aquarian Press, 1986.
65. Twitchell, J. P. *The Shariyat-Ki-Sugmad*. 2 vols. Menlo Park, Cal.: Illuminated Way Press, 1971–2.
66. Twitchell, J. P. *ECKANKAR, The Key to Secret Worlds*. New York: Lancer Books, 1969.
67. Vorilhon, C. ['Rael']. *Sensual Meditation: Awakening the Mind by Awakening the Body*. Tokyo: AOM, 1987.
68. Vorilhon, C. ['Rael']. *The Message Given to Me by Extra-Terrestrials: They Took Me To Their Planet*. Tokyo: AOM, 1986.
69. Wierwille, V. P. *Jesus Christ is Not God*. New Knoxville, Ohio: American Christian Press, 1975.
70. Wierwille, V. P. *Power for Abundant Living*. New Knoxville, Ohio: American Christian Press, 1971.
71. Williams, J. L. *Victor Paul Wierwille and the Way International*. Chicago: Moody Press, 1979.

[XX] North American Indian Religions

Compiled by Stephen Reno

1. Armstrong, Virginia I. (ed.), *I Have Spoken: American History Through the Voices of the Indians*. Chicago: Swallow, 1971.
2. Bailey, Paul. *Wovoka, The Indian Messiah*. Los Angeles: Westernlore, 1957.
3. Barnett, H. G. *Indian Shakers: A Messianic Cult of the Pacific Northwest*. Carbondale, Ill., 1957.
4. Dockstader, Frederick J. *Great North American Indians*. New York: Van Norstrand Reinhold, 1977.
5. Drake, Benjamin. *Life of Tecumseh and of His Brother the Prophet. With an Historical Sketch of the Shawnee Indians*. Philadelphia: Quaker City Publishing House, 1856.
6. Hebard, Grace. *Washakie*. Glendale: Clark, 1930.
7. Heckewelder, John. *History, Manners, and Customs of the Indian Nations*. Philadelphia: Historical Society of Pennsylvania, 1876.
8. Jackson, Clyde L., and Jackson, Grace. *Quanah Parker, Last Chief of the Comanches: A Study in Southwestern Frontier History*. New York: Exposition Press, 1963.
9. Leipold, L. Edmond. *Famous American Indians*. Minneapolis: Denison, 1967.
10. Mooney, James. *The Ghost Dance Religion and the Sioux Outbreak of 1890*, ed. A. F. C. Wallace. Chicago: University of Chicago Press, 1965.
11. Neihardt, John G. *Black Elk Speaks*. Lincoln: University of Nebraska Press, 1932. Repr. 1961.
12. Nicolar, Joseph. *The Life and Traditions of the Red Man*. Fredericton: Saint Annes Point Press, 1979.
13. Underhill, Ruth. *Red Man's Religion*. Chicago: University of Chicago Press, 1965.
14. Walker, Deward E., Jr. *The Emergent Native Americans*. Boston: Little Brown, 1972.
15. Wallace, Anthony F. C. *The Death and Rebirth of the Seneca*. New York: Knopf, 1970.
16. Weslayer, Clarence A. *The Delaware Indians: A History*. New Brunswick: Rutgers University Press, 1972.

[XXI] Pacific Religions

Compiled by Gary Trompf

1. Bos, R. 'The Congress: A New Movement in Aboriginal Christianity'. In *The Cultured Pearl*, ed. J. Houston. Melbourne, 1986. pp. 166–75.
2. Bos, R. 'The Dreaming and Social Change in Arnhem Land'. In *Aboriginal Australians and Christian Missions*, ed. T. Swain and D. B. Rose. Adelaide, 1988. pp. 422–37.
3. Brown, S. *Men from under the Sky*. Rutland: 1973.
4. Burridge, K. *New Heaven, New Earth*. Oxford, 1969.
5. Champ, C. 'The Peli Association and the New Apostolic Church'. In *Religious Movements in Melanesia*. Vol. 1, ed. W. Flannery. Point Series, no. 2. Goroka, 1983. pp. 78–93.
6. Clark, M. T. *Pastor Doug: The Story of Sir Douglas Nicholls, Aboriginal Leader*. Adelaide, 1975.

7. Clark, M. T. *The Boy from Cumeroogunga: The Story of Sir Douglas Rolph Nicholls, Aboriginal Leader*. Sydney, 1979.
8. Durack, M. N. *Kings in Grass Castles*. London, 1967.
9. Elsemore, B. *Like Them that Dream*. Tauranga, 1985.
10. Freeman, J. D. 'The Joe Gimlet or Siovili Cult'. In *Anthropology in the South Seas*, eds. J. D. Freeman and W. G. Geddes. New Plymouth, 1959. pp. 185–200.
11. Gesch, P. *Initiative and Initiation*. Studia Instituti Anthropos, no. 33. St Augustin, 1985.
12. Gesch, P. 'The Cultivation of Surprise and Excess'. In *Cargo Cults and Millenarian Movements*, ed. G. W. Trompf. Religion and Society Series. Berlin, 1989. pp. 213–38.
13. Gilson, R. P. *Samoa, 1830–1900*. Melbourne, 1970.
14. Gray, F. du P. *Hawaii: The Sugar Coated Fortress*. New York, 1972.
15. Gondarra, D. *Series of Reflections of Aboriginal Theology*. Darwin, 1986.
16. Gondarra, D. 'Father You Gave Us the Dreaming'. *Compass Theology Review*, 22 (1988), pp. 6–8.
17. Gondarra, D. 'Aboriginal Theology and the Future'. In *From Here to Where?*, ed. A. Dutney. Melbourne, 1988. pp. 149–54.
18. Griffin, J., Nelson, H., and Firth, S. *Papua New Guinea*. Melbourne, 1979.
19. Greenwood, W. *The Upraised Hand*. Wellington, 1942.
20. Harding, T. G., and Wallace, B. *Cultures of the Pacific*. New York, 1970.
21. Harris, C. 'Reflections on the Challenges to the Churches'. *Compass Theology Review*, 22 (1988), pp. 4–5.
22. Henderson, J. *Ratana*. Wellington, New Zealand, 1963.
23. Hume, L. 'Christianity Full Circle'. In *Aboriginal Australians and Christian Missions*, T. Swain and D. B. Rose. Adelaide, 1988. pp. 250–62.
24. Lawrence, P. *Road belong Cargo*. Manchester, 1964.
25. Lini, W. *Beyond Pandaemonium*. Wellington, New Zealand, 1980.
26. Malcolm, A., *et al. Love Speaks Out*. Sydney, 1990.
27. Metge, J. *The Maoris of New Zealand*. Rev. edn. London, 1976.
28. Momis, J. 'The Christian Vision of a New Society'. In *The Gospel is Not Western*, ed. G. W. Trompf. Maryknoll, NY, 1987, pp. 157–65.
29. Morauta, L. *Beyond the Village*. LSE Monographs in Social Anthropology, no. 49. London, 1974.
30. Mulholland, J. F. *Hawaii's Religions*. Rutland: 1970.
31. Murphy, P. 'Momis's Theology of Politics Interpreted'. *Catalyst*, 5/3 (1975), pp. 19–45.
32. Narokobi, B. *The Melanesian Way*. Port Moresby, 1983.
33. Paliau Maloat. 'Histori Bilong Mi'. In *The Politics of Melanesia*, ed. M. Ward. Canberra, 1970, pp. 145–61.
34. Paliau Maloat and Lukas, P. *Kalopeu: Manus Kastam Kaunsol: Stori*. Lae [?], *c*. 1982.
35. Papua New Guinea Government. *Biographies of Ministers in the Namaliu Government, 1988*. Port Moresby, 1988.
36. Roxborough, I. *The Ringatu Movement*. New Zealand, 1958.
37. Rowse, T. 'Were You Ever Savages?'. *Oceania*, 58/2 (1987), pp. 81–99.
38. Scarr, D. *Fragments of Empire*. Canberra, 1967.
39. Schwartz, T. *The Paliau Movements in the Admiralty Islands*. Anthropology Papers of the American Museum of Natural History, no. 49/2. New York, 1968.
40. Shaw, B. *Banggaiyerri*. Canberra, 1983.
41. Shaw, B. *Countrymen*. Canberra, 1986.
42. Shears, R. *The Coconut War*. Sydney, 1980.
43. Simpson, T. *Te Riri Pakeha*. Martinborough, New Zealand, 1979.
44. Trompf, G. W. 'The Life and Work of Paliau Maloat'. In *Melanesian and Judaeo-Christian Traditions*, ed. G. W. Trompf. Port Moresby, 1975. Vol. 2, pp. 39–53.
45. Trompf, G. W. 'The Theology of Beig Wen, the Would-be Successor to Yali'. *Catalyst*, 6/3 (1976), pp. 166–74.
46. Trompf, G. W. 'Jimmy Stevens as Betrayer of a Faith'. *Pacific Islands Monthly*, 51/11 (1980), pp. 29–33.
47. Trompf, G. W. 'Independent Churches in Melanesia'. *Oceania*, 54/1 (1983), pp. 51–72.
48. Tuza, E. 'Silas Eto of New Georgia'. In *Prophets of Melanesia*, ed. G. W. Trompf. Port Moresby, 1986.

[XXII] Roman Religion

Compiled by Roger Beck

1. Athanassiadi-Fowden, P. *Julian and Hellenism: An Intellectual Biography*. London: Oxford University Press, 1981.
2. Bailey, C. *Phases in the Religion of Ancient Rome*. Berkeley: University of California Press, 1932.
3. Bailey, C. *Religion in Virgil*. London: Oxford University Press, 1935. Repr. New York: Barnes & Noble, 1969.
4. Behr, C. A. *Aelius Aristides and the Sacred Tales*. Amsterdam: Hakkert, 1968.
5. Birley, A. R. *Marcus Aurelius*. London: Eyre & Spottiswoode, 1966.
6. Boissier, G. *Étude sur la vie et les ouvrages de M. Terentius Varron*. Hachette: Paris, 1861.
7. Bowersock, G. W. *Julian the Apostate*. Cambridge, Mass.: Harvard University Press, 1978.
8. Browning, R. *The Emperor Julian*. London: Weidenfeld & Nicolson, 1976.
9. Bruwaene, M. van der. *La Théologie de Cicéron*. Louvain: Bureaux de Recueil, Bibliothèque de l'Université, 1937.
10. Cardauns, B., ed. *M. Terrentius Varro: Antiquitates rerum divinarum*. 2 vols. Wiesbaden: Steiner, 1976.
11. Dodds, E. R. *Pagan and Christian in an Age of Anxiety*. Cambridge: Cambridge University Press, 1965.
12. Dumezil, G. *Archaic Roman Religion*, trans. P. Krapp. 2 vols. Chicago: University of Chicago Press, 1970.
13. Dzielska, M. *Apollonius of Tyana in Legend and History*. Rome: Bretschneider, 1986.
14. Ferguson, J. *The Religions of the Roman Empire*. London: Thames & Hudson, 1970.
15. Festugière, A. J. *Personal Religion among the Greeks*. Berkeley: University of California Press, 1960.
16. Fowler, W. W. *The Religious Experience of the Roman People*. New York: Cooper Square, 1911. Repr. 1971.
17. Frank, T. *Vergil, a Biography*. New York: Holt, 1922. Repr. Russell, 1965.
18. Frend, W. H. C. *Martyrdom and Persecution in the Early Church*. Oxford: Blackwell, 1965.
19. Griffin, J. *Virgil*. London: Oxford University Press, 1986.
20. Griffiths, J. Gwyn. *Apuleius of Madauros: The Isis Book*. Leiden: Brill, 1975.
21. Jones, C. P., trans. *Philostratus: Life of Apollonius* (abridged), with an introduction by G. W. Bowersock. Harmondsworth: Penguin, 1970.
22. Knight, W. F. J. *Roman Vergil*. 2nd edn. London: Faber, 1944. Rev. edn. Harmondsworth: Penguin, 1966.
23. Lane Fox, R. *Pagans and Christians*. New York: Knopf, 1987.
24. Liebeschuetz, J. H. W. G. *Continuity and Change in Roman Religion*. London: Oxford University Press, 1979.
25. Nock, A. D. *Conversion*. London: Oxford University Press, 1933.
26. Ogilvie, R. M. *The Romans and their Gods in the Age of Augustus*. New York: Norton, 1969.
27. Penella, R. J., trans. *The Letters of Apollonius of Tyana*. Leiden: Brill, 1979.
28. Perrin, B., ed. and trans. *Plutarch's Lives*. Vol. I, Cambridge, Mass.: Harvard University Press, 1959.
29. Rawson, E. *Cicero: A Portrait*. London: Allen Lane, 1975.
30. Rawson, E. *Intellectual Life in the Late Roman Republic*. Baltimore: Johns Hopkins University Press, 1985.
31. Rose, H. J. *Religion in Greece and Rome*. New York: Harper Row, 1959.
32. Sandbach, F. H. *The Stoics*. London: Chatto & Windus, 1975.
33. Staniforth, M., ed. and trans. *Marcus Aurelius: Meditations*. Harmondsworth: Penguin, 1964.
34. Stevenson, J., ed. *A New Eusebius: Documents Illustrative of the Church to A.D. 337*. Rev. edn. London: SPCK, 1960.
35. Syme, R. *The Roman Revolution*. Rev. edn. London: Oxford University Press, 1956.
36. Tatum, J. *Apuleius and The Golden Ass*. Ithaca, NY: Cornell University Press, 1979.
37. Taylor, L. R. *The Divinity of the Roman Emperor*. Middletown, Conn.: American Philological Association, 1931.
38. Wardman, A. *Religion and Statecraft among the Romans*. Baltimore: Johns Hopkins University Press, 1982.
39. Williams, S. *Diocletian and the Roman Recovery*. London: Batsford, 1985.
40. Winkler, J. J. *Auctor & Actor: A Narratological Reading of Apuleius's Golden Ass*. Berkeley: University of California Press, 1985.

[XXIII] Sikhism

Compiled by Hew McLeod

1. Baldev Raj Nayar. *Minority Politics in the*

Punjab. Princeton, NJ: Princeton University Press, 1966.
2. Banerjee, A. C. *Guru Nanak and his Times*. Patiala: Punjabi University, 1971.
3. Banerjee, A. C. *Guru Nanak to Guru Gobind Singh*. New Delhi: Rajesh Publications, 1978.
4. Banerjee, A. C. *The Khalsa Raj*. New Delhi: Abhinav Publications, 1985.
5. Banerjee, A. C. *The Sikh Gurus and the Sikh Religion*. New Delhi: Munshiram Manoharlal, 1983.
6. Barrier, N. Gerald. *The Sikhs and their Literature*. Delhi: Manohar Book Service, 1970.
7. Bhagat Singh. *Sikh Polity in the Eighteenth and Nineteenth Centuries*. New Delhi: Oriental Publishers, 1978.
8. Bikrama Jit Hasrat. *Life and Times of Ranjit Singh*. Nabha: author, 1977.
9. Cole, W. Owen. *Sikhism and its Indian Context, 1469–1708*. London: Darton Longman & Todd, 1984.
10. Cole, W. Owen, and Piara Singh Sambhi. *The Sikhs: Their Religious Beliefs and Practices*. London: Routledge & Kegan Paul, 1978.
11. Court, H., trans. *History of the Sikhs*. Lahore: Civil & Military Gazette, 1888.
12. Cunningham, J. D. *A History of the Sikhs*. London: John Murray, 1849.
13. Fauja Singh. *After Ranjit Singh*. New Delhi: Master Publishers, 1982.
14. Fauja Singh. *Guru Amar Das: Life and Teachings*. New Delhi: Sterling Publishers, 1979.
15. Fauja Singh, ed. *Papers on Guru Nanak*. Patiala: Punjabi University, 1969.
16. Fauja Singh and Arora, A. C., eds. *Maharaja Ranjit Singh: Politics, Society and Economy*. Patiala: Punjabi University, 1984.
17. Fauja Singh and Gurbachan Singh Talib. *Guru Tegh Bahadur: Martyr and Teacher*. Patiala: Punjabi University, 1975.
18. Fauja Singh Bajwa. *Kuka Movement*. Delhi: Motilal Banarsidass, 1965.
19. Fox, Richard B. *Lions of the Punjab: Culture in the Making*. Los Angeles: University of California, 1985.
20. Ganda Singh. *Life of Banda Singh Bahadur*. Amritsar: Sikh History Research Department, 1935.
21. Ganda Singh, ed. *Bhagat Lakshman Singh: Autobiography*. Calcutta: Sikh Cultural Centre, 1965.
22. Ganda Singh, ed. *Early European Accounts of the Sikhs*. Calcutta: R. K. Maitra, 1962.
23. Ganda Singh, ed. *Sources of the Life and Teachings of Guru Nanak*. Patiala: Punjabi University, 1969.
24. Gobind Singh Mansukhani. *Guru Ramdas: His Life, Work and Philosophy*. New Delhi: Oxford & IBH, 1979.
25. Gokul Chand Narang. *Transformation of Sikhism*. Lahore: Tribune Press, 1914.
26. Gopal Singh. *A History of the Sikh People, 1469–1978*. New Delhi: World Sikh University Press, 1979.
27. Grewal, J. S. *From Guru Nanak to Maharaja Ranjit Singh; Essays in Sikh History*. Amritsar: Guru Nanak Dev University, 1972.
28. Grewal, J. S. *Guru Nanak in History*. Chandigarh: Panjab University, 1969.
29. Grewal, J. S. *The Reign of Maharaja Ranjit Singh*. Patiala: Punjabi University, 1981.
30. Grewal, J. S., and Bal, S. S. *Guru Gobind Singh: A Biographical Study*. Chandigarh: Panjab University, 1967.
31. Grewal, J. S., and Indu Banga, eds. *Maharaja Ranjit Singh and his Times*. Amritsar: Guru Nanak Dev University, 1980.
32. Gurbachan Singh Talib. *Guru Nanak: His Personality and Vision*. Delhi: Gur Das Kapur & Sons, 1969.
33. Gurmukh Nihal Singh. *Guru Nanak: His Life, Time and Teaching*. Delhi: Guru Nanak Foundation, 1969.
34. Harbans Singh. *Bhai Vir Singh*. Delhi: Sahitya Akademi, 1972.
35. Harbans Singh. *Guru Gobind Singh*. 2nd rev. edn. New Delhi: Sterling Publishers, 1979.
36. Harbans Singh. *Guru Nanak and the Origins of the Sikh Faith*. Bombay: Asia Publishing House, 1969.
37. Harbans Singh. *Guru Tegh Bahadur*. New Delhi: Sterling Publishers, 1982.
38. Harbans Singh. *The Heritage of the Sikhs*. 2nd rev. edn. New Delhi: Manohar, 1983.
39. Harbans Singh and Barrier, N. Gerald, eds. *Punjab Past and Present: Essays in Honour of Dr Ganda Singh*. Patiala: Panjab University, 1976.
40. Hari Ram Gupta. *History of the Sikhs*. Vol. 1: *The Sikh Gurus (1469–1708)*. 2nd rev. edn. New Delhi: Munshiram Manoharlal, 1984.
41. Hari Ram Gupta. *History of the Sikhs*. Vol. 2: *Evolution of Sikh Confederacies (1708–1769)*.

3rd rev. edn. New Delhi: Munshiram Manoharlal, 1978.
42. Hari Ram Gupta. *History of the Sikhs*. Vol. 3: *Sikh Domination of the Mughal Empire (1764–1803)*. 2nd rev. edn. New Delhi: Munshiram Manoharlal, 1980.
43. Hari Ram Gupta. *History of the Sikhs*. Vol. 4: *The Sikh Commonwealth or Rise and Fall of Sikh Misls*. New Delhi: Munshiram Manoharlal, 1982.
44. Indubhusan Banerjee. *Evolution of the Khalsa*. 2 vols. Calcutta: University of Calcutta, 1936.
45. Jeffrey, Robin. *What's Happening to India?* London: Macmillan, 1986.
46. Kailash Chander Gulati. *The Akalis Past and Present*. New Delhi: Ashajanak Publications, 1974.
47. Khushwant Singh. *A History of the Sikhs*. Vol. 1. Princeton, NJ: Princeton University Press, 1963.
48. Khushwant Singh. *A History of the Sikhs*. Vol. 2. Princeton, NJ: Princeton University Press, 1966.
49. Lakshman Singh. *Sikh Martyrs*. Madras: Ganesh, 1923.
50. Loehlin, C. H. *The Granth of Guru Gobind Singh and the Khalsa Brotherhood*. Lucknow: Lucknow Publishing House, 1971.
51. Loehlin, C. H. *The Sikhs and their Scripture*. Lucknow: Lucknow Publishing House, 1958.
52. Macauliffe, M. A. *The Sikh Religion: Its Gurus, Sacred Writings and Authors*. 6 vols. in 3. Oxford, 1909.
53. McLeod, W. H. *Early Sikh Tradition: A Study of the Janam-Sākhīs*. Oxford: Clarendon Press, 1980
54. McLeod, W. H. *The Evolution of the Sikh Community*. London: Oxford University Press, 1976.
55. McLeod, W. H. *Gurū Nānak and the Sikh Religion*. Oxford: Clarendon Press, 1968.
56. McLeod, W. H. *The Sikhs: History, Religion and Society*. New York: Columbia University Press, 1989.
57. McLeod, W. H. *Who is a Sikh?: The Problem of Sikh Identity*. Oxford: Clarendon Press, 1989.
58. McLeod, W. H., trans. *The B40 Janam-sa ̄khī*. Amritsar: Guru Nanak Dev University, 1980.
59. McLeod, W. H., trans. and ed. *Textual Sources for the Study of Sikhism*. Chicago: University of Chicago Press, 1990.
60. Mohinder Singh. *The Akali Struggle: A Retrospect*. New Delhi: Atlantic Publishers & Distributors, 1988.
61. Narendra Krishna Sinha. *Ranjit Singh*. Calcutta: A. Mukherji, 1951.
62. Narendra Krishna Sinha. *Rise of the Sikh Power*. Calcutta: University of Calcutta, 1946.
63. Niharranjan Ray. *The Sikh Gurus and the Sikh Society*. Patiala: Punjab University, 1970.
64. O'Connell, J. D., *et al.*, eds. *Sikh History and Religion in the Twentieth Century*. Toronto: University of Toronto Centre for South Asian Studies, 1988.
65. Rajiv A. Kapur. *Sikh Separatism: The Politics of Faith*. London: George Allen & Unwin, 1986.
66. Surjit Hans. *A Reconstruction of Sikh History from Sikh Literature*. Jalandhar: ABS Publications, 1988.
67. Surjit Kaur Jolly. *Sikh Revivalist Movements*. New Delhi: Gitanjali Publishing House, 1988.
68. Surjit Singh Gandhi. *History of the Sikh Gurus*. Delhi: Gur Das Kapur & Sons, 1978.
69. Surjit Singh Gandhi. *The Struggle of the Sikhs for Sovereignty*. Delhi: Gur Das Kapur & Sons, 1980.
70. Teja Singh. *Essays in Sikhism*. Lahore: Sikh University Press, 1944.
71. Teja Singh and Ganda Singh. *A Short History of the Sikhs*. Vol. 1. Bombay: Orient Longmans, 1950.
72. Tuteja, K. L. *Sikh Politics (1920–40)*. Kurukshetra: Vishal Publications, 1984.
73. Webster, John C. B. *The Nirankari Sikhs*. Delhi: Macmillan, 1979.
74. *Sikhism and Indian Society*. Transactions of the Indian Institute of Advanced Study, vol. 4. Simla: Indian Institute of Advanced Study, 1967.
75. *The Sikh Religion: A Symposium by M. Macauliffe, H. H. Wilson, F. Pincott, J. Malcolm, and Sardar Kahan Singh*. Calcutta: Susil Gupta, 1958.

[XXIV] South American Religions

Compiled by Lawrence Sullivan

1. Bartolomé, L. J. 'Movimientos milenaristas de los aborigenes chaqueños entre 1905 y 1933'. *Suplemento antropológico* (Asun-

ción, Paraguay) 7 (1972), pp. 107–20.

2. Manuela Carneiro da Cunha. 'Logique du mythe et de l'action: Le mouvement messianique canela de 1963'. *L'Homme*, 13 (1973), pp. 5–37.
3. William H. Crocker. 'The Canela Messianic Movement: An Introduction'. In *Atas do simpósio sôbre a biota amazônica*. Vol. 2: *Antrologia*. Rio de Janeiro, 1967, pp. 69–83.
4. Demarest, A. A. *Viracocha: The Nature and Antiquity of the Andean High God*. Cambridge, Mass., 1981.
5. Flores-Galindo, A., ed. *Tupac Amaru II: Antología*. Lima, 1976.
6. Hemming, J. *The Conquest of the Incas*. New York, 1970.
7. Métraux, A. 'A Quechua Messiah in Eastern Peru'. *American Anthropologist*, 44 (1942), pp. 721–5.
8. Métraux, A. *Religions et magies indiennes d'Amérique du sud*. Paris, 1967.
9. Montenegro, A. F. *Antonio conselheiro*. Fortaleza, Brazil, 1954.
10. Ossio, J. M., ed. *Ideología mesiánica del mundo andino*. Lima, 1973.
11. Pease, F. *El dios creador andino*. Lima, 1973.
12. Pereira de Queiroz, M. I. 'O Movimento messianico do Contestado'. *Revista Brasileira de Estudos Politicos*, 9 (1960), pp. 118–39.
13. Rowe, J. 'Inca Culture at the Time of the Spanish Conquest'. *Bulletin of the Bureau of American Ethnology*, 143/2 (1946), pp. 183–330.
14. Schaden, E. 'Le messianisme en Amérique du sud'. In *Histoire des religions*. Vol. 3, ed. Henri-Charles Puech. Paris, 1976.
15. Siegel, B. J. 'The Contestado Rebellion, 1912–1916: A Case Study in Brazilian Messianism and Regional Dynamics'. In *The Anthropology of Power: Ethnographic Studies from Asia, Oceania, and the New World*, ed. R. D. Fogelson and R. N. Adams. New York, 1977.
16. Sullivan, L. E. *Icanchu's Drum: An Orientation to Meaning in South American Religions*. New York, 1988.
17. Szeminski, J. *La utopía tupamarista*. Lima, 1984.
18. Teixeira d'Assumpção, H. *A campanha do Contestado*. 2 vols. Belo Horizonte, Brazil, 1917.
19. Urton, G. 'The History of a Myth: Pacariqtambo and the Origin of the Incas'. *Revista Andina* (July 1989).
20. Varese, S. *La sal de los cerros: Notas etnográficas e históricas sobre los Campa de la selva del Perú*. Lima, 1968.
21. Wright, R. M., and Hill, J. D. 'History, Ritual, and Myth: Nineteenth-century Millenarian Movements in the Northwest Amazon'. *Ethnohistory*, 33 (1986), pp. 31–54.
22. Zuidema, R. T. *The Ceque System of Cuzco*. Leiden: E. J. Brill, 1964.

[XXV] Tibetan and Central Asian Religions, excluding Buddhism

Compiled by Per Kvaerne

1. Hoffmann, H. *The Religions of Tibet*. London: George Allen & Unwin, 1961.
2. Karmay, Samten G. *The Treasury of Good Sayings: A Tibetan History of Bon*. London Oriental Series, vol. 26. London: Oxford University Press, 1972.
3. Kvaerne, Per. 'Peintures tibétaines de la vie de sTon-pa-gçen-rab'. *Arts asiatiques*, 41 (1986), pp. 36–81.

[XXVI] Zoroastrianism

Compiled by Mary Boyce and John R. Hinnells

1. Anonymous. *Famous Parsis*. Madras: Natesan, 1930.
2. Anklesaria, Bahramgore T. *Vichītīkā ī Zāt-sparam*. Bombay, 1964.
3. Bailey, H. W. *Zoroastrian Problems in the 9th Century Books*. Oxford, 1943. Repr. 1971.
4. Bidez, J., and Cumont, F. *Les mages hellénisés*. 2 vols. Paris, 1938.
5. Boyce, M. *A History of Zoroastrianism*. Vol. 1. Leiden, 1975. Vol. 2. Leiden, 1982. Vol. 3, with F. Grenet and R. Beck. Leiden, 1990.
6. Boyce, M. 'Manekji Limji Hataria'. *K. R. Cama Oriental Institute Golden Jubilee Volume*. Bombay, 1969, pp. 19–31.
7. Boyce, M., ed. *Textual Sources for the Study of Zoroastrianism*. Manchester: Manchester University Press, 1984.
8. Boyce, M. *Zoroastrianism: Its Antiquity and Chronic Vigour*. Columbia University Iranian Lectures, 1985. In preparation.

9. Boyce, M. *Zoroastrians, their Religious Beliefs and Practices*. 3rd rev. edn. London, 1987.
10. Braun, O., trans. *Ausgewählte Akten persischer Märtyrer*. Bibliothek der Kirchenväter, vol. 22. 1915.
11. *Cambridge History of Iran*. Vol. 3, ed. E. Yarshater. Cambridge, 1983. Vol. 4, ed. R. N. Frye. Cambridge, 1975.
12. *Cambridge History of Judaism*. Vol. 1, ed. W. D. Davies and L. Finkelstein. Cambridge, 1984.
13. Chiniwalla, F. S. *Essential Origins of Zoroastrianism*. Bombay, 1942.
14. Christensen, A. *L'Iran sous les Sassanides*. 2nd edn. Copenhagen, 1944.
15. Dastoor, K. N. *Zarathushtra, the yazata*. Bombay, 1984.
16. Dhabhar, B. N., trans. *The Persian Rivayats of Hormazyar Framarz and others*. Bombay, 1922.
17. Dhalla, M. N. *An Autobiography*, trans. G. and B. Rustomji. Karachi, 1975.
18. Dhalla, M. N. *History of Zoroastrianism*. New York, 1938. Repr. 1977.
19. Edwardes, S. M. *Kharshedji Rustamji Cama, 1831–1909: A Memoir*. Oxford, 1923.
20. *Encyclopaedia Iranica*, ed. E. Yarshater. London, 1982–.
21. Gignoux, P., ed. and trans. *Le Livre d'Ardā Vīrāz*. Paris, 1984.
22. Gnoli, G. *Zoroaster's Time and Homeland*. Naples, 1980.
23. Herodotus. *Histories*. Penguin: London.
24. Hinnells, J. R. *Persian Mythology*. 2nd edn. London, 1985.
25. Hinnells, J. R. 'Social Change and Religious Transformations among Bombay Parsis in the Early Twentieth Century'. In *Traditions in contact and change*, ed. P. Slater and D. Wiebe. Winnipeg, 1983.
26. Hinnells, J. R., with Writer, R. *Living Flame: Zoroastrians in Britain*. Manchester University Press, in preparation.
26a. Hinnells, J. R. 'Parsis and the British'. *Journal of the K. R. Cama Oriental Institute*. 46 (Bombay, 1978), pp. 2–92.
27. Hodivala, S. H. *Studies in Parsi History*. Bombay, 1920.
28. Hoffmann, G., trans. *Auszüge aus syrischcen Akten persischer Märtyrer*. Leipzig, 1880. Repr. 1966.
29. Huff, D. 'Recherches archéologiques à Takht-i Suleiman, centre religieux royal sassanide'. *Comptes-rendus de l'Académie des Inscriptions et Belles-lettres* (1978), pp. 776–89.
30. Humbach, H., trans. *Die Gathas des Zarathustra*. 2 vols. Heidelberg, 1959.
31. Insler, S., trans. *The Gāthās of Zarathustra*. Acta Iranica, vol. 8. Leiden, 1975.
32. Jackson, A. V. W. *Zoroaster, the Prophet of Ancient Iran*. New York, 1899. Repr. 1965.
33. Jaeger, W. *Aristotle, Fundamentals of the History of his Development*, trans. R. Robinson. 2nd edn. Oxford, 1948.
34. Karaka, D. F. *History of the Parsis*. 2 vols. London, 1884.
35. Kellens, J., and Pirart, E. *Les Textes vieil-avestiques*. Vol. 1, intro., text and trans. Wiesbaden, 1988.
36. Kingsley, P. 'The Greek Origin of the Sixth-Century Dating of Zoroaster'. *BSOAS*, 53 (1990), pp. 245–65.
37. Kulke, E. *The Parsees in India: A Minority as Agent of Social Change*. Munich, 1974.
38. Lommel, H. *Die Religion Zarathustras nach dem Awesta dargestellt*. Tübingen, 1930. Repr. 1971.
39. Mama, N. F. *A Mazdaznan Mystic*. Bombay, 1944.
40. Masani, P. S. *Zoroastrianism Ancient and Modern*. Bombay, 1917.
41. Masani, R. P. *The Grand Old Man of India*. London, 1938.
42. Menant, D. *Les Parsis*. Annales du Musée Guimet, no. 7. 1898. Repr. Osnabrück, 1975.
43. Mody, J. J. *K. R. Cama*. Bombay, 1932.
44. Mody, J. R. P. *Jamsetjee Jejeebhoy: The First Indian Knight and Baronet*. Bombay, 1959.
45. Molé, M. *La légende de Zoroastre selon les textes pehlevis*. Paris, 1967.
46. Moos, M. M. *Life of Ustad Saheb Behramshah Nowroji Shroff*. Bombay, 1981.
47. Moulton, J. H. *Early Zoroastrianism*. London, 1913. Repr. 1972 [with a translation of the *Gāthās*, essentially from the German of C. Bartholomae, pp. 343–90].
48. Nöldeke, T., trans. *Geschichte der Perser und Araber zur Zeit der Sasaniden aus der arabischen Chronik des Ṭabari*. Leiden, 1879.
49. Paymaster, R. B. *Biography of Mulla Feroze bin Mulla Kaus Jalal*. Bombay, 1931. [in Gujarati].
50. Schmidt, E. *Persepolis*. Vol. 3. University of Chicago Oriental Institute Publications, no. 70. Chicago, 1971.
51. Skjaervø, P. O. '"Kirdir's Vision": Translation and Analysis'. *Archaeologische Mitteilungen aus Iran*, 16 (1983), pp.

269–306.

52. Stronach, D. *Pasargadae, a Report on the Excavations Conducted from 1961 to 1963*. Oxford, 1978.
53. Wadia, J. H., ed. *Sir Jamsetjee Jejeebhoy Parsi Benevolent Institution Centenary Volume*. Bombay, 1950.
54. Warner, A. G. and E., trans. *Shahname*. 9 vols. London, 1912–25.
55. West, E. W., trans. *The Dādistān ī denig and Epistles of Mānushchīhr ī Goshnjam*. *SBE*, 18 (Oxford, 1882). Repr. Delhi, 1965.
56. Wilson, J. *The Parsi religion . . . Unfolded, Refuted and Contrasted with Christianity*. Bombay, 1843.
57. Zaehner, R. C. *Zurvan: A Zoroastrian dilemma*. Oxford, 1955.

Maps

ICELAND
Borgarfjordur
Skalaholl
Oddi
SCOTLAND
Arendal
Armagh
IRELAND
Kildare
Cashel
Jarrow
WALES
ENGLAND
Menevia
Carmarthen
Glamorgan
Cambridge
Oxford
London
Ockham
Canterbury
Amsterdam
Leiden
HOLLAND
Utrecht
Zwolle
Hamburg
Bremen
Deventer
Hanover
GERMANY
Cologne
Kassel
Echternacht
Marburg
Frankfurt
Rouen
Reims
Bingen
Trier
Mainz
Worms
R. Seine
Paris
Domrémy
Strasbourg
Heidelberg
Troyes
R. Loire
Orleans
Clairvaux
Augsburg
Basel
Cappel
Lausanne
Berne
Zurich
Geneva
Glarus
Einsiedeln
FRANCE
(GAUL)
Cluny
Bergamo
Milan
Brescia
Padua
Bologna
Leon
Lourdes
Toulouse
Avignon
Arles
Valladolid
Medina del Campo
Avila
Segovia
PORTUGAL
CASTILE
Madrid
Alcala
Toledo
SPAIN
Manresa
Barcelona
Fiesole
Florence
Pisa
Siena
Valencia
Seville
Cordova
Murcia
Granada
Majorca
Carthage

Europe

Trondheim
NORWAY
FINLAND
Valaam
St. Petersburg
Uppsala
Birka
Stockholm
SWEDEN
ESTONIA
Novgorod
Yaroslavl
Pskov
Zagorsk
Moscow
LATVIA
Jelling
Lund
BALTIC SEA
Kaluga
LITHUANIA
Vilnius (Vilna)
Optina
Tula
USSR
Minsk
Voronezh
BYELORUSSIA
Berlin
POLAND
Warsaw
Halle
Leipzig
Görlitz
Dresden
Lublin
Vladimir
Mülhausen
Berdichev
Kiev
Kharkov
Breslau
Arnstadt
Prague
Krakow
Wadowice
Lvov
UKRAINE
Zwickau
Radonice
MORAVIA
Poltava
CZECHOSLOVAKIA
MOLDAVIA
Vienna
AUSTRIA
HUNGARY
Suceava
Neamt
Pentele
Aquilea
GOTHIA
ROMANIA
Sirmium
WALLACHIA
YUGOSLAVIA
SERBIA
R. Danube
BLACK SEA
Assisi
Ras
BULGARIA
Nursia
Subiaco
Pec
Philipropolis
Sinope
Rome
Palestrina
Rila
Paroria
Constantinople
Aquino
Gaeta
Ohrid
Prespa
CAPPADOCIA
ITALY
ALBANIA
Metapontum
Athos
Mt. Olympus
GREECE
ASIA MINOR
Smyrna
Athens
Mt. Latros
Acragas (Agrigentum)

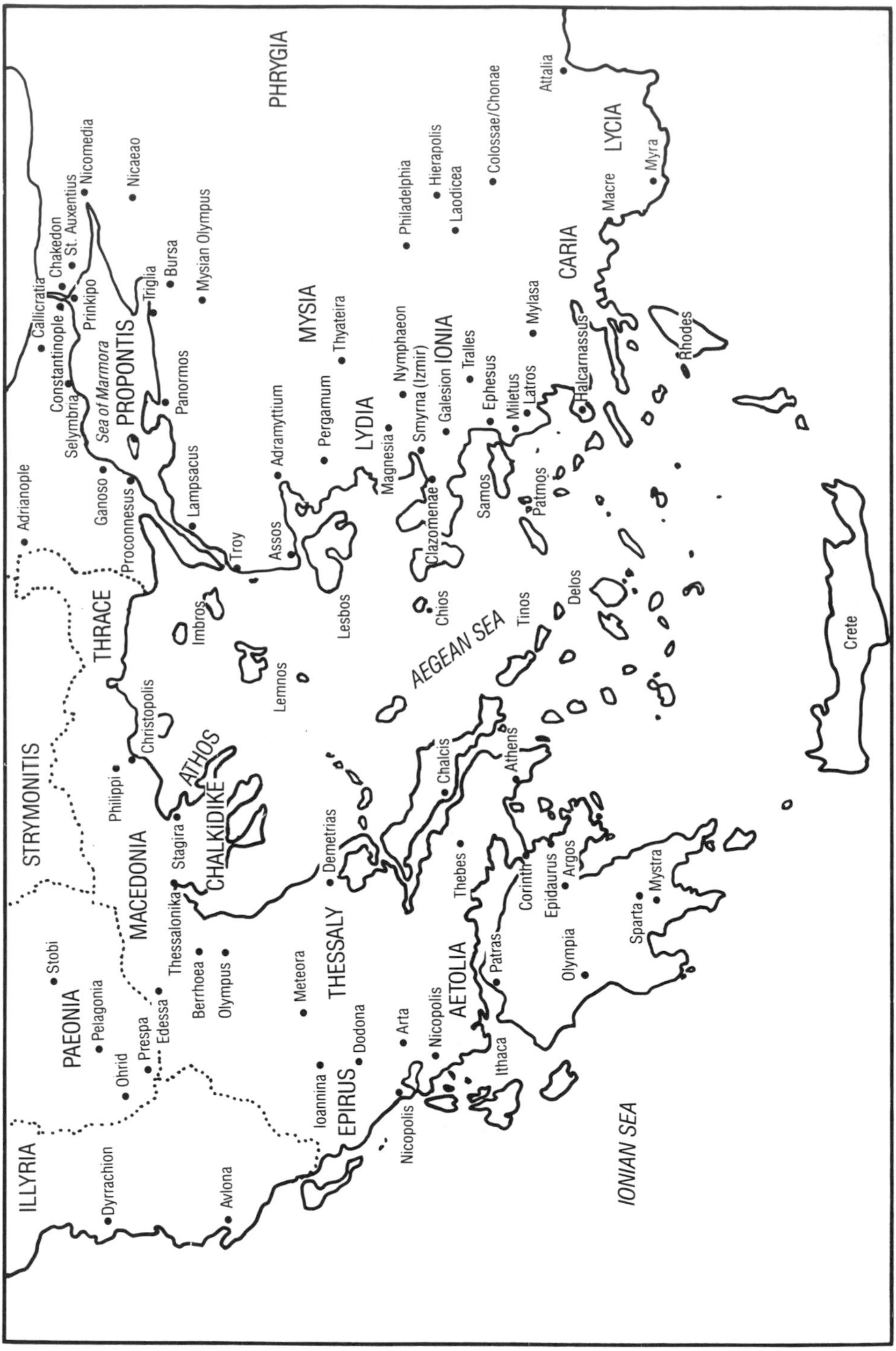
PHRYGIA
Attalia
Colossae/Chonae
LYCIA
Myra
Hierapolis
Laodicea
Philadelphia
Macre
Nicomedia
Nicaeao
St. Auxentius
Chakedon
Mysian Olympus
Bursa
Triglia
Callicratia
Constantinople
Prinkipo
PROPONTIS
Sea of Marmora
Selymbria
Panormos
MYSIA
Thyateira
Nymphaeon
IONIA
CARIA
Mylasa
Tralles
Smyrna (Izmir)
Galesion
Ephesus
Miletus
Latros
Halcarnassus
Rhodes
Adramyttium
Pergamum
LYDIA
Magnesia
Adrianople
Ganoso
Proconnesus
Lampsacus
Troy
Assos
Clazomenae
Samos
Patmos
Lesbos
Chios
THRACE
Imbros
Lemnos
AEGEAN SEA
Tinos
Delos
Crete
STRYMONITIS
Christopolis
Philippi
ATHOS
CHALKIDIKE
MACEDONIA
Stagira
Thessalonika
Chalcis
Athens
Demetrias
Thebes
Corinth
Epidaurus
Argos
Mystra
Sparta
Olympia
Patras
AETOLIA
THESSALY
Meteora
Olympus
Berrhoea
Edessa
Prespa
Stobi
PAEONIA
Pelagonia
Ohrid
Nicopolis
Arta
Dodona
Ioannina
EPIRUS
Ithaca
IONIAN SEA
ILLYRIA
Dyrrachion
Avlona

Greece

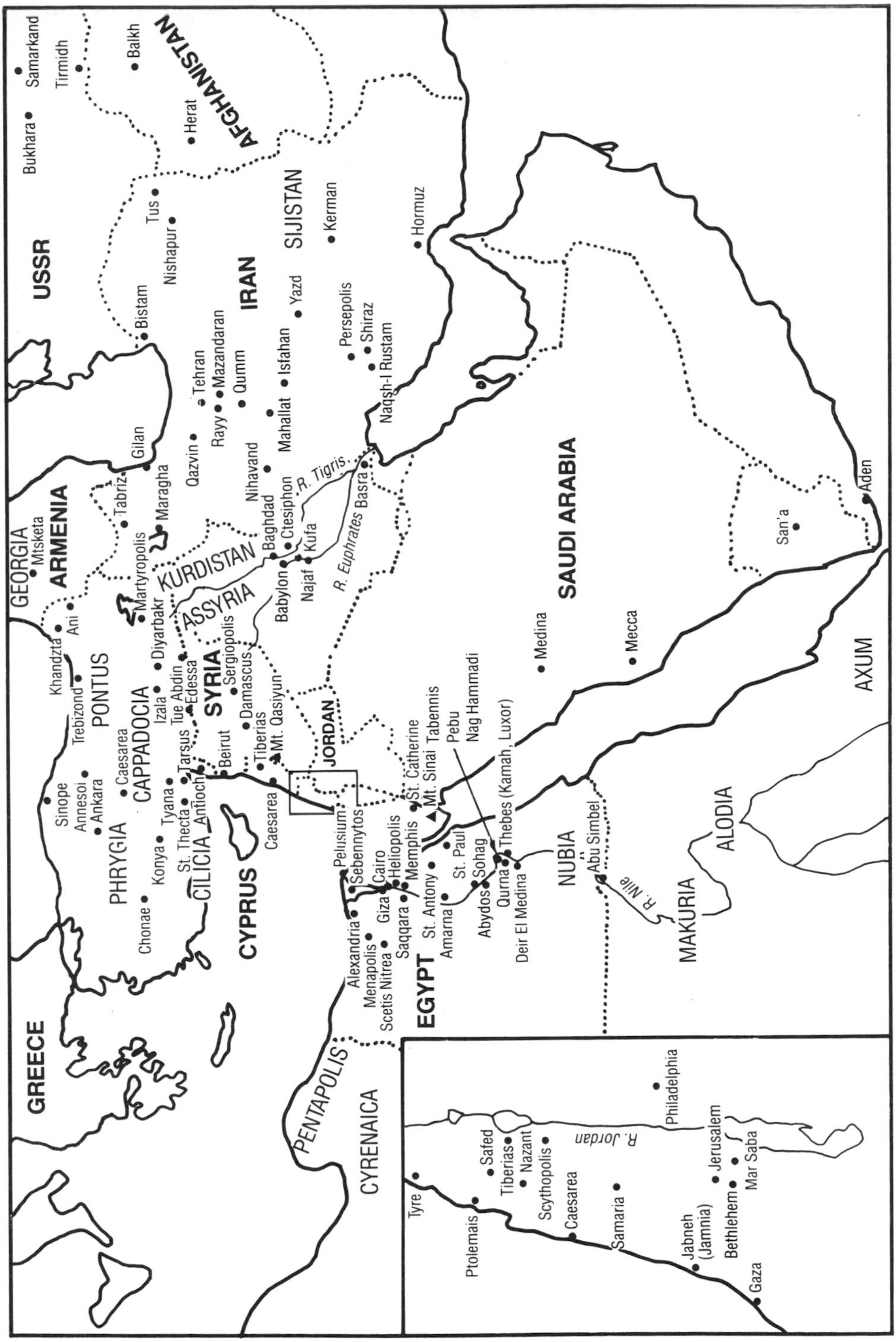

West Asia and Saudi Arabia, Egypt and Israel

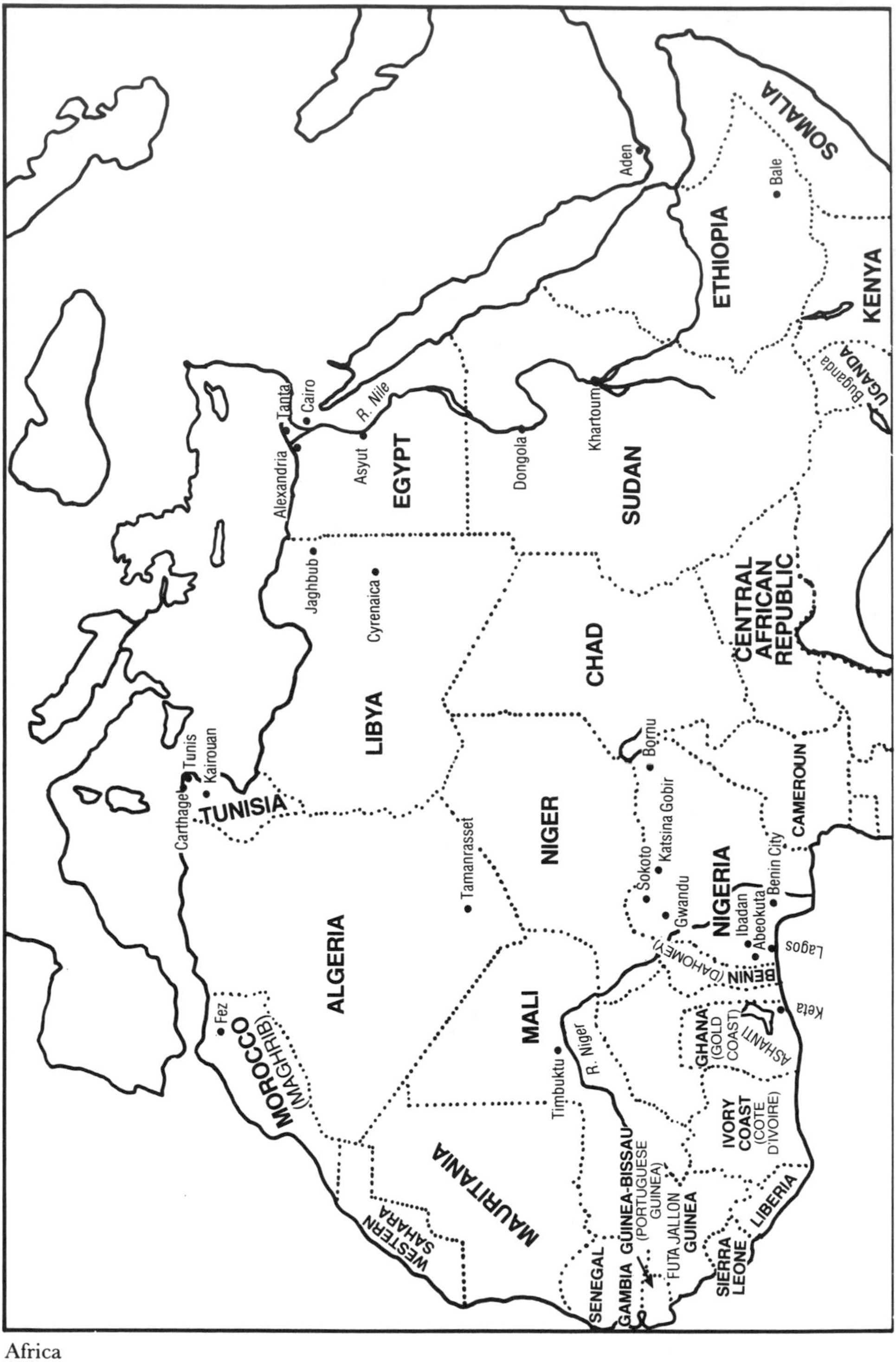
SOMALIA
ETHIOPIA
KENYA
UGANDA
Buganda
Aden
Bale
SUDAN
Khartoum
Dongola
EGYPT
Cairo
Tanta
Alexandria
Asyut
R. Nile
LIBYA
Jaghbub
Cyrenaica
CHAD
CENTRAL AFRICAN REPUBLIC
CAMEROUN
NIGER
Tamanrasset
Bornu
Katsina Gobir
Sokoto
Gwandu
NIGERIA
Benin City
Ibadan
Abeokuta
Lagos
BENIN (DAHOMEY)
Keta
GHANA (GOLD COAST)
ASHANTI
IVORY COAST (COTE D'IVOIRE)
LIBERIA
SIERRA LEONE
GUINEA
FUTA JALLON
GUINEA-BISSAU (PORTUGUESE GUINEA)
GAMBIA
SENEGAL
MALI
Timbuktu
R. Niger
MAURITANIA
WESTERN SAHARA
MOROCCO (MAGHRIB)
Fez
ALGERIA
TUNISIA
Tunis
Kairouan
Carthage

Africa

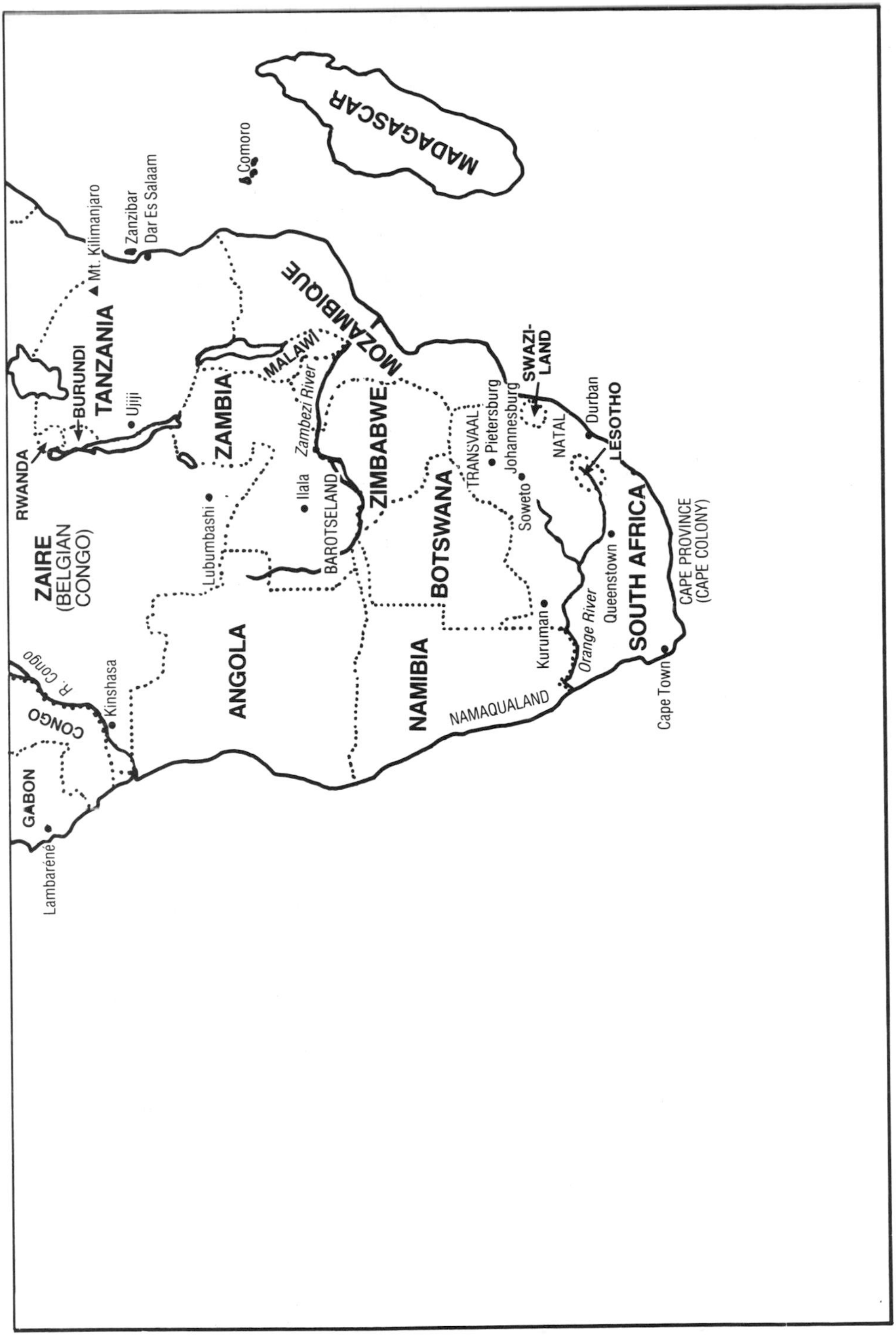
MADAGASCAR
Comoro
Zanzibar
Dar Es Salaam
Mt. Kilimanjaro
TANZANIA
BURUNDI
RWANDA
Ujiji
MOZAMBIQUE
MALAWI
ZAMBIA
Zambezi River
ZIMBABWE
Ilala
BAROTSELAND
ZAIRE
(BELGIAN
CONGO)
Lubumbashi
ANGOLA
Kinshasa
R. Congo
CONGO
GABON
Lambaréné
NAMIBIA
BOTSWANA
TRANSVAAL
Pietersburg
Johannesburg
Soweto
SWAZI-
LAND
NATAL
Durban
LESOTHO
Kuruman
Orange River
Queenstown
SOUTH AFRICA
NAMAQUALAND
CAPE PROVINCE
(CAPE COLONY)
Cape Town

AFGHANISTAN
PAKISTAN
Peshawar
Rawalpindi
Quandahar
Sialkot
Srinagar
R. Chenab
Kartarpur
R. Beas
Lahore
Amritsar
Bakala
Sultanpur
Anandpur
Ludhiana
Sirhind
Shimla
Patiala
Badarinath
R. Satling (Satluj)
Rishikesh
R. Saraswati
R. Indus
Delhi
Vrindaban
Aligarh
Mathura
Agra
Sambhar
Kanpur
R. Jumna
Karachi
Chittor
Jhansi
Allahabad
Idar
Patan
Ahmedabad
Ujjain
Dwarka
Rajkot
Baroda
R. Narmada
Porbanda
Surat
Diu
Navsari
Udwada
Wardha
Nasik
Sanjan
Aurangabad
Nander
Bombay
Pune (Poona)
R. Godavari
Pandharpur
R. Krishna
Dornakal
Raichur
R. Kistna
Pagan
(Amaravati)
Goa
Srngeri
Sravana Belgola
Belur
Udipi
Madras
Mangalore

India

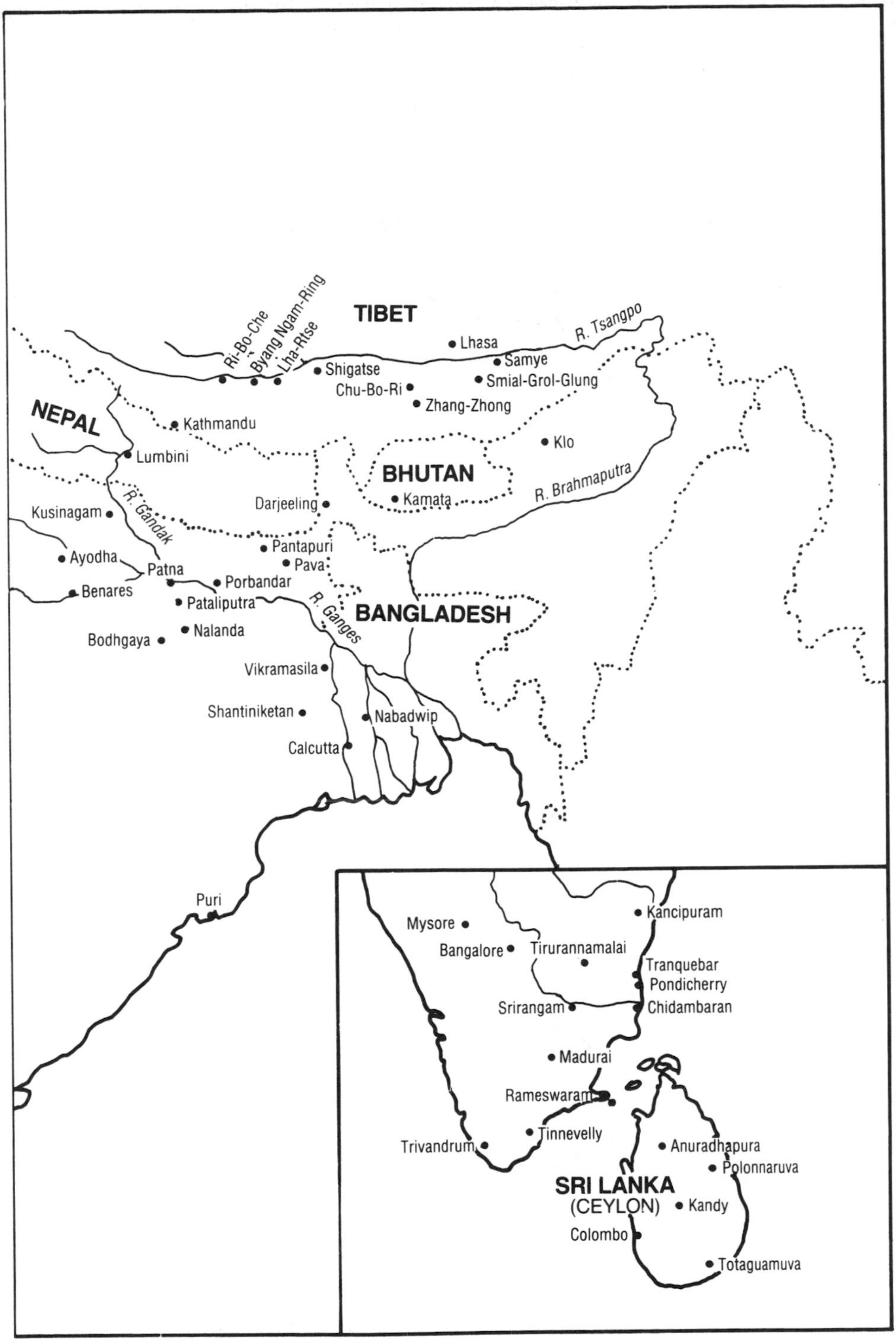
TIBET
Ri-Bo-Che
Byang Ngam-Ring
Lha-Rtse
Lhasa
R. Tsangpo
Samye
Shigatse
Chu-Bo-Ri
Smial-Grol-Glung
Zhang-Zhong
NEPAL
Kathmandu
Lumbini
Klo
BHUTAN
Kamata
R. Brahmaputra
Darjeeling
R. Gandak
Kusinagam
Pantapuri
Pava
Ayodha
Patna
Porbandar
Benares
Pataliputra
R. Ganges
BANGLADESH
Nalanda
Bodhgaya
Vikramasila
Shantiniketan
Nabadwip
Calcutta
Puri
Mysore
Kancipuram
Bangalore
Tirurannamalai
Tranquebar
Pondicherry
Srirangam
Chidambaran
Madurai
Rameswaram
Tinnevelly
Trivandrum
Anuradhapura
Polonnaruva
SRI LANKA
(CEYLON)
Kandy
Colombo
Totaguamuva

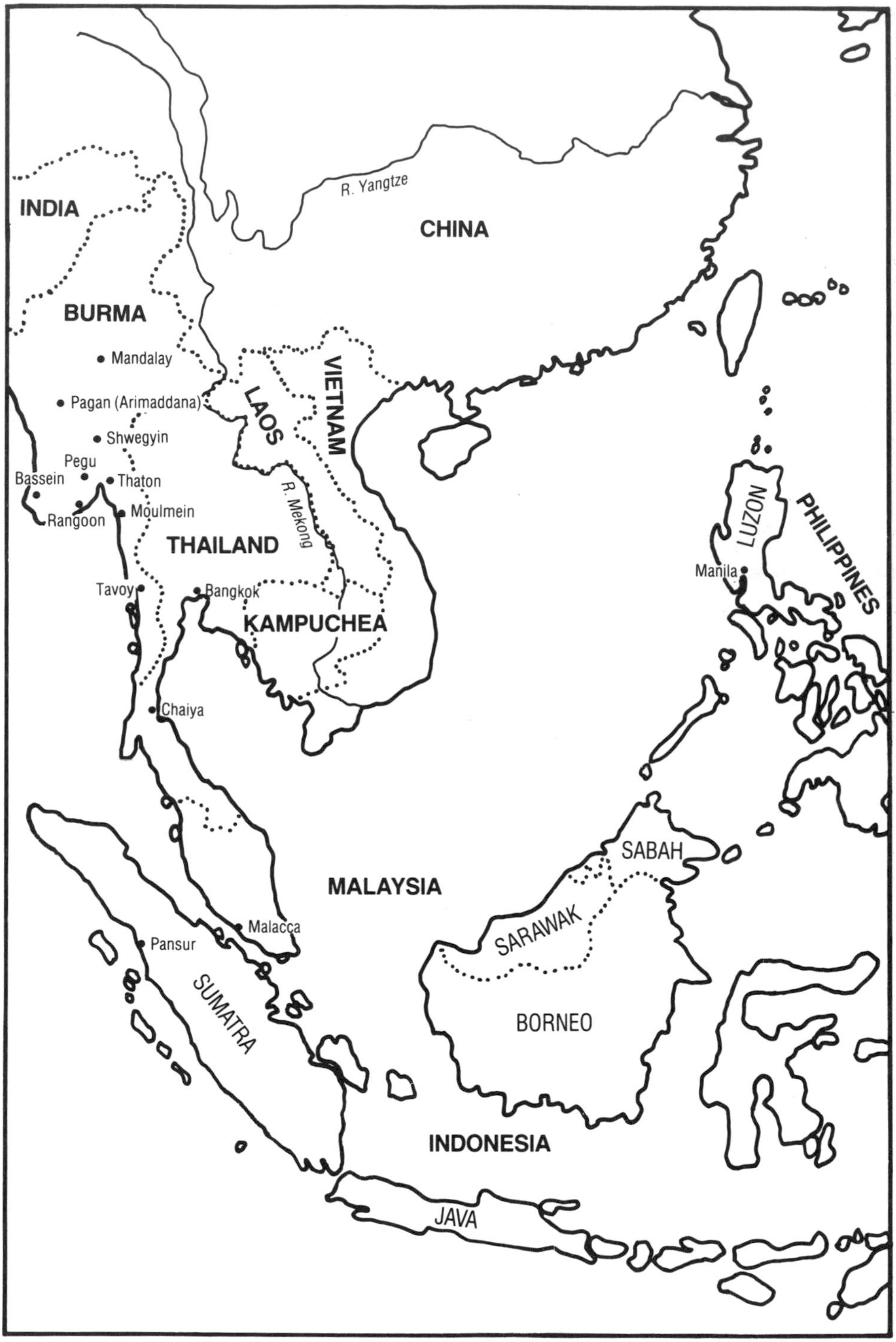

R. Yangtze
CHINA
INDIA
BURMA
Mandalay
Pagan (Arimaddana)
Shwegyin
Pegu
Bassein
Thaton
Rangoon
Moulmein
LAOS
VIETNAM
R. Mekong
THAILAND
Tavoy
Bangkok
KAMPUCHEA
Chaiya
LUZON
PHILIPPINES
Manila
SABAH
MALAYSIA
SARAWAK
Malacca
Pansur
SUMATRA
BORNEO
INDONESIA
JAVA

South Asia

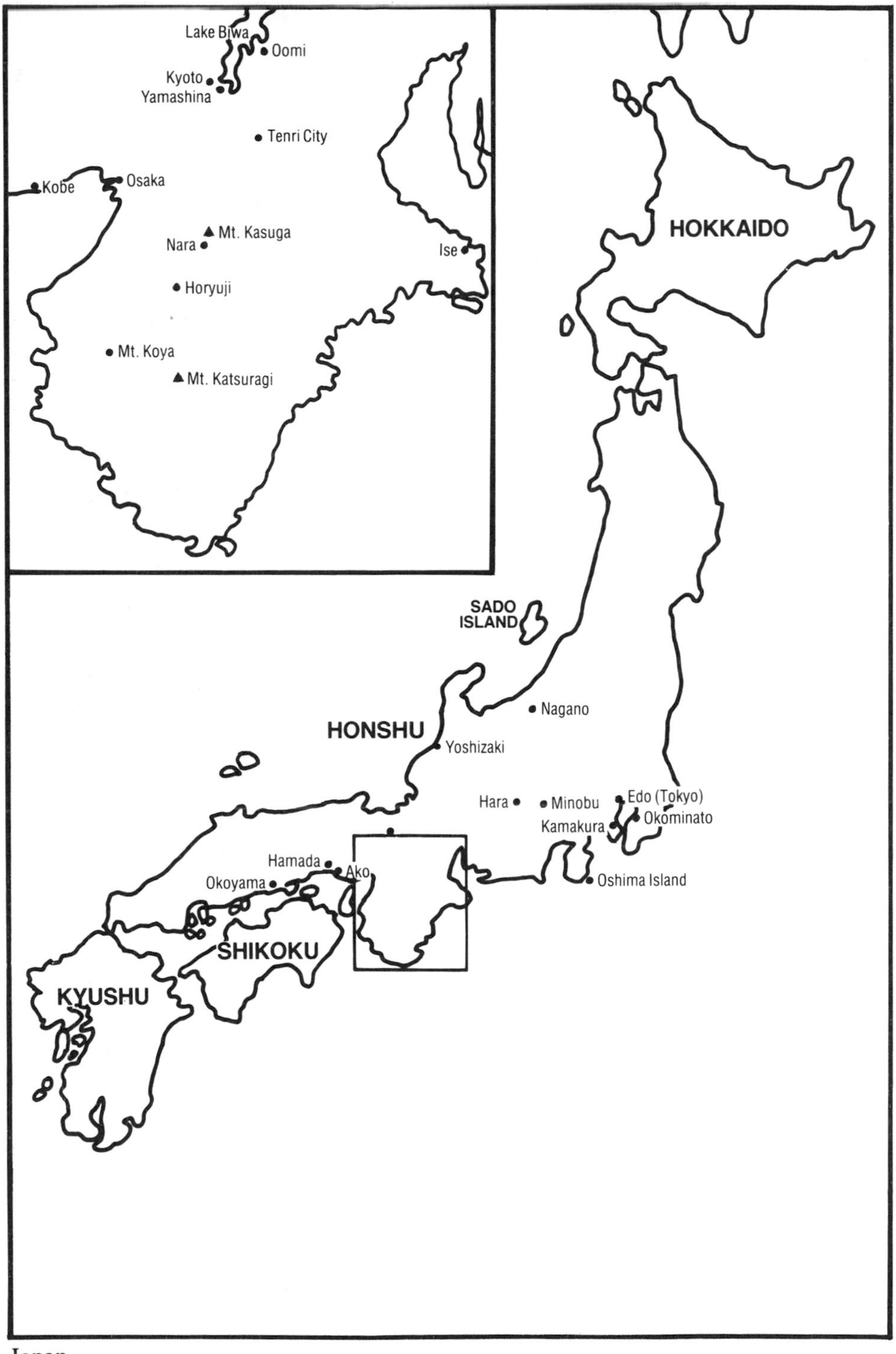
Lake Biwa
Oomi
Kyoto
Yamashina
Tenri City
Kobe
Osaka
Mt. Kasuga
Nara
Ise
Horyuji
Mt. Koya
Mt. Katsuragi
HOKKAIDO
SADO ISLAND
Nagano
HONSHU
Yoshizaki
Hara
Minobu
Edo (Tokyo)
Okominato
Kamakura
Hamada
Ako
Okoyama
Oshima Island
SHIKOKU
KYUSHU

Japan

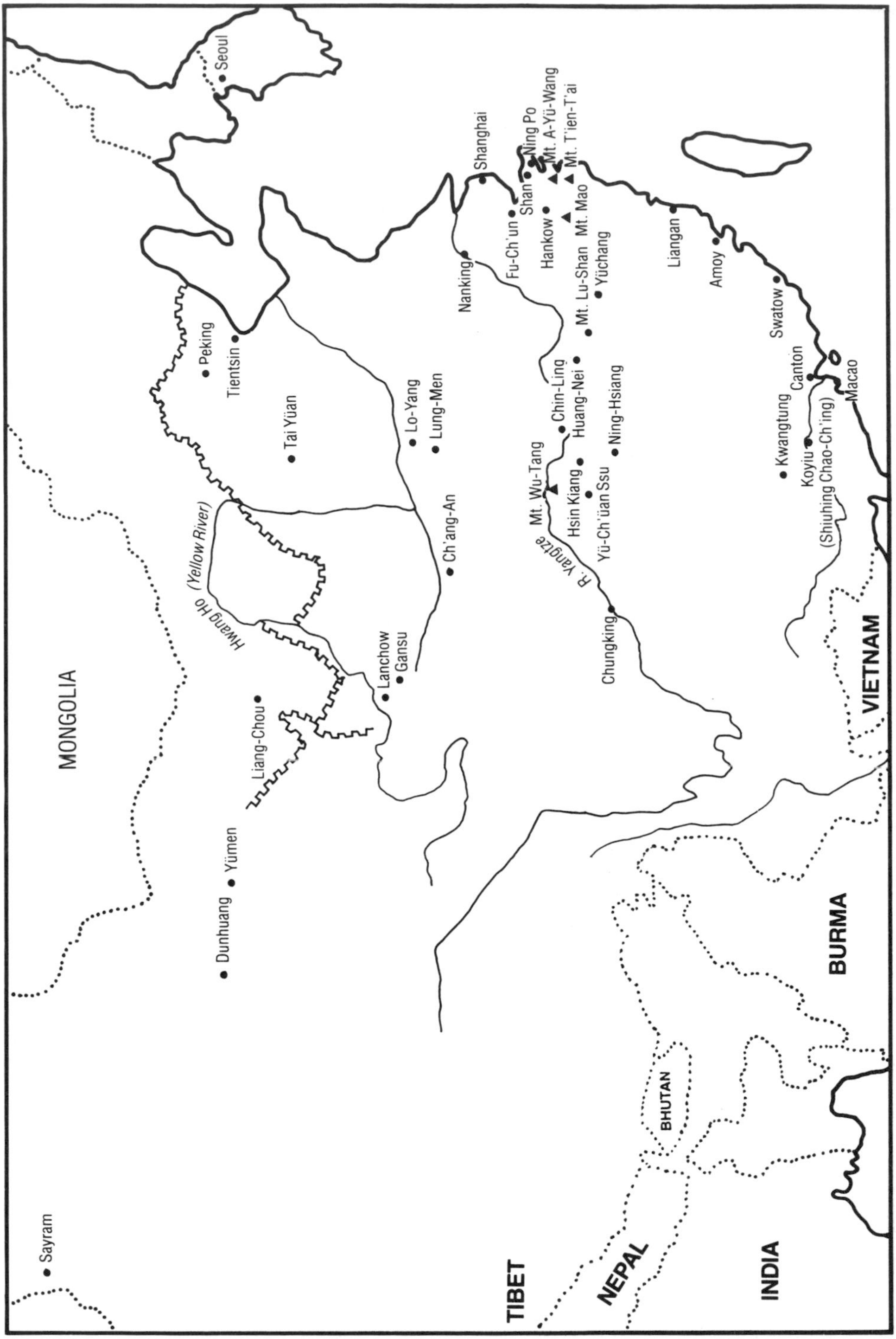

Seoul
Shanghai
Ning Po
Mt. A-Yü-Wang
Mt. T'ien-T'ai
Shan
Fu-Ch'un
Hankow
Mt. Mao
Mt. Lu-Shan
Yüchang
Nanking
Liangan
Amoy
Swatow
Canton
Macao
Kwangtung
Koyiu
(Shiuhing Chao-Ch'ing)
Peking
Tientsin
Tai Yüan
Lo-Yang
Lung-Men
Chin-Ling
Huang-Nei
Ning-Hsiang
Mt. Wu-Tang
Hsin Kiang
Yü-Ch'üan Ssu
Ch'ang-An
R. Yangtze
Chungking
Hwang Ho
(Yellow River)
Lanchow
Gansu
Liang-Chou
MONGOLIA
Yümen
Dunhuang
Sayram
VIETNAM
BURMA
BHUTAN
TIBET
NEPAL
INDIA

China

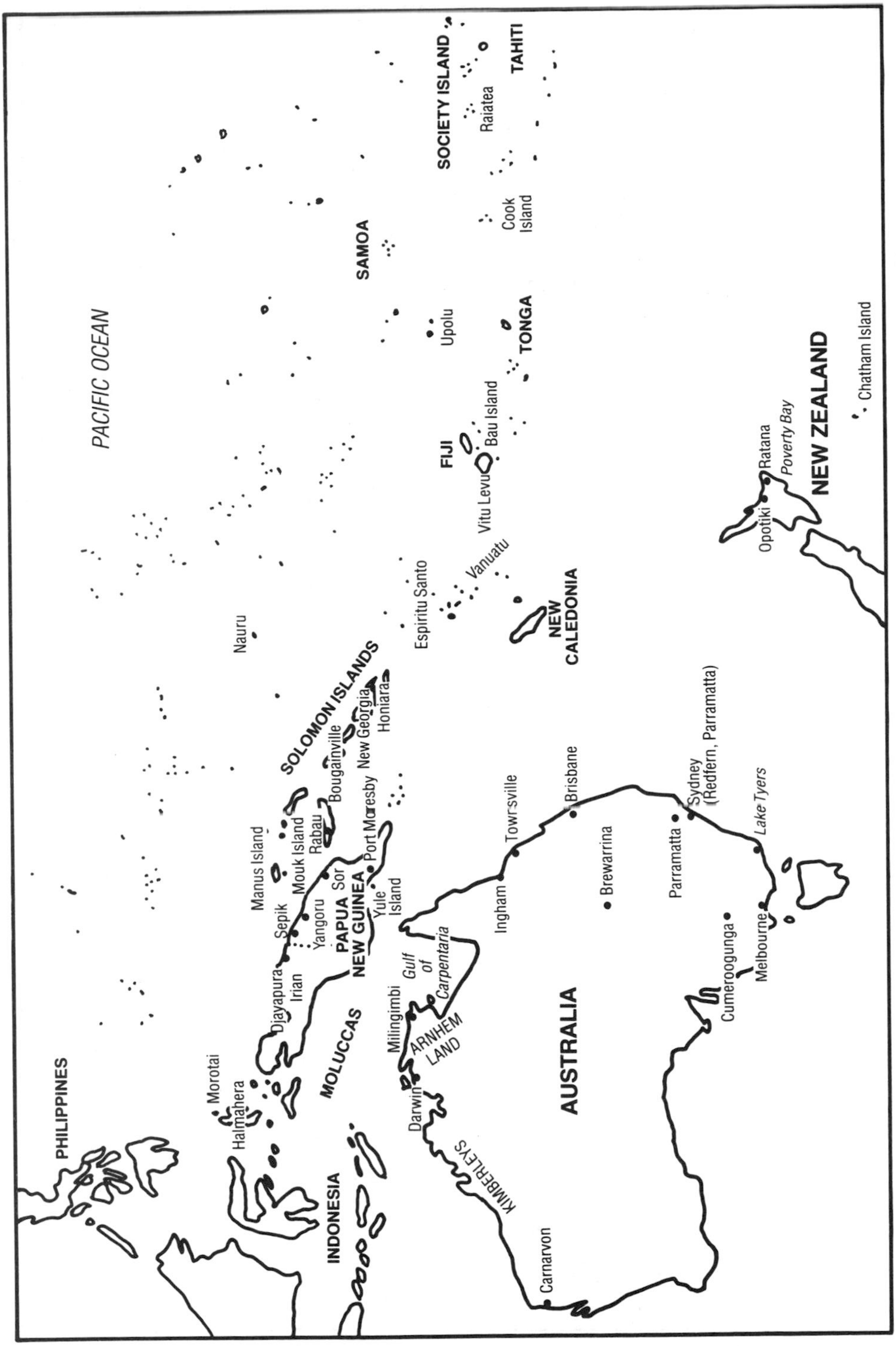

South-West Pacific and Australasia

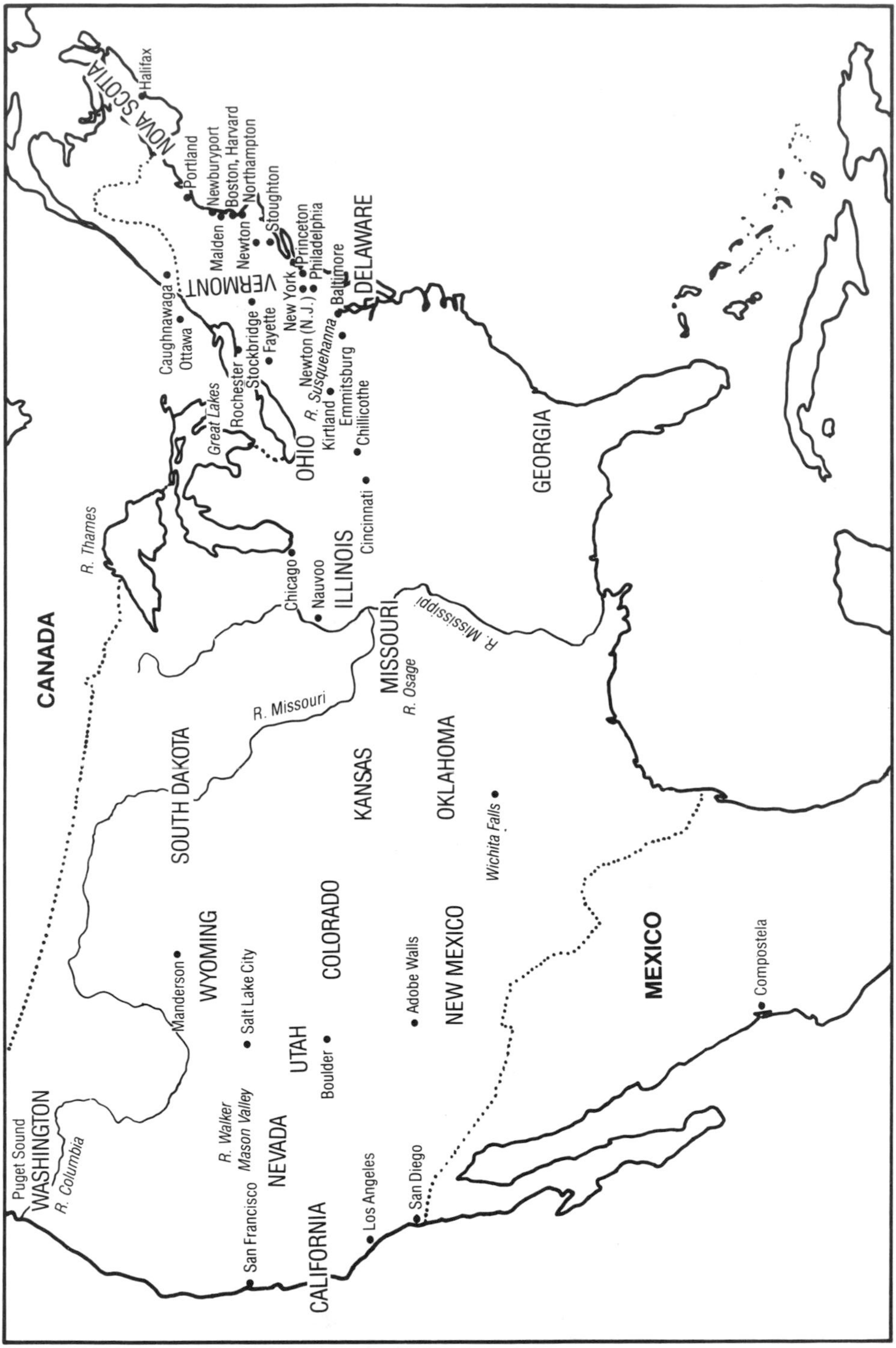

United States of America

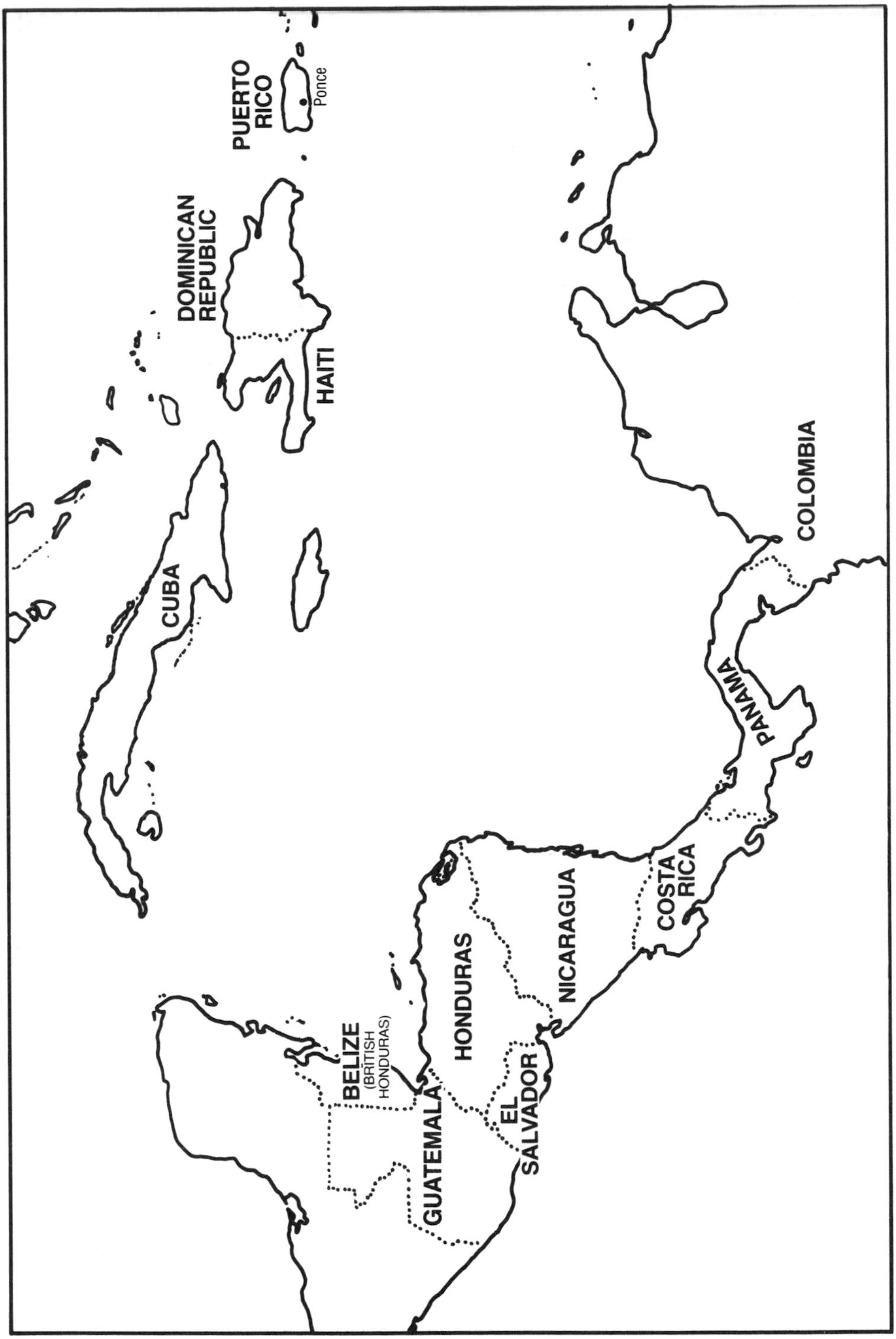

Central America

South America

Synoptic Index

[I] African Religions

[II] Ancient Near Eastern Religions

[III] Bahāʾī

[IV] Buddhism

[V] Chinese Religions, excluding Buddhism

[VI] Christianity

[VII] Egyptian Religion, Ancient

[VIII] European Religions, Ancient

[IX] Gnosticism

[X] Greek Religion, Ancient

[XI] Hinduism

[XII] Islam

[XIII] Jainism

[XIV] Japanese Religions, excluding Buddhism

[XV] Judaism

[XVI] Korean Religions, excluding Buddhism

[XVII] Magic and the Occult

[XVIII] Meso-American Religions

[XIX] New Religious Movements in the West

[XX] North American Indian Religions

[XXI] Pacific Religions

[XXII] Roman Religion

[XXIII] Sikhism

[XXIV] South American Religions

[XXV] Tibetan and Central Asian Religions, excluding Buddhism

[XXVI] Zoroastrianism

General Index

Please note that this Index is supplementary to the Alphabetical sequence of the main text and the Synoptic Index. Names which are headings in the main sequence are *not* listed again in the General Index unless there are other page references to indicate. Such names are distinguished by * and the main page reference is given first in italic type.

The Synoptic Index provides a guide to major religions and they are not included in the General Index unless it seems convenient to indicate page references more precisely: e.g. China, Buddhism, which supplements Synoptic Index V, Chinese religions. Individual movements and sects (except eponymous) are, however, listed in detail. Movements named after their founders can be traced through their founders' names.

The heading 'Women' lists the names of female headings in the main text. They are also indexed individually, as are also many other women mentioned in the text.